Leading Issues in
Economic Development

Leading Issues in Economic Development

EIGHTH EDITION

GERALD M. MEIER
Stanford University

JAMES E. RAUCH
University of California, San Diego

New York   Oxford
OXFORD UNIVERSITY PRESS
2005

Oxford University Press

Oxford   New York
Auckland   Bangkok   Buenos Aires   Cape Town   Chennai
Dar es Salaam   Delhi   Hong Kong   Istanbul   Karachi   Kolkata
Kuala Lumpur   Madrid   Melbourne   Mexico City   Mumbai
Nairobi   São Paulo   Shanghai   Taipei   Tokyo   Toronto

Copyright © 2005 by Oxford University Press, Inc.

Published by Oxford University Press, Inc.
198 Madison Avenue, New York, New York 10016
http://www.oup.com

Oxford is a registered trademark of Oxford University Press

ISBN 13: 978-0-19-517960-6
ISBN: 0-19-517960-9

Printing (last digit) 9 8 7 6 5 4 3 2 1

Printed in the United States of America
on acid-free paper

To the next generation of development economists.
–G.M.M.

To Doris
–J.E.R.

CONTENTS

EXHIBITS

PREFACE

The economics of development is one of the most exciting subjects in social science. Why, two centuries after the Industrial Revolution, are poverty and its attendant ills so prevalent in most of the world? And what can be done about it? Nobel Prize–winning economist Robert Lucas wrote of the questions addressed by development economics, "Once one starts to think about them, it is hard to think about anything else" ["On the Mechanics of Economic Development," *Journal of Monetary Economics* 22 (July 1988), p. 5].

Development economics is also a very frustrating subject. Unlike most areas within economics, there exists no consensus on what the student should know. Two scholars can with equal justification write two completely different textbooks.

The aim of this book is to convey as much of the excitement of development economics and as little of the frustration as possible. To this end we have avoided writing the ordinary type of textbook, instead culling the most insightful readings from the diffuse field of development and bringing them into conceptual order. By using this distinctive approach we allow for a variety of perspectives while keeping in sight the most important overarching themes. The section "Using This Book" (p. xvii) describes our strategy of combining excerpted readings ("Selections") with our own "Overviews," "Notes," "Comments," and "Exhibits."

After his seven editions over 40 years, Professor Meier now transfers all upgrading in this eighth edition to Professor Rauch. The most important analytical and quantitative dimensions of economic issues are now emphasized, and insights for future policy problems are demonstrated. The better analysis from this edition is appreciated.

In addition to a thorough updating, there have been several important changes in this eighth edition relative to the seventh edition:

- A comprehensive set of statistical Exhibits organized by country ranking on the Human Development Index (HDI) has been added. Some of these Exhibits contain information not available in print elsewhere.
- There is coverage of the new empirical microeconomics of development that emphasizes natural experiments and randomized trials in areas such as education and health.
- The representation in the Selections of articles from leading professional journals has increased.

We wish to express our appreciation to the authors and publishers who have granted permission to use excerpts from publications for which copyrights exist. Specific acknowledgment is given with each Selection. Some parts of the original versions of the excerpted materials have been omitted out of consideration for relevance and to avoid repetition. In some instances, tables and diagrams have been renumbered and the footnotes have been deleted or renumbered.

We would like to thank a number of extremely busy people who generously took time out to provide advice or to comment on portions of the manuscript: Mark Rosenzweig, Christopher Udry, Jeffrey Vincent, and Stephen Weymouth. We would also like to acknowledge the valuable research assistance of Maximilian Auffhammer and Jennifer Poole. James Rauch wishes to thank his wife, Doris Bittar, for making room in her life for this book during its final months of preparation. Terry Vaughn has been a very helpful and patient editor. Finally, we are grateful to the entire profession of social scientists whose writings on development provide the foundation for this volume.

USING THIS BOOK

Instructors and students can use this book more like a main text or more like a supplementary reader. To facilitate the latter approach the contents have been designed to allow individual freedom of choice in deciding what chapters and Selections to read and in what sequence. If the former approach is taken, the organizational and thematic guidance of the chapter Overviews can be followed and the chapters can be read in numerical order.

The chapters include the following materials:

Overviews: These are introductory essays that show how the subsequent chapter materials fit together and elucidate one or more overarching themes. They sometimes contain ideas that are not explicitly presented by the other chapter materials.

Selections: These are the core of the book. They present a broad sample of the major contributions by scholars and practitioners on the central issues in economic development. Each Selection has been edited for the sake of brevity and to highlight the points of greatest relevance for the chapter in which it appears.

Notes: These serve two purposes. One is to expound important ideas that are extant in the literature but are not presented as clearly or simply as we would like. The other is to present more original material that complements the Selections.

Comments: Like the Notes, these serve two purposes. One is to clarify or expand upon the immediately preceding Selection. The other is to suggest additional readings on the subject of the immediately preceding Selection.

Exhibits: These are tables and charts that provide empirical illustrations and data on topics under discussion.

Starting with Selection IV.A.5, some Selections include regression tables. Readers without econometric training are urged to refer to the Appendix to get the most insight from these Selections.

World Map of Human Development Index

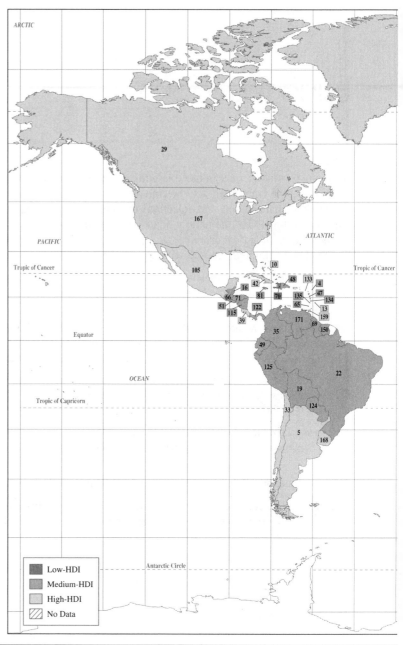

Low-HDI
Medium-HDI
High-HDI
No Data

Country Name (HDI Ranking)[a]

1	Albania (81)	19	Bolivia (62)	37	Congo (36)	55	Ethiopia (7)	73	Hungary (138)
2	Algeria (69)	20	Bosnia and Herzegovina (110)	38	Congo, Dem. Rep. of the (9)	56	Fiji (95)	74	Iceland (174)
3	Angola (12)	21	Botswana (51)	39	Costa Rica (134)	57	Finland (162)	75	India (49)
4	Antigua and Barbuda (120)	22	Brazil (111)	40	Côte d'Ivoire (15)	58	France (159)	76	Indonesia (64)
5	Argentina (142)	23	Brunei Darussalam (145)	41	Croatia (129)	59	Gabon (58)	77	Iran, Islamic Rep. of (70)
6	Armenia (76)	24	Bulgaria (119)	42	Cuba (124)	60	Gambia (25)	78	Ireland (164)
7	Australia (172)	25	Burkina Faso (3)	43	Cyprus (151)	61	Georgia (88)	79	Israel (154)
8	Austria (160)	26	Burundi (5)	44	Czech Republic (144)	62	Germany (158)	80	Italy (155)
9	Azerbaijan (87)	27	Cambodia (46)	45	Denmark (165)	63	Ghana (47)	81	Jamaica (98)
10	Bahamas (127)	28	Cameroon (34)	46	Djibouti (23)	64	Greece (152)	82	Japan (167)
11	Bahrain (139)	29	Canada (168)	47	Dominica (108)	65	Grenada (83)	83	Jordan (86)
12	Bangladesh (37)	30	Cape Verde (73)	48	Dominican Republic (82)	66	Guatemala (57)	84	Kazakhstan (100)
13	Barbados (149)	31	Central African Republic (8)	49	Ecuador (79)	67	Guinea (19)	85	Kenya (30)
14	Belarus (123)	32	Chad (11)	50	Egypt (56)	68	Guinea-Bissau (10)	86	Korea, Rep. of (146)
15	Belgium (170)	33	Chile (133)	51	El Salvador (71)	69	Guyana (84)	87	Kuwait (130)
16	Belize (109)	34	China (72)	52	Equatorial Guinea (60)	70	Haiti (26)	88	Kyrgyzstan (74)
17	Benin (17)	35	Colombia (112)	53	Eritrea (21)	71	Honduras (61)	89	Lao People's
18	Bhutan (40)	36	Comoros (42)	54	Estonia (135)	72	Hong Kong, China (SAR) (150)		Dem. Rep. (41)

[a]Countries are ranked based on the 2003 United Nations Human Development Index (HDI) from lowest to highest, 1=lowest HDI ranking and 175=highest HDI ranking.

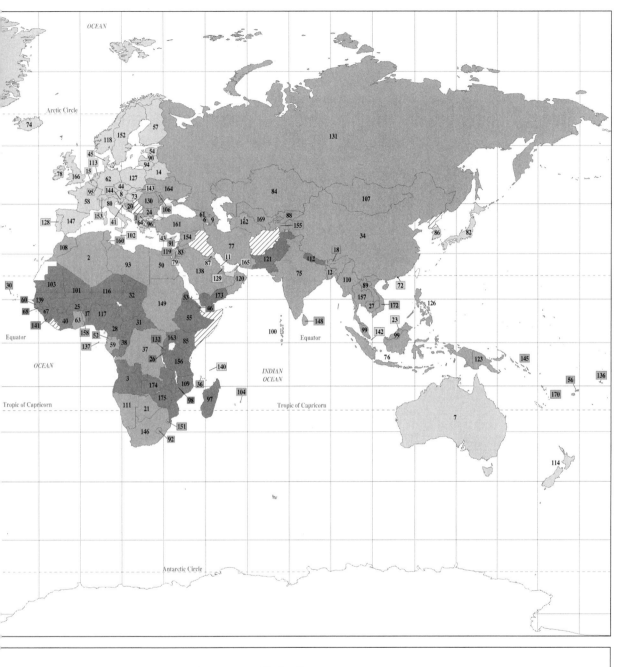

Leading Issues in
Economic Development

CHAPTER 1

Introduction

Overview

The subject of this book is the economics of less developed countries, sometimes called "developing countries." Yet we must admit from the start that there is no universally accepted definition of "less developed country" (LDC). Roughly speaking, the definition in use by the writers whose work is excerpted in this book is the countries of Latin America, North Africa and the Middle East, sub-Saharan Africa, and Asia minus Japan and the countries that were formerly members of the Soviet Union—in short, what used to be called the Third World. When the border that separated East and West Germany became obsolete, so did the boundaries that separated the classification "Second World" from the classifications "First World" and "Third World." Yet the countries of Eastern Europe and the former Soviet Union, no matter how poor, were labeled "transition" countries rather than "less developed" countries, and were the subject of "transition economics" rather than "development economics." Moreover, a number of formerly Third World countries such as Israel, Singapore, and Taiwan would appear to have graduated to "more developed" or "industrialized" status.

In attempting to define "less developed country" it would clearly be helpful to have an accepted measure of "development." In recent years a consensus has been gathering around the Human Development Index (HDI) as the preferred measure of development. The HDI is based on a country's per capita income, life expectancy, and educational attainment and effort. Exhibit I.A.1 shows the exact method of calculating the HDI used by the United Nations Development Program in its annual *Human Development Report.* Exhibit I.A.2 compares the rankings of countries by HDI to their rankings by per capita income in U.S. dollars, which was the preferred measure of development in the past. Note I.A.1 describes how the HDI evolved in response to criticisms of the adequacy of U.S. dollar per capita income as a measure of development.

The United Nations Development Program classifies countries with HDI less than 0.5 as "low human development," countries with HDI of at least 0.5 but less than 0.8 as "medium human development," and countries with HDI of at least 0.8 as "high human development." We can then call the low- and medium-human development countries the "less developed countries" and the high-human development countries the "more developed countries" or simply "developed countries." If we set the bar for developed country classification a bit higher, at an HDI of 0.85, then we can see from Exhibit I.A.2 that the only country from the former Third World with a population greater than 10 million that would be classified as "developed" is the Republic of Korea (South Korea). (Taiwan would be another such country, but it is not included in United Nations statistics.)

The per capita income component of the HDI is constructed using per capita GDP in "international dollars" or "purchasing power parity dollars" rather than U.S. dollars. As described in Note I.A.1, this is done because of evidence that the purchasing power of U.S. dollars is greater in poor countries than it is in rich countries. Exhibit I.A.3 shows that this "correction" of exchange-rate converted per capita income tends to be greater, the poorer the country relative to the United States. Selection I.A.1 by Jagdish Bhagwati and the following Comment attempt to explain why services are so much cheaper relative to commodities in poor countries than in rich countries, cheaper services being the chief reason why the purchasing power of the dollar is greater in poor countries.

Development has sometimes been measured by the reduction of poverty. In addition to other basic country data, Exhibit I.A.4 contains two indicators of poverty that are used to supplement the HDI as a measure of development. The construction of these internationally comparable poverty lines is discussed in Selection I.A.2 by the World Bank. The following Comment argues forcefully for use of an absolute poverty line, rather than a poverty line that is defined relative to the average income in a given society and therefore varies from country to country.

The first section of this chapter concludes with Note I.A.2, which discusses two important systematic differences between LDCs and developed countries that are not captured by the HDI or measures of poverty. First, population growth is higher in LDCs. Second, the share of the labor force engaged in agriculture is much higher in LDCs than in developed countries, and unfortunately it is also the case that productivity in agriculture relative to the rest of the economy is much smaller in the typical LDC than in the typical developed country.

The next section reviews the economic performance of LDCs in the recent past. It begins with Selection I.B.1 by William Easterly, who describes how the 1980s and 1990s were "lost decades" of economic growth for the typical LDC, despite the adoption of numerous "Washington consensus" policy reforms that were chosen precisely because they were expected to increase economic growth. Note I.B.1 takes a less pessimistic view, pointing out that Exhibit I.B.1 shows that life expectancy and educational attainment in the typical LDC continued to increase even as per capita income stagnated. Exhibit I.B.2 shows that the growth performance of the 1980s and 1990s looks much better when one examines the growth of population-weighted per capita income instead of giving each LDC equal weight regardless of population, and Exhibit I.B.3 reminds us that despite the disappointments of the recent past, it is possible for LDCs not only to grow rapidly but even to catch up to the per capita incomes of the countries of Northern Europe, where modern economic growth began.

The reason that weighting by population changes the growth rate so much in Exhibit I.B.2 is that the two largest countries in the less developed world, China and India, began growing much faster than the typical LDC in the 1980s and 1990s. In Selection I.B.2, Yingyi Qian describes how China did not adopt the Washington consensus package of liberalization and privatization but instead developed a set of "transitional institutions" that facilitated its transformation from a centrally planned economy to a more market-oriented economy. J. Bradford DeLong argues in Selection I.B.3 that Indian economic growth benefited from a Washington consensus-style wave of reform in the early 1990s, yet benefited equally from much weaker policy changes adopted in the mid-1980s. The latest boost to Indian economic growth appears to be coming from India's exports of computer software and "back office" services such as call centers and data processing, as described in Srinivasan and Tendulkar (2003, pp. 58–63).

More typical of recent LDC experience with economic reforms have been the results for the nine Latin American and Caribbean countries summarized in Selection I.B.4. Even though this Selection was written before the collapse of the Argentine economy in 2002, the authors conclude that the reforms had at best a small positive impact on growth in per capita income, offset by small negative impacts on employment and equality of income distribution. In Selection I.B.5 on sub-Saharan Africa, Paul Collier and Jan Willem Gunning divide the possible explanations for the dismal economic performance of this region into "bad" policies, which are amenable to reform, and unfavorable climatic and geographic characteristics, which are not. They note that by the mid-1990s policies had "improved" in many countries and growth rates had become more dispersed (though this was not necessarily linked to changes in policies), so that "sub-Saharan Africa" was becoming less meaningful as a category.

The section that concludes this introductory chapter concerns development economics as a discipline. Note I.C.1 discusses the evolution of the discipline from the late 1940s to the 1980s, and Comment I.C.1 examines its "classical" antecedents. Comment I.C.2 addresses the question of how development economics is different from the rest of economics. This question has perhaps become more urgent with the rise of "new" or "endogenous" growth theory in the late 1980s and early 1990s, which is described in Note I.C.2. Endogenous growth theory has changed the relationship of development economics to the neoclassical mainstream, both by bringing ideas from development economics into the mainstream and by allowing the mainstream to analyze economic growth in less developed countries more effectively. As will be evident to readers of this book, however, development economics is much broader than growth theory, old or new.

Reference

Srinivasan, T. N., and Tendulkar, Suresh D. 2003. *Reintegrating India with the World Economy* (Washington, DC: Institute for International Economics).

I.A. MEASURING DEVELOPMENT

Exhibit I.A.1. The Human Development Index (HDI)

The HDI is a summary measure of human development. It measures the average achievements in a country in three basic dimensions of human development:

• A long and healthy life, as measured by life expectancy at birth.
• Knowledge, as measured by the adult literacy rate (with two-thirds weight) and the combined primary, secondary and tertiary gross enrolment ratio (with one-third weight).
• A decent standard of living, as measured by GDP per capita (PPP US$).

Before the HDI itself is calculated, an index needs to be created for each of these dimensions. To calculate these dimension indices —the life expectancy, education and GDP indices—minimum and maximum values (goalposts) are chosen for each underlying indicator.

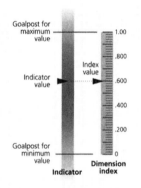

Performance in each dimension is expressed as a value between 0 and 1 by applying the following general formula:

$$\text{Dimension index} = \frac{\text{actual value} - \text{minimum value}}{\text{maximum value} - \text{minimum value}}$$

The HDI is then calculated as a simple average of the dimension indices. The box at right illustrates the calculation of the HDI for a sample country.

Goalposts for calculating the HDI

Indicator	Maximum value	Minimum value
Life expectancy at birth (years)	85	25
Adult literacy rate (%)	100	0
Combined gross enrolment ratio (%)	100	0
GDP per capita (PPP US$)	40,000	100

Calculating the HDI

This illustration of the calculation of the HDI uses data for Albania.

1. Calculating the life expectancy index
The life expectancy index measures the relative achievement of a country in life expectancy at birth. For Albania, with a life expectancy of 73.4 years in 2001, the life expectancy index is 0.807.

$$\text{Life expectancy index} = \frac{73.4 - 25}{85 - 25} = 0.807$$

2. Calculating the education index
The education index measures a country's relative achievement in both adult literacy and combined primary, secondary and tertiary gross enrolment. First, an index for adult literacy and one for combined gross enrolment are calculated. Then these two indices are combined to create the education index, with two-thirds weight given to adult literacy and one-third weight to combined gross enrolment. For Albania, with an adult literacy rate of 85.3% in 2001 and a combined gross enrolment ratio of 69% in the school year 2000/01, the education index is 0.798.

$$\text{Adult literacy index} = \frac{85.3 - 0}{100 - 0} = 0.853$$

$$\text{Gross enrolment index} = \frac{69 - 0}{100 - 0} = 0.690$$

Education index = 2/3 (adult literacy index) + 1/3 (gross enrolment index)
= 2/3 (0.853) + 1/3 (0.690) = **0.798**

3. Calculating the GDP index
The GDP index is calculated using adjusted GDP per capita (PPP US$). In the HDI income serves as a surrogate for all the dimensions of human development not reflected in a long and healthy life and in knowledge. Income is adjusted because achieving a respectable level of human development does not require unlimited income. Accordingly, the logarithm of income is used. For Albania, with a GDP per capita of $3,680 (PPP US$) in 2001, the GDP index is 0.602.

$$\text{GDP index} = \frac{\log(3,680) - \log(100)}{\log(40,000) - \log(100)} = 0.602$$

4. Calculating the HDI
Once the dimension indices have been calculated, determining the HDI is straightforward. It is a simple average of the three dimension indices.

HDI = 1/3 (life expectancy index) + 1/3 (education index)
+ 1/3 (GDP index)
= 1/3 (0.807) + 1/3 (0.798) + 1/3 (0.602) = **0.735**

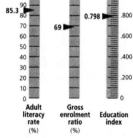

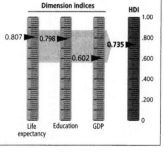

Source: From United Nations Development Program, *Human Development Report 2003* (New York: Oxford University Press, 2003), p. 341. Reprinted by permission.

Exhibit I.A.2. Human Development Index Rankings Compared to U.S. Dollar Per Capita GDP Rankings

Country Name (listed from lowest to highest HDI)	Real GDP Per Capita[a] (U.S.$) 2001	Real GDP Per Capita (PPP$) 2001	Life Expectancy at Birth (Years) 2001	Adult Literacy Rate[b] (Percent aged 15 and older) 2001	Combined First-, Second- and Third-Level Gross Enrollment Rate[c] (Percent) 2001	GDP Index[d]	Life Expectancy Index	Education Index	Human Development Index (HDI) Value	HDI Rank minus U.S.$ Per Capita GDP Rank[e]
Low-human development countries										
Sierra Leone	158	470	35	36	51	0.26	0.16	0.41	0.275	−4
Niger	208	890	46	17	17	0.36	0.34	0.17	0.292	−7
Burkina Faso	250	1,120	46	25	22	0.40	0.35	0.24	0.330	−10
Mali	292	810	48	26	29	0.35	0.39	0.27	0.337	−14
Burundi	141	690	40	49	31	0.32	0.26	0.43	0.337	2
Mozambique	213	1,140	39	45	37	0.41	0.24	0.43	0.356	−4
Ethiopia	121	810	46	40	34	0.35	0.34	0.38	0.359	5
Central African Republic	339	1,300	40	48	24	0.43	0.26	0.40	0.363	−16
Congo, Dem. Rep. of the	85	680	41	63	27	0.32	0.26	0.51	0.363	8
Guinea-Bissau	206	970	45	40	43	0.38	0.33	0.41	0.373	2
Chad	230	1,070	45	44	33	0.40	0.33	0.41	0.376	0
Angola	525	2,040	40	42	29	0.50	0.25	0.38	0.377	−33
Zambia	405	780	33	79	45	0.34	0.14	0.68	0.386	−18
Malawi	163	570	39	61	72	0.29	0.22	0.65	0.387	8
Côte d'Ivoire	715	1,490	42	50	39	0.45	0.28	0.46	0.396	−41
Tanzania, U. Rep. of	197	520	44	76	31	0.28	0.32	0.61	0.400	9
Benin	424	980	51	39	49	0.38	0.43	0.42	0.411	−18
Rwanda	253	1,250	38	68	52	0.42	0.22	0.63	0.422	4
Guinea	613	1,960	49	41	34	0.50	0.39	0.39	0.425	−31
Senegal	629	1,500	52	38	38	0.45	0.46	0.38	0.430	−31
Eritrea	156	1,030	53	57	33	0.39	0.46	0.49	0.446	17
Mauritania	502	1,990	52	41	43	0.50	0.45	0.41	0.454	−20
Djibouti	777	2,370	46	66	21	0.53	0.35	0.51	0.462	−34
Nigeria	257	850	52	65	45	0.36	0.45	0.59	0.463	8
Gambia	382	2,050	54	38	47	0.50	0.48	0.41	0.463	−3
Haiti	354	1,860	49	51	52	0.49	0.40	0.51	0.467	0
Madagascar	253	830	53	67	41	0.35	0.47	0.58	0.468	12
Yemen	316	790	59	48	52	0.34	0.57	0.49	0.470	9
Uganda	355	1,490	45	68	71	0.45	0.33	0.69	0.489	2
Kenya	325	980	46	83	52	0.38	0.36	0.73	0.489	8

Zimbabwe	559	2,280	35	89	59	0.52	0.17	0.79	0.496	−16
Pakistan	517	1,890	60	44	36	0.49	0.59	0.41	0.499	−12
Nepal	248	1,310	59	43	64	0.43	0.57	0.50	0.499	21
Cameroon	696	1,680	48	72	48	0.47	0.38	0.64	0.499	−20
Median	***304***	***1,095***	***46***	***48***	***40***	***0.40***	***0.35***	***0.45***	***0.417***	***−4***
Medium-human development countries										
Togo	322	1,650	50	58	67	0.47	0.42	0.61	0.501	14
Congo	792	970	49	82	57	0.38	0.39	0.73	0.502	−22
Bangladesh	386	1,610	61	41	54	0.46	0.59	0.45	0.502	8
Sudan	328	1,970	55	59	34	0.50	0.51	0.51	0.503	15
Lesotho	563	2,420	39	84	63	0.53	0.23	0.77	0.510	−9
Bhutan	554	1,833	63	47	33	0.49	0.62	0.42	0.511	−6
Lao People's Dem. Rep.	465	1,620	54	66	57	0.46	0.48	0.63	0.525	2
Comoros	433	1,870	60	56	40	0.49	0.59	0.51	0.528	5
Swaziland	1,529	4,330	38	80	77	0.63	0.22	0.79	0.547	−36
Papua New Guinea	897	2,570	57	65	41	0.54	0.53	0.57	0.548	−18
Myanmar	317	1,027	57	85	47	0.39	0.53	0.72	0.549	28
Cambodia	421	1,860	57	69	55	0.49	0.54	0.64	0.556	26
Ghana	1,174	2,250	58	73	46	0.52	0.54	0.64	0.567	13
Vanuatu	477	3,190	68	34	54	0.58	0.72	0.41	0.568	−24
India	1,436	2,840	63	58	56	0.56	0.64	0.57	0.590	9
Morocco		3,600	68	50	51	0.60	0.72	0.50	0.606	−25
Botswana		7,820	45	78	80	0.73	0.33	0.79	0.614	−69
Namibia	4,130	7,120	47	83	74	0.71	0.37	0.80	0.627	−47
Solomon Islands	2,383	1,910	69	77	50	0.49	0.73	0.68	0.632	4
Sao Tome and Principe	587	1,317	69	83	58	0.43	0.74	0.75	0.639	29
Nicaragua	344	2,450	69	67	65	0.53	0.73	0.66	0.643	2
Egypt	1,229	3,520	68	56	76	0.59	0.72	0.63	0.648	−17
Guatemala	1,554	4,400	65	69	57	0.63	0.67	0.65	0.652	−24
Gabon	4,378	5,990	57	71	83	0.68	0.53	0.75	0.653	−64
Mongolia	430	1,740	63	99	64	0.48	0.64	0.87	0.661	23
Equatorial Guinea	1,578	15,073	49	84	58	0.84	0.40	0.76	0.664	−22
Honduras	711	2,830	69	76	62	0.56	0.73	0.71	0.667	6
Bolivia	944	2,300	63	86	84	0.52	0.64	0.85	0.672	−2
Tajikistan	420	1,170	68	99	71	0.41	0.72	0.90	0.677	30
Indonesia	1,034	2,940	66	87	64	0.56	0.69	0.80	0.682	−3
South Africa	4,068	11,290	51	86	78	0.79	0.43	0.83	0.684	−54
Syrian Arab Republic	796	3,280	72	75	59	0.58	0.77	0.70	0.685	7
Viet Nam	390	2,070	69	93	64	0.51	0.73	0.83	0.688	37
Moldova, Rep. of	678	2,150	69	99	61	0.51	0.72	0.86	0.700	16

Exhibit I.A.2. (Continued)

Country Name (listed from lowest to highest HDI)	Real GDP Per Capita[a] (U.S.$) 2001	Real GDP Per Capita (PPP$) 2001	Life Expectancy at Birth (Years) 2001	Adult Literacy Rate[b] (Percent aged 15 and older) 2001	Combined First-, Second- and Third-Level Gross Enrollment Rate[c] (Percent) 2001	GDP Index[d]	Life Expectancy Index	Education Index	Human Development Index (HDI) Value	HDI Rank minus U.S.$ Per Capita GDP Rank[e]
Algeria	1,616	6,090	69	68	71	0.69	0.74	0.69	0.704	−17
Iran, Islamic Rep. of	1,714	6,000	70	77	64	0.68	0.75	0.73	0.719	−21
El Salvador	1,757	5,260	70	79	64	0.66	0.76	0.74	0.719	−21
China	878	4,020	71	86	64	0.62	0.76	0.79	0.721	11
Cape Verde	1,550	5,570	70	75	80	0.67	0.75	0.77	0.727	−7
Kyrgyzstan	417	2,750	68	97	79	0.55	0.72	0.91	0.727	42
Uzbekistan	512	2,460	69	99	76	0.53	0.74	0.91	0.729	32
Armenia	1,068	2,650	72	99	60	0.55	0.78	0.86	0.729	7
Sri Lanka	876	3,180	72	92	63	0.58	0.79	0.82	0.730	17
Occupied Palestinian Territories			72	89	77	0.56	0.79	0.85	0.731	8
Ecuador	1,155	3,280	71	92	72	0.58	0.76	0.85	0.731	3
Turkey	1,478	5,890	70	86	60	0.68	0.75	0.77	0.734	−27
Albania	2,873	3,680	73	85	69	0.60	0.81	0.80	0.735	15
Dominican Republic	2,077	7,020	67	84	74	0.71	0.70	0.81	0.737	−12
Grenada	3,579	6,740	65	94	63	0.70	0.67	0.84	0.738	−31
Guyana	942	4,690	63	99	84	0.64	0.64	0.94	0.740	21
Tunisia	2,562	6,390	73	72	76	0.69	0.79	0.73	0.740	−16
Jordan	1,639	3,870	71	90	77	0.61	0.76	0.86	0.743	−2
Azerbaijan	460	3,090	72	97	69	0.57	0.78	0.88	0.744	49
Georgia	499	2,560	73	100	69	0.54	0.81	0.89	0.746	47
Turkmenistan	1,587	4,320	67	98	81	0.63	0.69	0.92	0.748	5
Maldives	1,938	4,798	67	97	79	0.65	0.70	0.91	0.751	−3
Philippines	1,165	3,840	70	95	80	0.61	0.74	0.90	0.751	20
Paraguay	1,703	5,210	71	94	64	0.66	0.76	0.84	0.751	3
Lebanon	2,890	4,170	73	87	76	0.62	0.80	0.83	0.752	−15
Peru	2,311	4,570	69	90	83	0.64	0.74	0.88	0.752	−4
Fiji	2,763	4,850	69	93	76	0.65	0.74	0.88	0.754	−9
Saint Vincent and the Grenadines	2,737	5,330	74	89	58	0.66	0.81	0.79	0.755	−7
Oman		12,040	72	73	58	0.80	0.79	0.68	0.755	−35
Jamaica	2,171	3,720	76	87	74	0.60	0.84	0.83	0.757	3
Suriname	1,036	4,599	71	94	77	0.64	0.76	0.88	0.762	31

Kazakhstan	1,712	6,500	66	99	78	0.70	0.68	0.92	0.765	10
Ukraine	986	4,350	69	100	81	0.63	0.74	0.93	0.766	36
Thailand	2,853	6,400	69	96	72	0.69	0.73	0.88	0.768	−4
Saudi Arabia	6,614	13,330	72	77	58	0.82	0.78	0.71	0.769	−33
Romania	1,393	5,830	71	98	68	0.68	0.76	0.88	0.773	30
Saint Lucia	3,771	5,260	72	90	82	0.66	0.79	0.88	0.775	−12
Samoa (Western)	1,500	6,180	70	99	71	0.69	0.74	0.89	0.775	28
Venezuela	3,326	5,670	74	93	68	0.67	0.81	0.84	0.775	−6
Dominica	3,291	5,520	73	96	65	0.67	0.80	0.86	0.776	−3
Belize	3,189	5,690	72	93	76	0.67	0.78	0.88	0.776	0
Bosnia and Herzegovina	1,584	5,970	74	93	64	0.68	0.81	0.83	0.777	27
Brazil	4,633	7,360	68	87	95	0.72	0.71	0.90	0.777	−13
Colombia	2,277	7,040	72	92	71	0.71	0.78	0.85	0.779	16
Russian Federation	2,609	7,100	67	100	82	0.71	0.69	0.93	0.779	11
Mauritius	4,352	9,860	72	85	69	0.77	0.78	0.80	0.779	−7
Libyan Arab Jamahiriya		7,570	72	81	89	0.77	0.79	0.84	0.783	3
Macedonia, TFYR	2,417	6,110	73	94	70	0.72	0.81	0.86	0.784	16
Panama	3,243	5,750	74	92	75	0.69	0.82	0.86	0.788	7
Malaysia	4,708	8,750	73	88	72	0.68	0.80	0.83	0.790	−8
Bulgaria	1,630	6,890	71	99	77	0.75	0.76	0.91	0.795	32
Antigua and Barbuda	9,015	10,170	74	87	69	0.77	0.82	0.81	0.798	−19
Median	*1,515*	*4,350*	*69*	*87*	*69*	*0.63*	*0.74*	*0.83*	*0.731*	*3*

High-human development countries

Mexico	3,739	8,430	73	91	74	0.74	0.80	0.86	0.800	5
Trinidad and Tobago	5,553	9,100	72	98	67	0.75	0.78	0.88	0.802	−8
Belarus	1,493	7,620	70	100	86	0.72	0.74	0.95	0.804	46
Cuba		5,259	77	97	76	0.66	0.86	0.90	0.806	39
Saint Kitts and Nevis	6,535	11,300	70	98	70	0.79	0.75	0.89	0.808	−10
Latvia	2,816	7,730	71	100	86	0.73	0.76	0.95	0.811	21
Bahamas		16,270	67	96	74	0.85	0.70	0.88	0.812	−14
United Arab Emirates		20,530	74	77	67	0.89	0.82	0.73	0.816	−24
Croatia	5,355	9,170	74	98	68	0.75	0.82	0.88	0.818	2
Kuwait	13,345	18,700	76	82	54	0.87	0.86	0.73	0.820	−15
Lithuania	2,308	8,470	72	100	85	0.74	0.79	0.94	0.824	34
Qatar		19,844	72	82	81	0.88	0.78	0.82	0.826	−18
Chile	5,385	9,190	76	96	76	0.75	0.85	0.89	0.831	5
Costa Rica	3,900	9,460	78	96	66	0.76	0.88	0.86	0.832	16
Estonia	4,707	10,170	71	100	89	0.77	0.77	0.96	0.833	10
Uruguay	5,870	8,400	75	98	84	0.74	0.83	0.93	0.834	3
Slovakia	4,405	11,960	73	100	73	0.80	0.80	0.90	0.836	14

Exhibit I.A.2. (Continued)

Country Name (listed from lowest to highest HDI)	Real GDP Per Capita[a] (U.S.$) 2001	Real GDP Per Capita (PPP$) 2001	Life Expectancy at Birth (Years) 2001	Adult Literacy Rate[b] (Percent aged 15 and older) 2001	Combined First-, Second- and Third-Level Gross Enrollment Rate[c] (Percent) 2001	GDP Index[d]	Life Expectancy Index	Education Index	Human Development Index (HDI) Value	HDI Rank minus U.S.$ Per Capita GDP Rank[e]
Hungary	5,540	12,340	72	99	82	0.80	0.77	0.93	0.837	9
Bahrain	11,070	16,060	74	88	81	0.85	0.81	0.86	0.839	-3
Seychelles	5,939	17,030	73	91		0.86	0.80	0.87	0.840	6
Poland	3,716	9,450	74	100	88	0.76	0.81	0.95	0.841	26
Argentina	7,468	11,320	74	97	89	0.79	0.81	0.94	0.849	5
Malta	10,098	13,160	78	92	76	0.81	0.88	0.87	0.856	3
Czech Republic	5,583	14,720	75		76	0.83	0.83	0.91	0.861	13
Brunei Darussalam		19,210	76	92	83	0.88	0.85	0.89	0.872	-3
Korea, Rep. of	13,502	15,090	75	98	91	0.84	0.84	0.96	0.879	0
Slovenia	11,984	17,130	76	100	83	0.86	0.85	0.94	0.881	4
Singapore	27,118	22,680	78	93	75	0.91	0.88	0.87	0.884	-12
Barbados	8,610	15,560	77	100	89	0.84	0.87	0.96	0.888	11
Hong Kong, China (SAR)	24,505	24,850	80	94	63	0.92	0.91	0.83	0.889	-9
Cyprus	14,592	21,190	78	97	74	0.89	0.88	0.90	0.891	2
Greece	13,669	17,440	78	97	81	0.86	0.89	0.93	0.892	5
Portugal	13,109	18,150	76	93	93	0.87	0.85	0.97	0.896	9
Israel	16,576	19,790	79	95	90	0.88	0.90	0.93	0.905	3
Italy	21,144	24,670	79	99	82	0.92	0.89	0.93	0.916	0
New Zealand	18,425	19,160	78		99	0.88	0.88	0.99	0.917	2
Spain	17,595	20,150	79	98	92	0.89	0.90	0.97	0.918	4
Germany	32,813	25,350	78		89	0.92	0.88	0.96	0.921	-11
France	30,492	23,990	79		91	0.91	0.90	0.96	0.925	-3
Austria	33,172	26,730	78		92	0.93	0.89	0.97	0.929	-10
Luxembourg	56,382	53,780	78		73	1.00	0.88	0.90	0.930	-14
Finland	32,121	24,430	78		103	0.92	0.88	0.99	0.930	-6
United Kingdom	22,697	24,160	78		112	0.92	0.88	0.99	0.930	7
Ireland	29,401	32,410	77		91	0.96	0.86	0.96	0.930	3
Denmark	38,710	29,000	76		98	0.95	0.86	0.99	0.930	-7
Switzerland	47,064	28,100	79		88	0.94	0.90	0.95	0.932	-8
Japan	44,458	25,130	81		83	0.92	0.94	0.94	0.932	-6
Canada	23,080	27,130	79		94	0.94	0.90	0.97	0.937	11

United States	31,592	34,320		77	0.97	94	0.86	0.97	0.937	4
Belgium	31,218	25,520		79	0.92	107	0.89	0.99	0.937	7
Netherlands	31,333	27,190		78	0.94	99	0.89	0.99	0.938	7
Australia	24,203	25,370		79	0.92	114	0.90	0.99	0.939	14
Sweden	31,627	24,180		80	0.92	113	0.91	0.99	0.941	7
Iceland	32,060	29,990		80	0.95	91	0.91	0.96	0.942	7
Norway	38,298	29,620		79	0.95	98	0.90	0.99	0.944	4
Median	*14,131*	*19,160*	*f*	*77*	*0.88*	*86*	*0.86*	*0.94*	*0.884*	*4*

a The data are expressed in constant 1995 U.S. dollars.

b The Human Development Index is calculated using a value of 99 percent for countries for which adult literacy rates are higher than 99 percent or are not reporting because adult literacy is not a problem.

c Gross enrollment rate is the total enrollment rate in a specific level of education, regardless of a students' age. It is expressed as a percentage of the official school-age population corresponding to the same level of education in a given school year and can exceed 100 because the numerator, unlike the denominator, is not limited to youths of a given age. Early entry into school and grade repetition are among the reasons that the numerator may include youths outside the appropriate age range.

d The GDP index refers to the data expressed in international PPP dollars.

e Countries are first ranked from lowest to highest and given a number from 1 to 175 for both the human development index (HDI) and GDP per capita in U.S. dollars. This column subtracts the GDP per capita in U.S. dollars ranking from the human development ranking. A positive figure indicates that the HDI ranking is higher than the GDP per capita ranking, a negative figure indicates the opposite. Countries with missing U.S. dollar GDP data were inserted into the U.S. dollar GDP ranking using the PPP GDP ranking.

f There is no reliable median for the adult literacy rate in high-human development countries due to the lack of reporting, but insofar as the authorities are not reporting because literacy is high, then the true median is likely to be higher than would be expressed in the table.

Complete reference information can be found in the source publication.

Sources: United Nations Development Program, *Human Development Report 2003* (New York: Oxford University Press, 2003); World Bank, World Development Indicators, 2003.

Note I.A.1. The Evolution of Measures of Development

The traditional yardstick for development is per capita income measured in U.S. dollars. The World Bank labels countries with Gross National Income (GNI) per capita in 2002 less than U.S. $736 as "low-income," countries with GNI per capita in 2002 greater than U.S. $9,075 as "high-income," and all countries in between as "middle-income." It would thus be traditional to call the low- and middle-income groups "less developed countries" and the high-income group "more developed countries."

The first column of Exhibit I.A.2 shows Gross Domestic Product (GDP) per capita in U.S. dollars. GDP is defined as the total final outputs of goods and services (value-added) produced within a country's territory by residents and nonresidents. GNI equals GDP plus factor incomes accruing to residents from abroad, less the income earned in the domestic economy accruing to nonresidents. GNI per capita is the correct measure of income per head, but GDP per capita is often easier to estimate.

Per capita income is an average over all the residents of a country, and as such can obscure important regional differences. For example, according to an estimate for 1975, per capita income in the southeast region of Brazil was double that in the northeast region even after correcting for differences in cost of living (World Bank 1991, p. 41). This problem extends to all attempts to measure development at the national level. This practice has persisted nevertheless because many countries lack reliable regional-level data and because most crucial policy decisions are made at the national level.

In the 1970s various attempts were initiated to correct, supplement, or replace per capita income in U.S. dollars as a measure of development. These attempts were motivated by three major problems with this measure:

1. As is obvious to anyone who has spent time in poor countries, the purchasing power of U.S. dollars is much greater there than in rich countries. GDP per capita in U.S. dollars therefore gives an exaggerated estimate of the differences in average standards of living between poor and rich countries.

2. Per capita GDP is a "one dollar, one vote" average. Even if the majority of the population is very poor, a rich minority can raise per capita GDP to a relatively high level.

3. Per capita GDP does not directly measure well-being. Populations in countries with similar per capita GDPs may differ widely in average levels of health, for example.

To understand the first problem it is helpful to start by showing why we might expect the purchasing power of a dollar to be *equal* across countries. Consider the dollar cost of purchasing commodity i in the United States versus country j. Suppose the price of commodity i in the United States equals P_i^{US}, measured in U.S. dollars, the price of commodity i in country j equals P_i^j, measured in the currency of country j, and the exchange rate equals e, measured in U.S. dollars per unit of currency of country j. Then the dollar cost of purchasing commodity i is the same in the United States and in country j if

$$P_i^{US} = eP_i^j. \tag{1}$$

Equation (1) is known as the *law of one price*. Why should we expect this "law" to hold? Suppose it does not. If $P_i^{US} > eP_i^j$, then one could buy commodity i in country j, resell it in the United States, and make a guaranteed profit. This process, known as *international commodity arbitrage*, will bid up the price of commodity i in country j and bid down the price of commodity i in the United States until equation (1) holds. International commodity arbitrage also rules out $P_i^{US} < eP_i^j$.

Implicit in the preceding argument is the assumption that international trade is perfectly free: there are no transport costs, tariffs, or other trade barriers. Since this assumption does not hold in the real world, dollar prices may in fact differ across countries. In particular, most services have extremely high transportation costs. If haircuts are cheaper in country j than in the United States, it is impossible for an arbitrageur to buy haircuts in country j and resell them in the United States, and extremely expensive for a consumer to fly from the United States to country j to get a cheap haircut. Housing and local transportation are similar to haircuts in this regard, though many business services such as accounting can be cheaply transported electronically. If the dollar prices of services are much lower in poor countries, while the dollar prices of goods are kept close across countries by international commodity arbitrage, than the overall cost of a standardized basket of goods and services will be lower in poor countries.

Selection I.A.1 by Bhagwati gives two explanations for why nontraded services should be cheaper in poor countries. Both explanations essentially boil down to the following: wages are lower in poor countries, labor is a major input to production of services, and technology for producing services does not differ dramatically across countries, so that lower wages translate into lower costs of production.

In the 1970s the International Comparison Project (ICP) under the direction of Kravis, Heston, and Summers (1982) collected price data in 34 countries. As expected, the prices of services relative to goods tended to rise with per capita income, as shown in Figure 1 and Table 1 of the Bhagwati selection. Using a rather involved procedure described fully in their book, Kravis, Heston, and Summers went on estimate per capita GDP for all 34 countries measured in "international dollars" whose purchasing power is, in theory, the same everywhere. In Exhibit I.A.3 the ratio of per capita GDP measured in international dollars to per capita GDP measured in U.S. dollars, labeled the "exchange-rate-deviation index," is plotted against per capita GDP in international dollars (measured relative to the United States). There is a strong tendency for the exchange-rate-deviation index to rise as "real per capita GDP" falls. In other words, the poorer the country, the more its per capita GDP measured by exchange-rate conversion of local currency into U.S. dollars tends to underestimate the average purchasing power of its citizens relative to U.S. citizens.

In Exhibit I.A.2 the work of the ICP has been extended to produce estimates of 2001 per capita GDP in international dollars (also known as Purchasing Power Parity or PPP dollars) for all 175 countries in the Exhibit. We can illustrate the large difference that adjustment for purchasing power can make with an admittedly extreme example. The country with the highest per capita GDP in U.S. dollars is Luxembourg and the country with the lowest per capita GDP in U.S. dollars is the Democratic Republic of the Congo. The ratio of their U.S. dollar per capita GDPs is \$56,382/\$85 = 663. In contrast, the ratio of their PPP dollar per capita GDPs is \$53,780/\$680 = 79, which is smaller by a factor of 8. We can see from Exhibit I.A.3 that a more typical correction factor when comparing a high-income to a low-income country would be about 3.

Measuring per capita GDP in PPP dollars does not change the fact that it is an average over the entire population and thus does not address the second problem with using per capita GDP as a measure of development described above. If we think a major goal of development is reduction of poverty, we might want to supplement (if not replace) per capita GDP with a measure of the extent of poverty. Attempts to develop internationally comparable "poverty lines" and measure the extent of poverty across countries are described in Selection I.A.2 by the World Bank. In Exhibit I.A.4 the poverty lines of one PPP dollar a day and two PPP dollars a day are used, and estimates of the percentage of each country's population living below the respective poverty lines are given. It is clear that averages do indeed conceal a great deal. For example, the 2001 per capita GDPs measured in PPP dollars for Ghana and Vietnam are \$2,250 and \$2,070, respectively, but 44.8 percent of Ghana's population was living on less than one PPP dollar a day compared to only 17.7 percent of Vietnam's population.

Just as one can find countries that have similar average incomes but differ greatly in the extent of poverty, so one can find countries with similar average incomes that differ greatly in life expectancy and literacy. The 2001 per capita GDPs measured in PPP dollars for

Guatemala and Sri Lanka are $4,400 and $3,180, respectively, yet Guatemalan life expectancy at birth was only 65 years and 69 percent of Guatemalan adults were literate, compared to Sri Lankan life expectancy of 72 years and adult literacy of 92 percent. This kind of observation motivated some in the 1970s to advocate discarding income-based measures of development altogether in favor of direct measurement of the extent to which the "basic needs" of the population were being met. A major effort in this direction was development of the Physical Quality of Life Index or PQLI (Morris 1979). This index was based on a country's life expectancy, infant mortality rate, and literacy rate. The successor to the PQLI is the Human Development Index (HDI) devised by the United Nations Development Program. As shown in Exhibit I.A.1, the HDI uses life expectancy as its only indicator of health rather than including the infant mortality rate as does the PQLI. The HDI also adds school enrollment rates to the literacy rate to form a weighted index of educational attainment that is averaged into the overall index. The most important difference between the HDI and the PQLI, however, is that the HDI gives a one-third weight to an index based on per capita GDP measured in PPP dollars, although the index uses the logarithm of income to account for diminishing marginal utility (another dollar of income is valued much less by someone earning $100,000 annually than by someone earning $1,000). The HDI is thus intended to be a more comprehensive measure of development than either the PQLI or per capita income.

Exhibit I.A.2 ranks 175 countries from lowest to highest 2001 HDI values, and shows the differences between their rankings by per capita GDP measured in U.S. dollars and their HDI rankings. Many of the biggest positive differences (countries ranked much higher by HDI than by per capita income) are for socialist or formerly socialist countries, and many of the biggest negative differences (countries ranked much higher by per capita income than by HDI) are for countries that are major oil exporters. The former observation can be partly explained by the more equal distribution of income in these countries. If one takes $1,000 annually from someone earning $100,000 and gives it to someone earning $1,000, the health of the first person is unlikely to suffer, while the health of the second person may improve significantly. However, it is likely that the more important reason the socialist and formerly socialist countries have high HDI values relative to their per capita incomes is that their governments both made provision of educational and health services a very high priority and commanded the share of national resources needed to deliver these services. The latter observation that major oil exporters have low HDI values relative to their per capita incomes can be partly explained by the fact that a major mineral discovery or sharp increase in the price of a mineral (such as the quadrupling of the price of oil that occurred during 1973–74) can make a country wealthy almost literally overnight, while it takes time for that higher income to generate greater health and educational attainment. A more recent and ominous cause for countries to be ranked much lower by HDI than by per capita income is the AIDS crisis, which has sharply reduced life expectancy in some sub-Saharan African countries, as reported in Selection IV.B.3.

One should, however, not let individual cases exaggerate the differences in ranking between per capita GDP in U.S. dollars and the Human Development Index: the correlation coefficient between the two rankings is 0.92.

References

Kravis, Irving B., Alan Heston, and Robert Summers. 1982. *World Product and Income: International Comparisons of Real Gross Product* (Baltimore: Johns Hopkins University Press).

Morris, Morris David. 1979. *Measuring the Condition of the World's Poor: The Physical Quality of Life Index* (New York: Pergamon Press).

World Bank. 1991. *World Development Report 1991* (New York: Oxford University Press).

Exhibit I.A.3. Exchange-Rate-Deviation Index in Relation to Real GDP Per Capita, Thirty-four Countries, 1975

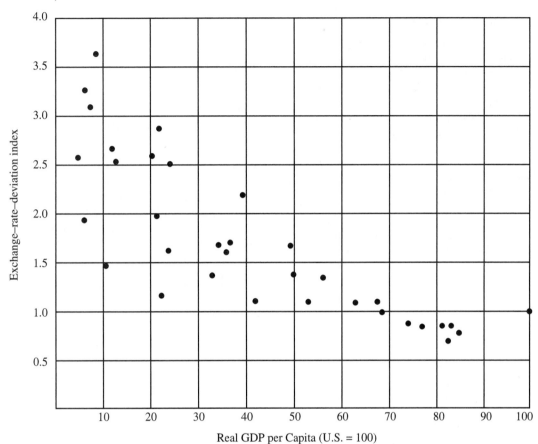

Real GDP per Capita (U.S. = 100)

Source: Kravis, Irving B., Alan Heston, and Robert Summers, *World Product and Income: International Comparisons of Real Gross Product* (Baltimore: Johns Hopkins University Press, 1982), p. 11.

Selection I.A.1. Why Are Services Cheaper in the Poor Countries?*

I. The Empirical Phenomenon

In their important work on international comparisons of national incomes and of comparative price structure, Kravis, Heston and Summers (1982, p. 8) have noted that "services are much cheaper in the relative price structure of a typical poor country than in that of a rich country."

This phenomenon has been documented now fairly systematically by the data, gathered under their guiding hand, of the United Nations International Comparison (ICP) which covers 34 countries. Table 1 reproduced from their work (1982), and Fig. 1 based on rows 3 and 11–13, indeed show this tendency for the relationship between relative service prices and real per capita GDP in this Kravis–Heston–Summers 34-country 6-group sample. The tendency is strongly evident except for the intermediate groups III and IV.

II. The Kravis–Heston–Summers Explanation: International Productivity Differences

An explanation of this phenomenon was provided by Kravis–Heston–Summers as follows:

As a first approximation it may be assumed for purposes of explaining the model that the prices of traded goods, mainly commodities, are the same in different countries. With similar prices for traded goods in all countries, wages in the industries producing traded goods will differ from country to country according to differences in productivity–a standard conclusion of Ricardian trade theory. In each country the wage level established in the traded goods industries will determine wages in the industries producing nontraded goods, mainly services. Because international productivity differences are smaller for such industries, the low wages established in poor countries in the low-productivity traded goods industries will apply also to the not-so-low productivity service and other nontraded goods industries. The consequences will be low prices in low-income countries for services and other nontraded goods (1982, p. 21).

This is an interesting explanation and indeed is to be found also in Balassa (1964) and Samuelson (1964) and, as Kravis has pointed out to me, in a splendid early analysis in Harrod (1933, chap. IV). Kravis et al. explore it further and insightfully. But it does raise, within the parameters of its own approach, the question whether we cannot formalise

it in general equilibrium, also extending the formalisation beyond the excessively limiting Ricardian framework of a single factor, labour, so that we get closer to a more realistic and meaningful formulation.

This can indeed be done, drawing on two elements of general-equilibrium analysis as practised by international trade theorists: (i) the use of the Lerner diagrammatic technique relating goods to factor prices, as used to advantage in analysing technical change in the 2-good case by Findlay and Grubert (1959) and the pattern of comparative advantage and the Heckscher–Ohlin theorem in the many-good case by Bhagwati (1972) and Deardorff (1979); and (ii) the notion that we can go beyond the single-factor Ricardian theory by taking multifactor production functions with Hicks-neutral productivity differences internationally, this generalisation having been proposed in Bhagwati (1964).[1]

Then, to formalise the Kravis–Heston–Summers argument in a general equilibrium, 2-factor model, take Fig. 2. X and Y are two "traded" commodities; S is the non-traded service. Suffixes R and P refer to the Rich and Poor countries respectively. Assume the standard restrictions on constant-returns-to-scale production functions in each activity. Putting a wage-rental price line, ω, tangent to the corresponding isoquants then defines, as shown by Lerner, the corresponding goods price vector. Evidently, $\bar{X}_R$ will exchange for $\bar{Y}_R$ and each, in turn, for $\bar{S}_R$, in the Rich country.[2]

The Kravis–Heston–Summers argument assumes that in the Poor country, if the same traded-goods prices prevail due to free trade and productivity is indeed lower by λ in the traded sector, $\lambda\bar{X}_P$, exchanges for $\lambda\bar{Y}_P$ yielding, of course, the same $X{:}Y$ price ratio. But the service sector is equally productive as in the Rich country. Hence, $\lambda\bar{X}_P$ exchanges for $\lambda\bar{Y}_P$ but for $\bar{S}_P$. Hence, trade will link the Rich and the Poor countries but lead to $\bar{S}_R = \lambda\bar{S}_P$ $(\lambda > 1)$, yielding therefore the observed

---

*From Jagdish N. Bhagwati, "Why Are Services Cheaper in the Poor Countries?" *Economic Journal* 94 (June 1984): 279–285. Reprinted by permission.

[1]Thus, if I and II are countries, and X and Y are two activities using factors K and L, let

$$X^{\mathrm{I}} = \phi^{\mathrm{I}}(K_x, L_x) \text{ and } X^{\mathrm{II}} = \lambda\phi^{\mathrm{I}}(K_x, L_x).$$

If $\lambda > \mathrm{I}$, country II has Ricardian-style neutral productivity advantage in producing good X. The Ricardian theory of comparative advantage is then reformulated in Bhagwati (1964) in terms of comparative λ differences across trading countries.

[2]Evidently, since they are tangent to the same factor price line, $P_x\bar{X}_R = P_y\bar{Y}_R = P_s\bar{S}_R (= \omega OQ$ worth of wages). Therefore $p_x/p_y = \bar{Y}_R/\bar{X}_R$, etc.

Table 1. Nominal and Real per Capita Absorption of GDP in the Form of Services and Commodities, and Price Indexes, by Real per Capita GDP Group, 1975

	Income group					
	I	II	III	IV	V	VI
1. Number of countries	8	6	6	4	9	1
Real GDP per capita (U.S. = 100)						
2. Range	0–14.9	15–29.9	30–44.9	45–59.9	60–89.9	90 and over
3. Mean	9.01	23.1	37.3	52.4	76.0	100.0
Per capita expenditures converted at exchange rate						
4. GDP (U.S. = 100)	3.7	12.1	24.2	38.7	82.3	100.0
5. Commodities (U.S. = 100)	5.0	15.2	31.1	50.6	92.7	100.0
6. Services (U.S. = 100)	2.0	8.1	15.5	23.4	69.1	100.0
7. Share of services	22.2	28.4	27.4	25.6	36.8	43.9
Per capita quantity indexes (based on PPP-conversion of expenditures)						
8. Commodities (U.S. = 100)	8.8	23.4	37.5	53.8	77.4	100.0
9. Services (U.S. = 100)	9.4	22.7	37.0	49.2	73.0	100.0
10. Share of services	33.8	31.7	31.8	30.3	31.2	32.3
Price indexes (U.S. = 100)						
11. GDP	40.6	51.7	64.7	73.5	107.5	100.0
12. Commodities	57.2	65.9	83.1	94.0	119.0	100.0
13. Services	20.7	34.1	41.2	46.3	94.6	100.0
14. 13/12	0.36	0.52	0.49	0.49	0.79	1.00

Line 2 $\dfrac{\text{(expenditure in domestic currency/population)} \div \text{purchasing power parity}}{\text{GDP in U.S./U.S. population}} \times 100.$

Line 3 Simple average of values within each income class.

Line 4 $\dfrac{\text{(expenditures in domestic currency/population)} \div \text{exchange rate}}{\text{GDP in U.S./U.S. population}} \times 100.$

Lines 6, 7, 9, 10, and 13 include public consumption as well household expenditures.

Lines 11–13 purchasing power parity $\div$ exchange rate $\times$ 100.

Source: Kravis–Heston–Summers (1982).

phenomenon that the relative price of the service sector is lower in the Poor country.

This theoretical, general-equilibrium[3] formulation of the Kravis–Heston–Summers argument is based on a more satisfactory notion of "productivity" advantage than simply labour productivity and is fully rigorous. But it does also imply at least two other unrealistic consequences: that the wage-

[3]A conventional demand side can be readily added to the model to close it. Evidently, the configuration of demand and factor endowments must be such that, within each country, the wage-rental ratio is the same, as in the argument formalised via Fig. 1. With presumably the relative endowment of labour higher in the poor countries, this implies that the argument permits demand there to be skewed more in favour of services. Line 10 in Table 1, and private conversation with Kravis, suggest however that the share of services in total expenditure is not differentially greater in the poor countries. Demand differences have been discussed also by Samuelson (1964) in the context of the purchasing power parity doctrine.

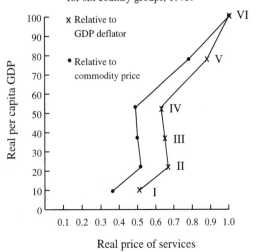

Figure 1. Relative price of services and per capita GDP for six country groups, 1975.

Figure 2

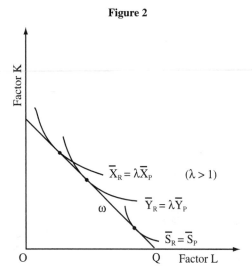

rental ratio, ω, is equal across countries and that K/L ratios are also equal across countries within each activity. One *could* weaken some of these implications by, for example, parametrically shifting the $\bar{X}$ and $\bar{Y}$ isoquants for the Poor country to the right, to allow for the observed fact that Poor countries seem to have lower K/L ratios in each activity than Rich countries. But that would be surely an *ad hoc* procedure.

Besides, it is not evident to me at all that the non-traded sectors do have "productivity" parity in the proper theoretical sense (as against simply looking at labour productivity differences) whereas the traded sectors are technologically inferior, in the Poor countries relative to the Rich countries. It is arguable that technology diffuses fairly substantially through sale of technology, direct investment, etc. in the traded sectors and that this implies that the λ parameter in Fig. 2 is not important. On the other hand, services today are not by any means technically stagnant and hence there is probably a not insignificant λ in the services sector in favour of the Rich countries.

Can we therefore build an explanation of the observed phenomenon of real price of services being lower in Poor countries *without* resorting to a particular specification of comparative-productivity ranking between countries in their traded (commodity) and non-traded (services) sectors, while *also* explaining the *labour*-productivity rankings? I believe it is indeed possible to do so, as shown immediately below. In fact, I propose to develop an explanation which, while altogether ignoring differential ("true") productivity differences across sectors between countries, manages to "explain"

simultaneously a number of related empirical observations in Kravis, Heston, and Summers (1982) as also the fact that groups III and IV in Table 1 do not conform to the central phenomenon being discussed in this paper.

III. An Alternative Explanation

Consider then the same basic model as in Fig. 1. But now assume, as in Fig. 3, that the Rich and Poor countries have identical production functions in each sector: "productivity" differences are thus assumed to be non-existent. Let ω_R be the wage–rental ratio obtaining in the Rich country, implying that $\bar{X}_R$ exchanges for $\bar{Y}_R$ for $\bar{S}_R$.

If, however, the Poor country were to have this wage–rental ratio, its overall endowment ratio $(\bar{K}/\bar{L})_P$ for all employment would have to be spanned by OA and OC, with AOC (not drawn) constituting the McKenzie–Chipman diversification cone. But if, as in Fig. 3, $(\bar{K}/\bar{L})_P$ lies outside this diversification cone, ω_R is not feasible and the Poor country, being so abundantly endowed with labour, would have to have a *lower* wage–rental ratio such as ω_P. The consequence is that production of X is no longer possible at the goods price ratio $\bar{X}_R = \bar{Y}_R$ given from the Rich country, whereas $\bar{Y}_P$ will now exchange, *not* for $\bar{S}_P$ but for $\bar{S}_P$, the choice of K/L ratios being OE and OD respectively in the Poor country. The new diversification cone defined by EOD, of course, spans $(\bar{K}/\bar{L})_P$. This immediately means that the relative price of services is cheaper in the Poor country, since $\bar{S}_P > \bar{S}_P$.

But, aside from yielding the central phenomenon to be explained, my construct also shows that one may find that labour productivity in services

Figure 3

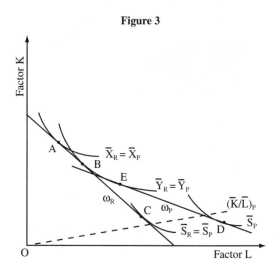

relative to labour productivity in commodities is higher in consequence in the Poor country. For, at ω_P relative to ω_R, these are *two* effects lowering K/L ratio in commodities (and hence lowering the labour productivity in them) whereas there is only *one* effect lowering it in services. The two effects in commodities are: (i) the elimination of X, the most K-intensive good, from production; and (ii) the substitution effect from B to E in Y-production. The one effect in services is simply the corresponding substitution effect from C to D. . . .

It is, in fact, remarkable that this is precisely what Kravis, Heston, and Summers (1982) report:

Kuznets' own work relating first to 1950 and later to 1960 and the independent work of Chenery and Syrquin (1975) summarizing the period 1950–70 show clearly that the productivity of the service sector relative to the commodity sector tends to be inversely related to the income level of the country. This finding is confirmed when sectoral productivity indexes, circa 1975 are regressed against real per capita GDP for the 20 ICP Phase III countries for which data for such indices were available. In the following regression, productivity in the service industries (SP) relative to productivity in the commodity industries (CP) of each country is taken as the dependent variable and the ICP estimate of 1975 real per capita GDP (r) is the independent variable (standard errors are shown in parenthesis):

$$\ln(SP/CP) = 7.3988 - 0.3100 \ln r \quad \bar{R}^2 = 0.618$$
$$(0.4349) \ (0.0550) \quad \text{S.E.E.} = 0.198$$
$$\text{n} = 20$$

The coefficient of r is negative and highly significant. The higher the country's per capita income, the lower its service sector productivity relative to its commodity sector productivity.

My explanation also implies that, as $\bar{K}/\bar{L}$ endowment ratio rises, and therefore GDP per capita increases, the wage–rental ratio would tend to rise and hence for K/L ratios in each sector to rise. I.e., in Fig. 3, the (K/L) ratio at OE in the Poor country is exceeded by those at OB and OA in the Rich country; also, that at OD is exceeded by that at OC. This again is observed statistically by Kravis, Heston, and Summers (see Table 2).

Finally, it is clear that these effects, both the central phenomenon of the relative service decline with GDP per capita and the associated comparative labour productivity observations between sectors and within sectors across countries, depend in my construct on the fact that, for the pair of countries being compared, their comparative factor endowments are sufficiently apart so as not to permit them to be at the same wage–rental ratio and hence to be in the same diversification cone. If therefore

Table 2. Capital/Labour Ratios*

Income group	Commodities	Services
I	4.39	2.48
II	9.24	5.16
III	5.64	6.21
IV	6.91	6.32
V	16.27	9.44
VI	21.94	10.96

*$1000 worth of capital per man-year.

two countries or groups of countries are close together, in GDP per capita, we would expect that the several correlative phenomena explained in this paper would also be correspondingly weak.

And this seems more or less to be so. Thus, if we examine Table 2, it is evident that the capital/labour ratios in the two "sectors" (commodities and services) are not substantially changed between country groups II–IV. This would suggest that these lie more or less within the same diversification cone and hence we would not expect to observe substantial change in the relative price of services within the range of per capita GDP variation defined by these groups. It is therefore somewhat remarkable that, as Table 1 and Fig. 1 show, the relative price of services is indeed fairly constant over groups II–IV! My explanation, therefore, seems yet additionally compelling.[4]

[4]Kravis has kindly drawn my attention to Kravis and Lipsey (1983) where a "factor proportions" explanation, consonant with that advanced in this paper, is stated.

References

Balassa, B. (1964). "The purchasing-power parity doctrine: a reappraisal." *Journal of Political Economy,* vol. 72 (December), pp. 584–96.

Bhagwati, J. N. (1964). "The pure theory of international trade: a survey." Economic Journal, vol. 74 (March), pp. 1–84.

——— (1972). "The Heckscher–Ohlin theorem in the multi-commodity case." *Journal of Political Economy,* vol. 80 (September/October), pp. 1052–5.

Chenery, H. and Syrquin, M. (1975). *Patterns of Development 1950–1970.* London: Oxford University Press.

Deardorff, A. (1979). "Weak links in the chain of comparative advantage." *Journal of International Economics,* vol. 9 (May), pp. 197–209.

Findlay, R. and Grubert, H. (1959). "Factor intensities, technological progress and the terms of trade." *Oxford Economic Papers,* vol. 11 (March), pp. 111–21.

Harrod, R. F. (1933). *International Economics.* Cambridge Economic Handbooks. London: Nisbet & Cambridge University Press.

Kravis, I., Heston, A., and Summers, R. (1982). "The share of services in economic growth" (mimeograph). In *Global Econometrics: Essays in Honor of Lawrence R. Klein* (ed. F. G. Adams and Bert Hickman). Cambridge: MIT Press.

Kravis, I. and Lipsey, R. (1983). "Toward an explanation of national price levels." Princeton Studies in International Finance, No. 52.

Samuelson, P. A. (1964). "Theoretical notes on trade problems." *The Review of Economics and Statistics,* vol. 46 (May), pp. 145–54.

Comment I.A.1. The Productivity and Factor Proportions Explanations Again

The preceding selection by Bhagwati uses graphical tools from international trade theory to present two explanations of why services are cheaper relative to commodities in poor than in rich countries, the first based on differences between productivity in rich and poor countries and the second based on differences between factor proportions in rich and poor countries. The intuition behind the productivity difference explanation is given in the quotation at the beginning of the selection. No comparable intuition is given for the factor proportions explanation, however, so we provide the following. Suppose the fact that poor countries have less physical capital per worker than rich countries leads to a higher cost of capital relative to labor in poor countries than in rich countries. Suppose further that commodities use more capital relative to labor in production than do services, as Table 2 of the selection indicates. One then expects commodities to be produced more expensively relative to services in poor than in rich countries. If prices reflect costs of production, then services will be cheaper relative to commodities in poor than in rich countries.

Exhibit I.A.4. Basic Data

Country Name (listed from lowest to highest HDI)	Population (Thousands) 2000	Surface Area (Square Kilometers)	Population Density (Per Square Kilometer) 2000	Per Capita Income Growth Rates:[a] 1960–1980	1980–2000	Poverty Survey Year	Percent of Population Living Under $1 per Day[b]	Percent of Population Living Under $2 per Day[b]	Average Years of Education[c] 1999	Children Under Age 5 Mortality Rate (Per 1,000 live births) 2000
Low-human development countries										
Sierra Leone	5,031	71,740	70	-1.8	-1.3	1989	57.0	74.5	2.0	316
Niger	10,832	1,267,000	9	0.1	1.1	1995	61.4	85.3	0.8	270
Burkina Faso	11,274	274,000	41	-0.2	0.1	1994	61.2	85.8		198
Mali	10,840	1,240,190	9	1.7	-1.8	1994	72.8	90.6	0.8	233
Burundi	6,807	27,830	265	-1.7	-0.4	1998	58.4	89.2		190
Mozambique	17,691	801,590	23	1.0	-0.1	1996	37.9	78.4	1.2	200
Ethiopia	64,298	1,104,300	64	-1.0		1999–2000	81.9	98.4		174
Central African Republic	3,717	622,980	6	-1.5		1993	66.6	84.0	2.1	180
Congo, Dem. Rep. of the	50,948	2,344,860	22		2.1				3.2	205
Guinea-Bissau	1,199	36,120	43	0.2	-2.9					215
Chad	7,694	1,284,000	6	1.5						200
Angola	13,134	1,246,700	11	-1.2						260
Zambia	10,089	752,610	14	0.1	-1.6	1998	63.7	87.4	5.4	202
Malawi	10,311	118,480	110	2.2	0.9	1997–1998	41.7	76.1	2.6	188
Côte d'Ivoire	16,013	322,460	50	2.2	-1.5	1995	12.3	49.4		173
Tanzania, U. Rep. of	33,696	945,090	38	2.3	-1.1	1993	19.9	59.7		165
Benin	6,272	112,620	57	-0.3	1.0				2.1	160
Rwanda	7,709	26,340	345	0.8	-1.0	1983–1985	35.7	84.6	2.0	187
Guinea	7,415	245,860	30	-0.3	0.4					175
Senegal	9,530	196,720	49	-1.1	0.5	1995	26.3	67.8	2.2	139
Eritrea	4,097	117,600	41							114
Mauritania	2,665	1,025,520	3	3.0		1995	28.6	68.7		183
Djibouti	632	23,200	27							146
Nigeria	126,910	923,770	139	0.8	-2.7	1997	70.2	90.8		184
Gambia	1,303	11,300	130	1.7	-0.2	1998	59.3	82.9	1.9	128
Haiti	7,959	27,750	289						2.7	125
Madagascar	15,523	587,040	27	-0.7	-1.3	1999	49.1	83.3		139
Yemen	17,507	527,970	33			1998	15.7	45.2		117
Uganda	22,210	241,040	113	-1.2	3.8	1996	82.2	96.4	2.9	127
Kenya	30,092	580,370	53	2.2	0.0	1997	23.0	58.6	4.0	120
Zimbabwe	12,627	390,760	33	3.8	-0.3	1990–1991	36.0	64.2	4.9	117
Pakistan	138,080	796,100	179	3.0	2.8	1998	13.4	65.6	2.5	110

Exhibit I.A.4. (Continued)

Country Name (listed from lowest to highest HDI)	Population (Thousands) 2000	Surface Area (Square Kilometers)	Population Density (Per Square Kilometer) 2000	Per Capita Income Growth Rates:[a] 1960–1980	Per Capita Income Growth Rates:[a] 1980–2000	Survey Year	Poverty: Percent of Population Living Under $1 per Day[b]	Poverty: Percent of Population Living Under $2 per Day[b]	Average Years of Education[c] 1999	Children Under Age 5 Mortality Rate (Per 1,000 live births) 2000
Nepal	23,043	147,180	161	0.5	2.6	1995	37.7	82.5	1.9	95
Cameroon	14,876	475,440	32	1.2	-0.2	1996	33.4	64.4	3.2	154
Median	*10,836*	*433,100*	*41*	*0.5*	*-0.2*		*41.7*	*82.5*	*2.2*	*175*
Medium-human development countries										
Togo	4,527	56,790	83	2.2	-2.3				2.8	142
Congo	3,018	342,000	9	5.8	0.7				4.7	108
Bangladesh	131,050	144,000	1,007	-0.4	2.7	2000	36.0	82.8	2.4	82
Sudan	31,095	2,505,810	13						1.9	108
Lesotho	2,035	30,350	67	3.3	0.8	1993	43.1	65.7	4.5	133
Bhutan	805	47,000	17							100
Lao People's Dem. Rep.	5,279	236,800	23			1997–1998	26.3	73.2		128
Comoros	558	2,230	250	0.4	-1.4					82
Swaziland	1,045	17,360	61						5.7	142
Papua New Guinea	5,130	462,840	11	1.8					2.4	95
Myanmar	47,749	676,580	73						2.4	110
Cambodia	12,021	181,040	68							135
Ghana	19,306	238,540	85	1.6	0.6	1999	44.8	78.5	4.0	102
Vanuatu	197	12,190	16							44
India	1,015,923	3,287,260	342	1.6	3.8	1999–2000	34.7	79.9	4.8	95
Morocco	28,705	446,550	64	4.1	1.1	1999	2.0	14.3		46
Botswana	1,675	581,730	3	6.4		1993	23.5	50.1	5.4	101
Namibia	1,757	824,290	2			1993	34.9	55.8		69
Solomon Islands	419	28,900	15							25
Sao Tome and Principe	148	960	154							75
Nicaragua	5,071	130,000	42	0.3	-2.7	1998	82.3	94.5	4.4	45
Egypt	63,976	1,001,450	64	2.5	2.7	2000	3.1	43.9	5.1	45
Guatemala	11,385	108,890	105	2.7	-0.2	2000	16.0	37.4	3.1	59
Gabon	1,230	267,670	5	5.5	-0.4					90
Mongolia	2,398	1,566,500	2			1995	13.9	50.0		78
Equatorial Guinea	457	28,050	16							156
Honduras	6,417	112,090	57	1.5	-0.5	1998	23.8	44.4	4.1	40
Bolivia	8,329	1,098,580	8	1.3	-0.6	1999	14.4	34.3	5.5	80

Tajikistan	6,193	143,100	44	3.5	3.3	1998	10.3	50.8	4.7	117
Indonesia	206,265	1,904,570	114	2.4	-0.3	2000	7.2	55.4	7.9	48
South Africa	42,801	1,221,040	35	3.8	1.6	1995	2.0	14.5	5.7	70
Syrian Arab Republic	16,189	185,180	88				17.7	63.7		29
Viet Nam	78,523	331,690	241	2.9	0.1	1998	22.0	63.7		34
Moldova, Rep. of	4,278	33,850	130	2.1	2.0	2001	2.0	15.1		33
Algeria	30,385	2,381,740	13	1.1	0.3	1995	2.0	7.3	4.7	50
Iran, Islamic Rep. of	63,664	1,648,200	39	2.2	6.3	1998	21.4	45.0	4.7	44
El Salvador	6,276	21,040	303	3.3	3.6	1997	16.1	47.3	4.5	40
China	1,262,460	9,598,050	135			2000			4.2	40
Cape Verde	435	4,030	108				2.0	34.1		40
Kyrgyzstan	4,915	199,900	26			2000	19.1	44.2	5.7	66
Uzbekistan	24,746	447,400	60			1998	12.8	49.0		66
Armenia	3,112	29,800	135			1998	6.6			38
Sri Lanka	18,467	65,610	286	1.5	3.1	1995–1996		45.4	6.1	19
Occupied Palestinian Territories	2,966									26
Ecuador	12,646	283,560	46	3.7	-1.0	1995	20.2	52.3	5.2	32
Turkey	67,420	774,820	85	2.3	2.3	2000	2.0	10.3	4.8	43
Albania	3,134	28,750	114						6.5	26
Dominican Republic	8,373	48,730	173	2.7	3.0	1998	2.0	2.0		48
Grenada	99	340	291		3.6					26
Guyana	761	214,970	4	2.0		1998	2.0	6.1	6.0	74
Tunisia	9,564	163,610	62	2.9	2.2	1995	2.0	10.0	4.2	29
Jordan	4,887	89,210	55		-0.2	1997	2.0	7.4	7.4	34
Azerbaijan	8,049	86,600	93			2001	3.7	9.1		97
Georgia	5,262	69,700	77			1998	2.0	12.4		29
Turkmenistan	5,285	488,100	11			1998	12.1	44.0		88
Maldives	274	300	913							80
Philippines	76,627	300,000	257	2.5	0.2	2000	14.6	46.4	7.6	40
Paraguay	5,270	406,750	14	3.1	0.2	1998	19.5	49.3	5.7	31
Lebanon	4,328	10,400	423							32
Peru	25,939	1,285,220	20	2.1	-0.3	1996	15.5	41.4	7.3	40
Fiji	812	18,270	44	2.6					8.0	22
Saint Vincent and the Grenadines	115	390	295		4.1					20
Oman	2,410	309,500	8							14
Jamaica	2,573	10,990	238	1.1	0.3	2000	2.0	13.3	5.2	20
Suriname	417	163,270	3							33
Kazakhstan	15,059	2,724,900	6			1996	1.5	15.3		92
Ukraine	49,501	603,700	85			1999	2.9	45.7		20
Thailand	60,728	513,120	119	4.6	4.6	2000	2.0	32.5	6.1	29

Exhibit I.A.4. (Continued)

Country Name (listed from lowest to highest HDI)	Population (Thousands) 2000	Surface Area (Square Kilometers)	Population Density (Per Square Kilometer) 2000	Per Capita Income Growth Rates:[a] 1960–1980	Per Capita Income Growth Rates:[a] 1980–2000	Survey Year	Poverty Percent of Population Living Under $1 per Day[b]	Poverty Percent of Population Living Under $2 per Day[b]	Average Years of Education[c] 1999	Children Under Age 5 Mortality Rate (Per 1,000 live births) 2000
Saudi Arabia	20,723	2,149,690	10							29
Romania	22,435	238,390	97			2000	2.1	20.5		23
Saint Lucia	155	620	255		3.4					19
Samoa (Western)	172	2,840	61							26
Venezuela	24,170	912,050	27	0.1	-1.1	1998	15.0	32.0	5.6	23
Dominica	72	750	96		3.9					14
Belize	240	22,960	11							41
Bosnia and Herzegovina	3,977	51,130	78							18
Brazil	170,100	8,547,400	20	4.9	0.6	1998	9.9	23.7	4.6	38
Colombia	42,299	1,138,910	41	2.7	1.1	1998	14.4	26.5	5.0	24
Russian Federation	145,555	17,075,400	9			2000	6.1	23.8		21
Mauritius	1,187	2,040	585	3.0	4.4				5.5	20
Libyan Arab Jamahiriya	5,290	1,759,540	3							20
Macedonia, TFYR	2,026	25,710	80			1998	2.0	4.0		17
Panama	2,854	75,520	38	4.2	0.6	1998	7.6	17.9	7.9	26
Malaysia	23,270	329,750	71	4.2	3.6	1997	2.0	9.3	7.9	11
Bulgaria	8,125	110,910	74			2001	4.7	23.7		16
Antigua and Barbuda	68	440	155							16
Median	*5,275*	*181,040*	*64*	*2.5*	*0.8*		*10.1*	*39.4*	*5.1*	*40*
High-human development countries										
Mexico	97,966	1,958,200	51	3.3	0.7	1998	8.0	24.3	6.7	30
Trinidad and Tobago	1,301	5,130	254	3.9	0.8	1992	12.4	39.0	7.6	20
Belarus	10,005	207,600	48			2000	2.0	2.0		20
Cuba	11,188	110,860	102							9
Saint Kitts and Nevis	44	360	122							24
Latvia	2,372	64,600	38			1998	2.0	8.3		17
Bahamas	305	13,880	30							17
United Arab Emirates	2,905	83,600	35							9
Croatia	4,380	56,540	78			2000	2.0	2.0		9
Kuwait	1,984	17,820	111						7.1	12
Lithuania	3,506	65,200	54			2000	2.0	13.7		11
Qatar	585	11,000	53							16

Chile	15,211	756,630	20	1.7	3.0	1998	*2.0*	*8.7*	7.9	12
Costa Rica	3,810	51,100	75	2.2	0.4	1998	*6.9*	*14.3*	6.0	12
Estonia	1,370	45,100	32			1998	*2.0*	*5.2*		11
Uruguay	3,337	176,220	19	1.6	0.9	1998	*2.0*	*2.0*	7.2	17
Slovakia	5,401					1996	*2.0*	*2.4*		10
Hungary	10,122	93,030	110		1.2	1998	*2.0*	*7.3*	8.8	11
Bahrain	648	710	913	5.0					6.1	16
Seychelles	81	450	181		1.1					14
Poland	38,648	323,250	127	1.8	1.4	1998	*2.0*	*2.0*	9.9	11
Argentina	37,032	2,780,400	14		0.2				8.5	20
Malta	390	320	1,219						7.6	8
Czech Republic	10,273	78,870	133	5.8		1996	*2.0*	*2.0*		6
Brunei Darussalam	338	5,770	64							8
Korea, Rep. of	47,008	99,260	476		6.0	1998	*2.0*	*2.0*	10.5	6
Slovenia	1,989	20,250	99	8.3		1998	*2.0*	*2.0*		7
Singapore	4,018	620	6,587	5.5	2.4				8.1	5
Barbados	267	430	621	7.0	3.8				9.1	17
Hong Kong, China (SAR)	6,665			4.8					9.5	
Cyprus	757	9,250	82	5.2	1.0				8.8	9
Greece	10,560	131,960	82	4.8	2.8		*2.0*		8.5	8
Portugal	10,008	91,980	109	3.6	2.0	1994		*0.5*	4.9	8
Israel	6,233	21,060	302	4.0	1.8				9.2	7
Italy	57,690	301,340	196	1.1	1.4				7.0	7
New Zealand	3,831	270,530	14	4.5	2.3				11.5	7
Spain	40,500	505,990	81						7.3	6
Germany	82,210	357,030	230	3.6	1.6				9.7	6
France	58,893	551,500	107	3.8	2.0				9.3	6
Austria	8,110	83,860	98	2.1	4.5				8.8	6
Luxembourg	438			3.7	2.1					6
Finland	5,172	338,150	17	2.0	2.2				10.1	5
United Kingdom	58,720	242,910	244	3.3	4.9				10.1	7
Ireland	3,794	70,270	55	2.5	1.9				9.0	7
Denmark	5,340	43,090	126	2.0	0.8				8.8	6
Switzerland	7,180	41,290	182	6.2	2.3				10.4	6
Japan	126,870	377,800	348	3.0	1.7				9.7	5
Canada	30,770	9,970,610	3	2.8	2.2				11.4	7
United States	282,224	9,629,090	31	3.7	1.9				12.2	9
Belgium	10,252	33,100	312	2.8	2.0				8.7	7
Netherlands	15,919	41,530	470	2.4	2.0				9.2	7
Australia	19,182	7,741,220	2						10.6	7

Exhibit I.A.4. (Continued)

Country Name (listed from lowest to highest HDI)	Population (Thousands) 2000	Surface Area (Square Kilometers)	Population Density (Per Square Kilometer) 2000	Per Capita Income Growth Rates:[a] 1960–1980	Per Capita Income Growth Rates:[a] 1980–2000	Survey Year	Poverty — Percent of Population Living Under $1 per Day[b]	Poverty — Percent of Population Living Under $2 per Day[b]	Average Years of Education[c] 1999	Children Under Age 5 Mortality Rate (Per 1,000 live births) 2000
Sweden	8,869	449,960	22	2.6	1.6				11.4	4
Iceland	280	103,000	3	4.0	1.5				8.7	6
Norway	4,491	323,880	15	3.6	2.4				11.9	5
Median	*5,401*	*83,730*	*90*	*3.6*	*1.9*		*d*	*d*	*8.8*	*8*

United Nations Human Development Index countries are included in the Exhibit only if they have data available.

[a]Calculated from Heston, Summers, & Aten (2002) Penn World Tables Version 5.6.

[b]Dollars are in 1993 purchasing power parity terms. Data in italics (2.0) are meant to signify that less than two percent of the population are living under the respective poverty lines. Data are for the most recent year available between 1989 and 2001.

[c]Calculated by Barro & Lee (1996) for the population over 25 years of age.

[d]There is no reliable median for the percent of the population living under $1 and $2 per day in high-human development countries due to the lack of reporting, but insofar as the authorities are not reporting because poverty is low, then the true median is likely to be lower than would be expressed in the table.

Sources: Robert Barro and Jong Wha Lee, "International Comparisons of Educational Attainment." Journal of Monetary Economics, December 1993. Vol. 32. No. 3, pp. 364–393, recent updates available at http://www.cid.harvard.edu/ciddata.html; Alan Heston, Robert Summers and Bettina Aten, Penn World Table Version 5.6, Center for International Comparisons at the University of Pennsylvania (CICUP), October 2002; Population Division of the Department of Economic and Social Affairs of the United Nations Secretariat, *World Population Prospects: The 2002 Revision*, 2002; World Bank, World Development Indicators, 2003.

Selection I.A.2. Income Poverty*

Using monetary income or consumption to identify and measure poverty has a long tradition. Though separated by a century, Seebohm Rowntree's classic study of poverty in the English city of York in 1899 and the World Bank's current estimates of global income poverty share a common approach and a common method (Box 1). Based on household income and expenditure surveys, the approach has become the workhorse of quantitative poverty analysis and policy discourse. It has several strengths. Because it is based on nationally representative samples, it allows inferences about the conditions and evolution of poverty at the national level. Moreover, since household surveys collect information beyond monetary income or consumption, the approach makes it possible to obtain a broader picture of well-being and poverty, investigate the relationships among different dimensions of poverty, and test hypotheses on the likely impact of policy interventions.

Poverty measures based on income or consumption are not problem free. Survey design varies between countries and over time, often making comparisons difficult. For example, some countries ask respondents about their food spending over the past month, while others do so for the past week. One-month recall data tend to result in higher poverty estimates than one-week recall data. Converting the information on income or consumption collected in household surveys into measures of well-being requires many assumptions, such as in deciding how to treat measurement errors and how to allow for household size and composition in converting household data into measures for individuals. Poverty estimates are very sensitive to these assumptions. . . .

Moreover, income or consumption data collected at the household level have a basic shortcoming; they cannot reveal inequality within the household, so they can understate overall inequality and poverty. One study that disaggregated household consumption by individual members found that relying only on household information could lead to an understatement of inequality and poverty by more than 25 percent. In particular, the conventional household survey approach does not allow direct measurement of income or consumption poverty among women. That is one reason why data on education and health, which can be

collected at the individual level, are so valuable—they allow a gender-disaggregated perspective on key dimensions of poverty.

A key building block in developing income and consumption measures of poverty is the poverty line—the critical cutoff in income or consumption below which an individual or household is determined to be poor. The internationally comparable lines are useful for producing global aggregates of poverty (see Box 1). In principle, they test for the ability to purchase a basket of commodities that is roughly similar across the world. But such a universal line is generally not suitable for the analysis of poverty within a country. For that purpose, a country-specific poverty line needs to be constructed, reflecting the country's economic and social circumstances. Similarly, the poverty line may need to be adjusted for different areas (such as urban and rural) within the country if prices or access to goods and services differs. The construction of country profiles based on these country-specific poverty lines is now common practice.

Once a poverty line has been specified, it remains to be decided how to assess the extent of poverty in a particular setting. The most straightforward way to measure poverty is to calculate the percentage of the population with income or consumption levels below the poverty line. This "headcount" measure is by far the most commonly calculated measure of poverty. But it has decided disadvantages. It fails to reflect the fact that among poor people there may be wide differences in income levels, with some people located just below the poverty line and others experiencing far greater shortfalls. Policymakers seeking to make the largest possible impact on the headcount measure might be tempted to direct their poverty alleviation resources to those closest to the poverty line (and therefore least poor).

Other poverty measures, which take into account the distance of poor people from the poverty line (the poverty gap) and the degree of income inequality among poor people (the squared poverty gap), can be readily calculated. In comparing poverty estimates across countries or over time, it is important to check the extent to which conclusions vary with the selection of poverty measure. . . .

The Evolution of Poverty

What are the magnitudes and patterns of poverty in the developing world? How has poverty

*From World Bank, *World Development Report 2000/2001* (New York: Oxford University Press, 2001), pp. 16–18, 21–24. Reprinted by permission.

Box 1   Measuring Income Poverty: 1899 and 1998

In a classic study first published in 1901, Seebohm Rowntree calculated that 10 percent of the population of the English city of York in 1899 was living in poverty (below minimum needed expenditures). As we enter the next century, he World Bank calculates that a fourth of the population of the developing world—about 1.2 billion people—is living in poverty (below $1 a day). These two calculations of income poverty are separated by a century and have very different coverage. Nevertheless, the basic concepts and methods they embody have strong similarities.

Rowntree's Approach

Rowntree's method was to conduct a survey covering nearly every working-class family in York to collect information on earnings and expenditures. He then defined poverty as a level of total earnings insufficient to obtain the minimum necessities for the maintenance of "merely physical efficiency," including food, rent, and other items. He calculated that for a family of five—a father, mother, and three children—the minimum weekly expenditure to maintain physical efficiency was 21 shillings, 8 pence; he proposed other amounts for families of different size and composition. Comparing these poverty lines with family earnings, he arrived at his poverty estimate.

The World Bank's Approach

The World Bank has been estimating global income poverty figures since 1990. The latest round of estimation, in October 1999, used new sample survey data and price information to obtain comparable figures for 1987, 1990, 1993, 1996, and 1998 (the figures for 1998 are preliminary estimates). The method is the same as in past estimates (World Bank 1990, 1996).

Consumption. Poverty estimated are based on consumption or income data collected through household surveys. Data for 96 countries, from a total of 265 nationally representative surveys, corresponding to 88 percent of the developing world's people, are now available, up from only 22 countries in 1990. Of particular note is the increase in the share of people covered in Africa from 66 to 73 percent, a result of extensive efforts to improve household data in the region.

Consumption is conventionally viewed as the preferred welfare indicator, for practical reasons of reliability and because consumption is thought to better capture long-run welfare levels than current income. Where survey data were available on incomes but not on consumption, consumption was estimated by multiplying all incomes by the share of aggregate private consumption in national income based on national accounts data. This procedure, unchanged from past exercises, scales back income to obtain consumption but leaves the distribution unchanged.

Prices. To compare consumption levels across countries, estimates of price levels are needed, and the World Bank's purchasing power parity (PPP) estimates for 1993 were used. These estimates are based on new price data generated by the International Comparison Program (ICP), which now covers 110 countries, up from 64 in 1985, and a more comprehensive set of commodities.

Poverty lines. The 1990 calculations of the international poverty lines had to be updated using 1993 price data and the 1993 PPP estimates. In 1990 national poverty lines for 33 countries were converted into 1985 PPP prices, and the most typical line among the low-income countries for which poverty lines were available was selected. In 1999 the same lines were converted into 1993 PPP prices, and the new line was obtained as the median of the 10 lowest poverty lines. That line is equal to $1.08 a day in 1993 PPP terms (referred to as "$1 a day" in the text). This line has a similar purchasing power to the $1 a day line in 1985 PPP prices, in terms of the command over domestic goods. The upper poverty line (referred to as "$2 a day") was calculated by doubling the amount of the lower poverty line, as in 1990, reflecting poverty lines more commonly used in lower-middle-income countries.

Estimates for 1998. To obtain consumption levels for 1998 where survey data were not yet available, estimated growth rates of per capita private consumption from national accounts statistics were used to update consumption data from the latest survey year to 1998. This meant assuming that the distribution of consumption did not change from the time of the last survey to 1998. The per capita private consumption growth rates came from estimates based on the model used for other World Bank forecasts (World Bank 1999). Surveys were available for 1997 or 1998 only for Belarus, China, India, Jordan, Latvia, Nigeria, Pakistan, Panama, Russia, Thailand, and Yemen. So the 1998 figures should be considered tentative, and trends should be interpreted cautiously, particularly in light of the controversy surrounding Indian data.

Country-specific poverty lines. The $1 and $2 a day poverty estimates described here are useful only as indicators of global progress, not to assess progress at the country level or to guide country policy and program formulation. Country-specific poverty lines, reflecting what it means to be poor in each country's situation and not affected by international price comparisons, are used in country-level analysis.

Source: Chen and Ravallion 2000.

Table 1. Income Poverty by Region, Selected Years, 1987–98

Region	Population covered by at least one survey (percent)	People living on less than $1 a day (millions)				
		1987	1990	1993	1996	1998[a]
East Asia and Pacific	90.8	417.5	452.4	431.9	265.1	278.3
Excluding China	71.1	114.1	92.0	83.5	55.1	65.1
Europe and Central Asia	81.7	1.1	7.1	18.3	23.8	24.0
Latin America and the Caribbean	88.0	63.7	73.8	70.8	76.0	78.2
Middle East and North Africa	52.5	9.3	5.7	5.0	5.0	5.5
South Asia	97.9	474.4	495.1	505.1	531.7	522.0
Sub-Saharan Africa	72.9	217.2	242.3	273.3	289.0	290.0
Total	88.1	1,183.2	1,276.4	1,304.3	1,190.6	1,198.9
Excluding China	84.2	879.8	915.9	955.9	980.5	985.7

Region	Share of population living on less than $1 a day (percent)				
	1987	1990	1993	1996	1998[a]
East Asia and Pacific	26.6	27.6	25.2	14.9	15.3
Excluding China	23.9	18.5	15.9	10.0	11.3
Europe and Central Asia	0.2	1.6	4.0	5.1	5.1
Latin America and the Caribbean	15.3	16.8	15.3	15.6	15.6
Middle East and North Africa	4.3	2.4	1.9	1.8	1.9
South Asia	44.9	44.0	42.4	42.3	40.0
Sub-Saharan Africa	46.6	47.7	49.7	48.5	46.3
Total	28.3	29.0	28.1	24.5	24.0
Excluding China	28.5	28.1	27.7	27.0	26.2

Note: The poverty line is $1.08 a day at 1993 PPP. Poverty estimates are based on income or consumption data from the countries in each region for which at least one survey was available during 1985–98. Where survey years do not coincide with the years in the table, the estimates were adjusted using the closest available survey and applying the consumption growth rate from national accounts. Using the assumption that the sample of countries covered by surveys is representative of the region as a whole, the number of poor people was then estimated by region. This assumption is obviously less robust in the regions with the lowest survey coverage. For further details on data and methodology see Chen and Ravallion (2000).

[a]Preliminary.

Source: World Bank 2000.

Figure 1. Poverty in the developing world is shifting toward South Asia and sub-Saharan Africa.

Distribution of population living on less than $1 a day

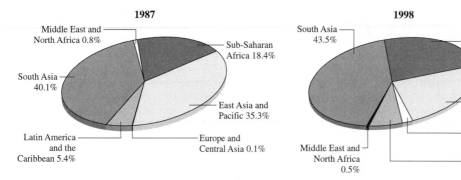

Source: Chen and Ravallion 2000.

evolved over the past decade? The answers to these questions are important in framing the challenge of attacking poverty. . . .

Between 1987 and 1998 the share of the population in developing and transition economies living on less than $1 a day fell from 28 percent to 24 percent (Table 1). This decline is below the rate needed to meet the international development goal of reducing extreme income poverty by half by 2015.

Because of population growth, the number of people in poverty hardly changed. But there are large regional variations in performance. East Asia and the Middle East and North Africa have reduced their numbers in poverty—East Asia dramatically so. But in all other regions the number of people living on less than $1 a day has risen. In South Asia, for example, the number of poor people rose over the decade, from 474 million to 522 million, even though the share of people in poverty fell from 45 percent to 40 percent. In Latin America and the Caribbean the number of poor people rose by about 20 percent.

Two regions fared particularly badly. In Europe and Central Asia the number in poverty soared from 1.1 million to 24 million. In Sub-Saharan Africa the number of poor people increased from an already high 217 million to 291 million over the same period, leaving almost half the residents of that continent poor.

These variations in regional performance are leading to a shift in the geographical distribution of poverty. In 1998 South Asia and Sub-Saharan Africa accounted for around 70 percent of the population living on less than $1 a day, up 10 percentages points from 1987 (Figure 1).

While these numbers provide a sense of broad trends, they should be treated with caution in light of the shortcomings of the data mentioned above and the fact that figures for 1998 are tentative because of the limited number of surveys available (see Box 1).

References

Chen, Shaohua, and Martin Ravallion. 2000. "How Did the World's Poorest Fare in the 1990s?" Policy Research Working Paper, World Bank, Washington, D.C.

World Bank. 1990 *World Development Report 1990: Poverty.* New York: Oxford University Press.

———. 1996. *Poverty Reduction and the World Bank: Progress and Challenges in the 1990s.* Washington, D.C.

———. 1999. *Global Economic Prospects and the Developing Countries 2000.* Washington, D.C.

———. 2000. *World Development Indicators 2000.* Washington, D.C.

Comment I.A.2. Capabilities and Entitlements
In delimiting the nature of poverty, Amartya Sen has stated that

> poverty is not just a matter of being relatively poorer than others in the society, but of not having some basic opportunities of material well-being—the failure to have certain minimum "capabilities." The criteria of minimum capabilities are "absolute" not in the sense that they must not vary from society to society, or over time, but people's deprivations are judged absolutely, and not simply in comparison with the deprivations of others in that society. If a person is seen as poor because he is unable to satisfy his hunger, then that diagnosis of poverty cannot be altered merely by the fact that others too may also be hungry (so that this person may not be, relatively speaking, any worse off than most others). . . . A person's advantage is judged in this approach by his capabilities, viz., what he can or cannot do, can or cannot be. The relevant capabilities are of many different kinds (e.g., being free from starvation, from hunger, from undernourishment; participating in communal life; being adequately sheltered; being free to travel to see friends; and so on). The ranking of "capability vectors" can be used to rank people's advantages vis à vis others. But in the context of poverty analysis, it is a question of setting certain absolute standards of minimum material capabilities relevant for that society. Anyone failing to reach that absolute level would then be classified as poor, no matter what his relative position is vis a vis others. Poverty, in this view, is not ultimately a matter of incomes at all; it is one of a failure to achieve certain minimum capabilities. The distinction is important since the conversion of real incomes into actual capabilities varies with social circumstances and personal features.[1]

Sen has also maintained that the most important thematic deficiency of traditional development economics is its concentration on national product, aggregate income, and total supply of particular goods rather than on the "entitlements" of people and the "capabilities" that these entitlements generate. Entitlement refers to the set of alternative commodity bundles that a person can command in a society using the totality of rights and opportunities that he or she has.

For an elaboration of entitlements and capabilities, see Amartya K. Sen, "Development: Which Way Now?" *Economic Journal* (December 1983), *Poverty and Famines: An Essay on Entitlement and Deprivation* (1981), *Choice, Welfare and Measurement* (1982), "Poor, Relatively Speaking," *Oxford Economic Papers* (July 1983), and *Commodities and Capabilities* (1985).

The case for a "capabilities-oriented" rather than a "goods-oriented" social welfare function is also argued by K. Griffin and J. Knight, "Human Development: The Case for Renewed Emphasis," *Journal of Development Planning* (1989).

---

[1]Amartya Sen, "A Sociological Approach to the Measurement of Poverty: A Reply to Professor Peter Townsend," *Oxford Economic Papers* (December 1985): 669–70.

Note 1.A.2. Other Important Differences Between Developed and Less Developed Countries

For convenience of use of the Exhibits in this book, let us consider the high-HDI countries to be developed countries (DCs) and the low-HDI and medium-HDI countries to be less developed countries (LDCs), with the low-HDI countries being the "least developed" LDCs. There are at least two important differences between DCs and LDCs that do not follow automatically from their differences in per capita incomes, health, and educational attainment documented in Exhibit I.A.2. The first important difference is that population growth is higher in LDCs. The median average annual growth rates of population for the low-HDI and medium-HDI countries in the period 1995–2000 are 2.6 percent and 1.8 percent, respectively (see Exhibit IV.C.1). This figure falls to 0.5 percent for the high-HDI countries. The cause of more rapid population growth in LDCs is easily traced to an incomplete "demographic transition" from high birth rates and death rates to low birth rates and death rates. The median average annual birth rates for the period 1995–2000 for the low-HDI and medium-HDI countries are 43.1 and 25.5 births per thousand persons, respectively (see Exhibit IV.C.1). This figure falls to 12.5 for the high-HDI countries. In contrast, the median average annual death rates for the period 1995–2000 for the low-HDI and medium-HDI countries are only 17.8 and 6.8 deaths per thousand persons, respectively, compared to 8.6 for the high-HDI countries. (The death rate for the high-HDI countries is greater than for the medium-HDI countries because the average age is higher in the former countries.) Thus population growth is more rapid in LDCs because death rates have dropped to near the level of DCs but birth rates have not.

A key factor in bringing down death rates in LDCs was control of major infectious diseases. This control was fostered by international aid agencies and its success did not require high incomes in the recipient countries. The most important factor keeping birth rates high in LDCs is the high number of children per woman rather than a high number of women of childbearing age. The median number of children per woman during the period 1995–2000 was 6.1 and 3.2 for the low-HDI and medium-HDI countries, respectively, compared to 1.6 for the high-HDI countries (see Exhibit IV.C.1). One consequence of the much higher birth rates in LDCs is that their populations tend to be much younger than in DCs, already noted in passing above. The median share of the population less than 15 years old was 45.1 percent and 34.2 percent for the low-HDI and medium-HDI countries, respectively, compared to 19.8 percent for the high-HDI countries (see Exhibit IV.C.1).

The second important difference between developed and less developed countries that does not follow automatically from their differences in per capita incomes, health, and educational attainment is the much higher proportion of the labor force engaged in agriculture in LDCs. The median shares of the labor force in agriculture for the low-HDI and medium-HDI countries in 2000 are 75.2 percent and 30.3 percent, respectively (see Exhibit VII.A.1). This figure falls to 5.2 percent for the high-HDI countries. Reasons for this enormous difference include the tendency of poor households to spend a much higher fraction of their incomes on food than rich households and the tendency of poor countries to export cash crops in exchange for manufactures. (The historical origins of the latter tendency and its contemporary persistence are described in Chapters II and III, respectively.) It is also the case that productivity in agriculture relative to the rest of the economy is much smaller in the typical LDC than in the typical DC. The median ratios of the value of nonagricultural to agricultural value-added per worker in 2000 were respectively 7.1 and 2.5 for the low-HDI and medium HDI countries, compared to 1.8 for the high-HDI countries. The reasons that LDCs have had such exceptional difficulty in raising agricultural productivity are explored in Chapter VII.

Our claim that a high agricultural labor force share is not automatically associated with low incomes, poor health, and lack of education is supported by the existence of numerous farming communities in temperate zone countries from Canada to New Zealand with the opposite characteristics. Yet it is also true that even in developed countries it is difficult and expensive to provide adequate schools and hospital services to rural areas. We might therefore expect that a high agricultural labor force share will be associated with low life expectancy and educational attainment even controlling for the level of per capita income. This expectation can be confirmed using the data in Exhibit I.A.2: a regression of either the life expectancy index or the education index on the GDP index and the agricultural labor force share yields a negative (and highly statistically significant) coefficient on the agricultural labor force share in addition to a positive coefficient on the GDP index. (This result holds even if other functions of per capita GDP are substituted for the GDP index.) This could reflect a negative causal relationship from agricultural work and rural location to health care and education.

I.B. ECONOMIC PERFORMANCE OF LESS DEVELOPED COUNTRIES: THE RECENT PAST

Selection I.B.1. The Lost Decades: Developing Countries' Stagnation in Spite of Policy Reform 1980–1998*

Growth regressions have become a standard tool for explaining variations in growth. Yet they fail to explain the following remarkable facts. In 1960–79, the median per capita growth in developing countries was 2.5 percent. In 1980–1999, the median per capita growth of developing countries was 0.0 percent.[1] In contrast, the standard determinants of growth in growth regressions like financial development, black market premiums, real over-valuation, educational attainment, life expectancy, fertility, and infrastructure got steadily more favorable for growth from the 60s through the 90s, as I will document. The fitted value from a growth regression on these factors diverges dramatically from actual growth in the 1980s and 1990s (Figure 1a).

The improvement in policy variables included in growth regressions reflect the sea-change beginning around 1980 towards increased emphasis on market-friendly economic policies by developing country governments. The development consensus shifted away from state planning towards markets, away from import substitution towards outward orientation, away from state controls of prices and interest rates toward "getting the prices right."

. . . For whatever reasons, the response of developing country growth rates to the policy reforms of the 80s and 90s has not been what could have been expected from previous empirical work on growth. Zero per capita growth on average after major reforms is a disappointing outcome whatever the cause. As a result of the poor countries' stagnation, poor and rich countries' income diverged over 1980–98. . . .

1. Policy Trends

This section will describe the trends in national economic policies, as well as in indirect indicators of policies like educational attainment, life expectancy, infrastructure, and fertility. If the country characteristics that are supposed to affect growth in cross-country regressions trended upward, then obviously they cannot explain the slowdown in growth in the 80s and 90s.

There is much work documenting the effects of financial depth on growth.[2] Figure 1 documents the trends in several relevant indicators. We see in Figure 1b that the ratio of M2/GDP rises steadily over time, and so was better in 1980–98 than in 1960–79 (in this and all the succeeding graphs, I show the 95 percent confidence bands for the median). The breakpoint for financial development was about 1985, after which it leveled off.

Figure 1c gives some insight as to how increasing financial depth came about, as real deposit rates in developing countries improved from the 70s to the 90s. The common practice of "financial repression," where governments controlled interest rates at a level below that of inflation, had increasingly disappeared by the 80s and 90s.

Another huge improvement in "getting the prices right" in developing countries was in correcting overvaluation of the real official exchange rate. I take the index of overvaluation for 1976–85 that Dollar 1992 calculates. Dollar's calculation was based on Summers-Heston purchasing power parity comparisons, measuring the extent of general overvaluation controlling for the level of income. He found this to be a significant determinant of growth rates (the more overvaluation, the less growth). I convert this into an annual series by calculating the real exchange rate as (Domestic CPI)/(Exchange Rate Domestic Currency per Dollar* US CPI). I benchmark this series for each country by adjusting the level such that the average for 1976–85 equals Dollar's calculation.

Figure 2 shows the resulting aggregate trend in the real exchange rate. The median official real exchange rate was overvalued in the 60s and 70s, then was devalued steadily through the 80s and

*From William Easterly, "The Lost Decades: Developing Countries' Stagnation in Spite of Policy Reform 1980–1998." *Journal of Economic Growth* 6 (June 2001): 135–136, 138–145. Reprinted by permission.

[1]The median weights all countries equally, which seems appropriate if we treat each country as an observation of a given set of country policies and characteristics. The median is 0.0 for both the 80s and 90s taken separately. The weighted average growth rate shows less of a decline, because of accelerated growth in India and China in 1980–98. The 1980–98 figures include the ex-Communist countries in Europe and Central Asia that had strong output declines. Excluding developing countries from Europe and Central Asia, the median per capita growth 1980–98 was still only 0.3 percent.

[2]King and Levine (1993a,b), Levine and Zervos (1998), Levine, Loayza, and Beck (1999).

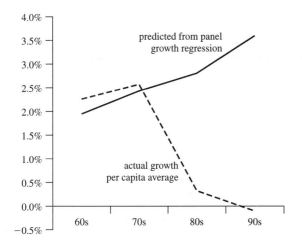

Figure 1a. Predicted vs actual per capita growth for developing countries (assuming constant intercept across decades).

Figure 1b. Confidence interval for median M2/GDP in developing countries.

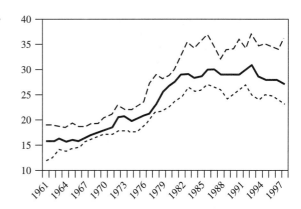

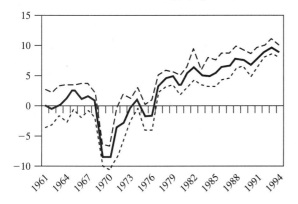

Figure 1c. Confidence interval for median real interest rate in developing countries.

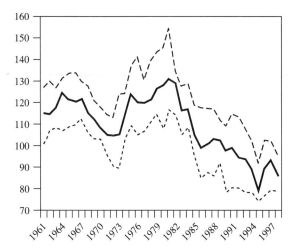

Figure 2. Confidence interval for median real exchange rate in developing countries.

90s. By the end of the period, the median real exchange rate was slightly undervalued in purchasing power parity terms.

But the strongest policy improvement of all in the developing world was in the outcomes for health, education, infrastructure, and fertility that resulted from national policies and technological progress. Figure 3a shows the huge improvement over time in secondary enrollment, whose initial value is often used as an explanatory variable in growth regressions (see Levine and Renelt, 1992; Barro and Sala-i-Martin, 1995; and Barro, 1998). Other educational indicators sometimes used in growth regressions, like primary enrollment and educational attainment, showed similar improvements.

Figure 3a also shows the huge improvement in life expectancy, which is also used as an explana-

tory variable in growth regression (e.g. Barro (1998)), from the 60s through the 90s. Figure 3b shows similarly breathtaking improvement in the density of telephone networks, which has also been used as an explanatory variable in growth regressions (Easterly and Levine, 1997; Canning and Fay, 1993), from the 60s through the 90s. Figure 3c shows the drop in fertility in developing countries, which should have had a positive effect on growth according to the results of Barro (1998). Health, education, infrastructure, and fertility improvements should have led to an acceleration of developing country growth from the 60s through the 90s, not stagnation in 1980–98.

The government budget balance is significantly correlated with growth in previous research (Easterly and Rebelo, 1993; Fischer, 1993). Figure 4a shows the fiscal deficit excluding grants worsened

Figure 3a. Median human capital measures in developing economies.

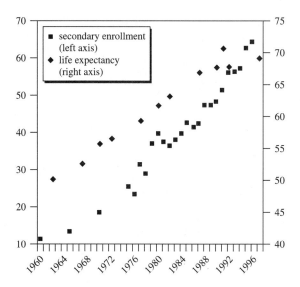

Figure 3b. Median telephone lines per 1000 population.

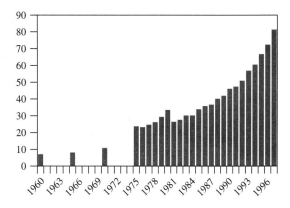

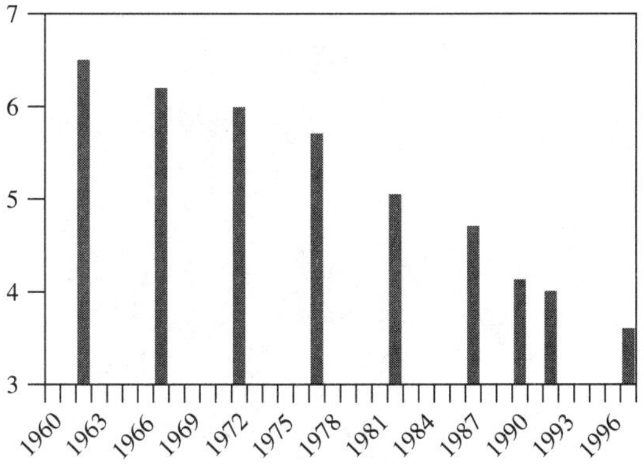

Figure 3c. Median fertility rate in developing countries (births per woman).

in the 70s, reached a nadir in the early 1980s, and has then showed a steady improvement in the 80s and 90s.

Figure 4b shows the fiscal deficit including grants with similar trends, although the trends are less pronounced. The trends in budget balance should have predicted improving growth in the 80s and 90s, but it did not happen.

Institutional factors have been suggested as important determinants of long-run growth (Knack and Keefer, 1994). We unfortunately have institutional indicators only back to 1984, but the data that we have show an improvement in institutional quality (Figure 5). There is nothing here to explain the lost decades.[3]

There were other policy indicators that did not necessarily show a clear improvement in the 80s and 90s, but fail to show the kind of deterioration that would explain the lost decades. Figure 6a, b, and c shows the trends (or lack thereof) in the black market premium, the inflation rate, and openness. The black market premium does not dis-

play a strong trend, although its cross-country variance has decreased over time—by 1997, most countries had low black market premia (Figure 6a). Since the distribution of the black market premium is skewed, its mean (in this case, geometric mean) lies above the median.[4] The mean declined steadily in the 90s. Inflation shifted up in the 70s, which is the wrong timing to explain the growth slowdown that began in the 80s (Figure 6b). Also the median inflation remained at 15 percent or below, whereas the cross country evidence finds a negative correlation between growth and inflation only at higher levels.[5] Since inflation, like the black market premium, is skewed to the right, its mean lies above the median. There was a sharp increase in the mean in the first half of the 90s, reflecting a small number of hyperinflation episodes,

[3]I also checked a measure of political instability, revolutions per year, but it displays no trend over 1960–93.

[4]The geometric mean is calculated as EXP(MEAN(LOG(P(t)/P(t − 1))) − 1.

[5]Bruno and Easterly (1998) find no robust evidence of a negative correlation between inflation and growth below 40 percent per annum; Barro (1998) finds a lower breakpoint of 15 percent per annum, below which there is no significant correlation between growth and inflation.

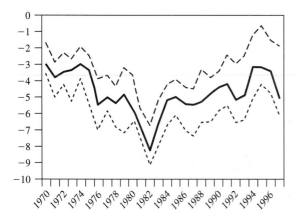

Figure 4a. Confidence interval for median budget balance (excluding grants) in developing countries.

Figure 4b. Confidence interval for median budget balance (including grants) in developing countries.

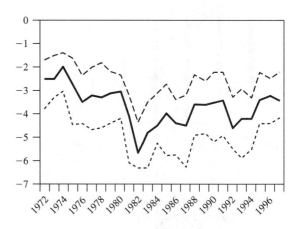

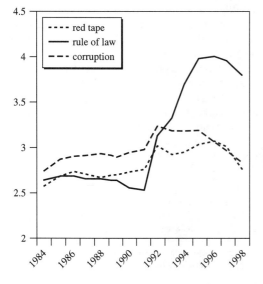

Figure 5. Median institutional measures in developing countries.

Figure 6a. Confidence interval for median black market premium in developing countries.

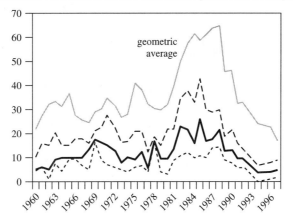

Figure 6b. Confidence interval for median inflation in developing countries.

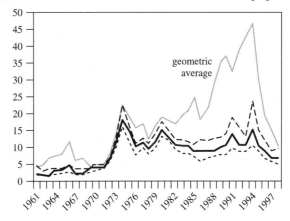

Figure 6c. Median export to GDP ratio in developing countries.

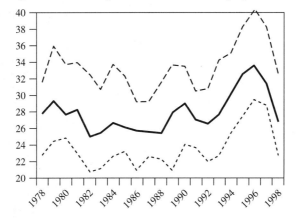

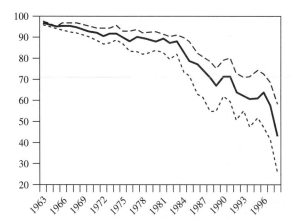

Figure 6d. Share of commodities in merchandise exports in developing countries.

but then inflation declined again by the end of the 90s. The median is probably more informative about the experience of the typical country and so inflation fails to explain the median growth stagnation of 1980–98.

Figure 6c shows the behavior of openness (measured as the export to GDP ratio). Openness does not show strong trends over time; it rose in the early 90s and then fell in 1997–98 with the East Asia crisis. There is nothing here to explain the lost decades.

Part of the growth literature has focused on political economy variables that affect policy-making. One political economy variable said to be adverse for growth is income inequality (see literature review above). The median Gini coefficient for our sample falls from 49 in the 1960s to 41 in the 1990s. According to most empirical research, this should have prompted increased growth in the sample. A related political economy variable is dependence on commodity exports, which is said to be adverse for growth by various mechanisms, such as lacking the externalities associated with manufacturing or setting off a frenzy of rentseeking. Dependence on commodity exports has fallen sharply in developing countries, with commodity exports as a share of total merchandise exports strongly trending downward over 1963–98 (figure 6d). The political economy environment for growth should have improved from the 1960s through the 1990s, according to measures standard in the literature.

In conclusion, poor policies are not a plausible candidate for explaining the lost decades. Policies either got better or remained the same throughout the period 1960–98.

References

Barro, R. J. (1998). *Determinants of Economic Growth: A Cross Country Empirical Study.* Cambridge, MA: MIT Press.

Barro, R. J., and X. Sala-i-Martin. (1995). *Economic Growth.* New York: McGraw-Hill.

Bruno, M., and W. Easterly. (1998). "Inflation Crises and Long-run Growth," *Journal of Monetary Economics* 4, 3–26.

Canning, D., and M. Fay. (1993). "The Effect of Transportation Networks on Economic Growth." Discussion Paper Series, Columbia University, Dept. of Economics.

Easterly, W., and R. Levine. (1997). "Africa's Growth Tragedy: Policies and Ethnic Divisions," *Quarterly Journal of Economics.*

Easterly, W., and S. Rebelo. (1993). "Fiscal Policy and Economic Growth: an Empirical Investigation," *Journal of Monetary Economics* 32, 417–458.

Fischer, S. (1993). "The Role of Macroeconomic Factors in Growth," *Journal of Monetary Economics* XXXII, 485–511.

King, R. G., and R. Levine. (1993a). "Finance and Growth: Schumpeter Might be Right," *Quarterly Journal of Economics* 108, 717–737.

King, R. G., and R. Levine. (1993b). "Finance, Entrepreneurship, and Growth: Theory and Evidence." *Journal of Monetary Economics* 32, 513–542.

Knack, S., and P. Keefer. (1995). "Institutions and Economic Performance: Cross-Country Tests Using Alternative Institutional Measures," *Economics and Politics* 7, 207–227.

Levine, R., and D. Renelt. (1991). "Sensitivity Analysis of Cross-Country Growth Regressions." *American Economic Review* XXC, 942–963.

Note 1.B.1. No Easy Answers, Yet All Is Not Lost

The preceding Selection shows that "market-friendly" economic reforms in LDCs have failed to deliver the acceleration in economic growth promised for them. These reforms, however, were undertaken partly in response to the perceived failure of more state interventionist policies that preceded them, which were seen to have led to the 1982 debt crisis and the deep recession that followed in many LDCs. It seems that neither state guidance nor laissez-faire provides an easy answer to the question of how to accelerate growth in per capita income.

Indeed, it now appears that the study of economic growth in LDCs is not as advanced as had been previously supposed. To use a medical analogy, it is as though we are in the early stages of the study of a disease, when a cure has yet to be discovered and research is concentrated on the characteristics and mechanisms that distinguish a healthy organism from a sick one. At this point we are still trying to understand what causes the differences between a healthy LDC economy (that is growing rapidly) and a sick one (that is growing slowly or not at all). We are not ready to prescribe a program of treatment (policies) with any confidence of success.

Easterly gloomily titles the article from which Selection I.B.1 is drawn "The Lost Decades," yet Exhibit I.B.1 shows that the 1980s and 1990s were not completely lost to LDCs. Although per capita income stagnated, median life expectancy increased by 10 years, the same amount it had increased during the 1960s and 1970s, and median educational attainment increased by 2 years, double the increase during the 1960s and 1970s. Thus health and knowledge of the residents of the typical LDC increased even though their power to purchase goods and services did not.

Moreover, the picture for per capita income growth changes considerably when one shifts perspective from the average less developed *country* to the average less developed country *resident,* that is, when one considers the growth of the population-weighted average of per capita income. (This is equivalent to computing growth of income per capita in the less developed world as though it were one big country.) Exhibit I.B.2 shows that from this latter perspective per capita income growth did not decrease at all during the 1980s and 1990s, and may even have increased relative to the 1960s and 1970s. The reason is that growth in the two largest LDCs, China and India, accelerated in the last two decades, offsetting the stagnation in most of the rest of the less developed world. This accelerated growth will be the subject of our next two selections.

Finally, Exhibit I.B.3 reminds us that it is possible for LDCs to catch up to the per capita incomes of the countries where the industrial revolution began two centuries ago. Japan was the first country that was neither European nor settled by Europeans to accomplish this feat, and South Korea and Taiwan remain on a path to be the next such countries with populations larger than 10 million to do so, despite the setback of the 1997–98 East Asian financial crisis. The combined message of Selection I.B.1 and Exhibit I.B.3 can be summarized as follows: Economic miracles do happen, but as yet we do not know how to make them.

Exhibit I.B.1. Life Expectancy and Educational Attainment Versus Per Capita GDP
Recent Performance of Less Developed Countries[a]

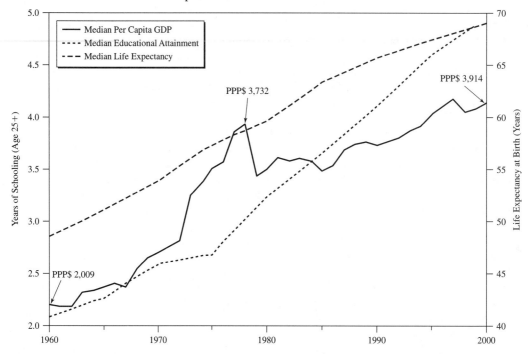

[a]Countries from Asia (minus Japan), Latin America and the Caribbean, the Middle East and North Africa, and Sub-Saharan Africa were included if they had data available for all three indicators. These countries include: Algeria, Argentina, Bangladesh, Barbados, Bolivia, Brazil,
Cameroon, Chile, Colombia, Costa Rica, Dominican Republic, Ecuador, El Salvador, Ghana, Guatemala, Honduras, India, Indonesia, Iran, Ja-
maica, Kenya, Korea, Lesotho, Malawi, Malaysia, Mali, Mauritius, Mexico, Mozambique, Nepal, Nicaragua, Niger, Pakistan, Panama,
Paraguay, Peru, Philippines, Senegal, South Africa, Sri Lanka, Syria, Thailand, Togo, Trinidad and Tobago, Tunisia, Turkey, Uganda, Uruguay,
Venezuela, Zambia, and Zimbabwe.

Sources: Robert Barro and Jong Wha Lee, "International Comparisons of Educational Attainment." Journal of Monetary Economics, December 1993. Vol. 32, No. 3, pp. 364–393. Recent updates available at http://www.cid.harvard.edu/ciddata/ciddata.html; Alan Heston, Robert Summers and Bettina Aten, Penn World Table Version 6.1, Center for International Comparisons at the University of Pennsylvania (CICUP), October 2002; World Bank, World Development Indicators, 2003.

Exhibit I.B.2. Country Average Versus Population-Weighted[a] Per Capita GDP Growth Rates[b]
Recent Performance of Less Developed Countries[c]

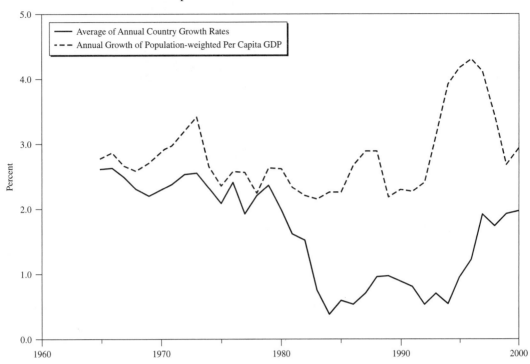

[a]The growth rate of population-weighted per capita GDP is defined as the growth rate of the ratio of the sum of the countries' total GDP to the sum of the countries' total populations.

[b]The graph shows five-year moving averages of annual growth rates based on the preceding five years. For example, the growth rate for 1965 is the average of the growth rates for 1960–1, 1961–2, 1962–3, 1963–4, and 1964–5.

[c]Countries from Asia (minus Japan), Latin America and the Caribbean, the Middle East and North Africa, and Sub-Saharan Africa were included if they had data available for the full time series. The sample of countries included are Algeria, Argentina, Bangladesh, Barbados, Benin, Bolivia, Brazil, Burkina Faso, Burundi, Cameroon, Cape Verde, Chad, Chile, China, Colombia, Comoros, Republic of Congo, Costa Rica, Côte d'Ivoire, Dominican Republic, Ecuador, Egypt, El Salvador, Equatorial Guinea, Ethiopia, Gabon, The Gambia, Ghana, Guatemala, Guinea-Bissau, Honduras, India, Indonesia, Islamic Republic of Iran, Jamaica, Jordan, Kenya, Republic of Korea, Lesotho, Madagascar, Malawi, Malaysia, Mali, Mauritius, Mexico, Morocco, Mozambique, Nepal, Nicaragua, Niger, Nigeria, Pakistan, Panama, Paraguay, Peru, Philippines, Romania, Rwanda, Senegal, Seychelles, South Africa, Sri Lanka, Syrian Arab Republic, Thailand, Togo, Trinidad and Tobago, Turkey, Uganda, Uruguay, Venezuela, Zambia, and Zimbabwe.

Source: Alan Heston, Robert Summers and Bettina Aten, Penn World Table Version 6.1, Center for International Comparisons at the University of Pennsylvania (CICUP), October 2002.

Exhibit I.B.3. Catching Up to the Core

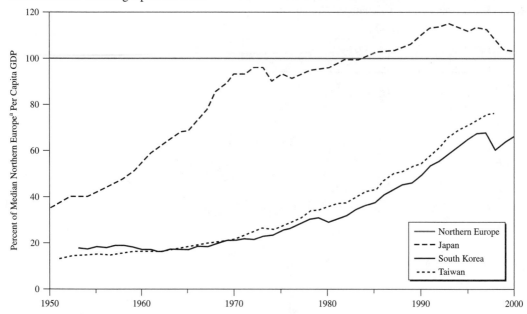

[a]Northern Europe includes: Austria, Belgium, Denmark, Finland, France, Germany, Ireland, Netherlands, Norway, Sweden, Switzerland, and the United Kingdom.

Source: Alan Heston, Robert Summers and Bettina Aten, Penn World Table Version 6.1, Center for International Comparisons at the University of Pennsylvania (CICUP), October 2002.

Selection I.B.2 How Reform Worked in China*

A Puzzling Reform That Worked

In the last 22 years of the 20th century, China transformed itself from a poor, centrally planned economy to a lower-middle-income, emerging market economy. With total gross domestic product (GDP) growing at an average annual rate of about 9 percent, China's per capita GDP more than quadrupled during this period. The benefits of growth were also shared by the people on a broad basis: the number of people living in absolute poverty was substantially reduced from over 250 million to about 50 million, a decline from a one-third to a twenty-fifth of its population; and life expectancy increased from 64 in the 1970s to over 70 in the late 1990s. Both the formal statistics and casual tourist impressions tell the same story: China's growth is real. Two decades ago, few economists would have bet on the outcome in China today. At the time, coming out of the disastrous decade of the Cultural Revolution, China was poor, overpopulated, short of human capital and natural resources, and was constrained by an ideology hostile toward markets and opposed to radical reform. Growth of this kind under such initial conditions is a surprise.

China's phenomenal growth is not just another successful growth story because China is not a "typical" country, although in cross-country regressions China can only represent one data point, the same as Singapore or Ireland or Botswana. China is the largest transition and developing economy. As an economy in transition from plan to market, China has a population three times greater than all other transition economies combined, including the 15 former Soviet Republics. In 2000, its $1 trillion economy was already bigger than all other transition economies combined. As a developing economy, China has a population almost three times that of all eight high-performing East Asian economies of Japan, South Korea, Taiwan, Hong Kong, Singapore, Malaysia, Thailand, and Indonesia. It has managed to match the growth record of these economies during their heyday, but with a much larger population. The cumulative effects of the two decades' growth are significant when comparing China with its two largest neighbors: in total GDP terms, in 1988 China was less than half of Russia, but ten years later Russia was

less than half of China. On per capita basis, two decades ago China and India were about equal, but now China is about twice as rich as India.

China's growth is unlikely to end any time soon. In the first half of 2001, China's economy ignored the global slowdown and continued to grow at an annual rate of about 8 percent. Defying the perception that China has reached a plateau of growth, more and more economists are starting to believe that the best part of China's growth has not come yet. With entry into the World Trade Organization (WTO), they suspect that China's economy is on the verge of the next boom.

According to Maddison's (1998) calculation, China might overtake the United States in total GDP in terms of "purchasing power parity" by 2015.[1] If Maddison is right, China would be the only economy, excluding the European Union, capable of surpassing the U.S. economy (in purchasing power parity) within the next two decades. And this would make China the largest economy in the world, regaining the historical position that it lost in the middle of the nineteenth century. No wonder Lawrence Summers speculated in the early 1990s: "It may be that when the history of the late 20th century is written in a hundred years the most significant event will be the revolutionary change in China" (1992, 7).

On the ground of economic growth and improving living standard, there is no question that China's reform has worked. But this reform is puzzling. In the early 1990s, the economics profession and policymakers reached a striking degree of unanimity on the recipe for transition from plan to market. Simply put, it calls for stabilization, liberalization, and privatization, following political democratization. Although many economists may not consider this recipe sufficient, few would question its necessity. Theoretically, it is difficult to imagine how a reform would work without these essential ingredients. Empirically, the fresh memory of the frustrated reform experience in Hungary, Poland, and the former Soviet Union prior to 1990

---

*From Yingyi Qian, "How Reform Worked in China." In Dani Rodrik, ed., *In Search of Prosperity* (Princeton: Princeton University Press, 2003), pp. 297–302, 305–306, 324–326. Reprinted by permission.

[1]In terms of purchasing power parity, China's per capita GDP in 1995 was about 11 percent of that of the United States. Because China had a population approximately 4.5 times as large as the United States, China's total GDP, in terms of purchasing power parity, was about one-half that of the United States in 1995. If China continues to grow four percentage points faster than the United States annually, then China's total GDP will be larger than that of the United States in 20 years.

suggests that a reform will fail if it does not follow these recommendations.

The Chinese path of reform and its associated rapid growth is puzzling because it seems to defy this conventional wisdom. Although China has adopted many of the policies advocated by economists—such as being open to trade and foreign investment and sensitive to macroeconomic stability—violations of the standard prescriptions are striking. For the most part of the past two decades, China's reform succeeded without complete liberalization, without privatization, and without democratization. One might have reasoned that coexistence of the planning mechanism with partial liberalization would only cause more distortion and become a source of disruption, not growth. Without privatization and secure private property rights, how could there be genuine market incentives? Without democracy, economic reform lacks a political basis and commitment to a market and thus is vulnerable. The actual performance of the Chinese reform provides a striking contrast to these expectations. Why has China grown so fast, ask Blanchard and Fischer (1993), when conditions thought to be necessary for growth were absent?

It is not surprising that China's reform has been viewed as an anomaly and thus has been unappreciated by mainstream economists. For example, *From Plan to Market: World Development Report 1996* on transition economies (World Bank 1996) gave China short shrift because it couldn't figure out where to put China on the various measurement parameters. China simply does not fit into the general description of the report.

Those who do not find China's reform puzzling often misunderstand it. Two types of misperceptions of China's economic success are common. The first is to regard foreign direct investment (FDI) and exports as the driving force for China's success. In this connection the roles of overseas Chinese and of Hong Kong and Taiwan are often emphasized. The simplicity of the argument adds to its power, and the tacit message—it is the foreigners and foreign markets that made China grow—finds an appreciative audience outside China. However, the argument loses its plausibility as soon as one considers a parallel experience in Germany. If Hong Kong or Taiwan could play such a powerful role in mainland China, West Germany should have been even more effective in East Germany, given that West Germany is much larger and stronger than Taiwan and Hong Kong combined, and East Germany is much smaller than mainland China.

The role of FDI in China is vastly overstated in the press. For the entire 1980s, FDI in China was tiny. FDI only started to increase substantially in 1993, and at its peak it accounted for about 10 percent of total investment. On per capita basis, China's FDI was not high by international standards. It is true that China's exports expanded very fast, but that cannot be the main story. The direct contribution of foreign trade and investment to large countries cannot be quantitatively as important as to small countries.

Like FDI, China's exports were very concentrated in coastal provinces. However, contrary to a popular perception, China's growth was not just a phenomenon of coastal provinces—it is across the board, both coastal and inland. Inland provinces are growing fast, though coastal provinces are growing faster. Anyone who has traveled to inland cities such as Xi' an or Guiyang cannot fail to notice their vibrant local economies. Indeed, if each China's provinces were counted as a distinct economy, about 20 out of the top 30 growth regions in the world in the past two decades would be provinces in China, many of which did not receive much foreign investment and did not depend on exports. Table 1 shows GDP growth by province in China and refutes the perception that growth in China is only coastal.

If focusing on FDI and foreign trade tends to downplay the entire reform process and the role of indigenous institutions, then a simple-minded view on trade and foreign investment creates obstacles to the understanding of growth in any country. This is because the effect of openness has to work through corresponding internal changes. Russia became very open after reform, more so than China, but neither higher growth nor more FDI ensued. Even in small East Asian countries, an export-oriented policy worked through domestic changes in investment and human capital accumulation. Therefore, it could well be the case that it is not exports that drive growth, but that the same forces of domestic change drive both exports and domestic growth.

The second common misperception about China's success is to attribute it exclusively to the agricultural reform in the early 1980s. To be sure, China's agricultural reform was a huge success. And the reason for it is pretty much a standard story of family farming plus market liberalization, although research has shown that the story is more complicated than that. For example, there seemed to be significant contributions from the rural R&D and infrastructure investments made in the 1970s toward the agriculture productivity growth in the 1980s (Huang and Rozelle 1996); and the state institutions for marketing also played important

Table 1. GDP Growth Rates by Province (precent)

Province	1978–90	1978–95	Province	1978–90	1978–95
Beijing	9.0	9.8	Henan	12.6	10.9
Tianjin	7.7	8.9	Hubei	9.4	10.5
Hebei	8.5	10.2	Hunan	7.7	8.7
Shanxi	8.2	8.8	Guangdong	12.3	14.2
Inner Mongolia	9.8	13.0	Guangxi	7.2	9.9
Liaoning	8.1	8.8	Hainan	10.1	12.3
Jilin	8.9	9.5	Sichuan	8.6	9.5
Heilongjiang	4.9	4.8	Guizhou	9.2	9.1
Shanghai	7.4	9.1	Yunan	9.7	9.9
Jiangsu	11.0	12.8	Tibet	7.7	8.3
Zhejiang	11.7	13.8	Shaanxi	9.0	9.1
Anhui	9.3	10.7	Gansu	8.2	8.6
Fujian	11.5	13.7	Qinghai	6.5	6.8
Jiangxi	9.0	10.4	Ningxia	9.2	8.9
Shangdong	10.0	11.9	Xinjiang	10.8	11.1

Source: *China Statistical Yearbook.*

roles in rural development (Rozelle 1996). Nevertheless, economists are generally comfortable with the Chinese agriculture reform because it fits their models of the world.

This way of thinking becomes a myth when one regards agricultural reform as the only successful reform in China. Often it carries two implicit messages: China did not do well in nonagricultural sectors because it did not follow the conventional advice, and China did well in agriculture reform because it was—and still is—a poor, agricultural country. The truth is that the agricultural reform was the first reform success in China, but its bigger achievements lie elsewhere. At the outset of reform in the late 1970s, over 70 percent of China's labor force was employed in agriculture. By 2000, China's agriculture labor force had already declined to below the 50 percent mark, which is impossible without successful development outside the agriculture sector. In the late 1990s, the agricultural share of China's GDP was at 16 percent, about the same level as in Poland and the Soviet Union in the early 1980s. Table 2 provides evidence showing that most of China's growth came from the nonagricultural sector—the industrial and tertiary sectors.

The agricultural sector can have important indirect effects on nonagricultural sectors. For example, successful agricultural reform provides sources of savings and labor to boost industrialization. But in order for this mechanism to work, reform of the nonagricultural sector is necessary. The fact that today China is no longer a poor, agricultural country demonstrates that the main success of China's reform lies outside agriculture.

One cannot understand China's growth without understanding how its reform worked in the domestic, nonagriculture sector, which is the focus of this Selection.

. . . Underlying China's reform is a series of institutional changes in the novel form of transitional institutions. These institutions work because they achieve two objectives at the same time—they improve economic efficiency on the one hand, and make the reform compatible for those in power on the other. They also take into consideration Chi-

Table 2. Growth Rates of GDP and GDP Components (percent)

Year	GDP	Agriculture	Industry	Tertiary
1979	7.6	6.1	8.2	7.8
1980	7.8	−1.5	13.6	5.9
1981	5.5	7.0	1.9	10.4
1982	9.1	11.5	5.6	13.0
1983	10.9	8.3	10.4	15.2
1984	15.2	12.9	14.5	19.4
1985	13.5	1.8	18.6	18.3
1986	8.8	3.3	10.2	12.1
1987	11.6	4.7	13.7	14.4
1988	11.3	2.5	14.5	13.2
1989	4.1	3.1	3.8	5.4
1990	3.8	7.3	3.2	2.3
1991	9.2	2.4	13.9	8.8
1992	14.2	4.7	21.2	12.4
1993	13.5	4.7	19.9	10.7
1994	12.6	4.0	18.4	9.6
1995	10.5	5.0	14.1	8.0

Note: Data on industry includes construction.
Source: *China Statistical Yearbook.*

na's specific initial conditions. At one level, one could argue that China's transitional institutions merely unleashed the standard forces of incentives, hard budget constraints, and competition. This is true, but such an economic rationale is inadequate. The transitional institutions are not created solely for increasing the size of a pie, they are also created to reflect the distributional concerns of how the enlarged pie is divided and the political concerns of how the interests of those in power are served. Rudimentary political logic readily predicts the existence of inefficiency, but it has difficulties in explaining why inefficient institutions are replaced by more efficient ones. China's reform shows that when the growth potential is large, with intelligence and will reformers can devise efficiency-improving institutional reforms to benefit all, including and especially those in power. There is apparently more room than we thought for institutional innovations to address both economic and political concerns, that is, for reforms to improve efficiency while remaining compatible with the interests of those in power.

The general principle of efficiency-improving and interest-compatible institutional change is simple, but the specific forms and mechanisms of transitional institutions often are not. Successful institutional reforms usually are not a straightforward copy of best-practice institutions. They need not be and sometimes should not be. They need not be because room exists for efficiency improvement that does not require fine tuning at the beginning. They should not be because the initial conditions are country- and context-specific, requiring special arrangements. Therefore, inevitably, transitional institutions display a variety of nonstandard forms. Furthermore, because these institutions are often responses to the initial institutional distortions, the mechanisms of their functioning can be intricate. Understanding these mechanisms sometimes needs an appeal to the counter-intuitive "second-best argument," which states that removing one distortion may be counterproductive in the presence of another distortion. For all these reasons, studying institutions in transition requires careful, and sometimes imaginative, analysis.

I study the general principle and the specific mechanisms underlying China's transitional institutions through the analysis of four successful reforms and one failure. Together, these five examples cover a broad spectrum of institutional reforms of the market, firms, and the government.

The first example is market liberalization through the so-called dual-track approach under which prices were liberalized at the margin while inframarginal plan prices and quotas were maintained. This approach is unconventional but shows in the simplest way how a reform can simultaneously improve efficiency and protect existing rents. The dual track reveals both the economic and political rationale, and also illustrates how a market-oriented reform can utilize existing institutions, which were designed for central planning.

The second example concerns an innovative form of ownership of firms—local government ownership in general and rural township-village enterprises (TVEs) in particular. This form is not standard, neither private nor state (i.e., national government) ownership. Yet TVEs were China's growth engine until the mid-1990s. The nonstandard ownership form worked to improve efficiency in an adverse environment characterized by insecure private property rights. At the same time, the equity stake of local governments served the interests of both local and national governments by giving them a higher share of revenue relative to the standard private ownership form.

The third example is one of making fiscal federalism productive. China's fiscal contracting between the central and local governments has worked to provide the incentives for local governments to pursue economic prosperity. By granting high marginal retention rates, this innovative arrangement has aligned the interests of local governments with local business, and played a fundamental role in turning local governments into "helping hands" for local business. Local governments responded to incentives by supporting productive nonstate enterprises and reforming nonproductive state enterprises.

The fourth example demonstrates a way to constrain the government in order to protect private incentives in the absence of rule of law. The institution of anonymous banking is not only unconventional but also contrary to the principle of transparency. But it has an economic logic: when other institutional means are not working, it limits government predation by reducing the amount of information available to it. The government accepts such a constraint because in benefits from the revenue out of the banking system through its control over interest rates and capital flow. Although such a practice of financial repression violates usual policy recommendations, it plays a crucial role in inducing the government to give up discretionary taxes on individuals.

Not all China's reforms worked. One miserable failure is the reform of large-scale state-owned enterprises (SOEs). After many experiments, no reforms of SOEs have been found to improve economic efficiency in a fashion compatible with the interests of those in power. The institution of Party appointment of top managers is a key obstacle. This failure reform is very costly to China. But fortunately it is not fatal, as SOEs now account for less than one-quarter of the entire economy, and their role is diminishing.

From Transitional Institutions to Best-Practice Institutions

. . . From the early 1990s, the planned track of the dual track in product markets was gradually phased out. By 1996, the plan track was reduced to 16.6 percent in agricultural goods, 14.7 percent in industrial producer goods, and only 7.2 percent in total retail sales of consumer goods. These numbers became even smaller in the late 1990s, and the planned track in those markets almost ceased to exist. On January 1, 1994, planed allocation of foreign exchange was completely abolished, and the planned track and the market track were merged into a single market track. Two direct factors have contributed to the smooth transition to a single track market.

First, because of the fast growth of the market track, the planned track became less significant as compared to the market track. For example, steel production under the planned track dropped to 30 percent in 1990 from the level of 52 percent in 1981. Similarly, in 1978, 97 percent of total retail sales were under the planned track, but only 31 percent in 1989. In the foreign exchange markets, at the time when the planned track of the foreign exchange was finally abolished in January 1994, the share of centrally allocated foreign exchange had already fallen to less than 20 percent of the total. With rapid growth, the plan track becomes a matter of little consequence to most potential losers, which in turn reduces the cost required for compensating them.

Second, when the plan track was abolished, potential losers were explicitly compensated. For example, although consumers have been able to buy food-stuffs in the market since 1980, urban food coupons (for purchasing grain, meat, oil, etc.) were finally removed only in the early 1990s. Guangzhou completed the removal of the above coupons in 1992 and spent on average 103 yuan in 1988, 113 yuan in 1990, and 43 yuan in 1992 per urban resident for compensation *(Guangzhou Statistical Yearbook)*. Beijing also spent 182 yuan in 1990, 185 yuan in 1991, and 123 yuan in 1994 per head before eliminating the coupons *(Beijing Statistical Yearbook)*. At the time of abolishment of the central allocation of foreign exchange in 1994, annual lump-sum subsidies sufficient to enable the purchase of the prereform allocation of foreign exchange were offered for a period of three years for those organizations that used to receive cheap foreign exchange.

After reaching the peak in the early 1990s, TVEs were being privatized throughout the 1990s. Privatization of TVEs accelerated in 1998 after the Chinese constitution was amended to regard the private sector as "an important component" of the economy. Wuxi in southern Jiangxu province was often regarded as the model for TVEs for the whole country, and it was the subject of almost all major studies on TVEs, including the important one by the World Bank (Byrd and Lin 1990). Until mid-1990s, TVEs were dominant in Wuxi. And private enterprises were almost nonexistent. Correspondingly, the income from TVEs was the chief revenue source for the township and village governments there. However, throughout the late 1990s, TVEs were being privatized in all the three counties in Wuxi, and by the year 2000 over 90 percent of TVEs had been privatized (author's interview, March 2001).

Three changes have played significant roles in increasing the gains from privatization of TVEs or the costs for the local government to continue to run TVEs. First, an important benefit of TVE ownership is the political protection of local government in order to secure property rights. In the late 1990s, private ownership of enterprises gained more legitimacy, as evidenced by the aforementioned constitutional amendment and the increased share of the private sector in the economy. Therefore, the benefit of TVEs in terms of more secure property right decreased. Second, the cost of TVE ownership, mainly the lack of managerial incentives, became more important as the economy became increasingly marketized and both product and labor market competition intensified. In the product market, fast entry of firms changed the previous seller's market to a buyer's market, eroding the profit margins TVEs enjoyed in the 1980s as early starters. Indeed, in the 1990s, the profitability of many TVEs deteriorated, while private enterprises started to boom in the same location. In the labor market, TVEs also started to lose good managers to foreign and joint venture firms when the latter gave the managers high salaries or even company shares. Third, the reforms in the monetary and banking systems made local bank branches more independent of local governments. TVEs found more difficulty in obtaining credit from the banking system.

The potential social gains from privatization will not automatically lead to privatization unless the local governments have the incentives to do it. [T]he significant benefits of TVE ownership to local governments are the tax revenues they extract from TVEs. After privatization, the township and village governments were able to keep all the privatization revenue. They were also able to continue to levy fees on all local private firms, usually 1.5 percent of total sales. This "local tax" is not shared with the higher level government; instead, township and village governments usually pay a fixed amount. Therefore, local governments support, rather than oppose, privatization out of their own interests.

China's fiscal contracting system played a positive role of providing fiscal incentives for local governments. But the fiscal contracting was an ad hoc arrangement and was not rule-based. On January 1, 1994, China introduced major tax and fiscal reforms that are more aligned with international best practices. Previously, China had never had a national tax bureau; there was no need because all taxes were collected by local governments and shared with the central government. The 1994 reform established formal fiscal federalism by introducing a clear distinction between national and local taxes and by establishing a national tax bureau and local tax bureaus, each responsible for its own tax collection. The reform also set up fixed rules between the national and local governments. For example, under the new system, the value-added tax is shared by the national and local government at a fixed ratio of 75:25.

Although the new tax and fiscal institutions are more in line with international best practice, they might hurt the interests of some local governments, which kept larger marginal shares of revenue under the previous fiscal contracting system. Why did the local governments accept such a change? Although some local governments (such as Guangdong province) benefited tremendously from the earlier fiscal contracting system, they also recognized that the ad hoc nature of the contracting system created many uncertainties and that the political pressures from other provinces had increased. The potential gain by moving to a rule-based tax system instead of the ad hoc contracting system is in their long-term interests. Moreover, the central government compensated the local governments for their potential revenue losses in the short run in the following way: Local government expenditures in the subsequent three years wold be guaranteed to stay at the 1993 levels. This is why in the fourth quarter of 1993

local expenditure exploded because local governments wanted to increase the base for compensation. The move from the fiscal contracting system to fiscal federalism turned out to be quite successful.

On April 1, 2000, China introduced "real name" household deposits under which all the bank deposits require a depositor's ID. This is an important step in moving from anonymous banking to real-name banking, an international practice. As in Korea, this change was not designed to increase tax revenue but to reduce political corruption by making the flow of money transparent. What is interesting is the particular way China introduced real-name banking: It followed a dual-track approach. The real-name policy only applies to new deposits made after April 1, 2000. Withdrawals from existing deposits, which amounted to about 6 trillion yuan (or more than 60 percent of China's GDP), continued to be anonymous. This drastically reduced opposition to this reform. By following the dual-track approach, the existing bank deposits were "grandfathered" and thus protected, and only the new deposits were required to follow the new rule.

The Chinese experience of institutional changes shows that transitional institutions can be superseded by conventional best-practice institutions when more development and reform take place. Transitional institutions do not necessarily lead to a partial reform trap, and incremental reforms do not always create obstacles to further reforms. However, China's experience also shows that this pattern will not develop automatically. It depends on the nature of early reforms, future gains, and especially, compensation schemes.

References

Beijing Statistical Yearbook. Various years. Beijing: China Statistical Publishing House.

Blanchard, Olivier, and Stanley Fischer. 1993. Editorial. *NBER Macroeconomics Annual, 1993.* Cambridge: MIT Press.

Byrd, William, and Qingsong Lin, eds. 1990. *China's Rural Industry: Structure, Development, and Reform.* Oxford: Oxford University Press.

China Statistical Yearbook. Various years. Beijing: China Statistical Publishing House.

Guangzhou Statistical Yearbook. Various years. Beijing: China Statistical Publishing House.

Huang, Jikun, and Scott Rozelle. 1996. "Technological Change: Rediscovery of the Engine of Productivity Growth in China's Rural Economy." *Journal of Development Economics* 49: 337–69.

Maddison, Angus. 1998. *Chinese Economic Performance in the Long Run.* Paris: OECD Development Centre.

Rozelle, Scott. 1996. "Gradual Reform and Institutional Development: The Keys to Success of China's Rural Reforms." In *Reforming Asian Socialism: The Growth of Market Institutions,* ed. John McMillan and Barry Naughton. Ann Arbor: University of Michigan Press.

Summers, Lawrence. 1992. "The Rise of China." *Transition Newsletter* (World Bank), 3, no. 6: 7.

World Bank. 1996. *From Plan to Market: World Development Report, 1996.* Oxford: Oxford University Press.

Selection I.B.3. India Since Independence*

The conventional narrative of India's post–World War II economic history begins with a disastrous wrong turn by India's first prime minister, Jawaharlal Nehru, toward Fabian socialism, central planning, and an unbelievable quantity of bureaucratic red tape. This "license raj" strangled the private sector and led to rampant corruption and massive inefficiency. As a result, India stagnated until bold neoliberal economic reforms triggered by the currency crisis of 1991, and implemented by the government of Prime Minister Narasimha Rao and Finance Minister Manmohan Singh, unleashed its current wave of rapid economic growth—at a pace that promises to double average productivity levels and living standards in India every sixteen years (Table 1).

Yet if you look at the growth performance of India during its first postindependence generation under the Nehru dynasty in the context of the general cross-country pattern, India does not appear to be an exceptional country. Its rate of economic growth appears average. Moreover, its values of the proximate determinants of growth appear average as well.

Simple growth theory tells us that the proximate determinants of growth are *(a)* the share of investment in GDP (to capture the effort being made to build up the capital stock), *(b)* the rate of population growth (to capture how much of investment effort has to be devoted to simply equipping a larger population with the infrastructure and other capital needed to maintain the current level of productivity, and *(c)* the gap between output per worker and the world's best practice (to capture the gap between the country's current status and its steady-state growth path, and also to capture the magnitude of the productivity gains possible through acquisition of the world's best-practice technologies). Neither India's investment share nor its rate of population growth are in any sense unusually poor for an economy in India's relative position as of independence.

The fact that pre-1990 India appears "normal," at least as far as the typical pattern of post—World War II economic growth is concerned, places limits on the size of the damage done to Indian eco-

nomic growth since World War II by the Nehru dynasty's attraction to Fabian socialism and central planning. India between independence and 1990 was not East Asia as far as economic growth was concerned, to be sure. But it was not Africa either.

One possibility is that the constraints placed on growth by the inefficiencies of the Nehru dynasty's "license raj" were simply par for the course in the post–World War II world: perhaps only exceptional countries were able to avoid inefficiencies like those of the license raj. A second possibility is that the failure of economic policies in promoting efficiency was in large part offset by successes in mobilizing resources: India in the first decades after World War II had a relatively high savings rate for a country in its development position.

Yet a third possibility is that the destructive effects of inefficiency-generating policies were offset by powerful advantages—a large chunk of the population literate in what was rapidly becoming the world's lingua franca, cultural patterns that placed a high value on education, the benefits of democracy in promoting accountability and focusing politicians' attention on their constituents' welfare, or some other factors—that should and would with better policies have made India one of the fastest-growing economies of the world not just in the 1990s but in previous decades as well.

If Indian economic growth before the past decade appears more or less ordinary, no one believes that Indian economic growth in the past decade and a half is anything like ordinary. In the 1990s India was one of the fastest-growing economies in the world. At the growth pace of the 1990s, Indian average productivity levels double every sixteen years. If the current pace of growth can be maintained, sixty-six years will bring India to the real GDP per capita level of the United States today. The contrast between the pace of growth in the 1990s and the pace of growth before 1980—with a doubling time of fifty years, and an expected approach to America's current GDP per capita level not in 2066 but in 2250—is extraordinary.

Moreover, this acceleration in Indian economic growth has not been "immiserizing." Poverty has not fallen as fast as anyone would wish, and regional and other dimensions of inequality have grown in the 1990s. But it is not the case that India's economic growth miracle is being fueled by the further absolute impoverishment of India's poor. Ahluwalia (1999) quotes Tendulkar (1997) as finding a 7 percent decline in the urban and a 20

*From J. Bradford DeLong, "India Since Independence." In Dani Rodrik, ed., *In Search of Prosperity* (Princeton: Princeton University Press, 2003), pp. 184–186, 194–197, 199–203. Reprinted by permission.

Table 1. Indian Rates of Economic Growth, 1950–2000

	1950–80	1980–90	1990–2000
Annual real GDP growth	3.7%	5.9%	6.2%
Annual real GDP per capita growth	1.5%	3.8%	4.4%

Source: IMF.

percent decline in the rural poverty gap[1] between 1983 and 1988, followed by a further 20 percent decline in both the urban and rural poverty gaps between 1988 and 1994. According to the Indian Planning Commission, the years between 1994 and 1999 saw a further 20 percent decline in the nation's poverty gap, leaving the best estimate of the proportional poverty gap today at 54 percent of its value back in 1983.

What are the sources of India's recent acceleration in economic growth? Conventional wisdom traces them to policy reforms at the start of the 1990s. In the words of Das (2000), the miracle began with a bang:

In July 1991 . . . the announcement of sweeping liberalization by the minority government of P. V. Narasimha Rao . . . opened the economy . . . dismantled import controls, lowered customs duties, and devalued the currency . . . virtually abolished licensing controls on private investment, dropped tax rates, and broke public sector monopolies. . . . [W]e felt as though our second independence had arrived: we were going to be free from a rapacious and domineering state.

Yet the aggregate growth data tells us that the acceleration of economic growth began earlier, in the early or mid-1980s, long before the exchange crisis of 1991 and the shift of the government of Narasimha Rao and Manmohan Singh toward neoliberal economic reforms.

Thus apparently the policy changes in the mid- and late-1980s under the last governments of the Nehru dynasty were sufficient to start the acceleration of growth, small as those policy reforms appear in retrospect. Would they have just produced a short-lived flash in the pan—a decade or so of fast growth followed by a slowdown—in the absence of the further reforms of the 1990s? My hunch is

that the answer is yes. In the absence of the second wave of reforms in the 1990s it is unlikely that the rapid growth of the second half of the 1980s could be sustained. But hard evidence to support such a strong counterfactual judgment is lacking.

The Indian Growth Miracle

The Value of India's Example

. . . The fact that India's growth performance seemed too *ordinary* in world context for the first three postindependence decades makes India's acceleration of economic growth since then much more exciting. With other countries that have experienced growth miracles, it is very difficult to imagine how to translate their experience into lessons for other developing countries. How is a country that seeks to emulate the Italian growth miracle to reproduce the close transport and trade links with the northwest European core? How is a country that seeks to repeat the growth miracle of Taiwan to attain the initial condition of an astonishingly equal distribution of land? How is a country that seeks to follow the Japanese model to assemble—in Japan's case, more than one hundred years ago—the national consensus for structural transformation and economic development that obtained among those who ruled in the name of Emperor Meiji?

It cannot be done. That is why the Indian case is so interesting, because it shows an example of an economy that was relatively stagnant and suffered from mammoth growth blockages yet managed to turn all that around, and in a short period of time.

Structural Breaks

To the extent that we trust aggregate national-level income accounts, it is clear that by 1985 Indian aggregate economic growth had undergone a structural break (Figure 1). Whether we should look for key causes of India's growth acceleration in the years immediately before 1985 depends on how we conceptualize that structural break. Was it the result of a once-and-for-all change that put the economy on a new, different path? Or when we say "structural change," are we referring to an ongoing process of waves of reform, each of which requires that the political coalition behind reform be reassembled, each of which could fail—with that failure capable of returning Indian growth to its pre-1980 pace?

Depending on how you answer this question, you focus on one of two time periods. If you seek a

---

[1] The percentage gap between the expenditure levels of all poor households, and what the expenditure levels of all poor households would be if they were pulled up to the poverty line.

Figure 1. Indian real GDP per capita level and 1962–80 trend.

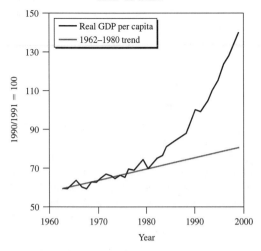

Source: International Monetary Fund.

single structural break, you look at the last years of Indira Gandhi's rule and at Rajiv Gandhi's administration, the years when economic reform and economic liberalization became ideologically respectable within the Indian government along with policies that a development-seeking government ought to pursue to some degree.

If you wish to identify ongoing waves of reform, each of them debated and debatable, then you are more likely to focus on the early 1990s—when the exchange crisis served as a trigger for larger-scale reforms by the government of Narasimha Rao than had been previously contemplated—and today, when one key item on the table is reform of India's budget, so that claims on social resources in excess of production do not lead to an inflation crisis.

The Last Nehru-Gandhi Government

Rajiv Gandhi's Congress party won 77 percent of the seats in the Lok Sabha in the election that followed his mother's assassination by her bodyguards. Party discipline was not overwhelmingly strong, but the magnitude of the majority—and the association of most members of parliament with Rajiv—meant that a relatively underdeveloped apparatus for enforcing party discipline did not matter. During Rajiv Gandhi's administration India came as close to an *elected* dictatorship as it has ever been. And as the visible representative of a new Indian generation—uncorrupt, interested in reform, focused on applying modern managerial techniques—this last Nehru-Gandhi government

ought to have had the power to carry out whatever plans of reform its leader could decide on.

Winning 48 percent of the national vote in the December 1984 election, and with 415 out of 545 seats in the Lok Sabha, this last government of the Nehru dynasty had the overwhelming majority needed for substantial reform. Moreover, the fact that Rajiv Gandhi himself was a new politician with his own circle of advisors and his own priorities meant that his government met the preconditions for a strong reforming executive: his government had the "relative autonomy" needed for it to have a good chance to transform the economy, rather than—as is usually the case—finding itself pulled back to the "political mainstream" by the standard pressures of politics.[2]

For the first time, private industry executives found it easy to move into powerful ministerial positions in an Indian government. Prime Minister Rajiv Gandhi himself spoke of how his government would pursue "deregulation, import liberalization, and . . . access to foreign technology" and invoked the example of Japan, which had in less than a generation moved from a country whose products were "synonymous with shoddy goods" to "a byword for the best available" (see Varshney 1999). The first budget of the Rajiv Gandhi government sought to reduce marginal tax rates, reduce tariffs, make restrictions on imports transparent by replacing quotas with tariffs, remove restrictions on large firms that had been imposed in 1969 as part of India's antitrust policy, and begin the process of eliminating license restrictions on manufacturing industries.[3]

The economic reform program that Rajiv Gandhi's government decided upon focused on (a) encouraging capital imports and commodity exports, (b) a modest degree of industrial deregulation, and (c) a modest degree of tax system rationalization. In the government's first year it eliminated quantitative controls on imports of industrial machinery and cut tariffs on imports of capital goods by 60 percent. (I know: it is hard to think of a reason for a country like India to have any tariffs or restrictions on imports of capital goods whatsoever. But you have to crawl before you can walk.) Taxes on profits from exports were halved as well. Subsidies were reduced (arousing bitter political opposition: Varshney (1999) cites Kothari (1986) as an example). The government reduced the number of industries subject to government capacity licensing from

---

[2]This is Varshney's (1999) judgment, relying on the typology of economic reform set out by Haggard and Webb (1994).

[3]The requirements that businesses obtain government licenses before they could build a plant or expand their capacity.

77 to 27 in 1988. And—although only in its last days—the government began to end price controls on industrial materials like cement and aluminum.

Yet somehow, somewhat paradoxically, the political power of Rajiv Gandhi's government was not transformed into rapid structural reform. Factions within the Congress Party seemed not to believe that their interests were bound up with the success of their leader and his policies, but were instead threatened by the potential backlash against an administration that was concerned with the prosperity of the rich rather than alleviating poverty: the Rajiv Gandhi regime had, after all, tried to increase the profits of businesses and cut marginal tax rates on food, kerosene, and fertilizer. Thus the reform plans carried out under Rajiv Gandhi were less bold than one would have expected given the rhetoric of his initial speeches.

The consequence of this first wave of economic reform was an economic boom. Real GDP growth averaged 5.6 percent per year over the Rajiv Gandhi government, while real rupee exports grew at 15 percent per year. By the end of the 1980s Indian aggregate labor productivity was one-third higher than a simple extrapolation of the pre-1980 trend would have predicted.

. . . Much conventional wisdom claims that the boom crated by Rajiv Gandhi's reforms was "unsustainable" and in some way "fictitious" because the late-1980s boom ended in an exchange rate crisis. The country's net capital import bill rose to 3 percent of GDP by the end of the 1980s. This growing foreign indebtedness—more than a quarter of exports were going to pay international debt service by the end of the 1980s—set the stage for the exchange crisis of 1991. Nevertheless, it is hard to argue that India would have been better off in the 1980s had it not borrowed from abroad. (It is easy to argue that it would have been better off had it followed a more realistic exchange rate policy in 1989 and 1990.) With limited exports, foreign borrowing is an extremely valuable way to finance capital-goods imports. If Lee (1995) is correct in arguing that such capital-goods imports are extraordinarily productive sources of technology transfer, then even extreme vulnerability to international financial crises as a result of foreign borrowing is a cost that weighs lightly in the balance relative to the benefits of one's firms being able to buy more foreign-made capital on the world market.

The Narasimha Rao Government

. . . Narasimha Rao's Congress Party won only 43 percent of the seats in the Lok Sabha in the 1991 election. For five years, however, he maintained his hold on the prime ministership and a narrow working majority. Varshney (2000) points out that in some respects the failure of the Congress Party to achieve a majority in the Lok Sabha in 1991 is deceptive and understates the strength of Rao's government. By 1991 the Hindu nationalist BJP had come to prominence in Indian national politics (see Hansen 1999). It was the second largest party in the Lok Sabha after the 1991 election. All of the other minor parties—the Janata Dal, the Communist Party of India (Marxist) (CPI(M)), and so forth—had to reckon that upsetting the Rao government and the Congress Party might well lead to the coming to power of the BJP, which was not to any of their tastes. Challenging any of the decisions of the Rao government might bring it down. Hence, as Echeverri-Gent (1998) puts it, because it was so weak—because it was a minority government—the Rao government could be very strong.

Under the Rao government, tariffs were reduced from an average of 85 percent to 25 percent of import value. The rupee became convertible. By the mid-1990s total foreign trade—imports plus exports—amounted to more than 20 percent of GDP. Foreign direct investment was encouraged and grew from effectively zero in the 1980s to $5 billion a year by the mid-1990s. The government walked rapidly down the path of reform that Rajiv Gandhi's government had tiptoed cautiously onto.

On the macroeconomic side, attention was focused on limiting money growth and thus controlling inflation. The government attempted—unsuccessfully—to erase the extremely high budget deficits of the past. And the government attempted—successfully—to build up its foreign exchange reserves.

The Rao government took the steps that the Rajiv Gandhi government had proposed to encourage foreign investment: it provided automatic government approval for FDI joint ventures in which foreigners held up to 51 percent of the equity; it provided automatic government approval for agreements licensing foreign technology as long as royalty payments to foreigners were kept at or below 5 percent of total sales.

And the Rao government carried through to completion a number of initiatives begun during the Rajiv Gandhi government to replace quantitative restrictions on imports by tariffs, to lower tariffs, to reduce the scope of licensing, and to attempt to reduce the scope of publicly owned monopolies.

The Vajpayee Government

. . . The governments that succeeded the Rao government have, in a move that many commentators found somewhat surprising, continued the reform process. After the Rao government, reform had become politically popular—indeed, inescapable for governments that wanted to take their share of credit for India's relatively rapid economic growth.

Most recently the BJP-led government of Prime Minister Vajpayee has removed capacity-licensing restrictions from the fossil-fuel and oil-cracking industries, from bulk pharmaceuticals, and from the sugar industry. The government has attempted to make sure that the remains of its old-fashioned industrial policy do not hobble the rapidly expanding Indian information technology industry. The government has gingerly taken steps toward establishing private industry and competition in electricity and telecommunications. The process by which licensing restrictions are removed from imports has continued. And further steps have been taken to try to rationalize the tax system.

The net effect of all of these reform policies has been a decade and a half of growth at the "new Hindu rate of growth" of 6 percent per year for overall real GDP, and of 3.5–4 percent per year for labor productivity. Such a pace of growth has made India one of the world's fastest-growing large economies—behind only China.

Reforms have had an effect not only on the policies notionally followed by the government, but on how those policies are implemented—on the amount of red tape and inefficiency generated by the government. The *Economist* reports that the head of General Electric's Indian subsidiaries, Scott Bayman, tells its reporters that the proportion of his time he spends in government offices has fallen from 70 percent to less than 5 percent.

Conclusion

What comes next for India? The governments that followed the Rao government—first the United Front and now the BJP-led coalition—have continued reform and liberalization, albeit not as rapidly as one might have hoped given the pace of economic reform in the first half of the 1990s. But the amount that is still left to be done is staggering.

For example, consider the electricity sector. The State Electricity Boards generate electricity and distribute it to consumers. Many consumers, including farmers and the politically favored, pay virtually nothing for their electricity. Many others steal it: losses in transmission and distribution amount to 35 percent of all electricity generated. The State Electricity Boards finance their operations by overcharging industrial and commercial consumers—giving them an incentive not to use higher-productivity electricity-intensive means of production. The rest of the State Electricity Boards' funding comes from the government. According to the *Economist,* the year-2000 losses of State Electricity Boards amounted to more than 1 percent of GDP, and accounted for 12 percent of the total public sector deficit. And the electricity provided is of miserable quality, with frequent blackouts and voltage spikes that have driven a third of industrial consumers to establish their own—small-scale, technically inefficient—private electricity generation facilities.

For another example, consider that India still has internal customs barriers. Trucks making a 500-mile journey may well have to pay internal tariffs at three different stops.

Moreover, India's government is a federal government. Much red-tape reduction needs to be accomplished not at the national but at the provincial level. And there are many provinces with huge populations and large shares of India's poor—Uttar Pradesh, Bihar, Orissa—in which the political establishment does not believe that increased governmental efficiency and reduced red tape should be a priority.

In the second half of the 1990s, India's governments have failed to make progress in bringing social claims on output into balance with productivity. The total deficits of the public sector—state and local governments, national government, and state-owned enterprises together—now amount to more than 10 percent of GDP. Unless this budget deficit is reduced and the rate of growth of the debt-to-GDP ratio brought under control, an inflation crisis at some point in the future seems likely once potential lenders to the Indian government decide that its debt-to-GDP ratio has risen too high for comfort.

Whether Indian real economic growth continues at the rapid pace of the past decade even if reform slows down and government budget deficits continue will tell us much about the resiliency of the growth process.

If Indian real economic growth does continue to be rapid even in the face of erratic public-sector performance, that will suggest to us that the most important factors were those that changed in India in the 1980s. What changed in the 1980s were three things. The first was a shift toward integration with the world economy—both the encouragement of exports, and the recognition that foreign investment and foreign-made capital goods had enormous potential as carriers of new and improved technology. The second was a shift in entrepreneurial attitudes: the fact that Rajiv Gandhi had not spent his life as a politician and the fact that his powerful ministers included ex-businessmen may have functioned as the Indian equivalent of Deng Xiaping's catch-phrase: "To get rich is glorious!" The third was a belief that the old Nehru dynasty order had come to an end, and that the rules of the economic game had changed. It may well be that these deeper changes had more importance for Indian growth than did individual policy moves.

On the other hand, if reform stagnates—or even continues at its current not very rapid pace—it may well be that Indian real growth will slow over the next decade. If so, that will suggest that the potential benefits in terms of higher growth from each act of policy liberalization are quickly taken up and exhausted. In that case successful reform will require not just that reformers be strong at one moment but that they institutionalize the reform and liberalization process over generations.

In either case, the world's economists now have an example of an economy that did *not* have remarkably favorable initial conditions but that has sustained rapid economic growth over two decades. To those for whom the East Asian miracle seemed out of reach—for whom the advice to emulate South Korea seemed so unattainable as to lead to despair—advice to emulate India may well prove more useful.

References

Ahluwalia, Montek. 1999. "India's Economic Reform: An Appraisal." In *India in the Era of Economic Reforms,* ed. Jeffrey Sachs, Ashutosh Varshney, and Nirupam Bajpai. New Delhi: Oxford University Press.

Das, Gurcharan. 2000. *India Unbound: A Personal Account of a Social and Economic Revolution.* New York: Knopf.

Echeverri-Gent, John. 1998. "Weak State, Strong Reforms: Globalization, Partisan Competition, and the Paradoxes of Indian Economic Reform." University of Virginia. Typescript.

Haggard, Stephan, and Steven Webb, eds. 1994. *Voting for Reform.* Oxford: Oxford University Press.

Kothari, Rajni. 1986. "The Flight into the Twenty-first Century: Millions Will Be Left Behind." *Times of India,* April 27, 1986.

Lee, Jong-Wha. 1995. "Capital Goods Imports and Long-Run Growth." *Journal of Development Economics* 48:91–110.

Tendulkar, S. 1997. "Indian Economic Policy Reform and Poverty." In *India's Economic Reforms and Development: Essays for Manmohan Singh,* ed. I. J. Ahluwalia and I. M. D. Little. Oxford: Oxford University Press.

Varshney, Ashutoth. 1999. "India's Economic Reforms in Comparative Perspective." In *India in the Era of Economic Reforms,* ed. Jeffrey Sachs, Ashutosh Varshney, and Nirupam Bajpai. New Delhi: Oxford University Press.

———. 2000. "Mass Politics or Elite Politics? India's Economic Reforms in Comparative Perspective." In *India in the Era of Economic Reforms,* ed. Jeffrey Sachs, Ashutosh Varshney, and Nirupam Bajpai. New Delhi: Oxford University Press.

Selection I.B.4. The Impact of the Economic Reforms in Latin America and the Caribbean*

All nine project countries [Argentina, Bolivia, Brazil, Chile, Colombia, Costa Rica, Jamaica, Mexico, and Peru] effected major changes in development strategy and public policies. A set of "first generation" reforms—import liberalization, domestic financial liberalization, capital account opening, privatization, and tax reform—was adopted to open the economies and to increase the role of market forces. In addition, macroeconomic policies became more equilibrated, and social expenditure increased substantially. Despite the generally similar policy trends, however, countries differed considerably in the extent to which they implemented the reforms and the style in which they were introduced. The reforms were instituted to varying degrees in the nine countries because of differences in initial conditions, especially inflation rates, past growth performance, and economic distortions. Countries with especially negative initial conditions—namely, Argentina, Bolivia, Chile, and Peru—turned out to be aggressive reformers. Presumably thinking they had little to lose and much to gain, they implemented many reforms in rapid order. Other countries, which had done well in previous periods and wanted to preserve certain elements in their societies and economies, became cautious reformers. This group—including Brazil, Colombia, Costa Rica, Jamaica, and Mexico—adopted a more gradual, selective approach to the reforms.

The reform results were neither as positive as supporters predicted nor as negative as opponents feared. Indeed, the reforms per se seem to have had a surprisingly small impact at the aggregate level, based on calculations using regional averages. It is only when we move to the country, sectoral, and microeconomic levels that the magnitude of the changes begins to become apparent. The principal aggregate level results can be summarized in five points.

—Growth recovered with respect to the 1980s, but there was no generalized surge (or decline) in output; many countries grew below their rates in the 1950–80 base period. Econometric evidence suggests that the impact of the reforms was positive, but small.

—Exports increased substantially, but imports grew even faster, leading to enlarged trade deficits.

—Investment and productivity recovered the ground that was lost in the 1980s, but no big gains occurred. As with growth, the reforms played a positive, but minor, role.

—Employment lagged behind the modest growth rates, and the quality of new jobs presented serious problems. The reforms appear to have played a negative role with respect to the quantitative aspects of job creation, but once again it was small.

—Inequality increased slightly, although serious measurement problems prevent a precise analysis of distribution trends. The reforms played a small, negative role, as with employment.

The biggest policy changes in a generation thus resulted in fairly modest changes in performance at the aggregate level. [Five] propositions provide elements for solving this puzzle. First, the reforms worked slowly, especially with respect to investment, because of the great uncertainty they generated; this was frequently exacerbated by macroeconomic instability. Uncertainty gave rise to three phases in the post-reform investment process: an initial decline, a recovery, and—only after the transitory factors that produced the first two phases had dissipated—a consolidation to normal levels. Second, the reforms and policies were frequently inconsistent, which increased the uncertainty that investors had to face. Third, international variables, especially volatile capital flows, contributed to both inconsistency and uncertainty. Fourth, different actors (that is, countries and firms) had different capacities to respond to the reforms; only a few could move quickly to take advantage of new opportunities, which contributed to slow change and inequality. Fifth, the reforms were incomplete and need complementary policies to make them function properly. Only now are most countries beginning to implement a "second generation" of reforms that involve improvement of regulation, public administration, the judiciary, and particularly education.

Proponents of the reforms expected that growth, employment, and equity outcomes would demonstrate a consistent, positive relation as a result of the policy changes. The reforms were expected to increase the efficiency of the economies and provide incentives for more investment. Investment and increased productivity would raise growth rates. In turn, higher growth would lead to more

*From Barbara Stallings and Wilson Peres, *Growth, Employment, and Equity: The Impact of the Economic Reforms in Latin America and the Caribbean* (Washington, D.C.: Brookings Institution Press, 2000), pp. 202–210. Reprinted by permission.

employment, especially for unskilled labor, and ultimately result in increased equity. Table 1 provides a very rough set of qualitative indicators that summarize performance results in comparison to these expectations.

Of the nine countries in the project, only Chile has come near to fulfilling the broad expectations held out for the reforms. It is essential to point out, however, that the Chilean economy went through multiple crises in the first decade after the initiation of the reforms. Significant policy adjustments were made starting in the mid-1980s, and these were deepened after the resumption of democratic rule in 1990, leading to the performance described in the table. What has Chile achieved? In quantitative terms, it has greatly increased investment and productivity with respect to its own past and to the rest of the region in the present. It has also kept its external accounts in order through an emphasis on exports and high domestic savings. These factors led to rapid and stable growth (until the crisis of the late 1990s revealed some previously ignored weaknesses on the external front and with respect to macroeconomic consistency). With GDP growth averaging about 7 percent per year for nearly fifteen years, employment creation was strong and poverty alleviation was notable. Household income concentration remained stubbornly high, but primary distribution became somewhat more equal and social services expanded. In qualitative terms, innovative macroeconomic policies were geared to maintaining stability and restraining volatility. Equally important, incentives were provided to the

private sector to stimulate the investments that were needed to continue the economic expansion.

The experiences of the other eight project countries are a mix of partial successes and pending challenges. They can be divided into three groups, based on the nature of their achievements and the problems they still face. First, Argentina, Bolivia, and Peru also improved their growth records in the 1990s in comparison with their past performance. Like Chile, they were all aggressive reformers that initially faced overwhelming problems including hyperinflation, poor economic performance, highly distorted economies, and serious problems of governability. All this represented enormous opportunities for improvement once new policies— both reforms and macroeconomic stabilization— were implemented and gained credibility. High GDP growth was achieved through a combination of factor accumulation or strong productivity growth. Nonetheless, all three economies are still fragile, and the societies have serious social problems, especially unemployment in Argentina and poverty in Bolivia and Peru.

A second group had less success in matching its past growth performance, but was nonetheless highly successful regarding exports and employment. The primary example is Mexico, closely followed by Costa Rica. Both countries were able to break into the markets of the industrialized countries, particularly the United States. Their higher participation in those markets was achieved mainly through labor-intensive exports from the *maquila* (in-bond) plants, which are part of the production

Table 1. Relation Between Reforms and Outcomes in the 1990s

Country	Reforms	Investment[a]	Productivity[b]	Growth[c]	Employment[d]	Equity[e]
Argentina	Aggressive	=	+	+	−	−
Bolivia	Aggressive	+	−	+	+	−
Brazil	Cautious	−	−	−	−	=
Chile	Aggressive	+	+	+	+	+
Colombia	Cautious	+	−	−	−	−
Costa Rica	Cautious	+	−	−	+	+
Jamaica	Cautious	n.a.	n.a.	−	=	n.a.
Mexico	Cautious	=	−	−	+	−
Peru	Aggressive	=	+	+	−	+

[a]Investment: + means that a country had a higher investment coefficient in the 1990s than in the base period (1950–80); − means that it had a lower coefficient; = means there was little change.

[b]Productivity: + means that growth of total factor productivity was higher in the 1990s than in the base period (1950–80); − means that it was lower; = means there was little change.

[c]Growth: + means that a country grew faster in the 1990s than in the base period (1950–80); − means that it grew more slowly.

[d]Employment: + means that the country ranked high on the labor market index; − means than it ranked low; = means that there was little change.

[e]Equity: + means that primary income distribution in the latest available year was more equal than the pre-reform period; − means that it was less equal; = means that there was little change.

chains that integrate the northern part of the hemisphere. Costa Rica and Mexico generated a substantial amount of employment through these exports. Real wages rose rapidly in Mexico until the peso crisis in 1994–95, but they have been stagnant since them. In Costa Rica, wages are among the most dynamic found in the project countries. Both countries turned in surprisingly strong performances in the face of the international financial crisis that buffeted the region in the late 1990s, based largely on the strength of the U.S. economy. On the social front, the improvement of basic services, together with relatively better initial conditions, allowed Costa Rica to deal with issues of equity more successfully than Mexico.

The remaining countries are mainly characterized by the multifaceted challenges they face. Brazil, Colombia, and Jamaica make up this group, although the lack of information on Jamaica makes it very difficult to judge what is happening there. Brazil and Colombia were strong performers in an earlier period; they have undertaken significant reforms without yet consolidating a new model to replace the one that served them well in the past. Serious ongoing macroeconomic problems, including fiscal deficits, external deficits, and high interest rates, have made the private sector very reluctant to participate in moving the economies forward. Low growth rates have begun to increase unemployment and other social problems, which undermine the governments' ability to find solutions to the challenges they face.

The type of aggregate analysis that is possible at the regional and country levels leaves many unanswerable questions. Moving to the sectoral and microeconomic levels provides additional insights and offers leverage to draw conclusions about probable future trends. It also offers a contrast to the aggregate analysis, since here we find evidence of stronger impact of the reforms. Beginning with the sectoral level, two reforms—namely, trade liberalization and privatization—had an important impact on investment, productivity, and employment.

—Investment was concentrated in a relatively small number of sectors. Only one sector (telecommunications) saw dynamic investment in all countries, and only one country (Chile) increased investment in all major sectors. Manufacturing investment was particularly dynamic in some capital-intensive subsectors (for example, cement, steel, petrochemicals, and chemicals). Nonetheless, investment coefficients in manufacturing as a whole were, at best, slightly higher than in the pre-reform period.

—Productivity gains were more evenly spread across broad sectors, but heterogeneity increased within sectors, for example, between commercial and family agriculture. Likewise, within manufacturing, some subsectors performed very well but others lagged behind. Despite productivity growth in manufacturing as a whole, the productivity gap vis-à-vis the United States did not narrow in the 1990s.

—Trade liberalization led to two different patterns of export growth in the 1990s: integration into the North American market through manufactured exports in Mexico, Central America, and the Caribbean versus a strong concentration in natural resource-based commodities in South America. The difference was due to trade arrangements such as the North American Free Trade Agreement (NAFTA) and the Caribbean Basin Initiative. To a lesser extent, subregional trade agreements in South America have also been instrumental in fostering manufactured exports. Strong local supplier linkages have not accompanied export growth in either of the two patterns: the *maquila* plants use few domestic inputs, and modernization of commodity production led to higher imports of capital goods.

—Privatization was instrumental to investment recovery and to modernization when other necessary conditions were also present. It fostered investment in certain tradables (for example, mining and natural gas), although linkages with the rest of the economy continued to be weak. In nontradables, the biggest increases in investment were in telecommunications; results were mixed in electricity. Privatization alone did not guarantee efficient performance. Strengthening property rights proved to be an important factor for attracting foreign investment in mining, while increasing competitive pressures were necessary to ensure efficient market outcomes in the services sectors, like telecommunications.

—When the concentration of growth in capital-intensive activities created few jobs, services became the residual source of employment. Services had a heterogeneous performance: high-quality jobs were created in telecommunications, banking, and finance, but the bulk was in low-skill services. Overall, employment generation was jointly determined by secular trends and the impact of the reforms. Agriculture continued its long-term decline in total employment, and manufacturing generally lost share, except for the *maquila*.

The old-style "triple alliance" among transnational corporations (TNCs), large domestic firms, and the state has broken down. The state privatized most of its firms, and local capital lost out to TNCs in the late 1990s. TNCs are less exposed to strategic uncertainty about opening new markets and using new technologies than are large domestic firms. They also have access to international finance under better conditions than even the largest domestic firms. The reforms that had the most important impact at the microeconomic level were privatization and the greater welcome for foreign direct investment.

—Large corporations led the investment process, and TNCs gained share in sales among the larger firms. Restructuring of corporate ownership was increasingly important in the second half of the 1990s. Nonetheless, the large firms contributed relatively little to the generation of employment since they tended to be highly capital-intensive.

—Despite the common perception that small and medium-size enterprises (SMEs) have done extremely poorly, they maintained their share in total production and employment. The fact that they did not grow rapidly, however, had negative implications for job creation.

—In the manufacturing sector, most new jobs were created by small firms and microenterprises. These were the only firms that increased employment in countries like Argentina, Brazil, Chile, and Costa Rica, where they accounted for more that 100 percent of the net job creation, because larger firms posted a net job loss as a result of the downsizing that accompanied modernization. Only in Mexico were large manufacturing firms more dynamic than smaller ones; the *maquila* played a very positive role in this outcome.

—Although the labor productivity of larger companies is three or four times higher than that of SMEs, the latter increased their efficiency and in some countries even narrowed the gap. Nonetheless, the productivity gap widened between large and medium-size firms, on the one hand, and small firms and microenterprises, on the other. Thus a large share of job creation took place in firms whose efficiency declined or at best stagnated.

—Wage differentials between larger firms and microenterprises increased, particularly in the second half of the 1990s. This is consistent with a widening productivity gap between the two groups of firms. All else equal, this wage differential contributed to increased inequality.

By the end of the 1990s, regional economies had more or less recovered what they had lost during the 1980s in terms of investment and production

tivity levels.[1] The new investments were more efficient than the ones they replaced, but they were highly concentrated in a few sectors, namely, natural resources, resource-based manufactured products, automobiles, and the *maquila.* Many subsectors in these industries are growing slowly in the world market, face falling terms of trade, or are technologically mature. Moreover, the expected rates of return on these investments are likely to be lower than before the reforms were introduced, due to greater competition and less state support. Labor productivity also returned to its pre-crisis levels, but this implies that the gap in Latin America and the Caribbean with respect to the member countries of the Organization for Economic Cooperation and Development (OECD) and the newly industrializing economies of East Asia increased. While a number of individual sectors did very well, their dynamism was not transmitted to the economies as a whole. This was partly due to weak or nonexistent supplier relations.

These weak domestic supplier networks have both advantages and disadvantages. Weaker links may be an advantage for exporting firms because their competitiveness increases when they are able to select the most efficient source of inputs, irrespective of domestic or foreign origin. When imported inputs grow as fast as total exports, however, trade surpluses in exporting activities are not sufficient to compensate for deficits in other sectors. The opportunity for technological progress is lost since it tends to concentrate in the user-supplier interface, and employment creation is weakened because of the destruction or non-creation of domestic suppliers.

Given this constellation of factors, a significant increase in growth rates in the next decade cannot be taken for granted. Lacking strong growth, unemployment rates are likely to remain high, which will exacerbate social problems and hinder attempts to lower the very high rates of inequality that characterize the region. External vulnerability, which has probably risen because of increased globalization together with trade and financial liberalization, makes solutions more complex. This outlook surely justifies the consideration of policy changes to improve expected outcomes. Or, as one ECLAC economist has put it, there is a need "to reform the reforms."

---

[1]It is important to recall that we are using simple averages to prevent Brazil and Mexico from overwhelming our results. Weighted averages would show that investment has yet to return to the 1980 peak.

Selection I.B.5. Why Has Africa Grown Slowly?*

In the 1960s, Africa's future looked bright. On the basis of Maddison's (1995) estimates of per capita GDP for a sample of countries, during the first half of the century Africa had grown considerably more rapidly than Asia; by 1950, the African sample had overtaken the Asian sample. In the 1950s there were uncertainties of political transition, but after 1960 Africa was increasingly free of colonialism, with the potential for governments that would be more responsive to domestic needs. During the period 1960–73, growth in Africa was more rapid than in the first half of the century. Indeed, for this period, African growth and its composition were indistinguishable from the geographically very different circumstances of south Asia (Collins and Bosworth, 1996). Political self-determination in Africa and economic growth seemed to be proceeding hand-in-hand.

However, during the 1970s both political and economic matters in Africa deteriorated. The leadership of many African nations hardened into autocracy and dictatorship. Africa's economies first faltered and then started to decline. While Africa experienced a growth collapse, nations of south Asia modestly improved their economic performance. A good example of this divergence is the comparison of Nigeria and Indonesia. Until around 1970, the economic performance of Nigeria was broadly superior to that of Indonesia, but over the next quarter-century outcomes diverged markedly, despite the common experience for both countries of an oil boom in a predominantly agricultural economy. Since 1980, aggregate per capita GDP in sub-Saharan Africa has declined at almost 1 percent per annum. The decline has been widespread: 32 countries are poorer now than in 1980. Today, sub-Saharan Africa is the lowest-income region in the world. Figure 1 and Table 1, taken together, offer a snapshot of Africa today. Figure 1 is a map of the continent. Table 1 gives some basic information on population, GDP, standard of living, and growth rates for countries of sub-Saharan Africa. We focus on the sub-Saharan countries, setting aside the north African countries of Algeria, Egypt, Libya, Morocco and tunisia. This is conventional for the studies of this area, since the north African countries are part of a dif-ferent regional economy—the Middle East—with its own distinctive set of economic issues. It is clear that Africa has suffered a chronic failure of economic growth. The problem for analysis is to determine its causes.

The debate on the causes of slow African growth has offered many different explanations. These can be usefully grouped into a two-by-two matrix, distinguishing on the one hand between policy and exogenous "destiny" and, on the other, between domestic and external factors. Table 2 compares Africa to other developing regions, using this grouping. Until recently it has largely been accepted that the main causes of Africa's slow growth were external, with the debate focusing upon whether external problems were policy-induced or exogenous. Especially during the 1980s, the World Bank, the International Monetary Fund and bilateral donors came to identify exchange rate and trade policies as the primary causes of slow growth in Africa. Table 2 offers some evidence that official exchange rates in sub-Saharan Africa have been more overvalued relative to (often illegal) market rates than is common for other less developed economies of Asia and Latin America. Tariffs and quantitative trade restrictions have also been higher in Africa than elsewhere. The rival thesis, often favored by African governments, was that the crisis was due to deteriorating and volatile terms of trade, and as Table 2 shows, terms of trade have indeed been more volatile for Africa than for other less developed economies. Jeffrey Sachs and his co-authors have emphasized a further adverse external "destiny" factor: Africa's population is atypically landlocked. As shown in Table 2, a high proportion of the population is remote from the coast or navigable waters.

Recently, attention has shifted to possible domestic causes of slow growth within African nations, but the debate as to the relative importance of policy-induced and exogenous problems has continued. Sachs and his co-authors have attributed slow growth to "the curse of the tropics." Africa's adverse climate causes poor health, and so reduces life expectancy below that in other regions, which puts it at a disadvantage in development. The adverse climate also leads to leached soils and unreliable rainfall, which constrains African agriculture. African nations also appear to have more ethnic diversity than other poor nations

*From Paul Collier and Jan Willem Gunning, "Why Has Africa Grown Slowly?" *Journal of Economic Perspectives* 13 (Summer 1999): 3–16, 19–20. Reprinted by permission.

Figure 1. The political geography of Africa.

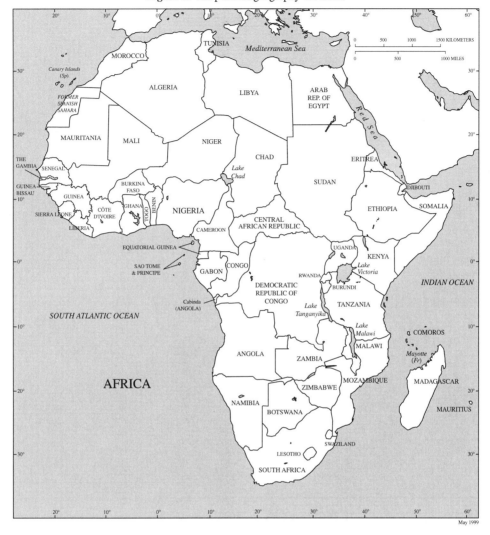

May 1999

of the world, which may make it harder to develop an interconnected economy. In contrast to the domestic destiny argument, Collier and Gunning (1999) have emphasized domestic policy factors such as poor public service delivery. African governments have typically been less democratic and more bureaucratic than their Asian and Latin American counterparts.

Of course, once the conditions for slow growth are established by any combination of these reasons, they can become self-reinforcing in an endogenous process. Weak economic growth helps explain a lower saving rate and a higher proportion of flight capital for Africa compared to the less developed nations of Asia and Africa. Richer coun-

tries tend to see their population growth rates drop off, so the poverty of Africa has helped to keep its birth rates high, even as compared to the world's other less developed economies. Similarly, poverty may have increased the incidence of Africa's numerous civil wars, as well as being a consequence of them.

In the discussion that follows, we assess the policy/destiny and domestic/external distinctions in various combinations. During the mid-1990s, African performance started to improve, with a few countries growing quite rapidly. We conclude by assessing these different explanations as guides to whether this improvement is likely to be transient or persistent.

Table 1. The Economies of Sub-Saharan Africa

Country	Population (millions) 1997	GDP US$m at 1990 Prices 1997	GNP per capita (PPP $) 1997	GNP average annual % growth per capita 1965–97	Life expectancy at birth (years) 1995	% of Population below $1 a day (early 1990s)	Trade as % of GDP (in PPP) 1997
Angola	11.6	9,886	728	. . .	48	. . .	77
Benin	5.7	2,540	1,240		48	. . .	17
Botswana	1.5	4,458	7,440	7.7	66	33	. . .
Burkina Faso	11.1	3,643	936	0.9	47	. . .	7
Burundi	6.4	939	661	1.1	51	. . .	5
Cameroon	13.9	11,254	1,739	1.4	57	. . .	13
Cape Verde	0.4	393	. . .	. . .	66	. . .	. . .
Central African Republic	3.4	1,420	1,254	−1.2	50	. . .	10
Chad	6.7	1,492	978	0.1	49	. . .	4
Comoros	0.7	251	. . .	. . .	57	. . .	. . .
Congo	2.7	2,433	1,275	1.7	53	. . .	80
Congo, Dem. Rep.	48.0	6,094	698	−3.7	. . .	. . .	7
Côte d'Ivoire	14.3	13,320	1,676	−0.9	50	18	30
Djibouti	0.4	384	. . .	. . .	49	. . .	. . .
Equatorial Guinea	0.4	541	. . .	. . .	49	. . .	. . .
Eritrea	3.4	1,010	990	. . .	52	. . .	. . .
Ethiopia	60.1	11,327	493	−0.5	49	46	7
Gabon	1.1	7,280	6,480	0.4	55	. . .	58
Gambia	1.0	332	1,372	0.5	46	. . .	30
Ghana	18.3	7,892	1,492	−0.9	57	. . .	19
Guinea	7.6	3,699	1,763	. . .	46	26	14
Guinea Bissau	1.1	306	1,041	0.1	45	88	13
Kenya	28.4	9,879	1,150	1.3	55	50	16
Lesotho	2.1	998	2,422	3.2	62	49	. . .
Liberia	2.5	. . .	. . .	. . .	57	. . .	. . .
Madagascar	15.8	3,187	892	−1.9	58	72	11
Malawi	10.1	2,480	688	0.5	45	. . .	21
Mali	11.5	3,132	715	0.5	47	. . .	19
Mauritania	2.4	1,346	1,654	−0.2	53	31	28
Mauritius	1.1	3,755	9,147	3.8	71	. . .	37
Mozambique	18.3	2,144	541	−0.1	47	. . .	15
Namibia	1.6	3,141	4,999	0.7	60	. . .	. . .
Niger	9.8	2,776	824	−2.5	48	62	9
Nigeria	118.4	34,418	854	0.0	51	31	23
Rwanda	5.9	1,979	643	0.1	47	46	9
Sao Tome & Principe	0.1	56	. . .	. . .	. . .	. . .	. . .
Senegal	8.8	6,708	1,670	−0.5	50	54	11
Seychelles	0.1	435	. . .	. . .	. . .	. . .	. . .
Sierra Leone	4.4	. . .	401	−1.4	40	. . .	24
Somalia	10.4	. . .	. . .	. . .	48	. . .	. . .
South Africa	43.3	117,089	7,152	0.1	64	24	23
Sudan	27.9	13,119	. . .	−0.2	54	. . .	. . .
Swaziland	0.9	1,031	. . .	. . .	59	. . .	. . .
Tanzania	31.5	4,956	608	. . .	52	11	14
Togo	4.3	1,726	1,408	−0.6	56	. . .	24
Uganda	20.8	6,822	1,131	. . .	44	69	6
Zambia	8.5	3,564	900	−2.0	48	85	26
Zimbabwe	11.7	7,904	2,207	0.5	52	41	21

Sources: African Development Report (1998); and *World Development Indicators* (1999).

Table 2. Africa Compared with Other Developing Regions (figures are unweighted country averages)

	Sub-Saharan Africa	Other LDCs
Domestic-Destiny		
Life expectancy in 1970 (years)	45.2	57.3
Income in 1960 (1985 $ PPP-adjusted)	835.5	1855.2
Ethnic Fractionalization	67.6	32.7
Domestic-Policy		
Political Rights, 1973–90	6.0	4.0
Bureaucracy	1.38	1.72
External-Destiny		
Population <100 km from the sea or river (%)	21.0	52.0
Terms of trade volatility	16.4	12.8
External-Policy		
Parallel market exchange rate premium	40.0	26.0
Average tariffs 1996–98 (%)	21.0	13.0
Quantitative Restrictions, 1988–90 (%)	46.0	21.0
Endogenous		
Growth of GDP per capita, 1965–90	0.5	1.7
Investment rate in 1997 (%)	18.0	25.0
Population growth rate, 1980–97 (%)	2.8	1.8
Capital flight/private wealth, 1990 (%)	39.0	14.0

Sources: Life expectancy, World Development Indicators, 1998. Income and growth: Penn World Tables 5.6. The index of eth-no-linguistic diversity is on the scale 0–100 with 0 being homogenous (Mauro, 1995). The Gastil index of political rights is on the range 1–7 with 1 being fully democratic.

The index of bureaucracy is on the scale 0–6 with high score indicating better quality (Knack and Keefer, 1995). Population living less than 100 km from the sea or a navigable river, from Bloom and Sachs (1999), Table 2, (other LDCs is the weighted average for Asia and Latin America). Terms of trade volatility is the standard deviation of annual log changes 1965–92, (Collins and Bosworth, 1996). Parallel exchange rate premium (%), (Easterly and Levine, 1997).

Average tariff: simple average, computed by IMF, we would like to thank Robert Sharer for these numbers. QRs: weighted average incidence of non-tariff measures over product lines; other LDCs is simple average of Latin America and East Asia; from Rodrik (1999, Table 12).

Investment rate and population growth rate, World Development Indicators, 1999 Capital flight/private wealth as of 1990 (Collier and Pattillo, 1999).

Four Types of Explanation

Domestic-Destiny

Africa has several geographic and demographic characteristics which may predispose it to slow growth. First, much of the continent is tropical and this may handicap the economy, partly due to diseases such as malaria and partly due to hostile conditions for livestock and agriculture. Life expectancy has historically been low, with the population in a high-fertility, high infant-mortality equilibrium. With the advent of basic public health measures, population growth became very high. In particular, Africa has not been through the demographic transition whereby fertility rates decline which occurred in Asia and Latin America over the past 40 years. On one estimate, Africa's low life expectancy and high population growth account for almost all of Africa's slow growth (Bloom and Sachs, 1998). The argument is not clear-cut, however. Low life expectancy and high

fertility are consequences of low income as well as causes, so the estimates are likely to be biased upwards. The household-level evidence suggests that the effects of poor health on income are small, although these in turn will be biased downwards by the omission of large-scale changes in economic activity which cannot be detected at the household level.

Whether or not Africa's past demographic characteristics have contributed to its slow growth, some African countries seem certain to go through a distinctive and disastrous demographic transition during the next two decades. As a result of AIDS, adult mortality rates will rise dramatically. In Africa, AIDS is a heterosexual disease. During the 1980s in parts of Africa it spread rapidly across the population before the risks became apparent, with up to 20–25 percent of adults now HIV-positive in some countries (World Bank, 1997). This human tragedy will have substantial economic effects during the next decade, especially since infection rates appear to be higher among the more educated, but it does not account for historically slow growth.

A second key characteristic of Africa which may predispose it to slow growth is that soil quality is poor and much of the continent is semi-arid, with rainfall subject to long cycles and unpredictable failure. Soils derive disproportionately from a very old type of rock ("Basement Complex"), which is low in micronutrients and varies considerably between localities. The application of additional macronutrients, which is the fertilizer package associated with the Green Revolution, is generally ineffective with low levels of micronutrients. Africa probably has scope for its own agricultural revolution, but it will depend upon locality-specific packages of micronutrients (Voortman et al., 1999). Since the 1960s, the semi-arid areas of Africa have been in a phase of declining rainfall (Grove, 1991). While there are no estimates of the output consequences of this decline, it may be significant, since agriculture is typically about one-quarter of GDP in this region. Given the lack of irrigation, the unpredictability of rainfall implies high risks in agriculture. With incomplete insurance and a high rate of time preference, households have to use assets for purposes of consumption-smoothing rather than investment. Households can thus become trapped in low-income, high-liquidity equilibria (Dercon, 1997).

A third relevant characteristic of Africa's economies, which can be seen as a result of these semi-arid conditions, is that the continent has very low population density. One by-product is high costs of transport which in turn have added to risk: poor market integration has hampered the use of trade for risk sharing. Another consequence of low population density is that Africa has relatively high natural resource endowments per capita (Wood and Mayer, 1998). High levels of natural resources can cause several problems. High levels of exported natural resources may lead to an appreciation of the exchange rate, which in turn makes manufacturing less competitive. Yet manufacturing may offer larger growth externalities, such as learning, than natural resource extraction. Natural resources may also increase "loot-seeking" activities. Collier and Hoeffler (1998) find that a dependence on natural resources strongly increases the risk of civil war, which has been a widespread phenomenon in Africa.

A further consequence of low population density is that African countries have much higher ethno-linguistic diversity than other regions; when groups come together less, there is less mingling and merging. Easterly and Levine (1997) find that this high level of diversity is the most important single cause of Africa's slow growth. There are various interpretations of this result. A common perception is that Africa's high ethnic diversity accounts for its high incidence of civil war. This turns out to be false: high levels of ethnic and religious diversity actually make societies significantly safer (Collier and Hoeffler, 1999). The effects of ethnic diversity on growth turn out to be contingent upon the political system; diversity has deleterious effects only when it occurs in the context of governments which are undemocratic. Collier (1999) finds that in democratic societies, ethnic diversity has no effect on either growth or the quality of public projects, but that in dictatorships, high levels of diversity reduce growth rates by 3 percentage points and double the rate of project failure relative to homogeneity. Dictatorships tend not to transcend the ethnic group of the dictator, so that the more ethnically fragmented the society, the more narrowly based a dictatorship will be, whereas democratic governments in such societies must be ethnically cross-cutting. In turn, the more narrowly based the government, the greater the payoff to predation relative to the inducement of generalized growth. Africa's problem was thus not its ethnic diversity but its lack of democracy in the context of diversity.

A fourth characteristic of Africa that may hinder its growth prospects is that because of its colonial heritage, Africa has much smaller countries in terms of population than other regions. Sub-Saharan Africa has a population about half that of India, divided into 48 states. These many states, combined with low levels of income, make Africa's national economies radically smaller that those of other regions. Very small states might be economically disadvantaged for several reasons. If government has some fixed costs, either in its administrative role or as a provider of services, then it may be hard for a small state to perform at minimum cost. Moreover, the society may forfeit much more extensive scale economies if it combines small scale with isolation. Some domestic markets will be too small even for the minimum efficient scale of production of single producer; all domestic markets taken alone will be less competitive than in larger economies. Small economies are also perceived by investors as significantly more risky (Collier and Dollar, 1999). Finally, they may have a slower rate of technological innovation; Kremer (1993) argues the incidence of discoveries may be broadly proportional to the population, so that if discoveries cannot readily spread between societies, low-population societies will have less innovation. However, in aggregate these effects cannot be large, because growth regressions generally find that state size does not affect a nation's rate of economic growth.

Domestic-Policy

For much of the post-colonial period, most African governments have been undemocratic. The median African government during the 1970s and 1980s was close to autocracy, and far less democratic than the median non-African developing country (as measured by the Gastil scale of political rights shown in Table 2). A typical pattern was that governments were captured by the educated, urban-resident population, with few agricultural or commercial interests. They expanded the public sector while imposing wide-ranging controls on private activity. These choices have been economically costly.

Public employment was expanded, often as an end in itself. For example, in Ghana by the late 1970s the public sector accounted for three-quarters of formal wage employment (Ghana Central Bureau of Statistics, 1988), and even in a more market-oriented economy like Kenya, the figure was 50 percent as of 1990 (Kenya Central Bureau of Statistics, 1996). Indeed, economic decline may have increased pressure for public sector employment. The large number of public sector employees was reconciled with limited tax revenue by reducing wage rates and non-wage expenditures. The ratio of wage to non-wage expenditures in African governments is double that in Asia, and this has lowered the quality of public services; for example, in education, teaching materials are often lacking. The large, ill-paid public sector became the arena in which ethnic groups struggled for resources. For example, in the Ghanaian public sector, the locally dominant ethnic group received a wage premium of 25 percent over other groups after controlling for worker characteristics, and cognitive skills were completely unrewarded (Collier and Garg, 1999). The combination of low wage levels and payment structures, which rewarded social connections rather than skill, made it difficult for managers to motivate staff, and the difficulties of service delivery were compounded by the low ratio of non-wage to wage expenditures.

Since public sector employment was the main priority, managers were not under severe pressure for actual delivery of services from their political masters. Because of the lack of democracy, neither were they accountable to the broader public. As a result, Africa experienced a paradox of poor public services despite relatively high public expenditure (Pradhan, 1996). Poor service delivery handicapped firms through unreliable transport and power, inadequate telecommunications networks, and unreliable courts. For example, manufacturing firms in Zimbabwe need to hold high levels of inventories, despite high interest rates, due to unreliable delivery of inputs tied to poor transportation infrastructure (Fafchamps et al., 1998). A survey of Ugandan firms found that shortage of electricity was identified as the single most important constraint upon firm growth; indeed, the provision of electricity by firms for their own use was almost as large as the public supply of electricity (Reinikka and Svensson, 1998). A study in Nigeria found that own generators accounted for three-quarters of the capital equipment of small manufacturers (Lee and Anas, 1991). The poor state of African telecommunications was estimated to reduce African growth rates by 1 percentage point, according to Easterly and Levine (1997). (However, since telecommunications was the main infrastructure variable which they could quantify, and since lack of different kinds of infrastructure is probably highly correlated, their estimate is probably a proxy for a wider range of infrastructural deficiencies.) African commercial courts are more corrupt than those in other regions (Widner, 1999). As a result, firms face greater problems of contract enforcement. Some firms can overcome these by relying upon their social networks to screen potential clients, but it is common to restrict business to long-standing clients (Bigsten et al., 1999). Ethnic minorities, such as Asians in East Africa and Lebanese in West Africa, tend to have more specialized social networks and so are better able than African firms to screen new clients (Biggs et al., 1996). The problem of contract enforcement thus makes markets less competitive and reduces the potential gains from trade, while tending to perpetuate the dominant position of minorities in business.

Poor public service delivery also handicapped households through inefficient education, health and extension services. A survey of primary education expenditures in Uganda found that, of the non-wage money released by the Ministry of Finance, on average, less than 30 percent actually reached the schools (Ablo and Reinikka, 1998). The expansion of the public sector has reduced private initiative. Since major areas of economic activity were reserved for the public sector—often including transport, marketing and banking—and African elites looked to the public sector rather than the private sector for advancement, Africa was slow to develop indigenous entrepreneurs.

African governments built various economic control regimes. A few nations, such as Ethiopia, Angola and Tanzania, had wide-ranging price controls under which private agents had an incentive to reduce production—at least officially marketed production. These governments often attempted to counterbalance these incentives with coercive production targets, but the net effect was usually dramatic declines in economic activity. More commonly, firms were subject to considerable regulation. For example, for many years manufacturing firms wishing to set up in Kenya had to acquire letters of no objection from existing producers, which resulted in a predictably low level of competition. In Uganda, when the government removed the requirement that coffee could only be transported by rail, the market for road haulage expanded sufficiently to induce new entry, which in turn broke an existing cartel, nearly halving haulage rates. Similarly, in Tanzania during the long period when agricultural marketing was heavily regulated, marketing margins for grain were double what they were both before regulation and after deregulation (Bevan et al., 1993). In this period, food prices became much more volatile: between 1964 and 1980 the coefficient of variation (that is, the ratio of the standard deviation to the mean) of maize prices at regional centers doubled, falling again sharply when markets were liberalized.

Government interventions undermined the functioning of product markets in many countries. Private trading, which was often associated with ethnic minorities such as the Indians in East Africa and the Lebanese in West Africa, was sometimes banned. A particularly damaging intervention, practiced even in relatively market-friendly economies such as Kenya, was to ban private interdistrict trade in food. Where government marketing monopolies were focused on ensuring the food supply to urban areas, this provision discouraged farmers from specializing in non-food export crops, since they could not rely on being able to buy food locally.

Since the political base of governments was urban, agriculture was heavily taxed and the public agronomic research needed to promote an African green revolution, based on locally-specific packages of micronutrients, was neglected. The main source of agricultural growth has been the gradual adoption of cash crops by smallholders, a process slowed down by government pricing policies (Bevan et al., 1993). While governments favored man-

ufacturing, the basis for industrial growth in this area was also undermined, since trade and exchange rate policies induced industrial firms to produce under uncompetitive conditions and only for small and captive domestic markets.

The same urban bias initially led governments to favor the urban wage labor force. In the immediate post-colonial period, minimum wages rose and unions acquired influence, so that wages increased substantially. However, post-independence inflation has usually eroded minimum wages, so that in most of Africa, wage rigidities in the labor market are not currently a significant impediment to the growth process. The exceptions are South Africa, where the labor market may just be going through such a real wage adjustment now, and the low inflation environments of Ethiopia and the countries in the "franc zone," the 13 former colonies of France in west and central Africa which had currencies pegged to the French franc. While high wage levels are not normally a hindrance to African economies, the job matching process appears to be inefficient, so that job mobility offers unusually high returns (Mengistae, 1998). This is an instance of the high costs of market information; for example, newspapers are expensive and have low circulation.

Financial markets were heavily regulated, with bank lending directed to the government, public enterprises or "strategic" sectors, very limited financial inter-mediation and virtually no competition between financial institutions. A common proxy for the extent of financial intermediation, known as "financial depth," is the broad money supply, M2, relative to GDP. But although Africa has even less financial depth than other developing areas, currently available evidence suggests that this may have had only a modest impact on its growth. For example, Easterly and Levine (1997) estimate that lack of financial depth reduced the annual growth rate by only 0.3 percentage points. Similarly, microeconomic survey evidence on manufacturing firms indicates that the lack of external finance is not currently the binding constraint on industrial investment (Bigsten et al., 1999).

External-Destiny

Africa is better located than Asia for most developed economy markets. However, most Africans live much further from the coast or navigable rivers than in other regions and so face intrinsically higher transport costs for exports (as shown in Table 2). Further, much of the population lives in countries which are land-locked, so that problems of distance are compounded by political barriers. Even a relatively open border like the one between Canada and the United States appears to be a substantial impediment to trade, in the sense that trade across Canadian provinces or across U.S. states is far greater than trade of equal distance between Canada and the United States (McCallum, 1995). Landlocked countries face national borders on all sides, which may constitute an irreducible barrier to trade even if they have good relations with their neighbors. Typically, growth regressions find that being landlocked reduces a nation's annual growth rate by around half of 1 percent.

A further aspect of external destiny is that Africa's exports are concentrated in a narrow range of commodities, with volatile prices that have declined since the 1960s. The deterioration in the terms of trade for such commodities has undoubtedly contributed to Africa's growth slowdown. However, there is controversy over whether its atypical exposure to terms of trade volatility has been damaging. Deaton and Miller (1996) find little evidence of detrimental effects in the short run. However, case study evidence suggests that shocks have often had longer-run deleterious effects. Investment has been concentrated into short periods, during which construction booms have raised the unit cost of capital, and government budgets have been destabilized, with spending rising during booms but being difficult to reduce subsequently (Schuknecht, 1999; Collier and Gunning, 1999b).

Africa has attracted much more aid per capita than other regions. Donor allocation rules have typically favored countries which have small populations and low incomes, and were recent colonies—and African countries met all three criteria.

. . . Excluding South Africa and the oil exporters (whose terms of trade have improved), the net aid inflows since 1970 have been around 50 percent greater than the income losses from terms of trade deterioration. The combination was thus somewhat analogous to an increase in export taxation: the terms of trade losses taking money from exporters, while the aid provided money to governments.

External-Policy

In recent decades, African governments adopted exchange rate and trade policies which were atypically anti-export and accumulated large foreign debts. On a range of indicators, Africa has had much higher trade barriers and more misaligned exchange rates than other regions (Dollar, 1992; Sachs and Warner, 1997). Exchange rates were commonly highly overvalued, reflecting the interest of the political elite in cheap imports. Tariffs and export taxes were higher in Africa than in other regions of the world, partly because of the lack of other sources of tax revenue to finance the expansion of the public sector. Exports were sharply reduced as a result of export crop taxation. For example, Dercon (1993) shows that Tanzanian cotton exports would have been 50 percent higher in the absence of taxation. Quantitative restrictions on imports were also used much more extensively, despite yielding no revenue. They often arose because of the difficulties of fine-tuning import demand in a situation where government was attempting to keep exchange rates fixed with few reserves. They probably persisted because they generated large opportunities for corruption, since someone could often be bribed to circumvent the quantitative limits.

The international growth literature has reached a consensus that exchange rate overvaluation and light trade restrictions are damaging, but controversy continues over the effects of more moderate trade restrictions (Rodrik, 1999). However, there are reasons why Africa's poor export performance may have been particularly damaging. Since 1980, African export revenue per capita has sharply declined, which in turn has induced severe import compression of both capital goods and intermediate inputs. Moreover, because African economies are so much smaller than other economies, external barriers of a given height have been significantly more damaging (Collier and Gunning, 1999).

By the 1990s, several African economies had accumulated unsustainable international debts, largely from public agencies. Clearly, this is one way in which poor decisions of the past become embedded in the present. There is a good theoretical argument that high indebtedness discourages private investment due to the fear of the future tax liability. There is some supporting evidence for this claim, although since poor policies lower GDP, using high debt/GDP as an explanatory variable may simply be a proxy for poor policies more broadly (Elbadawi et al., 1997).

Policy or Destiny?

The dichotomy between policy and destiny is of course an oversimplification: some apparently exogenous features of Africa have often been induced by policy, and conversely, African policies may reflect exogenous factors.

Consider, first, some of the "exogenous" factors that we have discussed under destiny. For example, the claim by Sachs and Warner (1997) that geography and demography almost fully account for Africa's slow growth rests largely upon the lack of a demographic transition to lower fertility rates in Africa, as has happened in most of Latin America and Asia. However, it is more plausible to regard these continuing high fertility rates as a consequence of slow growth than a cause. The lack of employment opportunities for young women has prevented the opportunity cost of children from rising, and the low returns to education in an environment where many of the "good" jobs are allocated by political criteria have reduced the incentive for parents to educate their children.

Similarly, the argument that the concentration of Africa's population in the interior is an external force holding down growth can also be seen as an endogenous outcome; specifically, the population has remained in the interior because of the failure of Africa's coastal cities to grow. In turn, this is partly because the failure to industrialize has slowed urbanization, and partly because policy has often been biased against coastal cities; for example, in both Nigeria and Tanzania the capital was relocated from the coast to the interior. Where policy was less biased, as in the Côte d'Ivoire during the 1970s, the coastal population grew so rapidly that it supported massive emigration from the landlocked economy of Burkina Faso: at its peak, around 40 percent of the Ivorien population were immigrants.

Further, being landlocked need not be an economic disadvantage. Developed landlocked economies, such as Switzerland, have atypically low international transport costs because they have oriented their trade towards their neighbors. By contrast, Africa's landlocked economies trade with Europe, so that neighboring countries are an obstacle rather than a market. These patterns of trade are partly a legacy of the colonial economy, but they also reflect the high trade barriers within Africa erected by post-independence governments, and the slow rate of growth. Ultimately, landlocked economies were faced with neighboring markets that were both inaccessible and unattractive, which did not make it desirable to reorient the economy to trade with them. Finally, Africa's continued export concentration in a narrow range of primary commodities, which we discussed earlier as reflecting the destiny of resource endowments, probably also reflects a number of public policy decisions. Other export activities have been handicapped either directly through overvalued exchange rates, or indirectly, through high transaction costs. Poor policy has given Africa a comparative disadvantage in "transaction-intensive" activities such as manufacturing.

Now consider the reverse situation; that is, how some of the dysfunctional policies that we have discussed can also be considered the outcome of exogenous forces. The anti-export policies which we argue hindered growth can be viewed as a consequence of the fact that most of the population lives far from the coast (Gallup and Sachs, 1999). In such societies, it might be argued that the elasticity of growth with respect to openness is lower and so the incentive for openness is reduced. However, at present Africa offers little evidence for this hypothesis. According to the World Bank's standardized ratings of policy (currently confidential), all five of the worst-rated countries on the continent are coastal whereas many of the best-rated countries are landlocked. As another example, it is possible that restrictive import policies are adopted, at least initially, in response to trade shocks like those created by an external dependence on commodity exports (Collier and Gunning, 1999b). The prevalence of natural resources may bring forth a variety of other policy errors, as well. For example, it may worsen policy by turning politics into a contest for rents or, through crowding out manufactured exports, prevent the emergence of potentially the most potent lobby for openness.

Along with being endogenous to fixed effects like geography, policies are also affected by experience. Societies which have experienced high levels of economic risk may place a higher priority on income-sharing arrangements such as expanded opportunities of public employment, rather than focusing on income generation. Societies also learn from past failure. The African nations which have recently implemented the strongest economic reforms, such as Ghana and Uganda, tended to be those which had earlier experienced the worst economic crises. However, African countries facing the challenge of reversing economic failure have lacked significant role models within the continent. In east Asia, Hong Kong, Singapore, Taiwan and Korea provided early role models, as did Chile since the late 1970s in Latin America. Within-continent models may be important because the information is both closer to hand and more evidently pertinent. Once Africa develops examples of success, the scope for societal learning across the continent will make it unlikely that Africa is "destined" to poor policies by its geography: although its geographic characteristics may have given it some weak tendencies towards poor policies in the initial post-independence period.

Conclusion: Will Africa Grow?

. . . During the mid-1990s, average African growth accelerated and performance became more dispersed. A few countries such as Uganda, Côte D'Ivoire, Ethiopia and Mozambique started to grow very fast, whereas others such as the Democratic Republic of the Congo and Sierra Leone descended into social disorder. "Africa" became less meaningful as a category. Both the improvement in the average performance and the greater dispersion among countries were consistent with what had happened to policy. During the 1990s many of the most egregious exchange rate, fiscal and trade policies were improved. By 1998, although Africa still ranked as the region with the worst policies on the World Bank ratings, it was also the region with by far the greatest policy dispersion.

However, the faster growth coincided not only with better policies but with improvements in the terms of trade. Further, investment in Africa as a share of GDP is currently only 18 percent. This is much lower than other regions: for example, 23 percent in South Asia and 29 percent on average in lower middle-income countries. Even these figures may understate Africa's true investment shortfall. Capital goods are more expensive in Africa than the international average, so that once the investment share is recalculated at international relative prices it approximately halves. Although it is not possible to disaggregate investment into its public and private components with complete accuracy, estimates suggest that the shortfall in African investment is due to low private investment. Thus, growth may be unsustainable unless there is a substantial increase in private investment.

On an optimistic interpretation of the evidence, Africa's slow growth from the early 1970s into the 1990s has been due to policies which reduced its openness to foreign trade. Since these policies have largely been reversed during the last decade, if this is correct then Africa should be well-placed for continued growth.

The pessimistic interpretation is that Africa's problems are intrinsic, often rooted in geography. This view implies that economic progress in Africa will be dependent upon international efforts to make its environment more favorable, such as research to eradicate tropical diseases, and finance to create transport arteries from the coast to the interior. The thesis that Africa's economic problems are caused by ethno-linguistic fractionalization has similarly intractable implications.

References

Ablo, Emanuel and Ritva Reinikka. 1998. "Do Budgets Really Matter? Evidence from Public Spending on Education and Health in Uganda." Policy Research Working Paper No. 1926, World Bank.

African Development Bank. 1998. *African Development Report.* Oxford: Oxford University Press.

Bevan, David. L., Paul Collier and Jan Willem Gunning. 1993. *Agriculture and the policy environment: Tanzania and Kenya.* Paris: OECD.

Biggs, T., M. Raturi and P. Srivastava. 1996. "Enforcement of Contracts in an African Credit Market: Working Capital Financing in Kenyan Manufacturing." RPED Discussion Paper. Africa Region, World Bank.

Bigsten, Arne, P. Collier, S. Dercon, B. Gauthier, J. W. Gunning, A. Isaksson, A. Oduro, R. Oostendorp, C. Pattillo, M. Soderbom, M. Sylvain, F. Teal and A. Zeufack. 1999, forthcoming. "Investment by Manufacturing Firms in Africa: a Four-Country Panel Data Analysis." *Oxford Bulletin of Economics and Statistics.*

Bloom, John and Jeffrey Sachs. 1998. "Geography, Demography and Economic Growth in Africa." *Brookings Papers in Economic Activity.* 2, 207–95.

Collier, Paul. 1999. "The Political Economy of Ethnicity," in *Proceedings of the Annual Bank Conference on Development Economics.* Pleskovic, Boris and Joseph E. Stiglitz, eds. World Bank, Washington, D.C.

Collier, Paul and David Dollar. 1999. "Aid, Risk and the Special Concerns of Small States." Mimeo, Policy Research Department, World Bank, Washington DC.

Collier, Paul and Ashish Garg. 1999, forthcoming. "On Kin Groups and Wages in the Ghanaian Labour Market." *Oxford Bulletin of Economics and Statistics,* 61:2, pp. 131–51.

Collier, P. and J. W. Gunning. 1999. "Explaining African Economic Performance." *Journal of Economic Literature.* March, 37:1, 64–111.

Collier, P. and J. W. Gunning. 1999a, forthcoming. "The IMF's Role in Structural Adjustment." *Economic Journal.* World Bank, Washington, DC.

Collier, P. and J. W. Gunning with associates. 1999b. *Trade Shocks in Developing Countries: Theory and Evidence.* Oxford: Oxford University Press (Clarendon).

Collier, Paul and Anke Hoeffler. 1998. "On the Economic Causes of Civil War." *Oxford Economic Papers.* 50, pp. 563–73.

Collier, Paul and Anke Hoeffler. 1999. "Loot-Seeking and Justice-Seeking in Civil War." Mimeo, Development Research Department, World Bank, Washington DC.

Collier, Paul and Catherine Pattillo, eds. 1999. *Investment and Risk in Africa*. Macmillan: London.

Collins, S. and B. P. Bosworth. 1996. "Economic Growth in East Asia: Accumulation versus Assimilation." *Brookings Papers in Economic Activity*, 2, pp. 135–203.

Deaton, A. and R. Miller. 1996. "International Commodity Prices, Macroeconomic Performance and Politics in Sub-Saharan Africa." *Journal of African Economies*. 5 (Supp.), pp. 99–191.

Dercon, Stefan. 1997. "Wealth, Risk and Activity Choice: Cattle in Western Tanzania." *Journal of Development Economics*. 55:1, pp. 1–42.

Dercon, Stefan. 1993. "Peasant supply response and macroeconomic policies: cotton in Tanzania." *Journal of African Economies*. 2, pp. 157–94.

Dollar, David. 1992. "Outward-Oriented Developing Economies Really do Grow More Rapidly: Evidence from 95 LDCs 1976–85." *Economic Development and Cultural Change*. 40, pp. 523–44.

Easterly, William and Ross Levine. 1997. "Africa's Growth Tragedy: Policies and Ethnic Divisions." *Quarterly Journal of Economics*. CXII, pp. 1203–1250.

Elbadawi, Ibrahim A., Benno J. Ndulu, and Njuguna Ndung'u. 1997. "Debt Overhang and Economic Growth in Sub-Saharan Africa," in *External Finance for Low-Income Countries*. Iqbal, Zubair and Ravi Kanbur, eds. IMF Institute, Washington, DC.

Fafchamps, Marcel, Jan Willem Gunning and Remco Oostendorp. 1998. "Inventories, Liquidity and Contractual Risk in African Manufacturing." Department of Economics, Stanford University, mimeo.

Gallup, John L. and Jeffrey D. Sachs. 1999. "Geography and Economic Growth," in *Proceedings of the Annual World Bank Conference on Development Economics*. Pleskovic, Boris and Joseph E. Stiglitz, eds. World Bank, Washington, DC.

Ghana Central Bureau of Statistics. 1988. *Quarterly Digest of Statistics*. Accra.

Grove, A. T. 1991. "The African Environment," in *Africa 30 Years On*. Rimmer, Douglas, ed. London: James Currey.

Kenya Central Bureau of Statistics. 1996. *Statistical Abstract*. Nairobi.

Knack, Stephen and Philip Keefer. 1995. "Institutions and Economic Performance: Cross-Country Tests Using Alternative Institutional Measures." *Economics and Politics*. 7:3, pp. 207–28.

Kremer, Michael. 1993. "Population Growth and Technological Change: One Million B.C. to 1990." *Quarterly Journal of Economics*. 108:3, pp. 681–716.

Lee, K. S. and A. Anas. 1991. "Manufacturers' Responses to Infrastructure Deficiencies in Nigeria: Private Alternatives and Policy Options," in *Economic Reform in Africa*. Chibber, A. and S. Fischer, eds. World Bank, Washington DC.

Maddison, Angus. 1995. *Monitoring the World Economy*. Paris: OECD.

Mauro, P. 1995. "Corruption and Growth." *Quarterly Journal of Economics*. 110, pp. 681–712.

McCallum, J. 1995, "National Borders Matter: Canada-U.S. Regional Trade Patterns." *American Economic Review*. 85, pp. 615–23.

Mengistae, Taye. 1998. "Ethiopia's Urban Economy: Empirical Essays on Enterprise Development and the Labour Market." D.Phil. Thesis, University of Oxford.

Pradhan, Sanjay. 1996. "Evaluating Public Spending." World Bank Discussion Paper 323, Washington DC.

Reinikka, Ritva and Jakob Svensson. 1998. "Investment Response to Structural Reforms and Remaining Constraints: Firm Survey Evidence from Uganda." Mimeo, Africa Region, World Bank.

Rodrik, Dani. 1999. *Making Openness Work: The New Global Economy and the Developing Countries*. Overseas Development Council, Washington DC.

Sachs, J.D. and Mark Warner. 1997. "Sources of Slow Growth in African Economies." *Journal of African Economies*. 6, pp. 335–76.

Schuknecht, Ludger. 1999. "Tying Governments' Hands in Commodity Taxation." *Journal of African Economies*. 8:2, 152–81.

Voortman, R.L., B.G.J.S. Sonneveld and M.A. Keyzer. 1999. "African Land Ecology: Opportunities and Constraints for Agricultural Development." Mimeo, Centre for World Food Studies, Free University, Amsterdam.

Widner, Jennifer, A. 1999. "The Courts as Restraints," in *Investment and Risk in Africa*. Collier, Paul and Catherine Pattillo, eds. London: Macmillan.

Wood, Adrian and J. Mayer. 1998. "Africa's Export Structure in Comparative Perspective," forthcoming in the UNCTAD series *Economic Development and Regional Dynamics in Africa: Lessons from the East Asian Experience*.

World Bank. 1997. *Confronting Aids*, Policy Research Report. Oxford University Press.

World Bank. 1999. *World Development Indicators*. Development Data Center, Washington, D.C.

I.C. THE DISCIPLINE OF DEVELOPMENT ECONOMICS

Note I.C.1. Evolution of Development Economics

Modern development economics arose in the late 1940s as an economic counterpart to the political independence of the emerging countries of Asia, Africa, and the Caribbean. Its influence spread rapidly to Latin America and other low-income areas. Regions that had been considered in the eighteenth century as "rude and barbarous," in the nineteenth century as "backward," and in the prewar period as "underdeveloped" now became the "less developed countries" or the "poor countries"—and the "emergent countries" and "developing economies."

But how was the development to be achieved? Although political independence can be legislated, economic independence cannot. An understanding of the forces of development was necessary, and the design of appropriate policies to support these forces was essential. To accomplish this, the creative participation of economists was needed.

The new development economics had some relation to the old growth economics of classical economists (Smith, Malthus, Ricardo)—a concern with the heavy variables of capital, population, and the objective of what Adam Smith termed the "progress of opulence" in the progressive state.[1]

But the new development economists went beyond their classical and neoclassical predecessors to consider the kinds of policies that an active state and the international community could adopt to accelerate a country's rate of development. And the new development economics, with its concern for economic theory and policy analysis, became more analytic than the prewar phase of colonial economics, which had been characterized by narrow institutional studies and economic anthropology.

The term "economic development" constituted a persuasive definition: an increase in real income per head as a desirable objective. During the 1950s and early 1960s, development policies emphasized the maximization of growth of GNP through capital accumulation and industrialization based on import substitution. In view of a distrust of markets and a belief in the pervasiveness of market failure, governments also turned to central planning. There was general optimism with respect to what could be accomplished by emphasizing planned investment in new physical capital, utilizing reserves of surplus labor, adopting import-substitution industrialization policies, embracing central planning of change, and relying on foreign aid. But there was pessimism regarding the external conditions of development—the international environment within which the national development process would have to progress—and the export of primary products: low price elasticities of demand, low income elasticities of demand, fluctuations in export revenue, deteriorating terms of trade—all these pessimistic views regarding primary-product exports reinforced the inward-looking import-substitution policies.[2]

Policy makers were adopting these policies not simply because of advice from economists, but also because of ideology and political economy.[3] Chapter IX considers from the perspective of political economy the more general problem of why governments of developing countries do what they do—either in accordance with or contrary to professional economic advice. Nonetheless, much of the thinking in the new development economics could be appealed to in support of these policies. A "big push"[4] or "critical minimum effort"[5] was believed necessary to break out of a "low level equilibrium trap."[6] An increase in the proportion of national income invested above 10 percent was advocated for a "take-off," with industry as the leading sector.[7] "Balanced growth"—the synchronized application of capital to a wide range of industries—was advocated by Nurkse:

> A frontal attack—a wave of capital investments in a number of different industries—can economically succeed while any substantial application of capital by an individual entrepreneur in any particular industry may be blocked or discouraged by the limitations of the preexisting market. . . . [T]hrough the application of capital over a wide range of activities, the general level of economic activity is raised and

the size of the market enlarged. . . . [Balanced growth] is a means of getting out of the rut, a means of stepping up the rate of growth when the external forces of advance through trade expansion and foreign capital are sluggish or inoperative.[8]

Hirschman, however, advocated unbalanced growth in order to maximize induced decision making and to take advantage of forward and backward linkages in the production process.[9] Unlike the neoclassical economists, who assumed a smoothly working market-price system, some of the early development economists adopted a more structuralist approach to development problems. Structuralist analysis attempted to identify specific rigidities, lags, shortages and surpluses, low elasticities of supply and demand, and other characteristics of the structure of developing countries that affect economic adjustments to development policy. The structuralist view also was pessimistic about the responsiveness of agents to price signals and incentives. Instead of neoclassical flexibility and substitutability, the structuralist view emphasized low elasticities of supply and market imperfections that limit the mobility of factors and the responsiveness of agents. Myrdal, Prebisch, and Singer were especially prominent in reinforcing the pessimistic view with respect to exports of primary products.[10]

During the late 1960s and early 1970s came a second phase of development economics, which focused more directly on poverty and inequality. It was argued that growth in GNP is not a sufficient condition for the removal of poverty: income was not trickling down to the lowest income groups, and the number of people living in absolute poverty was increasing in many countries. The very meaning of development was questioned, and instead of worshiping at the altar of GNP, many economists added other dimensions to the objectives of development. The World Bank emphasized redistribution with growth.[11] The International Labor Organization (ILO) concentrated on basic human needs.[12] Much of the development literature turned from an emphasis on industrial development to one on rural development. Impressed by studies of human capital formation,[13] economists also shifted their attention from physical capital to human resources. And the concern with appropriate technology broadened the problem of what could or should be borrowed from the more developed countries.[14]

The most substantial change in the content of development economics came during the 1970s and 1980s—decades marked by the resurgence of neoclassical economics.[15] There was increasing criticism of policy-induced distortions and the nonmarket failures associated with the implementation of public policies. This led to a critique of comprehensive and detailed administrative controls. With the renewed attention to the application of neoclassical economics, price distortions were to be removed: "'Getting prices right' is not the end of economic development. But 'getting prices wrong' frequently is."[16] It had long since become evident that economic rationality characterizes agents in the less developed countries as well as in the more developed.[17] Beyond the removal of price distortions, neoclassical economics advocated getting all policies right. Markets, prices, and incentives became central. Inward-looking strategies of development were to give way to liberalization of the foreign-trade regime and export promotion. Inflation was to submit to stabilization programs. State-owned enterprises were to be privatized. A poor country was now considered poor because of inappropriate policies, and good economics—that is, neoclassical economics—was good for the developing country.

In the 1950s, the pioneers in development had asked why underdeveloped countries were underdeveloped, and they formulated grand theories and general strategies. In contrast, the focus in the 1970s and 1980s became increasingly directed to the heterogeneity of the developing countries and to an explanation of differential rates of country performance. Analysis moved from highly aggregated growth models to disaggregated micro models. More emphasis was placed on applied research that was country-specific, based on empirical data, and on the application of neoclassical principles to policy issues. In an increasing number of countries, these changes in development thought produced an improvement in agricultural policies, a liberalization of the foreign-trade regime, and a professionalism in project appraisal.[18]

In contrast to the position of the early development economists, who eschewed the universal use of neoclassical economics and thought the "special case" irrelevant for development policy, many economists now emphasize the universality of neoclassical economics and dismiss the claim that development economics is a special subdiscipline in its own right. Hirschman, for instance, has written provocatively about the rise and decline of development economics.[19] So, too, does Kreuger state:

> Once it is recognized that individuals respond to incentives, and that "market failure" is the result of inappropriate incentives rather than of nonresponsiveness, the separateness of development economics as a field largely disappears. Instead, it becomes an applied field, in which the tools and insights of labor economics, agricultural economics, international economics, public finance and other fields are addressed to the special questions and policy issues that arise in the context of development.[20]

Many other students of development, however, believe that an obituary of development economics is not in order. Thus Sen argues that there is still much relevance in the broad policy themes that traditional development economics has emphasized: (1) industrialization, (2) rapid capital accumulation, (3) mobilization of underemployed manpower, and (4) planning and an economically active state.[21] And Lewis recognizes that "the overlap between Development Economics and the Economics of the Developed is bound to be great, but there are also differences that are rather large, which is why each also has some tools of its own."[22]

Perhaps the issue of the relevance of neoclassical economics to developing countries can be best resolved by concluding that the task of development economists is made difficult not because they must start afresh with a completely new set of tools or because they confront problems that are wholly different from those in advanced countries, but because they must acquire a sense of the different assumptions that are most incisive for analyzing a problem within the context of a poor country. In particular, this calls for special care in identifying different institutional relations, in assessing the different quantitative importance of some variables, and in allowing some elements that are usually taken as givens—such as population, "state of the arts," institutions, and supply of entrepreneurship—to become endogenous variables in development analysis.

Notes

1. For more detailed reference to early growth economists, see G.M. Meier and R.E. Baldwin, *Economic Development: Theory, History, Policy* (1957); G.M. Meier, *Emerging from Poverty* (1984), chap. 5; William J. Baumol, *Economic Dynamics* (1959); Irma Adelman, *Theories of Economic Growth and Development* (1961); and Lionel Robbins, *Theory of Economic Development in the History of Economic Thought* (1968).

2. See Jagdish Bhagwati, "Development Economics: What Have We Learned?," *Asian Development Review* 2, no. 1 (1984): 24–29.

3. See, for example, Albert O. Hirschman, "Political Economy of Import Substituting Industrialization," *Quarterly Journal of Economics* (February 1968).

4. P.N. Rosenstein-Roden, "Problems of Industrialization of Eastern and Southeastern Europe," *Economic Journal* (June–September 1943).

5. Harvey Leibenstein, *Economic Backwardness and Economic Growth* (1957), chap. 8.

6. Richard R. Nelson, "A Theory of the Low-Level Equilibrium Trap in Underdeveloped Economies," *American Economic Review* (December 1956): 894–908.

7. W. W. Rostow, *The Stages of Economic Growth* (1960).

8. Ragnar Nurkse, *Problems of Capital Formation in Underdeveloped Countries* (1953), pp. 13–15.

9. Albert O. Hirschman, *The Strategy of Economic Development* (1958).

10. Gunnar Myrdal, *Economic Theory and Underdeveloped Regions* (1957); Raúl Prebisch, "The Economic Development of Latin America and Its Principal Problems," *Economic Bulletin for Latin America* 7 (1950); Hans Singer, "Gains and Losses from Trade and Investment in Underdeveloped Countries," *American Economic Review* (May 1950).

11. World Bank, *Redistribution with Growth* (1974).

12. International Labor Organization, *The Basic Needs Approach to Development* (1977).

13. T.W. Schultz, "Investment in Human Capital," *American Economic Review* (March 1961): 1–17.

14. Frances Stewart, *Technology and Underdevelopment* (1977).

15. I.M.D. Little, *Economic Development* (1982), chap. 9.

16. C. Peter Timmer, "Choice of Techniques in Rice Milling in Java," *Bulletin of Indonesian Economic Studies* (July 1973).

17. The usual postulates of rationality and the principles of maximization or minimization have quite general applicability. For illustrative evidence, see P. T. Bauer and B. S. Yamey, *The Economics of Under-Developed Countries* (1957), pp. 91–101; W. J. Barber, "Economic Rationality and Behavior Patterns in an Underdeveloped Area: A Case Study of African Economic Behavior in the Rhodesias," *Economic Development and Cultural Change* (April 1960): 237–51; and W. O. Jones, "Economic Man in Africa," *Food Research Institute Studies* (May 1960): 107–34.

18. Gerald M. Meier, "On Getting Policies Right," in *Pioneers in Development*, 2d ser., ed. Gerald M. Meier (1987), pp. 3–11.

19. Albert O. Hirschman, "Rise and Decline of Development Economics," in *Essays in Trespassing* (1981).

20. Anne O. Krueger, "Aid in the Development Process," *World Bank Research Observer* (January 1986): 62–63.

21. Amartya K. Sen, "Development Which Way Now?" *Economic Journal* (December 1983).

22. W. Arthur Lewis, "The State of Development Theory," *American Economic Review* (March 1984): 2.

Comment I.C.1. Classical Growth Theory

Prior to the neoclassical marginalist revolution in the 1870s, classical economists had been very much interested in economic growth—Adam Smith's "progressive state." According to Smith, the level of output per head, together with the growth of output, "must in every nation be regulated by two different circumstances: first by the skill, dexterity, and judgement with which its labor is generally applied; and, secondly, by the proportion between the number of those who are employed in useful labor, and that of those who are not so employed."

The major sources of growth are (1) growth in the labor force and stock of capital, (2) improvements in the efficiency with which capital is applied to labor through greater division of labor and technological progress, and (3) foreign trade that widens the market and reinforces the other two sources of growth.

Once begun, the growth process becomes self-reinforcing in the progressive state. As long as the growth in wealth favors profits, there are savings and additional capital accumulation, and hence further growth. And with capital accumulation, the demand for labor rises, and a growing labor force is absorbed in productive employment.

Smith also attributed overwhelming importance to the division of labor, in the broad sense of technical progress. The division of labor entails improved efficiency of labor, and increasing specialization leads to rising per capita income. By extending the division of labor, improvements in production reduce the amount of input per unit of output. According to Smith, however,

> the division of labor is limited by the extent of the market. . . . When the market is very small, no person can have any encouragement to dedicate himself entirely to one employment, or want of power to exchange all that surplus part of the produce for his own labor, which is over and above his own consumption, or such parts of the produce of other men's labor as he has occasion for.

The division of labor increases wealth, which, in turn, widens the market, enabling the division of labor to be carried further forward.

If capital accumulation, division of labor, and foreign trade are sources of a nation's economic growth, then—according to Smith—growth can be promoted through the extension of market institutions and the activity of competition.

Some of Smith's insights retain much relevance. To Smith and the modern economists, growth is the outcome of a logical process. Both search for some laws and generalizations.

Modern economists emphasize, as did Smith, capital accumulation as a driving force in the growth process. So, too, do they concentrate on increasing productivity. They also point to the possibilities for development based on foreign trade. And at the forefront of development discussions, economists seek to find a proper division between reliance on the market-price system and dependence on governmental actions.

Among the classical economists, the development views of Thomas Malthus, David Ricardo, and John Stuart Mill are also significant.

From the 1870s to the 1930s, the theory of value and resource allocation dominated economic thought. Economic analysis turned its attention to the conditions that would make possible various optima rather than the conditions that would allow an economy to achieve ever-changing optima of ever-increasing range. Not the movement of aggregate output in the entire economy, but the movement of particular lines of production toward an equilibrium position became the neoclassicist's concern. To tighten up the economy and avoid inefficiency was the neoclassicist's objective. Rigorous analysis of individual markets and of price formation was the neoclassicist's hallmark. In *The Theory of Economic Growth* (1955), W. Arthur Lewis could therefore say that "no comprehensive treatise on the subject has been published for about a century. The last great book covering this wide range was John Stuart Mill's *Principles of Political Economy,* published in 1848."

For studies of the classical economists' views on economic growth, see Lionel Robbins, *The Theory of Economic Development in the History of Economic Thought* (1968); William J. Baumol, *Economic Dynamics* (1959); Irma Adelman, *Theories of Economic Growth and Development* (1961); G. M. Meier and R. E. Baldwin, *Economic Development: Theory, History, Policy* (1957); G. M. Meier, *Emerging from Poverty* (1984), chap. 5.; G. M. Meier, ed., *From Classical Economics to Development Economics* (1994).

Comment I.C.2. Development Economics as a Special Subject

In the years following World War II, the subject of development economics was formulated in its own right. Investigating issues that went beyond the earlier growth economics of classical economists (Smith, Malthus, Ricardo), a "new development economics" began to be formulated by a number of economists. For the outstanding contributions made in the formative period of the 1950s, see Gerald M. Meier and Dudley Seers, eds., *Pioneers in Development* (1984). Also, H. W. Arndt, *Economic Development: The History of an Idea* (1989).

Several retrospective papers have considered the evolution of development thought over the past four decades. Most useful in tracing the changing views of development economists are Albert Hirschman, "The Rise and Decline of Development Economists," in *Essays in Trespassing* (1981); Ian Livingstone, "The Development of Development Economics," *O.D.I. Review,* no. 2 (1981); Amartya Sen, "Development: Which Way Now?" *Economic Journal* (December 1983); Jagdish Bhagwati, "Development Economics: What Have We Learned?" *Asian Development Review* 2 (1984); W. Arthur Lewis, "The State of Development Theory," *American Economic Review* (March 1984); and "The Methodological Foundations of Development Economics" [special issue], *World Development* (February 1986).

Although development economists now rely much more on standard neoclassical principles that apply to rich and poor countries alike, the subject of development economics still has sufficient distinctive characteristics to distinguish it as a special subdiscipline in economics. This distinction is recognized in two recent surveys of the subject. Nicholas Stern's "Survey of Development," *Economic Journal* (September 1989) is addressed to "economists and students of economics who do know the tools of their trade but not necessarily how they have been applied to and fashioned for the analysis of the economics of developing countries." Bliss also argues that

> general economic principles are precisely too general to give us insights into applications for less developed economies. Alone, the parts of economic theory and method that apply more or less universal-

ly tell us less than we need in particular application. To give them life they have to be enlarged and translated. When this is done a specialty is created. Development economics consists in part of the refinement of general economics to deal with questions which arise in the context of development, and partly of certain special ideas which have proved useful in studying developing countries.[1]

---

[1]Christopher Bliss, *Handbook of Development Economics* (1989), p. 1188.

Note I.C.2. New Endogenous Growth Theory

At various times in the history of thought, economists have stressed increasing returns as an endogenous explanation for economic growth. Adam Smith did so in emphasizing that growth in productivity was due to the division of labor, which depends upon the extent of the market. Alfred Marshall also emphasized that the role of "nature" in production may be subject to diminishing returns, but the role of "man" is subject to increasing returns. And again, in an earlier period, J. M. Clark also observed that "knowledge is the only instrument of production that is not subject to diminishing returns."[1] Allyn Young also related economic progress to increasing returns that were external to the firm as a result of the progressive division and specialization among industries and the use of roundabout methods of production.[2]

Nobel laureate Kenneth Arrow gave a dynamic interpretation to increasing returns by emphasizing "Learning by Doing."[3] This was an early attempt to render technological progress endogenous in growth models by making the productivity of a given firm an increasing function of cumulative aggregate investment for the industry. (Note that Arrow emphasized cumulative investment, not cumulative output.)

Most recently, new endogenous growth models have gone beyond Robert Solow's neoclassical growth model that exhibited diminishing returns to capital and labor separately and constant returns to both inputs jointly, and that left technological progress as a residual.[4] The new growth theory examines production functions that show increasing returns because of specialization and investment in "knowledge" capital. Technological progress and human capital formation are endogenized within general equilibrium models of growth. New knowledge is generated by investment in the research sector. The technological progress residual is accounted for by endogenous human capital formation. With knowledge being treated as a public good, spill-over benefits to other firms may then allow aggregate investment in knowledge to exhibit increasing returns to scale. This in turn allows investment in knowledge capital to persist indefinitely and to sustain long-run growth in per capita income. A policy implication is that governments can promote growth by providing incentives to agents in the knowledge-producing, human capital–intensive sectors. Developing countries can also be aided by the international transfer of technology. See Paul M. Romer, "Increasing Returns and Long-run Growth," *Journal of Political Economy* (October 1986), and "Endogenous Technological Change," *Journal of Political Economy* (October 1990); and Robert Lucas, Jr., "On the Mechanics of Economic Development," *Journal of Monetary Economics* (July 1988).

For less developed countries, the implication of the new growth theory is to place more emphasis on human capital—even more than on physical capital, and to emphasize the benefit from the exchange of ideas that comes with an open economy integrated into the world economy. A discussion of the implications of new growth theory for the ability of government policies to affect long-run growth in LDCs is contained in the Overview to Chapter V.

It is also suggested by some empirical studies that the new endogenous growth models conform better to the evidence on diversity in growth rates among countries over the past three or four decades then does the neoclassical growth model. See Isaac Ehrlich, "The Problem of Development: Introduction," *Journal of Political Economy* (October 1990): S2–S3, S7; and Jati K. Sengupta, "Growth in NICs in Asia: Some Tests of New Growth Theory," *Journal of Development Studies* (January 1993): 342–57.

In contrast to the critics of the Solow model, another study of cross-country variation in income explains much of the variation in terms of an augmented neoclassical production-function model that includes accumulation of human capital as well as physical capital, but maintains the Solow assumption of decreasing returns to scale in capital. Even when denying the new growth theory's emphasis on externalities to capital accumulation, the augmented Solow model can explain most of the international variation in income per capita by differences in saving, education, and population growth. See N. Gregory Mankiw, David Romer, and David N. Weil, "A Contribution to the Empirics of Economic Growth," *Quarterly Journal of Economics* (May 1992): 407–37. We are still left, however, with the challenge to understand the determinants of saving, population growth, and worldwide technological change that remain as exogenous variables in neoclassical growth models.

For an evaluation of different models of growth, see the symposium "New Growth Theory," *Journal of Economic Perspectives* (Winter 1994): 3–72.

Notes

1. J. Maurice Clark, *Studies in the Economics of Overhead Costs* (1923), p. 120.

2. Allyn A. Young, "Increasing Returns and Economic Progress," *Economic Journal* (December 1928): 527–42.

3. Kenneth Arrow, "The Economic Implications of Learning by Doing," *Review of Economic Studies* (June 1962): 155–73.

4. Robert M. Solow, "A Contribution to the Theory of Economic Growth," *Quarterly Journal of Economics* (February 1956): 65–94.

CHAPTER II

Historical Perspective

Overview: The Division of the World

In order to analyze the problems of contemporary poor countries it is essential to understand how they became "less developed" than today's rich countries and how they have attempted to catch up. The main focus of this chapter is on the division of the world into agricultural and industrialized countries, with the latter located until recently entirely outside the tropics.

The first selection, by Lloyd Reynolds, examines economic growth of large countries (1980 population at least 10 million) in Asia, Latin America, North Africa and the Middle East, and sub-Saharan Africa during the period 1850–1980. Reynolds begins by noting that prior to this period many countries in these regions had for a century or more been experiencing what he calls "extensive growth," meaning growth in output that is absorbed by growth in population, leaving per capita income unchanged. He argues that developments during the period of extensive growth provided "important conditioning factors" such as nation-building for later growth in per capita income. When this "intensive growth" began in many countries during the "world economic boom" from 1850–1914, it was invariably led by exports of primary products to Europe and North America. This was by no means inevitable, since many countries in Western (but not Central) Europe responded to the industrial revolution that began in Britain in the late eighteenth century through imitation rather than trade. The question of why imitation did not take hold in the countries studied by Reynolds leads us to the second selection, by W. Arthur Lewis.

Lewis states his argument with an elegance and economy that cannot be improved:

> In a closed economy, the size of the industrial sector is a function of agricultural productivity. Agriculture has to be capable of producing the surplus food and raw materials consumed in the industrial sector, and it is the affluent state of the farmers that enables them to be a market for industrial products. If the domestic market is too small, it is still possible to support an industrial sector by exporting manufactures and importing food and raw materials. But it is hard to begin industrialization by exporting manufactures. Usually one begins by selling in a familiar and protected home market and moves on to exporting only after one has learnt to make one's costs competitive.
>
> The distinguishing feature of the industrial revolution at the end of the eighteenth century is that it began in the country with the highest agricultural productivity—Great Britain—which therefore already had a large industrial sector. The industrial revolution did not create an industrial sector where none had been before. It transformed an industrial sector that already existed by introducing new ways of making the same old things. The revolution spread rapidly in other countries that were also revolutionizing their agriculture, especially in Western Europe and North America. But countries of low agricultural productivity, such as Central and Southern Europe, or Latin America, or China had rather small industrial sectors, and there it made rather slow progress.

The assumption that "it is hard to begin industrialization by exporting manufactures" is crucial to Lewis's argument. We examine this assumption in detail in Note II.1. The assumption of a closed economy is also made in the next two selections, respectively by Kiminori Matsuyama and by Kevin Murphy, Andrei Shleifer, and Robert Vishny, which can be seen as formalizing and extending different aspects of Lewis's argument.

Matsuyama's model makes it clear that an income elasticity of demand for agricultural output (food) that is less than 1 (a well-established empirical regularity known as Engel's Law) is necessary for Lewis's argument to work. Otherwise, an increase in agricultural productivity would, by increasing income, cause a more than proportionate increase in demand for agricultural output that would require a greater share of the labor force to be employed in agriculture, shrinking rather than expanding the industrial sector. This assumption is only implicit in Lewis's argument—the "surplus food" that agriculture has to be capable of producing is a surplus over an assumed subsistence requirement that causes people with low incomes to spend a high proportion of their incomes on food.

Matsuyama also extends Lewis's argument by claiming that manufacturing is the locus of economic growth because only there does productivity increase through learning-by-doing take place. Higher agricultural productivity thus increases not only the level but also the rate of growth of income, because it leads to employment of a larger share of the labor force in manufacturing and thus more rapid learning-by-doing. Two important assumptions are that learning-by-doing is not subject to diminishing returns (there is no tendency to run out of things to learn), and that no individual manufacturing firm has an incentive to increase employment and output to learn more, because each firm is small relative to the industry as a whole and benefits from learning-by-doing in the entire industry. The learning-by-doing model of productivity increase will be discussed in more detail in Note III.A.2.

It is important to note what happens in Matsuyama's model when the assumption of a closed economy is removed. Now any shortage of agricultural output relative to domestic demand can be met by imports in exchange for exports of manufactures. High agricultural productivity is no longer needed to free up labor for manufacturing and generate demand for manufacturing output. On the contrary, high agricultural productivity allows farmers to attract workers out of the manufacturing sector and thus *lowers* the rate of income growth. The "curse" of abundant arable land and mineral resources will be extensively discussed in Note III.A.1.

The model of Murphy, Shleifer, and Vishny makes clear the importance of increasing returns to scale in the "new ways of making the same old things." Because of larger fixed costs, factory production cannot yield lower unit cost than handicraft production unless the volume of output is sufficiently large. With a closed economy, achieving a large volume of output depends on domestic demand. Murphy, Shleifer, and Vishny argue further that domestic demand is not only a function of average income (and thus average agricultural productivity), but also of the distribution of income. A small group of wealthy plantation owners might generate a demand for sterling silver cooking utensils too small to justify investment in a factory to make them, but the same income spread over a middle class of owner-cultivators may generate a volume of demand for flatware sufficient to support factory production. Thus both high agricultural productivity and a relatively equal distribution of agricultural income promote the introduction of modern manufacturing techniques in place of traditional handicrafts.

In Selection II.5, Stanley Engerman and Kenneth Sokoloff argue that climate and soil conditions in the temperate and tropical parts of the New World led to agricultural practices that generated a relatively equal distribution of income in the former (Canada and the United States) and a relatively unequal distribution of income in the latter (Latin America). Selection VIII.B.1 will show that location in the tropics remains a strong predictor of high income inequality to this day.

Returning to the selection by Lewis, he addresses how the tropical countries fared once they settled into the pattern of development through exports of primary products. He begins by noting that this development attracted immigration of about 50 million people from China and India to work on plantations, in mines, or in construction projects. He argues that the prices of tropical primary products could therefore not rise above the level that supported a Chinese or Indian standard of living, so that export production was not a way out of the trap of low tropical food productivity. (A number of reasons why tropical food productivity is so low will be given in Selection VII.A.1.) Lewis's argument assumes that the land needed to grow tropical cash crops was abundant, so that tropical farmers could not get rich from the rent on their land. This assumption does not hold for mineral-bearing lands, but the rents on these lands went to foreign investors. In contrast, the prices of primary product exports such as wool and frozen meat from the temperate countries of recent settlement, Canada, Argentina, Chile, Australia, New Zealand, and South Africa, had to sustain a European standard of living. Lewis's model of relative wage and price determination in the temperate and tropical worlds is presented in detail in Note II.2.

The period of favorable conditions for export-led growth came to an end with World War I, which initiated what Reynolds calls "the longest depression" from 1914–45. Only a handful of countries in Reynolds's sample began intensive growth in this period marked by two world wars and the Great Depression. Following World War II was the period Reynolds calls "the greatest boom," which ended in 1973. Both the initiation of intensive growth in countries including China and India and its continuation in many other countries in Reynolds's sample was now led by industrial production for the home market rather than exports of primary products. Governments played a key role in this change and indeed tended to expand their influence in every sphere of economic life. This part of the Reynolds selection is very wide ranging and provides an excellent background for issues that will be treated in much greater detail in the remaining chapters of this book.

As indicated in section I.B, the role of government has been scaled back in many less developed countries since 1983 when Reynolds wrote his article. Comment II.1 addresses one aspect of this retreat, the privatization of state-owned enterprises.

The delay in the onset of intensive growth in what we now call less developed countries relative to Western Europe, combined with slower intensive growth in many of these countries, led to a huge divergence in per capita incomes between the leading countries and all others. This divergence is documented in the final selection by Lant Pritchett. He estimates that the ratio of per capita income of the 17 richest countries to all others increased from 2.4 in 1870 to 4.5 in 1990. A concluding Comment following this Selection describes opposing views regarding whether this divergence will ever be reversed.

Selection II.1. The Spread of Economic Growth to the Third World: 1850–1980*

First, I deal only with growth in the simplest sense of capacity to produce. This is not meant to minimize the importance of how the product is distributed. But that is another large subject to include which would have stretched my study entirely too thin.

Second, I have excluded all countries with a 1980 population of less than 10 million people, which excludes about eighty countries at one stroke. Again, this does not mean that small countries are uninteresting, or that they do not differ in significant ways from larger countries. I can plead only the need to spare effort.

The countries included, forty-one in number, are as follows:

Latin America:	Argentina, Brazil, Chile, Colombia, Cuba, Mexico, Peru, Venezuela.
North Africa and Middle East:	Algeria, Egypt, Iran, Iraq, Morocco, Sudan, Turkey.
Africa (sub-Saharan):	Ethiopia, Ghana, Ivory Coast, Kenya, Mozambique, Nigeria, Tanzania, Uganda, Zimbabwe, Zaire, Zambia.
Asia:	Afghanistan, Bangladesh, Burma, China, Indonesia, India, South Korea, Malaysia, Nepal, Pakistan, Philippines, Japan, Sri Lanka, Taiwan, Thailand.

. . . An increase in capacity to produce may be "absorbed" either in population growth, or in a rise of per capita income, or both. A situation in which increased capacity is fully absorbed by population, with no uptrend in per capita income, I define as *extensive growth*. This does not imply that the increase in capacity precedes a "choice" as to how it shall be absorbed. Rather, there is a (largely) exogenous growth of population, which stimulates a growth of productive capacity, initially through cultivation of additional land, often followed by intensification of cultivation methods.

A situation in which capacity to produce is rising appreciably faster than population, so that there is a sustained rise in per capita income, I define as *intensive growth. . . .* The time at which extensive growth turns into intensive growth, a change which is not inevitable and in some countries has not yet occurred, I call the *turning point. . . .*

II. The Era of Extensive Growth

A. *Economic Organization*

The era in which population and output are growing at about the same rate is a long one. It typically lasts for a century or more, and in some countries has been documented over several centuries.[1] . . .

It is better to say that the economy is dominated at this stage by *household production*. Each family produces not only most of its own food, but most of its housing and clothing, plus a wide range of services—education, healing, recreational activity, religious observance. We commonly observe that at this stage 80 to 90 percent of the population live in rural areas—isolated farms, or small villages close to farmland. This was true in Europe in 1700. The 80 percent ratio is still true in China today. This is sometimes wrongly regarded as indicating the size of the "agricultural sector." All it really means is that most economic activity is family activity. A careful record of time use by rural family members will reveal that agricultural activities take perhaps 50 to 60 percent of the total, the remainder going to "industrial" and service activities.

A corollary is that the apparent shrinkage of the agricultural sector and the expansion of other sectors as economic growth proceeds is partly fictitious. In part, it represents a transfer of household activities to specialized commercial producers whose activities are more readily detected and measured. But people always have clothes and they always have housing, no matter how these goods are produced.

So household production is central during the period of extensive growth. But this is not inconsistent with a substantial amount of marketed output, a widespread development of markets, and trade

---

*From Lloyd G. Reynolds, "The Spread of Economic Growth to the Third World," *Journal of Economic Literature* 21 (September 1983): 941–975. Reprinted by permission.

[1]Some scholars suggest that, for countries now considered developed, the era of extensive growth lasted from about 1500 to 1800 (cf. Maddison, 1982, p. 6).

and transport over long distances. Nor is it inconsistent with substantial changes in commodities, techniques, market organization, and trade routes over the course of time. What some might view as a "primitive" economy is, in fact, quite complex, sophisticated, and responsive to change.

As regards West European countries, this view would be readily accepted. It is well known that these economies become increasingly diversified, commercialized, and linked by trade relations during the sixteenth and seventeenth centuries, well before the industrial era. There was substantial development of towns and town markets, extensive development of manufacturing by handicraft methods, substantial interchange of goods between town and country, creeping technical progress in agriculture, internal trade along rivers and canals, overseas trade around the shores of the Mediterranean and the Baltic and North Seas.

There is a tendency, however, to assume that similar statements cannot be made about third-world countries, that their pre-turning point economies were more primitive, static, agriculture-oriented than their European counterparts. As evidence to the contrary, consider first the case of China, as documented by Albert Feuerwerker (1969), Dwight Perkins (1975), Alexander Eckstein (1977), and others. The period before 1949 can be considered one of extensive growth, which had been going on more or less continuously since establishment of the Ming dynasty in 1368. Over the years 1368–1949, the population of the country increased about eight times. Crop acreage increased about four times, while yields per acre doubled. What did the economy look like in these earlier centuries?

Agriculture was central, but far from all-important. Feuerwerker estimates that agricultural output was about two-thirds of national output in the 1880s. This is close to Eckstein's estimate of 65 percent for 1933, suggesting the absence of significant structural change before 1940. Rural *population,* of course, was substantially higher—perhaps 80 percent of the total, as indeed it is today. But the rural population was doing many things other than growing foodstuffs.

"Industry," which at this stage meant handicrafts, produced perhaps 7–8 percent of national output. This work was done overwhelmingly in individual farm households. But there was also cooperative activity by a number of households in rice milling, wheat milling, salt and pottery production; and there were some larger workshops in urban areas. Trading activities constituted another 7–8 percent, and transport perhaps 5 percent of national output. Government in the late nineteenth century was raising in taxes about 7 1/2 percent of national output, a figure not out of line with tax ratios in European countries during the nineteenth century.

Trade was carried on in a stable hierarchy of markets, ranging from local to international in scope. Perhaps three-quarters of total trade went on in some 70,000 basic local markets, in which peasants and handicraftsmen exchanged their surplus produce. This local trade absorbed perhaps 20 percent of total farm output, and this proportion seems not to have changed much over the centuries. Trade was thoroughly monetized and commercialized but restricted in geographic scope.

Longer-distance trade was restricted by transport costs, and involved only objects of sufficient value to warrant the cost. Trade moved mainly along waterways, notably the vast Yangtze network, and by vessels ranging from tiny sampans to large freighters. In North China, less well-supplied with waterways, most goods had to move by carts, which was slow and expensive. It is estimated that only 5–7 percent of national output went into interprovincial trade, and perhaps 1–2 percent into foreign trade. Even by 1900 the trade network had changed only a little at the seacost fringes, and scarcely at all within the country.

The government apparatus which presided over this economic activity was a meritocracy populated by the small educated elite. Perhaps because of the sheer size of the country, provincial and local governments were relatively more important than in smaller countries. Regular (or irregular) tribute was paid to the Emperor, but the Emperor was far away. Even in the 1890s, scholars estimate that only 40 percent of tax revenues went to the central government. Government did little to promote economic growth, but it was adequate for maintenance of the economy at a relatively constant level of per capita output.

A more surprising illustration comes from West Africa. One might visualize the economic organization of this region in pre-colonial times as unusually primitive and culture-bound. But evidence assembled by A. G. Hopkins (1973) suggests that the reality was rather different.

While rural villages predominated, there was also considerable urbanization. For example, Ibadan in the mid nineteenth century had a population of 70,000 and city walls with a circumference of 24 miles. There was much mobility of population, associated mainly with shifting pasturage of livestock and with trading activities. While production occurred mainly within the household there was an active market for nonfamily labor, though for the most part this was a slave rather than a hired-labor market. (Slaves were preferred because the cost of acquiring and maintaining them was less than the cost of hiring wage labor.)

Agriculture was the basic economic activity, with cereals predominating in the savanna and root crops, which yield more calories per acre, predominating in the forest. The early food crops had come mainly from Asia by way of the Middle East. After the beginnings of European contact many new crops were introduced, especially from South America. Successful innovations included corn, cassava, groundnuts, tobacco, and cocoa. The crops which survived and spread did so for the good reason that the value of output exceeded the cost of production. This responsiveness to change refutes the idea of a static "traditional" economy.

As regards industry, Hopkins (1973, p. 48) notes that "pre-colonial Africa had a range of manufacturing industries which closely resembled that of pre-industrial societies in other parts of the world . . . based on clothing, metal working, ceramics, construction, and food processing." Kano was a major textile center, a kind of Manchester of West Africa. Leather goods were prominent in cattle-raising areas. Pottery production was widely diffused throughout the region. While most of these handicraft activities were smallscale and carried on within family units, they were often regulated by guild rules which any European would have recognized as familiar.

The extensive development of trade and markets should be emphasized, as an offset to stereotypes of purely subsistence production. Local trade was carried on in regular town markets, to which people walked from a radius of ten miles or so, bringing in foodstuffs and carrying back craft products. Nearby towns arranged to rotate their market days to avoid overlapping. Perhaps more surprising, there was a highly organized network of long-distance trade routes, extending as far as from the Lake Chad area to Dakar, and from Kano to the Mediterranean coast. Long-distance trade usually moved in caravans, which individual traders could join for part or all of their journey, and which provided protection from bandits as well as other external economies. There were recognized trade centers along these routes for the assembly, break-up, or re-export of shipments. There was an elaborate system of local agents and commission men, banking and credit facilities, even a code of commercial morality. All in all, there was no lack of economic motivation and business ability. . . .

B. Population and Food Supply

During the era of extensive growth, population is increasing by definition; and this increase begins very early. Durand estimates that population was growing at a low rate almost everywhere in the world from at least 1750 onward (Population Problems, 1967, pp. 136–59). (A possible exception is tropical Africa, for which estimates before 1900 are dubious.) Growth rates were low by modern standards. In Europe, the average growth rate was about 0.7 percent per year from 1800–1850 and 0.8 percent from 1850–1900. Kuznets' estimate for the less developed countries places their average population growth at 0.35 percent from 1800–1850 and 0.56 percent from 1850–1900 (Richard A. Easterlin, 1980, pp. 471–516).

The great killers are famine, war, and plague. Once these are somewhat under control, population tends to grow through a modest excess of births over deaths. At this stage of development, the fertility rate is mainly the result of uncontrolled reproduction. People are not sure that they will be able to have as many surviving children as they would prefer to have. In Easterlin's terminology, the desired number of children, C_d, is greater than the natural fertility rate, C_n; so the former is dominant, and there is no incentive to population control (Tilly, ed. 1978, pp. 57–134).

To speak of a "natural fertility rate" does not imply that this is a universal constant for all countries. Even the uncontrolled birth rate is influenced by such things as: (1) the percentage of women who marry; (2) average age at marriage, which varies presently from around 30 in Ireland to 25 in the United States to 20 in tropical Africa; (3) the rate at which fecundity declines with age; (4) the average interval between births, which is influenced by social factors such as breastfeeding customs and taboos on intercourse during breast feeding, and so may vary from less than two years to more than three years; (5) the probability of husband or wife dying before the end of the child-bearing period. Because of these factors, uncontrolled birth rates range from about 35 to 55 per thousand.

The mortality rate is somewhat influenced by economic factors. Famine, traditionally an important cause of death, has been gradually eliminated by reductions in the cost of transporting food within and among countries. More recently, improvements in nutrition, sanitation, and literacy have reduced child mortality from diarrhea and other diseases. To a large extent, however, the determinants of mortality are exogenous, related to the progress of medical science; and this progress is somewhat discontinuous. Techniques developed during the two world wars to reduce mortality among soldiers later proved applicable to civilian populations. Thus after a gradual sag of mortality rates up to 1914, we see a marked drop after 1920 and another marked drop after 1945.

Even during the period of extensive growth one often observes a slight acceleration in the population growth rate. This seems to be due to a (largely exogenous) secular decline in mortality. Fertility rates fluctuate somewhat with good or bad harvests; but they do not show any marked secular trend during the period of extensive growth.

We have defined extensive growth as a situation in which population growth is matched by growth of national output and in particular of food supply. When we see population growing, how do we know that this second condition is met? The data for some of the larger third-world countries such as Brazil, India, China, and Indonesia have been worked over with considerable care. These studies suggest that food output per capita was either stationary or rising very slowly in the pre-modern period. Usually, however, we have to resort to negative reasoning. *If* population growth had been accompanied by marked deterioration of living standards, one would expect this to have been reported by informed observers. While reports of short-term hardship arising from drought and other natural disasters are common in the literature, reports of a secular decline in living standards are rare. In general, growing populations manage to feed themselves at a near-stationary level.

How is this feat accomplished? Least interesting, though very important historically, is simply extension of the cultivated area. As of 1900, most countries in our sample still had substantial reserves of unused land, which shrank only gradually in succeeding decades. The spreading out of population over a larger area, with at least a proportionate increase in agricultural output, is familiar from experience in "areas of new settlement," such as North America, South America and Australia, and presents no analytical problems.

More interesting is intensification of cultivation, which tends to accompany acreage expansion and becomes dominant when the frontier finally closes. Using length of the fallow period as an intensity indicator, one can lay out a spectrum of cultivation systems, ranging from "slash-and-burn" through bush fallow to short fallow, annual cropping with no fallow period, and multicropping. Ester Boserup (1965 and 1981) has argued persuasively

that movement along this spectrum is a normal response to exogenous population growth. The population increase which requires larger food supplies also tends to produce them by bringing about a shift toward more intensive land use. She uses cross-section analysis across countries to test the relation between population density and the cultivation system, with good results.

More intensive cultivation systems, of course, require larger factor inputs per unit of land. Labor inputs present no problem. More mouths to feed are accompanied by more hands to cultivate, reaching a high point in Chinese or Javanese rice-growing, which resembles gardening more than farming. When the soil is no longer allowed to recuperate through fallow periods, larger fertilizer inputs also become necessary—at this stage, mainly organic rather than chemical fertilizer. Multicropping, and even annual cropping in areas of deficient rainfall, typically requires large investments of labor time in drainage and irrigation facilities.

In this way it is possible to raise crop yields *per acre* in the most intensive cultivation systems several times over yields in less intensive systems. Yield *per farm worker* will tend to fall, but perhaps not very much. Shigeru Ishikawa (1981) has made cross-country studies of rice cultivation in which yield per hectare on the vertical axis is charted against available hectares per farm worker on the horizontal axis. The results conform quite closely to a rectangular hyperbola, sometimes called an "Ishikawa curve." Data for the same country, such as Japan or Taiwan, in successive time periods show a similar pattern. A country moves upward to the left along the Ishikawa curve as land availability decreases.

A further possibility is changes in the agricultural product mix. Potatoes and other root crops yield substantially more calories per acre than do most grain crops, and thus a reallocation of land among crops can substantially raise caloric availability. Another way in which densely populated countries adjust is through de-emphasis of livestock production. Boserup finds a strong inverse relation between population density and pasture area/cultivated area and livestock/person ratios. Large animals are a very inefficient way of converting acreage into calories, though pigs and chickens are somewhat more efficient. Densely populated areas tend to get a high proportion of their animal protein from fish.

Several of these possibilities can be illustrated from the experience of China, which has been analyzed by Dwight Perkins (1969). As we noted earlier, over the period 1349–1949 China's population increased about eight times, its cultivated acreage only about four times. But yields per acre roughly doubled, indicating that this "traditional economy" was not immune to technical change. Perkins notes several kinds of change:

i.   Some improvement of seeds, partly developed and diffused within China, partly imported from abroad.
ii. Introduction of new crops from America after 1600. Corn and potatoes were especially important, partly because they could be grown in areas not hospitable to other crops. As the frontier gradually closed and the man/land ratio rose after 1850, farmers adjusted to this partly by shifting to crops (including cash crops such as cotton and raw silk) which yielded more food or income per acre and at the same time required more labor for their cultivation.
iii. A gradual extension of double cropping, accompanied by irrigation projects to provide the necessary control of water supply. By 1900 irrigation had been extended to almost all the feasible acreage. Population growth in a sense *produced* more double-cropping by providing more labor both for seasonal peaks of cultivation and for water-control projects.
iv. An increase of inputs, notably fertilizer inputs. More people produced more nightsoill. So did more pigs, whose numbers apparently kept up with population growth. Perkins suggests that without this side-benefit, pork production would have been unprofitable.

This is not meant to suggest that adaptation of agriculture to population growth was entirely painless. But the possibilities of adaptation, even in pre-modern times, were apparently greater than one might have anticipated.

C. The Non-Agricultural Sectors

Industrial output grows along with population and agricultural output; and there is a gradual shift in the locus of manufacturing activity from the household to specialized workshops and cottage industry. Since clothing is a major consumer good, textiles tend to take the lead in this process. The "putting-out system," in which a merchant supplies materials to home spinners and weavers and then collects and markets their product, is familiar to readers of European economic history; but it was by no means confined to that continent. Quite similar systems existed in China, India, and many other third-world countries. In addition to textiles,

one typically finds an array of other handicraft industries supplying household necessities.

Handicraft production in turn gives way eventually to factory production, with textiles and raw materials processing in the lead. Handicraft products are often forced to compete first with imported factory goods, and later on with the output of domestic factories. Whether factory production appears during the period of extensive growth depends on the era we are discussing. In the substantial number of countries which reached the turning point before 1900, factories were almost absent at the turning point, and did not become important for five or six decades thereafter. This is why, for these countries, it is wrong to take the onset of industrialization as marking the beginning of intensive growth. But when we come to the years 1900–1950, by which time modern industrial techniques were increasingly well known throughout the world, we find considerable industrial development in countries such as Egypt, Turkey, India, and China which were still in the extensive growth phase. And since 1950 efforts to initiate intensive growth have been strongly identified with forced-draft industrial development.

Even during the extensive growth period the economy has trade relations with other countries, typically exchanging primary products for manufactured consumer goods. The volume of trade grows along with the size of the economy, but it may not grow any faster. A marked rise in the export/GNP ratio occurs only after the turning point—indeed, we rely heavily on this ratio in dating the turning point.

Governmental systems varied widely among the three continents we are discussing. In Latin America, the first half-century of independence was a period of nation-building. While Brazil's transition to independence was relatively peaceful, in most other countries there was a prolonged period of civil wars among rival factions of the élite. Not until around 1850, and in some countries not until around 1880, did stable governments emerge. These were oligarchies, with a change of regime meaning replacement of one élite group by another; but there was enough continuity and domestic order to permit expansion of private economic activity. In Asia, most of the countries in our sample were colonies, though China, Thailand, and the Ottoman Empire remained independent. . . .

In Africa, while there were a few substantial kingdoms, political units were generally small and fragmented along tribal lines. The "countries" which emerged with the partition of Africa among the European powers in the late nineteenth century were synthetic creations lacking any natural legitimacy in the eyes of the population; and the fragility of these creations may be partly responsible for relatively poor African performance since independence.

Nineteenth-century governments, whether indigenous or colonial, collected only a small percentage of national income, mainly from head taxes, land taxes, and trade taxes. Expenditures were mainly for the Army, the civil service, and consumption of the ruling group, with little remaining for economic or social purposes. But there was some building of roads, railroads, ports and warehouses for trade and military purposes. Interestingly enough, some colonial governments were more active on this front than were most independent countries. . . .

D. The Question of Preconditions

To what extent can developments during the period of extensive growth be regarded as a preparation for, or a pre-requisite for, the turning-point to intensive growth?

. . . Important conditioning factors during the period of extensive growth include: (1) nation-building, which in many countries is a recent and precarious process, still going on with varying degrees of success; (2) small technical changes which add up to what we might call "the importance of the unconspicuous"; (3) changes in crops, water control systems, and cultivation methods which enable food output to at least keep up with population, and which lay a foundation for eventually leaping ahead of population; (4) gradual reduction of transport costs and extension of long-distance trade; (5) growth of manufacturing production outside the household, or even within the household through the "putting-out system."

These factors are perhaps especially important for countries which have *recently* embarked on intensive growth, and which had a long prior exposure to the world economy. For example, India in 1947 had a tradition of national unity and democratic government, a well-staffed civil service, a substantial educational system, much physical infrastructure, a long tradition of handicraft manufacturing, and the beginnings of factory industry, notably in textiles. Some of these things could be said also of China, Pakistan, Egypt, Turkey, and other recent developers. They were taking off, not from a situation of stagnation, but from an economy already visibly in motion. . . .

Table 1. A Turning-point Chronology

1840	Chile	1900	Cuba
1850	Brazil	1910	Korea
1850	Malaysia	1920	Morocco
1850	Thailand	1925	Venezuela
1860	Argentina	1925	Zambia
1870	Burma	1947	India
1876	Mexico	1947	Pakistan
1880	Algeria	1949	China
1880	Japan	1950	Iran
1880	Peru	1950	Iraq
1880	Sri Lanka	1950	Turkey
1885	Colombia	1952	Egypt
1895	Taiwan	1965	Indonesia
1895	Ghana	—	Afghanistan
1895	Ivory Coast	—	Bangladesh
1895	Nigeria	—	Ethiopia
1895	Kenya	—	Mozambique
1900	Uganda	—	Nepal
1900	Zimbabwe	—	Sudan
1900	Tanzania	—	Zaire
1900	Philippines		

III. The Turning Point

The striking fact which emerges from Table 1 is that about two-thirds of the countries which have thus far achieved a turning point (22 out of 34) had done so by around 1900. The years 1900–1945 are a "hollow period," during which only four countries appear on the list. After 1945 the procession speeds up again, with eight countries reaching the turning point soon thereafter. We shall argue that this chronology stems from three major epochs in the world economy, which will be reviewed briefly.

(1) World Economic Boom, 1850–1914. It is clear in retrospect that this era was unusually favorable to world-wide diffusion of economic growth. Output in the early developing countries of Europe and North America was rising rapidly, and with it their demand for imports of primary products. Kuznets (1966) estimates the median growth rate of output in these countries from 1860–1914 at about 3 percent per year, which meant median growth of about 2 percent a year in per capita terms.

Rapid economic growth in Europe and North America opened up the possibility of enlarged trade with other continents. But this possibility could scarcely have been realized without an improvement and cheapening of transport. This involved replacement of sailing ships by steam-driven steel ships, which reduced ocean freight rates by 1913 to about 30 percent of their 1870 level; a world-wide railroad boom, which peaked in the years 1870–1914, and which produced even more spectacular reductions in overland transport costs; and building of a worldwide telegraph network linking would-be sellers and buyers. Completion of the Suez Canal in 1869 was a particularly important development for Asian countries trading with Europe.

Available estimates of growth in the volume of international trade have been analyzed by Kuznets (1967). They show the sum of exports and imports growing at an average rate of 50.3 percent per decade from 1850–1880, and 39.5 percent per decade from 1881–1913. The ratio of world trade to world output was thus rising quite rapidly. Kuznets estimates that this ratio had reached 33 percent by 1913.

Trade was of course dominated by the countries of Europe and North America, which accounted for about three-quarters of combined exports and imports. Latin America, Africa, and Asia accounted for about 20 percent of trade in 1876–1880 and 22 percent in 1913, not far from their proportion in recent decades. The implication is that third-world countries were keeping up with the general pace of world trade. This is confirmed by the investigations of Lewis (1969), who finds that the volume of tropical exports grew at 3.6 percent per year from 1883–1913. Agricultural exports grew a bit slower than this, but mineral exports grew faster. Indeed, during this period total exports from the tropical countries grew at almost exactly the same rate as industrial production in the advanced countries. While terms of trade between primary products and manufactures show short-term fluctuations, Lewis (1970) concludes that there was no appreciable trend over the period as a whole.

The third-world countries which embarked on intensive growth during this period fall into three groups: (a) all of the Latin American countries in our sample with the exception of Venezuela. The turning point dates in most cases mark the beginning of political stability after the prolonged civil wars which followed independence. Growth was invariably export-led, the nature of the exports varying from case to case. Argentina and Chile were able to grow and export wool, wheat, meat, and other temperate-zone products. Brazil relied on tropical products, initially sugar with coffee becoming dominant from the 1840s onward. Coffee also dominated the early export trade of Colombia. Minerals were important in Chile—at first nitrates, later copper. Minerals dominated Mexico's nine-

teenth-century exports, though agricultural products, cattle, and timber grew gradually in importance. Peru also had a combination of agricultural and mineral exports. Cuba was a sugar island. But everywhere exports, directed mainly toward European and North American markets, were the key to economic expansion.

(b) Four of the Asian countries which were drawn into the world export boom lie in an arc from Ceylon through Burma and Malaya to Thailand. Their turning points can be dated generally from the 1850s, though Ceylon had large and growing coffee exports from the 1830s onward. In Burma and Thailand a rising flow of rice exports came mainly from peasant producers expanding into uncultivated land, a pattern to be repeated later in West Africa. In Malaya the early export product was tin, produced mainly by relatively small entrepreneurs of Chinese origin, but by 1900 rubber had emerged as a second major product. Ceylon's exports came initially from large foreign-owned plantations—coffee plantations from 1830–1970, tea plantations after the coffee trees had been ruined by plant disease. Toward the end of the century, however, smallholder production of coconuts, rubber, and other crops became increasingly important, and by 1913 the export list was quite diversified.

Next there is the case of Japan, which did not appear unusual at the time, and which seems exceptional in retrospect only because of that country's ability to sustain and accelerate its growth rate over the subsequent century. This case is so well documented that details would be superfluous. But it is worth noting that Japan, like the other countries listed, showed a consistently strong export performance. Exports plus imports were about 10 percent of GNP in the 1870s, but had risen to 30 percent by 1910–1913. Over the years 1881–1914, Japanese exports grew about twice as rapidly as world exports. Up to 1900 this is mainly the story of raw silk, after 1900 mainly the story of cotton textiles.

To round out the Asian experience, Taiwan was ceded to Japan after China's defeat in the Sino-Japanese war of 1894–1895; and Japan set out energetically to turn the island into a rice bowl for the home country. The Philippines passed under American control after Spain's defeat in the Spanish-American War of 1898. There followed a period of rapid export-led growth, dominated by sugar and aided by a preferential trade agreement with the United States.

(c) Toward the end of the century several areas of Africa were drawn into the intensive growth process. Algeria in North Africa; Nigeria, Ghana, and Ivory Coast in West Africa; Kenya, Uganda, and Tanganyika in East Africa; and Southern Rhodesia (Zimbabwe) in Central Africa. To speak of these as "countries" is to speak of colonial creations. Europeans drew the boundaries, established unified administration over numerous tribal areas, and created an impression of nationhood which, while it took on some substance over the years, was never as strong as in the ancient kingdoms of Asia.

Most of the Asian and Latin American countries mentioned participated in the pre-1914 boom for periods of forty to sixty years. The new African colonies were latecomers, who participated for a generation or less. They nevertheless got in on the tail-end of the boom. Their exports rose sharply up to 1914; and this gave them an initial momentum which they never entirely lost. Wheat, fruits, and wine from Algeria; palm products, cocoa, coffee, and timber from West Africa; cereals from Kenya, cotton from Uganda, sisal and coffee from Tanganyika; cereals, gold, and other minerals from Southern Rhodesia—all flowed into international trade in growing volume. Exports from Ghana, Nigeria, Ivory Coast, and Uganda came almost entirely from African smallholders, who brought additional land under cultivation in the pattern observed earlier in Southeast Asia. In Algeria, Kenya, and Southern Rhodesia, on the other hand, substantial white settlements created dualistic economies in which most of the exports came from European-owned farms.

(2) The Longest Depression, 1914–1945. This phrase, borrowed from Lewis (1978a), is adequately descriptive. It was a bleak period for the world economy, marked by two world wars, the Great Depression, and a marked slowdown in the growth of world production and trade. The growth rate of industrial production in the "developed" countries fell from 3.6 percent in 1883–1913 to 2.7 percent in 1913–1929 and 1.3 percent in 1929–1938. This is significant in view of Lewis' finding that the growth rate of primary exports from tropical countries is closely related to growth of industrial production in the advanced economies. And in fact the growth rate of tropical exports fell from 3.7 percent per year in 1883–1913 to 3.2 percent in 1913–1929 and 1.9 percent in 1929–1937. This decline in export volume was accompanied by a mild sagging of primary products' terms of trade against manufactures even before 1929, and a sharp drop after 1929. The import capacity of third-world countries was sharply reduced.

Under these depressed conditions, countries which had been growing quite rapidly before 1914 now grew more slowly. It is significant, too, that only four additional countries reached the turning point during this period, and these cases can be attributed to special circumstances. Korea was formally taken over by Japan in 1910 and, as in the earlier case of Taiwan, Japan set about to develop the country as an auxiliary to the Japanese economy. A French protectorate was established in Morocco in 1912 as part of a deal among the European powers, and effective control over most of the territory had been gained by 1920. Here, as earlier in Algeria, French settlers in effect implanted a new "modern" economy on top of the indigenous economy, initiating a growth process whose benefits went disproportionately to the Europeans.

In Venezuela, which had remained a stagnant backwater dominated by military dictators and an agricultural oligarchy, the discovery of oil in the early twenties set off a rapid transformation of both the economy and the political structure. Venezuela was the first great oil exporter and remains a key member of OPEC, which it took the initiative in founding in the 1960s. In Zambia (then Northern Rhodesia), rich copper deposits began to be exploited by foreign-owned companies in the late twenties. While these properties have now passed from foreign to national ownership, copper remains a dominant factor in the economy.

(3) The Greatest Boom, 1945–1973. The evolution of the world economy during this period is still fresh in mind and can be reviewed very briefly. The years 1945–1973 saw an unprecedented boom in world production and trade, a "second golden age" with growth rates well above those of the "first golden age" of 1870–1914. The average annual growth rate of GNP in the OECD countries from 1950–1973 was 4.9 percent, compared with an 1870–1913 average of 2.5 percent and a 1913–1950 figure of 1.9 percent. These high output rates, plus reduction of trade barriers, plus continued reduction of transport costs (supertankers, container ships, jet aircraft, great expansion of road mileage and truck transport) produced an even faster growth in the volume of international trade. Angus Maddison (1982) shows the export volume of the OECD countries rising at 8.6 percent per year from 1950–1973. Thus export/GNP ratios rose substantially.

Exports from third-world countries, while still growing rapidly by historical standards, grew somewhat less rapidly than developed country exports, so that their percentage of world exports fell from 25.3 percent to 17.7 percent. There was some diversification of the export mix. Manufactured goods formed only 7.6 percent of third-world exports in 1955, but by 1970 this had risen to 16.7 percent (and the percentage was to double again by 1980). Meanwhile exports of foodstuffs had fallen from 36.7 percent to 26.5 percent of the total, reflecting not only demand constraints but also increasing domestic food consumption associated with population growth and rising per capita incomes. The great grain-surplus areas are now the United States, Canada, Australia, and Europe. Thus the old distinction between "developed" exporters of manufacturers and "less developed" exporters of primary products has become increasingly blurred. The terms of trade between primary products and manufactures show no marked trend over the period 1945–1973. . . . Eight additional countries reached the turning point in the 1950–1980 period; and this includes the two Asian giants, China and India, plus Pakistan and Indonesia. In both China and undivided India one could make a case for a slight rise in per capita income from 1900–1940. But the increase, if present at all, is so slight that in our judgment the turning point for India and Pakistan should be dated from independence in 1947, and for China from the revolution of 1949.

Four additional countries—Egypt, Turkey, Iraq and Iran—lie in an arc across the Middle East. There is some ambiguity about the correct dating for these countries. They experienced some political and economic modernization from the 1920s onward. But the 1929 depression and the 1939 war followed so soon afterwards that they had scarcely made a significant beginning before 1945. It seems most reasonable, then, to locate their turning points in the postwar period.

The case of Indonesia is also complex and somewhat ambiguous. Exports from Indonesia rose from 1880–1930 at a quite respectable rate. But to an unusual degree these exports came from foreign-owned mines and plantations, and a large share of the proceeds remained in foreign hands. Particularly in densely-populated Java, the benefits to the local population seem to have been meagre. As a matter of judgment, then, we prefer to locate Indonesia's turning point after the achievement of independence. Even then, GNP per capita did not begin to rise perceptibly until the overthrow of President Sukarno and installation of the present regime in the mid-sixties.

(4) Some Laggards. We note finally that seven countries in our sample remain in the phase of extensive growth and show no sign of a sustained rise in per capita income. These countries are Afghanistan, Nepal, Bangladesh, Ethiopia, Sudan, Mozambique, and Zaire. There does not seem to be any single reason for their failure to achieve intensive growth. This failure results rather from varying combinations of geographic remoteness (Afghanistan, Nepal, most of Ethiopia, Zaire, and Sudan), absence of transport facilities and other infrastructure (all seven countries except Bangladesh), internal political turmoil (absent only in Nepal and post-1970 Sudan), colonial authorities who fled the country with no real preparation for independence (Mozambique, Zaire), primitive governments (Afghanistan, Ethiopia, Nepal), and massive misgovernment (Zaire). . . .

IV. Intensive Growth: Then and Now

. . . In the long era before 1940 the early developing countries followed a broadly similar growth pattern, which we shall try to characterize. The years after 1945 brought substantial changes in the political and economic setting. Countries which had reached the turning point before 1940 continued to grow, usually at an accelerated rate, but with significant changes in the growth pattern. Further, countries reaching the turning point after 1945 set off on a somewhat different course from the outset.

A. *Intensive Growth Before 1940*

(1) Population and Food Supply. Nineteenth-century population growth rates were low, typically below one percent. Kuznets estimates the average rate of population increase in third-world countries at only about 0.6 percent per year from 1850–1900 (Easterlin, ed., 1980, pp. 471–516). There was some acceleration after 1920, however, due mainly to a reduction of mortality rates associated with medical progress, Kuznets' estimate of average third-world population growth in the twenties is 1.3 percent.

Growing population and rising per capita income imply growing demand for food, at a rate which can be estimated from income elasticities of demand. Closed-economy growth models typically suggest that, unless food output rises at the minimum required rate, the internal terms of trade will turn in favor of agriculture. Rising food prices will put upward pressure on money wage rates, and this will choke off industrial growth in Ricardian fashion. In actual open economies, however, the situation is different. A country with flourishing exports of oil, minerals, timber, rubber, cotton, or whatever can trade these products for food, thus relaxing the domestic food supply constraint.

Pre-1940 experience in this respect is mixed. Many countries, perhaps most, did manage to keep food output rising in line with the moderate growth of demand. This was done mainly by extending the cultivated area. Crop yields usually did not change significantly, though extension of irrigation and multiple-cropping raised yields in Egypt and China, while improved seeds and other technical changes did so in Japan, Taiwan, and Korea.

What is rather surprising is how many countries fell into the habit of trading non-food exports for food imports, allowing not only the absolute volume of imports but the imported percentage of domestic consumption to rise over time. Notable examples were Chile, Peru, Mexico, Venezuela, Sri Lanka, Burma, Malaysia, Egypt, Iraq, and Iran. This could in some cases be regarded as a sensible exploitation of comparative advantage. But the main explanation seems to be government inattention to agriculture. Where government did have an active agricultural policy, as in Japan and its colonies, good results were achieved despite serious land constraints.

(2) Manufacturing. The development of manufacturing after the turning point follows a standard pattern, as regards both organization of production and type of product. As agricultural production becomes more labor-absorbing and more profitable, and as manufactures can be purchased from outside on more favorable terms, the rural family sheds some of its goods-producing functions and passes them over to specialized producers. Indeed, not only goods production but production of many services—education, healing, religion, dispute settlement—tends to move outside the family, which becomes more strictly a producer of *agricultural* goods rather than a multi-purpose producer of everything.

The manufacturing activities displaced from the household are taken over in the first instance by individual artisans and small-scale "rural industries." In almost every country this was the dominant form of manufacturing organization throughout the period we are considering. Opening of the economy to trade, of course, means that these local industries are early forced to compete with factory-made imports. But even in India, often cited as the classic case, and also in Southeast Asia and elsewhere, the extent of "handicraft destruction" has often been exaggerated. It was most pronounced in textiles, and especially in spinning, where the factory's technical superiority is very large. It was notably less in

other goods, particularly heavy or bulky goods where transport costs provide some natural protection. Costs of inland transport also meant that import competition was most severe in port cities, less so in the interior. The typical outcome was that handicraft production continued to grow, but at a rate below that of domestic consumption, so that the imported *share* of total supply rose.

As imports penetrate and reveal the market, this leads in time to initiation of local factory production. But time is required. The prospective market must be large enough to absorb the output of at least one plant of minimum efficient size. And even then, capital and entrepreneurship does not appear automatically. There is typically a lag, often of forty or fifty years, between the beginning of intensive growth and the appearance of large factories with power-driven equipment. Even in the Latin American countries, with relatively high per capita income and independent governments able to levy tariffs, factory industry was still very limited as of 1900. By 1940 it was more substantial; and an initial manufacturing base had been established also in India, China, Taiwan, Korea, and the Philippines. In most of the African countries, however, as well as in Sri Lanka, Burma, Malaysia, and Thailand, factory industry was virtually absent. For the third world as a whole, handicraft production must still have provided more than half of manufacturing output, and much more than half of manufacturing employment.

As regards type of product, textiles are normally the leading sector, because clothing is a basic need and the potential market is large. Further, the capacity to produce cotton and other fibers is widely distributed throughout the world, so that domestic raw materials are usually available. In addition to an assured domestic demand—often demonstrated initially by large cloth imports—the emergence of textiles is facilitated by relatively small minimum efficient scale of plant, a well-known technology, ready availability of used as well as new textile machinery, and limited requirements of skilled labor.

Other early industries are concerned mainly with agricultural processing for home use or for export—rice mills, flour mills, sawmills, palm oil extraction, and so on. These are followed by light consumer goods industries such as shoes, clothing, beverages, leather goods, ceramics, furniture, and household utensils, as well as building materials and simple agricultural implements. As the market continues to grow, additional industries appear in a sequence charted by Walther Hoffman (1958) and Hollis Chenery (1960, 1979). "Middle industries" such as chemicals and petroleum products appear, followed eventually by "late" or heavy-goods industries, dominated by metals, machinery, and transport equipment.

As of 1940 most third-world countries had proceeded only a short distance through this sequence. Most were at the stage of raw material processing, with at most a small development of textiles. Even the dozen or so more industrialized countries were producing mainly finished consumer goods, with capital goods and intermediates forming only a small percentage of manufacturing output.

(3) The Foreign Sector. Little need be added to what was said about exports in earlier sections. Typically, exports rose considerably faster than population or national output. During the 1850–1914 era, countries which had reached the turning point had population growth rates somewhat below 1 percent, GNP growth rates of perhaps 2 to 3 percent, but export growth of 3 to 4 percent, and occasionally even higher. From 1914–1945, output and export growth rates were lower; and there were also large short-term fluctuations associated with war and depression.

The largest import items were usually foodstuffs and cotton cloth, with other consumer goods making up most of the balance. Except for railroad equipment and other infrastructure requirements, capital goods imports were usually small, though by 1920–1940 industrial development in some Latin American countries was far enough along to require substantial machinery imports.

Private capital (mainly British and French up to 1914, with the United States prominent after 1920) flowed to these countries through several channels. The British were the main railroad builders all over the world, providing not only finance but physical equipment and engineering and construction skills, often followed by ownership and management of the completed lines. There was substantial direct investment in mineral exploitation and plantation agriculture. There was also private portfolio investment, particularly in Latin American government securities. Little foreign capital went into manufacturing, which was largely indigenous as regards both financing and entrepreneurship. When we say "indigenous," of course, we must recall the prominence of ethnic Chinese entrepreneurs throughout Southeast Asia. There were also foreign-owned manufacturing firms—Japanese and British textile mills in China, American firms in Cuba and the Philippines, British firms in India and other colonial areas. But these were rarely dominant. The textile and steel pioneers in India were Indians, not British.

(4) The Public Sector. The years before 1940 were an era of small government. Colonial administrations typically raised perhaps 5 percent of GNP through readily collectible trade and excise taxes, and spent the proceeds on a limited array of public services—roads, urban streets and sewerage, a small development of primary education and health facilities, a police force. But independent governments in Latin America and elsewhere were scarcely more enterprising. It is doubtful that the public goods/GNP percentage was higher in these countries than in the colonies. It is doubtful also that there was an uptrend in this percentage before 1914, with perhaps a slight uptrend from 1914–1940.

Government was more active as regards capital formation, particularly railroad building. Colonial administrators typically floated loans for this purpose in the home market, committing the colony to meet interest and principal repayments from tax revenue. Latin American governments also took the initiative in financing railroad building in one way or another—issuing government bonds, guaranteeing private bond issues, occasionally giving land concessions to the railroad companies. . . .

B. The Post-1945 Environment and Some Consequences

The years around 1945 mark a watershed in several respects:

i. About half the countries in our sample were decolonized and became independent countries.

ii. There was a marked change of political climate in most parts of the world, with much more emphasis on the economic functions of government. Economic growth was no longer something that happened or failed to happen, but something to be planned and promoted.

iii. The pace of scientific and technical progress quickened, especially in the fields of medicine and agriculture, accompanied by improved channels for diffusion of technical progress.

iv. There was a marked increase in the flow of capital from richer to poorer countries. In the first instance this was mainly "official" capital flowing through government-to-government channels; but private long-term investment and commercial bank lending grew in relative importance over the course of time.

v. Finally, there was the unprecedented growth of output and trade in the "developed" countries, which did more than any other single factor to generate rapid growth in the third world.

This changed environment, as suggested earlier, had two kinds of consequence: countries which were growing before 1940 tended to grow faster, but along somewhat different lines; and, in countries which reached the turning point only after 1945, intensive growth showed a somewhat different pattern than that followed by early developers. The growth of Pakistan from 1950–1980 looks more like Brazil from 1950–1980 than like Brazil from 1850–1900. These points can best be explained through a sector-by-sector review.

(1) Population and Food Supply. There was substantial technical progress before and during World War II in anti-insect chemicals, antibiotics, and other branches of medical science. After 1945 these new techniques were disseminated rapidly by the World Health Organization and national aid agencies, at low or zero cost to the recipient countries. The result was a striking decline in mortality rates, even in the poorest countries, and a corresponding rise in rates of natural increase. The Kuznets estimates for all third-world countries cited earlier show the average rate of natural increase rising from 1.3 percent in 1920–1930 to 2.0 percent in 1950–1955 and 2.6 percent in 1970–1975. The average crude death rate fell from 31 per thousand in 1937 to 16 per thousand in 1970–1975.

It is worth noting that a number of third-world countries already show signs of retracing the demographic pattern observed earlier in the "developed" countries, in which the birth rate follows the death rate downward with a considerable lag. Indeed, twenty-four of our forty countries show a significant drop in the crude birth rate between 1960 and 1980. Drops of 10 points or more have occurred in

Brazil (43–30)	Colombia (46–30)
Chile (37–22)	Peru (47–36)
Venezuela (46–35)	Cuba (32–18)
South Korea (43–24)	Taiwan (40–21)
Philippines (46–34)	Indonesia (46–35)
Thailand (44–30)	Malaysia (45–31)
Turkey (43–32)	

Declines of 8 points have occurred in Mexico and India. China's energetic population control program is said to have achieved substantial success. Even if these declines continue, however, the eventual steady state population numbers projected by demographers are startlingly large.

Higher population growth rates since 1945 mean that required rates of food output growth are now considerably higher. At the same time reserves of uncultivated land are smaller, and in China and South Asia are virtually zero. Governments have become more active in agriculture, but this activity has often taken unfavorable forms. The post-1950 tendency to regard industrialization as the key to growth has led in many countries to trade and exchange policies which turned the internal terms of trade sharply against agriculture. A desire to ensure cheap food for industrial workers and other city people has often led to farm price controls which discouraged production. Experiments with socialized agriculture, a tenure form not favorable to high productivity, have disorganized production in some countries.

The most encouraging postwar development has been rapid technical progress in rice, wheat, corn, and a number of other crops. Countries which have moved energetically to incorporate these developments in their agricultural systems have been able to achieve remarkable yield increases within a few years. It is probably fair to say also that, in most countries, government policies were more favorable to agriculture in the seventies than in the fifties. The glitter of rapid industrialization is somewhat tarnished, the importance of agricultural output is more widely appreciated, and the requirements for agricultural progress are better understood.

Country performance since 1950 has been variable. Countries which have done outstandingly well, with increases of 30 to 60 percent in *per capita* food output between the early fifties and 1980, are Brazil, Mexico, Malaysia, Taiwan, Thailand, Sri Lanka, and Venezuela. India and China have achieved a slight gain in per capita output despite population pressure and land scarcity. Of the remaining 32 countries in our sample, 17 show a modest increase in per capita output over the period, the median increase being about 15 percent. But the other 15 countries have been falling behind, showing a median *decrease* of 15 percent in food output per capita. It is not surprising that there is a marked relation between agricultural performance and overall economic performance. Of the twelve countries which rank lowest in terms of 1950–1980 GNP growth rate, ten also show a decline in food output per capita. Eight of these countries are in Africa, the others being Afghanistan and Nepal.

(2) The Public Sector. Economic growth before 1940 was largely private enterprise growth, though government's infrastructure contribution was usu-

ally substantial. But since 1945, private enterprise in most third-world countries has been in retreat. Public ownership, government regulation, economic planning, and the welfare state are in vogue. This world-wide tendency has been reinforced in some countries by nationalist sentiment. Where many of the private enterprisers are foreigners (and in Southeast Asia, even Chinese long resident in the country are "foreigners," as are Indians in East Africa), while the indigenous population controls the government, transferring economic activities from foreign to indigenous control is naturally interpreted as requiring transfer to government control.

This increased prominence of government takes several forms:

i. A marked rise in the public consumption share of GNP. We suggested earlier that before 1940 this share may have averaged 5 percent. By 1980 the median for countries in our sample was 15 percent, and a half-dozen countries were already in the 20–25 percent range. There are several reasons for this uptrend. Partly because of international demonstration effects, there has been insistent public demand for expansion of education, health facilities, housing and urban amenities, and other public services; and independent governments are under stronger pressure to respond to these demands than were the colonial administrators. Some countries have chosen the popular course of subsidizing urban food consumption and, more recently, consumption of petroleum products. There has been a tendency toward over-staffing and over-payment of government employees, again understandable on political grounds. And some countries have continued to enlarge their military establishments, which often control the government.

ii. A marked increase in public ownership of economic activities, extending beyond infrastructure to mining, manufacturing, finance, and trade. The reasons, in addition to ideological and nationalistic considerations, include the vogue of industrialization in the fifties and sixties, and the urge to launch large new enterprises in a situation where government seemed best able to mobilize the necessary investment funds. Rapid, government-propelled industrialization was preferred to the slower pace which would have resulted from relying on private initiative and finance.

iii. A marked increase in government investment expenditure. GDCF/GNP ratios have risen substantially, and in most countries of our sample now exceed 20 percent. Government is typically responsible for half or more of national capital formation, and its capital expenditures often rival current expenditures in size. Accelerated economic growth has increased the need for investment in roads, electric power, and other infrastructure facilities; and in addition government is typically the main source of finance for manufacturing investment.

iv. A tendency toward increasingly complex regulation of private economic activity. In addition to foreign trade and exchange controls, one finds licensing systems for new private enterprises, price controls for farm products, government marketing systems for these products, urban price controls sometimes accompanied by rationing, interest rate and wage rate regulations, and much else besides. In the best cases, this reflects an effort at coherent economic planning. But in many cases it comes closer to random interventionism, which can scarcely promote growth. In some countries, too, the structure of public administration is incapable of enforcing the complex controls, and private initiative reasserts itself through smuggling, black marketing, and other evasions of control.

(3) Manufacturing. All of the late developing countries except Indonesia and Pakistan already had by 1950 a modest base of factory industry developed during the period of extensive growth. India and China, in particular, had sizeable textile industries dating from the nineteenth century, as well as the beginnings of light consumer goods and engineering industries. Several of the early developers, too, had a substantial industrial base by 1950, including Argentina, Brazil, Chile, Mexico, Egypt, and the Philippines. In many other countries, however, and particularly in Africa, handicrafts greatly predominated, and factory industry was starting almost from zero.

One would have expected the high growth rate of per capita income after 1950 to stimulate industrial growth. It is well documented that, as per capita income rises, both the broader "industrial" share and the narrower manufacturing share of GNP increase steadily. Both import substitution and growth of domestic consumption contribute to this result. Chenery's (1960) analysis yields "growth elasticities" with respect to per capita income of 1.31 for consumer goods output, 1.50 for intermediate goods, and 2.16 for capital goods. Import substitution accounts for most of the relative increase in output of investment goods and intermediate goods. For consumer goods, on the other hand, growth of final demand is the dominant factor.

Manufacturing output did in fact grow rapidly in most countries, substantially raising its share of GNP. In 1950, the median manufacturing share in the countries of our sample was a bit below 10 percent. By 1980 the median had risen to 16 percent and twelve countries were in the 20–30 percent range, that is, approaching the structure characteristic of "developed countries." This group includes the major Latin American countries plus Egypt, Turkey, Sri Lanka, Philippines, Taiwan, South Korea, and China. In addition, India, Pakistan, and Thailand were only slightly below the 20 percent level. The data also show the expected shift toward heavier types of industry. In most of the growing economies of Asia and Latin America, though not in Africa, import substitution in consumer goods is now substantially complete—indeed, a half-dozen countries have substantial *exports* of consumer goods. Except in China and Brazil, import substitution in intermediates and capital goods is less far along, many countries still importing one-third to two-thirds of their requirements.

During the fifties and sixties manufacturing was the fair-haired child of most third-world governments. In addition to mobilizing capital for manufacturing investment and building supporting infrastructure, governments promoted industrialization by familiar techniques—high rates of effective protection, often accompanied by quantitative import restrictions; foreign exchange licensing and an overvalued exchange rate; preferential treatment in imports of materials and machinery; preferential access to capital through government lending institutions; a variety of tax holidays and tax rates for new industries; and pegging of interest rates at low, even negative, levels. These policies often involved substantial resource costs in terms of ill-conceived projects, implicit taxation of agriculture which discouraged farm production, and discrimination against exports. As this became evident, some countries moved from the early sixties onward toward a more outward-looking policy stance, involving trade and exchange policies which were more nearly neutral as between exports and import-substituting activities, plus higher interest rates and more realistic and flexible exchange rates. Notable examples are Brazil, Colombia, Taiwan, South Korea, Pakistan, and (recently) Sri Lanka. The growing efficiency of manufacturing industries in these countries, and their increasing success in export markets, can be traced partly to this policy shift.

The question of how far post-1950 manufacturing growth was a "normal" response to growth of domestic markets, and how far it was accelerated by government promotional efforts, would need to be examined country by country. Overall, my impression is that the effect of market expansion may have been underestimated in the literature, while the effect of promotional policies may have been overstated, especially in view of the fact that these policies had negative as well as positive effects.

An important aspect of post-1950 manufacturing expansion is the marked increase in the public-sector share of assets and output. Before 1940, third-world manufacturing industries were almost entirely in private hands. Since 1950, in most countries, government has not only been the main source of industrial finance through government investment banks, commercial banks, and direct budget allocations, but has gone beyond this to ownership and management of manufacturing establishments. The public-sector share of manufacturing is often 20 to 25 percent, and sometimes reaches 75 to 80 percent. The reasons vary from country to country: a long-standing statist tradition, as in Turkey and other remnants of the Ottoman Empire; socialist ideology of the British Labor Party type, as in India; a desire to transfer industry from foreign to national ownership, which tended to be interpreted as public ownership, as in Egypt or Burma; and a perhaps natural tendency for government investment banks to acquire majority equity ownership and thus responsibility for management, as in Mexico or Brazil.

In most countries, however, the private manufacturing sector, even when discriminated against by public policy, has enough vitality to remain important; and in perhaps half of our countries it is predominant. Multinational investment is important in a few of the most industrialized countries. But in general local entrepreneurship predominates, with capital being accumulated in classical fashion by reinvestment of earnings.

In most countries the structure of manufacturing remains quite dualistic. There is a strong persistence of small-scale industry, in the face of policies which usually discriminate against it; and even a marked persistence of handicraft activity in the countryside. There are still many countries in which handicraft and small-scale industries provide more than half of manufacturing employment, though a considerably smaller share of manufacturing output and capital stock. This very gradual replacement of the old by the new is not unlike what was happening a century ago.

(4) The Foreign Sector. Exports continue to be an important part of the growth story. In most

countries of our sample exports form 20 percent or more of GNP. In most countries, too, the export GNP ratio was stable or rising from 1950–1980. Exceptions include India, Egypt, Turkey, and several African countries with poor overall performance.

The primary export pessimism voiced by Prebisch and others in the fifties has turned out to be unwarranted. Primary products as a whole have done well. The export elasticities with respect to industrial output in the "developed" countries which Lewis calculated for 1883–1965 seem still to hold good. The behavior of terms of trade is always debateable, depending somewhat on the choice of series and of a base year. But there is no clear evidence that the terms of trade between primary products and manufactures have moved appreciably against primary products since 1945.

Growth of primary exports has been accompanied in many countries by a healthy diversification of exports, reducing the risks associated with any one crop. Notable examples are Thailand, Malaysia, Ivory Coast, Brazil, and Colombia. Further, a growing number of countries have been able to diversify into manufactured exports, sometimes termed "export substitution." This requires prior development of an industrial base. But it also requires the shift described earlier to outward-looking trade policies, and can be aided further by correct pricing of capital, labor, and foreign exchange. Some countries made this transition successfully during the sixties, but many have not yet done so. As a result, about half of third-world exports of manufactures come from a Far Eastern "gang of four" (Taiwan, South Korea, Hong Kong, Singapore), while another quarter comes from a Latin America "gang of four" (Brazil, Argentina, Mexico, Colombia).

Before 1940 export proceeds were used mainly to finance consumption. Since 1950 they have been used increasingly to finance investment. Except for food, consumer goods are a small and declining percentage of imports in most countries. Capital goods, fuels, and intermediates dominate the import list.

Comparing international capital flows from 1950–1980 with, say, 1850–1914, we note two main differences. First, recent capital transfers have been larger not only in absolute amount but relative to GNP and capital formation in the recipient countries; and second, long-term capital now flows mainly from governments to governments rather than through private channels. This institu-tional fact of life may be partly responsible for the relative expansion of the public sector in most third-world countries since 1950.

A country-by-country analysis would no doubt reveal that the productivity of foreign capital has varied widely from case to case, depending on the country's "absorptive capacity," which may reflect mainly the economic competence of government. In well-managed economies, foreign borrowing has no doubt been helpful in raising capital formation rates well above the pre-1940 level. But poorly-governed countries which lack the internal requisites for growth have (rightfully) had difficulty in borrowing; and where grant money has been poured into these countries, the returns have often been close to zero.

(5) GDP Growth Rates. For almost all countries in our sample there are official estimates of GDP and its components from about 1950 onward. But this is not as great an advantage as may appear. First, the quality of the data is highly variable and, if a rating scale could be constructed, many countries would probably deserve a C or D. Second, the estimates have several sources of upward bias. Two biases emphasized by Kuznets (1972) are: (1) that the ratio of industrial to agricultural prices is substantially higher in the LDCs than in developed countries, leading to overweighting of the fast-growing industrial sector; (2) that the estimated growth of service outputs is partly spurious, since it contains the "regrettable necessities" arising from urbanization, industrialization, and (in some countries) militarization. One suspects also that faster-growing activities such as large-scale manufacturing and infrastructure are overweighted simply because they are more visible and easier to measure than is household production in the countryside.

Taking the data at face value, they show a median growth rate of real GDP for the countries in our sample of 4.9 percent over the period 1950–1980. Because of relatively high population growth rates, the median rate of increase in real GDP per capita was only 2.3 percent. This is clearly below the median for the OECD countries over the same period. In this sense, the first-world/third-world gap has increased.

Perhaps more significant, however, is the marked variation of growth rates *among* third-world countries. At the top of the league are South Korea, Taiwan, Brazil, Thailand, and Malaysia with 1960–1980 growth rates of real per capita income above 4 percent. These countries have been gaining on the OECD countries, while at the same time pulling farther ahead of other third-world economies. At the bottom of the league are Ghana, Nepal, Sudan, Uganda, and Zaire, whose per capita income growth since 1950 has been zero or negative. This growing disparity of income levels makes it less and less meaningful to speak of all third-world economies as a group.

C. Concluding Comment

We shall not try to summarize what is already a very condensed argument. But several points seem worth making:

(1) Yes, things are different now. Intensive growth before 1940 was leisurely and intermittent, invariably export led, with moderate population growth, food output growing mainly through acreage expansion rather than technical progress, factory industry absent in most countries and only modestly developed in others, a low capital formation rate, and a small public sector. Since 1950, in both early and recent developers, population has grown considerably faster, per capita income in most countries has also grown faster, there are cases of non-export led growth, increases in agricultural output have relied increasingly on technical progress as land reserves shrink, factories have proliferated and in many countries now dominate the manufacturing sector, capital formation rates have doubled or more, and government's economic role has greatly expanded.

(2) At the same time there are strong elements of continuity with the pre-1940 period. Among these we may note: continuing pressure of growing population and food demand on agricultural output; continuing importance of exports, and the tendency for a high growth rate to be associated with export success; importance of infrastructure development, which has always been the responsibility of government; a broadly unchanged sequence of manufacturing development, as regards both form of organization and type of product; and the importance of international linkages through trade, capital flows, and technological transfer.

References

Boserup, Ester. *The conditions of agricultural growth. The economics of agrarian change under population pressure.* London: Allen and Unwin; Chicago: Aldine Pub. Co., 1965.

———. *Population and technological change: A study of long term trends.* Chicago: U. of Chicago Press, 1981.

Chenery, Hollis. "Patterns of Industrial Growth," *Amer. Econ. Rev.,* Sept. 1960, *50,* pp. 624–54.

———. *Structural change and development policy.* Oxford: pub. for the World Bank by Oxford U. Press, 1979.

Durand, J. Dana. *Historical estimates of world population: An evaluation.* Philadelphia: Population Studies Center, U. of Pennsylvania, 1974.

Easterlin, Richard A., ed. *Population and economic change in developing countries: A conference report.* Universities-National Bureau Committee for economic research; No. 30. Chicago: U. of Chicago Press, 1980.

Eckstein, Alexander. *China's economic revolution.* London and NY: Cambridge U. Press, 1977.

Feuerwerker, Albert. *The Chinese economy, ca 1870–1911.* Ann Arbor: Michigan papers in Chinese Studies, no. 5. U of Michigan, Centre for Chinese Studies, 1969.

Hoffman, Walther. *The growth of industrial economies.* Manchester: U. of Manchester Press, 1958.

Hopkins, A. G. *An economic history of West Africa.* NY: Columbia U. Press, 1973.

Ishikawa, Shigeru. *Essays on technology, employment and institutions in economic development: Comparative Asian experience.* Tokyo: Kinokuniya Bookstore Co., 1981.

Kuznets, Simon. *Modern economic growth: Total output and production structure.* New Haven: Yale U. Press, 1966.

———. "Quantitative Aspects of the Economic Growth of Nations: X. Level and Structure of Foreign Trade: Long-term Trends," *Econ. Develop. Cult. Change,* Jan 1967, *15*(2, Part II), pp. 1–140.

———. "Problems in Comparing Recent Growth Rates for Developed and Less Developed Countries." *Econ. Develop. Cult. Change,* Jan. 1972, 20, pp. 185–209.

Lewis, W. Arthur. *Aspects of tropical trade, 1883–1965.* Stockholm: Almqvist & Wiksell, 1969.

———. *Tropical development, 1880–1913: Studies in economic progress.* London: Allen & Unwin, 1970.

———. *Growth and fluctuations, 1870–1913.* London and Boston: Allen & Unwin, 1978a.

Maddison, Angus. *Phases of capitalist development.* Oxford: Oxford U. Press, 1982.

Perkins, Dwight M. *Agricultural development in China, 1368–1968.* Chicago: Aldine Press, 1969.

———, ed. *China's modern economy in historical perspective,* Stanford: Stanford U. Press, 1975.

Tilly, Charles, ed. *Historical studies of changing fertility.* Princeton: Princeton U. Press, 1978.

Comment II.1. State-owned Enterprises and Privatization

For a variety of reasons—not only economic, but also historical, ideological, and sociopolitical—governments of LDCs have often relied on public enterprise to try to achieve their development goals. In many LDCs, state-owned enterprises (SOEs) account for 10 to 40 percent of GDP. The major economic reasons for establishing state-owned enterprises have been to mobilize savings, create employment, provide public goods, and invest in large-scale capital-intensive projects that are natural monopolies or are subject to economies of scale or are especially risky for private investors.

There has, however, been growing concern about the performance of SOEs. One reason is that SOEs make large and growing claims on the budget and may resort to external debt for financing. In a number of countries, the public-enterprise deficit has been identified as a proximate cause of excessive credit creation, leading to monetary expansion, price inflation, and, ultimately, balance-of-payments pressures. SOEs also often undertake policies of controlling prices of public services, food grains, and other basic wage goods, which often prevent the public enterprises from covering their costs, with corresponding fiscal and monetary repercussions. For an elaboration of these macroeconomic aspects of SOEs, see Robert H. Floyd et al., *Public Enterprise in Mixed Economies: Some Macroeconomic Aspects* (1984).

At the micro level, there is also much concern about efficiency in production, profitable investment decisions, and nondistorting pricing policies. Various ways of improving SOE efficiency are now being emphasized—from the provision of systems for monitoring and evaluating performance to the sale of state-owned enterprises and promotion of privatization programs. On problems of management and control, see World Bank, *World Development Report, 1983* (1983), chap. 8.

Other instructive references are Deepak Lal, "Public Enterprises," in *Policies for Industrial Progress in Developing Countries,* ed. John Cody, Helen Hughes, and David Wall (1980); Leroy P. Jones, *Public Enterprise in Less Developed Countries* (1982); Tony Killick, "Role of the Public Sector in the Industrialization of African Developing Countries," *Industry and Development* (1985); Malcolm Gillis, "Role of State Enterprises in Economic Development," *Social Research* (Summer 1980); George Yarrow, "Privatization in Theory and Practice," *Economic Policy* (April 1984); and Gabriel Roth, *Private Provision of Public Services in Developing Countries* (1987).

In recent years, there have been numerous cases of privatizing state-owned enterprises—in terms of either ownership or management—in an effort to improve their efficiency and reduce their financial burden on the government's budget. For an appraisal of these cases, see Steve H. Hanks, ed., *Privatization and Development* (1987); Paul Cook and Colin Kirkpatrick, eds., *Privatization in LDCs* (1988); John Vickers and George Yarrow, *Privatization: An Economic Analysis* (1988); William Glade, ed., *Privatization of Public Enterprises in Latin America* (1991); Mary Shirley and John Nellis, *Public Enterprise Reform: Lessons of Experience* (1991); Sunita Kikeri et al., *Privatization: The Lessons of Experience* (1992); Leroy Jones et al., *Selling Public Enterprises: A Cost–Benefit Methodology* (1990); and Paul H. Boeker, ed., *Latin America's Turnaround: Privatization, Foreign Investment and Growth* (1993).

The study by Vickers and Yarrow (1988) is especially instructive in demonstrating how ownership of a firm will have significant effects on its behavior and performance, since changes in property rights will alter the structure of incentives faced by decision makers in the firm.

Selection II.2. The Division of the World and the Factoral Terms of Trade*

The Division of the World

How did the world come to be divided into industrial countries and agricultural countries? Did this result from geographical resources, economic forces, military forces, some international conspiracy, or what?

In talking about industrialization, we are talking about very recent times. England has seen many industrial revolutions since the thirteenth century, but the one that changed the world began at the end of the eighteenth century. It crossed rapidly to North America and to Western Europe, but even as late as 1850 it had not matured all that much. In 1850 Britain was the only country in the world where the agricultural population had fallen below 50 percent of the labor force. Today some 30 Third World countries already have agricultural populations equal to less than 50 percent of the labor force—17 in Latin America, 8 in Asia not including Japan, and 5 in Africa not counting South Africa. Thus, except for Britain, even the oldest of the industrial countries were in only the early stages of structural transformation in 1850.

At the end of the eighteenth century, trade between what are now the industrial countries and what is now the Third World was based on geography rather than on structure; indeed India was the leading exporter of fine cotton fabrics. The trade was also trivially small in volume. It consisted of sugar, a few spices, precious metals, and luxury goods. It was then cloaked in much romance, and had caused much bloodshed, but it simply did not amount to much.

In the course of the first half of the nineteenth century industrialization changed the composition of the trade, since Britain captured world trade in iron and in cotton fabrics; but the volume of trade with the Third World continued to be small. Even as late as 1883, the first year for which we have a calculation, total imports into the United States and Western Europe from Asia, Africa, and tropical Latin America came only to about a dollar per head of the population of the exporting countries.[1]

There are two reasons for this low volume of trade. One is that the leading industrial countries—Britain, the United States, France, and Germany—were, taken together, virtually self-sufficient. The raw materials of the industrial revolution were coal, iron ore, cotton, and wool, and the foodstuff was wheat. Between them, these core countries had all they needed except for wool. Although many writers have stated that the industrial revolution depended on the raw materials of the Third World, this is quite untrue. Not until what is sometimes called the second industrial revolution, at the end of the nineteenth century (Schumpeter's Third Kondratiev upswing based on electricity, the motor car and so on), did a big demand for rubber, copper, oil, bauxite, and such materials occur. The Third World's contribution to the industrial revolution of the first half of the nineteenth century was negligible.

The second reason why trade was so small is that the expansion of world trade, which created the international economic order that we are considering, is necessarily an offshoot of the transport revolutions. In this case, the railway was the major element. Before the railway the external trade of Africa or Asia or Latin America was virtually though not completely confined to the seacoasts and rivers; the railway altered this. Although the industrial countries were building railways from 1830 on, the railway did not reach the Third World until the 1860s. The principal reason for this was that, in most countries, railways were financed by borrowing in London—even the North American railways were financed in London—and the Third World did not begin to borrow substantially in London until after 1860. The other revolution in transport was the decline in ocean freights, which followed the substitution of iron for wooden hulls and of steam for sails. Freights began to fall after the middle of the century, but their spectacular downturn came after 1870, when they fell by two-thirds over thirty years.

For all these reasons, the phenomenon we are exploring—the entry of the tropical countries significantly into world trade—really belongs only to the last quarter of the nineteenth century. It is then that tropical trade began to grow significantly—at about four percent a year in volume. And it is then that the international order that we know today established itself.

Now it is not obvious why the tropics reacted to the industrial revolution by becoming exporters of agricultural products.

*From W. Arthur Lewis, "The Division of the World and The Factoral Terms of Trade," *The Evolution of the International Economic Order* (Princeton, NJ: Princeton University Press, 1978), pp. 4–20. Reprinted by permission.

[1]For the sources of this and other statistics used here, and generally for more detailed historical analysis, the reader may consult my book, *Growth and Fluctuations 1870–1913*, Allen and Unwin, London 1978.

As the industrial revolution developed in the leading countries in the first half of the nineteenth century it challenged the rest of the world in two ways. One challenge was to imitate it. The other challenge was to trade. As we have just seen, the trade opportunity was small and was delayed until late in the nineteenth century. But the challenge to imitate and have one's own industrial revolution was immediate. In North America and in Western Europe, a number of countries reacted immediately. Most countries, however, did not, even in Central Europe. This was the point at which the world began to divide into industrial and non-industrial countries.

Why did it happen this way? The example of industrialization would have been easy to follow. The industrial revolution started with the introduction of new technologies in making textiles, mining coal, smelting pig iron, and using steam. The new ideas were ingenious but simple and easy to apply. The capital requirement was remarkably small, except for the cost of building railways, which could be had on loan. There were no great economies of scale, so the skills required for managing a factory or workshop were well within the competence and experience of what we now call the Third World. The technology was available to any country that wanted it, despite feeble British efforts to restrict the export of machinery (which ceased after 1850), and Englishmen and Frenchmen were willing to travel to the ends of the earth to set up and operate the new mills.

Example was reinforced by what we now call "backwash." A number of Third World countries were exporting manufactures in 1800, notably India. Cheap British exports of textiles and of iron destroyed such trade, and provided these countries an incentive to adopt the new British techniques. India built its first modern textile mill in 1853, and by the end of the century was not only self-sufficient in the cheaper cottons, but had also driven British yarn out of many Far Eastern markets. Why then did not the whole world immediately adopt the techniques of the industrial revolution?

The favorite answer to this question is political, but it will not wash. It is true that imperial powers were hostile to industrialization in their colonies. The British tried to stop the cotton industry in India by taxing it. They failed because the Indian cotton industry had the protection of lower wages and of lower transportation costs. But they did succeed in holding off iron and steel production in India till as late as 1912. The hostility of imperial powers to industrialization in their colonies and in the "open door" countries is beyond dispute. But the world

was not all colonial in the middle of the nineteenth century. When the coffee industry began to expand rapidly in Brazil around 1850, there was no external political force from Europe or North America that made Brazil develop as a coffee exporter instead of as an industrial nation. Brazil, Argentina, and all the rest of Latin America were free to industrialize, but did not. India, Ceylon, Java, and the Philippines were colonies, but in 1850 there were still no signs of industrialization in Thailand or Japan or China, Indo-China or the rest of the Indonesian archipelago. The partition of Africa did not come until 1880, when the industrial revolution was already a hundred years old. We cannot escape the fact that Eastern and Southern Europe were just as backward in industrializing as South Asia or Latin America. Political independence alone is an insufficient basis for industrialization.

We must therefore turn to economic explanations. The most important of these, and the most neglected, is the dependence of an industrial revolution on a prior or simultaneous agricultural revolution. This argument was already familiar to eighteenth-century economists, including Sir James Steuart and Adam Smith.

In a closed economy, the size of the industrial sector is a function of agricultural productivity. Agriculture has to be capable of producing the surplus food and raw materials consumed in the industrial sector, and it is the affluent state of the farmers that enables them to be a market for industrial products. If the domestic market is too small, it is still possible to support an industrial sector by exporting manufactures and importing food and raw materials. But it is hard to begin industrialization by exporting manufactures. Usually one begins by selling in a familiar and protected home market and moves on to exporting only after one has learnt to make one's costs competitive.

The distinguishing feature of the industrial revolution at the end of the eighteenth century is that it began in the country with the highest agricultural productivity—Great Britain—which therefore already had a large industrial sector. The industrial revolution did not create an industrial sector where none had been before. It transformed an industrial sector that already existed by introducing new ways of making the same old things. The revolution spread rapidly in other countries that were also revolutionizing their agriculture, especially in Western Europe and North America. But countries of low agricultural productivity, such as Central and Southern Europe, or Latin America, or China had rather small industrial sectors, and there it made rather slow progress.

If the smallness of the market was one constraint on industrialization, because of low agricultural productivity, the absence of an investment climate was another. Western Europe had been creating a capitalist environment for at least a century; thus a whole new set of people, ideas and institutions was established that did not exist in Asia or Africa, or even for the most part in Latin America, despite the closer cultural heritage. Power in these countries—as also in Central and Southern Europe—was still concentrated in the hands of landed classes, who benefited from cheap imports and saw no reason to support the emergence of a new industrial class. There was no industrial entrepreneurship. Of course the agricultural countries were just as capable of sprouting an industrial complex of skills, institutions, and ideas, but this would take time. In the meantime it was relatively easy for them to respond to the other opportunity the industrial revolution now opened up, namely to export agricultural products, especially as transport costs came down. There was no lack of traders to travel through the countryside collecting small parcels of produce from thousands of small farmers, or of landowners, domestic or foreign, ready to man plantations with imported Indian or Chinese labor.

And so the world divided: countries that industrialized and exported manufactures, and the other countries that exported agricultural products. The speed of this adjustment, especially in the second half of the nineteenth century, created an illusion. It came to be an article of faith in Western Europe that the tropical countries had a comparative advantage in agriculture. In fact, as Indian textile production soon began to show, between the tropical and temperate countries, the differences in food production per head were much greater than in modern industrial production per head.

Now we come to another problem. I stated earlier that the industrial revolution presented two alternative challenges—an opportunity to industrialize by example and an opportunity to trade. But an opportunity to trade is also an opportunity to industrialize. For trade increases the national income, and therefore increases the domestic market for manufactures. Import substitution becomes possible, and industrialization can start off from there. This for example is what happened to Australia, whose development did not begin until the gold rush of the 1850s, and was then based on exporting primary products. Nevertheless by 1913 the proportion of Australia's labor force in agriculture had fallen to 25 percent, and Australia was producing more manufactures per head than France or Germany. Why did this not happen to all the other agricultural countries?

The absence of industrialization in these countries was not due to any failure of international trade to expand. The volume of trade of the tropical countries increased at a rate of about 4 percent per annum over the thirty years before the first world war. So if trade was the engine of growth of the tropics, and industry the engine of growth of the industrial countries, we can say that the tropical engine was beating as fast as the industrial engine. The relative failure of India tends to overshadow developments elsewhere, but countries such as Ceylon, Thailand, Burma, Brazil, Colombia, Ghana, or Uganda were transformed during these thirty years before the First World War. They built themselves roads, schools, water supplies, and other essential infrastructure. But they did not become industrial nations.

There are several reasons for this, of which the most important is their terms of trade. Thus, we must spend a little time analyzing what determined the terms of trade.

The Factoral Terms of Trade

The development of the agricultural countries in the second half of the nineteenth century was promoted by two vast streams of international migration. About fifty million people left Europe for the temperate settlements, of whom about thirteen million went to what we now call the new countries of temperate settlement: Canada, Argentina, Chile, Australia, New Zealand, and South Africa. About the same number—fifty million people—left India and China to work mainly as indentured laborers in the tropics on plantations, in mines, or in construction projects. The availability of these two streams set the terms of trade for tropical and temperate agricultural commodities, respectively. For temperate commodities the market forces set prices that could attract European migrants, while for tropical commodities they set prices that would sustain indentured Indians. These were very different levels.

A central cause of this difference was the difference in agricultural productivity between Europe and the tropics. In Britain, which was the biggest single source of European migration, the yield of wheat by 1900 was 1,600 lbs. per acre, as against the tropical yield of 700 lbs. of grain per acre. The European also had better equipment and cultivated more acres per man, so the yield per man must have been six or seven times larger than in tropical regions. Also, in the country to which most of the

European migrants went (the United States), the yield differential was even higher, not because of productivity per acre, which was lower than in Europe, but because of greater mechanization. The new temperate settlements could attract and hold European immigrants, in competition with the United States, only by offering income levels higher than prevailed in Northwest Europe. Since Northwest Europe needed first their wool, and then after 1890 their frozen meat, and ultimately after 1900 their wheat, it had to pay for those commodities prices that would yield a higher-than-European standard of living.

In the tropical situation, on the other hand, any prices for tea or rubber or peanuts that would offer a standard of living in excess of the 700 lb. of grain per acre level were an improvement. Farmers would consider devoting idle land or time to producing such crops; as their experience grew, they would even, at somewhat higher prices, reduce their own subsistence production of food in order to specialize in commercial crops. But regardless of how the small farmer reacted, there was an unlimited supply of Indians and Chinese willing to travel anywhere to work on plantations for a shilling a day. This stream of migrants from Asia was as large as the stream from Europe and set the level of tropical prices. In the 1880s the wage of a plantation laborer was one shilling a day, but the wage of an unskilled construction worker in Australia was nine shillings a day. If tea had been a temperate instead of a tropical crop, its price would have been perhaps four times as high as it was. And if wool had been a tropical instead of a temperate crop, it could have been had for perhaps one-fourth of the ruling price.

This analysis clearly turns on the long-run infinite elasticity of the supply of labor to any one activity at prices determined by farm productivity in Europe and Asia, respectively. This is applied to a Ricardian-type comparative cost model with two countries and three goods. The fact that one of these goods, food, is produced by both countries determines the factoral terms of trade, in terms of food. As usual one can elaborate by increasing the number of goods or countries, but the essence remains if food production is common to all.

One important conclusion is that the tropical countries cannot escape from these unfavorable terms of trade by increasing productivity in the commodities they export, since this will simply reduce the prices of such commodities. Indeed we have seen this quite clearly in the two commodities in which productivity has risen most, sugar and rubber. The factoral terms of trade can be improved only by raising tropical productivity in the common commodity, domestic foodstuffs.

There are interesting borderline cases where the two groups of countries compete. Cotton is an example. In the nineteenth century, the United States was the principal supplier of cotton, but the crop could also grow all over the tropics. The United States maintained its hold on the market despite eager British efforts to promote cotton growing in the British colonies. The U.S. yields per acre were about three times as high as the Indian or African yields, but this alone would not have been enough to discourage tropical production. The United States could not have competed with tropical cotton had southern blacks been free to migrate to the North and to work there at white Northern incomes. It was racial discrimination in the United States that kept the price of cotton so low; or, to turn this around, given the racial discrimination, American blacks earned so little because of the large amount of cotton that would have flowed out of Asia and Africa and Latin America at a higher cotton price.

Cotton was one of a set of commodities where low agricultural productivity excluded tropical competition. The tropics could compete in any commodity where the difference in wages exceeded the difference in productivity. This ruled out not only cotton and tobacco, which fell to the ex-slaves in North America, but also maize, beef, and timber, for which there were buoyant markets, and ground was lost steadily in sugar as beet productivity increased. This left a rather narrow range of agricultural exports and contributed to the overspecialization of each tropical country in one or sometimes two export crops. Low productivity in food set the factoral terms of trade, while relative productivity in other agriculture determined which crops were in and which were out.

Minerals fall into this competing set. Labor could be had very cheaply in the tropical countries, so high productivity yielded high rents. These rents accrued to investors to whom governments had given mining concessions for next to nothing, and the proceeds flowed overseas as dividends. Mineral-bearing lands were not infinitely elastic, but the labor force was. With the arrival of colonial independence over the last two decades, the struggle of the newly independent nations to recapture for the domestic revenues the true value of the minerals in the ground, whether by differential taxation, by differential wages for miners, or by expropriation, has been one of the more bitter aspects of the international confrontation.

Given this difference in the factoral terms of trade, the opportunity that international trade presented to the new temperate settlements was very different from the opportunity presented to the tropics. Trade offered the temperate settlements high income per head, from which would immediately ensue a large demand for manufactures, opportunities for import substitution, and rapid urbanization. Domestic saving per head would be large. Money would be available to spend on schools, at all levels, and soon these countries would have a substantial managerial and administrative elite. These new temperate countries would thus create their own power centers, with money, education, and managerial capacity, independent of and somewhat hostile to the imperial power. Thus, Australia, New Zealand, and Canada ceased to be colonies in any political sense long before they acquired formal rights of sovereignty, and had already set up barriers to imports from Britain. The factoral terms available to them offered them the opportunity for full development in every sense of the word.

The factoral terms available to the tropics, on the other hand, offered the opportunity to stay poor—at any rate until such time as the labor reservoirs of India and China might be exhausted. A farmer in Nigeria might tend his peanuts with as much diligence and skill as a farmer in Australia tended his sheep, but the return would be very different. The just price, to use the medieval term, would have rewarded equal competence with equal earnings. But the market price gave the Nigerian for his peanuts a 700-lbs.-of-grain-per-acre level of living, and the Australian for his wool a 1600-lbs.-per-acre level of living, not because of differences in competence, nor because of marginal utilities or productivities in peanuts or wool, but because these were the respective amounts of food that their cousins could produce on the family farms. This is the fundamental sense in which the leaders of the less developed world denounce the current international economic order as unjust, namely that the factoral terms of trade are based on the market forces of opportunity cost and not on the just principle of equal pay for equal work. And of course nobody understood this mechanism better than the working classes in the temperate settlements themselves, and in the United States. The working classes were always adamant against Indian or Chinese immigration into their countries because they realized that, if unchecked, it would drive wages down close to Indian and Chinese levels.[2]

[2]I have borrowed passages from my paper "The Diffusion of Development" in Thomas Wilson, Editor, *The Market and the State,* Oxford University Press, Oxford 1976.

Note II.1. Why Not Export First?

In the selection by W. Arthur Lewis, Lewis states that "it is hard to begin industrialization by exporting manufactures. Usually one begins by selling in a familiar and protected home market." In this Note the word we want to accent is *familiar*. It is one thing to export a homogeneous product like sugar. If a trader sees that the price differential between the home and foreign market is sufficient to cover the customs and transportation costs, he ships the product. Prices convey all the relevant information. It is another thing to export a differentiated product like garments or shoes. A trader cannot act on the price differential between domestic and foreign shoes because they bundle together different characteristics. Your shoes may be a poor fit (so to speak) for foreign consumers and thus sell (if they sell at all) for a price well below your expectations. Learning about foreign markets is an expensive process, and a continuous one, because styles and specifications are always changing.

This point is best illustrated by Japan, the only country *not* populated by Western Europeans to industrialize successfully during the "world economic boom" period 1850–1914. In Selection II.1 Reynolds notes that Japan began intensive growth as a raw silk exporter, but that by 1900 its exports were dominated by cotton textiles. Japan solved the problem of breaking into foreign markets by developing the general trading companies known as the *sogo shosha*. These trading companies were unique, among both developed and less developed countries, in both their size and their scope until imitations began in Korea and Turkey in the 1970s and 1980s, respectively. In their book on the sogo shosha, Yoshino and Lifson write of their operation in the late nineteenth and early twentieth centuries (1986, p. 23):

> Particularly important . . . was the role the sogo shosha played in providing export opportunities for the myriad small Japanese firms in cottage industries, which, like their counterparts in developing countries today, faced many problems in trying to break into the world market. The sogo shosha fed them market information, helped them design products, extended credit, and, most important, developed foreign outlets for their products.

An alternative to expensive cultivation of foreign markets is to establish export-oriented manufacturing through foreign direct investment (FDI). Writing about industrialization of the British West Indies, Lewis (1950) advised, "since it is difficult and expensive to break into a foreign market by building up new distribution outlets, this is most likely to succeed if the islands concentrate on inviting manufacturers who are already well established in foreign markets." Since Lewis wrote these words there has indeed been substantial export-oriented manufacturing FDI in less developed countries, and in fact many smaller LDCs could be said to have begun industrialization in this manner. Typically such FDI begins with assembly of components imported from the source country (Gereffi 1994). More integrated manufacturing in the host country comes later, if at all.

Could such an industrialization strategy have worked in the tropics in the 1850–1914 period? There is reason for doubt. First, the wage differential between the host and source countries was much smaller than it is now, and transportation costs were much larger, so FDI in export-oriented assembly operations may not have been profitable. Second, investments in agro-processing, mining, and infrastructure (especially railroads) associated with primary-product exports may have seemed like such good bets that few foreigners willing to risk their capital in far-off countries could have been persuaded to try export-oriented manufacturing instead. We conclude that, at least during the late nineteenth and early twentieth centuries, it is reasonable to take the size of the domestic market to be a key variable determining the ability of countries to industrialize.

References

Gereffi, Gary. 1994. "The International Economy and Economic Development." In Neil J. Smelser and Richard Swedberg, eds., *The Handbook of Economic Sociology* (Princeton, N.J.: Princeton University Press and Russell Sage Foundation), pp. 206–33.

Lewis, W. Arthur. 1950. "The Industrialization of the British West Indies." *Caribbean Economic Review* (May).

Yoshino, M. Y., and Thomas B. Lifson. 1986. *The Invisible Link: Japan's* Sogo Shosha *and the Organization of Trade* (Cambridge, Mass.: MIT Press).

Note II.2. The Lewis Model of the World Economy

In *Aspects of Tropical Trade, 1883–1965,* W. Arthur Lewis (1969) presents in much more detail the model of determination of the factoral and commodity terms of trade sketched in the preceding selection. He gives a series of numerical examples to illustrate his results. Here we adopt more general notation that allows us to present his results more compactly.

We begin with a table showing fixed outputs per labor hour (labor productivities) in manufactures, food, and cash crops:

Table 1. Output per Labor Hour

	Cash Crops	Food	Manufactures
Region 1	q_C^1	q_F^1	
Region 2		q_F^2	q_M^2

Region 1 represents either the tropical countries of Africa, Asia, and Latin America or the temperate countries of recent settlement such as Australia and Canada. Region 2 represents the industrialized "core" consisting of Western Europe and the United States. For the time being we ignore the possibility that region 1 could produce manufactures or that region 2 could grow cash crops (or produce synthetic substitutes for them).

It is assumed that all three goods are freely traded, that labor is perfectly mobile within regions but immobile across them, and that food is always produced in both regions. This last assumption is especially crucial, because it means that productivity in food determines the opportunity cost of labor in both regions. In other words, labor can be had for production of cash crops within region 1 or manufactures within region 2 only by paying wages sufficient to attract workers out of food production. This requirement, combined with competition, determines the prices of cash crops and manufactures in terms of food.

More formally, if labor is paid its marginal value product in all sectors (equal to its average value product in this model), perfect intraregional mobility of labor implies:

$$p_C q_C^1 = q_F^1 = w^1 \quad \text{or} \quad p_C = \frac{q_F^1}{q_C^1} \tag{1}$$

and

$$p_M q_M^2 = q_F^2 = w^2 \quad \text{or} \quad p_M = \frac{q_F^2}{q_M^2} \tag{2}$$

where p denotes price and w denotes wage. It follows immediately that the factoral terms of trade, the rate at which region 1 labor hours implicitly exchange for region 2 labor hours, are given by

$$\frac{w^1}{w^2} = \frac{q_F^1}{q_F^2} \tag{3}$$

and that the commodity terms of trade, the rate at which cash crops exchange for manufactures, are given by

$$\frac{p_C}{p_M} = \frac{q_F^1/q_C^1}{q_F^2/q_M^2} \tag{4}$$

We see that a region can only improve its factoral or commodity terms of trade by increasing its productivity in food. Productivity increases in a region's specialty only serve to drive down its price. Lewis (1969) documents the sharp decreases in the prices of rubber and sugar that took place from 1880–84 to 1960–64. He claims these were the only two tropical crops that showed dramatic productivity increases during this period. Letting region 1 represent the tropics, equation (4) shows that increases in cash crop productivity must drive down the price of tropical cash crops relative to manufactures. By the same token, if a cash crop is grown with unchanged productivity in a region with higher food productivity, its price must be proportionately higher. Suppose that food productivity in the temperate countries of recent settlement were four times higher than in the tropics. If region 1 now represents these temperate countries, the numerators of both equation (3) and equation (4) must be increased by a factor of 4. This explains Lewis's statement in the preceding selection, "If tea had been a temperate instead of a tropical crop its price would have been perhaps four times as high as it was. And if wool had been a tropical instead of a temperate crop it could have been had for perhaps one-fourth of the ruling price."

Above all, the standard of living within a region is primarily determined by its food productivity. From equations (1) and (2) we see that, for example, if the tropics (represented by region 1) were to double its productivity in food, its wage would double not only in terms of food but in terms of manufactures as well, whereas if the tropics were to double its productivity in cash crops, its wage would double only in terms of cash crops. This explains Lewis's statement in the preceding selection that "the market price gave the Nigerian for his peanuts a 700-lbs-of-grain-per-acre level of living, and the Australian for his wool a 1600-lbs-per-acre level of living, not because of differences in competence, nor because of marginal utilities or productivities in peanuts or wool, but because these were the respective amounts of food that their cousins could produce on the family farms."

A puzzling feature of this analysis is that demand plays no role in the determination of prices. Suppose, for example, that consumer preferences in the industrialized world were to change so that demand for tea or wool increased at given prices and incomes. With tea or wool output unchanged, its price would increase, increasing the marginal value product of labor in tea or wool production and attracting labor out of food production. This leads to an expansion of tea or wool output, which as we have seen must continue until the price of tea or wool is driven down to its original level (given by equation (1)) *provided the wage in food production is unchanged.* Would it not be the case, however, that the marginal product of labor in food production would increase as pressure on scarce food-producing land is reduced? The answer suggested by the preceding selection is that the labor supply of China and India is too large for the increased demand for labor in tea production to significantly reduce the labor-land ratios there, but could we say the same of the labor supply of Britain, the source of immigrants to Australia? A more credible answer, we believe, is to simply extend to food-producing land the assumption of abundance that Lewis makes for land suitable for cash crop production. Land cannot become less scarce if it is not scarce to begin with, so any tendency for the opportunity cost of immigrant labor to rise would be checked by region 1 residents leaving their food-producing land to work in cash crop production. The assumption of an unlimited supply of food-producing land can also be applied to region 2 if we think of it as including the United States.

We now allow for the possibilities that region 1 could produce manufactures and that region 2 could grow cash crops, or produce synthetic substitutes for them. We modify Table 1 appropriately:

Table 2. Output per Labor Hour

	Cash Crops	Food	Manufactures
Region 1	q_C^1	q_F^1	q_M^1
Region 2	q_C^2	q_F^2	q_M^2

Under what conditions does the pattern of trade above still apply? Consumers in region 1 must find imported manufactures cheaper than domestically produced output, and consumers in region 2 must find imported cash crops cheaper than domestically produced output. These conditions are given by, respectively,

$$p_M^2 = \frac{q_F^2}{q_M^2} < \frac{q_F^1}{q_M^1} = p_M^1 \tag{5}$$

and

$$p_C^1 = \frac{q_F^1}{q_C^1} < \frac{q_F^2}{q_C^2} = p_C^2 \tag{6}$$

where we have now superscripted the prices of cash crops and manufactures to indicate which region is producing them. Under these conditions region 1 does not produce manufactures and region 2 does not produce cash crops, just as in the model with which we started. We see that, as expected, these conditions are more likely to hold, the higher is the productivity of region 2 in manufactures relative to region 1 and the higher is the productivity of region 1 in cash crops relative to region 2. In contrast, an increase in a region's food productivity raises its cost of labor and thus makes it less likely that region will continue to export its specialty. For example, an increase in region 2 food productivity makes it less likely that condition (5) will hold. Lewis (1969) therefore notes that "a relative rise in food productivity in the temperate world forces the tropical countries to industrialize."

Reference

Lewis, W. Arthur. 1969. *Aspects of Tropical Trade, 1883–1965* (Stockholm: Almqvist and Wicksell).

Selection II.3. Agricultural Productivity, Comparative Advantage, and Economic Growth*

For many years, economists have discussed the role of agricultural productivity in economic development. Generations of development economists have stressed improving agricultural productivity as an essential part of successful development strategy. For example, Nurkse (1953, p. 52) argued that "[e]veryone knows that the spectacular industrial revolution would not have been possible without the agricultural revolution that preceded it," and Rostow (1960, p. 8) stated that "revolutionary changes in agricultural productivity are an essential condition for successful take-off." A casual reading of recent development textbooks suggests that this view seems to have achieved almost the status of an axiom in development economies.[1]

According to this conventional view, which is based in part on the experiences of the Industrial Revolution in Britain, there are *positive* links between agricultural productivity and industrialization. First, rising productivity in food production makes it possible to feed the growing population in the industrial sector. With more food being produced with less labor, it releases labor for manufacturing employment. Second, high incomes generated in agriculture provide domestic demand for industrial products. Third, it increases the supply of domestic savings required to finance industrialization.

However, a comparative look at some regional experiences of industrialization tells a different story. For example, why were Belgium and Switzerland the first to become leading industrial countries in continental Europe, while the Netherlands lagged behind and did not take off until the last decades of the nineteenth century? Or why did industrialization of the United States during the antebellum period, mainly in the cotton textile industry, occur in New England, not in the South? Economic historians who studied these experiences found their answer in the Law of Comparative Advantage, which implies a *negative* link between agricultural productivity and industrialization; see Mokyr's (1976) comparative study of industrialization in Belgium and the Netherlands, and Field (1978) and Wright (1979) for industrialization in New England and the South. According to this view, the manufacturing sector has to compete with the agriculture sector for labor. Low productivity in agriculture implies the abundant supply of "cheap labor" which the manufacturing sector can rely on.

The key to understanding these two conflicting views can be found in the difference in their assumptions concerning the openness of economies. Note that the logic behind the conventional wisdom crucially rests on the implicit assumption that the economy is an effectively closed system. This assumption, which may be appropriate for Britain during the half-century of the Seven Year War, the War of American Independence, the French Revolution, and the Napoleonic Wars, should not be taken for granted for many developing countries.[2] In an open trading system, where prices are mainly determined by the conditions in the world markets, a rich endowment of arable land (and natural resources) could be a mixed blessing. High productivity and output in the agricultural sector may, without offsetting changes in relative prices, squeeze out the manufacturing sector. Economies which lack arable land and thus have the initial comparative (but not necessarily absolute) advantage in manufacturing, on the other hand, may successfully industrialize by relying heavily on foreign trade through importing agricultural products and raw materials and exporting manufacturing products, as recent experiences in the newly industrialized economies in East Asia suggest.[3]

In an attempt to highlight the point made above, this paper presents a two-sector model of endogenous growth. The model is essentially of the Ricardo–Viner–Jones variety, with one mobile factor (called labor) combined with diminishing returns technologies. There are two additional features. First, preferences are non-homothetic and

---

*From Kiminori Matsuyama, "Agricultural Productivity, Comparative Advantage, and Economic Growth," *Journal of Economic Theory* 58 (December 1992): 317–322. Reprinted by permission.

[1] My samples include Gillis et al., 1983, Hayami and Ruttan 1985, Herrick and Kindleberger 1983, Timmer 1988, and Todaro 1989. Timmer claims that this view "has not been challenged (p. 277)."

[2] The effect of continuous wars on the British Industrial Revolution remains in dispute. In particular, the extent to which trade in food was disrupted has been questioned, given the closer integration of the Irish and British economies during the period; see Thomas 1985.

[3] Although my main concern here is output growth, I found the empirical findings reported in Rauch 1989 highly suggestive. He found that per capita consumption growth will be slower in countries with relatively large endowments of land per capita.

the income elasticity of demand for the agricultural good is less than unitary. Second, manufacturing productivity rises over time because of learning-by-doing. For the closed economy case, an exogenous increase in agricultural productivity shifts labor to manufacturing and thereby accelerates economic growth. The model therefore provides a formalization of the conventional wisdom, which asserts that agricultural revolution is a precondition for industrial revolution. For the open economy case, however, there exists a negative link between agricultural productivity and economic growth. An economy with less productive agriculture allocates more labor to manufacturing and will grow faster. For a sufficiently small discount rate, it will achieve a higher welfare level than the rest of the world. The productive agricultural sector, on the other hand, squeezes out the manufacturing sector and the economy will de-industrialize over time, and, in some cases, achieve a lower welfare level. The model is also used to illustrate the Dutch disease phenomena.

Once stated, the contrast between the results in the closed and open economies is quite intuitive, but has often escaped the attention that it deserves. It suggests that the openness of economies should be an important factor to be kept in mind when planning development strategies and predicting growth performances. At the turn of the century, those schooled in the conventional wisdom might have predicted that Argentina, with her fertile and vast pampas land, would grow faster than Japan, with her mountainous land and limited natural resources. To them, what happened to these two economies during the last 90 years may be puzzling. Or, to many, it provides prima-facie evidence that cultural or political factors are important determinants of economic development.[4] The result for the open economy case arguably offers an economic explanation for this "puzzle." . . .

The economy consists of two sectors: manufacturing and agriculture. Both sectors employ labor. Abstracting from the issue of population growth, the size of the population is constant and equal to L. The total labor supply is also constant and normalized to one. . . . Technologies in the two sectors are given by

$$X_t^M = M_t F(n_t),$$

$$F(0) = 0, F' > 0, F'' < 0, \qquad (1)$$

$$X_t^A = AG(1 - n_t),$$

$$G(0) = 0, G' > 0, G'' < 0, \qquad (2)$$

where n_t is the fraction of labor employed in manufacturing as of time t (time is continuous). Both sectors operate under diminishing returns. Agricultural productivity, A, which may reflect the level of technology, land endowment, and climate, among other things, is constant over time and treated as an exogenous parameter. On the other hand, productivity in the manufacturing sector, M_t, which represents knowledge capital as of time t, is predetermined, but endogenous. Knowledge accumulates as a by-product of manufacturing experience, as follows:[5]

$$\dot{M}_t = \delta X_t^M, \quad \delta > 0. \qquad (3)$$

These learning-by-doing effects are purely external to the individual firms that generate them. With complete spillovers, each manufacturing firm treats M_t as given when making production and employment decisions. Thus, competition between the two sctors for labor leads to the equilibrium condition in the labor market,

$$AG'(1 - n_t) = p_t M_t F'(n_t), \qquad (4)$$

where p_t is the relative price of the manufacturing good.

All consumers in this economy share identical preferences given by

$$W = \int_0^\infty [\beta \log(c_t^A - \gamma) + \log(c_t^M)] \, e^{-\rho t} \, dt,$$

$$\beta, \gamma, \rho > 0, \qquad (5)$$

where c_t^A and c_t^M denote consumption of the agriculture good (food for simplicity) and the manufacturing good, as of time t. The parameter γ represents the subsistence level of food consumption and satisfies

$$AG(1) > \gamma L > 0. \qquad (6)$$

The first inequality states that the economy's agricultural sector is productive enough to provide the subsistence level of food to all consumers. With a positive γ, preferences are non-homothetic and the

---

[4]For example, one political scientist argues that liberal theory, by which he means economies as commonly taught in North American universities, "tends to neglect the political framework, . . . , yet the process of economic development cannot be divorced from political factors." He then asks "How else can one explain the remarkable economic achievements of resource-poor Japan and the troubles of resource-rich Argentina? (Gilpin (1987) p. 269)"

[5]For simplicity, it is assumed that knowledge capital never depreciates. Introducing a depreciation generates possibility of a growth trap in this model.

income elasticity of demand for food is less than unitary. The low income elasticity is introduced partly because of its central role in the logic behind the conventional view and partly because of the empirically indisputable Engel's law; see Crafts (1985). It is also assumed that all consumers have enough income to purchase more than γ units of food. Then, from (5), demand for the two goods by a consumer satisfies $c_t^A = \gamma + \beta p_t c_t^M$. Aggregation over all consumers yields

$$C_t^A = \gamma L + \beta p_t C_t^M, \tag{7}$$

where the upper case letters denote aggregate consumption.

To proceed further, let us assume that the economy is a closed system. This requires that $C_t^M = X_t^M = M_t F(n_t)$ and $C_t^A = X_t^A = AG(1 - n_t)$. Combining them with Eqs. (4) and (7) yields

$$\phi(n_t) = \frac{\gamma L}{A}, \tag{8}$$

where $\phi(n) \equiv G(1 - n) - \beta G'(1 - n)F(n)/F'(n)$, which satisfies $\phi(0) = G(1)$, $\phi(1) < 0$, and $\phi' < 0$. From (6), (8) has a unique solution in $(0,1)$. Since the right-hand side is decreasing in A, this solution can be written as

$$n_t = v(A), \quad \text{with} \quad v'(A) > 0.$$

Thus, the employment share of manufacturing is constant over time and positively related to A. From (3), output in manufacturing grows at a constant rate, $\delta F(v(A))$, also positively related to A. Aggregate food consumption and production stay constant at the level given by

$$C^A = X^A = AG(1 - v(A))$$
$$= \frac{\gamma L + A\beta G'(1 - v(A))\, F(v(A))}{F'(v(A))},$$

which is also increasing in A. Under the closed economy assumption, the model predicts that an increase in agricultural productivity releases labor to manufacturing and immediately increases its output and accelerates its growth. It also causes a permanent increase in the level of food production. Therefore, the utility of the representative consumer, who consumes C^A/L and C_t^M/L, unambiguously increases with agricultural productivity. These results can thus be considered as a formalization of the conventional wisdom, which asserts that agricultural revolution is a precondition for industrial revolution and supports the development strategy that emphasizes the Green Revolution. Although the underlying mechanism is very simple, this is, to my best knowledge, the first attempt to

model a positive link between agricultural productivity and the growth *rate* of the economy. . . . Engel's law plays a crucial role here. If γ is zero, the solution to (8) is independent of A, and thus agricultural productivity has no effect on growth. If γ is negative, and so food is a luxury good, then a rise in agricultural productivity slows down the economy.

References

N. F. R. Crafts. Income clasticities of demand and the release of labor by agriculture during the British industrial revolution: A further appraisal, *J. Europ. Econ. Hist.* 9 (1980), 153–168; reprinted in J. Mokyr (Ed.), "The Economics of the Industrial Revolution," Rowman & Allanheld, Totawa, NJ, 1985.

A. J. Field, Sectoral shifts in Antebellum Massachusetts: A reconsideration, *Exploration Econ. Hist,* 15 (1978), 146–171.

M. Gillis. D. Perkins, M. Roemer, and D. Snodgrass, "Economics of Development," Norton, New York, 1983.

R. Gilpin, "The Political Economy of International Relations," Princeton Univ. Press, Princeton, NJ, 1987.

Y. Hayami and V. W. Ruttan, "Agricultural Development: An International Development," rev. expanded edition, Johns Hopkins Univ. Press, Baltimore, MD, 1985.

B. Herrick and C. Kindleberger, "Economic Development," 4th ed., McGraw-Hill, New York, 1983.

J. Mokyr, "Industrialization in the Low Countries, 1795–1850," Yale Univ. Press, New Haven, CT., 1976.

R. Nurkse, "Problems of Capital Formation in Underdeveloped Countries," Oxford Univ. Press, New York, 1953.

J. E. Rauch, "The Question of International Convergence of Per Capita Consumption," UCSD Working paper, August 1989.

W. W. Rostow, "The Stages of Economic Growth: A Non-Communist Manifesto," Cambridge Univ. Press, Cambridge, UK, 1960.

B. Thomas, Food supply in the United Kingdom during the Industrial Revolution, *Agr. Hist.* 56 (1982), 328–342; reprinted in J. Mokyr (Ed.), "The Economics of the Industrial Revolution," Rowman & Allanheld, Totawa, NJ, 1985.

C. P. Timmer, The agricultural transformation, *in* "Handbook of Development Economics" Vol. I (H. Chenery and T. N. Srinivasan, Eds.), North-Holland, Amsterdam, 1988.

M. P. Todaro, "Economic Development in the Third World," 4th ed., Longman, New York, 1989.

G. Wright, Cheap labor and Southern textiles before 1880, *J. Econ. Hist.* 39 (1979), 655–680.

Comment II.2. Income Elasticity of Demand for Food in the Matsuyama Model

Readers who enjoy mathematical economic models may find Matsuyama's model simpler and more convincing than the summary presented in the Overview for this chapter. For these readers we add a few details to the demonstration that the preferences given by equation (5) yield an income elasticity of demand for agricultural output (food) less than 1.

To maximize the integral given in equation (5), at every point in time the consumer must set the ratio of the marginal utility from consumption of manufactures to the marginal utility from consumption of food equal to the price ratio p_t, yielding $(c_t^A - \gamma)/\beta c_t^M = p_t$. This aggregates to equation (7). Moreover, consumers cannot save in Matsuyama's model, so at every point in time they consume their entire aggregate income, which we denote by Y_t: $C_t^A + p_t C_t^M = Y_t$. Combining this last equation with equation (7) and eliminating C_t^M gives us aggregate consumption of food as a function of aggregate income: $C_t^A = (\beta Y_t + \gamma L)/(1 + \beta)$. Finally, income elasticity $(dC_t^A/dY_t)(Y_t/C_t^A) = \beta Y_t/(\beta Y_t + \gamma L)$, which is less than 1 as long as γ is positive.

Selection II.4. Income Distribution, Market Size, and Industrialization*

We present a model of industrialization caused by an increase in agricultural productivity or by an export boom, that raises incomes and therefore demand for domestic manufactures. As domestic markets become larger, increasing returns production technologies that could not break even in smaller markets come into profitable use and industry expands. The key role of productive agriculture or exports for generating domestic demand for manufactures has been emphasized in earlier work of Rosenstein-Rodan [1943], Nurkse [1953], Lewis [1953, 1954], Ranis and Fei [1961], and especially Fleming [1955]. Empirically, Ohkawa and Rosovsky [1960] document the great increases in agricultural productivity in turn of the century Japan, and Johnston and Mellor [1961] note the importance of the demand from farmers for growth of industry during that period. Similarly, Thorbecke [1979] and Ranis [1979] present evidence for the dramatic progress of agriculture in postwar Taiwan, and Ranis in particular stresses the role of demand by farmers at the initial stages of Taiwan's industrialization. Lewis [1953] makes increases in farm productivity and in cash crop exports a cornerstone of his proposed development strategy for the Gold Coast, on the theory that increased rural purchasing power would foster industrialization.

The vibrancy of domestic agriculture or exports is not, however, always sufficient to bring about any industrialization. In some cases, although farm or export income is generated, it does not go to potential customers of domestic industry, and the relevant markets remain as narrow as ever. For industrial markets to expand, the composition of demand must concentrate buying power in the hands of consumers of manufactures. Large population, homogeneous tastes, and concentrated population all help to create large markets for manufactures.[1] But also of great importance to industrialization is the distribution of income, since the middle class are the natural consumers of manufactured goods. As has been pointed out by Baldwin [1956] and North [1959], extreme concentration of wealth in the hands of the very rich will manifest itself in the demand for handmade and imported luxuries rather than for domestic manufactures, even when farm or export income grows. The necessity of a middle class as the source of the buying power for domestic manufactures is the central message of our paper.

The effects of income distribution on the extent of industrialization seem to be important in a number of historical episodes. For example, in the first half of the nineteenth century, the United States greatly surpassed England in the range of consumer products it manufactured using mass production techniques. In contrast to high quality handmade creations of the English artisans, American producers offered standardized mass-produced utilitarian items such as rifles, cutlery or balloon-frame houses (which an English architect called bare, bald white cubes). This difference in production techniques seems to be accounted for by the difference in the composition of demand [Rosenberg, 1972]. Whereas in England manufactures were demanded by the quality-conscious upper class, that could not have possibly generated a large market, the American demand came from a large number of relatively well-off farmers. The large demand from this land-rich middle class enabled American manufactures to profitably sustain mass production.

This difference in the composition of demand and of techniques of production in the two countries have been described in the catalog for the 1851 London Crystal Palace exhibition (cited in Rosenberg [1972] p. 50):

The absence in the United States of those vast accumulations of wealth which favor the expenditure of large sums on articles of mere luxury, and the general distribution of the means of procuring the more substantial conveniences of life, impart to the productions of American industry a character distinct from that of many other countries. The expenditure of months or years of labour upon a single article, not to increase its intrinsic value, but solely to augment its cost and its estimation as the object of *virtu*, is not common in the United States. On the contrary, both manual and mechanical labour are applied with direct reference to increasing the number or the quantity of articles suited for the wants of a whole people, and adapted to promote the enjoyment of that moderate competency that prevails upon them.

In the model presented below, the U. S. experience can be understood in terms of distribution of returns from farming and the demand by farmers for industrial goods.

Perhaps the best example of a country in which the distribution of rewards from a boom in a lead-

*From Kevin M. Murphy, Andrei Shleifer, and Robert W. Vishny. "Income Distribution, Market Size, and Industrialization," *Quarterly Journal of Economics* 104 (August 1989): 537–545. Reprinted by permission.

[1]Chenery, Robinson, and Syrquin [1987] report that industrialization usually begins at a much lower level of income in high-population countries.

ing sector has led first to the failure and then to the success of industrialization is Colombia in the second half of the nineteenth century. In the 1850s and 1860s Colombia experienced a large boom in tobacco exports, which, however, failed to lead to widespread economic development. From about 1880 to 1915, Colombia went through a boom in coffee exports, the effect of which on industrialization has been much more widely pronounced. Harbison [1970] explains the difference between the two episodes by the fact that, technologically, tobacco had to be grown on large plantations and hence the income from the boom went to a very small number of plantation owners who spent it on luxury imports, whereas coffee was grown on small family enterprises with the result that income accrued to a large number of people who then demanded domestic manufactures. Harbison's [1970] analysis of Colombia illustrates precisely the point developed in our work:

The lion's share of increased prosperity generated by coffee production was enjoyed by the large poor rural *mestizo campesino* class, not the small group of rich white urban landlords. These peasants, in turn, certainly did not buy for themselves and their children foreign travel and foreign education or other luxury imports. . . . Since such items could not be produced in Colombia, the use of tobacco-generated incomes to purchase these luxury imports had resulted in a long-term depression and decline in Colombian artisan manufacture without compensating growth in another domestic sector. But coffee generated incomes in the hands of Antioqueno farmers who spend precisely on those necessities. . . . The rapid expansion of coffee production redistributed income toward that segment of the population most likely to spend the incremental income on items characterized by high potential for generating domestic incomes—i.e. on domestic goods whose large-scale production could utilize modern low-cost technology—and not on imports.

Colombia's experience with the two leading sector booms thus shows exactly how income distribution affects the consequences of such booms.

The central economic assumption underlying our interpretation of these examples is the relevance of local demand composition, as opposed to the world markets, for the choice of techniques. If world trade is costless and free of barriers, this assumption is untenable. In practice, however, transport costs, difficulties of penetrating foreign markets, and especially protectionism make the sizes of local markets relevant for a wide range of goods in many countries. In this paper we first focus on the case of a closed economy with agriculture serving as the source of high-powered demand for manufactures, and then let this role be played also by mineral or cash crop exports. . . . [In our model] each consumer spends all of his income on food until he gets z units of it. If he has income left over, he spends all of it on manufactures. He expands the menu of manufactures he buys in order of marginal utility per unit price. Richer consumers end up with a superset of manufactures bought by poorer consumers. . . .

Each [manufactured] good q is assumed to be produced in a separate sector that is small relative to the economy. Two technologies are assumed to be available for producing each good q. First, $\alpha >$ 1 units of labor can be applied to produce one unit of output of any good q using the constant returns to scale (CRS), or "backstop," technology. In addition, good q can be produced with a fixed investment of C units of labor and a variable labor requirement of one per unit of output. The idea of two alternative technologies has been used by Shleifer [1986] and Shleifer and Vishny [1988] to illustrate the importance of market size in promoting the switch to IRS technology. Here, since the size of the market for q is equal to the number of consumers whose menu includes q (customer base), income distribution will determine the profitability of producing q with increasing returns.

Industrialization in this paper is taken to be substitution of increasing returns technologies for constant returns technologies in production of some goods. It seems very plausible to associate increasing returns with events that are commonly linked to industrialization, such as mass production, escape from the farm, concentration of labor in the same location, etc. . . .

In the equilibrium we propose, all sectors producing goods 0 through Q for some Q industrialize. The entering monopolists displace the fringe in these sectors, but do not cut prices. The price of each manufacturing good is therefore αw, regardless of whether it is produced in an industrialized or a backstop sector. . . .

When all sectors $(0, Q)$ industrialize, and prices in all of them are kept at αw, the sector Q for whose monopolist it is marginally profitable to enter is one where variable profits just cover the fixed cost. Denote by N^* the sales of that sector, equal to the minimum efficient scale. For this sector, the break-even condition is

$$(\alpha w - w) N^* = Cw, \qquad (1)$$

or

$$N^* = \frac{C}{(\alpha - 1)}. \qquad (2)$$

Since the range of goods consumed declines with income, consumers of Q are the N^* richest people in the economy.

References

Baldwin, Robert E., "Patterns of Development in Newly Settled Regions," *The Manchester School,* XXIV (1956), 161–79.

Chenery, Hollis B., Sherman Robinson, and Moshe Syrquin. *Industrialization and Growth: A Comparative Study* (New York: Oxford University Press, 1987).

Fleming, J. Marcus, "External Economies and the Doctrine of Balanced Growth," *Economic Journal,* LXV (1955), 241–56.

Harbison, Ralph W., "Colombia," in *Tropical Development 1880–1913,* W. A. Lewis, ed. (Evanston: Northwestern University Press, 1970), pp. 64–99.

Johnston, Bruce F., and John W. Mellor, "The Role of Agriculture in Economic Development," *American Economic Review,* LI (1961), 566–93.

Lewis, W. Arthur, *Report on the Industrialization of the Gold Coast* (Accra: Government Printing Office of the Gold Coast, 1953).

———, "Economic Development with Unlimited Supplies of Labor," *The Manchester School,* XXII (1954), 139–91.

North, Douglass C., "Agriculture in Regional Economic Growth," *Journal of Farm Economics,* LI (1959), 943–51.

Nurkse, Ragnar, *Problems of Capital Formation in Underdeveloped Countries* (Oxford: Basil Blackwell, 1953).

Ohkawa, Kazushi, and Henry Rosovsky, "The Role of Agriculture in Modern Japanese Economic Development," *Economic Development and Cultural Change,* IX part 2 (1960), 43–68.

Ranis, Gustav, "Industrial Development," in *Economic Growth and Structural Change in Taiwan,* Walter Galenson, ed. (Ithaca and London: Cornell University Press, 1979).

Ranis, G., and J. C. H. Fei, "A Theory of Economic Development," *American Economic Review,* LI (1961), 533–65.

Rosenberg, Nathan, *Technology and the American Economic Growth* (New York: M. E. Sharpe, 1972).

Rosenstein-Rodan, Paul N., "Problems of Industrialization of Eastern and South-eastern Europe," *Economic Journal,* LIII (1943), 202–11.

Shleifer, Andrei, "Implementation Cycles," *Journal of Political Economy,* XCIV (1986), 1163–90.

———, and Vishny, Robert W. "The Efficiency of Investment in the Presence of Aggregate Demand Spillovers," *Journal of Political Economy,* XCVI (1988), 1221–31.

Thorbecke, Eric, "Agricultural Development," in *Economic Growth and Structural Change in Taiwan,* Walter Galenson, ed. (Ithaca and London: Cornell University Press, 1979).

Comment II.3. Minimum Market Size in the Murphy–Shleifer–Vishny Model

Here we link equation (2) to the discussion of the Murphy–Shleifer–Vishny model in the Overview. The fixed cost C of introducing factory production of a given manufacture must be spread out over a sufficient number of units to make the average cost of factory production at least as low as that of handicraft production. Average cost of factory production equals $(C/N + 1)w,$ where N is the number of units produced and w is the wage rate, and αw is the average cost of handicraft production. Solving the equation $(C/N + 1)w = \alpha w$ for N yields equation (2). As we would expect, the minimum number of units N^* depends positively on the fixed cost C and negatively on α, the number of labor hours needed to produce one unit of output using handicraft methods. Given the consumer preferences assumed by Murphy, Shleifer, and Vishny, N^* is also the minimum number of consumers above the level of income such that they demand one unit of the manufacture in question, that is, the minimum market size for successful introduction of factory techniques for this manufacture.

Selection II.5. Factor Endowments, Inequality, and Paths of Development Among New World Economies*

Our view highlights the fundamental importance of the extreme differences across the New World societies in the extent of inequality in the distributions of wealth, human capital, and political influence that were present from the early histories of the colonies and due primarily to their respective factor endowments (or initial conditions more generally).[1]

Some, such as the colonies established in the Caribbean or Brazil, enjoyed a climate and soil conditions that were extremely well suited for growing crops, such as sugar, that were highly valued on world markets and most efficiently produced on large slave plantations. Their populations came to be dominated by large numbers of slaves obtained through the international slave market, and they quickly generated vastly unequal distributions of wealth, human capital, and political power. Spanish America was likewise characterized early by extreme inequality, in large degree because of its factor endowments. The extensive native populations in the regions colonized by the Spanish (namely, Mexico and Peru) and the Spanish practices (significantly influenced by preexisting Native American organizations in those areas) of awarding claims on land, native labor, and rich mineral resources to members of the elite were powerful factors leading to extreme inequality.[2]

In contrast, small, family-sized farms were the rule in the northern colonies of the North American mainland, where climatic conditions favored a regime of mixed farming centered on grains and livestock that exhibited quite limited economies of scale in production and used few slaves. There were, moreover, relatively few Native Americans on the East Coast where the English, French, and Dutch colonies on the mainland were based. These regions do not appear to have been very attractive to Europeans during the first quarter of a millennium after they began to colonize the New World, since only a small fraction of the migrants to the New World opted to locate there. However, the circumstances fostered relatively homogeneous populations with relatively equal distributions of human capital and wealth.

These initial differences in the degree of inequality—which can be attributed largely to factor endowments, broadly conceived—had profound and enduring effects on the paths of development of the respective economies. Previous treatments of the impact of inequality on growth typically focus on the impact of inequality on savings or investment rates. Our hypothesis, however, concerns the possibility that the extreme differences in the extent of inequality that arose early in the history of the New World economies may have contributed to systematic differences in the ways institutions evolved. The logic is that great equality or homogeneity among the population led, over time, to more democratic political institutions, to more investment in public goods and infrastructure, and to institutions that offered relatively broad access to economic opportunities. In contrast, where there was extreme inequality, as in most of the societies of the Americas, political institutions were less democratic, investments in public goods and infrastructure were more limited, and the institutions that evolved tended to provide highly unbalanced access to economic opportunities and thereby greatly advantaged the elite. This mechanism, through which the extent of inequality affects the way institutions evolve, not only helps to explain the long-term persistence of differences in inequality among the respective societies, but it may also play a role in ac-

*From Stanley L. Engerman and Kenneth L. Sokoloff, "Factor Endowments, Inequality, and Paths of Development Among New World Economies." *Economia* 3 (Fall 2002): 44–46, 56–64, 66–71. Reprinted by permission.

[1]Engerman and Sokoloff (1997).

[2]The pattern of European organized settlement and population growth differed quite considerably from the patterns in the Native American period. It is estimated that just prior to the coming of Columbus, the distribution of the Native American population was roughly 35 percent in South America; 10 percent in the Caribbean; 47 percent in Mexico and Central America; and 8 percent in what would become the United States and Canada. Mexico alone had 37 percent of the "aboriginal" American population. The early colonizers, Spain and Portugal, went to the regions most heavily populated at that time: Spain went to Mexico, Peru, and elsewhere in South America and the Caribbean, and Portugal went to Brazil. Only the less densely populated areas of the United States, Canada, and the Caribbean were still available when the later colonizers, such as the British and French, arrived (see Denevan 1976, pp. 289–92). Prior to the arrival of the Spanish, the societies of Mexico and Peru were quite sophisticated economically and politically. Agricultural production was high, permitting urbanization, and the control of both native-born and captive labor served as the basis for productive agricultural and mining sectors. The direct adoption of Native American institutions by the conquering Spanish to provide for a labor force in

these sectors was limited because of the large demographic decline triggered by European settlement, but much in terms of production methods and labor supply was later adapted by the Spanish.

counting for the differences in the growth rates of per capita income over the last two centuries. If the processes of early industrialization were based on broad participation in the commercial economy, as suggested by evidence from the three leaders in that process (England, the United States, and the Netherlands), then economies with institutions that provided narrow access might have been less capable of realizing the potential of the new technologies, markets, and other economic opportunities that developed over the nineteenth century.[3]

. . . In explaining the logic and empirical basis for our view, it is convenient to distinguish between three types of New World colonies. The usefulness of this abstraction from the uniqueness of each society must be judged ultimately by how meaningful and coherent our stylized types are and by the explanatory power they help provide.

Our first category encompasses those colonies with climates and soils that were well suited for the production of sugar and other highly valued crops characterized by extensive scale economies associated with the use of slaves. Most of these sugar colonies, including Barbados, Cuba, and Saint Domingue, were in the West Indies, but some were also located in South America, mainly Brazil. They specialized in the production of such crops early in their histories, and through the persistent working of technological advantage, their economies came to be dominated by large slave plantations and their populations by slaves of African descent. The overwhelming fraction of the populations that came to be black and slave in such colonies, as well as the greater efficiency of the very large plantations, typically made their distributions of wealth and human capital extremely unequal. Even among the free population, such economies exhibited greater inequality than those on the North American mainland.[4]

The predominance of an elite class in such colonies may have derived from the enormous advantages in sugar production available to those able to assemble a large company of slaves, as well as the extreme disparities in human capital between blacks and whites, but the long-run success and stability of the members of this elite was also undoubtedly aided by their disproportionate politi-

cal influence. When abolition brought an end to the legally codified gross inequality intrinsic to slavery, great inequality in wealth remained and undoubtedly contributed to the evolution of institutions that commonly protected the privileges of the elite and restricted opportunities for the broad mass of the populations.[5]

The second category of New World colonies comprises only the Spanish colonies such as Mexico and Peru, which were characterized both by a substantial native population surviving contact with the European colonizers and by the distribution among a privileged few of claims to often enormous blocs of land, mineral resources, and native labor. The resulting large-scale estates and mines, established early in the histories of these colonies, were to some degree based on preconquest social organizations in which Indian elites extracted tribute from the general population, and the arrangements endured even when the principal production activities were lacking in economies of scale. Although small-scale production was typical of grain agriculture during this era, the essentially nontradable property rights to tribute (in the form of labor and other resources) from rather sedentary groups of natives gave large landholders the means and the motive to operate at a large scale. For different reasons, therefore, this category of colonies was rather like the first in generating very unequal distributions of wealth. The elites relied on the labor of Native Americans instead of slaves, but like the slave owners, they were racially distinct from the bulk of the population, and they enjoyed higher levels of human capital and legal standing.[6]

---

[5]Social mobility, and economic progress generally, in these post-emancipation economies may also have been hampered by the difficulties of adjusting to the loss of the productive technology on which they had long been based. See Engerman (1982).

[6]The existence of scale economies in slavery did not support the competitive success or persistence of the largest units of production in this second class of colonial economies. Rather, large-scale enterprises were sustained by the natives' inability or disinclination to evade their obligations to the estate-owning families or to obtain positions that allowed them to participate fully in the commercial economy. Lockhart and Schwartz (1983) provide an excellent and comprehensive overview of the *encomienda* and the evolution of large-scale estates, with their relation to preconquest forms of social organization in different parts of Spanish America. The paths of institutional development varied somewhat across Spanish colonies, reflecting significant differences between Indian populations in social capabilities and other attributes. For example, the preconquest forms of social organization for Indians in highland areas were quite different from those of populations on the plains or in the jungle. For a fascinating discussion of the workings of the early *encomienda* system in Peru, including differences in the system across colonies, the different interests of early and late arrivals, and the relevance of mineral resources, see Lockhart (1994).

---

[3]Our analysis has some antecedents in the work of Baldwin (1956); Domar (1970); Lewis (1955).

[4]On the early Caribbean sugar plantations, see Dunn (1972); Sheridan (1974); Moreno Fraginals (1976). For a detailed examination of the distribution of wealth among free household heads on a sugar island, see the analysis of the 1680 census for Barbados in Dunn (1972, chap. 3).

The first major export products from Spanish America were not agricultural products, but silver and gold mined primarily in Mexico, Peru, and what is now Bolivia. These mines had existed and been used by various groups of Native Americans prior to Spanish settlement. Mining had long relied on some variant of coerced labor, and the pattern in Spanish America was no different. The labor force consisted largely of Native Americans, who were nominally free but were coerced by various mechanisms to serve in the mines. Without this compulsion, mining output would, no doubt, have been quite limited, as labor in mines was exhausting and associated with high death rates. This was not of primary concern to the ruling elite, however. Indeed, the great value that Spanish policy-makers placed on silver and gold meant that areas without mines, such as the colonies in the Caribbean and Argentina, were of secondary interest and were forced to deal with policies that had been framed to support the colonies with mines. This typically meant limitations on shipping and trade that held back development in these outlying areas.

To almost the same degree as in the colonial sugar economies, the economic structures that evolved in this second group of colonies were greatly influenced by the factor endowments, viewed in broad terms. The fabulously valuable mineral resources and the abundance of low-human-capital labor certainly contributed to the extremely unequal distributions of wealth and income that generally came to prevail in these economies. Moreover, without the abundant supply of native labor, the generous awards of property and tribute to the earliest settlers would either not have been worth so much or not been possible, and it is highly unlikely that Spain would have introduced the tight restrictions on European migration to its colonies that resulted in the small share of European descendants in the population. The early settlers in Spanish America had endorsed, and won, formidable requirements for obtaining permission to go to the New World—a policy that surely limited the flow of migrants and helped to preserve the political and economic advantages they enjoyed.[7]

The path of development observed in Mexico is representative of virtually all of the Spanish colonies that retained substantial native populations.[8] In the initial phase of conquest and settlement, the Spanish authorities allocated *encomiendas,* or claims on labor and tribute from natives, and land grants to a relatively small number of individuals. The value of these grants was somewhat eroded over time by reassignment or expiration, new awards, and the precipitous decline of the native population over the sixteenth century that necessarily decreased the amount of tribute to be extracted. These *encomiendas* had powerful lingering effects, however, and ultimately gave way to large-scale *estancias* or *haciendas,* which obtained their labor services partially through obligations from natives and, increasingly, through local labor markets. Although the processes of transition from *encomienda* to *hacienda* are not well understood, it is evident that large-scale agriculture remained dominant, especially in districts with linkages to extensive markets. It is also clear that the distribution of wealth remained highly unequal, because elite families were able to maintain their status over generations. These same families generally acted as *corregidors* and other local representatives of the Spanish government in the countryside, wielding considerable local political authority.[9]

The final category of New World colonies is best typified by the colonies on the North American mainland, chiefly those that became the northern United States, but also Canada. These economies were not endowed either with substantial native populations able to provide labor or with a climate and soils that gave them a comparative advantage in the production of crops characterized by major economies of scale in using slave labor. Their growth and development, especially north of the Chesapeake, were therefore based on laborers of European descent who had similar, relatively high levels of human capital. Owing to the abundant land and low capital requirements, the great majority of adult men were able to operate as independent proprietors. Efforts to implant a European-style organization of agriculture based

---

[7]Because of the differences in settlement patterns, the fights for control between *criollos* and *peninsulares* in Spanish America took a quite different form from the colonial-metropolitan conflicts of British America. For a discussion of a more traditional form of conflict between the colonies and the metropolis with respect to the empire's trade policy, see Walker (1979). For a discussion of early Peru, see Lockhart (1994).

[8]Striking similarities are found even in colonies that did not retain substantial native populations. In formulating policies, the Spanish authorities seem to have focused on circumstances in major colonies like Mexico and Peru, and then applied them systemwide. Hence, policies like restrictions on migration from Europe and grants of large blocs of land, mineral resources, and native labor to the early settlers were generally in effect throughout Spanish America. See Lockhart and Schwartz (1983); Lockhart (1994).

[9]In addition to Lockhart and Schwartz (1983), see treatments of Mexico and Peru in Chevalier (1963); Van Young (1983); Lockhart (1994); Jacobsen (1993, chaps. 1–4).

on concentrated ownership of land combined with labor provided by tenant farmers or indentured servants, as when Pennsylvania and New York were established, invariably failed: the large landholdings unraveled because even men of rather ordinary means could set up independent farms when land was cheap and scale economies were absent. William Penn, for example, who was a central member of the elite, was not able to get what he wanted in such an environment despite his enormous wealth.

Conditions were somewhat different in the southern colonies, where crops such as tobacco and rice exhibited limited scale economies. Even so, the size of the slave plantations, the share of the population composed of slaves, and the degree of inequality in these colonies were quite modest by the standards of Brazil or the sugar islands. The South thrived in terms of output per capita, and it attracted the bulk of migrants to the British colonies on the mainland through the eighteenth century. It lagged behind the North, however, both before and after the Civil War, in evolving a set of political institutions that were conducive to broad participation in the commercial economy. The South was thus an intermediate case: it displayed many parallels with other New World economies that relied on slavery early in their histories, but it ultimately realized a record of development more like those of the northern United States or Canada.

Spain also had several colonies that might be considered to fall between categories. Most notable among them is Argentina.[10] The region is not suited for growing sugar as a major crop, and the country ultimately flourished as a grain producer. Yet substantial inequality in the distributions of land, human capital, and political influence is clearly apparent in Argentina by the second half of the nineteenth century. Argentina remained sparsely populated at the time of independence, largely as a result of Spanish restrictions on immigration and trade. (Spain directed shipping to its colonies in South America through Mexico and Peru until the Bourbon reforms of the late eighteenth century.) The initial development of inequality probably came with the massive grants of land made to favored families and military leaders during the first half of the nineteenth century. These large landholdings might have been expected to splinter over time in an environment of extreme labor scarcity, but this tendency appears to have been at least partially offset by several factors: the public lands disposed of in these early al-

locations proved to be among the most valuable throughout the country in terms of both fertility and location; scale economies in raising (or harvesting) the cattle that ran wild on the pampas made it feasible to make productive use of enormous parcels of land with little labor; and the country lacked a land policy that was oriented toward improving access to land (in contrast to Canada or the United States).[11] Indeed, despite protracted political debate on the connection between land policy and immigration, Argentina continued to dispose of its public lands through large allotments to the military or private development companies until late in the nineteenth century.[12] Substantial inequality was thus in place here, too, before the development of the economy was very far along, although it was not nearly as extreme as in most of the other Spanish American societies and the process by which it evolved was more complicated.

Finally, another way of illustrating that the marked differences in the extent of inequality across New World economies emerged early and were due primarily to factor endowments (or initial conditions) is to specifically address the issue of whether national or religious heritage was the fundamental determinant of the respective path of institutional and economic development. Clearly, they did have impacts, but we contend that the importance of adjustments that individuals and societies made in response to new or changing environments has not been sufficiently appreciated. Scholars too often presume that institutions are inflexible, even across very different circumstances or over a long period of time. As already noted, the idea that the distinctiveness of the North American mainland colonies was largely due to the effects of the British institutional heritage seems inconsistent with the observation that there was extraordinary diversity in paths of development across the many other New World societies with a British heritage. Most did not fare quite so well, and they generally resemble their neighbors that began with similar factor endowments but with other national heritages (Guyana, Belize, and Jamaica, for example). Perhaps the most striking example is the contrast between the two colonies established simultane-

[10]The others include Costa Rica and Uruguay.

[11]The record of land policy in Argentina is discussed below; see also Castro (1971) and Adelman (1994, 1999).

[12]For most of the period, the dominant political faction, with support based in Buenos Aires, opposed the implementation of policies that would have provided for broad access to land. See Castro (1971) for extensive discussion of this issue and the linkages between the debates over immigration and land policies.

ously by the Puritans early in the seventeenth century: Providence Island (off the coast of Nicaragua and now part of Colombia) and the more famous Massachusetts Bay Colony. Although the eventual overrunning of Providence Island makes for a shorter time series than analysts would prefer, Karen Kupperman's comparative study demonstrates that the paths of the two Puritan colonies diverged radically right from the beginning.[13] While we are all familiar with the intense work ethic of the Puritans that settled in the cold harsh New England environment, the Puritans that located on Providence Island quickly determined that manual labor was for Native Americans, slaves, and indentured servants—not them.

The range of experiences of the French colonies in the Americas further accentuates the importance of environment and factor endowment. French settlements fell into two distinct types. The French sugar islands in the Caribbean, particularly Saint Domingue, grew rapidly over the eighteenth century. They eventually became more populous than the British islands, with slaves accounting for more than 90 percent of the population. The French islands produced more output per capita (principal crops being sugar and coffee) than their British neighbors, and most contemporaries believed that they were more efficient in sugar production.[14] The basic institutions of the French colonies in the Caribbean, like those of the British, were centered on large slave plantations producing sugar. Canada was the other major French colony in the New World. Its climate made it seem less valuable than the northeastern regions of the British colonies, to say nothing of the colonies in the Caribbean. The French began settlement with an attempt to introduce a seignorial system for landholdings, but it gave way to a structure of small farms producing grains. The region received very few immigrants, as did the British colonies in New England, which had negative net migration over the colonial period.

The Role of Institutions in the Persistence of Inequality

We have suggested that various features of the factor endowments of three categories of New World economies, including soils, climates, and the size or density of the native population, predisposed them to very different degrees of inequality in wealth, human capital, and political power, and thus toward particular paths of institutional and economic development. Although these conditions might reasonably be treated as exogenous at the beginning of European colonization, such an assumption becomes increasingly tenuous the further one moves beyond the initial settlement. The factor endowment and the degree of inequality may influence the directions in which institutions evolve, but these institutions, in turn, can affect the evolution of the factor endowment and of the distributions of human capital, wealth, and political power. The initial conditions had long-lasting effects, however, not only because they were difficult to change, but also because government policies and other institutions tended generally to foster their persistence.

More specifically, in societies that began with extreme inequality, the elites were both inclined and able to establish a basic legal framework that ensured them a disproportionate share of political power and to use that influence to establish rules, laws, and other government policies that gave them greater access to economic opportunities than the rest of the population, thereby contributing to the persistence of the high degree of inequality. In societies that began with greater equality in wealth and human capital or homogeneity among the population, the elites were either less able or less inclined to institutionalize rules, laws, and other government policies that grossly advantaged them, and thus the institutions that evolved tended to provide more equal treatment and opportunities, thereby contributing to the persistence of the relatively high degree of equality.

. . . A prime example of the ways in which institutions may have contributed to the persistence of inequality over the long run is land policy. Virtually all the economies in the Americas had ample supplies of public lands well into the nineteenth century and beyond. Since the respective governments of each colony, province, or nation were regarded as the owners of this resource, they were able to influence the distribution of wealth, as well as the pace of settlement for effective production, by implementing policies to control the availability of land, set prices, establish minimum or maximum acreages, provide credit for such purposes, and design tax systems. Because agriculture was the dominant sector throughout the Americas, questions of how best to employ this public resource for the national interest, and how to make the land available for private use, were widely recognized as highly important and often became the

---

[13]Kupperman (1993).

[14]See the discussion in Eltis (1997). The end of French power in this area was not related to trade or production misfortunes, but rather to a successful uprising of the slave population in 1791 in what was to become Haiti, leading to independence in 1804.

subject of protracted political debates and struggles. Land policy was also used as a policy instrument to affect the labor force, either by encouraging immigration through making land readily available or by influencing the regional distribution of labor (or supply of wage labor) through limiting access and raising land prices.

The United States never experienced major obstacles in this regard, and the terms of land acquisition became easier over the course of the nineteenth century.[15] The well-known Homestead Act of 1862, which essentially made land free in plots suitable for family farms to all those who settled and worked the land for a specified period, was perhaps the culmination of this policy of promoting broad access to land. Canada pursued similar policies: the Dominion Lands Act of 1872 closely resembled the Homestead Act in both spirit and substance. Argentina and Brazil instituted similar changes in the second half of the nineteenth century as a means to encourage immigration, but these efforts were much less directed and thus less successful at getting land to smallholders than the programs in the United States and Canada.[16] In Argentina, for example, a number of factors explain the contrast in outcomes. First, the elites of Buenos Aires, whose interests favored keeping scarce labor in the province if not the capital city, were much more effective at weakening or blocking programs than were their urban counterparts in North America; this outcome may have resulted from the relatively greater economic prominence and power of Buenos Aires within the national arena. Second, even those policies nominally intended to broaden access tended to involve large grants to land developers (with the logic that allocative efficiency could best be achieved through exchanges between private agents) or transfers to occupants who were already using the land (including those who were grazing livestock). They thus generally conveyed public lands to private owners in much larger and concentrated holdings than did the policies in the United States and Canada. Third, the processes by which large landholdings might have broken up in the absence of scale economies may have operated very slowly in Argentina: once the land was in private hands, the potential value of land in grazing may have set too high a floor on land prices for immigrants and other ordinary would-be farmers to manage, especially given the underdevelopment of mortgage and financial institutions more generally.[17]

Argentina, Canada, and the United States all had an extraordinary abundance of virtually uninhabited public lands to transfer to private hands in the interest of bringing this public resource into production and serving other general interests. In societies such as Mexico, however, the issues at stake in land policy were very different. Good land was relatively scarce, and labor was relatively abundant. Here the lands in question had long been controlled by Native Americans, but without individual private property rights. Mexico was not unique in pursuing policies, especially in the final decades of the nineteenth and the first decade of the twentieth century, that had the effect of conferring ownership of much of this land to large non-Native American landholders.[18] The 1856 Ley Lerdo and the 1857 Constitution had set down methods of privatizing these public lands in a manner that could originally have been intended to help Native American farmers enter a national lands market and commercial economy. Under the regime of Porfirio Díaz, however, these laws became the basis for a series of new statutes and policies that effected a massive transfer of such lands (over 10.7 percent of the national territory) between 1878 and 1908 to large holders such as survey and land development companies, either in the form of outright grants for services rendered by the companies or for prices set by decree.

In Table 1, we present estimates for these four countries of the fractions of household heads, or a near equivalent, that owned land in agricultural areas in the late nineteenth and early twentieth cen-

---

[17]Because the major crops produced in the expansion of the United States and Canada were grains, the land could be profitably worked on relatively small farms, given the technology of the times. This may help explain why such a policy of smallholding was implemented and effective. See Atack and Bateman (1987); Danhof (1969). In Argentina, however, small-scale wheat production coincided with ownership of land in large units, thereby maintaining a greater degree of overall inequality in wealth and political power. See Solberg (1970, 1987). In addition to grains, livestock production on large landholdings also increased dramatically in the late nineteenth century, and scale economies in the raising of livestock may have helped maintain the large estates. For an example of a Spanish American country that came to be characterized by small-scale agriculture and followed a path of institutional development more like that in the United States, see the discussion of Costa Rica in Woodward (1976); Perez-Brignoli (1989).

[18]For further discussion of Mexico, see McBride (1923); Tannebaum (1929); Holden (1994).

---

[15]See Gates (1968) for a comprehensive overview of U.S. land policy. Discussions of Canadian land policy include Solberg (1987); Pomfret (1981, pp. 111–19); Adelman (1994, chap. 2).

[16]See Dean (1971); Viotti da Costa (1985, chap. 4); Solberg (1987); Solberg's essay in Platt and di Tella (1985); and the excellent discussions in Adelman (1994).

Table 1. Landholding in Rural Regions of Mexico, the United States, Canada, and Argentina in the Early 1900s in percent

Country, year, and region	Proportion of household heads who own land[a]
Mexico, 1910	
North Pacific	5.6
North	3.4
Central	2.0
Gulf	2.1
South Pacific	1.5
Total rural Mexico	2.4
United States, 1900	
North Atlantic	79.2
South Atlantic	55.8
North Central	72.1
South Central	51.4
Western	83.4
Alaska/Hawaii	42.1
Total United States	74.5
Canada, 1901	
British Columbia	87.1
Alberta	95.8
Saskatchewan	96.2
Manitoba	88.9
Ontario	80.2
Quebec	90.1
Maritime[b]	95.0
Total Canada	87.1
Argentina, 1895	
Chaco	27.8
Formosa	18.5
Missiones	26.7
La Pampa	9.7
Neuquén	12.3
Río Negro	15.4
Chubut	35.2
Santa Cruz	20.2
Tierra del Fuego	6.6

Source: For Mexico: computed by the authors from the 1910 census figures reported in McBride (1923, p. 154); for the United States: U.S. Census Office (1902, part, I, pp. lxvi–lxxxv); for Canada: Canada Bureau of Statistics (1914, vol. 4, page xii, table 6); for Argentina: computed by the authors from 1895 census figures reported in Carcano (1925) and Comisión Directiva del Censo de la República Argentina (1898, p. clvii, table IVd).

[a]Landownership is defined as follows: in Mexico, household heads who own land; in the United States, farms that are owner operated; in Canada, total occupiers of farm lands who are owners; and in Argentina, the ratio of landowners to the number of males between the ages of 18 and 50.

[b]The Maritime region includes Nova Scotia, New Brunswick, and Prince Edward Island.

turies. The proportion of landowners is far from an ideal measure of the extent of inequality, and it is sensitive to the mix of products produced in the respective areas. Nevertheless, the number does provide useful insight into the impact or effectiveness of the land policies pursued, and one can assemble a set of estimates that are comparable across a broad range of economies. The figures indicate enormous differences across the countries in the prevalence of land ownership among the adult male population in rural areas. On the eve of the Mexican Revolution, the figures from the 1910 census suggest that only 2.4 percent of household heads in rural Mexico owned land. The number is astoundingly low. The basic qualitative result of extreme inequality is confirmed by the observation that the figure varies across regions (as well as states) in the way one would expect: inversely with the proportion of the population that was Native American. The dramatic land policy measures in Mexico at the end of the nineteenth century may have succeeded in privatizing most of the public lands, but they left the vast majority of the rural population without any land at all. The evidence obviously conforms well with the idea that in societies that began with extreme inequality, such as Mexico, institutions evolved so as to greatly advantage the elite in access to economic opportunities, and they thus contributed to the persistence of that extreme inequality.

In contrast, the proportion of adult males that owned land in rural areas was quite high in the United States, at just below 75 percent in 1900. Although the prevalence of land ownership was markedly lower in the South, where blacks were disproportionately concentrated, the overall picture is one of land policies such as the Homestead Act providing broad access to this fundamental type of economic opportunity. Canada had an even better record, with nearly 90 percent of household heads owning the agricultural lands they occupied in 1901. The estimates of landholding in these two countries support the notion that land policies made a difference, especially when compared to Argentina. The rural regions of Argentina constitute a set of frontier provinces, where one would expect higher rates of ownership than in Buenos Aires. The numbers, however, suggest a much lower prevalence of land ownership than in the two North American economies.[19] Nevertheless, all of

[19]Our preliminary work with the data from the 1914 census yields the same qualitative results. It is worth noting that the proportions of families that owned land are exaggerated by the 1895 census figures. A close examination of the manuscripts indicates that double counting, in which both the husband and wife were listed as landowners, was prevalent in many parts of Argentina.

these countries were far more effective than Mexico in making land ownership available to the general population.

The contrast between the United States and Canada, with their practices of offering easy access to small units of land, and the rest of the Americas (as well as the contrast between Argentina and Mexico) is consistent with our hypothesis that the initial extent of inequality influenced the way in which institutions evolved and in so doing helped foster persistence in the degree of inequality over time. The same pattern seems to extend across a wide spectrum of institutions. The design of the U.S. patent system provides another example of how the U.S. government set rather low fees and established low thresholds for access to economic opportunities; similarly, the state governments in that country moved dramatically in the first half of the nineteenth century to ensure relatively free entry and otherwise limit concentrations of power through their requirements for the formation of financial institutions, including modest capital requirements and administrative routines.[20] This pattern stands in rather stark contrast to those in the many New World societies that had begun with much greater inequality, such as Mexico and Brazil.[21] In these countries, the rights to organize corporations and financial institutions or to develop intellectual capital were narrowly framed to favor the wealthy and influential. Of course, members of wealthy elites almost always enjoy privileged positions, but the paths of institutional development in these societies were unusual in the degree to which they advantaged elites.

---

[20]For discussions of these policies in the United States, see, for example, Khan and Sokoloff (1998); Hammond (1957).

[21]Haber (1989, 1991, 1997); Beatty (2001). For a comparison of patent systems that shows how a wide range of countries in Central and South America—from different national heritages—had among the highest fees in the world (as well as other features favorable to members of the elite), see Khan and Sokoloff (2001).

References

Adelman, Jeremy. 1994. *Frontier Development: Land, Labor, and Capital on Wheatlands of Argentina and Canada, 1890–1914.* Oxford University Press.

———. 1999. *Republic of Capital: Buenos Aires and the Legal Transformation of the Atlantic World.* Stanford University Press.

Atack, Jeremy, and Fred Bateman. 1987. *To Their Own Soil: Agriculture in the Antebellum North.* Ames: Iowa State University Press.

Baldwin, Robert E. 1956. "Patterns of Development in Newly Settled Regions." *Manchester School of Economic and Social Studies* 24 (May): 161–79.

Beatty, Edward. 2001. *Institutions and Investment: The Political Basis of Industrialization in Mexico before 1911.* Stanford University Press.

Canada Bureau of Statistics. 1914. *Census of Canada, 1911.* Ottawa: J. de la Tache.

Carcano, Miguel Angel. 1925. *Evolución histórica del régimen de la tierra pública: 1810–1916.* Buenos Aires: Juan Roldán y C.

Castro, Donald. 1971. *The Development of Argentine Immigration Policy, 1852–1914.* Ann Arbor: University of Michigan Press.

Chevalier, François. 1963. *Land and Society in Colonial Mexico: The Great Hacienda.* Berkeley: University of California Press.

Comisión Directiva del Censo de la República Argentina. 1998. *Segundo censo del la República Argentina, levantado el 10 de mayo de 1895,* 3 vols. Buenos Aires: Taller Tipográfico de la Penitenciaria Nacional.

Danhof, Clarence H. 1969. *Change in Agriculture: The Northern United States, 1820–1870.* Cambridge, Mass: Harvard University Press.

Dean, Warren, 1971. "Latifundia and Land Policy in Nineteenth Century Brazil." *Hispanic American Historical Review* 51 (November): 602–25.

Denevan, William M., ed. 1976. *The Native Population in the Americas in 1492.* Madison: University of Wisconsin Press.

Domar, Evsey E. 1970. "The Causes of Slavery or Serfdom: A Hypothesis." *Journal of Economic History* 30 (March): 18–32.

Dunn, Richard S. 1972. *Sugar and Slaves: The Rise of the Planter Class in the English West Indies, 1624–1713.* Chapel Hill: University of North Carolina Press.

Eltis, David. 1997. "The Slave Economies of the Caribbean: Structure, Performance, Evolution, and Significance." In *UNESCO General History of the Caribbean,* vol. 3, edited by Franklin W. Knight, 105–37. London: Macmillan.

Engerman, Stanley L. 1982. "Economic Adjustments to Emancipation in the United States and the British West Indies." *Journal of Interdisciplinary History* 12 (Autumn): 191–220.

Engerman, Stanley L., and Kenneth L. Sokoloff. 1997. "Factor Endowments, Institutions, and Differential Paths of Growth among New World Economies: A View from Economic Historians of the United States." In *How Latin America Fell Behind,* edited by Stephen Haber, 260–304. Stanford University Press.

Gates, Paul W. 1968. *History of Public Land Law Development.* U.S. Government Printing Office.

Haber, Stephen H. 1989. *Industry and Underdevelopment: The Industrialization of Mexico. 1890–1940.* Stanford University Press.

———. 1991. "Industrial Concentration and the Capital Markets: A Comparative Study of Brazil, Mexico, and the United States, 1830–1930." *Journal of Economic History* 51 (September): 559–80.

———. 1997. "Financial Markets and Industrial Development: A Comparative Study of Governmental Regulation, Financial Innovation, and Industrial Structure in Brazil and Mexico, 1840–1930." In *How Latin America Fell Behind,* edited by Stephen Haber, 146–78. Stanford University Press.

Hammond, Bray. 1957. *Banks and Politics in America, from the Revolution to the Civil War.* Princeton University Press.

Holden, Robert. 1994. *Mexico and the Survey of Public Lands. The Management of Modernization, 1876–1911.* Dekalb: Northern Illinois University Press.

Jacobsen, Nils. 1993. *Mirages of Transition: The Peruvian Altiplano.* Berkeley: University of California Press.

Khan, B. Zorina, and Kenneth L. Sokoloff. 1998. "Two Paths to Industrial Development and Technological Change." In *Technological Revolutions in Europe, 1760–1860,* edited by Maxine Berg and Kristine Bruland, 292–314. Cheltenham: Edward Elgar.

———. 2001. "The Innovation of Patent Systems in the Nineteenth Century: A Historical Perspective." University of California at Los Angeles.

Kupperman, Karen Ordahl. 1993. *Providence Island, 1630–1641: The Other Puritan Colony.* Cambridge University Press.

Lewis, W. Arthur. 1955. "Economic Development with Unlimited Supplies of Labor." *Manchester School of Economic and Social Studies* 23 (May): 139–91.

Lockhart, James. 1994. *Spanish Peru: 1532–1560. A Social History,* 2d ed. Madison: University of Wisconsin Press.

Lockhart, James, and Stuart B. Schwartz. 1983. *Early Latin America: A History of Colonial Spanish America and Brazil.* Cambridge University Press.

McBride, George McCutchen. 1923. *The Land Systems of Mexico.* New York: American Geographical Society.

Moreno Fraginals, Manuel. 1976. *The Sugarmill: The Socioeconomic Complex of Sugar in Cuba.* New York: Monthly Review Press.

Perez-Brignoli, Hector. 1989. *A Brief History of Central America.* Berkeley: University of California Press.

Platt, D. C. M., and Guido di Tella, eds. 1985. *Argentina, Australia, and Canada: Studies in Comparative Development, 1870–1965.* London: Macmillan.

Pomfret, Richard. 1981. *The Economic Development of Canada.* Toronto: Methuen.

Sheridan, Richard. 1974. *Sugar and Slavery: An Economic History of the West Indies, 1623–1775.* Barbados: Caribbean Universities Press.

Solberg, Carl E. 1970. *Immigration and Nationalism: Argentina and Chile, 1890–1914.* Austin: University of Texas Press.

———. 1987. *The Prairies and the Pampas: Agrarian Policy in Canada and Argentina, 1880–1913.* Stanford University Press.

Tannebaum, Frank. 1929. *The Mexican Agrarian Revolution.* New York: Macmillan.

U.S. Census Office. 1902. *Twelfth Census of the United States, Taken in the Year 1900: Agriculture.* U.S. Government Printing Office.

Van Young, Eric. 1983. "Mexican Rural History since Chevalier: The Historiography of the Colonial Hacienda." *Latin American Research Review* 18: 5–62.

Viotti da Costa, Emilia. 1985. *The Brazilian Empire: Myths and Histories.* University of Chicago Press.

Walker, Geoffrey J. 1979. *Spanish Politics and Imperial Trade, 1700–1789.* Bloomington: Indiana University Press.

Woodward, Ralph Lee. 1976. *Central America: A Nation Divided.* Oxford University Press.

Divergence in relative productivity levels and living standards is the dominant feature of modern economic history. In the last century, incomes in the "less developed" (or euphemistically, the "developing") countries have fallen far behind those in the "developed" countries, both proportionately and absolutely. I estimate that from 1870 to 1990 the ratio of per capita incomes between the richest and the poorest countries increased by roughly a factor of five and that the difference in income between the richest country and all others has increased by an order of magnitude.[1] This divergence is the result of the very different patterns in the long-run economic performance of two sets of countries.

One set of countries—call them the "developed" or the "advanced capitalist" (Maddison, 1995) or the "high income OECD" (World Bank, 1995)—is easily, if awkwardly, identified as European countries and their offshoots plus Japan. Since 1870, the long-run growth rates of these countries have been rapid (by previous historical standards), their growth rates have been remarkably similar, and the poorer members of the group grew sufficiently faster to produce considerable convergence in absolute income levels. The other set of countries, called the "developing" or "less developed" or "nonindustrialized," can be easily, if still awkwardly, defined only as "the other set of countries," as they have nothing else in common. The growth rates of this set of countries have been, on average, slower than the richer countries, producing divergence in relative incomes. But amongst this set of countries there have been strikingly different patterns of growth: both across countries, with some converging rapidly on the leaders while others stagnate; and over time, with a mixed record of takeoffs, stalls and nose dives. . . .

Calculating a Lower Bound for Per Capita GDP

There is no historical data for many of the less developed economies, and what data does exist has enormous problems with comparability and reliability. One alternative to searching for historical

*From Lant Pritchett, "Divergence, Big Time," *Journal of Economic Perspectives* 11 (Summer 1997): 3–4, 6–12. Reprinted by permission.

[1]To put it another way, the standard deviation of (natural log) GDP per capita across all countries has increased between 60 percent and 100 percent since 1870, in spite of the convergence amongst the richest.

data is simply to place a reasonable lower bound on what GDP per capita could have been in 1870 in any country. Using this lower bound and estimates of recent incomes, one can draw reliable conclusions about the historical growth rates and divergence in cross-national distribution of income levels.

There is little doubt life was nasty, brutish and short in many countries in 1870. But even deprivation has its limit, and some per capita incomes must imply standards of living that are unsustainably and implausibly low. After making conservative use of a wide variety of different methods and approaches, I conclude that $250 (expressed in 1985 purchasing power equivalents) is the lowest GDP per capita could have been in 1870. This figure can be defended on three grounds: first, no one has ever observed consistently lower living standards at any time or place in history; second, this level is well below extreme poverty lines actually set in impoverished countries and is inconsistent with plausible levels of nutritional intake; and third, at a lower standard of living the population would be too unhealthy to expand.

Before delving into these comparisons and calculations, it is important to stress that using the purchasing power adjustments for exchange rates has an especially important effect in poor countries. While tradable goods will have generally the same prices across countries because of arbitrage, nontradable goods are typically much cheaper in poorer countries because of their lower income levels. If one applies market exchange rates to convert incomes in these economies to U.S. dollars, one is typically far understating the "true" income level, because nontradable goods can be bought much more cheaply than market exchange rates will imply. There have been several large projects, especially the UN International Comparisons Project and the Penn World Tables, that through the collection of data on the prices of comparable baskets of goods in all countries attempt to express different countries' GDP in terms of a currency that represents an equivalent purchasing power over a basket of goods. Since this adjustment is so large and of such quantitative significance, I will denote figures that have been adjusted in this way by P$. By my own rough estimates, a country with a per capita GDP level of $70 in U.S. dollars, measured in market exchange rates, will have a per capita GDP of P$250.

The first criteria for a reasonable lower bound on GDP per capita is that it be a lower bound on measured GDP per capita, either of the poorest countries in the recent past or of any country in the distant past. The lowest five-year average level of per capita GDP reported for any country in the Penn World Tables (Mark 5) is P$275 for Ethiopia in 1961–65; the next lowest is P$278 for Uganda in 1978–82. The countries with the lowest level of GDP per capita ever observed, even for a single year, are P$260 for Tanzania in 1961, P$299 for Burundi in 1965 and P$220 for Uganda in 1981 (in the middle of a civil war). Maddison (1991) gives estimates of GDP per capita of some less developed countries as early as 1820: P$531 for India, P$523 for China and P$614 for Indonesia. His earliest estimates for Africa begin in 1913: P$508 for Egypt and P$648 for Ghana. Maddison also offers increasingly speculative estimates for western European countries going back much further in time; for example, he estimates that per capita GDPs in the Netherlands and the United Kingdom in 1700 were P$1515 and P$992, respectively, and ventures to guess that the average per capita GNP in western Europe was P$400 in 1400. Kuznets's (1971) guess of the trough of the average per capita GDP of European countries in 900 is around P$400.[2] On this score, P$250 is a pretty safe bet.

A complementary set of calculations to justify a lower bound are based on "subsistence" income. While "subsistence" as a concept is out of favor, and rightfully so for many purposes, it is sufficiently robust for the task at hand. There are three related calculations: poverty lines, average caloric intakes and the cost of subsistence. Ravallion, Datt and van de Walle (1991) argue that the lowest defensible poverty line based on achieving minimally adequate consumption expenditures is P$252 per person per year. If we assume that personal consumption expenditures are 75 percent of GDP (the average for countries with GDP per capita less than P$400) and that mean income is 1.3 times the median, then even to achieve median income at the lowest possible poverty line requires a per capita income of $437.[3]

As an alternative way of considering subsistence GDP per capita, begin with the finding that estimated average intake per person per day consistent with working productively is between 2,000 to 2,400 calories.[4] Now, consider two calculations. The first is that, based on a cross-sectional regression using data on incomes from the Penn World Tables and average caloric intake data from the FAO, the predicted caloric consumption at P$250 is around 1,600.[5] The five lowest levels of caloric availability ever recorded in the FAO data for various countries—1,610 calories/person during a famine in Somalia in 1975; 1,550 calories/person during a famine in Ethiopia in 1985; 1,443 calories/person in Chad in 1984; 1,586 calories/person in China in 1961 during the famines and disruption associated with the Cultural Revolution; and 1,584 calories/person in Mozambique in 1987—reveal that nearly all of the episodes of average daily caloric consumption below 1,600 are associated with nasty episodes of natural and/or man-made catastrophe. A second use of caloric requirements is to calculate the subsistence income as the cost of meeting caloric requirements. Bairoch (1993) reports the results of the physiological minimum food intake at $291 (at market exchange rates) in 1985 prices. These calculations based on subsistence intake of food again suggest P$250 is a safe lower bound.

That life expectancy is lower and infant mortality higher in poorer countries is well documented, and this relation can also help establish a lower bound on income (Pritchett and Summers, 1996). According to demographers, an under-five infant

---

poverty lines as not far above our lower bound, because many individuals can be in poverty, but not very far below the line. For instance, in South Asia in 1990, where 33 percent of the population was living in "extreme absolute poverty," only about 10 percent of the population would be living at less than $172 (my estimates from extrapolations of cumulative distributions reported in Chen, Datt and Ravallion, 1993).

[4]The two figures are based on different assumptions about the weight of adult men and women, the mean temperature and the demographic structure. The low figure is about as low as one can go because it is based on a very young population, 39 percent under 15 (the young need fewer calories), a physically small population (men's average weight of only 110 pounds and women of 88), and a temperature of 25°C (FAO, 1957). The baseline figure, although based on demographic structure, usually works out to be closer to 2,400 (FAO, 1974).

[5]The regression is a simple log-log of caloric intake and income in 1960 (the log-log is for simplicity even though this might not be the best predictor of the level). The regression is

ln (average caloric intake) = 6.37 + .183*ln (GDP per capita),

(59.3)(12.56).

with t-statistics in parentheses, $N = 113$, and R-squared = .554.

---

[2]More specifically, Kuznets estimated that the level was about $160, if measured in 1985 U.S. dollars. However, remember from the earlier discussion that a conversion at market exchange rates—which is what Kuznets was using—is far less than an estimate based on purchasing power parity exchange rates. If we use a multiple of 2.5, which is a conservative estimate of the difference between the two, Kuznets's estimate in purchasing power equivalent terms would be equal to a per capita GDP of $400 in 1985 U.S. dollars, converted at the purchasing power equivalent rate.

[3]High poverty rates, meaning that many people live below these poverty lines, are not inconsistent with thinking of these

Figure 1. Simulation of divergence of per capita GDP, 1870–1985 (showing only selected countries).

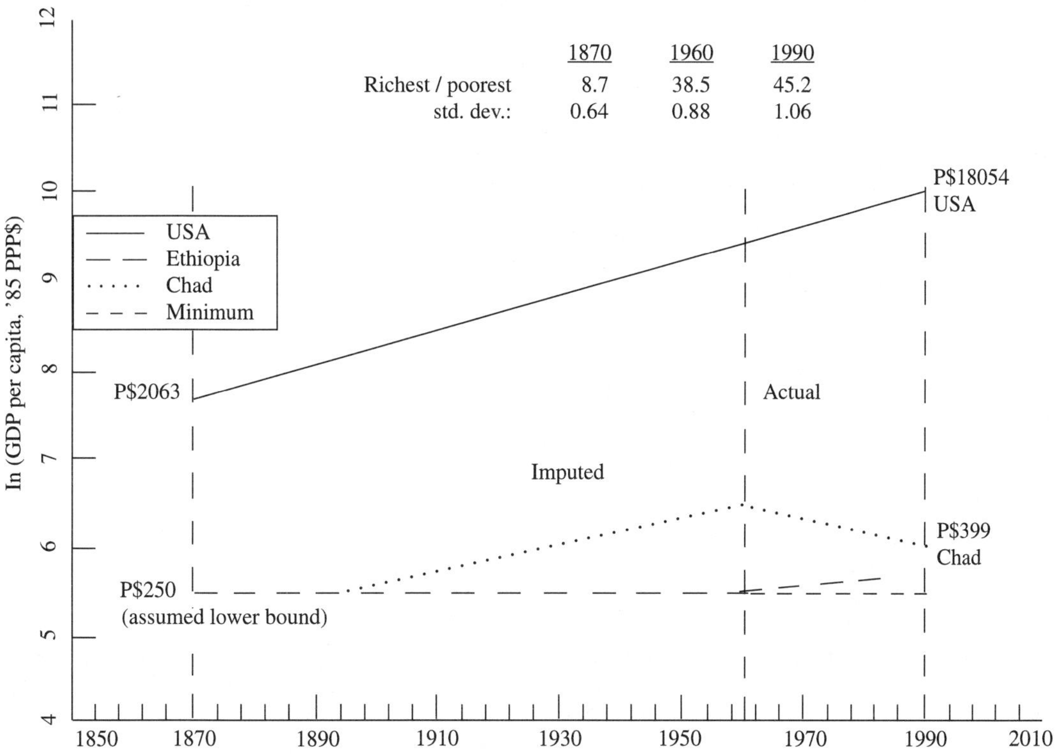

	1870	1960	1990
Richest / poorest	8.7	38.5	45.2
std. dev.:	0.64	0.88	1.06

mortality rate of less than 600 per 1000 is necessary for a stable population (Hill, 1995). Using a regression based on Maddison's (1991) historical per capita income estimates and infant mortality data from historical sources for 22 countries, I predict that infant mortality in 1870 for a country with income of P\$250 would have been 765 per 1000.[6] Although the rate of natural increase of population back in 1870 is subject to great uncertainty, it is typically estimated to be between .25 and 1 percent annually in that period, which is again inconsistent with income levels as low as P\$250.[7]

[6]The regression is estimated with country fixed effects:

$$\ln (\text{IMR}) = -.59 \ln (\text{GDP per capita}) - .013*\text{Trend}$$
$$\quad (23.7) \qquad\qquad (32.4)$$

$$- .002*\text{Trend}*(1 \text{ if} > 1960)$$
$$(14.23)$$

N = 1994 and t-statistics are in parentheses. The prediction used the average country constant of 9.91.

[7]Livi-Basci (1992) reports estimates of population growth in Africa between 1850 and 1900 to be .87 percent, and .93 percent between 1900 and 1950, while growth for Asia is estimated to be .27 1850 to 1900, and .61 1900 to 1950. Clark (1977) estimates the population growth rates between 1850 and 1900 to be .43 percent in Africa and India and lower, .33 percent, in China.

Divergence, Big Time

If you accept: (a) the current estimates of relative incomes across nations; (b) the estimates of the historical growth rates of the now-rich nations; and (c) that even in the poorest economies incomes were not below P\$250 at any point—then you cannot escape the conclusion that the last 150 years have seen divergence, big time. The logic is straightforward and is well illustrated by Figure 1. If there had been no divergence, then we could extrapolate backward from present income of the poorer countries to past income assuming they grew at least as fast as the United States. However, this would imply that many poor countries must have had incomes below P\$100 in 1870. Since this cannot be true, there must have been divergence. Or equivalently, per capita income in the United States, the world's richest industrial country, grew about four-fold from 1870 to 1960. Thus, any country whose income was not fourfold higher in 1960 than it was in 1870 grew more slowly than the United States. Since 42 of the 125 countries in the Penn World Tables with data for 1960 have levels of per capita incomes below \$1,000 (that is, less than four times \$250), there must have been substantial divergence between the top and bottom.

Table 1. Estimates of the Divergence of Per Capita Incomes Since 1870

	1870	1960	1990
USA (*P$*)	2063	9895	18054
Poorest (*P$*)	250	257	399
	(assumption)	(Ethiopia)	(Chad)
Ratio of GDP per capita of richest to poorest country	8.7	38.5	45.2
Average of seventeen "advanced capitalist" countries from Maddison (1995)	1757	6689	14845
Average LDCs from PWT5.6 for 1960, 1990 (imputed for 1870)	740	1579	3296
Average "advanced capitalist" to average of all other countries	2.4	4.2	4.5
Standard deviation of natural log of per capita incomes	.51	.88	1.06
Standard deviation of per capita incomes	P$459	P$2,112	P$3,988
Average absolute income deficit from the leader	P$1286	P$7650	P$12,662

Notes: The estimates in the columns for 1870 are based on backcasting GDP per capita for each country using the methods described in the text assuming a minimum of *P$250*. If instead of that method, incomes in 1870 are backcast with truncation at *P$250*, the 1870 standard deviation is .64 (as reported in Figure 1).

The figure of *P$250* is not meant to be precise or literal and the conclusion of massive divergence is robust to any plausible assumption about a lower bound.

Consider some illustrative calculations of the divergence in per capita incomes in Table 1. I scale incomes back from 1960 such that the poorest country in 1960 just reaches the lower bound by 1870, the leader in 1960 (the United States) reaches its actual 1870 value, and all relative rankings between the poorest country and the United States are preserved.[8] The first row shows the actual path of the U.S. economy. The second row gives the level of the poorest economy in 1870, which is *P$250* by assumption, and then the poorest economies in 1960 and 1990 taken from the

Penn World Tables. By division, the third row then shows that the ratio of the top to the bottom income countries has increased from 8.7 in 1870 to 38 by 1960 and to 45 by 1990. If instead one takes the 17 richest countries and applies the same procedure, their average per capita income is shown in the fourth row. The average for all less developed economies appearing in the Penn World Tables for 1960 and 1990 is given in the fifth row; the figure for 1870 is calculated by the "backcasting" imputation process for historical incomes described above. By division, the sixth row shows that the ratio of income of the richest to all other countries has almost doubled from 2.4 in 1870 to 4.5 by 1990.

The magnitude of the change in the absolute gaps in per capita incomes between rich and poor is staggering. From 1870 to 1990, the average absolute gap in incomes of all countries from the leader had grown by an order of magnitude, from $1,286 to $12,662, as shown in the last row of Table 1.

[8]The growth rate of the poorest country was imposed to reach *P$250* at exactly 1870, and the rate of the United States was used for the growth at the top. Then each country's growth rate was assumed to be a weighted average of those two rates, where the weights depended on the scaled distance from the bottom country in the beginning period of the imputation, 1960. This technique "smushes" the distribution back into the smaller range between the top and bottom while maintaining all cross country rankings. The formula for estimating the log of GDP per capita (GDPPC) in the ith country in 1870 was

$$GDPPC_i^{1870} = GDPPC_i^{1960} * (1/w_i)$$

where the scaling weight w_i was

$$w_i = \frac{(1 - \alpha_i) * \min(GDPPC^{1960})}{P\$250 \; + \alpha_i * GDPPC_{\text{USA}}^{1960}/GDPPC_{\text{USA}}^{1870}}$$

and where α_i is defined by

$$\alpha_i = \frac{(GDPPC_i^{1960} - \min(GDPPC^{1960}))}{(GDPPC_{\text{USA}}^{1960} - \min(GDPPC^{1960}))}.$$

References

Bairoch, Paul, *Economics and World History: Myths and Paradoxes.* Chicago: University of Chicago Press, 1993.

Chen, Shaohua, Gaurav Datt, and Martin Ravallion, "Is Poverty Increasing in the Developing World?" World Bank Policy Research Working Paper No. 1146, June 1993.

Clark, Colin, *Population Growth and Land Use.* London: Macmillan, 1977.

FAO, *Calorie Requirements: Report of the Second Committee on Calorie Requirements.* Rome: FAO, 1957.

FAO, *Handbook on Human Nutritional Requirements.* Rome: Food and Agriculture Organization and World Health Organization, 1974.

Hill, Kenneth, "The Decline of Childhood Mortality." In Simon, Julian, ed., *The State of Humanity.* Oxford: Blackwell, 1995, pp. 37–50.

Kuznets, Simon, *Economic Growth of Nations: Total Output and Production Structure.* Cambridge, Mass.: Belknap Press, 1971.

Livi-Basci, Massimo, *A Concise History of World Population.* Cambridge, Mass: Blackwell, 1992.

Maddison, Angus, *Dynamic Forces in Capitalistic Development: A Long-Run Comparative View.* New York: Oxford University Press, 1991.

Maddison, Angus, *Monitoring the World Economy, 1820–1992.* Paris: Development Centre of the Organisation for Economic Co-operation Development, 1995.

Pritchett, Lant, and Lawrence H. Summers, "Wealthier is Healthier," *Journal of Human Resources,* 1996, 31:4, 841–68.

Ravallion, Martin, Gaurav Datt, and Dominique van de Walle, "Quantifying Absolute Poverty in the Developing World," *Review of Income and Wealth,* 1991, 37:4, 345–61.

World Bank, *World Development Report: Workers in an Integrating Economy.* Washington, D.C.: Oxford University Press for the World Bank, 1995.

Comment II.4   Will the Poor Countries Catch Up?

There is a lively debate among economists regarding whether the per capita incomes of the currently poor countries will ever catch up or "converge" to those of the currently rich countries. There exist compelling theoretical arguments and empirical results to support both positive and negative answers to this question.

On the negative side, there are many theoretical models that yield a "low-level equilibrium trap" for poor countries. For example, consider a model in which household saving finances accumulation of physical capital, which in turn generates growth in per capita income. Households have a minimum consumption level, so if their incomes fall below this level they cannot save. Household incomes will fall below the minimum level if the initial stock of physical capital per head is too small. Thus we have a trap: a country that starts with a low stock of physical capital per head cannot save and increase this stock, leaving it stuck with a low per capita income forever. Theoretical predictions of multiple equilibria have received empirical support from the work of Danny Quah, who provides evidence that the world distribution of income is evolving toward "twin peaks," with one group of countries concentrated ("trapped") at low levels of per capita income and another group of countries concentrated at high levels of per capita income. See Danny Quah, "Empirical Cross-Section Dynamics in Economic Growth," *European Economic Review* 37 (1993): 426–434.

On the positive side, Robert Lucas has formulated one of the more interesting models predicting that per capita incomes of currently poor countries will converge toward the levels of rich countries. In "Some Macroeconomics for the 21st Century," *Journal of Economic Perspectives* 14, no. 1 (Winter 2000): 159–168, Lucas argues that countries can be thought of as being "released from the starting gate" onto a path of sustained growth at different times. Countries that started early are now rich; countries that started late (or have yet to start) are now poor. When some countries begin sustained growth and others do not, we observe the divergence documented in Selection II.6. However, Lucas assumes that when the lagging countries begin sustained growth, they will grow faster than the leading country in proportion to the gap between their incomes and the income of the leader, perhaps because they will learn from the leader. As a result the lagging countries will catch up, and eventually all countries will leave the starting gate and converge toward the per capita income of the leader. Michael Kremer, Alexei Onatski, and James Stock provide evidence supporting the predictions of Lucas's model. In particular, they show that once countries enter the top income group, they do not exit (with the possible exception of Argentina): countries that discover the "elixir of growth" do not forget it. See Michael Kremer, Alexei Onatski, and James Stock, "Searching for Prosperity," *Carnegie-Rochester Series on Public Policy* 55 (2001): 275–303, and the following response by Danny Quah.

CHAPTER III

International Trade and Technology Transfer

Overview

The division of the world described in Chapter II established a pattern of international trade in which poor, mainly tropical countries exported primary products to rich temperate countries in exchange for manufactures. Exhibit III.A.1 shows the extent to which this pattern has continued in the present when countries are ranked by the Human Development Index. We see that primary products account for 84 percent of the value of merchandise exports for the typical (median) low human development country, 60 percent of the value of merchandise exports for the typical medium human development country, and only 26 percent of the value of merchandise exports for the typical high human development country. Moreover, countries whose exports are dominated by primary products also tend to have their exports concentrated in a small number of commodities (the correlation between the primary product export share and the index of export concentration in Exhibit III.A.1 is 0.67).

In Note III.A.1 we recognize the strong association between high primary product export shares and abundant natural resources per capita, and summarize the empirical evidence and theoretical arguments that link natural resource abundance to slow economic growth. We go on to ask, if the empirical evidence and theoretical arguments are correct, can countries with abundant natural resources find a way around their negative effects? Some answers are suggested for regions with relatively high education levels (Latin America) and regions with relatively low education levels (sub-Saharan Africa).

In the period following World War II virtually every LDC government capable of implementing a coherent economic policy attempted to encourage industrialization by protecting domestic manufacturing from import competition. Among their motivations were the perception that exports of primary products were a dead end and some form of the infant-industry argument presented in Note III.A.2. As a result, in Selection III.A.1 Gustav Ranis looks at what follows the first phase of import-substituting industrialization to find differences in trade policies and economic performance across countries. He argues that countries that were able to complete the process of substitution for imports of labor-intensive, low-technology goods such as consumer nondurables faced a choice between two ways of continuing rapid growth of manufacturing production. They could remove protection for consumer nondurables producers in the hope that the infants had grown up and could expand into foreign markets, or they could extend protection to more capital-intensive, high-technology goods such as consumer durables. South Korea and Taiwan took the first path and the more advanced countries of Latin America took the second. Ranis suggests that, in part, the first path was forced on South Korea and Taiwan by lack of natural resources needed to generate exports sufficient to finance the imports of intermediate and capital goods still needed during the next phase of import substitution. Auty (1994) argues that China and India took the same path as Latin America despite poor resource endowments because they were "market-rich": their huge populations made their domestic markets large enough to allow economies of scale to be achieved even in the capital-intensive industries protected in the second phase of import substitution.

By the 1970s, South Korea, Taiwan, and Latin American countries such as Brazil and Mexico appeared to have wound up in the same place, with diversified industrial structures and substantial exports of labor-intensive manufactured goods. Ranis claims, however, that as a result of the different paths taken, both light and heavy industry in Korea and Taiwan were internationally competitive while Latin American industry suffered from high costs, requiring subsidies to push out manufactured exports and continued tariff and quota protection for the domestic market. Latin America (and India) ultimately felt compelled to undertake substantial liberalization in the 1980s and 1990s. The delay in liberalization relative to East Asia has been blamed for Latin America's relatively high income inequality and for the severity of the 1982 debt crisis and the lost decade of growth that followed (and for the prolonged slow growth of India prior to the 1980s).

Ranis argues that the introduction of more capital-intensive and technologically sophisticated industry in South Korea and Taiwan was much more of a market process in East Asia than in Latin America. The selection by Alan Deardorff and the following Comment show how such a market process might work. Accumulation of physical and human capital drives down the costs of renting capital equipment and employing skilled labor relative to the cost of employing unskilled labor, thereby reducing the cost of producing goods that make intensive use of physical and human capital relative to goods that make intensive use of unskilled labor. When this accumulation proceeds far enough, domestic production of the former goods can be profitable even at international prices.

In the selection by Bela Balassa, the consequences of overriding market signals are alleged to be particularly severe in the second stage of import-substituting industrialization. Essentially this is due to the much larger minimum efficient scale in capital-intensive than in labor-intensive industries. For intermediate goods such as petrochemicals and steel, efficient plant size is large. For consumer durables such as automobiles and refrigerators, the network of upstream suppliers of components needs to be large, and downstream assemblers are more efficient if they can dedicate separate plants to separate models. Domestic markets in most LDCs were too small to support the efficient levels of plant size and horizontal and vertical specialization for industries protected in the second stage of import substitution, making international cost competitiveness and the consequent ability to export imperative. LDC consumers also suffered from lack of competition and poor-quality products because of the limited number of domestic firms that could exist in small domestic markets, given economies of scale.

In Selection III.A.4, Dani Rodrik disputes the claim that the move of South Korea and Taiwan into capital-intensive industry was primarily a market process, and argues that a reduction in the relative cost of skilled labor is at best a precondition rather than sufficient for LDCs to advance beyond production of consumer nondurables. He asserts that exactly the characteristics of capital-intensive industry emphasized in the selection by Balassa—the need for large plants and large networks of component suppliers—induce a need for coordination of investments among upstream and downstream firms. The Korean and Taiwanese governments intervened to facilitate this coordination, while reliance on the market may have led to a coordination failure where (for example) potential automobile assemblers did not build plants because of inadequate supply of parts and potential suppliers of parts did not build plants because of inadequate demand by assemblers.

Rodrik assumes that domestic assemblers cannot import foreign components and domestic component suppliers cannot export to foreign assemblers, thereby avoiding coordination failure. The possibility that supplier networks could be located abroad also weakens Balassa's case against establishment of production of consumer durables for the domestic market only. In the Note that concludes section III.A we evaluate whether the assumption that intermediate goods are nontraded is appropriate and point out that an industrialization strategy that relies heavily on backward and forward linkages may create growth-reducing bottlenecks.

In section III.A trade is viewed as an arm's-length form of exchange. Trade may also be associated with more direct and personal contact such as repeated movement of engineers and other skilled personnel between developed country buyers and LDC suppliers. In the first Note of section III.B we argue that this contact is a major source of transfer of technology and managerial know-how, and discuss the organization of this contact through international production networks or "global commodity chains." In Selection III.B.1 Howard Pack describes how Korea and Taiwan moved beyond technology transfer from foreign buyers to more systematic means of acquiring foreign technology, including encouragement of large firms to obtain technology licenses (Korea) and establishment of central technology diffusion institutions (Taiwan).

Foreign direct investment (FDI) is also an important form of contact between more and less developed countries. In Selection III.B.2 Ann Harrison reports her findings that in Morocco and Venezuela firms with foreign equity participation exhibit much higher levels of productivity, but that there appeared to be no technology spillovers to domestically owned firms. On the other hand, she found that in Mexico location near multinational exporters increased the likelihood that domestically owned firms would export, possibly indicating spillovers of knowledge regarding foreign markets.

In Note III.B.2 we conclude this chapter by drawing on material from both sections to describe three views of the effect of international trade on the economic growth of less developed countries. The theme of the determinants of economic growth in LDCs will be taken up again in the first note of Chapter IV.

Reference

Auty, Richard M. 1994. "Industrial Policy Reform in Six Large Newly Industrializing Countries: The Resource Curse Thesis." *World Development* 22 (January): 11–26.

III.A. TRADE

Exhibit III.A.1. Share of Primary Products in Merchandise Exports and Index of Export Concentration

Country Name (listed from lowest to highest HDI)	Primary Product Export Share[a]		Export Concentration[b]
	Survey Year	Percent	
Low-human development countries			
Niger	1995	95.4	0.599
Burkina Faso	1995	79.9	0.534
Mali	1990	98.5	0.664
Burundi	2000	84.2	0.526
Mozambique	2001	91.4	0.540
Ethiopia	2000	85.6	0.386
Central African Republic	1995	54.9	
Guinea-Bissau	1995	99.8	
Angola	1990	99.9	
Zambia	1995	78.7	0.534
Malawi	1995	90.7	0.554
Côte d'Ivoire	2000	84.1	0.315
Tanzania, U. Rep. of	1999	60.8	0.288
Benin	1995	88.5	0.638
Rwanda	2001	97.9	0.520
Guinea	2001	56.9	0.575
Senegal	2001	70.9	0.246
Mauritania	1995	96.8	
Djibouti	1990	44.2	
Nigeria	2000	99.7	0.996
Gambia	1995	61.4	0.460
Haiti	1995	37.9	
Madagascar	1999	48.2	
Yemen	1995	99.5	
Uganda	2000	82.8	0.278
Kenya	2000	78.7	0.297
Zimbabwe	2000	85.3	0.289
Pakistan	2000	14.9	0.220
Nepal	2000	10.6	0.305
Cameroon	2001	95.3	0.466
Median		*84.1*	*0.493*
Medium-human development countries			
Togo	2000	50.3	0.336
Congo	1995	97.2	
Bangladesh	1995	8.3	0.308
Sudan	1995	92.9	0.733
Bhutan	1999	60.0	
Comoros	2000	88.7	0.881
Swaziland	2001	52.9	0.276
Papua New Guinea	2000	97.8	0.495
Ghana	2000	54.0	0.390
Vanuatu	2000	86.3	0.384
India	1999	22.4	0.130
Morocco	2000	35.1	0.167
Botswana	2000	9.1	0.828
Namibia	2001	46.5	0.368
Nicaragua	2000	82.5	0.239
Egypt	1999	60.2	0.287
Guatemala	2001	61.7	0.158
Gabon	1980	100.0	0.810
Mongolia	2001	65.2	0.367
Honduras	2000	71.2	0.256
Bolivia	2001	72.4	0.235
Tajikistan	2000	83.6	0.541
Indonesia	2001	43.3	0.126

Exhibit III.A.1. (Continued)

Country Name (listed from lowest to highest HDI)	Primary Product Export Share[a]		Export Concentration[b]
	Survey Year	Percent	
South Africa	2000	28.8	0.193
Syrian Arab Republic	2000	90.4	0.677
Moldova, Rep. of	2001	66.3	0.298
Algeria	2000	98.7	0.576
Iran, Islamic Rep. of	2000	90.3	0.804
El Salvador	2001	44.1	0.128
China	2000	11.1	0.077
Cape Verde	1995	3.5	0.482
Kyrgyzstan	1999	39.5	
Armenia	2000	49.9	0.188
Sri Lanka	1999	23.8	0.236
Ecuador	2001	88.9	0.390
Turkey	2000	17.5	0.086
Albania	2001	15.7	0.265
Dominican Republic	1995	19.5	
Grenada	1999	48.8	0.349
Tunisia	2000	19.2	0.194
Jordan	2001	34.0	0.191
Azerbaijan	2000	95.5	0.747
Georgia	2000	62.3	0.185
Turkmenistan	2000	91.6	0.526
Maldives	2001	57.7	0.385
Philippines	2000	8.8	0.387
Paraguay	2001	83.7	0.368
Lebanon	2001	29.1	0.107
Peru	2001	64.3	0.230
Fiji	2000	49.4	0.303
Saint Vincent and the Grenadines	2000	87.1	0.458
Oman	2000	87.4	0.681
Jamaica	2000	81.7	0.571
Suriname	2000	85.5	0.659
Kazakhstan	2000	82.0	0.478
Ukraine			0.145
Thailand	2000	22.3	0.100
Saudi Arabia	2000	90.8	0.894
Romania	2000	18.8	0.119
Saint Lucia	2001	79.1	0.557
Samoa (Western)	1990	96.4	
Venezuela	2001	89.0	0.605
Dominica	2000	42.5	0.428
Belize	1999	87.2	0.420
Brazil	2001	43.8	0.092
Colombia	2001	60.5	0.213
Russian Federation	2000	66.3	0.302
Mauritius	2001	25.2	0.290
Libyan Arab Jamahiriya	1990	95.3	
Macedonia, TFYR	2001	29.7	0.163
Panama	2000	86.7	0.286
Malaysia	2001	18.9	0.200
Bulgaria	2000	36.9	0.125
Median		*60.4*	*0.303*
High-human development countries			
Mexico	2001	14.9	0.132
Trinidad and Tobago	2000	57.2	0.325
Belarus	2000	30.0	0.149
Cuba	2001	90.1	

Exhibit III.A.1. (Continued)

Country Name (listed from lowest to highest HDI)	Primary Product Export Share[a]		Export Concentration[b]
	Survey Year	Percent	
Saint Kitts and Nevis	2000	26.7	0.624
Latvia	2001	41.1	0.177
Bahamas	1995	62.5	0.448
United Arab Emirates	1990	53.2	
Croatia	2001	26.7	0.143
Kuwait	1999	91.5	
Lithuania	2001	41.5	0.174
Qatar	1999	92.6	0.626
Chile	2000	79.3	0.268
Costa Rica	2000	37.5	0.204
Estonia	2001	25.1	0.181
Uruguay	2001	51.4	0.167
Slovakia	2001	15.7	0.130
Hungary	2001	12.3	0.116
Bahrain	2000	87.1	0.666
Seychelles	1995	98.8	
Poland	2000	18.7	0.081
Argentina	2001	65.7	0.136
Malta	2001	3.7	0.551
Czech Republic	2000	10.3	0.087
Brunei Darussalam	1990	99.5	
Korea, Rep. of	2001	9.2	0.140
Slovenia	2001	10.3	0.103
Singapore	2001	11.5	0.247
Barbados	2001	47.3	0.181
Hong Kong, China (SAR)	2001	4.1	0.207
Cyprus	2001	46.9	0.180
Greece	2000	47.0	0.108
Portugal	2000	13.2	0.113
Israel	2000	5.3	0.291
Italy	2001	10.2	0.055
New Zealand	2001	68.2	0.167
Spain	2000	20.9	0.122
Germany	2000	9.4	0.102
France	2001	16.1	0.082
Austria	2000	12.3	0.074
Luxembourg	2000	12.0	0.147
Finland	2001	13.9	0.221
United Kingdom	2001	15.3	0.101
Ireland	2001	8.7	0.206
Denmark	2001	29.5	0.086
Switzerland	2001	7.5	0.151
Japan	2001	3.1	0.135
Canada	2001	31.3	0.132
United States	2001	14.1	0.081
Belgium	2001	17.1	0.104
Netherlands	2000	29.7	0.096
Australia	2001	66.0	0.129
Sweden	2000	13.6	0.117
Iceland	2001	85.6	0.375
Norway	2001	74.5	0.445
Median		*25.9*	*0.143*

United Nations Human Development Index countries are included in the Exhibit only if they have data available.

[a]Primary products are the the the sum of all food items (SITC 0 + 1 + 22 + 4), agricultural raw materials (SITC 2 less (22 + 27 + 28)), fuels (SITC 3), and ores and metals (SITC 27 + 28 + 68). SITC = Standard International Trade Classification.

[b]Concentration is measured by the Hirschman-Herfindahl index normalized to range from 0 (minimum concentration) to 1 (maximum concentration). See p. 395 of Source for exact formula. Data are for 2001 or latest available year.

Source: United Nations Conference on Trade and Development. *UNCTAD Handbook of Statistics* (New York: United Nations), 2003.

Note III.A.1. Natural Resource Abundance, International Trade, and Economic Growth

Countries in Exhibit III.A.1 with high primary product export shares tend to have abundant natural resources (arable land or minerals) per capita, as we would expect. This tendency is illustrated in an especially striking way by the exceptions to the strong negative association between human development and primary product export share. Thus Bangladesh, one of the most densely populated countries in the world, has a primary product export share of 8.3 percent despite its relatively low level of human development, and Australia, one of the least densely populated countries in the world, has a primary product export share of 66.0 percent despite its very high level of human development. Both the negative association of primary product export share with human development and its positive association with natural resource abundance are supported by the cross-country regression analysis of Wood and Berge (1997). They show that the ratio of primary product to manufactures exports in the late 1980s depends negatively on the average years of schooling of the adult population and positively on land area per worker.

The association between exports of primary products and abundance of natural resources is sufficiently robust that the ratio of primary product exports to GDP is now used as the standard indicator of natural resource abundance in the cross-country statistical literature on determinants of per capita income growth (Asea and Lahiri 1999, Sachs and Warner 2001). These papers find that this indicator of natural resource abundance is strongly negatively associated with per capita income growth. This negative association remains even after controlling for many other potential determinants of economic growth such as climate, geography, economic policies, political institutions, and external shocks. Indeed, the ratio of primary product exports to GDP is considered one of the most robust determinants of growth in cross-country growth regressions (Sala-i-Martin 1997).

This cross-country evidence cannot be considered decisive—for example, natural resource abundance tends to decline over time as resources are depleted and population grows, yet Exhibit I.B.2 shows that per capita income growth rates have not tended to rise, at least not for less developed countries. However, there are also strong theoretical arguments for believing that natural resource abundance has a negative effect on economic growth.

The most popular argument is the "Dutch disease" model. In this model the wealth generated by exports of natural resources creates demand for nontraded goods (e.g., services). The nontraded goods sector competes with the manufacturing sector for scarce inputs such as skilled labor. Manufacturing in turn is assumed to be the engine of economic growth because it somehow yields positive externalities for the economy, perhaps through learning-by-doing spillovers as in Selection II.3. Another argument, also based on the idea that natural resources "crowd out" a desirable activity, is that abundant natural resources lower the return to obtaining an education by increasing wages for unskilled workers. In this argument, accumulation of human capital is assumed to be the engine of growth. Asea and Lahiri (1999) and Gylvason (2001) both present cross-country evidence that school enrollment is negatively associated with indicators of natural resource abundance. A third argument is based on political economy considerations. Governments in natural resource abundant countries are unable to resist the temptation to appropriate the earnings from natural resource exports for themselves, and are able to buy off opposition to this corruption using the part of export earnings that they do not consume. If good governance is the key to economic growth, as claimed in Selection IX.C.1, then natural resource abundance again leads to slow growth. Sala-i-Martin and Subramanian (2003) show that various indicators of natural resource abundance are negatively associated with measures of institutional quality in cross-country regressions.

Should we conclude that natural resource abundant countries are doomed to slow growth in per capita incomes? Governments have tried to counteract the Dutch disease by aiding the manufacturing sector, especially through protection from foreign competition. Unfortunately, this protection needs to be permanent, as opposed to the temporary protection called for by the infant-industry argument of Note III.A.2. By the 1990s, such protection was almost universally deemed to be too expensive, leading to a wave of trade liberalization.

Owens and Wood (1997) provide evidence that natural resource abundant countries that also have relatively abundant human capital are able to avoid the Dutch disease and become successful exporters of manufactures, specifically manufactures that make intensive use of natural resources. They distinguish a category of manufactures called "processed primary products"—fruit preserves instead of raw fruit, paper instead of logs. Figures 1 and 2 show that Latin America is the region of the less developed world that is relatively abundant in both natural resources and human capital and also the region with the highest share of processed primary products in total exports. At the same time, these figures show that the other natural resource abundant region of the less developed world, sub-Saharan Africa, is poor in human capital and has an export share of processed primary products much smaller than that of Latin America. (However, sub-Saharan Africans can take some comfort from the fact that natural resource abundance did not prevent Latin America from achieving a relatively high level of education, despite the disincentive to schooling alleged above.)

Recent experience in sub-Saharan Africa has shown that countries whose exports are dominated by primary products can still realize the kind of learning benefits and investment opportunities associated with manufacturing by upgrading quality and presentation. About the fresh vegetable business, Dolan, Harris-Pascal, and Humphrey (1999, p. 25) write:

> Export produce must enter an intricate cooling chain within a few hours of harvest and must remain in a temperature-controlled environment to avoid product damage. . . . [I]n both Kenya and Zimbabwe large exporters have invested in state of the art methods including chilled chlorinated water for washing. . . . Products packed in trays require more complicated machinery than products wrapped in cellophane packets. If they are also labeled and barcoded in the country of origin, this too requires further investment in equipment.

Figure 1. Regional factor endowments. The points are unweighted averages of the values for the countries in each group. 'HP' EAsia = "high-performing" East Asia: Hong Kong, Indonesia, Korea, Malaysia, Singapore, Taiwan, and Thailand.

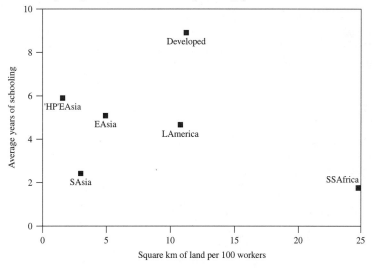

Source: Owens and Wood (1997, p. 1465). Reprinted by permission.

Figure 2. Regional export composition.

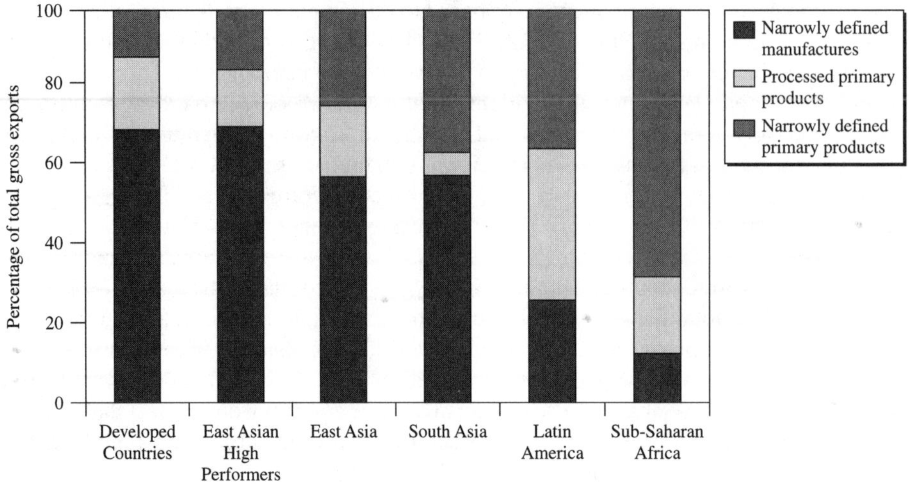

Source: Owens and Wood (1997, p. 1466). Reprinted by permission.

The need for management of these postharvest processes suggests that natural resource intensive production can provide more incentives to obtain an education than is conventionally believed.

Not all natural resource exports offer the same possibilities as vegetables, however. For mineral exports such as oil, the best policy may be to try to "neutralize" the negative effects on the economy while retaining the export proceeds. Gylfason (2001, p. 851) writes,

> Good policies can turn abundant natural resource riches into an unambiguous blessing. Norway, the world's second largest oil exporter (after Saudi Arabia), is a case in point. As Norway's oil wealth is a common-property resource by law, the Norwegian government takes in about 80 percent of the oil rent through taxes and fees. The government invests the revenues from oil in foreign securities in order to divide the oil receipts fairly between the present generation and future generations as well as to shield the domestic economy from too much income too quickly.

Another possibility is to earmark mineral wealth for education, thereby directly offsetting one of the alleged negative impacts of natural resource abundance on economic growth. The University of Texas is the richest public university in the United States thanks to its ownership of oil fields. Whether mechanisms can be designed to induce less developed country governments to adopt such policies rather than plunder mineral wealth for themselves remains to be seen.

References

Asea, Patrick K., and Amartya Lahiri. 1999. "The Precious Bane," *Journal of Economic Dynamics and Control* 23: 823–849.

Dolan, C., C. Harris-Pascal, and J. Humphrey. 1999. "Horticulture Commodity Chains: The Impact on the UK Market of the African Fresh Vegetable Industry." Institute of Development Studies Working Paper No. 96.

Gylvason, Thorvaldur. 2001. "Natural Resources, Education, and Economic Development." *European Economic Review* 45: 847–859.

Owens, Trudy, and Adrian Wood. 1997. "Export-Oriented Industrialization Through Primary Processing?" *World Development* 25, no. 9: 1453–1470.

Sachs, Jeffrey D., and Andrew W. Warner. 2001. "The Curse of Natural Resources." *European Economic Review* 45: 827–838.

Sala-i-Martin, Xavier X. 1997. "I Just Ran Two Million Regressions." *American Economic Review* 87, no. 2: 178–183.

Sala-i-Martin, Xavier X., and Arvind Subramanian. 2003. "Addressing the Natural Resource Curse: An Illustration from Nigeria." National Bureau of Economic Research Working Paper No. 9804 (June).

Wood, Adrian, and K. Berge. 1997. "Exporting Manufactures: Human Resources, Natural Resources, and Trade Policy." *Journal of Development Studies* 34, no. 1: 35–59.

Note III.A.2. Import-substituting Industrialization and the Infant-Industry Argument

The vast majority of countries that have become major exporters of manufactures initially protected their manufacturing sectors against foreign competition. Examples range from British protection against the cotton textiles of India in the eighteenth century through Taiwanese protection in the 1950s and early 1960s. The policy of government intervention to encourage domestic industrial production to replace imports has become known as *import-substituting industrialization,* or ISI. An important motivation for this policy is the *infant-industry argument.*

The infant-industry argument is deceptively simple. It states that industries in which a country has a long-run comparative advantage may be stifled by foreign competition if they are not protected from imports during an initial period in which firms learn to get their costs down. This sounds reasonable, but one may ask: if these firms are going to become internationally competitive, why do they not borrow to cover their losses during the learning period and repay the loans out of future profits, like any business start-up? Evidently a more sophisticated version of the infant-industry argument is required, one that explains why firms acting on their own will not achieve the socially optimal outcome, and how government policy can generate better results. Put differently, the existence of a "market failure" must be established, and it must be shown that the government can at least partially correct this failure.

There are many such versions of the infant-industry argument. The one presented here is based on Bardhan (1971). Consider a manufacturing industry in which firms are trying to adapt foreign production technology to the particular economic and social environment of their country. This is a trial-and-error process: the more any firm produces, the more it learns about what works and what does not, and the more efficient it becomes. This process is known as "learning-by-doing" and was a key feature of the Matsuyama model in Chapter II. An alternative way to describe a firm experiencing learning-by-doing is to say it is engaged in "joint production": it simultaneously produces commodities and knowledge. This kind of knowledge, however, cannot be patented. While the commodities can be sold, the knowledge easily leaks out to competing firms through many channels such as interfirm movement of personnel or the "watching and talking" that occurs in an industrial district. Here is the market failure: firms do not have to pay for the knowledge produced by their competitors, so each firm has an incentive to "free-ride" on the production of the industry as a whole.

Government can correct this market failure by granting each firm in the industry a subsidy per unit output, thereby compensating the firm for the value of the knowledge it generates for other firms as a by-product of its production process. Note that this policy is not identical to a policy of protecting domestic firms from foreign competition. Tariff or quota protection raises the price of imports and thereby raises the price domestic firms can charge for their output, which is equivalent to the effect of a production subsidy, but it also raises prices for domestic consumers. Nevertheless, the infant-industry argument is frequently used to justify taxes or quantitative restrictions on imports. One reason for this is ease of administration relative to production subsidies. All governments maintain customs services that collect trade taxes and enforce quotas and other regulations. LDC governments have especially limited administrative capacity, and it is easier to use an existing agency to implement protective tariffs or quotas than to create a new agency to administer production subsidies.

Finally, it is important to remember that the infant-industry argument supports a *temporary* policy to aid import-competing manufacturing. Once the learning process is complete, government help is no longer justified. One of the rebuttals made to the infant-industry argument is that an industry powerful enough to get government help when an infant will surely be powerful enough to retain that help when it is an adult. This is another reason a production subsidy is preferable to import protection: the former is a drain on the government budget while the latter adds to government revenues, so the government has a greater incentive to end subsidies when they are no longer needed.

Reference

Bardhan, Pranab K. 1971. "On Optimum Subsidy to a Learning Industry: An Aspect of the Theory of Infant Industry Protection." *International Economic Review* 12: 54–70.

Selection III.A.1. Typology in Development Theory: Retrospective and Prospects*

A Brief Demonstration of the Comparative Historical Analysis Approach

Consider the development record of three countries representing three distinct types: Kenya, as the relatively land surplus, natural resources rich, human resources deficient, "African type"; Mexico, as the moderately labor surplus, relatively natural resources and human resources rich, "Latin American type"; and Taiwan, as the heavy labor surplus, relatively natural resources poor, human resources rich, "East Asian type." I could devote much more space to spelling out these dimensions of the differences in the initial conditions, the precise degree of labor surplus measured by man-land ratios, the human-capital endowment measured by literacy or educational attainment rates, the natural resources endowment measured by the relative availability of exportable minerals or cash crops (see Table 1). Other dimensions—such as size, with Taiwan and Kenya fairly small, and Mexico somewhat intermediate—could be added as well, leading to a large potential number of typological cells. But this is not my purpose here. Instead, I want to demonstrate the approach at a rather elementary level in application to these three representatives of country types.

The beginning of the transition growth effort is set rather arbitrarily at the point when the system moves from its "colonial" pattern, during which it exports mainly primary products in return for the import of consumer nondurables, deployed to attract workers to the export enclave, and capital goods, deployed to permit the expansion of the export enclave. The next subphase almost invariably is an effort at primary import-substitution, once the newly independent country is able to get control of its foreign exchange earnings, supplemented by foreign capital. The beginning of the transition period has thus been placed around 1960 for Kenya, shortly before independence; in 1930 for Mexico, given that independence was much earlier and that the Great Depression gave a tremendous impetus to import substitution; and around 1952 for Taiwan after both retrocession from Japan and political separation from the mainland. According to Table 1, Kenya can be characterized as small in size, intermediate in labor surplus, poor in human capital, and poor in natural resources. The Latin American type, Mexico, may be viewed as intermediate in size, low in labor surplus, low in human capital, and rich in natural resources. The East Asian type, Taiwan, is small in size, heavy in labor surplus, rich in human capital, and poor in natural resources. . . .

Notice in Figure 1 (row 1) that during the colonial or pretransition era in the three countries under observation, the agricultural sector A is exporting traditional raw materials or mineral products X_A to the foreign country F and is importing producer goods M_P for the expansion of the enclave, along with manufactured consumer nondurables M_{CN} consumed, in addition to the food domestically produced D_F by the domestic households H. Export earnings may, of course, be supplemented by "private" foreign capital—Japanese foreign capital in Taiwan, U.S. foreign capital in Mexico, and British foreign capital in Kenya. The policy setting to sustain this modus operandi of the economy during the preindependence or colonial period in all three country cases includes an industrial policy specifying the role of domestic industry within the colonial system, with minimal infant-industry protection outside those narrow bounds and most colonial investments focused on overheads and services to facilitate the raw material or cash crop export.

There also are major differences in the colonial heritage of the three countries during this pretransition phase: the commodity content of the traditional export X_A was related to what the colonial power is basically interested in procuring. For example, in Kenya and Mexico agricultural research and such infrastructural investments as ports and railways by colonial and early postcolonial governments supported exports of traditional cash crops. In contrast, Japan was almost entirely interested in food production, and Taiwan's exports of rice and sugar were certainly instrumental in focusing attention on the provision of small-scale rural infrastructural investments, such as roads, irrigation, and electricity, and on such organizational innovations as land reform, as early as 1905, and the creation of farmers' associations. This helped prevent the development of a dualistic agriculture and an undue separation between agriculture and nonagriculture. It also set the stage for a dynamic rural economy.

---

*From Gustav Ranis, "Typology in Development Theory: Retrospective and Prospects," in Moshe Syrquin, Lance Taylor, and Larry E. Westphal, eds., *Economic Structure and Performance* (Orlando: Academic Press, 1984) pp. 29–37. Reprinted by permission.

Table 1. Initial Conditions[a]

	Size[b]	Labor surplus[c]	Human capital resources[d]	Mineral, fuel, and other natural resources
Kenya	8,017 (1960)	3.9 (1960)	20 (1962)	Moderate (no coal or oil but good in cash crops).
Mexico	16,589 (1930)	0.7 (1930)	30 (1930)	Rich (zinc, lead, copper, silver, iron ore, mercury, sulphur/oil reserves among largest in world).
Taiwan	7,981 (1950)	9.2 (1950)	50 (1950)	Poor (good coal, some natural gas, little oil).

[a]*Sources:* U.N. Demographic Yearbook (size), FAO Production Yearbook (arable land), UNESCO Statistical Yearbook (literacy), U.S. AID Data book (mineral and fuel resources).
[b]Population, in thousands.
[c]Man-arable land ratio, in hectares.
[d]Literacy rate (%).

The initial transition subphase (row 2 in Figure 1), almost universally adopted in contemporary LDCs, is primary import substitution (PIS).

The progress of PIS can be observed in the ratio of the value of M_{CN} to the value of total merchandise imports M over time, as D_{CN} gradually replaces M_{CN} (see Table 2). This ratio had already reached a low level plateau for Mexico by 1950, indicating that the inevitable termination of this subphase with the exhaustion of domestic markets had already been reached. Taiwan was nearing the completion of this subphase in the early 1960s, after about a decade. Kenya seems to be nearing the point of completing it at this stage. To protect and support the new infant industrial class, public policy effected the gradual displacement of the previously imported nondurable consumer goods M_{CN} by the domestically produced variety D_{CN} in all three cases. X_A continues to fuel the process, with the foreign exchange earnings now, however, used to import the producers' goods M_P needed for the construction of the nondurable-consumer-goods industries in the newly important nonagricultural sector (NA). This description corresponds rather closely to what Chenery (1979, p. 29) calls the early phase of the transition "characterized by the emphasis on primary exports, easy import substitution, and the availability of external aid on soft terms."

Once the initial subphase of transition has run out of steam, developing countries have a rather momentous political decision about the second subphase. The alternatives for the second subphase are illustrated by the divergence between Mexico and Taiwan in row 3 of Figure 1. (It is more instructive to concentrate in what follows on the comparison between Mexico and Taiwan—because of Kenya's much later start and less favorable initial conditions, especially its more limited industrial entrepreneurial capacity.) One possible strategy, adopted by Mexico and certainly representing the majority LDC case, is to shift to a secondary-import-substitution growth path. The (minority) Taiwan case stands in some contrast in that the primary-export-substitution subphase basically consists of exporting to international markets the same nondurable consumer goods (X_{CN}) previously supplied only to the domestic market; while any consumer durables required for final consumption are likely to be mainly imported (M_{CD}).

The third transition subphase (row 4 of Figure 1) follows more or less naturally from the choice of the second subphase. It is fair to say that the objective of all developing countries is ultimately to produce for the domestic market and to export a wide and increasingly sophisticated range of industrial products. In Taiwan this is likely to represent a natural sequel to the primary-export-substitution pattern in that, once the labor surplus has been exhausted, there is a natural tendency to shift toward the more capital-intensive and technology-intensive product mixes for the domestic market and, given its relatively small size, to export such commodities simultaneously, or at least soon. Thus the extent of simultaneity of the secondary-import-substitution/secondary-export-substitution (SIS/SES) growth subphase is very much a function of the size of the domestic market. Note that systems poor in natural resources, like Taiwan, will ultimately be food importers (row 4).

The SIS/EP (export promotion) growth path in Mexico, on the other hand (row 4), indicates the aforementioned desire to export industrial manufactured goods even if the labor-intensive industrial export phase has been "skipped." It is accomplished by superimposing industrial exports on the continued secondary import substitution structure

Figure 1. Comparative subphases of development: (1) colonial or pretransition; (2) initial transition; (3) second transition subphase; (4) third transition subphase. A, agricultural sector; D_{CD}, domestically produced consumer durables; D_{CN}, domestically produced consumer nondurables; D_F, domestically produced food; EP, export promotion; F, foreign country; H, households; M_{CD}, imports of consumer durables; M_{CN}, imports of consumer nondurables; M_F, imports of food-stuffs; M_p, imports of producer goods; NA, nonagricultural sector; PES, primary export substitution; PIS, primary import substitution; SES, secondary export substitution; SIS, secondary import substitution.

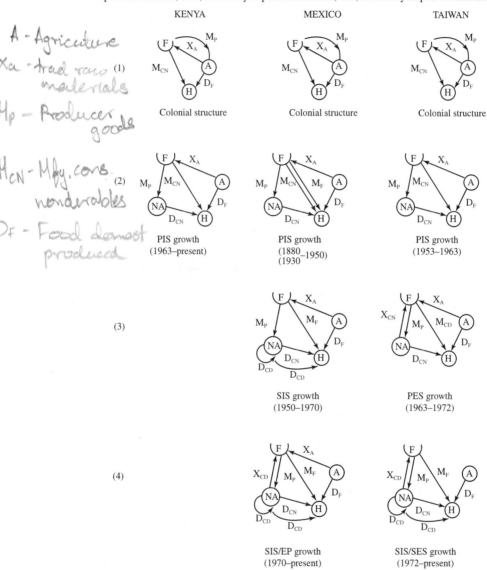

of sub-phase 2—which can be accomplished only through the direct or indirect subsidization of such exports. At a high level of aggregation of industrial exports, it is difficult to distinguish SIS/EP growth from SIS/SES growth. When manufacturing exports are decomposed further, however, it is found that 20% of Mexico's were consumer nondurables in 1970, compared with 41% of Taiwan's (Fei, Ranis, Kuo, 1979). To be emphasized, moreover, is that the Mexican development path continues to be clearly much less export oriented overall and gives evidence of a much lower proportion of manufactured exports than does Taiwan's, even if the focus is on changes over time rather than on absolute levels—thus reducing the impact of differences in country size.

In summary, traditional exports, recently augmented by oil and always by foreign capital, could

Table 2. Primary Import Substitution $(M_{CN}/M)^a$

	1950	1962	1970	1977
Kenya	—	16.4	14.3	6.9
Mexico	5.8	4.3	5.7	4.6
Taiwan	17.2 (53)[b]	8.1 (60)[b]	5.8	2.9

[a]Consumer nondurable industries = 61 leather, etc.; 64 paper, paper board, etc.; 65 textiles; 84 clothing; 851 foot-wear; 892 printed matter. Source: U.N. Yearbook of International Trade Statistics.

[b]Computation not completely comparable to others due to lack of Standard Industrial Classification data. Numbers in parentheses indicate the year to which the data refers.

continue to fuel the industrialization effort in Mexico, including the export of fairly sophisticated capital and consumer durables. In Taiwan the burden of financing continued industrialization was, in contrast, gradually shifted to exports of nondurable consumer goods during the crucial PES phase, thus getting industry to help increasingly in paying the way—in the foreign exchange allocation sense—for its continued expansion. . . .

I am entitled, in fact enjoined, to ask why there is such a deviation in pattern between the East Asian and Latin American types—or as Chenery might put it, why there is such a deviation of the "minority" East Asian type from the "majority" Latin American pattern approaching "average" regression performance. Partly, of course, the Latin American representative, Mexico, is substantially larger in size than the East Asian representative, Taiwan. And, as has already been indicated, it has a much lower level of labor surplus and a much better natural resource endowment. Consequently, even if policies had been identical in the two cases, a less pronounced and probably shorter primary export substitution phase could be anticipated in Mexico, given its generally higher levels of income and lower levels of labor surplus. Its relatively stronger natural resource endowment, even before petroleum became important, can be expected to yield a relatively stronger exchange rate and, by way of the "Dutch disease," be less favorable for potential labor-intensive manufacturing exports typical of the PES subphase.

In addition to these endowment-driven phenomena is the package of policy interventions that further curbed any underlying tendency to move toward more diversified production and exports by way of the PES subphase. This set of policies or strategies is based, in part, on economic forces but also deeply grounded in political economy. In other words, natural resource bonanzas and abundant capital inflows render the exchange rate strong and exert a politico-psychological effect,

making it not only feasible for the system to continue to afford heavy protectionism and the relatively inefficient growth path chosen but also politically difficult to deviate from that path. It is increasingly well understood that a shift from PIS to PES must overcome the resistance of (1) industrialists, reluctant to shift from certain and large unit-profit rates on a small volume in domestic markets to uncertain smaller unit-profit rates on a larger volume in export markets; and (2) the civil service, threatened with a reduction of its influence or power as controls are reduced. The shift also flies in the face of much of organized labor's tendency, especially in the Latin American case, to keep its eye on wage rates rather than the wage bill and the income of working families.

Thus, a country like Mexico, given the relative abundance of its natural resources and easy access to foreign capital, could afford to pay for the prolongation of import substitution and attempt to skip the primary export substitution subphase. It also found this politically much easier to do. Until recently Mexico thought it could afford the relatively costly choice of an SIS/EP growth path in the belief that its natural resources were plentiful enough, foreign capitalists responsive enough, and the employment-distribution outcomes tolerable enough. Unfortunately there now is considerable doubt at least about the second of these assumptions.

The East Asian cases, including the representative, Taiwan, on the other hand, did not have the same options from the outset. The agricultural sector could be viewed as a temporary, if important, source of fuel. But the system's long-run comparative advantage had to be sought else-where: first in its human resources, and then, increasingly, through the contribution of routinized science and technology as during the epoch of modern growth. The secular shortage of natural resources, in particular, and the unwillingness of foreign capital to support continued import substitution in a relatively small domestic market forced an early change in policy toward the use of human resources and away from land-based resources. Once a more market-oriented growth pattern had been established, it began to have its own modus operandi: one of flexibility, responsiveness to changing endowment conditions, and a changing international environment.

References

Chenery, H. B. (1979). *Structural Change and Development Policy*. New York: Oxford University Press.

Fei, J. C. H., G. Ranis, and S. Kuo (1979). *Growth with Equity: The Taiwan Case*. London: Oxford University Press.

Food and Agriculture Organization (1952, 1961). *Production Yearbook*. Rome: Food and Agriculture Organization.

UNESCO (United Nations Educational, Scientific and Cultural Organization) (1963). *Statistical Yearbook*. Paris: United Nations.

United Nations (1949–1950, 1980). *Demographic Yearbook*. New York: United Nations.

United Nations (1951, 1962, 1970, 1980). *Yearbook of International Trade Statistics*. New York: United Nations.

US AID (United States Agency for International Development) (1974, 1975). *Economic Data Book*. Washington, D.C.: Department of State, AID, Division of Statistics and Reports.

Selection III.A.2. An Exposition and Exploration of Krueger's Trade Model*

Krueger (1977) proposed a variant of the H–O model that is a hybrid of it with the specific-factors model.[1] Her model includes an agricultural sector that employs labour and land plus a manufacturing sector that employs labour and capital.[2] Capital and land are immobile between sectors, but capital is mobile within the manufacturing sector, which is modelled as capable of producing any of a large number of manufactured goods. These can be traded internationally, with a large number of countries among which factor prices are assumed to be unequal. The agricultural good—call it food—is also traded internationally.

Technologies in both agriculture and manufacturing are identical internationally and display constant returns to scale. Goods and factors are priced competitively, so that goods prices, together if necessary with factor endowments, determine factor prices in each country. Factor endowments are assumed to differ enough among countries to prevent factor price equalization even in the manufacturing sector. Thus world prices are such that, without interference, no country could produce more than a subset of the manufactured goods.

Countries at different levels of development may, depending also on their endowments of land, produce and perhaps export more or less capital-intensive manufactured goods. Also, unless they have very extreme factor endowments, they will import a variety of manufactured goods, some more capital intensive, and some less, than what they produce themselves. Finally, with exports of food also possible, a country with much land might import *all* manufactured goods, even when it produces only one of them.

All this can be seen in Figure 1. The figure combines Lerner–Pearce unit-value-isoquants for de-termining specialization within the manufacturing sector with the beaker-shaped diagram of the specific-factors literature. Together the two panels determine specialization and factor prices for a country with given factor endowments and facing given (free trade) prices of all goods.

To see how it is done, consider first the top panel, which is similar to figures in Deardorff (1979). Given world prices of three manufactured goods, p_1, p_2, and p_3, unit-value isoquants are drawn as M_1, M_2, and M_3 and are then connected by common tangents to form their convex hull.[3] This hull acts as a unit-value isoquant for manufacturing as a whole. Its slope indicates the ratio of the wage, w, to the rental on capital, r_K, that is implied by the marginal products of these factors in manufacturing. Along straight segments of the hull two goods[4] are produced in the sector, and marginal products of both factors are invariant with respect to small changes in the sector's employment of capital and labour.[5] Along curved portions of the hull, on the other hand, only one manufactured good is produced and marginal products of factors decline as their employment increases.

Given the capital stock $\bar{K}$, therefore, one can infer the behaviour of the manufacturing-sector wage as the level of employment in that sector, L_M, is varied. Moving to the right along the horizontal line at $\bar{K}$ in the top panel, one passes into and out of regions of specialization and non-specialization. For levels of manufacturing employment below L^0, for example, the sectoral capital-labour ratio is above the minimum k_3 needed for specialization in M_3. In this region the manufacturing wage, which is the value of labour's marginal product in manufacturing, V_L^M, is also its value marginal product in producing only M_3. As L_M rises in this region, the capital-labour ratio in M_3 falls, and so must the manufacturing wage. This is shown by the curve w_M in the lower panel.

*From Alan V. Deardorff, "An Exposition and Exploration of Krueger's Trade Model," *Canadian Journal of Economics* 17 (November 1984): 733–740. Reprinted by permission.

[1]The simple H—O model and the specific-factors model are both special cases of a generalized Heckscher–Ohlin model, in which there are arbitrary numbers of goods, factors, and countries. The generalized model retains some but not all of the properties of the simple model. See Deardorff (1979, 1982) and Ethier (1983). The Krueger model, too, is a special case of the generalized H—O model.

[2]The names "land" and "capital" are to indicate that these factors are not mobile between the agricultural and manufacturing sectors and need not otherwise have the properties of actual land and capital. The factor "land," in particular, could be thought of as representing a variety of factors that are specific to agriculture, including agricultural capital.

[3]The diagram can easily accommodate more than three goods, but three can make the points in this paper.

[4]I assume that world prices permit production of no more than two manufactured goods in any freely trading country. With only three manufactured goods in the sector, this is necessary in order to permit factor prices to differ internationally. With a larger number of goods that would not be necessary. The reader may think of figure 1 as including many additional undrawn isoquants, tangent to the hull along the straight segments.

[5]This of course is the familiar phenomenon of the factor-price equalization theorem of Samuelson (1949).

Figure 1

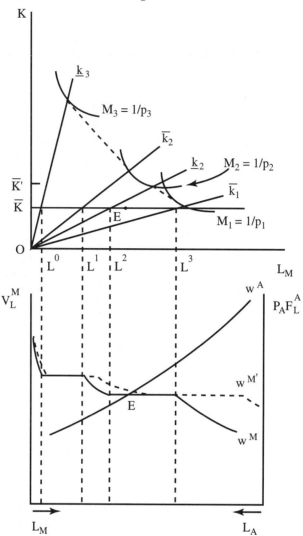

When L_M rises above L^0, the manufacturing sector begins production of M_2 as well as M_3. Factor prices become fixed, since the capital-labour ratio in the sector can now fall without changing the ratios $\underline{k}_3$ and $\bar{k}_2$ employed in each of the two industries. Thus the manufacturing wage in the lower panel becomes flat throughout this region of non-specialization—that is, between L^0 and L^1. Proceeding further to the right, the sector alternates between specialization and non-specialization, and the w_M curve below alternates downward sloping and horizontal segments.

Once constructed in this way, the w_M curve can be combined with another curve representing the agricultural wage, w_A, to determine the equilibrium allocation of labour between the sectors. This is the usual beaker-shaped diagram of the specific-factors model. The horizontal dimension of the beaker is the labour endowment, $\bar{L}$. Agricultural employment, L_A, is measured leftwards from the right-hand wall of the beaker. The agricultural wage must equal the value of the marginal product of labour in agriculture, $P_A F_L^A$. Given the endowment of land, $\bar{T}$, which is specific to that sector, and given also the world price of the agricultural good, P_A, that marginal product is a decreasing function of agricultural employment, as drawn.

Labour-market equilibrium with free mobility of labour between sectors requires the same wage in both. Thus equilibrium is at E, where the w_M

Figure 2

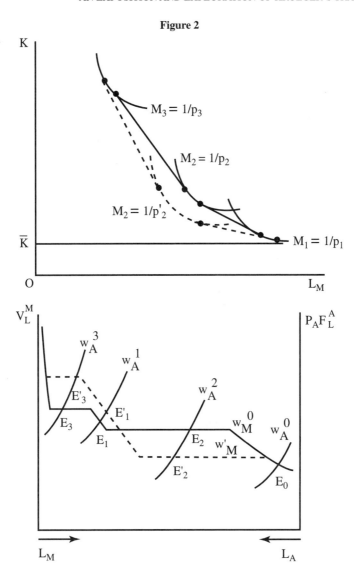

and w_A curves intersect. The pattern of specialization can be inferred from the segment of the w_M curve in which this intersection appears, and other behaviour in the manufacturing sector can be found in the upper panel.[6] As drawn, for example, the equilibrium entails production of both M_1 and M_2, using capital-labour ratios $\bar{k}_1$ and $\underline{k}_2$ in their production.

The diagram lends itself readily to comparative-static analysis and yields conclusions about effects of growth on trade that were a subject of Krueger's

paper. For example, an increase in the capital stock to $\bar{K}'$ shifts the w_M curve proportionately rightward, to w_M'. As drawn, this causes manufacturing to specialize completely in M_2. However, it is also clear that, for other initial equilibria, some capital accumulation can occur without changing the pattern of specialization, the wage, and total manufacturing employment. Note the contrast to the simpler specific factors model where accumulation of either specific factor necessarily raises the wage.

Comparison of economies with different endowments of land can also be done, although I leave the diagram to the reader. An increase in land shifts the w_A curve upward and causes an unambiguous decline in manufacturing employment, together with

[6]The point E in the upper panel could be used as the upper-right corner of an Edgeworth Box, showing allocation of capital and labour between industries M_1 and M_2.

Rybczynski-like effects on separate manufacturing outputs in regions of nonspecialization.[7] One can easily derive Krueger's interesting conclusion that a country with little capital may none the less produce quite capital-intensive manufactured goods if it is also well endowed with land. . . .

Consider now the effects of price increases due to tariffs. These can occur for any good, but I focus primarily on that manufactured good, M_2, of intermediate capital intensity. A rise in p_2 captures all the qualitative effects of any manufactured-good price increase, including what one would find in a model with a larger number of goods. I also briefly note the effects of an increase in the price of the agricultural good.

A rise in the price of M_2 shifts the unit-value isoquant for M_2 radially inward, as shown in Figure 2. The common tangents with the other two isoquants also adjust, rotating to maintain their tangencies. This alters all the capital-labour ratios at which these tangencies occur and thus changes the boundaries of all regions of specialization. The central region, for specialization in M_2, expands, while those for both M_1 and M_3 contract.

Factor prices are also altered by the price change in much of the diagram. Within regions of non-specialization these are most easily inferred from marginal products in M_1 and M_3, since their prices have not changed. In the lower region where M_1 and M_2 are produced, the capital-labour ratio in M_1 must fall. Thus, at world prices the wage falls and

the rental on capital rises. Just the opposite happens in the upper non-specialization region, since k rises in M_3. Finally, in the central region, where only M_2 is produced, all marginal products in terms of M_2 remain constant for given capital-labour ratios. Since the domestic price of M_2 has risen, however, both w and r_K rise in terms of world prices by the amount of the price increase.

These partial equilibrium effects on the wage are shown in the lower panel of figure 2 as altering the shape of the w_M curve from $w_M{}^0$ to $w_M{}'$. The horizontal portions of the curve shift vertically—one up, one down—while the downward sloping centre portion shifts up vertically by the amount of the price increase.

References

Deardorff, A. V. (1979) "Weak links in the chain of comparative advantage." *Journal of International Economics* 9, 197–209.

——— (1982) "The general validity of the Heckscher–Ohlin Theorem." *American Economic Review* 72, 683–94.

Ethier, W. J. (1983) "Higher dimensional trade theory." Chap. 3 of R.W. Jones and P.B. Kenen, eds, *Handbook of International Economics,* vol. 1 (Amsterdam: North-Holland).

Krueger, A. O. (1977) "Growth, distortions, and patterns of trade among many countries." *Princeton Studies in International Finance,* No. 40 (Princeton, NJ Princeton University).

Rybczynski, T. M. (1955) "Factor endowments and relative commodity prices." *Economica* 22, 336–41.

Samuelson, P. A. (1949) "International factor-price equalization once again." *The Economic Journal* (June), 181–97.

[7]For example, as manufacturing employment falls in the region between L^2 and L^3, output of M_2 rises and output of M_1 falls, much as in Rybczynski (1955).

Comment III.A.1. Moving Up the Ladder and Changes in Relative Costs of Factors of Production

Let us think of "capital" in the preceding selection as an aggregate of physical and human capital, as we did in Note III.1 on the AK model. Figure 1 can then be used to show how a country that is accumulating physical and human capital will "move up the ladder" from less to more capital- and skill-intensive goods (goods with higher value-added per worker) without the aid of government policy. The key is Deardorff's result that the w_M curve shifts right as the capital stock increases. Consider a country with a capital stock that is sufficiently small, and consequently a w_M curve that lies sufficiently far to the left, that the intersection of this curve with the w_A curve occurs on its rightmost downward-sloping portion associated with complete specialization of the manufacturing sector in production of M_1, the most labor-intensive good. Now allow this country to accumulate capital. The w_M curve shifts right, causing its intersection with the w_A curve to move up, corresponding to a higher wage and lower rental on capital. With the cost of capital falling relative to the cost of labor, eventually firms can introduce production of the more capital-intensive good M_2 and break even at its international price: the first kink in the w_M curve is reached. As capital continues to accumulate, its increased supply shifts the mix of manufacturing production toward M_2 and away from M_1 rather than driving down the rental rate. When the second kink in the w_M curve is reached, the manufacturing sector is completely specialized in production of M_2. Further accumulation of capital again causes the wage to rise and the rental on capital to fall, and the country gradually moves up to the next step on the ladder.

Protection can of course accelerate the introduction of more capital-intensive production. With a tariff on imports of M_2, firms can introduce its production when the economy has accumulated less capital: as shown in Figure 2, the first kink in the w_M curve occurs further to the right.

Note that Krueger's model, as set forth by Deardorff, assumes constant returns to scale in production of all goods. In contrast, the selections in this section by Balassa and Rodrik emphasize that increasing returns to scale are a very important feature of capital-intensive production. This is one reason why moving up the ladder to more capital- and skill-intensive goods may not be as smooth as Krueger's model suggests it can be.

Selection III.A.3. The Process of Industrial Development and Alternative Development Strategies*

Early Stages of Industrial Development

The Generation of a Surplus in the Primary Sector

Industrial development generally begins in response to domestic demand generated in the primary sector, which also provides investible funds for manufacturing industries. Demand for industrial products and investible savings represent possible uses of the surplus generated in agriculture (understood in a larger sense to include crops, livestock, fisheries, and forestry) or in mining as primary output comes to exceed subsistence needs. More often than not, the surplus generated in the primary sector is associated with export expansion. The effects of primary exports on industrial development, in turn, depend to a considerable extent on input-output relationships and on the disposition of incomes generated in the export sector.

Infrastructure in the form of ports, railways, and roads often represents important inputs for primary exports, and their availability may contribute to the development of industrial activities. In turn, the disposition of incomes generated in the export sector is affected by ownership conditions. In the case of foreign ownership, a substantial part of the surplus may be repatriated, although taxing the earnings of foreign capital does add to domestic incomes. There are leakages in the form of investing and spending abroad and consuming imported luxuries in the case of domestic ownership, too, in a system of plantation-type agriculture and large-scale mining. And, as Douglas North noted, plantation owners have little incentive to finance human investment in the form of general education.

By contrast, in cases where family-sized farms predominate, demand is generated for the necessities and the conveniences of life, as well as for education. This demand contributes to the development of domestic industry, which enjoys "natural" protection from imports in the form of transportation costs. It further contributes to the accumulation of human capital, which finds uses in manufacturing industries.

The process of industrial development may be accelerated if natural protection is complemented

by tariff or quota protection. This last point leads me to the next step in the industrialization process: the first, or "easy," stage of import substitution.

The First Stage of Import Substitution

With the exception of Britain at the time of the Industrial Revolution and Hong Kong more recently, all present-day industrial and developing countries protected their incipient manufacturing industries producing for domestic markets. There were differences, however, as regards the rate and the form of protection. While the industrial countries of today relied on relatively low tariffs, a number of present-day developing countries applied high tariffs or quantitative restrictions that limited, or even excluded, competition from imports.

At the same time, high protection discriminates against exports, through the explicit or implicit taxation of export activities. Explicit taxation may take the form of export taxes, while implicit taxation occurs as a result of the effects of protection on the exchange rate. The higher the rate of protection, the lower will be the exchange rate necessary to ensure equilibrium in the balance of payments, and the lower will be the amount of domestic currency exporters receive per unit of foreign exchange earned.

The adverse effects of high protection are exemplified by the case of Ghana, where import prohibitions encouraged inefficient, high-cost production in manufacturing industries; taxes on the main export crop, cocoa, discouraged its production; and other crops were adversely affected by the unfavorable exchange rate. Ghana's neighbor, the Ivory Coast, by contrast, followed a policy encouraging the development of both primary and manufacturing activities. As a result, it increased its share of cocoa exports, developed new primary exports, and expanded manufacturing industries.

Differences in the policies applied may largely explain why, between 1960 and 1978, per capita incomes fell from $430 to $390 in Ghana in terms of 1978 prices, compared with an increase from $540 to $840 in the Ivory Coast. This has occurred notwithstanding the facts that the two countries have similar natural-resource endowments and, at the time of independence, Ghana had the advantage of a higher educational level and an indigenous civil service.

Indeed, there is no need for high protection at the first stage of import substitution, entailing the

*From Bela Balassa, "The Process of Industrial Development and Alternative Development Strategies," Princeton University International Finance Section, Essays in International Finance No. 141 (December 1980): 4–12, 18–22, 24. Reprinted by permission.

replacement by domestic production of imports of nondurable consumer goods such as clothing, shoes, and household goods, and of their inputs, such as textile fabrics, leather, and wood. These commodities suit the conditions existing in developing countries when they begin the industrialization process: they are intensive in unskilled labor; the efficient scale of output is relatively low, and costs do not rise substantially at lower output levels; production does not involve the use of sophisticated technology; and a network of suppliers of parts, components, and accessories is not required for efficient operation.

The relative advantages of developing countries in these commodities explain the frequent references made to the "easy" stage of import substitution. At the same time, to the extent that the domestic production of these commodities generates external economies in the form of labor training, the development of entrepreneurship, and the spread of technology, there is an argument for moderate infant-industry protection or promotion.

Inward-oriented Industrial Development Strategies

In the course of first-stage import substitution, domestic production will rise more rapidly than domestic consumption, since it not only provides for increases in consumption but also replaces imports. Once the process of import substitution has been completed, however, the growth rate of output will decline to that of consumption.

Maintaining high industrial growth rates, then, necessitates either moving to second-stage import substitution or turning to the exportation of manufactured goods. This choice represents alternative industrial development strategies that may be followed after the completion of the first stage of import substitution. I first consider second-stage import substitution, representing the application of an inward-looking industrial development strategy, and subsequently examine an outward-oriented strategy that does not discriminate against exports, with favorable effects on the exporting of manufactured goods.

The Choice of Second-Stage Import Substitution

In the postwar period, second-stage import substitution was undertaken in several Latin-American countries, in some South Asian countries, particularly India, and in the Central and Eastern European socialist countries. In Latin America, the choice of this strategy reflected the ideas of Raul Prebisch, in whose view adverse foreign-market conditions for primary exports and the lack of competitiveness in manufactured exports would not permit developing countries to attain high rates of economic growth by relying on export production. Rather, Prebisch suggested that these countries should expand manufacturing industries oriented toward domestic markets. This purpose was to be served by industrial protection, which was said to bring additional benefits through improvements in the terms of trade.

Similar ideas were expressed by Gunnar Myrdal. Myrdal influenced the policies followed by India; they were also affected by the example of the Soviet Union, which chose an autarkical pattern of industrial development. And the European socialist countries faithfully imitated the Soviet example, attempting to reproduce it in the framework of much smaller domestic markets that also lacked the natural-resource base of the Soviet Union.

Second-stage import substitution involves the replacement of imports of intermediate goods and producer and consumer durables by domestic production. These commodities have rather different characteristics from those replaced at the first stage.

Intermediate goods such as petrochemicals and steel tend to be highly capital-intensive. They are also subject to important economies of scale: efficient plant size is large compared with the domestic needs of most developing countries, and costs rise rapidly at lower output levels. Moreover, the margin of processing is relatively small, and organizational and technical inefficiencies may contribute to high costs.

Producer durables, such as machinery, and consumer durables, such as automobiles and refrigerators, are also subject to economies of scale. But in these industries economies of scale relate not so much to plant size as to horizontal and vertical specialization, entailing reductions in product variety and the manufacture of parts, components, and accessories on an efficient scale in separate plants.

Reducing product variety will permit longer production runs that lower production costs through improvements in manufacturing efficiency along the "learning curve," savings in expenses incurred in moving from one operation to another, and the use of special-purpose machinery. Horizontal specialization is, however, limited by the smallness of domestic markets in the developing countries.

Similar conclusions apply to vertical specialization, which leads to cost reductions through the subdivision of the production process among plants of efficient size. General Motors, for example, has ten thousand subcontractors, each producing a part or component. This extended division of the production process has permitted General Motors to produce at a substantially lower cost than its U.S. competitors. A number of years ago, Martin Shubik reached the conclusion that without antitrust legislation only General Motors would survive in the United States, and he predicted the disappearance of several small American car producers. Some producers have in fact disappeared since, and without federal support Chrysler would have met a similar fate.

At the same time, the production of parts, components, and accessories has to be done with precision for consumer durables, and especially for machinery. This, in turn, requires the availability of skilled and technical labor and, to a greater or lesser extent, the application of sophisticated technology.

Given the relative scarcity of physical and human capital in developing countries that have completed the first stage of import substitution, they are at a disadvantage in the manufacture of highly physical-capital-intensive intermediate goods and skill-intensive producer and consumer durables. By limiting the scope for the exploitation of economies of scale, the relatively small size of their national markets contributes to high domestic costs in these countries. At the same time, net foreign-exchange savings tend to be small because of the need to import materials and machinery.

The domestic resource cost (DRC) ratio relates the domestic resource cost of production, in terms of the labor, capital, and natural resources utilized, to net foreign-exchange savings (in the case of import substitution) or net foreign-exchange earnings (in the case of exports). In the absence of serious distortions in factor markets, the DRC ratio will be low for exported commodities. It is also relatively low for consumer nondurables and their inputs, in the production of which developing countries have a comparative advantage. For the reasons already noted, however, DRC ratios tend to be high in the manufacture of intermediate goods and producer and consumer durables. The establishment of these industries to serve narrow domestic markets is therefore predicated on high protection, and the rates of protection may need to be raised as countries "travel up the staircase" represented by DRC ratios. This will occur as goods produced at earlier stages come to saturate domestic markets and countries embark on the production of commodities that less and less conform to their comparative

advantage. High protection, in turn, discriminates against manufactured and primary exports and against primary activities in general.

Characteristics of Inward-oriented Development Strategies

In the postwar period, several capitalist countries in Latin America and South Asia and the socialist countries of Central and Eastern Europe adopted inward-oriented industrial development strategies, entailing second-stage import substitution. Capitalist countries generally utilized a mixture of tariffs and import controls to protect their industries, while socialist countries relied on import prohibitions and industry-level planning. Notwithstanding these differences, the principal characteristics of the industrial development strategies adopted in the two groups of countries show considerable similarities.

To begin with, while the infant-industry argument calls for temporary protection until industries become internationally competitive, in both groups of countries protection was regarded as permanent. Also, in all the countries concerned, there was a tendency toward what a Latin-American economist aptly described as "import substitution at any cost."

Furthermore, in all the countries concerned, there were considerable variations in rates of explicit and implicit protection across industrial activities. This was the case, first of all, as continued import substitution involved undertaking activities with increasingly high domestic costs per unit of foreign exchange saved. In capitalist countries, the generally uncritical acceptance of demands for protection contributed to this result; in the absence of price comparisons, the protective effects of quantitative restrictions could not even be established. In socialist countries, the stated objective was to limit imports to commodities that could not be produced domestically or were not available in sufficient quantities, and no attempt was made to examine the implicit protection that pursuit of this objective entailed.

In both groups of countries, the neglect of intra-industry relationships further increased the dispersion of protection rates on value added in processing, or effective protection, with adverse effects on economic efficiency. In Argentina, high tariffs imposed on caustic soda at the request of a would-be producer made formerly thriving soap exports unprofitable. In Hungary, the high cost of domestic steel, whose production was based largely on imported iron ore and coking coals, raised costs for steel-using industries. Large investments in the steel industry, in turn, delayed the substitution of aluminum for steel, although Hungary had considerable bauxite reserves.

Countries applying inward-oriented industrial development strategies were further characterized by the prevalence of sellers' markets. In capitalist countries, the smallness of national markets limited the possibilities for domestic competition in industries established at the second stage of import substitution, while import competition was virtually excluded by high protection. In socialist countries, the system of central planning did not permit competition among domestic firms or from imports, so that buyers had neither a choice among domestic producers nor access to imported commodities.

The existence of sellers' markets provides little inducement to cater to users' needs. In the case of industrial users, it led to backward integration as producers undertook the manufacture of parts, components, and accessories themselves in order to minimize supply difficulties. This outcome, observed in capitalist as well as socialist countries, led to higher costs, since economies of scale were foregone.

Also, in sellers' markets, firms had little incentive to improve productivity. In capitalist countries, monopolies and oligopolies assumed importance; the oligopolists often aimed at the maintenance of market shares while refraining from actions that would invoke retaliation. In socialist countries, the existence of assured outlets and the managers' emphasis on short-term objectives discouraged technological change.

The managers' emphasis on short-term objectives in socialist countries had to do with uncertainty as to the planners' future intentions. In capitalist countries, fluctuations in real exchange rates (nominal exchange rates, adjusted for changes in inflation rates at home and abroad) created uncertainty for business decisions. These fluctuations, resulting from intermittent devaluations in the face of rapid domestic inflation, aggravated the existing bias against exports, because the domestic-currency equivalent of export earnings varied with the devaluations, the timing of which was uncertain.

In countries engaging in second-stage import substitution, distortions were further apparent in the valuation of time. In capitalist countries, negative real interest rates adversely affected domestic savings, encouraged self-investment—including inventory accumulation—at low returns, and provided inducements to transfer funds abroad. Negative interest rates also necessitated credit rationing, which generally favored import-substituting investments, whether the rationing was done by the banks or the government. In the first case, the lower risk of investments in production for domestic than for export markets gave rise to such a result; in the second case, the preference given to import-substituting investments reflected government priorities. Finally, in socialist countries, ideological considerations led to the exclusion of interest rates as a charge for capital and an element in the evaluation of investment projects.

There was also a tendency to underprice public utilities in countries following an inward-oriented strategy, either because of low interest charges in these capital-intensive activities or as a result of a conscious decision. The underpricing of utilities particularly benefited energy-intensive industries and promoted the use of capital.

In general, in moving to the second stage of import substitution, countries applying inward-oriented development strategies deemphasized the role of prices. In socialist countries, resources were in large part allocated centrally in physical terms; in capitalist countries, output and input prices were distorted, and reliance was placed on nonprice measures—import restrictions and credit allocation.

Effects on Exports and on Economic Growth

The discrimination in favor of import substitution and against exports did not permit the development of manufactured exports in countries engaging in second-stage import substitution behind high protection. There were also adverse developments in primary exports, because low prices for producers and consumers reduced the exportable surplus by discouraging production and encouraging consumption. In fact, instead of improving the external terms of trade, import protection turned the internal terms of trade against primary activities and led to a decline in export market shares in the countries in question. Decreases in market shares were especially pronounced in cereals, meat, oilseeds, and nonferrous metals, benefiting developed countries, particularly the United States, Canada, and Australia.

The volume of Argentina's principal primary exports, chiefly beef and wheat, remained, on average, unchanged between 1934–38 and 1964–66, while world exports of these commodities doubled. In the same period, Chile's share of world copper exports, which accounted for three-fifths of the country's export earnings, fell from 28 per cent to 22 per cent.

Similar developments occurred in socialist countries, where the allocation of investment favored industry at the expense of agriculture. In Hungary, exports of several agricultural commodities, such as goose liver, fodder seeds, and beans, declined in absolute terms, and slow increases in production made it necessary to import cereals and meat, which earlier were major export products.

The slowdown in the growth of primary exports and the lack of growth of manufactured exports did not provide the foreign exchange necessary for rapid economic growth in countries pursuing inward-oriented industrial development strategies. The situation was aggravated by the increased need for foreign materials, machinery, and technological know-how, which reduced net import savings. As a result, economic growth was increasingly constrained by the scarcity of foreign exchange, and intermittent foreign-exchange crises occurred when attempts were made to expand the economy at rates exceeding that permitted by the growth of export earnings.

The savings constraint became increasingly binding as high-cost, capital-intensive production at the second stage of import substitution raised capital-output ratios, requiring ever-increasing savings ratios to maintain rates of economic growth. At the same time, the loss of income because of the high cost of protection reduced the volume of savings and, in capitalist countries, negative interest rates contributed to the outflow of funds.

In several developing countries, the cost of protection is estimated to have reached 6 to 7 per cent of GNP. There is further evidence that the rate of growth of total factor productivity was lower in countries engaging in second-stage import substitution than in the industrial countries. Rather than reduce the economic distance between the industrial and the developing countries, then, infant-industry protection may have caused this lag to increase over time. . . .

The Choice of a Development Strategy: Lessons and Prospects

Inward- vs. Outward-oriented Development Strategies

The evidence is quite conclusive: countries applying outward-oriented development strategies performed better in terms of exports, economic growth, and employment than countries with continued inward orientation, which encountered increasing economic difficulties. At the same time, policy reforms aimed at greater outward orientation brought considerable improvement to the economic performance of countries that had earlier applied inward-oriented policies.

It has been suggested, however, that import substitution was a necessary precondition for the development of manufactured exports in present-day developing countries. In attempting to provide an answer to this question, a distinction needs to be made between first-stage and second-stage import substitution.

I have noted that, except in Britain and Hong Kong, the exportation of nondurable consumer goods and their inputs was preceded by an import-substitution phase. At the same time, there were differences among the countries concerned as regards the length of this phase and the level of protection applied. First-stage import substitution was of relatively short duration in the present-day industrial countries and in the three Far Eastern developing countries that subsequently adopted an outward-oriented strategy; it was longer in most other developing countries, and these countries also generally had higher levels of protection.

Nor did all nondurable consumer goods and their inputs go through an import-substitution phase before the Far Eastern countries began to export them. Synthetic textiles in Korea, plastic shoes in Taiwan, and fashion clothing in Singapore all began to be produced largely for export markets. Plywood and wigs, which were Korea's leading exports in the late sixties and early seventies, did not go through an import-substitution phase either.

Wigs provide a particularly interesting example, because they reflect the responses of entrepreneurs to incentives. Korea originally exported human hair to the industrial countries, especially the United States. Recognizing that human hair was made into wigs by a labor-intensive process, entrepreneurs began to exploit what appeared to be a profitable opportunity to export wigs, given the favorable treatment of exports in Korea and the limitations imposed by the United States on wigs originating from Hong Kong. The supply of human hair soon proved to be insufficient, however, and firms turned to exporting wigs made of synthetic hair. Wigs made with synthetic hair were for a time Korea's second-largest single export commodity, after plywood.

The example indicates that entrepreneurs will export the commodities that correspond to the country's comparative advantage if the system of incentives does not discriminate against exports. It also points to the need to leave the choice of exports to private initiative. It is highly unlikely that government planners would have chosen wigs as a potential major export or that they would have effected a switch from human to synthetic hair in making them. Even if a product group such as toys were identified by government planners, the choice of which toys to produce would have to be made by the entrepreneur, who has to take the risks and reap the rewards of his actions. At the same time, providing similar incentives to all export commodities other than those facing market limitations abroad and avoiding a bias against exports will ensure that private profitability corresponds to social profitability. This was, by and large, the case in countries pursuing an outward strategy.

These considerations may explain why Singapore and Taiwan did not need a planning or targeting system for exports. Export targets were in effect in Korea, but the fulfillment of these targets was not a precondition of the application of the free-trade regime to exports or of the provision of export incentives. While successful exporters were said to enjoy advantageous treatment in tax cases and export targets may have exerted pressure on some firms, these factors merely served to enhance the effects of export incentives without introducing discrimination among export products. At any rate, most firms continually exceeded their targets. A case in point is the increase in Korean exports by two-thirds between the second quarter of 1975 and the second quarter of 1976, exceeding the targets by a very large margin.

The reliance on private initiative in countries that adopted an outward-oriented development strategy can be explained by the need of exporters for flexibility to respond to changing world market conditions. Furthermore, government cannot take responsibility for successes and failures in exporting that will affect the profitability of firms. For these reasons Hungary, among socialist countries, gave firms the freedom to determine the product composition of their exports after the 1968 economic reform and especially after 1977.

In the Latin-American countries that reformed their incentive systems in the period preceding the 1973 oil crisis, the expansion of manufactured exports was not based on export targets either. The question remains, however, whether the development of exports in these countries was helped by the fact that they had undertaken second-stage import substitution.

This question can be answered in the negative as far as nondurable consumer goods and their inputs are concerned. Had appropriate incentives been provided, these commodities could have been exported as soon as first-stage import substitution was completed, as was the case in the Far Eastern countries. In fact, to the extent that the products in question had to use some domestic inputs produced at higher than world market costs, exporters were at a disadvantage in foreign markets. It can also be assumed that the inability to exploit fully economies of scale and the lack of sufficient specialization in the production of parts, components, and accessories in the confines of the protected domestic markets retarded the development of exports of intermediate products and producer and consumer durables.

More generally, as a Hungarian economist has pointed out, there is the danger that second-stage import substitution will lead to the establishment of an industrial structure that is "prematurely old," in the sense that it is based on small-scale production with inadequate specialization and outdated machinery. Should this be the case, any subsequent move toward outward orientation will encounter difficulties. Such difficulties were apparent in the case of Hungary and may also explain why, although exports grew rapidly from a low base, their share in manufacturing output remained small in the Latin-American countries that moved toward outward orientation from the second stage of import substitution.

In contrast, in the period following the oil crisis the Far Eastern countries increasingly upgraded their exports of nondurable consumer goods and began exporting machinery, electronics, and transport equipment. For several of these products, including shipbuilding in Korea, photographic equipment in Singapore, and other electronic products in Taiwan, exporting was not preceded by an import-substitution phase. There are even examples, such as color television sets in Korea, where the entire production was destined for foreign markets.

Intermediate goods, machinery, and automobiles require special attention, given the importance of economies of scale on the plant level for the first; the need for product (horizontal) specialization for the second; and the desirability of vertical specialization in the form of the production of parts, components, and accessories on an efficient scale for the third. In all these cases, production in protected domestic markets will involve high costs in most developing countries, and the establishment of small-scale and insufficiently specialized firms will make the transition to exportation difficult. This contrasts with the case of nondurable consumer goods and their inputs, where efficient production does not require large plants or horizontal and vertical specialization.

It follows that, rather than enter into second-stage import substitution as a prelude to subsequent exports, it is preferable to undertake the manufacture of intermediate goods and producer and consumer durables for domestic and foreign markets simultaneously. This will permit the exploitation of economies of scale and ensure efficient import substitution in some products, while others continue to be imported. At the same time, it will require the provision of equal incentives to exports and to import substitution instead of import protection that discriminates against exports. . . .

Policy Prescriptions and Prospects for the Future

The experience of developing countries in the postwar period leads to certain policy prescriptions. First, while infant-industry considerations call for the preferential treatment of manufacturing activities, such treatment should be applied on a moderate scale, both to avoid the establishment and maintenance of inefficient industries and to ensure the continued expansion of primary production for domestic and foreign markets.

Second, equal treatment should be given to exports and to import substitution in the manufacturing sector, in order to ensure resource allocation according to comparative advantage and the exploitation of economies of scale. This is of particular importance in the case of intermediate goods and producer and consumer durables, where the advantages of large plant size and horizontal and vertical specialization are considerable and where import substitution in the framework of small domestic markets makes the subsequent development of exports difficult. The provision of equal incentives will contribute to efficient exportation and import substitution through specialization in particular products and in their parts, components, and accessories.

Third, infant-industry considerations apart, variations in incentive rates within the manufacturing sector should be kept to a minimum. This amounts to the application of the "market principle" in allowing firms to decide on the activities to be undertaken. In particular, firms should be free to choose their export composition in response to changing world market conditions.

Fourth, in order to minimize uncertainty for the firm, the system of incentives should be stable and automatic. Uncertainty will also be reduced if the reform of the system of incentives necessary to apply the principles just described is carried out according to a time-table made public in advance.

Selection III.A.4. Getting Interventions Right: How South Korea and Taiwan Grew Rich*

The Coordination Failure Interpretation

The Argument

First, by 1960 Taiwan and South Korea shared a set of advantageous initial conditions relating to social infrastructure. In particular, both economics had a skilled labour force, relative to their physical capital stock and income levels. These initial conditions made both countries ready for economic take-off, in the sense that the latent return to capital accumulation was high.

Second, for a number of reasons, the economic take-off could not take place under decentralized market conditions. Chief among these reasons are the imperfect tradability of key inputs (and technologies) associated with modern-sector production, and some increasing returns to scale in these activities. These conditions created a situation of coordination failure. In other words, while the rate of return to coordinated investments was extremely high, the rate of return to individual investments remained low.

Third, governments in both countries undertook a set of measures starting in the late 1950s that not only removed some policy-induced distortions, but also served to coordinate and subsidize private investment. These measures included: credit subsidies, tax incentives, administrative guidance and public investment.

Fourth, this active government role helped remove the coordination failure that had blocked industrial growth. As private entrepreneurs responded to these measures, the resulting investments turned out to be profitable not only in financial terms, but in social terms as well.

Fifth, government intervention could be implemented in an effective manner (without leading to rent-seeking behaviour) because initial conditions, once again, had endowed the government in each country with an extraordinary degree of insulation from pressure groups, and with leadership capability over them. Among these initial conditions, a relatively equal distribution of income and wealth was critical.

Sixth, as investment rose as a share of GDP, so did imports of capital goods, as neither country had a comparative advantage in such goods. Thanks to

*From Dani Rodrik, "Getting Interventions Right: How South Korea and Taiwan Grew Rich," *Economic Policy* 20 (April 1995): 78–84, 88–91. Reprinted by permission.

appropriate macroeconomic and exchange rate policies, export supply was adequate to meet the increase in import demand, and rose alongside imports.

Seventh, as a consequence, the increase in exports played a critical role in paying for the imports of capital goods. But it is more appropriate to view this increase in exports as a consequence of the increase in investment demand, rather than the other way around.

A Framework of Analysis

There are two critical claims in this story: (1) both countries were ready for economic take-off by the early to mid-1960s, but economic growth was blocked by a coordination failure; (2) governments in both countries were able to undertake the measures needed to override this coordination failure. The evidence on the presence of a coordination failure is necessarily circumstantial. I think the case is reasonably compelling in view of the likelihood that all of the prerequisites for the existence of a coordination failure were met in the two countries. . . . I rely on an intuitive exposition of the economic logic.

Imagine a small open economy, initially specializing in the production of traditional goods. Alongside there exists a relatively capital-intensive modern sector, which yields higher factor returns when it is viable. The modern sector relies on specialized inputs (e.g. particular labour skills, technologies, intermediate inputs or capital goods). These inputs share the following features: (1) they require well-educated workers but at low cost; (2) they exhibit scale economies; and (3) they cannot be perfectly traded in international markets. The viability of the modern sector requires the local presence of these inputs, which in turn depends (in part) on the existence of a sufficiently well-educated workforce.

Such an economy is ready for take-off if there is enough skilled labour that the modern sector would be viable if a large enough share of the economy's resources were devoted to producing the specialized inputs. Yet there is no certainty that labour and capital move from the traditional sector to the modern sector, leading to specialization in the latter and to higher incomes. The reason is that, because of scale economies, only a large-scale movement of resources is guaranteed to be profitable. From the perspective of an individual investor, it will not pay to invest in the modern sector unless others are doing so as well. The profitability of the modern sector depends on the simultaneous presence of the specialized inputs; but the profitability of producing these inputs in turn depends on the presence of demand from a pre-existing modern sector. It is this interdependence of production and investment decisions that creates the coordination problem.

Coordination failure is least likely to happen when the economy is well endowed with both skilled labour and physical capital, for then production in the modern sector is profitable even when entrepreneurs act in an uncoordinated manner. For economies at the other end of the spectrum—lacking both skilled labour and capital—the coordination issue is moot because the modern sector is not viable in the first place. It is in the intermediate economies most reminiscent of Korea and Taiwan in the early 1960s—well endowed with skilled labour but poor in physical capital—that the coordination problem is most severe.

Markets are known to handle resource allocation poorly in the presence of scale economies and non-tradability: market prices reflect the profitability of different activities only as they are currently undertaken; they do not provide any signals about the profitability of activities that would require a large-scale reallocation of resources within the economy (which, after all, is what economic development is all about). These are, of course, old ideas that go back to Scitovsky's (1954) analysis of pecuniary externalities and Rosenstein-Rodan's (1943) advocacy of big-push policies. More recently, the arguments have been formalized in papers by Faini (1984), Pack and Westphal (1986), Murphy et al. (1989), Krugman (1991), Matsuyama (1991), Ciccone and Matsuyama (1993), Rodríguez-Clare (1993) and Rodrik (1993).

One problem with this literature has been that coordination failure is often presented as a generic problem affecting all kinds of economies. The present framework is more specific about the prerequisites. It highlights the following three prerequisites for a coordination failure to become a serious issue: (1) some degree of non-tradability in the technologies and/or goods associated with the modern sector; (2) economies of scale; (3) a reasonably skilled labour force (but a low endowment of physical capital). The last one clearly applies to the case of Korea and Taiwan. Scale economies are also plausible in many of the modern-sector activities. Hence, non-tradability is the feature that requires additional discussion.

Upon a moment's reflection, it should be clear

that some degree of non-tradability is necessarily associated with the types of goods produced by rich countries. Otherwise poor countries would not remain poor for long: arbitrage through trade would eliminate the disparities. In practice, the non-tradability of modern-sector inputs is observed in a number of different ways. Labour services are for the most part effectively non-traded, so that skilled and specialized workmanship must be locally available. The fixed costs often required to develop these skills lead to scale economies. Intermediate and capital goods are in principle tradable, but they sometimes require either geographic proximity to the final user (as when they are manufactured to suppliers' specifications) or the use of complementary local inputs before they can be put to use (as when skilled workers are needed to operate sophisticated imported machinery). Often, the requisite technologies also have a non-tradable element, in so far as much of the technological capability is tacit and not explicitly codified in designs and blueprints. As Pack and Westphal (1986) put it:

The tacitness of technology leads to problems in its communication over long distances and across social differences, problems which can be overcome—if at all—only at some cost . . . Moreover, knowledge that exists (somewhere in the world) does not exist everywhere simultaneously because there are costs in advertising its mere existence or in discovering its existence through search. Only knowledge that is "close by" is known to exist . . . Another significant channel for inter-industry externalities is the exchange of technological elements in transactions involving intermediate products and capital goods. Indeed many such exchanges leading to better utilization of local resources and to improvements in the design of capital goods have been observed. A salient aspect of these exchanges is the dependence of their outcome on extensive interaction between suppliers and users in iteratively changing both process and product characteristics.

Some examples drawn from the East Asian experience may help bring these points to life.

Case Studies: Hyundai and Lucky-Goldstar

The importance of specialized labour skills and the complementarities they generate across manufacturing activities is illustrated by the experience of Hyundai, one of Korea's huge conglomerates (*chaebol*). Hyundai first entered manufacturing in 1964 by building a cement plant. According to Amsden (1989):

Hyundai used its cement plant as a laboratory to train its managers with background in construction, before assigning them to other manufacturing affiliates. Trainees gained experience in inventory management, quality and process control, capacity planning, and so on, thus spreading basic production skills throughout the Hyundai organization. After Hyundai Cement, the next manufacturing affiliate in the group was founded in 1967 and named Hyundai Motors. Twenty years later it became the first independent automaker from a late-industrializing country to export globally. The first president of Hyundai Motors was a former president of Hyundai Cement.

Korean government policies were highly partial to conglomerates like Hyundai. By giving them access to subsidized capital, the government allowed them to internalize many of the labour market spillovers in the fashion described in the quote.

Hyundai's experience with shipbuilding provides a concrete instance of the imperfect tradability of technology (and its interaction with scale economies). The company started out by importing its basic design from a Scottish firm, but soon found that this was not working out. The Scottish design relied on building the ship in two halves because the original manufacturer had enough capacity to build only half a ship at a time. When Hyundai followed the same course, it found out that the two halves did not quite fit. Subsequent designs imported from European consulting firms also had problems, in that the firms would not guarantee the rated capacity, leading to costly delays. Engines were available from Japanese suppliers, but apparently only at a price higher than that obtained by Japanese shipyards. Moreover, ship buyers would often require design modifications, which Hyundai would be unable to undertake in the absence of an in-house design capability. Only with large enough capacity would it pay for Hyundai to integrate backwards (into design and engine building). In a highly volatile business, scale in turn depended on having access to a steady and reliable customer (a merchant marine). The Korean government provided Hyundai with substantial assistance, as well as an implicit guarantee of markets. Hyundai eventually integrated both backwards and forwards. The government's guarantee came in handy in 1975 when a shipping slump led to the cancellation of foreign orders. President Park responded by forcing Korean refineries to ship oil in Korean-owned tankers, creating a captive demand for Hyundai (Jones and Sakong, 1980).

The chairman of the Lucky-Goldstar group explains the success of his company in this way:

My father and I started a cosmetic cream factory in the late 1940s. At the time, no company could supply us with plastic caps of adequate quality for cream jars, so we had to start a plastic business. Plastic caps alone were not sufficient to run the plastic-moulding plant, so we added combs, toothbrushes, and soap boxes. The plastics business also led us to manufacture electrical and electronic products and telecommunication equipment. The plastics business also took us into oil refining which needed a tanker-shipping company. The oil-refining company alone was paying an insurance premium amounting to more than half the total revenue of the then largest insurance company in Korea. Thus, an insurance company was started. This natural step-by-step evolution through related businesses resulted in the Lucky-Goldstar group as we see it today. (cited in Amsden, 1989)

The quotation clearly illustrates the importance of local inputs and customers as well as of scale economies in fuelling the growth of *chaebol*. While the *chaebol* could thus internalize some of the coordination issues, they were greatly assisted in doing so by government policies which will be discussed in the next section.

In both Korea and Taiwan, the rate of return to capital and profitability in key manufacturing activities rose significantly from the late 1950s on. In Korea, Jones and Sakong (1980) report (based on Hong, 1977) steadily rising real rates of return to capital in manufacturing: the range is 9–18% in mid- to late-1950s, 9–26% in 1962–6, 16–38% in 1967–72, and 17–40% after 1972. The rate of profit in manufacturing steadily rose from 9% in 1951–3 to 16% in 1954–6, to 28% in 1957–62, and to 35% in 1963–70 (Hong, 1993, p. 347). Apparently, investment became more profitable as the investment rate rose.[1] In Taiwan, profitability rates rose in most of the private manufacturing industries after the late 1950s, with the notable exception of textiles and wood products, two major exporting industries (Lin, 1973). Interestingly, the greatest increase in profitability in the post-1963 period (outside food, beverages and tobacco) was experienced by public-sector manufacturing. As will be discussed in the next section, it was public enterprises that supplied many of the key intermediate inputs in Taiwan. This is how Lin (1973) explains the increase in their profits:

The domestic consumption of the output of these non-food industries (which produce petroleum products, chemical fertilizers, industrial chemicals, etc.) increased tremendously during the 1960s, due to increased demand from chemical-using industries (such as those making polyvinylchloride, monosodium glutamate, and paper and pulp for both the export and domestic market), as

---

[1]Little (1994) calculates that the annualized return to investment in Korea was 31.1% during the period 1963–73. However, his calculations also show a reduction in the rate of return subsequently, to 18.3% during 1974–9. He attributes the decline to the HCI drive.

well as from the agricultural sector and the transportation industry.

In other words, intermediate industries became profitable thanks to expanding linkages downstream.

We note finally that in both Korea and Taiwan the way policy-makers viewed the economy and their role in it has parallels with the logic of the co-ordination failure. As the discussion in the following section will make clear, the Korean government has always perceived itself as a mediating agent and a facilitator for bringing about industrial change, through arm-twisting, subsidies or public enterprises as the circumstances may demand. In the words of Pack and Westphal (1986):

In Taiwan, the basic philosophy underlying [the government strategy] is that an economy will undergo certain stages of development, and at each stage there are certain key industries (such as integrated steel mill, large shipyard, and petrochemical plants) which through various linkages will bring about development of the entire economy. This strategy also assumes that government officials know what those key industries are and what policy measures should be adopted to develop these industries. (Hou, 1988, cited in Hong, 1993)

Indeed, Taiwan's Fourth Plan (1965–8) stated:

For further development, stress must be laid on basic heavy industries (such as chemical wood pulp, petrochemical intermediates, and large-scale integrated steel production) instead of end product manufacturing or processing. Industrial development in the long run must be centred on export products that have high income elasticity and low transportation cost. And around these products there should be development of both forward and backward industries, so that both specialization and complementarity may be achieved in the interest of Taiwan's economy. (quoted in Wade, 1990)

Hence, what these governments thought they were doing has much in common with the ideas discussed here.

Government Policies to Subsidize and Coordinate Private Investment

Under the conditions discussed in the previous section, there exists a large role for government intervention. Such intervention can take many different forms. Most directly, policy-makers can coordinate private-sector production and investment decisions through their control over credit allocation, the tax regime and trade policy, as well as through "administrative guidance." Government policies to subsidize investment in the modern sectors of the economy have a large payoff because

they get the private sector to internalize the coordination externalities. The same outcome can also be obtained through investments by public enterprises themselves. The Korean and Taiwanese governments used a combination of these interventions, thereby raising the private return to capital in the modern sectors to the level of the social return. . . .

Direct Co-ordination of Investment Decisions

In addition to providing subsidies, the Korean and Taiwanese governments played a much more direct, hands-on role by organizing private entrepreneurs into investments that they may not otherwise have made. In Taiwan, it was the government that took the initial steps in establishing such industries as plastics, textiles, fibres, steel and electronics. In Korea, in the words of Amsden (1989), "[t]he initiative to enter new manufacturing branches has come primarily from the public sphere. Ignoring the 1950s . . . every major shift in industrial diversification in the decades of the 1960s and 1970s was instigated by the state."

Wade (1990) describes how Taiwan's first plastics plant for PVC was built under government supervision, and handed over to a private entrepreneur upon completion in 1957. In 1966, three more private firms began producing PVC. All four relied on an imported intermediate. Meanwhile, the state-owned Chinese Petroleum Corporation (CPC) produced ethylene, from which an intermediate suitable for processing into PVC could be derived at a cheaper price than the imported intermediate. "So the government forced the four private producers of PVC to merge in a joint venture with the Chinese Petroleum Corporation and another state-owned chemical company, in order to adopt a more efficient ethylene-using production method" (Wade, 1990). (While Wade is not explicit on this, there must have been some scale economies or complementarities that prevented CPC from unilaterally moving into the production of the ethylene-based intermediate, without waiting for a commitment from the downstream producers.) The story illustrates nicely the coordinating role of the government.

A similar account is given regarding fibres:

The government . . . decided to oversee the creation of a rayon-making plant as part of a plan to diversify the textile industry away from cotton fibre. With much help from US advisors it brought together an American synthetic fibre company with several local textiles from both public and private firms, and oversaw negotiations on the terms of the joint venture . . . The resulting corporation

... was the largest "private" firm on the island at the time [1957] ... In 1962, this same state-sponsored rayon company, together with a state financing agency, created another company to make nylon. It started production in 1964. (Wade, 1990)

Private firms soon followed after this state-led entry into synthetic fibres.

Finally, the role of the Taiwanese state was crucial in the early stages of the electronics industry. In 1974 the publicly owned Electronic Research and Service Organization (ERSO) was formed to bring in foreign technology and disseminate it to local firms. ERSO built the country's first model shop for wafer fabrication and entered a technology transfer agreement with RCA. It trained engineers, who later moved to private firms. The strategy led to many private-sector offshoots that commercialized the technology developed by ERSO (Wade, 1990).

It is interesting to note that the Taiwanese authorities' approach to selecting industries to nurture in this fashion was based on what Wade calls "engineering concepts," such as take-off, linkages, gaps, substitutions and incremental extensions—concepts which have little place in conventional welfare economics. Wade mentions that the justification for building a stainless steel plant in the early 1980s was to "fill a gap in Taiwan's infrastructure." Similarly, "[d]evelopments in electronics are being promoted with the aid of an input-output map which highlights gaps in the production structure within Taiwan." This concern with linkages may sit awkwardly with neoclassical development theory, but it does resonate with our emphasis on coordination failures.

In Korea, as we have seen, the presence of large conglomerates helped internalize some of the industrial complementarities that Taiwanese policymakers had to nurture through more direct interventions. But the Korean government was not hesitant to intervene in order to solve what it perceived to be larger-scale coordination problems:

The state masterminded the early import-substitution projects in cement, fertilizers, oil refining, and synthetic fibres, the last greatly improving the profitability of the overextended textiles industry. The government also kept alive some unprofitable factories inherited from the colonial period, factories that eventually provided key personnel to the modern general machinery and shipbuilding industries, which the state also promoted. The transformation from light to heavy industry came at the state's behest, in the form of an integrated iron and steel mill . . . [The government] was responsible for the Big Push into heavy machinery and chemicals in the late 1970s. (Amsden, 1989)

The case of shipbuilding has already been discussed in some detail. As in Taiwan, the government proceeded on the understanding that some industries and products were more "strategic" than others because they were the source of linkages with the rest of the economy. A recent account about how Daewoo got into the shipbuilding business provides yet another example: "Mr Kim [the founder of Daewoo] found himself in shipbuilding in 1978, when the government twisted his arm to take over a near-bankrupt project to build a giant shipyard at Okpo, on Koje island near the southern port of Pusan. "I did not have a chance to say no," says Mr Kim. Indeed, the government simply announced the move when he was out of the country" (*The Economist,* 26 November 1994, p. 81). The Okpo shipyard is now "at the heart of . . . [Korea's] achievement" in shipbuilding.

Use of Public Investment and Public Enterprise

Public enterprises played a very important role in enhancing the profitability of private investment in both countries (perhaps more so in Taiwan than in Korea). They did so by ensuring that key inputs were available locally for private producers downstream. In Taiwan, as we have seen, it was common for the state to establish new upstream industries and then either hand the factories over to selected private entrepreneurs (as happened in the case of glass, plastics, steel and cement) or run them as public enterprises. In Korea, the government established many new public enterprises in the 1960s and 1970s, particularly in basic industries characterized by a high degree of linkages and scale economies. In both countries, public enterprises were the recipient of favourable credit terms, as well as direct allocations from the government budget.

Not only did public enterprises account for a large share of manufacturing output and investment in each country, their importance actually increased during the critical take-off years of the 1960s. This can be seen clearly in Table 1, where data on three comparator countries are also listed. Public enterprises actually accounted for a larger share of GDP in Taiwan than in such "socialist" developing countries as India and Tanzania.

Jones and Sakong (1980) have analysed in detail the expansion of the public enterprise sector in Korea. They find that the Korean government had a coherent set of preferences with respect to where public enterprises should be set up. They summarize their results thus: "the industries chosen for

Table 1. The Importance of Public Enterprise in GDP and Investment (%)

| | | Public enterprise share of | |
	Year	GDP	Capital formation
South Korea	1963–4	6.7	31.2
	1971–2	9.1	21.7
Taiwan	1954–7	11.7	34.3
	1958–61	13.5	38.1
	1962–5	14.1	27.7
	1966–9	13.6	28.0
	1970–3	13.3	30.5
	1974–7	13.6	35.0
India	1966–9	6.5	29.6
Tanzania	1970–3	12.7	48.2
Argentina	1978–80	4.6	19.6

Sources: Wade (1990, Table 6.2), from original data in Short (1983), except for public enterprise share in GDP for Korea, which is from Jones and Sakong (1980, Table 24).

the public-enterprise sector [were] characterized by high forward linkages, high capital intensity, large size, output-market concentration, and production of non-tradables or import substitutes rather than exports." These are exactly the characteristics associated with a high potential for coordination failure.

The case of POSCO, Korea's state-owned integrated steel mill, is instructive (if not entirely representative). In the early 1970s, the Korean government was turned down by the World Bank when it applied for a loan to construct a steel plant. The World Bank's argument was that Korea did not have a comparative advantage in steel. The government was undeterred and went ahead nonetheless. The government provided POSCO with capital assistance as well as infrastructure subsidies (for the construction of water supply facilities, port facilities, an electricity generating station, roads and a railway line). In addition, the government supported downstream industries to ensure demand for POSCO's production. POSCO eventually became, by the World Bank's reckoning, "arguably the world's most efficient producer of steel" (cited in Wade, 1990), supplying Korean minimills with steel at below world prices. Moreover, the presence of POSCO stimulated in turn a wide range of upstream industries, ranging from capital goods to spare parts. Between 1977 and 1984, the local content of POSCO's output rose from 44 to 75%.

References

Amsden, A. H. (1989). *Asia's Next Giant: South Korea and Late Industrialization,* Oxford University Press, New York.

Ciccone, A. and K. Matsuyama (1993). "Start-up Costs and Pecuniary Externalities as Barriers to Economic Development," NBER Working Paper No. 4363.

Faini, R. (1984). "Increasing Returns, Non-Traded Inputs, and Regional Development," *Economic Journal.*

Hong, W. (1977). "Trade, Distortions and Employment in Korea," Korea Development Institute, Seoul.

—— (1993). "Trade and Development: The Experience of Korea and Taiwan," in G. Hasson (ed.), *International Trade and Development,* Routledge, London.

Hou, C.-M. (1988). "Strategy for Economic Development in Taiwan and Implications for Developing Economies," paper presented at the Conference on Economic Development Experiences of Taiwan, Taipei, 8–10 June.

Jones, Leroy and Il Sakong (1980). *Government, Business, and Entrepreneurship in Economic Development: The Korean Case,* Harvard University Press, Cambridge, MA.

Krugman, P. (1991). "History versus Expectations," *Quarterly Journal of Economics.*

Lin, C.-Y. (1973). *Industrialization in Taiwan, 1946–72: Trade and Import-Substitution Policies for Developing Countries,* Praeger, New York.

Little, I. M. D. (1994). "Trade and Industrialization

Revisited," unpublished paper, Nuffield College, Oxford.

Matsuyama, K. (1991). "Increasing Returns, Industrialization and Indeterminacy of Equilibrium," *Quarterly Journal of Economics.*

Murphy, K., A. Shleifer and R. Vishny (1989). "Industrialization and the Big Push," *Journal of Political Economy.*

Pack, H. and L. E. Westphal (1986). "Industrial Strategy and Technological Change: Theory versus Reality," *Journal of Development Economics.*

Rodríguez-Clare, A. (1993). "The Division of Labor and Economic Development," unpublished manuscript, Stanford University, CA.

Rodrik, D. (1993). "Coordination Failures and Government Policy in Intermediate Economies: A Model with Applications to East Asia and Eastern Europe," unpublished manuscript, Columbia University, New York.

Rosenstein-Rodan, P. (1943). "Problems of Industrialization of Eastern and South-Eastern Europe," *Economic Journal.*

Scitovsky, T. (1954). "Two Concepts of External Economies," *Journal of Political Economy.*

Short, R. (1983). "The Role of Public Enterprises: An International Statistical Comparison," International Monetary Fund, Washington, DC.

Wade, R. (1990). *Governing the Market: Economic Theory and the Role of Government in East Asian Industrialization,* Princeton University Press, Princeton, NJ.

Note III.A.3. Tradeability of Intermediate Goods, Linkages, and Bottlenecks

In the preceding selection Rodrik claims that the Taiwanese government intentionally and successfully fostered forward and backward "linkages" among domestic producers of intermediate and final goods. In contrast, Riedel (1976, p. 320) claims that Taiwan is a "prime example" of a country "characterized by a rather 'footloose,' import-dependent industrial structure" and states "it might be argued that Taiwan has been so successful precisely because its industrial structure lacks backward linkages." These differing perceptions of Taiwanese industry and trade reflect a more general difference of opinion regarding the tradeability of intermediate goods and the desirability of domestic linkages versus reliance on imports (or exports, if intermediate goods are produced domestically but then sold to foreign downstream users).

When intermediate goods are used to produce a final product, they must fit together, literally and figuratively. This may require that downstream and upstream producers be in regular consultation in order to make necessary modifications. As Rodrik points out, geographic proximity reduces the cost of such consultation. The relationships between downstream assemblers and upstream suppliers have been especially well studied for the automobile industry. Transnational auto companies from Europe, Japan, or the United States typically rely on their home suppliers when they begin production in LDCs (Dobson and Yue 1997), but often later try to establish supplier networks within the host country (see, e.g., Doner 1997, pp. 220–21), consistent with the need for geographic proximity.

The tolerance for "poor fit" among components may be much greater for labor-intensive industries such as apparel and toys than for capital-intensive industries such as automobiles, and components for the former set of industries may be more standardized. In these industries it may be considerably less difficult for a downstream producer to find the right inputs abroad or for an upstream producer to find a foreign assembler for which his part will work. (We discussed the relative ease of trading standardized versus differentiated products in Note II.1.) It may therefore be much more feasible to have an "unlinked," import-dependent structure for consumer nondurables than for consumer durables and machinery. This could explain why Riedel and Rodrik perceived Taiwan so differently. Riedel was writing in the mid-1970s when Taiwan could still be described as a "labor-abundant LDC" and its manufacturing production was more concentrated in light industry than it was two decades later when Rodrik was writing.

This discussion suggests that the case for a policy of promoting linkages is much weaker when appropriate imported inputs are easily available. Balassa (1980, p. 14) notes that the four Latin American countries engaged in second-stage import substitution that he studied (Argentina, Brazil, Colombia, Mexico) "did not, however, provide exporters with a free choice between domestic and imported inputs. Rather, in order to safeguard existing industries, exporters were required to use domestic inputs produced under protection." Forcing downstream firms to rely on domestic upstream production is risky, because if upstream production develops only slowly (due perhaps to difficulty in mastering the requisite technology), it becomes a bottleneck for expansion of all the downstream producers. One can also argue that diversification for its own sake reduces both static and dynamic economies of scale (the latter generated, for example, by learning-by-doing) achievable by any given industry. Weinhold and Rauch (1999) find that productivity growth in the manufacturing sector in LDCs is higher when production is more specialized.

References

Balassa, Bela. 1980. *The Process of Industrial Development and Alternative Development Strategies.* Princeton University International Finance Section, Essays in International Finance No. 141 (December).

Dobson, Wendy, and Chia Siow, Yue, eds. 1997. *Multinationals and East Asian Integration.* Singapore: IDRC Books and ISEAS.

Doner, Richard F. 1997. "Japan in East Asia: Institutions and Regional Leadership." In Peter J. Katzenstein and Takashi Shiraishi, eds., *Network Power: Japan and Asia.* (Ithaca, N.Y.: Cornell University Press), pp. 197–233.

Riedel, James. 1976. "A Balanced Growth Version of the Linkage Hypothesis: Comment." *Quarterly Journal of Economics* 90 (May): 319–22.

Weinhold, Diana, and James E. Rauch. 1999. "Openness, Specialization, and Productivity Growth in Less Developed Countries." *Canadian Journal of Economics* 32 (August): 1009–1027.

III.B. FOREIGN CONTACT AND TECHNOLOGY TRANSFER

Note III.B.1. Learning in International Production Networks

Economists have typically modeled technology transfer as an arm's-length phenomenon. Firms are not *taught* the new technology. Rather they engage in purposive imitative activity on their own (e.g., Grossman and Helpman 1991), employ machinery and equipment that embody foreign knowledge (e.g., Coe, Helpman, and Hoffmaister 1997), license the new technology, and so on. However, as Rodrik points out in his selection in the preceding subsection, it is difficult to learn new technology from a distance. Keller (forthcoming, pp. 9–10) writes, "Many careful studies of technology and how it is transferred conclude that only the broad outlines of technological knowledge are codified—the remainder remains 'tacit.' . . . [N]on-codified knowledge is usually transferred through demonstrations, through personal instructions, as well as through the provision of expert services." There is a growing body of evidence that for LDC firms in particular, a major and perhaps predominant source of technology transfer (and transfer of managerial know-how) is instruction by developed country buyers: producers seeking cheaper suppliers of inputs and distributors seeking cheaper suppliers of final goods. Pack and Page (1994, pp. 220–221) state:

> The motivation of the purchasers is to obtain still lower-cost, better quality products from major suppliers whose products account for a significant percentage of profits. To achieve this they are willing to transmit tacit and occasionally proprietary knowledge from their other OECD suppliers. Such transfers of knowledge are more likely to characterize simpler production sectors such as clothing and footwear or more generally those older technologies that are not hedged by restrictions adopted to increase appropriability, such as patents and trade secrets.

One example of such evidence is a study by Egan and Mody (1992), who surveyed U.S. buyers operating in LDCs, including "manufacturers, retailers, importers, buyers' agents, and joint venture partners" (p. 322). They found that

> [b]uyers also render long-term benefits to suppliers in the form of information on production technology. This occurs principally through various forms of in-plant training. The buyer may send international experts to train local workers and supervisors. . . . Buyers may also arrange short-term worker training in a developed country plant. (p. 328)

Rhee, Ross-Larson, and Pursell (1984) surveyed Korean exporters of manufactures. Their findings (p. 61) were similar to those of Egan and Mody:

> The relations between Korean firms and the foreign buyers went far beyond the negotiation and fulfillment of contracts. Almost half the firms said they had directly benefited from the technical information foreign buyers provided: through visits to their plants by engineers or other technical staff of the foreign buyers, through visits by their engineering staff to the foreign buyers.

The Rhee, Ross-Larson, and Pursell survey was conducted in 1975. More recently Korea and the other advanced East Asian countries have played the role for LDCs that foreign buyers used to play for them. The role of Korea in developing garment exports from Bangladesh is an especially interesting case that is studied in Rhee and Belot (1990). This case is part of the broader phenomenon of "triangle manufacturing" (Gereffi 1999) in East Asia: countries such as Korea and Taiwan continue to accept and fulfill the orders of developed country buyers for labor-intensive goods, but have "outsourced" the actual production to countries with lower wages.

This process of learning foreign technology can be thought of as taking place within international production networks or "global commodity chains" (Gereffi 1994, 1999). This theoretical framework predicts that once LDC firms are incorporated into the "bottoms" of the chains, their learning will continue by movement up the chains. There are two types of chains: "producer-driven" and "buyer-driven" (Gereffi 1994). In the former, large manufacturers play the central roles in coordinating the production networks. Producer-driven chains are typical in capital- and technology-intensive industries such as automobiles, aircraft, computers, semiconductors, and heavy machinery. In the latter, large retailers, branded marketers, and branded manufacturers play the coordinating roles. Buyer-driven commodity chains are typical in labor-intensive, consumer goods industries such as garments, footwear, toys, housewares, and consumer electronics. Profitability is highest at the tops of the chains where barriers to entry are greatest: scale and technology in producer-driven chains, design and marketing expertise in buyer-driven chains.

In buyer-driven commodity chains, one mode through which learning is predicted to continue is *organizational succession:* from assembler to original equipment manufacturer (OEM) to original brand-name manufacturer (OBM), which is from more subordinate, competitive, and low-profit positions to more controlling, oligopolistic, high-profit positions. In the apparel industry, Gereffi (1999) finds that LDC firms that have parts provided to them for assembly learn how to find on their own the parts needed to make the product according to the design specified by the buyer (and may then subcontract the assembly); firms that have reached this level learn how to design and sell their own merchandise, becoming branded manufacturers (and may then subcontract the production, becoming branded marketers). Additional study is needed to determine whether this pattern of learning is common in other consumer goods industries. At the same time, work is needed to reconcile the kind of findings discussed in this Note with econometric analyses (surveyed in Rodrik 1999, Chapter 2) that conclude that more productive firms export, but exporting does not make firms more productive.

In producer-driven commodity chains, one mode of learning is through "vertical linkages" established between foreign subsidiaries of the large manufacturers that coordinate the production networks and host country suppliers. Saggi (2002, p. 213) writes:

> Mexico's experience with FDI is illustrative of how such a process works. In Mexico, extensive backward linkages resulted from FDI in the automobile industry. Within five years of investments by major auto manufacturers there were 300 domestic producers of parts and accessories, of which 110 had annual sales of more than $1 million (Moran 1998). Foreign producers also transferred industry best practices, zero defect procedures, and production audits to domestic suppliers, thereby improving their productivity and the quality of their products.

References

Coe, David T., Elhanan Helpman, and Alexander W. Hoffmaister. 1997. "North-South R&D Spillovers." *Economic Journal* 107, no. 440: 134–149.

Egan, Mary Lou, and Ashoka Mody. 1992. "Buyer-Seller Links in Export Development." *World Development* 20, no. 3: 321–334.

Gereffi, Gary. 1994. "The Organization of Buyer-Driven Global Commodity Chains: How U.S. Retailers Shape Overseas Production Networks." In Gary Gereffi and Miguel Korzeniewicz eds., *Commodity Chains and Global Capitalism* ed. (Westport, CT: Praeger), pp. 95–122.

———. 1999. "International Trade and Industrial Upgrading in the Apparel Commodity Chain." *Journal of International Economics* 48, no. 1: 37–70

Grossman, Gene, and Elhanan Helpman. 1991. "Endogenous Product Cycles." *Economic Journal* 101, no. 408: 1214–1229.

Keller, Wolfgang. "International Technology Diffusion." *Journal of Economic Literature,* forthcoming.

Moran, Theodore. 1998. *Foreign Direct Investment and Development* (Washington, DC: Institute for International Economics).

Pack, Howard and John M. Page, Jr. June 1994. "Accumulation, Exports, and Growth in the High-performing Asian Economies." *Carnegie-Rochester Conference Series on Public Policy* 40: 199–257.

Rhee, Yung Whee, Bruce Ross-Larson, and Garry Pursell. 1984. *Korea's Competitive Edge: Managing the Entry into World Markets* (Baltimore: Johns Hopkins University Press).

Rhee, Yung Whee, and Therese Belot. 1990. "Export Catalysts in Low-Income Countries: A Review of Eleven Success Stories." World Bank Discussion Paper No. 72, Washington, DC.

Rodrik, Dani. 1999. *Making Openness Work: The New Global Economy and the Developing Countries* (Washington, DC: Overseas Development Council).

Saggi, Kamal. 2002. "Trade, Foreign Direct Investment, and International Technology Transfer: A Survey." *World Bank Research Observer* 17 no. 2: 191–235.

Selection III.B.1. Technology Gaps Between Industrial and Developing Countries: Are There Dividends for Latecomers?*

Firms have several alternatives for obtaining new technology that, if mastered, yield a higher level of TFP [total factor productivity] for any given capital-labor ratio. These alternatives include: (a) the purchase of new equipment; (b) direct foreign investment; (c) the purchase of technology licenses for domestic production of new products or the use of new processes; (d) the use of nonproprietary technology, including that obtained from purchasers of exports; (e) acquisition of knowledge from returning nationals who have been educated or have worked in industrial countries and from nationals who remain in industrial countries; and (f) domestic research and development and efforts in reverse engineering.

All these possibilities, except for the research and development efforts, represent an attempt to move toward international best practice by transferring technologies available abroad. The research and development alternative may have an element of aiding the identification, modification, and absorption of foreign technology rather than generating a completely indigenous technology.

The Experience of Two Successful Asian Economies

This section describes some of the means by which two of the fastest-growing newly industrializing economies—Korea and Taiwan (China)—were able to shift toward an international production function.[1]

Korea and Taiwan (China)

Until the mid- to late 1970s neither Korea nor Taiwan (China) employed explicit technology policies. The main exceptions were the restrictions placed on direct foreign investment and a fairly perfunctory review of technology licensing agreements in Korea. The ability of the two countries to close the initial productivity gaps was a result of firms' responses to the incentives contained in national economic policies. Among these policies

were: (a) the relative neutrality of the foreign trade regime with respect to profitability between domestic and foreign sales and the relatively low variance in protection across sectors; (b) export targeting in Korea and undervaluation of the real exchange rate in Taiwan (China) to encourage exports to a greater extent than would have been the case given the protection afforded to new industries in the domestic market; (c) a relatively undistorted labor market that, along with some movement toward market rates of interest (particularly in Taiwan, China), kept the wage-rental ratio closer to its scarcity value than in other developing countries.

The responses to these incentives led to a set of favorable but unintended technological consequences. For example, as a result of the rapid rates of export growth that these policies encouraged, there was a substantial inflow of nonproprietary technology, embodied in equipment and in the knowledge provided by customers (Westphal, Rhee, and Pursell 1981). This inflow was greater because exports and production increased most in older labor-intensive sectors in which technology from industrial countries was less protected. Technology and knowledge were relatively easy to acquire and absorb in these sectors even without a large stock of highly educated engineers. Much of the relevant information was based on mechanical knowledge rather than on electronic, biological, or chemical principles that would have required more formal education of employees.

Moreover, the machinery that was employed to manufacture the increased output was quite labor-intensive, in response to the low wage-rental ratio (Ranis 1979; Rhee and Westphal 1977). The simple equipment and the absence of continuous processing were conducive to minor innovations for increasing productivity, which were often suggested by blue-collar workers. Thus, the trade and factor price regimes were complementary and were conducive both to obtaining static gains in output and to fostering the move toward best practice. In this period, until the late 1970s, it is likely that much of the growth in productivity was the unplanned consequence of getting the prices right. Dollar and Sokoloff (1990) find that TFP growth in labor-intensive sectors in Korea exceeded that in the capital-intensive sectors. Technology policy was implicit in the standard economic policies, and technological learning complemented the conven-

*From Howard Pack, "Technology Gaps Between Industrial and Developing Countries: Are There Dividends for Latecomers?" *World Bank Economic Review Supplement* (1992): 295–99. Reprinted by permission.

[1]The evidence for the interpretations in this section is set forth in Dahlman and Sananikone (1990), Westphal, Rhee, and Pursell (1981), Pack and Westphal (1986), and Pack (1992).

tional economic responses, stimulating further growth in production and exports as a consequence of reduced production costs.

In the 1970s a more explicit policy toward technology acquisition appeared. This policy differed in the two economies. In Korea the growth of large local firms was encouraged by the use of selected credit and other instruments. As domestic real wages increased and newer lower-wage competitors entered the international market, large Korean firms were encouraged to acquire the technological capacity to enter sectors that were more capital- and technology-intensive and to achieve best-practice productivity (Pack and Westphal 1986). Information about production technology in these more complex producer goods sectors was likely to be more closely guarded than in the consumer goods industries, and importers in industrial countries were less likely to transfer such technology. The Korean government encouraged firms to obtain technology licenses, acquire advanced equipment, and engage in their own research and development.

In Taiwan (China) the transfer of knowledge in the consumer industries, in which the early export drive was concentrated, was similar to that in Korea (Pack 1992). As Taiwan entered newer areas, however, it did not encourage the growth of large-scale firms capable of substantial research and development. The industrial structure was characterized by many small firms, reflecting the prevalence of high interest rates and the limited use of selected credit directed to larger firms. Therefore Taiwan utilized central institutions such as the Industrial Technology Research Institute, as well as technology diffusion institutions such as the China Productivity Center, to introduce new technologies, develop new products and processes, diffuse knowledge of them, and scan international markets for both products and processes (see Dahlman and Sananikone 1990). Moreover, in the newest sectors the ability to attract back Taiwanese nationals or to utilize the knowledge of those who remain abroad has been critical (Pack 1992).

Efforts to obtain international knowledge will have lower payoffs if they are not accompanied by a growth in the stock of capital per worker. Capital, both physical and human, can be partly supplied by other countries in the form of direct foreign investment. The remarkable development of Singapore, for example, demonstrates the potency of externally provided capital and skills in facilitating a rapid movement to international best practice (Lim and Fong 1991). In the initial period of rapid growth of industrial productivity, Korea and Taiwan (China) benefited from both capital accumulation and the move toward international best practice.

It may be conjectured that the extent of the shift in the production function would have been less if the sectors in which exports grew had been those in which these countries were close to world best practice. In Chile, a more recent example of improved policies, TFP growth has been much slower. Part of the explanation for this may lie in its emphasis on primary exports, minerals, and agricultural products. It is likely that these sectors in Chile were much closer to international best practice than were the industrial growth sectors in Korea and Taiwan (China). Moreover, in some of the expanding export sectors, such as electronics, the best-practice frontier was itself shifting rapidly, and the two Asian economies were able to take advantage of this. If these conjectures are correct, early proponents of import-substituting industrialization such as Singer and Prebisch may have been correct in their intuition of the dynamic (TFP growth) benefits of industrialization. They were mistaken, however, in their emphasis on import substitution rather than export growth as the process for realizing these benefits.

In both economies, people (and the knowledge they embody) who have been educated abroad return because of the high wages made possible by growing exports. Purely domestically oriented firms with smaller sales bases could not have offered sufficiently high wages to attract them. The newly acquired international knowledge was embedded in a framework conducive to efficiency. Competitive pressures led to a search within plants for better productivity performance. As a result, imported practices were improved, and purely domestic efforts were made to increase productivity.

The Interaction of Knowledge Acquisition, Investment, and Human Capital

Both Korea and Taiwan (China) invested extensively in education and in the accumulation of substantial physical capital. The ratio of investment to GDP increased from relatively low levels to more than 30 percent in the 1980s. Figure 1 elucidates the process. Initially the economy is at point A on production function f_0. As physical and human capital accumulation proceed, it moves to point E on production function f_1. The shift to the higher production function is realized because of the growing utilization of international best practice. Note, however, that the benefit from this accumulation of knowledge would have been less—$AB < DE$—if capital per worker had not grown (Nelson 1973).

Figure 1

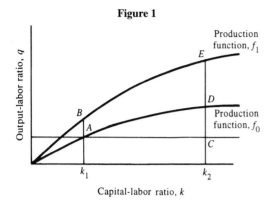

Thus the size of the benefit from the growing import of knowledge and from local efforts to increase productivity depends on the stock of physical investment and skills complementing local unskilled labor.

References

Dahlman, Carl J., and Ousa Sananikone. 1990. "Technology Strategy in the Economy of Taiwan (China): Exploiting Foreign Linkages and Investing in Local Capability." World Bank, Industry and Energy Department, Washington, D.C.

Dollar, David, and Kenneth Sokoloff. 1990. "Patterns of Productivity Growth in South Korean Manufacturing Industries, 1963–1979." *Journal of Development Economics* 33: 309–27.

Lim, Linda Y. C., and Pang Eng Fong. 1991. *Foreign Direct Investment and Industrialization in Malaysia, Singapore, Taiwan, and Thailand.* Development Centre Studies. Paris: Organization for Economic Cooperation and Development.

Nelson, Richard R. 1973. "Recent Exercises in Growth Accounting: New Understanding or Dead End?" *American Economic Review* 73: 162–68.

Pack, Howard. 1992. "New Perspectives on Industrial Growth in Taiwan." In Gustav Ranis, ed., *Taiwan: From Developing to Mature Economy.* Boulder, Colo.: Westview.

Pack, Howard, and Larry E. Westphal. 1986. "Industrial Strategy and Technological Change: Theory versus Reality." *Journal of Development Economics* 22: 87–128.

Ranis, Gustav. 1979. "Industrial Development." In Walter Galenson, ed., *Economic Growth and Structural Change in Taiwan.* Ithaca, N.Y.: Cornell University Press.

Rhee, Yung W., and Larry E. Westphal. 1977. "A Microeconometric Investigation of Choice of Technique." *Journal of Development Economics* 4: 205–38.

Westphal, Larry E., Yung W. Rhee, and Garry G. Pursell. 1981. "Korean Industrial Competence: Where it Came From." World Bank Staff Working Paper no. 469, Washington, D.C.

Selection III.B.2. The Potential Benefits of FDI for Less Developed Countries*

In 1993, direct foreign investment was the largest single source of external finance for developing countries, accounting for about half of all private resource flows. Following the virtual disappearance of commercial bank lending to these countries in the 1980s, many countries liberalized their restrictions on incoming foreign investment. Some countries even tilted the balance towards foreign firms by offering special incentives: in Czechoslovakia, joint ventures pay lower income taxes than domestic enterprises; foreign firms in much of the Caribbean receive income tax holidays, import duty exemptions and subsidies for infrastructure.

The pro-investment policies of the 1990s are very different from the wave of nationalizations which drove out foreign investment in many regions during the 1960s and 1970s. The new attitude is in part driven by the need for alternative sources of new capital, and in part driven by increasing skepticism about import-substituting trade and investment strategies. India, within one year, liberated both its trade regime and opened up its internal market to foreign investors, leading to what Indian Finance Secretary Montek Ahluwalia dubbed a "quiet economic revolution." [1]

Foreign Investment and Technology Transfer: Morocco and Venezuela

One reason to subsidize incoming foreign investors is the idea that they convey benefits which cannot be completely captured by the firm, such as new technology. Although technology transfer occurs through many different avenues, foreign investment could play an unusual role in several respects. New technology may not be commercially available and innovating firms may refuse to sell their technology via licensing agreements. In this case, alliances with innovating firms or close proximity to these firms may be the best means of learning about new technology. Foreign investment may also provide the competition necessary to stimulate technology diffusion, particularly if local firms are protected from import competition. Finally, foreign investors may provide a form of worker training which cannot be replicated in domestic firms or purchased from abroad, such as managerial skills. Technology diffusion may occur

through labor turnover as domestic employees move from foreign to domestic firms.

The studies on Morocco and Venezuela tested the magnitude of technology transfer from foreign subsidiaries (or joint ventures) to wholly domestically owned firms. [2] This is a working definition for the idea of a technology "spillover." I explored two related questions. First, to what extent do joint ventures or foreign subsidiaries perform better than domestic firms? Second, are there technology spillovers from firms with foreign equity investment to domestically owned firms?

Multinational enterprises (MNEs) are defined as any firm with foreign equity participation in the firm. Firm performance is measured as either labor productivity (output per worker) or a multi-factor productivity measure—which measures the productivity of all the firm's inputs simultaneously. Technological change is defined as an increase in output after taking into account all increases in the various inputs in production. Obviously, this concept of technological change is not an engineering concept. Technological change is synonymous with increases in observed productivity at the enterprise level.

In both Morocco and Venezuela, MNEs—firms with foreign equity participation—exhibit much higher levels of productivity. In Venezuela, increases in foreign equity participation also led to higher productivity growth. There is strong evidence that an infusion of foreign investment does more than simply provide additional capital to enterprises—it is also accompanied by knowledge transfers which lead to better firm performance.

Yet there is no evidence that the benefits accruing to joint ventures or local subsidiaries of multinationals are diffused to domestic firms. In other words, foreign investors provide direct benefits to those firms receiving the investment, but there are no "spillovers" to other plants. In fact, an increased multinational presence in Venezuela hurt the productivity of domestic competitors, in part because the multinationals took market share away from domestic plants.

These research results reinforce earlier case study evidence as well as interviews with plant managers in Morocco and Venezuela. The lack of technology transfer to domestic competitors can be explained by the limited hiring of domestic employees in higher level positions, very little labor mobility between domestic firms and foreign subsidiaries, limited subcontracting to local firms, no

*From Ann Harrison, "The Benefits of FDI," *Columbia Journal of World Business* (Winter 1994): 7–9. Reprinted by permission.

research and development by subsidiaries, and few incentives by multinationals to diffuse their knowledge to local competitors.

Foreign Investment and Breaking into Export Markets: Mexico

Anecdotal evidence, mostly derived from case studies in developing countries, suggests that the process of breaking into foreign markets can be very difficult. In order to export, firms must obtain information about foreign tastes and establish distribution channels in foreign markets. One obvious way for firms to learn about export markets is to observe other exporters who have already acquired experience selling abroad. Those exporters may be other domestic firms, or multinationals.

Case studies suggest that multinationals bring information about export markets to local producers, enabling them to access markets abroad. In Bangladesh, one Korean garment producer started a booming export business, triggering the entry into export markets of hundreds of new Bangladeshi garment producers. If this phenomenon is widespread, then governments may want to encourage foreign investors in sectors with high export potential but little know-how about foreign markets.

In a research project with Brian Aitken at the IMF and Gordon Hanson at the University of Texas, we test for the possibility that other exporters can reduce the cost of foreign market access for a firm contemplating the jump into export markets.[3] In particular, we examine whether locating near multinational exporters helps a firm to gain information about the export process.

Ours is the first study which provides statistical evidence on the role of foreign firms as "catalysts" for other exporters.[4] The basis for our study is 2,113 Mexican manufacturing plants over the period between 1986 and 1990. Following Mexico's trade reform in 1985, many Mexican manufacturers turned away from the previously protected domestic market towards outside markets. These changes during the 1980s allow us to identify the kinds of firms most likely to become exporters.

The analysis shows that multinational firms in Mexico do act as export catalysts. Domestic firms located near multinational exporters are much more likely to export than other firms. This suggests that foreign investors bring valuable information about export possibilities to developing countries—which then "spills over" to domestic rivals. One implication is that firms wishing to break into export markets should locate in areas with a concentration of multinational export activity. Another implication is that governments may wish to encourage exporters or potential exporters to locate near each other.

One policy option for developing countries is to encourage export processing zones (EPZs), special economic zones reserved for exporting firms. These zones often confer special benefits to exporters, such as duty-free imported inputs, tax holidays, or subsidized infrastructure. Our research suggests one unintended benefit of EPZs: by forcing potential exporters to locate near each other, they may help reduce the costs of breaking into foreign markets. However, EPZs need to be carefully designed to avoid isolating exporters from other enterprises. EPZs in countries like Jamaica, for example, are placed in fortress-like enclaves which isolates exporters from other enterprises.

Notes

1. Montek S. Ahluwalia, "India's Quiet Economic Revolution," *Columbia Journal of World Business* 29 (1), (Spring 1994): 6–12.

2. See: Mona Haddad and Ann Harrison, "Are there positive spillovers from direct foreign investment? Evidence from panel data for Morocco," *Journal of Development Economics* 42, (1993); and, Brian Aitken and Ann Harrison, "Do Domestic Firms Benefit from Foreign Direct Investment?" World Bank Policy Research Working Paper 1248, February 1994.

3. See: Brian Aitken, Gordon Hanson, and Ann Harrison, "Spillovers, Foreign Investment, and Export Behavior," World Bank, November 1994.

4. The term, export "catalyst," however, is not our creation. See the paper by Y. Rhee and T. Belot, "Export Catalysts in Low-Income Countries," World Bank, 1989, which presents case study evidence of this phenomena.

Note III.B.2. Trade as Enemy, Handmaiden, and Engine of Growth

The effect of international trade on the economic growth of less developed countries has long been one of the most passionately debated subjects in the field of development economics. In this concluding Note we describe three views that span the range from negative to positive, all of which can draw some support from this section and the preceding one.

It is easiest to make the case for trade as the enemy of growth by building on the open economy version of the Matsuyama model, already discussed in the Overview for Chapter II. Recall that in Matsuyama's model in Selection II.3 all productivity increase takes place through learning-by-doing in the manufacturing sector. Productivity in agriculture (or, more broadly, in the primary product sector) is constant by assumption. Now consider a country that is well endowed with natural resources compared with labor (and also relative to human and physical capital, if these are assumed to be used more intensively in manufacturing). Comparative advantage will lead this country to export primary products and import manufactures. Exports of primary products draw workers out of manufacturing and thereby reduce productivity growth both in that sector and in the aggregate (since there is no productivity growth in primary products). In this way trade reduces growth in per capita income in countries with abundant natural resources. It is interesting that the sociology literature on "dependency" and "world systems" comes to the same conclusion, that development of "peripheral" countries is hindered by their exports of primary products to "core" industrialized countries. For a summary of these arguments and a review of empirical studies see Crowly, Rauch, Seagrave, and Smith (1999).

We should note that the case for trade as the enemy of growth does not depend on the assumption that productivity in the primary product sector is constant. Obviously, learning-by-doing and other forms of productivity increase occur in this sector in the real world. What is crucial is only that this productivity increase tends to be substantially less rapid or less able to be sustained for a long period than it is in manufacturing.

The phrase "trade as handmaiden of growth" is from the title of an article by Kravis (1970). He states (p. 869),

> The term "engine of growth" is not generally descriptive and involves expectations which cannot be fulfilled by trade alone; the term 'handmaiden of growth' better conveys the notion of the role that trade can play. One of the most important parts of this handmaiden role for today's developing countries may be to serve as a check on the appropriateness of new industries by keeping the price and cost structures in touch with external prices and costs.

This supportive role can be usefully compared with that of financial development. As discussed in Chapter V, a well-developed financial system increases the efficiency of investment by helping to channel savings to the most profitable projects. One way that trade can increase the efficiency of investment is by helping to ensure that the most privately profitable projects are also the most socially profitable ones. Foreign competition discourages investors from attempting to establish monopoly positions in small domestic markets and from producing substandard goods. Other ways in which trade can increase the efficiency of investment are enabling producers to realize economies of scale through exporting, and relieving bottlenecks that might reduce the returns to well-conceived downstream investments or divert resources from them.

The view of trade as the engine of growth takes technological progress rather than investment to be the ultimate source of growth, and sees imported ideas as the main determinant of technological progress in LDCs. In other words, trade with more technologically advanced countries acts as a vehicle for the flow of knowledge from them and thereby drives growth in less advanced countries. Foreign direct investment from more to less developed countries plays the same role. (This contemporary view of trade as the engine of growth must be distinguished from the older view, in which growth is driven by expansion of land devoted to production of technologically stagnant primary products to meet the demand of industrialized countries.) This view is associated with the work of Romer (1993a, 1993b). Some specific mechanisms through which firms in LDCs absorb knowledge through contact with technologically advanced countries were discussed in the preceding Note and selections in this section.

The three views are not necessarily inconsistent with each other. Trade could be an enemy of growth for resource-abundant countries and a handmaiden or engine of growth for other countries. The mechanisms by which trade is said to operate as a handmaiden or engine of growth are not mutually exclusive.

References

Crowly, Angela M., James E. Rauch, Susanne Seagrave, and David A. Smith. 1998. "Quantitative Cross-National Studies of Economic Development: A Comparison of the Economics and Sociology Literatures." *Studies in Comparative International Development* 33 (Summer): 30–57.

Kravis, Irving B. 1970. "Trade as a Handmaiden of Growth: Similarities Between the Nineteenth and Twentieth Centuries." *Economic Journal* 80 (December): 850–72.

Romer, Paul M. 1993a. "Two Strategies for Economic Development: Using Ideas and Producing Ideas." *Proceedings of the World Bank Annual Conference on Development Economics 1992*. Washington, DC: World Bank.

Romer, Paul M. 1993b. "Idea Gaps and Object Gaps in Economic Development." *Journal of Monetary Economics* 32 (December): 543–73.

CHAPTER IV

Human Resources

Overview

Human development, as measured by the Human Development Index, involves not only economic growth but also raising educational attainment and improving health. Education and health are therefore the subjects of the first two sections of this chapter. The chapter continues with a section on population issues and concludes with a section on issues specific to women, who play a critical role not only in determining demographic outcomes but also in determining education and health outcomes.

Education is not just a contributor to human development in its own right but may also contribute to growth in per capita incomes. Education is a form of saving, causing accumulation of human capital and growth of aggregate output if human capital is an input in the aggregate production function. Taking a more disaggregated view, greater educational attainment helps a country to "move up the ladder" from production and export of less to more skill- and capital-intensive goods. An educated workforce is also better able to absorb foreign technology. We begin section IV.A on education with a Note that tries to trace these different views to differences in thinking about how education is used in production processes. A key distinction is whether education should be seen as a direct input to production or as a means of learning the production process and improving it to yield more output for given levels of inputs.

In the first selection, George Psacharopoulos summarizes evidence that social returns to investment in education in less developed countries are greatest for primary education and least for university education. The following Comment notes that he has updated his findings twice without changing this basic message. An additional Comment describes possible upward and downward biases from computing rates of return to educational investments using differences between earnings of more and less educated workers.

In Selection IV.A.2, the World Bank shows that the high-performing East Asian countries concentrated their educational expenditure on primary and secondary rather than university education, in effect following the prescription implied by the differences in returns to educational investment reported in the selection by Psacharopoulos. These East Asian countries have thereby achieved universal primary enrollment and higher rates of secondary enrollment than would be predicted given their income levels. This selection ends with a description of a massive school construction program in Indonesia that greatly increased primary school enrollment in rural areas. In the following selection, Esther Duflo confirms that children who received more schooling as a result of this program earned higher wages when they became adults.

If education is indeed important for development, how should countries go about it? In Selection IV.A.4 Eric Hanushek stresses the uncertain effectiveness of putting more resources into education. The studies of education in less developed countries that he surveys are especially negative concerning any benefits from higher teacher-pupil ratios. Anne Case and Angus Deaton in Selection IV.A.5 find, on the other hand, that higher teacher-pupil ratios (smaller class sizes) raised the enrollment, educational attainment, and numeracy test scores for black students under the apartheid system in South Africa. They argue that the special circumstances created for blacks by apartheid, including restrictions on residential choice by black parents and wide variations in class size, make their estimates more reliable than those surveyed by Hanushek. The effects of resources on educational outcomes in both more and less developed countries remain highly controversial, but Hanushek notes that there is broad agreement that schools make a difference: it is what makes a good school that is in doubt.

The extent of poor health and nutrition in the less developed compared to the more developed world is documented in Exhibit IV.B.1. In Selection IV.B.1, Michael Kremer notes that the tremendous advances in medical technology that occurred in the last century have made it possible for countries to achieve high life expectancy at relatively low levels of per capita income. Pharmaceuticals such as antibiotics and vaccines that control infectious diseases were a key part of these technological advances. Kremer shows, however, that in recent years few new drugs have been invented that address the disease burden in poor, tropical countries. He discusses reasons why pharmaceutical firms may lack incentives to invent such drugs, and what policies are appropriate to mitigate this problem.

Whereas Selection IV.B.1 focuses on problems with the supply of drugs for tropical diseases, Selection IV.B.2 by Edward Miguel and Michael Kremer focuses on problems with the demand for these drugs. There may be inadequate incentives to use the drugs that do exist because of "treatment externalities": other people benefit when an individual receives drug treatment for an infectious disease because he can no longer infect them, but his willingness to pay is determined only by the benefit to himself. Miguel and Kremer carefully measure externalities in rural Kenya from deworming treatment, and find that the health benefits from the external effects on untreated children are three times as large as the direct health benefits to children receiving treatment.

The infectious disease in less developed countries that is receiving the most publicity is AIDS. Selection IV.B.3 by the World Bank projects that by the year 2020 AIDS will account for 37.1 percent of LDC deaths from infectious diseases among people aged 15 to 59. The selection goes on to discuss the factors that contribute to the spread of AIDS and the policies that can bring this epidemic under control.

The section of this chapter on population begins with an Exhibit showing current demographic data such as birth and death rates and population age distributions. It also shows projected population growth by country and by geographic area for the period 2000–2050. World population is projected to grow from about 6 billion in 2000 to about 9 billion in 2050. The Note following this Exhibit draws a distinction between the effects on development of a large world population and a large average family size, the former the consequence and the latter a major cause of rapid population growth. It is perhaps surprising that a larger world population cannot be shown to have any negative impact on development, and if anything the contrary position is consistent with the evidence. On the other hand, in the following selection Nancy Birdsall notes the existence of substantial evidence that children from large families have lower educational attainment. Higher educational attainment is widely believed to make an essential contribution to economic growth, however much the exact mechanism may be in dispute. In the remainder of her selection Birdsall summarizes the findings of studies of the determinants of fertility, the major factor influencing family size. Female education above about four years has one of the strongest and most consistent negative associations with fertility. Family planning programs are also found to have some negative effect on fertility. Section IV.C concludes with a selection showing that continued high fertility in sub-Saharan Africa has led to a very young population and consequent low working age population per dependent. Sub-Saharan Africa has therefore not had the opportunity to benefit from the "demographic dividend" described in the following Comment, whereby a high number of workers per dependent stimulates saving and investment rates, potentially generating more rapid economic growth.

Women play an especially important role in determining health and family size. The previous two sections of this chapter thus lead naturally to the concluding section, IV.D, on gender and development.

In view of findings that more educated women have smaller and better nourished families, it is ironic that education of women in poor countries has lagged behind that of men. Selection IV.D.1 documents this "gender gap." It is largest in sub-Saharan Africa, South Asia, and the Middle East and North Africa. In Latin America and East Asia the gender gap in education has largely disappeared. The selection also discusses why the gender gap persists. Interactions of traditional practices with incentives provide part of the answer. For example, girls may be more valued in the home because by tradition they do much more housework than boys, and parents therefore have less incentive to send girls to school. Selection IV.D.1 also considers gender inequality in employment and earnings and political influence.

The most extreme manifestation of gender inequality is lower female survival rates. These give rise to the phenomenon of "missing women" in many less developed countries, where the ratio of women to men in the population is substantially below the level that would be expected in the absence of discrimination. In Selection IV.D.2, Stephan Klasen and Claudia Wink refine and update the estimates of the number of missing women, finding that both the percentage and absolute number of missing women are greatest in South Asia, followed closely by China. The main cause of missing women appears to be neglect of health care for girls, with sex-selective abortions a secondary cause that is increasing in importance.

Women are severely underrepresented in positions of political power in both more and less developed countries. Some countries have responded to this underrepresentation by imposing quotas for women in elected office. Since the mid-1990s, one-third of village council head positions in India have been randomly reserved for a woman: in these councils, only women can be elected to the position of head. In the final selection of this chapter, Raghabendra Chattopadhyay and Esther Duflo find that in rural areas administered by these councils, there is more investment in infrastructure such as provision of drinking water that is mostly demanded by women.

One theme that runs through most of this diverse chapter is the importance of government as a provider of services, whether the services are education, health care, or family planning. Selection IV.D.3 shows that governments are also becoming more involved in redressing discrimination against women. The leaders in this area, however, are mainly nongovernmental organizations (NGOs). For example, Selection IV.D.1 concludes with evidence that microfinance organizations have increased the bargaining power of women in their households by making it easier for them to get credit to finance small business ventures and acquire other valuable assets. In Chapter V, microfinance NGOs are discussed in detail in Selection V.5.

IV.A. EDUCATION

Note IV.A.1. Three Views of the Contribution of Education to Economic Growth

It is possible to think of the role of education in a production process in at least three different ways. These correspond to three different views of how education contributes to economic growth.

First, we can think of uneducated and educated workers as perfectly substitutable inputs to production. Two workers who have completed primary school, say, are equivalent to one worker who has completed secondary school. Put differently, labor is homogeneous and can be measured in terms of "efficiency units." Holding constant the number of actual workers, an increase in the average level of education of the labor force increases the size of the labor force measured in efficiency units. This increase in the number of efficiency units per worker generates greater output per worker since labor is an input to production. Growth in the average years of schooling per worker is thus associated with growth in output per worker.

Second, uneducated and educated workers can be seen as imperfectly substitutable inputs to production. In constructing a suspension bridge, say, three (or 30) workers with a primary school education cannot replace one civil engineer. With educated and uneducated labor treated as different inputs, different production processes can be thought of as making more or less intensive use of educated relative to uneducated labor. If the aircraft and the apparel industries face the same costs of hiring educated and uneducated labor, the aircraft industry will employ a higher ratio of educated to uneducated workers because of the nature of its production process compared with that of the apparel industry. As we saw in Selection III.A.2 by Deardorff and in the following Comment, increasing the number of educated workers helps a country to "move up the ladder" to production of more technologically sophisticated goods. Consider the following newspaper report on Thailand (Stier 1993):

> In the past decade, Thailand's economic growth has been fueled by export-oriented industries dependent on an abundance of low-skilled, low-wage workers. But those industries have lost much of their competitive advantage because Thai wage increases have outpaced labor costs in other developing Asian nations—including China, Indonesia, Vietnam and India—that are now competing in international trade. Thus within a relatively short period of industrialization, Thailand is under pressure to make a transition to more sophisticated, higher-skilled industries. . . . A serious problem for Thailand in taking the economy to a higher level is that the education and skill of the work force has not kept pace. More than 80% of Thai workers in a labor force of 34 million has a primary school education or less. Only about 4% of school-age youth make it through universities. Thailand has a shortage of skilled workers across the board—from doctors to auditors and engineers to middle managers. . . . Analysts say it could be years before Thailand's education system produces enough skilled workers for the next stage of industrialization.

Lack of educated workers is also seen as an obstacle to the continued rapid economic growth of Thailand in Selection IV.A.2 by the World Bank.

An industry's production process could make intensive use of educated labor because it requires sophisticated monitoring and quality control, say, or because technology is rapidly changing and highly educated workers are needed to learn it. Generalizing from the latter case, the role of educated labor in any production process can be seen as learning or creating technology that generates more output holding levels of inputs constant, rather than as an input itself. This leads to the third view of the contribution of education to the economic growth of less developed countries: it helps them absorb foreign technology.

Jess Benhabib and Mark M. Spiegel (1994) report evidence in favor of this third view and against the first view that education is a direct input to production. In cross-country regressions they found that growth of GDP per capita from 1965 to 1985 was not significantly affected by *growth* in average years of schooling in the labor force during that period, but was positively affected by the *level* of average years of schooling in 1965. They interpret the positive effect of the initial level of education as measuring the ability to absorb technology from abroad and create appropriate domestic technologies during the following 20 years, and interpret the lack of any effect of growth of education as showing that education is not a direct factor of production like physical capital. However, other research has cast doubt on both the results of Benhabib and Spiegel and their interpretation. Alan B. Krueger and Mikael Lindahl (2001) show that the measure of the growth of schooling used by Benhabib and Spiegel is unreliable, tending to bias estimates of its impact on growth of per capita GDP toward zero. Lant Pritchett (2003) argues that the failure of per capita GDP growth rates to increase despite the continued increase in the average level of schooling (see Exhibits I.B.1 and I.B.2) means that Benhabib and Spiegel's finding of a positive association between the initial level of education and subsequent growth must not reflect a true causal relationship.

In the international trade literature there is considerable evidence that as less developed countries catch up to the education levels of more developed countries, they "move up the ladder" from exports of products that intensively use uneducated workers to exports of products that intensively use educated workers (see, e.g., Romalis 2004). Yet little work has been done to connect this international trade evidence to growth in output per worker in manufacturing and ultimately to growth in GDP per capita. In conclusion, we judge that the three views of the contribution of education to economic growth described in this Note are as yet insufficiently precisely formulated and inadequately tested to inform educational policy.

References

Benhabib, Jess, and Mark M. Spiegel. 1994. "The Role of Human Capital in Economic Development: Evidence from Aggregate Cross-Country Data." *Journal of Monetary Economics* 34 (October): 143–173.

Krueger, Alan B., and Mikael Lindahl. 2001. "Education for Growth: Why and For Whom?" *Journal of Economic Literature* 39 no. 4: 1101–1136.

Pritchett, Lant. 2003. "Does Learning to Add Up Add Up? The Returns to Schooling in Aggregate Data." Kennedy School of Government Working Paper (November).

Romalis, John. 2004. "Factor Proportions and the Structure of Commodity Trade." *American Economic Review* 94 (March): 67–97.

Stier, Ken. 1993. "Thailand Caught Between Economic Levels." *Los Angeles Times* (November 8): D2.

Selection IV.A.1. Economic Impact of Education*

In this paper I review the evidence on the economic impact of education produced in the past thirty years and compile a number of lessons from the literature that might be useful to policy makers. And since no field is without controversy, I also review the major debates that have surrounded human capital theory and its applications.

The Evidence

The evidence on the economic impact of education can be divided into two distinct types: micro and macro.

Micro

If expenditure on education is a kind of investment leading to the formation of human capital, either for the individual or for society at large, one should be able to estimate the rate of return to this investment. In its most simplified form, the rate of return to investment in education (r) can be estimated by dividing the permanent annual benefits stream due to education ($Y_1 - Y_0$) by the cost of obtaining such education ($Y_0 + C_1$),

$$r = \frac{(Y_1 - Y_0)}{S(Y_0 + C_1)}$$

In this case Y_1 and Y_0 could refer to the mean earnings of workers who are literate and illiterate, respectively, S to the number of years of schooling it takes for someone to become literate, and C_1 to the annual cost of keeping someone in school. Note the appearance of Y_0 in the denominator of the expression, representing the opportunity cost of attending school rather than working in the labor market.

There are several ways to examine rates of return to education: by whether the returns refer to the individual investor or to society at large, namely, the private or social rate of return; by the country's level of economic development; by the type of curriculum—say, general or vocational secondary education; by type of economic sector the worker is in, say, modern wage employment or self-employment; and by gender.

Hundreds of studies have been conducted in the past thirty years on the profitability of investment

in education in a large number of countries across the dimensions cited above (for a summary see Psacharopoulos 1985). Figures 1 and 2 offer an impressionistic summary of the results of these studies. The figures are impressionistic in the sense that I want the reader to focus on the structure of the returns to education rather than the exact percentage points represented by the vertical axes. As a point of reference I give an illustrative 10 percent opportunity cost of capital or alternative discount rate. This might be more realistic in a developed country than in a developing country, although the 10 percent rate could be defended in a developing country setting if the country could borrow internationally for investment in education at this interest rate.

The first notable result of the application of rate of return studies to education is that the rates are not far off the yield of more conventional investments. The returns to investment in education in advanced industrial countries are roughly the same as those of investment in physical capital. By contrast, the returns to education in developing countries stand at a much higher level relative to industrial countries. This reflects both the continuing scarcity of human capital in poorer countries and barriers to the allocation of funds to human capital investment, so that the returns to any kind of capital (physical or human) equalize at the margin.

A typical pattern, found since the early days of rate of return estimation in education, is that returns decline by level of schooling. Thus, returns to primary education are higher relative to returns to secondary education, and the latter are higher than returns to university education. This finding, corroborated in study after study, has fundamental policy implications.

Another result worth noting is the difference between social and private rates of return. Because of the public subsidization of education in all parts of the world, private rates are typically several percentage points higher than social rates of return. By definition, the cost in a private rate-of-return estimation refers only to what the individual pays out of his or her pocket, whereas the cost in a social rate of return estimation refers to the full resource cost of someone attending school. The distortion incurred by the public subsidization of education means that, in some instances, individuals will find it profitable to pursue education to a given level whereas, from the point of view of society, this investment is not profitable. The maximum distor-

*From George Psacharopoulos, *The Economic Impact of Education: Lessons for Policymakers* (San Francisco: ICS Press, 1991), pp. 8–15. Reprinted by permission.

Figure 1. The returns to investment in education by level and country type.

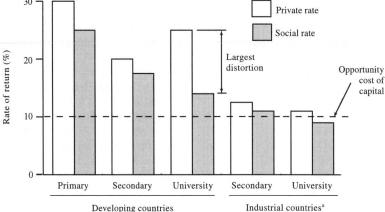

ᵃThe rate of return for primary education in industrial countries is undefined because of universal enrollment at this level of schooling.
Source: Based on Psacharopoulos 1985.

Figure 2. The returns to education by economic sector, curriculum type, and gender.

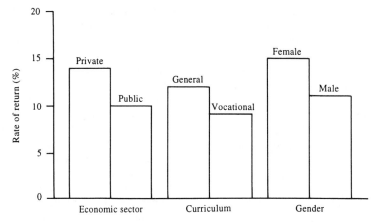

Source: Based on Psacharopoulos 1985.

tion between the private and the social rates refers to education at the university level. This level is more heavily subsidized in most countries relative to any other level.

Figure 2 presents three additional rate-of-return patterns that have been found in studies in many countries, irrespective of whether the rate of return is social or private. The first comparison shows that the return to education is typically higher in the private or competitive sector than in the public sector. It is well known that the public pay structure is very compressed, leading to a lower rate of return relative to estimates based on earnings in the private sector, where there is no limit to rewards. To the extent that private sector earnings truly approximate a worker's productivity, rates of return based

on earnings in the competitive sector provide a better fix for the scarcity of human capital than rates of return based on civil service pay scales. The latter, however, are very important for explaining the private behavior of individuals in seeking different levels and types of education. Given the dominance of the public sector in hiring university graduates in any kind of country, a private rate-of-return estimation using civil service data is very appropriate, if not a must, in understanding the demand for university education. However, a private earnings base would be more appropriate for setting priorities for educational investment in a given country.

The second pattern in Figure 2 provides a well documented yet highly counterintuitive finding:

within a given level of education, say, secondary schooling or university education, the more general the curriculum the higher the returns to education. This startling finding is due to two factors. First, the unit cost of vocational education, at any level, is higher than that of general education, because of the more specialized faculty and equipment that vocational education entails. Second, graduates of general programs are more flexible in fitting a wide spectrum of occupations—and perhaps are more easily trained on the job—than graduates of vocational programs that are earmarked to enter a particular occupation (to put it at the extreme, mechanical watch repairers).

The last pattern presented in Figure 2 refers to the worker's gender. Investment in the education of females often yields a higher rate of return than investment in the education of males. This finding could also be considered counter-intuitive, in the sense that males typically earn much more than females. One must remember that the rate of return to investment in education is a *relative* concept, comparing the *difference* between more- and less-educated workers with the cost of their education. A major component of the cost is the forgone earnings of the worker while studying, which can lead to a higher rate of return for females than for males.

Macro

If investment in education yields returns at the individual or social level, this must be reflected at the level of the economy. Growth accounting in the post-World War II period was based on the so-called aggregate production function.

Output = f(Land, Labor, Capital)

expressing a country's output (measured by gross domestic product) as a function of the traditional triad of factors of production: land, measured in terms of cultivated area; labor, measured in terms of the number of persons or man-hours worked; and capital, measured in terms of the value of the physical plant in operation. Fitting the above relationship to time-series data for the United States left a huge unexplained residual, named "the coefficient of our ignorance." Output grew much faster than increases in the traditional factors of production could account for. Relabeling the residual "technical change" was simply begging the question "what determines technical change?"

It was then that Schultz (1961) and Denison (1967), using computationally different although conceptually similar approaches, introduced the quality of labor or human capital into the traditional production function. Schultz, for example, plugged in the amount of investment represented by expenditures on education and explained a great part of the previously puzzling residual. The macro approach has been replicated by others over the past thirty years with similar results.[1]

Figure 3 shows that in Africa, investment in education explains nearly twice the proportion of economic growth that it does in more affluent Europe and North America. This macro result essentially replicates the rate-of-return structure by country type presented above, given that human capital is much scarcer in the poorer countries.

Beyond the results cited above, which have been generated by econometricians, economic historians took a stab at the matter by taking a much longer-term view than sophisticated statistical analysis permits. Thus it has been established that bouts of long-term economic growth were preceded by increases in the population's literacy level. The examples of Japan and Korea are the classic cases in which an educated population base has provided the necessary infrastructure for industrial advances to take place at a later date (see Saxonhouse 1977 and Easterlin 1981).

Wider Social Impact

Beyond the above "strict" or monetary impact of education, investment in human beings also has many other social values. Some come under the heading of externalities—namely, values captured by persons other than the individual investor. Others are labeled "nonmarket effects" (for a superb account of this see Haveman and Wolfe 1984). And others are simply means or mechanisms by which the overall impact of education is realized.

When a person becomes literate, this person will enjoy a higher lifetime consumption path, according to statistics for a large number of countries. Others will also benefit if the country has a more literate population—through lower transaction costs than if they were dealing with illiterates, for example.

Many educated females may choose not to participate in the labor force. This does not mean, however, that such females are not more productive (relative to their less educated counterparts) in the variety of goods and services produced within the household that are not readily marketable. For example, they may provide better sanitation conditions for all members of the family and more nutri-

---

[1] For a review see Psacharopoulos (1984).

Figure 3. The contribution of education to economic growth by continent.

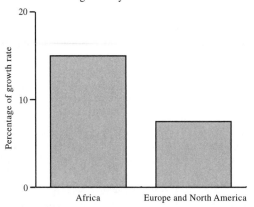

Source: Based on Psacharopoulos 1984.

tional meals. Such effects should be counted as part of the social impact of education.

Education increases the opportunity cost to a woman staying in the household and induces her to participate in the labor market. This contributes to overall efficiency in the economy to the extent that her market wage is higher than her implicit, shadow wage of being engaged in household activities.

Migration is an illustrative example of the means by which the returns to education are realized. To the extent that education makes the worker aware of employment opportunities elsewhere, or simply makes him or her employable in other contexts, it will instigate a more efficient allocation of labor to the most productive uses.

Health status is a very important part of human well-being. Several studies have shown that literacy and other measures of education are more closely correlated with life expectancy than per capita income is. The mechanism of this relationship is that education helps determine both the level of knowledge about how to combat disease and the ease with which it can be transmitted and utilized (Cochrane, O'Hara, and Leslie 1980).

The relationship between education and fertility is a very complex one, although most observers would agree that the link is negative—that increased literacy and school attendance in general delay marriage and increase the opportunity cost of having children. Consequently, families desire and have fewer children. This has been clearly demonstrated in urban areas on a global scale (see Cochrane 1979).

Last but not least, another often mentioned wider effect of education is that of having a more informed body of consumers and a literate electorate, leading to democratic government.

References

Cochrane, S. H. (1979). *Fertility and Education: What Do We Really Know?* Baltimore: Johns Hopkins University Press.

Cochrane, S. H., D. O'Hara, and J. Leslie (1980). *The Effects of Education on Health.* Staff Working Paper no. 405. Washington, D.C.: World Bank.

Denison, E. F. (1967). *Why Do Growth Rates Differ?* Washington D.C.: Brookings Institution.

Easterlin, R. (1981). "Why Isn't the Whole World Developed?" *Journal of Economic History* 41 (March): 1–19.

Haveman, R. H., and B. Wolfe (1984). "Schooling and Economic Well-being: The Role of Nonmarket Effects." *Journal of Human Resources* 19:377–407.

Psacharopoulos, G. (1984). "The Contribution of Education to Economic Growth: International Comparisons." In J. W. Kendrick, ed., *International Comparisons of Productivity and Causes of the Slowdown.* New York: Ballinger, pp. 335–60.

——— (1985). "Returns to Education: A Further International Update and Implications." *Journal of Human Resources* 20 (Fall): 583–604.

Saxonhouse, G. R. (1977). "Productivity Change and Labor Absorption in Japanese Cotton Spinning, 1881–1935." *Quarterly Journal of Economics* 91: 195–200.

Schultz, T. W. (1961). "Education and Economic Growth." In N. B. Henry, ed., *Social Forces Influencing American Education.* Chicago: University of Chicago Press.

Comment IV.A.1. Updated Estimates of Returns to Investment in Education

The author of this selection, George Psacharopoulos, has updated his findings twice: first in George Psacharopoulos, "Returns to Investment in Education: A Global Update," *World Development* 22, no. 9 (1994): 1325–1343, and second in George Psacharopoulos and Harry A. Patrinos, "Returns to Investment in Education: A Further Update," World Bank Policy Research Working Paper No. 2881 (September 2002). For the first update he concludes, "The results of this update are fully consistent with and reinforce earlier patterns. Namely, primary education continues to be the number one investment priority in developing countries, educating females is marginally more profitable than educating males, [and] the academic secondary school curriculum is a better investment than the technical/vocational track" (p. 1335). These conclusions are not changed by his second update.

In both updates Psacharopoulos takes care to distinguish between the returns to investment in education, as defined in this selection, and the percentage increase in earnings due to an additional year of schooling, which is conventionally called "the return to education" in the economics literature. The latter is equal to the coefficient on years of schooling in a regression of the logarithm of earnings on years of schooling and control variables. Neither the private nor the social cost of schooling is taken into account in these estimates of "the return to education."

Comment IV.A.2. Ability Differences, Spillovers, and the Returns to Investment in Education

The returns to investment in education reported by Psacharopoulos in Figure 1 of the preceding selection are computed using the differences in average earnings between workers with and workers without a given level of education. These computations are based on the implicit assumption that the average innate abilities of the more and less educated groups of workers are the same, and therefore have no effect on the average earnings differential. This assumption is accurate if the only cause of differences in educational attainment is differences in the resources to which the workers had access when students: for example, whether or not primary schools were present in their villages, as in Selection IV.A.3 by Esther Duflo. Suppose, to the contrary, that another cause of differences in educational attainment is differences in ability: high-ability students graduate from secondary school, say, while low-ability students drop out. In this case part of the higher earnings of secondary school graduates reflects their higher ability, and the return to secondary education is overestimated.

The ability bias argument suggests that the social returns to investment in education may not be as high relative to those on alternative investments as Figure 1 in Psacharopoulos's selection implies. However, this argument probably does not work against Psacharopoulos's claim that social returns to investment are greatest for primary education and least for university education. If anything, one would guess that ability bias in estimates of the return to education increases with the level of education, since the extent to which school attendance is compulsory decreases. We should also note that in the article from which Selection IV.A.3 is drawn, Esther Duflo finds no evidence of ability bias in the conventional estimates of the "return to education."

One can also argue that earnings differentials *under*estimate the social return to investment in education. People learn from those around them, so if I have an education I improve the learning environment for my co-workers. This positive spillover or "human capital externality" is not captured by the computations behind Figure 1 in Psacharopoulos's selection. Evidence for the existence of such spillovers in the United States is given by James E. Rauch, "Productivity Benefits from Geographic Concentration of Human Capital: Evidence from the Cities," *Journal of Urban Economics* (November 1993). He finds that workers earn more, the higher is the average level of education in their city, controlling for their individual characteristics and other important attributes of the city. Again, the implications of this argument for the relative returns to investments in different levels of education are unclear. If this spillover is most important for learning new technology it may have the greatest impact on the social return to university education.

Selection IV.A.2. Creating Human Capital*

Figures 1 and 2 present a stylized summary of the results of regressing primary and secondary enrollment rates on per capita national income for more than 90 developing economies for the years 1965 and 1987. Enrollment rates are higher at higher levels of per capita income. But the HPAE's [high-performing Asian economies] enrollment rates have tended to be higher than predicted for their level of income. At the primary level, this was most obvious in 1965, when Hong Kong, Korea, and Singapore had already achieved universal primary education, well ahead of other developing economies, and even Indonesia with its vast population had a primary enrollment rate above 70 percent. By 1987, East Asia's superior education systems were evident at the secondary level. Indonesia had a secondary enrollment rate of 46 percent, well above other economies with roughly the same level of income, and Korea had moved from 35 to 88 percent, maintaining its large lead in relative performance. Only in Thailand was the 28 percent secondary enrollment rate well below the income-predicted 36 percent and the 54 percent mean for middle-income economies. In recent years Thailand's weak educational performance has been felt, as serious shortages of educated workers have begun to threaten continued very rapid growth. . . .

Policies That Promoted Human Capital Formation

Higher shares of national income devoted to education cannot fully explain the larger accumulation of human capital in the HPAEs. In both 1960 and 1989, public expenditure on education as a percentage of GNP was not much higher in East Asia than elsewhere (see table 1). In 1960 the share was 2.2 percent for all developing economies, 2.4 percent for Sub-Saharan Africa, and 2.5 percent for East Asia. During the three decades that followed, the governments of East Asia markedly increased the share of national output they invested in formal education, but so did governments in other developing regions. In 1989 the share in Sub-Saharan Africa, 4.1 percent, was higher than the East Asian share, 3.7 percent,

which barely exceeded the average share for all developing economies, 3.6 percent.

Nor were initial conditions, for example the colonial legacy, decisive. While Korea did have much higher enrollment rates in 1950 than most developing economies, subsequent increases in primary and secondary enrollment rates account for Korea's present wide lead in enrollments over other middle-income economies. A comparison of Indonesia, a success story, and Pakistan, a laggard, is also illustrative. In 1987 Indonesia had achieved universal primary enrollment and a 48 percent secondary enrollment rate. By contrast, Pakistan's enrollment rates were 52 percent at the primary level and 19 percent at the secondary level. What proportion of these gaps is due to initial conditions? At the primary level, Indonesia increased its enrollment rate by nearly 80 percentage points since 1950, while Pakistan managed an increase of only 34 percentage points, implying that most of the current gap is explained by the pace of increase rather than initial conditions. For secondary schooling, Pakistan's enrollment rate in 1950 was actually higher than Indonesia's; all of the current gap is explained by the rates of increase during the past thirty-seven years.

Primary and Secondary Education

The allocation of public expenditure between basic and higher education is the major public policy factor that accounts for East Asia's extraordinary performance with regard to the quantity of basic education provided. The share of public expenditure on education allocated to basic education has been consistently higher in East Asia than elsewhere. Korea and Venezuela provide an extreme example that nicely illustrates the point. Table 2 indicates that in 1985 Venezuela allocated 43 percent of its education budget to higher education; by contrast, in the same year Korea allocated only 10 percent of its budget to higher education. Public expenditure on education as a percentage of GNP was actually higher in Venezuela (4.3) than in Korea (3.0). After subtracting the share going to higher education, however, public expenditure available for basic education as a percentage of GNP was considerably higher in Korea (2.5) than in Venezuela (1.3). Box 1 shows how Indonesia's emphasis on primary education, contrasted with Bolivia's relative neglect of primary schooling, is reflected in rural educational opportunities.

*From World Bank, "Creating Human Capital and Policies that Promoted Human Capital Formation," *The East Asian Miracle: Economic Growth and Public Policy* (Washington, D.C.: The World Bank, 1993), pp. 43–46, 198–201. Reprinted by permission.

Figure 1. Cross-economy regression for primary enrollment rates, 1965 and 1987.

Primary enrollment rates

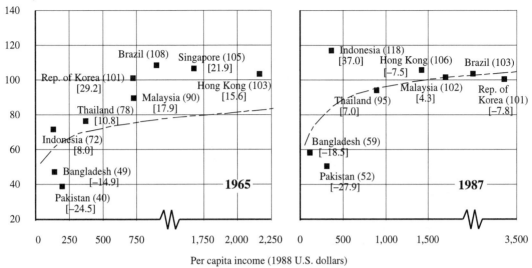

Per capita income (1988 U.S. dollars)

Note: Figures in parentheses are enrollment rates; bracketed numbers show residuals.
Source: Behrman and Schneider (1992).

Figure 2. Cross-economy regression for secondary enrollment rates, 1965 and 1987.

Secondary enrollment rates

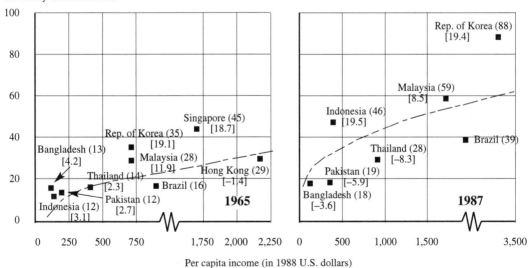

Per capita income (in 1988 U.S. dollars)

Note: Figures in parentheses are enrollment rates; bracketed numbers show residuals.
Source: Behrman and Schneider (1992).

Table 1. Public Expenditure on Education as a Percentage of GNP

Economy/region	1960	1989
HPAEs		
Hong Kong	—	2.8
Korea, Rep. of	2.0	3.6
Singapore	2.8	3.4
Malaysia	2.9	5.6
Thailand	2.3	3.2
Indonesia[a]	2.5	0.9
Average[b]	2.5	3.7
Other		
Brazil	1.9	3.7
Pakistan	1.1	2.6
Less developed economies[c]	1.3	3.1
Sub-Saharan Africa	2.4	4.1

—Not available

[a]Alternative sources of data indicate that expenditure on public education as a percentage of GDP was 3.0 percent in Indonesia in 1989.

[b]Average does not include Indonesia.

[c]Low- and middle-income economies.

Source: UNDP (1991).

The share of public funds allocated to tertiary education in East Asia has tended to be low, averaging roughly 15 percent during the past three decades. In Latin America the share has been roughly 24 percent. In South Asia, the share is close to the Latin American level. This had been the case in Sub-Saharan Africa as well, but in recent years the share has declined to East Asian levels.

By giving priority to expanding the primary and secondary bases of the educational pyramid, East Asian governments have stimulated the demand for higher education, while relying to a large extent on the private sector to satisfy that demand. In all developing regions the probability of going to university is markedly higher for secondary school graduates from high- than from low-income families. Typically, in low- and middle-income economies government subsidies of university education are not related to need, implying that they benefit families with relatively high incomes that

Table 2. Allocation of Education Budgets, 1985

Economy	Public expenditure on education as a percentage of GNP	Public expenditure on basic education as a percentage of GNP	Percentage of education budget allocated to higher education	Percentage of education budget allocated to basic education
Hong Kong	2.8	1.9	25.1	69.3
Indonesia[a]	2.3	2.0	9.0	89.0
Korea, Rep. of	3.0	2.5	10.3	83.9
Malaysia	7.9	5.9	14.6	74.9
Singapore	5.0	3.2	30.7	64.6
Thailand	3.2	2.6	12.0	81.3
Venezuela	4.3	1.3	43.4	31.0

[a]Alternative sources of data indicate that in Indonesia public expenditure on education as a percentage of GDP was 3.3 in 1984–85 and 4.3 in 1985–86, and that the percentage of the education budget allocated to basic education was 81 in 1984–85 and 80 in 1985–86.

Row percentages do not add up to 100 since three of the categories into which educational funding is channeled—pre-primary, other types, and not distributed—have not been included in this table.

Source: Column 1, UNDP (1990); columns 2 and 3, UNESCO (1989).

Box 1   Spending on the Kids: Primary Education in Bolivia and Indonesia

The impact of differing spending priorities within education budgets is starkly evident in a comparison of primary schools in Bolivia and Indonesia. Both economies are at roughly similar levels of development, and both have predominantly rural populations, national illiteracy rates of about 20 percent, and social and cultural factors that hinder the education of girls. Moreover, the proportion of national resources devoted to education at all levels is roughly similar. Bolivia has an annual per capita GNP of about $650; Indonesia, $610. Both spend 2.3 percent of their GDP on education. But while Bolivia devotes only 41 percent of its education budget to primary schools, Indonesia spends nearly 90 percent on basic education.

The resulting differences are striking. In Bolivia, the education system officially covers only 60 percent of children. But even that low figure overstates educational attainment. Only 45 percent of rural schools provide education through the fifth grade; the remainder, mostly in remote areas, offer only three years of instruction. Repetition and dropout rates are high, especially for girls, and only one in ten children has a textbook. Partly because of inadequate resources, teacher training is poor, and administrative corruption is widespread.

Indonesia, by contrast, has deliberately focused resources on primary education, to good effect. Beginning in 1974 with a massive school construction drive, and continuing in 1978 with the abolition of primary school fees, the government endeavored to make primary education available to all children. By 1987, 91 percent of children in rural areas were enrolled in primary school, only slightly less than the 92 percent enrolled nationwide. With near universal education, the gender gap in enrollments has disappeared. While dropout and repetition rates are higher in the countryside than in the cities, and large regional gaps in enrollment ratios and illiteracy rates persist, the focus on primary education has been an effective way to make the most of limited education resources.

Like other developing economies, Indonesia must balance the desire to fund more intermediate and advanced education against the reality that stretching education budgets means less for the lower grades. In 1987, the government expanded free education, which had previously covered up to the sixth grade, to include up to the ninth grade. Educational quality declined, however, and the government has since identified improvement of primary schooling as a key educational objective.

Sources: World Bank (1990; internal World Bank reports).

could afford to pay fees closer to the actual cost of schooling.

At the same time, in many economies, Brazil and Kenya being notable examples, low public funding of secondary education results in poorly qualified children from low-income backgrounds being forced into the private sector or entirely out of the education system. Because of the higher concentration on basic education in East Asia, public funds for education are more likely to benefit children of low-income families who might otherwise have difficulty remaining in school.

References

Behrman, Jere R., and Ryan Schneider. 1992. "An International Perspective on Schooling Investment in the Last Quarter Century in Some Fast-Growing Eastern and Southeastern Countries." Background paper for *The East Asian Miracle*. World Bank, Policy Research Department, Washington, D.C.

UNDP (United Nations Development Programme). 1991. *Human Development Report.* New York: Oxford University Press.

UNESCO. Various years. *Statistical Yearbook.* Paris.

World Bank. 1990. *Indonesia: Strategy for a Sustained Reduction in Poverty.* Washington, D.C.

Selection IV.A.3. Schooling and Labor Market Consequences of School Construction in Indonesia*

The questions of whether investments in infrastructure can cause an increase in educational attainment, and whether an increase in educational attainment causes an increase in earnings are basic concerns for development economists. A large body of literature investigates the impact of schooling infrastructure on schooling, as well as the returns to education in developing countries [see George Psacharopoulos (1994) and John Strauss and Duncan Thomas (1995) for surveys]. Estimated returns to education are, in general, larger in developing countries than in industrialized countries. However, most of the existing studies are based on simple correlations between years of education and wages. Family and community background are important determinants of both schooling and labor market outcomes in developing countries, and the bias in estimates that treat an individual's education level as exogenous could be important.

This paper exploits a dramatic change in policy to evaluate the effect building schools has on education and earnings in Indonesia, a country where the GDP per capita in 1995 was only $720, 3.5 percent that of the United States. In 1973, the Indonesian government launched a major school construction program, the Sekolah Dasar INPRES program. Between 1973–1974 and 1978–1979, more than 61,000 primary schools were constructed—an average of two schools per 1,000 children aged 5 to 14 in 1971. Enrollment rates among children aged 7 to 12 increased from 69 percent in 1973 to 83 percent by 1978. This was in contrast to the absence of capital expenditure and a decline in enrollment in the early 1970's.

Using a large cross section of men born between 1950 and 1972 from the 1995 intercensal survey of Indonesia (SUPAS), I linked an adult's education and wages with district-level data on the number of new schools built between 1973–1974 and 1978–1979 in his region of birth. The exposure of an individual to the program was determined both by the number of schools built in his region of birth and by his age when the program was launched. . . .

The estimates suggest that each new school constructed per 1,000 children was associated with an increase of 0.12 to 0.19 in years of education and

*From Esther Duflo, "Schooling and Labor Market Consequences of School Construction in Indonesia: Evidence from an Unusual Policy Experiment," *American Economic Review* 91, no. 4 (September 2001): 795–798, 812–813. Reprinted by permission.

1.5 to 2.7 percent in earnings for the first cohort fully exposed to the program. This implies estimates of economic returns to education ranging from 6.8 to 10.6 percent. . . .

The Sekolah Dasar INPRES Program

Starting in 1973, the Indonesian government emphasized the need for "equity" across provinces. Oil revenues were mobilized to finance centrally administered development programs, the "presidential instructions" (INPRES). The Sekolah Dasar INPRES was one of the first INPRES programs and by far the largest at the time it was launched (in 1973–1974). As a result of the oil boom, real expenditures on regional development more than doubled between 1973 and 1980, and the Sekolah Dasar INPRES program became extremely important. Between 1973–1974 and 1978–1979, 61,807 new schools were constructed, at a cost of over 500 million 1990 U.S. dollars (1.5 percent of the Indonesian GDP in 1973). This represented more than one school per 500 children aged 5 to 14 in 1971, which reportedly makes INPRES the fastest primary school construction program ever undertaken in the world (World Bank, 1990).

Once an INPRES school was established, the government recruited the teachers and paid their salaries (each school was designed for three teachers and 120 pupils). An effort to train more teachers paralleled the INPRES program (World Bank, 1990), and the proportion of teachers meeting the minimum qualification requirements did not worsen significantly between 1971 and 1978. The stock of schools multiplied by two over the period, and the stock of teachers grew by 43 percent. This contrasted with a freeze of capital expenditure and teacher recruiting prior to 1973 (Daroesman, 1971).

The program was designed explicitly to target children who had not previously been enrolled in school. The general allocation rule was that the number of schools to be constructed in each district was proportional to the number of children of primary school age *not enrolled in school* in 1972. . . .

Identification Strategy

The date of birth and the region of birth jointly determine an individual's exposure to the program. Indonesian children normally attend primary school between the ages of 7 and 12. All children born in 1962 or before were 12 or older in 1974, when the first INPRES schools were constructed. Thus, they did not benefit from the program, since they should have left primary school before the first INPRES schools were opened. Grade repetition and delayed school entry could lead a few of these children to benefit from the program during their last year in school. However, according to the 1993 Indonesian Family Life Survey (IFLS) data set (conducted in 1993 by RAND and the Demographic Institute at the University of Indonesia), less than 3 percent of the children born between 1950 and 1962 were still in primary school in 1974. For younger children, the exposure is an increasing function of their date of birth. Hence, the effect of the program should be close to 0 for children 12 or older in 1974 and increasing for younger children.

Because the program intensity was related to enrollment rates in 1972, which differed widely across regions, region of birth is a second dimension of variation in the intensity of the program. Region of birth is highly correlated with the region of education: 91.5 percent of the children in the IFLS sample were still living in the district where they were born at age 12. However, unlike region of education, it is not endogenous with respect to the program, given that all individuals in the sample were born before the program was started.

The basic idea behind the identification strategy can be illustrated using simple two-by-two tables. Table 1 shows means of education and wages for different cohorts and program levels. Regions are separated in "high program" and "low program" regions. The difference between the number of schools constructed per 1,000 children constructed in high and low program regions is 0.90. I compare the educational attainment and the wages of indi-

viduals who had little or no exposure to the program (they were 12 to 17 in 1974) to those of individuals who were exposed the entire time they were in primary school (they were 2 to 6 in 1974), in both types of regions. In both cohorts, the average educational attainment and wages in regions that received *fewer* schools are *higher* than in regions that received more schools. This reflects the program provision that more schools were to be built in regions where enrollment rates were low. In both types of regions, average educational attainment increased over time. However, it increased more in regions that received more schools. The difference in these differences can be interpreted as the causal effect of the program, under the assumption that in the absence of the program, the increase in educational attainment would not have been systematically different in low and high program regions. An individual young enough, born in a high program region, received on average 0.12 more years of education, and the logarithm of his wage in 1995 was 0.026 higher. These differences in differences are not significantly different from 0. This simple estimator suggests that one school per 1,000 children contributed to an increase in education by 0.13 years (0.12 divided by 0.90) and wages by 0.029 for children aged 2 to 6 when the program was initiated. The Wald estimate of returns to education is the ratio of these two estimates. . . .

Conclusion

The findings reported here are important because they show that an unusually large government-administered intervention was effective in increasing both education and wages in Indonesia. This intervention was meant to increase the *quantity* of education. It is sometimes feared

Table 1. Means of Education and Log(Wage) by Cohort and Level of Program Cells

	Years of education			Log(wages)		
	Level of program in region of birth			Level of program in region of birth		
	High (1)	Low (2)	Difference (3)	High (4)	Low (5)	Difference (6)
Aged 2 to 6 in 1974	8.49 (0.043)	9.76 (0.037)	−1.27 (0.057)	6.61 (0.0078)	6.73 (0.0064)	−0.12 (0.010)
Aged 12 to 17 in 1974	8.02 (0.053)	9.40 (0.042)	−1.39 (0.067)	6.87 (0.0085)	7.02 (0.0069)	−0.15 (0.011)
Difference	0.47 (0.070)	0.36 (0.038)	0.12 (0.089)	−0.26 (0.011)	−0.29 (0.0096)	0.026 (0.015)

Notes: The sample is made of the individuals who earn a wage. Standard errors are in parentheses.

that the deterioration in the quality of education that might result from this type of program could offset any gain in quantity. However, the estimates reported here suggest that the program was effective in increasing not only education levels but also wages. This suggests that the combined effect of quality and quantity changes in education was an increase in human capital.

This study concentrated on estimating the private returns to education. This large increase in the education of the young cohorts, however, may have had a broader impact on the Indonesian economy. How did the economy adjust to a shock in the supply of educated workers? Studying these effects will be the object of future work.

References

Daroesman, Ruth. "Finance of Education." *Bulletin of Indonesian Economic Studies,* December 1971, Pts. 1 and 2, 7(3), pp. 61–95.

Psacharopoulos, George. "Returns to Investments in Education: A Global Update." *World Development,* September 1994, 22(9), pp. 1325–43.

Strauss, John and Thomas, Duncan. "Human Resources: Empirical Modeling of Household and Family Decisions," in Jere Behrman and T. N. Srinivasan, eds., *Handbook of development economics.* Amsterdam: North-Holland, 1995, *3A*(9), pp. 1885–2023.

World Bank. "Indonesia: Strategy for a Sustained Reduction in Poverty." Washington, DC: World Bank Country Study, 1990.

Selection IV.A.4. Interpreting Recent Research on Schooling in Developing Countries*

Table 1 summarizes the effects of five educational inputs on student performance in developing countries on the basis of ninety-six studies: teacher-pupil ratio; teacher education, experience, and salary; expenditure per pupil. A more recent review (Velez, Schiefelbein, and Valenzuela 1993) contains a larger number of studies, but the general conclusions are the same. Table 1 shows which inputs have a statistically significant correlation (by sign of coefficient or direction of effect) and which are statistically insignificant. (The insignificant findings, unfortunately, cannot be divided by direction of effect.) In all cases, the reported correlations are those that hold after allowing for differences in the family backgrounds of students and in other educational inputs.

The evidence provides no support for policies to reduce class size. Of the thirty studies investigating teacher-pupil ratios, only eight find statistically significant results supporting smaller classes; an equal number are significant but have the opposite sign; and almost half are statistically insignificant. These findings qualitatively duplicate those in the U.S. studies, but are particularly interesting here. Class sizes in the developing-country studies are considerably more varied than those in the U.S. studies and thus pertain to a wider set of environments, providing even stronger evidence that the enthusiasm for policies to reduce class size is misplaced.

The effect of the teachers' experience yields results that are roughly similar to findings for the United States. Although 35 percent of the studies (sixteen out of forty-six) display significant positive benefits from more teaching experience (the analogous figure for the United States is 29 percent), the majority of the studies—twenty-eight out of forty-six—found this input statistically insignificant.

The results for teacher education, on the other hand, diverge in relative terms from those seen in the U.S. studies, with a majority (thirty-five out of sixty-three) supporting the conventional wisdom that more education for teachers improves student performance. (In the U.S. studies, teachers' education was the least important of all inputs.) Although these results are still surrounded by considerable uncertainty (twenty-six estimates are

*From Eric A. Hanushek, "Interpreting Recent Research on Schooling in Developing Countries," *World Bank Research Observer* 10 (August 1995): 230–231, 235–239, 243–244. Reprinted by permission.

insignificant and two display significantly negative effects), they do suggest a possible differentiation by stage of development and general level of resources available.

The evidence on teacher salaries in developing countries contains no compelling support for the notion that higher wages yield better teachers. Because these results aggregate studies across different countries, school organizations, and labor markets, however, it is difficult to take these results too far. For policy purposes, one would generally want information on what happens if the entire salary schedule is altered (as opposed to simply moving along a given schedule denominated, say, in experience, education, or some other attribute of teachers). But it is not possible with available studies to distinguish between the two effects.

Data on total expenditure per pupil are rarely available in analyses of developing countries, but the twelve studies that include such estimates are evenly split between statistically significant and statistically insignificant. Given questions about the quality of the underlying data, not too much should be inferred from these findings.

One of the clearest divergences between the findings in developing and industrial countries is the effect of facilities, suggesting that differences in the school environment are of some importance in developing countries. Twenty-two of the thirty-four investigations support the provision of quality buildings and libraries. The specific measures of facilities vary widely, however, so the interpretation almost certainly depends on local conditions.

Several other factors have been investigated in the course of the developing-country analyses, including an assortment of curriculum issues, instructional methods, and teacher training programs. Many of these inputs, however, are difficult to assess here because of the multicountry evidence and the probable importance of local institutions. One input—the provision of textbooks—has received widespread endorsement, although this support is as much for conceptual reasons as for solid empirical ones. The relationship of textbooks and writing materials to student performance is found to be important with reasonable consistency in developing countries, but relatively few studies are available (Lockheed and Hanushek 1988; Lockheed and Verspoor 1991). Investigations of technological or organizational differences have shown mixed results. In three extensive investiga-

Table 1. Summary of Ninety-six Studies on the Estimated Effects of Resources on Education in Developing Countries

Input	Number of studies	Statistically significant		Statistically insignificant
		Positive	Negative	
Teacher-pupil ratio	30	8	8	14
Teacher's education	63	35	2	26
Teacher's experience	46	16	2	28
Teacher's salary	13	4	2	7
Expenditure per pupil	12	6	0	6
Facilities	34	22	3	9

Source: Harbison and Hanushek 1992.

tions in Nicaragua, Kenya, and Thailand, interactive radio teaching, an approach to "distance education," has been found to be effective in teaching children in sparse settlements in rural areas. This result should not be generalized to all new technologies, however. In particular, there is little evidence at this time to support the widespread introduction of computers (Lockheed and Verspoor 1991). . . .

My own interpretation of existing evidence, based on results for both the United States and developing countries, is that schools differ in important ways, but we cannot describe what causes these differences very well. To take one example, Hanushek and Lavy (1994) investigated differences in the quality of schools across a sample of primary schools in Egypt. We defined school quality implicitly. After allowing for individual differences among students in achievement and in parental education, we labeled schools that had large gains in student achievement in a given year as high-quality schools; those with small gains, low quality. A continuous measure of school quality was developed by looking at growth in student achievement (after considering family and other influences on achievement growth). This exercise found enormous differences in the sixty sample schools. Table 2 shows the variation in the quality of schools by looking at achievement relative to a randomly chosen base school. The worst school shows an average achievement gain that is 62 percent below the base school, while the best school is 30 percent above. These results indicate dramatically that schools do differ in quality and that the difference is enough to be relevant to policymaking.

At the same time, measured attributes of teachers and schools explain only a small portion of these differences. From our estimation, only 16 percent of the variance in school quality is related to teacher attributes (such as education and gender) and school attributes (such as class size and facilities). Although we did not look further, I seriously doubt that adding more detailed measures of resources, or of pedagogy, or of curricular differences would have allowed us to explain the differences much more fully.

A similar approach undertaken in rural Brazil (Harbison and Hanushek 1992) pointed to very similar conclusions: schools show very large differences in their ability to improve student achievement, but these differences are not highly correlated with measured characteristics of teachers and schools.

In short, the findings summarized in Table 1 do *not* indicate that schools and teachers are all the same. Large differences exist, even though these differences are not captured by the simple measures commonly employed. Neither, it appears, are they captured by more detailed measures of classroom organization or pedagogical approach. This leads me to conclude that the educational process is very complicated and that we do not understand it very well. We cannot describe what makes a good or bad teacher or a good or bad school. Nor are we likely to be able to describe the educational process very well in the near future. My view is that we should learn to live with that fact: living with it implies finding policies that acknowledge and work within this fundamental ignorance.

Quality Versus Access

A third major aspect of current research relates to the importance of school quality and particularly to the perceived policy tradeoff between quality and access. The traditional concern goes something like this: given limited budgets for schools, and the commonly accepted twin objectives of expanding access and improving quality, policymakers face a particularly unpleasant dilemma. They must choose between expanding the availability of education or providing high-quality schools.

A second way of viewing these policy concerns, while apparently different, is actually quite closely related. Analyses of labor market implications and the rate of return to schooling in developing countries suggest strongly that schooling is a very good investment. A year of schooling typically shows a 25–30 percent real rate of return, which appears noticeably better than that of other investment alternatives. At the same time, school completion rates in low-income countries are very low (Lockheed and Verspoor 1991). These two facts are inconsistent. If education yields such a high rate of return, why are people not taking advantage of it?

Emerging analyses of school quality have something to say about both elements of education policy. I believe that the common conception of a simple tradeoff between access and quality is misleading—if not wrong; and I think that low school quality may frequently be an important explanation for the widespread failure to take advantage of the apparently high returns available from education.

The central theme here is that school quality is directly related to students' decisions about attending school and schools' decisions about promoting students. High-quality schools raise student achievement and speed students through primary (and perhaps secondary) school, thus saving costs. Additionally, students respond to higher school quality with lower dropout rates: they tend to stay in good schools and drop out of poor ones.

Both of these mechanisms indicate a direct relationship between the quantity of schooling attained and the quality of that schooling. Thus, studies of the rate of return to schooling that consider only the quantity of schooling produce a misleading estimate of the potential gains. Estimates of the rate of return to schooling that do not account for quality differences will systematically overstate the productivity gains that are associated with additional years of schooling, because the estimates will include quality differences that are correlated with quantity. The evidence shows that those who do not complete a given level tend to have attended poorer schools. If a policy simply pushes students to stay in school but makes no changes in the fundamental quality of the schools, the new school completers will get only the returns associated with years of schooling and not with quality. Thus, their rate of return on their investment in schooling will not be as high as the estimates suggest.

Many countries, concerned about very high grade repetition rates, directly intervene to ensure

Table 2. Distribution of Estimated School Quality in Egyptian Primary Schools

Distribution	All schools	Rural	Urban
Mean	−.084	−.111	−.057
Minimum	−.62	−.62	−.52
Maximum	.30	.30	.21

Note: Values indicate the average proportional achievement gain of a school in comparison with that of the arbitrarily chosen base school, Taha Hussein School.
Source: Hanushek and Lavy 1994.

regular promotion through school (Lockheed and Verspoor 1991), but they typically ignore school quality. Neglecting the quality of schools is a serious mistake. In studying primary school students in the rural northeast of Brazil, Ralph Harbison and I discovered a very direct relationship between what a student knows and the student's promotion probabilities. Students who learn more than the curriculum requires (as measured by specifically designed tests) are significantly more likely to be promoted through primary school than those who do not learn what is expected. Schools, not surprisingly, have an important impact on student achievement. These findings suggest that policies that improve the quality of schools—that is, that enhance student achievement—will simultaneously lead to more rapid progress by students through the grades.

The magnitude of the overall effects of improving school quality, when converted to a monetary metric, is remarkable. Hanushek, Gomes-Neto, and Harbison (1994) summarize the expected savings from two simple policies—improving the availability of textbooks and writing materials (software) or improving components of the facilities (hardware). They show that if $1 is invested in useful resources such as textbooks, an immediate savings of more than $12 is obtained from speeding students through school. (These savings are pure efficiency savings from getting through school more quickly and include none of the increased productivity benefits that typically justify schooling investments; increases in future productivity simply reinforce the efficiency gains.) Where facilities are lacking, each $1 improvement has an expected cost saving of more than $3.

These estimates of the savings that can be expected from quality improvements are subject to some uncertainty. Nonetheless, the lowest plausible savings still indicate substantial efficiency gains from improving the quality of schools. The availability of books and writing materials and school facilities is consistently important for student achievement and promotion.

These results highlight the importance of providing minimal resources for schools and are consistent with previous findings about the importance of basic textbooks, materials, and facilities. But these estimates—as startling as they are—may not represent the largest opportunities and are really lower-bound estimates of the potential for change. Specifically, all the research points to the importance of the teacher. Because the variations in teacher quality appear to be much more important than the variations in software or hardware, the savings from ensuring the former would almost certainly exceed those obtained from improvements in the latter. Unfortunately, because we do not know how to hire particularly effective teachers—nor what it would cost—we cannot calculate straightforward benefit-cost ratios.

Grade repetition is not entirely bad, because students do learn more with each time through the same grade, but it is an expensive way to improve student learning (Gomes-Neto and Hanushek 1994). One alternative explanation is that repetition reflects demand-side factors—that is, student choices that lead to low attendance during each school year. Little is actually known about attendance patterns, but anecdotal evidence suggests that normal crop cycles and requirements for children to work in the fields at planting and harvest times may be important in some settings. Such attendance patterns could severely constrain the chances of completing a given grade, at least in the likely absence of well-integrated, self-paced instruction. Dealing with these issues might require different policies aimed at lessening the current consumption constraints of families. In any event, however, the continued production of low-grade schools is no more effective in the face of such demand-side influences than without them.

In work on Egypt, Hanushek and Lavy (1994) pursue a related question: whether school quality affects students' decisions to drop out. In that analysis, the school quality estimates (Table 2) were included as one of the determinants of the decisions of individual students. Additionally, the analysis considered the students' own achievements and abilities as well as their earnings opportunities outside of school. If we hold achievement and opportunities constant, students going to high-quality schools are much more likely to stay in school than those going to low-quality schools. This makes sense. If a student is not going to get anything out of school, why waste the time?

The magnitude of the effect is particularly important. The primary schools sampled had average dropout rates in 1980 of 9.3 percent. If all the schools were at the quality level of the best one, the dropout rate would fall to 3.2 percent or less, a decline that indicates the huge impact of quality on school attainment.

Research in Brazil and Egypt points to similar conclusions. School quality has large and direct effects on school access and school attainment. These effects are complements, not substitutes, as suggested by the simple budgetary analysis that is commonly employed. And the research in both countries indicates that quality adds a dimension that is extremely important in thinking about schooling in developing countries. Finally, efforts to pursue quality improvement must confront the policy challenges described in the earlier sections. Inefficiency and general lack of knowledge about the production function in education imply that dealing with quality will require new and innovative approaches.

These conclusions are supported in Glewwe and Jacoby (1994), whose work on Ghana shows the direct relationship between school quality and school attainment. Improving the schools (in this case, the facilities) tends to hold students in school longer, other things equal. The authors do not obtain estimates of the total effects of school quality (as was done for Egypt), but the indication that measured effects have this influence confirms the quantity-quality correlation. This correlation in turn confirms the bias in rates of return flowing from analyses that ignore variations in school quality. . . .

Conclusions

The research into the educational process, both in the United States and in the developing world, promises some very distinct payoffs. In policy dimensions, we appear to have learned a great deal. At the same time, the results do not always conform to what was expected. Research conclusively demonstrates an inefficiency in the current organization of schools. Resources are being spent in unproductive ways—ways that do not contribute to improving student performance. Correcting these inefficiencies is not simple. There is no blueprint for a model school that can be reproduced and handed out to policymakers, and such a blueprint is unlikely to be developed in the near future. Instead, we must turn to new organizations and new incentives if we are to improve schools.

Research suggests that the most likely path to improvement involves the introduction of performance incentives. Although several ways to introduce incentives have been suggested, none has been tried extensively. An extensive and systematic program of experimentation and evaluation is thus in order.

Finally, the evidence underscores the importance of establishing good schools. Although translating this goal into policy will be difficult, there are powerful reasons to believe that providing quality schools should be very high on the policy agenda. The continued expansion of low-quality schools—often thought to be a step on the path both to high access and to high-quality schools—may actually be a self-defeating strategy.

References

Glewwe, Paul, and Hanan Jacoby. 1994. "Student Achievement and Schooling Choice in Low Income Countries: Evidence from Ghana." *Journal of Human Resources* 29(3):841–64.

Gomes-Neto, João Batista, and Eric A. Hanushek. 1994. "Causes and Consequences of Grade Repetition: Evidence from Brazil." *Economic Development and Cultural Change* 43(1):117–48.

Hanushek, Eric A., João Batista Gomes-Neto, and Ralph W. Harbison. 1994. "Self-financing Educational Investments: The Quality Imperative in Developing Countries." University of Rochester, Department of Economics, Rochester, N.Y. Processed.

Hanushek, Eric A., and Victor Lavy. 1994. *School Quality, Achievement Bias, and Dropout Behavior in Egypt*. Living Standards Measurement Study Working Paper 107. Washington, D.C.: World Bank.

Harbison, Ralph W., and Eric A. Hanushek. 1992. *Educational Performance of the Poor: Lessons from Rural Northeast Brazil*. New York: Oxford University Press.

Lockheed, Marlaine E., and Eric A. Hanushek. 1988. "Improving Educational Efficiency in Developing Countries: What Do We Know?" *Compare* 18(1):21–38.

Lockheed, Marlaine E., and Adriaan Verspoor. 1991. *Improving Primary Education in Developing Countries*. New York: Oxford University Press.

Velez, Eduardo, Ernesto Schiefelbein, and Jorge Valenzuela. 1993. "Factors Affecting Achievement in Primary Education." HROWP Working Paper 2. World Bank, Department of Human Resources Development and Operations Policy, Washington, D.C.

Selection IV.A.5. School Inputs and Educational Outcomes in South Africa*

One of the difficulties in estimating the impact of class size on outcomes is the potential endogeneity of school inputs. Parents who care about education may move to be close to good schools and may be willing to pay higher housing prices to do so. Parents who care about education will typically engage in political action to increase local school quality and funding. Such parents may also spend extra effort to ensure that their children are progressing well in school. In such cases, a positive relationship between school resources and outcomes for children may be due to unobserved parental tastes for education, and it is often difficult to disentangle the effects of such tastes from those of school inputs. . . .

In this paper we examine the relationship between educational inputs and school outcomes in South Africa immediately before the end of apartheid government, and, in doing so, we add to what is known about the impact of school quality on child outcomes. There are three features of the South African system that are particularly salient. First, Black households were severely limited in their residential choice under apartheid. Second, funding decisions for most Black schools were made centrally, by White-controlled entities on which Blacks were not represented and over which they had no control. These two features limited the two most obvious ways in which Blacks could affect the conditions under which their children were educated. Third, the allocations resulted in marked disparities in average class sizes even across areas as large as magisterial districts, with some districts averaging 20 children per teacher in Black schools, and others upwards of 80 children per teacher. The unusually large variation in pupil-teacher ratios provides an excellent opportunity to examine their effects on outcomes.[1]

Beginning early in the century, the White South African government pushed for a "Bantustan" system, in which Black families were assigned to "homelands" based upon their language, regardless of where the family had previously resided. This program gained momentum in 1970, with the passage of the "Black Homeland Citizenship Act." And South African government forced millions of Blacks into homelands, and made it extremely difficult for family members in a homeland to join a migrant working in a city or in a mine. Lack of mobility was consciously built into the South African migratory labor system. As a by-product, the system severely limited the ability of households to move to areas with better schools.

Under the apartheid regime, resources for Black schools were, with the exception of the "independent" homelands, centrally controlled. Funding for Black schools in the provinces that the White government wanted ultimately to comprise South Africa (Cape, Orange Free State, Natal, and Transvaal) was controlled centrally by a Department of Education and Training (DET), and was set apart from the bodies responsible for the education of the White population. School funds for the homelands that were slated to become independent (the so-called Self-Governing Territories (SGTs) of KwaZulu, Lebowa, Ganzankulu, KwaNdebele, KaNgwane, and Qwa-Qwa) were ear-marked centrally by the Minister of National Education. The "independent" homelands (Ciskei, Transkei, Bophuthatswana, and Venda) had more control over their budgets. However, most of the money these governments had to spend came through the South African Department of Foreign Affairs, which played an important role in determining how that money would be spent [Republic of South Africa 1994]. This system generated marked discrepancies in educational funding per pupil across racial groups and place of residence. Taking Blacks in the DET schools as unity, funding levels for Whites, Asians, Coloureds, Blacks in SGTs, and Blacks in homelands were, respectively, 1.85, 1.61, 1.59, 0.74, and 0.67 [South African Institute of Race Relations 1997]. Given the very limited control that the Black population had over location and resource allocation, an unusually large fraction of the variation in school resources across districts was independent of the variation in school resources across districts was independent of the educational choices of Black parents and their children.

We examine the effects of pupil-teacher ratios and school facilities on educational outcomes, including school attendance, educational attainment,

*From Anne Case and Angus Deaton. "School Inputs and Educational Outcomes in South Africa." *Quarterly Journal of Economics* 114, no. 3 (August 1999): 1047–1050, 1057–1058, 1060–1061, 1069–1073, 1075–1082. Reprinted by permission.

[1]In this paper we have little option but to follow the apartheid racial classifications of Black, Coloured, Asian, and White; we use capitals and the Anglicized spelling throughout to register the specialized use. Magisterial districts correspond roughly to counties: there are 363 in the country; the average (median) population in each is 100,000 (38,000).

and test scores. We use data from the South African Living Standards Survey (SALSS) that was carried out jointly by the South African Labor and Development Research Unit (SALDRU) and the World Bank in the last five months of 1993—just prior to the change of government. The survey was supplemented by a series of community questionnaires on local facilities, and by a literacy and numeracy survey administered to a subset of individuals in the base survey. We make use of both of these supplements, and of administrative data on pupil-teacher ratios by race and by magisterial district. The largest part of our paper is devoted to a national analysis of the relationship between pupil-teacher ratios and educational outcomes. Because we are not controlling for other school-based inputs, and because in South Africa, other inputs follow the supply of teachers, our purpose is not to assess the specific role of class size among other competing uses of resources, but to measure the effects of resources in general. Except when stated to the contrary, all subsequent references to the effects of pupil-teacher ratios should be understood in this sense.

Our empirical analysis shows marked effects of school quality as measured by pupil-teacher ratios, on outcomes for Black children. Controlling for household background variables—which themselves have powerful effects on outcomes, but have no effect on pupil-teacher ratios—we find strong and significant effects of pupil-teacher ratios on enrollment, on educational achievement, and on test scores for numeracy. . . .

That differences in pupil-teacher ratios may explain part of the fanning out in completed educa-

tion is clear from Figure 1, in which years of completed schooling are plotted against age at different pupil-teacher ratios for Black children aged ten to eighteen. Until roughly age thirteen we find little relationship in the raw data between the pupil-teacher ratio and completed education. Through age twelve, children in magisterial districts with average pupil-teacher ratios between 60 and 70 pupils per teacher advanced through school about as quickly as children in magisterial districts with average ratios between 20 and 30 pupils per teacher. Beyond that age, after which students must pass a provincewide examination in order to advance to the next grade, we see a pattern in which Black children in districts with fewer pupils per teacher advance more quickly. . . .

Figure 2 shows summary information for the pupil-teacher ratios. . . .

Apart from the obvious and very large difference in pupil-teacher ratios between Blacks and the other groups, the most notable feature of Figure 2 is that pupil-teacher ratios are much more dispersed within the Black population than is the case for the other groups. To some extent, this is a consequence of the fact that some groups—particularly Coloureds and Asians—are concentrated in a relatively small number of districts, but the differences are striking. . . .

Educational Inputs and Educational Outcomes: Econometric Analysis

Table 1 presents the results of an analysis of years of completed education for children aged ten to eighteen. The dependent variable in the regres-

Figure 1. Completed education by age at different pupil-teacher ratios, blacks 10–18.

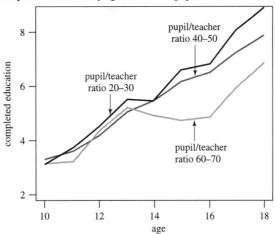

Figure 2.   Distributions of pupil-teacher ratios for school-age children in SALSS, by race, from district data.

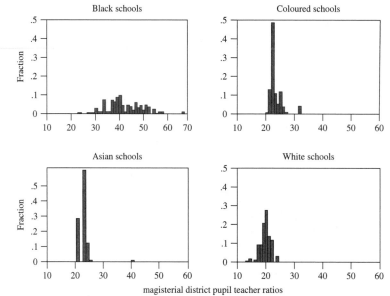

magisterial district pupil teacher ratios

sion in column (1) is educational attainment measured as years completed: among the explanatory variables, age is entered as a series of dummies, one for each year, with age ten omitted. Age is the immediate correlate of educational attainment for young people who are still in the educational system, and it is clearly the primary determinant of years of education attained. We also include a dummy variable for sex, various household socioeconomic characteristics, including the education of the head, household size, and a measure of household resources, as well as dummies for urbanization and provinces. In column (1) we show the regression for Whites and, in [the] subsequent column, regressions for Blacks only. There are 7103 Black children aged ten to eighteen in the SALSS with complete information, but only 629 Whites, and correspondingly fewer Coloureds and Asians, the results for whom we do not present.

The first two columns show how educational status rises with age, and the coefficients on the age dummies rise as we move down the columns. The differences between successive dummies would be unity if each child moved with certainty from one grade to the next, and this is essentially what happens in column (1) for Whites, where the differences are 0.81, 0.99, 1.06, 0.99, 1.04, 0.96, and 0.66, with the last figure presumably dropping off as some White children leave school at seventeen. Among Black children, however, the annual increments vary from 0.48 to 0.70, and average only a

little over 0.6, so that the average Black child obtains only two-thirds of a year of education for each additional year of age.

In both columns the pupil-teacher ratio has a negative impact on attainment for age, although the effect is small and insignificant for Whites; for Blacks it is −1.82 with a t-value of 4.3. According to this estimate, reducing the average Black class size from 40 to 30 pupils per teacher, or a quarter, for example, would raise average educational attainment by 0.52 years, equivalent to adding about ten months to age. Reducing it by 20, from the average Black to White ratio, would raise attainment by 1.26 years, about quarter of the actual years of education for a fourteen year old Black child.[2] One obvious interpretation of the difference in the effects between Whites and Blacks is that the effect of additional resources is nonlinear, and that decreases in the pupil-teacher ratio have a much larger effect when there are 40 (or 60) pupils per class than when there are 20. . . .

Gender and household characteristics have important effects in the regressions. Black female students have on average about half a year of educational attainment more than Black male students, and among Black students there are the expected positive effects of household resources and of the

[2] If the pupil-teacher ratio is used in place of its logarithm, the coefficient is −0.04 with a t-ratio of −3.6; this gives somewhat larger effects than those calculated above.

Table 1. Determinants of Years of Completed Education for Children Aged 10 to 18

	Whites (1)	Blacks (2)
Indicator: age = 11	.851	.393
	(10.3)	(7.0)
12	1.66	1.08
	(14.8)	(16.4)
13	2.65	1.70
	(17.8)	(23.8)
14	3.71	2.40
	(24.6)	(29.2)
15	4.70	3.08
	(28.5)	(35.1)
16	5.74	3.56
	(32.8)	(35.9)
17	6.40	4.26
	(25.3)	(39.5)
18	7.06	4.77
	(26.2)	(50.1)
Log (pupil-teacher ratio)	−.265	−1.82
	(0.4)	(4.3)
Female	−.007	.496
	(0.1)	(11.7)
Head of household's completed education	.061	.076
	(2.7)	(9.8)
Log (household size)	−.669	.188
	(1.6)	(2.6)
Indicator: female head	.136	.120
	(0.8)	(2.1)
Log (expenditure per household member)	−.086	.506
	(0.5)	(9.5)
Number of obs	629	7103

T-statistics are in parentheses. Regressions are estimated with robust standard errors, allowing for correlation between observations from the same cluster. Metro and province indicators are included in all regressions.

education of the household head. Head's education is a strong predictor of educational attainment among both Blacks and Whites; a head completing twelve years of education as opposed to eight years—the difference between completing primary school and completing secondary school—is predicted to raise the educational attainment of members of the household by a quarter of a standard. For Blacks the effect is about the same as that of reducing the pupil-teacher ratio by ten. This intergenerational influence will enhance the long-run benefits of lowering pupil-teacher ratios, since a better-educated current generation will have better-educated children.

For the purposes of this paper, the two most interesting contrasts are in the effects of resources, private resources through expenditure per head, and public resources through the pupil-teacher ratio. Household resources have no effect on the educational attainment of White children, but a marked positive effect on the education of Blacks. According to this, we might interpret the expenditure term as a resource effect; education is cheap enough so that funding is not a constraint for Whites but can be a serious constraint for the much poorer Blacks. The same appears to be true for the pupil-teacher ratio, whose strong negative effect is confined to Black pupils. The pupil-teacher ratio has no obvious effect on educational attainments of White children, among whom the pupil-teacher ratios are around nineteen. For the Black students, where the pupil-teacher ratios in primary and secondary schools are more than twice as big, higher pupil-teacher ratios have a strong and significant negative effect on attainment. . . .

Table 2 shows estimates of linear probability models for enrollment status. These are run for Blacks aged from eight through eighteen inclusive. A dummy variable equal to one for enrollment and zero otherwise is regressed on the pupil-teacher ratio and the family background variables, together with (not shown) a series of age indicators and urbanization dummies.

The results are qualitatively consistent with our findings on educational attainment in Table 1, particularly as concerns the effects of public and private resources on education. The log of the pupil-

Table 2. School Enrollment: Blacks Aged 8 to 18

Dependent variable: currently enrolled in school = 1	
Explanatory variables:	
Log (pupil-teacher ratio)	−.070
	(2.1)
Indicator: female	.010
	(1.6)
Household head's educ	.006
	(4.8)
Indicator: female head	.014
	(1.7)
Log (expend per hh mem)	.037
	(4.9)
Log (household size)	.029
	(2.6)
Number of obs	8958
R^2	.061

Linear probability model. Robust *t*-statistics are in parentheses, allowing for correlation between observations from the same cluster. Also included in the regressions are age indicators, urban, and rural indicators.

teacher ratio has a significant negative effect on the probability of being in school. Using the same example as before, a cut in the pupil-teacher ratio of a quarter would increase the probability of enrollment for Black students by 0.02 in a single year. The same cut is estimated in Table 1 to increase average educational attainment for ten to eighteen year olds by 0.52, which is larger than the prediction from the enrollment effects (between four and twelve years of risk times 0.02 per year). Enrollment and attainment are not mechanically linked; enrollment does not imply attendance, let alone passing on to the next grade, and dropouts can reenroll at various ages, so that it is hard to use the comparison as a cross-check. As with attainment, the effect of a four-year increase in head's education is about the same as a ten-pupil drop in the pupil-teacher ratio, and, in both cases, household resources enhance education. . . .

We now turn to the much smaller sample of individuals who took the comprehension and numeracy tests appended to the main survey. Since the selection of the adult sample of test-takers was problematic, and since the pupil-teacher ratio can only be reliably linked with those now in school, we confine our attention to those between thirteen and eighteen years of age, of which there are 763 Blacks, and 89 Whites. . . .

The results for the White subsample are presented in the first two columns of Table 3; there are no significant effects of any of the variables on either of the two scores. While this is consistent with the general lack of such findings in the literature,

the small sample size must be kept in mind; the estimated effects of the pupil-teacher ratio are insignificantly different from zero but are also consistent with the existence of a large negative influence of class size on test scores. For the larger sample of Black adolescents, the results are more precise. Columns 3 and 4 show the regressions with education omitted, columns 5 and 6 with years of completed education as a conditioning variable, and columns 7 and 8 with education included but without the family background variables. Since pupil-teacher ratios affect the amount of education, which in turn is likely to affect test scores, we are interested in regressions both unconditional and conditional on education. The conditional regression measures the direct effect of educational quality on test scores with quantity held constant, while the unconditional regression gives the total (reduced-form) effect of quality, both direct and indirect. In the absence of education, age has a positive effect on test scores, as does the education of the household head, household resources, and female headship. Higher pupil-teacher ratios negatively affect both scores, but the size of the effect is five times as large for the mathematics test scores as it is on the comprehension scores. The standard errors are much the same for both, so that only the effect on the math score is significantly different from zero.

Columns 5 and 6 include educational attainment as a regressor, which has a strong positive effect on test scores—four additional years generates one additional correct answer on the tests—and which

Table 3. Determinants of Literacy and Numeracy Test Scores

	Whites		Blacks		Blacks		Blacks	
	Literacy	Numeracy	Literacy	Numeracy	Literacy	Numeracy	Literacy	Numeracy
Years of completed education	.225 (1.5)	−.052 (0.3)	—	—	.225 (7.7)	.270 (8.7)	.273 (9.8)	.300 (10.2)
Age	.091 (0.5)	.355 (1.8)	.161 (4.6)	.146 (3.9)	.024 (0.6)	−.019 (0.5)	−.006 (0.2)	−.037 (0.9)
Log (pupil-teacher ratio)	1.15 (0.6)	3.24 (1.4)	−.156 (0.5)	−.778 (2.2)	.006 (0.0)	−.584 (1.7)	−.123 (0.4)	−.825 (2.5)
Head of household's completed educ	.078 (1.4)	.055 (0.9)	.072 (4.3)	.078 (4.3)	.053 (3.2)	.054 (3.1)	—	—
Log (expenditure per household member)	.569 (1.3)	.824 (1.7)	.392 (3.7)	.318 (2.8)	.231 (2.2)	.125 (1.1)	—	—
R^2	.200	.251	.132	.122	.125	.203	.175	.183
Number of obs	89	89	763	763	763	763	777	777

T-statistics are reported in parentheses. All regressions include metro indicators, log of household size, indicator for female-headed household, and an indicator that the respondent is female.

removes the effect of age. The estimated coefficients of pupil-teacher ratios are diminished (absolutely) by the exclusion of the indirect effect on educational attainment; there is no estimated direct effect of the pupil-teacher ratio on the comprehension score, and the reduction in the size of the effect on the math score leaves it significant only at the 10 percent level. The comparison between these results and those in columns 7 and 8 shows that the results are robust to the inclusion or exclusion of the background variables. In their absence, the pupil-teacher ratio has somewhat larger effects, and is more precisely estimated, but the difference is not very marked. . . .

Summary and Conclusions

On the eve of democratic elections in South Africa, . . . educational resources were . . . sharply different by race, with pupil-teacher ratios in Black schools more than twice as high as those in White schools. In this environment we find that poorly resourced schools, defined as those with high pupil-teacher ratios, discourage educational attainment conditional on age, lower test scores, and lower the probability of being enrolled in education. These results for educational attainment and enrollment are based on a large sample of pupils and schools; those for test scores on a much smaller subsample. The effects of the pupil-teacher ratio on attainment and enrollment are confined to Blacks, consistent with the view that at the small class sizes that characterize education for the other racial groups, reductions in class size have little or no effect. Pupils in better-off Black households do better in their education, and we find no parallel for Whites. That the education of Blacks but not Whites is constrained by financial resources is further supported by the fact that many Blacks who are not in school—but not Whites—report lack of resources as the reason. . . .

It should be reemphasized that our results apply to changes in the pupil-teacher ratio in South Africa that would hold constant the mix of teachers and other resources, and perhaps most importantly, that would hold constant the quality of teachers. We have little doubt that the positive effects of reducing class size would be reduced if the quality of teachers were to be reduced in an attempt to expand the number of teachers.

References

Republic of South Africa. *The Financing of Education in Terms of the Constitution of The RSA, 1983 (Act No. 110 of 1983),* National Education Policy Branch, Department of National Education, Report: NATED 02-329 (94/05), May 1994.

South African Institute of Race Relations, *South Africa Survey 1996/97* (Johannesburg: South African Institute of Race Relations, 1997).

Exhibit IV.B.1. Health Indicators

Country Name (listed from lowest to highest HDI)	Infant Mortality Rate (Per 1,000 live births) 2001	Prevalence of Malnutrition (Percent of children under 5)		Prevalence of Disease			Reproductive Health		Access to Health Care	
		By Height for Age[a]	By Weight for Age[a]	Adults Living with HIV/AIDS[b] (Percent of population aged 15–49) 2001	Malaria Cases[c] (Per 100,000 people) 2000	Tuberculosis Cases[d] (Per 100,000 people) 2001	Contraceptive Prevalence Rate[e] (Percent of women aged 15–49)	Maternal Mortality Ratio[f] (Per 100,000 live births)	Physicians[g] (Per 1,000 people)	Hospital Beds[g] (Per 1,000 people)
Low-human development countries										
Sierra Leone	182	35	27	7.0		258	4.0	1,800	0.1	1.2
Niger	156	40	40		1,693	150	8.2	590	0.0	0.1
Burkina Faso	104	37	34	6.5	619	157	11.9	480	0.0	1.4
Mali	141	49	27	1.7	4,008	295	7.0	580	0.1	0.2
Burundi	114	48	45	8.3	48,098	170	8.7		0.1	0.7
Mozambique	125	36	26	13.0	18,115	125	5.6	1,100	0.0	0.9
Ethiopia	116	52	47	6.4	556	179	8.1	870	0.0	0.2
Central African Republic	115	28	23	12.9	2,207	255	14.8	1,100	0.0	0.9
Congo, Dem. Rep. of the	129	45	34	4.9	2,960	184			0.1	1.4
Guinea-Bissau	130		25	2.8	2,421	135		950	0.2	1.5
Chad	117	29	28	3.6	197	168	4.1	910	0.0	0.7
Angola	154	53	41	5.5	8,773	197		830	0.1	1.3
Zambia	112	42	24	21.5	34,204	445	25.9	650	0.1	3.5
Malawi	114	49	25	15.0	25,948	242	30.6	1,100	0.0	1.3
Côte d'Ivoire	102	25	21	9.7	12,152	207	15.0	600	0.1	0.8
Tanzania, U. Rep. of	104	44	29	7.8	1,207	212	25.4	530	0.0	0.9
Benin	94	31	23	3.6	10,697	36	16.4	500	0.1	0.2
Rwanda	96	43	24	8.9	6,510	188	13.2	1,100	0.0	1.7
Guinea	109	41	33		75,386	134	6.2	530	0.1	0.6
Senegal	79	23	18	0.5	11,925	103	10.5	560	0.1	0.4
Eritrea	72	38	44	2.8	3,479	249	8.0	1,000	0.0	
Mauritania	120	35	32		11,150	209	8.0	750	0.1	0.7
Djibouti	100	26	18		715	382			0.1	2.5
Nigeria	110	34	31	5.8	30	196	15.3		0.2	1.7
Gambia	91	30	17	1.6	17,340	283			0.0	0.6
Haiti	79	23	17	6.1	15	190	28.1	520	0.2	0.7
Madagascar	84	48	40	0.3		158	19.4	490	0.1	0.9

Yemen	0.6	0.2	350	20.8	70	15,160	0.1	46	52	79
Uganda	0.9	0.0	510	14.8	187	46	5.0	23	39	79
Kenya	1.6	0.1	590	39.0	289	545	15.0	22	33	78
Zimbabwe	0.5	0.1	700	53.5	291	5,410	33.7	13	27	76
Pakistan	0.7	0.6		27.6	178	58	0.1	38	36	84
Nepal	0.2	0.0	540	29.0	135	33	0.5	48	51	66
Cameroon		0.1	430	19.3	96	2,900	11.8	22	29	96
Median	*0.8*	*0.1*	*595*	*14.8*	*188*	*3,220*	*6.0*	*27*	*37*	*104*
Medium-human development countries										
Togo	1.5	0.1	480	23.5	114	7,701	6.0	25	22	79
Congo	3.4	0.3			122	5,880	7.2	24	28	81
Bangladesh	0.3	0.2	400	53.8	211	40	0.1	48	45	51
Sudan	1.1	0.1	550	10.0	142	13,934	2.6	11	34	65
Lesotho		0.1		23.2	277	0	31.0	18	44	91
Bhutan	1.6	0.2	380	30.7	114	285	0.1	19	40	74
Lao People's Dem. Rep.	2.6	0.2	650	25.1	143	759	0.1	40	41	87
Comoros	2.8	0.1		21.0	49	1,930		25	34	59
Swaziland		0.2	230		627	2,835	33.4	10	30	106
Papua New Guinea	4.0	0.1	370	25.9	283	1,688	0.7	30	43	70
Myanmar	0.6	0.3	230	5.0	113	224		43	45	77
Cambodia	2.1	0.3	440	23.8	560	476	2.7	45	45	97
Ghana	1.5	0.1	210	22.0	145	15,344	3.0	25	26	57
Vanuatu	6.2	0.1			63	3,260		20	19	34
India	0.8	0.4	540	51.8	199	7	0.8	53	52	67
Morocco	1.0	0.5	230	59.0	47		0.1	10	24	39
Botswana	1.6	0.2	330	33.0	224	48,704	38.8	13	29	80
Namibia		0.3	270	29.0	221	1,502	22.5	26	29	55
Solomon Islands	2.7	0.1	553		52	15,172		21	26	20
Sao Tome and Principe	4.7	0.5			143			17	26	57
Nicaragua	1.5	0.9	150	60.3	35	402	0.2	12	25	36
Egypt	2.1	1.6	80	56.1	23		0.1	4	19	35
Guatemala	1.0	0.9	190	38.0	48	386	1.0	24	46	43
Gabon	3.2	0.2	520	32.7	187			12	21	60
Mongolia	11.5	2.4	150	59.9	124	2,148		13	25	61
Equatorial Guinea	2.8	0.2			102	2,744	0.1			101
Honduras	1.1	0.8	110	61.8	46	541	1.6	17	39	31
Bolivia	1.7	1.3	390	48.7	116	378	0.1	8	27	60
Tajikistan	8.8	2.0	65		83	303	0.1		31	91
Indonesia	0.7	0.2	380	57.0	321	920	0.1	25	42	33
South Africa		0.6		62.0	237	143	20.1	9	23	56

Exhibit IV.B.1. (Continued)

Country Name (listed from lowest to highest HDI)	Infant Mortality Rate (Per 1,000 live births) 2001	Prevalence of Malnutrition (Percent of children under 5) By Height for Age[a]	Prevalence of Malnutrition (Percent of children under 5) By Weight for Age[a]	Adults Living with HIV/AIDS[b] (Percent of population aged 15–49) 2001	Malaria Cases[c] (Per 100,000 people) 2000	Tuberculosis Cases[d] (Per 100,000 people) 2001	Contraceptive Prevalence Rate[e] (Percent of women aged 15–49)	Maternal Mortality Ratio[f] (Per 100,000 live births)	Physicians[g] (Per 1,000 people)	Hospital Beds[g] (Per 1,000 people)
Syrian Arab Republic	23	21	13			47	45.3	110	1.3	1.4
Viet Nam	30	37	34	0.3	95	93	75.3	95	0.5	1.7
Moldova, Rep. of	27			0.2		104	73.7	28	3.5	12.1
Algeria	39	18	6	0.1	2	23	50.8	140	1.0	2.1
Iran, Islamic Rep. of	35	15	11	0.1	27	32	73.0	37	0.9	1.6
El Salvador	33	23	12	0.6	11	36	59.7	120	1.1	1.6
China	31	14	10	0.1	1	107	83.0	55	1.7	2.4
Cape Verde	29	16	14			188	52.9	35	0.2	1.6
Kyrgyzstan	52	25	11	0.1		88	59.5	65	3.0	9.5
Uzbekistan	52	31	19	0.1	1	63	55.6	21	3.1	8.3
Armenia	31	13	3	0.2	4	47		35	3.2	0.7
Sri Lanka	17	20	33	0.1	1,110	50	62.0	90	0.4	2.7
Occupied Palestinian Territories	21					19	41.6		0.5	1.2
Ecuador	24	26	14	0.3	728	94	65.8	160	1.7	1.6
Turkey	36	16	8	0.1	17	25	63.9	130	1.3	2.6
Albania	23	15	14			21			1.3	3.2
Dominican Republic	41	11	5	2.5	6	88	64.0	230	2.2	1.5
Grenada	20					3		1	0.5	5.3
Guyana	54	10	12	2.7	3,074	65	31.0	110	0.2	3.9
Tunisia	21	8	4		1	18	60.0	70	0.7	1.7
Jordan	27	8	5	0.1	3	5	50.3	41	1.7	1.8
Azerbaijan	77	20	17	0.1	19	56	55.4	80	3.6	9.7
Georgia	24	12	3	0.1	5	58	40.5	50	4.4	4.8
Turkmenistan	69	22	12	0.1	1	56		65	3.0	11.5
Maldives	58	27	43	0.1		21		350	0.4	0.8
Philippines	29	32	32	0.1	15	226	47.0	170	1.2	1.1
Paraguay	26	14	4		124	43	57.4	190	1.1	1.3
Lebanon	28	12	3			11	61.0	100	2.1	2.7

Peru	30	25	7	0.4	258	94	68.9	190	0.9	1.5
Fiji	18	3	8	0.1		23	42.0	38	0.5	2.7
Saint Vincent and the Grenadines	22	24	20	0.1		5	23.7	43	0.9	1.9
Oman	12	23	23	1.2	27	3	65.0	14	1.3	2.2
Jamaica	17	4	4	1.2		44		95	1.4	2.1
Suriname	26			0.1	2,954	94		110	0.3	3.7
Kazakhstan	81	10	4	1.0		57	66.0	65	3.5	8.5
Ukraine	17	16	3	1.8		100	71.6	25	3.0	11.8
Thailand	24	13	18		130	27	72.0	44	0.4	2.0
Saudi Arabia	23			0.1	32	94	20.8		1.7	2.3
Romania	19	8	6			9	48.0	42	1.8	7.6
Saint Lucia	17					22	47.0	30	0.5	3.4
Samoa (Western)	20	13	4	0.5		22	18.0		0.3	4.4
Venezuela	19				94	9	62.0	60	2.4	1.5
Dominica	14					18	47.0	65	0.5	2.6
Belize	34		6	2.0	657	35		140	0.5	2.1
Bosnia and Herzegovina	15	11	4	0.1		44	77.0	10	1.4	1.8
Brazil	31	14	6	0.7	344	29	76.9	160	1.3	3.1
Colombia	19	13	7	0.4	250	93	34.0	80	1.2	1.5
Russian Federation	18	10	3	0.9	1	57	75.0	44	4.2	12.1
Mauritius	17	15	15	0.1	1	11	45.0	21	0.9	3.1
Libyan Arab Jamahiriya	16	5	5	0.2	2	26		75	1.3	4.3
Macedonia, TFYR	22	7	6	0.1		28	61.0	7	2.2	4.9
Panama	19	18	8	1.5	36	67	56.0	70	1.7	2.2
Malaysia	8			0.4	57	20		41	0.7	2.0
Bulgaria	14		20	0.1		3		15	3.4	7.4
Antigua and Barbuda	12	7	10					150	1.1	3.9
Median	*31*	*22*	*12*	*0.2*	*237*	*57*	*53.8*	*100*	*0.9*	*2.2*
High-human development countries										
Mexico	24	18	8	0.3	8	19	65.0	55	1.8	1.1
Trinidad and Tobago	17	5	7	2.5	1	9	53.0	70	0.8	5.1
Belarus	17			0.3		57		20	4.4	12.2
Cuba	7			0.1		6	70.0	33	5.3	5.1
Saint Kitts and Nevis	20					7	41.0	130	1.2	6.4
Latvia	17			0.4		43		45	2.8	10.3
Bahamas	13			3.5		19			1.5	3.9
United Arab Emirates	8		7			13		3	1.8	2.6
Croatia	7	1	1	0.1		40		6	2.3	5.9
Kuwait	9	3	2			27		5	1.9	2.8
Lithuania	8			0.1		48		18	4.0	9.2

Exhibit IV.B.1. (Continued)

Country Name (listed from lowest to highest HDI)	Infant Mortality Rate (Per 1,000 live births) 2001	Prevalence of Malnutrition (Percent of children under 5)		Adults Living with HIV/AIDS[b] (Percent of population aged 15–49) 2001	Malaria Cases[c] (Per 100,000 people) 2000	Tuberculosis Cases[d] (Per 100,000 people) 2001	Contraceptive Prevalence Rate[e] (Percent of women aged 15–49)	Maternal Mortality Ratio[f] (Per 100,000 live births)	Physicians[g] (Per 1,000 people)	Hospital Beds[g] (Per 1,000 people)
		By Height for Age[a]	By Weight for Age[a]							
Qatar	11	8	6			13	43.3	10	1.3	1.7
Chile	10	2	1	0.3		10		23	1.1	2.7
Costa Rica	9	6	5	0.6	42	7	68.0	29	0.9	1.7
Estonia	11			1.0		27		52	3.0	7.4
Uruguay	14	10	4	0.3		15		26	3.7	4.4
Slovakia	8			0.1		15		9	3.5	7.1
Hungary	8	3	2	0.1		22	72.5	15	3.2	8.2
Bahrain	13		7	0.3		34	61.8	46	1.0	2.9
Seychelles	13	5	6			26			1.3	6.3
Poland	8			0.1		23		8	2.2	4.9
Argentina	16	12	5	0.7	1	30		41	2.7	3.3
Malta	5			0.1		3			2.6	5.4
Czech Republic	4	2	1	0.1		7	68.9	9	3.1	8.8
Brunei Darussalam	6					24		0	0.8	3.0
Korea, Rep. of	5			0.1	9	48	77.0	20	1.3	6.1
Slovenia	4			0.1		12		11	2.3	5.7
Singapore	3			0.2		22	74.0	6	1.6	3.6
Barbados	12	7	6	1.2		11	55.0	0	1.3	7.6
Hong Kong, China (SAR)	3			0.1		39	81.0		1.3	4.9
Cyprus	5			0.3		5		0	2.6	5.1
Greece	5			0.2		11		1	4.4	4.9
Portugal	5			0.5		17	66.0	8	3.2	4.0
Israel	6			0.1		5		5	3.9	6.0
Italy	4			0.4		4		7	6.0	4.9
New Zealand	6			0.1		5		15	2.2	6.2
Spain	4			0.5		14	59.0	6	3.3	4.1
Germany	4			0.1		5	78.0	8	3.6	9.1
France	4			0.3		6	70.7	10	3.0	8.2

Austria	5			0.2	6	71.0	0	3.1	8.6
Luxembourg	5			0.2	6		6	3.1	8.0
Finland	4			*0.1*	5		7	3.1	7.5
United Kingdom	6			0.1	5	83.0		1.8	4.1
Ireland	6			0.1	6	60.0	6	2.3	9.7
Denmark	4			0.2	6		10	3.4	4.5
Switzerland	5			0.5	5	71.0	5	3.5	17.9
Japan	3	6	4	0.1	21	56.0	8	1.9	16.5
Canada	5			0.3	3	73.0		2.1	3.9
United States	7	2	1	0.6	2	64.2	8	2.8	3.6
Belgium	5			0.2	6	81.0		3.9	7.3
Netherlands	5			0.2	3	75.0	7	3.2	10.8
Australia	6	0	0	0.1	4	76.0		2.5	7.9
Sweden	3			0.1	2	78.0	5	2.9	3.6
Iceland	3			0.2	2			3.4	14.6
Norway	4			0.1	3		6	2.9	14.6
Median	*6*	*h*	*h*	*0.2*	*10*	*70.4*	*8*	*2.7*	*5.7*

United Nations Human Development Index countries are included in the Exhibit only if they have data available.

a Percentage of children under 5 years whose height (or weight) for age is less than minus two standard deviations from the median of the international reference population (children ages 0–59 months in the United States in 1983). Data are for the most recent year available between 1980 and 2001.

b Data in italics (*0.1*) are meant to signify that less than one tenth of a percent of the population is living with HIV/AIDS.

c Data refer to malaria cases reported to the World Health Organization and may represent only a fraction of the true number in a country because of incomplete reporting systems or incomplete coverage by health services, or both. Because of the diversity of case detection and reporting systems, country comparisons should be made with caution.

d Data refer to tuberculosis cases reported to the World Health Organisation and may represent only a fraction of the true number in a country because of incomplete coverage by health services, inaccurate diagnosis or deficient recording and reporting.

e Percentage of married women ages 15–49 who are practicing, or whose sexual partners are practicing, any form of contraception. Data are for the most recent year available between 1985 and 2001.

f The maternal mortality rates are those reported by national authorities. Data are for the more recent year available between 1985 and 2001.

g Data are for the most recent year available between 1980 and 2001.

h There is no reliable median for the prevalence of malnutrition or malaria in high-human development countries due to the lack of reporting, but insofar as the authorities are not reporting because the prevalence of malnutrition and malaria are low, then the true median is likely to be lower than would be expressed in the table.

Sources: United Nations Development Program. *Human Development Report 2003* (New York: Oxford University Press, 2003). World Bank, World Development Indicators, 2003.

Selection IV.B.1. Pharmaceuticals and the Developing World*

Pharmaceuticals have brought tremendous health benefits to developing countries, but existing pharmaceuticals are often underused or misused, and pharmaceutical R&D on health problems specific to poor countries is woefully inadequate.

The role of pharmaceuticals and medical technology in improving health in developing countries stands in contrast to the historical experience of the developed countries. Historically, health in currently developed countries improved largely due to higher incomes and consequent improvements in nutrition, sanitation and water supplies. Fogel (1986) finds that half of the decline in standardized British death rates and 70 percent of the decline in standardized American death rates between 1700 and 1980 occurred before 1911, in an era with few effective medicines. However, modern medical technologies allow tremendous improvements in health even at low income levels. The outward shift of the technological frontier is illustrated by Vietnam, which has a life expectancy of 69 years despite a per capita income that according to official statistics is less than one-tenth that of the United States in 1900, which had a 47-year life expectancy.[1] To take another example, per capita GDP in low-income sub-Saharan African nations decreased 13 percent from 1972 through 1992, but life expectancy increased by 10 percent, from 45 to 49 years, and infant mortality fell 30 percent, from 133 per thousand births to 93 per thousand births (World Bank, 2001b). (Unfortunately, since then, life expectancy in sub-Saharan Africa has fallen due to the AIDS pandemic.) Indeed, analysis of worldwide health trends in the twentieth century has found that most improvements resulted from technological advances rather than from income growth. Using the cross-sectional relationship between income and life expectancy, Preston (1975) estimated that income growth accounted for only 10 to 25 percent of the growth in world life expectancy between the 1930s and 1960s and suggested that the diffusion of technological advances was a major factor for the increase in life expectancy at any given income level. Jamison et al.

(2001) attribute 74 percent of the decline in infant mortality rates over the period from 1962 to 1987 to technical progress, 21 percent to greater education and only about 5 percent to income growth.

While other technological improvements—such as the development of oral rehydration therapy against diarrhea and the use of radios in public health campaigns—may have played a role in improving health, the development and dissemination of pharmaceuticals has played a key role. To take one example, about three-quarters of the world's children receive a standard package of cheap, off-patent vaccines through the World Health Organization's (WHO) Expanded Program on Immunization, and these vaccines are estimated to save 3 million lives per year (Kim-Farley, 1992). Though vaccination rates are uneven around the world, the World Bank (2001b) estimates that 70 percent of infants in low-income countries received the three-dose DTP (diphtheria, tetanus and pertussis) vaccine over the period from 1995 through 1999.

Yet many people in developing countries who could benefit from pharmaceuticals do not receive them. The failure of antiretroviral therapy to reach more than a tiny fraction of people with AIDS in developing countries has attracted wide-spread publicity, but even medicines that are far cheaper and easier to deliver are not reaching many of the people who need them. More than a quarter of children worldwide and over half of children in some countries do not receive the vaccines that are part of WHO's Expanded Program on Immunization, although these cost only pennies per dose and require no diagnosis. Three million lives are lost annually as a result (World Bank, 2001a). Only a small fraction of children in poor countries receive the newer hepatitis B and Haemophilus influenzae b (Hib) vaccines, which cost a dollar or two per dose. One in four people worldwide suffer from intestinal worms, although treatments only need to be taken once or twice per year, have virtually no side effects, and cost less than a dollar per year. These examples suggest that while intellectual property rights undoubtedly prevent some from obtaining needed pharmaceuticals, eliminating these rights would not help the majority of those without access to drugs.

While developing countries have obtained substantial benefits from pharmaceuticals originally developed for rich country markets, little research is conducted on diseases that primarily affect poor countries, such as malaria or tuberculosis. Pecoul

*From Michael Kremer, "Pharmaceuticals and the Developing World." *Journal of Economic Perspectives* 16, no. 4 (Fall 2002): 67–71, 75–76, 82–85. Reprinted by permission.

[1]Data are from Balke and Gordon (1989), Johnston and Williamson (2002), Kurian (1994) and World Bank (2001b). Even if GDP growth in the United States were underestimated by two percentage points annually, 1900 U.S. per capita GDP exceeds Vietnam's current per capita GDP.

et al. (1999) report that of the 1,233 drugs licensed worldwide between 1975 and 1997, only 13 were for tropical diseases. Of these, five came from veterinary research, two were modifications of existing medicines, and two were produced for the U.S. military. Only four were developed by commercial pharmaceutical firms specifically for tropical diseases of humans. According to WHO (1996), 50 percent of global health research and development in 1992 was undertaken by private industry, but less than 5 percent of that was spent on diseases specific to less developed countries. Even for diseases that affect both rich and poor countries, research tends to focus on products that are best suited for use in rich countries. For example, much research is conducted on sophisticated AIDS drugs that are useful in developed countries, but are too expensive and difficult to deliver to the majority of the population in the poorest countries. Much less research is conducted on vaccines, which are typically much more feasible to deliver than drugs in developing countries, since they often require only a few doses to deliver and can be delivered by personnel with limited medical training. . . .

Characteristics of the Pharmaceutical Market in Developing Countries

The market for pharmaceuticals in developing countries differs in several ways from that in the developed world.

Small Markets

The market for pharmaceuticals in the poorest countries is tiny. Connecticut spends more on health than the 38 low-income countries of sub-Saharan Africa combined (World Bank, 2001b; U.S. Census, 2000). In 1998, U.S. public and private health spending constituted 13 percent of its almost $32,000 per capita income, for a total of more than $4,000 per person. In contrast, low-income sub-Saharan African nations spent only 6 percent of their average $300 per capita GDP on health, or around $18 per person (World Bank, 2001b), though developing countries spend a higher percentage of their health budgets on pharmaceuticals than do developed countries. Drug developers often do not even bother to take out patents in small, poor countries (Attaran and Gillespie-White, 2001).

Middle-income country markets are small, but comprise a significant and growing source of revenue for pharmaceutical firms. The Pharmaceutical Research and Manufacturers of America (PhRMA) estimate that while only 1 percent of their market is

Table 1. World Pharmaceutical Market, Sales by Region, 1998

Region	Percentage of market
United States	39.6
Europe	26.1
Japan	15.4
Latin America	7.5
Southeast Asia & China	7.0
Canada	1.9
Africa	1.0
Middle East	0.9
Australasia	0.6

Source: PhRMA (2000, adapted from figure 7-2).

in Africa, including middle-income countries such as South Africa, 7 percent is in Southeast Asia and China, and 7.5 percent is in Latin America (PhRMA, 2000), as shown in Table 1.

Different Disease Environment

Developing countries face a significantly different disease environment than developed countries due to both their poverty and their geography. The burden of different diseases can be compared across countries using the concept of Disability Adjusted Life Years (Murray and Lopez, 1996). DALYs take into account not only the lives lost through disease, but also the number of years of disability caused. World Health Organization (2001) estimates imply that infectious and parasitic diseases account for one-third of the disease burden in low-income countries (in fact, for nearly half of Africa's disease burden), but only 3 percent of the burden in high-income countries, as seen in Table 2 (WHO, 2001). In contrast, the disease burden in high-income countries mainly consists of noncommunicable conditions like cancer and cardiovascular disease. Table 3 lists specific diseases for which more than 99 percent of the burden falls in low- and middle-income countries, which include malaria, schistosomiasis and leprosy (Lanjouw and Cockburn, 2001). . . .

Market Failures, Government Failures and Policy Implications

Clearly, the pharmaceutical market in developing countries is rife with market and government failures. Pharmaceutical use is sometimes suboptimal due to pricing above marginal cost and positive treatment externalities for infectious diseases; sometimes too great due to the failure of consumers to take into account externalities from drug

Table 2. Percentage of Disease Burden

Cause	World	Low-income countries	Middle-income countries	High-income countries
Infectious and parasitic diseases	23.1%	33.3%	13.9%	3.0%
Tuberculosis	2.4%	2.9%	2.2%	0.3%
HIV/AIDS	6.1%	9.7%	2.6%	0.7%
Malaria	2.7%	4.5%	1.0%	0.0%
Noncommunicable conditions	46.1%	33.2%	55.5%	82.7%
Malignant neoplasms (cancers)	5.3%	2.9%	6.7%	14.4%
Cardiovascular diseases	10.3%	7.7%	12.3%	16.4%

Sources: World Health Report (2001), World Bank (2001b).

Table 3. Diseases for Which 99 Percent or More of the Global Burden Fell on Low- and Middle-Income Countries in 1990

Disease	Disability adjusted life years (Thousands, 2000)	Deaths per year (2000)
Chagas disease	680	21,299
Dengue	433	12,037
Ancylostomiasis and necatoriasis (bookworm)	1,829	5,650
Japanese encephalitis	426	3,502
Lymphatic filariasis	5,549	404
Malaria	40,213	1,079,877
Onchocerciasis (river blindness)	951	—
Schistosomiasis	1,713	11,473
Tetanus	9,766	308,662
Trachoma	1,181	14
Trichuriasis	1,640	2,123
Trypanosomiasis	1,585	49,668
Leishmaniasis	1,810	40,913
Measles	27,549	776,626
Poliomyelitis	184	675
Syphilis	5,574	196,533
Diphtheria	114	3,394
Leprosy	141	2,268
Pertussis	12,768	296,099
Diarrhoeal diseases	62,227	2,124,032

Sources: Global Burden from WHO (1996), quoted in Lanjouw and Cockburn (2001, table 1). Figures updated from Lanjouw and Cockburn (2001), using WHO (2001).

resistance; and sometimes simply inappropriate due to information asymmetries between health care providers and their patients. Drug procurement is often inefficient and corrupt, and inappropriate regulation can hinder access. In addition, health care workers are politically powerful relative to patients.

However, the most severe distortions in developing country pharmaceutical markets probably involve dynamic issues. Pharmaceutical firms are reluctant to invest in R&D on the diseases that primarily affect developing countries not only because the poverty of the potential users reduces their willingness to pay, but also because the potential revenue from product sales is far smaller than the sum of customers' potential willingness to pay due to the lack of intellectual property protection and the tendency for governments to force prices down after firms have sunk their research and development costs. The underprovision of R&D on problems facing the poor, even relative to their incomes, implies that a redirection of foreign assistance from private goods, such as food, or even public goods, such as roads, to the international public good of R&D on health problems of the poor could make the poor better-off.

One reason why governments provide suboptimal R&D incentives is that pharmaceutical research and development is a global public good, so each country has an incentive to free ride on research financed by the governments of other countries or induced by their intellectual property rights protection. This is a general problem faced by all countries, not just developing ones. Indeed, the mystery is not why developing countries have historically offered little protection for intellectual property rights, but why small developed countries offer so much. A second reason for suboptimal R&D incentives is that the high fixed costs of R&D and low marginal costs of production for pharmaceuticals create a time-inconsistency problem for governments. Once products have been developed, governments have an incentive to set prices at or near marginal cost. Products are then consumed at the efficient level, and surplus is transferred from (typically foreign) producers to consumers. Governments are in a strong bargaining position because they are major pharmaceutical purchasers, they regulate products and often prices, and they are arbiters of intellectual property rights. However, if pharmaceutical firms anticipate low prices, they will be reluctant to invest. In a repeated game between nations and pharmaceutical producers, this time-inconsistency problem could potentially be overcome through reputation formation. Indeed, one reason why developed countries are developed may be that these countries were able to establish good reputational equilibria in a variety of areas, including research incentives. Developed countries typically have more stable governments that are more likely to invest in reputation formation for the long run.

Whatever the underlying causes, intellectual property rights for pharmaceuticals in developing countries are weak, and hence the private returns for developing products to fight diseases of developing countries are likely to be a tiny fraction of the social returns to these products. For example, consider a hypothetical future malaria vaccine. A standard way to assess the cost-effectiveness of a health intervention is the cost per Disability Adjusted Life Year saved. A common cost-effectiveness threshold for health interventions in the poorest countries is $100 per DALY. For comparison, health interventions are considered cost-effective in the United States at up to 500 to 1000 times this amount:

$50,000–$100,000 per year of life saved (Neumann et al., 2000). At a threshold of $100 per DALY, a malaria vaccine would be cost-effective even at a price of $40 per immunized person (Glennerster and Kremer, 2001), but based on the historical record of vaccine prices, the developer of a malaria vaccine would be lucky to receive payments of one-tenth or one-twentieth of that amount. . . .

R&D on Needed Products

As discussed earlier, current incentives for the development of products needed primarily by developing countries are inadequate. Vaccines for malaria, tuberculosis and the strains of AIDS prevalent in Africa are a prime example. Programs to encourage R&D can take two broad forms. "Push" programs subsidize research inputs—for example, through grants to researchers or R&D tax credits. "Pull" programs reward research outputs, for example, by committing in advance to purchase a specified amount of a desired product at a specified price. Both approaches have important roles, but current policy underutilizes pull programs.

Push programs are subject to asymmetric information between researchers and program administrators and between these groups and politicians and the public, giving rise to both moral hazard and adverse selection. Moral hazard arises because funders cannot perfectly monitor the actions of grant recipients, and grant recipients may have incentives to devote effort to pursuing general scientific research or preparing their next grant application rather than focusing on development of the desired product. In contrast, under a pull program, researchers will not receive payment unless a useable product is delivered, so researchers have incentives to focus on developing the desired product.

Adverse selection arises because researchers have more information than do funders about the probability that their research will lead to successful products. Research administrators and their ultimate employers—elected officials and the general public—may not be able to determine which research projects in response to certain diseases are worth pursuing, nor which diseases and products should be targeted. Decision makers may therefore wind up financing ideas with only a minute probability of success, or worse, failing to fund promising research because they do not have confidence that its backers are presenting objective information on its prospects. In contrast, under a pull program in which developers are rewarded only if they successfully produce the desired product, there is a strong incentive for firms considering research investments to assess the prospects for success realistically.

The moral hazard and adverse selection problems that plague push programs are illustrated by the U.S. Agency for International Development's (USAID) 1980s program to develop a malaria vaccine. During the USAID program, external evaluators suggested that additional funding should not be provided to two of the three research teams. However, as a result of information provided by the project director, USAID provided substantial new resources to all three teams and was sufficiently confident that vaccines would be developed that it even arranged to purchase monkeys for testing a vaccine. Two of three researchers diverted grant funds into their private accounts and were later indicted for theft and criminal conspiracy. The project director received kickbacks from the contract to purchase monkeys and eventually pleaded guilty to accepting an illegal gratuity, filing false tax returns and making false statements. In 1984, before the indictments, the agency claimed that there had been a "major breakthrough in the development of a vaccine against the most deadly form of malaria in human beings. The vaccine should be ready for use around the world, especially in developing countries, within five years" (Desowitz, 1991). By the end of the project, USAID had spent $60 million on its malaria vaccine effort with few results. While the example is extreme, it vividly illustrates the problems with push programs. . . .

In contrast, under pull programs, the public pays nothing unless a viable product is developed. Pull programs give researchers incentives to self-select projects with a reasonable chance of yielding a viable product and to focus on developing a marketable product. Under pull programs, governments do not need to "pick winners" among R&D proposals—they simply need to decide what success would be worth to society and offer a corresponding reward. Moreover, appropriately designed pull programs can help ensure that if new products are developed, they will reach those who need them. One kind of pull program is a purchase commitment in which sponsors would commit to purchase a specified number of doses at a specified price if a vaccine meeting certain specifications were developed. Purchase commitment programs are discussed in Kremer (2001a, b), World Bank (1999) and Batson and Ainsworth (2001), while shorter treatments of the idea in the popular press appear in Kremer and Sachs (1999) and Sachs

(1999).[2] An example of a purchase commitment would be for developed countries or private foundations to commit to purchase malaria vaccine at $5 per immunized person and to make it available to developing countries either free or for a modest copayment.

A key limitation of pull programs is that they require specifying the output in advance. A pull program could not have been used to encourage the development of the Post-It Note® or the graphical user interface, because these products could not have been adequately described before they were invented. Similarly, pull programs may not work well to encourage basic research, because it is typically difficult to specify the desired results of basic research in advance. (Of course, some basic research outputs, such as proving Fermat's last theorem, can be defined in advance.) Simply rewarding the development of applied products is not a good way to stimulate basic research, since a program that tied rewards to the development of a specific product would encourage researchers to keep their results private as long as possible to have an advantage in the next stage of research. Indeed, a key objective of basic research is to provide information to other researchers, rather than to develop products, and grant-funded academics and scientists in government laboratories have career incentives to publish their results quickly. In contrast to unanticipated inventions, like the Post-It Note®, or to basic research, it is comparatively easier to define what is meant by a safe and efficacious vaccine, especially as existing institutions, such as the U.S. Food and Drug Administration (FDA), are already charged with making these determinations.

Nonetheless, if donor governments, international organizations or private foundations commit to purchase a future vaccine, the eligibility rules they set will be key. Eligibility conditions for candidate products would likely include some minimal technical requirements. These technical requirements could include clearance by a regulatory agency, such as the U.S. FDA, or a waiver of regulatory approval in developed countries for products that would pass a risk-benefit analysis for use in developing, but not developed, countries. Products that pass these requirements might then be subject to

---

[2] An alternative push program design that has been proposed is to reward developers with extensions of patents on other pharmaceuticals. This would inefficiently and inequitably place the entire burden of financing development on patients who need these other pharmaceuticals. For example, giving a patent extension on Prozac for developing an HIV vaccine could prevent some people from getting needed treatment for depression.

market test: nations wishing to purchase products might be required to provide a modest copayment tied to their per capita income, so that countries would have an incentive to investigate carefully whether candidate products are appropriate for their local conditions. This provision would also help to assure that limited donor funds are allocated well and would increase incentives for developers by increasing the payment offered to the successful developer. On the other hand, it could reduce the confidence of potential vaccine developers in the program. A purchase commitment could also include a system of bonus payments for products that exceed the minimum requirements. Eligibility conditions should also specify who will have authority to judge whether the eligibility conditions have been fulfilled. Ideally, these adjudicators should be insulated from political pressure through long terms of service.

A well-written contract should also be credible to potential vaccine developers. Courts have held that similar public commitments to reward contest winners or to purchase specified goods constitute legally binding contracts and that the decisions of independent parties appointed in advance to adjudicate such programs are binding. For example, in the 1960s, the U.S. government pledged to purchase, at a minimum price, domestically produced manganese. After the world price of the commodity fell, the General Services Administration (GSA), the U.S. agency in charge of administering the program, attempted to renege, but U.S. courts forced the GSA to honor the commitment (Morantz and Sloane, 2001).

The total market promised by a purchase commitment should be large enough to induce substantial effort by vaccine developers, but less than the social value of the vaccine. The larger the market for a product, the more firms will enter the field, the more research leads each firm will pursue, and the faster a product will be developed. Given the enormous burden of diseases such as malaria, tuberculosis, and HIV/AIDS, it is important to provide sufficient incentive for many researchers to enter the field and to induce major pharmaceutical firms to pursue several potential leads simultaneously so that products can be developed quickly. There is little risk that payments made as a result of a purchase commitment could exceed the cost of saving the equivalent number of lives using today's treatments.

Prior work by the author and others suggests that an annual market of $250 million to $500 million is needed to motivate substantial research

(Kettler, 1999; Kremer, 2001b; Mercer Management Consulting, 1998). A commitment at this level to purchase vaccines for malaria, tuberculosis and HIV/AIDS would be extremely cost effective, costing nothing if a useable product was not developed and as little as $4 per year of life saved if a vaccine were developed.

References

Attaran, Amir and Lee Gillespie-White. 2001. "Do Patents for Antiretroviral Drugs Constrain Access to AIDS Treatment in Africa?" *Journal of the American Medical Association.* October 17, 286:15, pp. 1886–892.

Balke, Nathan S. and Robert J. Gordon. 1989. "The Estimation of Prewar Gross National Product: Methodology and New Evidence." *Journal of Political Economy.* February, 97, pp. 38–92.

Batson, Amie and Martha Ainsworth. 2001. "Private Investment in AIDS Vaccine Development: Obstacles and Solutions." *Bulletin of the World Health Organization.* 79:8, pp. 721–27.

Desowitz, Robert S. 1991. *The Malaria Capers: Tales of Parasites and People.* New York: W. W. Norton.

Glennerster, Rachel and Michael Kremer. 2001. "A Vaccine Purchase Commitment: Cost-Effectiveness Estimates and Pricing Guidelines." Unpublished Manuscript.

Jamison, Dean T. et al. 2001. "Cross-Country Variation in Mortality Decline, 1962–87: The Role of Country-Specific Technical Progress." CMH Working Paper No. WG1:4, April.

Johnston, Louis and Samuel H. Williamson. 2002 "The Annual Real and Nominal GDP for the United States, 1789-Present." Economic History Services, April, available at ⟨http://www.eh.net/hmit./gdp⟩.

Kettler, Hannah E. 1999. "Updating the Cost of a New Chemical Entity." London, Office of Health Economics.

Kim-Farley, R. and the Expanded Programme on Immunization Team. 1992. "Global Immunization." *Annual Review of Public Health.* 13, pp. 223–37.

Kremer, Michael. 2001a. "Creating Markets for New Vaccines: Part I: Rationale," in *Innovation Policy and the Economy.* Adam B. Jaffe, Josh Lerner, and Scott Stern, eds. Cambride: MIT Press, pp. 35–72.

Kremer, Michael. 2001b. "Creating Markets for New Vaccines: Part II: Design Issues," in *Innovation Policy and the Economy.* Adam B. Jaffe, Josh Lerner, and Scott Stern, eds. Cambride: MIT Press, pp. 73–118.

Kremer, Michael and Jeffrey Sachs. 1999. "A Cure for Indifference." *Financial Times.* May 5, available at ⟨http://www.brook.edu/views/oped/kremer/19990505.htm⟩.

Kurian, George Thomas. 1994. *Datapedia of the United States 1790–2000.* Lanham, Md.: Bernan Press.

Lanjouw, Jean O. and Iain M. Cockburn. 2001. "New Pills for Poor People? Empirical Evidence after GATT." *World Development.* 29:2, pp. 265–89.

Mercer Management Consulting. 1998. "HIV Vaccine Industry Study October-December 1998." World Bank Task Force on Accelerating the Development of an HIV/AIDS Vaccine for Developing Countries.

Morantz, Alison and Robert Sloane. 2001. "Vaccine Purchase Commitment Contract: Legal Strategies for Ensuring Enforceability." Mimeo, Harvard University.

Murray, Christopher J. L. and Alan D. Lopez. 1996. *The Global Burden of Disease: a Comprehensive Assessment of Mortality and Disability from Diseases, Injuries, and Risk Factors in 1990 and Projected to 2020. Global Burden of Disease and Injury Series, Volume 1.* Cambridge, Mass.: Published by the harvard School of Public Health on behalf of the World Health Organization and the World Bank, Distributed by harvard University Press.

Neumann, Peter J. et al. 2000. "Are Pharmaceuticals Cost-Effective? A Review of the Evidence." *Health Affairs* March/April. 19:2, pp. 92–109.

Pecoul, Bernard et al. 1999. "Access to Essential Drugs in Poor Countries: A Lost Battle?" *Journal of the American Medical Association.* January 27, 281:4, pp. 361–67.

PhRMA. 2000. *PhRMA Industry Profile 2000.* Available at ⟨http://www.phrma.org/publications/publications/profile00/⟩.

Preston, Samuel H. 1975. "The Changing Relation between Mortality and Level of Economic Development." *Population Studies.* July, 29:2, pp. 231–48.

Sachs, Jeffrey. 1999. "Helping the World's Poorest." *Economist.* August 14, 352;8132, pp. 17–20.

United States Census. 2000. Available at ⟨http://www.census.gov/dmd/www/2khome.htm⟩.

WHO (World Health Organization). 1996. *Investing in Health Research and Development: Report of the Ad Hoc Committee on Health Research Relating to Future Intervention Options.* Geneva: WHO.

WHO (World Health Organization). 2001. *World Health Report 2001.* Geneva: WHO.

World Bank. 1999. *Confronting AIDS: Public Priorities in a Global Epidemic.* Washington, D.C.: Oxford University Press.

World Bank. 2001a. *Immunization at a Glance.* Washington, D.C.: World Bank, November.

World Bank. 2001b. *World Development Indicators.* Washington, D.C.: Oxford University Press.

Selection IV.B.2. Identifying Impacts of Intestinal Worms on Health in the Presence of Treatment Externalities*

1. Introduction

Hookworm, roundworm, whipworm, and schistosomiasis infect one in four people worldwide. They are particularly prevalent among school-age children in developing countries. We examine the impact of a program in which seventy-five rural Kenyan primary schools were phased into deworming treatment in a randomized order. . . . We then identify cross-school externalities—the impact of deworming for pupils in schools located near treatment schools—using exogenous variation in the local density of treatment school pupils generated by the school-level randomization, and find that deworming reduces worm burdens among children in neighboring primary schools. . . .

Our approach can be distinguished from that in several recent studies in which treatment is typically randomized at the individual level. . . . These studies fail to account for potential externalities for the comparison group from reduced disease transmission. Moreover, if externalities benefit the comparison group, outcome differences between the treatment and comparison groups will understate the benefits of treatment on the treated. This identification problem is closely related to the well-known issue of contamination of experimental job programs in active labor markets, where programs have externality effects on program non-participants (typically by worsening their outcomes, as discussed in Heckman et al. 1999). . . .

2. Intestinal Helminth (Worm) Infections

Hookworm and roundworm each infect approximately 1.3 billion people around the world, while whipworm affects 900 million and 200 million are infected with schistosomiasis (Bundy 1994). While most have light infections, which may be asymptomatic, a minority have heavy infections, which can lead to iron-deficiency anemia, protein-energy malnutrition, abdominal pain, and listlessness.[1] Schistosomiasis can also have more severe consequences, for instance, causing enlargement of the liver and spleen.

Low-cost single-dose oral therapies can kill the worms, reducing hookworm, roundworm, and schistosomiasis infections by 99 percent, although single-dose treatments are only moderately effective against severe whipworm infections (Butterworth et al. 1991; Nokes et al. 1992; Bennett and Guyatt 2000). Reinfection is rapid, however, with worm burden often returning to eighty percent or more of its original level within a year (Anderson and May 1991), and hence geohelminth drugs must be taken every six months and schistosomiasis drugs must be taken annually. The World Health Organization has endorsed mass school-based deworming programs in areas with high helminth infections, since this eliminates the need for costly individual parasitological screening (Warren et al. 1993, WHO 1987), bringing cost down to as little as 49 cents per person per year in Africa (PCD 1999). Known drug side effects are minor, and include stomach ache, diarrhea, dizziness, and vomiting in some cases (WHO 1992). However, due to concern about the possibility that the drugs could cause birth defects (WHO 1992, Cowden and Hotez 2000), standard practice in mass deworming programs has been to not treat girls of reproductive age (Bundy and Guyatt 1996).[2]

Medical treatment could potentially interfere with disease transmission, creating positive externalities. School-aged children likely account for the bulk of helminth transmission (Butterworth et al. 1991). Muchiri, Ouma, and King (1996) find that school children account for 85 to 90 percent of all heavy schistosomiasis infections in nine eastern Kenyan villages. Moreover, conditional on infection levels, children are most likely to spread worm infections because they are less likely to use latrines and more generally have poor hygiene practices (Ouma 1987, Butterworth et al. 1991)."

Treatment externalities for schistosomiasis are likely to take place across larger areas than is typical for geohelminth externalities due to the differing modes of disease transmission. Geohelminth eggs are deposited in the local environment when children defecate in the "bush" surrounding their home or school, while the schistosomiasis parasite is spread through contact with infected fresh water. Children in the area are often infected with schistosomiasis by bathing or fishing in Lake Victoria,

*From Edward Miguel and Michael Kremer, "Worms: Identifying Impacts on Education and Health in the Presence of Treatment Externalities," *Econometrica* 72, no. 1 (January 2004): 159–162, 165, 172, 174–176, 184–188, 203–204. Reprinted by permission.

[1] Refer to Adams et al. (1994), Corbett et al. (1992), Hotez and Pritchard (1995), and Pollitt (1990).

[2] With a lengthening track record of safe use, this practice is now changing.

and children who live some distance from each other may bathe or fish at the same points on the lake. Moreover, the water-borne schistosome may be carried considerable distances by stream and lake currents, and the snails that serve as its intermediate hosts are themselves mobile. . . .

3. The Primary School Deworming Project in Busia, Kenya

We evaluate the Primary School Deworming Project (PSDP), which was carried out by a Dutch non-profit organization, Internationaal Christelijk Steunfonds Africa (ICS), in cooperation with the Busia District Ministry of Health office. The project took place in southern Busia, a poor and densely-settled farming region in western Kenya, in an area with the highest helminth infection rates in Busia district. The 75 project schools consist of nearly all rural primary schools in this area, and had a total enrolment of over 30,000 pupils between ages six to eighteen.

In January, 1988, the seventy-five PSDP schools were randomly divided into three groups of twenty-five schools each: the schools were first stratified by administrative sub-unit (zone) and by their involvement in other non-governmental assistance programs, and were then listed alphabetically and every third school was assigned to a given project group.[3] Due to ICS's administrative and financial constraints, the health intervention was phased in over several years. Group 1 schools received free deworming treatment in both 1998 and 1999, Group 2 schools in 1999, while Group 3 schools began receiving treatment in 2001. Thus in 1998, Group 1 schools were treatment schools while Group 2 and Group 3 schools were comparison schools, and in 1999, Group 1 and Group 2 schools were treatment schools and Group 3 schools were comparison schools. . . .

Health Outcome Differences Between Group 1 and Group 2 Schools

Before proceeding to formal estimation in Section 4, we present simple differences in health outcomes between treatment and comparison schools, although as we discuss below, these differences understate overall treatment effects if there are deworming treatment externalities across schools.

The Kenyan Ministry of Health conducted a parasitological survey of grade three to eight pupils in Group 1 and Group 2 schools in January and February 1999, one year after the first round of treatment but before Group 2 schools had been treated. Overall, 27 percent of pupils in Group 1 (1998 treatment) schools had a moderate-to-heavy helminth infection in early 1999 compared to 52 percent in Group 2 (1998 comparison) schools, and this difference is significantly different than zero at 99 percent confidence. The prevalences of moderate-to-heavy hookworm, roundworm, schistosomiasis, and whipworm infections were all lower in Group 1 (1998 treatment) schools than in Group 2 (1998 comparison) schools. The program was somewhat less effective against whipworm, perhaps as a result of the lower efficacy of single-dose albendazole treatments for whipworm infections.

Note that it is likely that substantial reinfection had occurred during the three to twelve months between 1998 deworming treatment and the 1999 parasitological surveys, so differences in worm burden between treatment and comparison schools were likely to have been even greater shortly after treatment. In addition, to the extent that pupils prone to worm infections are more likely to be present in school on the day of the parasitological survey in the Group 1 schools than the Group 2 schools due to deworming health gains, these average differences between Group 1 and Group 2 schools are likely to further understate true deworming treatment effects.

Group 1 pupils also reported better health outcomes after the first year of deworming treatment: four percent fewer Group 1 pupils reported being sick in the past week, and three percent fewer pupils reported being sick often (these differences are significantly different than zero at 95 percent confidence). Group 1 pupils also had significantly better height-for-age—a measure of nutritional status—by early 1999, though weight-for-age was no greater on average.[4] . . .

Health education had a minimal impact on behavior, so to the extent the program improved

---

[3]Twenty-seven of the seventy-five project schools were also involved in other NGO projects, which consisted of financial assistance for textbook purchase and classroom construction, and teacher performance incentives. . . .

[4]Although it is somewhat surprising to find height-for-age gains but not weight-for-age gains, since the latter are typically associated with short-run nutritional improvements, it is worth noting that Thein-Hlaing, Thane-Toe, Than-Saw, Myat-Lay-Kyin, and Myint-Lwin's (1991) study in Myanmar finds large height gains among treated children within six months of treatment for roundworm while weight gains were only observed after twenty-four months, and Cooper et al. (1990) present a similar finding for whipworm, so the result is not unprecedented.

health, it almost certainly did so through the effect of anthelmintics rather than through health education. There are no significant differences across treatment and comparison school pupils in early 1999 in three worm prevention behaviors: observed pupil cleanliness, the proportion of pupils wearing shoes, or self-reported exposure to fresh water.

4. Estimation Strategy

Econometric Specifications

Randomization of deworming treatment across schools allows estimation of the overall effect of the program by comparing treatment and comparison schools, even in the presence of within-school externalities. However, externalities may take place not only within, but also across schools, especially since most people in this area live on their farms rather than being concentrated in villages, and neighbors (and even siblings) often attend different schools since there is typically more than one primary school within walking distance. Miguel and Gugerty (2002) find that nearly one-quarter of all households in this area have a child enrolled in a primary school which is not the nearest one to their home. We estimate cross-school externalities by taking advantage of variation in the local density of treatment schools induced by randomization. Although randomization across schools makes it possible to experimentally identify both the overall program effect and cross-school externalities, we must rely on non-experimental methods to decompose the effect on treated schools into a direct effect and within-school externality effect.

We first estimate program impacts in treatment schools, as well as cross-school treatment externalities:

$$Y_{ijt} = a + \beta_1 \cdot T_{1it} + \beta_2 \cdot T_{2it} + X_{ijt}'\delta$$
$$+ \sum_d (\gamma_d \cdot N_{dit}^T) + \sum_d (\phi_d \cdot N_{dit})$$
$$+ u_i + e_{ijt}. \tag{1}$$

Y_{ijt} is the individual health or education outcome, where i refers to the school, j to the student, and $t \in \{1, 2\}$ to the year of the program; T_{1it} and T_{2it} are indicator variables for school assignment to the first and second year of deworming treatment, respectively; and X_{ijt} are school and pupil characteristics. N_{dit} is the total number of pupils in primary schools at distance d from school i in year t, and N_{dit}^T is the number of these pupils in schools ran-

domly assigned to deworming treatment. Individual disturbance terms are assumed to be independent across schools, but are allowed to be correlated for observations within the same school, where the school effect is captured in the u_i term.

Since local population density may affect disease transmission, and since children who live or attend school near treatment schools could have lower environmental exposure to helminths, which would lead to less re-infection and lower worm burdens, worm burden may depend on both the total number of primary school pupils (N_{dit}) and the number of those pupils in schools randomly assigned to deworming treatment (N_{dit}^T) within a certain distance from school i in year t of the program. Given the total number of children attending primary school within a certain distance from the school, the number of these attending schools assigned to treatment is exogenous and random. Since any independent effect of local school density is captured in the N_{dit} terms, the γ_d coefficients measure the deworming treatment externalities across schools. In this framework $\beta_1 + \sum_d(\gamma_d \overline{N}_{dit}^T)$ is the average effect of the first year of deworming treatment on overall infection prevalence in treatment schools, where $\overline{N}_{dit}^T$ is the average number of treatment school pupils located at distance d from the school, and $\beta_2 + \sum_d(\gamma_d \overline{N}_{dit}^T)$ is the analogous effect for the second year of deworming. β_1 and β_2 capture both direct effects of deworming treatment on the treated, as well as any externalities on untreated pupils within the treatment schools. . . .

5. Deworming Treatment Effects on Health

Estimation of equation (1) indicates that the proportion of pupils with moderate to heavy infection is 25 percentage points lower in Group 1 schools than Group 2 schools in early 1999 and this effect is statistically significant at 99 percent confidence (Table 1, regression 1). . . . Children who attend primary schools located near Group 1 schools had lower rates of moderate-to-heavy helminth infection in early 1999: controlling for the total number of (age and sex eligible) children attending any primary school within three kilometers, the presence of each additional thousand (age and sex eligible) pupils attending Group 1 schools located within three kilometers of a school is associated with 26 percentage points fewer moderate-to-heavy infections, and this coefficient estimate is significantly different than zero at 99 percent confidence. Each additional thousand pupils attending a Group 1 school located between three to six kilometers away is associated with 14 percentage points fewer

Table 1. Deworming Health Externalities Within and Across Schools, January to March 1999[†]

	Any moderate-heavy helminth infection, 1999 (1)	Moderate-heavy schistosomiasis infection, 1999 (2)	Moderate-heavy geohelminth infection, 1999 (3)
Indicator for Group 1 (1998 Treatment) School	−0.25***	−0.03	−0.20***
	(0.05)	(0.03)	(0.04)
Group 1 pupils within 3 km (per 1000 pupils)	−0.26***	−0.12***	−0.12*
	(0.09)	(0.04)	(0.06)
Group 1 pupils within 3–6 km (per 1000 pupils)	−0.14**	−0.18***	0.04
	(0.06)	(0.03)	(0.06)
Total pupils within 3 km (per 1000 pupils)	0.11***	0.11***	0.03
	(0.04)	(0.02)	(0.03)
Total pupils within 3–6 km (per 1000 pupils)	0.13**	0.12***	0.04
	(0.06)	(0.03)	(0.04)
Grade indicators, school assistance controls, district exam score control	Yes	Yes	Yes
Number of observations	2328	2328	2328
Mean of dependent variable	0.41	0.16	0.32

[†] Grade 3–8 pupils. Probit estimation, robust standard errors in parentheses. Disturbance terms are clustered within schools. Observations are weighted by total school population. Significantly different than zero at 99 (***), 95 (**), and 90 (*) percent confidence. The 1999 parasitological survey data are for Group 1 and Group 2 schools. The pupil population data is from the 1998 School Questionnaire. The geohelminths are hookworm, roundworm, and whipworm. We use the number of girls less than 13 years old and all boys (the pupils eligible for deworming in the treatment schools) as the school population for all schools.

moderate-to-heavy infections, which is smaller than the effect of pupils within three kilometers, as expected, and is significantly different than zero at 95 percent confidence (Table 1, regression 1). . . .

We estimate that moderate-to-heavy helminth infections among children in this area were 23 percentage points (standard error 7 percentage points) lower on average in early 1999 as a result of health spillovers across schools—over forty percent of overall moderate-to-heavy infection rates in Group 2 schools. To see this, note that the average spillover gain is the average number of Group 1 pupils located within three kilometers divided by 1000 $(\overline{N}_{03}^{T})$ times the average effect of an additional 1000 Group 1 pupils located within three kilometers on infection rates (γ_{03}), plus the analogous spillover effect due to schools located between three to six kilometers away from the school (refer to equation 1). Based on the externality estimates in Table 1, regression 1, this implies the estimated average cross-school externality reduction in moderate-to-heavy helminth infections is $[\gamma_{03}{}^*\overline{N}_{03,1}^{T} + \gamma_{36}{}^*\overline{N}_{36,1}^{T}] = [0.26{}^*454 + 0.14{}^*802]/1000 = 0.23$. . . . The existence of cross-school health externalities implies that the difference in average outcomes between treatment and comparison schools—a "naïve" treatment effect estimator—understates

the actual effects of mass deworming treatment on the treated. . . .

As discussed in Section 2, externalities are likely to operate over larger distances for schistosomiasis than for geohelminths. In fact, the cross-school externality effects are mainly driven by reductions in moderate-to-heavy schistosomiasis infections (Table 1, regression 2), while cross-school geohelminth externalities are negative and marginally significant within three kilometers but not significantly different than zero from three to six kilometers (regression 3). . . .

Health Cost Effectiveness

Annual government expenditure on health in Kenya was approximately five U.S. dollars per capita from 1990 to 1997 (World Bank 1999), so mass deworming is only one of many health interventions competing for scarce public resources. For example, the vaccination rate against measles and DPT (diptheria, pertussis, and tetanus) among Kenyan infants of less than one year of age was just 32 percent in 1997 (World Bank 1999), and these vaccinations are thought to be highly cost effective, at only 12 to 17 U.S. dollars per disability-adjusted life year (DALY) saved.

We use deworming program cost estimates from the Partnership for Child Development (PCD 1999), which reports costs of 0.49 US dollars per pupil per year in a large-scale government intervention in Tanzania. These costs are probably more relevant for potential large scale programs than the PSDP costs, since the PSDP was not able to fully realize economies of scale in drug purchase and delivery, and since it is difficult to disentangle evaluation and delivery costs in the PSD.[5]

According to the World Health Organization, schistosomiasis infections are associated with much greater disease burden per infected individual than geohelminths, on average.[6] Approximately 18 percent of those infected with helminths globally are thought to suffer morbidity as a result of their infection, and in our cost-effectiveness calculations we assume that the entire disease burden is concentrated among individuals with moderate-to-heavy infections (Bundy et al. 2001).[7]

In calculating the overall reduction in disease burden due to the program, we consider overall treatment effects (corrected for cross-school externalities) on the treated in treatment schools, externality effects (corrected for cross-school externalities) on the untreated in treatment schools, and externalities for untreated pupils in comparison schools. . . . Given the randomized design, we assume that the Group 3 schools (which lack 1999 parasitological data) experienced the same externality benefits as Group 2 schools through early 1999, when neither group had received deworming treatment.

Summing these three components of the treatment effect, the total number of DALY's averted as a result of the program is 649, which translates into a cost of approximately $5 per DALY averted, using the costs of the PCD program in Tanzania. This estimate still ignores the health spillover benefits for other untreated children and adults in the treatment area, thus underestimating cost-effectiveness. Even if the PCD costs were underestimated by a factor of two, deworming would still be among the most cost-effective health interventions for less developed countries.

The externality benefits of treatment (both within and across schools) account for 76 percent of the DALY reduction. A naïve treatment effect estimate that failed to take externalities into account would underestimate program treatment effects, not only because externalities would be missed, but also because gains among the treatment group would be underestimated. Consequently, the naïve estimate would overestimate the cost per DALY averted by a factor of four, leading to the mistaken conclusion that deworming does not meet the strictest cost-effectiveness standards.

The health gains are overwhelmingly attributable to reductions in the prevalence of moderate-to-heavy schistosomiasis: 99 percent of the total DALY reduction is due to averted schistosomiasis.

---

[5]Excluding the costs most clearly linked to the evaluation yields a cost per pupil treated through the PSDP in 1999 of 1.46 US dollars, with nearly half of this cost in drug purchases. However, the PSDP used trained nurses, held meetings to explain consent procedures, individually recorded the names of all pupils taking medicine, and was headquartered in Busia town, several hours drive away from many project schools. These costs might have been unnecessary in a large-scale program that did not include an evaluation component.

[6]Given data on the burden of disease in WHO (2000), and the number of people infected worldwide, the implied average DALY burden per person infected is 0.0097 for schistosomiasis, 0.0013 for hookworm, 0.0005 for whipworm, and 0.0004 for roundworm.

[7]Note that this implies that the burden of disease per infected individual in our sample is greater than the world average, which is appropriate, since levels of moderate-heavy infection are relatively high in this setting.

References

Adams, E.J., Stephenson, L.S., Latham, M.C., and Kinoti, S.N. (1994). "Physical Activity and Growth of Kenyan School Children with Hookworm, *Trichuris trichiura* and *Ascaris lumbricoides* Infections are Improved after Treatment with Albendazole." *The Journal of Nutrition,* 124 (8), 1199–1206.

Anderson, R.M., and R.M. May. (1991). *Infectious Diseases of Humans.* New York: Oxford University Press.

Bennett, Andrew, and Helen Guyatt. (2000). "Reducing Intestinal Nematode Infection: Efficacy of Albendazole and Mebendazole," *Parasitology Today,* 16 (2), 71–75.

Bundy, D.A.P. (1994). "The Global Burden of Intestinal Nematode Disease." *Transactions of the Royal Society of Tropical Medicine and Hygiene,* 88, 259–261.

Bundy, D.A.P., Chan M.S., Medley, G.F., Jamison, D. & Savioli, L. (2001). "Intestinal Nematode Infections." *The global epidemiology of infectious diseases,* (C. J. L. Murray and A. D. Lopez, eds). Cambridge: Harvard University Press.

Bundy, D.A.P., and Guyatt, H.L. (1996). "Schools for Health: Focus on Health, Education, and the School-age Child." *Parasitology Today,* 12 (8), 1–16.

Butterworth, A. E., R. F. Sturrock, J. H. Ouma, G. G. Mbugua, A. J. C. Fulford, H. C. Kariuki, and D. Koech (1991): "Comparison of Different Chemotherapy Strategies Against Schistosomiasis Mansoni in Machakos District, Kenya: Effects on Human Infection and Morbidity," *Parasitology,* 103, 339–355.

Cooper, E.S., D.A.P. Bundy, T.T. MacDonald, and M.H.N. Golden. (1990). "Growth Suppression in the Trichuris Dysentery Syndrome," *European Journal of Clinical Nutrition,* 44, 285–291.

Corbett, E.L., Butterworth, A.E., Fulford, A.J.C., Ouma, J.H., Sturock, R.F. (1992). "Nutritional Status of Children with Schistosomiasis Mansoni in Two Different Areas of Machakos District, Kenya." *Transactions of the Royal Society of Tropical Medicine and Hygiene,* 86, 266–273.

Cowden, John, and Peter Hotez. (2000). "Mebendazole and Albendazole Treatment of Geohelminth Infections in Children and Pregnant Women," *The Pediatric Infectious Disease Journal,* 19(7), 659–660.

Heckman, J., R. LaLonde, and J. Smith. (1999). "The Economics and Econometrics of Active Labor Market Programs," in O. Ashenfelter and D. Card (eds.), *Handbook of Labor Economics,* Vol. 3, 1865–2086. North Holland Press.

Hotez, P. J., and D. I. Pritchard (1995): "Hookworm Infection," *Scientific American,* 272, 68–75.

Miguel, Edward, and Mary Kay Gugerty. (2002). "Ethnic Diversity, Social Sanctions, and Public Goods in Kenya," mimeo., University of California, Berkeley and University of Washington.

Muchiri, Eric M., John H. Ouma, and Charles H. King. (1996). "Dynamics and Control of *Schistosoma Haematobium* Transmission in Kenya: An Overview of the Mwambweni Project," *American Journal of Tropical Medicine and Hygiene,* 55(5), 127–134.

Nokes, C., van den Bosch, C., and Bundy, D.A.P. (1998). *The Effects of Iron Deficiency and Anemia on Mental and Motor Performance, Educational Achievement, and Behavior in Children: A Report of the International Nutritional Anemia Consultative Group.* US-AID: Washington, DC.

Ouma, J.H. (1987). *Transmission of Schistosoma Mansoni in an Endemic Area of Kenya, with Special Reference to the Role of Human Defecation Behaviour and Sanitary Practices.* Ph.D. thesis, University of Liverpool.

Partnership for Child Development [PCD]. (1999). "The Cost of Large-Scale School Health Programmes which Deliver Anthelmintics in Ghana and Tanzania," *Acta Tropica,* 73, 183–204.

Pollitt, E. (1990). "Infection: Schistosomiasis", *Malnutrition and Infection in the Classroom,* Paris, Unesco.

Thein-Hlaing, Thane-Toe, Than-Saw, Myat-Lay-Kyin, and Myint-Lwin. (1991). "A Controlled Chemotherapeutic Intervention Trial on the Relationship between *Ascaria Lumbricoides* Infection and Malnutrition in Children," *Transactions of the Royal Society of Tropical Medicine and Hygiene,* 85, 523–528.

Warren, K.S., Bundy, D.A.P., Anderson, R.M., Davis, A.R., Henderson, D.A, Jamison, D.T., Prescott, N. and Senft, A. (1993). "Helminth Infections." In *Disease Control Priorities in Developing Countries* (ed. Jamison, D.T., Mosley, W.H., Measham, A.R. and Bobadilla, J.L.), 131–60. Oxford University Press.

World Bank. (1999). World Development Indicators (*www.worldbank.org*).

World Health Organization. (1987). *Prevention and Control of Intestinal Parasitic Infections. Report of the WHO Scientific Group.* WHO Technical Report Series: 749. WHO, Geneva.

World Health Organization. (1992). *Model Describing Information. Drugs Used in Parasitic Diseases.* WHO, Geneva.

World Health Organization. (2000). *The World Health Report 2000.* WHO, Geneva.

Selection IV.B.3. Confronting AIDS*

More than a decade after the human immunodeficiency virus (HIV) was first identified as the cause of acquired immune deficiency syndrome (AIDS), the disease has been reported in nearly all developing and industrial countries. UNAIDS, the United Nations joint program dedicated to combating the AIDS epidemic, estimates that at the end of 1996 about 23 million people worldwide were infected with HIV and more than 6 million had already died of AIDS. More than 90 percent of all adult HIV infections are in developing countries (Figure 1) About 800,000 children in the developing world are living with HIV; at least 43 percent of all infected adults in developing countries are women (AIDSCAP and others, 1996).

In many developing countries the HIV/AIDS epidemic is spreading rapidly. In major cities of Argentina, Brazil, Cambodia, India, and Thailand, more than 2 percent of pregnant women now carry HIV. These levels are similar to those found ten years ago in such African countries as Zambia and Malawi, where more than one in four pregnant women are now infected. In two African cities, Francistown, Botswana, and Harare, Zimbabwe, 40 percent of women attending antenatal clinics are infected. Figure 2 presents UNAIDS estimates of the number of new adult infections by region and over time. While new infections are thought to be leveling off in Sub-Saharan Africa as a whole, in some countries military conflict and civil unrest may be spreading the epidemic. Meanwhile, the disease is spreading rapidly in Asia. Extrapolation of the trends in Figure 2 leads some observers to think that Asia may already have surpassed Africa in the number of new infections per year. In Latin America and the Caribbean countries the number of new infections has been steady at about 200,000 per year for several years, while the countries of eastern Europe and central Asia are experiencing the initial stages of rapid spread (not shown). Only in North America and western Europe has the number of new infections declined from its peak in 1986, but even here the future of the epidemic is unclear as it invades lower-income populations whose education and access to health care more closely resemble those of the developing world.

AIDS is clearly taking an immense and growing human toll. The disease is catastrophic for the millions of people who become infected, get sick, and, in stark contrast to the recent hopeful news of treatment breakthroughs, die. It is also a tragedy for their families, who, in addition to suffering profound emotional loss, may be impoverished as a result of the disease. Because AIDS kills mostly prime-age adults, it increases the number of children who lose one or both parents; some of these orphans suffer permanent consequences, due to poor nutrition or withdrawal from school. Numbers cannot begin to capture the suffering caused by the disease. Each infection is a personal tragedy; Box 1 describes the experience of one of the nearly 30 million people who have contracted HIV.

AIDS is not alone in causing human suffering, however. In low-income countries in particular, many urgent problems compete for scarce skills and resources. In the year 2000, malnutrition and childhood diseases that can be prevented or treated much more easily than AIDS are expected to kill 1.8 million children in the developing world; tuberculosis (TB) is expected to kill more than 2 million people; and malaria, about 740,000. Worldwide, annual deaths from smoking are expected to increase from 3 million in 1990 to 8.4 million in 2020, and nearly all of this annual increase is expected to occur in developing nations (Murray and Lopez 1996). And disease is only one of many problems facing governments in improving the welfare of their citizens. About a billion people lack access to clean water, and about 40 percent of women and one-quarter of men in the developing world are illiterate. Throughout the world, inadequate transportation and communications hinder the efforts of billions of people to improve their lives. . . .

The Impact of AIDS on life Expectancy and Health

The most obvious impact of AIDS is on life expectancy and health. Measuring and predicting these impacts are difficult, not only because of the lack of quality data, but also because the relative size of an impact depends on many factors besides the spread of AIDS, including success in fighting other health problems. Available evidence discussed below suggests that in the most severely affected countries AIDS threatens to reverse a cen-

*From World Bank, *Confronting AIDS: Public Priorities in a Global Epidemic* (New York: Oxford University Press, 1999), pp. 13–16, 22–29, 31–33, 284–285, and 289. Reprinted by permission.

Figure 1. Estimated number of adults with HIV/AIDS, by region, December 1996.

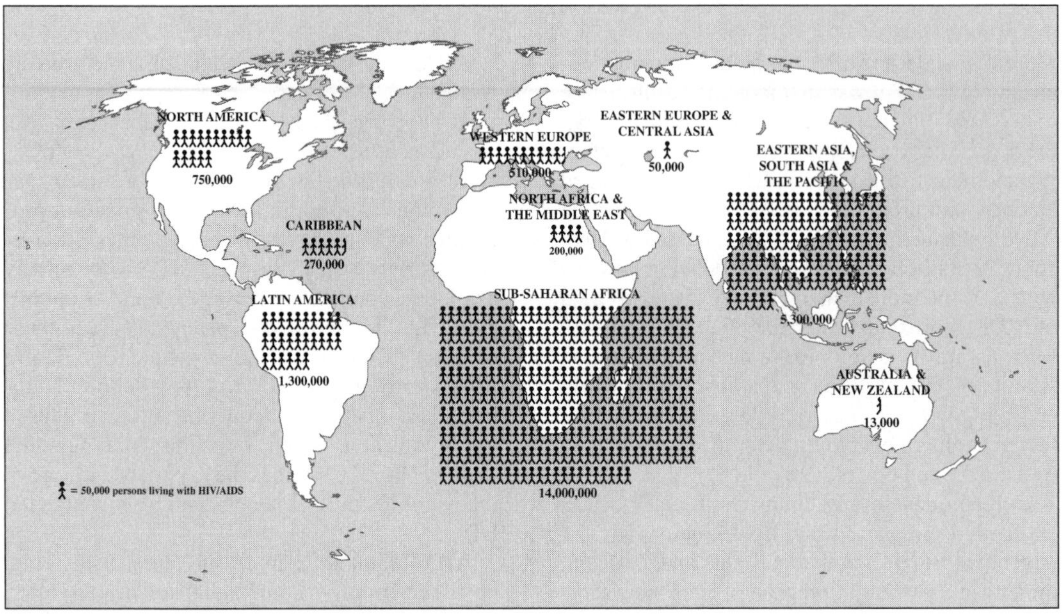

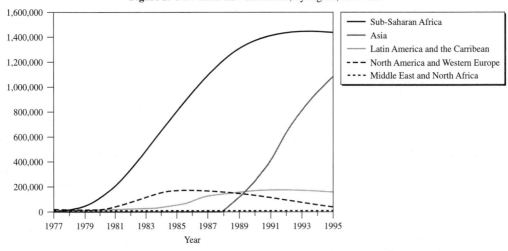

Source: UNAIDS

tury of progress in the fight against infectious diseases. Elsewhere, it is likely to account for an increased share of the infectious disease burden. Even so, AIDS is only one of many health problems confronting people in developing countries. Indeed, the poorer the country, the more likely it is that other problems—including easily treated

problems like malnutrition and diarrhea—account for a large share of the burden of disease.

Life Expectancy

Life expectancy is a basic measure of human welfare and of the impact of AIDS. From 1950 to

Figure 2. New adult HIV infections, by region, 1977–95.

Source: UNAIDS 1997.

Box 1 Pauline: One Woman's Story

Pauline, the youngest of seven children in a farm family in Ghana, was in her early twenties when an older cousin promised her work as a waitress in Abidjan, Côte d'Ivoire, and offered to lend her the bus fare. Because she was unable to make enough money to support herself trading fish near her home, she readily accepted.

"When I got there I found there was no job as a waitress. My cousin said I must work as a prostitute to pay back the bus fare. I lived in a house with several other women doing the same work.

"I did the business in the bars. There were so many other women there I couldn't count them. Some days I have about four or five men—the number depends on your beauty. But I didn't like the work, so I did it until I had enough for my food and rent and then I'd stop for a few days.

"If you didn't pay your rent the landlord would seize your belongings and throw you out. I only wanted to save up enough income to come home.

"After three months I had enough money and came home. That was two years ago. After a year a boil grew under my arm."

Pauline's sister took her to a herbalist who sold her a potion. When that failed to relieve her worsening symptoms she went to a private doctor and was admitted to a hospital, where she remained for three months. The doctors did not tell her that she had AIDS, only that she "must not go with men."

"I never used a condom while I was in Abidjan. Men never asked for them. I never even heard of AIDS until I returned home and met friends who had it," she said.

At the time of the interview, in 1991, Pauline was very thin, had septic ulcers on her chest and shoulders, and suffered from constant itching on her arms and legs. She is one of the six million people who have so far died of AIDS.

Source: Hampton 1991.

1990, dramatic progress in the fight against infectious disease raised life expectancy from 40 to 63 years in developing countries, narrowing the gap between these countries and industrial countries from 25 to 13 years. AIDS has slowed and in some countries reversed this trend. For example, life expectancy in Burkina Faso, a mere 46 years, is 11 years shorter than it would have been in the absence of AIDS (Figure 3). Life expectancy in several other hard-hit countries also has been pushed back to levels of more than a decade ago. The impact of AIDS on life expectancy in Thailand is less, because its infection rate is less than that of the other countries in the figure.

Disability-Adjusted Life Years (DALYs)

AIDS accounted for about 1 percent of all deaths worldwide in 1990; this proportion is likely to rise to 2 percent of all deaths in 2020 (Murray and Lopez 1996). However, the proportion of total deaths caused by a disease is an imperfect representation of its burden on society, because it ignores illness and does not distinguish among the deaths of people of different ages. Murray and

Lopez (1996) have estimated the cost of diseases in terms of disability-adjusted life years, or DALYs. Introduced by the *World Development Report 1993* (World Bank 1993), a DALY includes the disability as well as the mortality effects of disease and uses age weights to discount the importance of infant and elderly deaths. In 1990, poor health resulted in the loss of about 265 DALYs per thousand persons per year in developing countries, almost twice the 124 DALYs per thousand per year lost in industrial countries. Since HIV/AIDS deaths entail substantial disability before death and disproportionally strike prime-age adults, HIV/AIDS has a larger impact on health measured as DALYs than when measured as a share of total deaths. However, the difference is not large: Murray and Lopez (1996) project that HIV/AIDS would account for almost 3 percent of all DALYs lost in developing countries in the year 2020, up from 0.8 percent in 1990 (Table 1). One reason that HIV/AIDS does not account for a larger percentage of lost DALYs is that other causes of death in developing countries also entail substantial disability and premature death. Further, some of the increased impact of

Figure 3. The current impact of AIDS on life expectancy, six selected countries, 1996.

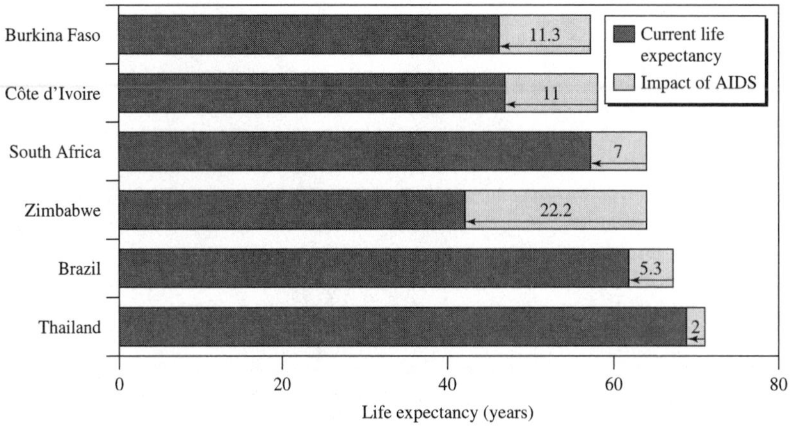

Source: U.S. Bureau of the Census, 1996, 1997.

Table 1. Annual Burden of Infectious Disease and HIV, as Measured by Deaths and Lost DALYs, the Developing World, 1990 and 2020

	1990		2020	
	Deaths	Lost DALYs	Deaths	Lost DALYs
Annual burden of disease	(percentage of total)		(percentage of total)	
Infectious disease (as percentage of total burden)	30.7	24.5	14.3	13.7
HIV (as percentage of total burden)	0.6	0.8	2.0	2.6
HIV (as percentage of infectious burden)	2.0	3.2	13.6	19.3
HIV plus a portion of TB (as percentage of infectious burden)[a]	2.8	3.8	20.3	25.3
Total burden per 1,000 people	9.7	265.2	8.6	186.2
Infectious burden per 1,000 people	3.0	64.9	1.2	25.5
HIV burden per 1,000 people	0.1	2.1	0.2	4.5

[a]The fourth row of the table is computed by adding 5 percent of the 1990 TB burden and 25 percent of the 2020 TB burden to the numbers for HIV. These percentages are the authors' estimates of the portion of HIV-negative TB deaths that would not have occurred had HIV-positive people not contributed to the spread of TB.

Source: Baseline scenario from Murray and Lopez (1996).

HIV/AIDS is offset by the decreasing share of prime-age adults in the population associated with the demographic transition.

HIV/AIDS as a Share of Infectious Diseases

The contribution of HIV/AIDS to the disease burden looms larger when we focus attention on infectious disease. Such a focus is particularly relevant to our overarching purpose—identifying the appropriate roles for developing country governments in the fight against AIDS—because economic theory, public health teaching, and longstanding practice all affirm that governments should play a significant role in preventing the spread of infectious disease.

By 2020 infectious diseases, which currently account for about 30 percent of deaths and one-quarter of lost DALYs in developing countries, will have declined to about 14 percent of both measures. But the contribution of HIV/AIDS to the infectious disease burden in developing countries is projected to increase sharply, from about 2 percent of deaths and 3 percent of lost DALYs to about 14 percent of deaths and nearly one-fifth of lost DALYs. Moreover, because HIV is an increasingly important factor in the spread of TB, it is estimated that about one out of four TB deaths *among HIV-negative people* in 2020 would not have occurred in the absence of the HIV epidemic. Adding a quarter of TB deaths among HIV-negative people to the deaths directly attributable to HIV/AIDS suggests

Figure 4. Breakdown of deaths from infectious diseases, the developing world, by disease category, 1990 and 2020 (percent).

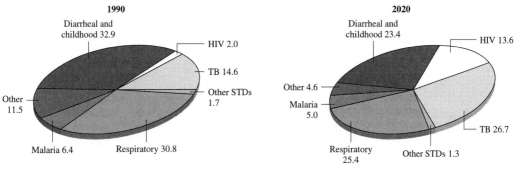

Source: Murray and Lopez 1996.

that HIV/AIDS will be responsible for about one-fifth of all infectious disease deaths in low-income countries in the year 2020.[1] In addition, HIV is likely to be responsible for a portion of deaths from several other infectious diseases (Figure 4).

HIV/AIDS as a Major Killer of Prime-Age Adults

Because HIV/AIDS is sexually transmitted, AIDS usually strikes prime-age adults—often people who are raising children and are at or near the peak of their income potential. In the absence of AIDS, prime-age adults tend to be less vulnerable to sickness and death than children, adolescents, or old people. Accordingly, AIDS casts an even larger shadow on the health of prime-age adults and the welfare of their dependents. In 1990, HIV was already third after TB and non-TB respiratory infections as a cause of adult death in the developing world; by 2020, HIV will be second only to TB as a killer of prime-age adults in developing countries (Figure 5). Adding one-quarter of TB deaths among HIV-negative prime-age adults makes

HIV/AIDS the largest single infectious killer of prime-age adults in the developing world in 2020, responsible for half of all deaths from infectious disease among this important group.

The HIV/AIDS share of the adult infectious disease burden varies widely across developing regions. In Africa, where other infectious diseases decline less quickly than in other regions and HIV/AIDS infection rates are assumed to be leveling off in many areas, HIV/AIDS will account for about one-third of these deaths (Figure 6). Because Latin America and the Caribbean countries are projected to make the most progress in reducing other infectious diseases, and HIV infection is predicted to continue to rise, HIV will be responsible for almost three-quarters of the infectious disease burden there.

AIDS and Development

Although the health impacts of the disease alone are ample cause for concern, there are additional reasons why the development community in general and policymakers in particular should be concerned about the HIV/AIDS epidemic. First, widespread poverty and unequal distribution of income that typify underdevelopment appear to stimulate the spread of HIV. Second, the accelerated labor migration, rapid urbanization, and cultural modernization that often accompany growth also facilitate the spread of HIV. Third, at the household level AIDS deaths exacerbate the poverty and social inequality that are conducive to a larger epidemic, thus creating a vicious circle. Policymakers who understand these links have the opportunity to break this cycle. . . .

[1] As this book was being finalized in the spring of 1997, the World Health Organization (WHO) announced that the new "directly observed treatment strategy" for TB (the DOTS approach) has been so effective that the global number of TB cases is projected to remain flat rather than to increase. A revision of the Murray and Lopez projections, which takes into account this new development, would decrease the number of TB deaths, including TB deaths among HIV-negative people, attributable to HIV. However, because the overall infectious disease burden would also decline, the relative importance of projected future deaths due directly to HIV/AIDS would increase. The same applies to projections for adult deaths caused by infectious diseases, discussed below.

Figure 5. Causes of death from infectious diseases among people ages 15 to 59, the developing world, 1990 and 2020 (percent).

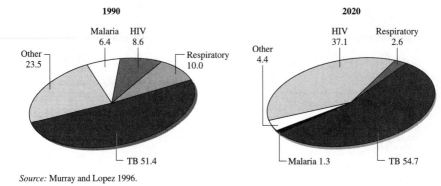

Source: Murray and Lopez 1996.

Figure 6. HIV/AIDS as a percentage of the infectious disease burden of adults, the developing world, 2020.

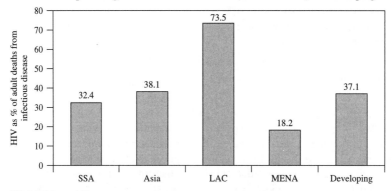

SSA Sub-Saharan Africa
LAC Latin America and the Caribbean Countries (total)
MENA Middle East and North Africa
Source: Murray and Lopez 1996.

Poverty and Gender Inequality Spread AIDS

While the determinants of an individual's sexual activity are subtle and complex, it is reasonable to expect that at the aggregate level social conditions would influence the frequency of risky sexual behavior and hence the size of the epidemic. One hypothesis is that poverty and gender inequality make a society more vulnerable to HIV because a woman who is poor, either absolutely or relative to men, will find it harder to insist that her sex partner

abstain from sex with other partners or use a condom or take other steps to protect herself from becoming infected with HIV. Poverty may also make a man more prone to having multiple casual partners, by preventing him from attracting a wife or by causing him to leave home in search of work. The idea that poverty and gender inequality exacerbate AIDS is supported by an exploratory analysis of national-level aggregate data on HIV infection rates.

Eight epidemiological, social, and economic variables can explain about two-thirds of the varia-

Figure 7. Relationship of four societal variables with urban adult HIV infections, 72 developing countries, circa 1995.

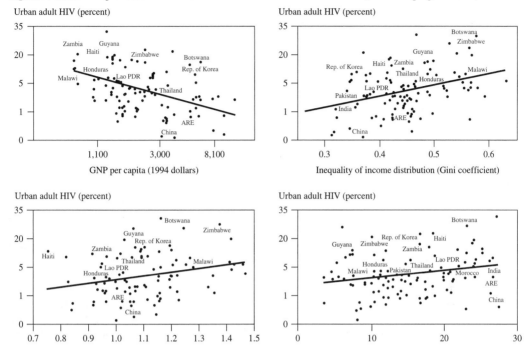

ARE Arab Republic of Egypt

Note: The vertical axis measuring HIV infection has been transformed to a logarithmic scale. Points on a given scatter plot represent the data for 72 individual countries after removing the effects of the other seven variables included in the regression analysis. Income inequality is measured by the Gini coefficient. The methodology and the detailed statistical results are presented in Over (*background paper,* 1997).

Source: Authors' estimates.

tion in cross-country HIV infection rates. Figure 7 shows the associations of four of these variables with the percentage of urban adults infected with HIV.[2] The top two panels of the figure demonstrate that, holding constant the other variables, both low income and unequal distribution of income are strongly associated with high HIV infection rates. For the average developing country a $2,000 increase in per capita income is associated with a reduction of about 4 percentage points in the HIV infection rate of urban adults. Reducing the index of inequality from 0.5 to 0.4, the difference in inequality between, for example, Honduras and Malawi is associated with a reduction in the infec-

tion rate by about 3 percentage points.[3] These findings suggest that rapid and fairly distributed economic growth will do much to slow the AIDS epidemic.[4]

When examining the influence of gender inequality on HIV infection, one must hold constant as much as possible other cultural influences, such

[2]Each panel of Figure 7 presents the relationship between one of the societal variables and HIV infection after purging the effects of the other seven explanatory variables. The figures were constructed by the *avplot* command in the 1997 STATA software package. See Over (*background paper,* 1997) for details and further results.

[3]The index of poverty used in the upper-right panel of Figure 7 is called the Gini coefficient and is defined on a scale from 0 to 1: 0 represents the perfectly equal distribution in which each person has exactly the same income and 1 represents the other extreme, absolute inequality such that all income is received by one person.

[4]Since the dependent variable is these regressions is transformed into a "logit" as described in Over (*background paper,* 1997), changes in the independent variables are associated with specific changes in these logits, which correspond to changes in the infection rate. All the results control for the age of the epidemic, which is statistically significant. In the average country, prevalence among urban residents at low risk is estimated to increase at the rate of 2.7 percentage points per year.

as Islam, which may be correlated with gender inequality across countries. The bottom two panels of Figure 7 show that, after controlling for the percentage of the population that is Muslim (as well as per capita gross national product (GNP), income inequality, and four other societal characteristics), two measures related to gender inequality are associated with higher HIV infection rates. The first of these, the ratio of males to females in urban centers, varies remarkably across countries: some countries have fewer male urban residents than female, and others have 40 percent more males. Other things being equal, one might suppose that commercial sex would be more common in cities where men greatly outnumber women, and that HIV levels would therefore be higher. The evidence of the lower left panel of Figure 7 is that cities in which men ages 20 to 39 greatly outnumber women do in fact have significantly higher HIV infection rates. For the average country, increasing the job opportunities for young women so that the ratio of males to females in urban areas falls, for example, from 1.3 to 0.9, would decrease the HIV infection rate by about 4 percentage points.

The second measure related to gender inequality included in the analysis is the gap between adult male and female literacy rates. Again, there is great variation across countries, the literacy rate among men being as much as 25 percentage points higher than among women in some countries. When women are much less literate than men, they may be less able to bargain effectively with men and thus be at greater risk in sexual encounters. Furthermore, illiterate women will have difficulty finding jobs and thus may depend more on sexual relationships for economic survival, again reducing their bargaining power. The lower right panel of Figure 7 supports these ideas, suggesting that the average country that reduces the literacy gap between genders by 20 percentage points can expect urban HIV infection to be about 4 percentage points lower. . . .

Sometimes a low-income society beginning rapid growth may face an increased risk of AIDS as a result of a broad shift from conservative social norms to more liberal attitudes; these attitudes often include greater individual freedom, especially for women. Lacking an objective measure of social conservatism, the regression used the percentage of the population that is Muslim as an imperfect proxy for a country's degree of social conservatism. Controlling for all other variables described above, a high degree of social conservatism is associated to a statistically significant degree with lower rates of HIV infection. This does not

necessarily imply that governments should attempt to instill or maintain social conservatism simply to minimize HIV; such broad social values may in any event be very difficult for governments to shape. However, the evidence does suggest the usefulness of an explicit government education policy that would help young people entering a rapidly modernizing society to recognize and avoid risky sexual encounters.

A final factor in the regression analysis that is not associated with development but can be readily affected by government policy is the level of militarization. In developing countries, military forces are often based near urban centers and consist predominantly of young, unmarried men. Using a variable that measures the number of men in the nation's armed forces as a percentage of its urban population, the regression analysis shows that, even after controlling for the ratio of male to female urban residents, countries with more soldiers will have higher infection rates. For the average country, reducing the size of the military from 30 to 12 percent of the urban population will reduce seroprevalence among urban adults by about 4 percentage points. An alternative . . . , which may be more feasible (and is reasonable regardless of the size of the military) is a vigorous HIV prevention program covering everyone in the military.

AIDS Has Little Net Macroeconomic Impact

Because HIV/AIDS is spreading rapidly and is nearly always fatal, some observers have concluded that it will significantly reduce population growth and economic growth; a few have suggested that populations in badly hit countries will decline in absolute terms and that there will be an associated collapse in economic output (Anderson and others 1991, Rowley, Anderson, and Ng 1990). However, the available evidence suggests that the impact of AIDS on these variables, although varying across countries, will generally be small relative to other factors. Moreover, at a very crude level, declines in population growth due to HIV/AIDS will tend to offset declines in economic growth, so that the net impact on gross domestic product (GDP) growth per capita will generally be small. . . .

The Role of Government

Experience has . . . shown that active government involvement is crucial if AIDS is to be overcome. Only governments have the means and mandate to finance the public goods necessary for the monitoring and control of the disease—epidemio-

logical surveillance, basic research on sexual ba-
havior, information collection for identifying high-
risk groups, and evaluation of the costs and effectiveness of interventions. Private individuals left to
their own devices would not invest adequately in
these activities. Governments also have a unique
responsibility to intervene to reduce the negative
externalities of high-risk behavior, while preventing discrimination that would inhibit behavioral
change. Without these government efforts, those at
high risk of contracting and spreading HIV are unlikely to reduce risky behaviors enough from the
perspective of the rest of society. The government
role extends to ensuring equity in access to HIV
prevention and treatment for the most destitute.

Other key functions that most governments are
already attempting to perform can also make an
important contribution to slowing the spread of
HIV: promoting labor-intensive economic growth
to reduce poverty; assuring basic social services,
law and order, human and property rights; and protecting the poor. Investing in female schooling and
ensuring equal rights for women in employment,
inheritance, divorce, and child custody proceedings are part of this broader mandate. These policies yield large development benefits in their own
right but are also important for preventing an HIV
epidemic and coping with its impact. . . .

An HIV/AIDS epidemic can be pre-empted, for
little cost, by promotion of safe injecting behavior
among injecting drug users and of safe sex and
STD prevention through condom use among those
with high levels of sexual activity. We know that
this can be done.

References

AIDSCAP/Family Health International, Harvard School
of Public Health, and UNAIDS. 1996. "The Status
and Trends of the Global HIV/AIDS Pandemic."
Final Report of a Satellite Symposium of the
Eleventh International Conference on AIDS, Vancouver, B.C., Canada. July 7–12. Family Health
International.

Anderson, Roy M., R. M. May, M. C. Boily, G. P. Gar-
nett, J. T. Rowley. 1991. "The Spread of HIV-1 in
Africa: Sexual Contact Patterns and the Predicted
Demographic Impact of AIDS." *Nature* 352 (6336):
581–89.

Hampton, Janie. 1991. *Meeting AIDS with Compassion:
AIDS Care and Prevention in Agomanya, Ghana.*
Strategies for Hope 4. London: ActionAid, in assoc.
with AMREF and World in Need.

Murray, Christopher J. L., and Allan D. Lopez. 1996.
"The Global Burden of Disease." *Global Burden of
Disease and Injury Series,* vol. 1. WHO, Harvard
School of Public Health, World Bank. Cambridge,
Mass.: Harvard University Press.

Over, Mead. 1997. "Societal Determinants of Urban
HIV Infection: An Exploratory Cross-country Regression Analysis." Background Paper for *Confronting AIDS.*

Rowley, Janet, Roy Anderson, and T. W. Ng. 1990. "Reducing the Spread of HIV Infection in Sub-Saharan
Africa: Some Demographic and Economic Implications." *AIDS* 4(1):47–56.

U.S. Bureau of the Census. 1996. "World Population
Profile 1996, with a Special Chapter Focusing on
Adolescent Fertility in the Developing World." U.S.
Department of Commerce. U.S. Government Printing
Office, Washington, D.C.

————. 1997. "Recent HIV Seroprevalence Levels by
Country: January, 1997." Research Note 23. Health
Studies Branch, International Programs Center, Population Division. U.S. Bureau of the Census, Washington, D.C.

World Bank. 1993. *World Development Report 1993: Investing in Health.* New York: Oxford University
Press.

Exhibit IV.C.1. Demographic Data and Population Forecasts, by Human Development Index and Geographic Region

Country Name (listed from lowest to highest HDI)	Population (Thousands) 2000	Projected Population (Thousands) 2050	Population Growth Rate 1995–2000	Population Growth Rate 2000–2050	Births per 1,000 Population[a]	Deaths per 1,000 Population[a]	Children per Woman[b]	Share of Population Aged 0–14 Years 2000	Share of Population Aged 15–64 Years 2000	Share of Population Aged 65 and Older 2000	Working Age Population per Dependent[c] 2000
Low-human development countries											
Sierra Leone	4,415	10,339	1.6	1.7	49.7	28.9	6.5	45.0	52.4	2.6	1.1
Niger	10,742	53,037	3.5	3.2	55.4	20.8	8.0	49.0	48.6	2.4	0.9
Burkina Faso	11,905	42,373	2.9	2.5	49.1	17.9	6.9	47.3	50.1	2.6	1.0
Mali	11,904	45,998		2.7				47.1	49.7	3.1	1.0
Burundi	6,267	19,459	0.8	2.3	43.1	22.2	6.8	46.3	51.0	2.6	1.0
Mozambique	17,861	31,275	2.3	1.1	43.0	21.4	5.9	43.1	53.2	3.7	1.1
Ethiopia	65,590	170,987	2.7	1.9	44.8	17.8	6.5	46.2	51.0	2.8	1.0
Central African Republic	3,715	6,563	2.0	1.1	40.0	20.3	5.3	42.5	54.0	3.4	1.2
Congo, Dem. Rep. of the	48,571	151,644	1.8	2.3	49.5	25.0	6.7	47.6	49.7	2.7	1.0
Guinea-Bissau	1,367	4,719	2.8	2.5	50.1	20.7	7.1	43.6	52.8	3.6	1.1
Chad	7,861	25,359	3.1	2.3	48.3	20.1	6.7	50.5	46.5	3.1	0.9
Angola	12,386	43,131	2.6	2.5	52.2	24.0	7.2	47.5	49.6	2.9	1.0
Zambia	10,419	18,528	2.1	1.2	44.7	25.2	6.1	45.3	52.5	2.1	1.1
Malawi	11,370	25,949	2.5	1.7	48.2	22.5	6.5	44.2	52.1	3.7	1.1
Côte d'Ivoire	15,827	27,572	1.9	1.1	37.1	18.5	5.3	42.4	55.0	2.5	1.2
Tanzania, U. Rep. of	34,837	69,112	2.4	1.4	42.5	16.9	5.7	45.5	52.2	2.4	1.1
Benin	6,222	15,602	2.6	1.8	43.4	14.4	6.1	46.3	50.9	2.7	1.0
Rwanda	7,724	16,973	8.2	1.6	44.5	25.5	6.2	48.6	48.2	3.2	0.7
Guinea	8,117	19,591	2.1	1.8	45.6	17.8	6.3	44.7	52.7	2.6	1.1
Senegal	9,393	21,589	2.4	1.7	38.4	13.5	5.4	44.9	52.5	2.7	1.1
Eritrea	3,712	10,539	2.9	2.1	42.1	12.6	5.9	45.4	52.0	2.6	1.1
Mauritania	2,645	7,497	2.8	2.1	42.6	15.5	6.0	44.1	52.7	3.2	1.1
Djibouti	666	1,395	3.2	1.5	42.3	17.2	6.1	43.4	53.6	3.0	1.2
Nigeria	114,746	258,478	2.8	1.6	41.7	13.5	5.9	44.0	53.4	2.5	1.1
Gambia	1,312	2,905	3.3	1.6	38.8	13.6	5.2	40.2	56.6	3.1	1.3
Haiti	8,005	12,429	1.3	0.9	31.6	15.4	4.4	40.7	55.7	3.6	1.3
Madagascar	15,970	46,292	2.9	2.1	44.0	14.7	6.1	45.2	51.8	3.0	1.1
Yemen	18,017	84,385	3.5	3.1	46.0	10.4	7.3	46.7	50.4	2.9	1.0
Uganda	23,487	103,248	2.9	3.0	50.3	20.3	7.1	49.0	49.0	1.9	1.0
Kenya	30,549	43,984	2.2	0.7	34.9	13.0	4.6	43.5	53.8	2.7	1.2
Zimbabwe	12,650	12,658	1.5	0.0	34.8	19.5	4.5	45.2	51.6	3.2	1.1

Pakistan	142,654	2.6	1.8	37.6	10.7	5.5	41.7	55.0	3.3	1.2
Nepal	23,518	2.3	1.5	35.3	11.1	4.7	41.0	55.2	3.7	1.2
Cameroon	15,117	2.4	1.0	37.7	13.8	5.1	42.0	54.3	3.7	1.2
Median	*11,637*	*2.6*	*1.7*	*43.1*	*17.8*	*6.1*	*45.1*	*52.3*	*2.9*	*1.1*
Total Low-HDI Population	*719,541*									
Share of World Population	*11.9*									

Medium-human development countries

Togo	4,562	3.3	1.6	40.7	13.8	5.8	44.3	52.6	3.2	1.1
Congo	3,447	3.2	2.3	44.4	15.0	6.3	46.3	50.4	3.3	1.0
Bangladesh	137,952	2.2	1.2	32.5	9.8	4.0	37.8	59.0	3.2	1.4
Sudan	31,437	2.3	1.3	36.0	12.1	4.9	40.1	56.4	3.4	1.3
Lesotho	1,785	1.2	-0.5	32.6	16.7	4.3	39.9	55.9	4.2	1.3
Bhutan	2,063	2.6	1.9	36.0	9.8	5.5	43.0	52.9	4.1	1.1
Lao People's Dem. Rep.	5,279	2.4	1.5	38.2	14.1	5.3	42.7	53.8	3.5	1.2
Comoros	705	2.9	1.9	38.6	9.4	5.4	43.9	53.6	2.5	1.2
Swaziland	1,044	2.1	-0.2	38.0	15.7	5.1	42.2	55.0	2.8	1.2
Papua New Guinea	5,334	2.5	1.5	35.9	10.7	4.6	40.1	57.5	2.5	1.4
Myanmar	47,544	1.5	0.6	26.5	11.5	3.3	33.1	62.3	4.6	1.7
Cambodia	13,147	2.7	1.6	36.8	10.4	5.3	43.9	53.3	2.8	1.1
Ghana	19,593	2.3	1.4	34.0	10.3	4.6	44.2	51.2	4.6	1.0
Vanuatu	197	2.7	1.6	33.7	6.1	4.6	41.6	55.8	2.5	1.3
India	1,016,938	1.8	0.8	27.0	9.1	3.5	35.5	61.5	5.0	1.6
Morocco	29,108	1.6	1.0	24.4	6.6	3.0	34.7	61.2	4.1	1.6
Botswana	1,725	2.1	-0.4	32.4	10.2	4.0	42.2	55.6	2.2	1.3
Namibia	1,894	2.8	0.7	38.0	12.3	5.2	41.6	54.6	3.8	1.2
Solomon Islands	437	3.1	1.8	36.3	5.3	5.0	44.6	53.0	2.4	1.1
Sao Tome and Principe	149	2.6	1.7	34.9	6.4	4.5	39.2	54.1	6.8	1.2
Nicaragua	5,073	2.7	1.5	35.3	5.6	4.3	42.6	54.3	3.1	1.2
Egypt	67,784	1.9	1.3	27.0	6.7	3.5	35.4	60.5	4.1	1.5
Guatemala	11,423	2.7	1.7	36.6	7.3	4.9	43.6	52.9	3.5	1.1
Gabon	1,258	2.5	1.4	34.5	11.9	4.5	40.2	54.1	5.8	1.2
Mongolia	2,500	0.9	0.8	24.3	8.1	2.7	34.0	62.0	4.0	1.6
Equatorial Guinea	456	2.6	1.9	43.1	17.3	5.9	43.5	52.7	3.7	1.1
Honduras	6,457	2.7	1.3	33.5	5.7	4.3	41.8	54.8	3.4	1.2
Bolivia	8,317	2.1	1.3	32.6	8.9	4.3	39.5	56.2	4.4	1.3
Tajikistan	6,089	1.2	0.9	28.8	6.7	3.7	39.7	56.0	4.4	1.3
Indonesia	211,559	1.4	0.7	22.5	7.6	2.6	30.6	64.9	4.5	1.8
South Africa	44,000	1.5	-0.2	24.6	10.0	2.9	32.4	62.9	4.7	1.7
Syrian Arab Republic	16,560	2.5	1.4	29.6	4.2	3.8	40.8	56.1	3.1	1.3
Viet Nam	78,137	1.4	0.8	21.5	7.0	2.5	33.2	61.5	5.3	1.6

Exhibit IV.C.1. (Continued)

Country Name (listed from lowest to highest HDI)	Population (Thousands) 2000	Projected Population (Thousands) 2050	Population Growth Rate 1995–2000	Population Growth Rate 2000–2050	Births per 1,000 Population[a]	Deaths per 1,000 Population[a]	Children per Woman[b]	Share of Population Aged 0–14 Years 2000	Share of Population Aged 15–64 Years 2000	Share of Population Aged 65 and Older 2000	Working Age Population per Dependent[c] 2000
Moldova, Rep. of	4,283	3,580	-0.3	-0.4	11.9	11.3	1.6	22.6	66.4	11.0	2.0
Algeria	30,245	48,667	1.6	1.0	24.1	6.0	3.2	36.1	60.0	3.9	1.5
Iran, Islamic Rep. of	66,443	105,485	1.3	0.9	19.5	5.4	2.5	33.8	61.5	4.7	1.6
El Salvador	6,209	9,793	1.8	0.9	27.7	6.0	3.2	35.6	59.4	5.0	1.5
China	1,275,215	1,395,182	0.9	0.2	16.2	7.0	1.8	25.4	67.6	7.0	2.1
Cape Verde	436	812	2.2	1.2	30.0	6.1	3.8	44.4	51.9	3.7	1.1
Kyrgyzstan	4,921	7,235	1.5	0.8	23.2	7.6	2.9	34.3	59.8	5.9	1.5
Uzbekistan	24,913	37,818	1.8	0.8	24.7	6.2	2.9	37.6	58.0	4.5	1.4
Armenia	3,112	2,334	-1.3	-0.6	11.2	7.3	1.4	24.1	67.0	9.0	1.5
Sri Lanka	18,595	21,172	0.9	0.3	17.1	6.4	2.1	26.3	67.4	6.3	2.1
Occupied Palestinian Territories								47.3	49.3	3.4	1.0
Ecuador	12,420	18,724	1.7	0.8	25.4	5.9	3.1	33.8	61.5	4.7	1.6
Turkey	68,281	97,759	1.6	0.7	23.0	6.3	2.7	28.5	65.8	5.7	2.0
Albania	3,113	3,670	-0.5	0.3	19.9	5.4	2.4	29.3	64.0	6.7	1.8
Dominican Republic	8,353	11,876	1.7	0.7	24.6	6.5	2.9	33.5	62.2	4.3	1.6
Grenada	81	63		-0.5				35.4	57.6	7.1	1.4
Guyana	759	507	0.5	-0.8	23.8	8.4	2.5	30.6	64.4	5.0	1.8
Tunisia	9,519	12,887	1.2	0.6	18.7	5.5	2.3	29.7	64.4	5.9	1.8
Jordan	5,035	10,154	3.4	1.4	30.9	4.6	4.1	38.6	58.4	3.0	1.4
Azerbaijan	8,157	10,942	0.9	0.6	19.7	5.9	2.3	29.2	63.8	7.0	1.8
Georgia	5,262	3,472	-0.3	-0.8	11.7	9.4	1.6	19.6	68.5	11.9	2.1
Turkmenistan	4,643	7,541	2.0	1.0	24.4	7.0	3.0	37.7	58.1	4.3	1.4
Maldives	291	819	3.0	2.1	37.0	6.9	5.8	42.0	54.0	4.0	1.2
Philippines	75,711	126,965	2.0	1.0	28.4	5.5	3.6	37.4	58.8	3.8	1.4
Paraguay	5,470	12,111	2.5	1.6	31.3	5.4	4.2	39.5	57.0	3.5	1.2
Lebanon	3,478	4,946	2.0	0.7	20.4	5.5	2.3	32.1	62.0	5.9	1.6
Peru	25,952	41,105	1.7	0.9	26.2	6.4	3.2	33.4	61.8	4.8	1.6
Fiji	814	969	1.2	0.3	25.9	5.6	3.2	33.4	63.3	3.3	1.7
Saint Vincent and the Grenadines	118	129	0.6	0.2	20.5	5.9	2.4	27.0	66.1	7.0	1.9
Oman	2,609	6,812	3.1	1.9	31.3	3.4	5.4	44.2	53.4	2.4	1.1
Jamaica	2,580	3,669	0.9	0.7	21.9	5.9	2.5	31.1	62.0	7.0	1.6
Suriname	425	459	0.8	0.2	23.9	6.1	2.6	29.7	65.0	5.3	1.9

Kazakhstan	15,640	13,941	–1.1	–0.2	16.9	9.8	2.1	27.0	65.8	7.2	1.9
Ukraine	49,688	31,749	–0.7	–0.9	8.8	14.6	1.3	17.6	68.4	14.0	2.2
Thailand	60,925	77,079	1.0	0.5	18.2	6.8	2.0	24.0	69.8	6.2	2.3
Saudi Arabia	22,147	54,738	3.1	1.8	32.9	3.9	5.1	40.9	56.2	3.0	1.3
Romania	22,480	18,063	–0.2	–0.4	10.4	11.6	1.3	18.3	68.4	13.3	2.2
Saint Lucia	146	163	0.8	0.2	21.1	6.2	2.4	32.2	62.0	5.8	1.6
Samoa (Western)	173	254	0.9	0.8	30.6	6.0	4.5	36.0	58.7	5.2	1.4
Venezuela	24,277	41,733	2.1	1.1	24.9	4.5	3.0	34.0	61.6	4.4	1.6
Dominica	78	76		–0.1				27.8	63.9	8.3	1.8
Belize	240	421	2.4	1.1	29.8	4.9	3.6	40.8	54.2	5.0	1.2
Bosnia and Herzegovina	3,977	3,564	3.0	–0.2	10.5	7.4	1.4	19.0	71.2	9.9	2.5
Brazil	171,796	233,140	1.4	0.6	20.7	7.0	2.3	28.8	66.1	5.1	1.9
Colombia	42,120	67,491	1.8	0.9	24.5	5.7	2.8	32.8	62.5	4.7	1.7
Russian Federation	145,612	101,456	–0.3	–0.7	8.9	14.3	1.3	18.1	69.6	12.2	2.3
Mauritius	1,186	1,461	1.1	0.4	17.6	6.7	2.1	25.7	68.2	6.1	2.1
Libyan Arab Jamahiriya	5,237	9,248	2.0	1.1	23.2	4.2	3.4	33.9	62.7	3.4	1.7
Macedonia, TFYR	2,024	2,156	0.6	0.1	14.7	8.2	1.9	22.6	67.4	10.0	2.1
Panama	2,950	5,140	2.0	1.1	24.1	5.0	2.8	31.3	63.1	5.5	1.7
Malaysia	23,001	39,551	2.4	1.1	25.5	4.8	3.3	34.0	61.9	4.1	1.6
Bulgaria	8,099	5,255	–0.8	–0.9	8.0	14.2	1.1	15.6	68.3	16.1	2.1
Antigua and Barbuda	72	77		0.1				20.6	72.1	7.4	2.6
Median	*5,279*	*10,154*	*1.8*	*0.8*	*25.5*	*6.8*	*3.2*	*34.2*	*61.3*	*4.6*	*1.6*
Total Medium-HDI Population	*4,063,264*	*5,495,495*									
Share of World Population	*66.9*	*61.6*									
High-human development countries											
Mexico	98,933	140,228	1.6	0.7	24.6	5.0	2.8	34.1	60.9	5.0	1.6
Trinidad and Tobago	1,289	1,221	0.4	–0.1	14.1	6.5	1.7	25.6	68.2	6.2	2.1
Belarus	10,034	7,539	–0.4	–0.6	9.0	13.5	1.3	18.7	67.9	13.4	2.1
Cuba	11,202	10,074	0.4	–0.2	13.1	6.8	1.6	21.6	68.5	9.9	2.2
Saint Kitts and Nevis	42	32		–0.5				27.3	59.1	13.6	1.4
Latvia	2,373	1,331	–1.0	–1.2	8.0	13.9	1.2	17.3	68.2	14.5	2.1
Bahamas	303	395	1.4	0.5	21.1	7.6	2.4	29.2	65.2	5.6	1.9
United Arab Emirates	2,820	4,112	2.4	0.8	19.0	2.3	3.2	26.8	70.7	2.5	2.4
Croatia	4,446	3,587	0.0	–0.4	10.9	11.2	1.6	17.0	68.1	14.9	2.1
Kuwait	2,247	4,926	5.6	1.6	22.8	1.9	2.9	33.1	64.7	2.2	1.8
Lithuania	3,501	2,526	–0.4	–0.7	9.8	11.5	1.4	19.6	66.9	13.5	2.0
Qatar	581	874	2.1	0.8	22.0	3.6	3.7	26.5	71.3	2.2	2.5
Chile	15,224	21,805	1.4	0.7	19.9	5.4	2.4	28.3	64.6	7.1	1.8
Costa Rica	3,929	6,512	2.5	1.0	21.4	3.8	2.6	31.9	62.5	5.6	1.7
Estonia	1,367	657	–1.1	–1.5	8.7	13.8	1.3	17.7	67.6	14.7	2.1

Exhibit IV.C.1. (Continued)

Country Name (listed from lowest to highest HDI)	Population (Thousands) 2000	Projected Population (Thousands) 2050	Population Growth Rate		Births per 1,000 Population[a]	Deaths per 1,000 Population[a]	Children per Woman[b]	Share of Population			Working Age Population per Dependent[c] 2000
			1995–2000	2000–2050				Aged 0–14 Years 2000	Aged 15–64 Years 2000	Aged 65 and Older 2000	
Uruguay	3,342	4,128	0.8	0.4	17.6	9.1	2.4	24.9	62.5	12.6	1.7
Slovakia	5,391	4,948	0.1	−0.2	10.8	10.2	1.4	19.8	68.9	11.3	2.2
Hungary	10,012	7,589	−0.4	−0.6	9.9	14.1	1.4	16.9	68.8	14.3	2.2
Bahrain	677	1,270	2.9	1.3	23.0	3.2	3.0	29.3	68.2	2.5	2.1
Seychelles	79	97		0.4				28.3	64.3	7.4	1.8
Poland	38,671	33,004	0.0	−0.3	10.6	9.8	1.5	19.3	68.6	12.1	2.2
Argentina	37,074	52,805	1.3	0.7	19.9	7.7	2.6	27.7	62.6	9.7	1.7
Malta	389	402	0.6	0.1	12.3	7.8	1.9	20.3	67.9	11.8	2.1
Czech Republic	10,269	8,553	−0.1	−0.4	8.8	11.0	1.2	16.5	69.8	13.7	2.3
Brunei Darussalam	334	685	2.5	1.4	25.3	2.9	2.7	32.5	65.1	2.4	1.9
Korea, Rep. of	46,835	46,418	0.8	0.0	13.7	5.5	1.5	21.7	71.6	6.7	2.5
Slovenia	1,990	1,569	0.0	−0.5	9.2	9.7	1.3	16.0	70.1	13.9	2.3
Singapore	4,016	4,538	2.9	0.2	13.9	4.8	1.6	21.9	70.9	7.2	2.4
Barbados	267	258	0.4	−0.1	12.9	8.3	1.5	21.0	68.5	10.5	2.2
Hong Kong, China (SAR)	6,807	9,431	1.9	0.7	10.0	5.5	1.1	17.2	71.7	11.1	2.5
Cyprus	783	892	1.0	0.3	13.8	7.4	2.0	23.2	65.1	11.6	1.9
Greece	10,903	9,814	0.8	−0.2	9.5	10.0	1.3	15.0	67.1	17.9	2.0
Portugal	10,016	9,027	0.2	−0.2	11.3	10.6	1.5	17.2	67.6	15.2	2.1
Israel	6,042	9,989	2.4	1.0	21.5	6.3	2.9	27.8	62.4	9.8	1.7
Italy	57,536	44,875	0.1	−0.5	9.2	10.4	1.2	14.3	67.6	18.2	2.1
New Zealand	3,784	4,152	1.0	0.4	14.9	7.3	2.0	22.6	65.7	11.7	1.9
Spain	40,752	37,336	0.4	−0.2	9.5	8.8	1.2	15.0	68.1	16.8	2.1
Germany	82,282	79,145	0.2	−0.1	9.5	10.6	1.3	15.5	68.5	16.0	2.2
France	59,296	64,230	0.4	0.2	12.6	9.3	1.8	18.8	65.1	16.1	1.9
Austria	8,102	7,376	0.1	−0.2	10.1	9.9	1.4	16.7	67.8	15.5	2.1
Luxembourg	435	716	1.4	1.0	13.2	8.2	1.7	18.9	66.2	14.8	2.0
Finland	5,177	4,941	0.3	−0.1	11.5	9.6	1.7	18.1	67.0	14.9	2.0
United Kingdom	58,689	66,166	0.3	0.2	12.3	10.8	1.7	18.8	65.2	16.0	1.9
Ireland	3,819	4,996	1.1	0.5	14.0	8.6	1.9	21.7	67.0	11.2	2.0
Denmark	5,322	5,273	0.4	0.0	12.5	11.6	1.8	18.4	66.8	14.9	2.0
Switzerland	7,173	5,810	0.2	−0.4	10.3	9.4	1.5	17.1	67.7	15.2	2.1
Japan	127,034	109,722	0.3	−0.3	9.6	7.6	1.4	14.6	68.2	17.2	2.1

Canada	30,769	39,085	0.9	0.5	11.6	7.2	1.6	19.1	68.4	12.5	2.2
United States	285,003	408,695	1.1	0.7	14.7	8.4	2.1	21.3	66.0	12.7	1.9
Belgium	10,251	10,221	0.2	0.0	11.2	9.9	1.6	17.4	66.1	16.6	1.9
Netherlands	15,898	16,954	0.6	0.1	12.4	8.8	1.6	18.5	67.9	13.6	2.1
Australia	19,153	25,560	1.2	0.6	13.5	7.0	1.8	20.7	67.4	11.9	2.1
Sweden	8,856	8,700	0.1	0.0	10.3	10.6	1.6	18.2	64.4	17.4	1.8
Iceland	282	330	1.1	0.3	15.4	6.8	2.1	23.6	64.6	11.8	1.8
Norway	4,473	4,895	0.5	0.2	13.3	10.1	1.9	20.0	64.8	15.2	1.8
Median	*5,391*	*5,810*	*0.5*	*0.1*	*12.5*	*8.6*	*1.6*	*19.8*	*67.6*	*12.6*	*2.1*
Total High-HDI Population	*1,186,274*	*1,360,774*									
Share of World Population	*19.5*	*15.3*									
World[d]	6,070,581	8,918,724	1.4	0.8	22.7	9.2	2.8	30.1	63.0	6.9	1.7
Africa	795,671	1,803,298	2.4	1.6	38.8	14.8	5.2	42.7	54.1	3.2	1.2
Eastern Africa	252,515	614,457	2.6	1.8	43.2	18.2	6.0	45.6	51.6	2.8	1.1
Middle Africa	92,960	266,301	2.2	2.1	47.0	21.9	6.4	46.0	51.0	3.0	1.0
Northern Africa	173,615	306,046	1.8	1.1	27.1	7.4	3.5	35.8	60.0	4.2	1.5
Southern Africa	50,448	46,602	1.5	-0.2	25.9	10.5	3.1	35.0	61.3	3.7	1.6
Sub-Saharan Africa	653,492	1,557,384	2.5	1.7	41.8	16.7	5.7	44.4	52.6	3.0	1.1
Western Africa	226,133	569,891	2.7	1.8	42.5	15.0	6.0	45.1	52.0	2.9	1.1
Asia	3,679,737	5,222,058	1.4	0.7	22.4	8.0	2.7	30.4	63.7	5.9	1.8
Eastern Asia	1,481,110	1,590,070	0.8	0.1	15.6	7.0	1.8	23.8	68.5	7.7	2.2
South-central Asia	1,486,049	2,463,916	1.8	1.0	28.3	9.3	3.7	35.6	59.8	4.6	1.5
South-eastern Asia	520,355	767,250	1.6	0.8	23.7	7.5	2.8	32.4	62.9	4.7	1.7
Western Asia	192,222	400,822	2.2	1.5	28.2	6.5	3.7	36.0	59.6	4.4	1.5
Latin America & The Caribbean	520,229	767,685	1.6	0.8	23.3	6.4	2.7	31.9	62.6	5.5	1.7
Central America	135,213	211,758	1.9	0.9	26.5	5.2	3.0	35.3	60.1	4.6	1.5
South America	347,343	510,113	1.5	0.8	22.3	6.7	2.6	30.8	63.6	5.6	1.7
Caribbean	37,673	45,814	1.0	0.4	20.7	8.6	2.5	29.5	63.4	7.1	1.7
Europe	727,986	631,938	0.0	-0.3	10.2	11.4	1.4	17.5	67.8	14.7	2.1
Eastern Europe	304,538	221,736	-0.4	-0.6	9.3	13.3	1.3	18.1	69.0	12.9	2.2
Northern Europe	94,123	100,072	0.3	0.1	11.9	10.8	1.7	19.1	65.3	15.6	1.9
Southern Europe	145,822	125,596	0.3	-0.3	10.1	9.7	1.3	15.7	67.9	16.4	2.1
Western Europe	183,502	184,534	0.3	0.0	10.9	9.9	1.5	17.1	67.0	15.9	2.0

Exhibit IV.C.1. (Continued)

Country Name (listed from lowest to highest HDI)	Population (Thousands) 2000	Projected Population (Thousands) 2050	Population Growth Rate		Births per 1,000 Population[a]	Deaths per 1,000 Population[a]	Children per Woman[b]	Share of Population			Working Age Population per Dependent[c] 2000
			1995–2000	2000–2050				Aged 0–14 Years 2000	Aged 15–64 Years 2000	Aged 65 and Older 2000	
North America	315,915	447,931	1.1	0.7	14.4	8.3	2.0	21.6	66.1	12.3	2.0
Oceania	31,043	45,815	1.4	0.8	18.7	7.5	2.5	25.8	64.4	9.8	1.8
Australia/New Zealand	22,937	30,072	1.1	0.5	13.7	7.1	1.8	20.9	66.9	12.2	2.0
Melanesia	6,996	13,968	2.4	1.4	34.2	9.5	4.4	40.4	57.0	2.6	1.3
Micronesia	499	863	1.6	1.1	27.8	5.4	3.8	36.3	59.1	4.6	1.4
Polynesia	611	912	1.1	0.8	26.1	5.8	3.5	35.5	59.9	4.6	1.5

United Nations Human Development Index countries are included in the Exhibit only if they have data available.

[a]The number of births or deaths in the 5-year period between 1995–2000 divided by the person-years lived by the population in the same 5-year period.

[b]The number of children in the 5-year period between 1995–2000 divided by the reproductive-years lived by women in the same 5-year period.

[c]The working age population per dependent is calculated as the ratio of population aged 15–64 year to population aged 0–14 plus population aged 65 and older.

[d]The sum of the individual country populations is less than the total world population because the Human Development Index is not computed for some small countries.

Sources: Population Division of the Department of Economic and Social Affairs of the United Nations Secretariat, World Population Prospects: The 2002 Revision; World Bank, World Development Indicators, 2003.

Note IV.C.1. The Size of the World's Population and the Size of the Average Family

Recently a growing "revisionist" literature has contradicted the commonly accepted view that rapid population growth is a hindrance to development. Especially influential was a report by the National Research Council of the National Academy of Sciences (1986), which identifies positive as well as negative impacts of population growth and claims that the net impact cannot be determined given current evidence.

The revisionist view has gained credence in part from the failed predictions of many non-economists (and a few economists) of dire consequences from an expanding world population. These predictions included famines and metal and mineral shortages. In fact, both food and metal and mineral prices fell between 1960 and 1995, and food production per person climbed steadily during the same period (*Economist* 1997). The rise in metal and mineral prices during the 1960s and early 1970s stimulated conservation, invention of substitute materials, and successful new exploration. Continued improvement in agricultural technology, practices, and infrastructure increased the supply of food. There is, however, reason to be less sanguine about the impact of an expanding world population on unpriced resources such as clean air (see Selection X.1).

One of the arguments in favor of a large world population is that it increases the worldwide rate of technological progress. This argument has been formalized in the endogenous growth literature. For example, Kremer (1993, p. 681) "constructs a highly stylized model in which each person's chance of being lucky or smart enough to invent something is independent of population, all else equal, so that the growth rate of technology is proportional to total population." Robinson and Srinivasan (1997, p. 1262) phrase the argument as, "larger populations have more geniuses, and . . . presumably, there are increasing returns to geniuses." The basis of this presumption is that ideas are "nonrival," in contrast to most goods and services: the use of an idea by one person does not make it more difficult for another person to use the idea, but when one person eats a peach another person cannot eat it as well.

The case for efforts to slow population growth through family planning programs, for example, is much stronger when we examine the microeconomic impact of large family size than when we focus on the macroeconomic impact of a large world population. Put simply, it is harder for parents to find the time and resources to educate a large family than a small one. Although the mechanisms through which education contributes to economic development are in dispute, there is little doubt that education is essential to development. Concerning the worldwide rate of technological progress, the World Bank (1984) points out that "ideas may be lost and Einsteins go undiscovered if many children receive little schooling." The next selection focuses on the effects of family size on educational attainment and health, and on the determinants of fertility (births per woman), the most important factor in family size.

References

The Economist. 1997. "Plenty of Gloom." *The Economist* 345 (December 20): 19–21.

Kremer, Michael. 1993. "Population Growth and Technological Change: One Million B.C. to 1990." *Quarterly Journal of Economics* 108 (August): 681–716.

National Research Council. 1986. *Population Growth and Economic Development: Policy Questions* (Washington, DC: National Academy Press).

Robinson, James A., and T. N. Srinivasan. 1997. "Long-Term Consequences of Population Growth: Technological Change, Natural Resources, and the Environment." In Mark R. Rosenzweig and Oded Stark, eds., *Handbook of Population and Family Economics* (Amsterdam: Elsevier).

World Bank. 1984. *World Development Report 1984* (New York: Oxford University Press).

Selection IV.C.1. Economic Approaches to Population Growth*

Health and Education

There is substantial evidence that children from large families have lower educational attainment and reduced levels of health, in developed as well as developing countries.[1] Though many studies have inadequate controls for parents' income and education, there is some evidence that the negative association is greater at lower levels of family income, and pertains especially after four children.[2] Since families in poor countries have on average lower income and higher family size than families in rich countries, in poor countries the negative association of large family size and reduced health and education of children, will have greater weight in the population as a whole.

However, the strong cross-section association should not be interpreted necessarily as a causal one—of family size on health and education. It is possible that parents decide jointly and simultaneously on both the number of children to have and the size of their parental investment in child health and education. Low income, low returns to education and health investments, and reasonable concern about their own long-term security could lead parents to choose simultaneously both large numbers of children and low investments per child. Thus, an exogenous shock which reduced the number of children—for example the unexpected death of a child—would not necessarily raise parental investments in the health and education of remaining children, in the absence of other changes in the family's environment.

The question thus arises whether parents consciously trade off more children against higher inputs per child, deciding jointly on the quantity and "quality" of children and viewing these as substitutes, or whether they invest in children taking the number as given. The question is an important one for policy. If there is a quantity–quality tradeoff, and parents are not "altruistic" toward their children, that is they do not incorporate into their own utility that of their children, then the negative relation of large families with children's health and education may signal a negative intertemporal externality (arising perhaps because parents do not believe they can capture the returns on investing in their children's health and education)—a market failure which could justify public intervention to discourage high fertility. But if parents are altruistic, then efforts to force parents into higher investments in child health and education through certain kinds of interventions, such as quantitative restrictions on numbers of children or imposition of mandatory school attendance, could simply reduce overall family welfare.[3] From a welfare point of view it is reasonable to assume, except in the case of "unwanted" children, that parents have another child only when they feel that the benefits of an additional child to the family as a whole, including to the children already born, exceed the costs.

Governments have generally taken the view that parents are altruistic (or at least that if they are not, they still retain total rights over their own reproductive lives), and that the decision regarding family size should be left to parents. The most widespread form of population policy is public support for family planning programs, justified as a means to assist parents avoid unwanted children for whom the private costs would add to any social costs of additional births. If some children are unwanted, then even altruistic parents must in effect take the number of children as given, and are forced into sequential decision-making and possibly lower investments in child health and education than they would otherwise have made. In a few countries, especially in Asia (where governments view the social costs of high fertility as substantially above the private costs), government spending on family planning is also justified to provide information and "education" to parents about the likely effects of their own high fertility on the health and education of their own children.

The best evidence that unwanted births do reduce parental investments in children is from a study of the effects of twins on children's school enrollment in India. Rosenzweig and Wolpin (1980) posit that the birth of twins is likely in at least some cases to constitute the exogenous imposition of an "unwanted" child; they report that children from families in which the most recent birth

*From Nancy Birdsall, "Economic Approaches to Population Growth," in Hollis Chenery and T. N. Srinivasan, eds., *Handbook of Development Economics, Volume I* (Amsterdam: North-Holland, 1988), 497–499, 514–521. Reprinted by permission.

[1] Work on the consequences of high fertility for child health and development has been largely the domain of psychologists, public health specialists and demographers. See Blake (1983) and Maine and McNamara (1985). For an economic view, see Birdsall and Griffin (1988).

[2] Birdsall (1980). See also studies cited in Birdsall (1977).

[3] A whole range of pricing policies could distort parental demand for the number and "quality" of children.

was of twins were significantly less likely to be in school. Here the causal link—from an exogenously-imposed extra birth to less child schooling—can easily be inferred. The implication is that the elimination of unwanted births, through for example a reduction in the cost of family planning, would raise average education levels among children. . . .

Female Education, Labor Force Participation, and Wages

There is some evidence that at low levels of education (e.g. between zero and three or four years), education's effect on fertility is positive [Cochrane (1979)]. This may be due to an increase in fecundity (supply of children) as education increases from very low levels in populations in which fertility is initially below desired fertility, as posited in the synthesis model. It may be that more education is associated with higher income (a variable often missing from studies Cochrane cites), and that the higher income is having a positive effect on fertility (by increasing fecundity or increasing the demand for children), without any offsetting change in a woman's shadow price of time (especially in the largely illiterate populations where this positive effect tends to obtain).

Female education above about four years, however, bears one of the strongest and most consistent negative relationships to fertility. Its negative effect is consistent with the price of time effect postulated in the household model, with a "taste" effect of education on a desire for fewer, more educated children postulated in the synthesis model, and with an efficiency effect, operating through a woman's improved efficiency in the use of contraception. Female education is also associated with a higher age at marriage, and may well have some intangible effect on a woman's ability to plan and on her taste for non-familial activities.

Distinguishing empirically among the postulated mechanisms by which education reduces fertility is difficult. For women who work, the wage rate in theory represents the price of time; but labor supply is endogenous to the fertility decision, and high labor supply and low fertility could result from the taste effect as well as the price of time effect of education. Using U.S. data, Rosenzweig and Seiver (1982) and Rosenzweig and Schultz (1985) have shown that at least part of the education effect operates through greater efficiency in contraceptive use. Rosenzweig and Schultz demonstrate that the efficiency effect operates through more effective use by educated

women of relatively ineffective methods (and their greater ability to decipher information about their own fecundity). Since education's effect is partly one of information-processing, schooling and birth control information programs are substitutes as public programs to encourage low fertility (and both are substitutes for birth control services). (No comparable studies using developing country data are known to this author. Insofar as birth control information is less available in developing countries, the efficiency effect of education may well be critical.)

Female education is also associated with entry by women into the formal market, especially into jobs in the modern sector. Participation in the labor market is negatively associated with fertility only for women in relatively high-wage modern sector jobs. Though there may be a causal effect of work in the formal labor market on fertility, virtually no studies in developing countries have allowed for the simultaneity of the fertility and labor supply decisions—for example, the possibility that women who have few children due to low fecundity decide to work more.[4] The identification problem in a simultaneous model is severe, since most factors that influence labor supply would also influence fertility.[5] Jobs outside the modern sector—in agriculture, cottage industry and so on—which do not take women far from the household and allow flexible hours, do not increase the time cost of raising children and are not associated with low fertility.[6]

As female education and female wages rise, the differential between female and child wages widens. This in itself tends to reduce fertility, since it means that the family's loss of the mother's income when children are young is not easily and quickly made up by children's work.

Child Schooling (the "Quality" of Children)

Though the effect of changing prices for child quality on quantity of children is a fundamental idea in the household demand model, only a few

---

[4]But see McCabe and Rosenzweig (1976).

[5]Fertility but not labor supply would be affected by the price of contraceptives. As Rosenzweig and Wolpin (1980) point out, in estimating a labor supply equation, if the only source of variation in fertility not due to preferences is the price of contraceptives, two-stage least squares in a simultaneous equations model is redundant. The contraceptive price variable should simply be included in a reduced-form labor supply equation.

[6]See Standing (1983) for a review of the literature on fertility and female labor force participation.

studies have rigorously explored this cross-price effect, i.e. the hypothesis that a decline in the price of child schooling (or child health) will reduce fertility. . . . Rosenzweig and Wolpin (1982) show that in India, households in villages with a school have, all other things the same, lower fertility than households in villages without a school. (They also confirm the converse cross-price effect.) Their study is a classic in its demonstration of the use of simple reduced-form ordinary least squares regressions to test the effects of various governmental interventions (more schools, more family planning) on various outcomes—direct own-price effects and indirect cross-price effects. In a subsequent study using the same Indian data, Rosenzweig (1982) shows that farm households more intensively exposed to (exogenous) new agricultural technologies have lower fertility and higher child schooling, similarly implying an alteration in the household's allocation of resources between child quantity and quality in the face of exogenous price changes.

Family Income and Income Distribution

In studies controlling for parents' education and taking into account the endogeneity of family income [e.g. Kelley (1980)], income has a positive effect on fertility.[7] This positive effect is consistent with the pure income effect of the household demand model,[8] and with the increased fecundity or supply of births postulated when income rises in low income households in the synthesis model. Within the same socioeconomic group, e.g. among small farmers, higher income parents also tend to have more children,[9] and in industrial countries, income growth in the short run is associated with higher fertility (e.g. in the United States in the 1950s). In the long run, however, income growth tends to be offset by social changes that reduce fertility—such as rising education, so that people with more income want and have fewer children.

As a result, the association of income and fertility tends to vary according to absolute levels of income. Below some minimum income, increases in income are associated with higher fertility. In the poorest countries of Africa and South Asia, many families are below that threshold. Above that

threshold, further increases in income are associated with lower fertility—for a given increase in income, the reduction is greater for low-income groups. Raising the incomes of the rich (be it of rich countries or of rich groups within countries) reduces fertility less than does raising the incomes of the poor. There is, however, no good evidence that the distribution of income has an independent effect on fertility; it is influential only to the extent that poor households usually have higher absolute incomes if their share of the total is higher.

Markets and Old-Age Security

An important feature of development is that markets enlarge and diversify. Contacts and kin begin to matter less as guarantors of jobs and help with the harvest; children begin to matter less as a form of old-age security. Children's greater geographical mobility in an expanding labor market makes them less dependable as a form of old-age support; at the same time, an expanding capital market means other instruments for old-age security, including private savings and social insurance, emerge.

The household and synthesis models of fertility emphasize the importance to fertility decline of increases in the relative costs of children, especially the time costs as women's education and wages increase and as the market for women's labor expands [see also Lindert (1980, 1983)]. Cain (1981, 1983), however, has criticized the failure of empirical studies based on these models to take into account the pension value of children as security in old age in societies where land and capital markets are poor and means of accumulation other than children are limited.[10] He examines, for example, the near-total reliance of women in societies such as Bangladesh on their sons' support should they be widowed, as an explanation of persistent high fertility that pertains irrespective of the rearing costs of children.

Williamson (1985) incorporates the effect of a poor capital market and an expanding labor market in a study of fertility decline in nineteenth-century England. He notes the importance of "default risk," i.e. the probability that adult children will emigrate from rural areas, and thus leave the par-

---

[7]Kelley shows that use of ordinary least squares, rather than two-stage least squares with income endogenous, produces a non-significant coefficient on income in a fertility regression.

[8]For a full discussion see Simon (1977).

[9]World Bank (1984, p. 108).

[10]Rosenzweig and Wolpin (1985) argue that Cain's approach requires an assumption of a poor capital and land market, but that in fact, the apparent absence of such markets (e.g. of land sales) may itself be simply a manifestation of an optimal implicit contract across generations which maximizes the gains from farm-specific knowledge; older people in effect trade information they have on own-farm characteristics, for support from children.

ents' household just as they become a net economic benefit at the margin, both to the net cost of a child and to a child's pension value.[11] Using data from nineteenth-century England on rural emigration rates, he shows that rising rates throughout the period reduced the present value of rural male children to parents (but not female children) by about 18 percent of farm wages (using a 5 percent discount rate).[12] The emigration rate matters only if remittances from absent children to parents were small; Williamson notes there is little evidence of remittances, and that capital markets that might have eased transfers were poor. His emphasis on the importance of rural emigration in explaining fertility decline thus relies on the combined assumptions of an increasingly integrated labor market and a poor capital market—a combination of assumptions that has not been explored in developing country settings.

Hammer (1986) has proposed that improvements in capital markets should lower fertility (and increase savings; he argues that increased savings per se are not the cause of lower fertility), and Nugent et al. (1983), using household data from India, show in a fully specified structural model that a weak local capital market is positively associated with higher fertility in nuclear households (and not in extended households, which presumably have greater access to capital through family networks).

Infant Mortality and Fertility

The demographic transition idea posits that a decline in infant mortality brings about a compensating decline in fertility. The exact nature of any causal link is not well understood, however. At the aggregate level, declines in fertility have tended to lag behind declines in mortality, producing in the 1950s through the early 1970s rapid rates of population growth. The real issue, however, is the effect of declining mortality at the individual and family level. At this level, several problems complicate empirical analyses of the effect of infant mortality on fertility behavior. First, at the family level, high mortality and high fertility may be jointly determined, so that ordinary least squares estimates will be biased. Only recently have analysts attempted to

isolate the family-specific exogenous component of life expectancy, in order to analyze the effect on fertility of exogenous changes in mortality; these effects appear much smaller than the endogenous mortality component [Olsen and Wolpin (1983)]. The problem of bias due to simultaneity can also occur because high fertility may cause high mortality, rather than vice versa, for example when the birth of a new child leads to rapid weaning (and poor nutritional status, diarrhea and death) of the preceding child.

Second, there is a biological as well as a behavioral effect of mortality on fertility, for example when with the death of a child a woman ceases breastfeeding, and is then more likely to become pregnant. To predict the long-run effects of declines in mortality on fertility, isolation of the behavioral effect is critical.

Schultz (1981, pp. 131–132) notes that knowledge that some fraction of children is likely to die has two offsetting effects on parents: it increases the cost per surviving child, and increases the number of births required to obtain a survivor. The effect on fertility of declines in the probability that children will die depends on the price elasticity of parental demand for surviving children; if demand is elastic, a reduction in the cost or "price" of births with a decline in (exogenous) mortality should increase the demand for children and raise fertility. If demand is inelastic, mortality decline should reduce fertility. The latter is likely if an exogenous reduction in mortality, by lowering the price of child "quality," encourages investment in child quality, i.e. in schooling and health, as allowed for in the quantity–quality model outlined above.

Finally, once a behavioral response to mortality decline is established, an additional question arises: whether the effect represents a reduction in "replacement" behavior (individual couples replacing lost children) or in "insurance" or "hoarding" behavior (couples having more births than they might otherwise have in order to insure against the possibility of loss). Replacement behavior is purported to be more prominent in populations at the highest and lowest levels of development, such as the industrial economies on the one hand, Bangladesh on the other [Preston (1975)]; for a country like Malaysia, replacement effects appear small [Wolpin (1984), Olsen (1983)].

On average, the evidence is that families do not completely replace a lost child, so that in the short run infant mortality reduces overall population growth, all other things the same. However, the indirect and long-run effect of reduced mortality is probably to reduce fertility in a more than compen-

---

[11]Caldwell's (1976, 1978) restatement of demographic transition theory emphasizes the shift from child-to-parent "wealth" transfers to parent-to-child transfers in explaining fertility decline, but does not refer explicitly to the "default risk" issue.

[12]The lower the discount rate the greater the relative effect of the default (or emigration rate) on the present value of children. Cain's view that the pension motive affects fertility in effect favors a low discount rate.

sating amount—as, with greater certainty about child survival, parents reduce "insurance" births and shift toward child "quality" investments. The need for hoarding or insurance births would appear limited, given the sequential nature of childbearing (which allows replacement); however, it is likely that in high mortality environments, couples begin childbearing earlier (which increases aggregate population growth), and have children more rapidly. Thus, hoarding effects appear to be greater than replacement effects [e.g. Olsen (1983)]. However, the likely root of the apparent long-run response of lower fertility to declining mortality is in the shift toward an entirely new pattern of child investment, as parents adjust their behavior in response to a new environment of costs and benefits of children, of which reduced mortality may be only one component.

Family Planning Programs and Fertility

Whether organized family planning programs, privately or publicly subsidized, contribute to fertility decline is of obvious policy interest; governments of many developing countries, especially in Asia, have subsidized family planning in an effort to reduce fertility, and donors, especially the United States, have supported such efforts financially.

Measuring the impact of family planning programs on fertility decline requires controlling for other possible causes of fertility decline discussed above—such as increases in education or declines in mortality. It also requires data on some exogenous change in the availability or quality of family planning to a household, community or nation. Any such exogenous change would correspond to a change (increase) in the price of child quantity in the household demand model or change (reduction) in the cost of fertility control in the synthesis model. Information on change in the use of services is generally more widely available than information on availability, but does not suffice, since use is endogenous to people's fertility goals.

Lack of good information on change of the "price" of family planning (i.e. in the availability and quality of information or services) meant that until about a decade ago it was difficult to resolve the debate about the relative importance to fertility decline of the supply of family planning services vs. the "demand" factors—increasing education, falling infant mortality and so on. Early family planning programs in Korea, Hong Kong, and other areas of East Asia had been established in countries where a marked fall in fertility was already in progress; some of the continued decline might have occurred even without official programs. In other countries (such as India and Pakistan), where programs were also established in the 1950s and 1960s, fertility was changing little during the 1960s.

More recently, however, such information has accumulated, especially at the national level, e.g. the nation-level measures of family planning program effort of Mauldin and Lapham (1985), and at the community level; and though this and other such measures remain controversial due to measurement problems, they have permitted analyses of fertility change taking into account both supply and demand factors.

In general, the evidence from these analyses is that family planning programs do matter, having some negative effect on fertility independent of demand factors. The negative effect is relatively weak where other factors do not encourage low fertility, but powerful where other factors do. Boulier (1985), for example, estimates a variant of the household demand model for a sample of developing countries, using the Mauldin and Lapham 1972 index of family planning as one variable explaining fertility change over the period 1965–75. Other variables include the change during the same period in life expectancy, in adult literacy, in income per capita, in the proportion of the population in cities of 100000 or more, and in fertility change 1960–65. The 1972 index is treated as an endogenous variable, statistically identified using pre-1965 socioeconomic data. (Boulier himself notes that this is rather arbitrary.) Fertility decline in the period 1960–65 turns out to be an important predictor of the 1972 index; it is plausible that fertility decline itself induces government officials to augment resources for encouraging more fertility decline, particularly if it represents real demand for more services. However, even taking into account that a stronger family planning program in 1972 is associated with prior fertility decline (in 1960–65), the effect of the program on fertility decline in the concurrent period (1965–75) is still positive.

In a similar analysis, Wheeler (1985) estimates the effect of change in the Mauldin–Lapham index between 1972 and 1982 on fertility change from 1970 to 1980. He experiments with various functional forms in a simultaneous equations model, and concludes that in explaining fertility change over this period in developing countries, it is the combination of family planning availability with female education which must be stressed, since specifications including the interaction of these two are the most powerful.

Studies within countries tend to complement these nation-level studies. Not surprisingly, cross-section studies of households, summarized by Boulier (1985), find that people are more likely to know about and use contraception the closer they live to a reliable source. Use of contraception does not necessarily reduce aggregate fertility, of course. However, Schultz (1973) in a study of administrative regions of Taiwan, found that fertility over the period 1964–69 declined more rapidly where health and family planning workers were more plentiful. Consistent with Wheeler's findings, the impact of workers was greater where child school enrollment rates were greater and infant mortality had declined more.

In another study, Rosenzweig and Wolpin (1982) examined the determinants of recent fertility among women in India in 1968–71, measuring family planning inputs by the fraction of villages having a family planning clinic in the district in which a woman resides. Holding constant wife's and husband's education, wife's age, farm and non-farm residence, and district level health, schooling, and sanitation characteristics, they reported that doubling the number of villages in a district with a family planning clinic (from 2 to 4 percent) would reduce fertility by 13 percent, as well as reducing child mortality and raising school attendance. In a later study [Rosenzweig and Wolpin (1986)], they examined the possibility that the availability of public services such as family planning and health to households cannot be treated as exogenous, given that governments may locate such services in specific places in an effort to compensate for or to complement "demand" factors. For the particular case they study, of the Philippines, they conclude that family planning services do reduce fertility; they also show that conventional tests could understate the true price effect of public programs in reducing fertility and improving health, since government appears to be following a compensatory strategy, locating services where other factors would mitigate against lower fertility and better health.

Finally, recent experimental studies testing the impact of family planning, summarized in World Bank (1984, pp. 119–121) suggest sustained programs can reduce fertility even in rural relatively uneducated populations; the most widely noted of these is that in Matlab, Bangladesh.

Greater availability or improved quality of family planning services, usually at no charge, reduces the overall price to potential users most obviously by reducing the cost of information or of travel. The economic models predict such a price re-duction will reduce fertility (except where demand for births still falls short of biological supply); the empirical evidence is consistent with the prediction.

References

Birdsall, N. (1977) "Analytical approaches to the relationship of population growth and development," *Population and Development Review,* 3:63–102.

Birdsall, N. (1980) "A cost of siblings: Child schooling in urban Colombia," in: J. Simon and J. DaVanzo, eds., *Research in population economics,* Vol. 2. Greenwich, CT: JAI Press.

Birdsall, N. and Griffin, C. C. (1988) "Fertility and poverty in developing countries," *Journal of Policy Modeling,* forthcoming.

Blake, J. (1983) "Family size and the quality of children," *Demography,* 18:421–442.

Boulier, B. L. (1985) "Family planning programs and contraceptive availability: Their effects on contraceptive use and fertility," in: N. Birdsall, ed., *The effects of family planning programs on fertility in the developing world.* World Bank Staff working paper no. 677, Washington, DC.

Cain, M. T. (1981) "Risk and insurance perspectives on fertility and agrarian change in India and Bangladesh," *Population and Development Review,* 7:435–474.

Cain, M. T. (1983) "Fertility as an adjustment to risk," *Population and Development Review,* 9:688–702.

Caldwell, J. C. (1976) "Toward a restatement of demographic theory," *Population and Development Review,* 2:321–366.

Caldwell, J. C. (1978) "A theory of fertility: From high plateau to destabilization," *Population and Development Review,* 4:553–577.

Cochrane, S. H. (1979) *Fertility and education: What do we really know?* World Bank Staff occasional paper, no. 26. Baltimore, MD: Johns Hopkins University Press.

Hammer, J. (1986) "Population growth and savings in LDCs: A survey article," *World Development,* 14:579–591.

Kelley, A. C. (1980) "Interactions of economic and demographic household behavior," in: R. A. Easterlin, ed., *Population and economic change in developing countries.* Chicago, IL: University of Chicago Press.

Lindert, P. H. (1980) "Child costs and economic development," in: R. A. Easterlin, ed., *Population and economic change in developing countries.* Chicago, IL: University of Chicago Press.

Lindert, P. H. (1983) "The changing economic costs and benefits of having children," in: R. A. Bulatao and R. D. Lee, eds., *Determinants of fertility in developing countries.* New York: Academic Press.

Maine, D. and McNamara, R. (1985) *Birth spacing and child survival.* New York: Columbia University.

Mauldin, W. P. and Lapham, R. J. (1985) "Measuring family planning effort in LDCs: 1972 and 1982," in: N. Birdsall, ed., *The effects of family planning programs on fertility in the developing world,* World Bank Staff working paper no. 677. Washington, DC: World Bank.

McCabe, J. and Rosenzweig, M. R. (1976) "Female labor force participation, occupational choice and fertility in developing countries," in: R. G. Ridker, ed., *Population and development: The search for selective interventions.* Baltimore, MD: Johns Hopkins University Press.

Nugent, J., Kan, K. and Walther, R. J. (1983) "The effects of old-age pensions on household structure, marriage, fertility and resource allocation in rural areas of developing countries," University of Southern California, mimeo.

Olsen, R. J. (1983) "Mortality rates, mortality events and the number of births," *American Economic Review,* 73:29–32.

Olsen, R. J. and Wolpin, K. I. (1983) "The impact of exogenous child mortality on fertility: A waiting time regression with dynamic regressors," *Econometrica,* 51:731–749.

Preston, H. (1975) "Health programs and population growth," *Population and Development Review,* 1:189–199.

Rosenzweig, M. R. (1982) "Educational subsidy, agricultural development and fertility change," *Quarterly Journal of Economics,* February: 67–88.

Rosenzweig, M. R. and Schultz, T. P. (1985b) "Schooling, information and non-market productivity: Contraceptive use and its effectiveness," Yale University, mimeo.

Rosenzweig, M. R. and Seiver, D. (1982) "Education and contraceptive choice: A conditional demand framework," *International Economic Review,* 23: 171–198.

Rosenzweig, M. R. and Wolpin, K. (1980a) "Testing the quantity-quality fertility model: The use of twins as a natural experiment," *Econometrica,* 48:227–240.

Rosenzweig, M. R. and Wolpin, K. (1982) "Governmental interventions and household behavior in a developing country," *Journal of Development Economics,* 209–225.

Rosenzweig, M. R. and Wolpin, K. (1985) "Specific experience, household structure and intergenerational transfers: Farm family land and labor arrangements in developing countries," *Quarterly Journal of Economics,* C (supplement): 961–988.

Rosenzweig, M. R. and Wolpin, K. (1986) "Evaluating the effects of optimally distributed public programs: Child health and family planning interventions," *American Economic Review,* 76:470–482.

Schultz, T. P. (1973) "Explanation of birth rate changes over time: A study of Taiwan," *Journal of Political Economy,* 31 (supplement): 238–274.

Schultz, T. P. (1981) *Economics of population.* Reading, MA: Addison-Wesley Publishing Company.

Simon, J. L. (1977) *The economics of population growth.* Princeton, NJ: Princeton University Press.

Standing, G. (1983) "Women's work activity and fertility," in: R. A. Bulatao and R. D. Lee, eds., *Determinants of fertility in developing countries,* Vols. 1 and 2. New York: Academic Press.

Wheeler, D. (1985) "Female education, family planning, income and population: A long-run econometric simulation model," in: N. Birdsall, ed., *The effects of family planning programs on fertility in the developing world,* World Bank Staff working paper no. 677. Washington, DC: World Bank.

Williamson, J. G. (1985) "Did rising emigration cause fertility to decline in 19th century rural England? Child costs, old-age pensions and child default," Harvard Institute for Economic Research, Harvard University, Cambridge, MA.

Wolpin, K. (1984) "An estimable dynamic stochastic model of fertility and child mortality," *Journal of Political Economy,* 92:852–874.

World Bank (1984) *World development report 1984.* New York: Oxford University Press. Also available as *Population change and economic development.* New York: Oxford University Press (1985).

Selection IV.C.2. Demographic Trends in Sub-Saharan Africa*

Delayed Demographic Transition

While most of the developing world has undergone a demographic transition from high fertility and high mortality to low fertility and low mortality, this process has stalled or progressed exceedingly slowly in Africa. As in most of the developing world, mortality declined sharply in Africa with the introduction of modern public health practices and health technologies after World War II.[1] The impact on child survival was particularly large, because antimicrobials are often powerful treatments for infectious diseases such as acute respiratory infections and diarrheal disorders.[2] Yet in contrast to other developing regions, Africa has not experienced corresponding declines in fertility to any appreciable degree (until, perhaps, very recently).

The combination of falling death rates, concentrated in the youth cohort, and stable birth rates have had two principal demographic consequences: rapid population growth and a skewing of the age structure toward the young ages. These trends are illustrated in Figure 1. Population growth averaged 2.3 percent in the 1950s, 2.4 percent in the 1960s, 2.7 percent in the 1970s, and 2.9 percent from 1980 to present. By contrast, in Asia and Latin America population growth has fallen, from rates of 2.4 percent and 2.7 percent, respectively, in the 1960s to rates of 1.5 percent and 1.7 percent, respectively, over 1990–95. Africa's current population growth rate, which implies a doubling of the population in less than twenty-five years, is huge by historical and comparative standards and is certainly not sustainable over the long run.

Figures 1 and 2 show that accelerating population growth has swelled the youth cohort, and consequently decreased the ratio of the working-age to dependent populations. The working-age population (between the ages of fifteen and sixty-four) is roughly half of the total population of Africa, and this share has actually fallen slightly since 1950. This contrasts with the higher (60 to 70 percent) and generally rising share found in other regions.

Cross-country data indicate that the working-age population in Africa grew at an almost identical rate to the total population from 1965 to 1990. In the rest of the world, by contrast, the working-age population grew, on average, 0.35 percent per year faster than the total population over the same period. This difference between African and world trends accounts for Africa's relatively high youth dependency ratio. Africa's youth dependency burden poses a significant impediment to the growth of income per capita, since labor force participation, productivity, and saving are low among the dependent population, relative both to the working-age population and to their own consumption and investment requirements.

Table 1, which reports total fertility rates and infant mortality rates across major world regions, demonstrates Africa's divergence from demographic trends elsewhere. It is striking that African fertility is so closely comparable to that observed in Asia and Latin America in the 1950s. Africa's demographic uniqueness, therefore, is not in the level of fertility but in the persistence of such a high level in the face of declining mortality rates. High fertility is the most salient feature of the continent's stalled demographic transition and the cause of its accelerating population growth and remarkably young age structure.

Contraceptive use increased modestly from a prevalence rate of 5 percent in 1960 to 17 percent in 1990. In East Asia contraceptive prevalence increased from 13 to 75 percent over the same period, and even in poorer South Asia, usage increased from 7 to 41 percent.[3] Table 2 summarizes fertility and contraceptive prevalence data collected in household surveys in seventeen African countries in the late 1980s and early 1990s. The most striking feature of the table is that in most countries not only total fertility rates but also "wanted" fertility rates, are above 5.0. Thus the provision of contraceptives is by itself unlikely to reduce fertility significantly. Africa's population problem is one of high desired fertility, rather than a need for contraceptive services. In contrast to other developing regions, eliminating unwanted fertility would have negligible to small effects on the achievement of replacement fertility levels (2.1 children per woman). Indeed, Africa's low levels of unwanted fertility are consistent with the pattern of extremely low rates of contraceptive prevalence among married women.

*From David E. Bloom and Jeffrey D. Sachs, "Geography, Demography, and Economic Growth in Africa," *Brookings Papers on Economic Activity,* 2 (1998): 243–251. Reprinted by permission.

[1]These health technologies include chloroquine, sulfa drugs, and powerful antibiotics such as penicillin and streptomycin, as well as DDT, which became available in 1943.

[2]While life expectancy increased by roughly 20 percent from 1960 to 1995, infant mortality fell by 40 percent, from 159 to 96 deaths per thousand births.

[3]Bongaarts (1994).

Figure 1. Age distribution in sub-Saharan Africa, 1950–95.

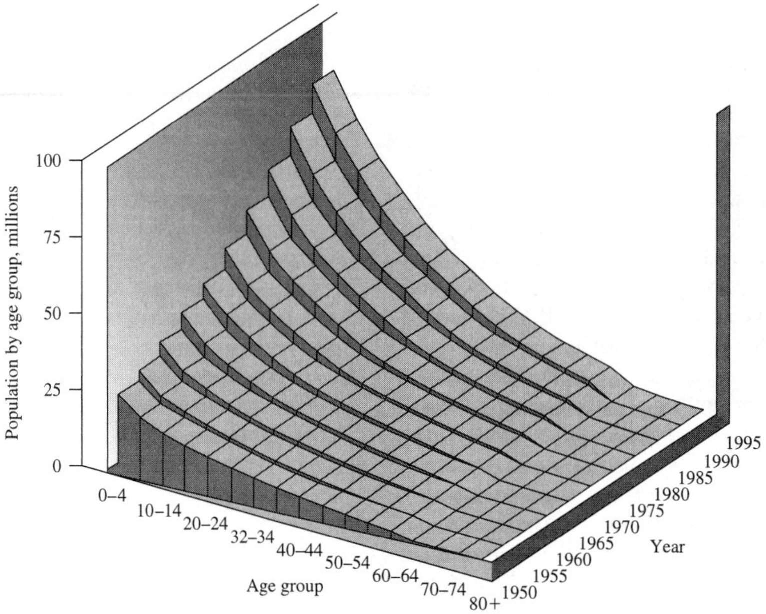

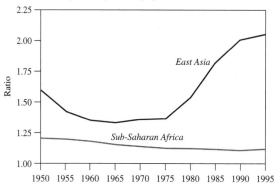

Source: United Nations (1996).

Figure 2. Ratio of working-age to dependent populations, Africa and East Asia, 1950–95.[a]

Source: United Nations (1992).

[a]Working-age population is between the ages of fifteen and sixty-four; dependent population includes all others.

Table 1. Fertility and Infant Mortality by Region

Region	1950–55		1990–95		Percent change in	
	Total fertility rate[a]	Infant mortality rate[b]	Total fertility rate[a]	Infant mortality rate[b]	Fertility	Infant mortality
Africa	6.6	185	5.7	94	−14	−49
Asia	5.9	180	2.8	62	−52	−66
East Asia	5.7	181	1.9	41	−67	−77
Oceania	3.8	69	2.5	26	−35	−62
Latin America and Caribbean	5.9	126	2.9	40	−50	−68
Europe	2.6	72	1.6	13	−39	−82
North America	3.5	29	2.0	9	−42	−69

[a]Births per woman.

[b]Deaths per 1,000 births.

Source: United Nations (1996).

Table 2. Fertility and Contraception, Selected Sub-Saharan African Countries

Country and year	Fertility rate[a]			Proportion of progress toward replacement level via wanted fertility rate[c]	Percentage of married women using contraception
	Total	Wanted[b]	Unwanted[b]		
Burkina Faso, 1993	6.9	6.0	0.9	0.19	7.9
Côte d'Ivoire, 1994	5.7	4.7	1.0	0.28	11.4
Ghana, 1988	6.4	5.5	0.9	0.21	12.9
Liberia, 1986	6.5	6.0	0.5	0.11	6.4
Madagascar, 1992	6.1	5.2	0.9	0.23	16.7
Malawi, 1992	6.7	5.7	1.0	0.22	13.0
Mali, 1987	6.7	6.9	. . .	. . .	4.7
Niger, 1992	7.4	7.1	0.3	0.06	4.4
Nigeria, 1990	6.0	5.8	0.2	0.05	6.0
Rwanda, 1992	6.2	4.4	1.8	0.44	21.2
Senegal, 1992–93	6.0	5.1	0.9	0.23	7.4
Sudan, 1989–90	5.0	5.9	. . .	. . .	8.7
Tanzania, 1991–92	6.3	6.4	. . .	. . .	10.4
1994	5.6	5.5	0.1	0.03	17.8
Togo, 1988	4.1	5.3	. . .	. . .	33.9
Uganda, 1988–89	7.3	6.8	0.5	0.10	4.9
Zambia, 1992	6.5	5.4	1.1	0.25	15.2
Zimbabwe, 1994	4.3	3.5	0.8	0.36	48.1

[a]Births per woman.

[b]A birth is "wanted" if the number of living children is less than or equal to the current ideal. Wanted fertility rates express the level of fertility that would prevail if all unwanted births were prevented. Unwanted fertility is total less wanted fertility. Note that in some cases, wanted fertility exceeds total fertility, possibly in part because some statistics refer to all women, while others refer only to currently married women.

[c]That is, progress toward fertility rate of 2.1 children per woman that would be achieved by reducing the total fertility rate to the wanted rate.

Source: Macro International (various years).

High fertility in Africa probably reflects a combination of low socioeconomic development (for example, in terms of education and gender inequality) and sociocultural practices that reinforce a preference for large families. There is an extensive literature on the determinants of fertility in Africa.[4] This literature notes that even after accounting for differences in infant mortality, income, education, and urbanization, Africa typically remains a positive outlier.[5] Explaining why this is so is an important research question.

We can identify two sets of factors that appear to be related to high fertility in Africa. First, in rural areas of Africa market activity is limited and corresponding financial institutions are poorly, if at all, developed, so that the scope for saving for old age is limited. Therefore children continue to be viewed as the current generation's main source of old age insurance. Similarly, formal labor market activity is limited, which tends to reduce the perceived costs to fertility. Children are also an important source of labor in rural settings, assisting both in small-holder cash crop agriculture, such as coffee, and in household work.[6] Second, sociocultural institutions and practices encourage large family sizes. The long history of low population densities and the ever-present struggle for survival in an environment of drought, low crop yields, slave trade, and infectious disease no doubt led to powerful norms of high fertility and large families, and these have changed only slowly in the face of rapidly declining infant mortality rates and rising population densities that limit the availability of farm land to divide among children.

Social structures that promote high fertility include fostering children, communal land tenure, and polygyny. The common practice of children being raised in households headed by someone other than their parents reduces the costs of raising children. John Caldwell and Pat Caldwell report that in West Africa as many as one-third of all children live in this way.[7] In addition, communal land tenure places a premium on family size, as village leaders distribute land according to family "need." In a system where there is no private title to land but land remains the primary factor of production,

having a large family is the best way to acquire access to increased resources. Finally, polygyny continues to be widely practiced in Africa, especially West Africa, and dilutes family and paternal bonds. Each wife comprises a discrete economic unit within the family, responsible for the care of her children. Husbands, while they have access to the fruits of their children's labor, have little responsibility for their welfare.

To test some of these hypotheses, we assembled an unbalanced panel data set for 103 countries at six points in time between 1960 and 1990. We regressed the log of the total fertility rate on income and income squared, infant mortality, schooling, gender gaps in schooling, geography, time, and financial market depth (measured by the ratio of liquid liabilities to GDP). The results reveal that fertility tends to increase with infant mortality and tropical location. They also reveal that fertility has tended to decline over time, and that it decreases with income, education, the degree of gender equality in schooling, and financial market depth. In addition, there is considerable fertility variation across geoclimatic regions, for example, tropical and subtropical wet and dry climates. Finally, an Africa dummy has a small but significant positive coefficient, consistent with other literature on the subject. These results imply that high fertility rates in Africa will decline as economic and social development proceeds.

Implications of Demographic Change in Africa

The dominance of youth in Africa's population creates enormous momentum for continued population growth. Even if the total fertility rate were immediately reduced to the replacement level of 2.1 children per woman, Africa's population would still increase to more than 1 billion (that is, by over 50 percent) during the next century, as today's children progress through their prime childbearing years.[8] Correspondingly, dependency ratios would remain high for decades, depressing the growth of income per capita. . . . Much of the most rapid population growth in Africa is occurring in the regions least suitable for rapid economic growth: rural, landlocked, and arid areas that are already under tremendous demographic stress.[9] Rising population densities in these low-productivity interior regions not only threaten economic growth but also intensify environmental degradation through de-

[4]See, for example, Boserup (1985); Caldwell and Caldwell (1987); Caldwell (1991, 1994); Bledsoe (1994); Ainsworth, Beegle, and Nyamete (1995); Pitt (1995).

[5]Chesnais (1992); Cohen (1993). Chesnais also provides a discussion of variance of socioeconomic "thresholds" and the onset of fertility decline in a not exclusively African context.

[6]Caldwell (1982, 1991).

[7]Caldwell and Caldwell (1987); see also Bledsoe (1994).

[8]Bongaarts (1999).

[9]Gallup and Sachs (1998).

forestation, soil erosion, and the depletion of aquifers.

Rapid population growth imposes a great burden on African governments in the provision of basic education. Indeed, Africa is the only region of the world in which school enrollment rates fell during recent decades (though the quality of the data is uncertain). According to the World Bank, between 1980 and 1993 primary school enrollment rates in sub-Saharan Africa fell from 68 percent to 65 percent of the primary school age cohort for females and from 90 percent to 78 percent of the cohort for males.[10] Nonetheless, increased numbers of primary school graduates (due to overall population growth) has led to increased demand for secondary education, which has also strained education budgets. In addition, it is extremely difficult to improve the low quality of education in Africa when the school-age population is growing so fast. For example, for the 106 developing countries with data for 1990, the correlation between the number of students per primary school teacher and the ratio of the dependent to total population is 0.52. Spending per primary school student in Africa, at an average of $126 per year (1985 PPP-adjusted), represents only 45 percent and 30 percent of that in Latin America and Asia, respectively. The number of students per teacher (forty-three) is much higher than in Latin America (twenty-eight) and Asia (thirty-two).[11]

[10]World Bank (1997).
[11]Barro and Lee (1997).

References

Ainsworth, Martha, Kathleen Beegle, and Andrew Nyamete. 1995. "The Impact of Female Schooling on Fertility and Contraceptive Use: A Study of Fourteen Sub-Saharan Countries." Living Standards Measurement Study Working Paper 110. Washington: World Bank.

Barro, Robert J., and Jong-Wha Lee. 1997. "Schooling Quality in a Cross-Section of Countries." Working Paper 6198. Cambridge, Mass.: National Bureau of Economic Research.

Bledsoe, Caroline. 1994. "'Children Are Like Young Bamboo Trees': Potentiality and Reproduction in Sub-Saharan Africa." In *Population, Economic Development, and the Environment,* edited by Kerstin Lindahl-Kiessling and Hans Landberg. Oxford University Press.

Bongaarts, John. 1994. "Population Policy Options in the Developing World." *Science* 263 (February): 771–76.

———. 1999. "Future Population Growth and Policy Options." In *Macroeconomics and Population Momentum,* edited by Andrew Mason, Thomas Merrick, and Paul Shaw. Washington: Economic Development Institute of the World Bank (forthcoming).

———. 1985. "Economic and Demographic Interrelationships in Sub-Saharan Africa." *Population and Development Review* 11(3): 383–97.

Caldwell, John C. 1982. *Theory of Fertility Decline.* London: Academic Press.

———. 1991. "The Soft Underbelly of Development: Demographic Transition in Conditions of Limited Economic Change." In *Proceedings of the World Bank Annual Conference on Development Economics 1990.* Washington: World Bank.

———. 1994. "Fertility in Sub-Saharan Africa: Status and Prospects." *Population and Development Review* 20(1): 179–87.

Caldwell, John C., and Pat Caldwell. 1987. "The Cultural Context of High Fertility in Sub-Saharan Africa." *Population and Development Review* 13(3): 409–37.

Chesnais, Jean-Claude. 1992. *The Demographic Transition: Stages, Patterns, and Economic Implications: A Longitudinal Study of Sixty-Seven Countries Covering the Period 1720–1984.* Oxford: Clarendon Press.

Cohen, Barry. 1993. "Fertility Levels, Differentials, and Trends." In *Demographic Change in Sub-Saharan Africa,* edited by Karen A. Foote and others. Washington: National Academy Press.

Gallup, John Luke, and Jeffrey D. Sachs. 1998. "Geography and Economic Development." Unpublished paper. Harvard Institute for International Development.

Pitt, Mark. 1995. "Women's Schooling, the Selectivity of Fertility, and Child Mortality in Sub-Saharan Africa." Living Standards Measurement Study Working Paper 119. Washington: World Bank.

United Nations. Various years. *World Population Prospects 1950–2050.* New York.

World Bank. 1997. *African Development Indicators.* Washington.

Comment IV.C.1. The "Demographic Dividend"

The preceding selection notes the contrast, during the period 1965–90, between the almost equal growth of the working-age and total populations in sub-Saharan Africa and the 0.35 percent faster growth of the working-age than total population in the rest of the world. Faster growth of working-age than total population results mechanically in a higher growth of GDP per capita for any given growth in productivity (GDP per worker). It has been argued, however, that an increased ratio of the working-age to the nonworking ("dependent") population has more than just this mechanical impact on the growth of per capita GDP. It is claimed by David E. Bloom and Jeffrey G. Williamson, "Demographic Transitions and Economic Miracles in Emerging Asia," *World Bank Economic Review* 12 (1998), that a higher ratio of working to dependent population increases growth by both raising savings rates and increasing demand for investment in housing and infrastructure. This effect of the increased number of workers per dependent has become known as the "demographic dividend."

The demographic dividend is a consequence of the demographic transition, previously discussed in Note I.A.2. The demographic transition begins with a fall in mortality rates that most strongly affects infants and children, leading to accelerated population growth and a decrease in the number of workers per young dependent. The next stage in the demographic transition is a fall in birth rates, reducing population growth and leaving a generational "bulge" from past high birth rates that works its way through the age distribution, increasing the number of workers per dependent until it reaches retirement age. These effects of the demographic transition on the ratio of working-age to dependent population were especially dramatic during the period 1950–95 for East Asia (China, Japan, South Korea, Singapore, and Taiwan), as can be seen from Figure 2 in the preceding selection. Exhibit IV.C.1 shows that the exceptionally high working-age population per dependent in these countries has persisted beyond the 1990s. Bloom and Williamson attribute as much as one-third of East Asia's per capita GDP growth during the period 1965–90 to the demographic dividend.

IV.D. GENDER AND DEVELOPMENT

Selection IV.D.1. Gender Inequality at the Start of the 21st Century*

Education

Education is central to one's ability to respond to the opportunities that development presents, but significant disparities remain in several regions (Figure 1). Disparities persist both in enrollment rates, which capture education flows, and in average years of schooling, which represent the stock of education in the population.

Female primary and secondary enrollment rates and average years of female schooling have generally risen over time. In several regions primary enrollment rates have flattened out at high levels—as in East Asia and Pacific, Latin America and the Caribbean, and Europe and Central Asia, where gross enrollment rates for females have reached or surpassed 100 percent.[1] Girls' primary enrollment rates have also leveled off in Sub-Saharan Africa— but at much lower levels. In Sub-Saharan Africa girls experienced strong gains in primary enrollment rates between 1970 and 1980, but those rates have since flattened out at 54 percent. Absolute levels of female enrollment and schooling remain lower in Sub-Saharan Africa than in other developing regions. Female secondary enrollment rates were just 14 percent in 1995, and average schooling attainment was just 2.2 years in 1990.

How do these trends compare with those for boys? Gender equality in school enrollments and average years of schooling has improved since 1970, as girls' schooling has generally increased faster than boys'. But the gender disparity and the speed in closing gender gaps have varied. As with rights, East Asia, Latin America, and Europe and Central Asia have the highest gender equality in education. In Europe and Central Asia and Latin America average female secondary enrollment rates now exceed male rates, and women have on average about 90 percent as many years of schooling as men.

Starting from lower initial levels of gender equality, South Asia, Sub-Saharan Africa, and the Middle East and North Africa have all registered noteworthy declines in gender disparities in primary and secondary enrollments between 1970 and 1995. Nonetheless, South Asia continues to have the lowest gender equality in education. Women in South Asia have on average only about half as many years of education as men, and female enrollment rates at the secondary level are still only two-thirds of male rates. Moreover, South Asia has larger gender inequalities in education than other developing regions where absolute levels of female education are lower (Filmer, King, and Pritchett 1998).

In Sub-Saharan Africa gender equality in enrollment rates has increased—although at the primary level improvements between 1980 and 1990 tended to reflect absolute declines in boys' enrollment rates rather than improvements in girls'. Moreover, in contrast to South Asia and the Middle East and North Africa, Sub-Saharan Africa made no real progress in closing the gender gap in average years of schooling between 1970 and 1990.

So, while there has been a clear trend toward gender equality in education since 1970, the gains have been slow and uneven for the poorest regions. Closing gender gaps in education—and closing them more quickly—are thus still important development challenges to policymakers, especially in South Asia, Sub-Saharan Africa, and some countries in the Middle East and North Africa. The challenges are particularly important as the world moves into the information age and knowledge-intensive output displaces traditional modes of production. Basic education is the foundation for developing the flexible skills needed to participate in knowledge-intensive economic activity. Those who lack access to basic education are likely to be excluded from the new opportunities, and where long-standing gender gaps in education persist, women will be at increasing risk of falling behind men in their ability to participate in development....

Employment and Earnings

Historically, men have had higher rates of participation in the labor force than women—a pattern that continues. But female labor force participation varies considerably across developing regions, with women's share of the labor force ranging

*From World Bank, *Engendering Development* (New York: Oxford University Press, 2001), pp. 41–44, 53–59, 63–66, 151–154, and 158–162. Reprinted by permission.

[1]Gross enrollment rate, the total enrollment in a specific level of education, regardless of students' age, expressed as a percentage of the official school-age population corresponding to the same level of education in a given school year, can exceed 100 because the numerator, unlike the denominator, is not limited to youths of a given age. Early entry into school and grade repetition are among the reasons that the numerator may include youths outside the appropriate age range.

Figure 1. Despite improvements, gender disparities persist in schooling in some regions.

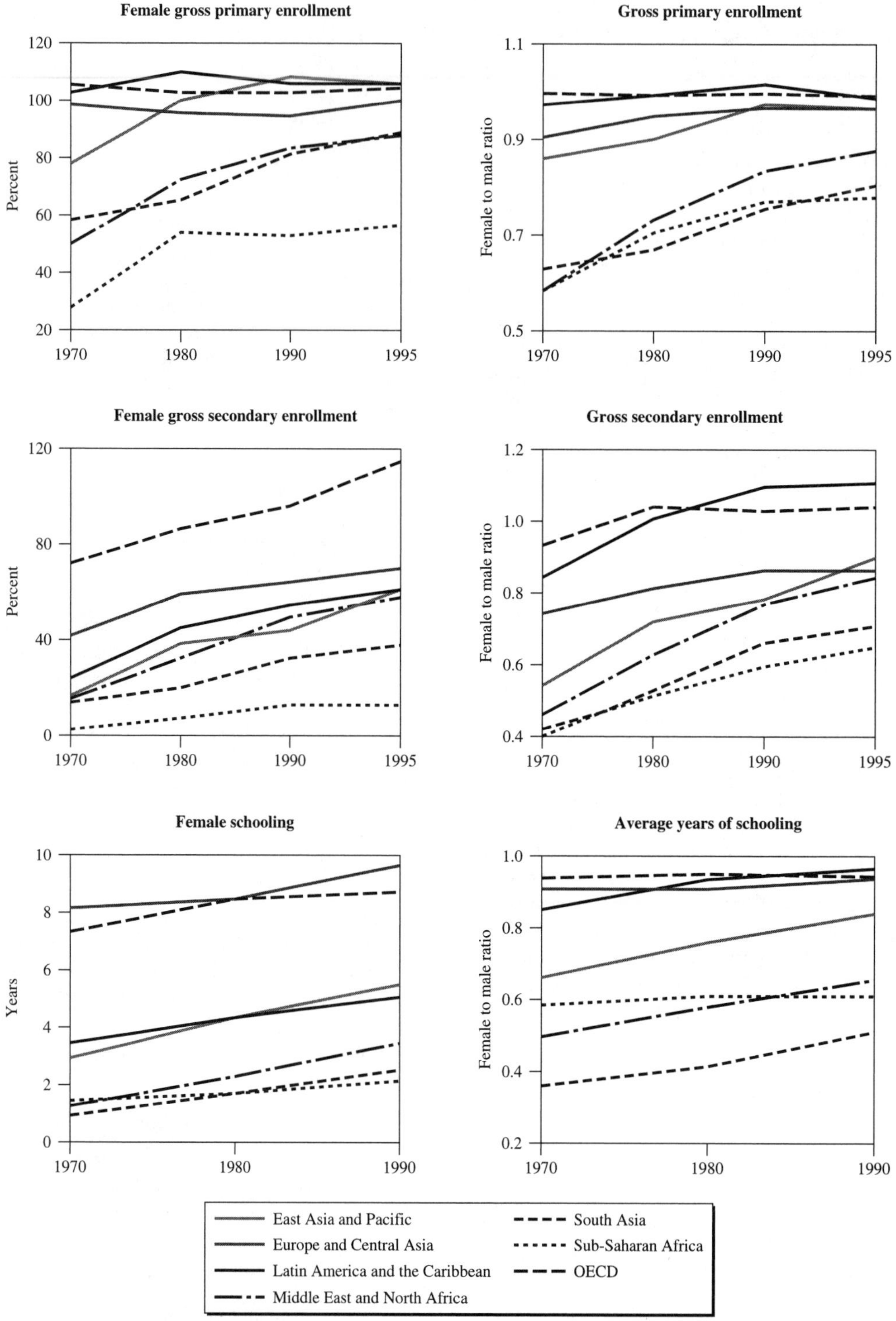

Sources: Years of schooling data from Barro and Lee (1994); population weights from World Bank (1999b).

Figure 2. Trends in female labor supply vary across regions.

Women as a share of total labor force

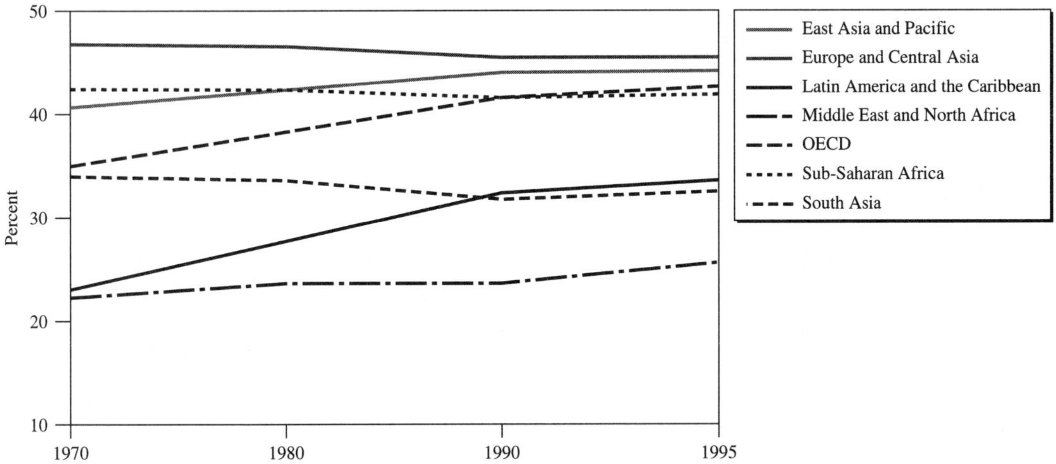

Source: World Bank (1999b).

from 25 percent in the Middle East and North Africa in 1995 to about 45 percent in Europe and Central Asia and in East Asia and Pacific (Figure 2). Regional trends also vary. Between 1970 and 1995 women's share of the labor force increased slightly in the Middle East and North Africa and in East Asia and Pacific, and considerably in Latin America and the Caribbean. In Sub-Saharan Africa women's relative participation rates were stable, but in South Asia and in Europe and Central Asia they declined slightly.[2]

In the labor force women and men commonly perform different tasks and work in different sectors. For example, women constitute the vast majority of production workers in the garment sector worldwide. There is persistent occupational segregation by gender in both developed and developing countries, with women underrepresented in better-paying formal sector jobs and overrepresented in the unpaid and informal sectors. Moreover, female employment is on average less secure than male employment, with women more often involved in subcontracting, temporary, or casual work, or work in the home.

One measure of occupational segregation by gender divides the proportion of all working women employed in a particular occupation by the proportion of all working men employed in that oc-

cupation. So, a ratio greater than one indicates that women are overrepresented, a ratio less than one that women are underrepresented. When this measure is applied to data from both developed and developing countries, several dimensions of occupational segregation emerge (Figure 3). For example, women are overrepresented in service occupations, professional and technical jobs, and clerical and sales jobs—in both developed and developing regions. And men are greatly overrepresented in production jobs as well as in higher-paying administrative and managerial positions.

There appears to have been some decline in employment and occupational segregation by gender over the past several decades. For example, a recent study by Tzannatos (1999) examines a measure of "employment dissimilarity" called the Duncan index and analyzes changes between the 1950s–60s and 1980s–90s. The study finds slight convergence in female and male employment profiles across industrial sectors, with faster convergence in wage employment than in self-employment or family work. There is also some evidence of convergence in occupational profiles between female and male wage employees, but little evidence of such convergence among self-employed or family workers. In developing countries, even with recent increases in the relative education and work experience of women in the labor force, occupational segregation remains a salient feature of labor markets.

Women also continue to earn less than men. Recent empirical studies from 71 countries indicate that on average in developed countries women earn

---

[2]Particularly in less developed countries, labor force statistics tend to understate female participation in economic activities. Some of the measured gender differences in labor force participation arise because much of women's work takes place in the home and is not captured in the labor force data.

Figure 3. Women and men hold different occupations.

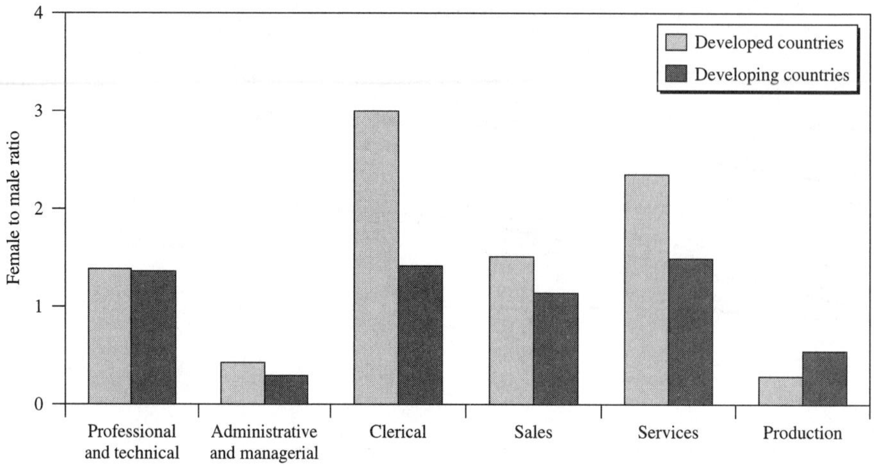

Source: Based on data from Anker (1998).

Table 1. Relative Earnings of Women and Men

	Female to male earnings ratio	Gender gap	Portion of gap unexplained (percent)
Developed countries (n = 19)	0.77	0.23	80.4
Developing countries (n = 42)	0.73	0.27	82.2

Note: The gender gap in earnings is the proportional difference between average female and male wages (1 minus the female to male earnings ratio). The unexplained portion of the gender gap in earnings is the portion not explained by an individual's characteristics, such as educational attainment and work experience, and by job characteristics.

Source: Various studies.

77 percent as much as men, and in developing countries, 73 percent as much (Table 1).[3] There averages, derived from the latest estimates available for these countries, mask wide variation across countries. Among developed countries, for example, the female to male earnings ratio ranges from 43 percent in Japan (1993–94) to 87 percent in Denmark (1995); among developing countries, it ranges from 43 percent in Nicaragua (1991) to 90 percent in Thailand (1989) and 101 percent in Chile (1996). While most studies do not measure the gender earnings ratio for exactly comparable groups of workers over time, evidence from several countries in Asia, Latin America, Sub-Saharan Africa, and the OECD suggests that female earnings tend to be rising relative to male earnings.

[3]The survey reviewed evidence from 19 developed countries and 42 developing and transition economies.

But comparing an unadjusted ratio of earnings for women and men can be misleading for three reasons. First, the average earnings (or Wage) data generally used to compute the ratio have not been adjusted for the characteristics of workers, such as education, work experience, and skills training. To the extent that women and men have different levels of education or experience, unadjusted ratios are not comparing earnings across similar types of workers. Second, data on earnings (or wages) reflect differences in occupations, and as previously shown, women and men tend to be concentrated in different types of occupations. And third, earnings figures often reflect differences in hours worked, since a larger proportion of men than women work full-time. If women work fewer hours per month for pay than men, a comparison of the monthly earnings of women and men would indicate lower relative earnings for women than would a comparison of hourly wages. The greater the gender differences in hours worked for pay, the lower the unadjusted gender earnings ratios will be relative to ratios that adjust for differences in hours worked.

Studies in developed and developing countries have analyzed the relative wages of women and men, controlling for such worker characteristics as education and experience. They usually decompose the gender gap in observed wages to separate the effect of discrimination from other factors. In the Republic of Korea women's wages are 51 percent of men's with half of the gap explained by differences in the characteristics of workers (Horton 1996). In Brazil women earn 70 percent of what men earn, but only 10 percent of this difference is due to differences in measured characteristics (Psacharopoulos and Tzannatos 1992). In Denmark, France, Germany, and the United Kingdom differences in measured human capital characteristics account for 20–30 percent of the earnings gap—and in Portugal and Spain, even less (Rice 1999). In general, workers' characteristics explain about a third or less of the gender earnings gap in developing countries. This suggests that although the way households allocate human capital investments between boys and girls has direct consequences for their children's prospects in the labor market, other important forces are at work.

Few studies of developing countries include measures of job attributes, usually because of lack of data. Those that do indicate that gender differences in job characteristics affect relative wages to some degree (controlling for worker characteristics)—but the impact appears to differ considerably across developed and developing countries. In developed countries adjusting the gender earnings gap for information on job characteristics significantly reduces the proportion of the gap that remains unexplained, confirming that men, on average, hold better-paying jobs (Rice 1999; Zabalza and Tzannatos 1985). Different patterns of employment explain up to a third of the gender wage gap in some countries (Tzannatos 1998). But occupational segregation appears to account for a relatively small share of the gender wage gap in developing countries. In Latin America employment differences between women and men appear to account for little, if any, of the earnings differences.

In sum, in developed and developing countries differences in observed worker and job characteristics explain only about 20 percent of the gender gap in earnings (See Table 1). The rest of the gap results from factors that are difficult to measure directly, such as differences in workers' abilities or differences in labor market treatment (discrimination).

Voice

Limited command over productive resources and weaker ability to generate incomes—whether in self-employed activities or in wage employment—constrain women's power to influence resource allocation and investment decisions within the home. Unequal rights and poor socioeconomic status relative to men also limit women's ability to participate in political processes as active agents and to influence decisions in their communities and at the national level. . . .

Women in the 20th century have gained the right to vote in nearly all countries. The gender gap in voting is declining, especially in countries where a high proportion of the population votes. Even so, substantial disparities still exist in more active forms of participation, such as demonstrations and boycotts. And women remain significantly less likely to discuss politics than men, especially among older cohorts and those with less education (Inglehart 1997).

Moreover, there still are large gender disparities in political participation and representation at all levels of government—from local councils to national assemblies and cabinets. Women continue to be vastly underrepresented in elected office (Figure 4). In all regions except East Asia and the Pacific and Europe and Central Asia, the average shares of parliamentary seats held by women remained at less than 10 percent between 1975 and 1995. In East Asia women's share has consistently been just less than 20 percent. The most dramatic change has occurred in Europe and Central Asia, where the high levels of female representation (relative to most of the rest of the would) fell dramatically in the late 1980s—from nearly 25 percent to 7 percent—following the start of the economic and political transition.[4] Substantial gender disparities also persist in local and regional assemblies.

Women also remain vastly underrepresented in the executive branch of government. In no developing region did women make up more than 8 percent of cabinet ministers in 1998 (UNDP 2000). In the Middle East and North Africa women held only 2 percent of cabinet positions, while in East Asia

---

[4]Time series data are lacking for most countries in Eastern Europe, so this pattern is based on data from only five countries: Albania, Bulgaria, Hungary, Poland, and Romania. The steep decline in female representation in parliament is attributed to the abolition of Eastern Europe's 25–33 percent quotas for women (UN 2000). This decline in female representation took place precisely at the time that national parliaments were beginning to play an active role in policymaking and governance in those countries.

Figure 4. Women are vastly underrepresented in parliaments.

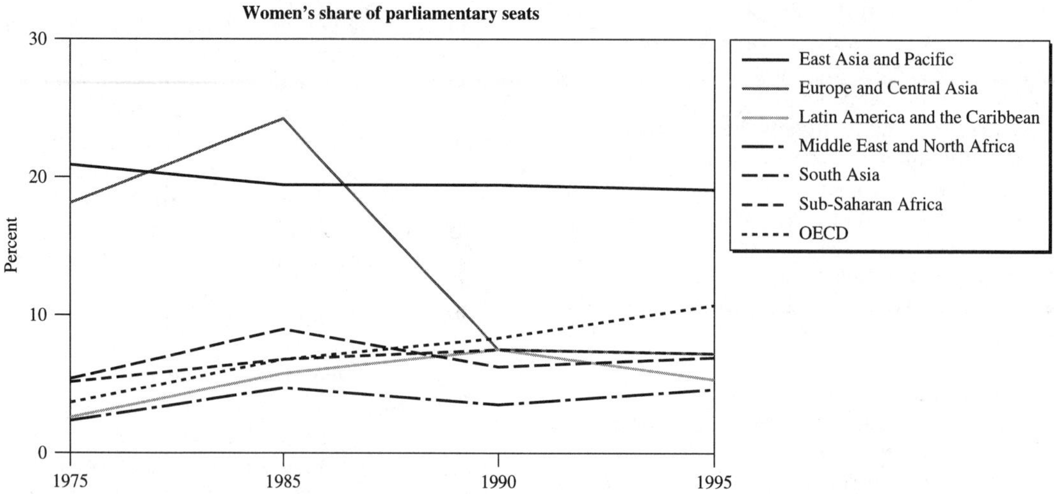

Women's share of parliamentary seats

Sources: Parliamentary data from WISTAT (1998); population weights from World Bank (1999a).

and Pacific they held 4 percent, and in South Asia and sub-Saharan Africa, roughly 6 percent. In Latin America and Eastern Europe and Central Asia women made up between 7 and 8 percent of cabinet ministers. Female representation in subministerial positions tends to be only slightly greater, and in South Asia, it is lower.[5]

Women who do hold cabinet appointments are more likely to be in ministries of women's or social affairs than ministries of finance, economics, or planning, which make mainstream policy and budgetary decisions. Of the 466 female ministers holding portfolios in 151 countries in early 2000, 95 (about 20 percent) were heads of ministries of women's and social affairs, but only 22 (just less than 5 percent) were heads of ministries of finance and of the economy and development (IPU 2000). . . .

Are Women Poorer Than Men?

Estimating the number of men and women living in poverty is difficult. Why? There is no adequate summary measure of individual welfare that can be compared for males and females. The most

commonly used indicator of poverty (or current welfare) is consumption. But most household-based surveys collect consumption data on households, not individuals. While this may partly reflect a traditional view of the household as the basic unit of economic decisionmaking . . . , it also reflects serious difficulties in measuring individual consumption. For example, many goods consumed by household members, such as housing and consumer durables, are consumed jointly. It is thus difficult, if not impossible, to assign some elements of household consumption to specific household members. This makes direct comparisons of consumption poverty between female and male members of the same household problematic.[6]

The lack of adequate data on individual consumption has led to a tendency to compare poverty

[5]In South Asia women held less than 1 percent of subministerial positions (UNDP 2000). Compare this with about 4 percent in the Middle East and North Africa, 6 percent in East Asia and the Pacific, approximately 8 percent in Sub-Saharan Africa and Eastern Europe and Central Asia, and 13 percent in Latin America and the Caribbean.

[6]Consumption data tend to be preferred to income data for measuring poverty, particularly in developing countries. For example, because income can vary from year to year (because of a variety of production shocks), while consumption is more stable, consumption is generally considered a better measure of long-term welfare. Moreover, income tends to be subject to more measurement error than consumption. For assessing the welfare of individuals within households, income and consumption data share some limitations. Particularly in rural areas of developing countries, many elements of household income are jointly produced, such as income from family-run farms or nonfarm enterprises. Therefore, like consumption, income is often difficult to assign to specific individuals within a household. And as with consumption, often little is known about how income is shared among different members of a single household.

between female-headed and male-headed households. The interest in such poverty comparisons has arisen from both substantive and statistical concerns. One substantive concern is that the proportion of female-headed households has been rising in several countries (Baden and Milward 1995; Bruce, Lloyd, and Leonard 1995). Another is that these households may be more vulnerable economically, both because they tend to have poorer access to productive inputs and because they have fewer working-age males who earn income, other factors being equal (Haddad and others 1996). . . .

It is difficult to draw hard conclusions about the gender dimension of poverty from standard headship analysis. Male- and female-headed households can be extremely heterogeneous in any society, ranging from young, single, well-educated men and women to two-parent nuclear or extended families to single-parent households and widows. Although households headed by widows or divorced women may be disproportionately represented among the poor, other female-headed households may be better off. For example, single-person households of young, unmarried women working in urban labor markets, or households to which an absent husband regularly sends remittances, may experience relatively low levels of poverty. Moreover, even sophisticated headship studies provide only limited information about poverty among females and males, since they tell little or nothing about the relative welfare of females in male-headed households or males in female-headed households.

A much smaller number of studies have analyzed data on individuals' food intake or nutrition to assess the relative welfare of females and males. This approach avoids the problem of assigning to individuals the house-hold goods that are jointly consumed. These studies have found gender disparities in nutrition in South Asia but little systematic evidence of gender differences in other regions (Appleton and Collier 1995; Alderman 2000). Even in South Asia the evidence is not uniform—in part because the extent of disparities can vary according to the season and because gender biases often manifest themselves in subtle ways. In Southern India there is gender discrimination in calorie intake only in the lean season, not in the surplus (Behrman 1988). And in Bangladesh apparent pro-male biases in calorie intake disappear after gender differences in caloric need or in energy exerted at work are taken into account (Chen, Huq, and D'Souza 1981; Pitt, Rosenzweig, and Hasssan 1990). Evidence from Bangladesh also indicates that the most severe gender in-equalities often are not in calories consumed, but in the distribution of preferred foods rich in micronutrients (Bouis 1998).

In sum, even while there is extensive evidence on persistent gender inequalities in rights, resources, and voice that affect the relative abilities of women and men to participate in and benefit from development, the evidence on how such disparities translate into poverty (measured by consumption) is still very limited. This argues for efforts to collect new types of data and to develop empirical methods better suited to capturing the gender dimensions of poverty (as traditionally defined). At the same time, the combined evidence makes clear the importance of focusing on a variety of dimensions of female and male well-being to understand the full implications of gender disparity (Box 1). . . .

Households Reproduce Gender Roles

No matter where they are or how they are organized, households regularly transmit gender roles to the next generations. Households are the first place of gender socialization, passing along knowledge, skills, and social expectations. Children acquire a gender identity that shapes the set of socially acceptable activities for women and men and the relations between them. Children are socialized through explicit instruction, through punishment for inappropriate behavior, and by observing and imitating their parents and other female and male role models in the family (Whiting and Edwards 1988).

Allocating resources is another way households shape gender roles. In extreme cases differences in the allocation of food, health care, and attention to young boys and girls mean greater female malnutrition, limiting girls' ability to learn and women's capacity to participate productively in society. But even in less extreme cases family decisions about investing in boys' or girls' education—or about involving sons in farming but daughters in household maintenance and care activities—all help reproduce and reinforce socially accepted gender roles.

The difference in girls' and boys' gender roles become more pronounced as children get older. In most of the world differences in household expenditure on girls' and boys' education tend to increase when children move from primary to secondary school. When girls reach adolescence they are generally expected to spend more time on such household activities as cooking, cleaning, collecting fuel and water, and caring for children. Meanwhile, boys tend to spend more time on farm or

Box 1 Are Women "Time Poor" Relative to Men?

Worldwide, women perform the bulk of child care and household maintenance. Women in most settings combine household work with market or nonmarket work to generate income or raise household consumption—work often not captured in traditional labor force statistics. And women tend to work significantly more hours than men when both market and household work are taken into account (Bevan, Collier, and Gunning 1989; Juster and Stafford 1991; Brown and Haddad 1995; UNDP 1995; Ilahi 2000).

The gender differences in time spent working vary across developing countries. But women commonly work an hour or more a day than men. In rural Kenya women work nearly three hours more a day than men. While few studies compare time use by gender across households at different income levels, evidence suggests that gender disparities in time use tend to be greater among the poor than the rich (Ilahi 2000).

This raises questions about how women's primary responsibility for household work, along with more total hours of work, affects their welfare relative to that of men. To the extent that the gender division of labor in the family means that women undertake household work at the expense of income-generating activities, this limits their bargaining power and decisionmaking capacity in the home. And that has implications for their well-being. Moreover, gender disparities in hours worked imply that even if there are no gender biases in consumption in a household, women will work more hours than men to achieve the same consumption (Lipton and Ravallion 1995).

wage work. When young children get sick, teenage girls, not boys, tend to increase their time providing care—often at the expense of their schooling (Pitt and Rosenzweig 1990; Ilahi 1999a). Meanwhile, boys are increasingly engaged in market work, preparing to become the main bread-winner of their own household.

This division of tasks by gender means that by the time girls and boys become adults and form new households, women generally work longer hours than men, have less experience in the labor force, and earn less income. In almost all countries—both developed and developing—there is a strikingly consistent gender division of labor, in which men work more in the market and women more in the home (Figure 5; UNDP 1995). Moreover, women often undertake multiple activities at once—such as taking care of children while working in the household or in home- or farm-based income-generating activities (Floro 1995).

Even when women work in the labor market they continue to do most of the unpaid work at home. For example, women in the former Soviet Union had a relatively high level of equality with men in labor force participation and occupational attainment, but they still tended to be responsible for most in-home child care (Lapidus 1993).

This division of time and tasks has important implications. For instance, if parents consider it unlikely that their daughters will join the labor force and earn income as adults, they may see less justification for sending their daughters to school. This is true whether or not women become part of their husband's family after marriage (a custom that reduces parents' incentives to invest in girls' schooling relative to boys'). In addition, lower education and labor force participation generally mean lower incomes for women—and thus limited power to influence resource allocation and investments in the home.

Since much of women's work in developing countries is unpaid and done inside the home, it is often "invisible" and not accounted for by policymakers.[7] But failing to recognize gender divisions of time and task allocations within households can result in policies that don't achieve their objectives or that produce unintended outcomes. For example, policies that increase demand for female labor may not elicit the expected supply response if

[7]By virtue of being outside the monetized economy, women's economic contribution tends to be undervalued (Elson 1992; Folbre 1998). For example, a much smaller proportion of female work than male work is captured in national income accounting systems. And the asymmetries, by gender, appear to be considerable. In industrial countries about two-thirds of men's total work time is spent in activities that are captured and valued in national accounts; this compares to about a third of women's total work time (UNDP 1995). In developing countries the gap is larger. More than three-quarters of men's total work time is spent in activities captured in national accounts, compared to about a third of women's total work time.

Figure 5. Men work more in the market, women more in the home.

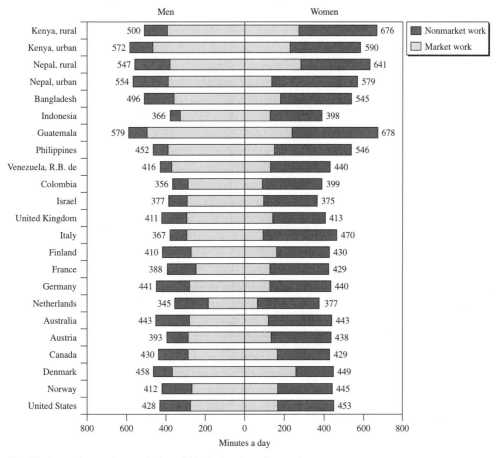

Note: The time use data pertain to productive activities, both market and nonmarket.
Source: UNDP (1995).

women cannot reduce their time on household maintenance or care activities. Or girls may be taken out of school to cover for mothers who enter the labor force (Grootaert and Patrinos 1999; Ilahi 1999b; Lokshin, Glinskaya, and Garcia 2000). Understanding how households allocate time and other resources by gender can thus provide the basis for more effective policies—and policies that generate fewer unintended and undesirable consequences. . . .

Resource Control and Bargaining Power Affect Household Allocations

Household Consumption Patterns

Studies from a diverse set of countries, including Bangladesh, Brazil, Canada, Côte d'Ivoire, Ethiopia, France, Indonesia, South Africa, Taiwan (China), and the United Kingdom, indicate that women's and men's relative control of resources has significant—and different—impacts on household consumption and expenditure. While the precise effects of female and male resource control differ from place to place, some consistent patterns emerge across countries. The most obvious: increases in the relative resources controlled by women generally translate into a larger share of household resources going to family welfare, and especially to expenditures on children—even after controlling for per capita income and demographic characteristics of the household. Greater resource control by women also leads to expenditure patterns and outcomes that strengthen women's well-being and status in the household.

How do women's contributions to household income affect household expenditure patterns? In Côte d'Ivoire increasing women's share of cash income in the household significantly increases the share of the household budget allocated to food, controlling for average per capita expenditure (income), household size, and demographic characteristics (Hoddinott and Haddad 1995). It also decreases the shares devoted to alcohol and cigarettes. In Brazil it is the same story. At the margin additional income in the hands of women results in a greater share of the household budget devoted to education, health, and nutrition-related expenditures (Thomas 1997).

Because the same factors that affect income control may affect household expenditure choices . . . , the Brazil and Côte d'Ivoire studies attempt to control econometrically for the possible "endogeneity" of current labor income using two-stage least squares. Moreover, the Brazil study analyzes both labor and nonlabor income. While not completely immune to concerns about endogeneity, nonlabor income may be less influenced by such factors as past or current labor supply choices that affect the outcomes of interest. In Brazil the finding that female and male income control have different effects on household expenditure patterns is robust to the choice of the income measure.

Another study analyzes the impact of assets brought to marriage by women and men and of relative education levels on resource allocation and investment in households in Bangladesh, Ethiopia, Indonesia, and South Africa (Quisumbing and Maluccio 1999). Comparable methodologies are used across countries. The data were collected specifically to analyze intrahousehold allocations and investments and to address concerns about the endogeneity of labor and nonlabor income. In particular, the assets and education men and women bring to marriage are exogenous to decisions made within the marriage.[8]

As in Brazil and Côte d'Ivoire the unitary household model is rejected in all four country cases. While the precise impact of female and male asset control and education differs across countries, the general patterns are consistent with those in the earlier studies. Additional resources and bargaining power in the hands of women have a greater impact on expenditure allocations toward the next generation—such as on education, health,

and nutrition—than additional resources in the hands of men.

A policy change in the United Kingdom that transferred income from fathers to mothers led to similar patterns. In the late 1970s the national Family Allowance program transferred control of a substantial child allowance benefit from fathers to mothers. This shift was followed by significant changes in household expenditure patterns that benefited women and children. Relative spending on women's and children's goods (such as clothing) rose, while relative spending on men's goods (clothing and tobacco) fell (Lundberg, Pollak, and Wales 1997; Ward-Batts 1997).

From Children's Well-being to Women's Empowerment

Female and male control of income, assets, and education affect more than household consumption patterns. In Brazil additional labor and nonlabor income in the hands of women tends to have a greater positive impact on child survival and nutrition than additional income in the hands of men (Thomas 1990, 1997). Regardless of who controls it, an increase in total household income is associated with improvements in child survival and nutrition (as measured by child height for weight and height for age). But at the margin, improvements are substantially larger if the mother controls the income.

Additional evidence on the gender-differentiated impacts of resource control on household outcomes comes from recent microfinance initiatives in Bangladesh.[9] Two related studies examine the impact of female and male borrowing—from Grameen Bank, the Bangladesh Rural Advancement Committee (BRAC), and government program RD-12—on such outcomes as per capita household expenditure (income) and girls' and boys' schooling and nutritional status (Khandker 1998; Pitt and Khandker 1998). The impacts often differ substantially based on whether the borrower is a woman or a man—and often the marginal impacts of borrowing are greater for women than for men.

---

[8]This is the case even if assets and education are endogenous due to marriage market selection. For further discussion on assets brought to marriage in the context of analyzing household bargaining behavior see Quisumbing and Maluccio (1999).

[9]Quantifying the impact of such programs as microfinance is often problematic. Researchers are rarely able to collect "experimental" data, which would allow them to make inferences that are not confounded by the effects of nonrandom program placement and self-selection of participants into the program. Nonetheless, several recent studies of microfinance programs in Bangladesh use data based on a "quasi-experimental" survey design that enable their authors to correct for these problems (Khandker 1998; Pitt and Khandker 1998; Menon 1999).

For all three microfinance programs the impact of female borrowing on per capita household expenditure (income) is about twice as large as the impact of male borrowing (Table 2). A 10 percent increase in female borrowing is associated with a roughly 40 percent increase in per capita expenditure—an effect that is strongly significant statistically. Compare this with a roughly 20 percent increase in per capita expenditure associated with the same percentage increase in male borrowing. Female borrowing also has a greater impact than male borrowing on households' ability to "smooth" consumption over time (Khandker 1998; Menon 1999).

As with other forms of resource control, female borrowing also appears to have a greater impact on child welfare than male borrowing does. For example, except for BRAC, female borrowing has a greater positive impact on children's school enrollments than male borrowing does. Moreover, in contrast to male borrowing, female borrowing has a large and statistically significant impact on children's nutritional well-being.

At the same time, male borrowing has a greater impact on household net worth than female borrowing. This suggests that while at the margin women seem to invest relatively more than men in the human capital of their children, men appear to invest more than women in physical capital.

Female and male borrowing also have different impacts on household reproductive behavior, suggesting that women and men do not share the same preferences relating to contraception or fertility. For example, female borrowing decreases contraceptive use and, except for Grameen Bank borrowing, increases fertility, whereas male borrowing increases contraceptive use and, except for BRAC borrowing, decreases fertility. At first glance the findings on the impact of female borrowing on contraceptive use and fertility may seem counterintuitive, since a body of empirical literature suggests that factors increasing the opportunity cost of women's time—such as increased education, wages, or labor market opportunities—tend to reduce fertility. But low-income women in Bangladesh may see additional children as assets capable of assisting them with what are often home-based, self-employment activities.

Increasing women's independent access to credit also empowers them in other dimensions. For example, female borrowing increases female control of nonland assets (Pitt and Khandker 1998; Khandker 1998). Women who participate in the credit programs report an increased role in household decisionmaking (Kabeer 1998) and greater acceptance by their husband of their participation in market-based economic activities (Agarwal 1997). A study of BRAC's microfinance program finds that female borrowing enhances women's ability to sell assets without asking their husband's permission (Zaman 1999). Specifically, women who have borrowed more than 10,000 taka are 46 percent more likely to be able to sell poultry without their husband's permission than members who have not borrowed. These borrowers are also twice as likely to be able to sell jewelry and 35 percent more likely to have control of their savings. And women who participate in credit programs have

Table 2. Impacts of Female and Male Borrowing on Selected Household Outcomes (percentage change for a 10 percent increase in borrowing)

Household outcome	German Bank		BRAC		RD-12	
	Male borrowing	Female borrowing	Male borrowing	Female borrowing	Male borrowing	Female borrowing
Per capita spending	0.18	**0.43**	0.19	**0.39**	**0.23**	**0.40**
Net worth	**0.15**	**0.14**	**0.20**	**0.09**	**0.22**	0.02
Boys' school enrollment	**0.07**	**0.61**	−0.08	−0.03	0.29	**0.79**
Girls' school enrollment	0.30	**0.47**	0.24	0.12	0.07	0.23
Boys' height for age[a]	−2.98	**14.19**	−2.98	**14.19**	−2.98	**14.19**
Girls' height for age[a]	−4.92	**11.63**	−4.92	**11.63**	−4.92	**11.63**
Contraceptive use	**4.25**	**−0.91**	0.40	**−0.74**	0.84	**−1.16**
Recent fertility	**−0.74**	−0.35	0.54	**0.79**	**−0.74**	0.50

Note: Figures in bold are based on coefficient estimates that are statistically significant at the 10 percent level or better.
[a]Percentage changes reported for boys' and girls' height for age represent average impacts across all three microfinance programs.
Source: Khandker (1998).

significantly higher demand for formal health care than women who do not (Nanda 1999).[10]

[10]There is a concern raised in the literature on microfinance in Bangladesh that female borrowing has led to increased violence against women in the home (Goetz and Sen Gupta 1996). Violence can erupt when men try to take control of their wife's credit resources or refuse to contribute to loan payments after they have used their wife's loans. Evidence on whether domestic violence has increased is mixed, however, with several studies suggesting that female membership in credit programs tends to be associated with less violence (Hashemi, Schuler, and Riley 1996; Schuler and others 1996; Kabeer 1998).

References

Agarwal, Bina. 1997. "'Bargaining' and Gender Relations: Within and Beyond the Household." Food Consumption and Nutrition Division Discussion Paper 27. International Food Policy Research Institute, Washington, D.C. Available online at *http://www.ifpri.cgiar.org/index1.htm*

Alderman, Harold. 2000. "Anthropometry." In Margaret Grosh and Paul Glewwe, eds., *Designing Household Survey Questionnaires for Developing Countries: Lessons from Fifteen Years of the Living Standards Measurement Study.* Oxford and New York: Oxford University Press.

Anker, Richard. 1998. *Gender and Jobs: Sex Segregation of Occupations in the World.* Geneva: International Labour Office.

Appleton, Simon, and Paul Collier. 1995. "On Gender Targeting of Public Transfers." In Dominique van de Walle and Kimberly Nead, eds., *Public Spending and the Poor: Theory and Evidence.* Baltimore, Md.: The Johns Hopkins University Press.

Baden, Sally, and Kirsty Milward. 1995. "Gender and Poverty." BRIDGE (Briefings on Development and Gender) Report 30. Institute of Development Studies, Brighton, U.K.

Barro, Robert J., and Jong-Wha Lee. 1994. "Sources of Economic Growth." *Carnegie-Rochester Conference on Public Policy* 40: 1–46.

Behrman, Jere R. 1988. "Intrahousehold Allocation of Nutrients in Rural India: Are Boys Favored? Do Parents Exhibit Inequality Aversion?" *Oxford Economic Papers* 40 (1): 32–54.

Bevan, David, Paul Collier, and Jan W. Gunning. 1989. *Peasants and Governments.* Oxford: Clarendon Press.

Bouis, Howarth. 1998. "Commercial Vegetable and Polyculture Fish Production in Bangladesh: Their Impacts on Income, Household Resource Allocation, and Nutrition." International Food Policy Research Institute, Washington, D.C.

Brown, Lynn R., and Lawrence Haddad. 1995. "Time Allocation Patterns and Time Burdens: A Gendered Analysis of Seven Countries." International Food Policy Research Institute, Washington, D.C.

Bruce, Judith, Cynthia B. Lloyd, and Ann Leonard. 1995. "Families in Focus: New Perspectives on Mothers, Fathers, and Children." Population Council, New York.

Chen, Lincoln C., Emdadul Huq, and Stan D'Souza. 1981. "Sex Bias in the Family Allocation of Food and Health Care in Rural Bangladesh." *Population and Development Review* 7 (1): 55–70.

Elson, Diane. 1992. "Male Bias in Structural Adjustment." In H. Afshar and C. Dennis, eds., *Women and Adjustment Policies in the Third World.* New York: St. Martin's Press.

Filmer, Deon, Elizabeth M. King, and Lant Pritchett. 1998. "Gender Disparity in South Asia: Comparisons between and within Countries." Policy Research Working Paper 1867. World Bank, Development Research Group, Washington, D.C. Available online at *http://wbln0018.worldbank.org/research/workpapers.nsf/policyresearch?openform*

Floro, Maria Sagrario. 1995. "Women's Well-Being, Poverty, and Work Intensity." *Feminist Economics* 1 (3): 1–25.

Folbre, Nancy. 1998. "The Neglect of Care-Giving." *Challenge* 41 (5): 45–58.

Goetz, Anne Marie, and Rina Sen Gupta. 1996. "Who Takes the Credit? Gender, Power and Control over Loan Use in Rural Credit Programs in Bangladesh." *World Development* 24 (1): 45–63.

Grootaert, Christian, and Harry Patrinos. 1999. *Policy Analysis of Child Labor: A Comparative Study.* New York: St. Martin's Press.

Haddad, Lawrence, Christine Pena, Chizuru Nishida, Agnes Quisumbing, and Alison Slack. 1996. "Food Security and Nutrition Implications of Intrahousehold Bias: A Review of Literature." Food Consumption and Nutrition Division Discussion Paper 19. International Food Policy Research Institute, Washington, D.C. Available online at *http://www.ifpri.cgiar.org/index1.htm*

Hashemi, Syed M., Sidney R. Schuler, and Ann P. Riley. 1996. "Rural Credit Programs and Women's Empowerment in Bangladesh." *World Development* 24 (4): 635–53.

Hoddinott, John, and Lawrence Haddad. 1995. "Does Female Income Share Influence Household Expenditures? Evidence from Côte d'Ivoire." *Oxford Bulletin of Economics and Statistics* 57 (1): 77–96.

Horton, Susan. 1996. *Women and Industrialization in Asia.* London and New York: Routledge.

Ilahi, Nadeem. 1999a. "Children's Work and Schooling: Does Gender Matter? Evidence from the Peru LSMS Panel Data." World Bank, Latin American and Caribbean Region, Poverty Reduction and Economic Management Unit, Washington, D.C.

———. 1999b. "Gender and the Allocation of Adult Time: Evidence from the Peru LSMS Panel Data." Background paper for *Engendering Development.* World Bank, Washington, D.C.

————. 2000. "Gender and the Allocation of Time and Tasks: What Have We Learnt from the Empirical Literature?" Background paper for *Engendering Development.* World Bank, Washington, D.C. Available online at *http://www.worldbank.org/gender/prr/wp13.pdf.*

Inglehart, Ronald. 1997. "Changing Gender Gaps." Paper presented at conference on *Representation and European Citizenship,* Rome, November. Institute for Social Research, University of Michigan.

IPU (Inter-Parliamentary Union). 2000. *Politics: Women's Insight.* Geneva.

Juster, F. Thomas, and Frank P. Stafford. 1991. "The Allocation of Time: Empirical Findings, Behavioral Models, and Problems of Measurement." *Journal of Economic Literature* 29 (June): 471–522.

Kabeer, Naila. 1998. "'Money Can't Buy Me Love'? Reevaluating Gender, Credit and Empowerment in Rural Bangladesh." IDS Discussion Paper 363. University of Sussex, Institute of Development Studies, Brighton.

Khandker, Shahidur R. 1998. *Fighting Poverty with Microcredit: Experience in Bangladesh.* Washington, D.C.: World Bank.

Lapidus, Gail W. 1993. "Gender and Restructuring: The Impact of Perestroika and Its Aftermath on Soviet Women." In Valentine M. Moghadam, ed., *Democratic Reform and the Position of Women in Transitional Economies.* Oxford: Clarendon Press.

Lipton, Michael, and Martin Ravallion. 1995. "Poverty and Policy." In Jere Behrman and T.N. Srinivasan, eds., *Handbook of Development Economics* Vol. 3. Amsterdam, New York, and Oxford: Elsevier Science Publishers.

Lokshin, Michael M., Elena Glinskaya, and Marito Garcia. 2000. "Effect of Early Childhood Development Programs on Women's Labor Force Participation and Older Children's Schooling in Kenya." Background paper for *Engendering Development.* World Bank, Washington, D.C. Available online at *http://www.worldbank.org/gender/prr/wp15.pdf*

Lundberg, Shelley, Robert A. Pollak, and Terence J. Wales. 1997. "Do Husbands and Wives Pool Their Resources? Evidence from the United Kingdom Child Benefit." *Journal of Human Resources* 32 (3): 463–80.

Menon, Nidhiya. 1999. "Micro Credit, Consumption Smoothing and Impact on Repayment Behavior: An Euler Equation Approach." Brown University, Department of Economics, Providence, R.I.

Nanda, Priya. 1999. "Women's Participation in Rural Credit Programmes in Bangladesh and Their Demand for Formal Health Care: Is There a Positive Impact?" *Health Economics and Econometrics* 8: 415–28.

Pitt, Mark M., and Shahidur R. Khandker. 1998. "The Impact of Group-based Credit Programs on Poor Households in Bangladesh: Does the Gender of Participants Matter?" *Journal of Political Economy* 106: 958–96.

Pitt, Mark M., and Mark R. Rosenzweig. 1990. "Estimating the Intrahousehold Incidence of Illness: Child Health and Gender-Inequality in the Allocation of Time." *International Economic Review* 31 (4): 969–80.

Pitt, Mark M., Mark R. Rosenzweig, and M. Nazmul Hassan. 1990. "Productivity, Health, and Inequality in the Intrahousehold Distribution of Food in Low-Income Countries." *American Economic Review* 80 (5): 1139–56.

Psacharopoulos, George, and Zafiris Tzannatos. 1992. *Women's Employment and Pay in Latin America: Overview and Methodology.* Washigton, D.C.: World Bank.

Quisumbing, Agnes R., and John Maluccio. 1999. "Intrahousehold Allocation and Gender Relations: New Empirical Evidence." Background paper for *Engendering Development.* World Bank, Washington, D.C. Available online at *http://www.worldbank.org/gender/prr/qm.pdf*

Rice, Patricia. 1999. "Gender Earnings Differentials: The European Experience." Background paper for *Engendering Development.* World Bank, Washington, D.C. Available online at *http://www.worldbank.org/gender/prr/rice.pdf*

Schuler, Sidney R., Syed M. Hashemi, Ann P. Riley, and Shireen Akhter. 1996. "Credit Programs, Patriarchy and Men's Violence against Woman in Rural Bangladesh." *Social Science and Medicine* 43 (12): 1729–42.

Thomas, Duncan. 1990. "Intrahousehold Resource Allocation: An Inferential Approach." *Journal of Human Resources* 25: 635–64.

————. 1994. "Like Father, Like Son; Like Mother, Like Daughter: Parental Resources and Child Height." *Journal of Human Resources* 29 (4): 950–88.

————. 1997. "Incomes, Expenditures, and Health Outcomes: Evidence on Intrahousehold Resource Allocation." In Lawrence Haddad, John Hoddinott, and Harold Alderman, eds., *Intrahousehold Resource Allocation in Developing Countries: Models, Methods, and Policy.* Baltimore, Md.: The Johns Hopkins University Press.

Tzannatos, Zafiris. 1999. "Women and Labor Market Changes in the Global Economy: Growth Helps: Inequalities Hurt and Public Policy Matters." *World Development* 27(3): 551–69.

UN (United Nations). 2000. *Review and Appraisal of the Implementation of the Beijing Platform for Action.* Report of the Secretary General. Advance Unedited Version. E/CN.6/2000/PC/2.

UNDP (United Nations Development Programme). 1995. *Human Development Report 1995.* New York: Oxford University Press.

————. 2000. *Human Development Report 2000.* New York: Oxford University Press.

Ward-Batts, Jennifer. 1997. "Modeling Family Expenditures to Test Income Pooling." University of Washington, Department of Economics, Seattle.

Whiting, B.B., and C.P. Edwards. 1988. *Children of Different Worlds: The Formation of Social Behavior.* Cambridge, Mass.: Harvard University Press.

WISTAT (Women's Indicators and Statistics Database). 1998. Version 3. Prepared by the United Nations Statistical Division. New York.

World Bank. 1999a. "Vietnam Development Report 2000: Attacking Poverty." Country Economic Memorandum, Poverty Reduction and Economic Management Unit, East Asia and Pacific Region, World Bank, Washington, D.C.

———. 1999b. *World Development Indicators 1999.* Washington, D.C.

Zabalza, Antoni, and Zafiris Tzannatos. 1985. *Women and Equal Pay: The Effects of Legislation on Female Employment and Wages in Britain.* Cambridge: Cambridge University Press.

Zaman, Hassan. 1999. "Assessing the Impact of Micro-Credit on Poverty and Vulnerability in Bangladesh." Policy Research Working Paper 2145. World Bank, Development Research Group, Washington, D.C. Available online at *http://wbln0018.worldbank.org/ research/workpapers.nsf/policyresearch?openform*

Selection IV.D.2. Missing Women*

I. Concept and Measurement Issues

There are principally two ways to examine the impact of gender bias in mortality. One is to compare actual age and sex-specific mortality rates with "expected" rates that we would obtain, given equal treatment of both sexes. If actual female mortality rates exceed expected rates, one may speak of "excess female mortality." Most microanalysis of gender bias in mortality have used these data to determine the extent of gender bias (e.g., D'Souza and Chen 1980; Jane Humphries 1991; Mamta Murthi, Anne-Catherine Guio, and Jean Drèze 1995; Stephan Klasen 1998).[1] The advantage of this approach is that it allows a more careful investigation of the age structure of gender bias in mortality, and thus helps to determine its proximate causes.

There are, however, two shortcomings of this approach. First, the data needed for such a detailed investigation are either not available or not reliable in many developing countries where gender bias in mortality is a serious issue. In particular, while there may be reliable data from small samples or surveys, reliable national age- and sex-specific mortality rates are not available for most countries, as these require a complete and reliable vital registration system. Second, such an analysis only yields a flow measure of gender bias in mortality, that is, how many females die in excess per year. It may, however, be of interest to have a stock measure that examines the total impact of past and present gender bias on the generations currently alive.

The second method, which was developed by Sen, is to compare the actual population sex ratio (the number of males divided by the number of females in the most recent census)[2] with an "expected" population sex ratio that we would obtain given equal treatment of the sexes in the distribution of survival-related goods. If the actual ratio exceeds the expected, the additional females that would have to be alive in order to equate the actual

with the expected sex ratios, would then be the number of "missing women" at that point in time.[3]

This measure does not share the shortcomings of an analysis based on mortality rates. It is based only on the population sex ratio which is likely to be the most reliable demographic figure in developing countries, as it "only" requires an accurate census count but no accurate monitoring of vital statistics.[4] Also, as a stock measure it allows an estimate of the cumulative impact of gender bias in mortality. Finally, as a measure that compares actual with expected sex ratios, it would include female victims of sex-selective abortions among the "missing women," which would not be included in an assessment of sex-specific mortality rates.

Clearly, however, this is a very aggregative statistic that does not allow a precise analysis of the mechanisms of gender bias in mortality. It can also be subject to biases, including sex-selective under-enumeration and sex-biased international migration (see Section III). Thus both methods complement each other and both are needed to arrive at a complete analysis of the magnitude of the phenomenon, as well as the details of its occurrence. As the focus of this paper is on "missing women," we will largely concentrate on the sex ratio statistic and will only draw on mortality data as supporting evidence where appropriate.

The critical question in the calculation of the number of "missing women" is the expected sex ratio in the absence of discrimination. Since no society in the world, past or present, has been entirely gender-neutral in the allocation of resources, opportunities, and behavioral patterns, it is quite difficult to speculate on what the sex ratio would be in the absence of gender discrimination. For example, the high female excess in European countries is not a sign of discrimination against males in the allocation of resources, but is, in part, related to male behavioral patterns, mainly smoking, drinking, dangerous driving, and a higher inci-

---

*From Stephan Klasen and Claudia Wink, "'Missing Women': Revisiting the Debate," *Feminist Economics* 9, nos. 2–3 (2003): 265–272, 274–278, 280–281. Reprinted by permission.

[1]There are difficult methodological issues to resolve, in particular regarding the "expected" mortality rates of women relative to men in the hypothetical case of "equal treatment." See Stephan Klasen (1998, 1999) for a discussion.

[2]In contrast to Coale and Klasen, Sen, in line with practice in India, always used the female–male ratio, the inverse of the sex ratio. To avoid confusion, we consistently use the sex ratio, i.e., the number of males divided by females, and have modified Sen's data accordingly.

[3]By holding the number of men constant in that hypothetical calculation, the implicit assumption (as also in the other method) is that the number of women could be increased without correspondingly reducing the number of males. Since the distribution of survival-related goods is, at least in part, a zero-sum game, it is not clear whether one could increase the number of females without at least somewhat reducing the number of males.

[4]As we show below, even censuses contain biases and (often sex-specific) under-registration. Apart from being the only national statistic available, they also tend to be more reliable, since vital registration data often have selective under-registration of births and/or deaths.

dence of violence against oneself and others, that reduce their life expectancy considerably vis-à-vis females (Ingrid Waldron 1993). Moreover, as will be clear below, the expected sex ratio in a society depends on the demographic make-up of that society, including its age structure and its overall mortality conditions.[5]

As a rough estimate, to provide "some idea of the enormity of the problem" (Amartya Sen 1992), Sen simply used the sex ratio then prevailing in Sub-Saharan Africa, where females outnumbered males by about 2 percent, as the expected sex ratio.[6] Given the similarity of circumstances between the developing region of Sub-Saharan Africa and the developing regions of South and East Asia and the Middle East, this appears a logical choice. It turns out, however, that the demographic conditions in Sub-Saharan Africa are quite different from those in Asia and the Middle East in three ways. First, fertility is much higher, which leads to a very different age structure with implications for the population sex ratio (see below). Second, mortality is also higher, which again has a differential impact on the expected mortality experience of males and females. And third, African populations have a slightly but significantly lower sex ratio at birth than other populations, which partly explains their comparatively low population sex ratio.[7] . . .

Coale (1991) then made the following assumptions to arrive at his estimate of "missing women." First, he assumed a sex ratio at birth of 1.059, which he derived as an average from the sex ratios at birth in rich countries. Second, he assumed that the populations with gender bias in mortality could be considered quasi-stable,[8] meaning that they have a roughly constant age structure of the population. This assumption allowed him to use the Model Life Tables for an estimate of "missing women" as they are generated for stable or quasi-stable populations. Third, he assumed that the "expected" mortality pattern in the absence of discrimination would conform to the Model Life Tables "West." They are based on 132 Model Life Tables detailing the mortality experience of Western European, and some Asian, Australian, and South African (white) populations, mostly from the late nineteenth to the mid-twentieth century. Fourth, he chose the Model Life Tables that corresponded to the mortality and population growth patterns these countries experienced in the early 1970s, to approximate the average mortality and fertility levels of the cohorts alive at the time of the census. Lastly, he ignored international migration, as did all other studies.

Based on these assumptions, Table 1 shows how Coale arrived at some 60 million "missing women" in the populations most affected by gender bias in mortality.[9] While this estimate was considerably

---

[5]In particular, since women have a large survival advantage in older age groups, the aging societies of the industrialized world are increasingly female-dominated. Another factor responsible for the high female excess in European countries is the legacy of World War II, which decimated male cohorts disproportionately.

[6]In some publications, Sen also used the sex ratio (males/females) prevailing in rich countries of 0.95 as an alternative benchmark (see, e.g., Sen 1990). This benchmark is more problematic than Sub-Saharan Africa for four reasons (see also Coale 1991). First, the low sex ratio in Europe is partly the result of World War II, which heavily decimated male cohorts. Second, and of increasing importance, is the large share of elderly among European populations compared to those of developing countries. Since women predominate among the elderly, a large share of the elderly reduces the sex ratio beyond the levels one would expect in the young societies of developing countries. Third, the behavioral patterns that lead to high mortality among males (compared to females) are particularly prevalent in rich countries where all population groups have widespread access to products which can cause death, such as automobiles, cigarettes, and alcohol. Fourth, the mortality resulting from these behavioral patterns constitutes a large share of overall mortality in these otherwise low-mortality populations, thus leading to particularly depressed sex ratios favoring females.

[7]This is not only apparent from data on sex ratios at birth in Africa, but also from Africans in the US and the Caribbean, and has been well-documented (e.g., Michael Teitelbaum 1970; Michael Teitelbaum and Nathan Mantel 1971; John W. Khoury, J. D. Erickson, and L. M. James 1983; Anoushe Chanazarian 1986; William James 1986). For a more detailed discussion, see Klasen (1994). While it is likely that sex ratios at birth in other

regions of the world differ slightly, and that, due to its high genetic diversity, the sex ratio at birth also likely differs within Africa, these differences have not been found to be large enough to be detected with any certainty in available demographic data. The precise biological reasons for these slight differences in the sex ratio are unclear; interestingly, they appear to be inversely related to twinning rates. For details, refer to James (1986) and Chanazarian (1986).

[8]Stable populations are those that have constant fertility and constant mortality rates and thus generate a stable age distribution. Quasi-stable populations are populations that have roughly constant fertility and constantly falling mortality and will also generate a stable age distribution. Coale assumed that the developing countries with missing women were quasi-stable. To adjust for the fact that most countries not only have falling mortality but also falling fertility levels, he did not take the fertility levels at the time of the census but rather the levels prevailing some twenty years earlier. This generates roughly average fertility levels for the cohorts alive at the time of the census. See Stephan Klasen and Claudia Wink (2002) for a discussion of this assumption.

[9]The expected sex ratio is calculated in the following manner. First, based on life expectancy some fifteen years earlier, the level of the life table is chosen from the "West" tables in Coale, Demeny, and Vaughan (1983). Then according to population growth some fifteen years earlier, the stable population structure is chosen for that level based on the same source. Finally, the indicator population size per births for males is multiplied by the sex ratio at birth (here assumed to be 1.059), and then divided by

Table 1. "Missing Women": Estimates by Sen, Coale, and Klasen in the Early 1990s

Country	Year	Number of women (millions)	Actual sex ratio	Sen's estimate based on the actual sex ratio in Sub-Saharan Africa			Coale's estimate based on Model Life Tables "West" and constant sex ratio at birth			Klasen's estimate based on Model Life Tables "East" and variable sex ratio at birth		
				Expected sex ratio	Missing women (m)	% missing	Expected sex ratio	Missing women (m)	% missing	Expected sex ratio	Missing women (m)	% missing
China	1990	548.7	1.066	0.977	49.98	9.11	1.010	30.42	5.54	0.993	40.14	7.32
India	1991	406.3	1.077	0.977	41.59	10.24	1.020	22.76	5.59	0.990	35.87	8.83
Pakistan	1981	40.0	1.105	0.977	5.24	13.10	1.025	3.12	7.80	1.002	4.09	10.23
Bangladesh	1981	42.2	1.064	0.977	3.76	8.90	1.025	1.61	3.80	0.969	4.13	9.78
Nepal	1981	7.3	1.050	0.977	0.55	7.47	1.025	0.18	2.44	0.980	0.52	7.13
West Asia	1985	55.0	1.060	0.977	4.67	8.50	1.030	1.60	2.91	1.005	3.01	5.47
Egypt	1986	23.5	1.047	0.977	1.68	7.16	1.020	0.62	2.65	0.996	1.20	5.12
Total		1,123.0			107.47	9.57		60.26	5.37		88.96	7.92

Source: Klasen (1994). The percent missing is arrived at by dividing the number of "missing women" by the actual number of women alive. These numbers are as they appeared in Klasen (1994) and do not take into account the impact of revised census counts and other adjustments.

smaller than Sen's, it supported the massive human toll of gender bias in mortality.

In a paper published in 1994, Klasen adopted Coale's general approach but questioned two of the assumptions. First, he argued that the use of the Model Life Tables "West" led to an underestimation of gender bias in mortality, particularly in high mortality environments, as the countries that formed the basis for those Model Life Tables had themselves experienced episodes of excess female mortality, particularly in the nineteenth century. He noted that the Model Life Tables "West" assumed that girls between 1 and 20 have higher mortality rates than boys in high mortality environments, which was contrary to the biological evidence and likely to be related to actual episodes of gender bias in mortality in the nineteenth century (e.g., Klasen 1998, 1999; Humphries 1991; K. McNay, Jane Humphries, and Stephan Klasen 1998). He then tried to correct these Model Life Tables for this gender bias in mortality. This increased the number of "missing women" by some 5 million, particularly in the high mortality countries of Bangladesh, Nepal, and India. When using the Model Life Tables "East," which did not show such pronounced excess female mortality among girls and showed a larger survival advantage for adult women, the number of "missing women" increased by a further 4 million, thus totaling 69.3 million.

Klasen's second criticism of Coale's method was the assumption of a constant sex ratio at birth in all countries. Based on long time series of sex ratios at birth, Klasen showed that there had been a secular upward trend in the sex ratio at birth in rich countries. The biological literature on the subject also suggested that improved overall health conditions should raise the sex ratio at birth since male fetuses disproportionately suffer from spontaneous abortions and stillbirths.[10] Whenever better health and nutrition lower the rates of such spontaneous abortions and miscarriages and reduce the incidence of stillbirths, the sex ratio at birth increases.

He then used available evidence on sex ratios at birth from around the world and found that they are indeed closely correlated with life expectancy. Based on this regression . . . , he then estimated that the expected sex ratio at birth in high mortality countries should be considerably below the 1.059 suggested by Coale. Lower male excess at birth would then reduce the expected population sex ratio and thus increase the resulting number of "missing women." As shown in the bottom panel of Table 1, using the Model Life Tables "East" and the revised assumptions about the sex ratio at birth, increased the number of "missing women" to about 89 million, which was slightly closer to Sen's 107 million than to Coale's 60 million. Clearly, the assumptions underlying the calculations make a large difference and there is considerable empirical support for the general approach by Coale with the two amended assumptions by Klasen. . . .

All of these calculations and discussions were based on demographic information from the 1980s and early 1990s. With new census information available, it is critical to know how gender bias in mortality, including its regional distribution, has changed over time.

II. Updating the Number of "Missing Women"

The actual sex ratios for Egypt, China, and India in Coale (1991) and Klasen (1994) were based on preliminary census figures. The final census figures led to some changes in the numbers. Most notably there was a downward revision of the sex ratio in China from 1.066 to 1.060 which thereby reduced the number of "missing women" by some 3.5 million (regardless of the assumption used to generate the expected sex ratio). In contrast, revisions to the figures from India and Egypt increased the number of "missing women" by 0.8 and 0.05 million, respectively.[11] Finally, we use a slightly revised assumption about the sex ratio at birth based on a

---

the population size per births for females. The population size per births is also found in the Model Life Tables. The procedure is explained with an example in Coale, Demeny, and Vaughan (1983). See also Klasen and Wink (2002) for further details.

[10]There is a large literature documenting that the sex ratio *in utero* is considerably higher than at birth, and that the sex ratio of miscarriages, spontaneous abortions, and stillbirths is much larger than the sex ratio at birth. As a result, improving health conditions that reduce the incidence of miscarriages and stillbirths will increase the sex ratio at birth, which is consistent with the secular trends in the sex ratio at birth. For a detailed discussion see Klasen (1994) and Chanazarian (1986).

[11]Moreover, Coale (1991), and, by implication, Klasen (1994) erroneously reported the sex ratio in West Asia in 1990, in the quoted source, to be 1.060 instead of the correct 1.073 (United Nations 1991). This increased the number of "missing women" there by about 0.7 million. Lastly, the life expectancy assumptions underlying the choice of life tables and the appropriate sex ratio at birth in Bangladesh in Klasen (1994) were too low. This led to an overestimation of the number of missing women in Bangladesh by some 0.5 million. This does not, however, invalidate the differences between Coale and Klasen in the relative assessment of gender bias in mortality in Bangladesh, especially vis-à-vis China.

more expanded analysis. All in all, the baseline to compare current figures is some 87 million "missing women" (or 7.7 percent of women) for the 1980s and early 1990s, instead of the 89 million reported in table 1. Similarly, some of the new census data (from China, India, Pakistan, Nepal, and Bangladesh) are based on preliminary census returns and might also be adjusted later.[12]

Coale (1991) and Klasen (1994) missed out on a few countries with possibly considerable excess female mortality. In particular, Iran, Afghanistan, Taiwan, South Korea, Algeria, and Tunisia were not included in the assessment despite having high sex ratios or showing other evidence of female disadvantage. They have now been included to generate a more complete assessment of the total number of "missing women" in the world.[13] Sri Lanka has also been added, as it used to have high sex ratios which have, however, fallen considerably recently. Finally, despite having comparatively low sex ratios, Sub-Saharan Africa might also suffer from excess female mortality, which is masked by the unusually low sex ratios at birth prevailing in African populations and populations of African descent (see Stephan Klasen 1994, 1996a, 1996b). Thus, one should also include this region in the list of candidates, particularly since the population sex ratios have been increasing considerably in recent years (Klasen 1996a, 1996b).[14] We not only include them in the current assessment but also estimate a baseline of "missing women" in the 1980s and early 1990s. Including these additional countries, the baseline is about 95 million for that time period, or 6.5 percent of all women in the countries affected (see Stephan Klasen and Claudia Wink 2002 for details). . . .

[In Table 2] we calculate a baseline estimate of the number of missing females in the world, based on the most recent census information and population estimates for all regions with presumed excess female mortality. Beginning with the global calculations, we present two figures. The first is just for the regions and countries considered in Coale

(1991) and Klasen (1994) (called "Total comparable"), while the second includes the additional countries.[15] The first figure shows an increase in the number of "missing women" from 87 million to 93 million. Thus, the cumulative impact of gender bias in mortality is exacting an increasing absolute toll on women world-wide. While this points to an *absolute* worsening, it suggests a slight *relative* improvement. The population in the countries suffering from excess female mortality increased by some 21 percent while the number of "missing women" increased by "only" about 7 percent. Thus gender bias in mortality has not increased in proportion to the population suggesting that, as a share of the female population, females now have slightly less unequal survival chances vis-à-vis males. This can also be seen in the share of "missing women" in the various countries considered. Compared to Table 1, this share has decreased in most regions, although the extent of the drop differs greatly between regions. The "total comparable" share of "missing women" has declined from 7.7 to 6.8 percent.

The largest drop, in percentage terms, occurred in Nepal, where results from the 2001 census suggest that the problem of "missing women" has all but disappeared. In fact, this drop had occurred already in the 1991 census and has held steady since. This sudden drop of the sex ratio is not very plausible, . . . so this result should be treated with some caution. The drop, in percentage terms, is also considerable in Bangladesh, Pakistan, and West Asia where the share of "missing women" (compared to the revised baseline) dropped by 3–5 percentage points. The fall is more modest in India and Egypt where it dropped by some 1–2 percentage points. In China, the share of "missing women" has actually increased by 0.4 percentage points to 6.7 percent (and the absolute number of missing females has increased to nearly 41 million), compared to the revised baseline where, after the census adjustments, the share was 6.3 percent and the absolute number of women stood at 35 million. As a result of improvements elsewhere, over 80 percent of the increase in the absolute number of "missing women" in the world is due to the increase in "missing women" in China. Owing to reductions in the share of "missing women" in Pakistan and Bangladesh, India now has the dubious distinction of having the largest share of "missing women"

---

[12]For example, the census figures for Bangladesh in 1991 have been adjusted several times, with implications for the sex ratio. While the preliminary count of the 1991 census found 105 million people and a sex ratio of 1.063, after two sets of adjustments, the population was fixed at 111 million and a sex ratio of 1.059 (see People's (Perspectives 1993).

[13]We also show figures for Syria and Turkey, although they are already included in the regional estimate for "missing women" in West Asia.

[14]Population estimates for the region as a whole are included, since censuses from individual countries are less reliable than elsewhere and migration within Africa is quite significant.

[15]Klasen and Wink (2002) provide a baseline estimate of "missing women" for these additional countries for the 1980s and early 1990s.

Table 2. Number of "Missing Women," Latest Estimate (based on Model Life Tables "East" and adjusted sex ratio at birth)

	Year	Actual number of women	Actual sex ratio	Expected sex ratio at birth	Expected sex ratio	Expected number of women	Missing women	% missing
China	**2000**	**612.3**	**1.067**	**1.050**	**1.001**	**653.2**	**40.9**	**6.7**
Taiwan	1999	10.8	1.049	1.052	1.002	11.3	0.5	4.7
South Korea	1995	22.2	1.008	1.047	1.000	22.4	0.2	0.7
India	**2001**	**495.7**	**1.072**	**1.039**	**0.993**	**534.8**	**39.1**	**7.9**
Pakistan	**1998**	**62.7**	**1.081**	**1.042**	**1.003**	**67.6**	**4.9**	**7.8**
Bangladesh	**2001**	**63.4**	**1.038**	**1.040**	**0.996**	**66.1**	**2.7**	**4.2**
Nepal	**2001**	**11.6**	**0.997**	**1.037**	**0.992**	**11.7**	**0.1**	**0.5**
Sri Lanka	1991	8.6	1.005	1.052	1.006	8.6	0.0	0.0
West Asia	**2000**	**92.0**	**1.043**	**1.042**	**1.002**	**95.8**	**3.8**	**4.2**
of which:								
Turkey	1990	27.9	1.027	1.047	1.003	28.5	0.7	2.4
Syria	1994	6.7	1.047	1.048	1.016	6.9	0.2	3.1
Afghanistan	2000	11.1	1.054	1.024	0.964	12.1	1.0	9.3
Iran	1996	29.5	1.033	1.039	0.996	30.6	1.1	3.7
Egypt	**1996**	**29.0**	**1.048**	**1.044**	**1.003**	**30.3**	**1.3**	**4.5**
Algeria	1998	14.5	1.018	1.043	1.005	14.7	0.2	1.2
Tunisia	1994	4.3	1.021	1.043	1.000	4.4	0.1	2.1
Sub-Saharan Africa	2000	307.0	0.987	1.017	0.970	312.5	5.5	1.8
Total (Comparable)		**1,366.7**					**92.8**	**6.8**
Total (World)		1,774.8					101.3	5.7

Notes: Total (Comparable) includes China, India, Pakistan, Bangladesh, Nepal, West Asia, and Egypt and shown in bold. Total (World) additionally includes Taiwan, South Korea, Iran, Algeria, Tunisia, and Afghanistan. Turkey and Syria are subsumed in West Asia and are therefore not added separately. Actual and expected sex ratios refer to the number of males per females in the entire population; the expected sex ratio at birth refers to the number of males per female at birth.

Sources: Registrar General (2001), United Nations (1999, 2000), State Statistical Bureau (2001), Statistical Bureau of Taiwan (2001), Mustak Hossain (2001), and Sanjaya Dhakal (2001).

among the comparable set of countries, followed closely by Pakistan.

When we consider the additional countries, the total number of "missing women" increases to some 101 million, or 5.7 percent of the female population in the countries affected. The largest relative problem appears in Afghanistan which has the highest share of "missing women" anywhere in the world. These figures are, however, the least reliable in the table, and are based on United Nations estimates. The last census took place in 1979, and since then wars, refugee flows, and regime changes are likely to have affected sex ratios. Also, policies by the recently deposed Taliban regime that sharply limit women's access to education, healthcare, and employment are likely to have worsened the mortality situation for women and girls considerably, so that even these estimates might understate the true state of affairs for women there. Taiwan also appears to have a considerable problem of gender bias in mortality, although the estimate suggests that it has improved over the past ten years. There are small shares of "missing women"

in South Korea, Sri Lanka, Tunisia, Algeria, Sub-Saharan Africa, and Iran.[16] In Sub-Saharan Africa, the figures are highly sensitive to the assumptions about the sex ratio at birth and should therefore be treated with some caution (see below and also Klasen 1994, 1996a, 1996b). In this expanded set of countries, the trend points to a falling share of "missing women," with the exception of South Korea where the problem appears to have worsened slightly from a previously negligible share of "missing women."

When examining the factors underlying this overall relative improvement, one can distinguish between changes in the expected sex ratio and changes in the actual sex ratio. With the exception of South Korea, the expected sex ratio has increased in all other countries included. This is

[16]The estimate for Iran might understate the true impact of gender bias in mortality since the Iran-Iraq war claimed the lives of more than a million men, and this artificially reduced the sex ratio and might therefore hide a considerable problem of gender bias in mortality.

mainly due to the increase in the expected sex ratio at birth, as a result of improved longevity. The higher longevity has a second effect on the expected sex ratio. In populations that are growing and thus have a large share of young people, expanded longevity actually increases the expected sex ratio since males, due to their greater vulnerability in infancy and childhood, benefit relatively more from an equiproportionate mortality decline, so that the male excess at birth persists to higher ages. Conversely, falling population growth rates in some (though not all) regions would have reduced the expected sex ratio as the populations would age and females would dominate more. Since the expected sex ratios increased everywhere except in South Korea, the first two effects dominate the third.

What, however, happened to the actual sex ratio? With the exception of China, South Korea, and Sub-Saharan Africa where it increased slightly, it has fallen in all other regions. The decrease varies considerably. The largest decrease (which appears implausible and suggests past or present enumeration problems) was in Nepal, but there were also substantial reductions in Pakistan, Bangladesh, Taiwan, Sri Lanka, and West Asia. In Egypt, Syria, Turkey, Afghanistan, Algeria, Tunisia, and India the decrease was slight.[17] In countries that were not included in Coale (1991) and Klasen (1994), most have also experienced a decrease in their sex ratio. It is particularly noteworthy that the sex ratio in Sri Lanka dropped from 1.04 in 1981 to an estimated 1.00 in 1991. This is all the more impressive since Sri Lanka had a sex ratio of about 1.15 in 1951, much worse than India's at the same time, after which it fell consistently (Klasen 1999).

If gender bias in mortality had remained constant in relative terms, we would have expected rising actual sex ratios in all regions except South Korea.[18] Combined with population growth, this would have led to drastically rising numbers of "missing women." In reality, the actual sex ratios dropped in most regions and these two factors combined are responsible for the more favorable relative picture, although existing population growth ensured that the *absolute* number of "missing women" increased in China, India, Pakistan,

South Korea, Afghanistan, Egypt, and Sub-Saharan Africa. . . .

III. Analyzing Trends in Gender Bias in Mortality

From [Table 1 and Table 2], we can generate the following stylized facts regarding trends in gender bias in mortality. While in absolute terms, the number of "missing women" has increased, in relative terms it is falling in most places. Sharp reductions, in relative terms, occurred in North Africa, and parts of South Asia, most notably Nepal, Bangladesh, and Pakistan (from very high levels) as well as West Asia. In Sri Lanka, gender bias in mortality disappeared entirely. Moderate reductions took place in India, Tunisia, Turkey, Syria, Iran, Afghanistan, and Egypt, while slight increases in the share of "missing women" occurred in South Korea and Sub-Saharan Africa. Lastly, China has experienced a significant increase in gender bias which is largely responsible for the world-wide increase in the absolute number of "missing women." . . .

It is important to briefly review the most important findings on both the mechanisms and the causal factors associated with excess female mortality. Most studies have shown that the most important process driving excess female mortality is unequal access to healthcare which leads to higher mortality of young girls (e.g., Chen, Huq, and D'Souza 1981; Alaka Basu 1992; Harold Alderman and Paul Gertler 1997; Ian Timaeus, Katie Harris, and Francesca Fairbairn 1998; Klasen 1999; Croll 2000; Gautam Hazarika 2000). In contrast, differences in access to nutrition appear to be a smaller factor, if present at all (e.g., Chen, Huq, D'Souza 1981; Sen and Sengupta 1983; Basu 1992; Kenneth Hill and Dawn Upchurch 1995; Elizabeth Somerfelt and Fred Arnold 1998; Hazarika 2000). This comparative neglect of female children, which is generally worse in rural areas, appears to be particularly severe for later-born girls and among them even worse for girls with elder sisters (Das Gupta 1987; Pradib Muhuri and Samuel Preston 1991; Drèze and Sen 1995; Klasen 1999).

In addition, sex-selective abortions seem to have played an increasing role in some countries experiencing "missing women," most notably China, South Korea, and recently also India (Judith Banister and Ansley Coale 1994; Chai Bin Park and Nam-Hoon Cho 1995; Croll 2000; Registrar General 2001). The most important evidence of this is the rising observed sex ratios at birth which appears to be due largely to sex-selective abortions

---

[17]The decrease in India might be due partly to a more accurate count of females in 2001, compared to 1991 (Tim Dyson 2001), in which case the high sex ratio in 1991 and the resulting number of missing females was somewhat overestimated. In any case, we no longer see a worsening of the sex ratio in India.

[18]In South Korea, the only country where we would have expected to see a decline in the sex ratio, we find an increase and thus the emergence of "missing women."

rather than the under-registration of female infants (Croll 2000; Banister and Coale 1994; Chu Junhong 2001; Registrar General 2001). While excess deaths due to unequal access to resources and sex-selective abortions have the same result, namely missing women, it is not clear whether the two processes should be seen as ethically equivalent. On the one hand, one may argue that female deaths due to sex-specific neglect are equivalent to abortions of female fetuses as they both terminat female life prematurely and are an outgrowth of discriminatory and demeaning attitudes towards women. In fact, one may argue that sex-selective abortions are more problematic as it leads to death (or prevention of female life) with certainty, while female neglect only increases the chance of female mortality. Moreover, sex-selective abortions are associated with late-term abortions which pose other health hazards to women. On the other hand, one may argue that sex-selective abortions are a somewhat lesser evil, as one should distinguish between pre-birth and post-birth interventions, with the latter usually judged wore than the former. This may be particularly the case if greater recourse to sex-selective abortions leads to a reduction of female neglect of those girls that end up being born, which some claim to be the case empirically (Daniel Goodkind 1996). Also, in the case of sex-selective abortions, interventions to combat the practice, such as (largely unenforced) bans on pre-natal sex determination in India and China, would have to balance the rights of a fetus with those of a woman. It is not possible to resolve this issue here, which is treated more fully elsewhere.[19] But it is important to note that the evaluation of "missing women" might depend on the process by which they went "missing" in the first place.

[19]See, for example, Stephan Klasen (2003, and the literature cited therein), Dolly Arora (1996), and Daniel Goodkind (1999). These questions might evolve further since new technologies, such as sperm sorting, are becoming increasingly available, which will also generate "missing women" but might raise different ethical questions. For a discussion, see Klasen (2003).

References

Alderman, Harold and Paul J. Gertler. 1997. "Family Resources and Gender Differences in Human Capital Investments: The Demand for Children's Medical Care in Pakistan," in Lawrence Haddad, John Hoddinott, and Harold Alderman (eds.) *Intrahousehold Resource Allocation in Developing Countries: Models, Methods, and Policy.* Baltimore, MD: Johns Hopkins University Press.

Arora, Dolly. 1996. "The Victimizing Discourse: Sex Determination Technologies and Policy." *Economic and Political Weekly* 31(7): 420–4.

Banister, Judith and Ansley J. Coale. 1994. "Five Decades of Missing Females in China." *Demography* 31(3): 459–79.

Basu, Alaka Malwade. 1992. *Culture, the Status of Women, and Demographic Behavior.* Oxford, UK: Oxford University Press.

Chanazarian, Anoushe. 1986. "Determinants of the Sex Ratio at Birth." PhD dissertation. Princeton University, NJ.

Chen, Lincoln, Emdadul Huq, and Stan D'Souza. 1981. "Sex Bias in the Family Allocation of Food and Health Care in Rural Bangladesh." *Population and Development Review* 7(1): 55–70.

Coale, Ansley. 1991. "Excess Female Mortality and the Balance of the Sexes." *Population and Development Review* 17(3): 517–23.

———, Paul Demeny, and Barbara Vaughan. 1983. *Regional Model Life Tables and Stable Populations.* Princeton, NJ: Princeton University Press.

Croll, Elizabeth. 2000. *Endangered Daughters.* London: Routledge.

Das, Gupta Monica. 1987. "Selective Discrimination against Females in Rural Punjab, India." *Population and Development Review* 13(1): 77–100.

Dhakal, Sanjaya. 2001. "More But Not Merrier." *Spotlight* 20, August 17–23.

Drèze, Jean and Amartya Sen. 1989. *Hunger and Public Action.* Oxford, UK: Clarendon Press.

——— and Amartya Sen. 1995. *India Economic Development and Social Opportunity.* Oxford, UK: Clarendon Press.

D'Souza, Stan and Lincoln C. Chen. 1980. "Sex Differences in Mortality in Rural Bangladesh." *Population and Development Review* 6: 257–70.

Dyson, Tim. 2001. "The Preliminary Demography of the 2001 Census in India." *Population and Development Review* 27: 341–56.

Goodkind, Daniel. 1996. "On Substituting Sex Preference Strategies in East Asia: Does Prenatal Sex Selection Reduce Postnatal Discrimination?" *Population and Development Review* 22: 111–25.

———. 1999. "Should Prenatal Sex Selection be Restricted? Ethical Questions and their Implications for Research and Policy." *Population Studies* 53: 49–61.

Hazarika, Gautam. 2000. "Gender Differences in Children's Nutrition and Access to Health Care in Pakistan." *Journal of Development Studies* 37(1): 73–92.

Hill, Kenneth and Dawn Upchurch. 1995. "Gender differences in child health: Evidence from the Demographic and Health Surveys." *Population and Development Review* 21: 127–151.

Hossain, Mustak. 2001. "Fourth Population Census 'Riddled with Inconsistencies'." *Daily Star,* September 3.

Humphries, Jane. 1991. "Bread and a Pennyworth of Treacle." *Cambridge Journal of Economics* 15: 451–73.

James, William H. 1986. "The Sex Ratio of Black Births." *Annals of Human Biology* 11: 39–44.

Junhong, Chu. 2001. "Prenatal Sex Determination and Sex-Selective Abortion in Rural Central China." *Population and Development Review* 27: 259–82.

Khoury, John W., J. D. Erickson, and L. M. James. 1983. "Paternal Effects on the Human Sex Ratio at Birth: Evidence from Interracial Cases." *American Journal of Human Genetics* 36: 1103–8.

Klasen, Stephan. 1994. "Missing Women Reconsidered." *World Development* 22(7): 1061–71.

———. 1996a. "Nutrition, Health, and Mortality in Sub Saharan Africa: Is There a Gender Bias?." *Journal of Development Studies* 32: 913–33.

———. 1996b. "Rejoinder." *Journal of Development Studies* 32: 944–8.

———. 1998. "Marriage, Bargaining, and Intrahousehold Resource Allocation." *Journal of Economic History* 58: 432–67.

———. 1999. "Gender Inequality in Mortality in Comparative Perspective." Mimeographed, University of Munich.

———. 2003. "Sex Selection." *Encyclopedia of Population.* (forthcoming).

——— and Claudia Wink. 2002. "A Turning Point in Gender Bias in Mortality? An Update on the Number of Missing Women." *Population and Development Review* 28(2): 285–312.

McNay, K., Jane Humphries, and Stephan Klasen. 1998. "Death and Gender in Victorian England and Wales: Comparisons with Contemporary Developing Countries." DAE Working Paper No. 9801. Department of Applied Economics, Cambridge University.

Muhuri, Pradib K. and Samuel H. Preston. 1991. "Effects of Family Composition on Mortality Differentials by Sex Among Children in Matlab, Bangladesh." *Population and Development Review* 17(3): 415–34.

Murthi, Mamta, Anne-Catherine Guio, and Jean Drèze. 1995. "Mortality, Fertility, and Gender Bias in India: A District-Level Analysis." *Population and Development Review* 21(4): 745–82.

Park, Chai Bin and Nam-Hoon Cho. 1995. "Consequences of Son Preference in a Low-Fertility Society:

Imbalance of the Sex Ratio at Birth." *Population and Development Review* 21(1): 59–84.

People's Perspectives 1993. "Population Clock and Census '91 in Bangladesh: Ticking Falsehood & Manipulating Numbers," *The People's Perspectives* No. 4–5, November–December, 1993.

Registrar General 2001. *Provisional Population Totals. Census of India Series 1, Paper 1 of 2001.* New Delhi: Ministry of Home Affairs.

Sen, Amartya. 1990. "Gender and Cooperative Conflict." in Irene Tinker (ed.) *Persistent Inequalities—Women and World Development,* pp. 123–49. New York: Oxford University Press.

———. 1992. "Missing Women." *British Medical Journal* 304: 586–7.

——— and Sunil Sengupta. 1983. "Malnutrition or Rural Children and the Sex Bias." *Economic and Political Weekly* 18: 855–64.

Somerfelt, Elizabeth and Fred Arnold. 1998. "Sex Differentials in the Nutritional Status of Young Children," in United Nations (ed.). *Too Young to Die—Genes or Gender?* New York: United Nations.

State Statistical Bureau. 2001. *Communique on Major Figures of the 2000 Population Census.* Beijing: National Bureau of Statistics.

State Statistical Bureau of Taiwan. 2001. *Population Estimates of Taiwan.* Taipeh: State Statistical Bureau.

Teitelbaum, Michael S. 1970. "Factors Affecting the Sex Ratio in Large Populations." *Journal of Biosocial Sciences,* Supplement 2: 61–71.

——— and Nathan Mantel. 1971. "Socio-Economic Factors and the Sex Ratio at Birth." *Journal of Biosocial Sciences* 3: 23–41.

Timaeus, Ian, Katie Harris, and Francesca Fairbairn. 1998. "Can Use of Health Care Explain Sex Differentials in Mortality in the Developing World?" in United Nations (ed.). *Too Young to Die—Genes or Gender?* New York: United Nations.

United Nations. 1991. *Demographic Yearbook.* New York: United Nations.

United Nations. 1999. *Demographic Yearbook.* New York: United Nations.

United Nations. 2000. *Demographic Yearbook.* New York: United Nations.

Waldron, Ingrid. 1993. "Recent Trends in Sex Mortality Ratios for Adults in Developed Countries." *Social Science Medicine* 36: 451–62.

Selection IV.D.3. Women as Policy Makers*

1. Introduction

Relative to their share in the population, women are under-represented in all political positions. In June 2000, women represented 13.8% of all parliament members in the world, up from 9% in 1987. Compared to economic opportunities, education and legal rights, political representation is the area in which the gap between men and women has narrowed the least between 1995 and 2000 (Norris and Inglehart (2000)). Political reservations for women are often proposed as a way to rapidly enhance women's ability to participate in policymaking. Quotas for women in assemblies or on parties' candidate lists are in force in the legislation of over 30 countries (World Bank (2001)), and in the internal rules of at least one party in 12 countries of the European Union (Norris (2001)).

Reservation policies clearly have a strong impact on women's representation, and there is evidence that women and men have different policy preferences (Lott and Kenny (1999), Edlund and Pande (2001)). This does not necessarily imply, however, that women's reservation has an impact on policy decisions. In a standard median voter model (e.g., Downs (1957)), where candidates can commit to a specific policy and have electoral motives, political decisions reflect the preferences of the electorate. Alternatively, in a Coasian world, even if the reservation policy increases women's bargaining power, only transfers to women should be affected; the efficient policy choices will still be made, and women will be compensated with direct transfers.

However, despite the importance of this issue for the design of institutions, very little is known about the causal effect of women's representation on policy decisions. The available evidence, based on cross-sectional comparison, is difficult to interpret, because the fact that women are better represented in a particular country or locality may reflect the political preferences of the group that elects them. The correlation between policy outcomes and women's participation then may not imply a causal effect from women's participation.[1]

Furthermore, even if we knew more about the causal effect of women's representation, this knowledge would not necessarily extend to the effects of quotas or other mechanisms to enforce greater participation of women in the political process. Ensuring women's representation through quotas may change the nature of political competition and thus have direct effects. For example, it may lower the average competence in the pool of eligible candidates, alter voter preferences for political parties, or increase the number of politicians that are new in office.

This paper studies the policy consequences of mandated representation of women by taking advantage of a unique experiment implemented recently in India. In 1993, an amendment to the constitution of India required the States both to devolve more power over expenditures to local village councils (Gram Panchayats, henceforth GPs) and to reserve one-third of all positions of chief (Pradhan) to women. Since then, most Indian States have had two Panchayat elections (Bihar and Punjab had only one, in 2001 and 1998 respectively), and at least one-third of village representatives are women in all major States except Uttar Pradesh, where only 25% of the village representatives are women (Chaudhuri (2003)). We conducted a detailed survey of all investments in local public goods in a sample of villages in two districts, Birbhum in West Bengal and Udaipur in Rajasthan, and compared investments made in reserved and unreserved GPs. As GPs were randomly selected to be reserved for women, differences in investment decisions can be confidently attributed to the reserved status of those GPs.

The results suggest that reservation affects policy choices. In particular, it affects policy decisions in ways that seem to better reflect women's preferences. The gender preferences of men and women are proxied by the types of formal requests brought to the GP by each gender. In West Bengal, women complain more often than men about drinking water and roads, and there are more investments in drinking water and roads in GPs reserved for women. In Rajasthan, women complain more often

*From Raghabendra Chattopadhyay and Esther Duflo, "Women as Policy Makers: Evidence From a Randomized Policy Experiment in India," *Econometrica* 72, no. 5 (September 2004): 1409–1414, 1423, 1425–1432, 1440. Reprinted by permission.

[1]For example, Dollar, Fisman, and Gatti (2001) find a negative correlation between representation of women in parliaments and corruption. Does this mean women are less corrupt, or that countries that are less corrupt are also more likely to elect women to parliament? Besley and Case (2000) show that worker compensation and child support enforcement policies are more likely to be introduced in states where there are more women in parliament, after controlling for state and year fixed effects. But they explicitly recognize that the fraction of women in parliament may be a proxy for women's involvement in politics, more generally.

than men about drinking water but less often about roads, and there are more investments in water and less investment in roads in GPs reserved for women. . . .

These results thus indicate that a politician's gender does influence policy decisions. More generally, they provide new evidence on the political process. In particular, they provide strong evidence that the identity of a decision maker does influence policy decisions. This provides empirical support to political economy models that seek to enrich the Downsian model (Alesina (1988); Osborne and Slivinski (1996); and Besley and Coate (1977)). The results are consistent with previous evidence by Levitt (1996), which shows that U.S. Senators' votes do not reflect either the wishes of their constituency or that of their party, and by Pande (2003), who shows that in Indian States where a larger share of seats is reserved for minorities in the State Legislative Assembly, the level of transfers targeted towards these minorities is also higher. Our paper presents the advantage of being based on a randomized experiment, where identification is entirely transparent. . . .

2. The Policy and Design of the Study

2.1. The Panchayat System

The Panchayat is a system of village level (Gram Panchayat), block level (Panchayat Samiti), and district level (Zilla Parishad) councils, members of which are elected by the people, and are responsible for the administration of local public goods. Each Gram Panchayat (GP) encompasses 10,000 people in several villages (between 5 and 15). The GP do not have jurisdiction over urban areas, which are administered by separate municipalities. Voters elect a council, which then elects among its members a Pradhan (chief) and an Upa-Pradhan (vice-chief). Candidates are generally nominated by political parties, but have to be residents of the villages they represent. The council makes decisions by majority voting (the Pradhan does not have veto power). The Pradhan, however, is the only member of the council with a full-time appointment.

The Panchayat system has existed formally in most of the major states of India since the early 1950s. However, in most states, the system was not an effective body of governance until the early 1990s. Elections were not held, and the Panchayats did not assume any active role (Ghatak and Ghatak (2002)). In 1992, the 73rd amendment to the Constitution of India established throughout India the framework of a three-tiered Panchayat system with regular elections. It gave the GP primary responsibility in implementing development programs, as well as in identifying the needs of the villages under its jurisdiction. Between 1993 and 2003, all major States but two (Bihar and Punjab) have had at least two elections. The major responsibilities of the GP are to administer local infrastructure (public buildings, water, roads) and identify targeted welfare recipients. The main source of financing is still the state, but most of the money which was previously earmarked for specific uses is now allocated through four broad schemes: The Jawhar Rozgar Yojana (JRY) for infrastructure (irrigation, drinking water, roads, repairs of community buildings, etc.); a small additional drinking water scheme; funds for welfare programs (widow's old age, and maternity pensions, etc); and a grant for GP functioning. The GP has, in principle, complete flexibility in allocating these funds. At this point, the GP has no direct control over the appointments of government paid teachers or health workers, but in some states (Tamil Nadu and West Bengal, for example), there are Panchayat-run informal schools.

The Panchayat is required to organize two meetings per year, called "Gram Samsad." These are meetings of villagers and village heads in which all voters may participate. The GP council submits the proposed budget to the Gram Samsad, and reports on their activities in the previous six months. The GP leader also must set up regular office hours where villagers can lodge complaints or requests.

In West Bengal, the Left Front (communist) Government gained power in 1977 on a platform of agrarian and political reform. The major political reform was to give life to a three-tiered Panchayat electoral system. The first election took place in 1978 and elections have taken place at five-year intervals ever since. Thus, the system that was put into place by the 73rd Amendment all over India was already well established in West Bengal. Following the Amendment, the GP was given additional responsibilities in West Bengal. In particular, they were entrusted to establish and administer informal education centers (called SSK), an alternative form of education for children who do not attend school (a instructor who is not required to have any formal qualification teaches children three hours a day in a temporary building or outdoors).

In Rajasthan, unlike West Bengal, there was no regularly elected Panchayat system in charge of distribution of state funds until 1995. The first election was held in 1995, followed by a second election in 2000. Since 1995, elections and Gram Samsads have been held regularly, and are well attended.

This setting is thus very different, with a much shorter history of democratic government. As in West Bengal, the Panchayat can spend money on local infrastructure, but unlike West Bengal, they are not allowed to run their own schools.

2.2. Reservation for Women

In 1992, the 73rd Amendment provided that one-third of the seats in all Panchayat councils, as well as one-third of the Pradhan positions, must be reserved for women. Seats and Pradhan's positions were also reserved for the two disadvantaged minorities in india, "scheduled castes" (SC) and "scheduled tribes" (ST), in the form of mandated representation proportional to each minority's population share in each district. Reservations for women have been implemented in all major States except Bihar and Uttar Pradesh (which has only reserved 25% of the seats to women).

In West Bengal, the Panchayat Constitution Rule was modified in 1993, so as to reserve one-third of the councilor positions in each GP to women; in a third of the villages in each GP, only women could be candidates for the position of councilor for the area. The proportion of women elected to Panchayat councils increased to 36% after the 1993 election. The experience was considered a disappointment, however, because very few women (only 196 out of 3,324 GPs) advanced to the position of Pradhan, which is the only one that yields effective power (Kanango (1998)). To conform to the 73rd amendment, the Panchayat Constitution Rule of West Bengal was again modified in April 1998 (Government of West Bengal (1998)) to introduce reservation of Pradhan positions for women and SC/ST. In Rajasthan, the random rotation system was implemented in 1995 and in 2000 at both levels (council members and Pradhans).

In both states, a specific set of rules ensures the random selection of GPs where the office of Pradhan was to be reserved for a woman. All GPs in a district are ranked in consecutive order according to their serial legislative number (an administrative number pre-dating this reform). They are then ranked in three separate lists, according to whether or not the seats had been reserved for a SC, for a ST, or is unreserved (these reservations were also chosen randomly, following a similar method). Using these lists, every third GP starting with the first on the list is reserved for a woman Pradhan for the first election.[2]

From discussions with the government officials at the Panchayat Directorate who devised the system and district officials who implemented it in individual districts, it appears that these instructions were successfully implemented. More importantly, in the district we study in West Bengal, we could verify that the policy was strictly implemented. After sorting the GPs into those reserved for SC/ST and those not reserved, we could reconstruct the entire list of GPs reserved for a woman by sorting all GPs by their serial number, and selecting every third GP starting from the first in each list. This verifies that the allocation of GPs to the reserved list was indeed random, as intended.[3]

Table 1 shows the number of female Pradhans in reserved and unreserved GPs in both states. In both states, all Pradhans in GPs reserved for a woman are female. In West Bengal, only 6.5% of the Pradhans are female in unreserved GPs. In Rajasthan, only one woman was elected on an unreserved seat, despite the fact that this was the second cycle. Women elected once due to the reservation system were not re-elected.[4] . . .

3. Data Collection and Empirical Strategy

3.1. Data Collection

We collected data in two locations: Birbhum in West Bengal and Udaipur in Rajasthan.

In the summer of 2000, we conducted a survey of all GPs in the district of Birbhum, West Bengal. Birbhum is located in the western part of West Bengal, about 125 miles from the state capital, Calcutta. At the time of the 1991 census, it had a population of 2.56 million. Agriculture is the main economic activity, and rice is the main crop cultivated. The male and female literacy rates were 50% and 37%, respectively. The district is known to have a relatively well-functioning Panchayat system.

There are 166 GPs in Birbhum, of which five were reserved for pre-testing, leaving 161 GPs in our study. . . . As expected, given the random selection of GPs, there are no significant differences between reserved and unreserved GPs. . . . Very few villages (3% among the unreserved GPs) have tap water, the most common sources of drinking water being hand-pumps and tube-wells. Most villages are accessible only by a dirt road. Ninety-one percent of villages have a primary school, but very

---

[2]For the next election, every third GP starting with the second on the list was reserved for a woman, etc. The Panchayat Constitution Rule has actual tables indicating the ranks of the GPs to be reserved in each election.

[3]We could not obtain the necessary information to perform the same exercise in Rajasthan. However, there too, the system appears to have been correctly implemented.

[4]The one woman elected on an unreserved seat had not been previously elected on a reserved seat.

Table 1. Fraction of Women Among Pradhans in Reserved and Unreserved GP

	Reserved GP	Non reserved GP
	(1)	(2)
West Bengal		
Total number	54	107
Proportion of female Pradhans	100%	6.5%
Rajasthan		
Total number	40	60
Proportion of female Pradhans	100%	1.7%

few have any other type of school. Irrigation is important: 43% of the cultivated land is irrigated, with at least some land being irrigated in all villages. Very few villages (8%) have any public health facility. . . .

Between August 2002 and December 2002 . . . , we collected the same village-level data . . . in 100 hamlets in Udaipur, Rajasthan, chosen randomly from a subset of villages covered by a local NGO. . . . Udaipur is a much poorer district than Birbhum. It is located in an extremely arid area with little irrigation and has male and female literacy rates of 27.5% and 5.5% respectively. Because the villages are bigger, they are more likely to have a middle school, a health facility and a road connection, compared to villages in West Bengal. As in West Bengal, we see no significant difference between the characteristics of reserved and unreserved villages before the reservation policy was implemented.

3.2. Empirical Strategy

Thanks to randomization built into the policy, the basic empirical strategy is straightforward. The reduced form effect of the reservation status can be obtained by comparing the means of the outcomes of interest in reserved and unreserved GPs. Note that this reduced form difference is not an estimate of the comparison between a system with reservation and a system without reservation. The policy decisions in unreserved GPs can be different than what they would have been if there was no reservation whatsoever. They will be different, for example, in the presence of dynamic incentives. What we are trying to estimate is the effect of being reserved for a woman, rather than not reserved, *in a system where there is reservation.* . . .

4. Results

4.1. Effects on the Political Participation of Women

Table 2 displays the effect of having a woman Pradhan on the political participation of women. In West Bengal, the percentage of women among participants in the Gram Samsad is significantly higher when the Pradhan is a woman (increasing from 6.9% to 9.8%). Since reservation does not affect the percentage of eligible voters attending the Gram Samsad, this corresponds to a net increase in the participation of women, and a decline in the participation of men. This is consistent with the idea that political communication is influenced by the fact that citizens and leaders are of the same sex. Women in villages with a reserved Pradhan are twice as likely to have addressed a request or a complaint to the GP Pradhan in the last 6 months, and this difference is significant.[5] The fact that the Pradhan is a woman therefore significantly increases the involvement of women in the affairs of the GP in West Bengal.

In Rajasthan, the fact that the Pradhan is a woman has no effect on women's participation at the Gram Samsad or the occurrence of women's complaints. Note that women participate more in the Gram Samsad in Rajasthan, most probably because the process is very recent, and the GP leaders are trained to mobilize women in public meetings.[6]

4.2. Requests of Men and Women

Table 3 shows the fraction of formal requests made by villagers to the Panchayat in the six months prior to the survey by type of good.[7]

In West Bengal, drinking water and roads were by far the issues most frequently raised by women. The next most important issue was welfare programs, followed by housing and eletricity. In Rajasthan, drinking water, welfare programs, and

---

[5]In the subsample of villages in which we conducted follow up surveys, we also asked whether men had brought up any issue in the previous six months. In all cases but one (a reserved GP), they had.

[6]Interestingly, women's participation is significantly higher when the position of council member *of the village* is reserved for a woman (results not reported to conserve space). This difference is probably due to the very long distance between villages in Rajasthan.

[7]We recorded the exact complaint or request: For example, the need to repair a specific well. We classified them ex post into these categories. In West Bengal, we had initially not asked about issues raised by men: A random subset of 48 villages was subsequently resurveyed later.

Table 2. Effect of Women's Reservation on Women's Political Participation

Dependent variables	Mean, reserved GP (1)	Mean, unreserved GP (2)	Difference (3)
West Bengal			
Fraction of women among participants in the Gram Samsad (in percentage)	9.80 (1.33)	6.88 (.79)	2.92 (1.44)
Have women filed a complaint to the GP in the last 6 months	0.20 (.04)	0.11 (.03)	0.09 (.05)
Have men filed a complaint to the GP in the last 6 months	0.94 (.06)	1.00	0.06 (.06)
Observations	54	107	
Rajasthan			
Fraction of women among participants in the Gram Samsad (in percentage)	20.41 (2.42)	24.49 (3.05)	−4.08 (4.03)
Have women filed a complaint to the GP in the last 6 months	0.64 (.07)	0.62 (.06)	0.02 (.1)
Have men filed a complaint to the GP in the last 6 months	0.95 (.03)	0.88 (.04)	0.073 (.058)
Observations	40	60	

Notes:

1. Standard errors in parentheses.

2. Standard errors are corrected for clustering at the GP level in the West Bengal regressions, using the Moulton (1986) formula.

roads were the issues most frequently raised by women. The issues most frequently raised by men in West Bengal were roads, irrigation, drinking water, and education. With the exception of irrigation, men have the same priorities in Rajasthan. A chi-square test rejects the hypothesis that the distributions of men's and women's complaints are the same (at less than 1% in West Bengal, and 9% in Rajasthan). Note that this pattern of revealed preferences is expected, in view of the activities of both men and women in these areas. Women are in charge of collecting drinking water, and they are the primary recipients of welfare program (maternity pension, widow's pension, and old age pension for the destitute, who tend to be women). In West Bengal, they are the main source of labor employed on the roads. In Rajasthan, both men and women work on roads, and the employment motive is therefore common. However, men travel very frequently out of the villages in search of work, while women do not travel long distance; accordingly, men have a stronger need for good roads.

In columns (5) and (11), we report the average across men and women of the fraction of complaints related to infrastructure . . . in West Bengal

and Rajasthan, respectively.[8] In columns (6) and (12), we report the difference between the fraction of issues raised by women and the fraction of issues raised by men. . . . We would expect more investments in drinking water and roads in reserved GPs in West Bengal, less investment in roads in Rajasthan, and less investment in education and irrigation in West Bengal.[9] . . .

4.3. Effects of the Policy on Public Goods Provision

Table 4 presents the effects of the Pradhan's gender on all public good investments made by the GP since that last election in West Bengal and in Rajasthan. As we aggregated investments in categories, these regressions reflect all the data we collected on public good investments.

Both in West Bengal and in Rajasthan, the gender of the Pradhan affects the provision of public

[8]These are the goods that are linked together by a budget constraint for the Panchayat, and therefore where we should see a trade-off.

[9]There are no Panchayat-run schools in Rajasthan.

Table 3. Issues Raised by Women and Men in the Last 6 Months

	West Bengal						Rajasthan					
	Women			Men	Average	Difference	Women			Men	Average	Difference
	Reserved	Unreserved	All				Reserved	Unreserved	All			
	(1)	(2)	(3)	(4)	(5)	(6)	(7)	(8)	(9)	(10)	(11)	(12)
Other programs												
Public works	0.84	0.84	0.84	0.85	0.84	-0.01	0.60	0.64	0.62	0.87	0.74	-0.26
Welfare programs	0.12	0.09	0.10	0.04	0.07	0.06	0.25	0.14	0.19	0.03	0.04	0.16
Child care	0.00	0.02	0.01	0.01	0.01	0.00	0.04	0.09	0.07	0.01	0.02	0.06
Health	0.03	0.04	0.04	0.02	0.03	0.02	0.06	0.08	0.07	0.04	0.03	0.03
Credit or employment	0.01	0.01	0.01	0.09	0.05	-0.08	0.06	0.06	0.05	0.04	0.09	0.01
Total number of issues	153	246	399	195			72	88	160	155		
Breakdown of public works issues												
Drinking water	0.30	0.31	0.31	0.17	0.24	0.13	0.63	0.48	0.54	0.43	0.49	0.09
Road improvement	0.30	0.32	0.31	0.25	0.28	0.06	0.09	0.14	0.13	0.23	0.18	-0.11
Housing	0.10	0.11	0.11	0.05	0.08	0.05	0.02	0.04	0.03	0.04	0.04	-0.01
Electricity	0.11	0.07	0.08	0.10	0.09	-0.01	0.02	0.04	0.03	0.02	0.02	0.01
Irrigation and ponds	0.02	0.04	0.04	0.20	0.12	-0.17	0.02	0.02	0.02	0.04	0.03	-0.02
Education	0.07	0.05	0.06	0.12	0.09	-0.06	0.02	0.07	0.05	0.13	0.09	-0.09
Adult education	0.01	0.00	0.00	0.01	0.00	0.00	0	0	0.00	0.00	0.00	0.00
Other	0.09	0.11	0.10	0.09	0.09	0.01	0.19	0.21	0.20	0.12	0.28	0.05
Number of public works issues	128	206	334	166			43	56	99	135		
Public works												
Chi-square	8.84		71.72				7.48		16.38			
p value	0.64		0.00				0.68		0.09			

Notes:

1. Each cell lists the number of times an issue was mentioned, divided by the total number of issues in each panel.

2. The data for men in West Bengal comes from a subsample of 48 villages.

3. Chi-square values placed across two columns test the hypothesis that issues come from the same distribution in the two columns.

Table 4. Effect of Women's Reservation on Public Goods Investments

	West Bengal			Rajasthan		
	Mean, reserved GP	Mean, unreserved GP	Difference	Mean, reserved GP	Mean, unreserved GP	Difference
Dependent variables	(1)	(2)	(3)	(4)	(5)	(6)
A. Village level						
Number of drinking water facilities	23.83	14.74	9.09	7.31	4.69	2.62
newly built or repaired	(5.00)	(1.44)	(4.02)	(.93)	(.44)	(.95)
Condition of roads (1 if in good	0.41	0.23	0.18	0.90	0.98	−0.08
condition)	(.05)	(.03)	(.06)	(.05)	(.02)	(.04)
Number of panchayat run education	0.06	0.12	−0.06			
centers	(.02)	(.03)	(.04)			
Number of irrigation facilities newly	3.01	3.39	−0.38	0.88	0.90	−0.02
built or repaired	(.79)	(.8)	(1.26)	(.05)	(.04)	(.06)
Other public goods (ponds, biogas,	1.66	1.34	0.32	0.19	0.14	0.05
sanitation, community buildings)	(.49)	(.23)	(.48)	(.07)	(.06)	(.09)
Test statistics: difference jointly significant			4.15			2.88
(p. value)			(.001)			(.02)
B. GP level						
1 if a new tubewell was built	1.00	0.93	0.07			
		(0.02)	(.03)			
1 if a metal road was built or repaired	0.67	0.48	0.19			
	(.06)	(.05)	(.08)			
1 if there is an informal education center	0.67	0.82	−0.16			
in the GP	(.06)	(.04)	(.07)			
1 if at least one irrigation pump was built	0.17	0.09	0.07			
	(.05)	(.03)	(.05)			
Test statistics: difference jointly significant			4.73			
(p. value)			(.001)			

Notes:

1. Standard errors in parentheses.

2. In West Bengal, there are 322 observations in the village level regressions, and 161 in the GP level regressions. There are 100 observations in the Rajasthan regressions.

3. Standard errors are corrected for clustering at the GP level in the village level regressions, using the Moulton (1986) formula, for the West Bengal regressions.

goods. In both places, there are significantly more investments in drinking water in GPs reserved for women. This is what we expected, since in both places, women complain more often than men about water. In West Bengal, GPs are less likely to have set up informal schools (in the village, this is significant only at the 10% level) in GPs reserved for women. Interestingly, the effect of reservation on the quality of roads is opposite in Rajasthan and in West Bengal: In West Bengal, roads are significantly better in GPs reserved for women, but in Rajasthan, this is the opposite. This result is important since it corroborates expectations based on the complaint data for men and women. The only unexpected result is that we do not find a significant effect of reservation for women on irrigation in West Bengal. The differences between investments in reserved and unreserved GP are jointly significant. In West Bengal, we run the same regression for GP-level investments (instead of village-level). The results, presented in panel B, are entirely consistent, and the effect on informal schooling is significant at the 5% level in the GP-level regression.

These results suggest that the reservation policy has important effects on policy decisions at the local level. These effects are consistent with the policy priorities expressed by women. . . .

5. Conclusion

Mandated representation of women has important effects on policy decisions in local government.

Women elected as leaders under the reservation policy invest more in the public goods more closely linked to women's concerns: drinking water and roads in West Bengal and drinking water in Rajasthan. They invest less in public goods that are more closely linked to men's concerns: education in West Bengal and roads in Rajasthan. . . .

These results contradict the simple intuition behind the Downsian model and the idea that political decisions are the outcomes of a Coasian bargaining process. In both of these views of the world, the fact that a woman is the head of the GP should not influence policy decisions. Indirectly, these results also confirm that the Panchayat has effective control over the policy decisions at the local level. These results suggest that direct manipulation of the identity of the policymaker can have important effects on policy.

The findings of this paper are thus important for two main reasons. First, as noted in the introduction, reservations for women are increasingly being implemented at various levels of government. The last country to have adopted such a policy was Morocco, which had a quota of 30% for women in the last parliamentary elections, and the new institutions in independent East Timor are such that for each local government level, one man and one woman must be elected. Second, these findings have implications beyond reservation policy, suggesting that, even at the lowest level of a decentralized government, all mechanisms that affect politician's identities (term limits, eligibility conditions, etc.) may affect policy decisions. This is important at a time in which many new decentralized institutions are being designed around the world.

References

Alesina, A. (1988): "Credibility and Policy Convergence in a Two-party System with Rational Voters," *American Economic Review,* 78(4), 796–805.

Besley, T., and A. Case (2000): "Unnatural Experiments? Estimating the Incidence of Endogenous Policies," *Economic Journal,* 110(467), F672–94.

Besley, T., and S. Coate (1997): "An Economic Model of Representative Democracy," *Quarterly Journal of Economics,* 112(1), 85–114.

Chaudhuri, S. (2003): "What Difference Does a Constitutional Amendment Make? The 1994 Panchayati Raj Act and the Attempt to Revitalize Rural Local Government in India," Mimeo, Columbia University.

Dollar, D., R. Fisman, and R. Gatti (2001): "Are Women Really the "Fairer" Sex? Corruption and Women in Government," *Journal of Economic Behavior and Organization,* 46(4), 423–429.

Downs, A. (1957): *An Economic Theory of Democray.* New York: HarperCollins.

Edlund, L., and R. Pande (2001): "Why Have Women Become Left-Wing? The Political Gender Gap and the Decline in Marriage," *Quarterly Journal of Economics,* 117(3), 917–961.

Ghatak, M., and M. Ghatak (2002): "Recent Reforms in the Panchayat System in West Bengal: Toward Greater Participatory Governance?," *Economic and Political Weekly,* pp. 45–58.

Government of West Bengal (1998): *The West Bengal Panchayat (Constitution) Rules, 1975* Department of Panchayats & Rural Development.

Kanango, S. D. (1998): "Panchayati Raj and Emerging Women Leadership: An Overview," in *People's Power and Panchayati Raj: Theory and Practice,* ed. by Bansaku. Indian Social Institute, chap. 5, pp. 77–95.

Levitt, S. D. (1996): "How Do Senators Vote? Disentangling the Role of Voter Preferences, Party Affiliation, and Senator Ideology," *American Economic Review,* 86(3), 425–441.

Lott, J. R., and L. W. Kenny (1999): "Did Women's Suffrage Change the Size and Scope of Government?," *Journal of Political Economy,* 107(6), 1163–1198.

Moulton, B. R. (1986): "Random Group Effects and the Precision of Regression Estimates," *Journal of Econometrics,* 32(3), 385–397.

Norris, P. (2001): "Breaking the Barriers: Positive Discrimination Policies for Women," in *Has Liberalism Failed Women: Parity, Quotas and Political Representation,* ed. by J. Klausen, and C. Maier. St Martins Press, chap. 10.

Norris, P., and R. Inglehart (2000): "Cultural Barriers to Women's Leadership: A Worldwide Comparison," IPSA 2000 paper.

Osborne, M. J., and A. Slivinski (1996): "A Model of Political Competition with Citizen-Candidates," *Quarterly Journal of Economics,* 111(1), 65–96.

Pande, R. (2003): "Can Mandated Political Representation Increase Policy Influence for Disadvantaged Minorities? Theory and Evidence from India," *American Economic Review,* 93(4), 1132–1151.

World Bank (2001): *Engendering Development: Through Gender Equality in Rights, Resources, and Voice.* Oxford University Press and World Bank.

CHAPTER V

Investment and Finance

Overview: Investment and Finance: The Engines of Growth?

Few doubt that investment in physical and human capital, financed primarily by domestic savings, is crucial to the process of economic development. Educational attainment is included in the Human Development Index discussed in Chapter I, making accumulation of human capital partially synonymous with development according to this measure. Achievement of high per capita incomes without accumulation of modern infrastructure, plant, and equipment seems a virtual impossibility, absent the kind of enormous mineral wealth that places a few oil-exporting countries among the high-income ranks. We are therefore not surprised to see the strong cross-country associations between rapid per capita income growth and high rates of fixed investment and school enrollment in Exhibit V.1. The importance of domestic savings follows from the well-known strong cross-country correlation between the savings and investment shares of GDP (Feldstein and Horioka 1980).

Whether or not savings and investment play a *leading* role in development, serving as "the engine of growth," has on the other hand been a source of controversy since the early days of development economics. The controversy centered on the role of saving to finance investment in physical capital. W. Arthur Lewis (1954, p. 155) wrote, "The central problem in the theory of economic development is to understand the process by which a community which was previously saving and investing 4 or 5 per cent of its national income or less, converts itself into an economy where voluntary saving is running at about 12 to 15 per cent of national income or more." Albert Hirschman (1958) took the opposite position, arguing that if opportunities for profitable projects were there, the requisite investable funds would be forthcoming. Saving could not create such opportunities, and would be wasted in their absence. For example, in an article entitled "The Vice of Thrift," the *Economist* (1998, p. 85) states, "it has become clear that the surge in investment in East Asia in the 1990s was a sign of weakness, not strength. Much of the money was wasted on speculative property deals or unprofitable industrial projects."

Outside of development economics, the received wisdom from growth theory was for many years that savings could not be the engine of growth because of diminishing returns to investment in physical capital. As the stock of physical capital per head increased, the rate of return on investment inevitably fell so low that the incentive for further saving was eliminated. An exceptionally thrifty population could only postpone the inevitable until a higher stock of capital per head was reached. Thus in the long run the propensity to save could only affect the level of per capita income, not its growth rate. The engine of growth was taken to be improvement in technology, which was considered to be exogenous to the saving and investment process. The impotence of savings extended to government policy. Policy could affect the rate of growth of per capita income only if it could affect the rate of technological progress.

The advent of "endogenous growth theory," described in section I.C, changed the message of growth theory regarding savings and policies. The accumulation of physical and human capital through saving was argued to be associated with an accumulation of knowledge that staved off diminishing returns. Without diminishing returns savings and investment could propel growth indefinitely, and policies that changed the rate of saving could change the rate of growth.

The debate over diminishing versus constant or increasing returns, and over exogenous versus endogenous growth theory, is of questionable relevance for development economics. One can argue that the level of capital per head in less developed countries is so low that diminishing returns do not apply, even if they are relevant for more developed countries. As Easterly, Kremer, Pritchett, and Summers state (1993, p. 479), "if countries are far from their steady states, models in which country characteristics determine income look similar to those in which country characteristics determine growth rates." Nevertheless, the development of endogenous growth theory gave a powerful new intellectual foundation to the position within development economics that savings is the engine of growth, and that growth rates can be changed by policies that affect the incentive to save. The AK model, attributable to Rebelo (1991), proved an especially useful vehicle for demonstrating how government policies could have effects on growth. Easterly, King, Levine, and Rebelo (1991) show how policies affect growth in the AK model either by changing the incentive to save or changing the efficiency of saving as measured by the extent to which the marginal private product of capital reflects its marginal social product. Note V.1, based loosely on pages 12–21 of their paper, shows how a simplified version of the AK model yields the results that growth is positively affected by the propensity to save, negatively affected by government income taxation to finance consumption, and ambiguously affected by government income taxation to finance investment in infrastructure.

Recent evidence has favored Hirschman's view that investment and saving tend to follow rather than lead growth. In Selection V.1, Magnus Blomström, Robert Lipsey, and Mario Zejan find that growth in per capita GDP helps to forecast the share of investment in GDP (growth "Granger-causes" investment) but investment does not help to forecast growth. Similar findings for savings, using both country- and individual-level data, are reported by Carroll and Weil (1994). These findings can be interpreted as evidence that growth creates opportunities that induce saving and investment, but unfortunately they do not tell us what causes growth in the first place.

A similar long-running controversy in development economics concerns the financial system: does its development lead or follow growth? One might think that if savings and investment follow growth, so must financial development. However, Ronald McKinnon (1986) claims that "the quality, if not the quantity, of investment improves significantly when interest rates are positive and financial intermediation is robust." It could be that growth is induced when improved financial intermediation allows savings to be channeled to the most profitable projects, even if an increase in the number of projects holding quality constant cannot have the same effect. Exhibit V.1 shows that both the ratio of liquid liabilities of the financial system (such as checking accounts) to GDP and the level of real interest rates (which attract savings into the banking system) are strongly positively correlated with growth in per capita GDP. In

Selection V.2, Ross Levine argues that this kind of correlation reflects a causal relationship from financial development to economic growth. In addition to economic theory and cross-country regression analysis, Levine lists a number of microeconomic studies using data at the firm level that support his argument. Arturo Galindo, Fabio Schiantarelli, and Andrew Weiss (2003) have done a more recent study along these lines using data from firms in twelve less developed countries, which shows that in most of these countries financial liberalization was associated with greater allocation of investment to firms with higher marginal returns to capital. This evidence supporting the hypothesis that financial development causes economic growth cannot be considered decisive, however, given the findings reported in Selection I.B.1 that financial development (as measured by M2/GDP) has improved in recent years yet growth in per capita income has declined.

Domestic investment can be financed by foreign as well as domestic savings. International capital flows can also finance consumption smoothing, i.e., countries can borrow abroad to maintain consumption when income is unusually low and repay these loans when income is higher. Reliance by less developed countries on foreigners to finance either consumption or investment has always been controversial because it leaves LDCs open to devastating crises if foreign lending suddenly dries up, the most spectacular recent example being the East Asian crisis of 1997–98. In Selection V.3, Barry Eichengreen argues that growing international capital mobility is unavoidable, but LDC governments can minimize the risk of crises by strengthening domestic financial markets and opening up to foreign direct investment before liberalizing the access of domestic firms and banks to foreign loans.

Another source of finance for LDCs is foreign aid, meaning loans (at concessional terms) and grants from foreign governments or international organizations such as the World Bank, as opposed to the private sector loans discussed in Selection V.3. William Easterly argues in Selection V.4 that foreign aid often yields poor results because neither the aid agencies nor the LDC governments have proper incentives to ensure that the aid actually raises the productive potential of the LDC citizens who need it the most. Given the perceived failure of large-scale foreign aid, a great deal of hope and excitement has been generated by "microfinance" programs such as the Grameen Bank in Bangladesh, which have used innovative lending techniques to bring the benefits of commercial banking to people previously considered too poor to be good credit risks. A major selling point of microfinance programs has been their very low default rates, yet Jonathan Morduch shows in Selection V.5 that the vast majority of these programs are not financially self-sufficient. Morduch points out that microfinance funds self-employment activities that most often supplement income for borrowers rather than generate new jobs for others. Rather than acting as an engine of growth, microfinance can be caricatured as a means to raise people out of destitution and into poverty. Such an assessment, however, would omit the social benefits of many microfinance programs such as "empowerment" of women that were emphasized in Selection IV.D.1.

References

Carroll, Christopher D., and David N. Weil. 1994. "Saving and Growth: A Reinterpretation." *Carnegie-Rochester Series on Public Policy* 40 (June): 133–192.

Easterly, William, Robert King, Ross Levine, and Sergio Rebelo. 1991. "How Do National Policies Affect Long-Run Growth? A Research Agenda." World Bank Working Paper No. 794 (October).

Easterly, William, Michael Kremer, Lant Pritchett, and Lawrence Summers. 1993. "Good Policy or Good Luck? Country Growth Performance and Temporary Shocks." *Journal of Monetary Economics* 32 (December): 459–483.

The Economist. 1998. "The Vice of Thrift." *The Economist* 346 (March 21): 85–86.

Feldstein, Martin S., and Charles Horioka. 1980. "Domestic Saving and International Capital Flows." *Economic Journal* 90 (June): 314–329.

Galindo, Arturo, Fabio Schiantarelli, and Andrew Weiss. 2003. "Does Financial Liberalization Improve the Allocation of Investment? Micro Evidence from Developing Countries." Processed (October): 2–7, 10–17.

Hirschman, Albert O. 1958. *The Strategy of Economic Development* (New Haven, Conn.: Yale University Press).

Lewis, W. Arthur. 1954. "Economic Development with Unlimited Supplies of Labour." *The Manchester School* 22: 139–191.

McKinnon, Ronald I. 1986. *Financial Liberalization in Retrospect: Interest Rate Policies in LDCs.* Center for Economic Policy Research Publication No. 74, Stanford University (July), processed.

Rebelo, Sergio, 1991. "Long Run Policy Analysis and Long Run Growth." *Journal of Political Economy* 99: 500–521.

Exhibit V.1. Investment and Financial Indicators in Fast and Slow Growth Economies[a] (Cross-Country Averages, 1960–2001)

Indicator (Percent)	Fast-growers	Slow-growers
Share of Investment in GDP	28.6	14.5
Secondary School Enrollment Rates	65.1	19.2
Primary School Enrollment Rates	105.2	70.6
M2/GDP	63.1	17.0
Real Interest Rate	4.5	−1.0

Countries are included if they had per capita GDP data available for the full time period, excluding Iraq, the former Soviet Republics, and all countries with population less than one million.

[a]The mean per capita growth rate for the countries in this sample is 1.9 percent. Fast growers are countries whose per capita growth rate is greater than or equal to the mean plus one standard deviation. The cutoff growth rate for fast growers was 3.6 percent and the number of fast growers is 12. Slow growers are countries with per capita growth rates that are less than or equal to the mean minus one standard deviation. The cutoff growth rate for slow growers was 0.2 percent and the number of slow growers is 11.

Definitions: Investment consists of outlays on additions to the fixed assets of the economy plus net changes in the level of inventories. The gross enrollment rate is the total enrollment rate in a specific level of education, regardless of a students' age, expressed as a percentage of the official school-age population corresponding to the same level of education in a given school year. It can exceed 100 because the numerator, unlike the denominator, is not limited to youths of a given age. Early entry into school and grade repetition are among the reasons that the numerator may include youths outside the appropriate age range. M2 is the sum of currency outside banks, demand deposits other than those of the central government, and the time, savings, and foreign currency deposits of resident sectors other than the central government. The real interest rate is the lending interest rate adjusted for inflation as measured by the GDP deflator.

Source: World Bank, World Development Indicators, 2003.

Note V.1. The AK Model

To begin, we express output per capita y as a function of an aggregate of physical and human capital per head k:

$$y = f(k) \tag{1}$$

Note that all economic activity has been aggregated into one sector that produces GDP or income. Unlike the models of Chapters II and III, no distinction is made between agriculture and industry. Next, we choose a very special functional form for the aggregate production function:

$$f(k) = Ak \tag{2}$$

where A is a constant that does not vary across time or countries. It follows that the marginal product of capital per head is constant rather than diminishing.

There are two time periods in the model: the present (period 1) and the future (period 2). Using equations (1) and (2), we can compute the rate of growth of per capita income g:

$$g = \frac{(y_2 - y_1)}{y_1} = \frac{(Ak_2 - Ak_1)}{Ak_1} = \frac{(k_2 - k_1)}{k_1} \tag{3}$$

where subscript denotes time period. We define investment $i \equiv k_2 - k_1$, the change in capital per head. Investment is assumed to be financed entirely by domestic savings per head s, so that $i = s$: there is no use of foreign savings by borrowing abroad (nor is domestic savings used to finance foreign investment). Substituting into equation (3) yields

$$g = \frac{s}{k_1} \tag{4}$$

Growth in income per capita is determined by savings in proportion to the initial stock of capital.

Since k_1 is inherited from the past and therefore fixed, we can close the model by determining the value of s. We assume that the choice of s is made by a consumer who represents all consumers in the sense that all consumers are assumed to have the same preferences and same income. The representative consumer has income y given by equation (1) and preferences given by

$$U(c_1, c_2) = \ln(c_1) + \frac{\ln(c_2)}{(1 + \rho)} \tag{5}$$

where c denotes consumption per head (i.e., consumption of the representative consumer), ln is the natural logarithm function, and ρ is a parameter called the "discount rate." The natural logarithm function yields diminishing marginal utility of consumption, discussed in connection with the Human Development Index in Chapter I, Section I.A. The discount rate is greater, the more the consumer values present relative to future consumption, that is, the more impatient the consumer is. Thus a lower discount rate is associated with a greater propensity to save.

Savings are given by the excess of present income over present consumption:

$$s = y_1 - c_1 = Ak_1 - c_1 \tag{6}$$

where we have used equations (1) and (2). We assume the capital stock is not consumable, and since there is no borrowing from abroad consumption cannot exceed income and $s \geq 0$. We will choose parameters so that this constraint on savings is never binding, however, and hence will ignore it in what follows. Since the capital stock is not consumable, and the consumer has no later period to save for, he or she will consume exactly his or her income in the future:

$$c_2 = y_2 = Ak_2 = A(k_1 + i) = A(k_1 + s) \tag{7}$$

where we have used equations (1) and (2). Substituting equations (6) and (7) into equation (5) yields the following expression for utility:

$$U = \ln(Ak_1 - s) + \frac{\ln(A(k_1 + s))}{(1 + \rho)} \tag{8}$$

We assume that the consumer chooses s so as to maximize utility. Using the fact that $d \ln x/dx = 1/x$ and rearranging, we obtain the first-order condition $Ak_1 - s = (1 + \rho)(k_1 + s)$, which we can solve for s to get

$$s = \frac{[A - (1 + \rho)]k_1}{2 + \rho} \tag{9}$$

We see that savings are increasing in A, the marginal product the consumer receives on the capital he or she invests, and decreasing in ρ, so that greater impatience yields lower propensity to save, as expected. This solution is valid (the constraint $s \geq 0$ is not violated) provided $A \geq 1 + \rho$.

Finally, substitution of equation (9) into equation (4) yields equilibrium growth in income per capita:

$$g = \frac{A - (1 + \rho)}{2 + \rho} \tag{10}$$

Two points should be made about this result. First, a thriftier (lower ρ) population will generate more rapid growth. Second, the rate of growth is independent of the initial level of capital per head: there is no tendency for richer countries to grow slower or faster than poor ones. Data for the period 1960–2000 actually show a weak *positive* correlation between growth in per capita GDP and the level of per capita GDP in 1960. However, when indicators such as those in Exhibit V.1 are controlled for, it is found that poor countries grow faster than rich ones, a result commonly termed "conditional convergence." Barro and Sala-i-Martin (2004, chap. 12) provide a good review of the evidence.

With savings as the engine of growth, we expect policies that reduce the incentive to save to lower the growth rate. Consider for example income taxation at rate τ to finance government consumption expenditure. In the real world government consumption expenditure might take a form such as food subsidies, but here it is simply a lump-sum grant t to the representative consumer. Although the government budget constraint ensures that $t = \tau y$, the representative consumer treats t as exogenous because it equals total tax receipts divided by the total population and is thus only negligibly affected by his or her own income. Individual savings affect the consumer's after-tax future income but not the size of his or her future government grant, hence the incentive to save is reduced by the fact that the consumer keeps only $1 - \tau$ of the return on his or her investment.

Because the representative consumer's present income and present government grant are both exogenous, equation (6) is unchanged:

$$s = (1 - \tau)y_1 + t_1 - c_1 = (1 - \tau)y_1 + \tau y_1 - c_1 = y_1 - c_1 = Ak_1 - c_1 \tag{6$'$}$$

In equation (7), on the other hand, the representative consumer's future after-tax income is determined by his or her savings, while the future government grant is still exogenous:

$$c_2 = y_2 = (1 - \tau)y_2 + t_2 = (1 - \tau)Ak_2 + t_2 = (1 - \tau)A(k_1 + i) + t_2 = (1 - \tau)A(k_1 + s) + t_2 \tag{7$'$}$$

Substituting equations (6$'$) and (7$'$) into equation (5) yields a new expression for utility:

$$U = \ln(Ak_1 - s) + \frac{\ln((1 - \tau)A(k_1 + s) + t_2)}{(1 + \rho)} \tag{8$'$}$$

We obtain the new first-order condition $(1 - \tau)A(Ak_1 - s) = (1 + \rho)[(1 - \tau)A(k_1 + s) + t_2]$. Substituting for t_2 using the government budget constraint, we can solve for s to get

$$s = \frac{[(1 - \tau) A - (1 + \rho)]k_1}{2 + \rho - \tau} \qquad (9')$$

Note that this solution is valid (the constraint $s \geq 0$ is not violated) provided $(1 - \tau)A \geq 1 + \rho$. Finally, substitution of equation (9′) into equation (4) yields the new equilibrium growth in income per capita:

$$g = \frac{[(1 - \tau)A - (1 + \rho)]}{2 + \rho - \tau} \qquad (10')$$

As expected, growth is lower, the higher is the income tax rate:

$$\frac{dg}{d\tau} = \frac{-(1 + \rho)(1 + A)}{(2 + \rho - \tau)^2} \qquad (11')$$

This result is consistent with the evidence in Barro and Sala-i-Martin (2004, chap. 12) that countries with high ratios of government consumption (such as expenditure on food subsidies) to GDP grow slower than countries where this ratio is low, provided that this higher expenditure is financed by higher taxes that reduce the incentive to save. Barro and Sala-i-Martin also find that fast- and slow-growing countries do not differ in their ratios of *total* government expenditure to GDP. We can understand this finding in terms of the AK model if we think of income tax revenue as financing government investment in infrastructure that is complementary to private capital as well as financing government consumption. A high tax rate then reduces the incentive to save directly, but can increase the incentive to save indirectly by financing accumulation of a larger stock of government-owned capital that increases the return to investment in privately owned capital. Thus a low share of government expenditure in GDP might correspond to inadequate infrastructure, while a high share might correspond to excessive taxation, leading on average to no difference between the government expenditure share of slow- and fast-growing countries. Readers who would like to see this result demonstrated in a formal model should see Easterly, King, Levine, and Rebelo (1991, p. 21).

References

Barro, Robert J., and Xavier Sala-i-Martin. 2004. *Economic Growth, Second Edition* (Cambridge, MA: MIT).

Easterly, William, Robert King, Ross Levine, and Sergio Rebelo. 1991. "How Do National Policies Affect Long-run Growth? A Research Agenda." World Bank Working Paper No. 794 (October).

Selection V.1. Is Fixed Investment the Key to Economic Growth?*

The strong relationship between fixed capital formation shares of GDP and growth rates since World War II has led many writers, such as De Long and Summers [1991, 1992], to conclude that the rate of capital formation or of capital formation in the form of equipment, determines the rate of a country's economic growth.[1] Yet, the strong association between fixed investment or equipment investment and growth, particularly over spans of fifteen to twenty years, does not prove causality. The effects may very well run from growth to capital formation, so that rapid growth leads to high rates of capital formation. An earlier study by Lipsey and Kravis [1987] found that for five-year periods within the longer spans, the rate of growth was more closely related to capital formation rates in succeeding periods than to contemporary or preceding rates. That result suggested that the observed long-term relationships were due more to the effect of growth on capital formation than to the effect of capital formation on growth.

In this paper we address that issue by again examining changes in capital formation and growth over successive five-year periods, but with more formal methods of studying the direction of causation. Our aim is to determine directions of influence and their timing between capital formation ratios and rates of growth. . . .

A first test of the timing issue is provided in the first part of Table 1, which shows simple regressions of five-year growth rates in per capita GDP on preceding, current, and succeeding period fixed capital formation rates (ratios of fixed capital formation to GDP).[2] The coefficients, t-statistics, and $\bar{R}^2$'s increase as one moves from the preceding period to the current one and then from there to the succeeding period. From this timing relationship we are led to suspect that the case for effects run-

ning from growth rates to subsequent capital formation is stronger than that for the effects running from capital formation to subsequent growth.

One risk in using pooled time series and cross-section data, is that the cross-sectional differences among countries reflect permanent characteristics of the countries that encourage or discourage both fixed investment and economic growth. Examples of such characteristics might be the efficiency of government, the degree of corruption, the level of violence, or the attitude of governments and populations toward individual achievement or enterprise. Any such relationship could give a false impression that high fixed capital formation resulted in high growth, or vice versa. To eliminate any such bias, we include country dummies. The effect is to remove cross-sectional differences among countries, leaving only time-series variations to be explained. The main result persists when inter-country differences are eliminated: growth seems to precede capital formation (see the second part of Table 1).

A more formal way of examining the direction of causality is to apply tests in the Granger-Sims causality framework [Granger 1969; Sims 1972]. We first estimate the following equations:

(i) $RGDPC_t = f(RGDPC_{t-1}, RGDPC_{t-2})$

(ii) $RGDPC_t = f(RGDPC_{t-1}, RGDPC_{t-2}, INV_{t-1})$,

where $RGDPC$ is growth in real income per capita, INV is the ratio of fixed capital formation to GDP, and t is the period (see Table 1). We interpret investment to be Granger-causing growth when a prediction of growth on the basis of its past history can be improved by further taking into account previous period's investment.

Estimating (i) and (ii) gives the following results (t-values are in parentheses):

$$RGDPC_t = 0.661 + 0.227\ RGDPC_{t-1}$$
$$(7.0)\quad (3.7)$$

$$+\ 0.142\ RGDPC_{t-2}$$
$$(2.1)$$

$$\bar{R}^2 = 0.06 \quad n = 303$$

$$RGDPC_t = 0.660 + 0.228\ RGDPC_{t-1}$$
$$(6.7)\quad (3.5)$$

$$+\ 0.142\ RGDPC_{t-2} - 0.002\ INV_{t-1}$$
$$(1.9)\qquad\qquad (0.02)$$

$$\bar{R}^2 = 0.06 \quad n = 303$$

*From Magnus Blomström, Robert E. Lipsey, and Mario Zejan, "Is Fixed Investment the Key to Economic Growth?" *Quarterly Journal of Economics* 111 (February 1996): 269–273. Reprinted by permission.

[1] See Levine and Renelt [1992] for a survey of the literature.

[2] We chose five-year periods, partly to dilute cyclical influences, partly to maximize the number of countries included and to use most of the years of the ICP benchmark surveys (the basis for the Summers and Heston estimates), for which the data should be most reliable. However, there is no theoretical basis for this interval, and it might be worthwhile to experiment with others also. Much shorter intervals might, however, give results reflecting business cycle developments rather than the longer term influences that are important for development.

A list of the 101 countries included in the study is provided in Blomström, Lipsey, and Zejan [1994].

Table 1. Regressions of Growth in Real GDP per Capita on Fixed Capital Formation Ratios Without and with Country Dummies

	Fixed capital formation/GDP		
	Preceding period	Current period	Following period
Country dummies excluded			
Coefficient	0.30	0.60	0.80
t-statistic	(3.42)	(5.71)	(8.94)
$\bar{R}^2$	0.03	0.07	0.16
No. of obs.	404	404	404
Country dummies included			
Coefficient	–1.00	–0.01	1.65
t-statistic	(3.95)	(0.04)	(6.78)
$\bar{R}^2$	0.16	0.12	0.23
No. of obs.	404	404	404

Real GDP per capita growth, 1965–1970, 1970–1975, 1975–1980, and 1980–1985 (ratio of end year over initial year).

Ratio of fixed capital formation to GDP, measured in current purchasing power parities, averaged over five-years periods (1960–1965, 1965–1970, 1970–1975, 1975–1980, 1980–1985, and 1983–1988).

Source: Summers and Heston (1991).

Thus, we cannot reject the null hypothesis that capital formation in the preceding period has no explanatory power with respect to growth in the current period, given the past history of growth in that country. The past history of growth is a poor predictor of current growth, but lagged investment does not improve the prediction.

We can then reverse the question to ask whether past growth has an effect on current capital formation rates, given the history of capital formation rates. The results are as follows (t-values are in parentheses):

$$INV_t = 2.48 + 0.948\, INV_{t-1} - 0.075\, INV_{t-2}$$
$$(4.6)\quad (15.3)\qquad\qquad (1.27)$$

$$\bar{R}^2 = 0.79 \quad n = 303$$

$$INV_t = -7.35 + 0.828\, INV_{t-1} - 0.012\, INV_{t-2}$$
$$(4.9)\quad (13.7)\qquad\qquad (0.21)$$

$$+\, 9.49\, RGDPC_{t-1}$$
$$(6.9)$$

$$\bar{R}^2 = 0.82 \quad n = 303.$$

The significant t-statistic on $RGDPC_{t-1}$ suggests that past growth has a significant effect on current capital formation even after past capital formation is taken into account. Even though the past history of capital formation rates predicts current rates well, past growth rates improve the prediction. . . .

In sum, informal and formal tests using only fixed investment ratios as independent variables give evidence that economic growth precedes capital formation, but no evidence that capital formation precedes growth. Thus, the causality seems to run in only one direction, from economic growth to capital formation.

References

Blomström, Magnus, Robert E. Lipsey, and Mario Zejan, "Is Fixed Investment the Key to Economic Growth?" NBER Working Paper No. 4436, 1993.

Blomström, Magnus, Robert E. Lipsey, and Mario Zejan, "What Explains the Growth of Developing Countries?" in William Baumol, Richard Nelson, and Edward Wolff, eds., *International Convergence of Productivity* (London: Oxford University Press, 1994), pp. 243–59.

De Long, J. Bradford, and Lawrence Summers, "Equipment Investment and Economic Growth," *Quarterly Journal of Economics,* CVI (1991), 445–502.

De Long, J. Bradford, and Lawrence Summers, "Equipment Investment and Economic Growth: How Strong Is the Nexus?" *Brookings Papers on Economic Activity* (1992), 157–211.

Granger, C. W. J., "Investigating Causal Relations by Econometric Models and Cross-Spectral Methods," *Econometrica,* XXXVII (1969), 424–38.

Levine, Ross, and David Renelt, "A Sensitivity Analysis of Cross-Country Growth Regressions," *American Economic Review,* LXXXII (1992), 942–63.

Lipsey, Robert, and Irving Kravis, *Saving and Economic*

Growth: Is the United States Really Falling Behind? (New York: The Conference Board, 1987).

Sims, Christopher A., "Money, Income and Causality," *American Economic Review,* LXII (1972), 540–52.

Summers, Robert, and Alan Heston, "The Penn World Table (Mark 5): An Extended Set of International Comparisons, 1950–1988," *Quarterly Journal of Economics,* CVI (1991), 327–68.

Selection V.2. Financial Development and Economic Growth*

A Parable

Consider Fred, who has just developed a design for a new truck that extracts rocks from a quarry better than existing trucks. His idea for manufacturing trucks requires an intricate assembly line with specialized labor and capital. Highly specialized production processes would be difficult without a medium of exchange. He would find it prohibitively costly to pay his workers and suppliers using barter exchange. Financial instruments and markets that *facilitate transactions* will allow and promote specialization and thereby permit him to organize his truck assembly line. Moreover, the increased specialization induced by easier transactions may foster learning-by-doing and innovation by the workers specializing on their individual tasks.

Production requires capital. Even if Fred had the savings, he would not wish to put all of his savings in one risky investment. Also, he wants ready access to savings for unplanned events; he is reluctant to tie up his savings in the truck project, which will not yield profits, if it does yield profits, for a long time. His distaste for risk and desire for liquidity create incentives for him to (a) diversify the family's investments and (b) not commit too much of his savings to an illiquid project, like producing a new truck. In fact, if Fred must invest disproportionately in his illiquid truck project, he may forgo his plan. Without a mechanism for managing risk, the project may die. Thus, *liquidity, risk pooling, and diversification* will help him start his innovative project.

Moreover, Fred will require outside funding if he has insufficient savings to initiate his truck project. There are problems, however, in mobilizing savings for Fred's truck company. First, it is very costly and time consuming to collect savings from individual savers. Fred does not have the time, connections, and information to collect savings from everyone in his town and neighboring communities even though his idea is sound. Banks and investment banks, however, can mobilize savings more cheaply than Fred due to economies of scale, economies of scope, and experience. Thus, Fred may seek the help of a financial intermediary to *mobilize savings* for his new truck plant.

Two additional problems ("frictions") may keep savings from flowing to Fred's project. To fund the truck plant, the financial intermediaries—and savers in financial intermediaries—require information about the truck design, Fred's ability to implement the design, and whether there is a sufficient demand for better quarry trucks. This information is difficult to obtain and analyze. Thus, the financial system must be able to acquire *reliable information* about Fred's idea before funding the truck plant. Furthermore, if potential investors feel that Fred may steal the funds, or run the plant poorly, or misrepresent profits, they will not provide funding. To finance Fred's idea, outside creditors must have confidence that Fred will run the truck plant well. Thus, for Fred to receive funding, the financial system must monitor *managers and exert corporate control.*

While this parable does not contain all aspects of the discussion of financial functions, it provides one cohesive story of how the five financial functions may interact to promote economic development. . . .

The Level of Financial Development and Growth: Cross-Country Studies

Consider first the relationship between economic growth and aggregate measures of how well the financial system functions. The seminal work in this area is by Goldsmith (1969). He uses the value of financial intermediary assets divided by GNP to gauge financial development under the assumption that the size of the financial system is positively correlated with the provision and quality of financial services. Using data on 35 countries from 1860 to 1963 (when available) Goldsmith (1969, p. 48) finds:

(1) a rough parallelism can be observed between economic and financial development if periods of several decades are considered; [and]
(2) there are even indications in the few countries for which the data are available that periods of more rapid economic growth have been accompanied, though not without exception, by an above-average rate of financial development.

Goldsmith's work, however, has several weaknesses: (a) the investigation involves limited observations on only 35 countries; (b) it does not systematically control for other factors influencing economic growth (Levine and David Renelt 1992); (c) it does not examine whether financial develop-

*From Ross Levine, "Financial Development and Economic Growth: Views and Agenda," *Journal of Economic Literature* 35 (June 1997): 701–709. Reprinted by permission.

ment is associated with productivity growth and capital accumulation; (d) the size of financial intermediaries may not accurately measure the functioning of the financial system; and (e) the close association between the size of the financial system and economic growth does not identify the direction of causality.[1]

Recently, researchers have taken steps to address some of these weaknesses. For example, King and Levine (1993a, 1993b, 1993c) study 80 countries over the period 1960–1989, systematically control for other factors affecting long-run growth, examine the capital accumulation and productivity growth channels, construct additional measures of the level of financial development, and analyze whether the level of financial development predicts long-run economic growth, capital accumulation, and productivity growth. (Also, see Gelb 1989; Gertler and Rose 1994; Roubini and Sala-i-Martin 1992; Easterly 1993; and the overview by Pagano 1993.) They use four measures of "the level of financial development" to more precisely measure the functioning of the financial system than Goldsmith's size measure. Table 1 summarizes the values of these measures relative to real per capita GDP (RGDP) in 1985. The first measure, DEPTH, measures the size of financial intermediaries and equals liquid liabilities of the financial system (currency plus demand and interest-bearing liabilities of banks and non-bank financial intermediaries) divided by GDP. As shown, citizens of the richest countries—the top 25 percent on the basis of income per capita—held about two-thirds of a year's income in liquid assets in formal financial intermediaries, while citizens of the poorest countries—the bottom 25 percent—held only a quarter of a year's income in liquid assets. There is a strong correlation between real per capita GDP and DEPTH. The second measure of financial development, BANK, measures the degree to which the central bank versus commercial banks are allocating credit. BANK equals the ratio of bank credit divided by bank credit plus central bank domestic assets. The intuition underlying this measure is that banks are more likely to provide the five financial functions than central banks. There are two notable weaknesses with this measure, however. Banks are not the only fi-

nancial intermediaries providing valuable financial functions and banks may simply lend to the government or public enterprises. BANK is greater than 90 percent in the richest quartile of countries. In contrast, commercial banks and central banks allocate about the same amount of credit in the poorest quartile of countries. The third and fourth measures partially address concerns about the allocation of credit. The third measures, PRIVATE, equals the ratio of credit allocated to private enterprises to total domestic credit (excluding credit to banks). The fourth measure, PRIVY, equals credit to private enterprises divided by GDP. The assumption underlying these measures is that financial systems that allocate more credit to private firms are more engaged in researching firms, exerting corporate control, providing risk management services, mobilizing savings, and facilitating transactions than financial systems that simply funnel credit to the government or state owned enterprises. As depicted in Table 1, there is a positive, statistically significant correlation between real per capita GDP and the extent to which loans are directed to the private sector.

King and Levine (1993b, 1993c) then assess the strength of the empirical relationship between each of these four indicators of the level of financial development averaged over the 1960–1989 period, F, and three growth indicators also averaged over the 1960–1989 period, G. The three growth indicators are as follows: (1) the average rate of real per capita GDP growth, (2) the average rate of growth in the capital stock per person, and (3) total productivity growth, which is a "Solow residual" defined as real per capita GDP growth minus (0.3) times the growth rate of the capital stock per person. In other words, if $F(i)$ represents the value of the ith indicator of financial development (DEPTH, BANK, PRIVY, PRIVATE) averaged over the period 1960–1989, $G(j)$ represents the value of the jth growth indicator (per capita GDP growth, per capita capital stock growth, or productivity growth) averaged over the period 1960–1989, and X represents a matrix of conditioning information to control for other factors associated with economic growth (e.g., income per capita, education, political stability, indicators of exchange rate, trade, fiscal, and monetary policy), then the following 12 regressions are run on a cross-section of 77 countries:

$$G(j) = \alpha + \beta F(i) + \gamma X + \varepsilon \qquad (1)$$

There is a strong positive relationship between each of the four financial development indicators,

---

[1]Goldsmith (1969) recognized these weaknesses, e.g., "there is no possibility, however, of establishing with confidence the direction of the causal mechanisms, i.e., of deciding whether financial factors were responsible for the acceleration of economic development or whether financial development reflected economic growth whose mainsprings must be sought elsewhere" (p. 48).

Table 1. Financial Development and Real Per Capita GDP in 1985

Indictors	Very rich	Rich	Poor	Very poor	Correlation with real per capita GDP in 1985	(P-value)
DEPTH	0.67	0.51	0.39	0.26	0.51	(0.0001)
BANK	0.91	0.73	0.57	0.52	0.58	(0.0001)
PRIVATE	0.71	0.58	0.47	0.37	0.51	(0.0001)
PRIVY	0.53	0.31	0.20	0.13	0.70	(0.0001)
RGDP85	13053	2376	754	241		
Observations	29	29	29	29		

Very rich: Real GDP per Capita > 4998
Rich: Real GDP per Capita > 1161 and < 4998
Poor: Real GDP per Capita > 391 and < 1161
Very poor: Real GDP per Capita < 391

DEPTH = Liquid liabilities to GDP
BANK = Deposit money bank domestic credit divided by deposit money bank + central bank domestic credit
PRIVATE = Claims on the non-financial private sector to domestic credit
PRIVY = Gross claims on private sector to GDP
RGDP85 = Real per capita GDP in 1985 (in constant 1987 dollars)
Source: King and Levine (1993a)

$F(i)$, and the three growth indicators $G(j)$, long-run real per capita growth rates, capital accumulation, and productivity growth. Table 2 summarizes the results on the 12 β's. Not only are *all* the financial development coefficients statistically significant, the sizes of the coefficients imply an economically important relationship. Ignoring causality, the coefficient of 0.024 on DEPTH implies that a country that increased DEPTH from the mean of the slowest growing quartile of countries (0.2) to the mean of the fastest growing quartile of countries (0.6) would have increased its per capita growth rate by almost one percent per year. This is large. The difference between the slowest growing 25 percent of countries and the fastest growing quartile of countries is about five percent per annum over this 30 year period. Thus, the rise in DEPTH alone eliminates 20 percent of this growth difference.

Finally, to examine whether finance simply follows growth, King and Levine (1993b) study whether the value of financial depth in 1960 predicts the rate of economic growth, capital accumulation, and productivity improvements over the next 30 years. Table 3 summarizes some of the results. In the three regressions reported in Table 3, the dependent variable is, respectively, real per capita GDP growth, real per capita capital stock growth, and productivity growth averaged over the period 1960–1989. The financial indicator in each of these regressions is the value of DEPTH in 1960. The regressions indicate that financial depth in 1960 is significantly correlated with each of the growth indicators averaged over the period 1960–

1989.[2] These results, plus those from more sophisticated time series studies, suggest that the initial level of financial development is a good predictor of subsequent rates of economic growth, physical capital accumulation, and economic efficiency improvements over the next 30 years even after controlling for income, education, political stability, and measures of monetary, trade, and fiscal policy.[3]

The relationship between the initial level of financial development and growth is large. For ex-

[2]There is an insufficient number of observations on BANK, PRIVATE, and PRIVY in 1960 to extend the analysis in Table 3 to these variables. Thus, King and Levine (1993b) use pooled, cross section, time series data. For each country, data permitting, they use data averaged over the 1960s, 1970s, and 1980s; thus, there are potentially three observations per country. They then relate the value of growth averaged over the 1960s with the value of, for example, BANK in 1960 and so on for the other two decades. They restrict the coefficients to be the same across decades. They find that the initial level of financial development is a good predictor of subsequent rates of economic growth, capital accumulation, and economic efficiency improvements over the next ten years after controlling for many other factors associated with long-run growth.

[3]These broad cross-country results hold even when using instrumental variables—primarily indicators of the legal treatment of creditors taken from LaPorta et al. 1996—to extract the exogenous component of financial development (Levine 1997). Furthermore, though disagreement exists (Woo Jung 1986 and Philip Arestis and Panicos Demetriades 1995), many time-series investigations find that financial sector development Granger-causes economic performance (Paul Wachtel Rousseau 1995). These results are particularly strong when using measures of the value-added provided by the financial system instead of measures of the size of the financial system (Klaus Neusser and Maurice Kugler 1996).

Table 2. Growth and Contemporaneous Financial Indicators, 1960–1989

Dependent variable	DEPTH	BANK	PRIVATE	PRIVY
Real per capita GDP growth	0.024***	0.032***	0.034***	0.032
	[0.007]	[0.005]	[0.002]	[0.002]
R^2	0.5	0.5	0.52	0.52
Real per capita capital stock growth	0.022***	0.022**	0.020**	0.025***
	[0.001]	[0.012]	[0.011]	[0.001]
R^2	0.65	0.62	0.62	0.64
Productivity growth	0.018**	0.026**	0.027***	0.025***
	[0.026]	[0.010]	[0.003]	[0.006]
R^2	0.42	0.43	0.45	0.44

*significant at the 0.10 level, **significant at the 0.05 level, ***significant at the 0.01 level.
[p-values in brackets]
Observations = 77

DEPTH =   Liquid liabilities to GDP
BANK =   Deposit bank domestic credit divided by deposit money bank + central bank domestic credit
PRIVATE =   Claims on the non-financial private sector to total claims
PRIVY =   Gross claims on private sector to GDP
Productivity Growth = Real per capita GDP growth – (0.3) * Real per capita capital stock growth

Other explanatory variables included in each of the 12 regressions: log of initial income, log of initial secondary school enrollment rate, ratio of government consumption expenditures to GDP, inflation rate, and ratio of exports plus imports to GDP.
Source: King and Levine (1993b)

Table 3. Growth and Initial Financial Depth, 1960–1989

	Per capita GDP growth, 1960–1989	Per capita capital growth, 1960–1989	Per capita productivity growth, 1960–1989
Constant	0.035***	0.002	0.034***
	[0.001]	[0.682]	[0.001]
Log (real GDP per person in 1960)	−0.016***	−0.004*	−0.015***
	[0.001]	[0.068]	[0.001]
Log (secondary school enrollment in 1960)	0.013***	0.007***	0.011***
	[0.001]	[0.001]	[0.001]
Government consumption/GDP in 1960	0.07*	0.049*	0.056*
	[0.051]	[0.064]	[0.076]
Inflation in 1960	0.037	0.02	0.029
	[0.239]	[0.238]	[0.292]
(Imports plus exports)/GDP in 1960	−0.003	−0.001	−0.003
	[0.604]	[0.767]	[0.603]
	0.028***	0.019***	0.022***
DEPTH (liquid liabilities) in 1960	[0.001]	[0.001]	[0.001]
R^2	0.61	0.63	0.58

*significant at the 0.10 level, ** significant at the 0.05 level, *** significant at the 0.01 level.
[p-values in brackets]
Observations = 57
Source: King and Levine (1993b)

ample, the estimated coefficients suggest that if in 1960 Bolivia had increased its financial depth from 10 percent of GDP to the mean value for developing countries in 1960 (23 percent), then Bolivia would have grown about 0.4 percent faster per annum, so that by 1990 real per capita GDP would have been about 13 percent larger than it was.[4] Thus, finance does not merely follow economic activity. The strong link between the level of financial development and the rate of long-run economic growth does not simply reflect contem-

[4]These examples do not consider causal issues or how to increase financial development.

poraneous shocks that affect both financial development and economic performance. There is a statistically significant and economically large empirical relationship between the initial level of financial development and future rates of long-run growth, capital accumulation, and productivity improvements. Furthermore, insufficient financial development has sometimes created a "poverty trap" and thus become a severe obstacle to growth even when a country has established other conditions (macroeconomic stability, openness to trade, educational attainment, etc.) for sustained economic development (Berthelemy and Varoudakis 1996).

Some recent work has extended our knowledge about the causal relationships between financial development and economic growth. For example, Rajan and Zingales (1996) assume that financial markets in the United States are relatively frictionless. This benchmark country then defines each industry's efficient demand for external finance (investment minus internal cash flow). They then examine industries across a large sample of countries and test whether the industries that are more dependent on external finance (in the United States) grow relatively faster in countries that begin the sample period with better developed financial systems. They find that industries that rely heavily on external funding grow comparatively faster in countries with well-developed intermediaries (as measured by PRIVY) and stock markets (as measured by stock market capitalization) than they do in countries that start with relatively weak financial systems. Similarly, using firm-level data from 30 countries, Demirguçs-Kunt and Maksimovic (1996) argue that firms with access to more developed stock markets grow at faster rates than they could have grown without this access. Furthermore, when individual states of the United States relaxed intrastate branching restrictions, this boosted bank lending quality and accelerated real per capita growth rates even after controlling for other growth determinants (Jayaratne and Strahan 1996). Thus, using firm- and industrial-level data for a broad cross-section of countries and data on individual states of the United States, recent research presents evidence consistent with the view that the level of financial development materially affects the rate and structure of economic development.

Not surprisingly, these empirical studies do not unambiguously resolve the issue of causality. Financial development may predict growth simply because financial systems develop in anticipation of future economic growth. Furthermore, differences in political systems, legal traditions (LaPorta et al. 1996), or institutions (Engerman and Sokoloff 1996; North 1981) may be driving both financial development and economic growth rates. Nevertheless, the body of evidence would tend to push many skeptics toward the view that the finance-growth link is a first-order relationship and that difference in financial development can alter economic growth rates over ample time horizons.

References

Berthelemy, Jean-Claude and Varoudakis, Aristomene. "Economic Growth, Convergence Clubs, and the Role of Financial Development," *Oxford Econ. Pap.,* Apr. 1996, *48*(2), pp. 300–28.

Demirgüçs-Kunt, Asli and Maksimovic, Vojislav. "Financial Constraints, Uses of Funds, and Firm Growth: An International Comparison." World Bank mimeo, 1996.

Easterly, William. "How much Do Distortions Affect Growth?" *J. Monet. Econ.,* Nov. 1993, *32*(4), p. 187–212.

Engerman, Stanley L. and Sokoloff, Kenneth L. "Factor Endowments, Institutions, and Differential Paths of Growth Among New World Economies: A View from Economic Historians of the United States," in *How Latin America fell behind.* Ed.: Stephen Haber. Stanford, CA: Stanford U. Press, 1996, pp. 260–304.

Gelb, Alan H. "Financial Policies, Growth, and Efficiency." World Bank PPR Working Paper No. 202, June 1989.

Gertler, Mark and Rose, Andrew. "Finance, Public Policy and Growth," in Gerard Caprio, Jr., Izak Atiljas, and James A. Hanson. *Financial Reform.* New York: Cambridge Univ. Press, 1994, pp. 13–45.

Goldsmith, Raymond, W. *Financial structure and development.* New Haven, CT: Yale U. Press, 1969.

Jayaratne, Jith and Strahan, Philip E. "The Finance-Growth Nexus: Evidence from Bank Branch Deregulation" *Quart. J. Econ.,* Aug. 1996, *111*(3), pp. 639–70.

King, Robert G. and Levine, Ross. "Financial Intermediation and Economic Development," in *Financial intermediation in the construction of Europe.* Eds.: Colin Mayer and Xavier Vives. London: Centre for Economic Policy Research, 1993a, pp. 156–89.

———. "Finance and Growth: Schumpeter Might Be Right," *Quart. J. Econ.,* Aug. 1993b, *108*(3), pp. 717–37.

———. "Finance, Entrepreneurship, and Growth: Theory and Evidence," *J. Monet. Econ.,* Dec. 1993c, *32*(3), pp. 513–42.

Laporta, Rafael et al. "Law and Finance." National Bureau of Economic Research Working Paper No. 5661. July 1996.

Levine, Ross and Renelt, David. "A Sensitivity Analysis of Cross-Country Growth Regressions," *Amer. Econ. Rev.,* Sept. 1992, *82*(4), pp. 942–63.

North, Douglass C. *Structure and change in economic history.* New York: Norton, 1981.

Pagano, Marco. "Financial Markets and Growth: An Overview," *Europ. Econ. Rev.,* Apr. 1993, 37(2–3), pp. 613–22.

Rajan, Raghuram G. and Zingales, Luigi. "Financial Dependence and Growth." U. of Chicago mimeo, May 1996.

Roubini, Nouriel and Sala-i-Martin, Xavier. "Financial Repression and Economic Growth." *J. Devel. Econ.,* July 1992, 39(1), pp. 5–30.

Selection V.3. Taming International Capital Flows

1. Introduction

There are two extreme views on the question of international capital flows. One is that redeploying capital from rich to poor countries promises to dramatically enhance economic efficiency. Assume following Lucas (1990) that output per person in the United States is 15 times that in India and that production in both countries obeys a Cobb-Douglas production function with a common intercept and an elasticity with respect to the capital/labor ratio of 0.4. Then the marginal product of capital in India is fully 58 times its value in the United States. A little capital mobility then goes a long way; it has the capacity to produce a lot of additional output. Moreover, for those who insist that output per person is lower in India than the United States not simply because India has a less capital per worker but also because its government follows more distorting policies, capital mobility applies pressure for reform. It promises to intensify the pressure for governments to follow sound and stable policies by imposing harsh penalties, in the form of capital flight, on those failing to do so. It promises to align domestic interest rates with world interest rates, just as free trade promises to align domestic prices with prices in the rest of the world.

At the opposite extreme, analysts like Rodrik (1998) and Bhagwati (1998) dispute these conclusions chapter and verse. There is no evidence, they insist, that opening an emerging market to foreign financial inflows significantly raises its output or rate of growth. If output per person differs, this is not so much because capital/labor ratios differ but because the parameters of the production function—the intercept capturing overall efficiency and also the elasticity with respect to the capital/labor ratio—differ across countries, reflecting differences in cultural context, institutional inheritance, and technological capacity. In addition, even if the marginal product of capital differs in different uses, it cannot not simply be assumed that financial liberalization will result in resources being redeployed from low-to high-marginal-productivity uses, financial markets being riddled with information asymmetries. The analogy between free trade and free capital mobility, in other words, is fundamentally flawed. To the extent that international capital markets are a source of market discipline,

*From Barry Eichengreen, "Taming Capital Flows," *World Development* 28, no. 6 (2000): 1105–1110. Reprinted by permission.

that discipline is arbitrary and erratic. International investors are prone to overlook weaknesses in the domestic policy environment until they are abruptly brought to their attention, at which point markets overreact. Creditors panic, and the country suffers a devastating financial crisis. The punishment, as Calvo and Mendoza (1996) have put it, is disproportionate to the crime.

The policy advice that flows from these positions is straightforward. Throw open the capital account, adherents to the first view advise, the sooner the better, or be prepared to bring up the rear of the Penn World Tables. Liberalize the capital account at your peril, those who subscribe to the second view warn, or run the risk of repeated crises.

Then there is the messy middle. Output per worker differs across countries, its occupants acknowledge, for both sets of reasons elucidated above. A higher capital/labor ratio therefore promises to raise output, but not necessarily to the extent implied by Lucas's identical-technologies logic. To be sure, capital-account liberalization also heightens countries' vulnerability to crises, but their incidence is neither arbitrary nor capricious. The problem for policy is thus to find an appropriate balance of risks and returns—that is, to liberalize flows just to the point where the benefits, in terms of additional stimulus to growth, continue to dominate the risks, in the form of susceptibility to financial disruptions. It is to find policies toward the capital account with the capacity to shift the frontier of feasible growth-stability combinations outward. It is not whether to live with international capital flows; rather, it is how to tame them.

2. The Messy Middle

Inhabitants of the messy middle find it hard to accept that inward foreign investment is without benefits. Foreign investment was integral to the development of the overseas regions of recent European settlement in the 19th century, when it financed the construction of railways, ports, and urban infrastructure. It came bundled with managerial and technological knowledge. Significantly, the majority of this capital transfer took the form of portfolio investment (Bordo, Eichengreen & Irwin, 1999). It is not obvious from this experience, in other words, that while direct investment has benefits, portfolio investment has only costs. Twentieth century history points to the same conclusion: all of the now-rich economies have open capital accounts and borrow and lend internationally. Why should sauce for the goose not be sauce for the gander?

Moreover, the notion that international financial liberalization is costly is hard to square with evidence that domestic financial liberalization is efficiency enhancing. In principle, the case for domestic financial liberalization should carry over to international capital markets. Indeed, capital-account liberalization itself contributes to the process of financial sector deepening that has proven integral to economic development. By intensifying competition, it undermines rent-seeking and monopoly distortions in domestic financial markets. . . .

Neither is it easy to swallow the opposing view that capital-account liberalization is always and everywhere benign. In the presence of other distortions, removing barriers to capital inflows can reduce welfare (Brecher & Bhagwati, 1982), as predicted by the theory of the second best. In particular, government guarantees for domestic banks and other enterprises can lead to excessive inflows into the sectors receiving the guarantees, creating a serious misallocation of resources (McKinnon & Pill, 1997).

The literature on information asymmetries casts particular doubt on the presumption that financial liberalization results in a superior allocation of resources by showing that this specific distortion can create adverse selection and moral hazard. Adverse selection can occur when lenders have imperfect knowledge of borrower quality and borrowers who are bad credit risks have a strong incentive to seek out loans. When incomplete information prevents lenders from being able to evaluate credit quality, they will only be willing to pay a price for a security that reflects the average quality of firms issuing securities, where that price is likely to be less than the fair market value for high-quality firms but above fair market value for low-quality firms. Because owners and managers of high-quality firms realize that their securities are undervalued (equivalently, credit costs are excessive), they will not wish to borrow on the market. The only firms that will wish to sell securities will be low quality because they know that the price of their securities is greater than their value. Since high-quality firms will issue few securities, many projects with a positive net present value will not be undertaken, while other projects whose net present value is lower than the opportunity cost of funds will in fact be financed. Under these circumstances, a liberalized capital market will not deliver an efficient allocation of resources.

Moral hazard can occur under asymmetric information because borrowers are capable of altering their behavior after the transaction has taken place. Borrowers will wish to invest in relatively risky projects in which they do well if the project succeeds but the lender bears most of the loss if the project fails; lenders, in contrast, will wish to limit the riskiness of the project. Hence, borrowers will attempt to alter their projects in ways that increase their risk after the financial transaction has taken place, and information asymmetries will facilitate their efforts to do so. Under these circumstances, many of the investment projects actually undertaken will be excessively risky. Lenders, anticipating this, will be reluctant to make loans, and levels of intermediation and investment will be suboptimal.

Finally, information asymmetries can aggravate financial instability and heighten crisis risk. This makes it no coincidence that the 1990s were a decade not just of capital-account liberalization but also of financial crises. In markets with incomplete information, lenders may engage in herding which results in sudden market movements. Herding can be rational in the presence of information cascades, when agents optimally infer information from the actions of other agents and therefore act alike. It can arise in an environment of incomplete information when incompletely-informed investors infer that a security is of lower (or higher) quality than previously thought from the decisions of other, presumably better informed, investors to sell (or buy) it. It is clear how such behavior can work to amplify price movements and precipitate crises. Insofar as information asymmetries are likely to be particularly severe where geographical and cultural distance is greatest, there is special reason to be wary of this phenomenon in international markets. Calvo and Mendoza (1997) provide a model of this form of herding: their argument is that financial globalization, by increasing the menu of assets available to investors and promoting portfolio diversification, reduces the returns to investing in acquiring information on individual assets and thereby aggravates incomplete-information problems. It is therefore conducive to herding and volatility. . . .

To be sure, crises have occurred in countries with both open and closed capital accounts. But there is an accumulation of evidence that capital-account liberalization heightens the risk of currency crises (see, e.g., Rossi, 1999) and that it raises the costs when things go wrong.[1] "The

---

[1] In contrast, Rossi (1999) does not report a correlation between capital-account liberalization and banking crises. Credit booms are, however, a reliable leading indicator of banking crises (Caprio, Atiyas & Hanson, 1994), and domestic credit booms are often a side-effect of capital-account liberalization.

greater frequency and cost of currency and twin crises," as the World Bank (1999, pp. 125–126) dryly puts it, "have been associated with surges in international capital inflows—especially private-to-private flows—to developing countries and the growing integration of these economies with world financial markets." This is not to imply that currency speculators strike randomly. Like an infectious disease, they are likely to pick off the weak and not the strong. But as with any plague, even robust health is no guarantee of survival.

All this suggests that optimal policy is neither to throw open the capital account nor to nail it shut. The question is not whether to liberalize but how to do so in a way that maximizes the benefits and minimizes the costs.

3. National Responses

Emerging markets can hope for multilateral assistance and for reforms of the international financial architecture, but at the end of the day they must fend for themselves. For inhabitants of the messy middle, this means adopting the following guidelines for policy.

(a) Open the Capital Account Only After Financial Markets Have Been Liberalized and Decontrolled

This may seem obvious, the point having been made in the 1980s (see, e.g., McKinnon & Mathieson, 1981; Edwards, 1984), but it is worth repeating in light of the international community's indifference and even encouragement of premature capital-account opening in the 1990s.

The 1980s version of the argument was that if capital flows are liberalized when domestic interest rates are capped, as has repeatedly been the case in developing countries, then capital account liberalization is a recipe for capital flight (as in Argentina in the early 1980s). The 1990s version points instead to the need to first strengthen the domestic financial sector, remove implicit guarantees, and impose hard budget constraints on domestic financial institutions. If bank capitalization is inadequate, management will have incentives to engage in excessive risk-taking and use the offshore funding available through the capital account to lever up its bets. If banks' liabilities are guaranteed by the authorities, on the grounds that widespread bank failures would be devastating to a financial system heavily dominated by banks, foreign investors will not hesitate to provide the requisite funding. A simple explanation for why the resolution costs of

banking crises have been larger in the 1990s than in earlier decades and larger in emerging than in advanced economies is the coincidence of these domestic financial weaknesses with premature capital-account opening.

Liberalization of the capital account thus should not precede recapitalization of the banking sector, significant strengthening of prudential supervision and regulation, and the removal of blanket guarantees. The danger is that maintaining barriers to capital flows and foreign financial competition will diminish the pressure for restructuring. But recent experience in Asia and elsewhere casts serious doubt on the notion that capital account liberalization which increases the urgency of complementary financial reforms will necessarily deliver meaningful reform before crisis strikes. Crisis itself can breed reform, of course, but at a price.

(b) Liberalize Foreign Direct Investment First

FDI is the form of foreign investment that most plausibly comes packaged with managerial and technological expertise. It is the form of foreign investment least likely to aggravate weaknesses in the domestic banking system. It is less footloose than portfolio capital and less likely to flee in a creditor panic. All this points to the wisdom of liberalizing inward foreign investment early in the capital-account-opening process.

Again, this advice would seem obvious but for the large number of governments that have failed to heed it. As of 1996, 144 of 184 countries surveyed by the IMF still maintained controls on FDI. One element of the Korean crisis was the government's reluctance to allow inward FDI and its readiness, in the face of foreign pressure, to instead open other components of the capital account. Admittedly, Thailand's lifting of most restrictions on inward FDI in import-competing industries in the 1970s and on export industries in the 1980s did not prevent a serious crisis. But the problem there was that the country also opened the capital account to portfolio flows without strengthening its financial system and rationalizing prudential supervision.

Skeptics such as Dooley (1996) question whether FDI is any more stable than other forms of foreign investment. Data on the volatility of flows (see World Bank, 1999) do not suggest a strong contrast with portfolio capital. But there is an obvious sense in which a foreign direct investor cannot easily unbolt machines from the factory floor in order to participate in a creditor panic. To be sure, direct investors have a particular incentive to hedge by purchasing other financial assets which they can liquidate in a crisis. They can borrow on domestic markets in order to sell short the domestic financial assets needed to take positions in anticipation of a currency crash. The implication is that the share of inward foreign investment in the form of FDI will offer some protection against financial instability in the early stages of capital account liberalization—that is, before the rest of the capital account has been opened and direct foreign investors, like others, can take positions on securities markets to hedge their exposures. But the more open the capital account, the easier it becomes to arbitrage different instruments, and the less the share of FDI in total capital inflows is likely to matter.

The case for liberalizing FDI early in the process of opening the capital account extends to the banking system. Entry by international banks is a way of upgrading management and its risk-management capacity in particular. The same knowledge spillovers that figure in discussions of other forms of FDI apply to financial sector. Insofar as home-country regulation applies, opening the banking sector to foreign investment should raise the average quality of prudential supervision. Insofar as international banks are better capitalized, they are unlikely to engage in excessive risk-taking. For all these reasons, permitting early entry by foreign banks can contribute to the upgrading of domestic financial arrangements that should be a precondition for further capital account liberalization (Demirguc-Kunt, Levine & Min, 1998).

Two caveats should be noted. First, foreign entry tends to squeeze margins and intensify the pressure on weak domestic intermediaries. If gambling for redemption is a problem, that problem is likely to worsen as entry gets underway. Thus, the stabilizing impact of opening the banking system may be less initially than subsequently. This points again to the need to strengthen the domestic financial system at the start of the process of capital account opening. Second, entry by foreign banks will undermine the effectiveness of measures to limit portfolio flows. International banks with local branches and an ongoing relationship with domestic broker-dealers will find it easier than other international investors—hedge funds, for example—to borrow the domestic securities needed to short the currency, controls or not.

can jeopardize the stability of the banking system. When foreign investors liquidate their positions in stock and bond markets, in contrast, their actions simply show up in the prices of securities. In reality, of course, things are not so simple. A stock- or bond-market crash can damage the balance-sheet position of banks and others who themselves hold stocks and bonds. It can make life difficult for entities, including the government, with funding needs and for whom the prices of their liabilities are an important signal of credit worthiness. But the single most reliable predictor turned up by the copious literature on leading indicators of currency crises is the term structure of portfolio capital inflows (Rodrik & Velasco, 1999). This suggests liberalizing foreign access to domestic stock and bond markets before freeing banks to fund themselves abroad.

Unfortunately, securitized markets are almost always and everywhere late to develop. Their informational requirements are formidable. This is why developing countries rely disproportionately on banks for intermediation services, banks having a comparative advantage through their long-term relationships with clients in bridging information gaps. Creating an active stock market requires putting in place a regulatory framework requiring disclosure, discouraging insider trading, and protecting the rights of minority shareholders. This is not easily done in countries with limited administrative capacity, which helps to explain the relative undercapitalization of securities markets in, inter alia, Eastern Europe and the former USSR (Eichengreen & Ruehl, 1998). Corporate bond markets develop only once a deep, liquid and reliable market has first grown up in a benchmark asset, typically treasury bonds. That, in turn, requires a government with a record of sound and stable macroeconomic and financial policies. Where that record is lacking, banks are captive customers for government bond placements, which is not good for their balance sheets and in return for which they receive other favors, which give rise to the domestic financial sector problems alluded to above.

Thus, opening domestic securities markets to foreign investors does not mean that they will beat down the doors instead of waiting for access to the banking system.

(c) Liberalize Stock and Bond Markets Next

Intuitively, foreign investment in securities poses fewer risks than short-term foreign deposits. Because bank deposits are a contractual obligation to repay at par, the withdrawal of foreign deposits

(d) Liberalize Offshore Bank Borrowing Last

Not to repeat, but this is the most fundamental lesson of the Asian crisis and, in a sense, of the literature on sequencing capital account liberalization. It is the message of Korea's crisis, which can-

Figure 1. Chile's external debt.

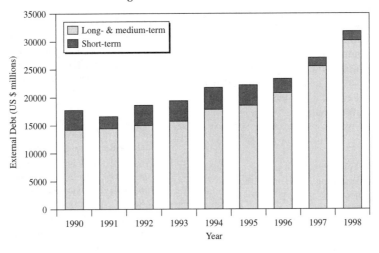

not be understood without reference to the decision to give the banks access to foreign funding before liberalizing other components of the capital account.

Equally, it is important to avoid creating artificial incentives for bank-to-bank lending. Thailand, as already noted, opened other components of the capital account first before giving banks access to offshore funds. But it then created the Bangkok International Banking Facility, under which Thai banks borrowing offshore (and onloaning the proceeds in foreign-currency terms) received favorable tax and licensing treatment. In part, this policy is to be understood as an attempt to develop Bangkok as an international financial center. In part it reflects the government's tendency to use the banks as an instrument of industrial policy. Either way it is indicative of policies that are incompatible with sound capital account liberalization.

(e) Rely on Market-Friendly Instruments for Managing the Capital Account

Advice like the preceding might be taken as encouragement for governments to micromanage the liberalization process. But efforts to fine tune the capital account carry their own dangers. They threaten to create a burdensome administrative bureaucracy conducive to rent-seeking and corruption. The development of financial markets makes it progressively easier for participants to evade the authorities' efforts by relabeling positions and repackaging obligations. Interventions which rely on markets instead of bureaucrats minimize these risks. This is the genius of the Chilean approach to

capital-import taxes. A 30% non-interest-bearing deposit for one year on all capital imports falls more heavily on investors with short horizons than on those prepared to stay for the duration. It is transparent and insulated from administrative discretion. There is less scope for evasion than of taxes on some forms of foreign investment but not others (see Figure 1).

Admittedly, there is an enormous debate over the effectiveness of these measures. Some warn that avoidance is still a problem. Others observe the lack of evidence that Chile's taxes limited the overall level of foreign borrowing. The second objection can be dismissed on the grounds that the goal was never to limit the level of foreign borrowing but to alter its average maturity, and on the maturity front the evidence is compelling (see Hernandez & Schmidt-Hebel, 1999).[2] As for the first objection, it is important to recall that such a measure, to effectively lengthen the maturity structure of the debt, need not be evasion free. The last word on this subject should go to Chile's finance minister, who has asked (I paraphrase), "If these capital-import taxes are so easily evaded, then why do we have so many non-interest-bearing foreign deposits at the central bank?"

---

[2]That studies of other countries that have employed similar policies reach analogous conclusions should be reassuring. See for example Cardenas and Barrera (1995) on Colombia. More generally, Calvo and Reinhart (1999) find in a 15-country panel, including Chile, that the presence of capital controls is significantly associated with portfolio plus short-term capital flows as a percentage of total flows. That they do not find the same when they look at portfolio flows alone suggests that the impact on short-term flows is doing all the work.

The same point applies to the outflow side: taxes are more efficient and less damaging to investor confidence than administrative controls. Thus, Malaysia in its wisdom has moved from comprehensive outflow controls to an exit tax on foreign capital satisfying a minimum-stay requirement. But not too much should be expected of outflow controls in times of crisis, given the strong incentives that then exist for avoidance.

References

Bhagwati, J. (1998). Yes to free trade, maybe to capital controls. *Wall Street Journal,* November 16, *A38.*

Bordo, M., Eichengreen, B., & Irwin, D. (1999). *Is globalization today really different than globalization a hundred years ago?* NBER Working Paper no. 7195, Cambridge, MA: NBER.

Brecher, R., & Bhagwati, J. (1982). Immiserizing transfers from abroad. *Journal of International Economics, 13,* 353–364.

Calvo, G., & Mendoza, E. (1996). Petty crime and cruel punishment: lessons from the Mexican debacle. *American Economic Review Papers and Proceedings, 96,* 170–175.

Calvo, G., & Mendoza, E., (1997). *Rational herd behavior and the globalization of securities markets.* Institute for Empirical Macroeconomics Discussion Paper no. 120–1, Federal Reserve Bank of Minneapolis.

Calvo, G., & Reinhart, C. (1999). *When capital inflows come to a sudden stop: consequences and policy options.* Unpublished manuscript, University of Maryland at College Park.

Caprio, G., Atiyas, I., Hanson, J. A. (1994). *Financial reform: theory and experience.* New York: Cambridge University Press.

Cardenas, M., & Barrera, F. (1995). *On the effectiveness of capital controls in Colombia.* Unpublished manuscript, Fedesarrollo.

Demirguc-Kunt, A., Levine, R., & Min, H.-G. (1998). Opening to foreign banks: issues of stability, efficiency, and growth. In *The implications of globalization of world financial markets* (pp. 83–115). Seoul: Bank of Korea.

Dooley, M. P. (1996). Capital controls and emerging markets. *International Journal of Finance and Economics, 1* (July), 197–205.

Edwards, S. (1984). *The order of liberalization of the external sector in developing countries.* Essays in International Finance no. 156, International Finance Section, Department of Economics. Princeton, NJ: Princeton University.

Eichengreen, B., & Ruehl, C. (1998). Financial institutions and markets in transition economies. In *Transition Report 1998* (pp. 93–105). London: European Bank for Reconstruction and Development.

Hernandez, L., & Schmidt-Hebel, K. (1999). *Capital controls in Chile: Effective? Efficient? Endurable?* Unpublished manuscript. Santiago: Central Bank of Chile.

Lucas, Jr., R. E. (1990). Why doesn't capital flow from rich to poor countries? *American Economic Review Papers and Proceedings, 90,* 92–96.

McKinnon, R., & Mathieson, D. (1981). *How to manage a repressed economy.* Essays in International Finance no. 145. International Finance Section, Department of Economics. Princeton, NJ: Princeton University.

McKinnon, R., & Pill, H. (1997). Credible economic liberalizations and overborrowing. *American Economic Review Papers and Proceedings, 87,* 189–193.

Rossi, M. (1999). *Financial fragility and economic performance in developing economies: do capital controls, prudential regulation and supervision matter?* IMF Working Paper no. 99/66. Washington, DC: IMF.

Rodrik, D. (1998). Who needs capital-account convertibility? In P. Kenen, *Should the IMF pursue capital-account convertibility?* Essays in International Finance no. 207, International Finance Section, Department of Economics. Princeton, NJ: Princeton University.

Rodrik, D., & Velasco, A. (1999). *Short-term capital flows.* Unpublished manuscript. Cambridge and New York: Harvard University and New York University.

World Bank (1999). *Global economic prospects and the developing countries,* 1998/99: *beyond financial crisis.* Washington, DC: The World Bank.

Selection V.4. Can Foreign Aid Buy Growth?

Aid Institutions: Moving the Money

The idea that "aid buys growth" is an integral part of the founding myth and ongoing mission of the aid bureaucracies. The aid bureaucracies define their final objective as "poverty reduction" (today's more politically correct name for "growth") and their immediate output as aid money disbursed. Sometimes they stress the immediate output of aid dispersed more than the final objective of poverty reduction or growth achieved. Judith Tendler's (1975) observation remains true today:

> A donor organization's sense of mission, then, relates not necessarily to economic development but to the commitment of resources, the moving of money. . . . The estimates of total capital needs for development assistance in relation to supply seem to have been the implicit standard by which donor organizations have guided their behavior and judged their performance . . . the quantitative measure has gained its supremacy by default. Other definitions of success and failure of development assistance efforts have been hard to come by.

Although voices have been raised throughout the years against "pushing loans" and "moving money," and change may actually have occurred, the continuity of stressing aid volume is more noticeable than the changes. The World Bank (1998) noted in its report *Assessing Aid* that a stress on disbursing aid had continued: "Disbursements (of loans and grants) were easily calculated and tended to become a critical output measure for development institutions. Agencies saw themselves as being primarily in the business of dishing out money." The World Bank's International Development Agency (IDA) continued to define itself in terms of volume in 2001: "IDA, as the largest source of concessional assistance to the world's poorest countries, plays a critical role in their efforts to achieve growth and poverty reduction." A World Bank (2001) publication, "Ten Things You Never Knew About the World Bank," advertised ten accomplishments of the organization—and all ten involved volumes of assistance for different purposes.

The stress on aid disbursements is understandable given the peculiar nature of the aid mechanism. The beneficiaries are supposed to be the poor of the world, who have little voice in their own governments, much less in the high-income coun-

*From William Easterly, "Can Foreign Aid Buy Growth?" *Journal of Economic Perspectives* 17, no. 3 (Summer 2003): 34–41. Reprinted by permission.

try governments who control the aid agencies. One has little or no feedback from the intended beneficiaries whether aid is in fact raising productive capacity. Moreover, the high-income country governments may have many different objectives for their aid besides poverty reduction, such as rewarding allies, promoting donor country exports or fighting drug trafficking. Multiple objectives often work against each other and weaken each other, so that aid may end up serving none of its multiple goals especially well.

The governments of the poor countries, through which the aid is directed, often have little incentive to raise the productive potential of the poor, especially when doing so might engender political activism that threatens the current political elite. The aid agencies themselves in this difficult environment do not have much incentive to achieve results, since the results are mostly unobservable. One can hardly monitor growth itself for a given country for a given year, since growth in any given year or even over a few years reflects too many other factors besides aid. In these circumstances, it is understandable the aid agencies prefer to emphasize an observable indicator of effort—namely, aid disbursements.

Even when economic performance is clearly deteriorating despite important and rising aid, as in the case of Africa illustrated in Figure 1, the aid bureaucracies try to finesse the issue by promising that better times are "just around the corner." The World Bank, for example, has been singing this refrain about Africa for over two decades. From a 1981 World Bank report, *Accelerated Development in Sub-Saharan Africa* (p. 133): "Policy action and foreign assistance . . . will surely work together to build a continent that shows real gains in both development and income in the near future." From a 1984 World Bank report, *Toward Sustained Development in Sub-Saharan Africa* (p. 2): "This optimism can be justified by recent experience in Africa . . . some countries are introducing policy and institutional reforms." From a 1986 World Bank report, *Financing Growth with Adjustment in Sub-Saharan Africa* (p. 15): "Progress is clearly under way. Especially in the past two years, more countries have started to act, and the changes they are making go deeper than before." From a 1989 World Bank report, *Sub-Saharan Africa: From Crisis to Sustainable Growth* (p. 35): "Since the mid-1980s Africa has seen important changes in policies and in economic performance." From a

Figure 1. Aid and Growth in Africa (10-year moving averages)

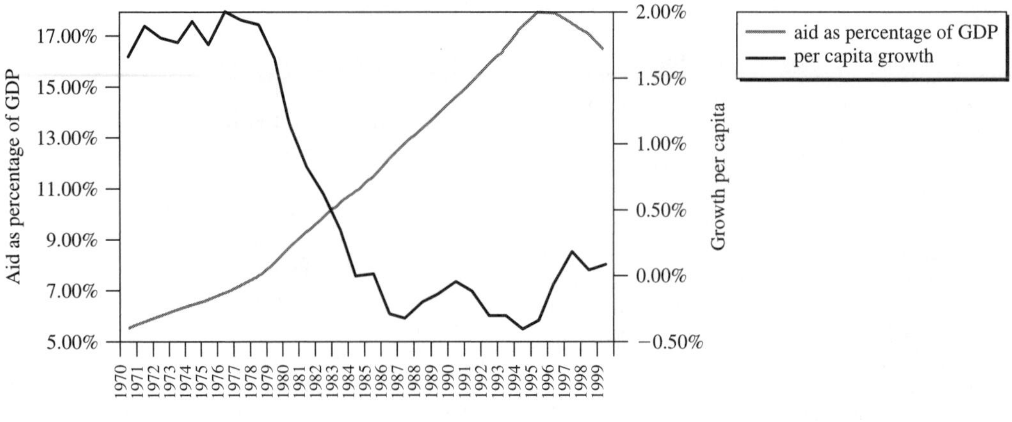

1994 World Bank report, *Adjustment in Africa* (p. 3): "African countries have made great strides in improving policies and restoring growth." From a 2000 World Bank report, *Can Africa Claim the 21ˢᵗ Century?:* "Since the mid-1990s, there have been signs that better economic management has started to pay off." From a 2002 World Bank press release on *African Development Indicators,* "Africa's leaders . . . have recognized the need to improve their policies, spelled out in the New Partnership for African Development (NEPAD)." . . .

Selectivity in Foreign Aid

In some cases foreign aid has been strikingly successful. For example, the World Bank's $70 million loan to the Ceara state government in the Brazilian northeast concluded in June 2001. The loan facilitated innovative government-led initiatives in land reform, rural electrification and water supply and a fall in infant mortality. There are countrywide success stories like Uganda, with heavy involvement by the World Bank and other aid agencies. Earlier success stories associated with aid included South Korea and Taiwan. There are also sectoral success stories, like the elimination of smallpox, the near elimination of river blindness, family planning and the general rise in life expectancy and fall in infant mortality, in which foreign assistance played some role.

However, there are also numerous examples of aid failing. Ferguson (1994) describes a Canadian aid project to help farmers in the mountains of Lesotho gain access to markets and develop modern methods of livestock management and grain production. The problem was that the beneficiaries mainly depended on migration to jobs in South Africa, and they already had access to markets where they had long since learned that grain production was not competitive given the region's poor agricultural conditions. The main long-run effect of the project seemed to be the building of roads that brought grain from South Africa *into* the region—driving the few existing local farmers out of business. An even more dispiriting example is the $45 million World Bank Roads Rehabilitation and Maintenance Project in Sierra Leone, disbursed in the middle of brutal civil war during 1998–2001. About 33 percent of the credit went to compensate contractors for lost time and destruction of their civil works. The rationality of financing infrastructure that was simultaneously being destroyed by rampaging armies is not immediately apparent.

How can scarce aid resources be directed away from less successful projects and toward those more likely to succeed? Aid agencies have two broad sets of tools for this task: imposing conditions on loans before they are granted and evaluating the effect of loans after they are completed. Virtually all observers of aid agencies agree that they allocate too little effort either to insuring that loan conditions were actually observed or to later evaluation of loan effectiveness.

Conditionality

Aid agencies often place conditions on loans and aid (the distinction between aid loans and aid grants is not very meaningful for low-income countries because the loans are heavily subsidized, so I will use "loans" and "aid" interchangeably here). These conditions typically include macroeconomic stability (low-budget deficits and inflation), noninterference with market pricing, privatization of state-owned enterprises and openness to international trade. However, the agencies then often provide additional future loans with little regard for the performance on previous loans. This problem arises for both the World Bank and the International Monetary Fund. The IMF likes to stress that it is not an aid agency. However, in low-income countries, especially in Africa, the IMF has delivered concessional loans on a sustained basis, part of which loans were later forgiven, which is observationally equivalent to delivering "aid" to these nations.

There was no progress on economic reform indicators from one adjustment loan to the next in the same country (Easterly, 2002; Van de Walle, 2001). A common reason for aid to be given even after conditions are violated is that with high political instability, a new government took power and was given a clean slate by the aid agencies. But there are a number of cases where aid was given repeatedly even to the same government in the same country. For example, World Bank reports on Kenya repeated a recommendation for increased funding for road maintenance in 1979, 1983, 1989, 1994, 1996 and 2000. A World Bank (1998) report noted that in Kenya, "the World Bank provided aid to support identical agricultural policy reforms five separate times." Yet the IMF and World Bank gave Kenya 21 adjustment loans during 1980–2000, all under the same regime of President Daniel Arap Moi. President Moi of Kenya got one conditional aid loan each from the World Bank and IMF in the year 2000, despite his poor track record and the new emphasis on selectivity.

Indeed, aid agencies have been repeatedly promising to be more selective for quite a while. Four decades ago, President John F. Kennedy (Message to Congress, April 2, 1963) described: "objective No. 1: To apply stricter standards of selectivity . . . in aiding developing countries." The attempt to foster "structural adjustment," including "structural" reforms such as removing price controls and macroeconomic "adjustments" such as reducing budget deficits, in the developing countries in the 1980s and 1990s was about directing aid money selectively to countries that met conditions of having good policies. The new selectivity is supposed to be about rewarding countries that reform on their own, in contrast to structural adjustment that is now alleged to have imposed reforms on countries. In both cases, aid and concessional loans are selectively available to countries that meet conditions, so if any practical difference exists, it is extremely subtle.

But the fundamental problem remains that both the success of past aid to follow conditions and the failure of past aid to follow conditions are both taken as justifications for future aid. For example, in 2002, a World Bank task force made recommendations on how to direct aid to states convulsed by predatory autocrats and corruption (the World Bank euphemism was "low income countries under stress"). In other words, a nation will selectively receive aid if it is a "good performer"—unless it is a bad performer, in which case it will receive aid from the "bad performer" fund. In these circumstances, the imposition of conditions is no more than a wistful hope, rather than a policy with consequences.

Evaluation

Despite the potential benefits of learning from past experience, aid agencies seem reluctant to promote honest evaluations that could lead to publicity about failures. Aid agencies typically give low priority to evaluating projects after completion. The World Bank reviews only 5 percent of its loans after three to ten years following the last disbursement for development impact (Meltzer Commission, 2000). Even these evaluations are based in part on self-evaluations by the staff in charge of the original projects and their implementing agencies, are done on a paltry budget, and are often sanitized as they are reviewed by management. The World Bank has done surveys of borrowing governments since the mid-1990s on how the bank has performed from the governments' point of view, but the bank has declined to make these surveys public, and there seems to be little mechanism for having managers learn from them (Wade, 2001).

Since what evaluation does take place uses reports from the very people who implemented the project, there are disconnects like that delicately described in OECD and UNDP (1999, p. 26) on Mali:

[I]t has to be asked how the largely positive findings of the evaluations can be reconciled with the poor development outcomes observed over the same period (1985–1995) and the unfavourable views of local people. Gauging the degree to which project objectives are achieved during the actual project period clearly fails to give a proper reflection of the lasting impact on standards of living.

Although I have concentrated here on World Bank experience because of my familiarity with its operations, this focus should not be taken to suggest that the World Bank compares poorly with other official aid agencies. U.N. agencies working on development issues do not have a stellar record; they often appear to spend most of their energies on large international summits that accomplish little beside preparing for further summits. Nor should nongovernmental organizations be automatically assumed to be superior to official aid agencies. There is virtually no systematic evaluation of projects by nongovernmental organizations, and they face some of the same incentives as official agencies to emphasize observable effort rather than focus on less observable results.

Increasing evaluation of the aid agencies need not be especially costly. In some cases, it may involve little more than specifying concrete and measurable objectives (not the dispersal of money) in advance. In other cases, case study information can be made available to outside scholars. In particular, aid agencies have almost never engaged in controlled experiments of particular interventions, despite the small amounts required relative to loan volume. The development literature has increasingly stressed scientific evaluation of interventions through controlled experiments. For example, Duflo (2001) studied an Indonesian school construction initiative that had a quasi-randomized design allowing scientific evaluation. She was able to derive estimates of the effect of school construction on learning and wages. Likewise, Kremer and Miguel (forthcoming) analyzed randomized controlled trials of treatment of intestinal parasites (worms) in school children. They found positive effects on children's school performance of a deworming program. Interventions whose value is confirmed by scientific evaluation are far from being the missing panacea, but it is clear that this kind of scientific rigor has been much too slow to find its way into the aid agencies.

In 1998, as part of legislation authorizing additional funds from the U.S. government to the International Monetary Fund, the U.S. Congress set up an advisory commission, chaired by Alan Meltzer, to consider the future roles of several international financial institutions. One of the recommendations of the Meltzer commission was that aid agencies like the World Bank undergo an independent evaluation (International Financial Institution Advisory Commission, 2000). Despite the good sense of this recommendation, it has yet to happen, maybe because the bank management feels it is being singled out. Perhaps aid agencies should collectively agree to an "Evaluation Compact" in which they all agree to an independent evaluation of their effectiveness.

The results of such evaluations could shed light on what makes aid institutions work well or less well, a subject on which there is surprisingly little knowledge after five decades of foreign aid. Aid agencies face a peculiar incentive problem: they spend one group of people's money on a different group of people. The intended beneficiaries have almost no voice in how the money is spent. There has been surprisingly little research thinking about how to design proper incentives for aid agencies to achieve results in this situation, as well as how the aid agencies can design contracts to create good incentives for recipients. Such research would likely involve principal-agent theory, organization theory, game theory and political economy.

A Realistic Vision for Foreign Aid

How to achieve a beneficial aggregate impact of foreign aid remains a puzzle. Aid agencies should set more modest objectives than expecting aid to "launch the takeoff into self-sustained growth." Aid agencies have misspent much effort looking for the Next Big Idea that would enable aid to buy growth. Poor nations include an incredible variety of institutions, cultures and histories; millennia-old civilizations in gigantic China and India; African nations convulsed by centuries of the slave trade, colonialism, arbitrary borders, tropical diseases and local despots; Latin American nations with two centuries of independence and five centuries of extreme inequality; Islamic civilizations with a long history of technical advance relative to the West and then a falling behind; and recently created nations like tiny East Timor. The idea of aggregating all this diversity into a "developing world" that will "take off" with foreign aid is a heroic simplification. World Bank President James Wolfensohn (2001) talked in 2001 about how "we" must act to achieve the goal of "ensuring a beneficial globalization" by doubling foreign aid. President George W. Bush said in his announcement of increased aid in March 2002: "We must include every African, every Asian, every Latin American, every Muslim, in an expanding circle of development." In virtually no other field of economics do economists and policymakers promise such large welfare benefits for modest policy interventions as "we" do in aid and growth. The macroeconomic evidence does not support these claims. There is no Next Big Idea that will make the small amount of foreign aid the catalyst for economic growth of the world's poor nations.

The goal of having the high-income people make some kind of transfer to very poor people remains a worthy one, despite the disappointments of the past. But the appropriate goal of foreign aid is neither to move as much money as politically possible, nor to foster societywide transformation from poverty to wealth. The goal is simply to benefit some poor people some of the time.

If some of the flaws noted in this article can be corrected, the international aid agencies could evolve into more effective and more accountable agencies, much as national governments in the now-rich countries gradually evolved from gangs of venal scoundrels to somewhat more effective and accountable civil servants (with plenty of further evolution still desirable in both cases!). In any case, improving quality of aid should come before increasing quantity. This step is difficult but not impossible.

I recently made a trip to Ethiopia, where amidst other business, I visited a project of a British aid organization called Water Aid, which receives funds from official aid agencies. Water Aid has put in a water pipe to carry clean water from springs on top of the mountains bordering the Great Rift Valley to villages down in the Valley. The project was run entirely by Ethiopians, with representatives from the villages on the board of the agency. At a bustling water tap in one village, the villagers watered their cattle and collected drinking water for a nominal fee paid to Water Aid, to be used for maintenance of the system. Previously, the villagers had walked every other day two miles to collect water from a polluted river that transmitted disease. Children had been kept out of school, farmers kept out of farming, all to pursue the all-consuming and back-breaking task of fetching water. With the new water pipe, life was better. I don't know if this experience is replicable on a broader scale or even if this anecdote of Water Aid offers any insight into how to make aid more effective. But I am glad that some aid dollars can reach some very needy people some of the time.

References

Duflo, Esther. 2001. "Schooling and Labor Market Consequences of School Construction in Indonesia: Evidence from an Unusual Policy Experiment." *American Economic Review.* September, 91:4, pp. 795–813.

Easterly, William. 2002. "What Did Structural Adjustment Adjust? The Association of Policies and Growth with Repeated IMF and World Bank Adjustment Loans." Working paper, Center for Global Development; available at (www.cgdev.org).

Ferguson, James. 1994. *The Anti-Politics Machine: "Development," Depoliticization and Bureaucratic Power in Lesotho.* Minneapolis: University of Minnesota Press.

Kremer, Michael and Edward Miguel. 2001. "Worms: Identifying Impacts on Education and Health in the Presence of Treatment Externalities." NBER Working Paper No. 8481. Forthcoming, *Econometrica.*

Meltzer Commission Report. 2000. March; available at ⟨http://www.house.gov/jec/imf/meltzer.pdf⟩.

OECD and UNDP. 1999. *Improving the Effectiveness of Aid Systems: The Case of Mali.* OECD: Paris.

Tendler, Judith. 1975. *Inside Foreign Aid.* Baltimore, Md.: Johns Hopkins University Press.

Van de Walle, Nicolas. 2001. *African Economies and the Politics of Permanent Crisis, 1979–99.* Cambridge: Cambridge University Press.

Wade, Robert. 2001. "The U.S. Role in the Malaise at the World Bank: Get Up Gulliver!" G-24 Discussion Paper Series, September.

Wolfensohn, James. 2001. World Bank President James Wolfensohn, remarks to G-20 Finance Ministers and Central Bank Governors, November 17; available at ⟨http://www.worldbank.org/html/extdr/???extme/jdwsp111701.htm⟩.

World Bank. 1981. *Accelerated Development in Sub-Saharan Africa: An Agenda for Action.* Washington, D.C.: World Bank.

World Bank. 1984. *Toward Sustained Development in Sub-Saharan African: A Joint Program of Action.* Washington, D.C.: World Bank.

World Bank. 1986. *Financing Adjustment with Growth in Sub-Saharan Africa, 1986–90.* Washington, D.C.: World Bank.

World Bank. 1989. *Sub-Saharan Africa: From Crisis to Sustainable Growth—A Long Term Perspective Study.* Washington, D.C.: World Bank.

World Bank. 1994. *Adjustment in Africa: Reforms, Results, and the Road Ahead.* Washington, D.C.: World Bank.

World Bank. 1998. *Assessing Aid: What Works, What Doesn't, and Why.* Washington, D.C.: World Bank.

World Bank. 2000. *Can Africa Claim the 21st Century?* Washington, D.C.: World Bank.

World Bank. 2001. *Ten Things You Never Knew About the World Bank.* Washington, D.C.: World Bank.

World Bank. 2002. *African Development Indicators.* Press Release, April 11.

Selection V.5. The Microfinance Promise

1. Introduction

About one billion people globally live in households with per capita incomes of under one dollar per day. The policymakers and practitioners who have been trying to improve the lives of that billion face an uphill battle. Reports of bureaucratic sprawl and unchecked corruption abound. And many now believe that government assistance to the poor often creates dependency and disincentives that make matters worse, not better. Moreover, despite decades of aid, communities and families appear to be increasingly fractured, offering a fragile foundation on which to build.

Amid the dispiriting news, excitement is building about a set of unusual financial institutions prospering in distant corners of the world—especially Bolivia, Bangladesh, and Indonesia. The hope is that much poverty can be alleviated—and that economic and social structures can be transformed fundamentally—by providing financial services to low-income households. These institutions, united under the banner of microfinance, share a commitment to serving clients that have been excluded from the formal banking sector. Almost all of the borrowers do so to finance self-employment activities, and many start by taking loans as small as $75, repaid over several months or a year. Only a few programs require borrowers to put up collateral, enabling would-be entrepreneurs with few assets to escape positions as poorly paid wage laborers or farmers.

Some of the programs serve just a handful of borrowers while others serve millions. In the past two decades, a diverse assortment of new programs has been set up in Africa, Asia, Latin America, Canada, and roughly 300 U.S. sites from New York to San Diego (*The Economist* 1997). Globally, there are now about 8 to 10 million households served by microfinance programs, and some practitioners are pushing to expand to 100 million poor households by 2005. As James Wolfensohn, the president of the World Bank, has been quick to point out, helping 100 million households means that as many as 500–600 million poor people could benefit. Increasing activity in the United States can be expected as banks turn to microfinance encour-

aged by new teeth added to the Community Reinvestment Act of 1977 (Timothy O'Brien 1998).

The programs point to innovations like "group-lending" contracts and new attitudes about subsidies as the keys to their successes. Group-lending contracts effectively make a borrower's neighbors co-signers to loans, mitigating problems created by informational asymmetries between lender and borrower. Neighbors now have incentives to monitor each other and to exclude risky borrowers from participation, promoting repayments even in the absence of collateral requirements. The contracts have caught the attention of economic theorists, and they have brought global recognition to the group-lending model of Bangladesh's Grameen Bank. . . .

Advocates who lean left highlight the "bottom-up" aspects, attention to community, focus on women, and, most importantly, the aim to help the underserved. It is no coincidence that the rise of microfinance parallels the rise of nongovernmental organizations (NGOs) in policy circles and the newfound attention to "social capital" by academics (e.g., Robert Putnam 1993). Those who lean right highlight the prospect of alleviating poverty while providing incentives to work, the nongovernmental leadership, the use of mechanisms disciplined by market forces, and the general suspicion of ongoing subsidization.

There are good reasons for excitement about the promise of microfinance, especially given the political context, but there are also good reasons for caution. Alleviating poverty through banking is an old idea with a checkered past. Poverty alleviation through the provision of subsidized credit was a centerpiece of many countries' development strategies from the early 1950s through the 1980s, but these experiences were nearly all disasters. Loan repayment rates often dropped well below 50 percent; costs of subsidies ballooned; and much credit was diverted to the politically powerful, away from the intended recipients (Dale Adams, Douglas Graham, and J. D. von Pischke 1984).

What is new? Although very few programs require collateral, the major new programs report loan repayment rates that are in almost all cases above 95 percent. The programs have also proven able to reach poor individuals, particularly women, that have been difficult to reach through alternative approaches. Nowhere is this more striking than in Bangladesh, a predominantly Muslim country tra-

*From Jonathan Morduch, "The Microfinance Promise," *Journal of Economic Literature* 37 (December 1999): 1569–1571, 1573–1576, 1578–1580, 1582–1585, 1587–1589, 1592–1594, 1609–1610. Reprinted by permission.

ditionally viewed as culturally conservative and male-dominated. The programs there together serve close to five million borrowers, the vast majority of whom are women, and, in addition to providing loans, some of the programs also offer education on health issues, gender roles, and legal rights. The new programs also break from the past by eschewing heavy government involvement and by paying close attention to the incentives that drive efficient performance.

But things are happening fast—and getting much faster. In 1997, a high profile consortium of policymakers, charitable foundations, and practitioners started a drive to raise over $20 billion for microfinance start-ups in the next ten years (*Microcredit Summit Report 1997*). Most of those funds are being mobilized and channeled to new, untested institutions, and existing resources are being reallocated from traditional poverty alleviation programs to microfinance. With donor funding pouring in, practitioners have limited incentives to step back and question exactly how and where monies will be best spent.

The evidence described below, however, suggests that the greatest promise of microfinance is so far unmet, and the boldest claims do not withstand close scrutiny. High repayment rates have seldom translated into profits as advertised. As Section 4 shows, most programs continue to be subsidized directly through grants and indirectly through soft terms on loans from donors. Moreover, the programs that are breaking even financially are not those celebrated for serving the poorest clients. A recent survey shows that even poverty-focused programs with a "commitment" to achieving financial sustainability cover only about 70 percent of their full costs (*MicroBanking Bulletin* 1998). While many hope that weak financial performances will improve over time, even established poverty-focused programs like the Grameen Bank would have trouble making ends meet without ongoing subsidies.

The continuing dependence on subsidies has given donors a strong voice, but, ironically, they have used it to preach against ongoing subsidization. The fear of repeating past mistakes has pushed donors to argue that subsidization should be used only to cover start-up costs. But if money spent to support microfinance helps to meet social objectives in ways not possible through alternative programs like workfare or direct food aid, why not continue subsidizing microfinance? Would the world be better off if programs like the Grameen Bank were forced to shut their doors? . . .

2. New Approaches

Received wisdom has long been that lending to poor households is doomed to failure: costs are too high, risks are too great, savings propensities are too low, and few households have much to put up as collateral. Not long ago, the norm was heavily subsidized credit provided by government banks with repayment rates of 70–80 percent at best. In Bangladesh, for example, loans targeted to poor households by traditional banks had repayment rates of 51.6 percent in 1980. By 1988–89, a year of bad flooding, the repayment rate had fallen to 18.8 percent (M. A. Khalily and Richard Meyer 1993). Similarly, by 1986 repayment rates sank to 41 percent for subsidized credit delivered as part of India's high-profile Integrated Rural Development Program (Robert Pulley 1989). These programs offered heavily subsidized credit on the premise that poor households cannot afford to borrow at high interest rates.

But the costs quickly mounted and the programs soon bogged down government budgets, giving little incentive for banks to expand. Moreover, many bank managers were forced to reduce interest rates on deposits in order to compensate for the low rates on loans. In equilibrium, little in the way of savings was collected, little credit was delivered, and default rates accelerated as borrowers began to perceive that the banks would not last long. The repeated failures appeared to confirm suspicions that poor households are neither credit-worthy nor able to save much. Moreover, subsidized credit was often diverted to politically-favored non-poor households (Adams and von Pischke 1992). Despite good intentions, many programs proved costly and did little to help the intended beneficiaries.

The experience of Bangladesh's Grameen Bank turned this around, and now a broad range of financial institutions offer alternative microfinance models with varying philosophies and target groups. Other pioneers described below include BancoSol of Bolivia, the Bank Rakyat Indonesia, the Bank Kredit Deas of Indonesia, and the village banks started by the Foundation for International Community Assistance (FINCA). The programs below were chosen with an eye to illustrating the diversity of mechanisms in use, and Table 1 highlights particular mechanisms.

The Grameen Bank, Bangladesh

The idea for the Grameen Bank did not come down from the academy, nor from ideas that started in high-income countries and then spread

Table 1. Characteristics of Selected Leading Microfinance Programs

	Grameen Bank, Bangladesh	Banco-Sol, Bolivia	Bank Rakyat Indonesia *Unit Desa*	Badan Kredit Desa, Indonesia	FINCA Village banks
Membership	2.4 million	81,503	2 million borrowers; 16 million depositors	765,586	89,986
Average loan balance	$134	$909	$1007	$71	$191
Typical loan term	1 year	4–12 months	3–24 months	3 months	4 months
Percent female members	95%	61%	23%	—	95%
Mostly rural? Urban?	rural	urban	mostly rural	rural	mostly rural
Group-lending contracts?	yes	yes	no	no	no
Collateral required?	no	no	yes	no	no
Voluntary savings emphasized?	no	yes	yes	no	yes
Progressive lending?	yes	yes	yes	yes	yes
Regular repayment schedules	weekly	flexible	flexible	flexible	weekly
Target clients for lending	poor	largely non-poor	non-poor	poor	poor
Currently financially sustainable?	no	yes	yes	yes	no
Nominal interest rate on loans (per year)	20%	47.5–50.5%	32–43%	55%	36–48%
Annual consumer price inflation, 1996	2.7%	12.4%	8.0%	8.0%	—

Sources: Grameen Bank: through August 1998, www.grameen.com; loan size is from December 1996, calculated by author. BancoSol: through December 1998, from Jean Steege, ACCION International, personal communication. Interest rates include commission and are for loans denominated in bolivianos; base rates on dollar loans are 25–31%. BRI and BKD: through December 1994 (BKD) and December 1996 (BRI), from BRI annual data and Don Johnston, personal communication. BRI interest rates are effective rates. FINCA: through July 1998, www.villagebanking.org. Inflation rate: World Bank, *World Development Indicators 1998.*

broadly. Programs that have been set up in North Carolina, New York City, Chicago, Boston, and Washington, D.C. cite Grameen as an inspiration. In addition, Grameen's group lending model has been replicated in Bolivia, Chile, China, Ethiopia, Honduras, India, Malaysia, Mali, the Philippines, Sri Lanka, Tanzania, Thailand, the U.S., and Vietnam. When Bill Clinton was still governor, it was Muhammad Yunus, founder of the Grameen Bank (and a Vanderbilt-trained economist), who was called on to help set up the Good Faith Fund in Arkansas, one of the early microfinance organizations in the U.S. As Yunus (1995) describes the beginning:

Bangladesh had a terrible famine in 1974. I was teaching economics in a Bangladesh university at that time. You can guess how difficult it is to teach the elegant theories of economics when people are dying of hunger all around you. Those theories appeared like cruel jokes. I became a drop-out from formal economics. I wanted to learn economics from the poor in the village next door to the university campus.

Yunus found that most villagers were unable to obtain credit at reasonable rates, so he began by lending them money from his own pocket, allow-

ing the villagers to buy materials for projects like weaving bamboo stools and making pots (*New York Times* 1997). Ten years later, Yunus had set up the bank, drawing on lessons from informal financial institutions to lend exclusively to groups of poor households. Common loan uses include rice processing, livestock raising, and traditional crafts.

The groups form voluntarily, and, while loans are made to individuals, all in the group are held responsible for loan repayment. The groups consist of five borrowers each, with lending first to two, then to the next two, and then to the fifth. These groups of five meet together weekly with seven other groups, so that bank staff meet with forty clients at a time. According to the rules, if one member ever defaults, all in the group are denied subsequent loans. The contracts take advantage of local information and the "social assets" that are at the heart of local enforcement mechanisms. Those mechanisms rely on informal insurance relationships and threats, ranging from social isolation to physical retribution, that facilitate borrowing for households lacking collateral (Besley and Coate 1995). The programs thus combine the scale advantages of a standard bank with mechanisms long used in traditional, group-based modes of informal finance, such as rotating savings and credit associations (Besley, Coate, and Glenn Loury 1993).[1]

The Grameen Bank now has over two million borrowers, 95 percent of whom are women, receiving loans that total $30–40 million per month. Reported recent repayment rates average 97–98 percent, . . . relevant rates average about 92 percent and have been substantially lower in recent years.

Most loans are for one year with a nominal interest rate of 20 percent (roughly a 15–16 percent real rate). Calculations . . . suggest, however, that Grameen would have had to charge a nominal rate of around 32 percent in order to become fully financially sustainable (holding the current cost structure constant). The management argues that such an increase would undermine the bank's social mission (Shahidur Khandker 1998), but there is little solid evidence that speaks to the issue. . . .

Kredit Desa, Indonesia

The Bank Kredit Desa system (BKDs) in rural Indonesia . . . is much less well-known. . . . Loans are made to individuals and the operation is financially viable. At the end of 1994, the BKDs generated profits of $4.73 million on $30 million of net loans outstanding to 765,586 borrowers.

Like Grameen-style programs, the BKDs lend to the poorest households, and scale is small, with an emphasis on petty traders and an average loan size of $71 in 1994. The term of loans is generally 10–12 weeks with weekly repayment and interest of 10 percent on the principal. Christen et al. (1995) calculate that this translates to a 55 percent nominal annual rate and a 46 percent real rate in 1993. Loan losses in 1994 were just under 4 percent of loans outstanding (Johnston 1996).

Also as in most microfinance programs, loans do not require collateral. The innovation of the BKDs is to allocate funds through village-level management commissions led by village heads. This works in Indonesia since there is a clear sys-

tem of authority that stretches from Jakarta down to the villages. The BKDs piggy-back on this structure, and the management commissions thus build in many of the advantages of group lending (most importantly, exploiting local information and enforcement mechanisms) while retaining an individual-lending approach. The commissions are able to exclude the worst credit risks but appear to be relatively democratic in their allocations. . . .

3. Microfinance Mechanisms

The . . . programs above highlight the diversity of approaches spawned by the common idea of lending to low-income households. Group lending has taken most of the spotlight, and the idea has had immediate appeal for economic theorists and for policymakers with a vision of building programs around households' "social" assets, even when physical assets are few. But its role has been exaggerated: group lending is not the only mechanism that differentiates microfinance contracts from standard loan contracts.[2] The programs described above also use dynamic incentives, regular repayment schedules, and collateral substitutes to help maintain high repayment rates. Lending to women can also be a benefit from a financial perspective.

As shown in Table 1, just two of the five programs use explicit group-lending contracts, but all lend in increasing amounts over time ("progressive" lending), offer terms that are substantially better than alternative credit sources, and cut off borrowers in default. Most also require weekly or semi-weekly repayments, beginning soon after loan receipt. . . .

Dynamic Incentives

. . . Programs typically begin by lending just small amounts and then increasing loan size upon satisfactory repayment. The repeated nature of the interactions—and the credible threat to cut off any future lending when loans are not repaid—can be exploited to overcome information problems and improve efficiency, whether lending is group-based or individual-based.[3]

Incentives are enhanced further if borrowers can anticipate a stream of increasingly larger loans.

---

[1]In a rotating savings and credit association, a group of participants puts contributions into a pot that is given to a single member. This is repeated over time until each member has had a turn, with order determined by list, lottery, or auction. Most microfinance contracts build on the use of groups but mobilize capital from outside the area. ROSCA participants are often women, and in the U.S. involvement is active in new immigrant communities, including among Koreans, Vietnamese, Mexicans, Salvadorans, Guatemalans, Trinidadians, Jamaicans, Barbadans, and Ethiopians. Involvement had been active earlier in the century among Japanese and Chinese Americans, but it is not common now (Light and Pham 1998). Rutherford (1998) and Armendariz and Morduch (1998) describe links of ROSCAs and microfinance mechanisms.

[2]Ghatak and Guinnane (1999) provide an excellent review of group-lending contracts. Monica Huppi and Gershon Feder (1990) provide an early perspective. Armendariz and Morduch (1998) describe the functioning of alternative mechanisms.

[3]See the general theoretical treatment in Bolton and Scharfstein (1990) and the application to microfinance contracts in Armendariz and Morduch (1998).

(Hulme and Mosley 1996 term this "progressive lending," and the ACCION network calls it "step lending.") . . . Keeping interest rates relatively low is critical, since the advantage of microfinance programs lies in their offering services at rates that are more attractive than competitors' rates. Thus, the Bank Rakyat Indonesia (BRI) and BancoSol charge high rates, but they keep levels well below rates that moneylenders traditionally charge. . . .

Dynamic incentives will also work better in areas with relatively low mobility. In urban areas, for example, where households come and go, it may not be easy to catch defaulters who move across town and start borrowing again with a clean slate at a different branch or program. BRI has faced greater trouble securing repayments in their urban programs than in their rural ones, which may be due to greater urban mobility.

Relying on dynamic incentives also runs into problems common to all finite repeated games. If the lending relationship has a clear end, borrowers have incentives to default in the final period. Anticipating that, the lender will not lend in the final period, giving borrowers incentives to default in the penultimate period—and so forth until the entire mechanism unravels. Thus, unless there is substantial uncertainty about the end date—or if "graduation" from one program to the next is well-established (ad infinitum), dynamic incentives have limited scope on their own.

One quite different advantage of progressive lending is the ability to test borrowers with small loans at the start. This feature allows lenders to develop relationships with clients over time and to screen out the worst prospects before expanding loan scale (Parikshit Ghosh and Debraj Ray 1997).

Dynamic incentives can also help to explain advantages found in lending to women. Credit programs like those of the Grameen Bank and the Bangladesh Rural Advancement Committee (BRAC) did not begin with a focus on women. In 1980–83, women made up 39 percent and 34 percent of their respective memberships, but by 1991–92, BRAC's membership was 74 percent female and Grameen's was 94 percent female (Anne Marie Goetz and Rina Sen Gupta 1996). As Table 2 shows, many other programs also focus on lending to women, and it appears to confer financial advantages on the programs. At Grameen, for example, 15.3 percent of male borrowers were "struggling" in 1991 (i.e., missing some payments before the final due date) while this was true for just 1.3 percent of women (Khandker, Baqui Khalily, and Zahed Kahn 1995).

The decision to focus on women has some obvious advantages. The lower mobility of women may

be a plus where ex post moral hazard is a problem (i.e., where there is a fear that clients will "take the money and run"). Also, where women have fewer alternative borrowing possibilities than men, dynamic incentives will be heightened.[4]

Thus, ironically, the financial success of many programs with a focus on women may spring partly from the *lack* of economic access of women, while, at the same time, promotion of economic access is a principal social objective (Sidney Ruth Schuler, Syed Hashemi, and Ann P. Riley 1996).

Regular Repayment Schedules

One of the least remarked upon—but most unusual—features of most microfinance credit contracts is that repayments must start nearly immediately after disbursement. In a traditional loan contract, the borrower gets the money, invests it, and then repays in full with interest at the end of the term. But at Grameen-style banks, terms for a year-long loan are likely to be determined by adding up the principal and interest due in total, dividing by 50, and starting weekly collections a couple of weeks after the disbursement. Programs like BancoSol and BRI tend to be more flexible in the formula, but even they do not stray far from the idea of collecting regular repayments in small amounts.

The advantages are several. Regular repayment schedules screen out undisciplined borrowers. They give early warning to loan officers and peer group members about emerging problems. And they allow the bank to get hold of cash flows before they are consumed or otherwise diverted, a point developed by Stuart Rutherford (1998).

More striking, because the repayment process begins before investments bear fruit, weekly repayments necessitate that the household has an additional income source on which to rely. Thus, insisting on weekly repayments means that the bank is effectively lending partly against the household's steady, diversified income stream, not just the risky project. This confers advantages for the bank and for diversified households. But it means that mi-

---

[4]Rahman (1998) describes complementary cultural forces based on women's "culturally patterned behavior." Female Grameen Bank borrowers in Rahman's study area, for example, are found to be much more sensitive to verbal hostility heaped on by fellow members and bank workers when repayment difficulties arise. The stigma is exacerbated by the public collection of payments at weekly group meetings. According to Rahman (1998), women are especially sensitive since their misfortune reflects poorly on the entire household (and lineage), while men have an easier time shaking it off.

Table 2. Performance Indicators of Microfinance Programs

	Observations	Average loan balance ($)	Avg. loan as % of GNP per capita	Average operational sustainability	Average financial sustainability	Avg. return on equity	Avg. percent of portfolio at risk	Avg. percent female clients	Avg. number of active borrowers
Sustainability									
All microfinance institutions	72	415	34	105	83	-8.5	3.3	65	9,035
Fully sustainable	34	428	39	139	113	9.3	2.6	61	12,926
Lending method									
Individual lending	30	842	76	120	92	-5.0	3.1	53	15,226
Solidarity groups	20	451	35	103	89	-3.0	4.1	49	7,252
Village bank	22	94	11	91	69	-17.4	2.8	92	7,833
Target group									
Low end	37	133	13	88	72	-16.2	3.8	74	7,953
Broad	28	564	48	122	100	1.2	3.0	60	12,282
High end	7	2971	359	121	76	-6.2	1.9	34	1,891
Age									
3 to 6 years	15	301	44	98	84	-6.8	2.2	71	9,921
7 or more years	40	374	27	123	98	-2.4	4.1	63	16,557

Source: Statistical appendix to *MicroBanking Bulletin* (1998). Village banks have a "B" data quality; all others are graded "A". Portfolio at risk is the amount in arrears for 90 days or more as a percentage of the loan portfolio. Averages exclude data for the top and bottom deciles.

crofinance has yet to make real inroads in areas focused sharply on highly seasonal occupations like agricultural cultivation. Seasonality thus poses one of the largest challenges to the spread of microfinance in areas centered on rainfed agriculture, areas that include some of the poorest regions of South Asia and Africa. . . .

4. Profitability and Financial Sustainability

Microfinance discussions pay surprisingly little attention to particular mechanisms relative to how much attention is paid to purely financial matters. Accordingly, this section considers finances, and social issues are taken up again in Section 5.

How well in the end have microfinance programs met their financial promise? A recent survey finds 34 profitable programs among a group of 72 with a "commitment" to financial sustainability (*MicroBanking Bulletin* 1998). This does not imply, however, that half of all programs worldwide are self-sufficient. The hundreds of programs outside the base 72 continue to depend on the generosity of donors (e.g., Grameen Bank and most of its replicators do not make the list of 72, although BancoSol and BRI do). Some experts estimate that no more than 1 percent of NGO programs worldwide are currently financially sustainable—and perhaps another 5 percent of NGO programs will ever cross the hurdle.

The other 95 percent of programs in operation will either fold or continue requiring subsidies, either because their costs are high or because they choose to cap interest rates rather than to pass costs on to their clients. Although subsidies remain integral, donors and practitioners have been reluctant to discuss optimal subsidies to alleviate poverty, perhaps for fear of appearing retrograde in light of the disastrous experiences with subsidized government-run programs. Instead, rhetoric privileges financial sustainability.

International Evidence

Table 2 gives financial indicators for the 72 programs in the *MicroBanking Bulletin* survey.[5] The 72 programs have been divided into nonexclusive categories by age, lending method, target group, and level of sustainability.[6] (There is considerable overlap, for example, between the village bank category and the group targeting "low end" borrowers.)

The groups, divided by lending method and target group, demonstrate the diversity of programs marching behind the microfinance banner. Average loan balances range from $94 to $842 when comparing village banks to those that lend exclusively to individuals. The focus on women varies from 92 percent to 53 percent. The target group category makes the comparison starker, with average loan balances varying from $133 to $2971. Averages for the 34 fully sustainable institutions are not, however, substantially different from the overall sample in terms of average loan balance or the percentage of female clients.

Sustainability is generally considered at two levels. The first is *operational sustainability*. This refers to the ability of institutions to generate enough revenue to cover operating costs—but not necessarily the full cost of capital. If unable to do this, capital holdings are depleted over time. The second level of concern is *financial sustainability*. This is defined by whether or not the institution requires subsidized inputs in order to operate. If the institution is not financially sustainable, it cannot survive if it has to obtain all inputs (especially capital) at market, rather than concessional, rates.

Most of the programs in the survey have crossed the operational sustainability hurdle. The only exceptions are the village banks and those with low end targets, both of which generate about 90 percent of the required income.

Many fewer, however, can cover full capital costs as well. Overall, programs generate 83 percent of the required income and the village bank/low end target groups generate about 70 percent. Strikingly, the handful of programs that focus on "high end" clients are just as heavily subsidized as those on the low end. Similarly, the financial performance of programs with individual loans is roughly equivalent to that of programs using solidarity groups, even though the former serve a clientele that is more than twice as rich.

The greatest financial progress has been made by broad-based programs like BancoSol and BRI that serve clients across the range. Financial progress also improves with age (although com-

---

[5]The project started as a collaboration with the American Economic Association's Economics Institute in Boulder, Colorado.

[6]Those with low end target groups have average loan balances under $150 or loans as a percentage of GNP per capita under 20 percent (they include, for example, FINCA programs).

Those with broad targets have average balances that are 20–85 percent of GNP per capita (and include BancoSol and the BRI *unit desa* system). The high end programs make average loans greater than 120 percent of GNP per capita. The solidarity group methodology is based on groups with 3–5 borrowers (like BancoSol). The village banks have groups with over five borrowers.

parisons of young and old groups can only be suggestive as their orientations tend to differ).[7]

The returns to equity echo the data on financial sustainability. The numbers give profits relative to the equity put into the programs. The table shows that this is not a place to make big bucks. While average returns to equity of 9.3 percent for the financially-sustainable programs are respectable, they do not compete well with alternative investments and often carry considerable risk. At the same time, social returns may well be high even if financial returns are modest (or negative). On average, the broad-based programs, for example, cover all costs and serve a large pool of clients with modest incomes, most of whom are women. Wall Street would surely pass by the investment opportunity, but socially-minded investors might find the trade-off favorable. . . .

If donors tire of footing the bill for microfinance, achieving financial sustainability and increasing returns to equity is the only game to play. The issue is: will donors tire if social returns can be proven to justify the costs? Answering the question puts impact studies and cost–benefit analyses high on the research agenda. It also requires paying close attention to the basis of self-reported claims about financial performance. . . .

5. Costs and Benefits of Credit Subsidies

Nearly all programs espouse financial sustainability as a key principle. At the same time, nearly all programs rely on subsidies of one sort or another. These subsidies are typically viewed as temporary aids that help programs overcome start-up costs, not as ongoing program features. It is the familiar "infant industry" argument for protection.

The anti-subsidy stance springs from a series of worries. First, donors can be fickle, and programs that aim to exist into the future feel the need for independence. Second, donor budgets are limited, restricting the scale of operations to the size of the dole. Self-sufficient programs, on the other hand, can expand to meet demand. Third, subsidized programs run the risk of becoming inefficient without hard bottom lines. Fourth, in the past subsidies have ended up in the wrong hands, rather than helping poor households.

The view that subsidies should just be temporary has meant that calculating the costs and bene-

fits of subsidies has not been an important part of microfinance practice, and there have been no careful cost–benefit studies to date. But the fact is that subsidies are an ongoing reality: some "infants" are getting old. Moreover, many of the worries about problems associated with subsidies can likely be overcome.[8]

It is true that donors can be fickle, but governments will remain committed to poverty alleviation well after international agencies have moved on to the next Big Idea. If subsidized microfinance proves to deliver more bang for the buck than other social investments, should subsidies be turned down?

Scale certainly matters, but often a small well-targeted program may do more to alleviate measured poverty than a large, poorly-targeted program. Consider this example from Morduch (2000). Assume that the typical client in a subsidized program has an income of, say, 50 percent of the poverty line, while the typical client of a sustainable (high interest rate) program has an income of 90 percent of the poverty line. To clarify the comparison, assume that the net impacts on income per borrower are identical for the programs (after repaying loans with interest).

Minimizing poverty as measured by the commonly-used "squared poverty gap" of James Foster, Joel Greer, and Erik Thorbecke (1984), for example, suggests that raising the poorer borrower's income by one dollar has five times greater impact than doing the same for the less poor borrower. If the sustainable program has 63,000 clients (roughly the size of Bolivia's BancoSol in the early 1990s), the subsidized program would need to reach just 12,600 clients to have an equivalent impact. The comparison is too simple, but it amply illustrates how social weights and depth of outreach can outweigh concerns with scale.

The third issue, the danger of slipping into inefficiency, has been demonstrated many times over by large public banks in low-income countries. But the key to efficiency is the maintenance of hard budget constraints, not necessarily profits. Several donors already use strict and explicit performance targets when lending to microfinance institutions, conditioning future tranches on performances to date. The lessons can be applied more widely and used to promote efficiency and improve targeting in a broader range of subsidized programs.

---

[7]None of the U.S. programs that I know of are profitable, and some are very far from financial sustainability, held back by legal caps on interest rates (Michael Chu 1996). None of the U.S. programs are included in the *MicroBanking Bulletin* survey.

[8]This section draws heavily on Morduch (2000). Adams, Graham, and von Pischke (1982) present a well-argued alternative perspective. Schreiner (1997) presents a framework for considering cost-effectiveness applied to BancoSol and the Grameen Bank.

Simple Cost-Benefit Ratios

How should costs and benefits be compared? A simple gauge can be formed by dividing the value of subsidies by a measure of benefits accruing to borrowers. For example, Khandker (1998) reports a cost-benefit ratio of 0.91 with respect to improvements in household consumption via borrowing by women from the Grameen Bank. This means that it costs society 91 cents for every dollar of benefit to clients. A similar calculation leads to a cost-benefit ratio of 1.48 for borrowing by men. The ratio is higher, since lending to men appears to have a smaller impact on household consumption (Mark Pitt and Khandker 1998), but Khandker stresses that even the ratio for male borrowers compares favorably to alternative poverty alleviation programs in Bangladesh, like the World Food Programme's Food-for-Work scheme (cost-benefit ratio = 1.71) and CARE's similar program (cost-benefit ratio = 2.62). The microfinance programs of the Bangladesh Rural Advancement Committee (BRAC) compare less favorably, however. Khandker (1998) reports ratios of 3.53 and 2.59 for borrowing from BRAC by women and men, respectively.

These calculations provide an important first-cut at taking costs and benefits seriously. They suggest that investing in microfinance is not a universal winner, but some programs beat alternatives. Like all quick calculations, though, they rest on a series of simplifications. Most immediately, only measurable benefits can be considered, thus excluding much-discussed social impacts like "gender empowerment." . . .

Simple cost-benefit ratios fail to capture dynamics. Imagine that borrowing allows a client to purchase a sewing machine. Owning the machine (and being able to set up a small-scale tailoring business) creates benefits into the future, and using impacts on current household consumption does not capture the full value of borrowing since cost is a stock variable, while benefit is a flow. In principle, costs should be compared to the present value of the flow of future impacts, not the current impact, and doing so will lower cost-benefit ratios.

Perhaps the most difficult problem—and the one most relevant from the vantage of the current debate into microfinance—is that simple cost-benefit calculations fail to provide insight about the relevant counterfactual scenario. Cost-benefit ratios might be improved (or worsened) by reducing subsidies slightly, and the simple cost-benefit ratios provide no sense of the optimality of such a move. Thus, while it might be that a dollar used to subsidize an existing microfinance program helps poor households more than other uses, it might *also* be that the microfinance program would ultimately help more poor people if it was *not* subsidized (or if it was subsidized at a much lower level). . . .

6. Conclusions

The microfinance movement has made inroads around the world. In the process, poor households are being given hope and the possibility to improve their lives through their own labor. But the "win-win" rhetoric promising poverty alleviation with profits has moved far ahead of the evidence, and even the most fundamental claims remain unsubstantiated.

Even if the current enthusiasms ebb, the movement has demonstrated the importance of thinking creatively about mechanism design, and it is forcing economists to rethink much received wisdom about the nature of poverty, markets, and institutional innovation. In the end, this may prove to be the most important legacy of the movement.

In particular, the movement has shown that, despite high transactions costs and no collateral, in some cases it is possible to lend profitably to low-income households. . . .

The microfinance movement has also lifted the profile of NGOs. While government failures become increasingly evident, NGOs have had the energy, dedication, and financial resources to pursue required legislative changes and institutional experimentation. Increasingly, NGOs can be expected to take over social tasks once the exclusive domain of state ministries, and international organizations like the World Bank are adapting accordingly.

This is all new, but some received wisdom holds. Most important, all else the same it remains far more costly to lend small amounts of money to many people than to lend large amounts to a few. As a result, the programs are highly cost-sensitive, and most rely on subsidies. Initiating a serious discussion about next steps necessitates first facing up to the exaggerated claims for financial performance that have characterized some leaders in the movement.

If the movement plans not to abandon the promise of substantial poverty alleviation through finance, it must make hard choices. One avenue is to take another hard look at management structures and mechanism design in order to lower costs while maintaining outreach. Doing so will be far from simple, and it is hard to imagine substantial progress without a second major wave of innovation. Donors can contribute by encouraging further experimentation and evaluation, rather than just replication and adherence to a narrow set of "best practices" based on existing programs.

The other path is to reopen the conversation on ways that ongoing subsidies can benefit both clients and institutions. The movement has shown some successes in coupling efficient operations with subsidized resources, and these lessons can be expanded. Some observers speculate that if subsidies are pulled and costs cannot be reduced, as many as 95 percent of current programs will eventually have to close shop. The remaining 5 percent will be drawn from among the larger programs, and they will help fill gaps in financial markets. But, extrapolating from current experience, the typical clients of these financially sustainable programs will be less poor than those in the typical program focused sharply on poverty alleviation.

No one argues seriously that finance-based programs will be the answer for truly destitute households, but the promise remains that microfinance may be an important aid for households that are not destitute but still remain considerably below poverty lines. The tension is that the scale of lending to this group is not likely to permit the scale economies available to programs focused on households just above poverty lines. Subsidizing may yield greater social benefits than costs here. . . .

This prospect is exciting, especially given the dearth of appealing alternatives, but the promise of microfinance should be kept in context. Even in the best of circumstances, credit from microfinance programs helps fund self-employment activities that most often supplement income for borrowers rather than drive fundamental shifts in employment patterns. It rarely generates new jobs for others, and success has been especially limited in regions with highly seasonal income patterns and low population densities. The best evidence to date suggests that making a real dent in poverty rates will require increasing overall levels of economic growth and employment generation. Microfinance may be able to help some households take advantage of those processes, but nothing so far suggests that it will ever drive them.

Still, by forging ahead in the face of skepticism, microfinance programs now provide promise for millions of households. Even critics have been inspired by this success. The time is right for assessing next steps with candor—and better evidence.

References

ACCION International. 1997. *Credit Lines* 3.1 (An Update of the ACCION U.S. Network), March.

Adams, Dale and J.D. von Pischke. 1992. "Microenterprise Credit Programs: Déja Vu," *World Devel.*, 20:10, pp. 1463–70.

Adams, Dale; Douglas Graham, and J.D. von Pischke. 1984. *Undermining Rural Development with Cheap Credit.* Boulder, CO: Westview Press.

Armendariz de Aghion, Beatriz and Jonathan Morduch. 1998. "Microfinance Beyond Group Lending," Harvard and Princeton, draft.

Besley, Timothy and Stephen Coate. 1995. "Group Lending, Repayment Incentives, and Social Collateral," *J. Devel. Econ.*, 46.

Besley, Timothy; Stephen Coate, and Glenn Loury. 1993. "The Economics of Rotating Savings and Credit Associations," *Amer. Econ. Rev.*, 83:4, pp. 792–810.

Bolton, Patrick and David Sharfstein. 1990. "A Theory of Predation Based on Agency Problems in Financial Contracting," *Amer. Econ. Rev.*, 80, pp. 93–106.

Christen, Robert Peck; Elizabeth Rhyne, Robert Vogel, and C. McKean. 1995. "Maximizing the Outreach of Microenterprise Finance: The Emerging Lessons of Successful Programs," USAID Program and Operations Assessment Report No. 10, Washington, DC.

The Economist. 1997. "Microlending: From Sandals to Suits," Feb. 1, p. 75.

Foster, James; Joel Greer, and Erik Thorbecke. 1984. "A Class of Decomposable Poverty Measures," *Econometrica*, 52:3, pp. 761–66.

Ghatak, Maitreesh and Timothy Guinnane. 1999. "The Economics of Lending with Joint Liability: Theory and Practice," *J. Devel. Econ.*, forthcoming.

Ghosh, Parikshit and Debraj Ray. 1997. "Information and Repeated Interaction: Application to Informal Credit Markets," Texas A&M and Boston U., draft.

Goetz, Anne Marie and Rina Sen Gupta. 1996. "Who Takes the Credit? Gender, Power, and Control over Loan Use in Rural Credit Programs in Bangladesh," *World Devel.* 24:1, pp. 45–63.

Grameen Bank (various years), *Annual Report.* Dhaka: Grameen Bank.

Hulme, David and Paul Mosley, eds. 1996. *Finance Against Poverty.* London: Routledge.

Huppi, Monica and Gershon Feder. 1990. "The Role of Groups and Credit Cooperatives in Rural Lending," *World Bank Research Obs.* 5:2, pp. 187–204.

Johnston, Don. 1996. "Notes on Bank Kredit Desa," Bank Rakyat Indonesia/Harvard Institute for Int. Development (Jakarta).

Khalily, M.A. and R. Meyer. 1993. "The Political Economy of Loan Recovery," *Saving and Devel.* 17:1, pp. 23–38.

Khandker, Shahidur. 1998. *Fighting Poverty with Microcredit: Experience in Bangladesh.* New York: Oxford U. Press for the World Bank.

Khandker, Shahidur R., Baqui Khalily, and Zahed Kahn. 1995. *Grameen Bank: Performance and Sustainability,* World Bank Discuss. Paper 306, Washington DC.

Light, Ivan and Michelle Pham. 1998. "Microcredit Credit and Informal Credit in the United States: New Strategies for Economic Development," *J. Devel. Entrepreneurship,* 3:1.

MicroBanking Bulletin. 1998. Boulder, CO: Economics Institute.

Microcredit Summit Report. 1997. Washington, DC: RESULTS Educational Fund.

Morduch, Jonathan. 2000. "The Microfinance Schism," *World Devel.,* forthcoming.

The New York Times. 1997. "Micro-loans for the Very Poor," (editorial), February 16.

O'Brien, Timothy. 1998. "For Banks, A Big Nudge to do More: Communities Fear Lending Drop-Off," *New York Times,* July 5, pp. D1, D9.

Pitt, Mark and Shahidur Khandker. 1998. "The Impact of Group-Based Credit Programs on Poor Households in Bangladesh: Does the Gender of Participants Matter?" *J. Polit. Econ.* 106:5, pp. 958–996.

Pulley, Robert. 1989. "Making the Poor Credit-worthy: A Case Study of the Integrated Rural Development Program in India," World Bank Discuss. Paper 58, Washington, DC

Putnam, Robert. 1993. *Making Democracy Work.* Princeton, NJ: Princeton U. Press.

Rahman, Aminur. 1998. "Microcredit Initiatives for Equitable and Sustainable Development: Who Pays?" *World Devel.* 26:12.

Rutherford, Stuart. 1998. *The Poor and Their Money,* draft manuscript.

Schreiner, Mark. 1997. A Framework For the Analysis of the Performance and Sustainability of Subsidized Microfinance Organizations with Application to BancoSol of Bolivia and Grameen Bank of Bangladesh. Unpublished Ph.D. Dissertation, The Ohio State U.

Schuler, Sidney Ruth, Syed M. Hashemi, and Ann P. Riley. 1996. "Rural Credit Programs and Women's Empowerment in Bangladesh," *World Devel.,* 24:4, pp. 635–53.

Yunus, Muhammad. 1995. Testimony before the House [of Representatives of the U.S.] Committee on Int. Relations, *Fed. News Service,* June 27.

CHAPTER VI

Urbanization and the Informal Sector

Overview

In Note I.A.2, we pointed out that the share of the labor force employed in agriculture is much smaller in developed countries than in less developed countries. Since agriculture is concentrated in rural areas and industry is typically concentrated in urban areas, we can expect substantial migration from rural to urban areas as a country develops. If one visits the major cities in many less developed countries, one gets a powerful impression that this urbanization process is not working very smoothly. The city centers are so congested that it seems impossible to get from one place to another, while outside the centers huge neighborhoods have no access to municipal services such as electricity, running water, and sewers. Judging by the abundance of farm animals, many of the residents of these neighborhoods are of rural origin. It is not surprising that many authors have concluded that the pace of urbanization in less developed countries is excessive.

The historical experience of developed countries provides one yardstick by which one can assess the current urbanization process of less developed countries. In 1875 the urban population share of the now-rich countries was very close to that of less developed countries in 1950. In the selection that begins the first section of this chapter, Samuel Preston reports that the increase in this share in less developed countries during the period 1950–75 was very similar to the increase that occurred in the now more developed countries during the period 1875–1900. What is unprecedented is the rate of growth of urban populations in less developed countries, which is due to the unprecedented overall rate of population growth in these countries rather than to an unprecedented rate of increase in the share of their populations living in urban areas.

As Vernon Henderson shows in Selection VI.A.2, rapid city growth creates a strong demand for public investment in urban infrastructure. Often the largest or primate city of a country absorbs a disproportionate share of this public investment, to the detriment of the quality of life in other cities. Controlling for country average income and metropolitan area population level and growth, Henderson finds that several indicators of the quality of life in nonprimate cities are adversely affected by the share of the primate city in a country's urban population. Two of these indicators are the child mortality rate and the percentage of households with access to potable water. Selection VI.A.3 points out that these are related, because young children are particularly vulnerable to water-related diseases. This selection concerns one of the suggestions for how to manage the strain on public investment created by rapid urban growth in LDCs: allowing private provision of infrastructure services. This is often accomplished by privatizing existing public utilities, sometimes through sale of assets and sometimes by granting long-term concessions. Privatization is often controversial, especially when the new private operators are foreign firms. In Argentina, concessions were granted to private firms to provide water and sewer services for many municipalities. Selection VI.A.3 provides evidence that this privatization reduced child mortality by decreasing the incidence of infectious and parasitic diseases and perinatal deaths, with the main impact being in poor municipalities. Careful regulation of the private service providers appears to have been a factor in this success.

In addition to overcrowding, the major cities in many less developed countries give an impression of massive underemployment. This is colorfully described in several of the selections in the second section of this chapter. W. Arthur Lewis speaks of "the young men who rush forward asking to carry your bag as you appear." Michael Todaro quotes another writer's description of "the urban in-migrant who, instead of doing absolutely nothing, joins Bombay's army of underemployed bootblacks or Delhi's throngs of self-appointed (and tippable) parking directors, or who becomes an extra, redundant salesman in the yard goods stall of the cousin." Gary Fields describes as representative "a woman sitting on a market street in Kuala Lumpur, garlics set out on a piece of newspaper in front of her for sale."

Official unemployment statistics are not a reliable way to measure the extent of this kind of underemployment because the underemployed are working. A crude way to measure underemployment is to label all self-employed workers and unpaid family labor as underemployed. (This is sometimes used as a measure of the size of "the informal sector." We will discuss the relationship between the concepts "informal sector" and "underemployment" later.) This is obviously an inaccurate measure, since the self-employed may own substantial firms or be highly educated professionals and unpaid family workers may earn their bed and board. Nevertheless, as shown in Exhibit VI.B.1, this measure of underemployment (as a share of the nonagricultural labor force) does decline sharply across countries as human development increases. (It should be noted that for the vast majority of countries, the share of self-employed workers and unpaid family labor is higher in agriculture than in nonagriculture, reflecting the influence of the age-old tradition of family farming.)

We would like, of course, not merely to describe and measure urban underemployment but to understand its causes and its links, if any, to rural-urban migration in less developed countries. There are two leading theories of underemployment in less developed countries. The first is described in Selection VI.B.1 by W. Arthur Lewis. Lewis argues that in less developed countries there is simply not enough demand for wage labor to employ all who want to work at the minimum wage needed for subsistence. The "surplus" labor survives through a combination of employment in family businesses (especially farms) that are willing to pay family members more than their marginal products, and low-productivity self-employment (again supplemented by family charity). For Lewis there is no conceptual difference between the urban and the rural underemployed, so for a given demand for wage labor rural-urban migration only serves to shift the location of the underemployed from rural to urban areas. A strong point of Lewis's theory is that it is consistent with the reduction of self-employment and unpaid family labor as per capita income increases suggested by Exhibit VI.B.1: the correlation coefficient between the share of self-employed workers and unpaid family labor in nonagriculture and PPP$ per capita GDP is –0.53. As capital accumulates in industry and per capita GDP increases, demand for wage labor increases and underemployed labor is absorbed into wage employment by nonfamily firms.

In Selection VI.B.2, Michael Todaro describes the second leading theory of underemployment in LDCs. Todaro starts from the premise that in LDCs wage employment in the urban "modern sector" provides a substantially higher income than rural employment, even adjusting for differences in cost of living, and that the urban underemployed cannot bid down modern sector wages. This wage differential causes migration from the countryside to the city, where the migrants spend some time underemployed in the urban "traditional sector" until they are lucky enough to obtain modern sector jobs. The larger is the number of underemployed seeking jobs in the urban modern sector, the longer a migrant can expect to wait before finding such a job, and the less attractive migration becomes. It follows that any attempt to reduce urban underemployment (by creating more modern sector jobs, for example) will be at least partially self-defeating because it will make rural-urban migration more attractive. As a proportion of the urban labor force, the underemployed will shrink only if the urban-rural income differential narrows.

Unfortunately, we cannot test Todaro's hypothesis using data on urban-rural income differentials or even nonagriculture-agriculture productivity gaps because for many countries these data are not available for the survey years in Exhibit VI.B.1. Data are available for agricultural value-added per worker for the survey years for nearly all the countries in the Exhibit, however, so we can perform a crude test of Todaro's hypothesis by checking whether the share of self-employment and unpaid family workers in nonagriculture decreases with agricultural value-added per worker, controlling for per capita GDP. A regression yields the results that not only is the coefficient on agricultural value-added per worker negative and statistically significant, but also the coefficient on per capita GDP falls to zero! (This is true whether per capita GDP is measured in PPP$ or US$, and is partly caused by very high multicollinearity between per capita GDP and agricultural value-added per worker.) For this reason, in Exhibit VI.B.1 we list agricultural value-added per worker alongside the share of self-employment and unpaid family labor in nonagriculture for the years corresponding to the labor force survey.

Todaro's theory of urban underemployment was incorporated into a larger model (and somewhat modified) by Harris and Todaro (1970). Harris and Todaro (p. 126) assume that the source of the urban-rural income differential is "a politically determined minimum urban wage at levels substantially higher than agricultural earnings." One can then see that the key difference between the Lewis and Harris–Todaro models of underemployment is that in the Lewis model the (subsistence) minimum wage holds in both agriculture and industry, while in the Harris–Todaro model the (politically determined) minimum wage is enforced only in industry. In Note VI.B.1 we put the Harris–Todaro and Lewis models of underemployment into a common diagrammatic framework. We observe that one consequence of the difference between the Lewis and Todaro (or Harris–Todaro) views of underemployment is sharply different predictions regarding the effects of expansion of urban labor demand on agricultural output: agricultural output must fall in the Harris–Todaro model but need not do so in the Lewis model.

In Selection VI.B.3, Gene Tidrick examines official unemployment in Jamaica rather than underemployment. Nevertheless, he finds that the Todaro theory has considerable explanatory power. For example, in the period Tidrick examines, the Jamaican urban economy was highly unionized, and wages of unskilled urban workers in occupations such as construction and transportation were much higher than wages of unskilled agricultural workers. The official unemployment rate never fell below 13 percent despite substantial growth in "modern" nonagricultural jobs and an almost stable labor force. Despite high unemployment, there were labor shortages in rural areas. An econometric study of Jamaican migration cited by Tidrick found that migration occurred largely in response to wage differentials and in spite of higher unemployment levels in high-wage areas. In Note VI.B.2, which follows Tidrick's selection, we discuss more recent econometric approaches to the study of rural-urban migration.

Subsequent to the writings of Lewis and Todaro, the concept of "underemployment" has fallen out of favor and been largely replaced by the concept of "the informal sector." The latter is most commonly defined as firms (including the self-employed) that operate outside the system of government benefits and regulations. This concept is already latent in the selection by Todaro and in Harris and Todaro (1970): one could view the "urban traditional sector" of Todaro as the part of the urban economy where the political forces that determine the minimum wage in the Harris–Todaro model do not apply. However, as the International Labour Office (ILO) makes clear (1972, pp. 5–8 and 503–508), "the informal sector" is seen as dominated not by the underemployed but rather by productive if small firms that supply essential goods and services. The ILO views urban economies in less developed countries as "dualistic," with a sharp distinction between informal activities that are small in scale, labor-intensive, and unregulated and formal activities that are large in scale, capital-intensive, and regulated. Other writers such as Livingstone (1991, pp. 667–668) extend this dualism from the supply to the demand side, stating that the informal and formal sectors cater to poor and well-off urban consumers, respectively.

In Selection VI.B.4, Gary Fields makes a distinction between the "easy-entry" informal sector and the "upper-tier" informal sector. Workers in the easy-entry informal sector resemble the underemployed of Lewis and Todaro and seek better positions in the formal sector. Workers in the upper-tier informal sector, on the other hand, prefer their positions to formal sector jobs and may even have received prior training in the formal sector before leaving to start informal sector businesses. Fields's characterization of the informal sector leaves open the possibility that the size of the easy-entry informal sector influences rural-urban migration in just the way that Todaro described: a smaller easy-entry informal sector encourages rural-urban migration by decreasing the time migrants expect to wait before landing a formal sector job.

In contrast to Fields, Biswajit Banerjee takes a strong position against the "probabilistic migration model" of Todaro in Selection VI.B.5. He argues that access to formal sector jobs is determined largely by one's contacts or social network, and that with good contacts one can line up a formal sector job directly from one's village without engaging in an urban-based job search, while without good contacts one is unlikely to obtain a formal sector job even after migrating to the city. Knowing this, rural workers do not see the number of formal sector jobs relative to the size of the informal wage sector as an important indicator of their chances of obtaining a formal sector job and do not migrate in response to this indicator. For more discussion of the importance of social structure in LDC labor markets, the reader can begin with Kannappan (1989, especially pp. 60–62) and the references therein.

References

Harris, John R., and Michael P. Todaro. 1970. "Migration, Unemployment and Development: A Two-Sector Analysis." *American Economic Review* 60 (March): 126–42.

ILO Mission. 1972. *Employment, Incomes, and Equality: A Strategy for Increasing Productive Employment in Kenya* (Geneva: International Labour Office).

Kannappan, Subbiah. 1989. "Employment Policy and Labour Markets in Developing Nations." In Bernard Salome, ed., *Fighting Urban Unemployment in Developing Countries* (Paris: OECD).

Livingstone, Ian. 1991. "A Reassessment of Kenya's Rural and Urban Informal Sector." *World Development* 19 (June): 651–70.

VI.A.   URBAN GROWTH AND INFRASTRUCTURE

Selection VI.A.1.   Urban Growth in Developing Countries: A Demographic Reappraisal*

In this review, we rely primarily upon material developed in the course of a United Nations study of urban and rural population change. This study assembled estimates of urban and rural population and of the population of cities larger than 100,000 from 1950 to the present. The study does not deal with all aspects of population distribution, but only with those demographic aspects that relate to distinctions between urban and rural areas and between places of differing size. Conclusions of this study are described here, and their bearing on distribution policy is considered.

(1) The rate of change in the proportion urban in developing countries is not exceptionally rapid by historical standards; rather it is the growth rates of urban populations that represent an unprecedented phenomenon.

The most common measure of the rate of urbanization is the annual change in the percentage of the population living in urban areas. According to this measure, urbanization in developing countries did not proceed with unusual speed in the quarter-century from 1950 to 1975. In this period the percentage urban grew from 16.7 to 28.0 in developing countries. While this is a rapid increase, it is very similar to the one that occurred in more developed countries during the last quarter of the nineteenth century. Between 1875 and 1900, the percentage urban of countries now more developed grew from 17.2 to 26.1. The slight difference from the growth in developing countries 75 years later is well within the margin of error of the estimates. The rates of net rural–urban migration required to achieve the observed increase in the urban percentage may even have been greater in more developed countries, in view of the higher rates of rural than of urban natural increase that typically prevailed at the time. That is, to achieve a certain increase in the urban percentage, higher rates of net rural–urban migration were required in developed countries than in developing countries, where rural-urban differences in rates of natural increase are far less significant.

*From Samuel H. Preston, "Urban Growth in Developing Countries: A Demographic Reappraisal," *Population and Development Review* 5 (June 1979): 196–199. Reprinted by permission.

Nor does it appear that rates of urbanization or of net rural–urban migration are accelerating in developing countries. Between 1950 and 1960 the proportion urban grew by 5.1 percentage points and between 1960 and 1975, a period 50 percent longer, by 6.2 percentage points. (These figures include China's uncertain estimates, which show decelerated urbanization.) The pace of urbanization has been accelerating in Africa but decelerating in Latin America. . . .

While the rate of urbanization (the rate of change in proportion urban) has not been unprecedented in developing countries, the growth rate of the urban population has been. Between 1875 and 1900, urban populations in now-developed countries grew by 100 percent and rural populations by 18 percent. While developing countries were traversing roughly the same range in proportions urban between 1950 and 1975, their urban populations grew by 188 percent and their rural ones by 49 percent. The growth factors of both rural and urban populations were much larger simply because rates of natural increase were much faster. Urban growth is currently exceptionally rapid in developing countries, but the explanation is not to be found in unusually rapid changes in the urban proportion produced by rural–urban migration but in the rapid changes in total population to which those proportions are applied.

(2) Urban growth through most of the developing world results primarily from the natural increase of urban populations.

This point is readily overlooked in the midst of scholarly and political concern with internal migration. It has been made before by Kingsley Davis, Eduardo Arriaga, Salley Findley, and the United Nations Population Division, and new findings on components of urban growth provide strong confirmation. Of the 29 developing countries whose data support a decomposition of the sources of urban growth during the most recent intercensal period, 24 had faster rates of urban natural increase than of net in-migration (the latter also including area reclassification). The mean percentage of urban growth attributable to natural increase for the 29 countries was 60.7 percent. Among the largest developing countries the percentage was 67.7 in India (1961–71), 64.3 in Indonesia

(1961–71), and 55.1 in Brazil (1960–70). There is apparently a slight tendency for the percentage of urban growth attributable to natural increase to grow over time. . . .

It should be noted that the coverage of African populations in the data set is very poor and that results pertain primarily to Latin America and Asia (except China). Judging from the unusually rapid urban growth in Africa, it is likely that rural–urban migration is a more important source of growth there than is implied by the above account.

Selection VI.A.2. Urban Primacy, External Costs, and Quality of Life*

1. Introduction

Urban concentration in a country is typically crudely measured by primacy—the share of the largest metro area in national urban population. . . . Very large primate cities in a country tend to demand excessive public investments and other public expenditures, as resources are devoted to try to prop up the deteriorating quality of life in such cities. The result is to divert resources that might go to non-primate cities, causing a quantifiable, significant deterioration in the quality of life in those cities. . . .

In the development literature (Williamson, 1965), as adapted to an urban context in Hansen (1990), a high degree of urban concentration in the early stages of economic development is viewed as essential to efficiency. By spatially concentrating industrialization, often in coastal cities, the economy conserves on "economic infrastructure"—physical infrastructure capital (transport and telecommunications) and managerial resources. As development proceeds, concentration eventually declines for two reasons. The economy can afford to spread economic infrastructure to hinterland areas. Second, the cities of initial high concentration become high cost, congested locations that are less attractive to producers and consumers.

There is an argument and, in some cases an absolute presumption, both that countries have a tendency to urban over-concentration, and that urban over-concentration is costly to economic growth. In the Williamson scenario, the initial concentrations become excessive; and deconcentration is delayed for too long. . . .

Often the basic political institutions in countries encourage over-concentration, or excessive urban primacy. The idea is that, in many countries, there is a lack of a level playing field across cities. The national government can choose to favor one (or two) cities over others. Typically such cities are national capitals (Bangkok, Mexico City, Jakarta, or Seoul, not to mention Paris); but they may also be a Sao Paulo, the seat of the national elite. Such favoritism can involve the allocation of local public services, where, for example, hinterland cities do not have the power to determine their own public service levels, either because the national constitution is strongly unitary or because local autonomy

has been suspended (as in South Korea from 1961 to the 1990). It can take the form of the national government choosing not to invest sufficiently in interregional transport and telecommunications, so that hinterland cities are not competitive locations for private producers. Favoritism, as in Indonesia (Henderson and Kuncoro, 1996; Kaiser, 1999), can also take the form of restrictions in capital markets, export/import markets, and licensing of production rights, all favoring firms which locate in the national capital, or sometimes other major cities.

The political economy analysis suggests national governments will choose to favor, in particular, the national capital. This allows central bureaucrats and politicians to extract rents in the allocation of loans and licenses, without competition from other locations. It allows such decision makers to favor their home city and themselves with special public services. Denying hinterland locations necessary transport and communications infrastructure benefits producers in the national capital, because competition from hinterland producers is deterred. . . .

All analyses tell us favored cities are over-sized with attendant efficiency losses for the country. Migrants and firms flow to a favored city, until it becomes so congested and costly to live in, that these costs offset the advantages of the favoritism. Apart from analyses and empirical work in economics, international agencies also take the view that many of the world's mega-cities are over-populated, at considerable cost to those economies. The UN (1993) asks how bad "the negative factors associated with very large cities" need to get "before (it is in the) self-interest of those in control to encourage development of alternative centers." The same report warns of "unbalanced urban hierarchies" and the crime, congestion, and social inequality in mega-cities. . . .

2. Effects of City Size and Primacy on Incomes, Cost-of-living, and Urban Quality of Life

Using a sample of about 90 metro areas worldwide, I explore how individual city sizes and population growth rates and national urban concentration affect city cost-of-living, and quality of life. The examination tries to separate out the internal costs of increasing any individual city's size, from the external costs that increases in primacy impose on other cities in the country. Primacy is the size of

*From Vernon Henderson, "Urban Primacy, External Costs, and Quality of Life," *Resource and Energy Economics* 24 (2002): 96–102, 104. Reprinted by permission.

the largest city in the country divided by national urban population. The cities in the study are almost exclusively non-primate cities. . . . The idea behind the external costs of primacy is that an excessive-size primate city absorbs a disproportionate share of public resources from the rest of the economy, leading to deteriorating conditions in average cities. So the reallocation of public resources caused by excessive primacy results in a deterioration in quality of life in non-primate cities.

I use a new dataset—the UNCHS data from the United Nations Center for Human Settlements (Habitat) in Nairobi—to find patterns of association between city size, primacy and urban costs. The UNCHS data covers almost 300 metro areas around the world for 1996, although for any particular dimension of quality of life, there are under 90 metro areas across 15–20 countries. . . .

I divide the examination into two parts. First, I examine determinants of the key components of urban costs-of-living—urban rents and commuting costs. Then I turn to determinants of aspects of urban quality of life, dealing with health and education. In each case, the general relationship being estimated takes the form

$$Y_{ij} = a + bX_{ij} + cZ_j + u_j + e_{ij}$$

where Y_{ij} is the outcome measure in city i in country j, X_{ij} is a determinant (e.g. city size) in city i in country j, Z_j is a country characteristic of country j (e.g. urban primacy), e_{ij} is an i.i.d. error term and u_j is a country random or fixed effect.

I generally estimate the equations by random effects which allows direct estimation of effects of country characteristics (Z_j). However, it is not unlikely that the u_j may affect the X_{ij} and Z_j. Thus, I also present country fixed effect estimates, which exclude direct estimates of the effects of Z_j variables. . . . With fixed effects estimation, the impacts of the Z_j may be recovered by regressing the Z_j on the estimated country fixed effects, from the country fixed effect regressions. Random and fixed effect estimates do differ as at least my priors would suggest, but on key dimensions—the effects of primacy—they are not dissimilar.

2.1. Cost-of-living

I estimate cost-of-living variables as a function of national income, metro area population and national primacy. Controlling for country income, or level of development, the idea is to distinguish the effect of own city-size on cost-of-living, from the effects of national urban primacy. The focus is on the random effects results. However, recognizing

that there are other country characteristics (education levels, trade, institutional and political system) which are not controlled for, and which may affect the covariates, I also did the country fixed effect estimates. There the only explanatory variable is metro area population (which gives the equation a different sample size since cities in countries with missing values on Z_j variables are no longer excluded in estimation). I then recover the country fixed effects from these regressions and regress them on primacy, as an alternative way to assess the effects of primacy on city costs of living. Those coefficients are in brackets.

Urban living costs are usually represented in urban models by commuting costs and housing rental costs. Here, I have the mean travel time to work in the metro area. For rents, I have the rent to income ratio. To try to standardize to get associations with rental prices, I control for income and floor space (despite its potential endogeneity). Turning to the effects of city size on local costs-of-living, in Table 1, in the first two columns, mean travel times appear to rise sharply with metro area size (an elasticity of 0.25), with random and fixed effect results being somewhat similar. In the housing rent equation, in the last two columns, again with an elasticity of around 0.25, rents rise with city size. To get a sense of magnitudes for large scale differences in city sizes, based on these coefficients, if metro area population increases from 250,000 to 2.5 million (well within the range of populations in our sample), that is associated with an 80% increase in both rents and commuting costs.

Turning to external effects, national urban primacy increases own city commuting times, potentially reflecting the drain of public resources away from investment in non-primate city transport infrastructure. A one-standard deviation increase in primacy (0.15) increases per person commuting costs in a typical (non-primate) city by 14% (for an elasticity of about 0.9, averaging the random and fixed effect estimates). For rents, primacy has no significant effect; but its coefficient is negative. That could simply reflect the negative effect of primacy on population skill mix and incomes in other cities.

Let's look more closely at why primacy matters for commuting costs. As noted above, given primacy appears to be excessive in many countries, that strains the urban sector. Larger cities are very costly to run, from both the point of view of needed urban infrastructure investments per capita and the difficulty of finding the human and political resources to manage increasingly complex, congested cities. That strain is reflected in national figures on public infrastructure investments.

Table 1. City Cost-of-living[a]

	log(mean travel time to work)		log(rent to income ratio)	
	(1) Country random effects	(2) Country fixed effects	(1) Country random effects	(2) Country fixed effects
log(GDP per capita)	–0.038 (0.050)		1.02** (0.242)	—
log(metro area size)	0.251** (0.038)	0.237** (0.040)	0.206* (0.108)	0.321** (0.136)
Primacy[b]	1.17** (0.572)	[0.748*] (0.413)	–1.41 (1.09)	[–2.03] (3.06)
log(average floor space per person)	—	—	0.111 (0.744)	1.04* (0.559)
Constant	1.64 (0.658)		–4.39 (1.45)	—
R^2	0.469	0.754	0.637	0.746
N (no. of countries)	73 (33)	78 (23)	52 (27)	43 (15)

[a]Column 1 estimates are OLS regressions, allowing for country random effects. Column 2 estimates are country fixed effect relationships between the dependent variables and city sizes. Then (the country invariant) primacy is used to explain country fixed effects, i.e. cross-country variations in costs-of-living.

[b]Country samples sizes in column 2 for the fixed effect primacy regression are 17 and 11, respectively.

The numbers in parentheses after table entries are the standard errors.

In Table 2, I use a dataset, which was put together for *Entering the 21st Century,* the World Development Report 1999/2000 (World Bank, 2000). While decomposing where investments go regionally within a country is not possible, Table 2 does show the determinants of the ratio of overall public investment (from IMF statistics on investments of national and sub-national governments) to GDP. In terms of the impact of primacy, a one-standard deviation increase (0.15) in national primacy increases the ratio by 18% from its mean of 0.033. The equation controls for the national urban growth rate, which raises the share of public investment significantly, as countries move from rural to urban societies with the attendant demands on infrastructure provision. The straining effects of both primacy and urban growth rates on national resources, and hence urban quality of life, are explored next.

2.2 *Urban Quality of Life*

I now turn to four measures of urban quality of life. The first two are of greatest interest—child mortality rate for children under 5 years old, and children per classroom in primary school—since they reflect health outcomes and schooling quality. The next two represent conditions which are related to health outcomes and the general neighborhood quality of life—percent of households with access (within 200 m) to potable water and percent of households with regular waste collection.

In Table 3, I present random effects regressions of the determinants of these variables in columns labeled 1. The variation in the dependent variables

Table 2. Public Investment Strain[a]

	Country random effects
log(GDP per capita)	0.0029 (0.0027)
National urban growth rate	0.094** (0.038)
National primacy	0.040** (0.016)
R^2 (no. of countries)	66 (38)

[a]National ratio: public investment to GDP. The sample is a mid-1980s and a mid-1990 for countries for which IMF data on national, state and local government capital investments are available.

is more across countries, than across cities within countries. As a result, country fixed effect estimates produce insignificant coefficients on all listed variables for each indicator. However, for country fixed effect estimates, I recover the fixed effects and regress primacy against them, reporting in the columns labeled 2 of Table 3, any significant relationships.

For these quality of life measures, a key determinant is average income. Metro area size for our sample of non-primate cities either has no effect per se, or it has a positive influence. Bigger cities often have a command of resources that allows them to invest in improved public service, health, and education outcomes. What lowers quality of life are items which strain the managerial and financial resources of individual cities and the urban system as a whole. Fast individual city growth rates hurt child mortality rates, access to potable water, and school class size. Fast city growth in some countries may be an inevitable aspect of the urbanization process, but it, at least temporarily, strains city capacities and hence quality of life.

Table 3. Urban Quality of Life and Primacy[a,b]

	Child mortality rate (under age 5)		Percent households access to potable water	Percent households regular waste collection		log(children per classroom)	
	(1) Country random effects	(2) Country fixed effects	(1) Country random effects	(1) Country random effects	(2) Country fixed effects	(1) Country random effects	(2) Country fixed effects
log(average income)	-0.0097** (0.0022)	—	0.048** (0.013)	0.090** (0.028)	—	-0.071** (0.021)	—
log(metro area population)	-0.0066** (0.0033)	—	0.029* (0.017)	0.023 (0.026)	—	-0.0026 (0.028)	—
Metro area annual population growth rate	0.540** (0.262)	—	-3.19* (1.64)	-2.25 (3.63)	—	6.43** (2.64)	—
National primacy	0.143** (0.034)	[0.152**] (0.032)	-0.245* (0.133)	-0.505** (0.197)	[-1.03**] (0.306)	0.468 (0.357)	[0.835**] (0.348)
Constant	0.110 (0.034)	-0.092 (0.0070)	0.493 (0.184)	0.176 (0.303)	0.679 (0.142)	3.79 (0.345)	-0.625 (0.132)
R^2	0.740	0.555	0.502	0.425	0.232	0.498	0.200
N (no. of countries)	56 (27)	18	67 (29)	57 (28)	18	61 (28)	18

[a]Column 2 estimates take country fixed effect estimates for the equation in Column 1 (excluding country invariant, primacy) for countries with two or more cities and estimate by OLS the effect of primacy on those fixed effects estimates. Results for equations with significant explanatory power are reported.

[b]The means and standard deviations of child mortality, access to potable water, regular waste collection, sewerage connection, class size, metro area growth rate and national primary are 0.064 (0.063), 0.844 (0.194), 0.516 (0.391), 0.687 (0.324), 0.029 (0.029) and 0.31 (0.15), respectively.

Primacy in either random effects regressions or in fixed effect country residual regressions hurts child mortality, access to potable water, regular waste collection, and school class size, in our sample of (mostly) non-primate cities. In general, a one-standard deviation increase in primacy hurts urban quality of life measures for typical cities by a magnitude equal to 20–35% of the quality of life standard deviations. This represents the costs for non-primate cities of the strain on national budgets and resources of excessive urban primacy. . . .

3. Conclusion

. . . Excessive primacy strains the whole urban system, absorbing resources that might go to other cities to improve the general quality of life. These resources are absorbed into high public infrastructure investments and high cost public service provision geared towards the primate city, trying to contain the congestion and environmental costs in that city. The result is strong deterioration in the quality of life in non-primate cities.

References

Hansen, N., 1990. Impacts of small and intermediate-sized cities on population distribution: issues and responses. Regional Development Dialogue 11, 60–76.

Henderson, J.V., Kuncoro, A., 1996. Industrial centralization in Indonesia. World Bank Economic Review 10, 513–540.

Kaiser, K., 1999. Pre- and Post-Liberalization Manufacturing Location in Indonesia (1975–1996), 5-27-99 mimeo, LSE.

UN, 1993. World Urbanization Prospects: The 1992 Revision. United Nations, New York.

Williamson, J., 1965. Regional Inequality and the Process of National Development, Economic Development and Cultural Change. pp. 3–45.

World Bank, 2000. Entering the 21st Century World Development Report 1999/2000. Oxford University Press, Oxford.

Selection VI.A.3. The Impact of the Privatization of Water Services on Child Mortality in Argentina*

We examine the impact of the privatization of water services on child mortality in Argentina. Our study focuses on young children because they are particularly vulnerable to water-related diseases due to weak body defenses, higher susceptibility, and greater exposure from inadequate knowledge of how to avoid risks (WHO, 2002a). There are two main disease transmission mechanisms generated by the lack of appropriate water systems: water-borne diseases that occur by drinking contaminated water, and water-washed diseases that occur when there is a lack of water and sanitation for household hygiene. Young children worldwide suffer from several deadly diseases that could easily be prevented through the interruption of these transmission mechanisms by access to safe and sufficient water supply and provision for the hygienic removal of sewage (WHO, 2000). For example, diarrhea alone accounts for approximately 15 percent of all child deaths worldwide (UNICEF, 2001). In Argentina, diarrhea, septicemia, and gastrointestinal infections are three of the top ten causes of death for children under five (Ministerio de Salud, 1999).

Our analysis takes advantage of the fact that local governments are responsible for delivering water services and only some municipalities privatized those services. During the 1990s, about 30 percent of municipalities covering approximately 60 percent of the population privatized their water services. This variation in ownership across time and space provides a potential instrument to identify the causal effect of privatization on child mortality.

A major methodological concern, however, is that local governments choose to privatize water services, and that choice may not be orthogonal to unobservable factors that also affect mortality. We address this concern in a number of ways that lead us to believe that the link between the privatization of water systems and child mortality is causal.

In the end, despite the concerns about potential negative health effects, we find that the privatization of water services is actually associated with a reduction in child mortality. Our main result is anticipated in Figure 1, which depicts the evolution of the child mortality rates for municipalities with privatized and non-privatized water companies.

During the first half of the decade, the mortality rates of the municipalities that eventually privatized their water systems decreased at the same rate as the mortality rates of the municipalities that did not privatize. However, after 1995 the mortality rates of the municipalities that privatized decreased faster than the mortality rates of those that did not privatize. . . . This timing is commensurate with the timing of privatization. Before 1995 only a few municipalities had privatized; whereas the bulk of privatizations occurred after 1995.

Our difference-in-differences models estimate that the effect suggested by Figure 1 corresponds to a reduction in child mortality of approximately 8 percent. Moreover, we find that most of the reduction in mortality occurred in low-income areas (26 percent), where the expansion of the water network was greatest. Finally, we scrutinize the validity of the causal interpretation of our estimates using cause specific mortality. While privatization is associated with significant reductions in deaths from infectious and parasitic diseases, it is uncorrelated with deaths from causes unrelated to water conditions.

1. The Economics of Water Systems

Water systems include both the supply of clean water and the treatment and removal of sewage. These services are a natural monopoly involving large fixed costs and significant economies of scale (Noll et al., 2000).[1] There is typically little competition to a well functioning water system from alternative sources (Foster, 1999; Estache et al., 2001). The main alternative is household self-provision through pumped wells, rainwater catchments, cesspools, and septic tanks. Self-provision suffers from low quality and high cost (Abdala and Spiller, 1999). Similarly, the sale of drinkable water from private vendors is substantially more costly and therefore does not present serious competition either. Finally, the average asset life of water systems' physical plant is very long and therefore impedes any potential dynamic competition.

The water sector is also characterized by the presence of significant externalities. Most water-related diseases are contagious. This generates positive externalities in the provision of clean wa-

*From Sebastian Galiani, Paul Gertler, and Ernesto Schargrodsky, "Water for Life: The Impact of the Privatization of Water Services on Child Mortality," *Journal of Political Economy,* forthcoming. Reprinted by permission.

[1]For example, fixed costs represent more than 80% of water service costs in the United Kingdom (Armstrong et al., 1994).

Figure 1. Evolution of Mortality Rates for Municipalities with Privatized vs. Non-Privatized Water Services

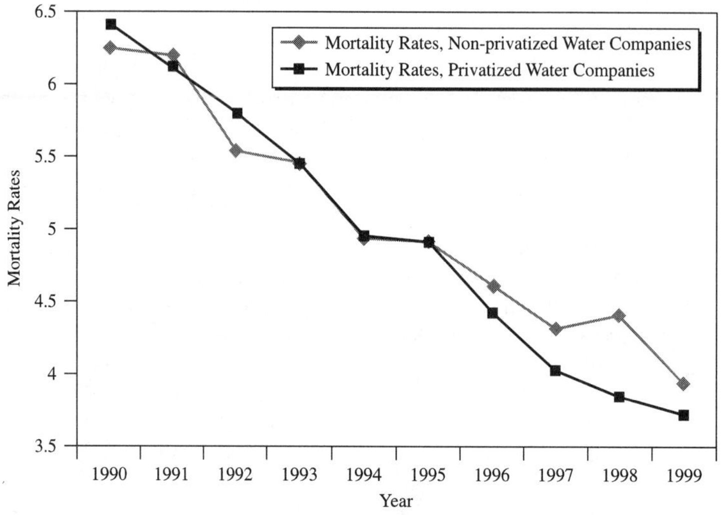

ter across society. Similarly, the proper elimination of sanitation residuals and treated industrial waste prevents negative externalities through the pollution of natural bodies of water and other natural resources.

Another special feature of water supply is that, as human life depends on access to drinkable water, the demand for water is perfectly price inelastic at survival levels. Of course, demand exhibits some price elasticity at levels for which water is used for other non-survival household and productive uses.

These features—natural monopoly, presence of significant externalities, and inelasticity of demand—have historically justified public intervention in the water sector. Most countries supply water services through the public sector, and private entry into water provision has been limited. However, there are growing calls to consider allowing a regulated private sector to deliver water services (World Bank, 2002).

Private supply has the advantage of providing strong incentives for cost reductions and other productivity enhancements. In contrast, these incentives are weak under public ownership, where typically agents cannot reap the results of their effort and innovation. In fact, empirical evidence from several sectors strongly suggests that service quality, productivity and profitability rise significantly following privatization (Megginson et al., 1994; Barberis et al., 1996; Frydman et al., 1999; La Porta and Lopez-de-Silanes, 1999).

Nonetheless, the weak efficiency incentives in public firms might be tolerable when cost reductions by private suppliers come at the expense of undesirable quality deterioration or reductions in access by the poor. In particular, unregulated pri-

vate providers may undersupply the socially optimal quality of water in the presence of externalities because they fail to take into account the marginal social benefits in their decisions. Similarly, private owners may exclude low-income households from the network by raising prices, strictly enforcing payment, and concentrating their investments in high-income areas.

However, the fear of quality deterioration or access exclusion can only be genuine when supply conditions are non-contractible (Shleifer, 1998). In the water industry, information asymmetries in service quality are relatively unimportant, and regulatory agencies can monitor water quality, pressure, repair delays, and shortages. Network expansions and universal coverage can also be enforced through regulation.

The arguments in favor of private provision are even stronger when we consider non-benevolent governments. Politicians may use the control of state firms to channel benefits for themselves and their supporters (Shleifer and Vishny, 1994). Excess employment, corruption, subsidies, and pork barreling are typical of state owned enterprises (SOEs) around the world. As Shleifer (1998) explains it, state companies not only are unproductive because of the lack of managerial incentives, but also because inefficiency results from the political use of SOE resources.

Finally, the process of resource allocation within the aggregated public sector does not guarantee the assignment of funds to the most profitable projects. The chronic under-investment in physical capital that plagues many SOEs is aggravated for debt-ridden governments with large fiscal deficits. Privatization can significantly improve the access of

Table 1. Change in Ownership of Water Systems 1990–1999

Ownership	Number of municipalities	Percentage
Always public	196	39.7%
Always private not-for-profit cooperative	143	28.9%
Transferred from public to private for-profit	138	27.9%
Always private for-profit	1	0.2%
No service or missing information	16	3.2%
Total	494	100.0%

Notes: In municipalities where more than one company provides water services, we defined the ownership status of the municipality as the ownership of the company supplying the largest fraction of the population.

firms to capital markets and therefore boost their ability to invest.

2. The Privatization of Water Services in Argentina

From 1870 through 1980, water services in Argentina were provided by the federal company Obras Sanitarias de la Nación (OSN) and a number of not-for-profit cooperatives. In 1980, OSN's jurisdiction was restricted to the federal district and 17 municipalities of the suburban Greater Buenos Aires area. While OSN remained under control of the federal government, the responsibility for public water services in the rest of the country was transferred to local governments (Artana et al., 2000). Most of the companies provided both water and sanitation; however, a few supplied only water. In these cases, there was no sewage service in the community.

In 1990, before privatization, public companies provided water services in two-thirds of the municipalities while not-for-profit cooperatives provided services in the remaining one-third. Between 1991 and 1999, about half of the public water companies servicing 28 percent of the country's municipalities and covering almost 60 percent of the country's population were transferred to private for-profit control (see Table 1). The remaining municipalities continued receiving water services from either public companies or nonprofit cooperatives.[2] . . .

3. The Effect of Privatization on Child Mortality

We evaluate the impact of the privatization of water services on the mortality of children under five. We focus on young children because they are

particularly vulnerable to water-related diseases due to weak body defenses, higher susceptibility, and greater exposure from inadequate knowledge of how to avoid risks; and because water related diseases can easily be prevented through access to clean drinking water, better hygiene and better sanitation (WHO, 2000).

The dependent variable in our analysis is the child mortality rate constructed from information contained in vital statistics registries compiled by the Argentine Ministry of Health. The database includes the 165,542 child deaths that occurred from 1990 through 1999, and is defined at the municipality level on an annual basis for 20 pathology groups.[3] . . .

Rather than using the probability that a child dies before she reaches age five, we prefer to use the probability that a child less than five years old dies in a given year. Therefore, we measure our dependent variable as the ratio of number of deaths of children less than five years old to the total number of children less than five alive at the beginning of the year. We estimate the total number of children using census data and the vital statistics records. Our results do not change when we use the more traditional definition. In that case, the estimated coefficients are equal to five times ours.

3.1. Main Results

Our objective is to identify the average effect of privatization on child mortality rates in the municipalities where the water supply system has been privatized (i.e. the average impact of treatment on the treated). Specifically, we are interested in comparing mortality when water services are privately provided compared to the counterfactual—i.e. mortality when services are publicly provided in

---

[2]The only exception is a small mining town in Jujuy, where a private mining company provided water service throughout the period of analysis.

[3]We exclude from the analysis 5,042 child deaths for which the municipality is unspecified. The mortality data is not available at the municipality level before 1990.

the treatment areas at the same point in time. Since the counterfactual is never observed, we must estimate it. In principle, we would like to randomly assign private and public ownership across municipalities and compare the average outcomes of the two groups. In the absence of a controlled randomized trial we are forced to turn to non-experimental methods that mimic it under reasonable conditions.

A major concern is that the municipalities that chose to privatize could be different from the municipalities that chose not to privatize, and that these differences may be correlated with mortality. For example, poorer urban areas where mortality rates were higher may have been the ones that privatize. In this case, the correlation between privatization and mortality would be confounded with the wealth effect. In principle, many of the types of (unobservable) characteristics that may confound identification are those that vary across municipalities, but are fixed over time. A common method of controlling for time-invariant unobserved heterogeneity is to use panel data and estimate difference-in-differences models.

Therefore, without the benefit of a controlled randomized trail, we turn to a difference-in-differences approach, which compares the change in outcomes in the treatment group before and after the intervention to the change in outcomes in the control group. By comparing changes, we control for observed and unobserved time-invariant municipality characteristics that might be correlated with the privatization decision as well as with mortality. The change in the control group is an estimate of the true counterfactual—i.e. what would have happened to the treatment group if there was no intervention. Another way to state this is that the change in outcomes in treatment areas controls for fixed characteristics and the change in outcomes in the control areas controls for time-varying factors that are common to both control and treatment areas. . . .

We present the estimation results for child mortality from all causes of death in Table 2. Each column reports the results from a different specification using the same dependent variable. The model in the first column includes no covariates except for municipality fixed effects and year dummies. We find that the privatization of water services is associated with a 0.33 reduction in the mortality rate, which amounts to a 5.3 percent reduction of the baseline rate.[4]

One concern with these results is that there may be observable or unobservable characteristics that vary across time and space, and that are correlated with both mortality and privatization. For example, it could be that the areas that privatized were also hit by positive economic shocks or there were improvements in the health care system or increases in public welfare programs at the time they privatized. . . .

We directly control for a number of observed time-varying characteristics. In the model reported in column 2 we include GDP per capita, unemployment, income inequality and local public spending. The public spending variable controls for the possibility that the impact of privatization is coming from correlated improvements in the local public programs. However, only inequality appears to be significantly correlated with child mortality at the ten percent level. More importantly, the estimated impact of privatization is unchanged.[5]

In column 3, we add dummy variables for the political party that controlled the local government. The same political parties that choose to privatize might run better administrations or have stronger preferences for child mortality reduction in ways not properly captured by the public spending variable. However, the estimated impact of privatization is unaffected. Overall, we find that privatization is associated with a significant reduction in the child mortality rate of about 5 percent using the full sample regardless of the choice of controls.

3.2. Results by Cause of Death

In spite of the robustness of our results to the inclusion of economic and political controls, it is still possible that at the time of privatization there may have been other unobserved changes in the municipalities that privatized that are correlated with mortality in general. For example, there may have been enhancements in the health care system or increases in public welfare programs not captured by the public spending or political variables. It is also possible that there were different migratory trends among treated and untreated municipalities correlated with privatization.

In order to rule out possible unobserved changes correlated with privatization, we examine the impact of privatization on mortality by cause of death. The mortality data in Argentina are disaggregated for 20 specific pathology groups. The privatization of water provision on child mortality should mainly operate by affecting deaths from infectious and par-

---

[4]Both the year and municipality fixed effects are jointly significantly different from zero. However, a Hausman test cannot reject the hypothesis that the fixed effect and random effect estimates are the same. This suggests that the treatment variable is uncorrelated with the fixed municipality characteristics.

[5]The results are unaffected if the control variables are lagged.

Table 2. The Impact of Water Services Privatization on Child Mortality

	Full sample		
	(1)	(2)	(3)
Private water services (=1)	–0.334	–0.320	–0.283
	(0.169)**	(0.170)*	(0.170)*
%Δ in mortality rate	–5.3%	–5.1%	–4.5%
Other covariates			
Real GDP per capita		0.007	0.009
		(0.005)	(0.006)
Unemployment rate		–0.555	–0.636
		(1.757)	(1.758)
Income inequality		5.171	5.085
		(2.868)*	(2.880)*
Public spending per capita		–0.028	–0.035
		(0.038)	(0.038)
Local government by radical party (=1)			0.482
			(0.267)*
Local government by peronist party (=1)			–0.202
			(0.191)
R-squared	0.1227	0.1254	0.1272
Number of observations	4732	4597	4597

Notes: Each column reports the estimated coefficients of a separate regression model where the dependent variable is the child mortality rate, whose mean was 6.25‰ in 1990. Standard errors are in parentheses. . . . All the regressions include year and municipality fixed effects. The sample includes the municipalities with always public, privatized and non-profit cooperative water companies (see Table 1). . . . The stars indicate statistical significance of the coefficients. *** Statistically different from zero at the 0.01 level of significance. ** Statistically different from zero at the 0.05 level of significance. * Statistically different from zero at the 0.1 level of significance.

asitic diseases. These deaths are classified into two of the pathology groups. If the death occurred after the first 28 days of life, it is classified in the Infectious and Parasitic Diseases group. However, all deaths that occurred during the first 28 days of life are placed into the Perinatal Deaths category, regardless of the cause. Thus, even if the death occurred from an infectious or parasitic disease it is assigned to the Perinatal Deaths during the first 28 days of life, and not to the Infectious and Parasitic Diseases category. Therefore, if the observed reduction in child mortality is operating through improved access and quality of water, then we should see significant negative effects on deaths in the Perinatal Deaths and Infectious and Parasitic Diseases categories, and negligible effects on deaths from other causes such as accidents, cardiovascular diseases, or cancer.

We estimate the difference-in-differences models using . . . all socio-economic and political controls for child mortality rates for each cause of death.[6] The results are reported in Table 3. As predicted, we find a statistically significant effect on mortality from infectious and parasitic diseases and perinatal deaths, but no statistically significant effect on mortality from any other cause either separately or in aggregate. The estimated effects correspond to a reduction of 18.2 percent in mortality from infectious and parasitic diseases, and a reduction of 11.5 percent on perinatal deaths.

The importance of this result cannot be overemphasized. Privatization could only be spuriously capturing the effect of unobservables if those uncontrolled variables are correlated with deaths from infectious and parasitic diseases, but not with deaths from any other cause. This result rules out the presence of almost any other plausible explanation of our main results and leads us to believe in their causal interpretation.

3.3. Impact by Socioeconomic Status

We hypothesize that privatization should have had a higher impact on child mortality in poor municipalities than in wealthier ones. Middle and high-income groups already had a high rate of connection to the water network prior to privatization. Even when they were not connected or when service quality was unsatisfactory, these income

[6]As we are analyzing child mortality, we exclude from this exercise the analysis of deaths from four causes that are only relevant for adults (suicides; homicides; other violent deaths; and pregnancy, labor, delivery and puerperal diseases). We also exclude the residual category of undefined causes.

Table 3. The Impact of Privatization on Child Mortality by Cause of Death

	1990 mean mortality rate	Estimated impact coefficients & standard errors	%Δ in mortality rate
Infectious and parasitic diseases	0.565	−0.103	
		(0.048)**	−18.2%
Perinatal deaths	2.316	−0.266	
		(0.105)**	−11.5%
All other causes in aggregate	2.565	−0.082	
		(0.114)	. . .
All other causes disaggregated			
Accidents	0.399	−0.004	
		(0.057)	. . .
Congenital anomalies	0.711	−0.022	
		(0.056)	. . .
Skin and soft tissues diseases	0.000	0.000	
		(0.001)	. . .
Blood and hematologic diseases	0.024	−0.002	
		(0.008)	. . .
Nervous system disorders	0.163	0.025	
		(0.026)	. . .
Cardiovascular diseases	0.236	0.006	
		(0.030)	. . .
Gastrointestinal tract disorders	0.051	−0.001	
		(0.010)	. . .
Genital and urinary diseases	0.020	−0.006	
		(0.007)	. . .
Osteoarticular and connective tissue diseases	0.003	−0.001	
		(0.001)	. . .
Respiratory diseases	0.511	−0.038	
		(0.051)	. . .
Immuno-deficiencies, endocrine and nutrition system diseases	0.376	−0.035	
		(0.033)	. . .
Mental disorders	0.002	0.001	
		(0.001)	. . .
Tumors	0.068	−0.006	
		(0.015)	. . .

Notes: Each cell reports the estimated coefficient on the Private Water Services dummy from a different difference-in-difference regression. Standard errors are in parentheses. . . . All the regressions include year and municipality fixed effects. . . . The stars indicate statistical significance of the coefficients. . . . *** Statistically different from zero at the 0.01 level of significance. ** Statistically different from zero at the 0.05 level of significance. * Statistically different from zero at the 0.1 level of significance.

groups enjoyed better access to substitutes such as pumped wells, septic tanks, or bottled water than poor households. The main beneficiaries of network expansions and service enhancements, therefore, were low-income households who also are the groups most vulnerable to child mortality.

In Table 4 we report the estimated impact of water privatization on child mortality at three different ranges of poverty at the municipality level. To estimate these heterogeneous impacts of privatization on child mortality, we interact the treatment dummy variable with a poverty indicator function from the 1991 Census. We construct three ranges

of poverty: municipalities with a percent of households suffering from Unmet Basic Needs (UBN) lower than 25%, municipalities with UBN between 25 and 50%, and municipalities with UBN higher than 50%.

We find that the privatization of water systems does not affect mortality in those municipalities with low levels of poverty (UBN lower than 25%). The effect on the remaining treated municipalities is increasing in the level of poverty and highly significant. In fact, the privatization of water systems is associated with a 26.5 percent reduction in child mortality in municipalities with high levels of

Table 4. The Impact of Privatization on Child Mortality by Poverty Level

	1990 mean mortality rate	Estimated impact coefficients & standard errors	%Δ in mortality rate
Non-poor municipalities	5.07	0.114 (0.233)	. . .
Poor municipalities	6.97	−1.004 (0.279)***	−14.4%
Extremely poor municipalities	9.11	−2.415 (0.544)***	−26.5%

Notes: Municipalities are divided into poverty groups using the government's index of Unmet Basic Needs (UBN) using data from the 1991 Census. Non-poor municipalities are defined as those in which less than 25% of households have Unmet Basic Needs. Poor municipalities are defined as those in which 25% to 50% of households have Unmet Basic Needs. Extremely poor municipalities are defined as those in which more than 50% of households have Unmet Basic Needs. The reported coefficients are the interaction of the Private Water Services dummy and UBN (recorded in a set of dummy variables in the three categories: below 25%, between 25% and 50%, and above 50%) in a difference-in-differences regression. . . . The regression includes year and municipality fixed effects, and the socioeconomic and political covariates used in the regression reported in Column 3 of Table 2. Standard errors are in parentheses. . . . The stars indicate statistical significance of the coefficients. . . . *** Statistically different from zero at the 0.01 level of significance. ** Statistically different from zero at the 0.05 level of significance. * Statistically different from zero at the 0.1 level of significance.

poverty (UBN greater than 50%). This result is consistent with the predictions of our causal model. The effect of privatization on child mortality should be stronger for the groups that are more vulnerable to water related diseases.

4. Pathways

There are a number of potential pathways by which the privatization of water systems might have induced the reduction in child mortality. First, privatization may have expanded the water supply and sewage network providing access to service to households that were not previously connected to water and sewage. Second, there may have been improvements in service quality in terms of reduced water and sewage spillage, faster repair rates, fewer shortages, cleaner water, and better water pressure and sewage treatment. All of these quality enhancements improve the epidemiological environment (WHO, 2002b). In this section, we present evidence that privatization affected these pathways.

A Case Study

The largest water company privatization was the transfer of the federal company OSN that provided service in the Buenos Aires metropolitan area. The analysis of this privatization, described in Abdala and Spiller (1999), Artana et al. (2000), Shirley (2000), and Alcazar et al. (2002), illustrates the changes experienced by water systems in Argentina after the transfer to private operation.

Rather than selling the assets to the private firms, water services in Argentina were transferred to the private sector through concessions.[7] In some cases, such as OSN, the royalty was set at zero and firms competed for the concession by offering the lowest tariff. In other cases, the privatized companies paid a canon to the government for the use of the public assets. For example, in the provinces of Cordoba and Corrientes, where a canon is paid on an annual basis, the royalty payments represented about 0.4% and 0.1% of the provincial revenues in 1999, respectively. Thus, the revenue from the water service privatization royalties constituted at best a very small share of the public budget.

In May 1993 Aguas Argentinas, a private consortium lead by the French company Lyonnaise des Eaux, won a 35-year concession to provide water services previously provided by OSN. The terms of the concession stipulated that 100% of households had to be connected to water service and 95% to sewage service by the end of the 35-year period. It also established service quality and waste treatment standards.

Water use fees in Buenos Aires were initially lowered by 26.9 percent as a result of the privatization bid. However, thirteen months after privatization, the regulator authorized a 13.5 percent in-

[7]This is the most common method of privatizing water services worldwide (Noll et al., 2000).

Table 5. Comparison of OSN (Public) vs. Aguas Argentinas (Private) Performance, 1980–1999

	OSN[a] (before privatization)	Aguas Argentinas[b] (after privatization)	Δ after privatization
Water production (1) (millions of cubic meters per day)	3.56	3.89	9.3%
Spilled water (2) (millions of cubic meters per day)	1.49[c]	1.27	−14.8%
Water supply (1–2) (millions of cubic meters per day)	2.07[c]	2.62	26.6%
Sewage drainage volume (millions of cubic meters per day)	2.18	2.45	12.4%
Water network extension (km of network)	10,148	13,287	30.9%
Sewage network extension (km of network)	6,875	8,312	20.9%
Average delay in attending repair requests (days)	180[d]	32[a]	−82.2%
Water leakages repaired per year	42,000[c]	96,383	129.5%
Sewage blockages repaired per year	100,000[c]	148,500	48.5%
Percentage of clients with appropriate water pressure	17[c]	54[f]	217.6%
Water turbidness (turbidness units)	7.5	2.3	−70%
Usage fee index[g]	100	84	−16%
Employees	9300	4000	−57%

Notes: (a) Average for the period 1980–1992. (b) Average for the period 1994–1999. (c) 1993 only. (d) 1992 only. (e) Average excludes 1994. (f) 1996 only. (g) Corresponds to the "K" tariff factor.

crease in the usage fee, and a significant increase in connection fees. This latter increase was particularly controversial as the connection fee almost reached a month's earnings for a household at the official poverty line. In response to protests, the connection fee was lowered to about one tenth of the previous level and a fixed charge was added to the water use bills for all clients as a cross-subsidy (Alcazar et al., 2002). Indeed, the Buenos Aires water concession has been criticized for its prompt and frequent renegotiations (Alcazar et al., 2002; Gerchunoff et al., 2003; Clarke et al., 2003).[8]

The enforcement of service payment was toughened after privatization. While delinquency was high for OSN, the private operator was allowed to cut service to customers with three unpaid bills (although it could be reconnected under the regulator's request). According to Artana et al. (2000) and Water World Vision (2000), over 90 percent of customers regularly pay the service fees, although only about 60 percent do it on time.

Privatization increased efficiency and profitability. Before privatization, OSN was overstaffed and absenteeism was high. During the first year under private management, the number of employees was

reduced from 7365 to 3800. The employment reduction, together with the increase in coverage and production, resulted in large productivity increases. In fact, after a first year of negative returns, Aguas Argentinas turned into a highly profitable company (Artana et al., 2000).

A major question was whether these efficiency gains were translated into service quality improvements. OSN had invested very little in infrastructure during the decade prior to privatization (Galiani et al., 2002). Low revenues and inefficiencies led to such low investment levels that they were not even sufficient to replace depreciating assets and maintain current supply. In 1985 OSN investment was 67.8 percent of what was needed to maintain current supply, and only 19.5 percent in 1990.[9] In the late 1980s, water coverage as a share of population was contracting, spilled water rates were very high, pressure and service quality were low, and summer shortages were frequent (Artana et al., 2000).

Things improved significantly after the privatization. The private company was able to invest a substantial amount in physical infrastructure and service quality. For the ten years before the privatization, OSN invested an average of 25 Million US dollars annually. From 1993 through 2000, Aguas Argentinas's investment jumped to around 200 Million per year. Table 5 shows large increases in water and sewage production, reductions in

---

[8]Renegotiations of water concessions seem to be pervasive. Guasch et al. (2003) reports that 70 percent of water concession contracts in Latin America have been renegotiated. Criticisms to the Buenos Aires water concession also refer to the obscure tariff system that was inherited from the public era. Water use bills for unmetered customers are a complex function of property characteristics (Alcazar et al., 2002). Aguas Argentinas increased fees for 17 percent of the customers through property reclassifications (Clarke et al., 2003).

[9]For the whole country, investment in the water sector as a percentage of total domestic investment fell from 1.5% during the 1960s to 0.5% in 1981–1993 (Rey, 2000).

Table 6. Network Expansion by Income Group in Greater Buenos Aires (1993–2000)

Income level	New connections	Percentage
High & upper middle income	90,200	15.4%
Lower middle income	282,250	48.3%
Low income	211,800	36.3%
Total	584,250	100.0%

Source: Subsecretaría de Recursos Hídricos, from Abdala and Spiller (1999).

spillage, and significant service enhancements. In addition, summer water shortages disappeared, repair delays shortened, and water pressure and cleanliness improved.[10]

The investments also paid off in terms of increased access to the network. The number of connections to the water and sewage networks in Buenos Aires expanded by 30 percent and 20 percent, respectively, after privatization. . . .

Moreover, the network expansion was concentrated in the poorer suburban areas of Greater Buenos Aires. Since 98% percent of households in the city of Buenos Aires were already connected to water services before privatization, most of the expansion in access necessarily had to be among lower income households in the suburban areas. Indeed, Table 6 shows that 84.6 percent of the new connections were to lower-middle and low-income households.

[10]Not all the water privatizations in Argentina were successful. In Tucumán, the provincial government privatized water provision in 1995. When prices doubled, public protests ignited and 80 percent of customers refused to pay their water bills. The concessionaire, a subsidiary of Vivendi, unilaterally rescinded the contract and filed a suit against the province. An international arbitration panel ruled in favor of the provincial government. In the Province of Buenos Aires, water provision was privatized in 1999. The concession was awarded to a subsidiary of Enron, which tendered three times the offer of the next bidder.

References

Abdala, M. and P. Spiller (1999): "Agua y Saneamiento," in *Instituciones, Contratos y Regulación en Argentina,* Buenos Aires: TEMAS.

Alcazar, L., M. Abdala and M. Shirley (2002): "The Buenos Aires Water Concession," in M. Shirley (ed.), *Thirsting for Efficiency: The Economics and Politics of Urban Water System Reform,* Amsterdam: Pergamon.

Armstrong, M., S. Cowan and J. Vickers (1994): *Regulatory Reform: Economic Analysis and British Experience,* Cambridge: MIT Press.

Artana, D., F. Navajas and S. Urbiztondo (2000): "Governance and Regulation in Argentina," in Savedoff, W. and P. Spiller (eds.), *Spilled Water,* Washington D.C.: IDB Press.

Barberis N., M. Boycko, A. Shleifer and N. Tsukanova (1996): "How Does Privatization Work? Evidence from the Russian Shops," *Journal of Political Economy* 104 (4), pp. 764–90.

Clarke, G., K. Kosec and S. Wallsten (2003): "Has Private Participation in Water and Sewerage Improved Coverage? Empirical Evidence from Latin America," forthcoming, Stanford Conference on Sector Reform in Latin America.

Estache, A., A. Gomez-Lobo and D. Leipziger (2001): "Utilities Privatization and the Poor: Lessons and Evidence from Latin America," *World Development,* 29 (7), pp. 1179–98.

Foster, V. (1999): "Literature Review for Regional Studies Project on Privatization and Infrastructure Services of the Urban Poor," mimeo, World Bank.

Frydman, R., C. Gray, M. Hessel and A. Rapaczynsku (1999): "When Does Privatization Work? The Impact of Private Ownership on Corporate Performance in the Transition Economies," *Quarterly Journal of Economics* 114 (4), pp. 1153–91.

Galiani, S., P. Gertler, E. Schargrodsky and F. Sturzenegger (2002): "The Benefits and Costs of Privatization in Argentina: A Microeconomic Analysis," forthcoming in Chong, A. and F. Lopez-de-Silanes (eds.), *The Benefits and Costs of Privatizations.*

Gerchunoff, P., E. Greco and D. Bondorevsky (2003): "Comienzos diversos, distintas trayectorias y final abierto: más de una década de privatizaciones en Argentina, 1990–2002," Serie Gestión Pública N° 34, ILPES-ECLAC.

Guasch, J., J. Laffont and S. Straub (2003): "Renegotiation of Concession Contracts in Latin America," *World Bank Policy Research Working Paper,* Washington, DC.

La Porta, R. and F. Lopez-de-Silanes (1999): "The Benefits of Privatization: Evidence from Mexico," *Quarterly Journal of Economics* 114 (4), pp. 1193–1242.

Megginson, W., R. Nash and M. van Randenborgh (1994): "The Financial and Operating Performance of Newly Privatized Firms: An Interpretational Empirical Analysis," *Journal of Finance* 49 (2), pp. 403–52.

Ministerio de Salud (1999): "Programa Nacional de Estadísticas de Salud, Defunciones de Menores de 5 Años, Argentina 1997," Buenos Aires: Ministerio de Salud.

Noll, R., M. Shirley and S. Cowan (2000): "Reforming Urban Water Systems in Developing Countries," in A. Krueger (ed.) *Economic Policy Reform: The Second Stage,* Chicago: University of Chicago Press.

Rey, O. (2000): *El Saneamiento en el Area Metropolitana: Desde el Virreinato a 1993,* Buenos Aires: Aguas Argentinas.

Shirley, M. (2000): "Reforming Urban Water Systems: A Tale of Four Cities," in L. Manzetti (ed.) *Regulatory Policy in Latin America: Post Privatization Realities,* Coral Gables: North-South Center Press, University of Miami.

Shleifer, A. and R. Vishny (1994): "Politicians and Firms," *Quarterly Journal of Economics* 109 (4), pp. 995–1025.

Shleifer, A. (1998): "State versus Private Ownership," *Journal of Economics Perspectives* 12 (4), pp. 133–50.

UNICEF (2001): *Estado Mundial de la Infancia,* New York: UNICEF.

Water World Vision (2000): "Informe Nacional sobre la Gestión del Agua en Argentina," mimeo.

WHO (2000): *Global Water Supply and Sanitation Assessment 2000 Report,* Geneva: World Health Organization.

WHO (2002a): *Children's Health and Environment: A Review of Evidence,* Copenhagen: European Environment Agency and World Health Organization, Regional Office for Europe.

WHO (2002b): *Water and Health,* Copenhagen: European Environment Agency and World Health Organization, Regional Office for Europe.

World Bank (2002): "Water—The Essence of Life," Development News, May 17.

VI.B. RURAL-URBAN MIGRATION AND THE INFORMAL SECTOR

Exhibit VI.B.1. Self-Employment[a] and Unpaid Family Workers

Country Name (listed from lowest to highest HDI)	Survey Year	Percent of Total Labor Force[b]	Percent of Non-Agricultural[c] Labor Force	Agricultural Value-Added Per Worker[d]
Low-human development countries				
Burundi	1990	93.6	29.1	177
Ethiopia	1999	83.9	84.1	137
Chad	1993	94.0	70.7	169
Rwanda	1996	93.9	36.9	268
Haiti	1990	69.5	38.1	
Pakistan	1998	61.0	58.1	704
Median		*88.7*	*48.1*	*177*
Medium-human development countries				
Bangladesh	1996	68.4	51.8	264
India	1991	5.3	12.7	339
Botswana	1991	23.6	10.0	787
Egypt	1999	35.7	31.8	1,266
Guatemala	1994	50.1	25.7	2,015
Honduras	1998	55.1	49.4	1,033
Bolivia	2000	64.0	64.4	755
Indonesia	1998	63.5	46.3	731
Syrian Arab Republic	1991	44.0	29.6	2,103
Moldova, Rep. of	2000	27.9	28.4	1,649
Iran, Islamic Rep. of	1991	47.2	33.7	2,850
El Salvador	1999	38.5	38.7	1,773
Cape Verde	1990	26.7	14.6	1,794
Ecuador	1998	37.7	37.9	1,788
Turkey	1998	53.1	25.7	1,979
Dominican Republic	1993	27.6	22.7	2,186
Maldives	1990	44.2	32.3	1,646
Philippines	1998	46.0	28.4	1,321
Paraguay	1994	36.9	35.9	3,238
Peru	2000[e]	45.7	45.8	1,876
Saint Vincent and the Grenadines	1991	20.2	10.1	2,624
Thailand	1998	61.2	33.8	892
Romania	1992	15.8	1.5	2,203
Samoa (Western)	1991	70.7	14.5	
Venezuela	1997	33.3	31.6	5,083
Belize	1991	24.2	15.6	3,976
Brazil	1997	32.9	26.4	4,091
Colombia	1994	30.6	30.5	3,355
Mauritius	1990	14.0	12.6	4,663
Macedonia, TFYR	1991	74.8	79.2	
Panama	1993	29.8	19.2	2,319
Malaysia	1998	26.6	17.9	6,482
Bulgaria	2000	11.6	9.7	7,960
Median		*36.9*	*28.4*	*1,979*
High-human development countries				
Mexico	2000	36.3	36.3	1,791
Trinidad and Tobago	1998	19.7	17.3	2,428
Latvia	2000	12.6	10.5	2,717
Croatia	1991	14.7	6.4	
Lithuania	2000	17.7	17.6	3,258
Chile	1998	28.6	26.2	5,754
Costa Rica	1998	27.8	25.0	5,027

Exhibit VI.B.1. (Continued)

Country Name (listed from lowest to highest HDI)	Survey Year	Percent of Total Labor Force[b]	Percent of Non-Agricultural[c] Labor Force	Agricultural Value-Added Per Worker[d]
Estonia	2000	8.2	7.0	4,347
Uruguay	2000	24.1	20.6	8,062
Slovakia	1993	90.2	89.5	2,813
Hungary	1992	13.3	12.3	4,177
Poland	2000[f]	23.8	23.4	1,560
Argentina	2000	26.8	24.0	10,260
Czech Republic	2000	14.1	12.3	6,306
Brunei Darussalam	1991	5.1	4.5	61,971
Korea, Rep. of	2000	36.1	35.6	13,758
Slovenia	2000	15.1	13.1	36,175
Singapore	1997	12.9	12.9	38,646
Hong Kong, China (SAR)	1998	9.9	9.7	
Cyprus	2000	22.9	22.6	
Greece	2000	37.4	32.2	14,285
Portugal	2000	24.6	20.5	7,469
Israel	1994	15.4	14.0	
Italy	1996	25.3	22.9	21,008
New Zealand	2000	19.4	17.4	29,288
Spain	1999	17.3	12.8	20,983
Germany	2000	10.2	8.1	32,629
France	1990	6.4	5.0	32,880
Austria	2000	12.7	10.2	31,396
Luxembourg	1991	9.7	7.2	
Finland	2000	12.5	9.6	41,686
Ireland	1991	19.6	11.0	
Denmark	2000	8.4	5.8	57,535
Japan	2000	15.8	16.1	31,791
Canada	2000	15.4	13.5	43,768
United States	2000	7.3	7.5	53,353
Belgium	2000	14.7	10.5	15,829
Netherlands	2000	11.6	7.5	59,346
Australia	1995	14.6	12.4	27,739
Sweden	2000	9.8	9.1	36,640
Iceland	1999	17.7	16.8	50,787
Norway	2000	7.1	7.2	35,211
Median		*15.2*	*12.8*	*20,996*

United Nations Human Development Index countries are included in the Exhibit only if they have data available.

[a]Self-employment is defined as own-account workers plus employers.

[b]The labor force includes all people identified by the International Labour Organization to be part of the economically active population.

[c]Industry classifications are based on the United Nations ISIC Revision 2. Agriculture corresponds to ISIC Revision 2 division 1 and includes forestry, hunting, and fishing as well as cultivation of crops and livestock production.

[d]Agriculture value added per worker is a measure of agricultural productivity. It is defined as the ratio of agricultural value added to the number of workers in agriculture. Value added in agriculture measures the output of the agricultural sector less the value of intermediate inputs. Industry classifications are based on the United Nations ISIC Revision 3. Agriculture corresponds to ISIC Revision 3 divisions 1–5 and includes forestry, hunting, and fishing as well as cultivation of crops and livestock production. Data are in constant 1995 U.S. dollars.

[e]Data are limited to urban areas only.

[f]Data for own-account workers also include members of producers' cooperatives.

Source: International Labour Organization; World Bank, World Development Indicators, 2003.

Selection VI.B.1. Economic Development with Unlimited Supplies of Labor*

In the first place, an unlimited supply of labour may be said to exist in those countries where population is so large relatively to capital and natural resources, that there are large sectors of the economy where the marginal productivity of labour is negligible, zero, or even negative. Several writers have drawn attention to the existence of such "disguised" unemployment in the agricultural sector, demonstrating in each case that the family holding is so small that if some members of the family obtained other employment the remaining members could cultivate the holding just as well (of course they would have to work harder: the argument includes the proposition that they would be willing to work harder in these circumstances). The phenomenon is not, however, by any means confined to the countryside. Another large sector to which it applies is the whole range of casual jobs—the workers on the docks, the young men who rush forward asking to carry your bag as you appear, the jobbing gardener, and the like. These occupations usually have a multiple of the number they need, each of them earning very small sums from occasional employment; frequently their number could be halved without reducing output in this sector. Petty retail trading is also exactly of this type; it is enormously expanded in overpopulated economies; each trader makes only a few sales; markets are crowded with stalls, and if the number of stalls were greatly reduced the consumers would be no whit worse off—they might even be better off, since retail margins might fall. Twenty years ago one could not write these sentences without having to stop and explain why in these circumstances, the casual labourers do not bid their earnings down to zero, or why the farmers' product is not similarly all eaten up in rent, but these propositions present no terrors to contemporary economists.

A little more explanation has to be given of those cases where the workers are not self-employed, but are working for wages, since it is harder to believe that employers will pay wages exceeding marginal productivity. The most important of these sectors is domestic service, which is usually even more inflated in over-populated countries than is petty trading (in Barbados 16 per cent. of the population is in domestic service). The reason is that in over-populated countries the code of ethical behaviour so shapes itself that it becomes good form for each person to offer as much employment as he can. The line between employees and dependents is very thinly drawn. Social prestige requires people to have servants, and the grand seigneur may have to keep a whole army of retainers who are really little more than a burden upon his purse. This is found not only in domestic service, but in every sector of employment. Most businesses in under-developed countries employ a large number of "messengers," whose contribution is almost negligible; you see them sitting outside office doors, or hanging around in the courtyard. And even in the severest slump the agricultural or commercial employer is expected to keep his labour force somehow or other—it would be immoral to turn them out, for how would they eat, in countries where the only form of unemployment assistance is the charity of relatives? So it comes about that even in the sectors where people are working for wages, and above all the domestic sector, marginal productivity may be negligible or even zero.

Whether marginal productivity is zero or negligible is not, however, of fundamental importance to our analysis. The price of labour, in these economies, is a wage at the subsistence level (we define this later). The supply of labour is therefore "unlimited" so long as the supply of labour at this price exceeds the demand. In this situation, new industries can be created, or old industries expanded without limit at the existing wage; or, to put it more exactly, shortage of labour is no limit to the creation of new sources of employment. If we cease to ask whether the marginal productivity of labour is negligible and ask instead only the question from what sectors would additional labour be available if new industries were created offering employment at subsistence wages, the answer becomes even more comprehensive. For we have then not only the farmers, the casuals, the petty traders and the retainers (domestic and commercial), but we have also three other classes from which to choose.

First of all, there are the wives and daughters of the household. The employment of women outside the household depends upon a great number of factors, religious and conventional, and is certainly not exclusively a matter of employment opportunities. There are, however, a number of countries where the current limit is for practical purposes only employment opportunities. This is true, for example, even inside the United Kingdom. The

*From W. Arthur Lewis, "Economic Development with Unlimited Supplies of Labor," *The Manchester School* 22(1954): 141–45. Reprinted by permission.

proportion of women gainfully employed in the U.K. varies enormously from one region to another according to employment opportunities for women. For example, in 1939 whereas there were 52 women gainfully employed for every 100 men in Lancashire, there were only 15 women gainfully employed for every 100 men in South Wales. Similarly in the Gold Coast, although there is an acute shortage of male labour, any industry which offered good employment to women would be besieged with applications. The transfer of women's work from the household to commercial employment is one of the most notable features of economic development. It is not by any means all gain, but the gain is substantial because most of the things which women otherwise do in the household can in fact be done much better or more cheaply outside, thanks to the large scale economies of specialisation, and also to the use of capital (grinding grain, fetching water from the river, making cloth, making clothes, cooking the midday meal, teaching children, nursing the sick, etc.). One of the surest ways of increasing the national income is therefore to create new sources of employment for women outside the home.

The second source of labour for expanding industries is the increase in the population resulting from the excess of births over deaths. This source is important in any dynamic analysis of how capital accumulation can occur, and employment can increase, without any increase in real wages. It was therefore a cornerstone of Ricardo's system. Strictly speaking, population increase is not relevant either to the classical analysis, or to the analysis which follows in this article, unless it can be shown that the increase of population is caused by economic development and would not otherwise be so large. The proof of this proposition was supplied to the classical economists by the Malthusian law of population. There is already an enormous literature of the genus: "What Malthus *Really* Meant," into which we need not enter. Modern population theory has advanced a little by analysing separately the effects of economic development upon the birth rate, and its effects on the death rate. Of the former, we know little. There is no evidence that the birth rate ever rises with economic development. In Western Europe it has fallen during the last eighty years. We are not quite sure why; we suspect that it was for reasons associated with development, and we hope that the same thing may happen in the rest of the world as development spreads. Of the death rate we are more certain. It comes down with development from around

40 to around 12 per thousand; in the first stage because better communications and trade eliminate death from local famines; in the second stage because better public health facilities banish the great epidemic diseases of plague, smallpox, cholera, malaria, yellow fever (and eventually tuberculosis); and in the third stage because widespread facilities for treating the sick snatch from the jaws of death many who would otherwise perish in infancy or in their prime. Because the effect of development on the death rate is so swift and certain, while its effect on the birth rate is unsure and retarded, we can say for certain that the immediate effect of economic development is to cause the population to grow; after some decades it begins to grow (we hope) less rapidly. Hence in any society where the death rate is around 40 per thousand, the effect of economic development will be to generate an increase in the supply of labour.

Marx offered a third source of labour to add to the reserve army, namely the unemployment generated by increasing efficiency. Ricardo had admitted that the creation of machinery could reduce employment. Marx seized upon the argument, and in effect generalised it, for into the pit of unemployment he threw not only those displaced by machinery, but also the self-employed and petty capitalists who could not compete with larger capitalists of increasing size, enjoying the benefits of the economies of scale. Nowadays we reject this argument on empirical grounds. It is clear that the effect of capital accumulation in the past has been to reduce the size of the reserve army, and not to increase it, so we have lost interest in arguments about what is "theoretically" possible.

When we take account of all the sources we have now listed—the farmers, the casuals, the petty traders, the retainers (domestic and commercial), women in the household, and population growth—it is clear enough that there can be in an over-populated economy an enormous expansion of new industries or new employment opportunities without any shortage of unskilled labour becoming apparent in the labour market. From the point of view of the effect of economic development on wages, the supply of labour is practically unlimited.

This applies only to unskilled labour. There may at any time be a shortage of skilled workers of any grade—ranging from masons, electricians or welders to engineers, biologists or administrators. Skilled labour may be the bottleneck in expansion, just like capital or land. Skilled labour, however, is only what Marshall might have called a "quasi-bottleneck," if he had not had so nice a sense of elegant language. For it is only a very temporary bottleneck, in the sense that if the capital is available for development, the capitalists or their government will soon provide the facilities for training more skilled people. The real bottlenecks to expansion are therefore capital and natural resources, and we can proceed on the assumption that so long as these are available the necessary skills will be provided as well, though perhaps with some time lag.

Selection VI.B.2. A Model of Labor Migration and Urban Unemployment in Less Developed Countries*

It is our opinion that a more realistic picture of labor migration in less developed countries would be one that views migration as a two-stage phenomenon. The first stage finds the unskilled rural worker migrating to an urban area and initially spending a certain period of time in the so-called "urban traditional" sector.[1] The second stage is reached with the eventual attainment of a more permanent modern sector job. This two-stage process permits us to ask some fundamentally important questions regarding the decision to migrate, the proportionate size of the urban traditional sector, and the implications of accelerated industrial growth and/or alternative rural-urban real income differentials on labor participation in the modern economy.

Employment Probability and the Decision to Migrate

In our model, the decision to migrate from rural to urban areas will be functionally related to two principal variables: (1) the urban-rural real income differential and (2) the probability of obtaining an urban job. Since it is this latter variable which will play a pivotal role in the analysis, it might be instructive at this point to explain briefly our reasons for incorporating this probability notion into the overall framework.

As pointed out above, an implicit assumption of typical labor transfer models is that any migrant who enters the modern sector is "absorbed" into the gainfully employed at the prevailing urban real wage. However, the important question to ask in this context is "how long" does the average migrant have to wait before actually obtaining a job. Even if

the prevailing real wage is significantly higher than expected rural income, the fact that the "probability" of obtaining a modern sector job, say within the next year or two, is very low must certainly influence the prospective migrant's choice as to whether or not he should leave the farm. In effect, he must balance the probabilities and risks of being unemployed or sporadically employed in the city for a certain period of time against the favorable urban wage differential. A 70 per cent urban real wage premium, for example, might be of little consequence to the prospective migrant if his chances of actually securing a job are, say, one in fifty. Nevertheless, even if expected urban real income is less than rural real income for a certain period following migration, it may still be economically rational from a longer-run point of view (e.g., from a discounted present value approach to the rural-urban work choice) for the individual to migrate and swell the ranks of the urban traditional sector. Our underlying behavioral model, therefore, will be formulated more in the spirit of permanent income theories than present wage differential theories.

To underline the fundamental role played by job opportunities and probabilities of employment in the actual migration decision-making process, we might cite two outstanding illustrations, one historical and one contemporary, which demonstrate the relative, and often overriding, importance of this variable. The first case concerns the movements of American unskilled laborers back and forth between agriculture and industry during the 1930 depression decade. In an extremely informative and well-documented study of American agriculture, Theodore Schultz (1945) argues that in 1932 when urban wages were still considerably higher and falling less rapidly than rural wages, there was a definite reversal of the historical flow of workers from the farm to the city. In fact, 1932 witnessed a net urban to rural labor migration (p. 90). Schultz attributes this seemingly paradoxical phenomenon to the severe lack of job opportunities in depressed urban factories and the more likely prospects of finding agricultural employment in rural areas even though there still existed a significant positive urban wage premium (p. 99).

The second, more contemporary case concerns an interesting experiment carried out in Kenya in 1964. In a modified version of a tactic suggested by the International Labor Office (1964) which advocated that governments of less developed countries

*From Michael P. Todaro, "A Model of Labor Migration and Urban Unemployment in Less Developed Countries," *American Economic Review* (March 1969): 139–147. Reprinted by permission.

[1]For the purposes of this paper, the urban traditional sector will encompass all those workers not regularly employed in the urban modern sector, i.e., the overtly unemployed, the underemployed or sporadically employed, and those who grind out a meagre existence in petty retail trades and services. J. P. Lewis provides an excellent description of this traditional sector which consists largely of "the urban in-migrant who, instead of doing absolutely nothing, joins Bombay's army of underemployed bootblacks or Delhi's throngs of self-appointed (and tippable) parking directors, or who becomes an extra, redundant salesman in the yard goods stall of the cousin, who according to custom, is going to have to provide him with bed and board anyway" (1962, p. 53). This description aptly fits a typical city in Africa and Latin America as well.

employ and, through taxes and subsidies, induce private enterprise to employ more labor than would be worthwhile on the basis of a comparison between productivity and wages, the government of Kenya instituted a "tripartite agreement" among itself, private employers, and trade unions. The avowed intention was to wipe out the considerable unemployment existing in the greater Nairobi area by having the two hiring participants agree to increase their employment immediately by 15 per cent. For their part the unions had to agree to forego any demands for general wage increases. In his analysis of this "agreement" Professor Harbison has observed that:

The effort was a colossal failure. The private employers did take on additional workers and *this acted like a magnet attracting new workers into the urban labor markets;* in a few months the working forces in most of the private establishments had dropped to their former levels through attrition not offset by new hires. In the end, the volume of unemployment, as a consequence of the expansion of the modern labor force *in response to the prospect of more jobs* was probably increased rather than decreased (1967, p. 183, fn**). (Italics not in original)

Here once again we can recognize the basic influence exerted by the probability of finding a job (whether real or anticipated) on the supply of rural workers into urban labor markets. . . .

Perhaps the most significant policy implication emerging from the model is the great difficulty of substantially reducing the size of the urban traditional sector without a concentrated effort at making rural life more attractive. For example, instead of allocating scarce capital funds to urban low cost housing projects which would effectively raise urban real incomes and might therefore lead to a worsening of the housing problem, governments in less developed countries might do better if they devoted these funds to the improvement of rural amenities. In effect, the net benefit of bringing "city lights" to the countryside might greatly exceed whatever net benefit might be derived from luring more peasants to the city by increasing the attractiveness of urban living conditions. Like Marshall's famous scissors analogy, the equilibrium level of nonparticipation in the urban economy is as much a function of rural "supply push" as it is one of urban "demand pull." Thus, as long as the urban-rural real income differential continues to rise sufficiently fast to offset any sustained increase in the rate of job creation, then even in spite of the long-run stabilizing effect of a lower probability of successfully finding modern sector employment, the lure of relatively higher permanent incomes will continue to attract a steady stream of rural migrants into the ever more congested urban slums. The potential social, political, and economic ramifications of this growing mass of urban unemployed should not be taken lightly.

References

F. Harbison, "The Generation of Employment in Newly Developing Countries," in J. Sheffield (ed.), *Education, Employment and Rural Development,* Nairobi 1967.

International Labor Office, *Employment and Economic Growth.* Geneva 1964.

J. P. Lewis, *Quiet Crisis in India.* Washington 1962.

T. W. Schultz, *Agriculture in an Unstable Economy.* New York 1945.

Note VI.B.1. The Lewis Versus the Harris–Todaro View of Underemployment in Less Developed Countries

How urban labor demand affe [handwritten annotation in margin]

These two enormously influential models make sharply different predictions regarding the effects of expansion of urban labor demand on underemployment and agricultural output. In this Note we will exposit the two views in a common diagrammatic framework in order to bring the sources of these different predictions into clear focus.

To better understand Lewis's model of underemployment and its predictions it is helpful to refer to Figure 1. The horizontal dimension of the figure is determined by the labor endowment $\bar{L}$ of the economy. We will treat total labor supply as fixed, so we will not consider the possibility that, for example, people might work more or less hours in response to higher wages. Agricultural employment L_A is measured to the right starting from O_A and industrial (manufacturing) employment L_M is measured to the left starting from O_M. The left vertical axis measures the marginal value product of labor in agriculture; the right vertical axis measures the marginal value product of labor in industry, which is assumed to be located in urban rather than rural areas. The prices of agricultural and manufacturing output, p_A and p_M, are assumed to be determined in international markets that the economy is too small to influence. This assumption allows us not to consider how the terms of trade between agriculture and industry might change as the relative outputs of the two sectors change. The marginal physical products of labor in agriculture and manufacturing, MPL_A and MPL_M, are determined by the respective technologies (the production functions) and by the ratio of labor to land in agriculture and the ratio of labor to capital equipment in industry. Land and capital stocks are assumed to be fixed, so the ratios of labor to land and labor to capital only change when employment in agriculture and industry changes, respectively. By diminishing returns, the marginal physical products of labor decrease as these ratios increase, hence the marginal value product of labor curve for agriculture AA slopes down to the right as L_A increases and the marginal value product of labor curve for industry MM slopes down to the left as L_M increases. Finally, $\bar{w}$ gives the subsistence wage mentioned by Lewis in his preceding selection, which is assumed to be equal for both agricultural and industrial (rural and urban) workers.

In Figure 1, farmers and manufacturing firms both find it worthwhile to hire labor until its marginal value product equals the subsistence wage, yielding employment $\hat{L}_A$ in agriculture and $\hat{L}_M$ in industry. This leaves a group of workers $U = \bar{L} - \hat{L}_A - \hat{L}_M$ who must eke out a living in some way other than employment by farmers or manufacturing firms. We call this group the underemployed.

Why do the underemployed not bid wages down below the subsistence level? A popular answer to this question is the nutrition-based efficiency wage model, which asserts that it is not profitable for employers to pay workers less than $\bar{w}$ because of adverse effects on employee nutrition and health. The idea is stated well by Swamy (1997, p. 86), who also provides a fine survey of the relevant literature: "employers do not lower the wage because the worker would then consume less, thereby lowering his productivity; paying a lower wage may raise the cost per efficiency unit of labor." (We should note that Swamy argues against the relevance of this model for rural India.)

How do the underemployed survive? The Malthusian answer is that they do not, or more precisely that they do not marry and reproduce. Over time, then, the horizontal dimension of Figure 1 ($\bar{L}$) will shrink until the marginal value product of labor curves in agriculture and industry intersect each other at rather than below $\bar{w}$, at which point the economy is in long-run equilibrium. Lewis had a very different answer: the underemployed would survive through family sharing, where by "family" we mean "extended family," not only one's parents and siblings. Some family members may earn an income above the subsistence level through ownership of assets other than unskilled labor such as land or capital equipment, and by altruism or tradition they may be willing to share some of this "extra" income with less fortunate family members who are underemployed. In terms of Figure 1, the areas $A\bar{w}a$ and $M\bar{w}m$

Figure 1. Underemployment in the Lewis model

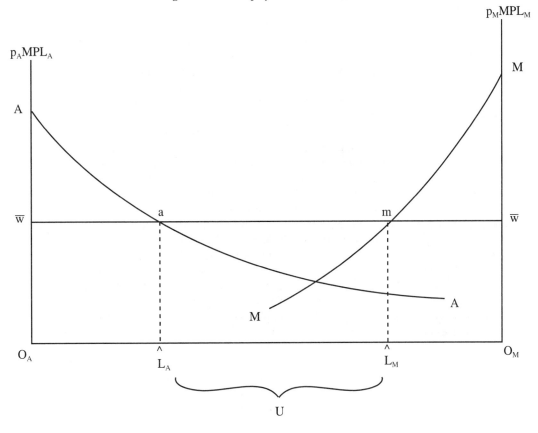

are potential sources of income the underemployed can receive through family sharing. There are a number of ways in which this family sharing can take place: the underemployed can be retained as workers on the family farm or in an urban family business and be paid more than their marginal products; or they can be self-employed (Lewis gives the example of petty retail trading) and receive supplemental income from family members (either in cash or in kind).

The model of Figure 1 generates powerful predictions concerning the effects of expansion of the manufacturing sector. Suppose that capital equipment accumulates, causing the marginal value product of labor curve for industry to shift to the left, but not so far as to raise its intersection with the marginal value product of labor curve in agriculture above $\bar{w}$. We first see that underemployment decreases: $\hat{L}_M$ increases while $\hat{L}_A$ remains constant, causing $U = \bar{L} - \hat{L}_A - \hat{L}_M$ to fall. Since $\hat{L}_A$ is constant, the only reduction in agricultural output is due to rural-urban migration of previously underemployed agricultural workers who were sustained by family sharing. Finally, the wages in both agriculture and industry remain constant, rather than increasing in response to the greater demand for labor. This last point was especially emphasized by Lewis, since it meant that earnings of owners of capital equipment (the area $M\bar{w}m$) would not be reduced by rising wages, and he believed that these earnings were the main source of savings that would finance further investment and drive economic growth. Nurkse (1953) argued that the resources used by families to support their underemployed constituted a source of "hidden savings" that were available to finance investment once these underemployed found jobs in the expanded manufacturing sector. Ranis and Fei (1961) noted that the reduction in underemployment could be viewed as a "commercialization" of the economy because the fraction of workers whose income was determined by market forces rather than family sharing increased.

We now turn to Figure 2, which is based on the model of Harris and Todaro (1970). We see that the marginal value product of labor curves from Figure 1 have been retained. The first major change in Figure 2 relative to Figure 1 is that the minimum wage now applies only to industry rather than to both industry and agriculture. It is therefore relabeled $\bar{w}_M$. Harris and Todaro view the minimum wage as determined not by the need for subsistence but rather by institutional forces such as government regulations and union contracts, which in turn are seen as effective in urban but not in rural areas. The notion of a subsistence wage is absent from the Harris–Todaro model entirely, so there is no floor underneath the agricultural wage. This raises the question, why does the agricultural wage not fall to w_A, at which agricultural employment $L_A = \bar{L} - \hat{L}_M$ and there is no underemployment? To answer we need to describe how the urban labor market functions in the Harris–Todaro model. We will then be able to generate the second major change in Figure 2 relative to Figure 1, the addition of the ii curve.

In the Harris–Todaro model the urban labor market can be described as a market for casual labor, in which every day employers hire anew the amount of workers they need that day. (This is more typically observed in construction or dock work than in manufacturing.) All workers picked on a given day receive the wage $\bar{w}_M$, and the remainder are unemployed that day and earn zero. Moreover, each day's drawing is random and independent of the previous day's drawing: being picked today does not make a worker more or less likely to be picked tomorrow. Every urban worker's odds of being picked on any day are thus equal to the ratio of total urban labor demand $\hat{L}_M$ to total urban labor supply L_U. It follows that every urban worker's income averages out to $(\hat{L}_M/L_U)\bar{w}_M$ in the long run. Returning to Figure 2, we see that if the agri-

Figure 2. Underemployment in the Harris–Todaro model

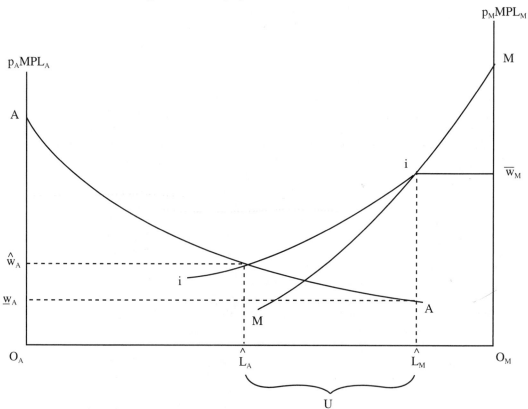

cultural wage is w_A, then the size of the urban labor force exactly equals $\hat{L}_M$, in which case every urban worker earns $\bar{w}_M$ on average. This is obviously preferable to earning w_A, so it will pay for agricultural workers to migrate to the city even though they will raise L_U above $\hat{L}_M$ and therefore obtain sporadic rather than regular employment. Agricultural employment must therefore fall below $L_A = \bar{L} - \hat{L}_M$ and the agricultural wage must rise above w_A.

To determine the level of underemployment that makes workers indifferent between remaining in the countryside and earning w_A and migrating to the city and earning $(\hat{L}_M/L_U)\bar{w}_M$ on average, we note that urban workers not picked on a given day are underemployed (actually, unemployed) so we can write $L_U = \hat{L}_M + U$. The condition for indifference is then:

$$w_A = \frac{\hat{L}_M}{\hat{L}_M + U}\,\bar{w}_M \qquad (1)$$

Equation (1) is depicted by the *ii* curve in Figure 2. It shows the agricultural wage for which a worker is indifferent between agricultural employment and migration to the city. This wage declines with U, given the levels of $\hat{L}_M$ and $\bar{w}_M$, hence the *ii* curve slopes down to the left starting from $w_A = \bar{w}_M$ at $U = 0$: as U increases, a worker is willing to stay in agriculture for lower and lower wages. At the intersection between the marginal value product of labor curve in agricultural and the *ii* curve, what agricultural employers are willing to pay equals what agricultural workers are willing to accept. (This depiction of labor market equilibrium in the Harris–Todaro model was introduced by Corden and Findlay (1975).)

Note that in the Harris–Todaro model every worker in agriculture is paid his marginal product. Lewis would argue that many of the agricultural workers who live with their families and work on the family farm are underemployed in the sense that their bed and board exceeds their marginal products. If there are well-functioning labor and land markets in rural areas, however, one could argue to the contrary that the families of any underemployed workers would insist that they get jobs on other farms or would rent land from other farms so that these workers could earn their keep. Thus the Harris–Todaro view that there is no underemployment in rural areas need not be inconsistent with the fact that there is a great deal of unpaid family labor in agriculture.

Let us now consider the effects in the model of Figure 2 of an increase in urban labor demand, just as we did for the model of Figure 1. Unfortunately graphical analysis is more complicated than in the earlier case, because the increase in $\hat{L}_M$ resulting from the leftward shift of the marginal value product of labor curve for industry also causes the origin of the *ii* curve to shift left. Let us instead turn to equation (1). We see that if we hold the agricultural wage w_A constant, an increase in urban employment $\hat{L}_M$ actually causes an increase rather than a decrease in urban underemployment U. The actual change in U depends on how fast the agricultural wage rises in response to the out-migration of agricultural workers induced by the increased income they can expect in the city. Could all of the increase in urban employment come from reduced urban underemployment, leaving the agricultural labor force unchanged? Clearly not, since then the ratio $\hat{L}_M/(\hat{L}_M + U)$ must increase, implying an increase in w_A by equation (1), which in turn requires a decrease in L_A. In sum, expansion of urban labor demand in the model of Figure 2 is much less beneficial than in the model of Figure 1: it need not reduce underemployment, whereas it must do so in the model of Figure 1, and it must reduce agricultural output (and raise the agricultural wage), whereas it need not do so in the model of Figure 1.

To conclude this Note, let us consider the effects in the model of Figure 2 of an increase in agricultural labor demand, caused for example by an increase in the quantity of irrigated land. Since the *ii* curve now remains stationary (because $\hat{L}_M$ and $\bar{w}_M$ do not change), when the marginal value product of labor curve for agriculture shifts right it must intersect the *ii* curve at a lower level of U. We have the paradoxical policy implication, emphasized by Todaro at the end of his preceding selection, that the surest way to reduce underemployment in the city is to improve employment opportunities in the countryside.

References

Corden, W. Max, and Ronald Findlay. 1975. "Urban Unemployment, Intersectoral Capital Mobility and Development Policy." *Economica* 42: 59–78.

Harris, John R., and Michael P. Todaro. 1970. "Migration, Unemployment and Development: A Two-Sector Analysis." *American Economic Review* 60 (March): 126–42.

Nurkse, Ragnar. 1953. *Problems of Capital Formation in Underdeveloped Areas* (New York: Oxford University Press).

Ranis, Gustav, and John C. H. Fei. 1961. "A Theory of Economic Development." *American Economic Review* 51 (September): 533–65.

Swamy, Anand V. 1997. "A Simple Test of the Nutrition-Based Efficiency Wage Model." *Journal of Development Economics* 53 (June): 85–98.

Selection VI.B.3. Wage Spillover and Unemployment in a Wage-Gap Economy: The Jamaican Case*

Jamaican Wage and Employment Patterns

A casual survey of urban unemployment levels in the Caribbean raises an intriguing question: Why does poor and stagnant Haiti seemingly have less open urban unemployment than comparatively rich and rapidly growing Jamaica, Puerto Rico, and Trinidad? There are no unemployment statistics for Haiti, but to all appearances open unemployment is lower than in the more prosperous islands. In Puerto Rico and Jamaica, unemployment has probably not fallen below 10 percent of the labor force since at least 1950, and Trinidad has more recently achieved this dubious distinction.[1] Why should the poorest of these structurally similar economies have the least unemployment problem? . . .

This is not the only perplexing question about Jamaican unemployment. Between 1953 and 1960 total output in real terms increased 76.8 percent while the labor force increased by only 2.5 percent (15,800 workers) due to massive emigration to the United Kingdom. "Modern" nonagricultural jobs[2]

*From Gene M. Tidrick, "Wage Spillover and Unemployment in a Wage-gap Economy: The Jamaican Case," *Economic Development and Cultural Change* (1975): 307–323. Reprinted by permission.

[1]On Puerto Rico, see Lloyd G. Reynolds and Peter Gregory, *Wages, Productivity, and Industrialization in Puerto Rico* (Homewood, Ill.: Richard D. Irwin, Inc., 1965); and for Trinidad, see Jack Harewood, *Employment in Trinidad and Tobago 1960* (Mona, Jamaica: Institute of Social and Economic Research, University of the West Indies, n.d.). For more recent figures, see David Turnham, *The Employment Problem in Less Developed Countries* (Paris: Development Centre of the OECD, 1971), p. 46. Employment data for Jamaica in this paper and some wage data are from Jamaica, Department [formerly Central Bureau] of Statistics, *Census of Jamaica and Its Dependencies, 1943; The Census of Jamaica: 7th April, 1960;* and *Report on a Sample Survey of the Population of Jamaica, Oct./Nov. 1953.* Other wage or average earnings data are from Jamaica, Department of Statistics, *Employment and Earnings in Large Establishments* and *Wage Rates, 1957–1965.* Output figures are from Jamaica, Department of Statistics, *National Accounts: Income and Expenditure,* 1950–1961, and *National Income and Product,* 1965–; and from Alfred P. Thorne, "Size, Structure, and Growth of the Economy of Jamaica," *Social and Economic Studies* 4, suppl. (December 1955): 1–156. For a detailed discussion of Jamaican wage, employment, and output data, and of the adjustments made to achieve comparability of data from different sources, see Gene M. Tidrick, "Wages and Unemployment in Jamaica" (Ph.D. diss., Harvard University, 1972), esp. chap. 3.

[2]For statistical purposes, the modern sector is defined to include all mining workers, factory workers in manufacturing, all other workers in secondary industries except own-account workers and employers in construction and distribution, and service workers excluding domestic service. Between 1942 and 1960,

increased by an estimated 50,000 during this same period. Yet unemployment fell only slightly from 98,000 to 88,100. Why did this spectacular output growth in the face of an almost stable labor force fail to cut unemployment more? Why did the relatively large increase in modern sector jobs not create more net employment in the economy as a whole? Why did migration not reduce unemployment, especially since so many of the migrants were unemployed?

Finally, what can we make of Jamaican wage behavior? Real average earnings (money earnings deflated by the cost-of-living index) rose by 2.6 percent per year between 1942 and 1960. In recent years the rate of increase has been more like 4 percent. The Jamaican economy is heavily unionized and output growth has been high, but these trends are still noteworthy for two reasons. First, the rate of open unemployment (where the definition of unemployment embraces all workers wanting work but working less than 1 day in a survey week) has remained extremely high since the 1930s. The lowest rate ever recorded was 13 percent in 1960. More importantly, wages in unorganized sectors of the economy rose by about the same amount as in unionized sectors. For example, real average earnings of female personal service workers (mostly domestic servants) rose 46.6 percent between 1942 and 1960 compared with an increase of 60 percent for all workers. Scattered evidence from the unorganized parts of agriculture suggests a similar pattern. Why were real wages not bid down in unorganized sectors? Moreover, despite rising rural wages and high overall unemployment, genuine labor shortages in rural areas have existed since the mid 1950s. How can we account for these shortages in the midst of high unemployment?

None of these puzzling features of Jamaican wage and employment patterns can be fully understood without reference to the distorted wage structure, that is, a wage structure in which workers of the same skill level receive different wages in different industries. The Jamaican wage structure is clearly distorted by this definition. Disparities among major sectors are dramatic. Unskilled bauxite mining workers earn about twice as much

modern jobs thus defined increased by 94,000 to 194,700, or about one-third of the labor force in 1960. Figures for the subperiod 1953–60 are not available, but output trends suggest that 50,000 plus or minus 10,000 is a reasonable estimate.

365

per week as unskilled workers in transportation or construction, the two next most highly paid industries. (In fact, unskilled mining workers earn more than skilled construction workers.) Unskilled construction workers, in turn, earn almost two and one-half times as much as agricultural workers. . . .

The Wage-Gap Model

. . . In figure 1, the demand for labor in the sugar sector (Ds) is measured from left to right. The demand for labor in the mining sector (Dm) is measured from right (at L') to left. The Dm is completely inelastic at $L'P$. In a competitive labor market, the allocation of the fixed supply of labor LL' between the two sectors and the equilibrium wage rate will be determined by the intersection of the two demand curves. In equilibrium, LP workers will be employed in sugar and $L'P$ will be employed in mining at a wage in both sectors of We. There is full employment and the equilibrium is stable. As long as the labor market is competitive, there is no tendency for the wage level to rise above We in either sector.

Assume, however, that in mining the wage is set at Wm, perhaps at the initiative of employers seeking better public relations or of government or unions who see an opportunity to raise mining wages without curtailing mining employment. Un-

der certain assumptions, the effect of setting the mining wage at Wm will be to create an incentive for some workers to withdraw from sugar employment to seek a job in the high-wage mining sector. The number who choose to withdraw from the sugar sector is a function of the wage gap between the two sectors. Thus, if the mining-sector wage is Wm and the sugar-sector wage is Ws, QP workers would choose to withdraw from sugar employment to seek mining employment. If the sugar wage were lower, more workers would withdraw, and if it were higher, fewer workers would withdraw. Only if the sugar-sector wage were also Wm would no workers withdraw from sugar employment. We can plot the succession of such points to obtain the supply curve of labor to the sugar sector, given a mining wage equal to Wm. The curve is labeled Ss in figure 1. If the sugar-sector labor market remains competitive and the mining wage remains fixed at Wm, the new "equilibrium" sugar wage will be Ws. Then LQ workers will be employed in sugar, $L'P$ will be employed in mining, and QP workers will be unemployed. If the mining wage were raised above Wm, the supply curve of labor to sugar would shift upward, thereby raising the equilibrium sugar wage above Ws and creating unemployment greater than QP.

To see this, assume that the fixed supply of labor is the result of a balanced flow of new entrants into

Figure 1

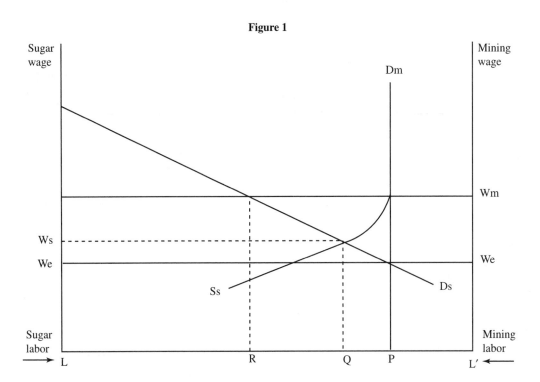

the labor force and of retirements. At any given time, therefore, there will be new job openings in mining. Assume, further, that the probability of getting a mining job is higher if a worker is not employed in sugar, perhaps because hiring is done at the gate and sugar and mining activities are located in different parts of the country. It will then be rational for a new entrant to remain unemployed rather than take a job in sugar, or for a sugar worker to quit his job in order to seek a job in mining so long as: (1) the present value of his forgone earnings in sugar is less than the expected lifetime earnings in mining and (2) he has some means of subsistence during his period of unemployment. Expected lifetime earnings in mining are simply the probability of having a mining job in each period times the mining wage summed over the worker's remaining work life, or

$$PVm = \sum_{t=0}^{n} \frac{P(t)Wm}{(1 + r)^t}, \qquad (1)$$

where PVm is the present value of lifetime earnings in mining and $P(t)$ is the probability of having a mining job at time t. For simplicity assume that $P(t)$ is the ratio of the number of hirings mining in period t, $H(t)$, to the number of unemployed workers, $U(t)$. That is,

$$P(t) = H(t)/U(t) \qquad (2)$$

The present value of lifetime earnings in sugar, PVs, is

$$PVs = \sum_{t=0}^{n} \frac{Ws}{(1 + r)^t}, \qquad (3)$$

and the equilibrium labor market condition is

$$PVs = PVm \qquad (4)$$

I defer the question of how the unemployed survive until a later section.

When the mining wage is raised, workers will leave sugar employment (or new entrants will remain unemployed) until the probability of getting a mining job is lowered sufficiently (unemployment raised sufficiently) to reestablish equality between PVs and PVm. In terms of figure 1, a rise in the mining wage to Wm will shift the supply curve of labor to sugar to Ss, cause the sugar wage to rise to Ws, and create unemployment of PQ. This supply-withdrawal unemployment is overt by any conventional measure. Workers could truthfully answer a labor force questionnaire that they wanted but could not obtain more work in either sector at the going wage. They could get a job in sugar at a lower wage rate, but their reserve supply price has risen and they would not accept it. They would take

a lower wage in mining and bid that wage down but are prevented from doing so by market imperfections. They are voluntarily unemployed with respect to sugar but involuntarily unemployed with respect to mining.

Even if an increased mining wage does not reduce employment directly in the mining sector itself, it will reduce employment (and output) indirectly in sugar. Moreover, the mining wage increase spills over into the sugar sector, raising the sugar wage. This effect does not depend on unionization. Wages rise in sugar even though sugar workers remain completely unorganized. . . .

An increase in mining employment will increase the probability of getting a high-wage job and hence the expected lifetime earnings of workers seeking mining employment. In figure 1, if the Dm curve shifts outward (to the left) at a constant wage Wm, the supply curve of labor to sugar will also shift farther upward as the increased probability of securing mining employment induces more workers to leave sugar employment. Thus, if mining employment increased to $L'Q$ in figure 1, unemployment would not be eliminated because the shift in the Dm curve would induce a shift in the supply curve of labor to sugar above Ss. Whether total unemployment would be less or greater than the original PQ after an increase in mining employment of QP depends on many factors, but it is clear that the net employment increase in the economy as a whole is less than the gross employment increase in mining in a wage-gap economy. Continued employment growth in mining at a constant wage Wm would not completely eliminate unemployment until mining employment was $L'R$. Outward shifts in the Ds curve would decrease unemployment by the amount that sugar employment increased, however. Net and gross employment effects are equal. . . .

The Sharing Mechanism

Unemployment is a rational response to a distorted wage structure only if the unemployed have some means of subsistence. The nature of the sharing mechanism will be an important determinant of the level of unemployment which the system can sustain. . . .

High-wage casual employment is a fairly important source of income for the "unemployed" in Jamaica. Counting opportunities in dock working, construction, tourism, and illegal activities, it is not hard to imagine that from a quarter to a half of unemployed males might earn at least as much or more over a year's time as a full-time wage earner in agriculture. The large number of casual jobs available also explains why unemployment is such a different phenomenon in less developed countries. A 10 percent unemployment rate is more likely to mean that 20 percent of the labor force is unemployed half the time.

Sharing mechanisms which allow the unemployed to subsist while looking for high-wage jobs are also undoubtedly important. . . . Assume that $L'P$ mining workers are hired on a full-time basis. Earnings in mining cannot be bid down as in a casual labor system, and it becomes rational for some workers to remain unemployed at a subsistence level while seeking permanent full-time employment in mining. The number who can afford to remain unemployed, and hence the number forced back into sugar, are determined by the sharing mechanism. . . . It is clear that an increase in mining wages or employment would increase the number of unemployed which the system could support, as well as raise expected lifetime earnings of those remaining temporarily unemployed.

Some sharing mechanisms may place a constraint on unemployment no matter how favorable the expected lifetime earnings differential. If the unemployed are supported largely by the low-wage sector, as in parts of Africa, increased wages or employment in the high-wage sector will not increase the capacity of the system to support unemployment as much as a high-wage-sector sharing mechanism. If the high-wage sector has a high propensity to share, however, support capacity will increase pari passu with the increased tendency of the system to generate unemployment. As suggested earlier, this is why Jamaica and Puerto Rico, with large high-wage sectors, can support more unemployment than Haiti.

The sharing mechanism helps determine not only how many but who will be unemployed. Where high-wage workers have a high propensity to share with dependents, for example, many of the unemployed will be new entrants whose reserve price is higher than the sugar wage because they live in a high-income household. This poses an interesting welfare issue. Since unemployment is voluntary with respect to low-wage employment, it appears that those who are worst off are not the unemployed but those forced to accept employment in the low-wage sector—the involuntarily employed as it were. . . .

Empirical Evidence

. . . The limited evidence from Jamaica on how the unemployed live suggests that many of the unemployed, though by no means all, may be better

off than those fully employed in the low-wage sector.

In the first place, there are many casual job opportunities in Jamaica, some at very high wages. The most extreme example is the water transport industry (mostly dock workers). In the 1960 census survey week, less than half of the 5,522 workers (nearly 1 percent of the labor force) in this industry worked 5 or more days and more than one-fourth worked only 1–2 days. Dock workers could earn more in 2 7-hour days in 1965 than the typical agricultural worker earned in a full week. In this extreme case, many workers registered as unemployed in a given week may have been better off over the course of a year than other fully employed workers. Second, in spite of the much larger population of unemployed in the Kingston Metropolitan Area, average household working-class income in the KMA in 1963–64 was about twice that in rural areas, a difference not nearly offset by the cost-of-living differential. More strikingly, only 10 percent of KMA households earned less than the median rural household income.[3]

Finally, 92 percent of the unemployed were dependents in 1960. Or, to put it in a different perspective, 98 percent of heads of households wanting work were employed. Of course, some might not have been heads of households because they were unemployed, rather than the other way around, but the presumption is that most were unemployed because they could afford to be.[4]

A closely related bit of evidence bearing on the presumed voluntary nature of unemployment comes from interviews with unemployed Jamaican workers. Two such surveys largely confirm the expectation that the reserve supply price of the unemployed is higher than the ruling wage in the low-wage sector. An official study of the rural labor shortage by M. G. Smith in 1955 found that over 90 percent of those looking for work in areas of "good" labor supply and over 80 percent in "bad" areas would not accept regular employment at the going agricultural wage rate in their respective areas.[5] A survey by Robert Kerton of unemployed men in the Kingston area in 1966–67 found that

---

[3]Jamaica, Department of Statistics, *Expenditure Patterns of Working Class Households* (Kingston: Department of Statistics, 1967), p. 10.

[4]Turnham, p. 55, cites similar evidence from Puerto Rico where a 1959 study showed "that family income tended to be higher than average for the families to which unemployed workers belonged and that such families, on average, included more working members."

[5]M. G. Smith, *A Report on the Labour Supply in Rural Jamaica* (Kingston: Government Printer, 1956), pp. 137–56.

one-third of those surveyed would not have accepted employment in the medium-wage, unskilled job of garbage collection and about two-thirds had a reserve supply price higher than the average weekly earnings on large farms.[6] Of course, garbage collection is a low-status and unpleasant job, but probably no less so in Jamaica than agricultural work, which paid only half as much. Moreover, for some of these men, their choice of residence in an urban area is evidence of their voluntary unemployment as far as agricultural work is concerned.

Kerton also found that the reserve supply price of the unemployed fell with age.[7] Again, this is what the wage-gap model predicts. Young workers have a longer lifetime over which to offset low earnings in the initial period of unemployment and a lower discount rate for future earnings because of fewer family responsibilities. Thus, the reserve supply price tends to fall with age, the unemployed tend to be disproportionately young, and workers in the low-wage sector tend to be older than average. All three age-structural characteristics are borne out by Jamaican data.

Finally, the most important evidence supporting the hypothesis that most Jamaican unemployment is generated by the wage gap is the pattern of migration flows within Jamaica. An econometric study by Nassau Adams[8] found that distance and wage differentials among the 14 Jamaican parishes explained almost all the variance (R^2 = .860 for Jamaican males age 15–54) of internal migration flows. Other variables—degree of urbanization, educational levels of sending areas, and unemployment levels—added negligibly to the explanation of migration flows. The unemployment level in receiving areas was positively (but insignificantly) correlated with migration rates, whereas the unemployment level in sending areas was positively (and significantly) associated with migration. The results confirm a central prediction of the wage-gap model. Migration occurs largely in response to wage differentials and in spite of higher unemployment levels in high-wage areas.

The size of the wage coefficient in receiving areas indicated that when wages in a high-wage area rose by 10 percent, the rate of migration rose by nearly 30 percent. Since Adams's study involved intercensal migration, this was cumulative migration over a number of years. Nevertheless, it implies a very powerful impetus to supply-withdrawal unemployment due to wage increases in the high-wage sector. Separate regressions for males age 15–29 and those age 30–54 showed a higher wage coefficient for the younger group, indicating both that the effect of wage differentials was more pronounced for younger workers and that the effect worked in a relatively short time period. . . .

Conclusion

The wage-gap model provides answers to the questions posed early in this paper and in the previous section.

Why does comparatively prosperous and rapidly growing Jamaica seemingly have more unemployment than poor and stagnant Haiti? Because the larger the high-wage modern sector, the more unemployed an economy can afford to support. In an economy without a high-wage sector, neither the incentive for nor the means to support unemployment may exist.

Why did employment growth in the high-wage sector and heavy migration abroad fail to reduce unemployment by a like amount? Because any reduction in the number of unemployed or any increase in the rate of hiring raises the probability of obtaining a high-wage job and induces further supply withdrawal from the low-wage sector.

Why did wages in unorganized, low-wage sectors rise along with wages in the unionized, high-wage sectors? Because the increased wage gap causes the supply curve of labor to the low-wage sector to shift. Why is there a long-standing labor shortage in agriculture when open unemployment levels have remained so high? Because the unemployed prefer unemployment and the uncertain prospect of a high-wage job to the certain prospect of low-wage steady employment.

Why do they prefer unemployment? Because their expected lifetime earnings are greater if they remain temporarily unemployed and because they have adequate means of support while searching for a high-wage job.

Why do migrants continue to pour into areas with high levels of unemployment? Because the higher wages the migrant will receive when he finally gets a job will more than compensate him for his forgone earnings in his place of origin.

[6]Robert Kerton, "Labour Theory and Developing Countries: The Individual's Supply of Effort in the Caribbean" (Ph.D. diss., Duke University, 1968), pp. 58–59.

[7]Ibid., p. 65.

[8]Nassau A. Adams, "Internal Migration in Jamaica: An Economic Analysis," *Social and Economic Studies* 18 (June 1969): 137–51.

Note VI.B.2. Econometric Studies of Migration

The key question of what determines rural-urban migration can be explored further in studies that set forth probabilistic job-search models and in empirical investigations of migration functions. Field studies and econometric analyses indicate the importance of the economic motive in the decision to migrate. Econometric estimates of migration functions have also demonstrated that the probability of urban employment, independent of the differences in actual rural and urban wages, contributes significantly to the explanation of variance among time periods and subgroups of the rural population in rates of urban migration.

In an excellent survey of numerous studies, however, Yap indicates several problems with the econometric functions that limit their usefulness for prediction.[1]

The basic form of the migration function is as follows:

$$\bar{M}_{ij} = f(Y_i, Y_j; U_i, U_g; Z_i, Z_j; d_{ij}; C_{ij})$$

The specification is usually log linear. Typical independent variables used to explain migration from place i to place j ($\bar{M}_{ij}$) include wage or income levels (Y), unemployment rates (U), the degree of urbanization (Z) for the population in areas i and j, the distance between i and j (d_{ij}), and the friends and relatives of residents of i in the destination j (C_{ij}). Population in areas i and j is sometimes included.

Limitations of these studies are: (1) the level of demographic and geographic aggregation masks different patterns of migration; (2) the migration variable used in some of the studies presents conceptual and econometric difficulties; and (3) the independent variables are often poorly measured, especially the income estimates.

According to Stark and Bloom,

> Recent empirical research on the economics of labor migration has benefited a great deal more from the development of new econometric techniques than from new theoretical ideas. The techniques that have substantially improved our ability to use micro data sets in the estimation of relatively standard models of labor migration include techniques for the analysis of qualitative dependent variables, techniques that correct for sample selection bias, and techniques for the analysis of longitudinal and pseudo-longitudinal data. At the micro level, most empirical studies have attempted to test simple microeconomic models of migration according to which individuals (or families) make locational decisions primarily by comparing their income opportunities at alternative locations. The key feature of recent studies of this type is their focus on the estimation of structural, as opposed to reduced-form, models of the migration decision.[2]

In his *The Migration of Labor* (1991), Stark extends portfolio investment theory to migration and to the remittance of earnings. Under this theory, migration decisions are ordered by family needs for stable income levels, provided by a diversified portfolio of laborers, both male and female, and the need to jointly insure the family's well-being. In brief, group decision making and objectives, rather than the wishes of individual migrants, determine migration patterns and remittance flows. Viewed in light of portfolio investment theory, families allocate their labor assets over geographically dispersed and structurally different markets to reduce risk. Research indicates that after migration, family members pool and share their incomes. This pooling, or co-insurance, covers risks of losing income in individual markets and allows the family to smooth its consumption.

As Yap concludes, additional empirical research on migration would be useful to define the migration rate appropriately, adjust for simultaneous equation biases, and include more policy variables to provide more predictive value.

Notes

1. L. Y. L. Yap, "The Attraction of Cities: A Review of the Migration Literature," *Journal of Development Economics* 4 (1977): 239–64.

2. Oded Stark and David E. Bloom, "The New Economics of Labor Migration," *American Economic Review* (May 1985): 176–77.

Selection VI.B.4. Labour Market Modelling and the Urban Informal Sector: Theory and Evidence*

The existence of earning opportunities in the informal sector gives each member of the labour force yet another search option: he might take up a job in the urban informal sector and search from there in the evenings, on weekends, or during the day when working hours are variable. In the typical developing country, most of the formal sector jobs are located in the cities. Urban informal sector workers would therefore be expected to have a better chance of obtaining an urban formal sector job than would an agricultural worker, if for no other reason than simple proximity to places of hiring. Writing in the early 1970s, based upon observation of the Kenyan situation, I characterized the search process as follows:

New arrivals in the cities ordinarily stay with friends or relatives who help house and feed them while they look for work. A dozen or more people crowded into one room is not uncommon. They need not live in housing which is rented or provided as part of job compensation. Squatter settlements and shanty towns house a substantial portion of urban populations, particularly in Africa.

Open unemployment is not very common. Additional household members are expected to contribute to their support. Frequently, they assist with the household chores by preparing meals, washing clothes, or caring for children. Simultaneously, they search for work (albeit on an irregular basis) and are classified as unemployed.

The most fortunate new migrants obtain a permanent modern-sector job as a clerk, messenger, or whatever. However, these are the best jobs and the typical migrant is forced to find some lesser means of earning a cash income. He may secure one or more typically a succession of wage jobs (e.g., house-servant, cook in a small lunch kiosk, assistant in a family shop) or engage in self-employment (e.g. selling produce, newspapers, curios, or shoe shines on the street corner).

The defining characteristics of the (informal) sector are ease of entry and the lack of a stable employer-employee relationship. The urban areas of less developed countries typically have a wide variety of such open entry, casual employment types of

jobs. For instance, a person can get started by buying some peas in the market, removing the pods at the side of the road, and selling podded peas to passers-by at a higher price. Prostitution is another occupation which has notoriously easy entry.

Workers in the (informal) sector are ordinarily classified as employed although they themselves and the statisticians who measure those things would be inclined to consider them underemployed. [Fields, 1975, pp. 171–172]

I would maintain that this characterization is equally valid today as a characterization of a broad range of economic activity, not only in Kenya but in a wide variety of developing countries.

Others agree. For example, Oberai and Singh (1984) conducted a study in Ludhiana in the Indian Punjab. They found (p. 509) "that more than 90 percent of migrants seeking work found a job within two months of their arrival, which means that migrants are being absorbed fairly quickly into the urban labour market." But much of this is free-entry self-employment. In Oberai and Singh's words (pp. 516–517): ". . . a fair proportion of migrants who take up self-employment on arrival start in the informal sector where they work as street vendors, porters, shoeshine boys and the like. Perhaps some of them also work in small family enterprises. All such employment requires little capital or skill. The proportion of migrants who are engaged in the formal sector as own-account workers or employers rises in most cases with length of stay; the increase is particularly sharp during the first few years." And in a study of Jamaica, Doeringer (1988) has written:

In particular, a distinction is drawn between those jobs (generally in what is often called the informal sector) where easy entry and work sharing are the principal determinants of income-earning opportunities, and those which are protected by formal sector internal labour markets. This distinction is critical for understanding how employment and productivity are affected by economic change, and by institutional forces in the workplace.

Thus, the main features of the urban informal sector, as I characterized it in my 1975 paper and as it remains characterized in many people's minds today are:

- *Free entry,* in the sense that all who wish to enter this sector can find some sort of work which will provide them with cash earnings;

*From Gary S. Fields, "Labour Market Modelling and the Urban Informal Sector: Theory and Evidence," in David Turnham, Bernard Salomé, and Antoine Schwartz, eds., *The Informal Sector Revisited* (Paris: OECD, 1990), 55–56, 64–68. Reprinted by permission.

- *Income-sharing,* because of the institutional circumstances of that sector's production and sales patterns;
- *Positive on-the-job search opportunities,* in that those who are engaged in the urban informal sector have a ~~non-zero~~ chance of finding a formal sector job;
- *An intermediate search probability,* in that those in the urban informal sector have a better chance of finding a formal sector job than do those in agriculture but a worse chance than those who are openly unemployed and searching full time; and
- *A lower wage in the urban informal sector than in agriculture,* arising endogenously as result of the higher on-the-job search opportunity here.

Free entry is the defining feature of the informal sector, and the other characteristics just listed are attributed of that sector in a typical developing economy. . . .

A Restatement of Results

. . . We may say that for some countries, the evidence shows:

i) Some of the activities which appear to be free-entry are not.
ii) The earnings of workers in small firms are lower on average than the earnings in large firms. However, the earnings in small firms are not uniformly lower. Rather, the two distributions overlap.
iii) The earnings of workers in small urban firms are not lower than the earnings of rural traditional workers.
iv) Those presently working in small firms, in firms not covered by social security, and in self-employment have been in those jobs for long periods of time.
v) Formal sector jobs are mostly filled by rural residents, not by informal sector workers.
vi) Many of those who are in small firms and in self-employment are there by choice.

When the studies are viewed this way—in terms of what the evidence actually shows rather than in terms of the labels and terminology of the authors—the early theoretical models are found for the most part not to be seriously challenged or contradicted by the empirical evidence.

There is one exception, though: contrary to the earlier theoretical models, empirical studies show that workers do indeed move into the informal sector by choice. Because this point leads to a major conclusion of this paper, I elaborate on it at some length below.

Some Economic Anthropology-Type Findings

To get a better handle on the the workings of the informal sector labour market, I led a research team in conducting a series of interviews with informal sector workers in the two cities: Kuala Lumpur, Malaysia and San José, Costa Rica. Three major findings emerged.

1. Diversity Within the Informal Sector

Informal activities prove to be quite diverse. Some are activities with easy entry and no fixed hours of operation. They may be characterized by self-employment or employment of unpaid family labour or of unskilled labour with non-specific work relations. By contrast, other informal activities exhibit limited entry due to higher set-up costs and/or complicated licensing requirements, irregular hours of operation, and employment of family labour and unskilled labour with semi-specified work relations. These contrast with formal sector enterprises, which are characterized by restricted entry, regular place and hours of operation, and employment of non-family labour with specific work-relations. These belong in the category of formal sector, even if they are very small in scale. One example would be professional services companies which, although small in scale, cannot be viewed in any meaningful way as part of the informal sector.

Some examples may help clarify the distinction between the three types of activities. In transportation, trishaws in Malaysia (pedi-cabs) are examples of easy entry activities. They require very little capital investment. They are usually operated and owned by one person. Their owners operate them at irregular hours and at negotiable prices. No particular skill is required to be a pedi-cab driver. Typical of the upper-tier informal activities are the individually owned and operated taxi-cabs. Taxis are much more expensive to purchase than trishaws and the operating costs of taxis are much higher. Hours of operation can be regular or irregular, and the owner may hire a second driver to operate at different times of day (such as the night shift). Finally, there are the large established taxi companies which own a fleet of vehicles and hire a number of drivers to operate them. The taxi-drivers are expected to report to work at regular, agreed-upon hours. Sometimes they are paid fixed wages, sometimes a percentage of the fares. These taxi companies are examples of formal sector activities.

In commerce, street-vending is an obvious representative of free-entry activities. Street-vending (e.g. a sugar cane juice stand or a fruit stand) requires relatively low set-up costs. There is no skill requirement to this work. Street-vending licenses are easily procured. Location rental fees are nominal. Hours of operation are irregular. Paid employees are rare; even unpaid family workers are not very numerous. For the upper-tier informal sector in the commerce industry, examples are small retail stores such as sundry shops. They face higher set-up costs than do street-vendors because of higher rental fees and also because more licenses are involved. Although these shops are opened and closed at the same hours on most days, they may without notice close up earlier or not open at all at the wish of their owners. These shops are usually family-run with some hired help. The hired workers can be non-relatives, although relatives are sometimes employed with semi-specified responsibilities. Supermarkets owned by a large company exemplify the formal sector in commerce.

In manufacturing, backyard industries belong to the easy entry informal sector. Entry is easy because capital costs are small and rental fees are minimal, since the owners live and work in the same house. These backyard industries use manual labour, sometimes with very few tools. Workers may have to put in long hours to fill an order, or when there is no order, the shop may have to close up. These workers are usually family members or paid relatives and are generally unskilled. The small manufacturing industries in the upper-tier informal sector have higher capital and property costs. Because of the kinds of machinery used and the larger number of workers hired in these activities, licensing requirements may be more complicated and time-consuming. Workers in the upper-tier informal sector are both family members and hired labourers who are either unskilled or semi-skilled. Work relations are semi-formal.

Thus, within the informal sector, we find considerable diversity. The UIS does not consist uniformly of free-entry, low-wage, unorganized enterprises and workers, although, some activities do indeed fit this characterization; I would refer to these as the easy entry informal sector. Others do not. These others have significant barriers to entry, higher capital or skill requirements, and fairly regular labour

relations arrangements; yet, they too may also be small, employ family labour, and operate at irregular hours and places. I shall refer to these as the upper-tier informal sector. In Malaysia and Costa Rica, there are really two urban informal sectors.

2. Voluntary Participation in Upper-Tier Informal Activities but Not Easy Entry Ones

Another major conclusion from the interviews is that many people are in informal activities by choice. When asked their reasons for doing what they were doing, many informal workers in Costa Rica gave the following answers most frequently: *i*) They felt they could make more money at the informal sector job they were doing than they could earn in the formal sector, or *ii*) Even though they made a little less money, they enjoyed their work more, because it allowed them to choose their own hours, to work in the open air, to talk to friends, etc.

Here are some examples of such people. One man, 46 years old, sells a peanut-sugar-butter candy called "melcochas" in downtown San José. He has been selling melcochas on the streets for 37 years, and before that his father made and sold them. He was very insistent that he was there voluntarily, doing what he likes to do, and that it pays better than formal sector work. His brother had, at one time, started up a small factory making melcochas, which he then sold to the public. The brother eventually gave up this factory because he realized that he could make more money selling in the streets himself. That is, the informal sector work paid better than formal sector work.

Another interview was with a 50-year-old man selling fruit on a corner. This man had worked in the United States in several paid positions, and could easily have become a formal sector job in Costa Rica. Yet he sold fruits, because he earned more money (US $36 a day) than in any other type of work he could get in San José.

These examples illustrate what I call the constrained voluntary nature of much upper-tier informal activity. That is, given the constrained choices open to them, a great many of informal sector workers are in that sector voluntarily. These people know that job opportunities are available in the urban formal sectors for people like themselves and that they could get such jobs. Yet, they choose not to seek such jobs, the foremost reason being that they prefer the combination of monetary rewards and psychic aspects of their informal sector jobs.

Of course, not all informal sector activities are of such a type. Many people face such severely constrained options that the informal sector involvement can only be seen as their making the best of a bad situation. Representative of this kind of informal sector activity is a woman sitting on a market street in Kuala Lumpur, garlics set out on a piece of newspaper in front of her for sale. She calls out the price of her products to shoppers who pass by. Whenever she sells off her garlics, she is ready to go home. If the market turns out to be slow for the day, she sometimes stays for longer hours; other times, she sells her products at a substantial discount. If it happens to be raining, she takes the day off. This kind of activity is clearly small in scale. It also has free entry; all anyone has to do to enter similar economic activity is buy a supply of garlics from a rack jobber. The owner is self-employed and manages her business in a very casual (though not necessarily inefficient) way. She is very poor.

3. Linkages Between the Formal Sector and Informal Sector Labour Markets

A third important conclusion is that the upper-tier informal sector and the easy-entry informal sector are linked to the formal sector in very different ways. Whereas most participants in the easy-entry sector reported themselves dissatisfied with their positions and sought better jobs in the formal sector, those in the upper-tier informal sector had typically come from the formal sector and were glad to leave the formal sector behind.

There are barriers to entry to many upper-tier informal sector activities. One needs skills and tools to repair shoes or watches. Even to sell fruit, one needs capital for the initial stock, contacts with fruit wholesalers in the market, and money to buy a license for a good street location. However, these barriers can be overcome by working in the formal sector.

The formal sector was found to provide training for workers to move into upper-tier small-scale employment. Examples are food industry workers who leave jobs in the formal sector to set up their own small food processing activities, office-workers who leave to work in small family stores, and repairmen who learn their trades in large work places and then leave to set up their own shops. In Costa Rica, a study by the Ministry of Planning found that more than 70 per cent of those self-employed in the informal sector had previously held wage or salary jobs in the formal sector. This finding was reaffirmed in our interviews of such workers in San José.

The formal sector also provides the opportunity for workers to accumulate savings to start up their own businesses. Examples are repairmen and small manufacturers who save part of their wages to buy their own machinery, tools, and raw materials for use in their own businesses. In Costa Rica, these savings from formal sector jobs are a much more important source of finance for new businesses than are loans from banks or other financial institutions.

At the other end of the spectrum, the formal sector was found to employ preferentially those workers who have acquired training in the easy entry segment of the informal sector. Examples are managers of appliance stores who had previously worked in small family businesses. These people tend to be young and well-educated. The growth of the formal sector enables workers to move out of the easy entry informal sector into newly-created formal sectors jobs. This is especially true in Malaysia, where the economy has been on a sustained positive economic growth path. It is much less the case in Costa Rica, where the severe economic crisis of the early 1980s led to a loss of formal sector employment. Examples in Malaysia are young people who start out in family stores but end up as clerks in fast-food restaurants or as mechanics in car-repair shops—jobs that have opened up due to the growth of the formal sector.

Although on balance the linkages between the informal sector and the formal sector were found to be positive, there is one identifiable group of losers among informal sector firms: those who fail to respond to the dynamic changes in the economy. Yet, a repeated finding from the interviews in Malaysia and Costa Rica, as surprising as it was consistent, is that those who do not respond often have deliberately decided not to. Many do not want to change. For example, proprietors of small family shops (often older people) prefer to go on operating them in much the same way as before despite growing competition from shopping centres. Another reason for losing out due to economic growth, much less common than the first, is technical change. An example is the reluctance of watch repairmen to enter new lines of work despite the fact that demand for their services has plummeted due to the advent of cheap digital watches which cost less to replace than to repair. It was rare for informal sector workers to report that they themselves or others in similar lines of work lost out because they were squeezed by formal sector firms.

References

Doeringer, Peter, "Market Structure, Jobs, and Productivity: Observations from Jamaica," *World Development,* Vol. 16, No. 4, April, 1988.

Fields, G., "Rural-Urban Migration, Urban Unemployment and Underemployment, and Job Search Activity in LDCs," *Journal of Development Economics,* June, 1975.

Oberai, A. S. and H. K. Manmohan Singh, "Migration, Employment and the Urban Labour Market: A Study in the Indian Punjab," *International Labour Review,* July–August, 1984.

Selection VI.B.5. The Role of the Informal Sector in the Migration Process: A Test of Probabilistic Migration Models and Labour Market Segmentation for India*

Attitude Towards the Informal Sector at Time of Entry

Seventy-one per cent of those who were absorbed in non-wage employment on arrival stated during the survey that they had come to the city with the specific intention of pursuing non-wage activity. The issue about the objectives of those who entered the informal wage sector cannot be resolved as easily, as the survey did not collect information on the type and size of establishments that migrants expected to join. However, some insight can be obtained from estimates of the prevalence of moving to the city with job prospects made certain from the rural area, and of job search after entering the informal wage sector.

Of those who entered the informal wage sector, 12 per cent had prearranged their urban jobs (in the sense that they had received *firm commitment* of employment from the *employer*), and 42 per cent had migrated on the suggestions of urban-based contacts.[1] For all practical purposes informal wage sector entrants who received suggestions from urban contacts have no uncertainty in their minds of getting a job in this sector on arrival at the urban centre. The survey data indicate that because of the responsibilities incurred, urban-based contacts are not likely to make suggestions until they have lined up specific jobs for their candidates or are sure of doing so.[2] Moreover, the ability of contacts to locate jobs for others outside their own sector is likely to be limited. Contacts have most influence with their own employers, and they are most knowledgeable about vacancies in their own occupations and establishments.

It can be argued that the evidence that many migrants expected to enter the informal wage sector and acquired such jobs through contacts does not establish that these migrants did not move to the city to engage in job search there. For it may be that they simply expected to start lower down the job ladder. However, the survey data suggest that this was not so. If informal sector entrants considered their job as a holding operation they would be looking for alternative employment. The continuation of job search after taking up first job was more prevalent among those who entered the informal wage sector, but the majority of migrants entering this sector did not search. Forty-one per cent of those who entered the informal wage sector continued job search, compared to 21 per cent and 20 per cent of those who entered the formal sector and non-wage employment respectively. Thus, it can be claimed with some confidence that a sizeable proportion, possibly one-half or more, of migrants who entered the informal wage sector and the non-wage sector had been attracted to the city by opportunities in these sectors, and did not consider employment there as a means of survival while waiting in the queue for formal sector jobs.

Mobility from the Informal Sector to the Formal Sector

Only 24 per cent of those who entered the informal wage sector on arrival and 6 per cent of the non-wage workers had found their way into the formal sector by the time of the survey. These figures represent the average experience of a large number of cohorts over varying periods of time. Thus they are not adequate measures of the degree of mobility, though the mobility from the non-wage sector is obviously on the low side. To overcome this deficiency, we suggested a comparison of the proportion of direct entrants in the formal sector in any particular year with the proportion of informal sector entrants in the previous year who moved to the formal sector within twelve months of arrival.

The results of such an exercise are presented in Table 1. The table shows that for migrants who entered the informal wage sector, the percentage who moved to the formal sector within twelve months of arrival was between 5 per cent and 15 per cent (col. 3). This was considerably lower than the percentage of all new arrivals and of those with no education who entered the formal sector directly. The percentage who had entered the formal sector directly varied from 38 per cent to 48 per cent for the entire sample (col. 1), and from 26 per cent to 46 per cent for migrants with no education (col.

*From Biswajit Banerjee, "The Role of the Informal Sector in the Migration Process: A Test of Probabilistic Migration Models and Labour Market Segmentation for India," *Oxford Economic Papers* 35 (1983): 411, 414–420. Reprinted by permission.

[1]These two categories of migrants overlap. In all, 48 per cent of the informal wage sector entrants had pre-arranged job and/or moved on the suggestion of a contact.

[2]This point is discussed in detail in Banerjee (1984).

Table 1. Direct Entry into the Formal Sector and Mobility from the Informal Sector, by Year of Arrival in Delhi

Year of arrival	Percentage of migrants who entered the formal sector directly (1)	Percentage of migrants with no education who entered the formal sector directly (2)	For those who entered the informal wage sector, the percentage who moved to the formal sector within 12 months of arrival (3)	For those who entered the informal wage sector, the percentage who were in the formal sector at the time of the survey (1975–76) (4)
1965	37.8	25.8	5.9	29.4
1966	44.3	32.0	7.1	31.0
1967	46.2	25.8	10.4	33.3
1968	45.4	43.9	4.8	20.6
1969	45.9	45.5	14.6	31.3
1970	43.9	29.5	11.6	30.4
1971	42.9	52.3	8.7	26.1
1972	41.8	37.2	12.5	20.8
1973	49.5	38.5	9.8	22.0
1974	40.5	35.7	14.3	16.7
1975	46.2	37.9	3.9[a]	3.9

[a]This figure is low because many of the new arrivals in 1975 had not completed 12 months of urban residence at the time of the survey.

2).[3] To give a specific example, of those migrants who had entered the informal wage sector in 1966, only 7.1 per cent had moved to the formal sector within twelve months of their arrival. But in 1967, 46.2 per cent of all new arrivals and 25.8 per cent of new arrivals with no education entered the formal sector directly. Thus in 1967 new arrivals were at least four to six times more likely to get formal sector employment than those who entered the informal wage sector in 1966. This suggests, in contrast to the assumption of probabilistic migration models, that the migrant labour market in Delhi is segmented.

It can be argued that in the context of Delhi the above criterion for judging segmentation is too stringent. Limiting the reference period to twelve months would be appropriate if job search was entirely urban based. But the survey data indicate that over one-half of the direct entrants to the formal sector had engaged in rural-based search. Therefore the reference period for measuring mobility from the informal sector ought to match the average length of rural-based search of formal sector entrants. Unfortunately, we are unable to do this as information on length of rural-based search was

[3]The percentage of direct formal sector entrants in any particular year has been calculated with respect to those who had arrived in the city that year and were living there at the time of the survey. This neglects those who had come in that year and had returned to their origin. To the extent these return migrants had entered the urban informal sector, the figures on direct formal sector entry are overestimates. But then, so also are the figures on mobility from the informal sector to the formal sector.

not collected in the survey. However, a consideration of mobility measured over a longer period (see col. 4) and the econometric evidence reported below on the influence of length of urban residence suggests that the conclusion of segmentation is still valid.

We now estimate the factors that contributed to mobility from the informal wage sector to the formal sector by estimating a binary logit model. The estimates, obtained by the maximum likelihood method, are presented in Table 2. The results indicate, contrary to the assertion of the segmentation model, that education has an important influence on mobility. In particular, having middle school- or intermediate college-level education increases the likelihood of mobility. However, age on arrival does not have any significant effect. Thus, the advantage that migrants who arrive between the age of 20 and 24 have over other age groups in gaining direct access to the formal sector is lost once they enter the informal wage sector.

As might be expected, the likelihood of mobility increases with duration of urban residence. Ceteris paribus, an additional year spent in the city increases the probability of an informal wage sector employee moving to the formal sector by 0.02, when evaluated at the aggregate predicted probability for mean values of the explanatory variables ($p = 0.18$).

The finding on the unmarried worker dummy is similar to that obtained in the model of sector of entry restricted to wage employees. This suggests that formal sector employers perhaps prefer to hire

Table 2. Logit Estimates of Mobility Between Sectors (Dependent variable: log of odds of moving to the formal sector from the informal wage sector)

Independent variable	Coefficient (asymptotic standard error)
Education dummies[a]	
Below primary	−0.06823 (0.34667)
Primary to below middle	−0.18347 (0.28831)
Middle to below matric	0.56045 (0.29552)†
Matric to below intermediate	0.43083 (0.35694)
Intermediate to below graduate	2.10030 (0.62826)*
Graduate and above	−25.71200 (237.00 × 10^3)[b]
Age on arrival dummies[c]	
20 to 24	0.11364 (0.25274)
25 to 29	0.33029 (0.32886)
30 to 39	0.13475 (0.38893)
40 and above	−0.19849 (0.68002)
Years of urban residence	0.14667 (0.03044)*
Unmarried	−0.42204 (0.22976)†
Scheduled caste	0.44327 (0.23079)†
Region of origin dummies[d]	
Haryana	−0.34077 (0.45692)
Punjab	−1.59160 (0.85051)†
Rajasthan	−0.43204 (0.51791)
Eastern Uttar Pradesh	0.09134 (0.33322)
Hill Uttar Pradesh	0.51610 (0.44980)
Central Uttar Pradesh	0.15181 (0.74723)
Western Uttar Pradesh	−1.06220 (0.39815)*
Constant	−2.04740 (0.44978)*
Log likelihood	−323.04
Likelihood ratio test	63.51
Degrees of freedom	20
(*N*)	(646)
Predicted probability at mean values of independent variables	0.18

[a]The omitted category was those with no education.

[b]There were very few observations in this education category, which has affected the size and reliability of the coefficient.

[c]The omitted category was those less than 19 years of age.

[d]The omitted category was those from "Rest of India."

*Significant at the 1 per cent level, using a two-tailed test.

†Significant at the 10 per cent level.

married workers or that informal sector employment is less acceptable to married than to unmarried workers. The evidence suggests that Scheduled caste migrants are more likely to move out of the informal wage sector to the formal sector than those who belong to other castes, reflecting their awareness and exploitation of the advantage they have from the government policy of reserving jobs for Scheduled castes.[4]

[4]For a detailed analysis of the influence of caste in the urban labour market see Banerjee and Knight (1982).

As for *potential mobility* from the informal sector to the formal sector, the probability appears to be low. At the time of the survey, only 15 per cent of the informal sector wage employees and 12 per cent of the non-wage workers were actively searching for alternative wage employment.

The lack of mobility from the non-wage sector and the lack of interest of non-wage workers in wage employment is not surprising given that the average monthly earnings of these workers were 47 per cent higher than those of workers in the formal sector. One reason for the low propensity of workers in the informal wage sector to seek alternative employment may be that the wage differential with the formal sector is not large enough to make it worthwhile to bother looking for formal sector employment. The informal sector migrants may currently be working together with their relatives and co-villagers, and may not like to sacrifice this working environment to seek employment elsewhere for slightly higher pay. Further, the cumulative loss from being in the informal sector rather than in the formal sector is minimal since education and experience are rewarded at similar rates in both sectors.[5] Another, and perhaps more important, reason may be that there are constraints on obtaining specific information and gaining access to formal sector employment. If information on formal sector opportunities is generally transmitted through contacts, informal sector employees will come to know of them only if they are able to widen their contacts after arrival. The widening of contacts is not easy, and is largely a matter of chance. The urban social network is based on kinship, caste membership, area of origin, and place of work. When jobs are scarce, social groups are likely to accommodate their own members first. An alternative way to obtain information would be to search personally at factory gates. But this search would have to be carried out during working hours, and may require giving up the current job. This option is therefore quite risky, and may not be preferred by many individuals. An additional consideration in rejecting this option may be the belief that jobs cannot be obtained without the influence of contacts. This belief may also inhibit individuals from searching for formal sector jobs through newspaper advertisement and employment exchange. Thus, migrants may not search because they do not know of any jobs that are available, or because they know that what is available cannot be obtained. The presence of contacts plays a crucial role in both these considerations. The role of contacts in mobility between sectors in Delhi is highlighted by individual level data: of those migrants in the sample who had moved from the informal wage sector to the formal sector, about 60 per cent came to know about their current employment from relatives and friends.

The above discussion suggests a reason why the proportion of new arrivals entering the formal sector was greater than the proportion of informal

wage sector workers moving to the formal sector. Informal sector wage employees were not aware of the formal sector vacancies which the new arrivals filled. Only if there was a perfect market mechanism for transmission of information would all persons have an equal chance to search.

Conclusions

A basic hypothesis of probabilistic migration models is that informal sector employment is a temporary staging post for new migrants on their way to formal sector employment. In this paper we have argued that there are no conclusive tests of probabilistic models in the empirical migration literature, and we then went on to examine evidence from a sample survey which tests the validity of the assumptions that underlie such models. We also tested some of the main hypotheses of the segmented labour market theory, a popular alternative to neo-classical theory for analyzing the structure of urban labour markets in developing countries. The empirical evidence indicates that the migration process postulated in probabilistic models does not seem to be realistic in the case of Delhi, and that the segmentation model is only partially valid.

Slightly more than one-half of the migrants in the sample joined the informal sector on arrival in Delhi, but only a small fraction entered non-wage employment. Not all informal sector entrants saw their job as a means of financing search for formal sector employment. A substantial proportion of informal sector entrants were attracted to Delhi by opportunities in the informal sector. About one-half of the informal wage sector entrants moved to Delhi after prearranging their job or on the suggestion of an urban-based contact, and nearly three-quarters of the non-wage sector entrants expected to set up such activities on arrival in the city. Only two-fifths of the informal wage sector entrants and one-fifth of the non-wage workers continued to search for alternative employment after finding their first job. The survey data also suggest that a majority of formal sector entrants too had engaged in rural-based search and had lined up their jobs from the rural area. These findings do not lend support to the basic assumptions of probabilistic migration models.

Actual mobility and potential mobility from the informal sector was low. Slightly less than one-quarter of informal wage sector entrants were able to move to the formal sector. The proportion who moved from the informal wage sector to the formal sector during any twelve month period was four to

[5]The superiority of the formal sector must not be gauged in terms of earnings differentials alone. This sector is likely to have greater non-pecuniary benefits and better terms and conditions of work than the informal sector.

six times lower than the proportion of all new arrivals and of those with no education during that period who entered the formal sector directly. Moreover, only a small proportion of informal sector wage employees were seeking alternative jobs at the time of the survey. This was interpreted as evidence of a segmented labour market, and was attributed in part to imperfect information flows, resulting from the importance of contacts in the recruitment process. Individual level data indicate that friends and relatives were heavily relied on to obtain employment by entrants to all sectors and by those who moved from the informal wage sector to the formal sector. Moreover, the dummy variables on region of origin, included as proxies for the influence of contacts, were statistically significant in the econometric analysis of earnings, sector of entry, and mobility between sectors.

An analysis of earnings of wage employees suggest that a meaningful distinction could be made between the formal sector and the informal wage sector. Earnings were lower in the informal wage sector and the process of wage determination in this sector differed from that in the formal sector. But, contrary to the assertion of the segmented labour market model, returns to education and experience were similar to both sectors. The differences observed were in the effect of employment status, nature of work, and caste on earnings. In the formal sector daily-wage workers, manual workers, and individuals belonging to the Scheduled castes had lower earnings, but there was no such discrimination in the informal sector. This suggests that the informal sector was, as might be expected, more competitive.

Informal sector entrants were, on the average, slightly less well educated than those who entered the formal sector, and the likelihood of moving from the informal to the formal sector was greater for those who had above middle school level education. The latter finding goes against the hypothesis of the segmentation model that human capital is not important in explaining mobility between sectors. However, this should not detract attention from the fact that over one-third of those with no education entered the formal sector directly on arrival in the city, and that the likelihood of uneducated informal sector entrants moving to the formal

sector was small. The probability of mobility increased with duration of urban residence but only by small magnitude, and it was higher for married migrants and those who belonged to the Scheduled castes.

The findings of this paper have important implications. The implication of the rejection of probabilistic models for policy decisions is that employment creation in the urban formal sector can play a part in the solution of the urban "employment problem," and that the contribution of migration to urban surplus labour and social costs is much less than is usually visualized. The importance of pre-arranging jobs and moving on the suggestion of contacts suggest that migration in response to job creation in the formal sector is not likely to exceed the number of openings by a large margin. Only those who have contacts in the formal sector and also have the necessary qualifications will receive information about new opportunities and stand some chance of obtaining employment. If jobs are created in establishments and occupations dominated by urban natives, induced migration will be particularly low. The findings also suggest that for migrants attracted to the city by informal sector opportunities, labour market segmentation is not a constraint on the achievement of their objectives formed at the time of migration. There is no reduction in the perceived increase in welfare through migration, arising out of segmentation of the market. Individuals in the informal sector are better off in the city than they were in the rural area, though their position could be even better if there was no segmentation. Further, the importance of education and experience in the determination of earnings of wage employees in the informal sector suggests that low earnings in this sector can be eliminated through human capital formation.

References

Banerjee, Biswajit (1984) "Information flow, expectations and job search: rural-to-urban migration process in India," *Journal of Development Economics* 15: 239–57.

Banerjee, Biswajit and Knight, J. B. (1982) "Caste discrimination in the Indian urban labour market," mimeo.

CHAPTER VII

Agriculture

Overview

Overview

The first section of this chapter begins with Exhibit VII.A.1, showing the share of agriculture in each country's labor force and each country's agricultural productivity relative to its non-agricultural productivity. Agricultural productivity in low human development countries is an even smaller fraction of that in high human development countries than is nonagricultural productivity, as we saw in Note I.A.2. Raising agricultural productivity is crucial for raising incomes of agricultural workers, who make up a large fraction or even the majority of the labor force in less developed countries. Increased agricultural productivity may yield other benefits for LDC economies such as reduced urban underemployment, as was claimed by Todaro in Selection VI.B.2.

What special characteristics of agriculture have made it so difficult to raise productivity? To begin, in a large LDC millions of individuals and households are making production decisions, while in other important industries the number of decision-makers might range from a handful to thousands. Next, the seasonality and geographical dispersion of agricultural production create the need for an extensive system of storage and transportation. The weather adds an extra element of uncertainty to the agricultural production process and contributes to exceptional volatility of output prices. All of these special characteristics, along with wide regional variation in climate in many countries, complicate the task of policymakers and increase the risk that government intervention will fail. Yet, as Timmer (1988, p. 301) points out, "Designing new technology and fostering its adoption is primarily a public sector activity because of the relatively small scale of individual farmers." The same could be said of rural infrastructure such as roads and irrigation projects.

The first selection of this chapter, by John Luke Gallup and Jeffrey D. Sachs, emphasizes another difficulty for raising agricultural productivity in many LDCs: the disadvantages of tropical climate and soils, and the inappropriateness of much research conducted for temperate countries for growing crops in tropical countries, given the climate and soil specificity of agricultural know-how. The following Note on food, hunger, and famine discusses studies of some of the more extreme consequences of agricultural problems. Given these special difficulties, how should less developed countries go about "transforming traditional agriculture" (Schultz 1964) or "getting agriculture moving" (Mosher 1966)? Selection VII.A.2 by C. Peter Timmer describes three different agricultural strategies: a free-market strategy of "benign neglect," an activist government strategy directed toward small farmers, and an intermediate strategy that recognizes government failures as well as market failures. The Note following this selection describes the theory of Hayami and Ruttan (1985) that the direction of technical and institutional change in agriculture toward saving labor or saving land is "induced" by relative scarcity of labor versus land. Also included in the Note is the less optimistic view, expressed by Braverman and Stiglitz (1986), that beneficial innovations may not be adopted and undesirable innovations may be given the structure of incentives in the landlord-tenant relationship. This Note is followed by Comment VII.A.1 on the "Green Revolution" in agricultural technology, in which high-yielding varieties of rice and wheat were introduced into less developed countries during the 1960s. Whether or not small farmers have benefited from diffusion of Green Revolution technology has been a subject of much controversy, and the Comment lists some of the key studies and issues.

Timmer writes that the intermediate agricultural strategy described in Selection VII.A.2 "incurs heavy analytical costs." The foundation for that analysis is given in Selection VII.A.3, in which Joseph Stiglitz lists the theoretical justifications for government intervention in agricultural markets and assesses the prospects that policies can succeed given the limited information that governments have available. The following selection by Timmer describes appropriate government interventions in the area of rural infrastructure, especially marketing infrastructure. The final selection of the first section of this chapter, by Abhijit Banerjee, evaluates a much more radical form of government intervention in the agricultural sector: redistributive land reform. Banerjee stresses the need to carefully take into account the nature of agricultural contracts and the incentives they generate when evaluating land reform. These same kinds of issues are explored more fully in the next section of this chapter, which covers the microeconomics of the rural sector.

In Selection VII.B.1, Joseph Stiglitz discusses the incentive effects of sharecropping arrangements that are widely used in less developed countries. Unlike a wage system, sharecropping provides an incentive for the tenant to work in the absence of monitoring by the landlord, and unlike a rental system, the landlord and tenant face the same risks. Hans Binswanger and Mark Rosenzweig in Selection VII.B.2 note the difficulty for contractual choice models of explaining "tenancy ladders" where workers first become sharecroppers, then fixed-rent tenants, and finally acquire land of their own. In the following selection Pranab Bardhan criticizes the tendency of researchers in this area to "explain" the existence of certain contractual arrangements by showing that they benefit the parties involved. Collective action and bargaining problems may allow inefficient institutions to persist, vitiating the power of such "explanations."

Complementary fixed capital investments are often required to achieve the maximum benefits from adopting technical innovations in agriculture, making effective provision of credit to small farmers a key ingredient in raising agricultural productivity. Avishay Braverman and J. Luis Guasch in Selection VII.B.4 review some of the fundamental problems with rural financial markets in less developed countries. In the following selection Inderjit Singh, Lyn Squire, and John Strauss try to capture in a formal model the complexity of agricultural household behavior. This complexity stems from the fact that the typical agricultural household must make decisions regarding production, family labor supply, and commodity consumption. They show that if the household is a price taker in all markets its production decisions are consistent with profit maximization and independent of the household's utility function. An important consequence is that output supply will increase with price. Empirical studies of the response of agricultural production to prices are listed in the Comment following this selection.

References

Braverman, Avishay, and Joseph Stiglitz. 1986. "Landlords, Tenants and Technological Innovations." *Journal of Development Economics* 23 (October): 313–32.

Hayami, Yujiro, and Vernon W. Ruttan. 1985. *Agricultural Development: An International Perspective,* revised and expanded edition (Baltimore: Johns Hopkins University Press).

Mosher, Arthur T. 1966. *Getting Agriculture Moving: Essentials for Development and Modernization* (New York: Praeger).

Schultz, Theodore W. 1964. *Transforming Traditional Agriculture* (New Haven, Conn.: Yale University Press).

Timmer, C. Peter. 1988. "The Agricultural Transformation." In Hollis Chenery and T. N. Srinivasan, eds., *Handbook of Development Economics, Volume I* (Amsterdam: North-Holland).

VII.A. DESIGNING AN AGRICULTURAL STRATEGY

Exhibit VII.A.1. Agricultural Labor Force and Productivity

Country Name (listed from lowest to highest HDI)	Total Labor Force[a] (Thousands) 2000	Percent of the Labor Force		Value-Added Per Worker[c]		Productivity Gap: Non-Agricultural to Agricultural Productivity[e] 2000
		In Agriculture[b] 1990	In Agriculture[b] 2000	In Agricultural Work[b] 2000	In Non-Agricultural Work[d] 2000	
Low-human development countries						
Sierra Leone	1,632	67.5	62.1	358	657	1.8
Niger	5,000	89.8	87.8	187	2,197	11.8
Burkina Faso	5,486	92.4	92.3	177	4,342	24.6
Mali	5,558	85.8	81.0	310	1,698	5.5
Burundi	3,344	91.6	90.4	150	1,527	10.1
Mozambique	9,586	82.7	80.5	128	1,285	10.1
Ethiopia	27,781		82.4	137	864	6.3
Central African Republic	1,752	80.2	72.7	493	1,316	2.7
Congo, Dem. Rep. of the	20,686	67.8	63.2	220	235	1.1
Guinea-Bissau	549	85.4	82.7	325	1,095	3.4
Chad	3,614	83.2	75.2	208	1,240	6.0
Angola	5,941	74.5	71.8	127	3,787	29.8
Zambia	4,398	74.4	69.1	197	2,484	12.6
Malawi	5,445	86.6	82.9	129	1,241	9.6
Côte d'lvoire	6,531	59.8	49.2	1,104	2,497	2.3
Tanzania, U. Rep. of	18,088	84.4	80.4	184	1,057	5.7
Benin	2,835	63.5	54.0	615	1,270	2.1
Rwanda	4,134	91.7	90.3	249	2,826	11.3
Guinea	4,047	87.2	83.8	271	5,461	20.2
Senegal	4,179	76.7	73.7	338	4,338	12.8
Eritrea	1,825		77.5	61	1,246	20.3
Mauritania	1,180	55.2	52.9	504	1,805	3.6
Nigeria	45,129	43.0	33.3	732	704	1.0
Gambia	668	81.8	79.0	297	2,326	7.8
Haiti	3,513	67.8	62.3			
Madagascar	7,632	78.1	74.2	154	1,497	9.7
Yemen	5,514	61.0	50.9	404	1,628	4.0
Uganda	11,397	84.5	80.1	341	2,035	6.0
Kenya	15,816	79.6	75.4	213	1,891	8.9
Zimbabwe	5,630	68.1	62.5	380	3,076	8.1
Pakistan	52,077	51.7	47.1	733	1,932	2.6
Nepal	10,870	93.5	93.0	201	4,672	23.3
Cameroon	6,104	69.7	59.4	1,184	2,320	2.0
Median	*5,466*	*79.6*	*75.2*	*260*	*1,752*	*7.1*
Medium-human development countries						
Togo	1,913	65.6	59.7	514	1,133	2.2
Congo	1,232	48.7	40.7	467	2,949	6.3
Bangladesh	69,611	65.2	55.6	315	1,189	3.8
Sudan	12,207	69.5	61.1			
Lesotho	864	39.9	37.8	552	1,742	3.2
Bhutan	1,005	94.1	93.7	150	4,562	30.5
Lao People's Dem. Rep.	2,625	78.2	76.5	617	1,846	3.0
Comoros	331	77.6	73.7	504	1,380	2.7
Swaziland	342	39.0	33.6	1,886	6,126	3.2
Papua New Guinea	2,313	79.2	74.1	856	5,701	6.7
Myanmar	25,682	73.3	70.2			
Cambodia	6,401	73.8	70.1	358	1,069	3.0

Exhibit VII.A.1. (Continued)

| Country Name (listed from lowest to highest HDI) | Total Labor Force[a] (Thousands) 2000 | Percent of the Labor Force | | Value-Added Per Worker[c] | | Productivity Gap: Non-Agricultural to Agricultural Productivity[e] 2000 |
		In Agriculture[b] 1990	In Agriculture[b] 2000	In Agricultural Work[b] 2000	In Non-Agricultural Work[d] 2000	
Ghana	9,508	59.3	56.9	566	1,199	2.1
India	442,156	64.0	59.6	395	2,035	5.2
Morocco	11,780	44.7	36.1	1,326	4,474	3.4
Botswana	673	46.5	44.6	563	17,201	30.5
Namibia	695	49.3	41.3	1,679	9,006	5.4
Solomon Islands	223	76.7	73.1			
Nicaragua	1,981	28.6	20.0			
Egypt	25,790	40.3	33.3	1,300	3,876	3.0
Guatemala	4,142	52.4	46.1	2,127	6,147	2.9
Gabon	555	51.4	37.7	2,048	14,326	7.0
Mongolia	1,295	32.0	24.2	1,432	589	0.4
Equatorial Guinea	189	74.7	70.4	920	10,860	11.8
Honduras	2,405	41.4	31.7	1,023	2,303	2.3
Bolivia	3,391	46.8	44.2	755	3,597	4.8
Tajikistan	2,400		33.8	1,411	779	0.6
Indonesia	102,561	55.2	48.4	746	3,252	4.4
South Africa	18,028	13.5	9.6	3,861	10,147	2.6
Syrian Arab Republic	5,165	33.2	27.8	2,602	2,444	0.9
Viet Nam	40,880	71.2	67.3	254	1,649	6.5
Moldova, Rep. of	2,180		22.8	1,649	1,134	0.7
Algeria	10,458	26.1	24.3	1,826	5,582	3.1
Iran, Islamic Rep. of	24,169	32.2	26.5	3,684	4,613	1.3
El Salvador	2,703	36.4	29.0	1,702	5,060	3.0
China	766,889	71.9	66.6	333	3,401	10.2
Cape Verde	174	31.0	23.0	2,607	4,221	1.6
Kyrgyzstan	2,163		25.7	1,616	661	0.4
Uzbekistan	10,756		27.6	1,085	1,164	1.1
Armenia	1,924		12.7	5,216	1,449	0.3
Sri Lanka	8,540	48.4	45.5	744	2,958	4.0
Ecuador	4,948	33.3	25.8	1,659	4,333	2.6
Turkey	31,212	53.6	46.2	1,909	10,600	5.6
Albania	1,558	54.6	48.2	2,121	1,827	0.9
Dominican Republic	3,625	24.8	16.7	3,169	5,060	1.6
Guyana	320	21.6	17.5	4,127	1,818	0.4
Tunisia	3,826	28.2	24.6	3,177	7,153	2.3
Jordan	1,566	15.1	11.4	1,265	5,541	4.4
Azerbaijan	3,625		26.6	775	997	1.3
Georgia	2,647					
Turkmenistan	2,047		33.4	1,481	4,505	3.0
Maldives	123	32.6	22.8	2,061	4,995	2.4
Philippines	31,355	45.8	39.5	1,426	3,721	2.6
Paraguay	2,075	38.9	34.4	3,312	5,127	1.5
Lebanon	1,256	7.3	3.7	29,061	9,218	0.3
Peru	9,713	35.6	30.2	1,876	8,152	4.3
Fiji	324	45.6	39.8			
Oman	721	44.7	35.8			
Jamaica	1,284	24.6	20.6	1,460	5,042	3.5
Suriname	159	21.2	18.9	2,091	2,697	1.3
Kazakhstan	7,998		17.7	1,545	3,090	2.0
Ukraine	25,274		14.4	1,494	1,799	1.2
Thailand	37,379	64.1	56.5	949	9,305	9.8

Exhibit VII.A.1. (Continued)

Country Name (listed from lowest to highest HDI)	Total Labor Force[a] (Thousands) 2000	Percent of the Labor Force		Value-Added Per Worker[c]		Productivity Gap: Non-Agricultural to Agricultural Productivity[e] 2000
		In Agriculture[b] 1990	In Agriculture[b] 2000	In Agricultural Work[b] 2000	In Non-Agricultural Work[d] 2000	
Saudi Arabia	6,095	19.1	9.8			
Romania	10,718	24.0	15.1	2,786	2,762	1.0
Venezuela	9,881	12.0	8.1	5,298	8,320	1.6
Belize	79	34.5	30.4	5,731	11,135	1.9
Bosnia and Herzegovina	1,859		5.2	7,634	3,026	0.4
Brazil	79,247	23.3	16.7	4,754	10,967	2.3
Colombia	18,213	26.6	20.4	3,642	5,734	1.6
Russian Federation	78,041		10.5	2,594	4,844	1.9
Mauritius	507	16.7	11.8	4,698	10,267	2.2
Libyan Arab Jamahiriya	1,794	11.0	6.0			
Macedonia, TFYR	937		12.8	4,395	5,656	1.3
Panama	1,205	26.2	20.3	2,742	9,061	3.3
Malaysia	9,432	27.4	18.7	6,849	12,978	1.9
Bulgaria	4,100	13.5	7.1	7,960	2,693	0.3
Median	*2,313*	*40.1*	*30.3*	*1654*	*4277*	*2.5*
High-human development countries						
Mexico	40,724	27.8	21.5	1,791	11,169	6.2
Trinidad and Tobago	578	11.1	8.7	3,075	12,827	4.2
Belarus	5,410		13.2	2,230	2,706	1.2
Cuba	5,552	18.2	14.1			
Latvia	1,330		12.0	2,717	4,904	1.8
Bahamas	156	5.6	3.8			
United Arab Emirates	1,362	7.8	4.9			
Croatia	2,196		8.5	9,452	10,338	1.1
Kuwait	807	1.2	1.1			
Lithuania	1,925		12.3	3,258	4,039	1.2
Qatar	313	2.8	1.3			
Chile	6,211	18.8	15.8	6,039	14,292	2.4
Costa Rica	1,629	26.1	20.1	5,255	10,179	1.9
Estonia	769		11.3	4,347	8,409	1.9
Uruguay	1,502	14.2	12.6	8,062	14,358	1.8
Slovakia	2,966		9.0	4,128	8,132	2.0
Hungary	4,769	15.2	10.7	5,161	12,148	2.4
Bahrain	299	1.8	1.0			
Poland	19,975	27.5	21.7	1,560	8,655	5.5
Argentina	14,996	12.1	9.8	10,260	20,544	2.0
Malta	148	2.3	1.4			
Czech Republic	5,765		8.2	6,306	9,882	1.6
Brunei Darussalam	148	1.8	0.7			
Korea, Rep. of	23,966	18.1	10.0	13,758	27,230	2.0
Slovenia	1,020		2.0	36,175	22,454	0.6
Singapore	2,013	0.4	0.1	44,744	56,829	1.3
Barbados	147	7.0	4.1	19,036	15,328	0.8
Hong Kong, China (SAR)						
Cyprus	385	13.6	8.6			
Greece	4,626	23.0	16.8	14,285	33,238	2.3
Portugal	5,103	17.8	12.7	7,469	27,939	3.7
Israel	2,589	4.1	2.7			
Italy	25,437	8.6	5.3	26,474	48,499	1.8
New Zealand	1,883	10.4	9.0	29,288	37,210	1.3
Spain	17,575	11.9	7.4	22,145	41,482	1.9

Exhibit VII.A.1. (Continued)

Country Name (listed from lowest to highest HDI)	Total Labor Force[a] (Thousands) 2000	Percent of the Labor Force		Value-Added Per Worker[c]		Productivity Gap: Non-Agricultural to Agricultural Productivity[e] 2000
		In Agriculture[b] 1990	In Agriculture[b] 2000	In Agricultural Work[b] 2000	In Non-Agricultural Work[d] 2000	
Germany	40,299	4.0	2.5	32,629	67,541	2.1
France	26,836	5.5	3.3	58,018	66,322	1.1
Austria	3,733	7.8	5.1	31,396	73,694	2.3
Luxembourg	184	3.6	2.2	52,580	135,600	2.6
Finland	2,602	8.4	5.5	41,686	64,846	1.6
United Kingdom	29,890	2.2	1.8	34,636	43,852	1.3
Ireland	1,605	14.3	10.2			
Denmark	2,935	5.6	3.8	57,535	70,505	1.2
Switzerland	3,807	5.5	4.2			
Japan	68,369	7.3	4.1	31,791	85,252	2.7
Canada	16,559	3.4	2.4	43,768	42,678	1.0
United States	145,105	2.8	2.1	53,353	62,117	1.2
Belgium	4,222	2.6	1.8	59,409	75,605	1.3
Netherlands	7,357	4.6	3.4	59,346	67,834	1.1
Australia	9,770	5.5	4.6	32,598	46,877	1.4
Sweden	4,793	4.4	3.2	36,640	58,683	1.6
Iceland	158	11.3	8.2	49,295	56,103	1.1
Norway	2,314	6.3	4.6	35,211	75,507	2.1
Median	*2,769*	*7.1*	*5.2*	*24,310*	*35,224*	*1.8*

United Nations Human Development Index countries are included in the Exhibit only if they have data available.

[a]The labor force includes all people identified by the Food and Agriculture Organization of the United Nations to be part of the economically active population.

[b]Agriculture corresponds to ISIC Revision 3 divisions 1–5 and includes forestry, hunting, and fishing, as well as cultivation of crops and livestock production.

[c]Data are in constant 1995 U.S. dollars.

[d]Non-agricultural value-added is defined as total gross domestic product less agricultural value-added. The non-agricultural labor force is defined as the total labor force less the agricultural labor force. This column reports the ratio of these two values

[e]The productivity gap is defined as the ratio of value-added per worker in non-agricultural work to value-added per worker in agricultural work.

Sources: Food and Agriculture Organization of the United Nations, FAOSTAT, 2003. World Bank, World Development Indicators, 2003.

Selection VII.A.1. Agriculture, Climate, and Technology: Why Are the Tropics Falling Behind?*

The disparity in agricultural productivity between the tropics and the temperate zones is even greater than the disparity in income levels. Income per capita in non-tropical countries was 3.3 times the level of income per capita in tropical countries in 1995, but agricultural output per worker in the non-tropical countries was 8.8 times the level in the tropics.

One would expect that the productivity of agricultural labor in poor tropical countries would be lower whether or not tropical climate or soils had an impact on agriculture. In poor countries, all labor has low wages so that a lot of labor is used in agriculture relative to other factors of production, ensuring low labor productivity in agriculture. Is poverty (due to other causes) rather than agricultural conditions responsible for low agricultural productivity in the tropics? Apparently not. When controlling for income level, labor productivity in tropical agriculture is still only 51% of labor productivity in non-tropical agriculture.[1]

Another way to look at the agricultural fecundity of the tropics is to compare crop yields, or the output per cultivated land area. The geographical tropics is a convenient classification for describing basic patterns, but it is the not the most appropriate way to distinguish zones of agro-ecological conditions. Much better are ecozone maps based on climatic data: temperature and precipitation. From detailed Köppen ecozones, one can distinguish four broad regions: Temperate, Tropical (the humid subset of the geographical tropics), Dry (most of the rest of the geographical tropics and the very dry non-tropical areas), and Cold (including high altitude areas).

Agricultural yields for all major crop categories are lower in the tropics (Table 1). The yields of six crop groups (wheat, maize, rice, pulses, root crops, and vegetables) and two livestock categories (beef

and pig) are generally lowest in Tropical ecozones, slightly higher in Dry ecozones, and substantially higher in Temperate and Cold ecozones. In 1998, all of the Tropical and Dry crop yields are lower than all the Temperate and Cold ecozones except for wheat yields in the Dry zone. Tropical ecozone crop yields range from 36% to 67% of Temperate zone yields, while Tropical livestock yields are about three quarters of Temperate zone yields.

Comparing crop yields in 1998 with yields in 1961 shows that the tropical disparity has actually gotten worse over the past four decades for all crops except for rice. Tropical ecozone crop yields in 1961 ranged from 48% to 77% of Temperate yields (excluding rice), while livestock yields ranges from 86% to 97% (Table 1). Comparing recent yields to those in 1961 also shows how much improvement there has been in crop yields everywhere. Foodgrain yields in particular have roughly doubled. Although the Tropical yields are further behind Temperate yields in 1998 than they were in 1961, Tropical yields in 1998 are near the level of Temperate yields in 1961 and surpass them in the case of cereals, wheat, and beef. Growth of cereals yields has been over 1% percent per year in the Tropical ecozones since 1961, and over 0.5% per year for the other crops.

Agricultural productivity of both labor and land are lower in the tropics, in the case of labor productivity, even after controlling for income levels. A more satisfactory way of examining the differences in agricultural productivity, though, is to take into account the whole range of inputs used in agriculture, which affect both labor and land productivities. This is done after considering several causal explanations for lower agricultural productivity in the tropics.

Why Should the Tropics Be Less Conducive to Agriculture?

The image of the humid tropics is the most fecund of environments, teeming with life. It is true that the humid tropics are teeming with biodiversity, but the conditions for biodiversity need not be related to conditions for optimal plant-growth. In many contexts biodiversity is negatively correlated with the fertility of the land [such as tree species diversity in Costa Rica (Huston, p. 514)]. Humid tropical forests are biologically productive [though often less than temperate forests (Huston, pp.

*From John Luke Gallop and Jeffrey D. Sachs, "Agriculture, Climate, and Technology: Why Are the Tropics Falling Behind?" *American Journal of Agricultural Economics* 82 (August 2000): 731–737. Reprinted by permission.

[1]The regression using 1995 data with *t*-statistics in parentheses below the coefficients is

$$\ln(\text{ag output/worker}) = -0.13 + 0.98^* \ln(\text{GDP per capita})$$
$$(0.18) \quad (12.12)$$
$$-0.67^*(\% \text{ land area in tropics})$$
$$(3.44)$$
$$N = 128 \quad R^2 = 0.77.$$

Table 1. Crop Yields and Yield Growth, 1961–1998

Crop Yields, 1998

Ecozones	Number of countries	Cereal (milled rice equivalent)	Wheat	Maize	Rice (paddy)	Pulses	Roots and tubers	Vegetables and melons	Beef carcasses	Pig carcasses
Cold	37	32.3	25.5	70.0	54.5	17.0	246.2	196.0	255.2	77.0
Dry	82	20.4	26.6	24.7	36.3	9.9	128.8	133.4	161.2	57.5
Temperate	71	33.7	26.1	53.6	58.1	13.7	253.8	200.1	223.5	73.2
Tropical	78	17.4	17.6	19.2	24.9	7.6	97.9	104.8	161.3	54.8
Tropical/temperate		51.6%	67.4%	35.8%	42.9%	55.5%	38.6%	52.4%	72.2%	74.9%

Crop Yields, 1961

Ecozones	Number of countries	Cereal (milled rice equivalent)	Wheat	Maize	Rice (paddy)	Pulses	Roots and tubers	Vegetables and melons	Beef carcasses	Pig carcasses
Cold	37	12.9	9.8	35.4	29.8	10.5	145.1	118.8	159.9	63.6
Dry	82	9.3	10.3	11.4	20.9	7.2	77.2	83.4	138.1	49.9
Temperate	71	14.5	11.6	21.7	37.8	9.6	130.4	106.5	159.9	58.5
Tropical	78	9.6	8.9	10.5	14.9	6.2	74.3	62.5	154.3	50.3
Tropical/temperate		66.2%	76.7%	48.4%	39.4%	64.6%	57.0%	58.7%	96.5%	86.0%

Yield Growth 1961–98 (Percent Per Year)

Ecozones	Number of countries	Cereal (milled rice equivalent)	Wheat	Maize	Rice (paddy)	Pulses	Roots and tubers	Vegetables and melons	Beef carcasses	Pig carcasses
Cold	37	2.48	2.58	1.84	1.63	1.30	1.43	1.35	1.26	0.52
Dry	82	2.12	2.56	2.09	1.49	0.86	1.38	1.27	0.42	0.38
Temperate	71	2.28	2.19	2.44	1.16	0.96	1.80	1.70	0.91	0.61
Tropical	78	1.61	1.84	1.63	1.39	0.55	0.75	1.40	0.12	0.23
Tropical/temperate		0.67	−0.35	−0.81	0.23	−0.41	−1.05	−0.31	−0.79	−0.37

Note: Yields are for 1998 in metric tons per hectare except for animal carcasses in kilograms per animal. The number of countries includes all countries which contain any agricultural land of the respective ecozones, where each country's contribution to the ecozone average is weighted by its share of the agricultural land in the ecozone and by the country's land area. Thus the total number of countries in the sample, 178, is less than the sum of countries containing each ecozone. The number of countries only applies strictly to cereal yields. The number of countries with data for the other crops and animals may be slightly more or less. Data source: FAO.

550–552)], but when the tree cover is stripped off and the land is farmed by conventional methods, it quickly loses its productivity.

Food plants are a small and particular subset of plants that need not be well suited to tropical conditions. According to Pingali (pp. 209–10), "In general, a system of farming that closely mimics the dense natural vegetation of the humid forests will work in the long run. . . . The humid and subhumid tropics are well suited to perennial crops such as bananas and to tree crops such as rubber, cocoa, and palm oil." None of these crops, with the possible exception of the banana, is a staple food crop.

Most explanations of the deficiencies of the humid tropics for agriculture focus on the soils (Weischet and Caviedes, Huston, and articles in Vosti and Reardon). Typical humid tropical soils (alfisols, oxisols, and ultisols) are low in nutrients and organic matter and are susceptible to erosion and acidification. In addition, application of synthetic fertilizers to improve the fertility of these soils is often ineffective and unsustainable, damaging the soil structure. The deficiencies of humid tropical soils are largely due to the long term effects of the tropical climate. High temperature and humidity cause organic matter in the soil to break down quickly, robbing the soil of nutrients as well as the structure needed to absorb fertilizers and slow erosion. High intensity rainstorms in humid tropical areas cause erosion, soil leaching, and compaction.

The rapid decomposition of organic matter makes soil fertility, a major investment of farmers, depreciate more quickly in the humid tropics. Hence the rates of return to farmer investments in soil are systematically lower in the humid tropics.

Humid tropical climates cover only a part of the geographical tropics. Much of the rest of the geographical tropics is made up of arid climates, with yields typically as low or lower than humid tropical yields. According to Weischet and Caviedes, the arid tropics have few problems with soil fertility, but cannot increase yields substantially without irrigation because of the high variability of rainfall and droughts. Irrigation, they argue, is limited by the general flatness of river valleys in the semi-arid tropics, so that irrigation dams must be impractically wide.

Most explanations of the geographical limitations of agriculture in the tropics focus on problematic soils in humid tropics, and rainfall variability and limited irrigation potential in the arid topics. Additional factors explaining lower agricultural potential in the tropics are pest and disease loads, and net photosynthetic potential differences.

The lack of freezing temperatures in the tropics causes a much greater number of agricultural pests in the tropics, including veterinary diseases like trypanosomiasis. Human tropical diseases such as malaria reduce agricultural labor productivity.

Although the tropics are generally warmer and sunnier throughout the year than temperate zones, the climate has disadvantages for photosynthesis. The humid tropics are often cloudy, blocking sunlight, and the high nighttime temperatures cause high respiration that slows plant growth. During the summer months, temperate zones have longer days than the tropics, giving an advantage to summer-season crops.

In light of the recent rapid change in agricultural yields in both the tropics and non-tropics, a differential role of agricultural technology across the two zones must also be considered. Empirical research to distinguish between these reasons for the tropical disadvantage in agriculture is scarce.

Quantification of the Tropical Disadvantage

. . . In Gallup and Sachs (1999) we estimate a cross-country Cobb-Douglas agricultural production function, correlating aggregate agricultural output per hectare with inputs per hectare of agricultural labor, education (as a measure of labor quality), agricultural capital (proxied by tractors and livestock), fertilizer; an indicator of the national level of technology (proxied by lagged GDP per person); an indicator of world technology level (a time trend); and shares of the agricultural land in Tropical, Dry, and Cold climates (with Temperate climate the left-out category). Data are available from 104 countries over the period 1961–94 for most countries.

Countries with Tropical and Dry climates all have significantly lower agricultural yields controlling for input and technology levels. The Tropical zones have 27% lower total factor productivity and the Dry zones have 42% lower productivity with respect to the Temperate regions. The higher productivity in the (moist) Tropical climatic zone is no comfort for the geographical tropics, though, because more of the geographical tropics are made up of Dry climatic zones (50.4%) than Tropical climatic zones (33.6%).

Yields of all crop categories in Table 1 have been rising since the 1960s, but generally have been rising much slower in the Tropical zones. Just as with the static yield differences across climatic zones, the yield growth changes could be due all or in part to differential changes in agricultural input use. Total factor productivity shows even more dra-

Table 2. Public Sector Agricultural Research Expenditures 1981–85

Ecozones	Research expenditures/ agricultural GDP (per billion)	Number of countries	Research expenditures/ agricultural laborer (1,000 1980 PPP $)	Number of countries
Temperate	18.0	22	231.2	30
Cold	36.9	6	511.3	7
Dry	8.9	29	12.9	34
Tropical	11.2	46	11.7	52
Total	16.0	103	147.4	123

Source: Pardey, Roseboom, and Anderson; World Bank (1998); FAO; and authors' calculations.

matic differences across climatic zones than simple crop yields. Controlling for inputs, Temperate zone productivity has risen by 1.1% per year from 1961 to 1994, but Tropical zone productivity *fell* by 0.6% per year and Dry zone productivity fell more by 1.0%.[2] The tropics failed to keep up with the productivity growth of the rest of the world, and in fact slipped back.

Geographical Destiny or Technology Conditioned by Geography?

. . . Tropical agriculture faces major limitations on transferring agricultural technology developed for the richer temperate-country markets to tropical climatic zones. Whereas innovations in machinery can be used interchangeably throughout the world, new crop varieties must be painstakingly adapted to each new ecological zone due to agriculture's dependence on local climate and soils.

Agricultural research is heavily concentrated outside of the tropics. Counting only public-sector agricultural research, 73% is performed in countries that have predominantly Temperate and Cold climates (calculated from Pardey, Roseboom, and Anderson). Private-sector agricultural research spending, which now dwarfs public research funding, is almost exclusively directed at Temperate and Cold climate zones because of their high income markets, so that worldwide public and private agriculture research is very heavily skewed toward the non-tropics. The research and development budget of the entire CGIAR [Consultative Group on International Agricultural Research] system of institutes studying developing world agricultural problems is less than half of the R&D bud-

get of one life-sciences multinational, Monsanto (Sachs, p. 19).

The Tropical and Dry climatic zones lag by almost any measure of agricultural research. In terms of public expenditures on agricultural research in 1981–85, the Dry and Tropical zones invested approximately half as much per dollar of agricultural output as Temperate zone countries (Table 2). The differences in research expenditure per agricultural laborer are gargantuan: Temperate countries spend nineteen times as much on research per laborer as Tropical and Dry zone countries. . . .

The large disparities in agricultural productivity between the regions of the world have worrying implications for agricultural development, especially in the tropics. Our estimates suggest that tropical agricultural output is at least one-third lower than the temperate regions when applying the same inputs. This is a huge disadvantage, and throws into question the viability of an "agriculture-led" development strategy in the mostly agricultural tropics.

References

FAO. *FAOStat Database,* 1994. http://apps.fao.org/default.htm.

Gallup, J.L., and J.D. Sachs. "Agricultural Productivity and the Tropics." Unpublished, Harvard Center for International Development, 1999.

Huston, M.A. *Biological Diversity: The Coexistence of Species on Changing Landscapes.* Cambridge UK: Cambridge University Press, 1994.

Pardey, P.G., J. Roseboom, and J.R. Anderson. "Appendix." *Agricultural Research Policy: International Quantitative Perspectives.* pp. 413–21. Cambridge UK: Cambridge University Press for ISNAR, 1991.

Pingali, P.L. "Agriculture-Environment-Poverty Interactions in the Southeast Asian Humid Tropics." *Sustainability, Growth and Poverty Alleviation: A Policy and Agroecological Perspective.* Stephen A. Vosti and

[2]This regression does not include lagged GDP per capita as a covariate to avoid confounding trends in national GDP and total factor productivity.

Thomas Reardon, eds., pp. 208–28. Baltimore MD: Johns Hopkins University Press, 1997.

Sachs, J. "Helping the World's Poorest." *The Economist* 352(14 August 1999):17–20.

Vosti, S.A., and T. Reardon, eds. *Sustainability, Growth and Poverty Alleviation: A Policy and Agroecological Perspective.* Baltimore MD: Johns Hopkins University Press, 1997.

Weischet, W., and C.N. Caviedes. *The Persisting Ecological Constraints of Tropical Agriculture.* New York: Longman Scientific and Technical, 1993.

World Bank. *World Development Indicators 1998,* CD-ROM. Washington DC: World Bank, 1998.

Note VII.A.1. Food, Hunger, Famine

Can developing countries attain levels of food consumption that will ensure adequate nutrition even for the lowest deciles in their income distribution? To guarantee adequate nutrition, agricultural development must be concerned simultaneously with the rate of increase in food production and the means by which production is increased. Unless a country's "pattern" of agricultural development facilitates the absorption of a large segment of the rural labor force into productive employment, even a large increase in food output will leave many households with inadequate access to food supplies.

Rather than being a race between food and population, the food equation is to be viewed as a dynamic balance in individual countries between food supply and food demand that depends on complex relationships among a number of variables. Equilibrium in this vital food equation can range from a low one—a small increase in food supplies and little purchasing power in the hands of the poor—to high levels of each. The level at which the food supply–food demand equation is balanced is largely dependent on the design and implementation of a country's development strategy, especially as it influences the rate of expansion of employment.

These views are presented in detail in John W. Mellor and Bruce F. Johnston, "The World Food Equation: Interrelations Among Development, Employment, and Food Consumption," *Journal of Economic Literature* (June 1984).

There is now deeper understanding of the causes and consequences of hunger and famine. The cause is not so much deficient food output as it is the absence of "entitlements" and the lack of "capability" for poor people without the financial means or political influence. This understanding follows from Sen's analysis in section I.A and is elaborated in Jean Drèze and Amartya Sen, *Hunger and Public Action* (1989).

Drèze and Sen also submit that capability and nutritional requirements encompass more than food intake—health care, basic education, clean drinking water, sewage, and adequate shelter. They point out that most of those who die in famines succumb to disease, not to starvation. Gender bias is also a cause.

Analyzing the Great Bengal Famine of 1943 and more recent famines in Bangladesh and Ethiopia, Sen has shown that it was not the decline in available food that was the major cause of famine. In Bengal, military expenditures in urban areas and the consequent inflation in food prices were responsible. Especially hard hit were landless agricultural laborers and self-employed rural artisans whose incomes lagged behind the inflation. When a threat of famine arises, relief works to provide employment and real purchasing power to the poorest can do much to avert famine. See A. K. Sen, *Poverty and Famines* (1981).

As demonstrated by India, famines can be averted, even in the event of harvest failure, by targeted and timely employment programs, direct relief to the unemployable, and careful use of food reserves. Drèze and Sen note that, in contrast to China, India's democratic political system and free press induced government action to avert famine. They contrast India, which has eliminated famine but retained chronic hunger, with China, which has reduced chronic undernutrition but has suffered famines.

For estimates of hunger and its causes and consequences, see also D. Gale Johnson and G. Edward Schuch, eds., *Role of Markets in the World Food Economy* (1983); Nicole Ball, *World Hunger* (1981); A. Macbean, "Achieving Food Security," in *Current Issues in Development Economics,* ed. U. N. Balasutramanyam and S. Lall (1991), chap. 4; and Paul Streeten, "Hunger," in *Equity and Efficiency in Economic Development,* ed. Donald J. Savoie and Irving Brecher (1992).

Selection VII.A.2. Agricultural Development Strategies*

Several main lessons have been learned in the last two decades about the functioning of the agricultural sector and its potential role in the development process: the emergence of the agricultural sector into a general equilibrium perspective; the recognition of the importance of macroeconomic policy for agricultural performance; the necessity (and feasibility because of the potential for technical change) of rapid economic growth to deal with the human welfare concerns that stem from poverty and hunger; and the superior performance of trade- and market-oriented systems in achieving this growth. These lessons do not define a single strategic approach to agricultural development, however. In fact, three sharply different paths would seem to be open for appropriate policies toward agriculture that view development of the sector as a means to an end—as part of the effort to speed the overall process of development—rather than as an end in itself.

The Alternatives

The first path has parallels to the philosophy of the 1950s, in which benign neglect of agricultural policy was thought to be sufficient for stimulating the process of economic growth. This perspective grows out of the recognition of the role of well-functioning markets and decision makers operating in a world of "rational expectations." In this view, most policy is irrelevant to farmers in more than a very transitory sense, and this is especially true of price policy. . . .

In this world, agricultural incomes are determined by employment opportunities outside agriculture, the agricultural sector *must* decline in proportional output terms and absolutely in the labor force, and the long-run decline in basic agricultural commodity prices due to technical change simply emphasizes that society is best served by getting resources out of agriculture as rapidly as possible. Although the clearest case for this view of the world is in the OECD countries, a host of middle-income countries, and even some quite poor countries, are also facing the problem of declining real incomes in the agricultural sector under the impact of rapid

technical change domestically and lower world prices for the resulting output. This perspective is obviously consistent with the view that open economies will show better performance than those with substantial trade barriers.

A sharply different path has been sketched by Mellor and Johnston (1984). Building on their earlier stress on balanced growth (1961), Johnston and Mellor call for an "interrelated strategy" that improves nutrition in one dimension while it fosters the broader growth process in the other. The approach calls for a major role of government in strategic design and program implementation, a role that is in marked contrast with the free-market approach sketched out above.

We have, therefore, emphasized that improvements in nutrition [one of Mellor and Johnston's key objectives for agricultural development] require a *set of interacting forces:* accelerated growth in agriculture; wage goods production; a strategy of development that structures demand towards high employment content goods and services; increased employment; and increased effective demand for food on the part of the poor. Agricultural growth not only satisfies the need for food to meet nutritional requirements (which is the other side of the wage-goods coin), but fosters a favorable employment-oriented demand structure as well. Agriculture's role in generating a structure of demand, favorable to rapid growth in employment, is central. (pp. 567–68, emphasis added)

Mellor and Johnston go on to summarize their earlier argument that agriculture can play this multiplicity of roles only if a unimodal development strategy is followed, that is, one in which a broad base of smallholders are the central focus of agricultural research and extension services and the recipient of the bulk of receipts from agricultural sales. The authors see the dualism inherent in bimodal strategies—those placing modernization efforts primarily on large, "progressive" farms while neglecting the "backward" smallholders—as the major obstacle to putting their set of interacting forces in motion.

The most common barrier to the interrelated strategy indicated is pronounced dualism in capital allocations—too much to industry and the unproductive elements of the private sector rather than to agriculture, and to capital intensive elements within those, as well as to large-scale and therefore capital-intensive allocations within agriculture. The outcome of the strategy will depend upon national-level decisions about macroeconomic policies, exchange rates, interest rates, and investment allocations among sectors and regions, not just within agriculture itself. Indeed, the whole strategy fails if it is viewed sim-

*From C. Peter Timmer, "The Agricultural Transformation," in H. Chenery and T. N. Srinivasan, eds., *Handbook of Development Economics,* Vol. I (Elsevier Science Publishers, North Holland Publishing Company, Amsterdam, 1988), pp. 321–28. Reprinted by permission.

ply as the responsibility of agriculture ministries. (Mellor and Johnston, 1984, p. 568)

This interrelated strategy must be directed by government planners; there is relatively little concern or role for the private sector, other than small farmers. The analysis leading to the strategy remains heavily influenced by closed economy considerations, and little attention is given to either domestic marketing activities or their relationship to international markets. Three key elements are suggested as essential to meeting all objectives of agricultural development—massive investment in human capital through nutrition, health, and family planning services in the countryside, creation of the complex, rural organizational structures seen in Japan and Taiwan that provide services to small farmers while also serving as a voice for their interests, and investment in rapid technical change appropriate to these small farmers in order to raise agricultural output and rural incomes simultaneously.

Notably missing in this list of key elements is significant concern for the structure of incentives for agriculture relative to industry or for the country's tradables relative to foreign competitors. Although it is realized that the macroeconomic setting is no doubt important to agriculture, it remains outside the scope of appropriate strategy for agricultural development. Not surprisingly, given the argument in Johnston and Clark (1982), the intellectual foundation for this strategy lies in rural development, not in a vision of agriculture linked to the macro economy and world markets by powerful market mechanisms. It is this latter vision which provides the third potential path for agricultural development strategy for the rest of the 1980s and into the 1990s.

The third approach contrasts with both the "free market" and "interrelated strategy" approaches. It calls for government policy interventions into market outcomes but uses markets and the private marketing sector as the vehicle for those policy interventions. This "market policy" approach recognizes widespread "market failures" in agriculture as well as extensive "government failures" in implementation of economic tasks. The strategic dilemma is how to cope with segmented rural capital and labor markets, poorly functioning land markets, the welfare consequences of sharp instability of prices in commodity markets, the pervasive lack of information about current and future events in most rural economies, and the sheer absence of many important markets, especially for future contingencies involving yield or price risks.

One powerful lesson of the postwar development record is that direct government interventions to correct market failures frequently make matters worse by inhibiting whatever market responses were possible in the initial circumstances, without providing greater output or more efficient utilization of resources. The agricultural sector in particular is vulnerable to well-intended but poorly conceived and managed state organizations that attempt a wide array of direct economic activities, including monopoly control of input supplies, capital-intensive state farms, and mandated control over crop marketing and processing. As Bates (1981) has demonstrated, these direct controls and agencies have a strong political economy rationale for a government that tries to reward its supporters and centralize power and resources in the hands of the state (see also Lipton, 1977).

The answer to the dilemma over making matters worse, in this approach, is to gain a much clearer understanding of the necessary interaction between the public and private sectors. . . . Political objectives for the performance of agriculture—its capacity to feed the population regularly and cheaply, or its ability to provide fair incomes to farmers caught in the pressures of successful structural transformation—are inevitable and, in some long-run sense, highly desirable.

The "market policy" path argues that these objectives are best served by making carefully considered interventions into the prices determined in markets, not by leaving markets alone or by striving to reach the objectives through direct activities by the government. If the "free market" approach incurs heavy political costs as markets relentlessly redistribute incomes to the winners in the course of economic development, and the "interrelated strategy" incurs heavy managerial and administrative costs as the government plays an active and direct economic role, the "market policy" approach incurs heavy analytical costs.

These analytical costs come from the need to understand each country's path of structural change, the workings of factor and commodity markets, and the potential impact of macro and commodity price interventions on these markets and ultimately on the structural path itself. It requires that government intervention be based on an empirical understanding of economic responses to a change in policy and the political repercussions from them. There is an important role for models in illuminating where to look for these responses, but the models themselves cannot provide the answers. This is especially true as attempts are made to build into the models the response of policy itself to changes in the economic environment. Such endogenous policy models may reveal some of the historical factors that accounted for policy shifts, but they seldom provide a sense of when the degrees of freedom for policy initiative are about to expand. Frequently, this is in times of crisis. Policy makers often embark on bold experiments in such times, and the payoff would be very high if sufficient analytical understanding already existed in order to anticipate the response to a policy change.

Agricultural Policy and Structural Change

Hayami and Ruttan (1985) have asked why agricultural growth has not been faster and more evenly spread around the world:

We indicated that the basic factor underlying poor performance was neither the meager endowment of natural resources nor the lack of technological potential to increase output from the available resources at a sufficiently rapid pace to meet the growth of demand. The major constraint limiting agricultural development was identified as the policies that impeded rather than induced appropriate technical and institutional innovations. As a result, the gap widened between the potential and the actual productive capacities of LDC agriculture. (p. 416)

This perspective, with its emphasis on the relationship between policy and agriculture's role in structural change, has provided the organizing theme for this selection. The progression of topics has followed from understanding why the agricultural sector is different from the industrial and service sectors and how the differences condition the nature of effective policy interventions. The factors needed for inducing the agricultural transformation, to "get agriculture moving," involves a complex mix of appropriate new technology, flexible rural institutions, and a market orientation that offers farmers material rewards for the physical effort they expend in their fields and households and for the risks they face from both nature and markets.

References

Bates, Robert H. 1981. *Markets and States in Tropical Africa: The Political Basis of Agricultural Policies.* Berkeley: University of California Press.

Hayami, Yujiro, and Vernon Ruttan. 1985. *Agricultural Development: An International Perspective* (revised and expanded edition). Baltimore and London: Johns Hopkins University Press.

Johnston, Bruce F., and William C. Clark. 1982. *Redesigning Rural Development: A Strategic Perspective.* Baltimore and London: Johns Hopkins University Press.

Johnston, Bruce F., and John W. Mellor. 1961. "The Role of Agriculture in Economic Development," *American Economic Review* 51, no. 4: 566–93.

Lipton, Michael. 1977. *Why Poor People Stay Poor: Urban Bias in World Development.* Cambridge, Mass.: Harvard University Press.

Mellor, John W., and Bruce F. Johnston. 1984. "The World Food Equation: Inter-relations Among Development, Employment, and Food Consumption." *Journal of Economic Literature* 22: 531–74.

Note VII.A.2. Induced Technical and Institutional Change

Hayami and Ruttan have presented an "induced innovation" model to explain growth in agricultural productivity:

> The model attempts to make more explicit the process by which technical and institutional changes are induced through the responses of farmers, agribusiness entrepreneurs, scientists, and public administrators to resource endowments and to changes in the supply and demand of factors and products.
>
> The state of relative endowments and accumulation of the two primary resources, land and labor, is a critical element in determining a viable pattern of technical change in agriculture. Agriculture is characterized by much stronger constraints of land on production than most other sectors of the economy. Agricultural growth may be viewed as a process of easing the constraints on production imposed by inelastic supplies of land and labor. Depending on the relative scarcity of land and labor, technical change embodied in new and more productive inputs may be induced primarily either (a) to save labor or (b) to save land.
>
> The nonagricultural sector plays an important role in this process. It absorbs labor from agriculture. And it supplies to agriculture the modern technical inputs that can be substituted for land and labor in agricultural production.
>
> The critical element in this process is an effective system of market and non-market information linkages among farmers, public research institutions, private agricultural supply firms, and political and bureaucratic entrepreneurs. It is hypothesized that the proper functioning of such interactions is a key to success in the generation of the unique pattern of technical change necessary for agricultural development in any developing economy.[1]

According to the theory of induced technical innovation, progress in agricultural technology is largely an endogenous phenomenon. As formulated by Hayami and Ruttan, the theory states that the high price associated with a scarce factor of production (e.g., land) induces farmers to choose technologies that conserve the scarce factor. A rise in the price of land relative to the price of labor induces the substitution of labor for land. Or mechanization relaxes labor constraints. Or new high-yield seeds and fertilizer relax land constraints. But the advance in technology is itself a function of institutional innovation. Therefore, farmers exert political pressure to induce institutional innovations that will advance technological change (e.g., by public research institutions or institutions of land reform). Shifts in the demand for institutional change are thus induced by changes in relative factor supply and technical change.

Evidence in support of the Hayami-Ruttan theory, however, has been questioned: see Michael Lipton with Richard Longhurst, *New Seeds and Poor People* (1989). Lipton and Longhurst also place more emphasis on the need for a global research and planning apparatus that will give more attention to the effects of modern agricultural technologies on the poor. In particular, they argue that research must focus not only on increasing output, but also on generating employment, on provision of cheap calories, and on the "full social systemic influences" of any new seed or technology.

Recognizing some special characteristics of the institutional structure of an agrarian economy, Braverman and Stiglitz have presented another interpretation of technological innovation in agriculture. They investigate two common beliefs: that landlords have used their control over the means of production to direct the development and adoption of technologies that have increased their own welfare at the expense of workers; and that interlinkage between credit and tenancy markets provides an impetus to the resistance of innovations: innovations that make tenants better off reduce their demand for loans, and thereby make landlords—as creditors—worse off.

Those who apply purely competitive models dismiss these beliefs, arguing that if an economy is competitive these results would not occur.

Braverman and Stiglitz, however, point out that, contrary to the competitive model in many

LDCs, sharecropping contracts are widely employed, widespread unemployment prevails, and there is not the full set of risk and capital markets required by the competitive paradigm.

Under these different institutional conditions Braverman and Stiglitz conclude that

(i) landlords may wish to—and can—resist innovations which unambiguously increase production whenever sharecropping contracts are employed.

(ii) conversely, landlords may adopt innovations which not only lower the welfare of workers, but even lower net national product.

(iii) the presence of interlinkage may, indeed, affect the adoption of a new technology; however, the reason for this is only partly related to the effect of innovations on tenants' borrowing. Indeed, innovations may increase as well as decrease the tenants' demand for borrowing.[2]

Notes

1. Yujiro Hayami and Vernon W. Ruttan, *Agricultural Development: An International Perspective,* rev. ed. (1985), pp. 4–5; for a detailed exposition, see also Vernon W. Ruttan, "Innovation and Agricultural Development," *World Development* (September 1989).

2. Avishay Braverman and Joseph Stiglitz, "Landlords, Tenants and Technological Innovations," *Journal of Development Economics* (October 1986): 313–32; see also Selection VII.A.3.

Comment VII.A.1. The Green Revolution

Studies of the Green Revolution include T. T. Poleman and D. K. Freebairn, eds., *Food, Population, and Employment: The Impact of the Green Revolution* (1973); Clive Bell, "The Acquisition of Agricultural Technology," *Journal of Development Studies* (October 1972); Bruce F. Johnston and J. Cownie, "The Seed-Fertilizer Revolution and Labor Force Absorption," *America Economic Review* (September 1969); John W. Mellor, *The New Economics of Growth* (1976); C. Wharton, "The Green Revolution: Cornucopia or Pandora's Box?" *Foreign Affairs* (April 1969); W. Ladejinsky, *Agrarian Reform as Unfinished Business* (1978); and Walter P. Falcon, "The Green Revolution: Second-Generation Problems," *American Journal of Agricultural Economics* (December 1978).

Radical political economists have argued that the Green Revolution's technology tends to be monopolized by large commercial farmers who have better access to new information and better financial capacity. A large profit resulting from the exclusive adoption of modern varieties of technology by large farmers stimulates them to enlarge their operational holdings by consolidating the farms of small nonadopters through purchase or tenant eviction. As a result, polarization of rural communities into large commercial farmers and landless proletariat is promoted. See Harry M. Cleaver, "The Contradictions of the Green Revolution," *American Economic Review* (May 1972); Ali M. S. Fatami, "The Green Revolution: An Appraisal," *Monthly Review* (June 1972); Keith Griffin, *The Political Economy of Agrarian Change* (1974); and Richard Grabowski, "The Implications of an Induced Innovation Model," *Economic Development and Cultural Change* (July 1979), and "Reply," *Economic Development and Cultural Change* (October 1981).

The Green Revolution is also often compared with the "Japanese model" of increases in agricultural productivity associated with the use of improved seed varieties, fertilizers, implements, and other complementary inputs within the framework of Japan's small-scale farming system. For a comparative study of Japan's experience and what has been brought about by the Green Revolution, see Kazushi Ohkawa, *Differential Structure and Agriculture—Essays on Dualistic Growth* (1972).

Experience with the Green Revolution has been mixed, with differential growth rates of agriculture in different countries or in agriculture in different regions within the same country.

This has been because of differences in the availability of inputs, extent of information, and attitude toward risks.

For an appraisal of the recent history of high-yielding cereals, see Michael Lipton with Richard Longhhurst, *New Seeds and Poor People* (1989). This study examines the impact of the new varieties on the poor and claims that the increases in food supplies have had little impact on the nutrition of the poor and on their poverty.

Selection VII.A.3. Some Theoretical Aspects of Agricultural Policies*

What are the legitimate reasons for government intervention in agricultural markets? In particular, what makes the market's own allocation either inefficient or otherwise "unacceptable"? There is a standard litany of such reasons; five are relevant to agriculture.

(1) *Incomplete markets in insurance futures and credit.* Farmers cannot get complete insurance against the big (output and price) risks they face. Rural credit markets, like agricultural insurance markets, are notoriously imperfect. Farmers' access to credit is limited, if they can obtain it at all. They often have to pay usurious interest rates, though this may have something to do with the likelihood of default.[1]

(2) *Public goods and increasing returns.* These provide the justification for governments to finance water projects. In some cases, the marginal cost of using irrigated water, once the dam has been built, is relatively low, and the cost of monitoring water usage is relatively high. Water projects therefore satisfy both the criteria of pure public goods. The provision of water is almost always a natural monopoly, and a common (though not universal) response to such monopolies is production by government.

(3) *Imperfect information.* Government supply of information can be thought of as a type of public good. (Where the government ascertains what crops grow best in a particular area, the information is best described as a local public good.) However, disseminating information is costly, and the benefits accrue mainly to those who receive it. So it is probably wrong to think of agricultural extension as a pure public service. It may be justified, however, by the next category of market failure.

(4) *Externalities.* The successful adoption of a new technology by one farmer conveys valuable information to his neighbors and hence gives them a significant externality. The existence of this externality has been used to justify subsidies for farmers to adopt new technologies.

(5) *Income distribution.* Perhaps the most important reason for government intervention in agriculture is concern with the distribution of income generated by free markets. Given the initial holdings of assets, this distribution need not, and often does not, satisfy society's ethical judgments. In particular, it may result in significant numbers of people having unacceptably low incomes or supplies of food. This suggests the government should design programs that increase the incomes of small farmers—and, for urban dwellers, a program of food subsidies.

Though this list provides various rationales for government action, the link between them and actual government policies may be tenuous. Thus, measures aimed at reducing risk (like price stabilization programs) may actually increase the riskiness of farmers' income, and they often entail large subsidies. Though government policies may be defended in terms of helping the small farmer, the main beneficiaries may be large farmers. And though governments may claim that their policies redistribute income, the net impact of the programs may be regressive.

Critics of government programs thus claim that market failures are matched by a corresponding list of government failures. The fact that markets face certain problems does not in itself justify government intervention; it only identifies the potential area for it. This caveat is particularly important in any assessment of public remedies for those market failures affected by imperfect information (for instance, imperfect credit markets), since the government is likely to face similar problems if it intervenes.[2]

To understand the nature of government interventions in agricultural markets, one must approach the problem from the perspective of the

---

*From Joseph E. Stiglitz, "Some Theoretical Aspects of Agricultural Policies," *World Bank Research Observer,* Vol. 2, No. 1 (January 1987), pp. 43–47, 49, 51. Reprinted by permission.

[1] Insurance markets are notoriously bad in many contexts other than agricultural markets. Particular problems in agricultural markets are adverse selection and moral hazard: the farmer is likely to be better informed about the hazards he faces than the insurer (this is referred to as the adverse selection problem); and there are actions the farmer can take that affect output (or, more generally, the insurance companies' expected liability; this is referred to as the moral hazard problem). Thus, though the farmer cannot affect whether there is a hailstorm, he can affect the losses he incurs if one happens, by taking precautionary action. Adverse selection and moral hazard problems need to be taken into account in the design of insurance contracts.

Government policies that ignore adverse selection and moral hazard may exacerbate the problems. Thus, government stabilization programs may induce farmers to increase their production of risky crops, thus imposing a greater cost on government than it would otherwise have to face.

[2] Indeed, the problems associated with distinguishing between good and bad borrowers and of monitoring the actions of borrowers enhance the scope for political abuse within subsidized credit schemes.

second best. Whether government or market failures are of greater importance may differ from country to country, and this will crucially affect the nature of the appropriate government policy. Failure to recognize this fact has given rise to much of the controversy over state intervention. Simplistic views—such as "governments should not intervene in free markets"—or even the more sophisticated view (based on optimal tax theory for developed countries) that "government should not impose trade taxes" become inappropriate once it is recognized that the government has limited instruments for collecting revenue (thus, some distortionary taxation is necessary) and for redistributing income (so that the surest way of improving the lot of the rural poor may be through trade taxes). But the prescription that the government use trade taxes to redistribute income may be inappropriate when the redistributive impact of trade taxes is likely to be regressive.

An analysis of the appropriate policy for a particular country must therefore begin by specifying the reasons for market failure and the instruments the government can use to remedy it. The role of general theories is to identify the circumstances under which one kind of policy is more likely to be appropriate, thereby developing a taxonomy for analyzing policies in different countries. The models for specific countries help to frame the policy discussion. They enable one to establish whether the source of disagreement over policy is differences in objectives (welfare weights associated with different groups or between current generations and future generations); or differences in views about the structure of the economy; or differences in views about the values of key parameters.

The following sections organize the evaluation of alternative policies around several themes: risk, credit, dynamic effects.

Risk

Most economists acknowledge that farmers face significant risks and have only limited opportunity to avoid them through insurance and other markets. However, appropriate remedies are the subject of theoretical and practical disagreement.

What is of crucial importance to farmers is stabilizing their *income,* not stabilizing the prices of their produce. If price and quantity are negatively correlated, stabilizing prices may actually exacerbate the fluctuations in income.

Some economists favor the use of futures markets. These have the advantage of allowing a farmer to choose how much of his crop to sell for-ward, to "adapt" the extent of price stabilization to his own circumstances and preferences. But futures markets have two important drawbacks. First, they involve bigger transactions costs than those price stabilization schemes that work through the market. To the extent that such schemes serve to stabilize incomes, they do so without any farmer taking special action for himself. Second, to the extent that crop sizes are uncertain, no farmer can completely hedge his position unless he purchases crop insurance (which in general is unavailable). These disadvantages are not necessarily as bad as those produced by schemes in which the government does not stabilize the market price, but makes separate agreements with different farmers to buy given amounts of a crop at a guaranteed price.

Despite their transactions costs, futures markets dominate most types of price stabilization schemes. The intuitive reason is that futures markets allow the farmer to choose how much he wishes to divest himself of price risk. However, even in developed countries in which futures markets exist, farmers have not (at least until recently) used these markets to any significant extent. Thus, it remains an open question whether futures markets could be an effective way of sparing small farmers from risks.

If governments decide to stabilize prices, they have several ways to do so. They can, for instance, use buffer stocks, which can be operated according to various rules. Perfect price stability is, in essence, impossible. Even simple rules, such as setting a band within which prices can move, are not immune to speculative attack. The only generally feasible rules involve prices being a function of the size of the current stock; as the amount in storage decreases, the government allows the price to rise.

The limited calculations done so far suggest that the welfare gains from well-designed rules may be significantly greater than those from certain simple rules, such as keeping prices within a band (even if that were possible). Indeed, questions may be raised about the significance of the latter gains altogether (Newbery and Stiglitz, 1982). As for buffer stocks, a major criticism is that it is usually more efficient to store general purchasing power than specific commodities—that is, to use savings and reserves—except when transport and transactions costs are large.

Another way for governments to try to affect price variability is to impose trade restrictions. These may have marked transactional advantages over other forms of price stabilization, though they may be less effective in stabilizing incomes. It is now widely recognized that, in the presence of uncertainty (and with limited governmental ability to respond to changing circumstances), quotas and tariffs are not interchangeable. Tariffs do not insulate a country from foreign-induced price fluctuations, but quotas may do so. Quotas are particularly effective when the source of price fluctuations is neither domestic demand nor supply; they can then completely insulate the producers from foreign shocks (at the cost, of course, of preventing a country from taking full advantage of its current comparative advantage). Quotas are also effective in the extreme case in which the only source of variability is domestic output; they then serve to raise prices whenever farmers are suffering from lower volume. Even in these circumstances, however, it is not clear that the gains from reducing risk exceed the costs of failing to take advantage of temporary comparative advantage. The calculations depend partly on supply responses.

With any price stabilization scheme, supply responses are a major uncertainty. How do farmers react to a reduction in risk? And to what extent do a government's price stabilization programs serve simply to replace the stabilizing (arbitrage) activities of the private sector? Little empirical work has been done on either of these issues, though the effects can clearly be large: some countries have had to restrict their farmers' production so as to limit the costs of government programs.

Though there often is a role for government intervention to reduce the risks faced by farmers, many of the programs justified on these grounds serve more to redistribute income than to stabilize it. Indeed, in some instances, they may actually increase the variability of income. The appeal of these programs may lie in the way that they conceal the size and allocation of subsidies. Were the subsidies provided more openly, they might not be politically acceptable.

Credit

It is a common observation that farmers in developing countries are unable to obtain credit, or that they can do so only at usurious interest rates. This is not, in itself, evidence of a market failure. Interest rates will be high if the probability of default is high—which is indeed often the case. At the same time, the fact that there is imperfect information on the credit risks of different individuals (the adverse selection problem) and on the actions of those individuals (the moral hazard problem)

means that the market equilibrium is not, in general, (constrained) Pareto efficient.

Nonetheless, government policies to boost credit for farmers need to take account of these adverse selection and moral hazard problems. The government is usually in no better (indeed, often worse) position for gathering information on the varying probabilities of default. Furthermore, a government credit program that involves some discretion in the granting of loans also contains scope for giving subsidies to particular individuals: whenever a "high-risk" farmer is granted a loan for which the interest rate has not been increased accordingly, he is obtaining an implicit subsidy. It is naturally difficult for an outsider to judge whether a subsidy has been granted; precisely for this reason, such programs are open to abuse.

Dynamic Effects

A justification for subsidizing inputs has to do with the adoption of new technologies. If peasants were perfectly rational and risk markets were perfect, then farmers would adopt the new technology if it increased their expected utility. No government subsidy would be needed.

Reality is different: risk markets are imperfect, and peasants are risk averse. Moreover, technologies that are riskier, but offer higher returns, yield more tax revenue for the government. Thus, the government has a real interest in encouraging the adoption of such technologies. If such technologies use a lot of fertilizer, for example, then a fertilizer subsidy may be an effective way of encouraging the adoption of the riskier technologies.

There is an added (and rather distinct) justification for governments to encourage the use of new technologies: when one farmer tries a new technology, he conveys a large amount of information to his neighbors. The presence of these informational externalities implies that farmers will have insufficient incentives for trying new technologies; the solution is to levy corrective (Pigovian) taxes or to provide subsidies.

The conflict between these dynamic efficiency objectives and distributional considerations raises a familiar problem. The farmers that are least risk averse are likely to be the large ones, so they are likely to be willing to try the new technology. Thus, subsidies for those who introduce the new technology are likely to be regressive. (The effect may be exacerbated if the new technologies are also capital intensive, and the larger farmers have easier access to capital markets or can borrow at lower interest rates.)

References

Newbery, David N., and Joseph E. Stiglitz. 1981. *The Theory of Commodity Price Stabilization.* London: Oxford University Press.

Newbery, David N., and Joseph E. Stiglitz. 1982. "Optimal Stockpiling Rules." *Oxford Economic Papers* 34, no. 3 (November): 403–27.

Selection VII.A.4. Rural Infrastructure*

Irrigation Investments

The appropriate mix between public and private investments becomes a lively issue in irrigation. Although there is no intrinsic reason why large-scale dams and delivery canals cannot be a private-sector activity, it seems to be beyond the capacity of private firms in developing countries to manage the substantial problems in coordination, design, finance, and execution. Only tube-well irrigation and low-lift pumps from rivers and canals are primarily a private activity in developing countries (and the developed world, for that matter).

With large-scale irrigation schemes almost always a public-sector activity, a number of policy issues arise. At one level, concerns exist over the public health and environmental impact of many irrigation facilities.[1] Diversion of water from natural flows inevitably has some consequences for the environment, including the potential for downstream salinity problems, the creation of breeding grounds for such public-health hazards as schistosomes and malarial mosquitoes, and depletion of underground aquifers that may be important water sources some distance away. These externalities should in principle be included in the evaluation of costs and benefits to the public-sector irrigation project. Indeed, the presence of such important externalities is a major reason why large-scale irrigation projects "should" be a public-sector activity. But the actual track record of incorporating environmental and public health costs into the design and evaluation of irrigation projects is dismal indeed, whether the projects were funded by external donors such as the World Bank or came directly from the country's own budget. . . .

Several issues exist with respect to water pricing. Simple concerns for allocative efficiency suggest that farmers should pay some type of fee related to the volume of water they use and the economic cost of delivering or replacing it. Bureaucratic efficiency in operation and maintenance of irrigation facilities by public-sector employees suggests that the fees paid by farmers should also be connected to the timeliness of water deliveries and the quality of water services. And a broader concern for the integrity of public-sector budgets suggests that full cost recovery from beneficiaries of public-sector irrigation projects is needed to provide the resources for continued investments.

Virtually none of these private charges is actually paid. Most countries have provided irrigation water free (or at modest fixed charges) to farmers, with both investment costs and operations and maintenance charges paid out of the budget of the central government (or sometimes by state or regional authorities). As a consequence, actual budgets for operations and maintenance are usually seriously inadequate even for an efficient bureaucracy. More important, there are no incentives to perform the operations and maintenance activities in a timely and effective manner, and most irrigation systems need complete rehabilitation well before their economic and technical designs would indicate. Investment costs are then spread much more thinly than is necessary, thus slowing the expansion of agricultural output.

These are precisely the sorts of government failures that have led to calls to privatize a greater proportion of development-related investments, including in the irrigation sector. But it is not easy to see how the private sector can overcome the barriers to its effective involvement either. Two kinds of compromise are possible. One draws on the best features of the two sectors to produce the right volume of irrigation projects, in the right places, and with appropriate concern for externalities, while design, construction, and operation are efficiently managed by the private sector. The other compromise, of course, combines the worst of the two sectors. Then public-sector funding subsidizes private investors to ignore cost-recovery issues, to scrimp on operations and maintenance programs, and to evade any responsibilities for negative externalities. The risk of the second approach is sufficiently large in most countries that efforts to improve public-sector capacity to design, finance, and manage their irrigation programs are probably better investments than trying to find new institutional arrangements that privatize most of these decisions.

Marketing Infrastructure

. . . For a rural marketing system to work efficiently, an entire set of interlinked components must be in place and mesh relatively smoothly. These components include farm to market roads, regional highways, railways, trucks, and rolling

*From C. Peter Timmer, "Agriculture and Economic Development," in Bruce L. Gardner and Gordon C. Rausser, eds., *Handbook of Agricultural Economics,* Vol. 2A (Amsterdam: Elsevier, 2002), pp. 1520–1524. Reprinted by permission.

[1]For a useful overview of the public health dimensions of agricultural development in Africa, see Ohse (1988).

stock; communications networks involving telephones, radios, and information-gathering capacity; reliable supplies of electricity for lighting, to operate office equipment, and to power rural industries; market centers and wholesale terminals with convenient access to both transport facilities and financial intermediaries; and a set of accepted grades and standards for traded commodities that permit reliable "arms-length" contracts to be written and enforced at low cost.[2]

Each individual component of a well-functioning marketing system has a major role for private-sector involvement, perhaps even to the exclusion of any necessary public role. Certainly trucking companies, warehouse operators, and rural and regional banks can be entirely in the private sector, and, indeed, the empirical record suggests that they should be if reasonable efficiency standards are to be maintained. But a marketing system is more than the sum of these private firms, partly because the *links* that connect these firms—the roads, railways, telephone networks, and so on—have important public good dimensions or problems of coordination that markets alone have a difficult time solving. A further part of the story, however, involves substantial economies of scale and externalities in the construction and operation of the marketing system itself. No private firm can hope to capture the full economic benefits accruing to an efficient marketing system, even when the firm's own investment is a crucial component needed to make the system work at all.

The existence of these externalities and system-wide scale economies that are not appropriable by individual private firms creates an important role for the public sector in guaranteeing that the basic rural infrastructure is in place and operates efficiently. Clearly, direct public investment, ownership, and operation is neither necessary or even desirable in many contexts, and regulation, indicative plans, and appropriate investment incentives may well be sufficient. But equally clearly, a direct public role may also be needed in many circumstances, especially in the building of roads, railroads, and communications networks. It is precisely these types of capital-intensive investments, however, that came under fire in the 1970s as failing to help the poor. Expanded funding for them, especially in the context of universally tighter public budgets, requires a clear rationale.

Investment in infrastructure has two important economic payoffs. Rural infrastructure, in the form of irrigation and drainage works, roads, ports and waterways, communications, electricity, and market facilities, provides the base on which an efficient rural economy is built. Much of the investment needed to provide this base comes from the public sector, even when the private sector is playing the predominant role in agricultural production and marketing. Without this public investment, rural infrastructure is seriously deficient in stimulating greater production of crops and livestock. Investment by the private sector is also less profitable in the absence of adequate rural infrastructure, thus further reducing rural dynamism. Public-sector investment in rural areas has a "crowding in" effect rather than a "crowding out" effect on private investment, and for this reason the main role of investments in infrastructure is this longer-run stimulation of agricultural production, which has important positive effects on rural employment and income distribution.

A second role needs to be stressed as well. The investments in infrastructure themselves can generate substantial rural employment directly, and this potential has not been lost on planners seeking both long-run employment creation and short-run work programs to alleviate rural poverty or even famine conditions. "Food for Work" and "Employment Guarantee" schemes almost always are designed to build rural infrastructure using low-cost or unemployed workers. Large-scale irrigation and road construction projects offer the potential to employ vast numbers of unskilled rural laborers if project designers are sensitive to employment issues in the choice of technique and are willing to address the managerial problems that arise from labor-intensive techniques in construction.

The progressive commercialization of agriculture—as more productive inputs are purchased and a greater share of output is marketed, made possible by the development of an efficient marketing system—is a major stimulus to agricultural productivity and creates substantial employment in the agriculturally related industries. In modern economies far more workers are engaged in agribusiness than in farming itself. In the less-developed agricultural economies, such nonfarm but agriculturally linked employment is not quite so important. Even so, the single most important sector of the industrial labor force is usually in agricultural processing. Employment in rice or wheat milling, jute mills, cotton spinning and weaving, and cigarette manufacture is often the main source of organized factory jobs. When small-scale traders, food wholesalers, retail-

---

[2]Chapter 4 of Timmer, Falcon and Pearson (1983) discusses at greater length these components of an efficient marketing system and analyzes the types of government policies that stimulate its development. Abbott (1993) also provides a broad review of the topic.

ers, and peddlers are also included, the volume of indirect employment begins to rival direct employment on farms. Many of the workers are the same, or at least live in the same household. Half of the income for farm households on Java now comes from off-farm labor. Not all of the jobs are in large- or small-scale agribusiness, of course, but most are linked via well-functioning commodity and factor markets to the health of the rural economy (and the strength of the urban construction industry). Such jobs are usually a critical step on the path out of poverty for many rural inhabitants [Mellor (1976, 2000)].

References

Abbott, J.C. (ed.) (1993), Agricultural and Food Marketing in Developing Countries: Selected Readings (CAB International).

Mellor, J.W. (1976), The New Economic of Growth: A Strategy for India and the Developing World (Cornell University Press, Ithaca, NY).

Mellor, J.W. (2000), "Agricultural growth, rural employment, and poverty reduction: Non-tradables, public expenditure, and balanced growth," prepared for the World Bank Rural Week 2000, March.

Ohse, T. (1988), "Epidemiology of hunger in Africa," in: D.E. Bell and M.R. Reich, eds., Health, Nutrition, and Economic Crises (Auburn House Publishing. Dover, MA) 223–240.

Timmer, C.P., W.P. Falcon and S.R. Pearson (1983), Food Policy Analysis (Johns Hopkins University Press for the World Bank, Baltimore, MD).

Selection VII.A.5. Prospects and Strategies for Land Reform*

Writing on a topic with as much emotional resonance as land reform is difficult. It is made all the more difficult by the multiple meanings of the term, from land reclamation to reforestation to a host of policy actions that affect land. To make the task more manageable, this analysis will limit *land reform* to its narrow definition of redistributing land to the rural poor. But even in this circumscribed definition, the case for land reform is multifaceted. And how we make the case influences what we think should be appropriate policy.

The case for land reform rests on two distinct arguments: first, that a more equitable distribution of land is desirable and second, that achieving more equitable distribution is worthwhile even after a careful consideration of the costs associated with redistributing land and the alternative uses to which the resources could have been put. Each of these arguments is explored in turn.

The Case for More Equitable Land Distribution

At the heart of the argument for more equitable land distribution is the observation that small farms in developing countries tend to be more productive than larger farms. Evidence for this relationship between size and productivity dates back to the 1940s and 1950s for India (Bhagwati and Chakravarty 1969). Berry and Cline (1979) summarize more recent evidence from a range of countries in Asia and Latin America (see also the many studies cited in Binswanger, Deininger, and Feder 1995).

The magnitude of the productivity difference is substantial. In Punjab, Pakistan, productivity on the largest farms (as measured by value added per unit of land) is less than 40 percent of that on the second smallest size group, while in Muda, Malaysia, productivity on the largest farms is just two-thirds of that on the second smallest size farms (Berry and Cline 1979). In the semi-arid region of India, profit-to-wealth ratios are at least twice as high on the smallest farms as on the largest farms (Rosenzweig and Binswanger 1993).

Scale Effects in Agriculture

Scale affects agricultural productivity in several ways. Technological factors appear to cause increasing returns to scale. Incentive effects tend to cause decreasing returns to scale.

Sources of Increasing Returns. From a purely technological point of view, the bias in agriculture is, if anything, toward increasing returns. It takes a certain minimum amount of land to make full use of a tractor or a harvester combine; even a draught team can be underused if there is too little land. Increasing returns may also emerge at the processing or marketing stage. Sugarcane crushers, for example, which are large (it takes thousands of acres of sugarcane to keep a single crusher fully employed), give large plantations an obvious advantage. Tea requires special marketing skills, which small farmers might have difficulty acquiring.

Some of the disadvantages of small size can be mitigated by clever contracting arrangements or better institutional design. The rental market for farm machinery and bullock teams, for example, allows small farmers to take advantage of better technologies without having to purchase them. Cooperatives allow sugar farmers to own crushers collectively, spreading the cost among many farmers. Contract farming, in which a single marketing organization contracts to purchase and market products from a large number of farmers, has been used in the fruit industry to allow farmers to take advantage of increasing returns in marketing.

On balance, however, small size probably remains a handicap, especially because the effectiveness of these alternative arrangements tends to be limited by agency problems and other transactions costs (see Banerjee and others 1998). Compounding the technological advantages of large farms is the fact that larger farms tend to have better access to credit and other inputs, partly because of increasing returns in lending. Larger farmers are also often able to capture more than a proportionate share of inputs that are politically regulated.[1] . . .

---

[1]Few historical phenomena share the remarkable uniformity found in the history of agrarian relations. The state, it appears, has intervened always and everywhere in the markets for land, agricultural labor, and other agricultural inputs and outputs in order to make life easier for larger farmers. See the appendix to Binswanger, Deininger, and Feder (1995) for an erudite account of this history.

*From Abhijit V. Banerjee, "Prospects and Strategies for Land Reform," in Boris Pleskovic and Joseph E. Stiglitz, eds., *Annual World Bank Conference on Development Economics 1999* (Washington, D.C.: World Bank, 2000), pp. 253–257, 260–265, 267–269, 271–272. Reprinted by permission.

Sources of Decreasing Returns. Incentive problems loom large in agriculture: by its very nature, agricultural work resists supervision. People work alone and at some distance from others. The work, while usually straightforward, often demands care and attention.

A potential source of decreasing returns is the fact that larger farms hire labor whereas smaller farms tend to be farmed by family members. Hired labor will be less productive than family labor unless it is effectively supervised (which may be very costly) or given the right incentives.

Agency theory helps us identify the conditions under which hired labor will face weaker incentives than those (implicitly) faced by family labor. A simple example is a situation in which there is a limit to how little someone can be left with. This limit could be physical (one cannot take away what someone does not have), social (most societies do not allow bonded labor, for example), or imposed by what is enforceable. Forcing tenants to give up more than this limit may be counterproductive—they may rebel or run away, making it costly to collect what they owe.

Such a limit sets a lower bound on how effectively a farm laborer can be punished for failure. Of course, workers could still be provided with the right incentives by offering them rewards for success, but rewards cost money. A rational landowner may choose to offer only a small reward in order to avoid having to pay it, settling instead for lower productivity.

This argument can be rephrased as follows: Ideally, landowners would like to sell hired laborers the right to be residuals (in other words, they would prefer fixed-rent tenants). The problem is that at the beginning of the season tenants are too poor to pay the rent landowners would like to charge. The alternative for landowners is to wait until after production, when tenants will have more money (at least on average). But production is uncertain; when crops fail, landowners still face the limit on how much they can collect from their tenants. This limit will set the bound on the fixed rent they can charge. (for a fixed rent to be meaningful, tenants have to be able to pay it even when their crops fail). If this lower bound is low enough, the landowners may not want a fixed rent; they would be better off charging their tenants more when the crop does well (and tenants are able to pay more) than when it fails. What emerges is a version of sharecropping, a contract by which landowners impose what is, in effect, a tax on their tenants' output. Tenants will react by putting less effort into production, and productivity will be lower than on

smaller farms that use only family labor. (For a theory of sharecropping along these lines, see Banerjee, Gertler, and Ghatak 1998.)

Thinking about the problem of incentives in this way makes it clear that the problem is not a missing market for credit or land. The landowner in our example has the option of offering the tenant a loan that the tenant could use to pay the rent. Providing credit simply shifts the problem from one of collecting rent to one of collecting on a loan, however. Unless limits on loans differ from limits on rents, the same limit on how much can be extracted from the tenant that made the rent contract unprofitable will now make the loan unprofitable. . . .

Agency problems can also arise in the absence of constraints on how much people can be made to pay. From the point of view of incentives, the ideal situation occurs when the tenant or laborer becomes the residual claimant. Unfortunately, this also means that tenants bear all the risk. If they are risk averse, they may not want to take on all of the risk, preferring to share the risk with landowners. As a result, it will be in both tenants' and landowners' interests to move away from a fixed-rent contract toward risk-sharing and lower incentives. (For a model of share tenancy based on these ideas, see Stiglitz 1974.)

Do these theories support the case for land reform? The two views of the agency problem seem superficially similar but are in fact quite different. In the first model, the size-productivity relationship is a direct consequence of the fact that owner farmers (who are the ones who crop small farms) face very different incentives from tenant farmers or hired laborers (who crop large farms). Landowners in this model are not doing anything useful; doing away with them thus has clear benefits and no costs.

In the second, risk aversion-based, model, landowners are indeed useful—they are acting as insurers to their tenants. To generate a size-productivity relation in this model, we need to assume that the demand for insurance (generated by the extent of risk aversion) varies among farmers. Owner farmers clearly tolerate much more risk than tenant farmers; we need to explain why they are prepared to do so. One explanation is that owner farmers and tenant farmers have different characteristics. Owner farmers are those who are willing to accept more risk in return for higher returns; tenant farmers settle for the relative safety of working for somebody else. . . . A second explanation recognizes the endogeneity of risk aversion, positing that owner farmers are those who happen to own some land and are therefore less risk averse.

The two versions of the risk aversion-based model have quite different implications for the effect of land reforms on productivity. Under the first, purely selection-based, view land reform should not affect erstwhile tenants' incentives. Like the previous landowners, the new owners will simply find someone with whom to share risk and returns; productivity will be unchanged. Under the second view, the new owners will be richer after land reform and therefore willing to take on more risk. Productivity will therefore rise.

It is important to emphasize that in all of these agency models, the incentive effect of redistribution occurs because land reform increases tenants' net worth. Incentives improve because tenants are richer, and it is easier to give incentives to richer tenants. *Any other way of making tenants richer could work just as well as redistributing land.* The fact that former tenants actually own the land after land reform is, in some sense, beside the point.

Ownership Effects. In the world of complete contracts we have been describing, ownership in itself has no incentive effect; some contractual incompleteness is necessary if there is to be a pure ownership effect. To see how that might work, consider the following rather commonsense variant on the agency story. Imagine that the input the agent chooses is not immediately useful, as we have been assuming, but pays off only after some time. Tenants who expect to be on the land for only a year or two would not purchase that input unless they were paid to do so by the landowner.[2] If the investment is difficult to contract—caring for a pump set, for example, keeping a well clean, not over-watering the land—the fact that tenants lack security of tenure will clearly affect their incentive to invest. The landowner could, of course, promise the tenant long-term tenure on the land. But without a legal system effective enough to enforce long-term contracts that specify both the length of tenure and the rents to be charged in the future, such a system would be problematic. Making the tenant the owner of the land clearly circumvents many of these problems and may therefore promote investment.

It is possible that the effect of ownership goes even farther. The arguments above implicitly assume that landowners make the best possible use of the land (given the various incentive con-

straints). In fact, people often own land for reasons other than making money from it. In India, where agricultural incomes are not taxed, land is a potential tax shelter. In Brazil land is an important form of collateral. In some rural societies land is a source of political power and social prestige. In some areas of India, for example, the person who controls the agricultural work teams reportedly also controls their votes (Elkins 1975). Such landowners may not try very hard to get the most out of their land. . . .

The Case for Redistributing Land

Redistribution is a goal in itself, quite apart from any efficiency gains that might result from a more equitable land distribution. The rural poor are among the poorest segments of the population in any country. Giving them any assets must therefore promote equity. Recent work has suggested that a more equitable distribution of wealth can promote efficiency (Galor and Zeira 1993; Banerjee and Newman 1993). With more assets the poor are able to obtain more credit and better insurance coverage, which helps them invest more effectively. The children of the beneficiaries of land reform may have better health and more education, which may make them more productive. They may also be better able to start small businesses of their own by using their land as loan collateral. . . .

None of this, however, implies that we ought to redistribute land. There are substantial costs of implementing redistribution, even if landowners are not compensated. Moreover, the opportunity cost of land redistribution might be high, since the government could expropriate the land, resell it, and redistribute the proceeds. In fact, giving these funds to the poor or using them to make public investments in education and health might benefit the poor more than redistributing land.

Why Give the Poor Land?

Regrettably, the current state of empirical knowledge is too primitive to allow us to compare the social benefits of investment in health or education with the benefits of land redistribution. On the question of whether we should redistribute land rather than money, the instinctive answer among economists is that redistributing money must be better, all else being equal, since beneficiaries could always use the money to purchase land. In fact, if the only reason the rural poor do not buy land is that they are too poor to do so, all poor rural residents would use a cash distribution to buy land

---

[2] The fact that tenants' incentives are distorted will mean that landowners may not want to pay for the input, even if, in a first-best world, doing so would be worthwhile (Braverman and Stiglitz 1986).

and the productivity gains from land reforms would be realized. The case for redistributing land could thus be based on the belief that all beneficiaries want land and that redistributing land directly would eliminate some transactions costs. In all other cases, one could argue, it would be better to distribute money.

Redistributing money may not always be the best option, however, for several reasons. One is that land reform may help keep people in rural areas instead of moving to cities. Giving the poor assets that are useful only in rural areas would be one way of discouraging migration. The problem with this argument is that the debate over whether cities are too large has been inconclusive. Until this issue is settled, it is hard to base an argument on this premise.

A more compelling argument is that land can be a permanent source of income for poor families. Heads of families may not always act in the collective interest of their families. If there are conflicts of interest within the family or between current and future generations, the goal of redistribution may be better served by giving the family an asset other than money. Doing so might, for example, prevent a husband from decamping with financial assets, leaving his wife and children destitute. Moreover, land may be a particularly good asset to inherit, because fewer skills are needed to make use of that asset than other fixed assets, such as factories or shops. Whichever family member is left with the land could probably earn a living from it (Agarwal 1996).

These arguments are obviously highly speculative. In the absence of better empirical support, they make what is at best a very tentative case for land redistribution as a way of benefiting the rural poor.

Why "Tax" Landowners?

It is possible to take a very different view of land reform, as simply an effective way of taxing the rural rich. The immediate goal of land reform is not to redistribute land to the poor but simply to raise resources. These resources could be given to the rural poor in the form of land, but there need not be a connection; the resources collected could go to the urban poor (or for that matter, to the urban rich). Conversely, resources to finance land transfers to the rural poor could be financed out of other taxes. The key here is to find the best way to raise resources.

One argument for using land reform as a tax is that taking land away from the rich, (perhaps) unlike taking factories away from the rich, has no direct efficiency cost. Moreover, as a tax on sunk capital, confiscating land has no short-run incen-

tive costs. If the government can credibly commit not to redistribute land again, the long-run costs of reform may also be limited.

A second argument for taxing landowners is based on the price effects of redistributing land. Large-scale land reform may be an effective way to convince landowners that there will be no more special subsidies for large farmers in the future (because the constituency of large farmers will be much depleted) and therefore to make them more willing to sell out. The importance of land ownership as a source of status and political influence may also be greater when there are many large landowners than when there are a few.

"Taxing" landowners can also have coordination benefits. One potential benefit of land reform is that it may forestall peasant unrest. In settings in which this is important, landowners who sell their land to peasants may be doing a favor to landowners who do not. It is possible as a result that in equilibrium too little land will be sold. A coordinated program of land transfers may therefore be in everyone's interest.

Although the potential benefits of land reform are compelling, actually redistributing land is difficult. The difficulty might seem counterintuitive. Land is, after all, the ultimate fixed asset—it can neither be hidden nor taken abroad. Land ownership is often less transparent than ownership of capital or other assets, however, partly because land records are often incomplete. Moreover, the structure of social relationships in many rural communities is such that the formal ownership of land is often irrelevant: Landowners can formally give away their land to members of their extended family, or even to farm servants, and yet retain effective ownership. Corruption in the bureaucracy entrusted with carrying out land reform is yet another problem. Landowners can simply pay the bureaucrats to look the other way. For all of these reasons, as Binswanger, Deininger, and Feder (1995, p. 2683) note, "Most large-scale land reforms were associated with revolts . . . or the demise of colonial rule. . . . Attempts at land reform without massive political upheaval have rarely succeeded in transferring much of a country's land."[3] The recent

---

[3]Bell (1990) also argues for pessimism about land reform in "normal" times. Peacetime reforms tend to fail for at least two reasons. First, landlords are probably more powerful in times of peace; by definition, revolts represent the times when the masses have managed to coordinate their efforts to resist. Second, peacetime reforms tend to respect de jure ownership—a problem because landlords may own much more land than legal records indicate. In contrast, during revolutionary times redistribution may be based on de facto ownership.

thrust in a number of countries, including Brazil, Colombia, and South Africa, toward market-assisted land reforms, in which the government uses general tax money to help the poor buy land, is perhaps the clearest proof that "taxing" agriculture has not proved easy.

The Design of a Land Reform Program

How should a land reform program be designed to achieve the efficiency and equity goals that are its ultimate justification? This section examines design issues that pertain to traditional land reform.

Should Land Reform Be Permanent?

Reforms differ in the extent to which they affect the long-term distribution of land. At one extreme are rules banning all transfers of redistributed land except through inheritance. More common and less extreme are permanent land ceiling regulations, which, if properly enforced, restrict the number of acres a landowner can own. At the other extreme are one-shot efforts that redistribute land without imposing any constraints on subsequent transactions. These programs could end up with the largest farmers eventually owning all of the land.

Permanent land reform is desirable for several reasons. First, permanent reform is less likely than a one-shot reform to be undone. Second, permanent reform reduces uncertainty. Following a one-shot reform, landowners fear future changes since other reforms can always follow if the distribution of land becomes too unequal. Lack of certainty about reform holds back investment. Moreover, fear of another round of reforms with possibly different rules may discourage landowners from renting out their land, even when doing so represents the most efficient choice. Third, permanent reform encourages the rural population to remain in rural areas.

Finally, and perhaps most important, if land has a natural tendency to become concentrated (as Binswanger, Deininger, and Feder 1995 have argued), the government should recognize that unless it takes steps to make the current reform permanent, there will be pressure for more redistribution in the future, when the current generation of beneficiaries are dead. Demands for such reform may be difficult to resist, since there is no obvious ethical reason why the next generation should suffer because their parents' generation managed to lose their land. Taking the cost of such future redistribution into account clearly strengthens the case for per-

manent reform. It is worth noting, however, that the government can limit the tendency toward land concentration in other ways. If, as Binswanger, Deininger, and Feder (1995) claim, distress sales are the main reason for increasing land concentration, preventing such sales by offering emergency income support programs (such as food-for-work programs) could help. Removing the distortions in the current system of taxes and transfers, which encourages the formation of large estates, would also counteract a tendency toward land concentration.

The most obvious objection to permanent reform is that it limits the extent of redistribution. The family that gets the land may be better off selling it or at least selling a part of it. But if, as argued above, long-term equity is better served by not allowing the sale of redistributed land, this tradeoff could be made more palatable by combining land reform with emergency income assistance, such as a food-for-work program. Such a policy, effectively implemented, would make it less likely that the peasant would need to sell land in an emergency.

Another potential disadvantage of a permanent reform is that it can stand in the way of efficient reallocation of land. In this respect, a land ceiling is less obtrusive than a ban on all sales, because it allows reallocation among landowners who own less than the maximum allowable acreage. . . .

A land ceiling could also prevent farmers from taking advantage of any increasing returns to scale. Increasing returns do not appear to be common in agriculture in developing countries, however. Moreover, banning land sales to large farmers does not imply that the use of the land cannot be transferred. Reverse tenancy—renting or leasing land to a large farmer on a yearly or even half-yearly basis—is still permissible and is widely practiced in many areas with enforced land ceilings. Given that large farmers who want extra land tend to have good access to credit and insurance, the efficiency loss from reverse tenancy should be relatively small in most settings (and indeed most of the reverse tenancy contracts tend to be fixed-rent contracts).[4]

It is possible, however, that increasing returns could become more important in agriculture in developing countries. If they do, the fact that a dynamic farmer could not come in, buy the needed land, and make the necessary investments could

[4]The efficiency loss could be exacerbated by banning the renting out of redistributed land, as the land ceiling act in Maharastra, India, does (Behuria 1997). The best argument for restricting rentals may be that rentals can be a way of making secret land sales.

hold back productivity growth. It should be possible, however, to limit the loss from this source by making it easier for current owners to make necessary investments. Publicly funded research on agricultural technology and agrobusiness, better extension services, public investments in infrastructure and marketing, and improvements in credit access should all be a part of a broader program that includes land reform. These investments would also make the redistributed land more valuable, thereby enhancing the extent of redistribution. . . .

Yet another problem with a permanent restriction on land transfers is that it makes it difficult or impossible to use land as collateral. Since land is typically the only asset the rural poor possess, banning the sale of land restricts their ability to obtain credit to finance consumption smoothing or investment. It is possible to limit the cost of such a restriction by providing alternative ways of smoothing consumption, such as food-for-work programs. Moreover, imposing a land ceiling rather than a ban on land sales would make it easier to use land as collateral, especially if lenders are permitted to hold on to the collateralized land for some period following a default, after which they must sell the land to someone who has not reached the land ceiling. (Selling the land immediately after default may be difficult, however, because defaults often occur as a result of shocks that are correlated across the area.) The government could agree to buy all land acquired in this way at a fixed price, thereby guaranteeing lenders a reasonable return. The government could then redistribute the land.

Finally, perhaps the most important problem with permanent reform is the need for a permanent bureaucracy. Land ceilings must be enforced and land sales monitored by bureaucrats, who would constantly be exposed to bribes. Any bureaucracy would find the task difficult. The limited bureaucratic resources available in developing countries make the task particularly difficult.

If, however, the alternative to permanent reform is implementing new land reforms every few years, permanent reform may nevertheless be desirable. While getting bureaucrats to monitor land transfers on an ongoing basis is difficult, it may be even harder to get them to carry out large-scale land transfers with the knowledge that their efforts will soon be undone. It may be possible to limit the bureaucratic demands of permanent reform by changing the style of enforcement. One possibility is to make greater use of the court system. Instead of monitoring all land transfers, the government could require that courts not enforce transfers that violate the land ceiling. Landowners who sell land

to buyers who already own the maximum holding would be given the right to reclaim the land without refunding the purchase price. Implementing such a policy would discourage potential buyers from exceeding the land ceiling.

Another option is to have the government stand willing to buy back any redistributed land at an attractive price, to be paid in the form of a guaranteed income. The government could then resell the land. If the price paid were high enough, it would attract a large fraction of true distress sales, thereby limiting the number of transactions the bureaucracy has to monitor. . . .

Should Landowners Be Compensated?

A key dimension of any land reform is compensation of landowners. At one extreme are programs of pure expropriation, as implemented in the postrevolutionary period in the Soviet Union and China. At the other extreme are programs in which landowners are generously (sometimes even excessively) compensated, as in Tsarist Russia or in the Philippines under Aquino, where landowners received 133 percent of the market value of their land (Riedinger 1995).

The tradeoff here is clear: landowners will resist reform less if they are generously compensated, but redistribution will be more limited if compensation must be paid. Reducing resistance to reform is beneficial; the landowner class tends to be well represented in the ruling elites of most countries, giving them enormous political power that they can use to block, stall, or undermine efforts to carry out land reforms. Generously compensating landowners clearly limits the benefits from the program, however. If the beneficiaries of reform pay the bulk of the compensation, the extent of effective redistribution—and therefore the equity gains from the reform—will be limited. Efficiency gains may also be limited, because from the point of view of the basic (complete contracting) agency model, what counts is not land ownership but the net asset position of the tenant. If tenants' net position changes only slightly because compensation payment liabilities have to be deducted from the value of the extra land they have acquired, their incentives and hence their productivity will also change little. Essentially, tenants will want to trade away a part of their share of the profits in order to reduce their borrowing costs or risk exposure. The fact that tenants' net asset position has not changed much also implies that their ability to borrow (and to take risks more generally) will not change much. We should not therefore expect to see large changes in other indicators, such as the health or education of tenants' children.

This is not to say that land reform cannot have a beneficial effect if the compensation payments that beneficiaries have to make are relatively generous. We have already argued that transfer of ownership can, by itself, have positive effects on productivity. Moreover, as already suggested, carrying out land transfers on a large enough scale could lower the price of the land and, more generally, make landlords more willing to reduce their landholdings.

The discussion so far assumes that beneficiaries pay most of the compensation, as the emancipated serfs did in Russia. But many modern reforms have included significant state subsidies. Often the state pays the compensation up front, with beneficiaries paying off the compensation over time, usually at a subsidized rate of interest. Since peasants often default on their amortization payments, which are then written off, the effective subsidy tends to be even larger than the nominal subsidy. Riedinger (1995), for example, reports that no more than 10 percent of the beneficiaries of the Marcos reforms were current on their amortization payments in the mid-1980s.

Subsidies, while they can enhance efficiency and equity benefits, are very costly. The extent of reform will be limited by the government's ability to mobilize additional resources from the rest of the economy.[5] In a country in which agriculture contributes 25 percent to GDP, the value of the nation's land may represent close to 25 percent of the national wealth. Redistributing land on any substantial scale and paying for it out of public resources will therefore require a very large transfer from the rest of the economy to the agricultural sector. (The problem here is not one of financing the transfer—which, in any case, can be facilitated by a loan from abroad—but of imposing a substantial and ongoing cut in the consumption stream of the nonagricultural sector.) A priori it is not clear that the political and economic costs of making such transfers are lower than those associated with

simply expropriating the land. Indeed, even if it were politically feasible, it is not obvious that the rural poor would be better off if the government paid for land reform by imposing an extremely heavy tax burden on the rest of the economy or by cutting back government spending. Moreover, once the government agrees to pay part of the compensation, the reform can turn into a bonanza for the landowner class if the government sets compensation too high.

The tradeoffs here are all unpleasant. Compensated reforms will tend to be politically easier but potentially less effective (and, if the government has to pay for them, less extensive) than uncompensated reforms. Some element of prior coalition building, which would make it easier to implement a less generously compensated reform, may have to be an integral part of a truly effective land reform.

Alternatives to Land Redistribution by the State

Redistributing land from those who own it to those who do not is not the only way of achieving land reform. Alternatives to traditional land reform can achieve the same goals without involving the state in physically redistributing land.

Market-Assisted Land Reform

Market-assisted land reform has emerged in recent years as a noncoercive alternative to traditional land reform in a number of countries, including Brazil, Colombia, and South Africa.

The basic idea is simple: the state gives qualified landless people a grant or a subsidized loan with which to buy land. Superficially, market-assisted land reform is therefore similar to a fully compensated land reform, with the government paying for a substantial part of the compensation. There are, however, key differences. First, market-assisted reform includes neither a fixed time-scale nor explicit targets for the kind of land distribution that will eventually be achieved. This probably means that the change in the land distribution will be less coordinated—both in time and in space—than in the case of a (successful) conventional land reform. For this reason, the coordination benefits of a market-assisted reform are likely to be smaller than those of a large-scale traditional land reform.

A second disadvantage of market-assisted reform is the uncertainty about how many landowners will sell. As a result, no landowner may want to be the first to sell out. Indeed, it is plausible that the

---

[5]In the short run, governments often finance these programs by issuing special bonds. This is a natural strategy if the reform is expected to generate productivity gains—the reform can, in effect, pay (at least in part) for itself. Some governments have also adopted the strategy of paying landlords, at least in part, with bonds. This approach gives landlords a stake in the success of the reform, since a failed reform and associated peasant unrest may cause the bonds to be devalued. Landlords are often reluctant to accept bonds from a government they do not trust, however. For this reason, at least in some situations, it may be better to pay cash to landlords by selling the bonds or obtaining an external loan.

price of land will go up when such a reform is introduced.

Supporters of market-assisted reform stress that it is demand driven. Instead of the government deciding who will benefit, potential beneficiaries decide whether they want to go through the various bureaucratic processes necessary to purchase land. This, presumably, generates better targeting, at least along some dimensions. People who want the land most and who know where to find the kind of land they are looking for should come forward first (although the fact that most of these programs do not forbid immediate resale may also attract buyers who have no interest in farming). Market-assisted reform may also raise productivity and placate the politically most volatile sections of the rural population, at least if there is some restriction on immediate resale. (It is less clear that this kind of procedure is the best way to promote equity; there is some reason to suspect that the nature of the bureaucratic process tends to discourage the weakest sections of the population. Encouraging and subsidizing NGOs to help those who would not otherwise be able to apply, as the South African program does, may resolve this problem.)

Another advantage of market-assisted reform is that beneficiaries pay a part of the price for the land, thereby presumably having stronger incentives for negotiating a low price than a bureaucrat entrusted to negotiate a compensation acceptable to the landowner. In this sense market-assisted land reform should be substantially less costly than a fully compensated traditional land reform. The market-assisted approach also avoids the substantial political costs of traditional reform.

The most important drawback of the market-assisted approach is one that it shares with traditional land reform programs that pay generous compensation—it is expensive (albeit not necessarily as costly as a fully compensated traditional program). The high cost of market-assisted reform means that it cannot be expected to achieve very substantial redistribution in the near future. (In the longer run, as the rest of the economy grows and agriculture becomes a less important part of the national product, making such transfers will be easier, albeit possibly less valuable.) Market-assisted reform may nevertheless be a useful policy tool, especially where the bureaucratic and political constraints are such that a traditional approach to land reform is doomed to failure. In particular, market-assisted reforms can be a way of giving some extra land to the most dynamic or volatile elements in the agricultural sector, thereby bringing about some measure of political peace in rural areas. Unlike ambitious traditional reform programs, however, market-assisted reform can only be a part of a much larger program for alleviation of rural poverty. . . .

Conclusion

After all these arguments and counterarguments, what are we left with? Although the evidence is hardly definitive, redistributive land reforms appear to promote equity and efficiency. Were implementation not a constraint, traditional (coercive) land reform would have a number of clear advantages over alternative types of land reform. Such reform will almost certainly be more extensive than noncoercive (market-assisted) reform. It also probably costs less and has a stronger effect on productivity. Implementation is a constraint, however, and may indeed be the binding constraint in many cases. In such cases, market-assisted reforms or tenancy reforms may provide better outcomes.

Where policymakers want to implement traditional reform, they should apply certain principles. Land reform programs should be accompanied by effective agricultural extension programs and by emergency support programs and other empowerment strategies. Such programs limit the need for emergency land sales, increase peasants' willingness to take risks, and improve the bargaining power of peasants who remain tenants. The government also needs to create an appropriate institutional environment for farmers cooperatives and contract farming. Reform beneficiaries should be permitted to rent out redistributed land. Land ceilings and any other laws applicable to tenancy should not discriminate on the basis of choices landowners can make (such as whether they return to cultivation, what crops they grow, and so on). Discrimination on the basis of past choices may be a good idea if the reform is implemented effectively and quickly. Tax distortions and distortions in the market for inputs that discriminate in favor of large farmers should be removed as a prelude to land reforms. Quick and coordinated implementation of the land transfer process may make it easier to commit to not reinstituting these or other distortions.

References

Banerjee, A., and A. Newman. 1993. "Occupational Choice and the Process of Development." *Journal of Political Economy* 101: 274–98.

Banerjee, A., P. Gertler, and M. Ghatak. 1998. "Empowerment and Efficiency: The Economics of Agrarian

Reform." Department of Economics, Massachusetts Institute of Technology, Cambridge, Mass.

Banerjee, A., D. Mookherjee, K. Munshi, and D. Ray. 1998. "Inequality, Control Rights, and Rent Seeking: Sugar Cooperatives in Maharashtra." Department of Economics, Massachusetts Institute of Technology, Cambridge, Mass.

Behuria, N. C. 1997. *Land Reforms Legislation in India: A Comparative Study.* New Delhi: Vikas Publishing.

Bell, C. 1990. "Reforming Property Rights in Land and Tenancy." *World Bank Research Observer* 5 (2): 143–66.

Berry, R. A., and W. R. Cline. 1979. *Agrarian Structure and Productivity in Developing Countries.* Baltimore, Md.: Johns Hopkins University Press.

Bhagwati, J., and S. Chakravarty. 1969. "Contributions to Indian Economic Analysis: A Survey." *American Economic Review* Supplement (September).

Binswanger, H., K. Deininger, and G. Feder. 1995. "Power, Distortions, Revolt, and Reform in Agricultural Land Relations." In J. Behrman and T. Srini-

vasan, eds., *Handbook of Development Economics.* Vol. III. New York: Elsevier.

Braverman, A., and J. Stiglitz. 1986. "Landowners, Tenants and Technological Innovations." *Journal of Development Economics* 23: 313–32.

Elkins, D. 1975. *Electoral Participation in a South Indian Context.* Durham, N.C.: Carolina Academic Press.

Galor, O., and J. Zeira. 1993. "Income Distribution and Macroeconomics." *Review of Economic Studies* 60: 35–52.

Riedinger, J. M. 1995. *Agrarian Reform in the Philippines: Democratic Transitions and Redistributive Reform.* Stanford, Calif.: Stanford University Press.

Rosenzweig, M. R., and H. P. Binswanger. 1993. "Wealth, Weather Risk and the Composition and Profitability of Agricultural Investments." *Economic Journal* 103: 56–78.

Stiglitz, J. E. 1974. "Incentives and Risk Sharing in Sharecropping." *Review of Economic Studies* 41: 219–55.

VII.B. MICROECONOMICS OF THE RURAL SECTOR

Selection VII.B.1. The New Development Economics*

There are a wide variety of institutional arrangements observed in different LDCs. One set that has been of long-standing interest to economists is sharecropping. Earlier views of sharecropping held that it was an inefficient form of economic organization: the worker received less than the value of his marginal product, and thus he had insufficient incentives to exert effort. The question was, how could such a seemingly inefficient form of economic organization have survived for so long (and why should it be such a prevalent form of economic organization at so many different places at different times?). For those who believe in even a modicum of economic rationality, some explanation had to be found.

One explanation that comes to mind is that peasants are more risk averse than landlords; if workers rented the land from the landlords, they would have to bear all of the risk. Though workers' risk aversion is undoubtedly of importance, it cannot be the entire explanation: there are alternative (and perhaps more effective) risk-sharing arrangements. In particular, in the wage system, the landlord bears all of the risk, the worker none. Any degree of risk sharing between the landlord and the worker can be attained by the worker dividing his time between working as a wage-laborer and working on his own or rented land.

The other central part of the explanation of sharecropping is that it provides an effective incentive system in the presence of costly supervision. Since in a wage system, the worker's compensation is not directly related to his output, the landlord must spend resources to ensure that the worker actual works. In a sharecropping system, since the worker's pay depends directly on his output, he has some incentives to work. The incentives may not be as strong as they would if he owned the land (since he receives, say, only half the product); but that is not the relevant alternative. Sharecropping thus represents a compromise between the rental system, in which incentives are "correct" but all the risk is borne by the worker, and the wage system, in which the landlord who is in a better position to bear risk, bears all the risk but in which effort can only be sustained through expenditures on supervision. This new view (Stiglitz, 1974) turns the traditional criticism of sharecropping on its head: it is precisely because of its incentive properties, relative to the relevant alternative, the wage system, that the sharecropping system is employed.

The contention that the rental system provides correct incentives is, however, not quite correct. The rental system provides correct incentives for effort decisions. But tenants make many decisions other than those involving effort; they make decisions concerning the choice of technique, the use of fertilizer, the timing of harvest, etc. These decisions affect the riskiness of the outcomes. For instance, many of the high-yielding seed varieties have a higher mean output, but a greater sensitivity to rainfall. Whenever there is a finite probability of default (that is, the tenant not paying the promised rent), then tenants may not have, with the rental system, the correct incentives with respect to these decisions. Of course, with unlimited liability, the worker could be made to bear all of the costs. But since the tenant might be unable to pay his rent even if he had undertaken all of the "right" decisions, and since it is often difficult to ascertain whether the individual took "unnecessary" risks, most societies are reluctant to grant unlimited liability, or to use extreme measures like debtor prisons, to ensure that individuals do not take unnecessary risks. Hence, in effect, part of the costs of risk taking by the tenant is borne by the landlord. With sharecropping, both the landlord and the tenant face the same risks.

Thus, sharecropping can be viewed as an institution which has developed in response to (a) risk aversion on the part of workers; (b) the limited ability (or desire) to force the tenant to pay back rents when he is clearly unable to do so; and (c) the limited ability to monitor the actions of the tenant (or the high costs of doing so).

The general theory has been extended in a number of directions, only three of which I can discuss here: cost sharing, interlinkage, and technical change.

In many situations, there are other important inputs besides labor and land, such as bullocks or fertilizer. How should these inputs be paid for? Clearly, if the worker pays all of the costs, but receives only a fraction of the benefits, he will have an insufficient incentive to supply these other inputs. Cost sharing is a proposed remedy. If the worker receives 50 percent of the output, and pays 50 percent of the cost, it would appear that he has

*From Joseph E. Stiglitz, "The New Development Economics," *World Development* 14, no. 2 (1986): 258–61. Reprinted by permission.

the correct incentives: both benefits and costs have been cut in half.

But in fact, though cost shares equal to output shares are common, they are far from universal. How do we explain these deviations from what seems both a simple, reasonable rule, and a rule which ensures economic efficiency? To find the answer, we again return to our general theoretical framework, which focuses on the role of imperfect information. First, it is clear that the landlord may want the tenant to supply more fertilizer than he would with a 50-50 rule, if increasing the fertilizer increases the marginal product of labor, and thus induces the worker to work harder. Remember, the central problem of the landlord is that he cannot directly control the actions of his worker; he must induce them to work hard. The reason that sharecropping was employed was to provide these additional incentives.

But if a cost-sharing arrangement can be implemented, it means that the expenditures can be monitored; and if the expenditures can be monitored, there is no necessity for engaging in cost sharing; rather the terms of the contract could simply specify the levels of various inputs. But workers typically have more information about current circumstances than the landlord (in the fashionable technical jargon, we say there is an asymmetry of information). A contract which specifies the level of inputs cannot adapt to the changing circumstances. Cost-sharing contracts provide the ability and incentives for these adaptations, and thus are more efficient contracts than contracts which simply specified the level of inputs.

Another aspect of economic organization in many LDCs is the interlinkage of markets: the landlord may also supply credit (and he may also supply food and inputs as well). How can we explain this interlinkage? Some have claimed that it is simply another way that landlords exploit their workers. We shall comment later on these alternative explanations. For now, we simply note that our general theory can explain the prevalence of interlinkage (both under competitive and noncompetitive circumstances). We have repeatedly noted the problem of the landlord in inducing the worker both to work hard and to make the "correct" decisions from his point of view (with respect to choice of technique, etc.). Exactly analogous problems arise with respect to lenders. Their concern is that the borrower will default on the loan. The probability of a default depends in part on the actions taken by the borrower. The actions of the tenant-borrower thus affect both the lender and the landlord. Note too that the terms of the contract with the landlord will affect the lender, and vice versa: if the landlord can, for instance, reduce the probability of default by supplying more fertilizer, the lender is better off. The actions of the borrower (both with respect to the effort and the choice of technique) may be affected by the individual's indebtedness, so that the landlord's (expected) income may be affected by the amount (and terms) of indebtedness. There appear to be clear and possibly significant externalities between the actions of the landlord and the actions of the lender. Whenever there are such externalities, a natural market solution is to internalize the externality, and that is precisely what the interlinkage of markets does.

Thus, interlinkage is motivated by the desire for economic efficiency, not necessarily by the desire for further exploitation of the worker.

Interlinkage has, in turn, been linked to the incentives landlords have for resisting profitable innovations. Bhaduri (1973) has argued, for instance, that landlords-cum-creditors may resist innovations, because innovations reduce the demand for credit, and thus the income which they receive in their capacity as creditors. Braverman and Stiglitz (1982) have shown that there is no presumption that innovations result in a reduction in the demand for credit. Credit is used to smooth income across periods, and under quite plausible conditions, innovations may either increase or decrease the aggregate demand for credit. But they argue further that what happens to the demand for credit is beside the point.

The central question is simply whether the innovation moves the economically relevant utilities possibilities schedule outward or inward. The utilities possibilities schedule gives the maximum level of (expected) utility to one group (the landlord) given the level of (expected) utility of the other (the workers). The economically relevant utilities possibilities curve takes into account the information problems which have been the center of our discussion thus far, for instance, the fact that with sharecropping, individuals' incentives are different from what they would be with costless monitoring. The utilities possibilities schedule with costless monitoring might move one way, the economically relevant utilities possibilities schedule the other. Thus, for instance, there are innovations which, at each level of input, increase the output, but which, at the same time, exacerbate the incentives-monitoring problem. Such innovations would not be socially desirable. Landlords would resist such innovations, as well they should, though from an "engineering" point of view, such innovations might look desirable.

The consequences of interlinkage for the adoption of innovations, within this perspective, are ambiguous. There are innovations which would be adopted with interlinkage, but would not without it, and conversely; but the effect of the innovation on the demand for credit does not seem to play a central role.

Though the landlord correctly worries about the incentive–monitoring consequences of an innovation, one should not jump to the conclusions either that the landlords collectively make decisions which maximize their own welfare, or that the landlord always makes the socially efficient decision. The landlord, within a competitive environment, will adopt an innovation if at current prices (terms of contracts, etc.) it is profitable for him to do so. Of course, when all the landlords adopt the innovation, prices (terms of contracts) will change, and they may change in such a way that landlords are adversely affected. In a competitive environment landlords cannot resist innovations simply because it is disadvantageous to them to do so. (By contrast, if they are in a "monopoly" position, they will not wish to resist such innovations, since presumably they will be able to capture all the surplus associated with the innovation.)

But just as the market allocation is not constrained Pareto efficient (even assuming a perfectly competitive economy) whenever there are problems of moral hazard, so too the market decisions concerning innovation are not constrained Pareto efficient. (We use the term *constrained Pareto efficient* to remind us that we are accounting for the limitations on information; we have not assumed the government has any information other than that possessed by private individuals.) Though in principle there exist government interventions which (accounting for the costs of information) could make everyone better off, whether such Pareto-improving interventions are likely to emerge from the political process remains a moot question.

Alternative Theories

In this section, I wish to present in summary form what I view to be the major competing approaches to understanding the organization of economic activity in the rural sector.

In many respects, I see my view as lying between other more extreme views. In one, the peasant is viewed as rational, working in an environment with reasonably complete information and complete and competitive markets. In this view, then, the differences between LDCs and more developed countries lies not so much in the differ-

ence between sophisticated, maximizing farmers and uneducated rule-bound peasants, as it does in differences in the economic environments, the goods produced by these economies, their endowments, and how their endowments are used to produce goods. In this view, sharecropping is a rational response to the problems of risk sharing; but there is less concern about the incentive problems than I have expressed; with perfect information and perfect enforceability of contracts, the sharecropping contract can enforce the desired level of labor supply and the choice of technique which is efficient. These theories have had little to say about some of the other phenomena which I have discussed: interlinkage, technical change, cost sharing. Interlinkage might be explained in terms of the advantages in transactions costs, but if transactions costs were central, one should only have observed simple cost-sharing rules (with cost share equalling output share).

By contrast, there are those who view the peasant as irrational, with his behavior dictated by customs and institutions which may have served a useful function at some previous time but no longer do so. This approach (which I shall refer to, somewhat loosely, as the institutional–historical approach) may attempt to describe the kinds of LDCs in which there is sharecropping, interlinkage, or cost sharing. It may attempt to relate current practices to earlier practices. In particular, the institutional–historical approach may identify particular historical events which lead to the establishment of the sharecropping system, or to the development of the credit system. But this leaves largely unanswered the question of why so many LDCs developed similar institutional structures, or why in some countries cost shares equal output shares, while in others the two differ. More fundamentally, a theory must explain how earlier practices developed; and to provide an explanation of these, one has to have recourse to one of the other theories. Thus, by itself, the institutional–historical approach is incomplete.

Still a third view emphasizes the departures from competitiveness in the rural sector, and the consequent ability of the landlords to exploit the workers. In some cases, workers are tied to their land; legal constraints may put the landlord in a position to exploit the worker. But in the absence of these legal constraints, one has to explain how the landlords exercise their allegedly coercive powers. In many LDCs there is a well-developed labor market. Many landlords need laborers at harvest time and at planting time. The worker chooses for whom he will work. It is important to recognize that the exploitation hypothesis fails to explain the mechanisms by which, in situations where there are many landlords, they exercise their exploitative power. More generally, it fails to explain variations in the degree of exploitation over time and across countries. The fact that wages are low is not necessarily evidence of exploitation: the competitive market will yield low wages when the value of the marginal product of labor is low.

The exploitation hypothesis also fails to explain the detailed structure of rural organization: why cost shares are the way they are, or why (or how) landlords who can exploit their workers use the credit market to gain further exploitative capacity.

There may be some grain of truth in all these approaches. Important instances of currently dysfunctional institutions and customs can clearly be identified. Institutional structures clearly to not adapt instantaneously to changed circumstances. Yet, as social scientists, our objective is to identify the systematical components, the regularities of social behavior, to look for general principles underlying a variety of phenomena. It is useful to describe the institutions found in the rural sector of LDCs, but description is not enough.

Therefore, I view the rationality hypothesis as a convenient starting point, a simple and general principle with which to understand economic behavior. Important instances of departures from rationality may well be observed. As social scientists, our objective is to look for *systematic* departures. Some systematic departures have been noted, for instance in the work of Tversky, in individuals' judgments of probabilities, particularly of small probability events; but as Binswanger's 1978 study has noted, departures from the theory appear less important in "important" decisions than in less important decisions. Many of the seeming departures from "rationality" that have been noted can be interpreted as "rational" decision-making in the presence of imperfect information.

I also view the competitiveness hypothesis as a convenient starting point. Many of the central phenomena of interest can be explained without recourse to the exploitation hypothesis. Some degree of imperfect competition is not inconsistent with the imperfect information paradigm: the imperfect information paradigm provides part of the explanation for the absence of perfect competition; it can help identify situations where the landlords may be in a better position to exploit the workers. Moreover, to the extent that imperfect information limits the extent to which even a monopoly landlord can extract surplus from his workers, the imperfect information paradigm can provide insights

into how he can increase his monopoly profits. The theory of interlinkage we have developed can thus be applied to the behavior of a monopolist landlord.

There is one other approach that has received some attention that is, in fact, closely related to the one I have advocated: the transactions cost approach, which attempts to explicate economic relations by focusing on transactions costs. Information costs are an important part of transactions costs (though information problems arise in other contexts as well). My reservations concerning the transactions cost approach lie in its lack of specificity: while the information paradigm provides a well-defined structure which allows one to derive clear propositions concerning, for instance, the design of contracts, the transactions cost paradigm does not. Thus, the transactions cost approach might provide some insight into why cost sharing is employed, but not into the terms of the cost-sharing agreement. The transactions cost paradigm might say that economies of scope provide an explanation for why the landlord also supplies credit, but it does not provide insights into when the landlord-cum-creditor would subsidize credit, or when he would "tax" it. Moreover, while the information paradigm identifies parameters which affect the magnitude of the externalities between landlords and creditors, and thus enables, in principle, the identification of circumstances under which interlinkage is more likely to be observed, the transactions cost paradigm can do little more than to say that there are circumstances in which the diseconomies of scope exceed the economies, and in these circumstances there will not be interlinkage.

References

Bhadari, A. (1973). "Agricultural Backwardness Under Semi-Feudalism." *Economic Journal* (March): 120–37.

Binswanger, H. P. (1978). "Attitudes Towards Risk: Implications and Psychological Theories of an Experiment in Rural India." Yale University Economic Growth Center DP 286.

Braverman, A., and J. E. Stiglitz (1982). "Sharecropping and the Interlinking of Agrarian Markets." *American Economic Review* (September): 695–715.

Stiglitz, J. E. (1974). "Alternative Theories of Wage Determination and Unemployment in LDCs: The Labor Turnover Model. *Quarterly Journal of Economics* 87 (May): 194–227.

Tversky, A. (1969). "Intransitivity of Preferences." *Psychological Review* 76: 31–48.

Selection VII.B.2. Contractual Arrangements, Employment, and Wages in Rural Labor Markets: A Critical Review*

In a world of perfect markets for all factors of production (including credit and insurance), a person's annual income would simply represent the employment of his or her factor endowments valued at the market rate per unit. In such a world, the initial distribution of endowments among people—for given tastes and aggregate quantities of each factor—would uniquely determine the distribution of income among people. Moreover, production—total output—would be not only maximal but unrelated to the distribution of factor ownership. Production techniques would be identical on all farms facing the same market environment and operating the same quality of land; for example, because output and employment per acre would be unrelated to farm size, barring scale economies, productive efficiency could not be improved by a rearrangement of factor uses or distributions. To explain labor earnings in a world of perfect markets with a given distribution of endowments requires that one explain the returns to each factor (wage rates, rent), a task for which the competitive supply-demand model has proved a powerful tool. The failure of one or more markets, however, would have important implications for the distribution of earnings and productive efficiency and would probably mean that more complex models would be required to understand earnings determination. An important, unresolved question is whether such models can outpredict the simpler, competitive models when only some markets are imperfect or absent.

Attention to market failure, however, is important not only for understanding the determination of earnings and the achievement of productive efficiency. It may also help us to understand the existence of and changes in the labor market's many and diverse institutional arrangements—different types of contracts and labor recruitment strategies and the interlinking of labor and one or more factors of production within one transaction. Indeed, because of the general nonindependence, or interrelatedness, of all factor markets, market failures anywhere in the rural sector may have a significant effect on labor market earnings or arrangements even if the market for labor operates perfectly. In these circumstances, explaining earnings requires

information beyond the determination of wages and labor supply.

In the rural economy, it is a fact that some labor is combined with land, not by the temporary sale of labor services but by the temporary acquisition of land. It is clear that the terms and arrangements associated with the market for land have a significant effect on the earnings of rural households and the production of aggregate output. . . . [This raises] two primary issues: First, what are the efficiency characteristics of a contract that provides laborers with a share of total agricultural output, an important contractual arrangement in the rural economy? Second, how do the welfare levels or earnings of such sharecroppers compare with those of laborers who work only for wages—that is, what determines the contractual terms?

Recent Tenancy Models

If the sales market for land is absent or involves very high transaction costs, landowners can hire all cooperating factors of production, including bullocks and management, in quantities that are optimal for their own land. Landowners can then rent out any nonland factors owned that are in excess of these optimal quantities. Productive efficiency—that is, equal factor ratios on all farms with land of equal quality—can still be achieved. Thus the absence of a sales market for land is not sufficient to force the use of tenancy. However, the institution of tenancy and the market for tenancies do substitute for the sales market. When there are no scale economies, at least one other factor market must be absent before the temporary rental of land becomes a necessary tool to achieve the most efficient factor ratios for all factors of production and all agents. The absent or incomplete markets (which involve high risks or high transaction costs) may be those for insurance, family labor, bullocks, or managerial skills. . . .

Cheung's (1968, 1969) work set the stage for the recent sharecropping literature in terms of the major reasons for share tenancy and the major issues to be addressed. His work both attacked the negative efficiency (incentive) implication of sharecropping and broadened the scope of inquiry of the sharecropping literature to include discussion of the manner in which size of tenancy and share of crop are determined. All writers from Cheung onward have regarded both tenancy size and share

*From Hans P. Binswanger and Mark R. Rosenzweig, *Contractual Arrangements, Employment and Wages in Rural Labor Markets: A Critical Review,* Agricultural Development Council, 1981, pp. 3–4, 21–27. Reprinted by permission.

level as endogenous to a particular model, while they have taken the wage rate as exogenously given. Contractual terms, but not the wage rate, are thus determined by economic forces, and the equilibrium solution to the contract choice problem involves maximization by both landlord and worker. The worker's equilibrium requires that "of the set of contracts available in the economy, there [exist] none which the individual worker prefers to the one which he has" (Stiglitz, 1974, p. 222). And landlord equilibrium implies that "there exists no subset [of the available contracts] which the landlord prefers to the subset which he employs" (ibid.).

Cheung also assigned *risk* and *risk aversion* a much larger role in determining share tenancy than others have accorded them. He did not include them, however, in his formal model. Clearly, under a wage labor system all the risks of cultivation are borne by the owner-cultivator; owner-cultivator income is the residual after payment of production costs at fixed wages. Under a fixed-rate tenancy, tenants bear all the risk since their income is the residual after payment of a fixed rent. Under share tenancy, however, the risk is divided between tenant and owner in proportion to the crop share of each.

As Jaynes (1979) has shown, however, Cheung's model achieves its efficiency outcome because it simply assumes away two problems—the negative incentives of sharing and the difficulty of monitoring effort. If these problems did not exist, we would not observe share tenancy. Thus Cheung must indeed introduce risk, risk aversion, and transaction costs in order to explain the existence of the contracts his formal model explores under conditions in which such sources of market imperfections do not exist.

With respect to risk aversion motivation for sharecropping, Newbery (1975) and Reid (1976) have shown that, with constant returns to scale, sharecropping provides no risk-sharing benefits that landlord and worker could not achieve by dividing a plot of land "into two subplots, one of which is rented out at a fixed rental R and the other is operated by the landlord who hires labor at a wage W" (Newbery and Stiglitz, 1979, p. 314). Thus a model in the Cheungian tradition—that is, one without problems of worker incentives—does not explain the existence of share tenancy, even in the presence of production risk and risk aversion. Sharecropping can, however, be a means of risk avoidance under more complex characterizations of risk. Newbery and Stiglitz (1979) have demonstrated that with a second independent source of

risk, such as wage rate risk in the labor market, share contracts are superior to a mixture of wage and fixed-rent contracts. If there are no incentive (monitoring) problems or economies of scale but there are multiple sources of risk, the sharecropping contract acts as the necessary instrument to achieve productive efficiency; that is, it prevents rather than creates an inefficient allocation of resources.

Another class of tenancy models focuses on the costliness of labor supervision as a cause of sharecropping—the *Marshallian inefficiency*. One of Stiglitz's (1974) models assumes costly supervision: the landlord sets the size of the tenancy just like the share, taking into account the impact of tenancy size on the tenant's input decision. The landlord can prevent the tenant from renting any other land or from working for wages, or he can include these restrictions in the contract and monitor and enforce them. The landlord thus has an extra control instrument and can, by means of maximization, control the contractual terms in such a way as to limit the tenant to his or her reservation utility—that is, the wage rate. Of course, given the effort monitoring problem, productive efficiency cannot be achieved in this model.

Braverman and Srinivasan (1979) have extended the Stiglitz model of costly supervision so as to allow tenant and landlord to engage in a simultaneous share-cum-credit contract, the credit being used for the tenant's consumption. Such a tied contract becomes superior to an untied contract if the landlord has access to credit from third parties at lower rates of interest than the tenant can obtain. The landlord sets four contractual terms: crop share, tenancy size, rate of interest to be charged the tenant, and proportion of credit requirements that the tenant borrows from the landlord. Given that the landlord has two extra instruments available, the landlord can almost always hold the tenant to the utility level the latter would obtain as a wage laborer. As a result, policies like tenancy reform or provision of credit to tenants at lower than market rates cannot improve the tenant's utility level. Nothing less than land redistribution, intervention in several markets, or rising alternative wage levels can improve tenants' welfare.

In the models discussed, costly supervision arises because of imperfect information. Information is asymmetrically distributed between landlord and tenant because only the tenant can know how much effort he or she will provide; the landlord cannot know this at sufficiently low cost. And a central planner, who shares the landlord's lack of information, cannot improve on the existing allocation. Such improvement can be achieved only if the central planner has cheaper means of monitoring effort than the landlord, which, in agriculture, is not likely. Alternatively, the central planner will have to redistribute land to tenants in order to overcome their inability to buy land in the land market, which inability has led to their status as tenants. Such a policy, however, will also improve efficiency in a decentralized economy. As long as the underlying constraints on information or land transfer remain in place, the share tenancy equilibrium achieved is optimal with respect to these constraints; that is, it is a second best optimum, relative to the set of informational constraints assumed in the model. This point is an important recurrent theme in the literature.

A problem that the models we have discussed so far fail to address explicitly is the coexistence in the same region of all forms of contracts: owner cultivation, share contracts, and fixed rent contracts. Moreover, *tenancy ladders* appear to be important in both developed and developing countries: workers first become sharecroppers, then fixed-rent tenants, and finally acquire land of their own.

There are three explanations for the coexistence of tenurial contractural arrangements: (1) differences in risk aversion, (2) screening of workers of different quality, and (3) market imperfections for inputs other than labor. But differential risk aversion cannot account for the tenancy ladder, since there is little reason to expect the same person to become completely risk neutral as he or she becomes older, even if the person accumulates assets. It must be recognized, therefore, that workers differ in other respects, such as ability, management skills, and capital endowments.

If productivity per hour of work differs among otherwise homogeneous workers but the productivity differences are known only to the workers and cannot be observed by the landlord without cost, landowners or workers face a screening cost. In this case, Hallagan (1978) and, independently, Newbery and Stiglitz (1979) have shown that the choice of contract conveys information about workers' perception of their abilities. "Individuals who believe they are most productive [as workers] will choose the rental contract; individuals who believe they are very unproductive will choose the wage contract and those in between will choose the share contract" (Newbery and Stiglitz, 1979,

p. 323). Each class of workers prefers its respective contract. Utility levels for the more able workers are higher than the levels they could achieve in a labor market without screening. Again, since information is asymmetrically distributed between landlord and workers, productive efficiency cannot be achieved. The implicit screening by means of contract choice again represents a second best improvement in efficiency over the situation without tenancy contracts. This model leads to coexistence of contracts but not to a tenancy ladder unless workers move to higher efficiency classes as they grow older.

The clearest route to the tenancy ladder, the social differentiation of laborers, and different types of tenants is through absent markets or imperfect markets for inputs other than labor.

References

Braverman, Avishay, and T. N. Srinivasan. Conference Paper, "Agrarian Reforms in Developing Rural Economies Characterized by Interlinked Credit and Tenancy Markets," 1979.

Cheung, S. N. S. "Private Property Rights and Sharecropping," *Journal of Political Economy,* Vol. 76, 1968, pp. 1117–1122.

Cheung, S. N. S. *The Theory of Share Tenancy* (Chicago: University of Chicago Press, 1969).

Hallagan, W. "Self-selection by Contractual Choice and the Theory of Sharecropping," *Bell Journal of Economics,* Vol. 9, 1978, pp. 344–54.

Jaynes, Gerald D. Conference Paper, "Economic Theory and Land Tenure," 1979.

Newbery, D. M. G. "The Choice of Rental Contracts in Peasant Agriculture" in Lloyd G. Reynolds (ed.), *Agriculture in Development Theory* (New Haven: Yale University Press, 1975).

Newbery, D. M. G., and J. E. Stiglitz. "Sharecropping, Risk Sharing and the Importance of Imperfect Information" in James A. Roumasset, Jean Marc Boussard, and Inderjit Singh (eds.), *Risk, Uncertainty, and Agricultural Development* (College, Laguna, Philippines and New York: Southeast Asian Regional Center for Graduate Study and Research in Agriculture and Agricultural Development Council, 1979).

Reid, Joseph D., Jr. "Sharecropping and Agricultural Uncertainty," *Economic Development and Cultural Change,* Vol. 24, 1976, pp. 549–76.

Stiglitz, Joseph E. "Incentives and Risk Sharing in Agriculture," *Review of Economic Studies,* Vol. 41, 1974, 209–56.

Selection VII.B.3. The New Institutional Economics and Development Theory*

In recent years two strands of non-Walrasian economic literature have developed well-articulated endogenous theories of institutions, and they are both getting to be prominent in the new microeconomics of development. One is the transaction cost school, flowing out of the famous paper by Coase (1960), . . . The other school is associated with the theory of imperfect information. . . . Although there is some family resemblance between the two strands, there are important differences in their points of emphasis. But they both deny the validity of some of the principal results of mainstream economics. For example, one of the main pillars of Walrasian neoclassical economies—the separability of equity and efficiency—breaks down when transaction costs and imperfect information are important; the terms and conditions of contracts in various transactions, which directly affect the efficiency of resource allocation, now crucially depend on ownership structures and property relations. Development economics, which deals with cases where market failure and incomplete markets (often the result of the substantive presence of transaction costs and information problems) are predominant, clearly provides hospitable territory for such institutional analysis.

According to the transaction cost school, institutions that evolve to lower these costs are the key to the performance of economies. These costs include those of information, negotiation, monitoring, coordination, and enforcement of contracts. When transaction costs are absent, the initial assignment of property rights does not matter from the point of view of efficiency, because rights can be voluntarily adjusted and exchanged to promote increased production. But when transaction costs are substantial, as is usually the case, the allocation of property rights is critical. In the historical growth process there is a trade-off between economies of scale and specialization on the one hand and transaction costs on the other. In a small, closed, face-to-face peasant community, for example, transaction costs are low, but the production costs are high, because specialization and division of labor are severely limited by the extent of market defined by the personalized exchange process of the small community. In a large-scale complex economy, as the network of interdependence widens the impersonal exchange process gives considerable scope for all kinds of opportunistic behavior (cheating, shirking, moral hazard) and the costs of transacting can be high. In Western societies over time, complex institutional structures have been devised (elaborately defined and effectively enforced property rights, formal contracts and guarantees, corporate hierarchy, vertical integration, limited liability, bankruptcy laws, and so on) to constrain the participants, to reduce the uncertainty of social interaction, in general to prevent the transactions from being too costly and thus to allow the productivity gains of larger scale and improved technology to be realized.

The imperfect–information theory of institutions is closely related to that of transaction costs, since information costs constitute an important part of transaction costs. But the former theory is usually cast in a more rigorous framework clearly spelling out assumptions and equilibrium solution concepts, drawing out more fully the implications of strategic behavior under asymmetric information, and sharply differentiating the impact of different types of information problems. Imperfect–information theory yields somewhat more concrete and specific predictions about the design of contracts, with more attention to the details of terms and conditions of varying contractual arrangements under varying circumstances, than the usual presentations of transaction cost theory.

The imperfect–information theory has been fruitfully used in modeling many key agrarian institutions which are seen to emerge as substitutes for missing credit, insurance, and futures markets in an environment of pervasive risks, information asymmetry, and moral hazard. It started with the literature on sharecropping, then on interlocking of transactions in labor, credit and land lease, on labor tying, on credit rationing, and so on. Radical economists have often cited some of these production relations as institutional obstacles to development in a poor agrarian economy, overlooking the microeconomic rationale of the formation of these institutions. Under a set of informational constraints and missing markets, a given agrarian institution (say, sharecropping or interlocking of contracts) may be serving a real economic function. Its simple abolition, as is often demanded on a radical platform, without taking care of the factors that gave rise to the institution in the first place, may not necessarily improve the conditions of the in-

*From Pranab Bardhan, "The New Institutional Economics and Development Theory," *World Development* 17, no. 9 (1989): 1390–94. Reprinted by permission.

tended beneficiaries of the abolition program. There may be some important political lessons here from what can be called the economics of second-best reformism.

The transaction–cost and imperfect–information theories are equally murky on the mechanism through which new institutions and property rights emerge. One gets the impression that more efficient institutions and governance structures evolve as the parties involved come to appreciate the new benefit-cost possibilities. The literature is marked by a certain ahistorical functionalism and even vulgar Darwinism on this point. An institution's mere function of serving the interests of potential beneficiaries is clearly inadequate in *explaining* it, just as it is an incompetent detective who tries to explain a murder mystery only by looking for the beneficiary and, on that basis alone, proceeds to arrest the heir of the murdered rich man. One cannot get away from the enormity of the collective action problem that limits the ability of potential gainers to get their act together in bringing about institutional changes. There are two kinds of collective action problems involved here: one is the well known free-rider problem about sharing the costs of bringing about change, the other is a bargaining problem where disputes about sharing the potential benefits from the change may lead to a breakdown of the necessary coordination.

A related question is that of the presumed optimality of persistent institutions. The transaction–cost (as well as the imperfect–information) school often unthinkingly implies the application of the market analogy of competitive equilibrium to the social choice of institutions or the biological analogy of natural selection in the survival of the fittest institution. In fact transaction costs themselves, by raising barriers to entry and exit, reduce pressures from any social selection process; sunk costs and asset-specificity insulate internal governance structures from market forces. As Greenwald and Stiglitz (1986) have shown, the market equilibrium under imperfect information and incomplete markets is, in general, constrained Pareto inefficient; and, as Farrell (1987) has shown, with imperfect information even bilateral relationships may not be efficient on account of complexity of private bargaining.

In the recent development literature the institution of interlocking of transactions (in labor, credit, and land relations) has been rationalized as a device to save transaction costs and to substitute for incomplete or nonexistent credit and insurance markets. But one should not overlook that such interlocking itself may act as a barrier to entry for third parties and be a source of additional monopoly power for the dominant partner (usually the employer-creditor-landlord) in such transactions. Personalized interlocking of labor commitments and credit transactions (involving selective exclusion of others) also divides the workers and emasculates their collective bargaining strength vis-à-vis employers, who use this as an instrument of control over the labor process.

As we all know from experience, dysfunctional institutions often persist for a very long period. Akerlof (1984) has built models to show how economically unprofitable or socially unpleasant customs may persist as a result of a mutually sustaining network of social sanctions when each individual conforms out of fear of loss of reputation from disobedience. In such a system, potential members of a breakaway coalition fear that it is doomed to failure and thus failure to challenge the system becomes a self-fulfilling prophecy. . . .

The biological analogy of survival of the fittest is particularly inappropriate as path dependence is assigned an important role in biological processes. To quote Gould (1980, p. 16): "Organisms are not billiard balls propelled by simple and measurable external forces to predictable new positions on life's pool table. . . . Organisms have a history that constrains their future in myriad, subtle ways. . . . Their complexity of form entails a host of functions incidental to whatever pressures of natural selection superintended the initial construction." The arguments against the operation of natural selection in social institutions are obviously much stronger.

References

Akerlof, G. (1984). *An Economic Theorist's Book of Tales.* Cambridge: Cambridge University Press.

Coase, R. (1960). "The problem of social cost." *Journal of Law and Economics* 3 (October): 144.

Farrell, J. (1987). "Information and the Coase theorem." *Journal of Economic Perspectives* 1 (Fall): 113–129.

Gould, S. J. (1980). *The Panda's Thumb.* New York: Norton.

Greenwald B., and J. E. Stiglitz (1986). "Externalities in economies with imperfect information and incomplete markets." *Quarterly Journal of Economics* 101 (May): 229–64.

Selection VII.B.4. Rural Credit Markets and Institutions in Developing Countries: Lessons for Policy Analysis from Practice and Modern Theory*

Until recently conventional wisdom held that imposing low ceilings on interest rates and allocating massive amounts of credit to rural financial markets would speed rural development and improve income distribution. But by and large policies directed along these lines have failed. Indeed, most often they have made matters worse. Low interest rate ceilings provide income transfers to loan recipients, distorting the real price ratio of investment opportunities by undervaluing the real cost of capital in different sectors. To the standard cost of distorted resource allocation, add the specific costs and consequences of implementing credit programs in rural financial markets for the full measure of impact. The record overwhelmingly shows credit programs' objectives have not been met.

These credit policy failures can be attributed to basic flaws intrinsic to formal rural credit markets out of which arise persistent problems as described in Table 1.

Informal lending was once the only form credit took in rural settings. Evidence suggests that as farm size increases, private credit sources, village moneylenders and pawnbrokers, chit funds with an array of implicit interest rates, and friends or relatives grow less important than banks. With the implementation of development plans, official lending complements but clearly does not supersede informal sources.

Sample surveys supply the information on the extent of informal lending practices. They indicate that its volume is far greater than that of organized institutions. It is characterized by a much shorter processing time, better screening techniques or enforcement devices (noted in the lower default rate), and higher interest rates, with a median around 50 percent and a variance much higher than institutionalized credit rate.

The lower delinquency rates reported in informal credit sources are to a large extent due to better assessment of creditworthiness, ability to exert social pressure for repayment, and the frequent practice of tying (interlinking) credit contracts with other input or output contracts. Documentation of the use and characteristics of the latter practice is quite extensive. Sharecropping contracts are quite often interlinked with credit contracts. . . . Credit contracts between landlords and tenants are often in the form of production loans and tied to the purchase of fertilizer, seeds, and other forms of capital with different tenants paying different interest rates on their loans. These interlinkage practices have been viewed as a way to address the adverse selection problem and the moral hazard problem indigenous to these markets.

Two approaches have been put forward in the past to explain why landlords (employers) transact with their tenants (workers) in credit. They are: (1) reduction of transaction costs and (2) exploitation of weaker agents by more powerful ones. Though both have merits under certain circumstances, they fail to explain such interlinkages under a wider range of circumstances. In particular, they do not pay attention to the particular information structure. Even though information costs are part of the transaction cost, it is essential to specify them in order to explain the details of the contractual equilibrium, for example, why some landlords may subsidize tenants' credit while others charge their tenants higher interest rates. The exploitation theory fails to explain why monopolist landlords choosing tenants (workers) from a pool of the "reserve army of the unemployed" need any extra instrument (credit) for exploitation beyond the rental (tenant) or wage (worker) contract.

The modern theory of contractual equilibrium under imperfect information focuses on the moral hazard and adverse selection features commonly found in rural developing economies. The "moral hazard" features as pertaining to the interlinking credit with labor and land contracts are:

(a) Individuals are not paid on the basis of their input (effort) in general since this is not observable and they often do not rent land for a fixed sum since that imposes too much risk on them. Hence the contractual arrangements involve at least some form of sharecropping; as a result, tenants do not obtain the full marginal product of their efforts.

(b) The landlord cannot completely specify the actions to be taken by the tenant: the tenant has considerable discretion both with respect to the allocation and level of effort, and the choice of production technique. Some of these decisions may be easily monitored by the landlord, but there are oth-

*From A. Braverman and J. L. Guasch, "Rural Credit Markets and Institutions in Developing Countries: Lessons for Policy Analysis from Practice and Modern Theory," *World Development*, Vol. 14, Nos. 10/11 (October/November 1986), pp. 1253–55, 1257, 1260–62. Reprinted by permission.

Table 1. Characteristics of Rural Financial Markets

Basic Flaws

Weakness of competitive forces.

Weak legal enforcement of contracts.

Corruption and lack of accountability in institutions, patronage and income transfer practices, which are partly due to poorly designed or non-existent incentive mechanisms to induce accountability on both sides of the market.

Significant information problems and uncertainty regarding the ability of borrowers to meet future loan obligations.

Inability to monitor the use of funds.

Lack of collateral often due to land tenure arrangements or ill-defined property rights (e.g. parts of Africa).

Lack of coherent financial savings mobilization program.

Higher opportunity cost of capital in other sectors because of interest rate ceilings.

Persistent Problems

Credit loans to wealthy farmers, small farmers rationed out of the credit market.

Loans for agricultural programs diverted to non-agricultural uses.

Credit policies that encourage consumption and discourage savings.

The term structure of agricultural loans contracts or fails to expand.

Low adoption rates of cost-savings technologies in agriculture and in financial services.

Low recovery rate.

Significant distortions in the optimal allocation of resources across markets.

Extensive use of interlinking credit contracts with labor and land contracts.

---

ers, perhaps equally important, for which the cost of monitoring would be very high.

The tenant's considerable discretion over his own actions combined with their significant impact on the landlord's expected profits have some further implications. In particular, the landlord has an incentive to *induce* tenants to behave as he wishes. This is attempted through influencing the amount and terms of credit the tenant borrows and by the goods he can purchase and the prices he pays.

The behavior affected includes the effort supplied by the tenant and the choice of technique (risk distribution) applied by him. For instance, if the landlord makes credit less expensive, under reasonable conditions the tenant will be induced to borrow more. If there are severe penalties associated with default (e.g., bonded labor), the tenant will then need to work harder to avoid this contingency.

Similarly the landlord may observe that his tenants are employing techniques of production which are too safe; the landlord's income might be increased if his tenants were willing to employ techniques with higher means and higher variances. He may note that his tenants are acting in a particularly risk-averse manner because of the consequences of defaulting on outstanding loans. To change their behavior, the landlord may require that his tenants only borrow from him. He may charge them interest above the market rate in order to induce them to limit their borrowing, and at the same time he may offer a tenancy contract which is much more attractive in some other dimensions. Such a phenomenon prevails both in competitive and non-competitive environments and shifts the utilities possibilities frontier. Since interlinking is really the internalization of the externality from the credit to the labor/land markets in the absence of a complete set of markets, the utilities possibilities frontier moves outward while the distribution effects of interlinkage are ambiguous. The rationale for interlinkage becomes even stronger where law or custom restricts certain contractual arrangements, for example usury laws or floors on tenants' crop shares.

Another rationale for interlinking is the "adverse selection" effect, where interlinking credit and tenancy contracts may screen the high-ability from the low-ability types. . . .

Braverman and Stiglitz have shown that there is no presumption that innovation results either in a reduction or in an increase in tenants' demand for credit. Whether the demand for credit itself is increased or decreased depends critically on both how the technical change affects the probability distribution of yields and on tenants' utility functions. The presence of interlinkage between credit and land markets does not preclude either resistance to or encouragement of the adoption of technological innovations. Either is possible. In some cases, it might actually encourage the adoption of some technologies which otherwise would not be adopted, even though the innovation itself reduces tenants' demand for credit.

As explained before, the amount borrowed affects the landlord's return (through its effect both on the tenants' effort and on his decisions concerning choices of technique), and conversely, the terms of the landlord's contract affect returns to the lender (through its effect on the likelihood of default). Interlinkage was a method by which these "externalities" could be internalized. What then concerns the landlord-cum-lender is the total impact of the innovation on his income; the decomposition of his income into a return as a lender, or return as a landlord, has no particular significance. So it becomes clear that the impact of an innovation on a landlord-cum-lender may be quite different from the impact of the same innovation on a landlord who does not control the borrowing activities of his tenants.

Selection VII.B.5. A Survey of Agricultural Household Models: Recent Findings and Policy Implications*

Efforts to predict the consequences of agricultural policies are often confounded by the complex behavioral interactions characteristic of semicommercialized, rural economies. Most households in agricultural areas produce partly for sale and partly for own-consumption. They also purchase some of their inputs—such as fertilizer and labor—and provide some inputs—such as family labor—from their own resources. Any change in the policies governing agricultural activities will therefore affect not only production but also consumption and labor supply.

Agricultural household models are designed to capture these interactions in a theoretically consistent fashion and in a manner that allows empirical applications so that the consequences of policy interventions can be illuminated. The existence of such models would enable the analyst to examine the consequences of policy in three dimensions.

First, one could examine the effects of alternative policies on the well-being of representative agricultural households. Well-being may be interpreted here to mean household income or some other measure such as nutritional status. For example, in examining the effect of a policy designed to provide cheap food for urban consumers, an agricultural household model would allow the analyst to assess the costs to farmers of depressed producer prices. The nutritional benefits for the urban population may be more than offset by the reduced nutritional status of the rural population that results from lower farm incomes.

Second, an understanding of the behavior of agricultural households would shed light on the spillover effects of government policies on other segments of the rural population. For example, since most investment strategies are designed to increase production, their primary impact is on the incomes of agricultural households. As a result, rural investment strategies may not reach landless households or households engaged in nonagricultural activities. A model that incorporates total labor demand and family labor supply, however, would allow the analyst to explore the effects of investment policy on the demand for hired labor and hence on the rural labor market and the incomes of landless households. Similarly, a model that incorporates consumer behavior would allow the analyst to explore the consequences of increased profits for agricultural households on the demand for products and services provided by nonagricultural, rural households. Since the demand for nonagricultural commodities is often thought to be much more responsive to an increase in income than the demand for agricultural staples, this spillover effect may well be important.

Third, governments are interested in the performance of the agricultural sector from a more macroeconomic perspective. For example, agriculture is often an important source of revenue for the public budget and a major earner of foreign exchange. In assessing the effects of pricing policy on the budget or the balance of payments, the government is obliged to consider how agricultural households will alter their production and consumption in response to changes in prices. A reduction in export taxes, for example, may increase earnings of foreign exchange and budget revenues if households market enough additional production. Since agricultural household models capture both consumption and production behavior, they are an appropriate vehicle for examining the effect of pricing policy on marketed surplus and hence on foreign exchange earnings and budget revenues.

The importance of agricultural households in the total population and the significance of sector policies combine to make the behavior of agricultural households an area warranting thorough theoretical and empirical investigation.

Modeling the Agricultural Household

In general, any analysis of the consumption or labor supply of agricultural households has to account for the interdependence of household production and consumption. Agricultural households combine the household and the firm, two fundamental units of microeconomic analysis. When the household is a price taker in all markets, for all commodities which it both consumes and produces, optimal household production can be determined independent of leisure and consumption choices. Then, given the maximum income level derived from profit-maximizing production, family labor supply and commodity consumption decisions can be made.

*From Inderjit Singh, Lyn Squire, and John Strauss, "A Survey of Agricultural Household Models: Recent Findings and Policy Implications," *World Bank Economic Review*, Vol. 1, No. 1, September 1986, pp. 149–50, 152–54. Reprinted by permission.

Given this sequential decisionmaking, the appropriate analytical framework is a recursive model with profit- and utility-maximizing components. Empirical analysis of both household consumption and production becomes considerably more tractable in a recursive model, which as a result has been used by most (but not all) empirical analyses.

In this section, a prototype static model is developed. (A more detailed treatment with derivations is found in Strauss, 1986.) For any production cycle, the household is assumed to maximize a utility function:

$$U = U(X_a, X_m, X_l) \qquad (1)$$

where the commodities are an agricultural staple (X_a), a market-purchased good (X_m), and leisure (X_l). Utility is maximized subject to a cash income constraint:

$$p_m X_m = p_a(Q_a - X_a) - p_l(L - F) - p_v V + E$$

where p_m and p_a are the prices of the market-purchased commodity and the staple, respectively; Q_a is the household's production of the staple (so that $Q_a - X_a$ is its marketed surplus); p_l is the market wage; L is total labor input; F is family labor input (so that $L - F$, if positive, is hired labor and, if negative, is off-farm labor); V is a variable input (for example, fertilizer); p_v is the variable input's market price; and E is any nonlabor, nonfarm income.

The household also faces a time constraint; it cannot allocate more time to leisure, on-farm production, or off-farm employment than the total time available to the household:

$$X_l + F = T$$

where T is the total stock of household time. It also faces a production constraint or production technology that depicts the relationship between inputs and farm output:

$$Q_a = Q(L, V, A, K)$$

where A is the household's fixed quantity of land and K is its fixed stock of capital.

In this presentation, various complexities are omitted. For example, the possibility of more than one crop is ignored. In addition, it is assumed that family labor and hired labor are perfect substitutes and can be added directly. Production is also assumed to be riskless. Finally, and perhaps most importantly, it is assumed that the four prices in the model—p_a, p_m, p_v, and p_l—are not affected by actions of the household. That is, the household is assumed to be a price taker in the four markets; as seen below, this will result in a recursive model.

The three constraints on household behavior can be collapsed into a single constraint. Substituting the production constraint into the cash income constraint for Q_a and substituting the time constraint into the cash income constraint for F yields a single constraint:

$$p_m X_m + p_a X_a + p_l X_1 = p_l T + \pi + E \qquad (2)$$

where $\pi = p_a Q_a (L, VA, K) - p_l L - p_v V$ and is a measure of farm profits. In this equation, the left-hand side shows total household "expenditure" on three items: the market-purchased commodity, the household's "purchase" of its own output, and the household's "purchase" of its own time in the form of leisure. The right-hand side is a development of Becker's concept of full income, in which the value of the stock of time ($p_l T$) owned by the household is explicitly recorded, as is any labor income. The extension for agricultural households is the inclusion of a measure of farm profits, $p_a Q_a - p_l L - p_v V$, with all labor valued at the market wage, this being a consequence of the assumption of pricetaking behavior in the labor market. Equations 1 and 2 are the core of all the studies of agricultural households reported in this article.

Equations 1 and 2 reveal that the household can choose the levels of consumption for the three commodities, the total labor input, and the fertilizer input into agricultural production. Maximization of household utility subject to the single constraint yields the following first-order conditions:

$$p_a \frac{\partial Q_a}{\partial L} = p_l \qquad (3a)$$

$$p_a \frac{\partial Q_a}{\partial V} = p_v \qquad (3b)$$

$$\frac{\partial U/\partial X_a}{\partial U/\partial X_m} = \frac{p_a}{p_m} \qquad (4a)$$

$$\frac{\partial U/\partial X_l}{\partial U_l/\partial X_m} = \frac{p_l}{p_m} \qquad (4b)$$

plus the constraint. Equations 3a and 3b show that the household will equate the marginal revenue products for labor and fertilizer to their respective market prices. An important attribute of these two equations is that they contain only two endogenous variables, L and V. The other endogenous variables, X_m, X_a, and X_l, do not appear and do not, therefore, influence the household's choice of L or V (provided second-order conditions are met). Accordingly, farm labor and fertilizer demand can be determined as a function of prices (p_a, p_l and p_v), the technological parameters of the production function, and the fixed area of land and quantity of capital. Since equations 3a and 3b depict the standard conditions for profit maximization, it can be concluded that the household's production decisions are consistent with profit maximization and independent of the household's utility function.

The maximized value of profits can be substituted into equation 2 to yield:

$$p_m X_m + p_a X_a + p_l X_l = Y^* \qquad (5)$$

where Y^* is the value of full income associated with profit-maximizing behavior. Equations 4a, 4b, and 5 can be thought of as the first-order conditions of a second maximization. That is, having first maximized profits (see equations 3a and 3b), the household then maximizes utility subject to its (maximized) value of full income. Equations 4a, 4b, and 5 can then be solved to obtain the demand equations for X_m, X_a, and X_l as functions of prices (p_m, p_a, p_l) and full income (Y^*). This demonstrates, given the assumptions made about markets, that even though the household's production and consumption decisions may be simultaneous in time, they can be modeled recursively (Nakajima, 1969; Jorgenson and Lau, 1969).

The presence of farm profits in equation 5 demonstrates the principal message of the farm household literature—that farm technology, quantities of fixed inputs, and prices of variable inputs and outputs affect consumption decisions. The reverse, however, is not true provided the model is recursive. Preferences, prices of consumption commodities, and income do not affect production decisions; therefore, output supply responds positively to own price at all times because of the quasi-convexity assumption on the production function. However, for consumption commodities (X_a) which are also produced by the household (Q_a), own-price effects are

$$\frac{dX_a}{dp_a} = \frac{\partial X_a}{\partial p_a} \bigg|_{Y^*} + \frac{\partial X_a}{\partial Y^*}\frac{\partial Y^*}{\partial p_a} \qquad (6)$$

The first term on the right-hand side of this expression is the standard result of consumer demand theory and, for a normal good, is negative. The second term captures the "profit effect," which occurs when a rise in the price of the staple increases farm profits and hence full income. Applying the envelope theorem to equation 6,

$$\frac{\partial Y^*}{\partial p_a} dp_a = \frac{\partial \pi}{\partial p_a} dp_a = Q_a dp_a \qquad (7)$$

that is, the profit effect equals output times the price increase and therefore is unambiguously positive. The positive effect of an increase in profits (and hence farm income), an effect totally ignored in traditional models of demand, will definitely dampen and may outweigh the negative effect of both income and substitution in standard consumer demand theory. The presence of the profit effect is a direct consequence of the joint treatment of production and consumption decisions.

References

Jorgenson, Dale, and Lawrence Lau. 1969. "An Economic Theory of Agricultural House-hold Behavior." Paper presented at Fourth Far Eastern Meeting of Econometric Society.

Nakajima, Chihiro. 1969. "Subsistence and Commercial Family Farms: Some Theoretical Models of Subjecture Equilibrium." In C. F. Wharton, Jr., ed., *Subsistence Agriculture and Economic Development.* Chicago: Aldine.

Strauss, John. 1986. "The Theory and Comparative Statics of Agricultural Household Models: A General Approach." In I. J. Singh, L. Squire, and J. Strauss, eds., *Agricultural Household Models: Extensions, Applications, and Policy.* Baltimore, Md.: Johns Hopkins University Press.

Comment VII.B.1. Supply Functions and Price Responsiveness

A number of empirical studies offer evidence on the positive supply elasticity of agricultural production in response to price incentives. An excellent summary of empirical estimates of supply elasticities is presented by Hossein Askari and John T. Cummings, *Agricultural Supply Response: A Survey of the Econometric Evidence* (1976). See also Raj Krishna, "Agricultural Price Policy and Economic Development," in *Agricultural Development and Economic Growth,* ed. Herman M. Southworth and Bruce F. Johnston (1967); Theodore W. Schultz, ed., *Distortions of Agricultural Incentives* (1978); Walter Falcon, "Farmer Response to Price in a Subsistence Economy," *American Economic Review, Papers and Proceedings* (May 1964); and K. Bardhan, "Price and Output Response of Marketed Surplus of Foodgrains," *American Journal of Agricultural Economics* (February 1970).

Considering the efficiency of farmer decision making, several studies have examined the allocational behavior of peasant producers from the viewpoint of efficiency across farm size groups, risk, pricing policy, credit, and marketing. See Theodore W. Schultz, *Transforming Traditional Agriculture* (1964); Amartya K. Sen, "Peasants and Dualism With or Without Surplus Labor," *Journal of Political Economy* (October 1966); D. W. Hopper, "Allocational Efficiency in Traditional Indian Agriculture," *Journal of Farm Economics* (August 1965); Michael Lipton, "The Theory of the Optimizing Peasant," *Journal of Development Studies* (August 1968); and M. Schluter and T. Mount, "Some Management Objectives of the Peasant Farmer," *Journal of Development Studies* (August 1977).

In an important study, *Palanpur: The Economy of an Indian Village* (1982), C. J. Bliss and N. H. Stern examine whether farmers' decisions about inputs and outputs can be explained by an optimizing model (whether farmers are rational profit- or utility-maximizing agents) and whether sharecropping tenancy is inefficient.

CHAPTER VIII

Income Distribution

Overview

This chapter begins with a Note that describes some of the problems involved in estimating the income distribution for a country and discusses the measures of inequality for a given distribution of income that are used in the subsequent selections. Exhibit VIII.1 presents income distribution data and three of the most commonly used inequality measures for all Human Development Index countries for which data are available.

The first section of this chapter concerns the impact of economic development on income distribution and in particular on measures of income inequality. It is theoretically possible, of course, that development has no impact on income distribution. For example, suppose it were the case that the distribution of income is determined entirely by the distribution of innate ability in the population. It is plausible that development will not change the distribution of innate ability, and therefore will not change the distribution of income. Against the hypothesis that development does not affect income distribution and therefore leaves income inequality unchanged, the alternative that has received by far the most attention is the hypothesis that income inequality first rises and then falls with development. A plot of inequality against a measure of development such as per capita income would then look like an inverted U. This hypothesis has therefore become known as the inverted-U hypothesis.

The inverted-U hypothesis originated with Simon Kuznets in the work featured in the first selection. Kuznets observed falling inequality in Germany and especially in the United Kingdom and the United States, beginning from roughly the last quarter of the nineteenth century for the United Kingdom and the First World War for Germany and the United States. He conjectured that inequality was falling after having risen during an earlier period, perhaps 1780 to 1850 in the United Kingdom and 1840 to 1890 in Germany and the United States. The reasoning behind his conjecture was that he believed that in these countries the distribution of income in agriculture was more equal than the distribution of income in urban areas, so that as development and urbanization proceeded, measured inequality overall should have risen. The subsequent fall in inequality that he actually observed was then due, he argued, to a decline in inequality within urban areas caused by better adaptation of the children of rural–urban migrants to city economic life and growing political power of urban lower-income groups to enact legislation favoring their interests.

Other researchers have sought to clarify the argument underlying Kuznets's original conjecture. Selection VIII.A.2 by Sherman Robinson considers a two-sector economy for which average income is higher in one sector. He shows that overall income inequality as measured by the variance in the logarithm of income follows an inverted U as the population is reallocated from one sector to another, provided that within-sector inequalities and the average sector log incomes are held constant. We can think of the two sectors as the rural and urban sectors, with average income and inequality both higher in the urban sector, but the point of Robinson's selection is that this interpretation is irrelevant: the inverted-U result holds regardless of which sector has higher average income or higher inequality. If the Gini coefficient rather than the log variance is used to measure income inequality, the inverted-U result can again be demonstrated in the special case where within-sector inequalities are zero, so that all inequality is attributable to the difference in incomes between the two sectors (see Knight 1976 and Fields 1979). Focusing on between-sector inequality yields a simple intuition for Robinson's result. When all of the population is in sector 1, between-sector inequality is zero. When some of the population has migrated to sector 2, between-sector inequality is positive. When all of the population has migrated to sector 2, between-sector inequality is again zero.

Robinson's result makes it appear that an inverted-U path of income inequality, should we observe it, is a rather uninteresting artifact of the way in which we measure inequality. This position is challenged in Selection VIII.A.3 by James Rauch and in the following Comment on the grounds that all individuals in Robinson's economy would prefer to be in the sector with higher average income, and that once the need for migration equilibrium is taken into account the cause of the inverted-U path of income inequality completely changes. Specifically, Rauch supposes that individuals are indifferent in equilibrium between earning the agricultural income with certainty or taking their chances in the urban sector, where they earn a high income if they are lucky and find a formal-sector job and a low income if they are unlucky and get stuck in informal-sector underemployment (which we can think of as the easy-entry informal sector described in Selection VI.B.4 by Fields). The main source of inequality in the Rauch model is not inequality between the rural and urban sectors but rather inequality within the urban sector between informally and formally employed workers. As urbanization increases the urban sector gains greater weight in the determination of overall inequality, causing it to rise, but at the same time the share of the underemployed in the urban population falls, eventually causing inequality within the urban sector and overall inequality to fall. The inverted U in income inequality is thus closely related to the growth and decline of the proportion of the population that falls into the poorest class, the underemployed. Rauch's result for overall income inequality is similar to Kuznets's original hypothesis that inequality should first increase with urbanization because population was being shifted from a sector with low inequality (agriculture) to a sector with high inequality and later decrease with urbanization because inequality within the urban sector would be reduced.

Exhibit VIII.1 does not provide evidence in support of the inverted-U hypothesis. Comparing the medians of the three inequality measures for the low, medium, and high human development countries, we see that all three measures steadily fall as development increases, rather than rising and then falling. In Selection VIII.A.4, Matthew Higgins and Jeffrey G. Williamson argue that an inverted U has been masked in the data by a "cohort size effect." Specifically, less developed countries tend to have a smaller proportion of their labor forces in the peak earning ages, 40–59, because of their incomplete demographic transitions and consequent higher population growth rates (discussed in Note I.A.2). The relative scarcity of these experienced workers in LDCs means that the jobs for which they are needed (e.g., administrative and managerial positions) will command higher wages, increasing inequality since these are already the most highly paid workers. The pattern of inequality we noted in Exhibit VIII.1 could therefore be explained by this cohort size effect. Higgins and Williamson show in Selection VIII.A.4 that once one controls for the cohort size effect, the inverted U emerges: inequality first rises and then falls as development measured by worker productivity increases.

A weakness of the evidence for the inverted-U hypothesis in Selection VIII.A.4 is that it is based on variation in inequality *across* countries, whereas the hypothesis predicts a rise followed by a fall in inequality *within* countries over time. In Comment VIII.A.2 we discuss the extent to which the evidence based on variation in inequality within countries over time also supports the inverted-U hypothesis.

The second section of this chapter reverses the arrow of causality in the first section and addresses the impact of income distribution on economic development. For many years the dominant view was that income inequality promoted domestic savings that financed investment and therefore promoted development. This opinion was closely linked to the view that investment is the engine of growth (see the Overview for Chapter V), and like that view it was succinctly expounded by W. Arthur Lewis (1954, pp. 156–157): "We are interested not in the people in general, but only say in the 10 percent of them with the largest incomes. . . . The remaining 90 percent of the people never manage to save a significant fraction of their incomes. . . . Saving increases relatively to the national income because the incomes of the savers increase relatively to the national income. The central fact of economic development is that the distribution of income is altered in favour of the saving class."

The view that inequality helps to generate rapid economic growth was called into question by the combination in the "high-performing East Asian economies" such as Korea and Taiwan of relatively equal distributions of income with rates of growth in per capita income (and with savings rates) that were among the world's highest. Selection VIII.B.1 by William Easterly investigates the hypothesis that a greater share of income received by the "middle class" (the middle three quintiles of the income distribution) promotes economic growth—just the opposite of Lewis's hypothesis. Easterly recognizes that a positive association between the middle-class income share and growth in per capita income does not show that the former causes the latter. For example, rapid growth could raise the return to education and thereby raise the middle-class income share. To avoid such problems of reverse causality, Easterly applies the hypothesis of Engerman and Sokoloff (Selection II.5) and estimates the middle-class income share as a function of commodity exporting, which in turn is a function of tropical location. He finds that tropical location predicts commodity exporting, which is negatively associated with the middle-class income share, as Engerman and Sokoloff would predict. Easterly then estimates a simultaneous equations system in which growth in per capita income is a function of the middle-class income share, which in turn is a (decreasing) function of commodity exporting that is predicted by tropical location. He finds a strong positive effect of the middle-class income share on economic growth, which cannot reflect reverse causality because growth cannot cause tropical location.

Why should economic growth be higher when the middle class receives a greater share of national income? Alberto Alesina and Roberto Perotti in Selection VIII.B.2 describe one possible mechanism and find evidence to support it using cross-country data. The key intervening variable in this mechanism is political instability: a low middle-class income share is hypothesized to cause political instability, which in turn is hypothesized to reduce investment. If investment is inhibited by political instability, it will be difficult to sustain development. In their sample of 71 countries during the period 1960–85, Alesina and Perotti find that their measure of the middle-class income share (the share of income received by the two quintiles just below the top) is negatively associated with an index of sociopolitical instability, and that this index in turn is negatively associated with the share of investment in GDP.

In the final section of this chapter we return to the impact of economic development on income distribution, but consider case studies rather than theory or cross-country statistical analysis. We consider one case of sharply rising inequality and one case of sharply falling inequality.

In Selection VIII.C.1, the World Bank reports that income inequality in China during the period 1981–95 rose by an amount greater than for any other country for which comparable data are available. An increased contribution of inequality between the rural and urban sectors appears to have been the main cause. This is the source of inequality highlighted by Robinson in Selection VIII.A.2. China's government has discouraged rural-urban migration, which might otherwise have tended to equalize average incomes between the rural and urban sectors and eliminate this source of inequality. The other major contributor to the rise in income inequality in China is increased inequality between coastal and interior provinces. This reflects the impact of "globalization" on China's economy, which has led to more rapid income growth in coastal provinces than interior provinces because the former are better positioned to engage in international trade and receive foreign direct investment.

In Selection VIII.C.2, Hal Hill reports that the Gini coefficient for rural Indonesia fell from 0.34 in 1978 to 0.26 in 1993, after showing no trend from 1964–65 to 1978. (He also reports that the Gini coefficient for all of Indonesia shows no trend over the entire period from 1964–65 to 1993). The key factor here appears to have been government policies that generated strong growth in rice output starting in the late 1970s. This reduced rural income inequality because rice is grown primarily by small farmers and is also one of the main items in their household budgets. The cases of both China and Indonesia thus demonstrate that government policies interacting with fundamental economic forces can yield strong changes in income inequality within a country over a relatively short period of time.

References

Fields, Gary S. "A Welfare Economic Approach to Growth and Distribution in the Dual Economy." *Quarterly Journal of Economics* 93 (August 1979): 325–53.

Knight, John B. "Explaining Income Distribution in Less Developed Countries: A Framework and an Agenda." *Oxford Bulletin of Economics and Statistics* 38 (August 1976): 161–77.

Lewis, W. Arthur. "Economic Development with Unlimited Supplies of Labour." *The Manchester School* 22 (1954): 139–91.

Note VIII.1. Measurement of Income Inequality

For a given distribution of income there are many ways to measure inequality. In this Note we will discuss only the measures that are used in the selections included in this chapter.

Estimation of the distribution of income presents many difficulties. Ideally we would like to use estimates of the incomes of all households in a country. By contrast, to estimate income or GNP per capita we only need estimates of two quantities: total income and total population. Because the data collection requirements are so great, countries rarely report estimates of their income distributions more frequently than every 10 years, and for many countries there exist no reliable estimates of income distribution at all. The estimates we do have are invariably based on the incomes of households in a given year rather than averaged over many years. (They are also almost always based on before-tax rather than after-tax incomes and are sometimes based on incomes received by individuals rather than households.) To see the problem this presents for measurement of inequality, consider a hypothetical country inhabited entirely by farmers, some of whom grow crops that benefit from above average rainfall and the rest of whom grow crops that benefit from below average rainfall. Suppose that all farmers within each group are identical, and that on average (that is, for average rainfall) these two groups of farmers earn the same household incomes. We would then want to say that there is no inequality in the distribution of income for this country. However, in any given year rainfall will differ from the average, and unequal incomes will be observed. Simon Kuznets lists the specifications for an ideal estimate of income distribution at the beginning of Selection VIII.A.1.

Ignoring these difficulties, we can measure inequality using the estimated income distributions that we have. Two popular measures are the ratio of the share of income received by the tenth *decile* (richest 10 percent) of households to the share of income received by the first decile (poorest 10 percent) of households, and the ratio of the share of income received by the fifth *quintile* (richest 20 percent) of households to the share of income received by the first quintile (poorest 20 percent) of households. Both of these measures are reported in Exhibit VIII.1. The quintile ratio is used in the empirical analysis of Matthew Higgins and Jeffrey G. Williamson in Selection VIII.A.4. The selections by William Easterly (VIII.B.1) and by Alberto Alesina and Roberto Perotti (VIII.B.2) label the shares of income received by the second, third, and fourth quintiles and by the third and fourth quintiles, respectively, as the "middle-class" income shares.

A more rigorous way to measure income inequality is to use *Lorenz curves.* A Lorenz curve plots the percentage of a country's income received by the poorest x percent of households against x. Thus in Figure 1, *OX* percent of households (the poorest group) receives a percent of income, and so on, giving the Lorenz curve *L*. Complete equality would occur only if a percent of households received a percent of income, yielding the curve of complete equality *E*. The curve of perfect inequality is *OGH,* with a right angle at *G*. This curve represents the case where one household has 100 percent of the country's income. In practice the Lorenz curve is typically fitted to data giving income shares by decile, that is, the points on the Lorenz curve that are actually observed are the percentage of income received by the poorest 10 percent of households, the percentage of income received by the poorest 20 percent of households, and so on. If the Lorenz curve for one income distribution α lies above that of another income distribution β for at least one point and never lies below it, that is, if distribution α *Lorenz dominates* distribution β, we say that distribution α is more equal than distribution β. It can be shown (see, e.g., Fields and Fei 1978) that if distribution α Lorenz dominates distribution β for the same level of income, α can be obtained from β by transferring positive amounts of income from the relatively rich to the relatively poor. If an additional dollar of income is worth less to the relatively rich than to the relatively poor (i.e., if there is diminishing marginal utility of income), we can judge that this transfer increases social welfare. In short, for a given

Figure 1. The Lorenz Curve

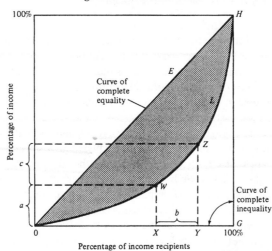

level of income, Lorenz dominance gives us a measure of income inequality that we can link to social welfare, with lower inequality implying higher welfare.

This feature makes measurement of income inequality using Lorenz curves very attractive. Unfortunately, it does not allow us to compare inequality of income distributions whose Lorenz curves cross. One way to deal with this problem is to measure inequality using the *Gini coefficient,* computation of which is illustrated in Figure 1. The shaded area in the figure, enclosed by the theoretical line of equality *E* and the observed Lorenz curve *L,* is known as the concentration area or area of inequality. The Gini coefficient is the ratio of this area to the total area under the line of equality. One way to compute the Gini coefficient is to take the sum of the areas of all "trapezoids" such as *WXYZ* and subtract it from the area under *E* to obtain the concentration area. The required ratio then follows. As a measure of income inequality, the Gini coefficient ranges from 0 to 1—the larger the coefficient, the greater the inequality. Thus 0 represents perfect equality, and 1 represents perfect inequality. It is clear that if one income distribution Lorenz dominates another, its Gini coefficient will be smaller, but the Gini coefficient also allows us to rank inequality for income distributions whose Lorenz curves cross. The Gini coefficient is reported in Exhibit VIII.1 and is a measure of income inequality used in the selections here by Higgins and Williamson (VIII.A.4), by the World Bank (VIII.C.1), and by Hal Hill (VIII.C.2).

A disadvantage of the Gini coefficient is that it cannot be decomposed into inequality within and inequality between groups, that is, the sum of inequality within and inequality between groups will not add up exactly to the overall Gini coefficient. This disadvantage is especially important when one wants to analyze a change in inequality that occurs over time, since one can often obtain a great deal of insight by analyzing how much of the change can be attributed to a change in within-group inequality and how much can be attributed to a change in between-group inequality. Many groupings are interesting, for example, by levels of education of the heads of households, but in the selections in this chapter attention is focused primarily on the division between rural and urban or agricultural and nonagricultural households.

The decomposable measure of income inequality that is used to analyze changes in inequality in the selections by Sherman Robinson (VIII.A.2) and by James Rauch (VIII.A.3) is the variance in the logarithm of income. Here we give the formula for the log variance using Robinson's notation. Let y_i equal the income of household or individual i and $Y_i = \ln(y_i)$. If there are n households or individuals in the country, the average of the logarithm of income or log mean is given by

$$Y = \sum_{i=1}^{n} Y_i/n$$

and the log variance is given by

$$\sigma^2 = \sum_{i=1}^{n} (Y_i - Y)^2/n$$

One reason for using the log variance rather than the variance is that it does not change when the units of measurement for income change, e.g., it is the same whether incomes are measured in dollars or cents. In Selection VIII.A.2 Robinson gives the decomposition formula for the log variance in the case of two groups. Another decomposable measure of income inequality is the Theil index, used by the World Bank in Selection VIII.C.1. The Theil index is given by

$$T = \sum_{i=1}^{n} s_i[\ln(s_i) - \ln(1/n)],$$

where s_i is the share of household or individual i in total national income. Note that if every household or individual has the same income, both the log variance and the Theil index equal zero. For a more thorough discussion of the advantages and disadvantages of various measures of inequality, see Foster (1985).

References

Fields, Gary S., and John C. H. Fei. 1978. "On Inequality Comparisons." *Econometrica* 46 (March): 303–16.

Foster, James. 1985. "Inequality Measurement." In Peyton Young, ed., *Fair Allocation* (Providence, R.I.: American Mathematical Society).

Exhibit VIII.1. Income Distribution and Inequality Measures

Country Name (listed from lowest to highest HDI)	Survey Year	Share of Income or Consumption[a] (Percent)						Inequality Measures		
		Poorest 10%	Poorest 20%	Middle 60%	Richest 20%	Richest 10%	Richest 10% to Poorest 10%[b]	Richest 20% to Poorest 20%[b]	Gini Index[c]
Low-human development countries[d]										
Sierra Leone	1989	0.5	1.1	35.5	63.4	43.6	87.2	57.6	62.9
Niger	1995	0.8	2.6	44.1	53.3	35.4	46.0	20.7	50.5
Burkina Faso	1998	1.8	4.5	34.8	60.7	46.3	26.2	13.6	48.2
Mali	1994	1.8	4.6	39.2	56.2	40.4	23.1	12.2	50.5
Burundi	1998	1.7	5.1	46.9	48.0	32.8	19.3	9.5	33.3
Mozambique	1996–97	2.5	6.5	47.0	46.5	31.7	12.5	7.2	39.6
Ethiopia	2000	0.7	2.4	36.8	60.8	43.8	59.7	24.8	48.6
Central African Republic	1993	0.7	2.0	33.0	65.0	47.7	69.2	32.7	61.3
Guinea-Bissau	1993	2.1	5.2	41.4	53.4	39.3	19.0	10.3	47.0
Zambia	1998	1.1	3.3	40.1	56.6	41.0	36.6	17.3	52.6
Malawi	1997	1.9	4.9	39.0	56.1	42.2	22.7	11.6	50.3
Côte d'Ivoire	1995	3.1	7.1	48.6	44.3	28.8	9.4	6.2	36.7
Tanzania, U. Rep. of	1993	2.8	6.8	47.7	45.5	30.1	10.8	6.7	38.2
Rwanda	1983–85	4.2	9.7	51.2	39.1	24.2	5.8	4.0	28.9
Guinea	1994	2.6	6.4	46.4	47.2	32.0	12.3	7.3	40.3
Senegal	1995	2.6	6.4	45.4	48.2	33.5	12.8	7.5	41.3
Mauritania	1995	2.5	6.4	49.5	44.1	28.4	11.2	6.9	37.3
Nigeria	1996–97	1.6	4.4	39.9	55.7	40.8	24.9	12.8	50.6
Gambia	1998	1.5	4.0	40.8	55.2	38.0	25.4	13.8	47.8
Madagascar	1999	2.5	6.4	48.8	44.8	28.6	11.4	7.0	46.0
Yemen	1998	3.0	7.4	51.4	41.2	25.9	8.6	5.6	33.4
Uganda	1996	3.0	7.1	48.0	44.9	29.8	9.9	6.4	37.4
Kenya	1997	2.3	5.6	43.2	51.2	36.1	15.6	9.1	44.5
Zimbabwe	1995	1.8	4.6	39.7	55.7	40.3	22.0	12.0	56.8
Pakistan	1998–99	3.7	8.8	48.9	42.3	28.3	7.6	4.8	33.0
Nepal	1995–96	3.2	7.6	47.6	44.8	29.8	9.3	5.9	36.7
Cameroon	1996	1.8	4.6	42.4	53.0	36.5	20.0	11.4	47.7
Median		*2.1*	*5.2*	*44.1*	*51.2*	*35.4*	*19.0*	*9.5*	*46.0*

Medium-human development countries[e]

Bangladesh	2000	3.9	9.0	49.7	41.3	26.7	6.8	4.6	31.8
Lesotho	1995	0.5	1.4	27.9	70.7	53.6	117.8	50.0	56.0
Lao People's Dem. Rep.	1997	3.2	7.6	47.4	45.0	30.6	9.7	6.0	37.0
Swaziland	1994[f]	1.0	2.7	32.9	64.4	50.2	49.7	23.8	60.9
Papua New Guinea	1996	1.7	4.5	39.0	56.5	40.5	23.8	12.6	50.9
Cambodia	1997	2.9	6.9	45.5	47.6	33.8	11.6	6.9	40.4
Ghana	1999	2.1	5.6	47.8	46.6	30.0	14.1	8.4	39.6
India	1997	3.5	8.1	45.8	46.1	33.5	9.5	5.7	37.8
Morocco	1998–99	2.6	6.5	46.9	46.6	30.9	11.7	7.2	39.5
Botswana	1993	0.7	2.2	27.5	70.3	56.6	77.6	31.5	63.0
Namibia	1993[f]	0.5	1.4	19.9	78.7	64.5	128.8	56.1	70.7
Nicaragua	1998	0.7	2.3	34.1	63.6	48.8	70.7	27.9	60.3
Egypt	1999	3.7	8.6	47.8	43.6	29.5	8.0	5.1	34.4
Guatemala	1998[f]	1.6	3.8	35.6	60.6	46.0	29.1	15.8	55.8
Mongolia	1998	2.1	5.6	43.2	51.2	37.0	17.8	9.1	44.0
Honduras	1998[f]	0.5	2.0	37.0	61.0	44.4	91.8	30.3	59.0
Bolivia	1999	1.3	4.0	46.9	49.1	32.0	24.6	12.3	44.7
Tajikistan	1998	3.2	8.0	52.0	40.0	25.2	8.0	5.0	34.7
Indonesia	2000	3.6	8.4	48.3	43.3	28.5	7.8	5.2	30.3
South Africa	1995	0.7	2.0	31.5	66.5	46.9	65.1	33.6	59.3
Viet Nam	1998	3.6	8.0	47.5	44.5	29.9	8.4	5.6	36.1
Moldova, Rep. of	2001	2.8	7.1	49.2	43.7	28.4	10.2	6.2	36.2
Algeria	1995	2.8	7.0	50.4	42.6	26.8	9.6	6.1	35.3
Iran, Islamic Rep. of	1998	2.0	5.1	45.0	49.9	33.7	17.2	9.7	43.0
El Salvador	1998[f]	1.2	3.3	40.3	56.4	39.4	33.6	17.3	50.8
China	1998[f]	2.4	5.9	47.5	46.6	30.4	12.7	8.0	40.3
Kyrgyzstan	2001	3.9	9.1	52.6	38.3	23.3	6.0	4.2	29.0
Uzbekistan	2000	3.6	9.2	54.5	36.3	22.0	6.1	4.0	26.8
Armenia	1998	2.6	6.7	48.2	45.1	29.7	11.5	6.8	37.9
Sri Lanka	1995	3.5	8.0	49.2	42.8	28.0	7.9	5.3	34.4
Ecuador	1995	2.2	5.4	44.9	49.7	33.8	15.4	9.2	43.7
Turkey	2000	2.3	6.1	47.2	46.7	30.7	13.3	7.7	40.0
Dominican Republic	1998[f]	2.1	5.1	41.6	53.3	37.9	17.7	10.5	47.4
Guyana	1999	1.3	4.5	45.8	49.7	33.8	25.9	11.1	44.6
Tunisia	1995	2.3	5.7	46.4	47.9	31.8	13.8	8.5	41.7
Jordan	1997	3.3	7.6	48.0	44.4	29.8	9.1	5.9	36.4
Azerbaijan	2001	3.1	7.4	48.1	44.5	29.5	9.7	6.0	36.5
Georgia	2000	2.2	6.0	48.8	45.2	29.3	13.4	7.6	38.9
Turkmenistan	1998	2.6	6.1	46.4	47.5	31.7	12.3	7.7	40.8

Exhibit VIII.1. (Continued)

Country Name (listed from lowest to highest HDI)	Survey Year	Share of Income or Consumption[a] (Percent)					Inequality Measures		
		Poorest 10%	Poorest 20%	Middle 60%	Richest 20%	Richest 10%	Richest 10% to Poorest 10%[b]	Richest 20% to Poorest 20%[b]	Gini Index[c]
Philippines	2000	2.2	5.4	42.3	52.3	36.3	16.5	9.7	46.1
Paraguay	1998[f]	0.5	1.9	37.4	60.7	43.8	91.1	31.8	57.7
Peru	1996[f]	1.6	4.4	44.4	51.2	35.4	22.3	11.7	46.2
Jamaica	2000	2.7	6.7	47.3	46.0	30.3	11.4	6.9	37.9
Kazakhstan	2001	3.4	8.2	52.2	39.6	24.2	7.1	4.8	31.2
Ukraine	1999	3.7	8.8	53.4	37.8	23.2	6.4	4.3	29.0
Thailand	2000	2.5	6.1	43.9	50.0	33.8	13.4	8.3	43.2
Romania	2000	3.3	8.2	53.4	38.4	23.6	7.2	4.7	30.3
Saint Lucia	1995[f]	2.0	5.2	46.5	48.3	32.5	16.2	9.2	42.6
Venezuela	1998[f]	0.6	3.0	43.6	53.4	36.3	62.9	17.9	49.1
Brazil	1998[f]	0.7	2.2	33.7	64.1	48.0	65.8	29.7	60.7
Colombia	1996[f]	1.1	3.0	36.1	60.9	46.1	42.7	20.3	57.1
Russian Federation	2000	1.8	4.9	43.8	51.3	36.0	20.3	10.5	45.6
Macedonia, TFYR	1998	3.3	8.4	54.9	36.7	22.1	6.8	4.4	28.2
Panama	1997	1.2	3.6	43.6	52.8	35.7	29.8	14.7	48.5
Malaysia	1997[f]	1.7	4.4	41.3	54.3	38.4	22.1	12.4	49.2
Bulgaria	2001[f]	2.4	6.7	54.4	38.9	23.7	9.9	5.8	31.9
Median		*2.3*	*5.8*	*46.4*	*47.8*	*32.3*	*13.6*	*8.4*	*41.3*
High-human development countries[g]									
Mexico	1998	1.2	3.4	39.0	57.6	41.6	34.6	17.0	51.9
Trinidad and Tobago	1992	2.1	5.5	48.6	45.9	29.9	14.4	8.3	40.3
Belarus	2000[h]	3.5	8.4	52.5	39.1	24.1	6.9	4.6	30.4
Latvia	1998	2.9	7.6	52.1	40.3	25.9	8.9	5.3	32.4
Croatia	2001[h]	3.4	8.3	52.1	39.6	24.5	7.3	4.8	29.0
Lithuania	2000[h]	3.2	7.9	52.1	40.0	24.9	7.9	5.1	36.3
Chile	1998	1.1	3.2	35.5	61.3	45.4	43.2	19.3	57.5
Costa Rica	1997	1.7	4.5	44.5	51.0	34.6	20.7	11.5	45.9
Estonia	1998	3.0	7.0	47.9	45.1	29.8	10.0	6.5	37.6
Uruguay	1998[i]	1.6	4.5	45.1	50.4	33.8	21.6	11.2	44.8
Slovakia	1996	3.1	8.8	56.4	34.8	20.9	6.7	4.0	25.8
Hungary	1998[h]	4.1	10.0	55.6	34.4	20.5	5.0	3.5	24.4
Poland	1998[h]	3.2	7.8	52.5	39.7	24.7	7.8	5.1	31.6

Czech Republic	1996	4.3	10.3	53.8	35.9	22.4	5.2	3.5	25.4
Korea, Rep. of	1998	2.9	7.9	54.6	37.5	22.5	7.8	4.7	31.6
Slovenia	1998	3.9	9.1	53.2	37.7	23.0	5.8	4.1	28.4
Singapore	1998	1.9	5.0	46.0	49.0	32.8	17.7	9.7	42.5
Hong Kong, China (SAR)	1996	2.0	5.3	44.0	50.7	34.9	17.8	9.7	43.4
Greece	1998	2.9	7.1	49.3	43.6	28.5	10.0	6.2	35.4
Portugal	1997	2.0	5.8	48.3	45.9	29.8	15.0	8.0	38.5
Israel	1997	2.4	6.9	48.8	44.3	28.2	11.7	6.4	35.5
Italy	1998	1.9	6.0	51.4	42.6	27.4	14.5	7.1	36.0
New Zealand	1997	2.2	6.4	49.8	43.8	27.8	12.5	6.8	36.2
Spain	1990	2.8	7.5	52.2	40.3	25.2	9.0	5.4	32.5
Germany	1998	2.0	5.7	49.6	44.7	28.0	14.2	7.9	38.2
France	1995	2.8	7.2	52.6	40.2	25.1	9.1	5.6	32.7
Austria	1995	2.3	7.0	55.1	37.9	22.4	9.8	5.5	30.5
Luxembourg	1998	3.2	8.0	52.3	39.7	24.7	7.7	4.9	30.8
Finland	1995	4.1	10.1	54.9	35.0	20.9	5.1	3.5	25.6
United Kingdom	1995	2.1	6.1	50.7	43.2	27.5	13.4	7.1	36.0
Ireland	1987	2.5	6.7	50.4	42.9	27.4	11.0	6.4	35.9
Denmark	1997	2.6	8.3	55.9	35.8	21.3	8.1	4.3	24.7
Switzerland	1992	2.6	6.9	52.8	40.3	25.2	9.9	5.8	33.1
Japan	1993	4.8	10.6	53.7	35.7	21.7	4.5	3.4	24.9
Canada	1997	2.7	7.3	53.4	39.3	23.9	9.0	5.4	31.5
United States	1997	1.8	5.2	48.4	46.4	30.5	16.6	9.0	40.8
Belgium	1996	2.9	8.3	54.4	37.3	22.6	7.8	4.5	25.0
Netherlands	1994	2.8	7.3	52.6	40.1	25.1	9.0	5.5	32.6
Australia	1994	2.0	5.9	52.8	41.3	25.4	12.5	7.0	35.2
Sweden	1995	3.4	9.1	56.4	34.5	20.1	5.9	3.8	25.0
Norway	1995	4.1	9.7	54.5	35.8	21.8	5.3	3.7	25.8
Median		*2.8*	*7.2*	*52.2*	*40.3*	*25.2*	*9.1*	*5.5*	*32.7*

United Nations Human Development Index countries are included in the Exhibit only if they have data available.

[a]The distribution of income is typically more unequal than the distribution of consumption. Data are for most recent year available between 1987 and 2001.

[b]Data show the ratio of the income or consumption share of the richest group to that of the poorest group.

[c]The Gini index measures inequality over the entire distribution of income or consumption. A value of 0 represents perfect equality, while a value of 100 represents perfect inequality.

[d]Low-human development country surveys are based on consumption, unless otherwise noted.

[e]Medium-human development country surveys are based on consumption, unless otherwise noted.

[f]Survey based on income.

[g]High-human development country surveys are based on income, unless otherwise noted.

[h]Survey based on consumption.

[i]Data refer to urban areas only.

Note: Because the underlying household surveys differ in method and in the type of data collected, the distribution data are not strictly comparable across countries.

Sources: United Nations Development Program, *Human Development Report 2003* (New York: Oxford University Press, 2003). World Bank, World Development Indicators, 2003.

VIII.A. THE IMPACT OF DEVELOPMENT ON INCOME DISTRIBUTION

Selection VIII.A.1. Economic Growth and Income Inequality*

The central theme of this paper is the character and causes of long-term changes in the personal distribution of income. Does inequality in the distribution of income increase or decrease in the course of a country's economic growth? What factors determine the secular level and trends of income inequalities?

These are broad questions in a field of study that has been plagued by looseness in definitions, unusual scarcity of data, and pressures of strongly held opinions. While we cannot completely avoid the resulting difficulties, it may help to specify the characteristics of the size-of-income distributions that we want to examine and the movements of which we want to explain.

Five specifications may be listed. First, the units for which incomes are recorded and grouped should be family-expenditure units, properly adjusted for the number of persons in each—rather than income recipients for whom the relations between receipt and use of income can be widely diverse. Second, the distribution should be complete, i.e., should cover all units in a country rather than a segment either at the upper or lower tail. Third, if possible we should segregate the units whose main income earners are either still in the learning or already in the retired stages of their life cycle—to avoid complicating the picture by including incomes *not* associated with full-time, full-fledged participation in economic activity. Fourth, income should be defined as it is now for national income in this country, i.e., received by individuals, including income in kind, before and after direct taxes, excluding capital gains. Fifth, the units should be grouped by *secular* levels of income, free of cyclical and other transient disturbances.

For such a distribution of mature expenditure units by secular levels of income per capita, we should measure shares of some fixed ordinal groups—percentiles, deciles, quintiles, etc. In the underlying array the units should be classified by average income levels for a sufficiently long span so that they form income-status groups—say a generation or about 25 years. Within such a period, even when classified by secular income levels, units may shift from one ordinal group to an-

other. It would, therefore, be necessary and useful to study separately the relative share of units that, throughout the generation period of reference, were continuously within a specific ordinal group, and the share of the units that moved into that specific group; and this should be done for the shares of "residents" and "migrants" within all ordinal groups. Without such a long period of reference and the resulting separation between "resident" and "migrant" units at different relative income levels, the very distinction between "low" and "high" income classes loses its meaning, particularly in a study of long-term changes in shares and in inequalities in the distribution. To say, for example, that the "lower" income classes gained or lost during the last twenty years in that their share of total income increased or decreased has meaning only if the units have been classified as members of the "lower" classes throughout those 20 years—and for those who have moved into or out of those classes recently such a statement has no significance. . . .

I. Trends in Income Inequality

Forewarned of the difficulties, we turn now to the available data. These data, even when relating to complete populations, invariably classify units by income for a given year. From our standpoint, this is their major limitation. Because the data often do not permit many size-groupings, and because the difference between annual income incidence and longer-term income status has less effect if the number of classes is small and the limits of each class are wide, we use a few wide classes. This does not resolve the difficulty; and there are others due to the scantiness of data for long periods, inadequacy of the unit used—which is, at best, a family and very often a reporting unit—errors in the data, and so on through a long list. Consequently, the trends in the income structure can be discerned but dimly, and the results considered as preliminary informed guesses.

The data are for the United States, England, and Germany—a scant sample, but at least a starting point for some inferences concerning long-term changes in the presently developed countries. The general conclusion suggested is that the relative distribution of income, as measured by annual income incidence in rather broad classes, has been moving toward equality—with these trends partic-

*From Simon Kuznets, "Economic Growth and Income Inequality," *American Economic Review* 45 (March 1955): 1–8, 16–19. Reprinted by permission.

ularly noticeable since the 1920's but beginning perhaps in the period before the first world war.

Let me cite some figures, all for income before direct taxes, in support of this impression. In the United States, in the distribution of income among families (excluding single individuals), the shares of the two lowest quintiles rise from 13 1/2 per cent in 1929 to 18 per cent in the years after the second world war (average of 1944, 1946, 1947, and 1950); whereas the share of the top quintile declines from 55 to 44 per cent, and that of the top 5 per cent from 31 to 20 per cent. In the United Kingdom, the share of the top 5 per cent of units declines from 46 per cent in 1880 to 43 per cent in 1910 or 1913, to 33 per cent in 1929, to 31 per cent in 1938, and to 24 per cent in 1947; the share of the lower 85 per cent remains fairly constant between 1880 and 1913, between 41 and 43 per cent, but then rises to 46 per cent in 1929 and 55 per cent in 1947. In Prussia income inequality increases slightly between 1875 and 1913—the shares of the top quintile rising from 48 to 50 per cent, of the top 5 per cent from 26 to 30 per cent; the share of the lower 60 per cent, however, remains about the same. In Saxony, the change between 1880 and 1913 is minor: the share of the two lowest quintiles declines from 15 to 14 1/2 per cent; that of the third quintile rises from 12 to 13 per cent, of the fourth quintile from 16 1/2 to about 18 per cent; that of the top quintile declines from 56 1/2 to 54 1/2 per cent, and of the top 5 per cent from 34 to 33 per cent. In Germany as a whole, relative income inequality drops fairly sharply from 1913 to the 1920's, apparently due to decimation of large fortunes and property incomes during the war and inflation; but then begins to return to prewar levels during the depression of the 1930's.[1]

Even for what they are assumed to represent, let alone as approximations to shares in distributions by secular income levels, the data are such that differences of two or three percentage points cannot be assigned significance. One must judge by the general weight and consensus of the evidence—which unfortunately is limited to a few countries. It justifies a tentative impression of constancy in the relative distribution of income before taxes, followed by some narrowing of relative income inequality after the first world war—or earlier.

Three aspects of this finding should be stressed. First, the data are for income before direct taxes and exclude contributions by government (e.g., relief and free assistance). It is fair to argue that both the proportion and progressivity of direct taxes and the proportion of total income of individuals accounted for by government assistance to the less privileged economic groups have grown during recent decades. This is certainly true of the United States and the United Kingdom, but in the case of Germany is subject to further examination. It follows that the distribution of income after direct taxes and including free contributions by government would show an even greater narrowing of inequality in developed countries with size distributions of pretax, ex-government-benefits income similar to those for the United States and the United Kingdom.

Second, such stability or reduction in the inequality of the percentage shares was accompanied by significant rises in real income per capita. The countries now classified as developed have enjoyed rising per capita incomes except during catastrophic periods such as years of active world conflict. Hence, if the shares of groups classified by their annual income position can be viewed as approximations to shares of groups classified by their secular income levels, a constant percentage share of a given group means that its per capita real income is rising at the same rate as the average for all units in the country; and a reduction in inequality of the shares means that the per capita income of the lower-income groups is rising at a more rapid rate than the per capita income of the upper-income groups.

The third point can be put in the form of a question. Do the distributions by annual incomes properly reflect trends in distribution by secular incomes? As technology and economic performance

---

[1] The following sources were used in calculating the figures cited:

United States. For recent years we used *Income Distribution by Size, 1944–1950* (Washington, 1953) and Selma Goldsmith and others, "Size Distribution of Income Since the Mid-Thirties," *Rev. Econ. Stat.*, Feb. 1954, XXXVI, 1–32; for 1929, the Brookings Institution data as adjusted in Simon Kuznets, *Shares of Upper Groups in Income and Savings* (New York, 1953), p. 220.

United Kingdom. For 1938 and 1947, Dudley Seers, The *Levelling of Income Since 1938* (Oxford, 1951) p. 39; for 1929, Colin Clark, *National Income and Outlay* (London, 1937) Table 47, p. 109; for 1880, 1910, and 1913, A. Bowley, *The Change in the Distribution of the National Income, 1880–1913* (Oxford, 1920).

Germany. For the constituent areas (Prussia, Saxony and others) for years before the first world war, based on S. Prokopovich, *National Income of Western European Countries*

(published in Moscow in the 1920's). Some summary results are given in Prokopovich, "The Distribution of National Income," *Econ. Jour.*, March 1926, XXXVI, 69–82. See also, "Das Deutsche Volkseinkommen vor und nach dem Kriege," *Einzelschrift zur Stat. des Deutschen Reichs*, no. 24 (Berlin, 1932), and W. S. and E. S. Woytinsky, *World Population and Production* (New York, 1953) Table 192, p. 709.

rise to higher levels, incomes are less subject to transient disturbances, not necessarily of the cyclical order that can be recognized and allowed for by reference to business cycle chronology, but of a more irregular type. If in the earlier years the economic fortunes of units were subject to greater vicissitudes—poor crops for some farmers, natural calamity losses for some nonfarm business units—if the over-all proportion of individual entrepreneurs whose incomes were subject to such calamities, more yesterday but some even today, was larger in earlier decades, these earlier distributions of income would be more affected by transient disturbances. In these earlier distributions the temporarily unfortunate might crowd the lower quintiles and depress their shares unduly, and the temporarily fortunate might dominate the top quintile and raise its share unduly—proportionately more than in the distributions for later years. If so, distributions by longer-term average incomes might show less reduction in inequality than do the distributions by annual incomes; they might even show an opposite trend.

One may doubt whether this qualification would upset a narrowing of inequality as marked as that for the United States, and in as short a period as twenty-five years. Nor is it likely to affect the persistent downward drift in the spread of the distributions in the United Kingdom. But I must admit a strong element of judgment in deciding how far this qualification modifies the finding of long-term stability followed by reduction in income inequality in the few developed countries for which it is observed or is likely to be revealed by existing data. The important point is that the qualification is relevant; it suggests need for further study if we are to learn much from the available data concerning the secular income structure; and such study is likely to yield results of interest in themselves in their bearing upon the problem of trends in temporal instability of income flows to individual units or to economically significant groups of units in different sectors of the national economy. . . .

II. An Attempt at Explanation

. . . An invariable accompaniment of growth in developed countries is the shift away from agriculture, a process usually referred to as industrialization and urbanization. The income distribution of the total population, in the simplest model, may therefore be viewed as a combination of the income distributions of the rural and of the urban populations. What little we know of the structures

of these two component income distributions reveals that: (a) the average per capita income of the rural population is usually lower than that of the urban; (b) inequality in the percentage shares within the distribution for the rural population is somewhat narrower than in that for the urban population—even when based on annual income; and this difference would probably be wider for distributions by secular income levels. Operating with this simple model, what conclusions do we reach? First, all other conditions being equal, the increasing weight of urban population means an increasing share for the more unequal of the two component distributions. Second, the relative difference in per capita income between the rural and urban populations does not necessarily drift downward in the process of economic growth: indeed, there is some evidence to suggest that it is stable at best, and tends to widen because per capita productivity in urban pursuits increases more rapidly than in agriculture. If this is so, inequality in the total income distribution should increase. . . .

We deal with two sectors: agriculture (A) and all others (B). . . . It seems most plausible to assume that in earlier periods of industrialization, even when the nonagricultural population was still relatively small in the total, its income distribution was more unequal than that of the agricultural population. This would be particularly so during the periods when industrialization and urbanization were proceeding apace and the urban population was being swelled, and fairly rapidly, by immigrants—either from the country's agricultural areas or from abroad. Under these conditions, the urban population would run the full gamut from low-income positions of recent entrants to the economic peaks of the established top-income groups. The urban income inequalities might be assumed to be far wider than those for the agricultural population which was organized in relatively small individual enterprises (large-scale units were rarer then than now).

If we grant the assumption of wider inequality of distribution in sector B, the shares of the lower-income brackets should have shown a downward trend. Yet the earlier summary of empirical evidence indicates that during the last 50 to 75 years there has been no widening in income inequality in the developed countries but, on the contrary, some narrowing within the last two to four decades. It follows that the intrasector distribution—either for sector A or for sector B—must have shown sufficient narrowing of inequality to offset the increase called for by the factors discussed.

This narrowing in inequality, the offsetting rise in the shares of the lower brackets, most likely occurred in the income distribution for the urban groups, in sector B. While it may also have been present in sector A, it would have had a more limited effect on the inequality in the countrywide income distribution because of the rapidly diminishing weight of sector A in the total. Nor was such a narrowing of income inequality in agriculture likely: with industrialization, a higher level of technology permitted larger-scale units and, in the United States for example, sharpened the contrast between the large and successful business farmers and the subsistence sharecroppers of the South. Furthermore, since we accept the assumption of *initially* narrower inequality in the internal distribution of income in sector A than in sector B, any significant reduction in inequality in the former is less likely than in the latter.

Hence we may conclude that the major offset to the widening of income inequality associated with the shift from agriculture and the countryside to industry and the city must have been a rise in the income share of the lower groups within the nonagricultural sector of the population. This provides a lead for exploration in what seems to me a most promising direction: consideration of the pace and character of the economic growth of the urban population, with particular reference to the relative position of lower-income groups. Much is to be said for the notion that once the early turbulent phases of industrialization and urbanization had passed, a variety of forces converged to bolster the economic position of the lower-income groups within the urban population. The very fact that after a while, an increasing proportion of the urban population was "native," i.e., born in cities rather than in the rural areas, and hence more able to take advantage of the possibilities of city life in preparation for the economic struggle, meant a better chance for organization and adaptation, a better basis for securing greater income shares than was possible for the newly "immigrant" population coming from the countryside or from abroad. The increasing efficiency of the older, established urban population should also be taken into account. Furthermore, in democratic societies the growing political power of the urban lower-income groups led to a variety of protective and supporting legislation, much of it aimed to counteract the worst effects of rapid industrialization and urbanization and to support the claims of the broad masses for more adequate shares of the growing income of the country. Space does not permit the discussion of demographic, political, and social considerations that could be brought to bear to explain the offsets to any declines in the shares of the lower groups, declines otherwise deducible from the trends suggested in the numerical illustration.

III. Other Trends Related to Those in Income Inequality

One aspect of the conjectural conclusion just reached deserves emphasis because of its possible interrelation with other important elements in the process and theory of economic growth. The scanty empirical evidence suggests that the narrowing of income inequality in the developed countries is relatively recent and probably did not characterize the earlier stages of their growth. Likewise, the various factors that have been suggested above would explain stability and narrowing in income inequality in the later rather than in the earlier phases of industrialization and urbanization. Indeed, they would suggest widening inequality in these early phases of economic growth, especially in the older countries where the emergence of the new industrial system had shattering effects on long-established pre-industrial economic and social institutions. This timing characteristic is particularly applicable to factors bearing upon the lower-income groups: the dislocating effects of the agricultural and industrial revolutions, combined with the "swarming" of population incident upon a rapid decline in death rates and the maintenance or even rise of birth rates, would be unfavorable to the relative economic position of lower-income groups. Furthermore, there may also have been a preponderance in the earlier periods of factors favoring maintenance or increase in the shares of top-income groups: in so far as their position was bolstered by gains arising out of new industries, by an unusually rapid rate of creation of new fortunes, we would expect these forces to be relatively stronger in the early phases of industrialization than in the later when the pace of industrial growth slackens.

One might thus assume a long swing in the inequality characterizing the secular income structure: widening in the early phases of economic growth when the transition from the pre-industrial to the industrial civilization was most rapid; becoming stabilized for a while; and then narrowing in the later phases. This long secular swing would be most pronounced for older countries where the dislocation effects of the earlier phases of modern economic growth were most conspicuous; but it might be found also in the "younger" countries like the United States, if the period preceding marked industrialization could be compared with the early phases of industrialization, and if the latter could be compared with the subsequent phases of greater maturity.

If there is some evidence for assuming this long swing in relative inequality in the distribution of income before direct taxes and excluding free benefits from government, there is surely a stronger case for assuming a long swing in inequality of income net of direct taxes and including government benefits. Progressivity of income taxes and, indeed, their very importance characterize only the more recent phases of development of the presently developed countries; in narrowing income inequality they must have accentuated the downward phase of the long swing, contributing to the reversal of trend in the secular widening and narrowing of income inequality.

No adequate empirical evidence is available for checking this conjecture of a long secular swing in income inequality;[2] nor can the phases be dated precisely. However, to make it more specific, I would place the early phase in which income inequality might have been widening, from about 1780 to 1850 in England; from about 1840 to 1890, and particularly from 1870 on in the United States; and, from the 1840's to the 1890's in Germany. I would put the phase of narrowing income inequality somewhat later in the United States and Germany than in England—perhaps beginning with the first world war in the former and in the last quarter of the 19th century in the latter.

[2]Prokopovich's data on Prussia, from the source cited in footnote 1, indicate a substantial widening in income inequality in the early period. The share of the lower 90 per cent of the population declines from 73 per cent in 1854 to 65 per cent in 1875; the share of the top 5 per cent rises from 21 to 25 per cent. But I do not know enough about the data for the early years to evaluate the reliability of the finding.

Selection VIII.A.2. A Note on the U Hypothesis Relating Income Inequality and Economic Development*

The purpose of this note is to demonstrate that the U hypothesis can be derived from a very simple model with a minimum of economic assumptions. One need only assume that the economy can be divided into two sectors with different sectoral income distributions and that there is a monotonic increase in the relative population of one of the sectors over time. . . .

Assume that the economy is divided into two sectors with different income distributions. The *log* mean and *log* variance of income in the two sectors are given by Y_1 and Y_2 and σ_1^2 and σ_2^2, respectively. Define the population shares of the two sectors as W_1 and W_2 with:

$$W_1 + W_2 = 1 \qquad (1)$$

The overall *log* mean income is given by:

$$Y = W_1 Y_1 + W_2 Y_2 \qquad (2)$$

and the overall *log* variance is given by:

$$\sigma^2 = W_1 \sigma_1^2 + W_2 \sigma_2^2 + W_1 (Y_1 - Y)^2$$
$$+ W_2 (Y_2 - Y)^2 \qquad (3)$$

The *log* variance is itself an increasing measure of income inequality. One need not use *log* means and *log* variances, but they are convenient since the *log* variance is a commonly used inequality measure. The arithmetic mean and variance would also do—the algebra is exactly the same.

Assuming that the within-sector distributions remain unchanged over time (σ_1^2, σ_2^2, Y_1, and Y_2 are constant), then from equation (3) inequality is a function only of sectoral population shares and overall *log* mean income. By equation (2), the overall *log* mean is itself a function of sectoral population shares.

*From Sherman Robinson, "A Note on the U Hypothesis Relating Income Inequality and Economic Development," *American Economic Review* 66 (June 1976): 437–438. Reprinted by permission.

Assume that sector 1 is the sector whose relative population share is increasing. Then, substituting (1) and (2) into (3) and doing a bit of algebra, one finally gets:

$$\sigma^2 = A W_1^2 + B W_1 + C \qquad (4)$$

where
$$A = -(Y_1 - Y_2)^2$$
$$B = (\sigma_1^2 - \sigma_2^2) + (Y_1 - Y_2)^2$$
$$C = \sigma_2^2$$

If one assumes that the *log* mean incomes are different in the two sectors, then inequality is a quadratic function of W_1. Since $A < 0$, the parabola has a maximum. As W_1 increases, inequality first increases, reaches a maximum, then decreases—precisely the U hypothesis.

There is one possible problem. Since by assumption $0 \leq W_1 \leq 1$, it is possible that the maximum value of σ^2 occurs for a value of W_1 outside the zero to one range. Setting the first derivative of (4) equal to zero, the maximum value of σ^2 occurs when W_1 is equal to $\hat{W}_1$:

$$\hat{W}_1 = \frac{\sigma_1^2 - \sigma_2^2}{2 \cdot (Y_1 - Y_2)^2} + 1/2 \qquad (5)$$

Thus, the more equal are the *log* variances, and the more different are the *log* mean incomes, the closer is $\hat{W}_1$ to 1/2. . . .

Some properties of these equations are interesting. The U hypothesis in no way depends on which sector has the higher income. If total income is to rise then Y_1 must be greater than Y_2, but the U hypothesis depends only on their being different. It also does not matter which sector has the more unequal distribution of within sector income. The difference between σ_1^2 and σ_2^2 affects $\hat{W}_1$, but not the existence of the U. If $\sigma_1^2 > \sigma_2^2$, then it will take longer for the distribution to start becoming more equal (for a given rate of change of sector population shares), but the turning point exists. It is interesting that even if people are moved from a sector with relatively more equality to one with less, the overall distribution will still become more equal.

Selection VIII.A.3. Economic Development, Urban Underemployment, and Income Inequality*

1. Introduction

Economic development invariably involves a transfer of labour from the agricultural to the non-agricultural sector, a process that for the purposes of this paper will be identified with urbanization. This transfer appears to take place monotonically over time. A check of the share of economically active population engaged in agriculture as reported in the Food and Agriculture Organization *Production Yearbook* showed a decline in every year for which data were available for all except one (Ireland) of 121 countries checked.[1] Kuznets (1955) saw this labour transfer as having important consequences for the size distribution of income over time. He hypothesized that income inequality will increase during the early stages of development as population shifts from the agricultural sector, where he believed incomes are more equally distributed, to the urban sector, where he believed incomes are less equally distributed. During the later stages of development this force for inequality is more than offset, he supposed, by growing equality of income distribution *within* the urban sector, owing to better adaptation of the children of rural-urban migrants to city economic life and growing political power of urban lower-income groups to effect "protective and supportive legislation" (17). A graph of income inequality against the urbanization rate or per capita income would therefore have the shape of an inverted U.

An important innovation in the formulation of Kuznets's hypothesis was made by Robinson (1976), who showed that, under the assumption of a constant difference between mean incomes in the rural and urban sectors, the inverted-U result required neither that urban income be more unequally distributed than rural income nor that urban income inequality decline as the urban share of the population increased. Specifically he showed that, if the within sector income distributions remain constant, then overall inequality as measured

by the variance of the logarithms of income is a quadratic function of the share of the population in the urban sector, and it achieves its maximum (under reasonable empirical assumptions) for a share between zero and one. The same result was established by Knight (1976) and independently by Fields (1979) for the Gini coefficient for the case where the difference in incomes between the two sectors is the *only* source of inequality.[2]

Their results led both Knight and Fields to question the importance of the inverted-U path of income inequality. Knight asks, "Should we be concerned about an increase in measured inequality [during the upswing of the inverted U] if it simply reflects a relative transfer of people from low- to high-income groups or sectors? No-one is made worse off—total income is allowed to increase—and some of the poor are made better off" (172–3). Before we accept the process described in the quotation as pertaining to real-world economic development, however, we must look more deeply into the situation described by Robinson, Knight, and Fields (hereafter called RKF).

The RKF assumptions are based on the numerous studies of LDCs (see, e.g., Tidrick 1975) that have shown that wages for comparably skilled labour tend to be higher in "formal" urban jobs than in rural jobs by a margin that is too large to be attributed to measurement error (such as failure to correct for lower cost of living in rural areas). These studies formed the basis for new models of LDC labour markets, beginning with Todaro (1969) and Harris and Todaro (1970), that themselves are absent from the RKF framework. Like the RKF economy, the Harris–Todaro economy consists of two sectors, which they label agriculture and urban manufacturing. Harris and Todaro argued that the wage in the urban manufacturing sector is set above the competitive equilibrium wage by institutional forces, which may in practice include trade unions, governments (e.g., through

*From James E. Rauch, "Economic Development, Urban Underemployment, and Income Inequality," *Canadian Journal of Economics* 26 (November 1993): 901–904, 912–915. Reprinted by permission.

[1] I am referring to data for the years 1960, 1970, and 1975–84. In 1985 the FAO appears to have revised its definitions, since many countries show a dramatic increase in the agricultural share of the economically active population. The 121 countries are the market economies covered in the study of Summers and Heston (1988).

[2] Since reliable time series on income inequality spanning several decades exist for extremely few countries, the Kuznets hypothesis has been empirically tested using cross-country data on the assumption that cross-country and intertemporal "Kuznets curves" are identical. In the most recent study of which I am aware, Papanek and Kyn (1986) find a statistically significant quadratic relationship between the Gini coefficient measure of income inequality and the log of per capita GNP using 145 observations for eighty-three countries. Inclusion of other economic, social, and regional explanatory variables did not weaken this relationship.

minimum wage legislation enforced only in urban areas), or both acting together. The key insight of Todaro (1969), used again in a different form in Harris and Todaro (1970), is that unlike the situation in the RKF economy, the equilibrium involving the minimum urban wage is *not* one where there is full employment, with all urban manufacturing jobs filled, and the remainder of the labour force employed in agriculture at a wage lower than the original competitive equilibrium wage. Instead, this equilibrium involves an excess supply of workers in the urban sector, with the resulting unemployment or underemployment acting to equate *expected utility* between the rural and urban sectors. It is this equation that allows labour market equilibrium to exist in the presence of rural-urban wage differentials.

Surprisingly, the way this equation is formulated in Harris and Todaro (1970) and in most of the subsequent theoretical work based on their paper implies that, in effect, there is *no* wage inequality within the urban sector or between the urban and rural sectors. It is assumed that in equilibrium the rural wage is equated to the expected urban wage, where the latter equals the urban minimum wage times the ratio of urban employment to the total urban labour force. This assumption can be justified by the following characterization of the urban labour market. Suppose we interpret the static Harris–Todaro equilibrium as a steady state persisting indefinitely in time. Suppose further that the labour market reopens in every period, at the beginning of which workers are drawn at random from the total urban labour pool for the given number of urban manufacturing jobs. Workers not drawn are unemployed during that period. If the draws are independent, then by the Law of Large Numbers, workers are certain to earn on average the expected wage described above, which should therefore be equal to the certain rural wage in equilibrium. Obviously there is no inequality in *lifetime* wage income in this model.

More recent research into the nature of LDC labour markets has shown that upon arriving in the city some rural migrants immediately obtain jobs in the protected labour market, while others wind up in what has become known as the "informal sector," meaning small businesses and self-employment that escape government and union intervention. The latter group earns less than comparably skilled workers in the former group (Banerjee 1983). While there is some mobility over time from the informal to the formal (protected) sector, most informal sector workers view their situations as permanent (Sethuraman 1981). This more recent research suggests that it is the risk of long-term underemployment in the informal sector that equates expected utility between the urban and rural sectors and thus allows for labour market equilibrium. The risk is substantial, since according to the studies surveyed by Sethuraman (appendix table 4, 213), the share of the urban labour force in LDC cities engaged in the informal sector ranges from 19 to 69 per cent, with a mean of roughly 41 per cent. If we modify the Harris–Todaro model in this way, we wind up with three classes of wage earners: rural (agricultural) workers, urban formal-sector workers, and urban informal-sector workers. I will thus address the evolution of income inequality by examining how the relative sizes and incomes of these three groups change during the course of economic development.

It turns out that the log variance measure of inequality in this economy tends to follow an inverted U. It rises when urbanization is low and consequent pressure on the land keeps rural incomes low, making agents willing to incur high risks of underemployment in the urban informal sector. It eventually falls after urbanization, and consequently rural incomes, has increased sufficiently to allow agents to make better than even bets in the industrial sector. This inverted U in inequality is associated with another inverted U in the share of the informal sector in the total labour force, the upswing of which is driven by the "Todaro paradox" that an increase in the number of urban manufacturing jobs may *increase* rather than decrease underemployment. . . .

2. Empirical Investigation of the Model: A Beginning

Is there evidence for my view of the causes of inverted-U behaviour of income inequality? We need incomes data reported by agricultural, urban formal, and urban informal sectors for a number of countries and years. Unfortunately, incomes data disaggregated by formal versus informal sector have typically been collected as part of one-time surveys of particular urban areas rather than as part of ongoing nationwide censuses. Moreover, the definitions of the informal sector tend to vary from survey to survey. While it therefore appears that the accuracy of our model's description of inequality behaviour cannot be assessed empirically at the present time, the model makes other predictions that are necessary though not sufficient for this description to be accurate. If they are supported by the stylized facts, I can at least claim that further investigation of my inequality results as better data become available is a promising direction for future research.

Underlying my inequality results are results on labour market behaviour. In particular, two predictions concerning the behaviour of the informal sector that can be checked against data emerge from the analysis. First, the informal sector share of the urban labour force $(1 - N_a - N_m)/(1 - N_a)$ should decrease with the level of urbanization. . . . Second, the informal sector share of the total labour force or underemployment rate $1 - N_a - N_m$ should follow an inverted U with urbanization. To facilitate the following empirical discussion of these predictions, I denote by URB and UNDER the variables used to measure $1 - N_a$ and $1 - N_a - N_m$, respectively. The ratio $(1 - N_a - N_m)/(1 - N_a)$ is measured by UNDER/URB, which is given the mnemonic SHARE.

Unlike the incomes data we would like, there do exist data on UNDER and URB (and therefore SHARE) that were collected for many countries on a nationwide basis using standardized definitions. This apparently unique data set was collected by PREALC (1982) under the direction of Victor E. Tokman, a leading scholar of the informal sector. It is based on the decennial censuses taken by almost every Latin American country. The variables of interest to us are defined as follows. URB is the non-primary share of the economically active population. It is further disaggregated into the classifications formal, informal, and wage-earning domestic service. Workers are classified as informal if they are either self-employed or unpaid family help, excluding professionals and technicians. This definition of UNDER is more restrictive than we would like, since it excludes the many wage earners in firms small enough to be bypassed by unions and government regulation.[3] We simply have to assume that the ratio of those omitted from UNDER to those included does not vary in any systematic way with URB.

The PREALC data cover seventeen Latin American countries[4] for the years 1950, 1960, 1970, and 1980. Perhaps more troubling than the obvious limitation resulting from inclusion in our sample of only one region of the globe is the fact that all the countries covered are classified by the World Bank

Table 1

Variable	Mean	Std dev.	Minimum	Maximum
URB	50.9	16.6	18.9	84.4
UNDER	11.3	3.4	4.5	20.4
SHARE	23.8	8.4	10.9	44.0

Note: All variables are expressed as percentages.

as either "lower-middle income" or "upper-middle income": no countries classified as low income or high income are included. Presumably this truncation of the sample at the low and high ends decreases the likelihood of finding an inverted U in UNDER. Nevertheless, table 1 shows that there is substantial variation in the data. The reader may also note from table 1 that the mean of SHARE is substantially below the figure of roughly 41 per cent (cited in the introduction to this paper) computed from the surveys of LDC cities listed by Sethuraman (1981). This result can be partly explained by the undercounting of the informal sector mentioned above, since the survey definitions, though not standardized, were typically more inclusive than the PREALC definition. Moreover, if my hypothesis concerning the decline of SHARE with URB is correct, the difference may also be explained by the inclusion of observations for several low-income countries (accounting for seven out of thirty-two observations, with a mean SHARE of 48 per cent) in the Sethuraman sample.

As in all studies that have checked for the existence of an inverted U in income distribution data (see the extensive references in Papanek and Kyn 1986), I shall seek to establish the stylized facts by applying ordinary least squares regressions to pooled data, a procedure that may be less troubling when one is working with a relatively homogeneous sample of countries such as Latin America. Table 2 shows that both predictions of my model concerning labour market behaviour are strongly supported by the PREALC data. Particularly impressive is the performance of the quadratic specification of the dependence of the underemployment rate on urbanization compared with the naïve linear specification that assumes that the urban informal sector expands pari passu with the rest of the urban sector.[5] The quadratic results imply that the peak of the inverted U in the underemployment rate occurs when 61.0 per cent of the labour force has left the primary sector. If these results are rep-

---

[3]Two studies of Latin American cities cited in Portes et al. (1989, 17, 97) expand the definition of the urban informal sector to include wage workers without social security protection. This change causes a shift from the formal to the informal sector of 3.1 per cent of the urban labour force in Montevideo in 1983 and 11.8 per cent in Bogotá in 1984.

[4]The countries included are Argentina, Bolivia, Brazil, Chile, Colombia, Costa Rica, Dominican Republic, Ecuador, El Salvador, Guatemala, Honduras, Mexico, Nicaragua, Panama, Peru, Uruguay, and Venezuela.

[5]Including $(URB)^2$ in the SHARE equation leads to statistically insignificant coefficients on both explanatory variables and a lower adjusted R^2.

Table 2

Variable	Dependent variable: SHARE	Dependent variable: UNDER	
	Coefficient (*t*-value)	Coefficient (*t*-value)	Coefficient (*t*-value)
CONSTANT	38.9	8.2	−3.0
	(14.5)	(6.3)	(0.8)
URB	−0.30	0.061	0.52
	(5.93)	(2.52)	(3.51)
			−0.0043
(URB)^2			(3.13)
R^2	0.35	0.09	0.21
$\hat{\sigma}$	6.8	3.3	3.1

Note: Number of observations = 68.

resentative of labour market behaviour in the world as a whole, they hold out considerable promise for future empirical support of my model's predictions concerning the source of inverted-U behaviour of income inequality.

3. Conclusions: Interpreting Inverted-U Behaviour of Income Inequality

For reasons noted in the introduction to this paper, Fields (1987) proposes that for the purpose of measuring change in income inequality during the course of economic development we discard the traditional indices in favour of ones that do not have the inverted-U property under the hypothetical conditions of pure "modern-sector enlargement" (expansion of the urban sector in the presence of a fixed rural-urban income differential). Moore (1990) argues against Fields's proposal. The present paper suggests that both sides of this debate may be misguided because they are using an incomplete economic model where there is no equilibrium condition that determines the intersectoral allocation of the labour force. In the complete model, the rise and fall of income inequality as measured by the log variance are closely related to the rise and fall of the proportion of the labour force that falls into the poorest class, the underemployed. Far from being an unimportant artifact of traditional inequality indices, then, the inverted U reflects the rise and fall of urban slums and of the share of the population with disappointed expectations, which are phenomena of political as well as economic significance.

Perhaps surprisingly, the model can be seen as a complement to the human-capital-based explanation of income inequality associated with the Uni-

versity of Chicago. According to this school of thought, exemplified by the work of Becker and Tomes (1979), inequality among identically endowed individuals is generated over time by differences in "market luck," which parents can pass on to their children by investing in the children's human capital. Market luck is exactly the source of inequality in the model: the lucky wind up in the formal sector, while the unlucky wind up in the informal sector. Over time, market luck first becomes more important, as the movement from an agrarian to an industrial society opens up more opportunities for both success and failure, and later becomes less important, simply because rising incomes in the agricultural sector provide a "safety net" that allows everyone to make much safer bets in the industrial sector. From this point of view, then, market luck is the driving force behind the inverted U, and the advantage of the model over the human capital model of income inequality is its ability to endogenize market luck. Its disadvantage is its inability to incorporate "inheritance" of market luck through parental investment in children. Overcoming this disadvantage should be a subject for future research.

References

Banerjee, Biswajit (1983) "The role of the informal sector in the migration process: a test of probabilistic migration models and labour market segmentation for India." *Oxford Economic Papers* 35, 399–422

Becker, Gary S., and Nigel Tomes (1979) "An equilibrium theory of the distribution of income and intergenerational mobility." *Journal of Political Economy* 87, 1153–89

Fields, Gary S. (1979) "A welfare economic approach to growth and distribution in the dual economy." *Quarterly Journal of Economics* 93, 325–53

——— (1987) "Measuring inequality change in an economy with income growth." *Journal of Development Economics* 26, 357–74

Harris, John R., and Michael P. Todaro (1970) "Migration, unemployment, and development: a two-sector analysis." *American Economic Review* 60, 126–42

Knight, John B. (1976) "Explaining income distribution in less developed countries: a framework and an agenda." *Oxford Bulletin of Economics and Statistics* 38, 161–77

Kuznets, Simon (1955) "Economic growth and income inequality." *American Economic Review* 45, 1–28

Moore, Robert E. (1990) "Measuring inequality change in an economy with income growth: reassessment." *Journal of Development Economics* 32, 205–10

Papanek, Gustav F., and Oldrich Kyn (1986) "The effect on income distribution of development, the growth rate and economic strategy." *Journal of Development Economics* 23, 55–65

Portes, Alejandro, Manuel Castells, and Lauren A. Benton, eds. (1989) *The Informal Economy: Studies in Advanced and Less Developed Countries* (Baltimore: Johns Hopkins University Press)

PREALC (Programa Regional del Empleo para Amèrica Latina y el Caribe) (1982) *Mercado de Trabajo en Cifras, 1950–1980* (Santiago: Oficina International del Trabajo)

Robinson, Sherman (1976) "A note on the u hypothesis relating income inequality and economic development." *American Economic Review* 66, 437–40

Sethuraman, S.V., ed. (1981) *The Urban Informed Sector*

in Developing Countries (Geneva: International Labour Office)

Summers, Robert, and Alan Heston (1988) "A new set of international comparisons of real product and price levels estimates for 130 countries, 1950–1985." *Review of Income and Wealth* 34, 1–25

Tidrick, Gene M. (1975) "Wage spillover and unemployment in a wage-gap economy: the Jamaican case." *Economic Development and Cultural Change* 23, 306–24

Todaro, Michael P. (1969) "A model of labor migration and urban unemployment in less developed countries." *American Economic Review* 59, 138–48

Comment VIII.A.1. The Informal Sector, Intraurban Inequality, and the Inverted U

As urbanization (*URB*) increases in the Rauch model, the informal sector share of the urban labor force (*SHARE*) falls, the informal sector share of the total labor force (*UNDER*) follows an inverted U, and inequality measured by the log variance also follows an inverted U. This Comment is intended to give the interested reader a better understanding of the sources of these results and the connections among them.

The labor market equilibrium condition in the Rauch model is that the expected utility from working in the agricultural sector is equal to the expected utility from working in the urban sector. This is analogous to the labor market equilibrium condition that holds in the Todaro and Harris–Todaro models of Chapter VI. Under the assumption of intertemporally log-linear utility (the same utility function used in Note III.1), this equilibrium condition boils down to an equality between the agricultural log wage and a weighted average of the log wages in urban informal and urban formal employment, where the weights are *SHARE* and 1 – *SHARE*, respectively. (This equality is consistent with a higher average wage in the urban sector measured in natural units.) It follows immediately that, since the population average log wage is equal across sectors, there is no contribution to the log variance measure of inequality from inequality between the agricultural and urban sectors. If the log variance measure of inequality follows an inverted U as the population is reallocated from one sector to the other, it cannot be because of changes in between-sector inequality as it was in Selection VIII.A.2 by Robinson.

As *URB* increases in the Rauch model the land-labor ratio in agriculture rises, increasing the marginal product of labor in agriculture and the agricultural wage. This is consistent with labor market equilibrium only if the weighted average log wage in the urban sector increases. This can only happen if *SHARE* (the weight on the smaller urban log wage) falls, because both the minimum wage enforced in urban formal employment and the self-employment wage of informal workers remain constant by assumption. The change in *UNDER* is then seen to be the result of two conflicting trends. On the one hand, holding *SHARE* constant the increase in *URB* must increase *UNDER*. On the other hand, *SHARE* falls as *URB* increases, tending to decrease *UNDER*. The first effect dominates when *URB* is low and the second effect dominates when *URB* is high, yielding an inverted u in *UNDER*. Intuitively, it is clear that the second effect must dominate when *URB* is sufficiently high because the agricultural wage must catch up to the urban formal wage, yielding *SHARE* equal to zero by the labor market equilibrium condition.

The same logic that leads to an inverted U in *UNDER* leads to an inverted U in the log variance measure of inequality in the Rauch model. Since between-sector inequality is zero, overall inequality is just a weighted average of inequalities within the rural and urban sectors, where the weights are the rural and urban population shares 1 – *URB* and *URB*, respectively.

Inequality within agriculture is zero but inequality within the urban sector is positive because of the difference in earnings between informally and formally employed workers. The change in overall inequality is then the result of the same two conflicting trends that determined the change in *UNDER*. Holding inequality within the urban sector constant, as *URB* increases overall inequality must increase because urban inequality is greater than rural inequality. Once *SHARE* shrinks below one-half, however, the further decline in *SHARE* as *URB* increases reduces inequality within the urban sector, tending to decrease overall inequality. This second effect eventually dominates the first effect, just as it did for *UNDER*. It can be shown, with an additional assumption on the agricultural production function, that the log variance measure of inequality cannot decline in the Rauch model until after *UNDER* declines.

Selection VIII.A.4. Explaining Inequality the World Round: Cohort Size, Kuznets Curves, and Openness*

I Reviewing the Three Hypotheses

Inequality and Cohort Size

The cohort-size hypothesis is simple enough: fat cohorts tend to get low rewards. When those fat cohorts lie in the middle of the age-earnings curve, where life-cycle income is highest, this labor market glut lowers their income, thus tending to flatten the age-earnings curve. Earnings inequality is moderated. When instead the fat cohorts are young or old adults, this kind of labor market glut lowers incomes at the two tails of the age-earnings curve, thus tending to heighten the slope of the upside and the downside of the age-earnings curve. Earnings inequality is augmented. This demographic hypothesis has a long tradition in the United States, starting with the entry of the baby boomers into the labor market when they faced such poor prospects [Easterlin 1980; Freeman 1979; Welch 1979], and it was surveyed recently by David Lam [1997: 1023–1024, 1044–1052]. Murphy and Welch [1992] and Katz and Murphy [1992] have now extended this work to include the 1980s. All of these studies have shown that relative cohort size has had an adverse supply effect on the relative wages of the fat cohort in the United States since the 1950s. . . .

If the cohort-size hypothesis helps explain U.S. postwar experience with wage inequality, it might do even better worldwide. After all, there is far greater variance in the age distribution of populations between regions and countries than there has been over time in the United States. Furthermore, the post-World War II demographic transition in the Third World has generated much more dramatic changes in relative cohort size than did the baby boom in the OECD countries. The higher demographic variance between countries at any point in time versus within countries over time can also be illustrated by a pair of summary statistics from the data set used in this analysis. Define the variable MATURE as the proportion of the adult population (taken to be persons in the age range 15–69) who are 40–59. When the standard deviation of MATURE is calculated between countries in the sample, we get a figure, 5.10, that far ex-

ceeds the standard deviation over time within countries for the sample, 1.66. Thus the variance in cohort size across countries and regions is more than nine times the variance for countries over time.

All of this suggests that cohort size is likely to matter in explaining inequality the world around since the 1950s, fat young-adult cohorts creating inequality whereas fat prime-age cohorts doing just the opposite. . . .

Inequality and Openness

The standard Heckscher-Ohlin two-factor, two-good trade model makes unambiguous predictions. Every country exports those products that use intensively abundant and cheap factors of production. Thus a trade boom induced by either declining tariffs or transport costs will cause exports and the demand for the cheap factor to boom too. Globalization in poor countries should favor unskilled labor and disfavor skilled labor; globalization in rich countries should favor skilled labor and disfavor unskilled labor. Lawrence and Slaughter [1993] used the standard Heckscher-Ohlin trade model to explore wage inequality and concluded that there is little evidence to support it. Instead, they concluded that technological change was the more important source of rising wage inequality. Hot debate ensued. . . .

Basing his results on insights derived from classical Heckscher-Ohlin theory extended by Stolper-Samuelson (hereafter cited as SS), Wood [1994] concluded that trade globalization could account for rising inequality in the rich North and falling inequality in the poor South. Wood's research has been met with stiff critical resistance. Since his book appeared, we have learned more about the inequality and globalization connection in the Third World. The standard SS prediction is that unskilled labor-abundant poor countries should undergo egalitarian trends in the face of globalization forces, unless those forces are overwhelmed by industrial revolutionary labor-saving events on the upswing of the Kuznets Curve [Kuznets 1955], or by young-adult gluts generated by the demographic transition [Bloom and Williamson 1997; 1998]. A recent review by Davis [1996] reports the contrary, and a study by Robbins [1996] of seven countries in Latin America and East Asia shows that wage inequality typically did not fall after

*From Matthew Higgins and Jeffrey G. Williamson, "Explaining Inequality the World Round: Cohort Size, Kuznets Curves, and Openness," *Southeast Asian Studies* 40, no. 3 (December 2002): 269–274, 276–288. Reprinted by permission.

trade liberalization, but rather rose.[1] This apparent anomaly has been strengthened by other studies, some of which have been rediscovered since Wood's book appeared. . . .

Strong Versus Weak Versions of the Kuznets Curve Hypothesis

Simon Kuznets [1955] noted that inequality had declined in several nations across the mid-twentieth century, and supposed that it probably had risen earlier. Furthermore, Kuznets thought it was demand-side forces that could explain his curve: that is, technological and structural change tended to favor the demand for capital and skills, while saving on unskilled labor. These laborsaving conditions eventually moderated as the rate of technological change (catching up) and the rate of structural change (urbanization and industrialization) both slowed down. Eventually, the laborsaving stopped, and other, more egalitarian forces were allowed to have their impact. This is what might be called the *strong version* of the Kuznets Curve hypothesis, that income inequality first rises and then declines with development. The strong version of the hypothesis is strong because it is unconditioned by any other effects. Factor demand does it all.

The *weak version* of the Kuznets Curve hypothesis is more sophisticated. It argues that these demand forces can be offset or reinforced by any other forces if they are sufficiently powerful. The forces of a demographic transition at home may glut the labor market with the young and impecunious early in development, reinforcing the rise in inequality. Or emigration to labor-scarce OECD or oil-rich economies may have the opposite effect, making the young and impecunious who stay home scarcer (while the old receive remittances). It depends on the size of the demographic transition and whether the world economy accommodates mass migration. A public policy committed to high enrollment rates and to the eradication of illiteracy may greatly augment the supply of skilled and literate labor, eroding the premium on skills and wage inequality. Or public policy may not take this liberal stance, allowing instead the skill premium to soar, and wage inequality with it. A commitment to liberal trade policies may allow an invasion of labor-intensive goods in labor-scarce economies,

thus injuring the unskilled at the bottom of the distribution. Or trade policies may protect those interests. And a commitment to liberal trade policies in industrializing labor-abundant countries may allow an invasion of labor-intensive goods in OECD markets, the export boom raising the demand for unskilled labor and thus augmenting incomes of common labor at the bottom. Or trade policies may instead protect the interests of the skilled in the import-competing industries. Finally, natural-resource endowment may matter since an export boom in economies having one will raise the rents on those resources and thus augment the incomes of those at the top who own those resources. . . .

II Inequality, Cohort Size, and Openness: The Data

Deininger and Squire [1996] subject their inequality data to various quality and consistency checks. In order to be included in their "high quality" data set, an observation must be drawn from a published household survey, provide comprehensive coverage of the population, and be based on a comprehensive measure of income or expenditure. The resulting data set covers 111 countries and four decades (the 1960s through the 1990s), yielding 682 annual observations. We exclude from our analysis here 19 countries with insufficient economic data, yielding a data set covering 92 countries and including a total of 600 annual observations. Although many countries contribute only one or two annual observations, 19 countries contribute ten or more, permitting the analysis of inequality trends over time.

We focus on two measures of inequality, the Gini coefficient (GINI) and the ratio of income earned by the top income quintile to income earned by the bottom quintile (Q5/Q1). . . .

To study Kuznets effects, we rely on real GDP per worker, measured at purchasing-power parity. Some earlier studies have relied on real GDP per capita rather than per worker, but we are persuaded that labor productivity is more closely connected to the Kuznets notion of stages of development. . . . Following many earlier studies, adding a quadratic GDP per worker term to the model captures the possibility that this inequality turning point appears at later stages of development. . . .

Our openness measure comes from Sachs and Warner [1995], who classify an economy as closed (dummy = 0) if it is characterized by any of the following four conditions: (1) a black market premium of 20 percent or more for foreign exchange, (2) an export-marketing board that appropriates

---

[1]An even more recent survey by Lindert and Williamson [2002] suggests some reasons why the SS result was not forthcoming at the time Robbins was writing but now is [Robertson 2001].

most foreign-exchange earnings, (3) a socialist economic system, or (4) extensive nontariff barriers on imports of intermediate and capital goods. The black market premium is generally the most decisive criterion of the four, by itself identifying the vast majority of countries considered closed. According to the Sachs-Warner index, the OECD region has been quite open since the 1960s. The Pacific Rim became open in the 1970s. Latin America waited until the first half of the 1990s to make a significant switch toward economic openness, whereas sub-Saharan Africa still remains closed. . . .

To capture the effects of cohort size, we rely on the fraction of the labor force in its peak earning years (MATURE). Because data concerning age-specific labor force participation rates are unavailable, we approximate this by the fraction of the adult population aged 40–59. This cohort size measure has been relatively stable within regions over the past three decades, but it varies substantially across regions, standing far higher in the developed world than elsewhere. . . . Evidently the mature adult share of the labor force rises substantially only during later stages of the demographic transition.

III Empirical Results

Our benchmark empirical model treats the data as decadal averages by country, following Deininger and Squire [1998]. We first estimate the standard unconditional Kuznets Curve, with only real output per worker and its square as explanatory variables. We then add measures of openness and cohort size to the conditional Kuznets Curve. . . . Our results provide considerable support for the hypotheses that inequality follows an inverted U as an economy's aggregate labor productivity rises, and that inequality falls as an economy's population matures. We find only limited support, however, for the hypothesis that economic openness brings increased inequality. Cohort size has a consistent and powerful effect throughout.

Pooled Estimates

Since the benchmark model relies on decadal averages, each country contributes between one and four observations. The average number of observations per country in our largest sample is 2.4, or about two and a half decades. All specifications include three dummy variables describing whether an inequality observation is (a) measured at the personal or household level, (b) based on income

or expenditure, or (c) based on gross or net income.[2] All specifications also include a dummy variable for the presence of a socialist government as well as decade dummies, the latter ensuring that the estimates are driven entirely by cross-sectional variation. The standard errors used to generate our test statistics are robust to heteroskedasticity of an unknown form.

We begin by estimating the unconditional Kuznets Curve—that is, a model containing only real output per worker and its square as explanatory variables (RGDPW and RGDPW^2), along with the various dummy variables. These initial results point to a relationship between inequality (GINI or Q5/Q1) and labor productivity, significant at the 1 percent level, but the relationship does not follow the expected inverted U (Table 1, columns 1 and 3). The estimated coefficients in GINI for RGDPW and RGDPW^2 are both negative, implying that inequality declines monotonically with the level of economic development. When inequality is measured instead by Q5/Q1, the inverted U does appear, but the individual coefficients are very imprecisely estimated, reflecting a high degree of collinearity between the two variables. Much the same holds true when the model is estimated for the four decades in our sample (not reported): for both the GINI and Q5/Q1 variables, RGDPW and RGDPW^2 are always jointly significant at the 1 percent level, but the estimated sign pattern is often perverse. Adding regional dummy variables for sub-Saharan Africa and Latin America changes these results but little (columns 2 and 4).

It is, of course, possible that the inverted U posited by Kuznets is masked by other forces, such as cohort size and economic openness. After all, economic relationships are seldom expected to hold unless other relevant influences are controlled.[3] In this spirit, we add to the model the measures of openness and cohort size discussed earlier, and when we do so the Kuznets Curve emerges (Table 2, columns 1 and 2, 4 and 5). RGDPW and RGDPW^2 are jointly and individually significant at the 1 percent level, and they display the expected sign pattern. It is worth noting, however, that the estimated inequality turning point is quite high, at

---

[2] Deininger and Squire [1996] note that measured inequality levels vary systematically along these dimensions, making it important to control for them in empirical work.

[3] The distinction between unconditional and conditional convergence in country income levels provides an apt analogy [Williamson 1998]. Numerous studies fail to find support for unconditional convergence, but they do find powerful evidence of convergence after controlling for determinants of steady-state income levels.

Table 1. The Unconditional Kuznets Curve

	Dependent variable			
	Gini coefficient		Q5/Q1 income ratio	
RGDPW	–7.14 E-02	–2.55 E-02	4.77 E-03	1.290 E-03
	(0.31)	(0.13)	(0.31)	(0.10)
RGDPW^2	–1.34 E-02	–9.52 E-03	–8.08 E-04	–4.22 E-04
	(2.01)	(1.67)	(1.87)	(1.16)
Joint significance	<.0001	<.0001	<.0001	.0013
Turning point	NA	NA	$2,952	$1,528
Africa dummy		10.64		0.614
		(6.22)		(5.45)
Latin dummy		12.63		0.751
		(10.99)		(8.94)
R^2 adj.	0.373	0.624	0.336	0.587
Observations	223	223	196	196

Note: The Q5/Q1 income ratio is measured in logs. Absolute *t*-statistics, in parentheses, are based on heteroskedasticity-corrected standard errors. Data are pooled by decade, with countries contributing between one and four observations. All specifications include the following dummy variables: (i) inequality data based on expenditure rather than income; (ii) inequality measured at household rather than personal level; (iii) inequality data based on gross rather than net income; (iv) socialist government; and (v)–(vii) decade. . . . NA—Not applicable.

about $15,000 evaluated at purchasing-power parity in 1985 prices.[4] For comparison, as of 1990, real output per worker stood at $36,800 in the United States, $16,000 in South Korea, and $6,800 in Thailand. . . .

Next, note that Table 2 reports emphatic support for a link between cohort size and aggregate inequality. The estimated coefficient for MATURE is negative and easily statistically significant at the 1 percent level for both the GINI and Q5/Q1 variables, indicating that a more experienced labor force is associated with reduced inequality, regardless of schooling levels or its distribution. The estimated quantitative impact is also large. According to the estimated coefficients, a one-standard deviation increase in this variable would lower a country's Gini coefficient by 6.5 and reduce the value of its Q5/Q1 variable by 2.8. We return below to the quantitative impact of these cohort-size effects, as well as of the other two explanatory variables; but these cohort-size effects appear to be very big.

Finally, note that Table 2 does not support the view that economic openness is closely connected with higher inequality. Nor does Table 2 support

the more complex predictions of standard trade theory, namely that poor countries that go open should become less unequal whereas rich countries that go open should become more unequal. There are two specifications each under GINI and Q5/Q1. The first specification interacts OPEN (here, the Sachs-Warner measure) with an indicator variable that equals 1 if a country was in the top third of the labor-productivity distribution in 1975–79; this new variable is called RICH. The second specification interacts OPEN with an indicator variable that equals 1 if a country was in the bottom third of the labor-productivity distribution in 1975–79; this new variable is called POOR. As Table 2 shows, OPEN × RICH and OPEN × POOR are always small and insignificant, indicating that the impact of openness (as measured here) does not vary with income, productivity, or human-capital endowment. Standard Stolper-Samuelson trade theory does not survive in these data. . . .

Our tests may simply lack statistical power against the null hypothesis that inequality is unrelated to openness. Remember, we interact the Sachs-Warner openness measure with a dummy variable that selects members of (depending on the specification) the top or the bottom third of the world-income distribution. It turns out that, by this measure, almost all countries in the top third of the world income distribution are rated as open, and almost all countries in the bottom third as closed. Because the available data may not permit a sharp

[4]Recall that these estimates are based on output per worker, which is generally about twice as high as output per capita. Also, developing country productivity levels evaluated at purchasing power parity are often more than twice as high as productivity levels evaluated at current prices and exchange rates [Summers and Heston 1991].

Table 2. The Kuznets Curve, Openness, and Cohort Size

	Dependent variable					
	Gini coefficient			Q5/Q1 income ratio		
RGDPW	0.739	0.801	0.580	4.61 E-02	5.14 E-02	3.07 E-02
	(3.22)	(3.63)	(2.77)	(2.90)	(3.51)	(2.29)
RGDPW^2	−2.57 E-02	−2.65 E-02	−2.01 E-02	−1.38 E-03	−1.49 E-03	−9.34 E-04
	(4.16)	(4.23)	(2.74)	(3.34)	(3.72)	(2.02)
Joint significance	<.0001	<.0001	.0002	.0030	.0010	.0441
Turning point	$14,377	$15,113	$14,428	$16,703	$17,248	$16,435
Open	−3.74	−3.71	−1.14	−0.152	−0.179	−2.04 E-02
	(2.30)	(2.47)	(0.92)	(1.50)	(1.93)	(0.24)
Open × Rich	1.10			2.08 E-02		
	(0.54)			(0.16)		
Open×Poor		1.58			0.177	
		(0.39)			(0.61)	
Mature	−1.15	−1.13	−0.852	−6.57 E-2	−6.52 E-2	−4.44 E-2
	(7.65)	(7.95)	(6.89)	(6.69)	(7.39)	(4.98)
Africa dummy			9.71			0.555
			(5.81)			(4.95)
Latin dummy			9.02			0.550
			(6.92)			(5.39)
R^2 adj.	0.554	0.554	0.688	0.494	0.496	0.627
Observations	219	219	219	193	193	193

Note: The Q5/Q1 income ratio is measured in logs. Absolute *t*-statistics, in parentheses, are based on heteroskedasticity-corrected standard errors. Data are pooled by decade, with countries contributing between one and four observations. All specifications include the following dummy variables: (i) inequality data based on expenditure rather than income; (ii) inequality measured at household rather than personal level; (iii) inequality data based on gross rather than net income; (iv) socialist government; and (v)–(vii) decade. . . .

test of the hypothesis that the openness-inequality relationship should vary with the level of development—and in light of the negative openness results reported above—the remainder of this article treats the openness-inequality relationship as independent of the level of development.

Turning to the direct effect of openness, the coefficient on the Sachs-Warner variable is negative and statistically significant at the 1 percent level for the GINI variable (columns 1 and 2), and negative but significant at the 10 percent level in only one of the two specifications for the Q5/Q1 variable. According to these estimated coefficients, an economy rated as fully open (dummy = 1) would have a Gini coefficient of 3.5 below that of an economy rated as fully closed (dummy = 0). Given that the cross-country standard deviation for Gini coefficients is close to 10, the maximum quantitative impact of 3.5 does not appear to be very large (and only 7 percent of the Latin American Gini in the 1990s). Similarly, according to the estimated coefficients, the Q5/Q1 variable is only 14 percent higher for a closed than for an open economy, a reduction of only about 1.3 percent evaluated at the sample average for the 1990s.

Checking Robustness

To evaluate the robustness of these results, we experiment with a number of alternative specifications. We begin by adding dummy variables for sub-Saharan Africa and Latin America to control for unobserved factors peculiar to these regions (Table 2, columns 3 and 6).[5] Now how do our three main hypotheses perform? First, and most important, the link running from older working-age populations to lower inequality remains significant at the 1 percent level. Second, the Kuznets Curve persists. . . . For the GINI variable, RGDPW and RGDPW^2 are easily significant at the 1 percent level, while the estimated productivity turning point falls slightly. For the Q5/Q1 variable, the statistical significance of the productivity variable falls from the 1 percent level, but still retains significance at the 5 percent level. Third, the evidence of any link between economic openness and inequality essentially disappears. The coefficient for

[5]We experimented with adding additional regional dummies for OECD and Pacific Rim economies. These dummy variables were statistically insignificant, and coefficient estimates for other variables remained essentially unchanged.

Table 3. Stability of Regression Estimates over Time

	Dependent variable							
	Gini coefficient				Q5/Q1 income ratio			
	1960s	1970s	1980s	1990s	1960s	1970s	1980s	1990s
RGDPW	1.20	1.29	0.565	0.175	6.32 E-02	9.810 E-02	4.05 E-02	–1.88 E-02
	(2.10)	(2.74)	(2.07)	(0.29)	(0.86)	(2.33)	(2.26)	(0.39)
RGDPW^2	–3.16 E-02	–4.32 E-02	–2.13 E-02	–9.91 E-03	–6.95 E-04	–2.92 E-03	–1.21 E-03	9.55 E-05
	(2.01)	(1.67)	(4.32)	(0.71)	(0.29)	(2.44)	(2.45)	(0.09)
Joint significance	.0997	.0124	.0029	.4023	.2799	.0498	.0480	.4894
Turning point	$18,987	$14,931	$13,263	$8,829	$45,468	$16,798	$16,736	NA
Open	–9.63	–4.55	–0.348	–1.23	–0.699	–0.178	1.23 E-02	–1.02 E-02
	(2.17)	(1.48)	(0.16)	(0.31)	(1.69)	(0.88)	(0.10)	(0.03)
Mature	–1.22	–1.09	–0.734	–1.39	–8.73 E-2	–7.09 E-2	–4.76 E-2	–8.74 E-2
	(2.08)	(2.77)	(2.93)	(4.43)	(1.34)	(2.30)	(3.24)	(3.85)
R^2 adj.	0.539	0.620	0.629	0.399	0.367	0.553	0.581	0.357
Observations	34	56	69	60	28	49	64	52

Note: The Q5/Q1 income ratio is measured in logs. Absolute t-statistics, in parentheses, are based on heteroskedasticity-corrected standard errors. All specifications include the following dummy variables: (i) inequality data based on expenditure rather than income; (ii) inequality measured at household rather than personal level; (iii) inequality data based on gross rather than net income; and (iv) socialist government. . . . NA—Not applicable.

OPEN retains its negative sign, but is far from significant statistically.

We next explore the stability of the empirical relationships over time, estimating the models separately for each decade.[6] The results lead to some softening of the evidence supporting the Kuznets Curve (Table 3). For the GINI variable, the coefficients for RGDPW and RGDPW^2 are of the expected signs and jointly statistically significant at or close to the 1 percent level for the 1970s and 1980s; they are also significant at the 10 percent level for the 1960s. However, there is no evidence of a Kuznets Curve in the 1990s. Similarly, for the Q5/Q1 variable, coefficients for RGDPW and RGDPW^2 are of the expected signs and jointly statistically significant at the 5 percent level for the 1970s and 1980s; but they switch signs and fall well short of statistical significance for the 1990s. In short, it seems wise to be tentative even about the emergence of a conditional Kuznets Curve in these data. After all, while the poor results for the 1960s may reflect the small sample size (in particular, there are few inequality observations for Africa or Latin America), the results for the 1990s are just plain negative.

Splitting the sample by decade tends to increase the already strong support for cohort-size effects on inequality. The MATURE variable attains 5 per-

[6]The estimates will also be influenced by decadal differences in the availability of the inequality data.

cent significance levels in all cases but one—for the Q5/Q1 variable in the 1960s, a period for which the sample size is small. In contrast, the Sachs-Warner openness measure—treated here as the simple additive variable OPEN because Table 2 rejected complex interactions—attains a conventional statistical significance level for only one specification, that for the GINI variable in the 1960s.

The extensive theoretical and empirical literature on inequality has identified many other potentially important inequality determinants. We further examine the robustness of our empirical results by adding a number of these other determinants to our bench-mark equations (Table 4). Bourguignon and Morrisson [1998] focus on the role of relative labor productivity in agriculture and non-agriculture to capture Kuznets's notion that the differential development of these sectors plays a key role in explaining inequality. These authors also include arable land per capita to capture a potential link between natural resource endowment and inequality, and the secondary-school enrollment ratio to capture the intuitive notion that broader access to education reduces inequality.

Table 4 confirms the importance of the Bourguignon-Morrisson agricultural variables in explaining inequality. The productivity ratio between industry and agriculture is statistically significant at the 1 percent level, bigger productivity gaps contributing to greater inequality. The estimated coef-

Table 4. Extending the Basic Regression Model

	Dependent variable			
	Gini coefficient		Q5/Q1 income ratio	
RGDPW	1.04	0.600	5.22 E-02	3.03 E-05
	(4.63)	(2.54)	(3.43)	(1.74)
RGDPW^2	−3.02 E-02	−1.94 E-02	−1.40 E-03	−8.52 E-10
	(4.54)	(2.88)	(3.19)	(1.79)
Joint significance	<.0001	.0126	.0028	.1893
Turning point	$17,219	$15,464	$18,643	$17,782
Mature	−1.15	−0.945	−8.95 E-2	−6.34 E-02
	(6.01)	(6.03)	(6.74)	(5.26)
Secondary enroll.	−6.61 E-2		−5.39 E-4	
	(1.74)		(0.22)	
Ind./agr. labor prod.	0.398	0.300	1.80 E-2	8.56 E-03
	(2.61)	(2.12)	(2.16)	(1.05)
Arable land/pop.	1.22	0.657	9.37 E-2	5.76 E-02
	(3.16)	(1.82)	(3.57)	(2.52)
Africa dummy		8.50		0.50
		(4.83)		(3.93)
Latin America dummy		7.76		0.41
		(5.50)		(3.49)
R^2 adj.	0.561	0.643	0.541	0.586
Observations	162	164	141	143

Note: The Q5/Q1 income ratio is measured in logs. Absolute *t*-statistics, in parentheses, are based on het-eroskedasticity-corrected standard errors. Data are pooled by decade, with countries contributing between one and four observations. All specifications include the following dummy variables: (i) inequality data based on expenditure rather than income; (ii) inequality measured at household rather than personal level; (iii) inequality data based on gross rather than net income: (iv) socialist government; and (v)–(vii) decade. . . .

ficient implies that a reduction in the productivity ratio from 7.0 to 1.5 (the values, respectively, for Peru and the United States in the early 1990s) would lower a country's Gini coefficient by 2.2, compared with a cross-sectional standard deviation of about 9.7. Similarly, a more abundant agricultural endowment is associated with higher inequality, supporting the view that abundant resources can be a social "curse" as well as a drag on growth [Sachs and Warner 1995].[7] The secondary-school enrollment ratio has the expected sign, but it is statistically significant at the 10 percent level for only the GINI inequality measure. For both the GINI and Q5/Q1 variables, however, the Kuznets Curve and cohort-size effects remain significant at the 1 percent level, with little change in the coefficient estimates. . . .

A final specification drops variables that are insignificant at the 10 percent level and adds dummy

variables for Latin America and Africa, with little effect on the results. . . .

The results described above provide emphatic support for the link between inequality and cohort size. They also offer strong, even if not unequivocal, support for a Kuznets Curve. Even so, our empirical models are not without their flaws. First, the estimates suffer from possible simultaneity bias, as is true of most other work in this area. The dearth of variables correlated with the relevant explanatory variables, and clearly uncorrelated with disturbances to inequality, makes it difficult to address this issue in a satisfactory way. Equally important, the estimates are likely to suffer from omitted-variable bias. Our strategy has been to address this issue by testing the robustness of our principal results to the inclusion of other variables identified in the literature as potential inequality determinants.

[7]We experimented by measuring natural resource abundance as the share of natural resource exports in GDP, rather than as agricultural land per capita. The alternative variable was statistically insignificant. Natural resource exports include fuels, minerals, and primary agricultural products.

References

Bloom, D.; and Williamson, J. G. 1997. Demographic Change and Human Resource Development. In

Emerging Asia: Change and Challenges, Ch. 3. Manila: Asian Development Bank.

————. 1998. Demographic Transitions and Economic Miracles in Emerging Asia. *World Bank Economic Review* 12: 419–455.

Bourguignon, F.; and Morrisson, C. 1998. Inequality and Development: The Role of Dualism. *Journal of Development Economics* 57 (2): 233–258.

Davis, D. R. 1996. *Trade Liberalization and Income Distribution.* NBER Working Paper No. 5693 (August). Cambridge, MA: National Bureau of Economic Research.

Deininger, K.; and Squire, L. 1996. A New Data Set Measuring Income Inequality. *World Bank Economic Review* 10: 565–591.

————. 1998. New Ways of Looking at Old Issues: Inequality and Growth. *Journal of Development Economics* 57 (2): 259–288.

Easterlin, R. A. 1980. *Birth and Fortune: The Impact of Numbers on Personal Welfare.* New York: Basic Books.

Freeman, R. B. 1979. The Effects of Demographic Factors on Age-Earnings Profiles. *Journal of Human Resources* 14: 289–318.

Katz, L.; and Murphy, K. 1992. Changes in Relative Wages, 1963–1987: Supply and Demand Factors. *Quarterly Journal of Economics* 107: 35–78.

Kuznets, S. 1955. Economic Growth and Income Inequality. *American Economic Review* 45: 1–28.

Lam, David. 1997. Demographic Variables and Income Inequality. In *Handbook of Population and Family Economics,* edited by Mark R. Rosenzweig and Oded Stark, pp. 1015–1059. Amsterdam: Elsevier Science B. V.

Lawrence, L.; and Slaughter, M. 1993. International Trade and American Wages in the 1980s: Giant Sucking Sound or Small Hiccup? *Brookings Papers on Economic Activity, Microeconomics* 2: 161–226.

Lindert, P. H.; and Williamson, J. G. 2002. Does Globalization Make the World More Unequal? In *Globalization in Historical Perspective,* edited by M. Bordo, A. M. Taylor, and J. G. Williamson. Chicago: University of Chicago Press.

Murphy, K.; and Welch, F. 1992. The Structure of Wages. *Quarterly Journal of Economics* 107: 285–326.

Robbins, D. 1996. Trade, Trade Liberalization and Inequality in Latin America and East Asia: Synthesis of Seven Countries. Harvard Institute for International Development, Cambridge, MA. (Mimeographed)

Robertson, R. 2001. Relative Prices and Wage Inequality: Evidence from Mexico. Unpublished paper (October). Macalester College, St. Paul, MN. 53p.

Sachs, J.; and Warner, A. 1995. Economic Reform and the Process of Global Integration. *Brookings Papers on Economic Activity* 1: 1–68.

Summers, R.; and Heston, A. 1991. The Penn World Table (Mark 5): An Expanded Set of International Comparisons, 1950–1988. *Quarterly Journal of Economics* 106: 327–368.

Welch, F. 1979. Effects of Cohort Size on Earnings: The Baby Boom Babies Financial Bust. *Journal of Political Economy* 87: S65–S97.

Williamson, J. G. 1998. Growth, Distribution, and Demography: Some Lessons from History. *Explorations in Economic History* 35 (3): 241–271.

Wood, A. 1994. *North-South Trade, Employment and Inequality: Changing Fortunes in a Skill-Driven World.* Oxford: Clarendon Press.

Comment VIII.A.2. Evidence for the Inverted U Across Countries Versus Within Countries over Time

The Kuznets inverted-U hypothesis is that income inequality will first rise and then fall as a country develops over time. The evidence supporting this hypothesis, however, has come from the pattern of income inequality that exists across countries rather than within countries over time. The movement of inequality within countries over time has offered little support for the inverted-U hypothesis. For example, Gary S. Fields finds that over time there is no tendency for income inequality in poor countries to increase rather than decrease and no tendency for income inequality in rich countries to decrease rather than increase (see his chapter, "Growth and Income Distribution," in George Psacharopoulos, ed., *Essays on Poverty, Equity, and Growth* [Oxford: Pergamon, 1991]).

The reason for negative results such as Fields's may be that inequality simply does not change very much over time within any given country, so that the variance in inequality data is dominated by variance across countries. In a working paper version of the article from which the preceding selection was drawn (National Bureau of Economic Research Working Paper No. 7224, July 1999, Table 7), Matthew Higgins and Jeffrey G. Williamson show that 87 percent of the variance in the Gini coefficient in their sample is explained by country dummies, also known as "fixed effects." Higgins and Williamson then go on to include these fixed effects in Table 8 of their working paper, which we have reproduced here as Table 1. We see that, con-

Table 1. Fixed-Effects Specifications

	Dependent variable							
	Gini coefficient				Q5/Q1 income ratio			
LDV			0.372	0.453			0.296	0.389
			(4.40)	(5.74)			(4.11)	(6.01)
RGDPW	3.98E-02	0.405	0.349	0.956	4.27E-03	1.76E-02	2.78E-02	5.06E-02
	(0.30)	(2.33)	(1.43)	(4.08)	(0.42)	(1.49)	(2.12)	(4.04)
RGDPW^2	−3.09E-03	−8.82E-03	−1.04E-02	−1.81E-02	−1.93E-04	−4.56E-04	−8.04E-04	−1.13E-03
	(1.12)	(2.69)	(2.52)	(3.97)	(1.03)	(2.11)	(3.43)	(4.22)
Joint significance	0.3014	.0227	.0029	.0002	0.4493	0.0902	<.0001	.0001
Turning point	$6,440	$22,959	$16,779	$26,409	$11,062	$19,298	$17,289	$22,389
Open		1.03	0.114	−0.385		−5.76E-3	2.13E-02	1.81E-02
		(1.47)	(.196)	(.458)		(0.111)	(0.526)	(0.432)
Mature		−0.183	−0.309	−0.462		−6.99E-3	−2.33E-02	−2.79E-02
		(2.21)	(2.96)	(4.84)		(1.01)	(3.75)	(4.43)
Secondary Enroll.		−6.56E-2	−.161	−0.202		−2.24E-3	−8.78E-03	−1.17E-02
		(3.00)	(3.89)	(4.41)		(1.47)	(3.29)	(4.33)
R^2 adj	0.909	0.915	0.957	0.921	0.872	0.880	0.946	0.939
DW Statistic	1.46	1.47	NA	NA	1.54	1.53	NA	NA
Countries	44	44	23	10	37	37	21	10
Observations	459	449	216	162	394	387	202	156

The Q5/Q1 income ratio is measured in logs. Absolute t-statistics, in parentheses, are based on heteroskedasticity-corrected standard errors. For the model without a lagged dependent variable (LDV), the panel was restricted to countries with at least four complete observations. For the LDV model, the panel was restricted to countries with at least three complete observations in columns three and six, and seven complete observations in columns four and eight. For the LDV model, note that coefficient estimates and absolute t-statistics (other than for the LDV itself) pertain to the *sum* of the estimated coefficients for the current variable value and its first lag. Similarly, the test for the joint significance of RGDPW and RGDPW^2 refers to the joint restriction that the coefficients for RGDPW and its first lag sum to zero, and that the coefficients for RGDPW^2 sum to zero. In addition to the fixed country effects, all models also included a set of year dummies.

trary to Fields, they continue to find support for the inverted-U hypothesis provided that they include the variable "Mature" in their regressions, just as in the tables in the preceding selection. These results must be treated with caution, however, because of econometric problems. As indicated by the Durbin-Watson statistic, serial correlation is present in the regression residuals when a lagged dependent variable (LDV) is not included, and the inclusion of a lagged dependent variable when fixed effects are also included is known to yield biased estimates of the regression coefficients. Higgins and Williamson could not correct the latter problem because the appropriate econometric techniques would have required a longer time dimension in the data.

VIII.B. THE IMPACT OF INCOME DISTRIBUTION ON DEVELOPMENT

Selection VIII.B.1. The Middle Class Consensus and Economic Development*

1. Literature Review and Discussion

The papers that directly inspired the present paper are Engerman and Sokoloff (1997) and Sokoloff and Engerman (2000). Engerman and Sokoloff link tropical commodity factor endowments (which had significant scale economies) in Latin American countries to the concentration of wealth in the hands of a small elite, which in turn led to their entrenchment in power. Once entrenched, the elite was reluctant to invest in mass human capital for fear that they would be displaced from power. . . . So Latin America was condemned to low human capital and low development. In contrast, the non-tropical land in North America lent itself to family farms, which implied greater equality and greater investment in mass human capital.

The second strand of the literature links ethnic divisions to poor growth and public good outcomes. While violence directed at or by ethnic groups is well-known, the more subtle economic effects of ethnic conflict have only recently attracted attention in the economics literature. The mechanism could be similar to that in the previous paragraph—an ethnically distinct group in power is reluctant to invest in public services for the other ethnic groups for fear that the other ethnic groups will be enabled to displace the first group from power. . . .

This paper brings together these two strands of the literature. I call a situation of relative equality and ethnic homogeneity a "middle class consensus." I argue that this middle class consensus facilitates higher levels of income and growth, as well as higher levels of public goods. Like Engerman and Sokoloff (1997) and Sokoloff and Engerman (2000), I link the existence of a middle class consensus to initial factor endowments, mainly a tropical endowment that lent itself to production of primary commodities, but I test their hypothesis with cross-country data. I find that a middle class consensus provides a remarkably parsimonious explanation of development outcomes. . . .

2. Empirical Testing on Commodity Endowment, Middle Class Consensus, and Development

2.1. Tropical Endowments, Commodity Exporting, and Inequality

I first test the hypothesis of Engerman and Sokoloff (1997) and Sokoloff and Engerman (2000) that a tropical endowment leads to commodity production, and that commodity production is associated with higher inequality. Their hypothesis has not been systematically tested with cross-country data as far as I am aware.[1] Establishing these facts will make these variables candidates to be instruments for inequality. I use the World Bank World Development Report classification of countries as non-oil commodity exporters. I should clarify that the commodities are not necessarily "tropical" like bananas; they could just as well be coal or iron ore that are also produced in industrial countries. Hence, the hypothesis that tropical location is associated with commodity exporting is far from tautological. For tropical location, I construct a dummy that takes on the value one if the country's mean absolute latitude is less than 23.5 degrees and 0 otherwise. Table 1 shows a probit equation for commodity production on tropical location.

Not too surprisingly, commodity exporting is strongly associated with the tropics. Table 2 classifies countries by whether they are commodity exporters and by whether they are tropical. The vast majority (85%) of commodity exporting nations are in the tropics. Tropical nations are five times more likely to be commodity exporters than temperate nations.

The next step is to see whether being commodity exporting is associated with higher inequality, as hypothesized by Engerman and Sokoloff. Here is a simple regression of the share of the middle three income quintiles on the commodity exporting dummy (in light of the foregoing regression, TROPICS is an instrument for COMMOD) and a dummy for oil exporting nations. Confirming the Engerman-

---

*From William Easterly, "The Middle Class Consensus and Economic Growth," *Journal of Economic Growth* 6, 2001: 318–320, 322–326. Reprinted by permission.

[1]After completing a previous draft, I become aware of the 1998–1999 report of the InterAmerican Development Bank (1999), which graphically shows correlations between commodity exports and income inequality and between latitude and income inequality. The advantage of my approach compared to theirs is that I make the endogenous variable (commodity exporting) respond to the exogenous variable (tropical location).

Table 1. Commodity Exporting and Tropical Location

Variable	Coefficient	Standard error	z-Statistic	Prob.
C	−1.471424	0.205586	−7.157227	0.0000
Tropics	1.130729	0.245913	4.598093	0.0000
Mean dependent var	0.222857	S.D. dependent var		0.417357
S.E. of regression	0.391207			
Obs. with Dep. = 0	136			
Obs. with Dep. = 1	39			

Notes: Dependent variable: Commodity exporting dummy; Method: ML—Binary Probit; Included observations: 175; Covariance matrix computed using second derivatives.

Table 2. Commodity Exporting and Tropical Location

	No. of countries		
	Tropical	Non-tropical	Total
Commodity exporter	33	6	39
Non-commodity exporter	58	78	136
Total	91	84	175
Percent of row totals			
Commodity exporter	36%	7%	
Non-commodity exporter	64%	93%	
Percent of column totals			
Commodity exporter	85%	15%	
Non-commodity exporter	43%	57%	

Sokoloff hypothesis, commodity production (including oil production) is associated with a lower share of income of the middle quintiles. The effect of commodity exporting is enormous, equal to nearly three standard deviations of the middle income share. Going from being a commodity exporter to being a non-commodity exporter explains two-thirds of the entire range of the middle class share variable, which only varies between 30 and 58 per-

cent. Oil production also moves the middle income share by a sizeable amount, more than one standard deviation (Table 3).

2.2. The Middle Class Consensus and Growth

I now have potential instruments for the middle income share to use in a regression of . . . growth on the middle income share and the ethnic fractionalization index. . . .

I use a system estimator, as shown in Table 4.

A one standard deviation increase in the middle class income share is associated with a growth increase of 0.42 standard deviations, equivalent to one additional percentage point of per capita growth. A movement from the minimum middle class income share to the maximum in the sample is associated with an enormous increase in growth—3.8 percentage points.

A one standard deviation increase in ethnic fractionalization is associated with a growth decrease of 0.21 standard deviations, equivalent to half of a percentage point of growth. A movement from the minimum ethnic fractionalization to the maximum is associated with a fall in growth of 1.5 percentage points.

Figure 1 shows the fall in the per capita growth rate as one goes from high to low middle class

Table 3. Middle Class Share and Commodity Exporting

Variable	Coefficient	Standard error	t-Statistic	Prob.
C	51.63167	1.058569	48.77496	0.0000
Commodity dummy	−19.62242	4.996424	−3.92793	0.0002
Oil dummy	−10.88073	3.315207	−3.282066	0.0014
S.E. of regression	9.308190	Mean dependent variable		46.75934
F-statistic	9.590131	S.D. dependent variable		7.121557
Prob(F-statistic)	0.000156			

Notes: Dependent variable: Middle class income share; Method: Two-Stage least squares; Included observations: 102; White Heteroskedasticity-Consistent Standard Errors & Covariance; Instrument list: C Tropics dummy, Oil dummy.

Figure 1. Growth as function of middle income share and ethnic diversity.

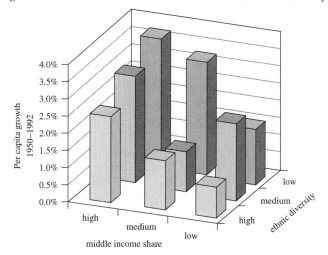

Table 4. System Estimation for Per Capita Growth as Dependent Variable

	Coefficient	Standard error	t-Statistic	Prob.
C(1)	51.0619	1.7443	29.27	0.000
C(2)	–19.1717	5.2902	–3.62	0.000
C(3)	–9.1976	3.7984	–2.42	0.017
C(4)	–0.0314	0.0238	–1.32	0.189
C(5)	0.0012	0.0005	2.51	0.013
C(6)	–0.0001	0.0001	–2.48	0.014

Notes: Estimation method: Three-stage least squares; Instruments: Ethnic fractionalization, oil dummy, Tropics Dummy, Constant; Equation: Middle Class Share = C(1) + C(2)* Commodity dummy + C(3)* Oil dummy; Observation: 80; Equation: Per Capita Growth (1950–1992) = C(4) + C(5)* Middle Class Share + C(6)*Ethnic Fractionalization; Observation: 80.

share, and from low to high ethnic diversity. The highest growth rate is with a high middle income share and low ethnic diversity; growth miracles Japan and Korea are in this group. The lowest growth is with a low middle income share and high ethnic diversity. Guatemala, Sierra Leone, and Zambia are examples of countries that fall in the low middle class share, high ethnic diversity part of the sample.

How robust are these results to other exogenous factors that have been mentioned in the literature? Bloom and Sachs (1998) and Sachs and Warner (1997) argue that being landlocked is a geographic disadvantage for development. When I introduce a landlocked dummy as an exogenous variable into . . . the . . . growth regression (and add it as an in-

strument in this and the following system regression), it is insignificant and the middle class share and ethnic fractionalization remain significant.

These authors also argue that tropical location is a development disadvantage. I agree with this thesis, but provide a structural explanation for why it matters—through the effect on inequality. I introduce the tropics dummy directly into the . . . growth equation controlling for middle class share and ethnic fractionalization. Although the tropics dummy weakens the significance of . . . the middle class share in the growth equation, the tropics dummy itself is not significant. . . . Still, insignificance does not prove the coefficient is zero, and the dependence of my results on the exclusion restriction on the tropics dummy should be kept in mind. . . .

References

Bloom, D. E., and J. D. Sachs. (1998). "Geography, Demography, and Economic Growth in Africa," *Brookings Papers on Economic Activity* 2.

Engermann, S., and Kenneth K. Sokoloff. (1997). "Factor Endowments, Institutions, and Differential Paths of Growth Among New World Economies: A View from Economic Historians of the United States." In Stephen Haber (ed.), *How Latin America Fell Behind.* Stanford CA: Stanford University Press.

Sachs, J., and A. Warner. (1997). "Fundamental Sources of Long-Run Growth," *American Economic Review Papers and Proceedings* 87(2), 184–188.

Sokoloff, K. L., and S. L. Engerman. (2000). "Institutions, Factor Endowments, and Path of Development in the New World," *Journal of Economic Perspectives* 14(3), 217–232.

Selection VIII.B.2. Income Distribution, Political Instability, and Investment*

1. Introduction

This paper studies the effects of income distribution on investment, by focusing on political instability as the channel which links these two variables. Income inequality increases social discontent and fuels social unrest. The latter, by increasing the probability of coups, revolutions, mass violence or, more generally, by increasing policy uncertainty and threatening property rights, has a negative effect on investment and, as a consequence, reduces growth.

Several authors have recently argued that income inequality is harmful for growth: in more unequal societies, the demand for fiscal redistribution financed by distortionary taxation is higher, causing a lower rate of growth.[1] Alesina and Rodrik (1993), Alesina and Rodrik (1994) and Persson and Tabellini (1994) present reduced form regressions supportive of this hypothesis.

An important question, still unresolved empirically, is what exactly is the channel through which inequality harms investment and growth. Perotti (1996) explicitly investigates the fiscal channel described above, with, however, rather inconclusive results.

In this paper we emphasize and test a different link from income inequality to capital accumulation: political instability. Therefore, our paper is related to the research on the effects of political instability on growth. For instance, Barro (1991), Alesina et al. (1996), and Mauro (1993) find an inverse relationship between political instability and growth or investment, using different techniques, approaches and data.[2] Venieris and Gupta (1986) identify an inverse relationship between political instability and the savings rate.

We estimate on a cross-section of 71 countries for the period 1960–85 a two-equation system in which the endogenous variables are investment in physical capital and a measure of political instability.[3] In our model, economic and political variables are jointly endogenous, an issue that has been generally ignored in the recent literature on the political economy of growth.[4] We are specifically interested in two questions:

1. Does income inequality increase political instability?
2. Does political instability reduce investment?

According to our findings, the answer to both questions is "yes." First, more unequal societies are more politically unstable: in particular, our results suggest that political stability is enhanced by the presence of a wealthy middle class. Second, political instability has an adverse effect on investment and, therefore, on growth. Furthermore, these two effects (from inequality to instability, and from instability to investment) are not only statistically significant, but also economically significant. . . .

2. Definition and Measure of Political Instability

. . . Socio-political instability is measured by constructing an index which summarizes various variables capturing phenomena of social unrest. . . . The index is constructed by applying the method of principal component to the following variables: *ASSASS,* the number of politically motivated assassinations; *DEATH,* the number of people killed in conjunction with phenomena of domestic mass violence, as a fraction of the total population; SCOUP, the number of successful coups; *UCOUP,* the number of attempted but unsuccessful coups; *DEM,* a dummy variable that takes the value of 1 in democracies, 0.5 in "semi-democracies" and 0 in dictatorships. A "democracy" is defined as a country with free competitive elections; a semi-democracy is a country with some form of elections but with severe restrictions on political rights (for instance, Mexico); a dictatorship is a country without competitive elections. All the variables are expressed as the average of annual values over the sample period, 1960–85. A

*From Alberto Alesina and Roberto Perotti, "Income Distribution, Political Instability, and Investment," *European Economic Review* 40 (June 1996): 1203–1219. Reprinted by permission.

[1]A non-exhaustive list of papers in this area includes Alesina and Rodrik (1993), Alesina and Rodrik (1994), Persson and Tabellini (1994), Bertola (1993) and Perotti (1993).

[2]Londregan and Poole (1990), and Londregan and Poole (1991) in related work do not seem to find such evidence. For a discussion of their results and comparisons with other literature see Alesina et al. (1996).

[3]The number of countries used in different specifications and different tests may vary slightly because of data availability. We have always chosen the largest sample of countries for which data were available.

[4]Some exceptions are Londregan and Poole (1990), Londregan and Poole (1991), and Alesina et al. (1996).

more detailed definition of the variables used in this paper, including sources, is in Table 1. . . .

Applying the method of principal components to the five variables listed above leads to the following index of socio-political instability:

$$SPI = 1.39 \, ASSASS + 1.21 \, DEATH$$
$$+ 7.58 \, SCOUP + 7.23 \, UCOUP$$
$$- 5.45 \, DEM \qquad (1)$$

3. Data and Sample Period

We perform cross-sectional regressions using a sample of 71 countries for the period 1960–1985. The binding constraint on the number of countries is the data availability. We have income distribution data for 74 countries, but for only 71 of these we have data on political instability and the other variables we use in our regressions, like investment shares in 1960–85 and GDP per capita in 1960.

We use the same dataset on income distribution assembled by Perotti (1996). The income distribution data consist of the income shares of the five quintiles of the population, measured as close as possible to the beginning of each sample period, 1960. In our framework, income distribution is predetermined; therefore, it is appropriate to measure this variable at the beginning of the sample pe-

riod. In fact, in the long run income distribution is likely to be endogenous, as it is arguably affected by such factors as land reforms, the savings behavior of the population etc. These problems of endogeneity are clearly hard to overcome: however, measuring income distribution at the beginning of the sample period is a way of minimizing them. . . .

The binding constraint on the initial date of the sample period is the availability of economic data. Our main sources for this variable is the Barro–Wolf and the Barro–Lee datasets, with the exceptions noted in Table 1. The end of our sample period (1985) is imposed by the availability of economic and socio-political variables. The list of these variables with their sources is included in Table 1, as well.

Table 2 reports the average of our *SPI* index for the sample 1960–85, ordered from the poorest to the richest country, in terms of their per capita income in 1960. This ordering immediately highlights a positive correlation between poverty and socio-political instability. Furthermore, a few countries suggest interesting observations. Japan has a much lower index of instability than countries at comparable level of development in 1960. Thirty years later this country is one of the richest in the world. The opposite observation holds for Argentina: it has the second highest *SPI* index and from 1960 to 1985 it has dropped several steps in

Table 1. Definition of Variables and Data Sources

GDP:	GDP in 1960 in hundreds of 1980 dollars;
PRIM:	Primary school enrollment rate in 1960, from Barro and Lee (1993);
SEC:	Secondary school enrollment rate in 1960, from Barro and Lee (1993);
MIDCLASS:	Share of the third and fourth quintiles of the population in or around 1960;
INV:	Ratio of real domestic investment (private plus public) to real GDP (average from 1960 to 1985);
PPPI:	PPP value of the investment deflator (U.S. = 1.0), 1960;
PPPIDE:	Magnitude of the deviation of the PPP value for the investment deflator from the sample mean, 1960;
SPI:	Index of socio-political instability, constructed using averages over 1960–85 of the variables that appear in the formula of Eq. 1;
SPIG:	Index of socio-political instability, constructed using annual data from the formula in Gupta (1990), average over 1960–85;
HOMOG:	Percentage of the population belonging to the main ethnic or linguistic group, 1960, from Canning and Fay (1993);
URB:	Urban population as percentage of total population in 1960. Source: World Bank Tables;
GOV:	Government consumption as share of GDP, average 1970–85;
DEATH:	Average number of deaths in domestic disturbances, per millions population, 1960–85, from Jodice and Taylor (1988);
ASSASS:	Average number of assassinations, 1960–85, from Jodice and Taylor (1988);
UCOUP:	Average number of unsuccessful coups, 1960–85, from Jodice and Taylor (1988);
SCOUP:	Average number of successful coups, 1960–85, from Jodice and Taylor (1988);
DEM:	Dummy variable taking the value 1 for democracies, 0.5 for semi-democracies, and 0 for dictatorships, average 1960–85, from Jodice and Taylor (1988).

This table describes the data used in the regressions. All the data are from the Barro and Wolf (1989) data set, except for the income distribution data which are mainly from Jain (1975) (see Perotti (1996) for a more detailed list of the original sources) or unless otherwise indicated.

Table 2. SPI Index (sample 1960–85)

Country	SPI	Country	SPI
Tanzania	−0.73	Panama	5.42
Malawi	−2.66	Brazil	−0.19
Sierra Leone	9.11	Colombia	−4.69
Niger	3.42	Jamaica	−11.60
Burma	1.58	Greece	2.41
Togo	6.80	Costa Rica	−11.76
Bangladesh	8.39	Cyprus	−5.55
Kenya	−0.72	Peru	7.46
Botswana	−9.68	Barbados	−11.76
Egypt	1.83	Iran	−1.13
Chad	7.61	Mexico	−4.15
India	−8.92	Japan	−11.68
Morocco	2.41	Spain	−2.77
Nigeria	12.69	Iraq	30.64
Pakistan	9.11	Ireland	−11.37
Congo	21.66	South Africa	−7.08
Benin	30.34	Israel	−11.67
Zimbabwe	−1.76	Chile	0.50
Madagascar	2.42	Argentina	30.54
Sudan	15.09	Italy	−8.10
Thailand	9.31	Uruguay	4.80
Zambia	−3.46	Austria	−11.68
Ivory Coast	−2.74	Finland	−11.76
Honduras	5.00	France	−9.44
Senegal	−0.98	Holland	−11.68
Gabon	4.05	U.K.	−7.63
Tunisia	−2.57	Norway	−11.76
Philippines	−4.14	Sweden	−11.68
Bolivia	44.19	Australia	−11.68
Dom. Republic	8.22	Germany	−11.45
Sri Lanka	−9.91	Venezuela	4.03
El Salvador	7.94	Denmark	−11.76
Malaysia	−11.21	New Zealand	−11.76
Ecuador	19.91	Canada	−11.68
Turkey	2.88	Switzerland	−11.76
		U.S.A.	−11.06

the income ladder. Not surprisingly, the most stable countries are OECD democracies, even though several LDCs, such as Botswana, are also relatively stable. The case of Venezuela is also interesting: in 1960 it had the fifth highest per capita income in the sample, but a much higher *SPI* index than the countries in the same group. . . .

4. Model Specification

Our hypothesis is that income inequality increases socio-political instability and the latter reduces the propensity to invest. A large group of impoverished citizens, facing a small and very rich group of well-off individuals is likely to become dissatisfied with the existing socio-economic sta-

tus quo and demand radical changes, so that mass violence and illegal seizure of power are more likely than when income distribution is more equitable. Several arguments justify the second link, from political instability to investment. Broadly speaking, political instability affects investment through three main channels. First, because it increases the expected *level* of taxation of factors that can be accumulated. . . . Second, because phenomena of social unrest can cause disruption of productive activities, and therefore a fall in the productivity of labor and capital. Third, because socio-political instability increases *uncertainty,* thereby inducing investors to postpone projects, invest abroad (capital flights) or simply consume more. In turn, a high value of the *SPI* index implies high uncertainty for two reasons. First, when social unrest is widespread, the probability of the government being overthrown is higher, making the course of future economic policy and even protection of property rights more uncertain. Second, the occurrence of attempted or successful coups indicates a propensity to abandon the rule of law and therefore, in principle, a threat to established property rights.

We capture these two links in a simple bivariate simultaneous equation model with *SPI* and investment as endogenous variables. The most basic specification of this model is as follows:

$$INV = \alpha_0 + \alpha_1 SPI + \alpha_2 GDP + \alpha_3 PPPIDE$$
$$+ \alpha_4 PPPI + \varepsilon_1, \tag{2}$$
$$SPI = \beta_0 + \beta_1 PRIM + \beta_2 INV$$
$$+ \beta_3 MIDCLASS + \varepsilon_2. \tag{3}$$

. . . As discussed above, we expect α_1 in the investment equation to be negative. In the same equation, we control for the initial level of GDP per capita, as it is common in the literature. Note that the sign of the coefficient of *GDP*, α_2, is a priori ambiguous: according to the exogenous growth theory, long-run convergence would imply a negative sign. However, as Levine and Renelt (1992) have shown, empirically *GDP* enters with a consistently positive sign in cross-country investment regressions, suggesting that the convergence in GDP per capita occurs through channels different from increases in physical investment. The two variables *PPPI* (the PPP value of the investment deflator in 1960 relative to that of the U.S.) and *PPPIDE* (the magnitude of the deviation of PPPI from the sample mean) capture the effects of domestic distortions which obviously would affect investment directly.

Table 3. Investment and SPI Equations, 1960–85[a]

	INV (1a)	SPI (1b)	INV (2a)	SPI (2b)
Constant	27.36 (9.34)	37.43 (4.54)	27.85 (9.49)	32.44 (3.02)
GDP	0.07 (1.09)		0.06 (0.91)	
SPI	–0.50 (–2.39)		–0.57 (–3.14)	
PPPI	–0.14 (–2.39)		–0.15 (–3.14)	
PPPIDE	0.04 (0.62)		0.05 (0.79)	
PRIM		–0.23 (–2.45)		–0.32 (–2.82)
MIDCLASS		–1.01 (–3.42)		–0.68 (–2.34)
INV		0.72 (1.30)		0.66 (1.38)
LAAM				9.89 (2.39)
ASIA				2.59 (0.38)
AFRICA				–3.17 (–0.76)
NOBS	71	71	71	71
s.e.e.	6.71	11.62	7.09	10.90

[a]2SLS. *t*-statistics in parentheses. Estimates using 3SLS are very similar.

Turning to the *SPI* equation, we included the variable *PRIM* (the enrollment ratio in primary school in 1960) as a proxy for human capital, on the ground that a higher level of education may reduce political violence and channel political action within institutional rules (see Huntington (1968) or Hibbs (1973)).[5] Therefore, we expect β_1 to be negative. Investment is also included to test whether rapidly growing economies tend to be more stable: on the one hand, more growth means more prosperity, less dissatisfaction and possibly more stability, implying a negative sign for β_2. On the other hand, periods of very high growth may temporarily lead to social disruptions and economic transformation which may actually *increase* political instability. Finally, as discussed at length above, we expect a positive relation between inequality and instability: accordingly, under the null hypothesis the sign of β_3 should be negative when an index of equality is used. . . .

5. Estimation of the Basic Specification

We start by estimating the basic specification of Eqs. (2) and (3) in columns (1a) and (1b) of Table 3. The two key coefficients are those that capture the effects of *SPI* on *INV* and of *MIDCLASS* on *SPI*. Both coefficients have the expected signs and are significant at the 5% level: socio-political

instability depresses investment and a rich middle class reduces socio-political instability. A "healthy" middle class is conducive to capital accumulation because it creates conditions of social stability. . . . the share of income of the middle class has a correlation of almost –1 with the share of the richest quintile; thus, a wealthier middle class implies more equality in the distribution of income.

An increase by one standard deviation of the share of the middle class is associated with a decrease in the index of political instability by about 5.7, which corresponds to about 48% of its standard deviation. This in turn is associated with an increase in the share of investment in GDP of about 2.85 percentage points. The effect of income distribution on investment implied by these estimates is definitely not negligible, since the difference between the highest and lowest value of *MIDCLASS* in the sample is about 4 standard deviations. In addition, an exogenous increase in the *SPI* index by one standard deviation causes a decrease in the share of investment in GDP of about 6 percentage points.

The coefficient on *PPPI* in the investment equation has the expected negative sign and is significant at high levels of confidence: market distortions do have negative effects on investment. The second proxy for market distortions, *PPPIDE,* is insignificant. Consistently with the results of the existing literature, initial GDP per capita has a positive, although insignificant, coefficient.[6]

The estimation results for the *SPI* equation are also very sensible. *PRIM* has a negative and signif-

[5]In addition to providing new measures of primary enrollment, Barro and Lee (1993) have recently estimated several stock measures of human capital, and they kindly made all their data available to us. We prefer to use their primary enrollment ratio which is not an estimate but a direct observation. When we use their estimated human capital stock our regressions are less successful, possibly because of measurement errors in the constructed stock variables.

[6]Note that our results in the investment equation are consistent with the reduced-form results in Barro (1991).

icant coefficient: as expected, countries with higher levels of education tend to be more stable.

In columns (2a) and (2b) we add three regional dummies, *ASIA* (for the East Asian countries), *LAAM* (for Latin American countries) and *AFRICA* (for Sub-Saharan countries), in the *SPI* equation. There are at least two reasons for this: first, cultural and / or historical reasons may influence the amount of socio-political unrest in different regions of the world. Second, in certain regions, particularly Africa, under-reporting of socio-political events can be particularly acute. Of the three regional dummies, only *LAAM* is significant: as expected, on average Latin American countries tend to be much more unstable than the other countries in the sample. The coefficient of *SPI* in the investment equation is very similar to that of column (1a), while the coefficient of *MIDCLASS* in the *SPI* equation drops (in absolute value) by about 30% to −0.68, although it remains strongly significant. This is hardly surprising, since the Latin America countries in the sample are more unstable than the average and, especially, have a particularly unequal distribution of income. Since regional dummies do appear to be important in our regressions, from now on we include them in all our reported estimates; it might be worthwhile nothing that, if we did not include them, in general our results on the income distribution variable would be *stronger* than the ones we report.

References

Alesina, Alberto and Dani Rodrik, 1993, Income distribution and economic growth: A simple theory and some empirical evidence, In: Alex Cukierman, Zvi Hercovitz and Leonardo Leiderman, eds., The political economy of business cycles and growth (MIT Press, Cambridge, MA).

Alesina, Alberto and Dani Rodrik, 1994, Distributive politics and economic growth, Quarterly Journal of Economics, 109, 465–490.

Alesina, Alberto, Sule Ozler, Nouriel Roubini and Philip Swagel, 1996, Political instability and economic growth, Journal of Economic Growth, forthcoming.

Barro, Robert J., 1991, Economic growth in a cross-section of countries, Quarterly Journal of Economics 106, 407–444.

Barro, Robert J. and Jong-Waa Lee, 1993, International comparisons of educational attainments, Unpublished (Harvard University, Cambridge, MA).

Barro, Robert J. and Holger Wolf, 1989, Data appendix for economic growth in a cross section of countries, unpublished (National Bureau of Economic Research, Cambridge, MA).

Bertola, Giuseppe, 1993, Market structure and income distribution in endogenous growth models, American Economic Review 83, 1184–1199.

Canning, David and Marianne Fay, 1993, Growth and infrastructure, Unpublished (Columbia University, New York).

Gupta, Dipak K., 1990, The economics of political violence (Praeger, New York).

Hibbs, Douglas, 1973, Mass political violence: A cross-sectional analysis (Wiley and Sons, New York).

Huntington, Samuel, 1968, Political order in changing societies (Yale University Press, New Haven, CT).

Jain, Shail, 1975, Size distribution of income: A compilation of data (World Bank, Washington, DC).

Jodice, D. and D. L. Taylor, 1988, World handbook of social and political indicators (Yale University Press, New Haven, CT).

Levine, Ross and David Renelt, 1992, A sensitivity analysis of cross-country growth regressions, American Economic Review 82, 942–963.

Londegran, John and Keith Poole, 1990, Poverty, the coup trap and the seizure of executive power, World Politics 92, 1–24.

Londegran, John and Keith Poole, 1991, Leadership turnover and unconstitutional rule, Unpublished.

Mauro, Paolo, 1993, Political instability, growth and investment, Unpublished (Harvard University, Cambridge, MA).

Ozler, Sule and Guido Tabellini, 1991, External debt and political instability, Mimeo.

Perotti, Roberto, 1993, Political equilibrium, income distribution, and growth, Review of Economic Studies, Sep.

Perotti, Roberto, 1996, Income distribution, democracy and growth: What the data say, Journal of Economic Growth, forthcoming.

Persson, Torsten and Guido Tabellini, 1994, Is inequality harmful for growth? Theory and Evidence, American Economic Review 84, 600–621.

Venieris, Yannis and Dipak Gupta, 1986, Income distribution and socio-political instability as determinants of savings: A cross-sectional model, Journal of Political Economy 96, 873–883.

VIII.C. CASE STUDIES

Selection VIII.C.1. Rising Inequality in China, 1981–1995*

As China's reforms have continued, its income distribution has become more unequal. In 1981 China was an egalitarian society, with an income distribution similar to that of Finland, the Netherlands, Poland, and Romania. But rapid economic growth has brought dramatic change, so that China's income inequality is now just about average by international standards (Figure 1). In 1981 China's Gini coefficient (a measure of inequality of income distribution ranging from 0, absolute equality, to 100, absolute inequality) was 28.8. By 1995 it was 38.8—lower than in most Latin American, African, and East Asian countries and similar to that in the United States, but higher than in most transition economies in Eastern Europe and many high-income countries in Western Europe.

The increase in China's Gini coefficient was by far the largest of all countries for which comparable data are available (Figure 2). Such a large change is unusual. Levels of inequality vary enormously by country, but income distributions are strikingly stable over time within a given country (Deininger and Squire 1996). When large changes do occur, they generally signal deep structural transformations in the underlying distribution of assets and in their rates of return. Recent examples come mainly from transition economies, but Brazil, Thailand, and the United Kingdom have also experienced substantial increases in inequality.

Still, China's recent experience stands out even in this crowd. Not even the transition economies of Eastern Europe and the former Soviet Union registered increases in inequality as large as those observed in China over the past fifteen years. Moreover, some East Asian countries actually saw inequality fall during this period.

Growing Unequal: National Trends

Regardless of how inequality is measured, China's income distribution has become more unequal (Figure 3). This conclusion holds despite the many shortcomings of China's household survey data. . . . The decile ratio (the ratio of the mean income of the top 10 percent of the population to the mean income of the bottom 10 percent) has been rising, especial-

*From World Bank, *Sharing Rising Incomes: Disparities in China* (Washington, D.C.: The World Bank, 1997), pp. 7–10, 15–17, 20, 22, 24–25. Reprinted by permission.

ly since 1990, suggesting increasing divergence between the richest and poorest groups.

Since the start of reforms China has experienced three distinct periods in the evolution of personal incomes (Box 1).[1] Between 1981 and 1984 all segments of society benefited from across-the-board improvements in welfare, with only a small rise in inequality. Between 1984 and 1989 personal incomes stagnated and became increasingly unequal, implying real losses in the standard of living for a large part of the population. Renewed growth in incomes between 1990 and 1995 appears to have reached the poorer (but not the poorest) segments of society but was accompanied by substantial increases in inequality. . . .

A look at the components of the worsening national income inequality reveals unique features in China's income distribution and points to the unfinished nature of transition. The widening gulf between rural and urban incomes is the biggest contributor to increased inequality. Regional disparities are responsible for a smaller but growing portion of inequality.

The Rural-urban Divide Is Growing

The income gap between China's rural and urban populations is large and growing. According to State Statistical Bureau data, rural-urban disparities accounted for more than one-third of inequality in 1995 and about 60 percent of the increase in inequality between 1984 and 1995 (Figure 4). Adjusting these data for some . . . shortcomings . . . reveals an even starker picture. Adjusted, rural-ur-

[1]The density distributions used to analyze these periods were generated by software designed to process distribution data—the Gini TookPak—developed by Yuri Dikhanov of the World Bank. State Statistical Bureau data in the *China Statistical Yearbook* include tabulations for the share of households with per capita income within a range, for rural households; and average per capita income for each decile (each 5 percent starting in 1989) of households, with corresponding share of total income ranked by per capita income, for urban households. The computations here convert household distributions into population distributions based on household size per income category, shown in the *China Statistical Yearbook* for the urban survey and supplied by the State Statistical Bureau for the rural survey (for 1985, 1990, and 1992–95, with interpolations for intervening years). Incomes are deflated using the urban or rural consumer price index (except for pre-1985 rural data, which were deflated by the rural retail price index). Rural and urban data are aggregated into the national distribution using population data (based on registration status) from the *China Statistical Yearbook*.

Figure 1. Since 1981 China's income distribution has become much less equal . . .

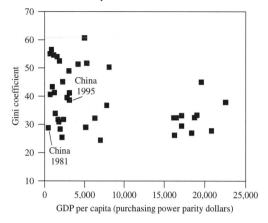

Note: The countries in the figure are chosen largely on the basis of availability of comparable data, but also with a view to representing different regions. Comparable statistics on income distribution are still not common and restricted the number of countries that could be included. All Ginis shown are based on income (not expenditure) distributions. China data are based on World Bank staff estimates. Data for all other countries are for years between 1988 and 1992.
Source: Deininger and Squire 1996; World Bank 1996; World Bank staff estimates.

Figure 2. . . . because of remarkable changes between 1981 and 1995

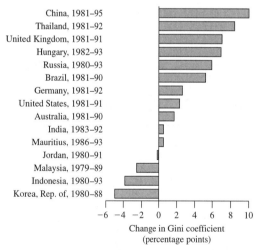

Note: The countries in the figure are chosen largely on the basis of availability of comparable data, but also with a view to representing different regions. Comparable statistics on income distribution are still not common and restricted the number of countries that could be included. All Ginis shown are based on income (not expenditure) distributions. China data are based on World Bank staff estimates. Data for all other countries are for years between 1988 and 1992.
Source: Deininger and Squire 1996; World Bank 1996f; World Bank staff estimates.

Figure 3. Other measures of inequality point to the same conclusion as the Gini index, 1981–95.

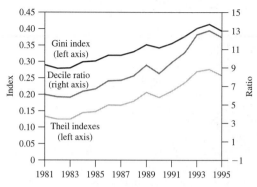

Note: The decile ratio is the ratio of the mean income of the top decile of the population to the mean income of the bottom decile. The Theil indexes (Theil 1 and 2, or mean log deviation) belong to the generalized entropy class of inequality measures, which are decomposable.
Source: State Statistical Bureau data and World Bank staff estimates.

ban disparities accounted for more than 50 percent of inequality in 1995 and explain 75 percent of the increase between 1984 and 1995. The data adjustments yield two important changes: they lower inequality within rural and within urban areas but maintain the trend increase, and they magnify rural-urban disparities. The overall impact of the changes is an increase in total inequality.

China's rural-urban income gap is large by international standards. Data for thirty-six countries show that urban incomes rarely are more than twice rural incomes; in most countries rural incomes are 66 percent or more of urban incomes (Yang and Zhou 1996). In China rural incomes were only 40 percent of urban incomes in 1995, down from a peak of 59 percent in 1983 (Figure 5). These figures do not take into account the differential increases in the cost of living between urban and rural areas. But even the deflated series reveals an unmistakable trend. Rural incomes grew rapidly during the early years of reform but in 1985 began to trail increases in urban incomes. This trend reversed only in 1995.

Two other variables affect the accurate assessment of rural-urban income disparities, and both have been incorporated in the adjusted data in Figure 4 and Table 1: cost of living differences between rural and urban areas and the underestimation of both rural and urban in-kind income.[2] Rural incomes were adjusted to include imputed rent and

---

[2] Deflating rural and urban incomes corrects for different increases in prices but does not adjust for differences in the level of prices between urban and rural areas in the initial year.

Box 1 China's income distribution, 1981–95: A tale of three periods

Growth with Equity

China started its economic reforms in 1978 with the introduction of the household responsibility system. The unleashing of rural productivity in response to the provision of incentives for personal gain are by now well-known. Between 1981 and 1984 the national income distribution shifted to the right (see top figure), indicating across-the-board benefits from reforms. Mean incomes increased by 12.6 percent a year (in real terms) during this period. The slightly flatter curve in 1984 indicates an increase in inequality relative to 1981, although the distribution of income re-

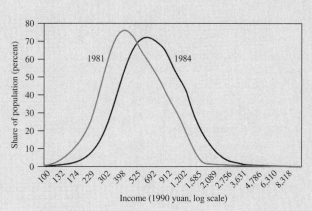

Source: World Bank staff estimates.

mained remarkably equal for such a large shift in average incomes. Between 1981 and 1984 the Gini coefficient increased slightly, from 28.8 to 29.7.

Inequality with Little Growth

Between 1984 and 1989 the income distribution curve shifted dramatically. Inequality became much more pronounced, with the shorter and wider 1989 curve reflecting a jump in the Gini coefficient from 29.7 in 1984 to 34.9 in 1989 (see middle figure). Interestingly, these large distributional shifts occurred despite stagnation in personal incomes. Between 1984 and 1989 average incomes increased by less than 1 percent a year. Although the mean income of the top decile of the population increased by 2.8 percent a year (shift to the right in the right tail), the mean income of the bottom decile dropped by 4.5 percent a year (shift to the left in the left tail).

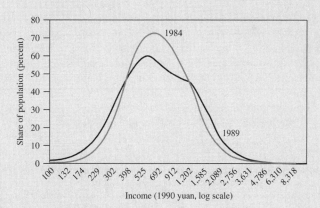

Source: World Bank staff estimates.

Positive income growth started occurring only with the sixth decile. These changes are reflected in a deterioration in poverty indicators during this period, which also saw an increase in rural-urban disparities (the bulge in the upper right side of the 1989 curve).

Growth with Inequality

Between 1990 and 1995 renewed growth in personal incomes (7.1 percent a year) was associated with substantial increases in inequality (see bottom figure). During this period the Gini coefficient increased from 33.9 to 38.8. Still, the benefits of growth reached people at the lower end of the income distribution, with the possible exception of those at the very bottom (incomes less than 190 yuan a year in 1990 prices). Incomes of the bottom decile (less than 337 yuan a year) increased by 1.7 percent a year between 1990 and 1995, but most of these gains were registered in 1994 and 1995, when the mean income of this group grew by 6.7 percent a year. Mean incomes of the top decile increased by 9.7 percent a year between 1990 and 1995

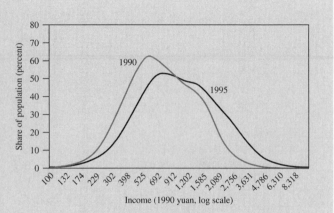

Source: World Bank staff estimates.

but by as much as 12.1 percent between 1990 and 1994. Growth in 1995 appears to have considerably equalized the distribution of incomes.

Source: State Statistical Bureau data and World Bank staff estimates.

urban incomes to include in-kind income for housing, education, health care, pensions and other subsidized services. In addition, a 15 percent cost differential was introduced between urban and rural areas. These adjustments lowered rural incomes to 31 percent of urban incomes in 1990—substantially less than the 50 percent suggested by official data.[3] The adjusted data also yield much higher national inequality (as measured by the Gini coefficient) because urban income increases more than compensate for the higher cost of living in urban areas.

The magnitude of the gap between China's rural and urban incomes points to imperfect mobility in factor markets, especially for labor. Despite in-

creasing accommodation of the swelling demand for rural emigration, impediments to labor mobility remain. These are motivated by the government's desire to control the pace of migration and ensure grain self-sufficiency. The costs of relocation, lack of job information, absence of a housing market, and limited access to social services in urban areas pose additional constraints to migration. Meanwhile, government policies continue to prop up urban standards of living. Urban citizens are subsidized in a variety of ways, including through the absence of hard budget constraints for state-owned enterprises (primarily to protect urban jobs), low-cost capital for urban enterprises, low-cost housing for urban residents, and generous pensions and health insurance schemes. Enterprise and financial sector reforms and fiscal constraints are challenging these acquired rights: some in-kind benefits have been eliminated while others are being monetized, as workers now pay higher rents and contribute more to their pension and medical benefits. This may account for part of the observed increase in the rural-urban income gap in official data. . . .

According to official data, both rural and urban inequality increased steadily between 1981 and 1995 (Figure 6). The urban Gini coefficient increased from 17.6 in 1981 to 27.5 in 1995, although it dropped during the recession years of 1989–91 and in 1995. The rural Gini increased from a much higher base of 24.2 in 1981 to 33.3 in 1995. It dipped in 1985 and in 1990 and has stabi-

[3]The State Statistical Bureau's urban household survey team estimated the monetary value of the main categories of in-kind income, including housing, health care, education, and pension contributions. The results increased the mean urban income in 1990 by some 80 percent. The bureau partly addressed the most important sources of underestimation of rural income in official data with the valuation of own-grain consumption at mixed prices, starting in 1990. Among the remaining areas requiring adjustment, an important one is imputed rent to reflect the value of owner-occupied housing. Based on household survey data for four provinces, Ravallion and Chen (1997) estimate this at about 6 percent of mean income. The changes in the rural-urban income ratio in this analysis are more pronounced than the ones found in Griffin and Zhao (1993). A 1988 household survey that corrected for a number of the concerns with official State Statistical Bureau data placed rural incomes at 41 percent of urban incomes and the national Gini coefficient at 38. The corresponding figures based on official data were 49 percent for the rural-urban income ratio and 33 for the Gini.

Figure 4. Rural-urban disparities account for the bulk of the increase in inequality.

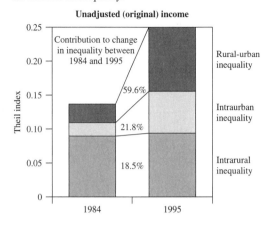

Figure 5. Rural per capita incomes are plummeting relative to urban per capita incomes, 1978–95.

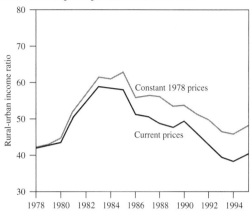

Note: Rural incomes deflated using the rural consumer price index for 1985–95. Pre-1985 rural incomes deflated using the rural retail price index. Urban incomes deflated using the urban consumer price index

Source: World Bank staff estimates based on State Statistical Bureau data.

The Gulf Between the Coast and the Interior Is Widening

Within China, much of the debate on inequality has focused on regional growth patterns. This is understandable given sharply widening regional disparities: interprovincial differences contributed 50 percent more to inequality in 1995 than in 1985, and the contribution of the coastal-interior gap doubled during the same period (Figure 7). Yet regional income inequality in China is still moderate. As much as two-thirds of total inequality remains *within* provincial borders.[4]

Provincial distributions for 1992 (the only year for which data are available) are telling (Figure 8). They show that the income gap between the coast and the interior is significant; in 1992 average incomes in coastal China were 50 percent higher than in interior provinces. But in the same year the rural-urban income gap was twice as large.[5]

Provincial income disparities are increasing for several reasons. Since the start of reforms, coastal

Note: Adjustments are only indicative and reflect various corrections made to these data. Changes to rural incomes are based on corrections made by Ravallion and Chen (1997) to rural household data from four provinces (Guanqxi, Guizhou, Guangdong, and Yunnan) for 1985–90. Here we assume that these adjustments can be generalized to the country's rural areas as a whole. We also assume that changes made to the State Statistical Bureau's methodology in 1990 correct fully for the undervaluation of own-grain consumption. Thus adjusted data after 1990 reflect only the impact of regional price differentials and assume that the impact of these on rural inequality in 1990–95 remains as in 1990. Adjustments to urban data are based on information provided by the State Statistical Bureau's household survey team for 1990 and 1995. They reflect the inclusion of in-kind benefits on urban income. We assume that the level and distribution of pre-1990 in-kind benefits were as in 1990, and interpolate for the years between 1990 and 1995. Finally, we introduce a 15 percent cost of living differential between urban and rural areas, based on 1990 prices.

Source: World Bank staff estimates based on State Statistical Bureau data.

lized since 1993. The declines in 1985 and 1990 almost certainly represent measurement effects because there were large adjustments to the State Statistical Bureau's household survey in both years. . . .

[4]In 1992 mean income in the wealthiest province (Guangdong) was only 2.8 times mean income in the poorest province (Guizhou), whereas the ratio of the top to bottom income decile was 4.7 in the most equal province (Jiangxi) and as much as 16.0 in the most unequal province (Ningxia).

[5]Rural residents in the interior have incomes that are much closer to coastal peasants than to urban residents in the interior. Similarly, people living in coastal cities have only mildly higher incomes than people living in interior cities but much higher incomes than people living in the coastal countryside. . . .

Table 1. Rural-urban Income Gap and Inequality with Data Adjustments, 1990

Measure	Rural-urban income ratio (percent)	National Gini coefficient	Contribution to national inequality (percent)
Official data	49.5	33.9	29.5
With 15 percent higher cost of living in urban areas	56.9	31.9	20.5
Plus in-kind incomes	30.5	40.6	51.8

Source: State Statistical Bureau urban household survey team and World Bank staff estimates.

Figure 6. Rural and urban inequality have increased steadily since reforms began.

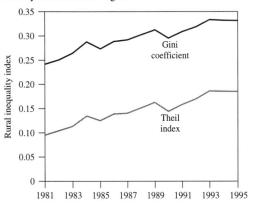

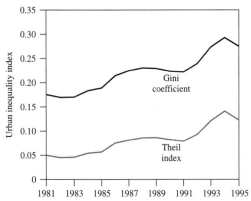

Source: World Bank staff estimates.

Figure 7. Interprovincial and coastal-interior disparities are widening but remain moderate.

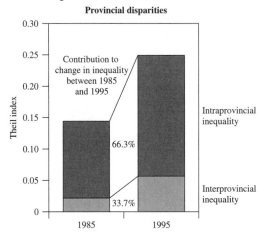

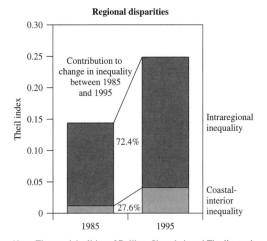

Note: The municipalities of Beijing, Shanghai, and Tianjin are included in the coast.

Source: World Bank staff estimates based on State Statistical Bureau data.

provinces have grown faster—and at an accelerating pace—than interior ones, fueling disparities in personal incomes. Coastal provinces grew 2.2 percentage points faster during 1978–94, 2.8 percentage points faster during 1985–94, and a remarkable 5 percentage points faster during 1990–94. Initial conditions, natural endowments, and preferential policies have combined to give coastal provinces a

boost over interior ones in taking advantage of the opportunities created by reforms.

First, the interior lags the coast in human capital development. Even before reforms, education and health levels were higher on the coast; the gap has

Figure 8. There is a clear income gap between the coast and the interior . . .

. . . but rural-urban disparities are much larger . . .

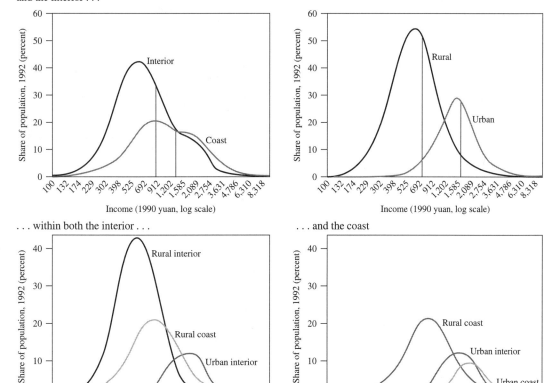

. . . within both the interior . . .

. . . and the coast

Source: World Bank staff estimates based on State Statistical Bureau data.

since widened. Literacy, school attendance, and infant mortality are all better on the coast. The presence of large ethnic minority populations in the interior likely contributes to this outcome. While primary school attendance is only slightly worse in the interior, high school attendance rates are significantly lower than on the coast.

Second, per capita investment levels on the coast are two and a half times those in the interior. And differences are not confined to levels of investment; they also extend to types of investment. In particular, the coast invests more in fast-growing industries, so more coastal residents work in industries that have seen high productivity gains. The coast also shows somewhat lower investment in state enterprises. More important, investment in fast-grow-

ing township and village enterprises accounts for nearly half of all non-state enterprise investment in most coastal regions, but less than a quarter in the interior. And these enterprises have grown faster on the coast than in the interior. Disparities in foreign direct investment and trade are even more striking. For example, in 1992 foreign direct investment in the coast accounted for more than 10 percent of total fixed investment; in the interior it accounted for less than 2 percent. And coastal regions received more than 85 percent of China's imports in 1993.

Third, as China has shifted from a closed and planned agricultural economy to an open, market-oriented industrial one, returns have increased to natural and geographical advantages. Natural advantages like harbors, transport corridors, proximity to world markets, and communication links have played a big role in spurring growth in coastal areas.

Fourth, regional policies have favored coastal areas by designating them for preferential treatment in foreign trade and investment. Credit has been allocated disproportionately to the coast, explaining in part investment differentials between the two regions. In addition, coastal provinces have often been the location of choice for pilot reform experiments.

References

China State Statistical Bureau. 1996. *China Statistical Yearbook 1996.* Beijing.

Deininger, Klaus, and Lyn Squire. 1996. "A New Data Set Measuring Income Inequality." *The World Bank Economic Review* 10 (3): 565–91.

Griffin, Keith, and Renwei Zhao, eds. 1993. *The Distribution of Income in China.* New York: St. Martin's Press.

Ravallion, Martin, and Shaohua Chen. 1997. "When Economic Reform Is Faster than Statistical Reform: Measuring and Explaining Inequality in Rural China." World Bank, China and Mongolia Department, Washington, D.C.

World Bank. 1996. *World Development Report 1996: From Plan to Market.* New York: Oxford University Press.

Selection VIII.C.2. Falling Inequality in Rural Indonesia, 1978–1993*

Rice

Rice has been the success story, dominated by the growth of *sawah* (wet rice): *Sawah* output rose by more than 250 per cent from 1966 to 1992, while apparent per capita consumption jumped by almost 80 per cent. Yields more than doubled over this period, and contributed almost 70 per cent of the increased production; the contrast with the minimal yield increases before 1966 is a stark one. Rice dominates the Indonesia diet, except in a few of the eastern provinces, and in the late 1960s had a weight of 31 per cent in the Jakarta 62-commodity CPI. It is therefore not surprising that rice became a major preoccupation of the government after the macroeconomic stabilization phase (1966–68) was completed. "Indeed food policy *was* rice policy" during *Repelita* I, according to Mears and Moeljono (1981, p. 23), although a decade later the government began to place more emphasis on food crop diversification.

Developments in rice reflect the interplay between longer-term policy and institutional factors, and shorter-term influences such as climatic conditions and pest attacks. The longer-term development strategy comprised principally the introduction of high yielding varieties (HYVs), rising input (fertilizer and pesticide) subsidies, output price stabilization and (at least in the 1980s) support, and the rehabilitation and development of irrigation and extension networks. It is the latter factors which explain Indonesia's dramatic rice success, while the shorter-term influences explain annual fluctuations around an improving trend line.

The regime inherited the agricultural extension efforts developed in the early 1960s, known as *Bimas*[1] (Penny, 1969). *Bimas* and several subsequent rice intensification efforts, together with the food procurement agency *Bulog*,[2] have been the institutional pillars of the government's rice promotion efforts. By the late 1960s an operational framework, first expounded systematically by Mears and Afiff (1969), involved the establishment by *Bulog* of floor and ceiling prices for paddy, with margins providing sufficient incentive for private traders to enter the market. The *Bimas* program, operating

through village cooperative units,[3] provided a package of seed and other inputs, together with credit from the government bank specializing in agriculture, Bank Rakyat Indonesia. *Inmas,* an intensification program without credit subsidies, was also introduced.

The first decade after 1966 saw mixed results, in terms of both output and yields (Figures 1 and 2). In some years output rose significantly, notably 1968 owing to increased fertilizer availability (from imports), and 1970 under the impetus of *Bimas* organizational reforms and good rainfall. But for much of the 1970s the record was indifferent. In 1972 a prolonged dry season resulted in falling output. *Bulog* was slow to act, and eventually was unable to defend its ceiling. It was later to enter international markets which in any case were characterized by shortages and rising prices. As a result, domestic rice prices doubled in the last four months of that year. Problems emerged again a few years later. Arrears under the *Bimas* credit program escalated. There was a prolonged drought in 1976. Outbreaks of the *wereng* (brown plant hopper) pest, which first appeared on a wide scale in the 1974/5 season, were particularly serious in 1977. From 1974 to 1977 output barely increased. It appeared then that Indonesia would never be able to achieve significant output expansion, much less the goal of self-sufficiency. By the late 1970s it was importing up to one-third of the world's traded rice, becoming something of a price-maker on thin and then volatile international markets. Mears and Moeljono (1981, p. 49) reflected authoritative thinking at the time, stating that "it seems that the goal of self-sufficiency in rice by 1985 (or any reasonable time thereafter) will be very hard to achieve."

Unlike the situation a decade earlier, by the mid-1970s Indonesia had ample foreign exchange reserves with which to purchase rice. But policymakers were concerned about the sluggish growth in rice production for at least two reasons: first, as real oil prices began to taper off, the prospect of continuing large imports in a thin international market was viewed with concern. The arguments invoked at that time to promote rice were in some respects similar to the justification for the November 1978 devaluation. That is, there needed to be

*From Hal Hill, *The Indonesian Economy, Second Edition* (Cambridge: Cambridge University Press, 2000), pp. 130–138, 196–198, 201–203. Reprinted by permission.

[1]*Bimas* is *Bimbingan Massal,* or Mass Guidance Program.

[2]*Bulog* is *Badan Urusan Logistik,* or State Logistics Board.

[3]These were the BUUD. *Badan Usaba Unit Desa,* or Village Organizational Unit, and KUD. *Kooperasi Unit Desa,* or Village Cooperative Unit.

Figure 1. Production of food crops, 1969–92

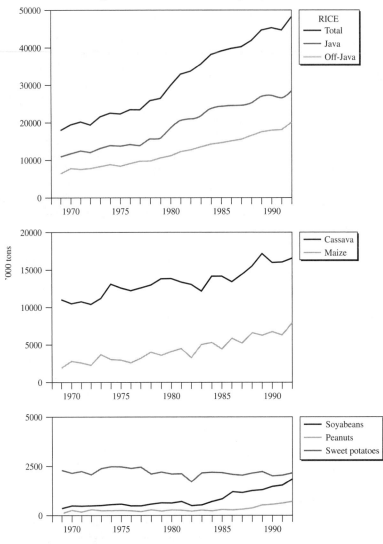

Note: Before 1987, data do not include East Timor.

Sources: BPS, *Statistik Indonesia* and *Indikator Ekonomi,* various issues.

exchange rate protection, or at least compensation, for the intersectoral effects of the Dutch disease.

Secondly, there was a political motive for intervention, to avoid a repetition of the damaging 1972 crisis and to ensure that the benefits of the oil boom were recycled into rural areas, especially the Javanese heartland. In this respect, Indonesia's political economy equations were and are quite unlike those of other OPEC countries, and indeed of much of the third world in general. The issue of why the country adopted a strong rural development strategy in the 1970s has been a question attracting much speculation but limited systematic analysis by political scientists. A fashionable ex-

planation, invoking Soeharto's rural origins, does appear to be quite convincing. Consider, for example, the following quote recorded in his semi-official biography: "It's natural that I pay greater attention to the problem of rural development. What's more, I am myself the son of a peasant" (Roeder, 1976, p. 218).[4] It may be misleading to invoke essentially anecdotal and highly personalized re-

---

[4]In a similar vein, Timmer (1993, p. 175) records the amazement of delegates to the Food and Agriculture Organization (FAO) at the President's detailed knowledge of technical, agronomic issues on the occasion of the latter's receipt of an international award in recognition of the country's rice production achievements.

Figure 2. Yields of major food crops, 1969–92

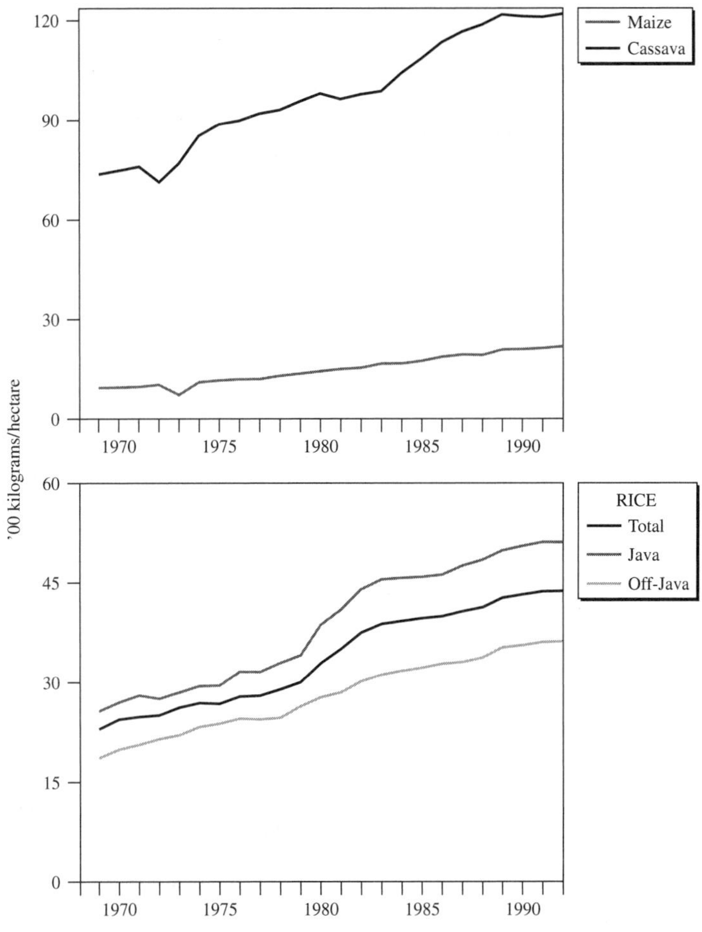

Note: Before 1987, data do not include East Timor.

Sources: BPS, *Statistik Indonesia,* and *Indikator Ekonomi,* various issues.

marks as the basis for understanding the political economy of rice in the New Order. But there does seem to be little doubt that the President's strong support for the rice program has been a major factor in its success.

Alternative explanations for Indonesia's pro-rural strategies might focus on the bases of the regime's political and military support, especially its Javanese power base, and the belief that security in this arena would ensure the New Order's popularity. The fact that rice has been heavily supported, in marked contrast to the poorly performing smallholder cash crop sector, located mainly off-Java, lends superficial support to the notion that the regime has been more "pro-Java" than "pro-rural" in general. But this is an issue on which more research by political scientists is required.

The mid-1970s was therefore something of a watershed in rice policy, the effects of which were to become evident by the end of the decade. A number of measures to be discussed shortly, had a dramatic impact on rice production. These initiatives had a delayed but relatively swift impact on production from the late 1970s. In 1977–78, rice production began to grow rapidly, from 23.3 million tons in 1977 to 29.7 million tons in 1980 and 38.1 million tons in 1984 (Figure 1). Good rainfall and the absence of pest problems facilitated the expansion, but the primary explanation was the concerted and comprehensive policy measures discussed above. In 1980, serious storage capacity problems emerged, indicative of the fact that the supply response caught even officials by surprise. The country weathered the 1982–83 drought, the most serious in a decade. Output growth resumed quickly in 1984 and 1985, once again leading to storage problems for *Bulog,* which was left with large quantities of deteriorating, low quality rice.

Figure 3. Rice: intensification and fertilizer use, 1969–92

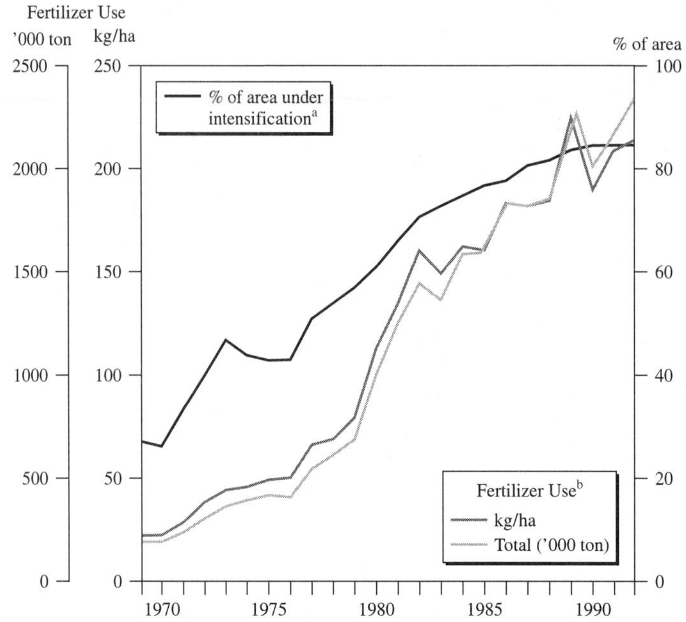

[a]Includes all intensification programs, "special" and "general," and various initiatives within these categories, such as Bimas, Inmas, and Insus.
[b]Includes the three principal fertilizers, N, P2O, and K2O. The data refer to fertilizer used for the entire food crop sector, whereas the land area includes only rice.

Source: Lampiran Pidato Kenegaraan, various issues.

In November 1985 President Soeharto announced that rice self-sufficiency had been achieved, on the occasion of an invited address to the 40th anniversary conference of the FAO. . . .

Figures 3 and 4 document the key policy instruments used to increase production over this period, all funded by the government's newly found oil wealth. First, there was a concerted effort to accelerate the spread of HYVs. The percentage of the rice area covered by various intensification programs is a reasonable proxy for the coverage of HYVs. The latter's share of rice crop plantings over the 1970–80 decade more than doubled, from about 26 per cent to 61 per cent (Figure 3). The percentage continued to rise strongly in the first half of the 1980s, before tapering off around 1987. Over this period, also, the extent of subsidy implicit in the intensification program began to diminish, especially as farmers began to pay interest rates approximating market levels.

A second instrument, and a key ingredient of the intensification program, was fertilizer. The new varieties are particularly responsive to fertilizer usage, and in the 1960s Indonesia's consumption of commercial fertilizer varieties was low. However, fertilizer application began to rise rapidly during the 1970s, by some five-fold over the

1970–80 decade, doubling again in the following decade (Figure 3). Given that the area under food crop cultivation expanded very slowly, these increases translated into greatly intensified fertilizer usage per hectare, rising by more than 12-fold from 1969 to 1992.[5] Expanding supplies were facilitated by the growth of the domestic industry, but most important, initially, by the availability of foreign exchange to finance imports. Increased usage was unquestionably desirable in the 1970s, and it made a major contribution to rising yields. However, fertilizer became a topic of intense economic and ecological debate in the late 1980s. The former concern was on the grounds of budgetary expense and the belief that application may have exceeded optimum rates.[6] The ecological concern

[5]It needs to be emphasized that the fertilizer data in Figure 3 refer to the entire food crop sector and not just rice. However rice has been by far the largest user, so the trends identified are broadly accurate.

[6]To quote the assessment of one careful analyst of fertilizer application rates: "There is serious technical and price inefficiency in the use of fertilizer in Indonesia. Average application rates on rice are excessive in many provinces when judged by nutrient uptake, agronomic recommendations, and economic criteria. The problem is most common on Java" (Roche, 1994, p. 16).

Figure 4. Rice: price ratios, 1969–92

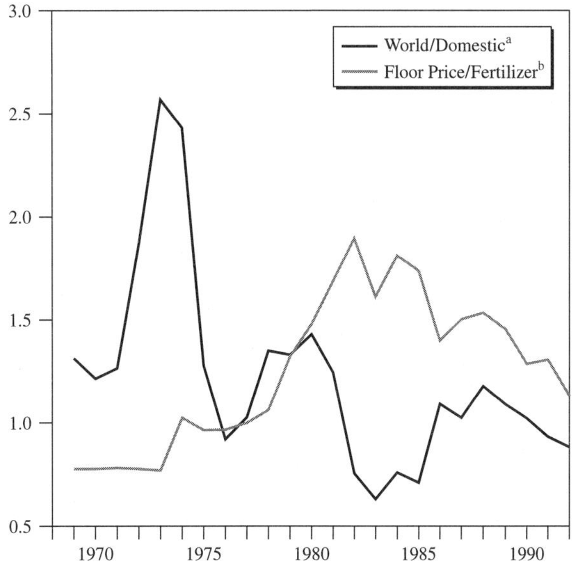

[a]Ratio of Bangkok (5% broken) price, allowing 15–25% CIF Jakarta, to an average of the domestic floor and ceiling prices
[b]Ratio of the floor price to the official fertilizer price.
Source: Data kindly supplied by Dr Erwidodo and Dr Ray Trewin, from various unpublished sources.

centred on the fact that low official prices were encouraging indiscriminate application, possibly leading to pollution of waterways and fisheries, and soil degradation.

. . . The fertilizer subsidy . . . rose from Rp 32 billion in 1977 to Rp 756 billion in 1987 before tapering off. But even in 1991, retail prices were, on average, 42 per cent below world prices and, in the important case of urea fertilizer, 50 per cent below (World Bank, 1992, p. 62). The pesticide subsidy also increased significantly, peaking at Rp 175 billion in 1987. However, in a major victory for both economic rationality and environmental management, it was abolished in the following year, and replaced with a program of integrated pest management.[7] The impact of the fertilizer subsidy is clearly evident in the rice-fertilizer price ratios (Figure 4). After being constant during the first Five Year Plan (1969–73), they began to rise appreciably in the mid-1970s, coinciding more or less exactly with the growth in the government's oil revenue. The sharp increase from 1978 to 1982,

the critical period in terms of achieving rice self-sufficiency, is particularly noticeable. The ratio began to fall after the mid-1980s as the value of the subsidy declined marginally. But even by 1990 it was higher than that of any year over the 1969–78 period.

The third component of rice strategy was price support. Indonesia has largely avoided the extremes of excessive rice protection or taxation. But especially in the 1970s, the government did attempt to insulate the domestic rice market from international fluctuations. During most of the 1970s, the world price exceeded the domestic price by a significant margin, peaking at a differential of more than two to one in 1973–74, when international prices were historically high (Figure 4). Already grappling with its first serious inflation problem since the restoration of price stability in 1968–69, the government sought to restrain domestic rice prices for fear that a significant increase would further fuel inflationary pressures. An additional factor was that this was also a period of domestic political uncertainty, following the January 1974 *Malari* riots, and so any sharp rise in the price of such a basic staple would have been unpopular with vocal urban opinion.

Thereafter, however, relative prices moved in favour of rice producers. After the traumatic expe-

[7]The latter figure is from Tabor (1992, pp. 177–83) who also points out that over the years 1985–86 to 1987–88 these subsidies exceeded the value of the agricultural and irrigation development budget. Moreover, the official fertilizer subsidy estimate understates the real economic subsidy owing to the concessional energy prices paid by fertilizer producers.

rience of 1972–73, *Bulog* began to build up its storage and stock capacity, which enabled it to influence domestic prices significantly. During the 1980s, domestic rice prices did not deviate significantly from world prices. Between 1982 and 1990 the ratio ranged from 0.63 to 1.19, and over this period world prices were, on average, some 91 per cent of domestic prices. Thus in a number of years rice producers received assistance both in the form of input subsidies and output protection.

There were other important components of the rice program which contributed to output growth. The irrigation infrastructure, mainly on Java, had been run down badly over the 1940–66 period (Booth, 1977). Major rehabilitation projects were initiated, many as part of foreign aid programs. Water rates incorporated significant public subsidy. The government stepped up its R&D efforts, building on the work of the International Rice Research Institute in the Philippines, particularly in the development of varieties which were resistant to local pest attacks. Finally, of course, very large subsidies flowed to the rice sector in the form of credit subsidies, both through below-market interest rates, and arrears on repayment, including outright default. These subsidies were channelled directly from the Central Bank to the two key implementing agencies, *Bulog* and Bank Rakyat Indonesia.

What was the magnitude in aggregate of these various forms of assistance? Quantification of the impact of all forms of intervention is virtually impossible. But it is useful to cite the results of one innovative study, by Morrisson and Thorbecke (1990), who provided a fresh perspective on these subsidies, by calculating the domestic agricultural surplus for Indonesia using a 1980 Social Accounting Matrix. Not surprisingly, though unusually for developing countries, they found that the surplus was negative, meaning that "the non-agricultural sector provided a net excess of goods and factors to agriculture . . . of Rp 74 billion" (p. 1086). Significantly, they estimated the net positive public transfer from the government to agriculture to be some Rp 175 billion.

Decomposing rice production growth into its principal components provides further insights into the bases of this sector's dynamics. First, rising yields have consistently been the most important factor in the expansion. Rice yields almost doubled from 1969 to 1992, from 2.25 tons per hectare to 4.35. Consequently, they account for most of the increased output, some 68 per cent over the 1970–90 period. The contribution was somewhat less in the 1980s, owing to considerable area expansion off-Java, but higher in the 1970s. . . .

Inequality and Poverty

Tables 1 and 2 provide a summary picture of trends in inequality and poverty.

The real success story appears to begin in the late 1970s. . . .

The rice economy began to expand dramatically. Each new round of household expenditure survey data (the *Susenas*) reported significant declines in poverty incidence, even during the recession of the mid-1980s, and the figures were quickly and prominently reported in the press. Moreover, the conclusions appeared to be robust, as more sophisticated quantitative analyses all pointed in the same direction. For example, one detailed study concluded that:

No matter where one draws the poverty line, or what poverty measures one uses (within a broad class), aggregate poverty (measured in terms of income) unambiguously fell between 1984 and 1987. (Ravallion and Huppi, 1991, p. 68)

What factors explain Indonesia's comparatively good record on distribution and poverty alleviation since 1966? While it is not possible to offer precise empirical quantification, at least three appear to have been critically important. The first, the legacy of history, is that initial conditions were favourable. In the mid-1960s, there were no major concentrations of private wealth, either in agriculture or in the commercial-industrial sectors. The colonial era and the first 20 years of Independence did not witness the accumulation of vast, land-based rural agglomerations. Moreover, what there were—mainly foreign-owned estates—were run down and later nationalized over the 1958–65 period. Thus the commanding heights of the economy in 1965, such

Table 1. Trends in the Gini Ratio, 1964–65 to 1993[a]

	Urban	Rural	Total
1964–65	0.34	0.35	0.35
1969–70	0.33	0.34	0.34
1976	0.35	0.31	0.34
1978	0.38	0.34	0.38
1980	0.36	0.31	0.34
1981	0.33	0.29	0.33
1984	0.32	0.28	0.33
1987	0.32	0.26	0.32
1990	0.34	0.25	0.32
1993	0.33	0.26	0.34

[a]Based on household expenditure data.

Sources: Unpublished BPS data for 1978–93, and Booth (1992, p. 335) for 1964–65 to 1976, based on *Susenas* data. . . .

Table 2. Trends in Poverty Incidence, 1976–93

	Numbers in poverty (millions)			% of population		
Year	Urban	Rural	Total	Urban	Rural	Total
1976	10.0	44.2	54.2	38.8	40.4	40.1
1978	8.3	38.9	47.2	30.8	33.4	33.3
1980	9.5	32.8	42.3	29.0	28.4	28.6
1981	9.3	31.3	40.6	28.1	26.5	26.9
1984	9.3	25.7	35.0	23.1	21.2	21.6
1987	9.7	20.3	30.0	20.1	16.4	17.4
1990	9.4	17.8	27.2	16.8	14.3	15.1
1993	9.1	16.4	25.5	14.2	13.1	13.5

Source: BPS (1991). . . .

as they were, were almost entirely in the hands of the state. In this respect, Indonesia was quite unlike the Latin American countries or, closer to home, the Philippines and Malaysia, with their large concentrations of private agricultural wealth. It has much more in common with Taiwan and Korea, both noted for their even income distribution. Indonesia's experience therefore appears to provide empirical confirmation for the proposition that initial conditions play a key role in determining subsequent distributional outcomes, and that it is much more difficult to redistribute once the process of rapid economic growth has commenced.[8]

A second factor is that Indonesia's growth trajectory has been conducive to equitable outcomes, in at least two important respects. The strong performance of the rice sector has been the first of these. The food crop sector tends to be associated inherently with more even distributions of wealth and income, owing to the technologies employed, to cultivation practices, and to the predominance of smallholders. The contrast with cash crops, particularly the plantation sector, is clearly evident. And, as we have seen, there is no evidence that the green revolution has exacerbated rural inequalities, so that a buoyant rice sector has directly injected purchasing power into rural households, rich and poor alike.

The other feature of Indonesia's post-1965 development with important employment and equity implications has been the growth of export-oriented, labour-intensive manufactures since the mid-1980s. Although criticized by some as a form

of exploitation and "sweated labour," this growth path has been critical to the success of the Asian NIEs in achieving equitable growth (World Bank, 1993). For the poor, who by definition lack any form of capital, the surest means of raising their living standards is through enhancing their earning capacity. This entails, on the supply side, improving education and health standards, and on the demand side expanding employment opportunities. The most effective means of hastening the approach of the "turning point" in the labour market, when conditions of labour surplus begin to disappear, is such a labour-intensive strategy.[9] Here also, therefore, Indonesia shares common features with Japan, Taiwan and Thailand, all states with comparatively good equity records.

A third important factor has been public policy. The New Order regime has been criticized for paying insufficient attention to poverty and inequality. These criticisms are justified in a number of areas. There has never been a serious attempt to introduce a progressive structure of taxation. The politically powerful receive all manner of special privileges and perquisites, some quite blatant in nature. The poor, lacking any political power, have sometimes been treated shamelessly, such as in the relocation of urban squatters, or the eviction of tenant farmers from their land.

Conversely, some government policies have been pro-poor. The rice success story is an obvious

[8]Morawetz (1977, p. 71), for example, advances such a proposition on the basis of his survey of the lessons of economic development from 1950 to 1975. Sundrum (1990, Ch. 16) provides a detailed survey and analysis of redistributive policies in developing countries.

[9]Oshima (1987) emphasizes both these points as being crucial to East Asia's good distributional outcomes, noting in particular that in the early stages of economic development intensive wet rice cultivation was rarely if ever associated with concentrated agricultural land holdings. Indonesia is the only major economy among the NIEs and ASEAN not included in this study, according to Oshima owing to deficiencies in its long-run economic statistics. Nevertheless, much of his analysis is highly relevant to Indonesia.

example, as was more generally the government's capacity to channel a significant proportion of the windfall oil revenues into rural areas, including local development projects and employment-generation programs. The major emphasis on education, and greatly improved standards of basic literacy, is another important example. Large investments in infrastructure have assisted poor farmers, by reducing marketing margins and thereby achieving higher returns. Such a point is emphasized in the three-village study of Hayami and Kawagoe (1993). These investments have also facilitated personal mobility, enabling the poor to migrate more easily in search of better employment opportunities. Another factor, frequently overlooked, is that firm macroeconomic management has indirectly assisted the poor, since it is generally this group which is least able to protect itself from the ravages of high inflation. In addition, the government made a concerted effort to insulate poorer households during the difficult period of fiscal stabilization of the mid-1980s. In sum, therefore, while the record could have been much better, public policies have played a not insignificant role in poverty alleviation since the mid-1960s.

References

(Note: *BIES* refers to the *Bulletin of Indonesian Economic Studies*)

Booth, A. (1977), "Irrigation in Indonesia, Parts I and II," *BIES*, 13(1), pp. 33–74; 13(2), pp. 45–77

Booth, A. (ed.) (1992). *The Oil Boom and After: Indonesian Economic Policy and Performance in the Soebarto Era,* Oxford University Press, Singapore

BPS, Biro Pusat Statistik, *National Accounts* Jakarta, various issues

Hayami, Y. and T. Kawagoe (1993), *The Agrarian Origins of Commerce and Industry: A Study of Peasant Marketing in Indonesia,* St Martin's Press, New York

Mears, L.A. and S. Afiff (1969), "An Operational Rice Price Policy for Indonesia," *Ekonomi dan Keuangan Indonesia,* 17(1), pp. 3–13

Mears, L.A. and S. Moeljono (1981), "Food Policy," in A. Booth and P. McCawley (eds.). *The Indonesian Economy During the Soebarto Era,* Oxford University Press, Kuala Lumpur, pp. 23–61

Morawetz, D. (1977), *Twenty-five Years of Economic Development 1950 to 1975,* Johns Hopkins University Press, for the World Bank, Baltimore

Morrisson, C. and E. Thorbecke (1990), "The Concept of Agricultural Surplus," *World Development,* 18(8), pp. 1081–95

Oshima, H.T. (1987), *Economic Growth in Monsoon Asia: A Comparative Survey,* University of Tokyo Press, Tokyo

Penny, D.H. (1969), "Indonesia," in R.T. Shand (ed.), *Agricultural Development in Asia,* Australian National University Press, Canberra, pp. 251–79

Ravallion, M. and M. Huppi (1991), "Measuring Changes in Poverty: A Methodological Case Study of Indonesia During an Adjustment Period," *World Bank Economic Review,* 5(1), pp. 57–82

Roche, F.C. (1994), "The Technical and Price Efficiency of Fertilizer Use in Irrigated Rice Production," *BIES,* 30(1), pp. 59–83

Roeder, O.G. (1976), *The Smiling General—President Soebarto of Indonesia,* 2nd edn, Gunung Agung, Jakarta

Sundrum, R.M. (1990), *Income Distribution in Less Developed Countries,* Routledge, London

Tabor, S.R. (1992), "Agriculture in Transition," in A. Booth (ed.), *The Oil Boom and After: Indonesian Economic Policy and Performance in the Soebarto Era,* Oxford University Press, Singapore, pp. 161–203

Timmer, C.P. (1993), "Rural Bias in the East and Southeast Asian Rice Economy: Indonesia in Comparative Perspective," *Journal of Development Studies,* 29 (4), pp. 149–176

World Bank (1992), *Indonesia: Agricultural Transformation: Challenges and Opportunities,* 2 vols., World Bank, Washington, D.C.

World Bank (1993), *The East Asian Miracle: Economic Growth and Public Policy,* World Bank. Washington, D.C.

CHAPTER IX

Political Economy

Overview

Since the origin of modern development economics in the 1950s, thinking about the state and economic development has gone through three phases. The first, most optimistic phase viewed the state as an essentially benevolent leader of the development process, an "omniscient social-welfare maximizer" in the words of Dani Rodrik in Selection IX.C.3. The second, most pessimistic phase views the state as a major obstacle to development, acting on behalf of narrow interest groups or on behalf of politicians and bureaucrats (i.e., on its own behalf) rather than for the greater good. Both the theoretical reasoning and the empirical findings constituting this second, ongoing phase are represented in section IX.B. The third phase identifies wide variations in state performance and seeks to explain them, focusing in particular on institutional determinants of "state capacity," meaning the ability of the state to formulate policy independent of corrupting influences and to implement policy effectively. The last section in this chapter is devoted to this newest phase.

While today few specialists in development believe in a benevolent and omniscient state, no one doubts the value of knowing what the state should do if its goal is to maximize social welfare. This is the subject of section IX.A. Under the implicit assumption that "government is well intentioned, well informed, and competent," Nicholas Stern in Selection IX.A.1 identifies five groups of arguments for state intervention: market failure, income distribution, rights to certain facilities or goods such as education, paternalism (relating to drugs, for example), and the rights of future generations. These arguments "point fairly directly to particular areas of government expenditure, notably education, health, social support, and the environment." Stern also states, "When we add to the list basic administration, law and order, and defence, we see that a substantial fraction of GDP will be involved." In Exhibit IX.A.1 he summarizes both reasons for market failure and problems with state intervention.

As noted in the first Comment following Stern's selection, comprehensive development planning has clearly fallen out of favor. Yet some argue for a more limited form of government guidance of the economy, often under the heading of "industrial policy." One of the most prominent advocates of this position is Robert Wade, whose views on "governing the market" are summarized in the Comment that concludes section IX.A. Disagreement regarding the desirability of industrial policy is the chief remaining controversy in what Fischer and Thomas (1990) describe as "the new consensus on development policy":

> The new consensus on development policy places greater stress than before on the central role of markets, and on the private sector (in some countries, the informal private sector) as the engine of growth. The role of the public sector is seen as the creation of a favorable enabling environment for economic activity. The enabling environment consists of the legal, institutional, and policy framework within which economic agents operate.
>
> A government that creates a favorable enabling environment has a large role to play, for instance in ensuring the provision of infrastructure, including social services, such as poverty alleviation, basic education, and access to health care; public security; a stable macroeconomic framework; and an efficient fiscal and regulatory system.
>
> The most difficult question about the role of the government is whether it should take an active part in promoting particular industries, that is, whether it should pursue an industrial policy. Some successful elements of an active policy are clear: export development and assistance in marketing, information, technology, and know-how. Expanding manufactured exports requires sustained efforts on both macroeconomic and microeconomic levels. Japan, Korea, and Taiwan have paid attention to the many nonprice requirements of export development. For a period of time, they also pursued export development while maintaining a certain degree of import protection.

We should note that priorities are not part of this new consensus. Given its limited resources, should the government build roads or schools first? Should the most attention of policymakers and the best and brightest civil servants be devoted to tax collection or macroeconomic management? How should these priorities differ depending on the level of development and other country characteristics? To date economists have had very little to say on this subject.

As evidence for failure of government leadership of the development process mounted, particularly in sub-Saharan Africa (see Selection I.B.5), the view of the state as a major obstacle to development gained momentum. Advocates of this view were hampered, however, by conventional welfare economics analysis that predicts that the "deadweight losses" generated by government interventions in the economy will be small relative to national income. In the first selection of the second section, Anne Krueger points out that when government interventions take the form of restrictions on economic activity that create rents, resources may be wasted in competing for these rents, causing these interventions to be much more costly than conventional analysis predicts. Under certain assumptions it can be shown that the value of the resources wasted by competitive rent seeking will equal the value of the rents; Krueger estimates the value of rents to have been 7.3 percent of Indian GNP in 1964 and roughly 15 percent of Turkish GNP in 1968. Krueger's selection is preceded by a Note explaining exactly what "rents" are and showing that rents and thus the cost of rent seeking can be large relative to deadweight losses. The first Comment following Krueger's selection shows how the Harris–Todaro model presented in Note VI.B.1 can be seen as an example of the complete rent dissipation predicted by Krueger. The second Comment clarifies the relationship between rent seeking and corruption.

In Krueger's analysis, rent seeking is an unintended side effect of well-intentioned (if sometimes misguided) state interventions in the economy. Other writers in the "neoclassical political economy" tradition have argued that these interventions are the result of lobbying by interest groups. For example, import quotas may be designed to protect politically powerful industries. Government failure is thus generated by interest groups that use their influence on the state to cause it to enact inefficient policies that redistribute income in their favor, and is amplified by the rent-seeking activities to which these policies give rise.

In recent years a wave of trade liberalization (mentioned in Selection I.B.1), including the membership of some less developed countries in the World Trade Organization, has greatly reduced the importance of import quotas as a source of rents. At the same time, many scholars have concluded that for most LDCs the "grabbing hand" of government mainly serves the government bureaucrats and politicians themselves rather than private sector special interests. Selection IX.B.2 reflects both of these developments, focusing on regulations of business entry rather than import quotas as a source of rents, and advocating the "tollbooth" hypothesis that state officials put licenses, permits, and other regulatory procedures in place because they give the officials the power to extract bribes. Entrepreneurs may be willing to pay bribes because regulations of business entry restrict competition and thereby create excess profits (rents) that the entrepreneurs want to obtain, or entrepreneurs could anticipate rents from entry because they have new innovations or market niches, in which case bribes serve to transfer some of these rents from the entrepreneurs to state officials.

We should emphasize that regulatory barriers to entry do not automatically induce bribes. As is mentioned in Selection IX.A.2, entrepreneurs may instead hire an expediter such as a legal advisory firm. Moreover, this selection reports evidence that legal traditions unrelated to any desire to extract bribes partly explain why some countries have more onerous regulatory procedures than others. The relationship between regulations of business entry and corruption is therefore an empirical question. In Selection IX.A.2, the number of regulatory procedures is found to be strongly associated with perceived government corruption, even after controlling for a country's per capita GDP.

Government failure has been especially pervasive in sub-Saharan Africa. It is a fact that sub-Saharan African countries are among the world's most ethnically fractionalized, and in Selection IX.B.3 William Easterly and Ross Levine argue that ethnically divided societies are more prone to government failure that includes but is not limited to generation of rents and rent seeking. For example, valuable infrastructure investments may not be made because groups cannot agree on large expenditures, perhaps because of different preferences or because of suspicions that one's own ethnic group will benefit least. In addition, if different ethnic groups control different branches of the government, there may be an especially strong tendency to enact rent-generating legislation, with each group believing its members can capture the rents while the costs fall on other groups. (One could also argue, following the reasoning of Bates [1983], that ethnically divided societies are more likely to adopt exceptionally inefficient project-based policies that can be targeted to co-ethnics.) Either of these arguments can be reversed—each group may agree to support infrastructure investments that benefit other groups in return for support of its favorite projects ("logrolling"), and each group may veto the rent-generating legislation of the other groups—so ultimately the effects of ethnic diversity on infrastructure expenditure and rent-generating legislation are empirical questions. Using data for roughly 100 countries, Easterly and Levine find that ethnic diversity is associated with lower school attainment, fewer telephones per worker, and a higher black-market exchange rate premium (a good source of rents). Through its impact on these and other policy indicators, ethnic diversity tends to reduce economic growth and thus account for much of the poor growth performance of sub-Saharan Africa.

The theoretical and empirical grounds for viewing the state as an obstacle to economic development appear very strong. Yet readers of this book will be able to recall a number of examples of beneficial state action, particularly in East Asia. In the first selection of the final section, Stephen Knack and Philip Keefer present more systematic evidence that state performance, rather than being uniformly bad, varies widely, and that this variation has substantial consequences for economic growth. As explanatory variables in cross-country growth regressions they use indices based on ratings compiled by two private international investment risk services of aspects of state performance such as rule of law, infrastructure quality, and bureaucratic delays. An increase of one standard deviation in either index is associated with an increase in average annual per capita GDP growth of more than 1.2 percentage points.

Writers seeking to explain government success as well as government failure in less developed countries reject the model of the state as a tool of narrow interest groups, but must then confront the issue of why "autonomous" states do not simply maximize the income of politicians and bureaucrats. Indeed, Peter Evans finds in Selection IX.C.2 that some LDC states, notably the government of the former Zaire, do use their autonomy for this purpose. The Korean and Taiwanese states, on the other hand, have worked hand in glove with the private sector to promote investment and enhance the capacity of private firms to enter international markets, earning these governments the moniker "developmental states." Evans argues that a necessary (but not sufficient) condition for a state to be "developmental" is professionalization of the state bureaucracy. Meritocratically recruited officials, partially insulated from society by civil service procedures, identify with the corporate goals of the state and seek to advance their self-interests not through corruption but rather by impressing their colleagues with superior performance and thereby moving up the bureaucratic hierarchy.

In Evans's view, bureaucratic professionalism may be adequate for the state to create the "favorable enabling environment" for private sector economic activity called for in the new consensus on development policy described earlier, but it is not sufficient for the state to pursue successfully the more controversial task of industrial policy. For this the state needs good communications networks with key private sector decision-makers, that is, it needs to be "embedded" in society yet maintain its autonomy—a difficult feat.

In Selection IX.C.3, Dani Rodrik focuses the discussion of state capacity around the ability of the government to successfully implement export subsidies. While he agrees with Evans regarding the importance of autonomy for the ability of the state to implement policy without being manipulated by interest groups, he is much less confident about what state characteristics cause this autonomy to be put to good use. Rather than citing "embeddedness" of bureaucrats as a complement to autonomy, Rodrik emphasizes the need for "coherence" of policy priorities set by the politicians at the top of the decision-making hierarchy.

In the final selection, James Rauch and Peter Evans seek to test Evans's hypothesis that bureaucratic professionalism improves state performance by examining the effects of measures of meritocratic recruitment, internal promotion and career stability, and competitive official salaries on ratings of corruption, bureaucratic quality, and bureaucratic delays collected by Knack and Keefer. To construct their measures Rauch and Evans surveyed three experts per country for 35 LDCs regarding personnel practices in those countries' core economic agencies. Controlling for country per capita income, level of education, and ethnic diversity, they find that their measure of meritocratic recruitment is positively associated with all three ratings of bureaucratic performance collected by Knack and Keefer, and that their measure of salary competitiveness is positively associated with one of these three ratings.

Looking back from the last to the first section of this chapter, it appears that development specialists are much closer to a consensus on what the government should do than they are on how to get the government to do what it should effectively.

References

Bates, Robert H. 1983. "Governments and Agricultural Markets in Africa." In D. Gale Johnson and G. Edward Schuh, eds., *The Role of Markets in the World Food Economy* (Boulder, CO: Westview).

Fischer, Stanley, and Vinod Thomas. 1990. "Policies for Economic Development." *American Journal of Agricultural Economics* 72 (August): 809–14.

IX.A. THE (PROPER) ROLE OF THE STATE IN LESS DEVELOPED COUNTRIES

Selection IX.A.1. Public Policy and the Economics of Development*

The Role of the State

Early writers on development, governments of recently independent developing countries, and many Western countries facing reconstruction after World War II saw a major role for the state in the production process. Behind these judgements were a pessimism about the market's ability to deliver economic change in key dimensions with the speed deemed necessary. . . . More recently the pendulum has swung the other way with a sizeable fraction of the herd of both politicians and economists charging in the direction of minimalist government, privatisation, and so on. I shall argue, on the basis of theory, of rights, and of experience, that the state's role should not be minimal. The state's emphasis, however, should not be on production. It should rather be on health, education, protection of the poor, infrastructure, and providing the right environment for entrepreneurial activity to flourish. When we add to the list basic administration, law and order, and defence, we see that a substantial fraction of GDP will be involved. It should be emphasised that the organisation and finance of this expenditure can take many forms, particularly concerning the tier of government and the relationship between government and community, but the discussion of these important issues would take us too far afield.

I begin with a brief review of what standard microeconomic theory has to say about market and government failures. First note that it would be a mistake to see the issue of the role of the state in terms of finding an appropriate balance along a single dimension such as the fraction of productive capacity owned by the state. Many activities and institutions have public and private aspects to them and many of the crucial policy issues involve finding an effective integration of the market and the government.

Five groups of arguments for state intervention in the economy may be distinguished:

(i) market failure, which may arise from many possible sources including externalities, missing markets, increasing returns, public goods, and imperfect information;

*From Nicholas Stern, "Public Policy and the Economics of Development," *European Economic Review* 35 (1991): 250–57. Reprinted by permission.

(ii) a concern to prevent or reduce poverty and/or to improve income distribution;
(iii) the assertion of rights to certain facilities or goods such as education, health, and housing;
(iv) paternalism (relating, for example, to education, pensions, and drugs); and
(v) the rights of future generations (including some concerns relevant to the environment).

The first two groups of arguments arise from standard welfare economics but the others arise rather differently. Strands from all five provide grounds for government action for both developed and developing countries although they are perhaps stronger for the latter. Together they point fairly directly to particular areas of government expenditure, notably education, health, social support, and the environment.

There is a further substantial role for government in improving market functioning and private sector activity through such measures as building infrastructure, providing a regulatory and legislative framework which allows competition to work effectively, and intervening selectively in industry and agriculture. The market failure arguments are especially persuasive concerning infrastructure, where increasing returns, public goods, and externalities can all be of considerable importance. The arguments therefore help identify important areas for state activity, but, as we have remarked, the case for direct state activity in the production of ordinary producer and consumer goods such as steel, cars, shoes, or ice cream does not appear to be strong, at least from the perspectives included here.

Until now, we have assumed implicitly that the government is well intentioned, well informed, and competent. Governments, however, may be craven or manipulated, they may be very badly informed, and they may be incompetent. In recent years much of the profession seems to have swung towards an emphasis on government failures in contrast to market failures (see, for example, the symposium in the June 1990 issue of the *Journal of Economic Perspectives*, in particular, Krueger 1990), and this shift in the climate of opinion has gone hand-in-hand with the reduction of government activities in a number of countries, although it is not clear that it is economic analysis that has led the way. There is no doubt, however, that failures of government are indeed important and are particularly severe for developing nations.

In the recent past there has been substantial attention in development economics given to the generation by government action (including quotas, prohibitions, restrictions, and the like) of rent-seeking and unproductive activities. It has been argued that this type of economic loss associated with government activity can be very large, relative to traditional calculations of deadweight losses (usually associated with government action in the form of taxes) of the "triangle" variety (or suitable general equilibrium generalisations) which have often been viewed as quite small (1% or so of GNP is a common figure for these losses).

Rent-seeking is no doubt important, but in my judgement the empirical evidence on its magnitude has been weak. Attempts, however insecure, to measure the size of rents are generally far more secure than estimates of the resources used in the pursuit of those rents. Those resources are usually estimated simply by the magnitude of the rents themselves. This rests on the rather dubious assumption that the competition for rents take place in a manner which is perfect in an important sense. Indeed, one of the complaints about the generation of rents is precisely that they are allocated in ways which favour certain groups (such as close relations of the President) and the market for them is not competitive. While this causes aggravation, it may imply that efficiency losses are much smaller than the rents themselves. The effects, however, of the creation of special privileges for certain groups by government may be rather more pernicious and long-term than is portrayed in the simple static descriptions embodied in the arguments just described. Rent-seeking is not limited to developing countries, of course. The New Yorkers see Washington as the rent-seeking capital of the world and the Milanese have a similar view of Rome.

Let us now turn to an examination of empirical evidence. Consideration of the expenditure figures shown in Table 1 indicates that health and social security receive relatively less attention in developing than in industrial nations while defence and general public services show a greater share. It is reasonable to ask why it is that industrial countries attach greater (proportional) weight to social security expending when problems of poverty are clearly far greater in developing nations. One can also argue the share of expenditure on infrastructure (proxied by Transport and Communications in Table 1) is too low given its backward state in many LDCs and its central role in generating growth and aiding market functioning. There appears to be considerable scope for alteration of the composition of expenditures in order to improve living standards and market functioning in developing countries. In support of this view evidence is provided on the impact of various type interventions drawn from a wide range of countries.

Health and Nutrition

The performance of China and Sri Lanka in reducing mortality rates and increasing life expectancy has been outstanding in relation to their incomes. This high performance appears largely to have been the result of public action. I shall describe some central elements briefly. China's life expectancy of 70 and infant mortality rate of 31 per thousand may be compared with India's of 58 and 97, respectively. It seems reasonable to relate this to the extensive social support system in China. Through in large part, a strong focus on the food supply and distribution system China has attained a high level of food consumption per capita (2,630 daily calories per person in 1986) as compared with India at 2,238 (World Bank 1990, table 28). In 1984 there were 1,000 people per physician China as compared with 2,520 in India and much greater attention was paid to maternal and child health care and support of the elderly.

Aggregate income would not appear to be the main issue here. Brazil with an income per capita of $2,160 (conventionally measured), as compared with $330 for China, has only managed a life expectancy of 65 and an infant mortality rate of 61, and the gains in life expectancy and infant mortality rate in China were achieved prior to the very rapid growth since the reforms began in 1979. The crude comparisons of aggregates understates the achievements of China's support system. Whereas China provides a fairly universal system of support, reaching all parts of the country, coverage in India and Brazil is haphazard. For example, the poorest part of Brazil, the north-east which contains most of the country's poor (but only a quarter of the population) receives few social services. Indeed, Brazil's population per physician (1,080) and food consumption per capita (2,656 calories) are similar to China's but the distribution is much worse. The distribution of services probably plays a major part in explaining the higher life expectancy and lower infant mortality rate—the weak and the old in China receive much better support than in most developing countries. Further, China has placed a great emphasis on preventive measures including education, the provision of pure water supply, and adequate sanitation.

The explanation behind Sri Lanka's outstanding performance is similar to that of China although

Table 1. Central Government Expenditures by Type (percent total expenditure, 1986–87)

Area	General public services	Defense	Education	Health	Social security	Transport and communication	Other economic services	Other	Central expenditures (% GDP)
Industrial	8.05	7.34	8.45	9.61	37.71	5.12	7.15	16.57	31.46
Developing	16.94	11.97	14.11	6.21	12.60	7.19	16.04	14.94	25.40
Africa	18.54	8.85	15.97	5.51	8.25	7.12	17.49	18.27	25.63
Asia	17.87	12.99	14.39	5.18	7.14	11.23	19.41	11.79	19.89
Europe	16.88	13.63	7.26	6.26	23.07	6.53	21.18	5.19	29.15
Middle East	13.29	26.69	12.54	4.85	13.22	3.71	11.06	14.64	33.12
Western Hemisphere	16.09	7.53	13.98	8.32	18.77	6.80	11.88	16.63	25.04

Source: International Monetary Fund, *Government Finance Statistics Yearbook* (1989).

Sri Lanka's advance came rather earlier (primarily prior to 1960). The subsidised rice system was introduced in 1942 and the promotion of primary education goes back to the early part of this century (see Drèze and Sen 1990, chap. 12). Like China, Sri Lanka has long had an emphasis on public health—a particularly important example being the eradication of malaria. Chile reduced its infant mortality from 103 per thousand in 1965 to 20 per thousand in 1988 in large part as a result of reforms begun in the early 1970s, including an expansion of primary health care with an emphasis on vulnerable groups (World Bank 1990, chap. 5).

Improved health and nutrition are important in their own right. They may also improve economic performance and there are a number of cases from, for example, Indonesia, Kenya, and India (see Berg 1987, chap. 6) where it has been claimed that improved nutrition in manual workers led to higher productivity.

Protection of Living Standards

To a major extent the reduction of age-specific mortality rates and the lengthening of life expectancy are achieved by protecting the poor from death and illness by, for example, providing clean water, adequate sanitation, and ensuring that they can obtain food. The protection of health and nutrition constitutes a central aspect of social support in developing countries. Over the last ten years or so we have come to understand much more about how protection can be provided (see, for example, Sen 1981, Drèze and Sen 1990, and Ahmad, Drèze, Hills, and Sen 1991). These authors have argued persuasively for careful integration of public action with the market. An important example is the employment-based famine prevention and poverty reduction schemes which have been effective where applied in India throughout this century—see Drèze (1988). The Employment Guarantee Scheme in Maharastra, as well as providing longer-term support, was also effective in meeting the threat of famine in the early 1970s. The cash-for-work element in these schemes embodies both the self-selection device of presentation for work and the provision of purchasing power to buy food. Markets seem effective in ensuring that the supply becomes available to meet the demand. Cash allows that demand to manifest itself.

Education

We have already discussed the Barro (1989a, b) results relating growth rates to human capital mea-

sured in terms of education. The *World Development Report 1990* (chap. 5) reports similar statistical relationships (although between the level of the real GDP and average years of education—Box 5.2) plus estimates of social returns to primary education in Sub-Saharan Africa (16%), Asia (27%), and Latin America (26%) based on Psacharopoulos (1985).

Infrastructure

Looking back over the World Bank's successes and failures (as seen through the eyes of its Operation Evaluation Department) in different areas of activity, Pohl and Mihaljek (1989) found investments in roads and irrigation to have been particularly productive. The *World Development Report 1990* (p. 85) indicates an economic rate of return, on average, for agricultural infrastructural projects of 17 percent. The *World Development Report 1987* noted a study of the Indian economy that put the costs of power cuts in the mid-1970s at 2 percent of GDP. In Bangladesh a study of sixteen villages found that those which had benefitted from public programmes for infrastructure (roads, power, and so on) displayed an increase in average household income approaching one-third (World Bank 1990, p. 60). . . .

The Environment for Economic Activity

Health, education, and infrastructure all play a critical role in the economic environment. So too does competition. Indeed one of the critical lessons of the British privatisation experience has been that competition seems to be of greater importance than whether an industry is publicly or privately owned (see Vickers and Yarrow 1988). A number of discussions of agriculture and the environment in Africa (for example, Platteau 1990) point to the importance of the establishment of clear property rights if investment and land development are to be encouraged. A similar interpretation may be attached to the substantial negative effect of political instability on growth in the Barro analysis. Reynolds (1983), in a study of comparative growth from a perspective of 100 years or so, suggests that the single most important explanatory variable is "political organisation and the administrative competence of government" (p. 978).

The role of government in encouraging private industry can involve much more than defining property rights and promoting a competitive environment. . . . To take some examples from developing countries which have exhibited rapid growth, the government has been very actively involved in channeling credit to selected industries in South Korea, Singapore, and Taiwan. It is interesting that in most of the countries just cited the strategies have involved neither the command economy nor the free market. In some cases international trade has been substantially less than free. One should not view the apparent collapse of the Eastern European economies and the success of Hong Kong together with the (strong) evidence on the beneficial effects of trade-oriented strategies (see, for example, Papageorgiou et al. 1990) as establishing an overwhelming case for minimalist government and a free trade policy. Looking to agriculture we see that governments, such as those of Mexico, India, and Indonesia, have been very influential in developing and disseminating the new technologies that created what is sometimes called "the green revolution." Economic coordination and the encouragement of new ideas and adoption do seem to be areas where the state can play a productive role in assisting the market.

References

Ahmad, E., J. P. Drèze, J. Hills, and A. K. Sen, eds. (1991). *Social Security in Developing Countries.* Oxford: Oxford University Press.

Barro, R. J. (1989a). "Economic Growth in a Cross Section of Countries." National Bureau of Economic Research, Working Paper no. 3120, September.

Barro, R. J. (1989b). "Economic Growth in a Cross Section of Countries." University of Rochester, Working Paper no. 201, September.

Berg, A. (1987). *Malnutrition: What Can Be Done? Lessons from World Bank Experience.* Baltimore: Johns Hopkins University Press.

Drèze, J. P. (1988). "Famine Prevention in India." Development Economics Research Programme Discussion Paper no. 3 (London School of Economics) February.

Drèze, J. P., and A. K. Sen. (1990). *Hunger and Public Action.* Oxford: Oxford University Press.

International Monetary Fund. (1989). *Government Finance Statistics Yearbook,* vol. 13 (Washington, D.C.: International Monetary Fund).

Krueger, A. O. (1990). "Government Failures in Development." *Journal of Economic Perspectives* 4:9–24.

Papageorgiou, D., M. Michaely, and A. M. Choksi (1990). *Liberalizing Foreign Trade.* Oxford: Basil Blackwell for the World Bank.

Platteau, J. Ph. (1990). *Land Reform and Structural Adjustment in Sub-Saharan Africa: Controversies and Guidelines.* Report prepared for the Food and Agricultural Organisation, August.

Pohl, G., and D. Mihaljek. (1989). *Project Evaluation in Practice: Uncertainty at the World Bank.* Economic Advisory Staff, The World Bank.

Reynolds, J. (1983). "The Spread of Economic Growth to the Third World, 1850–1980." *Journal of Economic Literature* 21: 941–80.

Sen, A. K. (1981). *Poverty and Famines.* Oxford: Oxford University Press.

Vickers, J., and G. Yarrow. (1988). *Privatisation: An Economic Analysis.* Cambridge, Mass.: MIT Press.

World Bank. (1987, 1990). *World Development Report.* Oxford: Oxford University Press/World Bank.

EXHIBIT IX.A.1. Market Failure and State Intervention

Reasons for Market Failure

   (i) Markets may be monopolised or oligopolistic.

  (ii) There may be externalities.

 (iii) There may be increasing returns to scale.

 (iv) Some markets, particularly insurance and futures markets, cannot be perfect and, indeed, may not exist.

  (v) Markets may adjust slowly or imprecisely because information may move slowly or marketing institutions may be inflexible.

 (vi) Individuals or enterprises may adjust slowly.

(vii) Individuals or enterprises may be badly informed about products, prices, their production possibilities, and so on.

(viii) Individuals may not act so as to maximise anything, either implicitly or explicitly.

 (ix) Government taxation is unavoidable and will not, or cannot, take a form which allows efficiency.

Some Problems of State Intervention

   (i) Individuals may know more about their own preferences and circumstances than the government.

  (ii) Government planning may increase risk by pointing everyone in the same direction—governments may make bigger mistakes than markets.

 (iii) Government planning may be more rigid and inflexible than private decision-making since complex decision-making machinery may be involved in government.

 (iv) Governments may be incapable of administering detailed plans.

  (v) Government controls may prevent private sector individual initiative if there are many bureaucratic obstacles.

 (vi) Organisations and individuals require incentives to work, innovate, control costs, and allocate efficiently and the discipline and rewards of the market cannot easily be replicated within public enterprises and organisations.

(vii) Different levels and parts of government may be poorly coordinated in the absence of the equilibrating signals provided by the market, particularly where groups or regions with different interests are involved.

(viii) Markets place constraints on what can be achieved by government, for example, resale of commodities on black markets and activities in the informal sector can disrupt rationing or other non-linear pricing or taxation schemes. This is the general problem of "incentive compatibility."

 (ix) Controls create resource-using activities to influence those controls through lobbying and corruption—often called rent-seeking or directly unproductive activities in the literature.

  (x) Planning may be manipulated by privileged and powerful groups which act in their own interests and further, planning creates groups with a vested interest in planning, for example, bureaucrats or industrialists who obtain protected positions.

 (xi) Governments may be dominated by narrow interest groups interested in their own welfare and sometimes actively hostile to large sections of the population. Planning may intensify their power.

Source: Nicholas Stern, "The Economics of Development," *Economic Journal* (September 1989), p. 616. Reprinted by permission.

Comment IX.A.1. *Development Planning*

Beginning in the early 1950s with India's first Five-Year Plan, many countries attempted to formulate a central plan for their economy's development. General introductions to development planning were provided by Maurice Dobb, *An Essay on Economic Growth and Planning* (1960); W. Arthur Lewis, *Development Planning* (1966); Jan Tinbergen, *Development Planning* (1967); K. Griffin and J. Enos, *Planning Development* (1971); and Michael P. Todaro, *Development Planning* (1971).

In the 1970s and 1980s, however, the failures of central planning were more widely recognized. Deficiencies in the formulation and especially the implementation of development plans became acute. One critic of the practice of development planning lists the following causes of poor plan performance:

1. Deficiencies in the plans: they tend to be over-ambitious; to be based upon inappropriately specified macro-models; to be insufficiently specific about policies and projects; to overlook important non-economic considerations; to fail to incorporate adequate administrative provision for their own implementation.

2. Inadequate resources: incomplete and unreliable data; too few economists and other planning personnel.

3. Unanticipated dislocations to domestic economic activity: adverse movements in the terms of trade; irregular flows of development aid; unplanned changes in the private sector.

4. Institutional weaknesses: failures to locate the planning agency appropriately in the machinery of government; failures of communication between planners, administrators, and their political masters; the importation of institutional arrangements unsuited to local circumstances.

5. Failings on the part of the administrative civil service: cumbersome bureaucratic procedures; excessive caution and resistance to innovations; personal and departmental rivalries; lack of concern with economic considerations. (Finance Ministries are a particularly frequent target, often said to undermine the planning agency by resisting the co-ordination of plans and budgets.)[1]

See also S. Chakravarty, "Development Planning: A Reappraisal," *Cambridge Journal of Economics* (March 1991).

Among the numerous country studies of development planning, of particular interest are those related to India: S. Chakravarty, *Development Planning: The Indian Experience* (1987); B. S. Minhas, "Objectives and Policy Frame of the Fourth Indian Plan," in *The Crisis in Planning,* vol. 2, ed. Mike Faber and Dudley Seers (1972); J. Bhagwati and P. Desai, *India—Planning for Industrialization* (1970); and P. Bardhan, *The Political Economy of Development in India* (1984).

[1]Tony Killick, "The Possibilities of Development Planning," *Oxford Economic Papers* (July 1976): 164.

Comment IX.A.2. Governing the Market

Although many developing countries have abandoned central planning of a comprehensive character, an active public sector still exercises substantial influence in most countries. Of special interest—and subject to varying interpretations—is the role of government in the high-performing economies of Asia. Some neoclassical economists read the success of these economies as having been the result of the "invisible hand"—little government intervention and neutral incentives across activities that promote allocative efficiency. A revisionist view, however, sees the visible hand of government in "picking winners," protecting infant industries, and promoting exports.

The latter view is presented by Robert Wade, *Governing the Market: Economic Theory and the Role of Government in East Asian Industrialization* (1990). He rejects the claims of those who interpret the East Asian story as a vindication of either free-market principles or the confinement of government intervention only to promoting exports and correcting market failures. Equally, he disputes those who maintain that it all resulted from government intervention. Instead of "market supremacy," Wade's interpretation emphasizes "government leadership"—that is,

> a synergistic connection between a public system and mostly private market system, outputs of each becoming inputs for the other, with the government setting rules and influencing decision-making in the private sector in line with its view of an appropriate industrial and trade profile for the economy. Through this mechanism, the advantages of markets (decentralization, rivalry, diversity and multiple experiments) have been combined with the advantages of partially insulating producers from the instabilities of free markets and of stimulating investment in certain industries selected by government as important for the economy's future growth. This combination has improved upon the results of free markets.[1]

Wade concludes that

[1]Robert Wade, *Governing the Market: Economic Theory and the Role of Government in East Asian Industrialization* (1990), p. 5.

a necessary but not sufficient condition for more rapid industrialization is state deployment of a range of industrial promotion policies, including ones to intensify the growth of selected industries within the national territory. This is not to say that effectiveness increases with the sheer amount of intervention, nor that it increases the more the state imposes its will on society, ignoring other groups. State effectiveness is a function of the range of options, given by the number and force of policy instruments, and the flexibility with which those policy instruments are used. Flexibility means that the capacity to intervene, as given by the number and force of policy instruments, is used to varying degrees, more in some industries than in others at any one time, and more in one industry at some times than at others, always with an eye on the costs of interventions in political as well as economic terms.[2]

What distinguishes the use of state power in the high-performing economies is that government intervened in accordance with market opportunities, national economic management was independent of interest groups, government was capable of undertaking an entire set of appropriate policies (especially monetary and fiscal as well as industrial), government and business had close consultations, and policy instruments were used promotionally rather than restrictively.

From the experience of the high-performing economies, we can conclude that the most important questions about the role of the state are not how large should be the public sector or how much government intervention there should be, but rather what kind of intervention. What can government do best? And in what types of policy instruments does government have a comparative advantage? Answers do not point to a minimalist state, but rather to a shift from policies of planning and control to policies that work through markets. See Tony Killick, *A Reaction Too Far* (1990), pp. 27–32.

A similar interpretation of market friendly interventionism is given by Christopher Colclough and James Manor. The problem is not "too much government" but too much of government doing the wrong things. "The task is to dismantle the disabling state . . . [and] . . . establish the enabling state."[3]

Being realistic, we should endorse the conclusion of Dwight Perkins:

Making markets work is a much more complex process than slogans such as "getting the prices right," "privatization," or "getting rid of controls" would imply. Making markets work involves fundamental changes in enterprise behavior in most cases and substantial changes in the way government itself carries out its functions. Finally, most developing nations are never going to be willing to turn as much over to the market as, say, Hong Kong. Nonmarket controls or hierarchical commands will continue to play a major role in many sectors of most economies. Reform, therefore, is not just a matter of getting rid of such commands. A high growth economy must learn to make both the market and the bureaucracy perform efficiently.[4]

---

[2]Ibid., pp. 370–71.

[3]Christopher Colclough and James Manor, eds., *States or Markets?* (1991), pp. 276–77.

[4]Dwight H. Perkins, *Reforming Economic Systems in Developing Countries* (1991), p. 45.

IX.B. RENT SEEKING AND GOVERNMENT FAILURE

Note IX.B.1. What Are Rents?

Economists use the term *rent* in two very different ways. Sometimes it has the same meaning as in everyday life: the payment one makes to use a piece of equipment or a structure one does not own. Other times it means *the return to an asset in excess of its best alternative earning.* This latter concept is often called "economic rent" to distinguish it from rent as conventionally defined. In the literature on the political economy of development, "rent" is always short for "economic rent." In fact, one can go further and state that in this literature "rent" is short for "economic rent created by government action."

To further clarify the concept of rent it helps to consider some examples of rents *not* created by government action. A classic example is the return earned by the holder of a piece of rich mineral-bearing land, the best alternative use of which is farmland. The difference between what the owner can earn by extracting the minerals and what he can earn by using the land to grow crops is the economic rent on the land. Another example is the earnings of an employee who has become extremely valuable to a particular firm by virtue of having learned all the ins and outs of its production process, but whose knowledge is of no special value to any other firm. The difference between his earnings at his current firm and what he would earn at another firm is the rent to his firm-specific knowledge. (If the employee is not actually paid more than his best alternative earning, this rent accrues to his employer rather than to him.)

From this second example it is easy to see one way in which the government can create rents. Suppose the government chooses to pay its employees more than they would earn in positions of comparable responsibility and skill in the private sector. The difference between the earnings in the government jobs and the earnings in comparable private sector employment are the rents received by holders of government jobs. It is also easy to see how this government action could give rise to rent-seeking behavior. We can expect that government jobs would be in excess demand, and that the government will need some way to choose among qualified applicants. One way might be to hire only applicants with college degrees, even though skills learned in college are not needed to perform the jobs. People might then attend college not in order to learn but rather as a means of obtaining access to rents on government jobs.

The most important way in which governments create rents is by issuing licenses or permits to engage in various forms of economic activity. Examples are a license to import some units of a particular good and a permit to make an investment by building a factory. Such licenses and permits have no alternative uses, hence insofar as they have any value to their holders we can consider this value to be rent. Rents will be generated only insofar as the licenses or permits effectively restrict the level of economic activity to below what it would be in their absence. For this reason it is often assumed that the existence of positive rents to holders of licenses or permits indicates that government policies are reducing economic efficiency. This need not be true. Consider a license, such as a patent, that gives the holder exclusive rights to produce and market a new product for a number of years. Without the rents generated by this license, there might be no incentive to expend the resources necessary to invent the new product in the first place. Similarly, rent seeking is often assumed to be a socially wasteful activity, as it was in the example at the end of the previous paragraph. Yet inventive activity pursued with the intent of securing a patent can also be labeled rent seeking.

The selection that follows by Anne Krueger concentrates on rents and rent seeking generated by import licenses. Figure 1 shows how the welfare effects of an import quota and the total rents obtained by holders of import licenses can be quantified. The figure shows the domestic market for an internationally tradeable commodity. Domestic supply is given by the upward-sloping schedule S and domestic demand is given by the downward-sloping schedule D. In the absence of international trade the domestic market clears at point a (for *autarky*). With free international trade the country can import the commodity at the world price P_w. We

Figure 1. Welfare Loss from a Tariff or Equivalent Quota

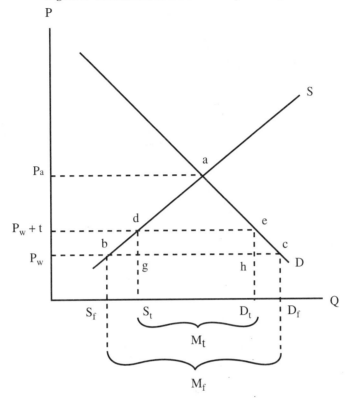

assume that the country is too small to affect the world price, so that P_w prevails regardless of how much the country imports. Under this assumption the country's consumers purchase D_f units of the commodity and its producers supply S_f units, leaving $M_f = D_f - S_f$ units of demand to be satisfied by imports.

We see that, compared with autarky, free trade increases consumer surplus (the area to the left of the demand curve) and decreases producer surplus (the area to the left of the supply curve). According to standard welfare analysis, national gains from international trade can be approximated by the sum of the changes in consumer and producer surplus. This sum is given by the trapezoid acP_wP_a less the trapezoid abP_wP_a, which equals the triangle abc. Now suppose the government imposes a tariff t per unit of imports. Under the assumption of perfect competition in import supply, the domestic price of the importable commodity will rise by exactly the amount of the tariff to $P_w + t$. Units purchased will fall to D_t, units supplied will rise to S_t, and imports will fall to $M_t = D_t - S_t$ units. Gains from trade shrink from abc to ade. However, the country also collects tariff revenue $t \times M_t$, equal to the rectangle $dehg$. The net loss in national welfare from the tariff policy (sometimes called the "deadweight loss") is therefore given by the sum of the triangles bdg and ceh.

Finally, suppose that instead of imposing a tariff the government imposes a quota that limits imports to M_t units. This creates an excess demand at the price P_w, causing the domestic price to be bid up to $P_w + t$, at which point demand for imports $D_t - S_t$ equals supply M_t. Holders of import licenses can purchase imports at the price P_w and resell them in the domestic market at the price $P_w + t$, earning a rent of t per unit. The total amount of quota rents equals $t \times M_t$, exactly equal to the tariff revenue collected by the government under the tariff policy. Note that if the quota had been set at M_f units (or higher), no excess demand at the price P_w would have been created and the domestic price would not have risen above the world price.

The quota licenses would then have been worthless: they would simply have conveyed the right to purchase imports at the price P_w and resell them at the same price. We see that licenses create rents only by restricting the level of economic activity (in this case, importing) to below what it would be in their absence.

Because the net loss in national welfare is the same whether the government imposes a tariff t or a quota M_t, these are sometimes called "equivalent" policies. One of the main points of Krueger's selection is that if resources are devoted to rent seeking (i.e., if resources are devoted to competing for quota licenses), the policies are not equivalent: the welfare loss from the quota policy will exceed the welfare loss from the tariff policy. Krueger argues that the value of the resources wasted in rent seeking will be roughly equal to the value of the rents themselves. A comparison of the rectangle *dehg* in Figure 1 with the triangles *bdg* and *ceh* suggests that if Krueger is right, the welfare cost of a quota could far exceed that of the "equivalent" tariff. In lieu of her model, in the Comment following her selection we demonstrate the result that the value of rents is completely dissipated for the Harris–Todaro model.

Selection IX.B.1. Political Economy of the Rent-Seeking Society*

In many market-oriented economies, government restrictions upon economic activity are pervasive facts of life. These restrictions give rise to rents of a variety of forms, and people often compete for the rents. Sometimes, such competition is perfectly legal. In other instances, rent seeking takes other forms, such as bribery, corruption, smuggling, and black markets.

It is the purpose of this paper to show some of the ways in which rent seeking is competitive, and to develop a simple model of competitive rent seeking for the important case when rents originate from quantitative restrictions upon international trade. In such a case 1) competitive rent seeking leads to the operation of the economy inside its transformation curve; 2) the welfare loss associated with quantitative restrictions is unequivocally greater than the loss from the tariff equivalent of those quantitative restrictions; and 3) competitive rent seeking results in a divergence between the private and social costs of certain activities. Although the analysis is general, the model has particular applicability for developing countries, where government interventions are frequently all-embracing. . . .

Competitive Rent Seeking

A. *Means of Competition*

When quantitative restrictions are imposed upon and effectively constrain imports, an import license is a valuable commodity. It is well known that under some circumstances, one can estimate the tariff equivalents of a set of quantitative restrictions and analyze the effects of those restrictions in the same manner as one would the tariff equivalents. In other circumstances, the resource-allocational effects of import licensing will vary, depending upon who receives the license.[1]

It has always been recognized that there are *some* costs associated with licensing: paperwork, the time spent by entrepreneurs in obtaining their licenses, the cost of the administrative apparatus necessary to issue licenses, and so on. Here, the argument is carried one step further: in many circumstances resources are devoted to competing for those licenses.

The consequences of that rent seeking are examined below. First, however, it will be argued that rent-seeking activities are often competitive and resources are devoted to competing for rents. It is difficult, if not impossible, to find empirically observable measures of the degree to which rent seeking is competitive. Instead, some mechanisms under which rent seeking is almost certain to be competitive are examined. Then other cases are considered in which it is less obvious, but perhaps equally plausible, that competition results.

Consider first the results of an import-licensing mechanism when licenses for imports of intermediate goods are allocated in proportion to firms' capacities. That system is frequently used, and has been analyzed for the Indian case by Jagdish Bhagwati and Padma Desai. When licenses are allocated in proportion to firms' capacities, investment in additional physical plant confers upon the investor a higher expected receipt of import licenses. Even with initial excess capacity (due to quantitative restrictions upon imports of intermediate goods), a rational entrepreneur may still expand his plant if the expected gains from the additional import licenses he will receive, divided by the cost of the investment, equal the returns on investment in other activities.[2] This behavior could be perfectly rational even if, for all entrepreneurs, the total number of import licenses will remain fixed. In fact, if imports are held constant as domestic income grows, one would expect the domestic value of a constant quantity of imports to increase over time, and hence installed capacity would increase while output remained constant. By investing in additional capacity, entrepreneurs devote resources to compete for import licenses.

A second sort of licensing mechanism frequently found in developing countries is used for imports of consumer goods. There, licenses are allocated pro rata in proportion to the applications for those licenses from importers-wholesalers. Entry is generally free into importing-whole-saling, and firms usually have U-shaped cost curves. The result is a larger-than-optimal number of firms, operating on the downward sloping portion of their

*From Anne Krueger, "The Political Economy of the Rent-Seeking Society." From *American Economic Review* 64 (June 1974): 291–294, 301–302. Reprinted by permission.

[1]This phenomenon is explored in detail in Bhagwati and Krueger.

[2]Note that: 1) one would expect to find greater excess capacity in those industries where rents are higher; and 2) within an industry, more efficient firms will have greater excess capacity than less efficient firms, since the return on a given amount of investment will be higher with greater efficiency.

cost curves, yet earning a "normal" rate of return. Each importer-wholesaler receives fewer imports than he would buy at existing prices in the absence of licensing, but realizes a sufficient return on those licenses he does receive to make it profitable to stay in business. In this case, competition for rents occurs through entry into the industry with smaller-than-optimally sized firms, and resources are used in that the same volume of imports could be efficiently distributed with fewer inputs if firms were of optimal size.

A third sort of licensing mechanism is less systematic in that government officials decide on license allocations. Competition occurs to some extent through both mechanisms already mentioned as businessmen base their decisions on expected values. But, in addition, competition can also occur through allocating resources to influencing the probability, or expected size, of license allocations. Some means of influencing the expected allocation—trips to the capital city, locating the firm in the capital, and so on—are straightforward. Others, including bribery, hiring relatives of officials or employing the officials themselves upon retirement, are less so. In the former case, competition occurs through choice of location, expenditure of resources upon travel, and so on. In the latter case, government officials themselves receive part of the rents.

Bribery has often been treated as a transfer payment. However, there is competition for government jobs and it is reasonable to believe that expected total remuneration is the relevant decision variable for persons deciding upon careers. Generally, entry into government service requires above-average educational attainments. The human capital literature provides evidence that choices as to how much to invest in human capital are strongly influenced by rates of return upon the investment. For a given level of educational attainment, one would expect the rate of return to be approximately equated among various lines of endeavor. Thus, if there appear to be high official-plus-unofficial incomes accruing to government officials and higher education is a prerequisite for seeking a government job, more individuals will invest in higher education. It is not necessary that government officials earn the same total income as other college graduates. All that is necessary is that there is an excess supply of persons seeking government employment, or that highly educated persons make sustained efforts to enter government services. Competition takes place through attaining the appropriate credentials for entry into government service and through ac-cepting unemployment while making efforts to obtain appointments. Efforts to influence those in charge of making appointments, of course, just carry the argument one step further back.

To argue that competition for entry into government service is, in part, a competition for rents does not imply that all government servants accept bribes nor that they would leave government service in their absence. Successful competitors for government jobs might experience large windfall gains even at their official salaries. However, if the possibility of those gains induces others to expend time, energy, and resources in seeking entry into government services, the activity is competitive for present purposes.

In all these license-allocation cases, there are means, legal and illegal, for competing for rents. If individuals choose their activities on the basis of expected returns, rates of return on alternative activities will be equated and, in that sense, markets will be competitive.[3] In most cases, people do not perceive themselves to be rent seekers and, generally speaking, individuals and firms do not specialize in rent seeking. Rather, rent seeking is one part of an economic activity, such as distribution or production, and part of the firm's resources are devoted to the activity (including, of course, the hiring of expediters). . . .

B. Are Rents Quantitatively Important?

Granted that rent seeking may be highly competitive, the question remains whether rents are important. Data from two countries, India and Turkey, suggest that they are. Gunnar Myrdal believes India may ". . . on the balance, be judged to have somewhat less corruption than any other country in South Asia" (p. 943). Nonetheless, it is generally believed that "corruption" has been increasing, and that much of the blame lies with the proliferation of economic controls following independence.[4]

Table 1 presents crude estimates, based on fairly conservative assumptions of the value of rents of all sorts in 1964. One important source of rents—investment licensing—is not included for lack of

[3] It may be objected that illegal means of competition may be sufficiently distasteful that perfect competition will not result. Three comments are called for. First, it requires only that enough people at the margin do not incur disutility from engaging in these activities. Second, most lines of economic activity in many countries cannot be entered without some rent-seeking activity. Third, risks of detection (especially when bribery is expected) and the value judgments associated with illegal activities differ from society to society. See Ronald Wraith and Edgar Simpkins.

[4] Santhanam Committee, pp. 7–8.

Table 1. Estimates of Value of Rents: India, 1964

Source of rent	Amount of rent (Rs. million)
Public investment	365
Imports	10,271
Controlled commodities	3,000
Credit rationing	407
Railways	602
Total	14,645

Sources:

1) Public investment: The Santhanam Committee, pp. 11–12, placed the loss in public investment at *at least* 5 percent of investment. That figure was multiplied by the average annual public investment in the *Third Five Year Plan.*

2) Imports: The Santhanam Committee, p. 18, stated that import licenses were worth 100 to 500 percent of their face value. Seventy-five percent of the value of 1964 imports was used here as a conservative estimate.

3) Controlled commodities: These commodities include steel, cement, coal, passenger cars, scooters, food, and other price- and/or distribution-controlled commodities, as well as foreign exchange used for illegal imports and other unrecorded transactions. The figure is the lower bound estimate given by John Monteiro, p. 60. Monteiro puts the upper bound estimate at Rs. 30,000 billion, although he rejects the figure on the (dubious) ground that notes in circulation are less than that sum.

4) Credit rationing: The bank rate in 1964 was 6 percent; Rs. 20.3 billion of loans were outstanding. It is assumed that *at least* an 8 percent interest rate would have been required to clear the market, and that 3 percent of bank loans outstanding would be equivalent to the present value of new loans at 5 percent. Data source: Reserve Bank of India, Tables 534 and 554.

5) Railways: Monteiro, p. 45, cites commissions of 20 percent on railway purchases, and extra-official fees of Rs. 0.15 per wagon and Rs. 1.4 per 100 maunds loaded. These figures were multiplied by the 1964 traffic volume; 203 million tons of revenue-paying traffic originated in that year. Third plan expenditure on railroads was Rs. 13,260 million. There were 350,000 railroad goods wagons in 1964–65. If a wagon was loaded once a week, there were 17,500,000 wagons of freight. At Rs. 0.15 per load, this would be Rs. 2.6 million; 100 maunds equal 8,228 pounds so at 1.4 Rs. per 100 maunds, Rs. 69 million changed hands; if one-fifth of railroad expenditures were made in 1964–65, Rs. 2652 million was spent in 1964; at 20 percent, this would be Rs. 530 million, for a total of Rs. 602 million.

any valid basis on which to estimate its value. Many smaller controls are also excluded. Nonetheless, it is apparent from Table 1 that import licenses provided the largest source of rents. The total value of rents of Rs. 14.6 billion contrasts with Indian national income of Rs. 201 billion in 1964. At 7.3 percent of national income, rents must be judged large relative to India's problems in attempting to raise her savings rate.

For Turkey, excellent detailed estimates of the value of import licenses in 1968 are available. Data on the c.i.f. prices of individual imports, their landed cost (c.i.f. price plus all duties, taxes, and landing charges), and wholesale prices were collected for a sizeable sample of commodities representing about 10 percent of total imports in 1968. The c.i.f. value of imports in the sample was TL

547 million and the landed cost of the imports was TL 1,443 million. The value at the wholesale level of these same imports was TL 3,568 million. Of course, wholesalers incur some handling, storage, and transport costs. The question, therefore, is the amount that can be attributed to normal wholesaling costs. If one assumes that a 50 percent markup would be adequate, then the value of import licenses was TL 1,404 million, or almost three times the c.i.f. value of imports. Imports in 1968 were recorded (c.i.f.) as 6 percent of national income. On the basis of Aker's data, this would imply that rents from import licenses in Turkey in 1968 were about 15 percent of *GNP.* . . .

Conclusions and Implications

While import licenses constitute a large and visible rent resulting from government intervention, the phenomenon of rent seeking is far more general. Fair trade laws result in firms of less-than-optimal size. Minimum wage legislation generates equilibrium levels of unemployment above the optimum with associated deadweight losses, as shown by John Harris and Michael Todaro, and Todaro. Ceilings on interest rates and consequent credit rationing lead to competition for loans and deposits and/or high-cost banking operations. Regulating taxi fares affects the average waiting time for a taxi and the percent of time taxis are idle, but probably not their owners' incomes, unless taxis are also licensed. Capital gains tax treatment results in overbuilding of apartments and uneconomic oil exploration. And so on.

Each of these and other interventions lead people to compete for the rents although the competitors often do not perceive themselves as such. In each case there is a deadweight loss associated with that competition over and above the traditional triangle. In general, prevention of that loss can be achieved only by restricting entry into the activity for which a rent has been created.

That, in turn, has political implications. First, even if they *can* limit competition for the rents, governments which consider they must impose restrictions are caught on the horns of a dilemma: if they do restrict entry, they are clearly "showing favoritism" to one group in society and are choosing an unequal distribution of income. If, instead, competition for the rents is allowed (or cannot be prevented), income distribution may be less unequal and certainly there will be less appearance of favoring special groups, although the economic costs associated with quantitative restrictions will be higher.

References

J. Bhagwati and P. Desai, *Planning for Industrialization: A Study of India's Trade and Industrial Policies Since 1950,* Cambridge 1970.

——— and A. Krueger, *Foreign Trade Regimes and Economic Development: Experience and Analysis,* New York forthcoming.

J. R. Harris and M. P. Todaro, "Migration, Unemployment, and Development: A Two-Sector Analysis," *Amer. Econ. Rev.,* Mar. 1970, *60,* 126–42.

J. B. Monteiro, *Corruption,* Bombay 1966.

G. Myrdal, *Asian Drama,* Vol. III, New York 1968.

M. P. Todaro, "A Model of Labor Migration and Urban Unemployment in Less Developed Countries," *Amer. Econ. Rev.,* Mar. 1969, *59,* 138–48.

R. Wraith and E. Simpkins, *Corruption in Developing Countries,* London 1963.

Santhanam Committee, *Report on the Committee on Prevention of Corruption,* Government of India, Ministry of Home Affairs, New Delhi 1964.

Comment IX.B.1. Complete Rent Dissipation Through Competitive Rent Seeking in the Harris–Todaro Model

At the end of her selection Krueger mentions the work of John Harris and Michael Todaro, "Migration, Unemployment, and Development: A Two-Sector Analysis," *American Economic Review* (March 1970), as an example of a model in which rent seeking leads to welfare losses. Since we have already presented their model in Note VI.B.1, we can build on that presentation here to demonstrate Krueger's result that when rent seeking is competitive the value of the resources wasted in rent seeking equals the value of the rents.

One interpretation of the Harris–Todaro model is that the government enforces a minimum wage $\bar{w}_M$ in urban areas that exceeds the market-clearing wage. Workers who obtain employment at this minimum wage can then be said to earn rents equal to the difference between $\bar{w}_M$ and their best alternative, the agricultural wage w_A. Migration into urban areas to obtain high-wage jobs constitutes the competitive rent-seeking behavior in the Harris–Todaro model. The unemployment of urban workers not chosen for the available high-wage jobs gives the quantity of resources wasted in rent seeking. To show the equality between the value of resources wasted in rent seeking and the value of the rents, we use the condition that determines the level of unemployment for which workers are indifferent between remaining in the countryside and migrating to the city, $w_A = [\hat{L}_M/(\hat{L}_M + U)]\bar{w}_M$, where $\hat{L}_M$ is urban employment at wage $\bar{w}_M$ and U is unemployment. This condition can be rearranged as $w_A U = (\bar{w}_M - w_A)\hat{L}_M$. The right-hand side of this equation gives the value of the rents earned by workers who obtain high-wage employment, while the left-hand side gives the value of the resources wasted when workers withdraw from agriculture to engage in rent seeking.

Comment IX.B.2. The Relationship Between Rent Seeking and Corruption

In her selection Krueger mentions "corruption" as a means of seeking rents. Later writers have often used the concepts of corruption and rent seeking interchangeably. Here we wish to clarify the relationship between the two concepts, partly by amplifying points already made in both the Krueger selection and the selection by Stern in the first section of this chapter.

Let us define corruption as the use of public office for private gain. This is typically illegal. Yet Krueger is quite clear that many forms of rent seeking are perfectly legal, so that rent seeking should not be seen as only a form of corruption. It is also easy to find examples in which corruption, rather than being a form of rent seeking, actually eliminates rent seeking. Consider again the case of import quota licenses. Suppose that the government official in charge of allocating import licenses gives them away to members of his extended family. No resources have been expended in competing for the quota rents, yet the official's action fits the definition of corruption. (It is possible that resources will be expended in competition for entrance to the official's extended family, however.)

As Krueger points out, insofar as corruption creates rents by raising the incomes of government officials above what they would earn in positions of comparable responsibility and skill in the private sector, it may give rise to rent seeking. Here it is more accurate to say that corruption causes rent seeking than to say that corruption and rent seeking are identical, and in this case the two are actually separate activities carried out by different groups of people.

Perhaps the most complex relationship between corruption and rent seeking occurs when officials enact restrictions on economic activity for the main purpose of creating rents which they can capture through rent-seeking bribery (or allocate to family, friends, and political supporters). This "toll booth" corruption may be the type most damaging to economic development. It is the subject of the next selection.

Selection IX.B.2. The Regulation of Entry*

I. Introduction

Countries differ significantly in the way in which they regulate the entry of new businesses. To meet government requirements for starting to operate a business in Mozambique, an entrepreneur must complete 19 procedures taking at least 149 business days and pay US$256 in fees. To do the same, an entrepreneur in Italy needs to follow 16 different procedures, pay US$3946 in fees, and wait at least 62 business days to acquire the necessary permits. In contrast, an entrepreneur in Canada can finish the process in two days by paying US$280 in fees and completing only two procedures.

. . . We describe the required procedures governing entry regulation, as well as the time and the cost of following these procedures, in 85 countries. We focus on legal requirements that need to be met before a business can officially open its doors, the official cost of meeting these requirements, and the minimum time it takes to meet them if the government does not delay the process. . . . We look at the official requirements, official cost, and official time—and do not measure corruption and bureaucratic delays that further raise the cost of entry. . . .

Our analysis of exhaustive data on entry regulation in 85 countries leads to the following conclusions. The number of procedures required to start up a firm varies from the low of 2 in Canada to the high of 21 in the Dominican Republic, with the world average of around 10. The minimum official time for such a start-up varies from the low of 2 business days in Australia and Canada to the high of 152 in Madagascar, assuming that there are no delays by either the applicant or the regulators, with the world average of 47 business days. The official cost of following these procedures for a simple firm ranges from under 0.5 percent of per capita GDP in the United States to over 4.6 times per capita GDP in the Dominican Republic, with the worldwide average of 47 percent of annual per capita income. For an entrepreneur, legal entry is extremely cumbersome, time-consuming, and expensive in most countries in the world. . . .

*From Simeon Djankov, Rafael La Porta, Florencio Lopez-di-Silanes, and Andrei Shleifer, "The Regulation of Entry," *Quarterly Journal of Economics* 117 (February 2002): 1–2, 4–15, 18–22, 26–29, 31–34. Reprinted by permission.

II. Data

A. *Construction of the Database*

This paper is based on a new data set, which describes the regulation of entry by start-up companies in 85 countries in 1999. We are interested in all the procedures that an entrepreneur needs to carry out to begin legally operating a firm involved in industrial or commercial activity. Specifically, we record all procedures that are officially required of an entrepreneur in order to obtain all necessary permits and to notify and file with all requisite authorities. We also calculate the official costs and time necessary for the completion of each procedure under normal circumstances. The study assumes that the information is readily available and that all governmental bodies function efficiently and without corruption.

We collect data on entry regulation using all available written information on start-up procedures from government publications, reports of development agencies such as the World Bank and USAID, and government web pages on the Internet. We then contact the relevant government agencies to check the accuracy of the data. Finally, for each country we commission at least one independent report on entry regulation from a local law firm, and work with that firm and government officials to eliminate disagreements among them.

We use official sources for the number of procedures, time, and cost. If official sources are conflicting or the laws are ambiguous, we follow the most authoritative source. In the absence of express legal definitions, we take the government official's report as the source. If several official sources have different estimates of time and cost, we take the median. Absent official estimates of time and cost, we take the estimates of local incorporation lawyers. If several unofficial (e.g., a private lawyer) sources have different estimates, we again take the median.

Our countries span a wide range of income levels and political systems. The sample includes fourteen African countries, nine East Asian countries including China and Vietnam, three South Asian countries (India, Pakistan, and Sri Lanka), all Central and Eastern European countries except for Albania and some of the former Yugoslav republics, eight former Soviet Union republics and Mongolia, ten Latin American countries, two Caribbean countries (Dominican Republic and Jamaica), six Middle Eastern countries (Egypt, Israel, Jordan, Lebanon, Morocco, and Tunisia), and all major developed countries.

We record the procedures related to obtaining all the necessary permits and licenses, and completing all the required inscriptions, verifications, and notifications for the company to be legally in operation. When there are multiple ways to begin operating legally, we choose the fastest in terms of time. In some countries, entrepreneurs may not bother to follow official procedures or bypass them by paying bribes or hiring the services of "facilitators." An entrepreneur in Georgia can start up a company after going through 13 procedures in 69 business days and paying $375 in fees. Alternatively, he may hire a legal advisory firm that completes the start-up process for $610 in three business days. In the analysis, we use the first set of numbers. We do so because we are primarily interested in understanding the structure of official regulation.

Regulations of start-up companies vary across regions within a country, across industries, and across firm sizes. For concreteness, we focus on a "standardized" firm, which has the following characteristics: it performs general industrial or commercial activities, it operates in the largest city[1] (by population), it is exempt from industry-specific requirements (including environmental ones), it does not participate in foreign trade and does not trade in goods that are subject to excise taxes (e.g., liquor, tobacco, gas), it is a domestically owned limited liability company,[2] its capital is subscribed in cash (not in-kind contributions) and is the higher of (i) 10 times GDP per capita in 1999 or (ii) the minimum capital requirement for the particular type of business entity, it rents (i.e., does not own) land and business premises, it has between 5 and 50 employees one month after the commencement of operations all of whom are nationals, it has turnover of up to 10 times its start-up capital, and it does not qualify for investment incentives. Although different legal forms are used in different countries to set up the simplest firm, to make comparisons we need to look at the same form.

Our data almost surely underestimate the cost and complexity of entry.[3] Start-up procedures in the provinces are often slower than in the capital. Industry-specific requirements add procedures. Foreign ownership frequently involves additional verifications and procedures. Contributions in kind often require assessment of value, a complex procedure that depends on the quality of property registries. Finally, purchasing land can be quite difficult and even impossible in some of the countries of the sample (for example, in the Kyrgyz Republic).

B. Definitions of Variables

We use three measures of entry regulation: the number of procedures that firms must go through, the official time required to complete the process, and its official cost. . . .

We keep track of all the procedures required by law to start a business. A separate activity in the start-up process is a "procedure" only if it requires the entrepreneur to interact with outside entities: state and local government offices, lawyers, auditors, company seal manufacturers, notaries, etc. For example, all limited liability companies need to hold an inaugural meeting of shareholders to formally adopt the Company Articles and Bylaws. Since this activity involves only the entrepreneurs, we do not count it as a procedure. Similarly, most companies hire a lawyer to draft their Articles of Association. However, we do not count that as a procedure unless the law requires that a lawyer be involved. In the same vein, we ignore procedures that the entrepreneur can avoid altogether (e.g., reserving exclusive rights over a proposed company name until registration is completed) or that can be performed after business commences.[4] Finally, when obtaining a document requires several separate procedures involving different officials, we count each as a procedure. For example, a Bulgarian entrepreneur receives her registration certificate from the Company Registry in Sofia, and then

---

[3]The World Economic Forum [2001] surveys business people on how important administrative regulations are as an obstacle to new business. Our three measures are strongly positively correlated with these subjective assessments.

[4]In several countries, our consultants advised us that certain procedures, while not required, are highly recommended, because failure to follow them may result in significant delays and additional costs. We collected data on these procedures, but did not include them in the variables presented here because we wanted to stick to the mandatory criterion. We have rerun the regressions discussed below including these highly recommended procedures. The inclusion does not have a material impact on the results.

---

[1]In practice, the largest city coincides with the capital city except in Australia (Melbourne), Brazil (Sao Paulo), Canada (Toronto), Germany (Frankfurt), Kazakhstan (Almaty), the Netherlands (Amsterdam), South Africa (Johannesburg), Turkey (Istanbul), and the United States (New York).

[2]If the Company Law allows for more than one privately owned business form with limited liability, we choose the more popular business form among small companies in the country.

has to pay the associated fee at an officially designated bank. Even though both activities are related to "obtaining the registration certificate," they count as two separate procedures in the data.

To measure time, we collect information on the sequence in which procedures are to be completed and rely on official figures as to how many business days it takes to complete each procedure. We ignore the time spent to gather information, and assume that all procedures are known from the very beginning. We also assume that procedures are taken simultaneously whenever possible, for maximum efficiency. Since entrepreneurs may have trouble visiting several different institutions within the same day (especially if they come from out-of-town), we set the minimum time required to visit an institution to be one day.[5] Another justification for this approach is that the relevant offices sometimes open for business only briefly: both the Ministry of Economy and the Ministry of Justice in Cairo open for business only between 11 a.m. and 2 p.m.

We estimate the cost of entry regulation based on all identifiable official expenses: fees, costs of procedures and forms, photocopies, fiscal stamps, legal and notary charges, etc. All cost figures are official and do not include bribes, which De Soto [1990] has shown to be significant for registration. Setup fees often vary with the level of start-up capital. As indicated, we report the costs associated with starting to operate legally a firm with capital equivalent to the larger of (i) ten times per capita GDP in 1999 or (ii) the minimum capital requirement stipulated in the law. We have experimented with other capital levels and found our results to be robust. . . .

Table 1 lists typical procedures associated with setting up a firm in our sample. The procedures are further divided by their function: screening (a residual category, which generally aims to keep out "unattractive" projects or entrepreneurs), health and safety, labor, taxes, and environment. The basic procedure in starting up a business, present everywhere, is registering with the Companies' Registry. This can take more than one procedure; sometimes there is a "preliminary license" and a "final" license. Combined with that procedure, or as a separate procedure, is the check for uniqueness of the proposed company name. Add-on pro-

cedures comprise the requirements to notarize the Company Deeds, to open a bank account and deposit of start-up capital, and to publish a notification of the company's establishment in an official or business paper. Additional screening procedures that include obtaining different certificates and filing with agencies other than the Registry may add up to 97 days in delays, as is the case in Madagascar. Another set of basic screening procedures, present in almost every country in the data set, covers certain mandatory municipal procedures, registrations with statistical offices and with Chambers of Commerce and Industry (or respective Ministries). In the Dominican Republic these procedures take seven procedures and fourteen days. There is large cross-country variation in terms of the number, time, and cost of screening procedures as the Company Registry performs many of these tasks automatically in the most efficient countries but the entrepreneur does much of the legwork in the less efficient ones.

Additional procedures appear in four areas. The first covers tax-related procedures, which require seven procedures and twenty days in Madagascar. The second is labor regulations, which require seven procedures and 21 days in Bolivia. The third area is health and safety regulations, which demand five procedures and 21 business days in Malawi. The final area covers compliance with environmental regulations, which take two procedures and ten days in Malawi if all goes well.

Figures 1 and 2 describe the number, time, and cost of the procedures needed to begin operating legally in New Zealand and France, respectively. New Zealand's streamlined start-up process takes only three procedures and three days. The entrepreneur must first obtain approval for the company name from the website of the Registrar of Companies, and then apply online for registration with both the Registrar of Companies and the tax authorities.

In contrast, the process in France takes 15 procedures and 53 days. To begin, the founder needs to check the chosen company name for uniqueness at the Institut National de la Propriété Industrielle (INPI). He then needs the mayor's permit to use his home as an office. (If the office is to be rented, the founder must secure a notarized lease agreement.) The following documents must then be obtained, each from a different authority: proof of a clean criminal record, an original extract of the entrepreneur's certificate of marital status from the City Hall, and a power of attorney. The start-up capital is then deposited with a notary bank or Caisse des Dépôts, and is blocked there until proof of registra-

---

[5] In the calculation of time, when two procedures can be completed on the same day in the same building, we count that as one day rather than two (following the urgings of officials in several countries, where several offices are located in the same building). Our results are not affected by this particular way of computing time.

Table 1. List of Procedures for Starting Up a Company

This table provides a list of common procedures required to start up a company in the 85 countries of the sample.

1. *Screening procedures*
   —Certify business competence
   —Certify a clean criminal record
   —Certify marital status
   —Check the name for uniqueness
   —Notarize company deeds
   —Notarize registration certificate
   —File with the Statistical Bureau
   —File with the Ministry of Industry and Trade, Ministry of the Economy, or the respective ministries by line of business
   —Notify municipality of start-up date
   —Obtain certificate of compliance with the company law
   —Obtain business license (operations permit)
   —Obtain permit to play music to the public (irrespective of line of business)
   —Open a bank account and deposit start-up capital
   —Perform an official audit at start-up
   —Publish notice of company foundation
   —Register at the Companies Registry
   —Sign up for membership in the Chamber of Commerce or Industry or the Regional Trade Association

2. *Tax-related requirements*
   —Arrange automatic withdrawal of the employees' income tax from the company payroll funds
   —Designate a bondsman for tax purposes
   —File with the Ministry of Finance
   —Issue notice of start of activity to the Tax Authorities
   —Register for corporate income tax
   —Register for VAT
   —Register for state taxes
   —Register the company bylaws with the Tax Authorities
   —Seal, validate, rubricate accounting books

3. *Labor/social security-related requirements*
   —File with the Ministry of Labor
   —Issue employment declarations for all employees
   —Notarize the labor contract
   —Pass inspections by social security officials
   —Register for accident and labor risk insurance
   —Register for health and medical insurance
   —Register with pension funds
   —Register for Social Security
   —Register for unemployment insurance
   —Register with the housing fund

4. *Safety and health requirements*
   —Notify the health and safety authorities and obtain authorization to operate from the Health Ministry
   —Pass inspections and obtain certificates related to work safety, building, fire, sanitation, and hygiene

5. *Environment-related requirements*
   —Issue environmental declaration
   —Obtain environment certificate
   —Obtain sewer approval
   —Obtain zoning approval
   —Pass inspections from environmental officials
   —Register with the water management and water discharge authorities

tion is provided. Notarization of the Articles of Association follows. A notice stating the location of the headquarters office is published in a journal approved for legal announcements, and evidence of the publication is obtained. Next, the founder registers four copies of the articles of association at the local tax collection office. He then files a request for registration with the Centre de Formalités des Entreprises (CFE) which handles declarations of existence and other registration-related formali-

Figure 1. Start-up procedures in New Zealand.

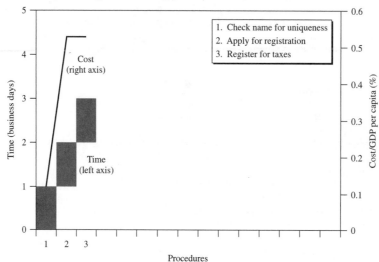

Procedures are lined up sequentially on the horizontal axis and described in the text box. The time required to complete each procedure is described by the height of the bar and measured against the left scale. Cumulative costs (as a percentage of per capita (GDP) are plotted using a line and measured against the right scale.

Figure 2. Start-up procedures in France.

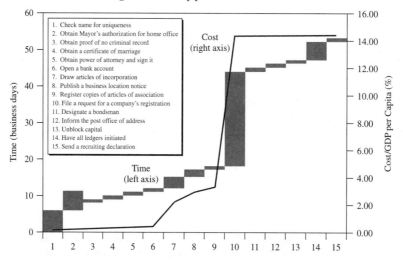

Procedures are lined up sequentially on the horizontal axis and described in the text box. The time required to complete each procedure is described by the height of the bar and measured against the left scale. Cumulative costs (as a percentage of per capita GDP) are plotted using a line and measured against the right scale.

ties. The CFE must process the documents or return them in case the request is incomplete. The CFE automatically enters the company information in the Registre Nationale des Entreprises (RNE) and obtains from the RNE identification numbers: numero SIRENE (Système Informatique pour le Répertoire des Entreprises), numero SIRET (Système Informatique pour le Répertoire des Etablissements), and numero NAF (Nomenclature des Activitées Francaises). The SIRET is used by, among others, the tax authorities. The RNE also publishes a notice of the company formation in the official bulletin of civil and commercial announcements. The firm then obtains a proof of registration form "K-bis," which is effectively its identity card. To start legal operations, the entrepreneur completes five additional procedures: inform the post office of the new enterprise, designate a bondsman or guarantee payment of taxes with a cash deposit, unblock the company's capital by filing with the bank a proof of registration (K-bis), have the firm's ledgers and registers initialed, and file for social security. The magazine L'Entreprise comments: "To be sure that the file for the Company Registry is complete, many promoters check it with a counselor's service, which costs FF200 in Paris (about US$30). But there's always something missing, and most entrepreneurs end up using a lawyer to complete the procedure."

III. Basic Results

Table 2 presents the basic information from our sample. Countries are ranked in ascending order first by the total number of entry procedures, then by the time it takes to complete them, and finally by the cost of entry. We classify each procedure as one of five types: safety and health, environmental, tax, labor, and a residual category which we label "screening," whose purpose . . . is to weed out the undesirable entrepreneurs. We then compute and report the total number of procedures and their breakdown into our five categories for each country. We also report the minimum number of business days that are officially required to comply with entry regulations, the costs arising from the official fees, and the total costs which impute the entrepreneur's time (as a fraction of GDP per capita). Finally, we take averages by income level and report t-tests comparing the regulation of entry across income groups.

The data show enormous variation in entry regulation across countries. The total number of procedures ranges from 2 in Canada to 21 in the Dominican Republic and averages 10.48 for the whole sample. Very few entry regulations cover tax and labor issues. The worldwide average number of labor and tax procedures are 1.94 and 2.02, respectively. Procedures involving environmental issues and safety and health matters are even rarer (0.14 and 0.34 procedures on average, respectively). Instead, much of what governments do to regulate entry falls into the category of screening procedures. The worldwide average number of such procedures facing a new entrant is 6.04.

The number of procedures is highly correlated with both the time and cost variables. . . . The correlation of the (log) number of procedures with (log) time is 0.83 and with (log) cost is 0.64. Translated into economic terms, this means that entrepreneurs pay a steep price in terms of fees and de-

lays in countries that make intense use of ex ante screening. For example, completing 19 procedures demands 149 business days and 111.5 percent of GDP per capita in Mozambique. In Italy the completion of 16 procedures takes up 62 business days and 20 percent of GDP per capita. The Dominican Republic is in a class of its own: completing its 21 procedures requires 80 business days and fees of at least 4.63 times per capita GDP. These figures are admittedly extreme within the sample, yet meeting the official entry requirements in the average sample country requires roughly 47 days and fees of 47 percent of GDP per capita.

When we aggregate time and out-of-pocket costs into an aggregate cost measure, the results for some countries become even more extreme. The world average full cost measure rises to 66 percent of per capita GDP, but varies from 1.7 percent of per capita GDP for New Zealand to 4.95 times per capita GDP in the Dominican Republic.

Panel B of Table 2 reports averages of the total number of procedures and its components, time and cost by quartiles of per capita GDP in 1999. Two patterns emerge. First, the cost-to-per-capita-GDP ratio decreases uniformly with GDP per capita. The average cost-to-per-capita-GDP ratio for countries in the top quartile of per capita GDP ("rich countries") is 10 percent and rises to 108 percent in countries in the bottom quartile of per capita GDP. This pattern merely reflects the fact that the income elasticity of fees (in log levels) is about 0.2. Second, countries in the top quartile of per capita GDP require fewer procedures and their entrepreneurs face shorter delays in starting a legal business than those in the remaining countries.[6] The total number of procedures in an average rich country is 6.8 which is significantly lower than the rest-of-sample average of 11.8 (t-statistics are reported in Panel C). Rich countries also have fewer safety and health, tax, and labor start-up procedures than the rest of the sample. Similarly, meeting government requirements takes approximately 24.5 business days in rich countries, statistically significantly lower than the rest-of-sample mean of 55.4 days. In contrast, countries in the other three quartiles of per capita income are not statistically different from each other in the number of procedures and the time it takes to complete them.

---

[6]One objection to this finding is that entrepreneurs in rich countries might face more postentry regulations than they do in poor countries. We have data on one aspect of postentry regulation, namely the regulation of labor markets (see Djankov et al. [2001]). The numbers of entry and of labor market regulations are positively correlated across countries, contrary to this objection.

Table 2. The Data

Panel A reports the total number of procedures and their breakup in the following five categories: (1) safety and health; (2) environment; (3) taxes; (4) labor; and (5) screening. The table also reports the time, direct cost (as a fraction of GDP per capita in 1999) associated with meeting government requirements, and direct cost plus the monetized value of the entrepreneur's time (as a fraction of GDP per capita in 1999) as well as the level of GDP per capita in dollars in 1999. Countries are sorted in ascending order on the basis of (1) the total number of procedures; (2) time; and (3) cost. Panel B presents means of the variables by quartiles of GDP per capita in 1999. Panel C presents t-statistics for differences in means across quartiles of per capita GDP in 1999. . . . .

	Number of procedures	Safety & Health	Environment	Taxes	Labor	Screening	Time	Cost	Cost + time	GDP/POP$_{1999}$
				Panel A: Data						
Canada	2	0	0	1	0	1	2	0.0145	0.0225	19,320
Australia	2	0	0	1	0	1	2	0.0225	0.0305	20,050
New Zealand	3	0	0	1	0	2	3	0.0053	0.0173	13,780
Denmark	3	0	0	1	0	2	3	0.1000	0.1120	32,030
Ireland	3	0	0	1	0	2	16	0.1157	0.1797	19,160
United States	4	0	0	1	1	2	4	0.0049	0.0169	30,600
Norway	4	0	0	1	1	2	18	0.0472	0.1192	32,880
United Kingdom	5	0	0	1	1	3	4	0.0143	0.0303	22,640
Hong Kong	5	0	0	0	1	4	15	0.0333	0.0933	23,520
Mongolia	5	0	0	1	0	4	22	0.0331	0.1211	350
Finland	5	0	0	1	3	1	24	0.0116	0.1076	23,780
Israel	5	0	0	2	1	2	32	0.2132	0.3412	15,860
Zimbabwe	5	0	0	2	1	2	47	0.1289	0.3169	520
Sweden	6	0	0	1	1	4	13	0.0256	0.0776	25,040
Jamaica	6	0	0	2	1	3	24	0.1879	0.2839	2,330
Zambia	6	0	0	2	1	3	29	0.6049	0.7209	320
Panama	7	0	0	1	1	5	15	0.3074	0.3674	3,070
Switzerland	7	0	0	2	1	4	16	0.1724	0.2364	38,350
Singapore	7	0	0	1	2	4	22	0.1191	0.2071	29,610
Latvia	7	0	0	2	1	4	23	0.4234	0.5154	2,470
Malaysia	7	0	0	1	1	5	42	0.2645	0.4325	3,400
Sri Lanka	8	0	0	1	1	6	23	0.1972	0.2892	820
Netherlands	8	0	1	2	0	5	31	0.1841	0.3081	24,320
Belgium	8	0	0	1	2	5	33	0.0998	0.2318	24,510
Taiwan, China	8	0	0	1	2	5	37	0.0660	0.2140	13,248
Hungary	8	0	0	1	1	6	39	0.8587	1.0147	4,650
Pakistan	8	0	0	2	1	5	50	0.3496	0.5496	470

Country										
Peru	8	0	0	2	2	4	83	0.1986	0.5306	2,390
South Africa	9	0	0	2	2	5	26	0.0844	0.1884	3,160
Kyrgyz Republic	9	0	0	1	1	7	32	0.2532	0.3812	300
Thailand	9	0	0	3	2	4	35	0.0639	0.2039	1,960
Nigeria	9	1	0	2	1	5	36	2.5700	2.7140	310
Austria	9	0	0	2	2	6	37	0.2728	0.4208	25,970
Tunisia	9	0	0	0	2	7	41	0.1722	0.3362	2,100
Slovenia	9	0	0	0	1	8	47	0.2103	0.3983	9,890
Lebanon	9	0	0	1	1	7	63	1.5672	1.8192	3,700
Uruguay	10	0	0	1	4	5	23	0.4949	0.5869	5,900
Bulgaria	10	0	0	2	0	8	27	0.1441	0.2521	1,380
Chile	10	0	0	3	2	5	28	0.1308	0.2428	4,740
Germany	10	1	0	1	2	7	42	0.1569	0.3249	25,350
Ghana	10	0	2	1	4	4	45	0.2175	0.3975	390
Lithuania	10	0	0	2	1	5	46	0.0546	0.2386	2,620
Czech Republic	10	0	0	1	2	7	65	0.0822	0.3422	5,060
India	10	0	0	3	3	4	77	0.5776	0.8856	450
Japan	11	0	0	2	2	7	26	0.1161	0.2201	32,230
Uganda	11	0	2	2	1	6	29	0.3040	0.4200	320
Egypt, Arab Rep.	11	0	0	2	1	8	51	0.9659	1.1699	1,400
Kenya	11	0	0	2	3	6	54	0.5070	0.7230	360
Armenia	11	0	0	1	1	9	55	0.1267	0.3467	490
Poland	11	0	2	3	3	5	58	0.2546	0.4866	3,960
Spain	11	0	0	4	4	5	82	0.1730	0.5010	14,000
Indonesia	11	0	0	2	1	8	128	0.5379	1.0499	580
Croatia	12	0	1	2	3	6	38	0.4503	0.6023	4,580
Kazakhstan	12	0	0	1	3	8	42	0.4747	0.6427	1,230
Portugal	12	0	0	2	2	8	76	0.1844	0.4884	10,600
Slovak Republic	12	0	0	2	3	7	89	0.1452	0.5012	3,590
China	12	0	0	5	2	5	92	0.1417	0.5097	780
Korea, Rep.	13	0	0	2	4	7	27	0.1627	0.2707	8,490
Tanzania	13	0	1	5	2	5	29	3.3520	3.4680	240
Ukraine	13	0	0	2	3	8	30	0.2569	0.3769	750
Turkey	13	0	0	2	2	9	44	0.1932	0.3692	2,900
Malawi	13	2	5	1	1	4	52	0.1886	0.3966	190
Morocco	13	0	1	3	3	6	57	0.2126	0.4406	1,200
Georgia	13	0	2	1	1	9	69	0.6048	0.8808	620
Burkina Faso	14	0	0	3	2	9	33	3.1883	3.3203	240
Philippines	14	0	0	5	5	8	46	0.1897	0.3737	1,020
Argentina	14	0	0	4	4	5	48	0.1019	0.2939	7,600
Jordan	14	0	1	2	1	10	64	0.5369	0.7929	1,500

Table 2. (Continued)

	Number of procedures	Safety & Health	Environment	Taxes	Labor	Screening	Time	Cost	Cost + time	GDP/POP$_{1999}$
Venezuela	14	1	1	3	3	6	104	0.1060	0.5220	3,670
Greece	15	0	0	4	2	9	36	0.5860	0.7300	11,770
France	15	0	0	3	1	11	53	0.1430	0.3550	23,480
Brazil	15	0	0	7	5	3	63	0.2014	0.4534	4,420
Mexico	15	1	2	2	3	7	67	0.5664	0.8344	4,400
Mali	16	1	0	3	2	10	59			240
Italy	16	0	0	5	3	8	62	0.2002	0.4482	19,710
Senegal	16	0	0	3	2	11	69	1.2331	1.5091	510
Ecuador	16	2	0	2	4	8	72	0.6223	0.9103	1,310
Romania	16	1	2	1	3	9	97	0.1531	0.5411	1,520
Vietnam	16	0	1	1	5	9	112	1.3377	1.7857	370
Madagascar	17	0	0	7	3	7	152	0.4263	1.0343	250
Colombia	18	2	0	4	5	7	48	0.1480	0.3400	2,250
Mozambique	19	4	0	1	3	11	149	1.1146	1.7106	230
Russian Federation	20	0	0	2	5	13	57	0.1979	0.4259	2,270
Bolivia	20	0	1	2	7	10	88	2.6558	3.0078	1,010
Dominican Republic	21	0	0	2	3	16	80	4.6309	4.9509	191
Sample average	**10.48**	**0.34**	**0.14**	**2.04**	**1.94**	**6.04**	**47.40**	**0.4708**	**0.6598**	**8.226**

Panel B: Means by Quartiles of GDP per capita in 1999

	Number of procedures	Safety & Health	Environment	Taxes	Labor	Screening	Time	Cost	Cost + time	GDP/POP$_{1999}$
1st Quartile	6.77	0.00	0.05	1.59	1.14	4.00	24.50	0.10	0.20	24,372
2nd Quartile	11.10	0.24	0.14	2.14	2.38	6.19	49.29	0.33	0.53	5,847
3rd Quartile	12.33	0.52	0.14	2.19	2.33	7.14	53.10	0.41	0.62	1,568
4th Quartile	11.90	0.62	0.24	2.24	1.95	6.90	63.76	1.08	1.34	349

Panel C: Test of means (t-statistics)

	Number of procedures	Safety & Health	Environment	Taxes	Labor	Screening	Time	Cost	Cost + time	GDP/POP$_{1999}$
1st vs. 2nd Quartile	-4.20[a]	-2.07[b]	-0.87	-1.35	1.14	-3.34[a]	-3.71[a]	-3.03[a]	-3.97[a]	12.03[a]
1st vs. 3rd Quartile	-4.58[a]	-3.02[a]	-0.87	-1.64[b]	2.38	-4.07[a]	-4.21[a]	-2.54[b]	-3.19[a]	16.35[a]
1st vs. 4th Quartile	-4.04[a]	-2.08[a]	-1.55	-1.61	2.33	-3.18[a]	-4.09[a]	-3.53[a]	-4.06[a]	17.31[a]
2nd vs. 3rd Quartile	-1.17	-1.34	0.00	-0.11	0.10	-1.51	-0.54	-0.52	-0.59	6.14[a]
2nd vs. 4th Quartile	-0.72	-1.17	-0.61	-0.21	1.10	-0.89	-1.46	-2.54[b]	-2.73[a]	8.05[a]
3rd vs. 4th Quartile	0.33	-0.27	-0.61	-0.11	0.82	0.26	-1.06	-2.17[b]	-2.27[b]	8.53[a]

[a]Significant at 1 percent; [b]significant at 5 percent; [c]significant at 10 percent.

Figure 3. Corruption and number of procedures.

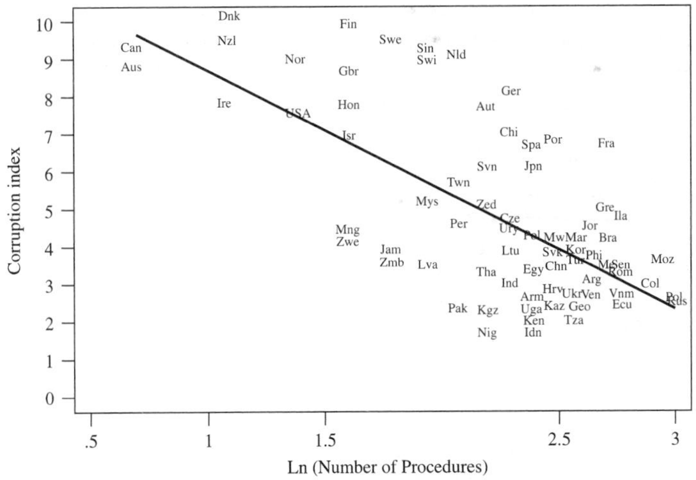

The scatter plot shows the values of the corruption index against the (log) number of procedures for the 78 countries in our sample with nonmissing data on corruption.

Table 3. Evidence on the Tollbooth Theory

The table presents the results of OLS regressions using corruption* as the dependent variable. The independent variables are (1) the log of the number of procedures; (2) the log of time; (3) the log of cost; and the log of per capita GDP in dollars in 1999. Panel A presents results for the 78 observations with available corruption data. Robust standard errors are shown in parentheses below the coefficients.

Panel A: Results for the whole sample

Independent variable	(1)	(2)	(3)	(4)	(5)	(6)
Number of procedures	−3.1811[a]	−1.8654[a]				
	(0.2986)	(0.2131)				
Time			−1.7566[a]	−0.8854[a]		
			(0.1488)	(0.1377)		
Cost					−1.2129[a]	−0.4978[a]
					(0.1206)	(0.1285)
Ln GDP/POP$_{1999}$		0.9966[a]		0.9765[a]		0.9960[a]
		(0.0864)		(0.1014)		(0.1118)
Constant	11.8741[a]	1.1345	11.0694[a]	0.0677	2.7520[a]	−4.0893[a]
	(0.7380)	(0.9299)	(0.5932)	(1.1176)	(0.2414)	(0.7867)
R^2	0.4656	0.8125	0.4387	0.7662	0.4256	0.7306
N	78	78	78	78	78	78

[a]Significant at 1 percent. . . .

*Corruption perception index for 1999. Corruption is defined broadly as "the misuse of public power for private benefits, e.g., bribing of public officials, kickbacks in public procurement, or embezzlement of public funds." The index averages the corruption scores given by the following sources: (1) Freedom House Nations in Transit (FH); (2) Gallup International (GI); (3) the Economist Intelligence Unit (EIU); (4) the Institute for Management Development, Lausanne (IMD); (5) the International Crime Victim Survey (ICVS); (6) the Political and Economic Risk Consultancy, Hong Kong (PERC); (7) The Wall Street Journal, Central European Economic Review (CEER); (8) the World Bank and University of Basel (WB/UB), (9) the World Economic Forum (WEF). Descending score from 1 (most corrupt) to 10 (least corrupt). *Source: Transparency International (www.transparency.de/).*

To summarize, the regulation of entry varies enormously across countries. It often takes the form of screening procedures. Rich countries (i.e., those in the top quartile of per capita GDP) regulate entry relatively less than do all the other countries. . . .

IV. Who Gets the Rents from Regulation?

A direct implication of the *tollbooth* hypothesis is that corruption levels and the intensity of entry regulation are positively correlated. In fact, since in many countries in our sample politicians run businesses, the regulation of entry produces the double benefit of corruption revenues and reduced competition for the incumbent businesses already affiliated with the politicians. Figure 3 presents the relationship between corruption and the number of procedures without controlling for per capita GDP.[7] Table 3 shows statistically that, consistent with the *tollbooth* theory, more regulation is associated with worse corruption scores. The coefficients are statistically significant (with and without controlling for income) and large in economic terms. The estimated coefficients imply that, controlling for per capita GDP, reducing the number of procedures by ten is associated with a reduction in corruption of .8 of a standard deviation, roughly the difference between France and Italy. The results using the cost and the time of meeting the entry regulations as independent variables are also statistically significant, pointing further to the robustness of this evidence in favor of the tollbooth theory. . . .

V. Who Regulates Entry?

In this section we . . . classify countries based on the origin of their commercial laws into five broad groups: English, French, German, Scandinavian, and Socialist. . . .

In Table 4 we present the results of regressing the number of procedures on a constant, . . . the political variables, . . . and the log of per capita income. . . .

Holding per capita income constant, countries of French, German, and Socialist legal origin have more regulations than English legal origin coun-

[7]We have tried a number of measures of corruption, all yielding similar results. We have made sure that our results do not depend on "red tape" being part of the measure of corruption.

Table 4. Evidence on Regulation and Political Attributes

The table presents . . . results [using] the log of the number of procedures as the dependent variable. . . . Robust standard errors are shown in parentheses below the coefficients.

French legal origin	0.7245[a]
	(0.0916)
Socialist legal origin	0.4904[a]
	(0.1071)
German legal origin	0.7276[a]
	(0.1363)
Scandinavian legal origin	–0.0085
	(0.1733)
Ln GDP/POP$_{1999}$	–0.1434[a]
	(0.0270)
Constant	2.9492[a]
	(0.1955)
R^2	0.6256
N	85

[a]Significant at 1 percent. . . .

tries, while countries of Scandinavian legal origin have about the same. . . . Civil law countries (with the exception of those in Scandinavia) regulate entry more heavily.

References

Djankov, Simeon, Rafael La Porta, Florencio Lopez-de-Silanes, and Andrei Shleifer, "The Regulation of Labor," Harvard University manuscript in preparation, 2001.

De Soto, Hernando, *The Other Path* (New York, NY: Harper and Row, 1990).

World Economic Forum, *The Global Competitiveness Report 2001,* Klaus Schwab et al., eds. (New York, NY: Oxford University Press, 2001).

Selection IX.B.3. Africa's Growth Tragedy: Policies and Ethnic Divisions*

I. Introduction

Africa's economic history since 1960 fits the classical definition of tragedy: potential unfulfilled, with disastrous consequences. In the 1960s a leading development textbook ranked Africa's growth potential ahead of East Asia's, and the World Bank's chief economist listed seven African countries that "clearly have the potential to reach or surpass" a 7 percent growth rate. Yet, these hopes went awry. On average, real per capita GDP did not grow in Africa over the 1965–1990 period, while, in East Asia and the Pacific, per capita GDP growth was over 5 percent and Latin America grew at almost 2 percent per year. Much of Africa has even suffered negative per capita growth since 1960, and the seven promising countries identified by the World Bank's chief economist were among those with negative growth (Figure 1). Sub-Saharan Africa's growth tragedy is reflected in painful human scars. The typical African mother has only a 30 percent chance of having all of her children survive to age five. Average life expectancy for a person born in 1980 in Sub-Saharan Africa is only 48 years compared with 65 in Latin America, and daily calorie intake is only 70 percent of Latin America's and East Asia's.

Although an enormous literature points to a diverse set of potential causes of Sub-Saharan Africa's ills, ranging from bad policies, to poor education, to political instability, to inadequate infrastructure,[1] existing work does not explain why some countries choose growth-enhancing policies

*From William Easterly and Ross Levine, "Africa's Growth Tragedy: Policies and Ethnic Divisions," *Quarterly Journal of Economics* 112 (November 1997): 1203–1219, 1223–1227, 1230–1236, 1241. Reprinted by permission.

[1]See Bevan, Collier, and Gunning [1993], Collier and Gunning [1992], Soludo [1993], Husain and Faruqee [1994], Pack [1993], Lewis [1986], Wheeler [1984], Ndulu [1991], Elbadawi [1992], Elbadawi and Ndulu [1994], Helleiner [1986], Fosu [1992a, 1992b], Gyimah-Brempong [1991], Killick [1991], Berg [1993], Pickett [1990], Hadjimichael et al. [1994], and Rimmer [1991]. Chhibber and Fischer [1992] edited a book on economic reform in Sub-Saharan Africa that discusses changes in exchange rate, fiscal, financial sector, trade, educational, and regional integration policies that could potentially stimulate sustained growth in Africa. Other books include Blomstrom and Lundahl [1993], Borgin and Corbett [1982], Glickman [1988], Ravenhill [1986], Sadiq Ali and Gupta [1987], and Turok [1987]. From the World Bank, see World Bank [1981, 1989, 1994a]. A recent and thorough World Bank study on Sub-Saharan Africa is *Adjustment in Africa: Reforms, Results, and the Road Ahead* [World Bank 1994], with an update in Bouton, Jones, and Kiguel [1994].

and others adopt growth-retarding ones. Why did so many public policies all go so badly wrong in Africa? This paper examines a simple hypothesis: cross-country differences in ethnic diversity explain a substantial part of the cross-country differences in public policies, political instability, and other economic factors associated with long-run growth. This paper seeks a better understanding of cross-country growth differences by examining the direct effect of ethnic diversity on economic growth and by evaluating the indirect effect of ethnic diversity on public policy choices that in turn influence long-run growth rates. Though motivated by Africa's growth tragedy and its considerable ethnic diversity, none of the results is particular to Africa since we conduct the analysis on a broad cross section of countries. Thus, this paper examines the general proposition that ethnic diversity influences economic performance, and most of this effect works indirectly through public policies, political stability, and other economic factors. We illustrate the economic importance of ethnic diversity by demonstrating that it helps account for Africa's growth tragedy.

The paper first quantifies the empirical relationship between economic growth and a wide array of factors using data over the last 30 years. We include standard variables such as initial income to capture convergence effects, schooling, political stability, and indicators of fiscal, trade, exchange rate, financial sector policies, and infrastructure. We find that low school attainment, political instability, poorly developed financial systems, large black market exchange rate premiums, large government deficits, and inadequate infrastructure are significantly correlated with economic growth and enter the growth regressions with economically large coefficients. These variables account for about two-fifths of the growth differential between the countries of Sub-Saharan Africa and fast growing East Asia.

Next, the paper turns to its main focus: do higher levels of ethnic diversity encourage poor policies, poor education, political instability, inadequate infrastructure, and other factors associated with slow growth? While debate persists, an assortment of political economy models suggest that polarized societies will be both prone to competitive rent-seeking by the different groups and have difficulty agreeing on public goods like infrastructure, education, and good policies [Alesina and Tabellini 1989; Alesina and Drazen 1991; Shleifer and

Figure 1. Regional distribution of negative growth.

Countries that had negative per capita growth 1960–1988 are shaded gray.

Vishny 1993; Alesina and Rodrik 1994; Alesina and Spolaore 1997]. Alesina [1994, p. 38] recently argued that "society's polarization and degree of social conflict" are key factors underlying policy decisions. Ethnic diversity may increase polarization and thereby impede agreement about the provision of public goods and create positive incentives for growth-reducing policies, such as financial repression and over-valued exchange rates, that create rents for the groups in power at the expense of society at large.

To assess the hypothesis that ethnic divisions influence economic growth and public policies, we assemble a diverse set of measures of ethnic diversity. We focus most of our attention on a measure of ethnolinguistic diversity, ETHNIC, that measures the probability that two randomly selected individuals in a country belong to different ethnolinguistic groups. ETHNIC is derived from Soviet data collected in the early 1960s. . . .

The data indicate that high levels of ethnic diversity are strongly linked to high black market premiums, poor financial development, low provision of infrastructure, and low levels of education. Although ethnic diversity is not significantly correlated with every economic indicator, the evidence is consistent with the hypothesis that ethnic diversity adversely affects many public policies associated with economic growth. The evidence regarding the direct link between ethnic diversity and growth is more ambiguous. While some indicators of ethnic diversity remain significantly negatively correlated with growth after controlling for a diverse set of factors, other ethnic diversity measures are so strongly correlated with the other factors included in the regression that they lose their significance when entered jointly in cross-country growth regressions. The indirect link between ethnic diversity and public policies, however, is robust to alternative measures of ethnolinguistic diversity. While not fully accounting for Africa's growth performance, the extraordinarily high levels of ethnic diversity in Africa importantly contribute to our understanding of Africa's growth tragedy. Indeed, after accounting for the effects of ethnic diversity on education, political stability, financial depth, black market premiums, fiscal policy, and infrastructure development, ethnic diversity alone accounts for about 28 percent of the growth differential between the countries of Africa and East Asia. . . .

II. Using Cross-Country Regressions to Explain Growth

We begin by quantifying the empirical association between long-run economic growth and a wide variety of indicators. The goal here is not to establish that any particular economic or political indicator has an empirical relationship with long-run growth that is independent of other indicators. That is, the goal is not to establish "robustness" as defined by Levine and Renelt [1992]. Instead, this section shows that many indicators have a close association with growth and these indicators account for a substantial amount of the cross-country variation in growth rates over the last 30 years. This section sets the stage for the remainder of the paper, where we ask: why do countries select growth-retarding policy-packages?

A. Regression Framework

Since we are focusing on long-run growth, we attempt to abstract from business cycle fluctuations by studying economic performance over decades. Specifically, the explanatory variable in our regressions is the average annual growth rate of GDP per capita in the 1960s, 1970s, and 1980s for all countries with data (excluding Gulf Oil States). Thus, each country has three observations, data permitting. The equations are estimated using the technique of seemingly unrelated regressions, where each decade forms one-third of the system. This procedure allows for country random effects that are correlated across decades. It should be noted that the AR(1) coefficient across decades is typically smaller than 0.25, and the simple ordinary least squares results are virtually identical to those reported below.

To account for cross-country growth differences, we use an array of right-hand-side variables. Besides different intercept terms for each decade, we include dummy variables for Sub-Saharan Africa and Latin America and the Caribbean called AFRICA and LATINCA that Barro [1991] and many others have found to be significant and negative.

We include two variables to control for initial income (at the start of each decade) and thereby capture the convergence effect highlighted by Barro and Sala-i-Martin [1992]. This convergence result, however, is nonlinear, first rising and then falling with per capita income [Baumol, Blackman, and Wolff 1992; Easterly 1994]. Consequently, we include two terms: the logarithm of GDP per capita at the start of the decade and the

square of the logarithm of initial income at the start of each decade.

The cross-country growth regressions also include the logarithm of the average educational attainment variable constructed by Barro and Lee [1993], which is measured at the beginning of each decade. Also, we control for political instability by including a measure of political assassinations, which Barro [1991] found to be negatively associated with growth. We used other indicators of political instability, such as measures of civil liberties, the number of revolutions and coups, and the number of casualties from war, but these did not alter the results.

We include three economic indicators that have been linked to economic growth in past studies. First, we include a measure of the black market exchange rate premium, averaged over each decade. The black market exchange rate premium is frequently used as a general indicator of trade, exchange rate, and price distortions.[2] Second, we measure the fiscal stance of the country by including the central government surplus to GDP ratio, averaged over each decade.[3] Finally, we include a measure of financial depth that equals liquid liabilities of the financial system divided by GDP, averaged over each decade.[4] Unlike the black market premium and the fiscal surplus, financial depth is not directly linked to a policy lever. Collier and Mayer [1989] and Levine [1997], however, show that financial depth is closely linked with measures of financial sector policies and measures of the legal treatment of outside creditors developed by La Porta, López-de-Silanes; Shleifer, and Vishny [1996]. With the caveat that financial depth is not a policy lever, we sometimes refer to these three variables as policy indicators.[5]

---

[2]See Easterly [1994], Fischer [1993], and Levine and Zervos [1993].

[3]Fischer [1993] and Easterly and Rebelo [1993] find a negative relationship between government deficits and economic growth.

[4]King and Levine [1993a, 1993b] show that financial depth is closely associated with long-run growth. Furthermore, alternative measures of financial development, such as (1) the fraction of credit banks allocate to enterprises relative to the fraction of credit provided to central, state, and local governments and (2) the fraction of credit intermediated by commercial banks relative to credit intermediated by the central bank, produced similar results.

[5]We experimented with including measures of inflation and other variables frequently included in cross-country regressions, but these other variables did not enter significantly, nor did they alter this paper's conclusions. Trade or export shares are not significant as explanatory variables in cross-country growth studies. Helleiner [1986] has previously pointed out the lack of explanatory power of export shares for Africa specifically.

Table 1. Growth Regressions: Pooled Decades (1960s, 1970s, 1980s) (dependent variable: real per capita GDP growth)

Variable	(1)	(2)	(3)	(4)
Dummy for the 1960s	−0.142 (−1.66)	−0.169 (−1.96)	−0.246 (−2.60)	−0.267 (−2.82)
Dummy for the 1970s	−0.145 (−1.70)	−0.171 (−1.99)	−0.243 (−2.56)	−0.261 (−2.76)
Dummy for the 1980s	−0.165 (−1.93)	−0.191 (−2.22)	−0.259 (−2.74)	−0.277 (−2.93)
Dummy variable for Sub-Saharan Africa	−0.014 (−3.24)	−0.015 (−3.45)	−0.016 (−3.39)	−0.018 (−3.58)
Dummy variable for Latin America and the Caribbean	−0.021 (−5.58)	−0.019 (−5.21)	−0.015 (−4.22)	−0.016 (−4.56)
Log of initial income	0.047 (2.11)	0.055 (2.43)	0.079 (3.22)	0.090 (3.74)
(Log of initial income) squared	−0.003 (−2.26)	−0.004 (−2.60)	−0.006 (−3.59)	−0.007 (−4.58)
Log of schooling	0.012 (2.93)	0.013 (3.04)	0.011 (2.53)	0.009 (1.89)
Assassinations		−23.783 (−2.26)	−17.868 (−1.82)	−22.923 (−2.52)
Financial depth			0.018 (3.08)	0.013 (2.19)
Black market premium			−0.020 (−4.48)	−0.018 (−4.09)
Fiscal surplus/GDP			0.093 (3.00)	0.177 (4.93)
Log of telephones per worker				0.007 (2.71)
No. of observations	83; 89; 96	78; 88; 95	45; 72; 76	41; 70; 67
R^2	0.21, 0.18, 0.32	0.20, 0.18, 0.34	0.42, 0.43, 0.49	0.42, 0.49, 0.59

t-statistics are in parentheses.

Estimated using Seemingly Unrelated Regressions: a separate regression for each period.

B. Growth Regression Results

Regressions (1)–(3) in Table 1 present the results using these traditional measures of initial income, schooling, political stability, and policies. All of the variables are significant at the 0.05 significance level and of the anticipated sign. Countries with greater financial depth, larger fiscal surpluses, and lower black market exchange rate premiums grew significantly faster than countries with more shallow financial systems, large fiscal deficits, and sizable black market premiums. The regression also indicates that political assassinations are negatively correlated with long-run growth, while educational attainment is positively linked to growth.

The dummy variables for both Sub-Saharan African countries and Latin America and Caribbean countries are significant and negative. While the regressors are able to account for some of the poor growth performance of Africa, the regression does not explain all of it. Africa (and Latin America) grow more slowly than predicted by the cross-country growth regressions. A Chow test does not reject the hypothesis that the reported coefficients are the same for only the sample of Sub-Saharan African countries. Although the power of the Chow test is probably low, the data do not make us believe that the tragedy of Africa lies in different sensitivities to various economic indicators.

The coefficients on the catch-up variables, 0.079 on the logarithm of initial income and −0.006 on the logarithm of initial income squared in regression (3), imply that the catch-up effect is a concave function of initial income. For the given parameter values, the catch-up effect is strongest for countries with incomes of $1020.[6] Africa's initial per capita income (averaging over 1960, 1970, and 1980) is $883. Thus, the regression indicates that Africa should enjoy a catch-up effect, even though this effect will, on average, be slightly less pronounced for Africa than for countries right around the "convergence maximum" of about $1000.

Many studies of Africa cite the poor state of infrastructure. Low-quality infrastructure can hinder growth by depressing the marginal product of private investment. An influential study by Aschauer [1989] claimed that infrastructure had large effects on U.S. productivity growth; Canning and Fay [1993] and Easterly and Rebelo [1993] have similar findings for a cross-country sample, emphasizing transport and communication infrastructure.[7]

[6] To compute this, set the derivative of growth in the core regression with respect to INCOME equal to zero: 0 = 0.078936 − (0.005697)(2)(log of initial real per capita GDP). Thus, initial real per capita GDP with the maximum catch-up effect is exp{0.078936/(2*0.005697)} = $1020.

[7] Easterly and Rebelo [1993] used consolidated public sector investment in transport and communications; these data are available for too few African countries to be of use here.

Table 2. Economic Indicators: Africa Versus East Asia

Variable	Africa mean	East Asia mean
Log of schooling	1.031	1.574
Assassinations	1.13E-05	3.73E-06
Financial depth	0.240	0.474
Black market premium	0.450	0.054
Log of telephones per worker	2.436	3.538
Fiscal Surplus/GDP	–0.051	–0.025

As an indicator of the state of a country's infrastructure, we use Canning and Fay's [1993] measure of telephones per worker. We find a strong, positive link between growth and telephones per worker as shown in regression (4) of Table 1. . . .

The Table 1 results suggest that a variety of economic indicators are closely associated with economic growth in a cross section of economies. These indicators account for between 42 percent and 59 percent of the cross-country variance of growth rates depending on the decade.

To illustrate the importance of these public policy indicators in accounting for growth differences, we compare the most slowly growing region, Africa, with the most rapidly growing region, East Asia. Table 2 gives average values of the explanatory variables of regression (4) of Table 1 for East Asia and Africa. East Asia's country characteristics were uniformly more favorable for growth than those of Africa. East Asia's average years of school attainment at the beginning of each decade was 72 percent higher than Africa's. The number of assassinations in East Asia was one-third of those in Africa. East Asia had twice the financial depth and its black market premium was practically one-tenth that of Africa's. East Asia's government deficits were half the size of those in Africa. East Asia had three times as many telephones per worker as Africa. (Hong Kong had more telephones in 1960 than Nigeria, even though Nigeria's population was seventeen times larger. By 1980 Hong Kong had more telephones than all of Sub-Saharan Africa.) Thus, East Asia enjoyed substantially better country characteristics—from policies, to infrastructure, to political stability—than Africa. These country characteristics—budget deficits, black market premiums, financial depth, political instability, infrastructure, and human capital—account for a substantial amount of the cross-country variation in growth rates. Specifically, as we document below, these public policy indicators account for about 44 percent of the growth differential between Africa and East Asia. The importance of public policies in accounting for growth

differences, however, leaves open an important question: why did so many factors all go wrong in Africa? . . .

III. Ethnicity: Growth and Policy Choices

A. Ethnic Diversity: Concepts and Country Examples

The borders of African nations were determined through a tragicomic series of negotiations between European powers in the nineteenth century that split up ethnic groups and exacerbated preexisting high levels of ethnic and linguistic diversity.[8] A vast political science literature argues that these high levels of ethnic diversity have encouraged growth-impeding policies. For example, a leading Nigerian social scientist, Claude Ake, argues that a "conflict among nationalities, ethnic groups, and communal and interest groups" broke out after the independence of African nations. The resulting "struggle for power was so absorbing that everything else, including development, was marginalized" [Ake 1996, pp. 5, 7].[9]

Besides the analyses of political scientists, economic theories suggest that ethnically polarized societies are more likely to select socially suboptimal policies under many circumstances. Alesina

---

[8]Negotiations about African nation borders paid far more attention to where explorers of each European nationality had happened to wander than to existing ethnic borders, so that many ethnic groups were split between neighboring countries. For a popular historical treatment see Pakenham [1991].

[9]Scarritt [1993] concurs that in Africa, "The prevalent form of conflict . . . is competition over political and economic distribution in the context of unstable multiethnic coalitions" [p. 252]. The historian Davidson [1992] states flatly that African economic decline was due to the destruction caused by "rival kinship networks, whether of 'ethnic' clientelism or its camouflage in no less clientelist 'multiparty systems'" [p. 291]. Chazan [1988] says these ethnic groupings in Africa "have been proven to be effective channels for the extraction of state resources" [p. 134]. All of this contrasts, according to Gurr [1993], with Western democracies, which "have devised strategies that have contributed to a substantial decline in most kinds of ethnic conflict" [p. 290].

and Drazen [1991] describe how a war of attrition between interest groups can postpone macroeconomic stabilization. In this model, the first group to concede and accept stabilization bears a disproportionate share of the cost. The groups differ in the welfare loss they suffer from postponing stabilization, but their type is not known to the other group. The stabilization is delayed as the groups accumulate information on the other group's likelihood of conceding. Although they focus on inflation, the logic applies equally to any distortion such as a black market premium or financial repression. We see ethnic diversity entering their model by making it more likely that there will be polarized groups engaged in a war of attrition.

For another example, corruption may be particularly damaging when there is more than one bribe-taker [Shleifer and Vishny 1993]. If each independent bribe-taker does not internalize the effect of his bribes on the other bribe-taker's revenues, then the result is more bribes per unit of output and less output. Ethnically diverse societies may be more likely to yield independent bribe-takers since each ethnic group may be allocated a region or ministry in the power structure. Mauro [1995] has already demonstrated the empirical association between ethnic fragmentation and high corruption.

Moreover, ethnically diverse societies may produce situations formally analogous to Shleifer and Vishny's [1993] uncoordinated bribe-takers, beyond straight bribe collection. Specifically, uncoordinated ministries may each pursue a rent-seeking strategy without taking into account the effect of their actions on the other groups' rents. For example, one group may impose an overvalued exchange rate and strict exchange controls for the purpose of generating rents from reselling foreign exchange on the black market. Another group may impose very low interest rates (e.g., negative in real terms) on savers for the purpose of generating rents in the form of low-interest loans to their ethnic supporters. Different groups do not internalize the effects of their actions on other groups or society at large. For example, an overvalued official exchange rate creates incentives to smuggle local currency savings out of the country because of fear of devaluation, lowering the amount of financial savings that the other group can appropriate as low-interest loans. Likewise, highly negative domestic real interest rates create incentives to invest in foreign assets, giving exporters an additional incentive to underinvoice and keep foreign exchange outside of the country, lowering the amount of foreign exchange the group setting the official exchange rate can implicitly tax. As in Shleifer and Vishny, the results

from uncoordinated rent-seeking are lower output and higher "bribes"—in this case higher black market premiums and more financial repression—than would occur in a monolithic government.

More generally, separation of powers between distinct groups can lead to "common pool" problems, where each group seizes its share of the "pool" of rents until the pool is exhausted [Persson, Roland, and Tabellini 1997]. The common pool problem is alleviated only if checks and balances exist that give each group a veto over the other groups' rent appropriation. As we will see below, ethnically diverse societies not only by definition have distinct groups but are also empirically less likely to have the kind of political institutions that create effective checks and balances, i.e., democratic institutions and rule of law. To mix metaphors, the "common pool" story could help explain the otherwise inexplicable phenomenon of "killing the goose that lays the golden egg." It is not uncommon to observe in Africa some activity nearly taxed out of existence, that is, taxed far beyond the revenue-maximizing tax rate.

Other models tell us that polarized preferences lead to a low provision of public goods. In Alesina and Spolaore [1997] a public good like a school brings less satisfaction to everyone in an ethnically diverse situation because of the different preferences for language of instruction, curriculum, location, etc. So less of the public good is chosen by society, lowering the level of output or growth. Although this lower provision may be socially optimal, given the constraint that the school must reconcile very different preferences by ethnic groups, the existence of this constraint is costly for output and growth compared with a homogeneous society.

Some work on data from U.S. localities finds evidence for ethnic diversity affecting public goods choice. Poterba [1996] finds that a larger fraction of elderly in a jurisdiction leads to lower public spending on education and that "this reduction is particularly large when the elderly residents and the school age population are from different racial groups." Alesina, Baqir, and Easterly [1997] find that a variety of public goods—roads, schools, trash pickup, libraries—worsen or receive less funding with higher ethnic diversity in a sample of U.S. cities.[10]

---

[10]Other models in which it is more difficult to achieve a consensus for good policies in a polarized environment include Persson and Tabellini [1994], Alesina and Tabellini [1989], Lane and Tornell [1995], and Alesina and Rodrik [1994]. We should note that it is theoretically conceivable that the effect of diversity on public goods could go the other way. If each public good is purely "local" to each ethnic group, then the "common pool" type model could imply more public goods from ethnic fragmen-

A few country anecdotes help give a flavor of how ethnic divisions can foster growth-retarding policies. Kenya has more than 40 ethnic groups, including Kikuyu (21 percent of population), Luhya (13), Luo (13), Kalenjin (11), Kamba (11), Masai (2), and Somali (2). A large Indian business community and some remaining white Kenyans add to the complicated mix. The Kikuyu led the fight for independence and dominated politics under President Kenyatta until 1978, at first in alliance with the Luo and then with the Kamba. Since 1978 the Kalenjin group of President Moi has been prominent in government, in alliance with Kamba, Luhya, and smaller groups [Cohen 1995; Throup 1987]. In the 1992 presidential elections, the Luo candidate won 75 percent of the vote in the Luo region, the two Kikuyu candidates together received 96 percent of the vote in the Kikuyu region, and the Kalenjin candidate—President Moi—received 71 percent of the vote in the Kalenjin region.[11]

Barkan and Chege [1989] analyze the allocation of road-building investments in Kenya between what they consider to be the home regions of the Kenyatta and the Moi ethnic coalitions during their respective governments. Each regional grouping contains a third of Kenya's population. They report that after Moi took over in 1978, the road-building investment share of the Kenyatta coalition home regions fell from 44 percent in 1979–1980 to 16 percent in 1987–1988. The share of the Moi coalition home regions rose from 32 percent to 57 percent. The share of health expenditures in 1987–1988 going to the regions of the Kenyatta ethnic coalition was 18 percent, while the regions of the Moi coalition received 49 percent.[12]

The history of Ghana provides an illustrative example of how ethnic conflict over economic rents adversely affects policy choices. Ghana's main export crop is cocoa, production of which is concentrated in the region of the Ashanti group who make up 13 percent of the population. The Ashanti Empire was dominant in precolonial times, to the resentment of other groups such as the coastal Akan groups (30 percent of population). Beginning with the runup to independence in the 1950s, cocoa replaced historical resentments as a bone of interethnic contention [Mikell 1989].

In the early 1950s Kwame Nkrumah, himself from one of the coastal Akan groups, split off from the traditional Ashanti-based independence party. He pushed a bill through the colonial legislature in 1954 to freeze the producer price of cocoa. An Ashanti-based opposition party to Nkrumah ran against him in the 1956 elections with the slogan, "Vote Cocoa," while also pushing for secession. With most of the other groups favoring Nkrumah, these efforts failed. Nkrumah continued to tax cocoa heavily—through the Cocoa Marketing Board and through the growing overvaluation of the official exchange rate.

In 1969–1971 Kofi Busia led the only Ashanti-based government in modern Ghanaian history, having co-opted some of the coastal Akan groups as allies. One of Busia's first acts was to raise the producer price of cocoa. Later in his term, in 1971, he instituted a large devaluation that raised the domestic currency price of cocoa at a time when the world cocoa price was falling. The military overthrew him three days later and partially reversed the devaluation.

Though ethnic coalitions rotated with dizzying speed through the 1970s and early 1980s in Ghana, they all seemed to concur on punitive taxation of cocoa exports through the ludicrously overvalued official exchange rate (reflected in a high black market premium). Granting of permission to import goods at the official exchange rate was one way to dissipate these rents to political and ethnic supporters. The black market premium reached its historical peak in 1982, with the black market exchange rate at 22 times the official exchange rate [Wetzel 1995, p. 197]. The cocoa producers had received 89 percent of the world price of cocoa in 1949 [Bates 1981]. By 1983 they received 6 percent of the world price. Cocoa exports were 19 per-

---

tation. Under other models, like those that feature "log-rolling," each ethnic representative gets his favorite local public projects funded while agreeing in return to support the other representatives' projects and so the result is *excessive* spending on public goods. Whether these considerations are relevant is an empirical issue our results will address.

[11]Miller and Yeager [1994, p. 116]. Moi was elected with a plurality (36 percent) of the votes due to the splitting of opposition votes. Of course, ethnic bloc voting is hardly unique to Kenya, or to Africa. In Fiji's 1977 elections, 82 percent of people of Fijian origin voted for one party, while 86 percent of people of Indian origin voted for the other party [Milne 1981]. In Washington, DC's mayoral election in 1994, the white candidate got over 90 percent of the vote in the mostly white Ward 3, while the black candidate got over 90 percent of the vote in the mostly black Ward 8 (*Washington Post*).

[12]Background studies of parliamentarians find that "the one characteristic they share with their constituents is ethnicity," since communities "want to be sure that a candidate will represent their interests" [Miller and Yeager 1994, p. 77]. Cohen [1995] says the group in power has systematically manipulated the multiple exchange rate system to extract rents for its particu-

lar ethnic group, which illustrates "how brazen ethnic-based rent-seeking coalitions can become." See also Nyangira [1987], Throup [1987], Haugerud [1995], and Bates [1989] for other examples of ethnic distributional conflicts in Kenya.

Table 3. Ethnolinguistic Fractionalization Index (ETHNIC) (66 Countries, 1960)

Country	ETHNIC	Country	ETHNIC
15 most fractionalized		15 least fractionalized	
Tanzania	93	Haiti	1
Uganda	90	Japan	1
Zaire	90	Portugal	1
Cameroon	89	Hong Kong	2
India	89	Yemen	2
South Africa	88	Germany	3
Nigeria	87	Burundi	4
Ivory Coast	86	Dominican Republic	4
CAR	83	Egypt	4
Kenya	83	Ireland	4
Liberia	83	Italy	4
Zambia	82	Norway	4
Angola	78	Iceland	5
Mali	78	Jamaica	5
Sierra Leone	77	Jordan	5

ETHNIC measures the probability that two randomly selected persons from a given country will not belong to the same ethnolinguistic group. The more groups there are, the higher ETHNIC. The more equally distributed the groups, the higher the ETHNIC.

Source: Taylor and Hudson [1972].

cent of GDP in 1955; by 1983 they were only 3 percent of GDP. Ghanaian cocoa is one of the classic examples of "killing the goose that laid the golden egg." Reforms finally began in the mid-1980s. The case of Ghana suggests that the interethnic struggle over rents from a commodity like cocoa has something to do with the choice of growth-retarding policies—like an overvalued exchange rate resulting in a high black market premium.

Finally, in contrast to Ghana and Kenya, Botswana is an African success story with growth comparable to South Korea's. In terms of this paper's focus, it is noteworthy that Botswana has one of the most ethnically homogeneous populations in Africa and has adopted some of the best policies in Sub-Saharan Africa. . . .

B. Measuring Ethnic Diversity

Table 3 shows the most and the least ethnically diverse societies in the world according to the Soviets' measure of ETHNIC. Fourteen out of the fifteen most ethnically heterogeneous societies in the world are in Africa; eight countries classified as high-income countries by the World Bank's Development Report are among the most ethnically homogeneous, and no such rich countries are among the top-fifteen most ethnically diverse countries. Two of the East Asian fast growers (Japan and Hong Kong) are among the most ethnically homogeneous. . . .

C. Growth Regressions

The simple regression of growth on ETHNIC (with decade dummies) is highly significant, with a t-statistic of -4.4. The magnitude of the coefficient ($-.023$) indicates that going from complete homogeneity to complete heterogeneity is associated with a fall in growth of 2.3 percentage points.[13] A one-standard-deviation increase in ETHNIC is associated with a decrease in per capita growth of about 30 percent of a standard deviation in growth across countries. ETHNIC is not simply proxying for the Africa dummy here, because it also remains significant in the non-Africa sample (coefficient of

[13]We estimate this and the following regressions with the method of seemingly unrelated regressions with one equation for each decade. We believe the pooled decade average, cross section sample is useful despite the lack of intertemporal variability of ETHNIC so that we can—as we will see—capture the intertemporal variation in the other variables. If we run the simple correlation between growth and ETHNIC as a cross section by averaging the decade growth rates, the association remains highly significant.

Table 4. Ethnic Diversity and Long-Run Growth (Dependent Variable is Growth of per Capita real GDP)

Variable	(1)	(2)	(3)	(4)	(5)
Dummy for the 1960s	−0.072	−0.096	−0.186	−0.254	−0.224
	(−0.88)	(−1.15)	(−1.94)	(−2.66)	(−2.37)
Dummy for the 1970s	−0.074	−0.098	−0.182	−0.248	−0.217
	(−0.90)	(−1.17)	(−1.90)	(−2.59)	(−2.30)
Dummy for the 1980s	−0.094	−0.117	−0.198	−0.263	−0.232
	(−1.14)	(−1.40)	(−2.07)	(−2.76)	(−2.46)
Dummy variable for Sub-	−0.013	−0.014	−0.012	−0.013	−0.013
Saharan Africa	(−2.82)	(−2.98)	(−2.46)	(−2.53)	(−2.49)
Dummy variable for Latin	−0.022	−0.021	−0.017	−0.018	−0.019
America and the	(−6.52)	(−5.88)	(−4.74)	(−4.90)	(−5.22)
Caribbean					
Log of initial income	0.033	0.039	0.066	0.086	0.081
	(1.56)	(1.82)	(2.69)	(3.58)	(3.41)
(Log of initial income)	−0.003	−0.003	−0.005	−0.007	−0.006
squared	(−1.83)	(−2.09)	(−3.10)	(−4.25)	(−4.23)
Log of schooling	0.011	0.011	0.009	0.009	0.010
	(2.85)	(2.83)	(2.28)	(1.98)	(2.22)
Assassinations		−20.730	−14.874	−21.480	−21.862
		(−2.04)	(−1.56)	(−2.45)	(−2.45)
Financial depth			0.015	0.012	0.011
			(2.54)	(2.10)	(1.90)
Black market premium			−0.020	−0.019	−0.019
			(−4.63)	(−4.46)	(−4.52)
Fiscal surplus/GDP			0.088	0.171	0.158
			(2.88)	(4.82)	(4.40)
Log of telephones per				0.005	0.005
worker				(1.74)	(1.86)
ETHNIC	−0.020	−0.017	−0.016	−0.011	
	(−3.19)	(−2.74)	(−2.54)	(−1.53)	
AVG-ETHNIC					−0.020
					(−2.73)
No. of observations	78; 84; 90	75; 83; 89	44; 69; 72	40; 68; 64	41; 70; 67
R^2	0.31, 0.24, 0.35	0.27, 0.23, 0.36	0.43, 0.44, 0.51	0.43, 0.49, 0.61	0.45, 0.52, 0.60

t-statistics are in parentheses.

Estimated using Seemingly Unrelated Regressions: a separate regression for each period.

AVG-ETHNIC is the average value of ETHNIC and the Muller [1964], Roberts [1962], and two Gunnemark [1991] measures of ethnolinguistic diversity.

−.016 and *t*-statistic of −2.3). This simple, reduced-form regression is an important result because we will argue that many of the standard explanatory variables in growth regressions are themselves endogenous to ETHNIC.[14]

[14]Many readers have wondered whether the relationship between growth and ETHNIC was nonlinear; for example, maybe having two equal groups is just as damaging to political economy as four equal groups; alternatively, maybe ethnic diversity only matters when there are many small ethnic groups (the upper range of ETHNIC). Unfortunately, our efforts to estimate a spline regression were unavailing; we found no evidence of a change in slope at ETHNIC = .5 and at ETHNIC = .75, which may simply reflect our small sample.

Table 4 presents evidence on the empirical association between ETHNIC and economic growth, controlling for other factors. Regression (1) shows that ETHNIC is significantly correlated with growth after controlling for initial income and including dummy variables for countries in Sub-Saharan Africa and Latin America. In regression (2) we introduce measures of educational attainment and political stability. Ethnic diversity remains significant with little change in the coefficient. Moreover, ethnic diversity remains significantly negatively correlated with growth after controlling for financial depth, the fiscal surplus, and the black market exchange rate premium as shown in regression (3).[15] The economic magnitude of the coefficient on ETHNIC is substantial. Taken literally, the coefficient in regression (3) implies that if Nigeria had the sample mean value of ETHNIC (0.42) instead of its actual value of 0.87, its per capita growth rate over the 1960–1989 period would have been almost double its actual value of 0.7 percent per annum. In regression (4) we also include the logarithm of the number of telephones per worker as an indicator of national infrastructure. The significance of ethnic diversity weakens, and the coefficient diminishes when we also include the infrastructure measure. Apparently, ETHNIC is sufficiently correlated with public policy indicators such that it loses its independent association with long-run growth in regression (4) of Table 4. We get similar results when the analysis is restricted to the non-African countries. Thus, as suggested by theory and country studies, ETHNIC may primarily affect growth indirectly by influencing public policy decisions. . . .

D. Ethnic Diversity, Political Instability, and Policy Choices

Ethnically fragmented economies may find it difficult to agree on public goods and good policies. They also may be politically unstable. Table 5 presents evidence on the effects of ethnic diversity on political instability and policy choices. The simple relationship between ethnic diversity and assassinations is insignificant. There is no evidence that ethnic diversity affects this manifestation of political instability. This lack of correlation is not unique to this indicator—out of a set of nine indicators of political instability, we found only one (constitutional changes) to be correlated with ethnic diversity. A related observation is that Africa does *not* have significantly above average political instability by these measures, despite its well-documented ethnic conflicts.[16] These results suggest that, for

some countries, high levels of ethnic conflict coexist with governments that for long periods successfully suppress overt political opposition.

Although ethnic diversity is not significantly correlated with fiscal surpluses, ethnic diversity is significantly negatively correlated with school attainment, financial depth, and the number of telephones per worker, and ethnic diversity is significantly positively correlated with the black market premium.[17] (Ethnic diversity was also positively correlated with the other infrastructure measures mentioned earlier: electrical system losses and the percentage of roads that are unpaved.) Although the results do not hold for every policy indicator, the data are consistent with the view that ethnic diversity tends to slow growth by making it more difficult to agree on the provision of public goods and policies that foster economic growth. Since Africa is much more ethnically diverse than other regions, this feature of African economies helps explain their tendency to choose growth-retarding policies. . . .

Econometrically, the correlation between ETHNIC and the public policy indicators helps clarify why the partial correlation between long-run growth and some measures of ethnolinguistic diversity are not robust to the inclusion of the wide array of public policy indicators used in regression (4) of Table 4: ethnic diversity affects many of the explanatory variables used in standard growth regressions. Our interpretation of those results is *not* so much that one should throw one more variable—ETHNIC—into growth regressions.[18] Our interpretation is that ETHNIC helps explain some of the explanatory variables used in growth regressions and, through these policy indicators, growth itself.

E. Assessing Africa's Performance: The East Asia Comparison

We now put our results in context by comparing East Asia's growth miracle with Africa's growth

---

[15]We have already noted that war is associated with ethnic fragmentation. Over the past three decades, many military conflicts have occurred in Africa. To gauge whether our results merely reflect the economic disruptions caused by war, we examine the relationships between wars and growth and between wars and policy choices. We use a dummy variable, WAR, that takes on the value 1 when Sivard [1993] reports a war taking place on the territory of a given country in a given decade. When we include WAR in the pooled cross-country, decade growth regressions of Table 1 that include policy indicators (regressions (3)–(4)), WAR enters with a P-value of greater than 0.10 and the results on the other variables remain unaffected.

[16]The nine measures of political instability were antigovernment demonstrations, assassinations, cabinet changes, constitutional changes, coups, government crises, purges, revolutions,

and riots. The source, as in some of the measures used by Barro [1991] and Alesina, Ozler, Roubini, and Swagel [1996], was Banks [1994]. . . . Africa was below average for the whole sample on six of these measures, and above average for three of them; constitutional changes was the only indicator significantly above average for Africa.

[17]The associations between ETHNIC and telephones, black market premium, financial depth, and school attainment are also highly significant in a pure cross section.

[18]Here we are careful to hedge by using the phrase ". . . not so much . . ." because some measures of ethnolinguistic diversity maintain a robust independent partial correlation with growth after controlling for a wide array of public policy indicators.

Table 5. Determinants of Economic Indicators

Dependent variable	C	ETHNIC	R^2	Number of observations
Log of schooling	1.508	−0.991	0.08, 0.09, 0.10	83; 85; 91
	(17.12)	(−6.21)		
Assassinations	1.24E-05	1.03E-06	−0.01, −0.06, −0.02	98; 105;
	(1.52)	(0.07)		105
Financial depth	0.417	−0.266	0.09, 0.06, −0.02	94; 100;
	(11.44)	(−3.67)		103
Black market premium	0.070	0.252	0.05, 0.08; −0.04	97; 107; 106
	(1.82)	(3.39)		
Fiscal surplus/GDP	−0.026	−0.013	−0.14, −0.02, −0.13	55; 87; 82
	(−5.48)	(−1.37)		
Log of telephones per worker	4.331	−3.067	0.21, 0.23, 0.04	95; 103; 92
	(18.95)	(−7.17)		

t-statistics are in parentheses.

Equations estimated using Seemingly Unrelated Regression procedures.

tragedy. We start by ignoring the role of ethnicity and simply showing how much of the East Asia–Africa growth differential is accounted for by the public policy indicators used in regression (4) of Table 4. By subtracting Africa's value for each explanatory variable from East Asia's country value and multiplying this difference by the regression coefficient (from regression (4) in Table 4), we compute that part of the difference in growth rates between East Asian and African countries associated with each explanatory variable.[19] Table 2 gives the values for the public policy variables. Taken together, Africa's high budget deficits, financial shallowness, substantial black market exchange rate premiums, high political instability, weak infrastructure, and low human capital account for 2.6 percentage points of the 3.4 percentage point differential between East Asia and Africa (Table 6).[20] Although these factors appear to explain most of the East Asia–Africa growth difference, they are offset by one factor that was in Africa's favor. Africa's income at the beginning of each decade was much lower than East Asia's. This convergence effect predicts that Africa should have grown 1.1 percentage points faster than East Asia, so that on net, the non-ETHNIC explanatory variables in regression 4 of Table IV account for 1.5 percentage points (2.6 − 1.1) of the 3.4 percentage point growth differential. The non-ETHNIC variables account for about two-fifths of the growth difference.

Now consider the direct effect of ETHNIC on growth. As discussed above, this direct effect is relatively modest. The direct effect explains an additional 0.2 percentage points of the growth differential. Thus, all explanatory variables in regression (4) of Table 4 account for about half (1.7 percentage points) of the difference between East Asian and African growth rates. Of the unexplained differential, most is due to the Africa dummy, and the remainder to the positive East Asia residual.[21]

Next, consider the indirect effect of ETHNIC on growth: ETHNIC helps account for long-run growth differences by explaining public policy decisions. ETHNIC is 0.74 in the 27 observations for the Africa group included in this sample and 0.53 in the 19 observations for the East Asia group. (This sample excludes Korea and Hong Kong, as discussed earlier, so likely understates the difference in ethnic diversity between the two regions.) We use the policy regressions in Table 5 to explain how much of the East Asia–Africa policy differences are attributable to ETHNIC. Although these types of calculations may be sensitive to the simple linear functional form that we have used through-

[19]Recall that we demonstrated earlier that the coefficients on the explanatory variables are not significantly different for Africa from the rest of the sample.

[20]These decomposition results are virtually indential to those obtained from regression (4) of Table 1, which does not include ETHNIC. We use the regression results from Table 4 to facilitate comparisons across the different scenarios presented in Table 6.

[21]The positive East Asia residual reminds us that not all of the Africa dummy is necessarily due to "Africa." The Africa and Latin America dummies reflect how these two underachieving regions compare with the rest of the sample, which includes at least one overachieving region—East Asia. If we put for symmetry a dummy to measure how much of *East Asia's* performance is not fully captured by the regressions, then the Africa dummy is reduced in magnitude and significance compared with regressions (4) and (5) of Table 4. With the Soviet ETHNIC, AFRICA is just barely significant and with AVG-ETHNIC, the AFRICA dummy is no longer significant.

Table 6. Decomposition of Growth Differential Between Africa and East Asia (based on regression (4), Table 4 with Soviet ETHNIC measure)

	Africa–East Asia growth differential accounted for this variable	% of difference in each variable explained by ETHNIC	Growth differential implicitly explained by ETHNIC through this variable
Political/policy indicator RHS variables:			
Log schooling	0.5%	43%	0.2%
Assassinations	0.0%	3%	0.0%
Financial depth	0.3%	21%	0.1%
Black market premium	0.8%	13%	0.1%
Fiscal surplus/GDP	0.5%	11%	0.1%
Log telephones per worker	0.5%	60%	0.3%
(1) Total effect through political/policy indicator RHS variables on growth	2.6%	28%	0.7%
ETHNIC—Soviet (the partial effect of ETHNIC in regression (4), Table 4)	0.2%		0.2%
(2) Joint effect of all policy indicator and ETHNIC RHS variables	2.8%	34%	1.0%
Convergence effect (growth effect includes both linear and quadratic terms on initial income)	−1.1%		
(3) Joint growth effect of all RHS variables	1.7%	56%	1.0%
Residual	1.7%		
unexplained difference of which: Africa dummy	*1.3%*		
(4) Actual per capita growth differential, East Asia–Africa	3.4%	28%	1.0%
Ethnic diversity:			
Africa: 0.744			
East Asia: 0.527			

out this paper, we present these calculations to illustrate the potential importance of ethnic diversity on economic growth. We find that ETHNIC indirectly accounts for about 28 percent of the 2.6 percentage point growth difference attributable to political/policy indicators. When we include the direct effects of ETHNIC, ETHNIC alone explains about one percentage point of the 3.4 percentage point East Asia–Africa growth differential. . . .

IV. Conclusions

Understanding Africa's growth tragedy requires not only an accounting of the relationship between slow growth and unfavorable country characteristics, but also an understanding of why country characteristics were so unfavorable. Africa's poor growth—and resulting low income—is associated with low schooling, political instability, underdeveloped financial systems, distorted foreign exchange markets, high government deficits, and insufficient infrastructure. High ethnic diversity is closely associated with low schooling, underdevel-

oped financial systems, distorted foreign exchange markets, and insufficient infrastructure. While motivated by Africa, these results are not particular to Africa. In evaluating the extent to which cross-country differences in ethnic diversity explain cross-country differences in public policies and political stability, we conduct the analysis on a broad cross section of countries. The results lend support to theories that interest group polarization leads to rent-seeking behavior and reduces the consensus for public goods, creating long-run growth tragedies.

References

Ake, Claude, *Democracy and Development in Africa* (Washington, DC: The Brookings Institution, 1996).

Alesina, Alberto, "Political Models of Macroeconomic Policy and Fiscal Reforms," in Stephen Haggard and Steven Webb, eds. *Voting for Reform: Democracy, Political Liberalization, and Economic Adjustment* (New York, NY: Oxford University Press, 1994).

Alesina, Alberto, Reza Baqir, and William Easterly,

"Public Goods and Ethnic Divisions," Harvard University and World Bank mimeo, March 1997.

Alesina, Alberto, and Allen Drazen, "Why Are Stabilizations Delayed?" *American Economic Review,* LXXXI (1991), 1170–1188.

Alesina, Alberto, Sule Ozler, Nouriel Roubini, and Phillip Swagel, "Political Instability and Economic Growth," *Journal of Economic Growth,* I (1996), 189–211.

Alesina, Alberto, and Dani Rodrik, "Distributive Politics and Economic Growth," *Quarterly Journal of Economics,* CIX (1994), 465–490.

Alesina, Alberto, and Enrico Spolaore, "On the Number and Size of Nations," *Quarterly Journal of Economics,* CII (1997), 1027–1056.

Alesina, Alberto, and Guido Tabellini, "External Debt, Capital Flight and Political Risk," *Journal of International Economics,* XXVII (1989), 199–220.

Aschauer, David A., "Is Public Expenditure Productive?" *Journal of Monetary Economics,* XXIII (1989), 177–200.

Banks, Arthur S., "Cross-National Time Series Data Archive," Center for Social Analysis, State University of New York at Binghamton, 1994.

Barkan, Joel, with Michael Chege, "Decentralising the State: District Focus and the Politics of Reallocation in Kenya," *Journal of Modern African Studies,* XXVII (1989), 431–453.

Barro, Robert, "Economic Growth in a Cross Section of Countries," *Quarterly Journal of Economics,* CVI (1991), 407–443.

Barro, Robert, and Jong-Wha Lee, "International Comparisons of Educational Attainment," *Journal of Monetary Economics,* XXXII (1993), 363–394.

Barro, Robert, and Xavier Sala-i-Martin, "Convergence," *Journal of Political Economy,* C (1992), 223–251.

Bates, Robert H., *Markets and States in Tropical Africa: the Political Basis of Agricultural Policies* (Berkeley, CA: University of California Press, 1981).

——, *Beyond the Miracle of the Market: The Political Economy of Agrarian Development in Kenya* (Cambridge and New York: Cambridge University Press, 1989).

Baumol, William J., Sue Anne Batey Blackman, and Edward N. Wolff, *Productivity and American Leadership: The Long View* (Cambridge, MA: MIT Press, 1992).

Berg, Elliot, "L'Integration Economique en Afrique de l'Ouest: Problemes et Strategies," *Revue d'Economie du Developpement,* XCIII (1993), 51–82.

Bevan, David, Paul Collier, and Jan Willem Gunning, "Trade Shocks in Developing Countries: Consequences and Policy Responses," *European Economic Review,* XXXVII (1993), 557–565.

Blomstrom, Magnus, and Mats Lundahl, eds., *Economic Crisis in Africa: Perspectives on Policy Responses* (New York, NY: Routledge, 1993).

Borgin, Karl, and Kathleen Corbett, *The Destruction of a Continent: Africa and International Aid* (San Diego, CA: Harcourt Brace Jovanovich, 1982).

Bouton, Lawrence, Christine Jones, and Miguel Kiguel, "Macroeconomic Reforms and Growth in Africa: Adjustment in Africa Revisited," Working Paper Series No. 1394, Washington, DC, World Bank, 1994.

Canning, David, and Marianne Fay, "The Effect of Transportation Networks on Economic Growth," Discussion Paper Series, Columbia University, Department of Economics, 1993.

Chazan, Naomi, *The Precarious Balance: State and Society in Africa,* Naomi Chazan and Donald Rothchild, eds. (Boulder, CO: Westview Press, 1988).

Chhibber, Ajay, and Stanley Fischer, eds., *Economic Reform in Sub-Saharan Africa* (Washington, DC: World Bank, 1992).

Cohen, John M., "Ethnicity, Foreign Aid, and Economic Growth: The Case of Kenya," HIID Development Discussion Paper No. 520, 1995.

Collier, Paul, and J.W. Gunning, "Aid and Exchange Rate Adjustment in African Trade Liberalization," *Economic Journal,* CII (1992), 925–939.

Collier, Paul, and Colin Mayer, "Financial Liberalization, Financial Systems, and Economic Growth: The Assessment," *Oxford Review of Economic Policy,* V (1989), 1–12.

Davidson, Basil, *Black Man's Burden: Africa and the Curse of the Nation-State* (New York, NY: Times Books, 1992).

Easterly, William, "Economic Stagnation, Fixed Factors, and Policy Thresholds," *Journal of Monetary Economics,* XXXIII (1994), 525–557.

Easterly, William, and Sergio Rebelo, "Fiscal Policy and Economic Growth: An Empirical Investigation," *Journal of Monetary Economics,* XXXII (1993), 417–457.

Elbadawi, Ibrahim, "World Bank Adjustment Lending and Economic Performance in Sub-Saharan Africa in the 1980s: A Comparison of Early Adjusters, Late Adjusters, and Nonadjusters," Working Paper Series No. 1001, Washington, DC, World Bank, 1992.

Elbadawi, Ibrahim, and Benno Ndulu, "Long-Term Development and Sustainable Growth in Sub-Saharan Africa," AERC, mimeo, 1994.

Fischer, Stanley, "The Role of Macroeconomic Factors in Growth," *Journal of Monetary Economics,* XXXII (1993), 485–511.

Fosu, Augustin K., "Effect of Export Instability on Economic Growth in Africa," *Journal of Development Areas,* XXVI (1992a), 323–332.

——, "Political Instability and Economic Growth: Evidence from Sub-Saharan Africa," *Economic Development and Cultural Change,* XL (1992b), 829–841.

Glickman, Harvey, *The Crisis and Challenge of African Development* (New York, NY: Greenwood Press, 1988).

Gunnemark, Erik V., *Countries, Peoples and Their Languages: The Linguistic Handbook* (Gothenburg, Sweden: Lanstryckeriet, 1991).

Gurr, Ted Robert, *Minorities at Risk: A Global View of Ethnopolitical Conflicts* (Washington, DC: United States Institute of Peace Press, 1993).

Gyimah-Brempong, Kwabena, "Export Instability and Economic Growth in Sub-Saharan Africa," *Economic Development and Cultural Change,* XXXIX (1991), 815–28.

Hadjimichael, Michael T., Dhaneshwar Ghura, Martin Muhleisen, Roger Nord, and E.Murat Ucer, "Effects of Macroeconomic Stability on Growth, Savings, and Investment in Sub-Saharan Africa: An Empirical Investigation," IMF Working Paper 94/98, 1994.

Haugerud, Angelique, *The Culture of Politics in Modern Kenya* (Cambridge, MA: Cambridge University Press, 1995).

Helleiner, Gerald K, *Theory and Reality in Development: Essays in Honor of Paul Streeten,* Saniaya Lall, and Stewart Frances, eds. (New York, NY: St. Martin's Press, 1986).

Husain, Ishrat, and Rashid Faruqee, eds. *Adjustment in Africa: Lessons from Case Studies* (Washington, DC: World Bank, 1994).

Killick, Tony, "The Developmental Effectiveness of Aid to Africa," Working Paper Series No. 646, Washington, DC, World Bank, 1991.

King, Robert G., and Ross Levine, "Finance and Growth: Schumpeter Might Be Right," *Quarterly Journal of Economics,* CVIII (1993a), 717–738.

King, Robert G., and Ross Levine, "Finance, Entrepreneurship, and Growth: Theory and Evidence," *Journal of Monetary Economics,* XXXII (1993b), 513–542.

Lane, Philip, and Aaron Tornell, "Power Concentration and Growth," Harvard Institute of Economic Research, Discussion Paper No. 1720, Harvard University, 1995.

La Porta, Rafael, Florencio López-de-Silanes, Andrei Shleifer, and Robert W. Vishny, "Law and Finance," NBER Working Paper No. 5661, July 1996.

Levine, Ross. "Law, Finance, and Economic Growth," University of Virginia, mimeo, 1997.

Levine, Ross, and David Renelt, "Sensitivity Analysis of Cross-Country Growth Regressions," *American Economic Review,* LXXXII (1992), 942–963.

Levine, Ross, and Sara J. Zervos, "What We Have Learned about Policy and Growth from Cross-Country Regressions," *American Economic Review, Papers and Proceedings,* LXXXIII (1993), 426–30.

Lewis, John Prior, *Development Strategies Reconsidered* (New Brunswick, NJ: Transaction Books, 1986).

Mauro, Paolo, "Corruption and Growth," *Quarterly Journal of Economics,* CX (1995), 681–712.

Mikell, Gwendolyn, *Cocoa and Chaos in Ghana* (New York, NY: Paragon House, 1989).

Miller, Norman, and Rodger Yeager, *Kenya: The Quest for Prosperity* (Boulder, CO: Westview Press, 1994).

Milne, R. S. *Politics in Ethnically Bipolar States: Guyana, Malaysia, Fiji* University of British Columbia Press (Vancouver: 1981).

Muller, Siegfried H., *The World's Living Languages: Basic Facts of Their Structure, Kinship, Location, and Number of Speakers* (New York, NY: Ungar, 1964).

Ndulu, Benno J., *Economic Reform in Sub-Saharan Africa,* Ajay Chhibber and Stanley Fischer, eds. (Washington, DC: World Bank, 1991).

Nyangira, Nicholas, *The Political Economy of Kenya,* Michael G. Schatzberg, ed. (New York, NY: Praeger, 1987).

Pack, Howard, "Productivity and Industrial Development in Sub-Saharan Africa," *World Development,* XXI (1993), 1–16.

Pakenham, Thomas, *The Scramble for Africa* (New York, NY: Random House, 1991).

Persson, Torsten, Gérard Roland, and Guido Tabellini, "Separation of Powers and Accountibility," *Quarterly Journal of Economics,* CXII (1997), 1163–1202.

Persson, Torsten, and G. Tabellini, "Is Inequality Harmful for Growth?" *American Economic Review,* LXXXIV (1994), 600–621.

Pickett, James, "Low-Income Economies of Sub-Saharan Africa: Problems and Prospects," *African Development Bank, Economic Research Papers,* XII (1990), 1–48.

Poterba, James, M. "Demographic Structure and the Political Economy of Public Education," NBER Working Paper No. 5677, July 1996.

Ravenhill, John, ed., *Africa in Economic Crisis* (Basingstoke, NH: Macmillan, 1986).

Rimmer, Douglas, ed., *Africa 30 Years On* (London: Villiers Publications Ltd., 1991).

Roberts, Janet, "Sociocultural Change and Communication Problems," in *Study of the Role of Second Languages in Asia, Africa, and Latin America,* Frank A. Rice, ed. (Washington DC: Center for Applied Linguistics of the Modern Language Association of America, 1962), pp. 105–123.

Sadiq Ali, Shanti, and Anirudha Gupta, eds., *Africa: Dimensions of the Economic Crisis; An Analysis of the Problems and Constraints of Development* (New Delhi: Sterling Publishers, 1987).

Scarritt, James R., *Minorities at Risk: A Global View of Ethnopolitical Conflicts,* Ted Robert Gurr, ed. (Washington, DC: United States Institute of Peace Press, 1993).

Shleifer, Andrei, and Robert Vishny, "Corruption," *Quarterly Journal of Economics,* CVIII (1993), 599–617.

Sivard, Ruth L., *World Military and Social Expenditures: 1993,* 15th ed. (Washington, DC: World Priorities, 1993).

Soludo, Charles C., "Growth Performance in Africa: Further Evidence on the External Shocks versus Domestic Policy Debate," UNECA Development Research Paper Series No. 6 (November), United Nations, 1993.

Taylor, Charles Lewis, and Michael C. Hudson, *World Handbook of Political and Social Indicators,* 2nd ed. (New Haven, CT: Yale University Press, 1972).

Throup, David W., *The Political Economy of Kenya* Michael G. Schatzberg, ed. (New York, NY: Praeger, 1987).

Turok, Ben, *Africa: What Can Be Done?* (London: Zed Books, 1987).

Wetzel, Deborah L., *The Macroeconomics of Fiscal Deficits in Ghana: 1960–94,* Ph.D. thesis, Oxford University, 1995.

Wheeler, David, "Sources of Stagnation in Sub-Saharan Africa," *World Development,* XII (1984), 1–23.

World Bank, *Accelerated Development in Sub-Saharan Africa: An Agenda for Action* (Washington, DC: World Bank, 1981).

———, *Sub-Saharan Africa: from Crisis to Sustainable Growth—a Long-Term Perspective Study* (Washington DC: World Bank, 1989).

———, *Adjustment in Africa: Reforms, Results, and the Road Ahead* (New York, NY: Oxford University Press, 1994).

IX.C. STATE CAPACITY

Selection IX.C.1. Institutions and Economic Performance: Cross-Country Tests Using Alternative Institutional Measures*

The Institutional Data

The focus of this paper is on institutional indicators compiled by two private international investment risk services: International Country Risk Guide (ICRG) and Business Environmental Risk Intelligence (BERI). We use the first observations that these services have for any country; for BERI, the vast majority of observations are from 1972 and for ICRG, nearly all observations are from 1982. . . .

ICRG variables *Expropriation Risk,* measuring the risk of expropriation, and *Rule of Law,* measuring whether there are established peaceful mechanisms for adjudicating disputes, are interpreted here as proxies for the security of property and contract rights. If countries score low on these dimensions, they are likely to suffer a reduction in the quantity and efficiency of physical and perhaps even human capital investment. As the probability increases that investors will lose the proceeds from the investment, or the investment itself, investors reduce their investment and channel their resources to activities that are more secure from the threat of expropriation (trading rather than manufacturing, for example), although they may be less profitable.

Repudiation of Contracts by Government is another indicator of contract enforcement. It is likely that if private actors cannot count on the government to respect the contracts it has with them, they will also not be able to count on the government enforcing contracts between two private parties. In the absence of impartial state enforcement, the only impersonal exchanges taking place between private economic actors will be those that are "self-enforcing"—those in which the benefits of compliance exceed the gains from cheating or reneging. This restriction on economic activity severely limits the universe of possible Pareto-improving exchanges that would otherwise be undertaken.

Repudiation is also an indicator of government credibility. Regimes in which officials have the power unilaterally to modify or to repudiate contractual agreements will likely be unconstrained in numerous other areas that impinge on economic activity. In particular, entrepreneurs are likely to be suspicious about the institutional or other barriers on state officials that keep them from pursuing policies of confiscatory taxation (directly, or through inflation), or outright expropriation.[1]

The remaining two ICRG variables used in this paper are *Corruption in Government* and *Quality of Bureaucracy.* They are taken as proxies for the general efficiency with which government services are provided, and for the extent and damage of rent-seeking behavior. When countries score poorly (low) on these dimensions, it is a strong indication that a bureaucracy lacks procedural clarity or technical competence and is likely to introduce criteria other than efficiency into the determination of government policies or the allocation of public goods. In particular, the bureaucracy is likely to award contracts, business and trade licenses, police protection and so forth on the basis of criteria other than those of allocative and technical efficiency. In addition, bureaucracies where corruption is higher or competence is low are less likely to provide a strong bulwark against infringements on property rights. The resulting distortions in investment and trade may reduce the quantity and efficiency of capital investment and foreign technology introduced into the country.

Theoretically, the use of corrupt allocation schemes in the political marketplace need not produce less efficient results than other forms of political allocation. However, in those countries where ICRG records high levels of corruption, entrepreneurs are also beset by greater uncertainty regarding the credibility of government commitments. That is, the same institutions that allow public officials to demand large and arbitrary bribes, such as failed law enforcement systems, also inhibit those officials from credibly pledging not to renege on their future commitments. This discourages investment and encourages forms of economic activity that are less vulnerable to expropriation.[2]

---

[1]See Weingast (1993) and Keefer (1993) for a discussion of the effects of government credibility on investment and growth.

[2]The predominance of trading as the object of most new entrepreneurial effort in Russia during the transition is likely due not only to the high returns to trading, but also to the low returns to other forms of economic activity that are driven down by riskiness of investments and the difficulties of making credible deals with corrupt government officials.

*From Stephen Knack and Philip Keefer, "Institutions and Economic Performance: Cross-Country Tests Using Alternative Institutional Measures," *Economics and Politics* 7 (November 1995): 210–212, 214–222. Reprinted by permission.

The measures from BERI that are used for this paper are *Contract Enforceability* and *Infrastructure Quality*, which do not have close analogues in the ICRG data set, and *Nationalization Potential* and *Bureaucratic Delays*, which parallel the ICRG variables *Expropriation Risk* and *Quality of Bureaucracy*. The relevance of all the BERI variables is indicated by the foregoing discussion, with the exception of *Infrastructure Quality*. This variable allows some approximation to be made to the efficiency with which governments allocate public goods.

Because of strong correlations among these separate indicators, with the consequent risk of multicollinearity, and in order to avoid omitting any of them from the equation, the five ICRG variables and the four BERI variables have been aggregated to form an ICRG index (*ICRG82*) and a BERI index (*BERI72*) of the security of contractual and property rights. Although the aggregation is accomplished through simple addition, the results reported below do not change significantly when individual components of these indices are used, or when the indices are compiled with different weights. Higher values of the ICRG and BERI indices indicate better conditions for investment. . . .

The Growth Equation

. . . Barro (1991) is the specification that is relied upon below to compare the effects of political violence and institutional indicators on growth:

$$GR6085 = \alpha + \beta_1 GDP60 + \beta_2 SEC60$$
$$+ \beta_3 PRIM60 + \beta_4 GOVCONS$$
$$+ \beta_5 REVCOUP + \beta_6 ASSASS$$
$$+ \beta_7 PPI60DEV + \varepsilon_i \qquad (1)$$

Here, growth is a function of initial income,[3] secondary and primary school enrollment in 1960, the percent of government consumption in GDP, frequencies of revolutions and assassinations, and the magnitude of the deviation of the Summers and Heston investment deflator (U.S. = 100) from the sample mean. . . .[4]

[3]Other research has employed the log of initial GDP. The regressions reported below, employing initial GDP, were also run with the log of this variable. In nearly all cases the qualitative findings, that the institutional variables add significant additional information that explains growth, remain unchanged.

[4]Barro (1991) uses economic growth and investment data from Summers and Heston. For this paper, data on these variables come from the World Bank and are taken from Levine and Renelt (1992).

Unlike Barro (1991), this paper focuses on growth over the period 1974–1989 to mitigate the effects of possible measurement error in the ICRG and BERI indices that might have been introduced by evaluator bias. The evaluators of the investor services might be influenced by the level of income of the countries that they evaluate. Current levels of GDP are a product of past growth, naturally. To the extent that evaluators are influenced by the current level of GDP, estimates of the effect of property rights on growth might be biased upwards. This is a problem that afflicts all such measures, including the Gastil measures. Our choice of period reduces problems of simultaneity that might cloud inferences about the effect of property rights. . . .

Empirical Results—Growth

Equations (1) of Tables 1 and 2 are benchmark regressions for the ICRG and BERI samples, respectively, and include no institutional variables. Equations (2) add the political violence indicators, but not the ICRG and BERI indices. . . .

In equations (3) of Tables 1 and 2 the ICRG and BERI indices, respectively, replace the political violence indicators. Both are more significant than the political violence indicators. . . .

In the final equations of these two tables, the political violence indicators enter with either *ICRG82* or *BERI72*. In the regression with the ICRG index, the magnitude and statistical significance of the violence indicators drop substantially and *ICRG82* remains significant. *BERI72* performs less well, but still exhibits at least as much economic and statistical significance as the political violence indicators.[5]

Comparing these variables in terms of their economic impact also reveals the greater explanatory power of the ICRG/BERI indices relative to the political violence indicators. Since the units of the variables are not comparable, standardized estimates of their regression coefficients were calculated. These denote the change in the dependent variable, in standard deviation units, for a one unit change in the standard deviation of the independent variable. For the ICRG case in Table 1, the sum of the standardized estimates of *REVC7499* and *ASSN7489* in Equation (2) is –0.36. The standardized estimate of ICRG82 when it replaces

[5]Using log of initial income and the BERI sample of countries, and including the two political violence indicators along with *BERI72*, all three variables are statistically insignificant, although *BERI72* is more significant than *ASSN7489*, and the standardized estimate of *BERI72* is equal to the sum of the standardized estimates of the two political violence indicators.

Table 1. Growth, Institutions and Political Violence: ICRG

	(1)	(2)	(3)	(4)
Intercept	1.980	3.028	0.254	1.345
	1.980	*2.851*	*0.237*	*1.091*
ICRG82			0.092	0.072
			3.420	*2.499*
REVC7489		−1.630		−1.115
		−1.904		*−1.302*
ASSN7489		−3.486		−2.278
		−1.695		*−1.108*
GDP70	−0.401	−0.482	−0.692	−0.683
	−2.564	*−3.141*	*−4.055*	*−4.030*
SEC70	6.083	6.284	5.051	5.411
	3.819	*4.083*	*3.286*	*3.524*
PRIM70	−0.690	−0.959	−0.532	−0.752
	−0.758	*−1.072*	*−0.617*	*−0.862*
GCON7489	−5.222	−6.388	−4.289	−5.286
	−1.213	*−1.527*	*−1.051*	*−1.293*
PPI74DEV	−0.920	−0.985	−0.892	−0.941
	−2.243	*−2.482*	*−2.3*	*−2.439*
R-Square	0.198	0.270	0.291	0.318
N	97	97	97	97

Dependent variable: Average annual per capita GDP growth, 1974–1989.

Numbers in italics are t-statistics.

Table 2. Growth, Institutions and Political Violence: BERI

	(1)	(2)	(3)	(4)
Intercept	1.022	0.356	−0.977	−0.627
	0.644	*0.205*	*−0.545*	*−0.336*
BERI72			0.376	0.263
			2.111	*1.357*
REVC7489		−1.653		−1.630
		−1.304		*−1.300*
ASSN7489		−23.015		−14.695
		−1.710		*−1.003*
GDP70	−0.501	−0.594	−0.694	−0.721
	−2.751	*−3.277*	*−3.520*	*−3.566*
SEC70	5.376	4.624	4.047	4.026
	2.805	*2.411*	*2.083*	*2.067*
PRIM70	0.653	2.793	0.580	2.018
	0.377	*1.389*	*0.349*	*0.976*
GCON7489	−1.145	−1.508	−2.968	−3.052
	−0.183	*−0.249*	*−0.489*	*−0.500*
PPI74DEV	−0.929	−0.894	−0.711	−0.748
	−1.921	*−1.938*	*−1.495*	*−1.595*
R-Square	0.276	0.375	0.350	0.405
N	46	46	46	46

Dependent variable: Average annual per capita GDP growth, 1974–1989.

Numbers in italics are t-statistics.

these two variables in Equation (3) of Table 1, however, is 0.504: an increase of one standard deviation in ICRG82 leads to an increase in growth equal to 0.504 of its standard deviation. The standard deviation of the growth variable GR7489 is 2.465, indicating that an increase of one standard deviation in ICRG82 [equal to approximately 12 points on the 40 point scale, or the difference between the ICRG82 scores of Honduras (15) and Costa Rica (27), or of Argentina (25) and Italy (30)] increases growth by more than 1.2 percentage points. The importance of the effect of ICRG82 can be seen by comparing its standardized coefficient to the standardized coefficient on secondary education enrollment (SEC70), which is not much higher at 0.57. When ICRG82 and the political violence variables are all included in the same regression, the standardized estimate of ICRG82 is 0.393 and the sum of the standardized estimates of the violence indicators is −0.235. In all cases, the economic impact of ICRG82 is significant and greater than that of the political violence indicators.

A similar story can be told with regard to BERI172. Alone, the two political violence indicators have a combined standardized estimate of −0.47. When it replaces these variables, however, the BERI index has a standardized estimate of 0.54. When the three variables enter into the same regression, the combined political violence standardized estimate is −0.37 and the standardized estimate of BERI72 is 0.38.

These results were robust to a number of alternative specifications. The institutional variables were statistically and economically significant in growth regressions that included rates of factor accumulation (investment and labor force growth); that deleted OPEC members from the 1974–1989 period regressions; that substituted REVC6088 and ASSN6088 for their 1974–1988 counterparts in growth regressions; and that employed the log of initial income.

The coefficients on the institutional variables were somewhat lower when investment was included. This is to be expected; one way that insecure property rights hinder growth is by deterring investment, an effect that is captured by investment itself when it enters the regression. However, it is noteworthy that the institutional variables were still significant, even in the presence of an investment term. This suggests that institutions measured by the BERI and ICRG indices matter not only because secure property rights encourage fixed investments, but also because they encourage the efficient allocation of factor inputs. In response to expropriatory threats of one kind or another, entre-

Table 3. Investment, Institutions and Political Violence

Institutional Variable:	ICRG82			BERI72		
	(1)	(2)	(3)	(4)	(5)	(6)
Intercept	0.160	0.112	0.125	0.159	0.124	0.123
	5.188	*3.443*	*3.404*	*2.678*	*2.487*	*2.174*
Institut'l var.		0.002	0.001		0.014	0.014
		2.151	*1.741*		*3.087*	*2.554*
REVC7489	−0.017		−0.014	−0.011		−0.008
	−0.578		*−0.480*	*−0.216*		*−0.174*
ASSN7489	−0.083		−0.042	−0.560		−0.118
	−1.201		*0.072*	*−1.346*		*−0.281*
GDP70	−0.0002	−0.004	−0.004	−0.002	−0.009	−0.009
	−0.050	*−1.000*	*−0.942*	*−0.461*	*−1.754*	*−1.643*
SEC70	0.019	−0.002	−0.00007	0.033	0.007	0.005
	0.447	*−0.044*	*−0.002*	*0.528*	*0.131*	*0.085*
PRIM70	0.065	0.071	0.067	0.090	0.026	0.037
	2.529	*3.011*	*2.662*	*1.323*	*0.519*	*0.564*
GCON7489	0.005	0.043	0.048	−0.103	−0.215	−0.204
	0.043	*0.345*	*0.381*	*−0.527*	*−1.221*	*−1.105*
PPI74	−0.022	−0.019	−0.014	−0.014	−0.011	−0.011
	−2.549	*−2.325*	*−2.375*	*−1.329*	*−1.136*	*−1.099*
R-Square	0.312	0.338	0.345	0.215	0.356	0.359
N	69	69	69	38	38	38

Dependent variable: Average private investment/GDP, 1974–1989. Numbers in italics are t-statistics.

preneurs not only reduce investment, they also invest in less specialized capital (human and physical), which can be moved more easily from one activity to another. This has static efficiency effects, but also discourages dynamic gains from innovation, since innovation is most likely to thrive when specialization is encouraged. . . .

Empirical Results—Investment

Another basis for comparing the different institutional variables is in their ability to explain investment. Barro excludes investment from his growth estimations at least implicitly because many of the variables in the growth equation, including institutional variables, operate, at least in part, through factor accumulation. The importance of institutions, then, can also be examined through empirical estimates of the determinants of investment. Barro (1991) estimates variants of the following equation for private investment, for which cross country data is available beginning in the 1970s:

$$PINV7085 = \alpha + \beta_1 GDP60 + \beta_2 SEC60$$
$$+ \beta_3 PRIM60 + \beta_4 GOVCONS$$
$$+ \beta_5 REVCOUP + \beta_6 ASSASS$$
$$+ \beta_7 PPI60DEV + \beta_8 PPI60 + \varepsilon_i \quad (2)$$

where *PINV7085* is the average ratio of real private investment to real GDP over the period, equal to the ratio of real total investment over real GDP less the same ratio for real public investment. The 1960 purchasing power parity investment deflator (from Summers and Heston) is also employed.[6] Initial income, *GDP60*, enters as a proxy for initial capital stock. The higher the initial capital stock, the greater the effect of diminishing returns on investment, and the less investment that would be expected.

As before, the ICRG and BERI indices perform substantially better than the political violence variables: their statistical and economic significance is greater and the explanatory power of models that contain only the ICRG and BERI indices is greater than those that contain the political violence measures.

Table 3 summarizes the investment results comparing the political violence, ICRG and BERI indicators. Contrary to the Barro (1991) results for the time period 1960–1985, Table 3 indicates that for the time period 1974–1989 revolutions and assassi-

[6]Barro runs this model with and without dummy variables for Africa and Latin America. These dummies remain significant even in the presence of the ICRG and BERI indices. They disappear in the work on political instability by Alesina, et al. (1992), who attempt to take into account simultaneity that might exist between political instability and growth.

nations are statistically insignificant, alone or in combination with *ICRG82* and *BERI72,* while the institutional indicators are statistically significant wherever they appear.[7] Economically, as well, the institutional indicators offer a more powerful explanation of growth. The sum of the standardized coefficients for *REVC7489* and *ASSN7489* in regression (4) of Table 3 is –0.31. When the BERI variable enters alone, in regression (5), its standardized coefficient is 0.815. When the three variables enter together, the difference remains equally dramatic, –0.08 versus 0.77. The ICRG results are qualitatively the same, although the magnitude of the differences in absolute value is smaller: –0.20 versus 0.37 when they enter in separate equations,

and –0.12 versus 0.33 when they enter in the same equation.

References

Alesina, A., O. Sule, R. Nouriel, and P. Swagel, 1992, Political Instability and Growth. NBER Working Paper No. 173.

Barro, R., 1991, Economic Growth in a Cross Section of Countries. *Quarterly Journal of Economics* 106, 407–444.

Keefer, P., 1993, Institutions, Credibility and the Costs of Rent-seeking. Manuscript, The IRIS Center, University of Maryland.

Levine, R. and D. Renelt, 1992, A Sensitivity Analysis of Cross-Country Growth Regressions. *American Economic Review* 82, 942–963.

Weingast, B., 1993, The Political Foundations of Democracy and the Rule of Law. IRIS Working Paper No. 54.

---

[7]The ICRG/BERI variables are much weaker at predicting total investment. This is consistent with the theory, however. We would not expect public investment to be sensitive to risks of expropriation.

Selection IX.C.2. The State as Problem and Solution: Predation, Embedded Autonomy, and Structural Change*

Perspectives on the State

Even theories of development that privilege the market as an institution have always recognized that "the existence of the state is essential for economic growth,"[1] but the essential state was a minimal one, "restricted largely, if not entirely, to protecting individual rights, persons and property, and enforcing voluntarily negotiated private contracts."[2] In its minimal neoclassical form, the state was treated as an exogenous black box whose internal functionings were not a proper or worthy subject for economic analysis. Neoutilitarian political economists, however, became convinced that the negative economic consequences of state action were too important to leave the black box closed. To unravel its workings, they applied the "standard tools of individual optimization" to the analysis of the state itself.[3]

The exchange relation between incumbents and supporters is the essence of state action. Incumbents require political supporters to survive and the supporters, in turn, must be provided with incentives sufficient to prevent their shifting support to other potential officeholders. Incumbents may either distribute resources directly to supporters,

through subsidies, loans, jobs, contracts, or the provision of services, or use their rule-making authority to create rents for favored groups by restricting the ability of market forces to operate. Rationing foreign exchange, restricting entry through licensing producers, and imposing tariffs or quantitative restrictions on imports are all ways of creating rents. Incumbents may also exact a share of the rent for themselves. Indeed, it is hypothesized that "competition for entry into government service is, in part, a competition for rents."[4] In the economy as a whole, high returns from "directly unproductive profit-seeking" make investment in productive activities less attractive. Efficiency and dynamism decline.

In order to escape the deleterious effects of state action, the state's sphere should be reduced to the minimum, and bureaucratic control should be replaced by market mechanisms wherever possible. The range of state functions considered susceptible to marketization varies but some authors even speculate on the possibility of using "prizes" and other incentives to induce "privateers" and other private citizens to provide at least partially for the national defense.[5]

It would be foolish to deny that the neoutilitarian vision captures a significant aspect of the functioning of most states, perhaps the dominant aspect of the functioning of some states. Rent seeking, conceptualized more primitively as corruption, has always been a well-known facet of the operation of Third World states. Some states' apparatuses consume the surplus they extract, encourage private actors to shift from productive activities to unproductive rent seeking, and fail to provide collective goods. They have no more regard for their societies than a predator does for its prey and are legitimately called "predatory."[6]

*From Peter B. Evans, "The State as Problem and Solution: Predation, Embedded Autonomy, and Structural Change," in Stephan Haggard and Robert R. Kaufman, eds., *The Politics of Economic Adjustment* (Princeton, NJ: Princeton, 1992), pp. 143–179. Reprinted by permission.

[1]Douglas North, *Structure and Change in Economic History* (New York: Norton, 1981), p. 20.

[2]James M. Buchanan, Robert D. Tollison, and Gordon Tullock, eds., *Toward a Theory of the Rent-Seeking Society* (College Station, Tex.: Texas A&M University Press, 1980), p. 9.

[3]T. N. Srinivasan, "Neoclassical Political Economy, the State and Economic Development," *Asian Development Review* 3, no. 2 (1985): 38–58, 41. Among public choice theorists Nobel Laureate James Buchanan and his collaborators Tollison and Tullock are best known (see Buchanan, Tollison and Tullock, *The Rent-Seeking Society*). Others would include William A. Niskanen, *Bureaucracy and Representative Government* (Chicago: Aldine-Atherton, 1971); Richard D. Auster and Morris Silver, *The State as Firm: Economic Forces in Political Development* (The Hague: Martinus Nijhoff, 1979). The recent re-emergence of neoclassical political economy represents a similar, though usually less extreme, perspective. See David C. Colander, ed., *Neoclassical Political Economy: An Analysis of Rent-seeking and DUP Activities* (Cambridge, Mass.: Ballinger, 1984). Elements of the neoutilitarian view are also present in collective action perspectives, e.g., Mancur Olson, *The Rise and Decline of Nations* (New Haven, Conn.: Yale University Press, 1982), and the new institutional economics, which emphasizes property rights, e.g., Douglas North, *Structure and Change in Economic History.*

[4]Anne O. Krueger, "The Political Economy of the Rent-Seeking Society," *American Economic Review* 64, no. 3 (June 1974): 291–303, 293.

[5]Auster and Silver, *The State as Firm,* p. 102.

[6]It is important to note that this vernacular way of conceptualizing the predatory state is quite different from the way the term is used by it advocates. Deepak Lal, *The Hindu Equilibrium: Cultural Stability and Economic Stagnation, India c. 1500BC–AD1980,* vol. 1 (Oxford: Clarendon Press, 1988), and Margaret Levi, *Of Rule and Revenue* (Berkeley: University of California Press, 1988) both equate predatory behavior with revenue maximizing behavior. In Levi's use states may maximize revenue in ways that promote development or in ways that impede it. Thus, the term *predatory* in her usage has no necessary

Because it reintroduces politics, the neoutilitarian view should even be considered an improvement on the traditional neoclassical vision of the state as neutral arbiter. Indeed, the assumption that state policies "reflect vested interests in society" partially recaptures some of Marx's original insights into the biases that characterize state policy.[7] As an explanation of one pattern of the incumbent behavior which may or may not dominate in a particular state apparatus, neoutilitarian thinking is a useful contribution. As a monocausal master theory applicable to states generically, which the neoutilitarian view tends to become in the hands of its more dedicated adherents, the neoutilitarian model is problematic.

To begin with, it is hard to explain why, if officeholders are primarily interested in individual rents, they do not all "freelance." Neoutilitarian logic provides little insight into what constrains individual incumbents to work together as a collectivity at all. If we postulate that somehow the state solves its own collective action problem, there is no reason, within the logic of neoutilitarian arguments, for those who have a monopoly on violence to rest content being nightwatchmen and every reason for them to try to expand rental havens. In short, strict adherence to a neoutilitarian logic makes the existence of the state difficult to explain and the nightwatchman state almost a theoretical impossibility.[8]

At the same time, the neoutilitarian assumption that exchange relations are natural, that is epistomologically prior to other kinds of social relationships, is not well supported by empirical evidence. Detailed studies of real processes of exchange (as opposed to analytical summaries of their results) find that markets operate well only when they are supported by other kinds of social networks.[9] An efficient system of property relations is not enough. The smooth operation of exchange requires the dense, deeply developed medium of trust and culturally shared understandings, summarized by Durkheim under the deceptively simple heading of the "noncontractual elements of contract."

For better or worse, markets are always inextricably embedded in a matrix that includes both cultural understandings and social networks composed of polyvalent individual ties. In some cases support for exchange relations may be generated by informal interaction. In other cases, formal hierarchical organizations may "internalize" exchange relations.[10] If markets must be surrounded by other kinds of social structures in order to operate, then neoutilitarian attempts to free the market from the state may end up destroying the institutional underpinnings that allow exchange to operate. This is, of course, the position of the classic tradition of comparative institutionalist scholarship which emphasized the essential complementarity of state structures and market exchange, particularly in the promotion of industrial transformation.

This tradition has always been critical of the proposition that exchange was a natural activity that required only the most minimal institutional underpinnings. Forty years ago Polanyi argued, "The road to the free market was opened and kept open by an enormous increase in continuous, centrally organized and controlled interventionism."[11] From the beginning, according to Polanyi, the life of the market has been intertwined not just with other kinds of social ties, but with the forms and policies of the state.

Looking at established market societies, Weber carried this line of reasoning further, arguing that the operation of large scale capitalist enterprise depended on the availability of the kind of order that only a modern bureaucratic state could provide. As he put it: "Capitalism and bureaucracy have found each other and belong intimately together."[12] Weber's assumption of the intimate relation was, of course, based on a conception of the bureaucratic state apparatus that was the mirror image of the neoutilitarian view. Weber's bureaucrats were concerned only with carrying out their assignments and contributing to the fulfillment of the goals of the apparatus as a whole. Use of the prerogatives of

---

developmental implications. States that others call developmental could easily be labeled predatory under Levi's definition. Lal is more convinced of the negative relation between revenue maximization and development. For him, as for the neoutilitarians, the alternative to the predatory state is the minimal nightwatchman state and there is no analytical space for a developmental state.

[7]Colander, *Neoclassical Political Economy,* p. 2.

[8]It is important to note that this critique is intended to highlight some of the problems inherent in the thinking that supported the radical second wave approach to the state, not as a review of the wide variety of literature on the state that has emerged under the general rubric of rational choice. For one such review see Levi, *Of Rule and Revenue,* appendix.

[9]See Mark Granovetter, "Economic Action and Social Structure: The Problem of Embeddedness," *American Journal of Sociology* 91, no. 3 (November 1985): 481–510.

[10]Cf. Oliver E. Williamson, *Markets and Hierarchies: Analysis and Antitrust Implications* (New York: Free Press, 1975).

[11]Karl Polanyi, *The Great Transformation* (Boston: Beacon Press, 1957), p. 140.

[12]Max Weber, *Economy and Society,* ed. Guenter Roth and Claus Wittich (New York: Bedminster Press, 1968), p. 1395, n. 14.

office for maximizing private interests was, for Weber, a feature of earlier prebureaucratic forms.

For Weber, the state was useful to those operating in markets precisely because the actions of its incumbents obeyed a logic quite different from that of utilitarian exchange. The state's ability to support markets and capitalist accumulation depended on the bureaucracy being a corporately coherent entity in which individuals see furtherance of corporate goals as the best means of maximizing their individual self-interest. Corporate coherence requires that individual incumbents be to some degree insulated from the demands of the surrounding society. Insulation, in turn, is enhanced by conferring a distinctive and rewarding status on bureaucrats. The concentration of expertise in the bureaucracy through meritocratic recruitment and the provision of opportunities for long-term career rewards was also central to the bureaucracy's effectiveness. In short, Weber saw construction of a solid, authoritative framework as a necessary prerequisite to the operation of markets.

Later observers extended Weber's vision of the state's role. The ability to implement rules predictably, however necessary, is not sufficient. Gerschenkron's work on late developers complements Weber by focusing on the specific contributions of the state apparatus to overcoming problems created by a disjunction between the scale of economic activity required for development and the effective scope of existing social networks.[13] Late industrializers confronting production technologies with capital requirements in excess of what private markets were capable of amassing were forced to rely on the power of the state to mobilize the necessary resources. Instead of simply providing a suitable environment, as it did in Weber's model, the state was now actively organizing a crucial aspect of the market. Gerschenkron's argument also raises a new issue—the problem of risk taking. The crux of the problem faced by late developers is that institutions that allow large risks to be spread across a wide network of capital holders do not exist, and individual capitalists are neither able nor interested in taking them on. Under these circumstances the state must serve as surrogate entrepreneur.

Hirschman takes up this emphasis on entrepreneurship as the missing ingredient for development in much more detail. Based on his observations of the "late late" developers of the twentieth-century Third World, Hirschman argues that capital, in the sense of a potentially investable surplus, is not the principal ingredient that is lacking in developing countries. What is lacking is entrepreneurship in the sense of willingness to risk the available surplus by investing it in productive activities, or in Hirschman's own words, "the perception of investment opportunities and transformation into actual investments." If "maximizing induced decision-making" is the key as Hirschman argues it is, then the state's role involves a high level of responsiveness to private capital.[14] It must provide disequilibrating incentives to induce private capitalists to invest and at the same time be ready to alleviate bottlenecks that are creating disincentives to investment. . . .

The Gershenkronian/Hirschmanian vision makes the relationship between state capacity and insulation (or "autonomy") more ambiguous than a strictly Weberian perspective or, for that matter, a neo-Marxist one.[15] For the insulated state to be effective, the nature of a project of accumulation and the means of implementing it must be readily apparent. In a Gerschenkronian or Hirschmanian scenario of transformation, the shape of a project of accumulation must be discovered, almost invented, and its implementation demands close connections to private capital. A Prussian-style bureaucracy might well be effective at the prevention of force and fraud, but the kind of surrogate entrepreneurship that Gerschenkron talks about or the kind of subtle triggering of private initiative that Hirschman emphasizes would demand more than an insulated, corporately coherent administrative apparatus. It demands accurate intelligence, inventiveness, active agency and sophisticated responseness to a changing economic reality. Such arguments demand a state that is more embedded in society than insulated.[16]

Whatever the structural features that underlie state capacity, arguments for the central role of the state apply most strongly to situations in which structural transformation is the order of the day. In-

[14]Albert Hirschman, *The Strategy of Economic Development* (New Haven, Conn.: Yale University Press, 1958), pp. 35, 44.

[15]Neo-Marxist arguments for the necessity of relative autonomy from the particularistic demands of individual capitalists reinforce the idea of a positive relation between capacity and autonomy. Cf. Dietrich Rueschemeyer and Peter Evans, "The State and Economic Transformation: Toward an Analysis of the Conditions Underlying Effective State Intervention," in Peter Evans, Dietrich Rueschemeyer, and Theda Skocpol, eds., *Bringing the State Back In* (New York: Cambridge University Press, 1985), pp. 44–77.

[16]Cf. Granovetter, "Economic Action and Social Structure," for a discussion of embeddedness.

[13]Alexander Gerschenkron, *Economic Backwardness in Historical Perspective* (Cambridge, Mass.: Belknap, 1962).

dustrialization, which is the focus of the case studies that follow, is the classic example of this kind of transformation, but structural adjustment also requires more than incremental movement. It is also when transformation is on the agenda that the contrast between predatory and developmental states comes into sharpest relief. As Callaghy points out, the potential existence of a positive state role creates no logical necessity of the potential being realized. Societies and economies that "need" developmental states don't necessarily get them, as the case of Zaire amply demonstrates.

Zaire: An Exemplary Case of Predation

Since Joseph Mobutu Sese Seko gained control over Zaire in 1965, he and his coterie within the Zairian state apparatus have extracted vast personal fortunes from revenues generated by exporting the country's impressive mineral wealth. Over the next 25 years Zaire's GNP per capita *declined* at an annual rate of 2 percent a year, gradually moving the country toward the very bottom of the world hierarchy of nations and leaving the country's population in misery as bad or worse than that which they suffered under the Belgian colonial regime.[17] Zaire is, in short, a textbook case of a predatory state in which the preoccupation of the political class with rent-seeking has turned society into its prey.

Following Weber, Callaghy emphasizes the patrimonial qualities of the Zairian state; the mixture of traditionalism and arbitrariness that Weber argued retarded capitalist development.[18] True to the patrimonial model, control of the state apparatus is vested in a small group of personally connected individuals. At the pinnacle of power is the "presidential clique," which consists of "50-odd of the president's most trusted kinsmen, occupying the most sensitive and lucrative positions such as head of the Judiciary Council, secret police, Interior Ministry, President's office and so on."[19] Next is the "presidential brotherhood" who are not kin, but whose positions still depend on their personal ties with the president, his clique, and each other.

One of the most striking, and ironic, aspects of the Zairian state is the extent to which market relations dominate administrative behavior, again al-

most as a caricature of the neoutilitarian image of how rent-creating state apparatuses are likely to work. A Zairian archbishop described it as follows:

> Why in our courts do people only obtain their rights by paying the judge liberally? Why do the prisoners live forgotten in prisons? They do not have anyone who can pay the judge who has their dossiers at hand. Why in our office of administration, like public services, are people required to return day after day to obtain their due? If they do not pay the clerk, they will not be served.[20]

President Mobutu himself characterized the system in much the same way saying: "Everything is for sale, everything is bought in our country. And in this traffic, holding any slice of public power constitutes a veritable exchange instrument, convertible into illicit acquisition of money or other goods."[21]

The prevalence of such a thoroughgoing market ethic might at first seem inconsistent with what Callaghy characterizes as an "early modern absolutist state,"[22] but it is in fact quite consistent. Personalism and plundering at the top destroy any possibility of rule-governed behavior in the lower levels of the bureaucracy. Moreover, the marketization of the state apparatus makes the development of a bourgeoisie oriented toward long-term productive investment almost an impossibility by undermining the predictability of state action.

The persistence of the regime itself might be taken as evidence that Mobutu has managed to at least construct a repressive apparatus with the minimal amount of corporate coherence necessary to fend off potential competitors. It is not clear that even this is the case. As Gould puts it bluntly: "The bureaucratic bourgeoisie owes its existence to past and continued foreign support."[23] Aid from the World Bank as well as individual Western nations has played an important role, but French and Belgian troops at critical moments (e.g., in Shaba in 1978) have been the sine qua non of Mobutu's remaining in power.[24] Thus, Mobutu provides only a weak test of the limits to which rent seeking can be allowed to prevail without undermining even the repressive apparatus necessary for regime survival.[25]

[17]World Bank, *World Development Report, 1991* (New York: Oxford University Press, 1991), p. 204.

[18]Thomas Callaghy, *The State-Society Struggle: Zaire in Comparative Perspective* (New York: Columbia University Press, 1984), pp. 32–79.

[19]David Gould, "The Administration of Underdevelopment," in Guy Gran, ed., *Zaire: The Political Economy of Underdevelopment* (New York: Praeger, 1979), p. 93.

[20]Cited in Callaghy, *The State-Society Struggle,* p. 420.

[21]Crawford Young, "Zaire: The Unending Crisis," *Foreign Affairs* 57, no. 1 (Fall 1978): 172.

[22]Callaghy, *The State-Society Struggle.*

[23]Gould, "The Administration of Underdevelopment," p. 93.

[24]Galen Hull, "Zaire in the World System: In Search of Sovereignty," in Gran, *The Political Economy of Underdevelopment,* pp. 263–83.

[25]Obviously, a full analysis of both the original character of the regime and its persistence would require more careful attention to the nature of Zaire's social structure. For a general ap-

Zaire confirms clearly that it is not the bureaucracy that impedes development so much as the *absence* of a coherent bureaucratic apparatus. The "kleptopatrimonial" Zairian state is an amalgam of personalism and a thoroughly marketized administrative apparatus.[26] It is precisely the kind of exchange-dominated state that the neoutilitarians postulate and fear, but it is not only rampant rent seeking and distorted incentives that are produced. Weakness at the center of the political-economic system undermines the predictability of policy required for private investment. The state fails to provide even the most basic prerequisites for the functioning of a modern economy: predictable enforcement of contract, provision and maintenance of infrastructure, and public investment in health and education.

Zaire also poses some problems for conventional views of the importance of state autonomy in formulating coherent adjustment and growth strategies. On the one hand, since the state as a corporate entity is incapable of formulating coherent goals and implementing them, and since policy decisions are up for sale to private elites, the state might be seen as completely lacking in autonomy. This lack of autonomy is what permits pervasive rent seeking to prevail. At the same time, however, the Zairian state is strikingly unconstrained by society. It is autonomous in the sense of not deriving its goals from the aggregation of societal interests. This autonomy does not enhance the state's capacity to pursue goals of its own, but rather removes critical social checks on arbitrary rule. The Zairian case suggests that the relationship between capacity and autonomy needs rethinking. This becomes even more evident in looking at the developmental states of East Asia.

Developmental States

While states like Mobutu's were providing practical demonstrations of the perversions predicted by neoutilitarian visions of the state, a different set of nations halfway around the world were writing

historical records that confirmed institutionalist expectations. By the end of the 1970s, the economic success of the major East Asian newly industrialized countries (NICs), Korea and Taiwan, was increasingly interpreted as depending on the active involvement of the state,[27] even by observers with a neoclassical bent.[28] . . .

The Japanese Model

Looking for institutional bases on which to build rapid industrialization, the East Asian NICs drew on the regional model of the active state—Japan. Analyses of the Japanese case provide a nice starting point for understanding of the developmental state. Chalmers Johnson's account of the golden years of the Ministry of International Trade and Industry (MITI) provides one of the best pictures of the developmental state in action.[29] His description is particularly fascinating because it corresponds so neatly to what a sophisticated implementation of ideas from Gerschenkron and Hirschman might look like in practice.

In the capital-scarce years following World War II, the Japanese state acted as a surrogate for weakly developed capital markets, while inducing transformative investment decisions. State institutions from the postal saving system to the Japan Development Bank were crucial in getting the needed investment capital to industry. The state's centrality to the provision of new capital, in turn, allowed MITI to aquire a central industrial policy role. Given its role in the approval of investment loans from the Japan Development Bank, its authority over foreign currency allocations for industrial purposes and licenses to import foreign technology, its ability to provide tax breaks, and its capacity to articulate "administrative guidance cartels" that would regulate competition in an industry, MITI was in a perfect position to "maximize induced decision-making."[30]

---

proach to the question of the state and development which begins with an analysis of social structure see Joel Migdal, *Strong Societies and Weak States: State-Society Relations and State Capabilities in the Third World* (Princeton, N.J.: Princeton University Press, 1988).

[26] The conjunction of leviathan and the invisible hand is not as contradictory as it might seem but is, in fact, quite common. It does take different forms in different states. For example, in the less traditionally corrupt military regimes of Argentina and Chile, brutal, leviathan-like control over political dissension was combined with fierce imposition of market logic on the surrounding society.

[27] Alice Amsden, "Taiwan's Economic History: A Case of Etatisme and a Challenge to Dependency Theory," *Modern China* 5, no. 3 (1979): 341–80.

[28] For example, Leroy Jones and Sakong II, *Government, Business and Entrepreneurship in Economic Development: The Korean Case. Studies in Modernization of the Korean Republic, 1945–1975* (Cambridge, Mass.: Harvard University Press, 1980).

[29] Chalmers Johnson, *MITI and the Japanese Miracle: The Growth of Industrial Policy, 1925–1975* (Stanford, Calif.: Stanford University Press, 1982).

[30] See, for example, Johnson's description of MITI's nurturing of the petrochemical industry in the 1950s and 1960s, *MITI and the Japanese Miracle*, p. 236.

Some might consider Johnson's characterization of MITI as "without doubt the greatest concentration of brainpower in Japan" an exaggeration, but few would deny the fact that until recently, "official agencies attract the most talented graduates of the best universities in the country and positions of higher level official in these ministries have been and still are the most prestigious in the country."[31]

There is thus clearly a Weberian aspect to the Japanese developmental state. Officials have the special status that Weber felt was essential to a true bureaucracy. They follow long-term career paths within the bureaucracy and operate generally in accordance with rules and established norms. These characteristics vary somewhat across the Japanese bureaucracy, but the less bureaucratic, more clientelistic agencies like the Ministry of Agriculture are generally viewed as "pockets of conspicuous inefficiency."[32] If Japan confirms Weberian pronouncements regarding the necessity of a coherent, meritocratic bureaucracy, it also indicates the necessity of going beyond such prescriptions. All descriptions of the Japanese state emphasize the indispensability of informal networks, both internal and external, to the state's functioning. Internal networks, particularly the *gakubatsu,* or ties among classmates at the elite universities from which officials are recruited, are crucial to the bureaucracy's coherence.[33] These informal networks give the bureaucracy an internal coherence and corporate identity that meritocracy alone could not provide. The fact that formal competence, rather than clientelistic ties or traditional loyalties, is the prime requirement for entry into the network, makes it much more likely that effective performance will be a valued attribute among loyal members of the various *batsu.* The overall result is a kind of "reinforced Weberianism," in which the "nonbureaucratic elements of bureaucracy" reinforce the formal organizational structure in the same way that Durkheim's "noncontractual elements of contract" reinforce the market.[34]

External networks connecting the state and private powerholders are even more important. As Chie Nakane puts it, "the administrative web is woven more thoroughly into Japanese society than perhaps any other in the world."[35] Japanese industrial policy depends fundamentally on the ties that connect MITI and major industrialists.[36] Ties between the bureaucracy and private powerholders are reinforced by the pervasive role of MITI alumni, who through *amakudari* (the "descent from heaven" of early retirement), end up in key positions not only in individual corporations but also in the industry associations and quasi-governmental organizations that comprise "the maze of intermediate organizations and informal policy networks, where much of the time-consuming work of consensus formation takes place."[37]

The centrality of external ties has led some to argue that the state's effectiveness emerges "not from its own inherent capacity but from the complexity and stability of its interaction with market players."[38] This perspective is a necessary complement to descriptions like Johnson's, but it runs the danger of setting external networks and internal corporate coherence as opposing alternative explanations. Instead internal bureaucratic coherence should be seen as an essential precondition for the state's effective participation in external networks. If MITI were not an exceptionally competent, cohesive organization, it could not participate in external networks in the way that it does. If MITI were not autonomous in the sense of being capable of independently formulating its own goals and able to count on those who work within it to see implementing these goals as important to their individuals careers, then it would have little to offer the private sector. MITI's relative autonomy is what allows it to address the collective action problems of private capital, helping capital as a whole to reach solutions that would be hard to attain otherwise, even within the highly organized Japanese industrial system.

This embedded autonomy is the mirror image of the incoherent absolutist domination of the predatory state and constitutes the organizational key to the effectiveness of the developmental state. Em-

---

[31]Johnson, *MITI and the Japanese Miracle,* pp. 26, 20. Johnson reports that in 1977 only thirteen hundred out of fifty-three thousand passed the higher-level Public Officials Examination and cites an overall failure rate of 90 percent for the years 1928–43 (p. 57).

[32]Daniel I. Okimoto, *Between MITI and the Market: Japanese Industrial Policy for High Technology* (Stanford, Calif.: Stanford University Press, 1989), p. 4.

[33]In 1965 an astounding 73 percent of higher bureaucrats were graduates of Tokyo University Law School.

[34]Cf. Rueschemeyer and Evans, "The State and Economic Transformation."

[35]Cited in Okimoto, *Between MITI and the Market,* p. 170.

[36]Okimoto, *Between MITI and the Market,* p. 157, estimates that the deputy director of a MITI sectoral bureau may spend the majority of his time with key corporate personnel.

[37]Okimoto, *Between MITI and the Market,* p. 155.

[38]Richard J. Samuels, *The Business of the Japanese State: Energy Markets in Comparative and Historical Perspective* (Ithaca, N.Y.: Cornell University Press, 1987), p. 262.

bedded autonomy depends on an apparently contradictory combination of Weberian bureaucratic insulation with intense immersion in the surrounding social structure. How this contradictory combination is achieved depends, of course, on both the historically determined character of the state apparatus and the nature of the social structure in which it is embedded, as a comparison of Japan with the East Asian NICs illustrates.

Korea and Taiwan

Korea and Taiwan have different state structures linked to different social bases of support, different patterns of industrial organization, and different policy strategies.[39] Nonetheless, they share crucial features. In both, the policy initiatives that facilitated industrial transformation was rooted in coherent, competent bureaucratic organization. Though both of the East Asian NICs look more autonomous than the Japanese state, both reveal elements of the embedded autonomy that was crucial to Japan's success.

In comparing the Korean bureaucracy to Mexico's, Kim Byung Kook points out that while Mexico has yet to institutionalize exam-based civil service recruitment, meritocratic civil service examinations have been used for recruiting incumbents into the Korean state since A.D. 788, more than a thousand years.[40] Despite Korea's chaotic twentieth-century political history, the bureaucracy has been able to pick its staff from among the most talented members of the most prestigious universities. Data on the selectivity of the Higher Civil Service Examinations are almost identical to the data offered by Johnson for Japan. Despite a sevenfold increase in the annual number of recruits to the higher civil service between 1949 and 1980, only about 2 percent of those who take the exam are accepted.[41]

Along with similar recruitment patterns comes the inculcation of a particular corporate culture. Choi's discussion of the Economic Planning Board, for example, notes the same kind of confidence and esprit de corps that characterize MITI in Johnson's description.[42] Finally, as in Japan, meritocratic recruitment via elite universities and the existence of a strong organizational ethos creates the potential for constructing *batsu*-like solidary interpersonal networks within the bureaucracy. Looking at those who passed the civil service examination in 1972, Kim found 55 percent were graduates of Seoul National University and of these, 40 percent were graduates of two prestigious Seoul high schools.[43]

While the Korean bureaucracy seems an archetype, Korea's experience also shows the insufficiency of a bureaucratic tradition. In the 1950s under Rhee Syngman, the civil service exam was largely bypassed, with only about 4 percent of those filling higher entry level positions entering via the civil service exam. Nor were those who entered the higher civil service able to count on making their way up through the ranks via a standard process of internal promotion. Instead higher ranks were filled primarily on the basis of politically-driven "special appointments."[44]

The character of bureaucratic appointment and promotion under Rhee is, of course, quite consistent with the character of his regime. While Rhee presided over a certain amount of import-substituting industrialization, his regime was more predatory than developmental. Massive U.S. aid, in effect, financed substantial government corruption. Rhee's dependence on private sector donations to finance his political dominance made him dependent on clientelistic ties with individual businessmen and, not surprisingly, "rent-seeking activities were rampant and systematic."[45]

Without a deep, thoroughly elaborated, bureaucratic tradition, neither the Park regime's reconstruction of bureaucratic career paths nor its reorganization of the economic policy making apparatus would have been possible. Without some powerful additional basis for cohesion in the upper ranks of the state, the bureaucratic tradition would have remained ineffectual. Without both in combination it would have been impossible to transform the state's relationship to private capital.

Only with the ascension to power of a group with strong ideological convictions and close personal and organizational ties was the state able to "regain

[39]Cf. Tun-jen Cheng, "The Politics of Industrial Transformation: The Case of the East Asia NICs" (Ph.D. diss., Department of Political Science, University of California, 1987).

[40]Kim Byung Kook, "Bringing and Managing Socioeconomic Change: The State in Korea and Mexico" (Ph.D. diss., Department of Government, Harvard University, 1987), pp. 101–2.

[41]Kim, "Bringing and Managing Socioeconomic Change," p. 101.

[42]Choi Byung Sun, "Institutionalizing a Liberal Economic Order in Korea: The Strategic Management of Economic Change" (Ph.D. diss., Kennedy School, Harvard University, 1987).

[43]Kim, "Bringing and Managing Socioeconomic Change," p. 101.

[44]Ibid., pp. 101–2.

[45]Cheng, "The Politics of Industrial Transformation," p. 200.

its autonomy."[46] The junior officers involved in the coup led by Park Chung Hee were united by both reformist convictions and close interpersonal ties both on service experience and close *batsu*-like network ties originating in the military academy.[47] The super-imposition of this new brand of organizational solidary sometimes undercut the civilian state bureaucracy as military men were put in top posts but, in general, the military used the leverage provided by their own corporate solidarity to both strengthen and discipline the bureaucracy. Under Park the proportion of higher entry-level positions filled with Higher Civil Service examinees quintupled and internal promotion became the principal means of filling all ranks above them, with the exception of the highest political appointments.[48]

One of the features of the revitalized state bureaucracy was the relatively privileged position held by a single pilot agency, the Economic Planning Board (EPB). Headed by a deputy prime minister, the EPB was chosen by Park to be a "superagency" in the economic area.[49] Its power to coordinate economic policy through control of the budgetary process is enhanced by mechanisms like the Economic Ministers Consultation Committee and by the fact that its managers are often promoted into leadership positions in other ministries.[50] As in the Japanese case the existence of a pilot agency does not mean that policies are uncontested within the bureaucracy. The EPB and the Ministry of Trade and Industry (MTI) are often at loggerheads over industrial policy.[51] Nonetheless, the existence of a given agency with generally acknowledged leadership in the economic area allows for the concentration of talent and expertise and gives economic policy a coherence that it lacks in a less clearly organized state apparatus.

When the Park regime took power its goal seemed to be not just insulation from private capital but complete dominance over it. Criminal trials and confiscation were threatened and the leaders of

industry were marched through the street in ignominy as corrupt parasites. This soon changed as Park realized that he needed to harness private entrepreneurship and managerial expertise to achieve his economic goals.[52] Over time, and particularly in the 1970s, the ties between the regime and the largest *chaebol* (conglomerates) became so tight that visiting economists concluded that "Korea, Inc." was "undoubtedly a more apt description of the situation in Korea than is 'Japan, Inc.' "[53]

As in the case of Japan, the symbiotic relationship between the state and the *chaebol* was founded on the fact that the state had access to capital in a capital scarce environment.[54] Through its ability to allocate capital the state promoted the concentration of economic power in the hands of the *chaebol,* and "aggressively orchestrated" their activities.[55] At the same time, the Park regime was dependent on the *chaebol* to implement the industrial transformation that constituted its primary project and the basis for its legitimacy.

The embeddedness of the Korean state under Park was a much more top-down affair than the Japanese prototype, lacking the well-developed intermediary associations and focused on a much smaller number of firms. The size and diversification of the largest *chaebol* did give them interests that were relatively "encompassing" in sectoral terms so that the small number of actors did not limit the sectoral scope of the shared project of accumulation.[56] Still, the Korean state could not

[46]Ibid., p. 203.

[47]See for example Kang's (1988) description of the Hanahoe club, founded by members of the eleventh military academy class.

[48]Kim, "Bringing and Managing Socioeconomic Change," pp. 101–8.

[49]Ibid., p. 115.

[50]For example, according to Choi, "Institutionalizing a Liberal Economic Order," p. 50, "four out of five Ministers of the Ministry of Trade and Industry between December 1973 and May, 1982 were former Vice-Ministers of the EPB."

[51]Cheng, "The Politics of Industrial Transformation," p. 231–32, claims that the MTI rather than the EPB dominated industrial policy making in the early 1970s, but clearly by the late 1970s the EPB was again dominant.

[52]See Kim Eun Mee, "From Dominance to Symbiosis: State and *Chaebol* in the Korean Economy, 1960–1985" (Ph.D. diss., Department of Sociology, Brown University, 1987); Kim Myoung Soo, "The Making of the Korean Society: The Role of the State in the Republic of Korea (1948–1979)" (Ph.D. diss., Department of Sociology, Brown University, 1987).

[53]Mason et al., *The Economic and Social Modernization of the Republic of Korea* (Cambridge: Harvard University Press, 1980), cited in Bruce Cumings, "The Origins and Development of the Northeast Asian Political Economy: Industrial Sectors, Product Cycles and Political Consequences," in F. Deyo, ed., *The Political Economy of the New Asian Industrialism* (Ithaca, N.Y.: Cornell University Press, 1987), p. 73.

[54]The importance first of foreign aid and then of foreign loans, both of which were channeled through the state and allocated by it was a cornerstone of the state's control over capital. See Kim, "From Dominance to Symbiosis"; Woo Jung-en, *Race to the Swift: State and Finance in Korean Industrialization* (New York: Columbia University Press, 1991); and Barbara Stallings, "The Role of Foreign Capital in Economic Development," in Gary Gereffi and Donald L. Wyman, eds. *Manufacturing Miracles: Paths of Industrialization in Latin America and East Asia* (Princeton: Princeton University Press, 1990), pp. 55–89.

[55]Robert Wade, *Governing the Market: Economic Theory and the Role of Government in East Asian Industrialization* (Princeton: Princeton University Press, 1990), p. 320.

[56]Cf. Mancur Olson, *The Rise and Decline of Nations.*

claim the same generalized institutional relation with the private sector that the MITI system provided and never fully escaped the danger that the particularistic interests of individual firms might lead back in the direction of unproductive rent seeking. This, at least, was the perception of the Young Turk technocrats in the EPB at the beginning of the 1980s who felt that it was past time that the state begin to distance itself from resource claims of the largest *chaebol.*[57]

Korea is pushing at the limit to which embeddedness can be concentrated in a few ties without degenerating into particularistic predation. The opposite risk, of weak links to private capital threatening the state's ability to secure full information and count on the private sector for effective implementation, is represented by the region's second prominent pupil of the Japanese model, Taiwan.

In Taiwan, as in Korea, the state has been central to the process of industrial accumulation, channeling capital into risky investments, enhancing the capacity of private firms to confront international markets, and taking on entrepreneurial functions directly through state-owned enterprises. In Taiwan, as in Korea, the ability of the state to play this role depended on a classic, meritocratically-recruited, Weberian bureaucracy, crucially reinforced by extra-bureaucratic organizational forms. As in the case of the Korean state, the Kuomintang (KMT) regime is built on a combination of longstanding tradition and dramatic transformation, but differences in the historical experience of the two states led to very different patterns of relations with the private sector and, in consequence, very different patterns of state entrepreneurship. The transformation of the Kuomintang state following its arrival on Taiwan is as striking as the changes in Korea between the Rhee and Park governments. On the mainland the KMT regime had been largely predatory, riddled with rent seeking and unable to prevent the particular interests of private speculators from undermining its economic projects. On the island, the party remade itself. Freed of its old landlord base, and aided by the fact that the "most egregiously corrupt and harmful" members of the capitalist elite did not follow Chiang Kai Shek to the island,[58] the KMT was able to completely rework its ties with private capital. A corrupt and faction-ridden party organization came to approxi-

mate the Leninist party-state that it had aspired to be from the beginning,[59] thus providing the state bureaucracy with a reinforcing source of organizational cohesion and coherence more powerful and stable than could have been provided by military organization alone.

Within the reinforced governmental apparatus, the KMT put together a small set of elite economic policy organizations similar in scope and expertise to Japan's MITI or Korea's EPB.[60] The Council on Economic Planning and Development (CEPD) is the current incarnation of the planning side of the economic general staff. It is not an executive agency but "in Japanese terms lies somewhere between MITI and the Economic Planning Agency."[61] The Industrial Development Bureau (IDB) of the Ministry of Economic Affairs is staffed primarily by engineers and takes a more direct role in sectoral policies. Both of these agencies, like their counterparts in Korea and Japan, have traditionally been successful in attracting the best and the brightest. Staff members tend to be both KMT members and graduates of the country's elite Taiwan National University.[62]

Without negating the fundamental transformation in the character of the Kuomintang apparatus, it is also noteworthy that as in the case of Korea, the existence of a long bureaucratic tradition gave the regime a foundation on which to build. Not only was there a party organization that provided political cohesion at the top, but there was also an economic bureaucracy with considerable managerial experience. For example, the National Resources Commission (NRC), founded in 1932, had a staff of twelve thousand by 1944 and managed over one hundred public enterprises whose combined capital accounted for half of the paid-up capital of all Chinese enterprises. It was an island of relatively meritocratic recruitment within the mainland regime and its alumni eventually came to play a major role in managing industrial policy on Taiwan.[63]

The punishing experience of being undercut by the particularistic interests of private speculators on the mainland led the political leadership of the KMT as well as the alumni of the NRC to harbor a fundamental distrust of private capital and to take

---

[57]See Stephan Haggard and Chung-in Moon, "Institutions and Economic Policy: Theory and a Korean Case Study," *World Politics* 42, no. 2 (January 1990): 210–37.

[58]Tom Gold, *State and Society in the Taiwan Miracle* (New York: M.E. Sharpe, 1986), p. 59.

[59]Cheng, "The Politics of Industrial Transformation," p. 97.

[60]The discussion that follows draws primarily on Wade, *Governing the Market.*

[61]Wade, *Governing the Market,* p. 198.

[62]Ibid., p. 217.

[63]According to Wade, *Governing the Market,* pp. 272–73, the pool of NRC technocrats provided among other leading economic bureaucrats eight out of fourteen Ministers of Economic affairs.

seriously the anticapitalist elements of Sun Yat Sen's ideological pronouncements. These predilections were reinforced by the pragmatic fact that strengthening private capitalists on Taiwan involved increasing the power of an ethnically distinct, politically hostile private elite. It is therefore hardly surprising that instead of turning Japanese properties over to the private sector as its American advisors recommended, the KMT retained control, generating one of the largest state-owned sectors in the non-Communist world.[64] What is surprising is that Taiwan's state-owned enterprises (SOEs), in contrast to the pattern of inefficiency and deficit financing that is often considered intrinsic to the operation of such firms, were for the most part both profitable and efficient.[65]

On Taiwan, SOEs have been key instruments of industrial development. In addition to the banking sector, which was state-owned as in post-Rhee Korea, state-owned enterprises accounted for the majority of industrial production in the 1950s[66] and, after falling off a bit in the 1960s, their share expanded again in the 1970s.[67] SOEs are particularly important in basic and intermediary industries. China Steel, for example, has enabled Taiwan to successfully outcompete all Organization for Economic Cooperation and Development (OECD) steel exporters in the Japanese market.[68] The state enterprise sector not only makes a direct entrepreneurial contribution, but is also a training ground for economic leadership in the central state bureaucracy.[69] Thus, economic policy formation in Taiwan grows out of "a little understood but apparently vigorous policy network which links the central economic bureaus with public enterprises [and] public banks."[70]

What is striking in comparing Taiwan with Korea and Japan is the extent to which the Taiwanese private sector has been absent from economic policy networks. Even though the current trend is to "expand and institutionalize decision-making inputs from industrialists, financiers and others,"[71] historical relations between the KMT state and private (mainly Taiwanese) capital have been sufficiently distant to raise the question of whether embeddedness is really a necessary component of the developmental state.

The Taiwanese state unquestionably operates effectively with a less dense set of public-private network ties than the Korean or Japanese versions of the developmental state. Nonetheless, its lack of embeddedness should not be exaggerated. It is hardly isolated from the private sector. Gold has shown the close relations that existed between the government and the nascent textile sector in the 1950s, as well as the key intermediary role the government played in the development of the semiconductor industry in the 1970s. Wade notes that IDB officials spend a substantial portion of their time visiting firms and are engaged in something very much like MITI's "administrative guidance."[72] He provides a revealing example of the state's close interaction with private capital in his discussion of negotiations between raw materials producers and textile companies in the synthetic fiber industry. While the formal negotiations involved the downstream industry association (Manmade Fibers Association) and the upstream domestic monopolist (a state-MNC joint venture), state managers were continuously involved.[73] By engaging in this kind of negotiation state managers ensure that neither the Country's efforts at backward integration into intermediary products nor the export competitiveness of its textile producers is threatened by unresolved private conflicts. Informal public-private networks may be less dense than in the other two cases, but they are clearly essential to Taiwan's industrial policy.

In addition to defining the limits to which embeddedness can be reduced, the Taiwanese case highlights the symbiotic relationship between state autonomy and the preservation of market competition. The role of state autonomy in preserving market relationships is also crucial in Korea and Japan, but it is most apparent in the case of Taiwan.[74]

---

[64]See Cheng, "The Politics of Industrial Transformation," p. 107; Wade, *Governing the Market,* p. 302.

[65]Cf. Waterbury, chapter 4.

[66]Wade, *Governing the Market,* p. 78. Even in the 1980s, the state accounted for almost half of Taiwan's gross domestic capital formation and state enterprises accounted for two-thirds of the state's share (Cheng, "The Politics of Industrial Transformation," p. 166).

[67]Wade, *Governing the Market,* p. 97.

[68]P. Bruce, "World Steel Industry: The Rise and Rise of the Third World," *Financial Times* (London, 22 November 1983), cited in Wade, *Governing the Market,* p. 99.

[69]According to Wade, *Governing the Market,* p. 275, "most Ministers of Economic Affairs have had management positions in public enterprises."

[70]Wade, *Governing the Market,* p. 295.

[71]Ibid., p. 293.

[72]Ibid., p. 284.

[73]Ibid., p. 281.

[74]Cf. Stephan Haggard, *Pathways from the Periphery: The Politics of Growth in the Newly Industrializing Countries* (Ithaca, N.Y.: Cornell University Press, 1990), pp. 44–45.

The evolution of the textile industry offers the best illustration.[75] In the early 1950s, K. Y. Yin, ignoring the American-trained economists advising his government, decided that Taiwan should develop a textile industry. The result was the textile entrustment scheme that, by providing an assured market and raw materials, minimized the entrepreneurial risk involved in entering the industry and successfully induced the entry of private capital. In this initial phase, the state was supportive in a classic Hirschmanian way, inducing investment decisions and stimulating the supply of entrepreneurship.[76]

The entrustment scheme in itself is unusual only in the lengths to which the state was willing to go in order to ensure that entrepreneurship was forthcoming; otherwise it was very similar to the policies of most Latin American countries in the initial phases of industrialization. What is unusual is that the entrustment scheme did not become the instrument of the entrepreneurs it had created. Instead, the KMT regime progressively exposed its "greenhouse capitalists" to the rigors of the market, making export quotas dependent on the quality and price of goods, gradually shifting incentives toward exports, and finally diminishing protection over time.[77] Thus, the state was able to enforce the emergence of a free market rather than allowing the creation of rental havens. Without the autonomy made possible by a powerful bureaucratic apparatus, it would have been impossible to impose the unpleasantness of free competition on such a comfortable set of entrepreneurs.

The example reinforces the point made earlier in relation to embeddedness and autonomy in Japan. Private capital, especially private capital organized into tight oligopolistic networks, is unlikely to be a political force for competitive markets. Nor can a state that is a passive register of these oligopolistic interests give them what they are unwilling to provide for themselves. Only a state that is capable of acting autonomously can provide this essential collective good. Embeddedness is necessary for information and implementation, but without autonomy embeddedness will degenerate into a supercartel, aimed, like all cartels, at protecting its members from changes in the status quo.

A final, equally important characteristic of the developmental state is also well illustrated by the Taiwanese case. While the government has been deeply involved in a range of sectors, the Taiwanese state is extremely selective in its interventions. The bureaucracy operates in Wade's words as a "filtering mechanism," focusing the attention of policy makers and the private sector on products and processes crucial to future industrial growth.[78] Like most of the KMT's Taiwan strategy, selectivity was in part a response to previous experience on the mainland; having experienced the disasters of an overextended state apparatus, the KMT was determined to husband its bureaucratic capacity in its new environment.[79] Selectivity would, however, seem to be a general feature of the developmental state. Johnson describes how the Japanese state, having experimented with direct and detailed intervention in the pre-World War II period, limited itself to strategically selected economic involvement after the war,[80] and Okimoto goes so far as to note that in terms of its overall size, the Japanese state could be considered "minimalist."[81]

The Dynamics of Developmental States

The salient structural features of the development state should now be clear. Corporate coherence gives them the ability to resist incursions by the invisible hand of individual maximization by bureaucrats; internally, Weberian characteristics predominate. Highly selective, meritocratic recruitment and longterm career rewards create commitment and a sense of corporate coherence. Developmental states have benefited from extraordinary administrative capacities, but they also restrict their interventions to the strategic necessities of a transformative project, using their power to selectively impose market forces. The sharp contrast between the prebureaucratic, patrimonial character

[75]Cf. Peter Evans and Chien-kuo Pang, "State Structure and State Policy: Implications of the Taiwanese Case for Newly Industrializing Countries" (Paper presented at the International Conference on Taiwan: A Newly Industrialized Country, National Taiwan University, 3–5 September 1987).

[76]See Gold, *State and Society in the Taiwan Miracle,* p. 70; Pang Chien Kuo, "The State and Economic Transformation: The Taiwan Case" (Ph.D. diss., Department of Sociology, Brown University, 1987), pp. 167–69.

[77]The same strategy continues to be used. Wade, *Governing the Market,* pp. 207–8, recounts the IDB's efforts to induce local VCR production at the beginning of the 1980s. Two local companies were at first given a monopoly, but when, after a year and a half, they were still not producing internationally competitive products, Japanese firms were allowed to enter the market (with local joint venture partners) despite the protests of the original entrants.

[78]Wade, *Governing the Market,* p. 226.

[79]Johnson notes in his discussion of the Japanese case how the state apparatus, having attempted with very mixed success detailed and direct intervention in the pre-War period, limited itself to strategically chosen interventions after the war.

[80]Johnson, *MITI and the Japanese Miracle.*

[81]Okimoto, *Between MITI and the Market,* p. 2.

of the predatory state and the more closely Weberian character of developmental states should give pause to those who attribute the ineffectiveness of Third World states to their bureaucratic nature. Lack of bureaucracy may come closer to the correct diagnosis.

At the same time, the analysis of the East Asian cases has underlined the fact that the nonbureaucratic elements of bureaucracy may be just as important as the non-contractual elements of contract.[82] Historically deep, informal networks, or tightknit party or military organization have enhanced the coherence of the East Asian bureaucracies. Whether these ties are based on commitment to a parallel corporate institution or performance in the educational system, they reinforce the binding character of participation in the formal organization structure rather than undercutting in the way that informal networks based on kinship or parochial geographic loyalties do in the predatory pattern.

Having successfully bound the behavior of incumbents to its pursuit of collective ends, the state can act with some independence in relation to particularistic societal pressures. The autonomy of the developmental state is, however, of a completely different character from the aimless, absolutist domination of the predatory state. It is not just relative autonomy in the structural Marxist sense of being constrained by the generic requirements of capital accumulation. It is an autonomy embedded in a concrete set of social ties which bind the state to society and provide institutionalized channels for the continual negotiation and renegotiation of goals and policies.

In order to understand how this felicitous combination of autonomy and embeddedness emerged, it is necessary to set the developmental state in the context of a conjuncture of domestic and international factors. East Asian developmental states began the post-World War II period with legacies of long bureaucratic traditions and considerable prewar experience in direct economic intervention, in Korea and Taiwan under Japanese colonialism. World War II and its aftermath provided all these states with unusual societal environments. Traditional agrarian elites were decimated, industrial groups were disorganized and undercapitalized, and external resources were channeled through the state apparatus. The outcome of the war, including, ironically, American occupation in Japan and Korea, qualitatively enhanced the autonomy of these states vis-à-vis private domestic elites.[83] The combination of historically accumulated bureaucratic capacity and conjuncturally generated autonomy, placed them in an exceptional historical position.

At the same time, the state's autonomy was constrained by the international context, both geopolitical and economic. These states were certainly not free to make history as they chose. The international context excluded military expansion, but generated clear external threats. Economic expansion was not only the basis for shoring up legitimacy, but for maintaining defensive capabilities in the face of these threats. American hegemony on the one side and expansionary Asian communism on the other left them little choice but to rely primarily on private capital as the instrument of industrialization. The environment conspired to create the conviction that rapid, market-based industrialization was necessary to regime survival. Their small size and lack of resources made the place of export competitiveness in successful industrialization obvious.

Commitment to industrialization motivated these states to promote the growth of local industrial capital. Their exceptional autonomy allowed them to dominate (at least initially) the formation of the ties that bound capital and the state together. Out of this conjuncture the kind of embedded autonomy that characterized these states during the most impressive periods of their industrial growth emerged: a project shared by a highly developed bureaucratic apparatus and a relatively organized set of private actors who could provide useful intelligence and decentralized implementation.

. . . Recent developments suggest that embedded autonomy is not a static characteristic of the developmental state. In contrast to the absolutist domination of the predatory state, which seems self-reinforcing, embedded autonomy has been, to a surprising extent, its own gravedigger. The very success of the developmental state in structuring the accumulation of industrial capital has changed the nature of relations between capital and the state. As private capital has become less dependent on the resources provided by the state, the state's relative dominance has diminished. MITI influence in the 1980s cannot be compared to the golden era of the 1950s and early 1960s. Korean *chaebol* can now tap international capital markets directly[84] and

---

[82]Cf. Rueschemeyer and Evans, "The State and Economic Transformation."

[83]See Johnson, *MITI and the Japanese Miracle;* Pang, "The State and Economic Transformation."

[84]See Woo, *Race to the Swift.*

the state's ability to veto their projects has correspondingly eroded.[85]

The capacity of state apparatuses to command the loyalties of the most talented graduates of the best universities has also begun to erode as private careers become more rewarding. For example, Wade notes that the proportion of Masters and Ph.D.s entering government service in Taiwan has dropped substantially while the share entering the private sector has risen,[86] which is not surprising given the increasing salary differentials between the public and private sector. Whether the bureaucracy's traditional esprit de corps and corporate coherence can be preserved in the face of these trends remains to be seen. Even more fundamentally, the achievement of higher standards of living has made it more difficult to legitimize a national project justified solely on grounds of its contribution to the growth of GNP. Resurgent distributional demands, both political and economic, do not fit comfortably with the elite networks and bureaucratic structures which fostered the original project of industrial accumulation.[87]

There is no reason to presume that the developmental state will persist in the form that has been described here. Nor can we presume that if these state apparatuses persisted in their present form they would promote the satisfaction of future societal goals. They proved themselves formidable instruments for instigating the accumulation of industrial capital but, in all likelihood, they will have to be transformed in order to deal with the problems and opportunities created by the success of their initial project.

Brazil and India: "Intermediate" Cases

Having developed the contrast between the embedded autonomy of the East Asian developmental state and the incoherent absolutism of the predatory Zairian regime, it is time to look at how elements from these two ideal types can be combined in different ways to produce results that are neither purely predatory nor consistently developmental. Brazil and India provide ample illustration of how elements from the developmental ideal type may

be combined with characteristics that negate Weberian insulation and undercut embeddedness. . . .

Brazil

A plethora of historical and contemporary research make the differences between Brazil and the ideal typical developmental state clear.[88] The differences begin with the simple question of how people get government jobs. Barbara Geddes chronicles the unusually extensive powers of political appointment and the corresponding difficulty Brazil has experienced in instituting meritocratic recruitment procedures.[89] Ben Schneider points out that while Japanese prime ministers appoint only dozens of officials and American presidents appoint hundreds, Brazilian presidents appoint thousands.[90] It is little wonder that the Brazilian state is known as a massive *cabide de emprego* (source of jobs), populated on the basis of connection rather than competence.

The negative consequences of patronage are exacerbated by the character of the career patterns that such a system encourages. Instead of being

---

[85]See, for example, Kim, "From Dominance to Symbiosis," on the interaction of the state and the *chaebol* in the auto industry in the early 1980s.

[86]Wade, *Governing the Market,* table 7.1, p. 218.

[87]As Rueschemeyer and Evans, "The State and Economic Transformation," p. 53, argue, the state capacity required to implement distributional policies is likely to be significantly higher than that required to implement policies aimed at accumulation, further complicating prospects for success.

[88]Among historical studies those by Jose de Carvalho Murilo, "Elite and State-building in Brazil" (Ph.D. diss., Department of Political Science, Stanford University, 1974); and Fernando Uricoechea, *The Patrimonial Foundations of the Brazilian Bureaucratic State* (Berkeley: University of California Press, 1980) are particularly relevant to this discussion. Important recent contemporary studies include Sergio Abranches, "The Divided Leviathan: The State and Economic Policy Making in Authoritarian Brazil" (Ph.D. diss., Department of Political Science, Cornell University, 1978); Michael Barzelay, *The Politicized Market Economy: Alcohol in Brazil's Energy Strategy* (Berkeley: University of California Press, 1986); Frances Hagopian, "The Politics of Oligarchy: The Persistence of Traditional Elites in Contemporary Brazil" (Ph.D. diss., Department of Political Science, MIT, 1987); Barbara Geddes, *Economic Development as a Collective Action Problem: Individual Interests and Innovation in Brazil* (Ann Arbor, Mich.: University of Michigan Microfilms, 1986); Silvia Raw, "The Political Economy of Brazilian State-Owned Enterprises" (Ph.D. diss., Department of Economics, University of Massachusetts, 1986); Ben R. Schneider, "Politics within the State: Elite Bureaucrats and Industrial Policy in Authoritarian Brazil" (Ph.D. diss., Department of Political Science, University of California, 1987); Ben R. Schneider, "Framing the State: Economic Policy and Political Representation in Post Authoritarian Brazil," in John D. Wirth, Edson de Oliveira Nunes, and Thomas E. Bogenschild, eds., *State and Society in Brazil: Continuity and Change* (Boulder, Colo.: Westview Press, 1987); Helen Shapiro, "State Intervention and Industrialization: The Origins of the Brazilian Automotive Industry" (Ph.D. diss., Department of Economics, Yale University, 1988); and Eliza J. Willis, "The State as Banker: The Expansion of the Public Sector in Brazil" (Ph.D. diss., University of Texas at Austin, 1986). The discussion that follows draws especially on Schneider.

[89]Geddes, *Economic Development as a Collective Action Problem.*

[90]Schneider, "Politics Within the State," pp. 5, 212, 644.

tuned to the long-term gains via promotions based on organizationally relevant performance, Brazilian bureaucrats face staccato careers, punctuated by the rhythms of changing political leadership and periodic spawning of new organizations. A 1987 survey by Schneider of 281 Brazilian bureaucrats found that they shifted agencies very four or five years. Since the top four or five layers of most organizations are appointed from outside the agency itself, long-term commitment to the agency has only a limited return and construction of an ethos and of agency- and policy-relevant expertise is difficult. There is thus little to restrain strategies oriented toward individual and political gain.[91]

Unable to transform the bureaucracy as a whole, Brazilian leaders have tried to create pockets of efficiency (*bolsoes de eficiencia*) within the bureaucracy,[92] modernizing the state apparatus incrementally rather than through a broader transformation.[93] The National Development Bank (BNDE), favored especially by Kubitschek as an instrument of his developmentalism in the 1950s, was, until recently, a good example of a pocket of efficiency.[94] Unlike most of Brazil's bureaucracy, the BNDE offered "a clear career path, developmental duties and an ethic of public service."[95] Early in its institutional life (1956) the BNDE started a system of public examinations for recruitment. Norms grew up against arbitrary reversal of the judgments of the bank's technical personnel (*opiniao do tecnico*) by higher-ups. A solid majority of the directors was recruited internally, and a clear esprit de corps developed within the bank.[96]

Agencies like the BNDE are, not surprisingly, more developmentally effective than the traditional parts of the Brazilian bureaucracy.[97] According to Geddes those projects in Kubitschek's Target Plan that were both under the jurisdiction of executive groups or work groups and under the financial wing of the BNDE fulfilled 102 percent of their targets whereas those projects that were the responsibility of the traditional bureaucracy achieved only 32 percent.[98] Because the BNDE was a major source of long term investment loans, its professionalism was a stimulus to improving performance in other sectors.[99] Tendler notes, for example, that the necessity of competing for loan funds was an important stimulus to the improvement of proposals by Brazil's electrical power-generating companies.[100]

Unfortunately, the pockets of efficiency strategy has a number of disadvantages. As long as pockets of efficiency are surrounded by a sea of traditional clientelistic norms, they are dependent on the personal protection of individual presidents. Geddes, for example, chronicles the decline in the effectiveness of the Departmento Administrativo de Servico Publico (DASP) established by Vargas in 1938 as part of the Estado Novo once Vargas' protection was no longer available.[101] Willis emphasizes the dependence of the BNDE on presidential support, both in terms of the definition of its mission and in terms of its ability to maintain its institutional integrity.[102]

Incrementalism, or reform by addition, is likely to result in uncoordinated expansion and make strategic selectivity much more difficult to achieve. Having entered power with the intention of shrinking the state by as much as two hundred thousand positions, the Brazilian military ended up creating "hundreds of new, often redundant, agencies and enterprises" and expanding the federal bureaucracy from seven hundred thousand to 1.6 million.[103] Try-

[91]Ibid., p. 106. As Schneider points out, there are positive as well as negative features to this pattern. It discourages organizationally parochial perspectives and generates a web of inter-organizational ties among individuals. The main problem with these career patterns is that they provide insufficient counterweight either to the idiosyncratic decision-making from the top political leadership or to the tendencies toward individualized rent seeking.

[92]Geddes, *Economic Development as a Collective Action Problem*, p. 105.

[93]See Philippe Schmitter, *Interest Conflict and Political Change in Brazil* (Stanford, Calif.: Stanford University Press, 1971); Schneider, "Politics Within the State," p. 45.

[94]The BNDE later became the BNDES (National Bank for Economic and Social Development). Its history is discussed by both Geddes and Schneider, but the fullest discussions are Luciano Martins, *Estado Capitalista e Burocracia no Brasil Pos64* (Rio de Janeiro: Paz e Terra, 1985), and Willis, "The State as Banker."

[95]Schneider, "Politics Within the State," p. 633.

[96]Willis, "The State as Banker," pp. 96–126.

[97]Among the agencies highlighted by Geddes, *Economic Development as a Collective Action Problem*, p. 117, are the BNDES, CACEX, SUMOC, DASP, Itamaraty, Kubitscheks Executive Groups and Work Groups and the foreign exchange department of the Bank of Brazil.

[98]Geddes, *Economic Development as a Collective Action Problem*, p. 116.

[99]According to Willis, "The State as Banker," p. 4, the bank has "virtually monopolized the provision of long term credit in Brazil, often accounting for as much as 10 percent of gross domestic capital formation."

[100]Judith Tendler, *Electric Power in Brazil: Entrepreneurship in the Public Sector* (Cambridge, Mass.: Harvard University Press, 1968). See also Schneider, "Politics Within the State," p. 143.

[101]Geddes, *Economic Development as a Collective Action Problem*, p. 97.

[102]Willis, "The State as Banker."

[103]Schneider, "Politics Within the State," pp. 109, 575, 44. This was the goal of Roberto Campos (p. 575).

ing to modernize by piecemeal addition also undercuts the organizational coherence of the state apparatus as a whole. As new pieces are added, a larger and ever more baroque structure emerges. The resulting apparatus has been characterized as "segmented,"[104] "divided,"[105] or "fragmented."[106] It is a structure that not only makes policy coordination difficult, but encourages resort to personalistic solutions.

Just as the internal structure of the Brazilian state apparatus limits its capacity to replicate the performance of the East Asian developmental states, the character of its embeddedness makes it harder to construct a project of industrial transformation jointly with industrial elites. While the Brazilian state has been an uninterruptedly powerful presence in the country's social and economic development since colonial times, it is important to keep in mind that, as Fernando Urichochea, Jose Murilo de Carvalho and others have emphasized, "the efficiency of government . . . was dependent . . . on the cooperation of the landed oligarchy."[107] Despite the increasing weight of industrial capital in the economy, the persistent legacy of rural power continues to shape the character of the state. Hagopian argues that contemporary rural elites have turned increasingly to trying to use the state as an instrument for reinforcing their traditional clientelistic networks.[108] Thus, rather than being able to focus on its relationship with industrial capital, the state has always had to simultaneously contend with traditional elites threatened by the conflictful transformation of rural class relations.

At the same time, relations with industrial capital have been complicated by the early and massive presence of transnational manufacturing capital in the domestic market.[109] The threat of domination by transnational corporations (TNCs) created an atmosphere of defensive nationalism and made it more difficult to discipline domestic capital. It is much harder to force industrial capital to confront the market, as K. Y. Yin did with the Taiwanese textile industry, when transnational capital is the probable beneficiary of any gale of creative destruction.

Problems created by divisions in dominant economic elites were reinforced by the nature of state structures. The lack of a stable bureaucratic structure also made it harder to establish regularized ties with the private sector of the administrative guidance sort and pushed public-private interaction into individualized channels. Even the military regime, which had the greatest structural potential for insulation from clientelistic pressures, proved unable to construct an administrative guidance relationship with the local industrial elite.[110] The regime was "highly legitimate in the eyes of the local bourgeoisie, yet unconnected to it by any well-institutionalized system of linkages."[111] Instead of becoming institutionalized, relationships became individualized, taking the form of what Cardoso called "bureaucratic rings": small sets of individual industrialists connected to an equally small sets of individual bureaucrats, usually through some pivotal office holder.[112] As Schneider points out, the ad hoc, personalized character of these linkages makes them both undependable from the point of view of industrialists and arbitrary in terms of their outcomes.[113] They are, in short, quite the opposite of the sort of state-society ties that are described by Samuels and others in their discussions of the developmental state.

Overall, this reading of the internal structure and external ties of the Brazilian state is consistent with Schneider's lament that "the structure and operation of the Brazilian state should prevent it from fulfilling even minimal government functions."[114] But it is important to underline that despite its problems the Brazilian state has been entrepreneurially effective in a variety of industrial areas, and that these areas have undoubtedly contributed to its long-term growth and industrialization. These successes are, as we would expect, found in

[104]Barzelay, *The Politicized Market Economy.*

[105]Abranches, "The Divided Leviathan."

[106]Schneider, "Politics Within the State."

[107]Uricoechea, *The Patrimonial Foundations,* p. 52.

[108]Hagopian, "The Politics of Oligarchy."

[109]See Peter Evans, *Dependent Development: The Alliance of Multinational, State and Local Capital in Brazil* (Princeton: Princeton University Press, 1979); for a discussion of the consequences of foreign capital in Brazil, "Reinventing the Bourgeoisie: State Entrepreneurship and Class Formation in Dependent Capitalist Development," *The American Journal of Sociology* 88 (Supplement 1982): S210–47. For a more general contrast between Latin America and East Asia see Peter Evans, "Class, State and Dependence in East Asia: Some Lessons for Latin Americanists," in F. Deyo, ed., *The Political Economy of the New Asian Industrialism* (Ithaca, N.Y.: Cornell University Press, 1987); Stallings, "The Role of Foreign Capital in Economic Development."

[110]As a very cohesive corporate group whose lack of combat opportunities brought technocratic (i.e., educational) criteria for internal mobility to the fore, the Brazilian military approximated a KMT-style institutional reinforcement to the state's bureaucracy. See Alfred Stepan, *The Military in Politics: Changing Patterns in Brazil* (Princeton: Princeton University Press, 1971), and especially Geddes, *Economic Development as a Collective Action Problem,* chap. 7.

[111]Evans, "Reinventing the Bourgeoisie," p. S221.

[112]Fernando Henrique Cardoso, *Autoritarismo e Democratizacao* (Rio de Janeiro: Paz e Terra, 1975).

[113]Schneider, "Framing the State," pp. 230–31.

[114]Schneider, "Politics Within the State," p. 4.

areas where the relevant state organizations had exceptional coherence and capacity. These coherent state organizations, in turn, also rested on a more institutionally effective set of linkages with the private sector, the precise pattern visible in the developmental states of East Asia.

Shapiro's discussion of the role of the Grupo Executivo para Industria Automobilistica (GEIA) in the implantation of Brazil's auto industry during the late 1950s and early 1960s is a good example. She concludes that overall "the Brazilian strategy was a success" and that the planning capacity and subsidies provided by the state through the GEIA were crucial to inducing the required investments.[115] The GEIA served as a sectorally specific minipilot agency. Because it combined representation from all the different agencies that needed to pass on plans, it "could implement its program independently of the fragmented policy-making authority" that plagued the government as a whole.[116] Its ability to provide predictable timely decisions was critical to risk reduction as far as the TNCs that were being asked to invest were concerned. In addition, again much like MITI or the IDB, the GEIA "played a critical coordinating role between the assemblers and the parts producers."[117]

The later development of the petrochemical industry exhibited an even more potent variant of embedded autonomy.[118] Trebat concludes that state-led investment in the petrochemical industry saved foreign exchange[119] and was economically reasonable given the prevailing opportunity costs of capital.[120] At the heart of the initiative was Petrobras, the most autonomous and corporately coherent organization within the state enterprise system. Equally crucial to the explosive growth of Brazil's petrochemical capacity in the 1970s, however, was the dense network of ties that were constructed to link the Petrobras system to private capital, both domestic and transnational.

Out of these sectoral examples a clear overall difference between the Brazilian state and the ar-

chetypal developmental state emerges. Embedded autonomy is a partial rather than a global attribute, limited to certain pockets of efficiency. The persistence of clientelistic and patrimonial characteristics has prevented the construction of Weberian corporate coherence. Brazil's complex and contentious elite structure makes embeddedness much more problematic. It is hardly surprising that embedded autonomy remains partial.

India

The Indian state is even more ambiguously situated in the space between predatory and developmental than the Brazilian one. Its internal structure, at least at the apex, resembles the Weberian norm, but its relation to the country's convoluted social structure more thoroughly undercuts its capacity to act. Its harsher critics see it as clearly predatory and view its expansion as perhaps the single most important cause of India's stagnation.[121] Others, like Pranab Bardhan, take almost the reverse point of view, arguing that state investment was essential to India's industrial growth in the 1950s and early 1960s and that the state's retreat from a more aggressively developmental posture has been an important factor in India's relatively slow growth in the 1960s and 1970s.[122]

At the time of independence the Indian Civil Service (ICS) was the apex of a venerable bureaucracy. It was the culmination of a tradition that stretched back at least to the Mughal empire.[123] Its eleven hundred members formed a prestigious elite, providing "the steel frame of empire" for two hundred years.[124] Its successor, the Indian Administrative Service (IAS) has carried on the tradition. Entry is primarily via a nationwide examination which, historically at least, has been as highly competitive as its East Asian counterparts.[125] While educational training is not concentrated in a single national university in the way that it is in East Asia, solidary networks are enhanced by the fact that each class of recruits spends a

[115]Shapiro, "State Intervention and Industrialization," p. 57.

[116]Ibid., p. 111.

[117]Ibid., p. 58.

[118]See Evans, Dependent Development; "Reinventing the Bourgeoisie"; "Class, State and Dependence in East Asia"; and "Collectivized Capitalism: Integrated Petrochemical Complexes and Capital Accumulation in Brazil," in Thomas C. and Philippe Faucher Bruneau, eds., Authoritarian Brazil (Boulder, Colo.: Westview, 1981).

[119]Thomas Trebat, Brazil's State-Owned Enterprises: A Case Study of the State as Entrepreneur (Cambridge, England: Cambridge University Press, 1983).

[120]See Evans, "Collectivized Capitalism."

[121]E.g., Lal, The Hindu Equilibrium.

[122]Pranab Bardhan, The Political Economy of Development in India (Oxford: Basil Blackwell, 1984).

[123]See Lloyd I. Rudolf and Susanne Hoeber Rudolf, In Pursuit of Lakshmi: The Political Economy of the Indian State (Chicago, Ill.: University of Chicago Press, 1987).

[124]Richard P. Taub, Bureaucrats Under Stress: Administrators and Administration in an Indian State (Berkeley: University of California Press, 1969), p. 3.

[125]Taub, Bureaucrats Under Stress, p. 29, reports that in 1960 eleven thousand college graduates competed for one hundred places.

year together at the National Academy of Administration.[126]

Despite an historically deep tradition of solid state bureaucracy, the colonial traditions that the IAS inherited were by no means an unambiguous asset from the perspective of development. Assimilation of imperial culture and a humanistic training was an important criteria of acceptance into the ICS. Even after the English had departed, IAS exams still had three parts, English, English essay, and general knowledge.[127] An intelligent generalist might, of course, perform well, if career patterns provided the opportunity for the gradual acquisition of relevant technical knowledge and skills. Unfortunately, career patterns do not generally afford this kind of opportunity. Careers are characterized by the same kind of rapid rotation of people in jobs that characterize the Brazilian bureaucracy. Rudolf and Rudolf report, for example, that chief executives in the petrochemical industry have an average tenure in office of about fifteen months.[128] In addition to the problems of the IAS tradition itself, the extent to which the "steel frame" has remained uncorroded is questionable. The Rudolfs argue that there has been an "erosion of state institutions" at least since the death of Nehru.[129] Contemporary fieldstudies have found corruption not just endemic but overwhelming.[130] Erosion may be due in part to problems internal to the bureaucracy, but the difficulties of building connections to the surrounding social structure seem the more serious source of difficulty. In a "subcontinental, multinational state" like India state-society relations are qualitatively more complex than in the East Asian cases.[131] Given the diseconomies of scale inherent in administrative organizations, it would take a bureaucratic apparatus of truly extraordinary capacity to produce results comparable to what can be achieved on an island of twenty million people or a peninsula of forty million. Class, ethnic, religious, and regional divisions compound administrative difficulties.

From the time of independence, the political survival of Indian regimes has required simultaneously pleasing a persistently powerful rural landowning class and a highly concentrated set of industrial capitalists. The shared interests of larger landowners and the millions of "bullock capitalists" in the countryside give this group daunting political weight.[132] At the same time, the large business houses like the Tatas and Birlas must be kept on board.[133] Since business houses and landowners share no encompassing developmental project, the divided elite confronts the state in search of particularistic advantage. They comprise in Bardhan's terms, "a flabby and heterogeneous dominant coalition preoccupied in a spree of anarchical grabbing at public resources."[134]

The micropolitics of state-private interactions further diminish the possibility of the state leading a coherent developmental project. Historically, the stereotypical IAS veteran was an anglophile Brahman of Fabian socialist ideological leanings. The private capitalists with whom he was dealing were likely to be of lower caste, different cultural tastes, and opposing ideology. While these stereotypes have gradually changed over time, shared discourse and common vision, on the basis of which a common project might be constructed, are often still lacking, leaving the exchange of material favors as the only alternative to hostile stalemate. Policy networks that allow industry experts from within the state apparatus to collect and disseminate information, build consensus, tutor, and cajole are missing. Nor do we find sectorally specific networks comparable to the one that binds together the state and private capital in the Brazilian petrochemical industry. Unlike the developmental states, the Indian state cannot count on the private sector either as a source of information about what kind of industrial policy will fly or as an effective

---

[126]An example of the solidary created is the statement by one of Taub's (*Bureaucrats Under Stress,* p. 33) informants that he could "go anywhere in India and put up with a batch mate [member of his IAS class]," a possibility that the informant considered unheard of in terms of normal relations with nonkin.

[127]Take, for example, the question cited by Taub (*Bureaucrats Under Stress,* p. 30): "Identify the following: Venus de Milo, Mona Lisa, the Thinker, William Faulkner, Corbusier, Karen Hantze Susman, Major Gherman Titov, Ravi Shankar, Disneyland."

[128]Rudolf and Rudolf, *In Pursuit of Lakshmi,* p. 34.

[129]Ibid., chap. 2.

[130]E.g., Robert Wade, "The Market for Public Office: Why the Indian State Is Not Better at Development," *World Development* 13, no. 4 (1985): 467–97.

[131]Rudolf and Rudolf, *In Pursuit of Lakshmi.*

[132]Ibid.

[133]Dennis Encarnation, *Dislodging the Multinationals: India's Strategy in Comparative Perspective* (Ithaca, N.Y.: Cornell University Press, 1990), p. 286.

[134]Bardhan, *The Political Economy of Development in India,* p. 70. It is interesting to contrast this vision with a quite different social structural dilemma, equally difficult for a would-be developmental state. In Maurice Zeitlin and Richard E. Ratcliff's *Landlords and Capitalists: The Dominant Class of Chile* (Princeton: Princeton University Press, 1988), analysis of Chile they found not a split elite but one which united agrarian and industrial interests, thus ensuring that the elite as a whole would resist transformation of the agrarian sector and the kind of single-minded focus on industrialization that characterized East Asian cases.

instrument for the implementation of industrial policy.

It would be unfair and incorrect to say that the Indian state has made no developmental contribution. State investment in basic infrastructure and intermediate goods was a central element in maintaining a respectable rate of industrial growth in the 1950s and early 1960s. Even Deepak Lal admits that infrastructural investments and the increase in the domestic savings rate, both of which depended largely on the behavior of the state, were "the two major achievements of post-Independence India."[135] State investment in basic agricultural inputs, primarily irrigation and fertilizers, played an important role in increasing agricultural output. The state has invested effectively, if not always efficiently,[136] in basic and intermediate industries like steel and petrochemicals and even in more technologically adventurous industries like electrical equipment manufacture.[137]

Unfortunately, these are largely accomplishments of the past, of the 1950s and early 1960s. Increasingly, lack of selectiveness in state intervention has burdened the bureaucracy and helped propel the erosion of state institutions. The "license, permit, quota raj" has attempted to enforce detailed control over the physical output of a broad range of manufactured goods.[138] At the same time, the state is directly involved in production of a variety of goods greater than even relatively expansive states like Brazil have attempted. Indian SOEs produce not only computers but also televisions, not only steel but also automobiles.[139] The state-owned share of corporate assets moved from one-sixth to a half between 1962 and 1972,[140] as the number of state enterprises grew from five in 1951

to 214 in 1984.[141] Given the overwhelming demands created by the sheer task of supplying even minimalist governance, unselective state involvement is simply unsustainable.

Relative to Brazil, it might be argued that India suffers from excessive autonomy and inadequate embeddedness and consequently has more difficulty in executing the kind of sectoral projects that are the focus here. At the same time, the degree to which the "steel frame" still retains some residual coherence may help account for India's ability to avoid the disastrous excesses that Brazil has fallen prey to.

Given their continental scale, Brazil and India may appear as sui generis, and of limited comparative relevance. Yet their states share many of the same problems, both with one another and with many of the middle-income developing countries as well. Their bureaucracies, which are not patrimonial caricatures of Weberian structures as in the predatory case, still lack the corporate coherence of the developmental ideal type. Consistent career ladders that bind the individual to corporate goals while simultaneously allowing him to acquire the expertise necessary to perform effectively are not well institutionalized. India has a more thoroughly Weberian organizational structure, but lacks the ties that might enable it to mount a shared project with social groups interested in transformation.

With less well-developed bureaucratic capacity, these intermediate apparatuses must nevertheless confront more complex and divided social structures. Their ability to construct a project of industrialization is specifically complicated by the continuing social power of agrarian elites. In the Brazilian case the problem is complicated even further by the historical importance of foreign firms at the core of the industrial establishment. In the Indian case it is exacerbated by the cultural divergence between state managers and private capitalists. In both countries the state has tried to do too many things; it has been unable to strategically select a set of activities commensurate with its capacity. Lesser capacity and a more demanding array of tasks combine to make embedded autonomy impossible. . . .

State Structures and Adjustment

. . . The comparative evidence argues strongly in favor of focusing more on state capacity as an important factor in policy choice and outcomes and helps clarify the structures and processes that un-

[135]Lal, *The Hindu Equilibrium*, p. 237.

[136]For a good discussion of problems in the inefficiency of state investments in terms of extraordinarily high capital output ratios etc., see Isher Judge Aluwalia, *Industrial Growth in India: Stagnation since the Mid-Sixties* (Delhi: Oxford University Press, 1985).

[137]Ravi Ramamurti, *State-owned Enterprises in High Technology Industries: Studies in India and Brazil* (New York: Praeger, 1987).

[138]See Encarnation, *Dislodging the Multinationals.*

[139]This lack of selectivity is not always evident in aggregate comparisons. For example, the distribution of public enterprises in Korea and India looked quite similar when Leroy Jones and Edward S. Mason, "Role of Economic Factors in Determining the Size and Structure of the Public-Enterprise Sector in Less-developed Countries with Mixed Economies," in Jones, ed., *Public Enterprise in Less-developed Countries* (New York: Cambridge University Press, 1982), p. 22, considered manufacturing a single sector rather than disaggregating it.

[140]Encarnation, *Dislodging the Multinationals*, p. 283.

[141]Lal, *The Hindu Equilibrium*, p. 257.

derlie capacity. Most specifically, this analysis challenges the tendency to equate capacity with insulation. It suggests instead that transformative capacity requires a combination of internal coherence and external connectedness that can be called embedded autonomy.

The first and most obvious lessons to be extracted from these cases is that bureaucracy is in *under,* not over-, supply. This is not only a problem in the post-colonial societies of the sub-Sahara. Even in countries like Brazil that enjoy relatively abundant supplies of trained manpower and a long tradition of state involvement in the economy, predictable, coherent, Weberian bureaucracies are hard to find. The standard perception to the contrary flows from the common tendency for patrimonial organizations to masquerade as Weberian bureaucracies. There is an abundance of rule-making or administrative organizations, but most have neither the capability of pursuing collective goals in a predictable, coherent way nor an interest in doing so. Weber misled his successors by insisting that bureaucracy would naturally sweep all other forms before it. Just as markets are less natural than Smith would have had us believe, so bureaucracies need more nurturing than Weber led us to expect.

The second lesson is an extension of the first. The state's ability to perform administrative and other functions must be treated as a scarce good. Early visions of the developmental state seemed to assume that the resources necessary to undertake new tasks would be automatically generated by the performance of the tasks themselves, just as expanding firm sales generate resources for new production. The analogy is false. Unjudicious expansion of the menu of tasks leads too easily to a vicious cycle. State capacity grows more slowly than tasks expand. Administrative and organizational diseconomies of scale and scope lead to declining performance. Inadequate performance undercuts legitimacy and makes it hard to claim the resources necessary to increase capacity. The gap between capacity required and capacity available yawns wider until even the effective execution of nightwatchman duties is threatened.

Almost all Third World states try to do more than they are capable of doing. The contrasting balance of capacity and tasks that separates India and Brazil from the East Asian developmental states illustrates the point. The developmental states not only had higher levels of capacity but exercised greater selectivity in the tasks they undertook. They focused on industrial transformation and their strategies of promoting industry were designed to conserve administrative resources. . . .

Autonomy and corporate coherence, like insulation, are well within the Weberian tradition. Emphasis on embeddedness as the necessary complement to autonomy not only contradicts the notion that insulation is the most important feature of capacity, it also departs from a Weberian perspective. Embeddedness represents a different solution to the shortage of capacity. Embeddedness is necessary because policies must respond to the perceived problems of private actors and rely in the end on private actors for implementation. A concrete network of external ties allows the state to assess, monitor, and shape private responses to policy initiatives, prospectively and after the fact. It extends the state's intelligence and enlarges the prospect that policies will be implemented. Admitting the importance of embeddedness turns arguments for insulation on their head. Connections to civil society become part of the solution rather than part of the problem.

The obvious question is: Why doesn't embeddedness devolve into clientelism, corruption and undermining the effectiveness of the state? Most of the answer lies in the fact that embeddedness is assumed to have value only in the context of autonomy. In the absence of a coherent, self-orienting, Weberian sort of administrative structure, embeddedness will almost certainly have deleterious effects. . . . It is the *combination* of embeddedness and autonomy that works, not either on its own.

Selection IX.C.3. Taking Trade Policy Seriously: Export Subsidization as a Case Study in Policy Effectiveness*

Preliminary Considerations

There are three sets of economic models that I think are invaluable in thinking about policy formulation and implementation: (i) models of dynamic inconsistency of policy; (ii) models with irreversibilities and hysteresis; and (iii) models of rent seeking. Each of these has a distinct lesson for what makes policy effective.

The basic model of dynamic inconsistency points to the costs of discretionary behavior by government officials and brings out the advantage of rule-based policy regimes which entail high degrees of precommitment. Two significant applications of these ideas in the area of trade policy can be found in Staiger and Tabellini 1987 and Matsuyama 1990. The first of these papers shows the bias towards excessive protection on the part of governments that care about income distribution, while the second demonstrates the difficulties of disciplining firms by threatening to remove protection, a threat that is hardly credible ex post. In each case, a clear implication is that designing schemes that would enhance the commitment of policymakers to ex-ante rules would be desirable.

Models with irreversibilities demonstrate the importance of policy stability, or more accurately, predictability in coaxing the desired response from the private sector. When supply decisions are subject to sunk costs, unpredictability about future policy can seriously dampen the supply response to any policy change (Dixit 1989; Pindyck and Solimano 1993), and potentially render a prima-facie desirable policy change harmful (Rodrik 1991). Combined with Calvo's 1989 demonstration that a lack of credibility in trade policy amounts to an intertemporal distortion, this literature underscores the importance of building predictability into the policy making process.

Finally, the rent-seeking approach to trade policy, originating from Krueger's 1974 venerable article, reminds us that policies that create rents will also create rent seekers. This in turn generates incentives for bureaucrats to create rents in the first place (Shleifer and Vishny 1991). These ideas lie at the core of the neoclassical political-economy lit-

erature on trade policy, where rent-seeking interest groups and rent-providing policy makers interact to produce inefficient policy configurations (Grossman and Helpman 1992 provide a recent example[1]). The implications are bleak for policy making: policy interventions should be avoided as a rule, but if they cannot, they should be undertaken in manner that keeps private groups at arms length.

Taken together, these theoretical ideas yield quite a coherent story about what constitutes a good policy regime. Successful government programs are likely to contain the following characteristics:

- they apply simple and uniform rules, rather than selective and differentiated ones;
- they endow bureaucrats with few discretionary powers;
- they contain safeguards against frequent, unpredictable alteration of the rules;
- they keep firms and other organized interests at arms length from the policy formulation and implementation process.

These conclusions seem broadly reasonable, and lists like the above are often drawn in policy discussions.

When I first decided to take on export subsidies as a case study, I was expecting that the evidence on what makes some programs successful and others failures would validate these conclusions. I was wrong. While the models mentioned above *are* useful in understanding what happens, the broad generalizations that one is tempted to draw from them are much less so. In fact, as a first cut, these broad conclusions have more explanatory power when they are turned upside down! The two most successful programs of export subsidization I found, those in South Korea and Brazil, were highly complex and selective, differentiated by firm, subject to frequent changes, gave bureaucrats enormous discretionary powers, and entailed close interaction between bureaucrats and firms. On the other hand, the least successful programs in my sample, those in Kenya and Bolivia, consisted of simple, across-the-board, and non-selective subsidies.

What is going on here? I think the answer is that there is a lot that we do not know or understand

*From Dani Rodrik, "Taking Trade Policy Seriously: Export Subsidization as a Case Study in Policy Effectiveness," in Alan V. Deardorff et al., eds., *New Directions in Trade Theory* (Ann Arbor: University of Michigan, 1995), pp. 350–378. Reprinted by permission.

[1]However, they also allow the government to place an exogenous weight on aggregate efficiency.

about state capabilities and policy effectiveness. . . . With regard to export subsidies, there are two concepts that I have found useful in characterizing the differences in outcomes across countries. The first, and more fundamental, one is the notion of *state autonomy.* This refers to the degree to which the state and administrative apparatus of a society is insulated from organized private interests and, consequently, can exercise discipline over them.[2] The second useful notion is that of *policy coherence,* meaning a clearly articulated, stable, and non-conflicting set of policy priorities. I will be using these terms in a descriptive, rather than explanatory, fashion, as it remains unclear whether they can be operationalized in a meaningful manner.

The evidence from the case studies points to some simple conclusions. Policies work best when autonomy and coherence are both present; they fail when neither is. However, policy coherence on its own is worth something: coherent programs can be successfully formulated and implemented even when autonomy is lacking, but at the cost of some abuse. An important implication for economic analysis is the following one: while the state may not be an omniscient social-welfare maximizer, neither is it a tool of lobbying groups as in much of the recent political-economy literature. To understand where each case fits, we have to dig deeper than we are prone to do.

As mentioned above, the concept of state autonomy is borrowed from the political science literature. However, it has an important antecedent in Gunnar Myrdal's magisterial work on Asian development, *Asian Drama* 1968. In his study of Asian societies, Myrdal was struck by how little states asked of their citizens, and how incapable they were of eliciting compliance when they tried. The result was a pattern of economic policy making that was all carrots and no stick. Myrdal christened such states as "soft states," and contrasted them with their opposite, "strong states." This distinction, under different names, has survived. For example, Jones and Sakong's 1980 excellent study of policy making in South Korea harks back to this distinction, and the authors locate the key to that country's stellar performance in the presence of a "hard" state (more on this below).

State autonomy, as the term is usually used, is effectively a measure of how "strong" or "hard" a state is. Migdal 1988 is a good source on how political scientists have approached the issue of state strength and societal control, as well as on attempts to quantify these concepts. I find it helpful to think of autonomy as the extent to which the state can act as a Stackelberg leader over private groups, rather than as a Stackelberg follower; states that fall in the first category are strong, while states in the second category are weak.[3] The existing literature is not very helpful on where autonomy comes from and how it is acquired. Most studies point to distinctive historical experience: Migdal 1988, for example, emphasizes massive social dislocations, such as war, revolution, or mass migration, as a precondition to the existence of strong states.[4]

Going back to our list of what constitutes a good policy regime, then, these conclusions turn out to be too pessimistic about state capabilities in societies governed by strong states. On the other hand, they are too optimistic about the capabilities of weak states—and that is really bad news! In either case, they provide a bad fit.

I will expand on these points in the following sections. Export subsidization is a good area to try some of these ideas out for a number of reasons. For one thing, it is the policy on which the strategic trade policy literature has focussed. Second, it is very common: most countries have tried it at some time or another, and this provides a large sample. Third, the administration of export subsidies tends to be "organizationally demanding" (Levy 1993 p. 257), opening a window into contrasts in state capabilities. Finally, the received wisdom on export subsidies is that they have not been effective (Nogués 1990 and Thomas and Nash 1991).

Two Successful Cases: Korea and Brazil

Korea

Korea's phenomenal export boom starting in the early 1960s is well known. Less well known is the significant role played by the Korean government's micro-management of export incentives in produc-

---

[2]Occasionally the literature draws a distinction between the two parts of this definition, referring to the first as "autonomy" and the second as "capacity." See Barkey and Parikh 1991 pp. 525–26.

[3]See Rodrik 1992 for a first attempt to formalize this. Using a highly stylized model of interaction between the government and the private sector, I show that, compared to a strong state (the Stackelberg leader), a weak state (a Stackelberg follower) systematically underprovides economically desirable interventions, and systematically overprovides politically motivated (and economically harmful) interventions.

[4]As Migdal 1988 p. 269 puts it, "[a]ll these cases [Israel, Cuba, China, Japan, Vietnam, Taiwan, North Korea, and South Korea] of relatively strong states have occurred in societies in which major social disturbances rocked existing structures within the last half-century."

ing the boom. It is not a great exaggeration to say that the manner in which the Korean bureaucracy administered and coordinated the export push of the 1960s and 1970s is reminiscent of the way that the military command of a nation would run a war.

Under the Rhee government of the 1950s, Korean policy was preoccupied by largely political considerations, and the government attached no particular importance to either economic growth or exports (Jones and Sakong 1980 pp. 272–273). While there were some export subsidies, they were implemented haphazardly and often not budgeted at all (Frank et al. 1975 pp. 38–39). This changed dramatically after Park took over in a military coup on May 16, 1961. Park made exports his top priority, and aside from devaluing the won, greatly expanded the scope of export subsidization. Table 1 shows estimates of the combined ad-valorem equivalents of export subsidies during 1958–70. Two significant jumps in the subsidies are evident from the data, one in 1961–62 and another one in 1966–67.

Exporters had access to a bewildering array of subsidies in this period. Direct cash grants were important very early on, but they were phased out by 1965 and replaced by tax and import duty exemptions. In that year, the priority given to exporters in acquiring import licenses was formalized and expanded: exporters were allowed duty-free imports of raw materials and intermediate inputs up to a limit. This limit was determined administratively, on the basis of firm and industry input-output coefficients plus a margin of "wastage allowance." Since the imports acquired under the wastage allowance could be sold in the domestic market, this was a significant subsidy and was consciously used as such. Frank et al. 1975, p. 66 estimate that the wastage allowance alone provided an export subsidy of 4.6 percent in 1968 on average, and up to 17–21 percent in certain fabrics and footwear. Bureaucrats had virtually unrestricted discretion in setting wastage allowances, and their generosity varied from time to time (Frank et al. p. 50). Businesses and trade associations regularly lobbied for increased allowances.

Subsidized credit to exporters was another significant incentive. As Table 1 shows, it became particularly important after 1966. Frank et al. 1975 table 5-5 list twelve different types of preferential loans to exporters that were operative in the 1967–1970 period.

A noteworthy feature of the Korean export subsidies is that they applied not only to the final exporters, but to the indirect exporters as well (i.e., the firms that supplied the intermediate inputs used

in exportables). The available econometric evidence indicates that exports were highly sensitive to subsidies: Jung and Lee 1986 estimate that a 1 percent increase in export subsidies eventually led to more than a 2 percent increase in export supply. Intriguingly, they also find that the elasticity of export supply with respect to the real exchange rate was smaller than this.

These subsidies were disbursed against a background of highly unusual government-business relationship. One of the first acts of the Park regime was to arrest most of the country's leading businessmen and to threaten the confiscation of their assets under a recently passed Law for Dealing with Illicit Wealth Accumulation (Jones and Sakong 1980 p. 69).[5] A compromise was then arranged by which these businessmen would build factories and turn their shares over to the government in exchange for their release. The matter was eventually closed in December 1964 with most businessmen paying their fines in cash (with fines amounting to a total sum of $16 million). The planned transfer of ownership never took place. "Nonetheless," as Jones and Sakong remark (1980, p. 70), "the basic pattern was set, with businessmen in a decidedly subordinate role" to the state.

The ability of the government to elicit the desired response from firms by a combination of cajoling, arm-twisting, and threats was characteristic of the manner in which the export subsidies were administered. Westphal's description of the situation is worth quoting at length:

[T]he [Korean] government has not relied solely on market forces acting in response to incentives. It has also used publicly announced, quarterly export targets for individual commodities, markets, and firms. Contact between government and business in the day-to-day implementation of these targets has been close. Next to the responsible minister's office, an "export situation room" was established, laid out so that potential export shortfalls could be identified at a glance. A large staff has maintained almost daily contact with major exporters, and it has not been uncommon for the minister to intervene in difficult situations; for example, to obtain immediate customs clearance for inputs being delayed on some pretext. Progress towards targets and the current trade situation have been regularly reviewed at a Monthly Trade Promotion Conference, chaired by the president and attended by ministers, bankers, and the more successful exporters, large and small.

The highest export achievements have brought national awards as well as material benefits bestowed

---

[5]This law was actually passed by the short-lived Chang Myon regime intervening between the Rhee and Park years, but its implementation took place under Park's government.

Table 1. Export Subsidies in Korea, 1958–70 (%)

	Direct subsidies	Tax exemptions	Duty exemptions	Credit subsidies	Total
1958	0.00	0.00	0.00	2.30	2.30
1959	0.00	0.00	0.00	2.53	2.53
1960	0.00	0.00	0.00	1.85	1.85
1961	5.89	0.00	0.00	0.75	6.64
1962	7.94	4.35	3.58	0.66	16.54
1963	3.14	4.67	5.06	2.20	15.07
1964	1.36	3.86	4.66	2.80	12.68
1965	0.00	6.11	5.79	2.86	14.76
1966	0.00	7.54	7.85	3.79	19.18
1967	0.00	8.52	9.07	5.45	23.04
1968	0.00	8.27	14.32	5.50	28.10
1969	0.00	9.07	11.89	5.11	26.06
1970	0.00	9.61	12.66	5.57	27.84

Source: Calculated from Frank et al. 1975, Tables 5–8.

through discretionary means . . . [including] additional preferences in the general allocation of credit under a system of government directed bank lending and relaxed tax surveillance under a revenue system that gives government officials considerable latitude in determining tax liabilities. . . . Conversely, indolence has been deterred by the perception that discretion could be—indeed, sometimes was—exercised in ways that impose material costs or deny potential benefits in other areas of a firm's activity. (Westphal 1990 pp. 45–46)

There was a clear understanding on the part of firms that good export performance would be rewarded by various kinds of government benefits, while poor performance would bring forth penalties. Most notable among the penalties were tax inspection and collection applied more rigorously than usual (Rhee et al. 1984 p. 92).

As the passage quoted above makes clear, the government issued specific export targets for firms (as well as commodities and export markets). When the government first began to issue such targets, the heads of firms are reported to have willingly complied, "with the[ir] memory still fresh of their being jailed by the new regime for the illicit accumulation of wealth" (Rhee et al. 1984 p. 21). Eventually, firms began to set their own targets, but remained constrained by past performance as well as the vigilance of bureaucrats in extracting maximum export performance.[6,7]

The extent to which the government's priorities and resources were organized around export performance is striking. As mentioned in the passage by Westphal above, the monthly trade promotion conferences were chaired by President Park himself, and he often took decisions on the spot. Exports were monitored literally on a daily basis:

The head of the export promotion office in the Ministry of Commerce and Industry has at his side a computer printout of progress against targets by industry and by firms. The data is for the preceding day, which is all the more remarkable when it is considered that most developing countries do not have aggregate information on exports for many months. The printout is also broken down by geographic region. If sales in a region are not up to target, the Korean ambassadors there are recalled to find out what the problems are and what can be done to spur Korean sales. And in the foyer of the head office of the Korean Traders' Association is a big board tracking the progress of each industry towards its target. The export associations of each industry, the nodes for all information flows on exports, have their own boards tracking progress. So do firms on the shop floors, where workers—dressed in uniforms that give all of industry a paramilitary air—keep track of their firm's progress toward targets and of that by competitors down the street. (Rhee et al. 1984 p. 22)

The extreme discretion that trade officials had allowed them to be flexible and respond quickly to changes in circumstances. For example, export tar-

---

[6]Around half or more of the firms surveyed by Rhee et al. 1984 reported that the export targets had negative effects on the firm in terms of profitability or sales diversion. Enterprise-level export targets have also been used, apparently quite successfully, in China (see Panagariya 1993).

[7]As it turned out, most firms regularly exceeded their targets. Balassa 1978 reads this as evidence that targets did not play an

important role. However, that fact itself says nothing about how binding these requirements were ex ante: for one thing, Korean exports grew at a stupendous rate that would have been impossible to predict beforehand; secondly, there was a general expectation that failure to meet targets would attract penalties, creating strong incentives for fulfillment; and third, over-fulfillment brought rewards from the administration.

gets for automotive products were scaled down more than once during the 1970s (Westphal 1990 p. 54), and a survey by Rhee et al. 1984 found that nearly a third of the respondents had their targets revised during 1973–75.[8] But when asked whether a firm had any say in setting the export target for itself, 47 of the 97 firms replied negatively.

Without these two institutional innovations—the practice of setting and monitoring export targets and the holding of monthly trade promotion conferences—the export incentives themselves would arguably not have been as effective (Rhee et al. 1984). These were instrumental in communicating the top leadership's priorities to lower level bureaucrats and to firms alike, in resolving administrative problems quickly, and as a combined carrot-and-stick strategy more broadly. To the question of why firms did not systematically manipulate the incentives or set low targets (as in socialist economies), the simple answer is that state officials were on top of things. In turn, low-level corruption on the part of bureaucrats themselves was ruled out by the high priority given to the export drive by the top leadership.

The Korean state's strength (or autonomy) is usually ascribed to a number of distinctive circumstances. According to Amsden 1989 p. 54, "[t]he Korean state was able to consolidate its power in the 1960s because of the weakness of the social classes. Workers were a small percentage of the population, capitalists were dependent on state largesse, the aristocracy was dissolved by land reform, and the peasantry was atomized into smallholders." Others like Evans 1992 also stress the importance of a tradition of meritocratic bureaucracy. Such historical considerations, however, do not explain how the Korean state under Park was able to metamorphose itself from its poor cousin under Rhee.[9] We also need to take into account the *coherence* of export policies under Park—the consistent priority given to them at the expense of other objectives—and the lack thereof under Rhee.

Brazil

Brazil's economy has been so mismanaged since the early 1980s that it is hard to imagine the presence there of an effective program of export subsidies. Yet starting in the second half of the 1960s an extensive set of export incentives was successfully implemented and led—alongside a crawling exchange rate policy—to an impressive increase in manufactured exports. It was this export performance that prompted many observers to talk about a "Brazilian miracle," until the debt crisis of 1982 and macroeconomic mismanagement turned the economy into a big mess.

Prior to the military coup of 1964, government policy in Brazil did not attach particular attention to exports, in keeping with the bias towards import substitution. The incoming government, like Park's regime, developed a clear commitment to exports. There was some liberalization of import restrictions, a move (in 1968) to a crawling peg regime to maintain competitiveness, and the development of an extensive and generous system of export subsidies for manufactures. These subsidies included duty and tax rebates, income tax exemption, credit subsidies, and many others (see table 2). By the latter half of the 1970s, the combined value of these subsidies stood close to 50 percent of exports. As in Korea, these subsidy programs were implemented in a highly selective and discriminatory manner.[10] Export subsidization varied greatly from industry to industry, as well as from firm to firm. Almost without exception, the larger firms obtained a disproportionate share of the subsidies (Fasano-Filho et al. 1987 p. 66).

The effectiveness of these subsidies appears beyond question. In a survey of export subsidies in Latin America, Nogués 1990 lists only the Brazilian case as a success. Fasano-Filho et al. 1987 provide econometric evidence of their importance in export supply decisions. A World Bank study (1983 p. 121) credits the BEFIEX program (discussed below) for stimulating a significant amount of new investments oriented towards world markets. Perhaps most telling of all is that Brazilian manufactured exports expanded at an annual average rate of 38 percent during the 1970s.

Among the subsidies listed in table 2, one stands out in terms of effectiveness and distinctiveness. This is the BEFIEX program, introduced in 1972. (BEFIEX is the Brazilian acronym for Fiscal Benefits for Special Export Programmes.) According to

---

[8]Here is how Jones and Sakong 1980 p. 61 describe the down side of the discretionary environment: "Businessmen often complain about the sudden shifts in policy direction, and (at a decidedly lower level of importance) academics are regularly frustrated when their critiques of policy become outdated before reaching print." But according to Rhee et al. 1984 p. 36: "Firms . . . saw the flexibility and frequent adjustments in the incentive system not as characteristics that would create uncertainty about the automaticity and stability of that system. They saw them as part of the government's long-term commitment to keep exports profitable. . . ."

[9]Survey results reported in Jones and Sakong 1980 Table 22 show a striking difference in firms' perceptions with regard to the effectiveness and hardness of economic policies under the two regimes.

[10]Evans 1979 pp. 93–94 characterizes post-1964 Brazil as "a case of espousing liberal free enterprise while acting to increase vastly the economic role of the state, both regulatory and entrepreneurial."

Table 2. Export Subsidies in Brazil, 1969–1985 (%)

	Duty drawback	BEFIEX	Tax credit premium	Credit subsidies	Income tax exempt.	Total
1969	4.0	—	6.7	4.1	0.0	14.8
1970	4.0	—	13.5	7.5	0.0	25.0
1971	4.0	—	13.2	7.8	1.3	26.3
1972	4.9	n.a.	16.3	8.2	1.3	30.7
1973	7.2	n.a.	16.2	6.5	1.3	31.2
1974	12.6	n.a.	12.0	6.1	1.8	32.5
1975	8.3	n.a.	12.1	11.5	1.7	33.6
1976	11.8	3.6	11.7	15.9	1.3	44.3
1977	12.6	4.6	12.4	19.6	1.5	50.7
1978	9.1	5.0	12.8	17.0	1.8	45.7
1979	10.5	5.4	12.8	13.9	2.1	44.7
1980	9.0	8.1	0.0	2.0	1.9	21.0
1981	9.4	10.2	6.5	18.7	1.8	46.6
1982	10.3	7.7	9.1	21.7	1.6	50.4
1983	8.6	4.9	7.8	9.3	1.6	32.2
1984	9.1	4.3	7.8	2.7	1.6	25.5
1985	9.1	5.9	1.4	3.6	1.6	21.6

Source: Clements 1988 pp. 15–17, and GATT 1992 Table IV, pp. 14–15.

Fritsch and Franco 1992 p. 9, this was the most important of the export subsidies. The scheme was unusual in that it entailed the signing of long-term contracts (for usually 10 years) by participating firms detailing their export commitments. Aside from these export commitments, firms also had to satisfy minimum local-content requirements in order to qualify for BEFIEX incentives. The contracts were negotiated with the BEFIEX administration on the basis of detailed information on firms' activities and strategic plans. The incentives, in turn, typically included "90% reduction of import duties and the Industrialized Products Tax (IPI) on imported machinery and equipment; 50% reduction on import duties and IPI tax on imported raw materials, parts and components, and other intermediate products; exemption from the 'similarity' test; and income tax exemption on profits attributable to exports of manufactured products" (GATT 1992 p. 104).[11]

Between 1972–1985, 316 contracts were signed, mainly with multinational enterprises in the transport equipment and textile and clothing industries. In the automotive sector, GM, Ford, and VW each committed to $1 billion of exports over ten years, Fiat to $550 million, and Mercedes Benz to $500 million (Shapiro 1993 p. 213; World Bank 1983 p. 257). The effect of the program in this sector was nothing short of dramatic. As shown in figure 1, automotive exports rose from virtually nothing in

1972 to more than $1 billion in 1980. Total exports under BEFIEX contracts increased to $8.2 billion by 1990, at which time the program was phased out as part of an overall trade liberalization. According to a GATT study (1992, p. 104), BEFIEX-linked exports eventually covered about *half* of all manufactured exports.

To an economist, perhaps the most striking thing about BEFIEX is the apparent absence of gaming between firms and the government and of renegotiation of initial contract terms. Participation in BEFIEX meant that firms were under legal obligation to live up to their export commitments, irrespective of economic circumstances such as foreign demand conditions or exchange-rate fluctuations. These were tough terms, and firms apparently lived by them. In her study of the Brazilian automotive industry, Shapiro 1993 mentions instances in which multinationals had to make adjustments to their global strategies—by cutting back exports from third countries, for example—so as not to run afoul of BEFIEX export commitments.[12] This must be confounding to economists who generally believe that long-term contracts are not enforceable, especially when the government is on one side, and must

[11]The "similarity test" in the quote refers to the infamous law that prohibited the importation of foreign products when similar products were available domestically.

[12]In the late 1980s, GM headquarters allowed the Brazilian subsidiary to export engines to GM-Opel (Germany) for the first time, even though the firm's global strategy had assigned the European market to its Australian subsidiary. "GM was forced to grant Brazil access to the European market . . . [because otherwise] GMB [GM-Brazil] would not have been able to meet its export commitments. . . ." (Shapiro 1993 p. 222). Fiat began to export the Uno from Brazil, even though it would not have done so without BEFIEX (ibid. p. 223).

Figure 1. Brazilian automotive exports.

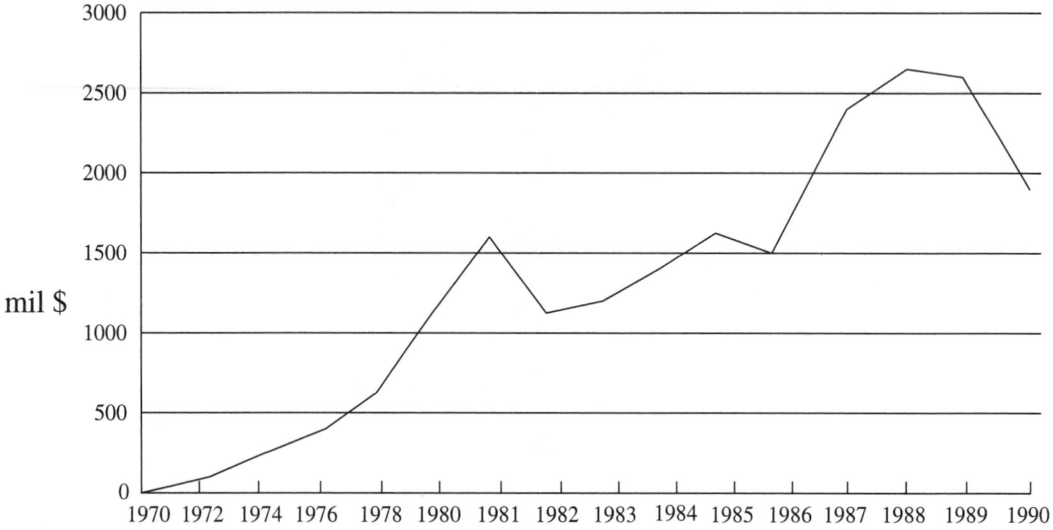

Source: Shapiro (1993, Table 5-4).

come under severe renegotiation pressure in response to unforeseen circumstances. In this instance the Brazilian state had the capacity to discipline firms and was perceived as such. It is difficult to envisage this kind of discipline being exerted in the countries that we will turn to next.[13]

Just as in the Korean case, the reasons for the Brazilian state's strength and autonomy in the area of export policy remain murky. Leff argues in his study of economic policy making during the earlier 1947–64 period that the Brazilian government could always act autonomously from special interest groups, and impose policy rather freely (Leff 1968). His description of Brazil is reminiscent of Jones and Sakong's 1980 analysis of Korea. On pre-1964 export policy, he writes: "policy here was made in direct opposition to the interests of major private groups, the exporters and the landed elites producing primary products, in deference instead to doctrines which commanded widespread influence among the government administrators and in elite opinion" (Leff 1968 p. 77).[14] He lists several reasons for the state's autonomy, and notes in particular the emergence of a strong government *prior* to the development of manufacturing interests.

Evans 1992 presents a rather different picture of the Brazilian state, much less autonomous, and having to contend with important social groups. Evans notes that clientelism was rampant, that the bureaucracy had (compared to Korea, for example) much less of a tradition of meritocracy, and that there was no policy coordination within the state. "Even the military regime, which had the greatest structural potential for insulation from clientelistic pressures, proved unable to construct an administrative guidance relationship with the local industrial elite" (Evans 1992 p. 170). However, he notes the presence of "important pockets of state efficiency," mentioning in particular the state's relationship with the auto sector. The co-existence of pockets of autonomy with general state weakness rings true in light of the macroeconomic crisis in which the Brazilian state—virtually alone in Latin America—still remains deeply mired. It suggests the possibility that state strength may vary not only across time but also across sectors and issues.

Two Failures: Kenya and Bolivia

Kenya

Kenya's export subsidization policy is undistinguished in many respects, including effectiveness. The only thing that recommends it to our attention is the presence of a good study by Patrick Low 1982, who observed it at close distance.

[13]Indeed, in Turkey's case export commitments were formally demanded, but remained on paper.

[14]Hence, Leff leaves no doubt that autonomy did not come with the military coup—it existed prior to 1964. This is important because it suggests that authoritarianism need not be a precondition for autonomy. Jones and Sakong also express doubt about the relationship between authoritarianism and autonomy in the case of Korea: "Until the early 1970s, the Park regime was both hard and reasonably democratic" (1980 p. 140).

Compared to the Korean and Brazilian programs we have just discussed, the Kenyan scheme was on paper an economist's dream: it could not have been simpler, less discretionary, or more uniform. The Local Manufactures (Export Compensation) Act of 1974 applied a straightforward 10 percent export subsidy to most manufactures. (The rate was increased to 20 percent in 1980.) The only restriction was that the value of imported goods could not amount to more than 70 percent of the value of the export. The subsidy was to be paid through commercial banks, after export proceeds were received and after government officials processed the subsidy claims.

The effects of the program were imperceptible. Low 1982 interviewed 55 firms and found that only 16 (29 percent) of them had responded by increasing exported output. The plurality of firms (17, or 31 percent) treated the subsidy simply as a windfall, while 7 firms (13 percent) did not even bother to claim the subsidy. Even more telling is Low's calculation that at the aggregate level less than 30 percent of eligible exports actually received the subsidy. A very large number of exporters either did not claim the subsidy or did not get it.

What seems to have happened is a bit of both. Government officials processing the subsidy claims exercised such zeal that many applications were rejected on trivial grounds. Low spent a day with these officials and observed two claims being rejected, "one because a date had been inadvertently omitted on a form and the other because the quadruplicate instead of the sextuplicate copy of the Export Entry form had been submitted with the claim" (1982 p. 297). The officials also took their time. More than a quarter of the firms interviewed by Low expected to wait more than six months after claims had been filed. And since the claims could not be filed before export proceeds were actually received, the total waiting time was even longer than this. The delay and unpredictability explain why many firms did not bother to claim, and why those that treated the subsidy as a lump-sum payment, did not allow it to influence their export decisions.

At a deeper level, the failure of this program must be attributed to the fact that the Kenyan government never clearly sorted out and prioritized its objectives as they impinged on the export subsidy policy. While encouraging exports (or more correctly reducing the anti-export bias due to import restrictions) was obviously an objective, it did not rank very high in the overall scheme of things. Neither was the apparent conflict with the negative fiscal implications of the program ever resolved. Note that the program was administered by the Customs

and Excise Department, a revenue-raising body. Since providing the subsidy was expensive, the program as it stood was subject to a clear time inconsistency: the dynamically consistent policy was to promise to pay the subsidy but not to do so (since payment was to occur *after* exports had gone out). There was no commitment to exports on the part of the top leadership (as in Korea or Brazil) that would help resolve this dilemma on the side of exports.

In partial recognition of these problems, the government reformed the program in 1980. The subsidy was raised to 20 percent, coverage of the scheme was expanded to almost all non-traditional exports, and an attempt was made to streamline administrative procedures. Two features of the reform deserve special mention. First, the increase in the subsidy was accompanied by an equivalent 10 percent surcharge on imports. This was intended to de-emphasize fiscal considerations in the implementation of the subsidy, but is also indicative of the incoherence of policy: by the Lerner symmetry theorem, the import surcharge served to cancel the effect of the increase in the export subsidy.[15] Second, administrative responsibility for the subsidy scheme was moved from the Customs and Excise Department to the Central Bank, an institution with less stake in revenue and greater reputation for bureaucratic efficiency.

Low's study does not extend to the period after 1980, so we do not have a good account of how these reforms fared. There is reason to be skeptical however. A recent account in *The Economist* (August 14, 1993, pp. 37–38) relates the scandalous story of a Kenyan firm called Goldenberg. This firm, the sole recipient of a license to export gold and jewelry, apparently received $54 million in export subsidies from the Central Bank (amounting to 5 percent of Kenya's total exports!). Not only was the firm paid a subsidy of 35 percent (rather than 20 percent, as the law requires), but the foreign firms to which Goldenberg claimed to have shipped its exports were either fictituous or had never heard of Goldenberg. Kenya's export policy has apparently moved from the Scylla of incentive-blunting diligence to the Charybdis of corrupt generosity.

Bolivia

Between 1987 and 1991, Bolivia had an export subsidy program similar to the Kenyan scheme, which also failed for virtually identical reasons. As the authorities never resolved the conflicting objec-

---

[15]Almost. The equivalence was not exact, of course, because there were prevailing tariffs that were generally higher than the pre-existing 10 percent export subsidy.

tives of safeguarding revenue versus stimulating exports, the exporters reacted by alternatively ignoring the scheme and badly abusing it.

The export subsidy introduced in July 1987 was in principle aimed at reimbursing exports for duties paid in imported inputs (hence the acronym CRA, standing for the initials for Tariff Refund Certificate in Spanish). However, rather than create an explicit drawback scheme which can be an administrative nightmare, the government sensibly set the subsidy at a uniform 10 percent for non-traditional exports and 5 percent for traditional exports. (The top rate was subsequently lowered to 6 percent in August 1990, following a tariff reduction.)

Bolivia had recently come out of a hyperinflation, with inflation running at more than 40,000 percent per annum and a budget deficit of more than 20 percent of GDP prior to the stabilization of August 1985. The authorities were naturally more than slightly nervous about the budgetary implications of the subsidy. Partly for that reason, the entry into force of the CRA was delayed. No CRA certificates were issued before April 1988, and a new regulation in September 1988 retroactively limited the benefits accruing to some of the exporters having earned CRA rights between July 1987 and April 1988. Apparently, no CRA payments were made until 1989 (see GATT 1993 table IV.8). And once payments began to be made, enterprising individuals and firms freely abused the system: there was a famous case of so-called tourist cows (*vacas turistas*) in which cow herds were led across the Bolivian borders several times, collecting CRA benefits at each crossing (GATT 1993 p. 93). The system was finally scrapped in April 1991, and replaced by a narrower scheme with lower financial benefits.

Hence we have once more a clear example of a uniform, transparent scheme which fails because: (i) delays in payments blunt incentive effects early on; and (ii) when payments are made, fraudulent practices take over and cannot be reined in. The government is then forced to narrow the scope of a scheme which has a large fiscal impact but little incentive effect.[16]

Two Intermediate Cases: Turkey and India

Turkey

Turkish economic policy experienced a radical shift to export orientation as a result of a dramatic package of measures undertaken in January 1980 by Turgut Özal (then a top technocrat, and subsequently prime minister and president). Undertaken in the midst of a macroeconomic crisis, the package included a devaluation, fiscal actions, and a series of measures designed to enhance export incentives. Alongside a flexible exchange-rate policy, the generous package of export subsidies did much to contribute to the export boom that ensued (see Arslan and van Wijnbergen 1990 and Uygur 1993 for econometric evidence linking subsidies to export supply). However, it also led to much abuse and a phenomenon that came to be called "fictitious exports"—various forms of fraud designed to take advantage of the financial incentives.

These subsidies were of many types. They comprised export tax rebates (supposedly to compensate for indirect taxes, but going well beyond them), sub-market export credits, foreign exchange allocations which conferred the right to duty-free imports, corporate tax reductions (after 1981), and additional tax rebates for enterprises exporting above a threshold (Milanović 1986, Krueger and Aktan 1992, Togan 1993). The combined ad-valorem equivalent of these subsidies rose to 34 percent in 1983, coming down thereafter to around 26 percent (see table 3). Exports were a top priority for Özal, to the point where "the success of the export drive became almost synonymous with the success of the stabilization program" (Milanović 1986 p. 73). He took pains to ensure that no obstacle stood between an exporter and his claim to a subsidy. One of his key institutional innovations was the centralization of export incentives, which had been previously dispersed among numerous government agencies, into a specific agency, the Directorate of Incentives and Implementation (TUD) within the State Planning Organization. Exporters now had to apply to the TUD to obtain an "export investment certificate," which served as the basis for receiving all the subsidies discussed above. This stood in stark contrast with previous practice whereby an exporter would have to establish his standing with each agency separately. The new system was simple and rapid, and exporters could get their certificates within weeks or days (Krueger and Aktan 1992 p. 76).[17]

---

[16]This combination of delays with fraudulent response is apparently quite general. Additional cases appeared in Senegal and Côte d'Ivoire during the second half of the 1980s, when the governments in both cases decided to undertake a simulated devaluation by increasing import tariffs and export subsidies simultaneously.

[17]There were occasional glitches though. In 1983 and 1984 shortage of government funds led to important arrears in both tax refunds due to exporters and interest rate rebates for export credits due to commercial banks (Milanovic 1986 p. 48).

Table 3. Export Subsidies on Manufactures in Turkey, 1980–86 (%)

	Tax rebates	Export credits	Foreign exchange retention & allocation	VAT exemption	Others	Total
1980	5.9	5.5	5.8	—	0.0	17.2
1981	3.6	6.4	4.9	—	4.0	15.3
1982	9.5	7.2	6.7	—	6.0	24.0
1983	11.8	7.9	13.0	—	1.5	34.2
1984	11.3	6.0	4.0	—	2.0	23.3
1985	3.1	3.2	3.9	10.0	5.8	26.0
1986	1.9	3.6	6.5	10.2	4.6	26.8

Source: Krueger and Aktan 1992 Table 14.

Obtaining the export certificate entailed the undertaking of a quantitative export commitment on whose realization the granting of incentives in principle depended (Milanović 1986 p. 6). In practice, this was a commitment that the government easily waived. According to Krueger and Aktan 1992 p. 247 fn. 5: "If, for some reason, the export was not realized, [the firms] simply notified TUD/TUB that they would not be exporting that amount, and there was no penalty." Firms believed that the authorities would impose penalties only in cases where the certificate had been obtained with no intent to export at all (ibid.).

As mentioned above, these subsidies led to widespread abuse. Documented cases included instances in which: (i) low-value items such as scrap metal or stones were exported under the guise of industrial products with high tax-rebate rates; (ii) low- or medium-grade items (such as common rugs) were over-invoiced as high-grade (silk rugs); (iii) the quantity shipped was overstated, as in the case of leather wallets whose number was blown up by a factor of 100;[18] and (iv) the most egregious of all, entire export operations took place on paper only, with no physical transaction ever taking place (these and other cases are detailed in a popular book by Çetin 1988).

An attempt to quantify the extent of over-invoicing and other mischief that took place is shown in figure 2. These estimates are based on comparisons of Turkish export statistics with OECD statistics for imports from Turkey. The presence of over-invoicing is unmistakable. Until 1981, the calculations reveal a small *under*-invoicing, which is not surprising in view of the black-market premium for foreign currency that existed prior to the 1980 sta-

bilization. But over the course of the first half of the 1980s, over-invoicing increased steadily, reaching more than 25 percent of export value by 1984. It thereafter decreased sharply, partly because of the decline in subsidies and partly because "fictitious exports" became a hot political issue and became risky for all but the most adventurous of firms. It should be mentioned, however, that the Turkish export boom of the 1980s looks only slightly less impressive when over-invoicing is taken into account. In other words, the boom was not a statistical illusion by any stretch of the imagination.

Özal, who was a brilliant technocrat, was fully aware of the abuses that the subsidies were giving rise to. State officials had large numbers of files on suspected abuses. But Özal firmly resisted the Turkish bureaucracy's inclination to tighten the regulations and prosecute the fraudulent cases (Çetin 1988). He feared that unleashing the bureaucracy on exporters would do more harm than good and discourage the legitimate exporter alongside the fictitious one. Put differently, unlike in the Korean and Brazilian cases, the Turkish bureaucracy could not be trusted to find the right balance between providing incentives and discouraging potential abusers. He thus understood very well the dilemma of a weak state: the carrot and the stick may not be available simultaneously, so one has to go with one or the other. A corollary is what we may call the second-best law for weak states: a weak state may become less effective in trying to act strong.

India

Until very recently, India was hardly known for its pro-export policies. Export subsidies of one kind or another have always been part of the Indian policy landscape, but these were greatly overshad-

---

[18]This case came to light because the exporting firm had neglected to raise the weight of the shipment by the same factor, leading to ridiculously low unit weights (Çetin 1988 p. 34).

Figure 2. Over-invoicing in Turkish exports to the OECD.

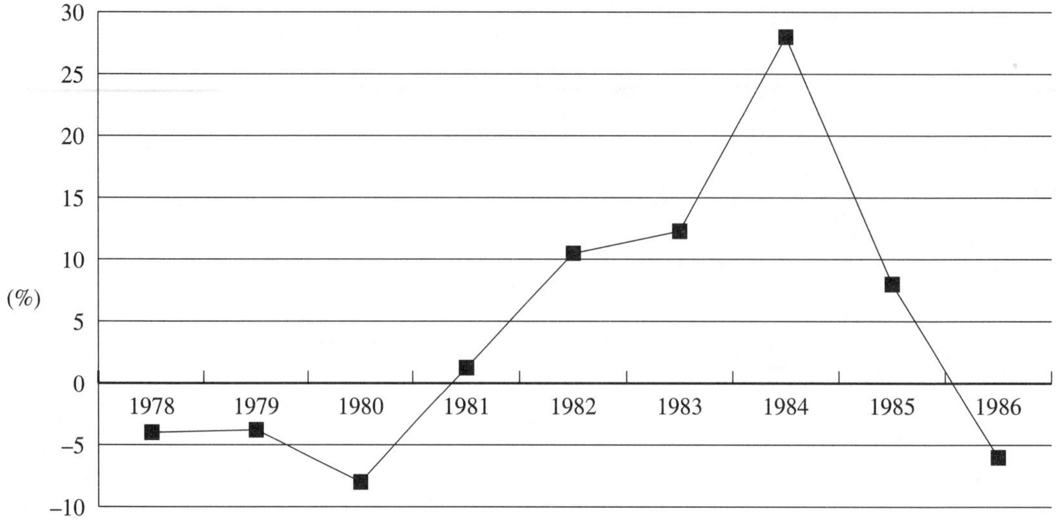

Source: Rodrik (1988).

owed by a highly restrictive import regime. Here I will focus on the period before the devaluation of 1966, on which we have the excellent and enormously detailed study by Bhagwati and Desai 1970. This is a case of mixed success, somewhat like Turkey's except less stark. The subsidies in place appear to have played a role in stimulating exports, but they also led to fraud.

Indian exporters had already access to a variety of fiscal subsidies during the late 1950s, but these were considerably strengthened in the course of the early 1960s. The most significant subsidy, on which I will concentrate, was an import entitlement scheme under which exporters were awarded import licenses in proportion to the value of their exports. According to Bhagwati and Desai 1970 p. 406, the average premiums for import licenses were of the order of 70–80 percent, so the incentive effect of this policy can be easily imagined.

Bhagwati and Desai characterize Indian state administration in the trade policy area as "ad hocism at the top and corruption at the bottom" (1970 p. 134). Yet the import entitlement scheme started out as a relatively non-discretionary program with well-defined rules. Two principles were laid down at the outset to govern the scheme's administration: (i) import entitlements would not exceed 75 percent of the f.o.b. value of exports; and (ii) subject to the previous constraint, the entitlement would equal only twice the value of an exporting firm's import content (ibid. p. 409). As it turned out, these rules were frequently flouted by the authorities who were anxious to demonstrate success on the export front. Note that since subsidies consisted of import licenses, they had no immediate fiscal impact (unlike in Bolivia and Kenya), and there was consequently little inherent resistance to awarding them. In turn, the officials were aided in this by exporters themselves who naturally lobbied for the most generous terms possible. As Bhagwati and Desai put it, the increasing subsidy "reflected the growing pressure to make exports more profitable, on the part of the exporters, combined with an accommodating Ministry whose objective was to maximize export earnings" (ibid. p. 426).

Given these pressures, the Indian export subsidy scheme eventually took on a perverse quality with subsidies awarded in inverse relationship to an exporter's competitiveness. That is, exporters could get a subsidy large enough to make their exports profitable by manipulating the government: "it became generally possible to ask the Ministry of International Trade for ad hoc entitlements, for chemical and engineering exports, to make up for any ostensible difference between the domestic sale price of a product and its supposed f.o.b. export price plus the subsidy normally available" (ibid. pp. 465–66). Bhagwati and Desai also note that the scheme resulted in significant over-invoicing, as in Turkey.[19]

[19]They point out that partner-country trade statistics were not helpful to get a sense of the magnitude of over-invoicing in this case because the over-invoicing occurred with free ports like Aden, Hong Kong, and Panama.

For all its problems, Bhagwati and Desai credit the export subsidies of the period as being "undoubtedly instrumental in sustaining the spurt in the Indian export performance during the Third Plan [April 1961–March 1966]" (ibid. p. 429).

Concluding Remarks

These stories reveal a wide variety of experience with export subsidies. Policies that look identical on the books often produce different results, and policies that appear ex ante well designed frequently result in failure. Perhaps the greatest surprise is that the most successful programs in our sample were the ones in which state officials exercised the greatest discretion, applied the least uniformity (at least ex ante), and interacted the most intensively with firms. The other cases, however, make clear that these successful experiences cannot easily be replicated in settings characterized by weak states.[20]

The message that comes out of the cases is both pessimistic and optimistic as regards state capabilities. On the one hand, the importance of state autonomy, which seems to be determined largely by historical and structural factors, underscores the point that the range of options open to most governments may be fairly limited. On the other hand, policy coherence alone counts for something: weak states can achieve some of their objectives if their priorities are sufficiently crystallized and if they are creative in designing appropriate institutional frameworks. Centralizing subsidy functions in a high-visibility agency (as in Turkey) or processing claims through the trade ministry rather than the finance ministry (as in India) are examples of institutional considerations that may make a large difference in practice. Priorities are most clearly articulated and communicated when there exists political commitment on the part of the top leadership: in Korea, Brazil, Turkey, success derived in part from the clear, unmitigated commitment to exports by new regimes. The case of export subsidies shows that normally incoherent states can produce coherent policies when they attach a sufficiently high priority to them. On the other hand, nothing is more distinctive about weak states than a multiplicity of conflicting government objectives.

---

[20]It is useful to interject here Hernando de Soto's poignant complaints about the unpredictability of policy-making in Peru: "It is simply untrue that, in Peru, we are all equal before the law, because no two people pay the same tax, no two imports are taxed in the same way, no two exports are subsidized in the same way, and no two individuals have the same right to credit. . . . Uncertainty is constant in the redistributive state, for the Peruvians are aware that the executive branch, which issues some 110 regulations and decisions each working day, can change the rules of the game at any moment without prior consultation or debate" (1989 pp. 195–199). These complaints ring true to anyone who has observed policy making in developing countries. The trouble is that, absent the reference to the redistributive state, this statement is equally valid for Korean policy making. Jones and Sakong resolve the paradox in the following manner: "the lesson of the Korean case is that in a hard state with leadership commitment to growth, the Myrdalian objections to discretionary controls on economic grounds may be obviated. Just as compulsion is necessary, so also is discretion. Both mechanisms are potentially subject to great abuse, and their use constitutes a high-risk/high-gain strategy which is feasible only in a Myrdalian hard state" (1980 p. 139).

References

Amsden, Alice H. 1989. *Asia's Next Giant: South Korea and Late Industrialization.* New York: Oxford University Press.

Arslan, İsmail, and Sweder van Wijnbergen. 1990. "Turkey: Export Miracle or Accounting Trick?" Washington, DC: World Bank Discussion Paper WPS 370.

Balassa, Bela. 1978. "Export Incentives and Export Performance in Developing Countries: A Comparative Analysis," *Weltwirtschaftliches Archiv* 114: 24–61.

Barkey, Karen, and Sunita Parikh. 1991. "Comparative Perspectives on the State," *Annual Review of Sociology* 17: 523–49.

Bhagwati, Jagdish N., and Padma Desai. 1970. *India: Planning for Industrialization.* London: Oxford University Press.

Calvo, Guillermo. 1989. "Incredible Reforms," in G. Calvo et al. (eds.), *Debt, Stabilization, and Development: Essays in Honor of Carlos Diaz-Alejandro.* New York: Basil Blackwell.

Clements, Benedict J. 1988. *Foreign Trade Strategies, Employment, and Income Distribution in Brazil.* New York: Praeger.

Çetin, Bilal. 1988. *Soygun: Hayali İhracatın Boyutları* [Hold-Up: Dimensions of Fictitious Exporting]. Ankara: Bilgi Yayınları.

De Soto, Hernando. 1989. *The Other Path: The Invisible Revolution in the Third World.* New York: Harper & Row.

Dixit, Avinash. 1989. "Trade and Insurance with Adverse Selection," *Review of Economic Studies* 56: 235–47.

Evans, Peter. 1979. *Dependent Development: The Alliance of Multinationals, State, and Local Capital in Brazil.* Princeton, NJ: Princeton University Press.

Evans, Peter. 1992. "The State as Problem and Solution: Predation, Embedded Autonomy, and Structural Change," in S. Haggard and R. Kaufman (eds.), *The Politics of Adjustment.* Princeton, NJ: Princeton University Press.

Fasano-Filho, Ugo, Bernard Fischer, and Peter Nunnenkamp. 1987. *On the Determinants of Brazil's Manufactured Exports: An Empirical Analysis.* Tubingen: J.C.B. Mohr (Paul Siebeck).

Frank, Charles R., Jr., Kwang Suk Kim, and Larry E. Westphal. 1975. *Foreign Trade Regimes and Economic Development: South Korea.* New York and London: Columbia University Press.

Fritsch, Winston, and Gustavo H.B. Franco. 1992. "Brazil as an Exporter of Manufacturers," unpublished manuscript.

GATT. 1992. *Trade Policy Review Mechanism: Brazil.* Geneva: GATT.

GATT. 1993. *Trade Policy Review Mechanism: Bolivia.* Geneva: GATT.

Grossman, Gene, and Elhanan Helpman. 1992. "Protection for Sale," unpublished manuscript, Princeton University.

Jones, Leroy P., and Il Sakong. 1980. *Government, Business, and Entrepreneurship in Economic Development: The Korean Case.* Cambridge, MA: Harvard University Press.

Jung, Woo S., and Gyu Lee. 1986. "The Effectiveness of Export Promotion Policies: The Case of Korea," *Weltwirtschaftliches Archiv* 122: 340–357.

Krueger, Anne O. 1974. "The Political Economy of the Rent-Seeking Society," *American Economic Review* 64: 291–303.

Krueger, Anne O., and Okan H. Aktan. 1992. *Swimming Against the Tide: Turkish Trade Reform in the 1980s.* San Francisco: ICS Press.

Leff, Nathaniel H. 1968. *Economic Policy-Making and Development in Brazil 1947–1964.* New York: John Wiley & Sons.

Levy, Brian. 1993. "An Institutional Analysis of the Design and Sequencing of Trade and Investment Policy Reform," *The World Bank Economic Review* 7: 247–262.

Low, Patrick. 1982. "Export Subsidies and Trade Policy: The Experience of Kenya," *World Development* 10: 293–304.

Matsuyama, Kiminori. 1990. "Perfect Equilibria in a Trade Liberalization Game," *American Economic Review* 80: 480–92.

Migdal, Joel. 1988. *Strong Societies and Weak States.* Princeton, NJ: Princeton University Press.

Milanović, Branko. 1986. *Export Incentives and Turkish Manufactured Exports, 1980–1984,* The World Bank, Staff Working Papers No. 768, Washington, DC.

Myrdal, Gunnar. 1968. *Asian Drama: An Inquiry into the Poverty of Nations.* New York: Pantheon.

Nogués, Julio. 1990. "The Experience of Latin America with Export Subsidies," *Weltwirtschaftliches Archiv* 126: 97–115.

Panagariya, Arvind. 1993. "Unravelling the Mysteries of China's Foreign Trade Regime," *The World Economy* 16: 51–68.

Pindyck, Robert S., and Andrés Solimano. 1993. "Economic Instability and Aggregate Investment," NBER Working Paper No. 4380.

Rhee, Yung Whee, Bruce Ross-Larson, and Garry Pursell. 1984. *Korea's Competitive Edge: Managing the Entry into World Markets.* Baltimore and London: The Johns Hopkins University Press.

Rodrik, Dani. 1991. "Policy Uncertainty and Private Investment in Developing Countries," *Journal of Development Economics* 36: 229–242.

Rodrik, Dani. 1992. "Political Economy and Development Policy," *European Economic Review* 36: 329–336.

Shapiro, Helen. 1993. "Automobiles: From Import Substitution to Export Promotion in Brazil and Mexico," in D. Yoffie (ed.), *Beyond Free Trade: Firms, Governments, and Global Competition.* Boston, MA: Harvard Business School Press.

Shleifer, Andrei, and Robert Vishny. 1991. "Pervasive Shortages under Socialism," NBER Working Paper No. 3791.

Staiger, Robert W., and Guido Tabellini. 1987. "Discretionary Trade Policy and Excessive Protection," *American Economic Review* 77: 823–837.

Thomas, Vinod, and John Nash. 1991. "Reform of Trade Policy: Recent Evidence from Theory and Practice," *The World Bank Research Observer* 6: 219–240.

Togan, Sübidey. 1993. "How to Assess the Significance of Export Incentives: An Application to Turkey," Bilkent University (forthcoming, *Weltwirtschaftliches Archiv*).

Uygur, Ercan. 1993. "Trade Policies and Economic Performance in Turkey in the 1980s," unpublished paper, Faculty of Political Science, Ankara University.

Westphal, Larry E. 1990. "Industrial Policy in an Export-Propelled Economy: Lessons from South Korea's Experience," *Journal of Economic Perspectives* 4: 41–59.

World Bank. 1983. *Brazil: Industrial Policies and Manufactured Exports.* Washington, DC.

Selection IX.C.4. Bureaucratic Structure and Bureaucratic Performance in Less Developed Countries*

I. Introduction

. . . In this paper we will be especially concerned with ratings of the performance of the central government bureaucracy. Knack and Keefer (1995) use ratings by the International Country Risk Guide (ICRG) of "corruption in government" and "bureaucratic quality" in one of their indices of institutional quality and use a rating by Business and Environmental Risk Intelligence (BERI) of "bureaucratic delays" in the other, and Mauro (1995) uses ratings by Business International (BI) of "bureaucracy and red tape" and "corruption" in his index of bureaucratic efficiency. Knack and Keefer find positive and significant effects of both of their institutional quality indices on growth in per capita GDP, and Mauro finds the same for his index of bureaucratic efficiency.

While the cross-country statistical evidence reinforces the idea that differential governmental performance may have an impact on economic growth, it tells us little about what kind of institutional characteristics are associated with lower levels of corruption or red tape. If the findings just listed are meaningful, it is worth identifying which characteristics of government bureaucracies lead to good ratings from the ICRG, BERI, and BI on the variables cited above. This is our aim in the present paper. . . .

Our data collection and analysis will be guided by what we call the "Weberian state hypothesis." Drawing on the original insight of Weber (1968 [1904–1911]), Evans (1992, 1995) argues that replacement of a patronage system for state officials by a professional state bureaucracy is a necessary (though not sufficient) condition for a state to be "developmental." The key institutional characteristics of what he calls "Weberian" bureaucracy include meritocratic recruitment through competitive examinations, civil service procedures for hiring and firing rather than political appointments and dismissals, and filling higher levels of the hierarchy through internal promotion.

To test the Weberian state hypothesis (actually several related hypotheses), we collected original data on various elements of bureaucratic structure for 35 countries. The next section of this paper describes our hypotheses more fully and contrasts them with other views of the determinants of bureaucratic performance. . . .

II. Theoretical Approach

In the economics literature, bureaucratic performance is typically addressed using a principal-agent model. The case studies described by Klitgaard (1988) leave little doubt that a powerful and determined outside monitor (principal) can reduce corruption and improve delivery of services by his bureaucratic agents. Milgrom and Roberts (1992) give a comprehensive theoretical treatment of the strategies a principal can use to elicit better performance from his agents, such as performance-based pay and (implicit) tournaments among employees for higher-level positions.[1] These strategies have been incorporated into "the new public management" (Aucoin 1990, Caiden 1988), which to date has been applied most extensively in New Zealand (Boston et al. 1991).

A drawback of the principal-agent approach is that to some extent it assumes away the problem, especially in an LDC context, because the political will to engage in vigorous monitoring and implement appropriate strategies is lacking, or worse yet the principal is himself corrupt. Rose-Ackerman (1997, p. 48) notes that "behind all proposals for civil service reform is an effective set of internal controls or of antibribery laws with vigorous enforcement," leaving one to wonder what can be done if vigorous enforcement is not available. It follows that reforms that make weaker demands on outside monitors or the political system for their implementation and enforcement are of considerable interest.

We believe that the reforms that constitute the Weberian state have this property. Enforcement of meritocratic recruitment requires verification of whether entry into government service has been conditioned on passage of a civil service exam or attainment of a university degree. Implementation of internal promotion requires that higher-level agency positions be filled by current agency employees or at least current members of the civil service. Maintenance of competitive salaries requires

*From James E. Rauch and Peter B. Evans, "Bureaucratic Structure and Bureaucratic Performance in Less Developed Countries," *Journal of Public Economics* 75 (January 2000): 49–62. Reprinted by permission.

[1]Another strand of the literature addresses the effects of interagency competition on corruption (Rose-Ackerman 1978, Shleifer and Vishny 1993). In this paper we examine only intraagency bureaucratic structure.

a simple comparison with private sector numbers. It is precisely the relative ease with which one can observe whether and to what extent these rules are being followed that makes possible our empirical analysis below. In contrast, consider the effort that must be made to evaluate "performance" in pay-for-performance schemes (Milgrom and Roberts 1992, pp. 464–469), or the initiative that must be taken to implement "strong financial management systems that audit government accounts and make financial information about the government public" (Rose-Ackerman 1997, pp. 49–50).

How do the ingredients of the Weberian state combine to produce good bureaucratic performance? We first present an argument based on Evans (1992, 1995). Making entry to the bureaucracy conditional on passing a civil service exam or attaining a university degree, and paying salaries comparable to those for private positions requiring similar skills and responsibility, should produce a capable pool of officials. The stability provided by internal promotion allows formation of stronger ties among them. This improves communication, and therefore effectiveness. It also increases each official's concern with what his colleagues think of him, leading to greater adherence to norms of behavior. Since the officials entered the bureaucracy on the basis of merit, effective performance is likely to be a valued attribute among them rather than, say, how much one can accomplish on behalf of one's clan. The long-term career rewards generated by a system of internal promotion should reinforce adherence to codified rules of behavior. Ideally, a sense of commitment to corporate goals and "esprit de corps" develop.

The work of Rauch (1995) attempts to marry the Weberian state hypothesis to a principal-agent framework. Internal promotion is defined as recruiting the principal from the ranks of the agents. Only the principal exercises power in the sense of deciding (or at least influencing) the mix of services the bureaucracy will supply. Individuals are assumed to differ in their desire to impose their preferences over collective goods on the public. Imposing preferences requires that the bureaucracy as a whole be effective in fulfilling its mission. A principal who values exercise of power highly will spend more time supervising her agents to ensure that they are carrying out their tasks (and thereby implementing her preferences), and less time looking for ways to line her own pockets. With internal promotion, agents who hope to exercise power themselves will be more responsive to any effective supervision in order to increase their chances of becoming principal. Since agents who care about power are more

likely to become principal, principals are more likely to care about power and therefore supervise their agents more closely. It follows that given any positive initial level of supervision, internal promotion generates a virtuous circle that increases (in expectation) the value the principal places on exercise of power, tending to increase the extent to which the bureaucracy as a whole carries out its assigned tasks of public goods provision and decrease the extent to which it implicitly taxes the private sector through large-scale corruption. Competitive salaries and meritocratic recruitment are of only secondary importance for bureaucratic performance in this model.

The arguments of both Evans (1992, 1995) and Rauch (1995) for the virtues of the Weberian state are based largely on the effects of selection and the development of norms. A more standard incentive-based analysis may reach different conclusions. Regarding meritocratic recruitment, a civil service system typically entails not only examinations but also civil service protection, and it could be argued that bureaucrats with civil service protection are less motivated to perform since it is more difficult to fire them. In other words, a civil service system entails worse monitoring conditions for the bureaucracy. . . . Exams and other credentials may not select for relevant skills but instead may function mainly as barriers to entry that shield incumbent officials from competition from qualified outsiders. Similarly, internal promotion may simply prevent the best candidates from being appointed to higher positions when they are open.[2] Only regarding the benefits of competitive salaries will the standard analysis agree, pointing in particular to the reduction in the incentives to take bribes given the presumed reduction in the marginal utility of income and increase in the disutility of being fired if one is caught in corrupt activity.

In the long run, however, we feel that there is no contradiction between the Weberian approach to bureaucratic reform and "the new public management." Instead, the former can be seen as part of the preconditions for implementing the latter, as suggested by the following quotation from a World Bank debate (Bale and Dale 1998, Schick 1998) over the applicability of New Zealand's reforms to LDCs (p. 116):

The following precedents formed the basis for the reforms adopted in New Zealand: a tradition of a politi-

---

[2]Overall, the Weberian state hypothesis is similar to a "Williamsonian" (1985) argument that governance structures that limit the extent of competition may sometimes have more than compensating benefits.

cally neutral, relatively competent civil service; little concern about corruption or nepotism; a consistent and well-enforced legal code, including contract law; a well-functioning political market; and a competent, but suppressed, private sector. The right reform mix for any developing country must reflect any major differences in these preconditions; New Zealand's reforms cannot simply be transplanted.

III. Collection of Original Data

Our collection of data on bureaucratic structure proceeded in three steps. First, we developed and pretested a survey to be filled out by country experts. Second, we identified a sample of countries for which we thought it was feasible to collect accurate data on the core economic agencies. Third, we sent out the final version of our survey with the goal of obtaining responses from at least three experts per country for purposes of cross-validation. We met this goal in all but three cases (see Table 1). . . .

Feasibility and maintenance of data quality required us to sample less than the entire universe of countries. The same concerns led us to restrict our coverage of agencies within a country. We chose to focus on the core economic agencies.[3]. . . Using our data on the bureaucratic structure of core economic agencies to explain the privately produced measures of bureaucratic performance cited in the Introduction creates a problem if these agencies are, for example, "pockets of efficiency" with bureaucratic structures that are more "Weberian" than is typical of the rest of the state bureaucracy. Since these measures of bureaucratic performance are intended to serve the needs of transnational investors, this problem may be somewhat mitigated if these investors mainly deal with officials who are employed by (or heavily influenced by) the core economic agencies. . . .

The [survey] questions that we deemed relevant for this study, and their codings, are reproduced in Table 2. We used the average of the coded expert responses for each country.[4] These questions were

[3]The respondents were asked to choose "the four most important agencies in the central state bureaucracy in order of their power to shape overall economic policy." The Ministry of Finance was the most commonly listed agency, followed at a distance by the Planning Ministry/Board and Ministry of Trade/Commerce/Industry. Other agencies represented include the President's/Prime Minister's office (or Royal Palace), Central Bank, and Ministry of Defense.

[4]For all questions used in the analysis below, the between-country variance far outweighed the variance among experts assessing the same country.

Table 1. Sample of 35 Countries World Bank Country ID and Number of Expert Survey Respondents Per Country

Country	ID	Number
Argentina	ARG	3
Brazil	BRA	4
Chile	CHL	4
Cote D'Ivoire	CIV	3
Colombia	COL	4
Costa Rica	CRI	3
Dominican Republic	DOM	5
Ecuador	ECU	3
Egypt	EGY	3
Greece	GRC	5
Guatemala	GTM	4
Haiti	HTI	4
Hong Kong	HKG	3
India	IND	3
Israel	ISR	3
Kenya	KEN	3
(S.) Korea	KOR	3
Malaysia	MYS	3
Mexico	MEX	4
Morocco	MAR	2
Nigeria	NGA	3
Pakistan	PAK	3
Peru	PER	5
Philippines	PHL	4
Portugal	PRT	4
Singapore	SGP	4
Spain	ESP	5
Sri Lanka	LKA	5
Syria	SYR	4
Taiwan	OAN	4
Thailand	THA	2
Tunisia	TUN	5
Turkey	TUR	4
Uruguay	URY	2
Zaire	ZAR	3

almost always answered in terms of an assessment of the period 1970–1990 as a whole. The questions virtually always require quantitative rather than qualitative answers in order to minimize the possibility that the expert responses would be influenced by their perceptions of bureaucratic performance, thereby introducing spurious correlation between our measures of bureaucratic structure and the ratings of bureaucratic performance we seek to explain.

Questions 4–5 in Table 2 address the extent to which recruitment is meritocratic at the entry level. *MERIT* is an equal-weight index of the two questions, where each question and the index itself have been normalized to lie in the range 0–1. Question 8,

Table 2. Construction of Bureaucratic Structure Indices from Survey Responses

[We are interested primarily in what these bureaucracies looked like in the recent past, roughly 1970–1990. In answering the following questions, assume that "higher officials" refers to those who hold roughly the top 500 positions in the core economic agencies you have discussed above.]

Q4. Approximately what proportion of the higher officials in these agencies enter the civil service via a formal examination system?
Codes: 1 = less than 30%, 2 = 30%–60%, 3 = 60%–90%, 4 = more than 90%

Q5. Of those that do *not* enter via examinations, what proportion have university or post-graduate degrees?
Codes: 1= less than 30%, 2 = 30%–60%, 3 = 60%–90%, 4 = more than 90%

$$MERIT \text{ index} = [(Q4 - 1)/3 + (Q5 - 1)/3]/2$$

Q6. Roughly how many of the top levels in these agencies are political appointees (e.g., appointed by the President or Chief Executive)?
Codes: 1 = none, 2 = just agency chiefs, 3 = agency chiefs and vice-chiefs, 4 = all of top 2 or 3 levels.

Q7. Of political appointees to these positions, what proportion are likely to already be members of the higher civil service?
Codes: 1 = less than 30%, 2 = 30%–70%, 3 = more than 70%

Q8. Of those promoted to the top 2 or 3 levels in these agencies (whether or not they are political appointees), what proportion come from within the agency itself or (its associated ministry(ies) if the agency is not itself a ministry)?
Codes: 1 = less than 50%, 2 = 50%–70%, 3 = 70%–90%, 4 = over 90%

Q10. What is roughly the modal number of years spent by a typical higher-level official in one of these agencies during his career?
Codes: 1 = 1–5 years, 2 = 5–10 years, 3 = 10–20 years, 4 = entire career

Q11. What prospects for promotion can someone who enters one of these agencies through a higher civil service examination early in his/her career reasonably expect? Assuming that there are at least a half dozen steps or levels between an entry-level position and the head of the agency, how would you characterize the possibilities for moving up in the agency?
Codes: 2, if respondent circled "if performance is superior, moving up several levels to the level just below political appointees is not an unreasonable expectation" or "in at least a few cases, could expect to move up several levels within the civil service and then move up to the very top of the agency on the basis of political appointments" and *not* "in most cases, will move up one or two levels but no more" or "in most cases, will move up three or four levels, but unlikely to reach the level just below political appointees"; 1 otherwise.

$$CAREER \text{ index} = [(4 - Q6)/3 + (Q7 - 1)/2 + (Q8 - 1)/3 + (Q10 - 1)/3 + (Q11 - 1)]/5$$

Q14. How would you estimate the salaries (and perquisites, not including bribes or other extralegal sources of income) of higher officials in these agencies relative to those of private sector managers with roughly comparable training and responsibilities?
Codes: 1 = less than 50%, 2 = 50%–80%, 3 = 80%–90%, 4 = comparable, 5 = higher

Q16. Over the period in question (roughly 1970–1990) what was the movement of legal income in these agencies relative to salaries in the private sector?
Codes: 1 = declined dramatically, 2 = declined slightly, 3 = maintained the same position, 4 = improved their position

$$SALARY \text{ index} = [(Q14 - 1)/4 + (Q16 - 1)/3]/2$$

and to a lesser extent questions 6, 7, and 11, pertain to the extent of internal promotion, whereas question 10 addresses career stability. *CAREER* is an equal-weight index of questions 6–8 and 10–11. Question 14 concerns the level and question 16 concerns the change of bureaucratic compensation relative to the private sector. *SALARY* is an equal-weight index of these two questions. . . .

IV. Testing the Weberian State Hypotheses

We will seek to explain the cross-country variation in the five measures of bureaucratic performance, cited in the Introduction, that are available to us from private ratings services. These are described in Table 3, listed in the order in which we will use them as dependent variables in the data

Table 3. Available Measures of Bureaucratic Performance

Variable	Country coverage	Time coverage	Definition
CORRUPT1 Source: ICRG Scored 0–6	complete	1982–1990	Low scores indicate "high government officials are likely to demand special payments" and "illegal payments are generally expected throughout lower levels of government" in the form of "bribes connected with import and export licenses, exchange controls, tax assessment, police protection, or loans" (quoted from Knack and Keefer 1995)
BURQUAL Source: ICRG Scored 0–6	complete	1982–1990	High scores indicate "autonomy from political pressure" and "strength and expertise to govern without drastic changes in policy or interruptions in government services"; also existence of an "established mechanism for recruiting and training" (quoted from Knack and Keefer 1995).
BURDELAY Source: BERI Scored 1–4	missing Costa Rica, Dominican Republic, Guatemala, Haiti, Hong Kong, Sri Lanka, Syria, Tunisia, and Uruguay	1972–1990	High scores indicate greater "speed and efficiency of the civil service including processing customs clearances, foreign exchange remittances and similar applications" (quoted from Knack and Keefer 1995).
REDTAPE Source: BI Scored 0–10	missing Costa Rica, Guatemala, Syria, and Tunisia	1981–1989; only certain years in this period for a few countries	Measures "the regulatory environment foreign firms must face when seeking approvals and permits; the degree to which government represents an obstacle to business" (quoted from Mauro 1995); lower scores indicate greater levels of regulation and/or government obstruction.
CORRUPT2 Source: BI Scored 0–10	missing Costa Rica, Guatemala, Syria, and Tunisia	1981–1989; only certain years in this period for a few countries	Measures "the degree to which business transactions involve corruption or questionable payments" (quoted from Mauro 1995); lower scores indicate greater levels of corruption.

analysis. Two of these measures require additional comment. First, the definition of *BURQUAL* indicates that it measures not only an aspect of bureaucratic performance but also some of the same elements of bureaucratic structure that are addressed by our survey. It follows that while a positive and significant effect of our indices on this variable provides some information, in the absence of similar effects on other measures of bureaucratic performance such a finding could not be considered important evidence in favor of our hypotheses. Second, it should be noted that unlike *CORRUPT1*, *CORRUPT2* is not necessarily an indicator of bureaucratic performance: it is not clear whether the "corruption or questionable payments" in the definition are made to government officials or to private sector managers such as purchasing agents. . . .

In attempting to explain these measures of bureaucratic performance, the question arises as to what control variables to include along with our measures of bureaucratic structure. Rauch and Evans (1999, Figure 1a) show a strong tendency for high income countries to have high bureaucratic performance ratings, and Weberian state characteristics are also likely to be positively correlated with country income, so it seems clear that we should control for level of development. Our measure of level of development, *RGDP,* will be GDP per capita at the beginning of the time period for which the dependent variable is available, corrected for differences in purchasing power across countries (Summers and Heston 1991). It also seems prudent to control for country level of education. Countries with higher levels of education may be more likely to adopt meritocratic recruitment procedures, and

Table 4. Testing the Weberian State Hypotheses

Dependent Variable	CORRUPT1	CORRUPT1	BURQUAL	BURQUAL	BURDELAY	BURDELAY	REDTAPE	REDTAPE	CORRUPT2	CORRUPT2
Intercept	0.762	0.751	1.344	1.391	0.724	0.783	1.986	3.621	2.588	2.487
	(0.542)	(0.344)	(0.526)	(0.354)	(0.248)	(0.176)	(1.024)	(0.513)	(1.190)	(0.756)
MERIT	2.175[c]	1.671[a]	2.287[b]	2.032[a]	0.067	0.589[b]	1.832		2.544	
	(1.108)	(0.542)	(1.074)	(0.558)	(0.521)	(0.267)	(2.138)		(2.485)	
CAREER	-0.876		-0.468		0.580		-0.514		-1.407	
	(1.391)		(1.349)		(0.592)		(2.513)		(2.921)	
SALARY	0.451		0.810		1.161[a]	1.220[a]	1.998		-1.368	
	(0.849)		(0.823)		(0.348)	(0.307)	(1.548)		(1.800)	
RGDP	0.000332[a]	0.000373[a]	0.000119	0.000136[b]	0.000010	0.000084[a]	0.000276	0.000509[a]	0.000370[c]	0.000382[b]
	(0.000097)	(0.000063)	(0.000094)	(0.000064)	(0.000058)	(0.000036)	(0.000178)	(0.000121)	(0.000207)	(0.000167)
HUMCAP	0.036		-0.009		0.099[c]		0.239		0.333	0.418[b]
	(0.101)		(0.098)		(0.052)		(0.189)		(0.220)	(0.198)
ETHFRAC	-0.0015		-0.0014		-0.000326		-0.0018		-0.0052	
	(0.0059)		(0.0058)		(0.0024)		(0.0112)		(0.0130)	
n	32	35	32	35	23	26	28	31	28	28
R²	0.672	0.666	0.505	0.442	0.698	0.636	0.558	0.378	0.545	0.507
Root MSE	0.825	0.754	0.799	0.776	0.289	0.281	1.432	1.534	1.664	1.587

1970 value of *HUMCAP* and *RGDP* for *BURDELAY*; 1980 value of *HUMCAP* and *RGDP* for all other dependent variables. Standard errors in parentheses.

[a]Significant at the one percent level.
[b]Significant at the five percent level.
[c]Significant at the ten percent level.

at the same time education could affect bureaucratic performance by enabling the population to better monitor the state bureaucracy, and may also help on the supply side by improving the pool of applicants for the officialdom. Our education measure, *HUMCAP*, is the average years of schooling in the population over age 25, as compiled by Barro and Lee (1993). This variable is available only at five-year intervals, is missing for three countries in our sample (Cote d'Ivoire, Morocco, and Nigeria), and is available only in 1975 for Egypt. Except for Egypt, we use the 1980 value to explain all dependent variables except *BURDELAY,* for which we use the 1970 value. (For consistency we also use the 1980 or 1970 values of *RGDP.*) Finally, we control for the ethnic diversity of a country. Easterly and Levine (1997) present both arguments and country anecdotes supporting the view that ethnic diversity generates more competition for government-created rents, leading to greater corruption and poorer bureaucratic performance generally. At the same time, if government patronage is organized along ethnic lines, ethnic diversity may make it more difficult to replace a clientelistic bureaucratic structure with a more rule-based one. We use the same measure of ethnolinguistic fractionalization used by Mauro (1995) and Easterly and Levine (1997), pertaining to the year 1960 and originally collected by the Department of Geodesy and Cartography of the State Geological Committee of the Soviet Union. The variable, *ETHFRAC,* measures the probability that two randomly selected individuals in a country will belong to different ethnolinguistic groups.

In Table 4 we report two ordinary least-squares regressions for each measure of bureaucratic performance, where the dependent variables are the time averages of the variables in Table 3. The first regression for each dependent variable contains all the bureaucratic structure indices and control variables, while the second regression is a more parsimonious specification that results from retaining all explanatory variables that are statistically significant in the first regression, plus any that is significant when added back individually to a regression containing only the significant variables. . . .

Table 4 shows that bureaucratic structure indices are statistically significant determinants of the bureaucratic performance measures produced by the ICRG and by BERI but not of the bureaucratic performance measures produced by BI. *MERIT* is retained in the more parsimonious specifications for the ICRG and BERI measure of bureaucratic performance while *SALARY* is retained in the more parsimonious specification for the BERI measure of bureaucratic performance only. Among the control variables, *RGDP* is retained in the more parsimonious specifications for all five measures of bureaucratic performance and *HUMCAP* is retained in the more parsimonious specification for *COR-RUPT2* only, though . . . it could have been retained instead of *RGDP* in the *BURDELAY* equation. *ETHFRAC* is not a statistically significant determinant of any measure of bureaucratic performance. . . .

These results indicate that meritocratic recruitment is the element of Weberian bureaucracy that is most important for improving bureaucratic performance. Internal promotion and career stability are at best of secondary importance, given that *CAREER* is a statistically significant determinant of bureaucratic performance only when *MERIT* is omitted. Whether or not competitive salaries have any effect on bureaucratic performance is unclear.

References

Aucoin, P., 1990. Administrative reform in public management: paradigms, principles, paradoxes, and pendulums. *Governance* 3(1), 115–137.

Bale, M., Dale, T., 1998. Public sector reform in New Zealand and its relevance to developing countries. *World Bank Research Observer* 13(1), 103–121.

Barro, R. J., Lee, J., 1993. International comparisons of educational attainment. *Journal of Monetary Economics* 32(3), 363–394.

Boston, J., Martin, J., Pallot, J., Walsh, P. (Eds), 1991. *Reshaping the State: New Zealand's Bureaucratic Revolution.* Oxford University Press, Auckland.

Caiden, G., 1988. The vitality of administrative reform. *International Review of Administrative Sciences* 54(3), 331–358.

Easterly, W., Levine, R., 1997. Africa's growth tragedy: policies and ethnic divisions. *Quarterly Journal of Economics* 112(4), 1203–1250.

Evans, P. B., 1992. The state as problem and solution: predation, embedded autonomy, and structural change. In: Haggard, S., Kaufman, R. R. (Eds), *The Politics of Economic Adjustment.* Princeton University Press, Princeton, NJ, pp. 139–191.

Evans, P. B., 1995. *Embedded Autonomy: States and Industrial Transformation.* Princeton University Press, Princeton, NJ.

Knack, S., Keefer, P., 1995. Institutions and economic performance: cross-country tests using alternative institutional measures. *Economics and Politics* 7(3), 207–227.

Klitgaard, R., 1988. *Controlling Corruption.* University of California Press, Berkeley, CA.

Mauro, P., 1995. Corruption and growth. *Quarterly Journal of Economics* 110(3), 681–712.

Milgrom, P., Roberts, J., 1992. *Economics, Organization, and Management.* Prentice-Hall, Englewood Cliffs, NJ.

Rauch, J. E., 1995. Choosing a dictator: bureaucracy and welfare in less developed polities. National Bureau of Economic Research Working Paper No. 5196.

Rauch, J. E., Evans, P. B., 1999. Bureaucratic structure and bureaucratic performance in less developed countries. UCSD Discussion Paper No. 99–06.

Rose-Ackerman, S., 1978. *Corruption: A Study in Political Economy.* Academic Press, New York.

Rose-Ackerman, S., 1997. The political economy of corruption. In: Elliott, K. A. (Ed), *Corruption and the Global Economy.* Institute for International Economics, Washington, D.C., pp. 31–60.

Schick, A., 1998. Why most developing countries should not try New Zealand's reforms. *World Bank Research Observer* 13(1), 123–131.

Shleifer, A., Vishny, R. W., 1993. Corruption. *Quarterly Journal of Economics* 108(3), 599–617.

Summers, R., Heston, A., 1991. The Penn World Table (Mark 5): an expanded set of international comparisons, 1950–1988. *Quarterly Journal of Economics* 106(2), 327–368.

Weber, M., 1968 [1904–1911]. *Economy and Society.* Roth, G., Wittich, C. (Eds), Bedminster Press, New York.

Williamson, O. E., 1985. *The Economic Institutions of Capitalism: Firms, Markets, Relational Contracting.* Free Press, New York.

World Bank, 1993. *The East Asian Miracle: Economic Growth and Public Policy.* Oxford University Press, New York.

CHAPTER X

Development and the Environment

Overview: Environmental Problems in Less Versus More Developed Countries

Concern with environmental degradation that began in the industrialized countries in the 1960s and 1970s extended to the less developed countries by the 1980s. The most pressing issues in the latter countries are not necessarily the same as in the former countries, however. A particularly dramatic example is "indoor air pollution," of which the World Bank states in the first selection of this chapter:

> For hundreds of millions of the world's poorer citizens, smoke and fumes from indoor use of biomass fuel (such as wood, straw, and dung) pose much greater health risks than any outdoor pollution. Women and children suffer most from this form of pollution, and its effects are often equivalent to those of smoking several packs of cigarettes a day.

Exhibit X.1 shows that access to safe water and improved sanitation facilities is a major problem in low human development countries and in many medium human development countries, but has almost disappeared as a problem in high human development countries.

The reason environmental problems differ so substantially between less and more developed countries is that few if any forms of environmental degradation tend to remain constant with economic growth. Figure 3 of the first selection shows that some environmental problems such as inadequate urban sanitation tend to improve as income increases, others such as urban air pollution initially worsen but then improve as incomes rise, and still others such as carbon dioxide emissions tend to worsen steadily with increasing income. The tendency of many forms of environmental degradation to follow an "inverted U" when plotted against income has been christened the "environmental Kuznets curve." The Comment that follows the first selection goes into the possible causes of the environmental Kuznets curve in more detail and suggests some additional readings on this subject.

The environmental problems of less and more developed countries are of course not completely independent of each other. If, as seems probable, the carbon dioxide emissions that come primarily from rich countries are causing greenhouse warming, less developed countries are affected. Loss of biodiversity due to destruction of tropical rainforests in less developed countries is a problem for more developed countries as well. Environmental problems and policies of less and more developed countries may also interact indirectly through international trade. If, for example, "dirty" industries locate in less developed countries and export to more developed countries, environmental degradation is worsened in the former and improved in the latter. By one view, such a pattern of trade is desirable because the demand for environmental quality or the (implicit) economic valuation of life is lower in LDCs. An opposing view holds that this pattern of trade is undesirable because weaker government regulation leads to a greater divergence between the private and social costs of environmental degradation in less than in more developed countries. Selection X.2 by Graciela Chichilnisky identifies a particularly clear theoretical case where international trade between poor and rich countries promotes socially inefficient environmental degradation. This case arises when property rights to a natural resource are better enforced in rich countries, leading to overexploitation of the natural resource in poor countries that is exacerbated by international trade. The Comment that follows Chichilnisky's selection reviews some of the empirical evidence regarding the impact of international trade on the environment in less developed countries.

Tropical deforestation is the chief example given by Chichilnisky of environmental degradation that is exacerbated by international trade in the presence of weak property rights in less developed countries. The link between property rights and deforestation (setting aside any effect of international trade) is given a systematic empirical investigation in Selection X.3 by Robert Deacon. We should note that Chichilnisky considers property rights within a harvest period, whereas Deacon considers property rights across harvest periods, yielding different though complementary arguments why better property rights will reduce deforestation. Chichilnisky's argument is essentially that if a forest is the private property of the harvester, he will take full account of the fact that each tree he harvests raises his cost of harvesting an additional tree (by forcing him deeper into the forest, say). This will lead to a lower overall level of harvesting than if the forest is unregulated common property harvested by many small producers, each of whom does not take into account the impact of his actions on the costs of the others. Deacon argues that preservation or restoration of forests is an act of investment and is therefore encouraged if those making the initial sacrifice feel confident that they will receive the future benefits. A harvester has a greater incentive to replant if he expects to have the rights to harvest the new trees. Deacon uses indicators of political instability and nonrepresentative government as proxies for the strength of property rights. These indicators should affect the security of any investment, not just investment in preservation or restoration of forests. Across countries they generally have the expected associations with deforestation, but it is not clear that these associations hold when population growth is controlled for. The weakness of Deacon's results may be due to lack of direct measures of forest property rights or of policies that specifically regulate use of forests.

As the first selection of this chapter points out, clarification and enforcement of property rights is a practical means of reducing some but not all types of environmental degradation. Other types of government policies are needed, such as pollution taxes or requirements to use emission control equipment. These kinds of regulation are quite weak in most less developed countries, which might lead one to expect production of uniformly high pollution intensity. In Selection X.4, Hemamala Hettige, Mainul Huq, Sheoli Pargal, and David Wheeler find to the contrary that there is wide variation in the pollution intensity of manufacturing production in the countries of South and Southeast Asia, with some plants even satisfying more developed country regulatory standards. They identify a number of different sources of this variation, such as whether a plant is state owned. A particularly interesting result is that higher per capita income in the community surrounding the plant is associated with greater installation of pollution control technologies or lower measured pollution intensity. This and related findings suggest that informal regulation in the form of community pressure can play a significant role in protecting the environment in less developed countries. Community pressure can also cause local governments to implement formal regulations. Some LDC cities, such as Taiyuan, China (*The Economist* 2002), are even experimenting with tradeable air pollution permits, one of the types of "market-based" pollution control policies listed by the World Bank in the first selection of this chapter.

The final selection concerns the issue of whether less developed countries are on "sustainable" development paths. Clearly if a country continually lives beyond its means in the sense of negative savings, its level of development will not be sustainable. In this selection, Kirk Hamilton and Michael Clemens adjust the standard, financial definition of savings downward to account for depletion of natural resources and for reduced social welfare due to pollution, and upward to account for increased human capital due to education. They find that both the sub-Saharan Africa and Middle East and North Africa regions have negative "genuine" savings during the 1980s and 1990s. Implicit in the idea of positive genuine savings as a condition for sustainable development is the assumption that increases in the man-made physical capital stock or the human capital stock can substitute for decreases in the "natural" capital stock. Some scholars would argue that decreases in certain components of the natural capital stock, such as biodiversity, cannot be made up by increases in other capital stocks, so that positive genuine savings is not sufficient to ensure that development is sustainable. Further discussion of the concept of sustainable development can be found in Pearce and Atkinson (1995).

References

The Economist. 2002. "Urban Air Pollution: A Great Leap Forward." *The Economist* 363, no. 8272 (May 11): 75.

Pearce, David, and Giles Atkinson. 1995. "Measuring Sustainable Development." In Daniel W. Bromley, ed., *The Handbook of Environmental Economics* (Oxford: Blackwell).

Exhibit X.1. Environmental Indicators

Country Name (listed from lowest to highest HDI)	Percentage of the Population with Access to		Emissions & Pollution			
	An Improved Water Source[a] 2000	Improved Sanitation Facilities[b] 2000	Fine Suspended Particulates[c] 1999	Total Industrial Carbon Dioxide Emissions[d] 1999	Carbon Dioxide Emissions Per Unit of PPP$ GDP[d] 1999	Annual Deforestation[e] (Annual Percent Change) 1990–2000
Low-human development countries						
Sierra Leone	57	66	63	542	0.26	2.9
Niger	59	20	164	1,136	0.13	3.7
Burkina Faso	42	29	108	1,015	0.09	0.2
Mali	65	69	194	498	0.06	0.7
Burundi	78	88	36	242	0.05	9.0
Mozambique	57	43	46	1,334	0.08	0.2
Ethiopia	24	12	88	5,503	0.12	0.8
Central African Republic	70	25	49	267	0.06	0.1
Congo, Dem. Rep. of the	45	21	51	2,143	0.06	0.4
Guinea-Bissau	56	56	86	260	0.25	0.9
Chad	27	29	161	121	0.02	0.6
Angola	38	44	125	10,270	0.38	0.2
Zambia	64	78	73	1,806	0.25	2.4
Malawi	57	76	46	769	0.13	2.4
Côte d'Ivoire	81	52	64	12,117	0.50	3.1
Tanzania, U. Rep. of	68	90	37	2,528	0.16	0.2
Benin	63	23	47	1,257	0.23	2.3
Rwanda	41	8	35	564	0.06	3.9
Guinea	48	58	69	1,264	0.09	0.5
Senegal	78	70	92	3,741	0.30	0.7
Eritrea	46	13	80	583	0.14	0.3
Mauritania	37	33	113	3,037	0.64	2.7
Djibouti	100	91		385	0.27	0.0
Nigeria	62	54	104	40,388	0.40	2.6
Gambia	62	37	93	253	0.11	−1.0
Haiti	46	28	50	1,414	0.10	5.7
Madagascar	47	42	47	1,898	0.16	0.9
Yemen	69	38	98	18,258	1.45	1.8
Uganda	52	79	16	1,370	0.05	2.0
Kenya	57	87	44	8,838	0.31	0.5
Zimbabwe	83	62	61	17,624	0.53	1.5
Pakistan	90	62	180	98,869	0.42	1.1
Nepal	88	28	50	3,320	0.12	1.8
Cameroon	58	79	85	4,694	0.21	0.9
Median	*58*	*48*	*69*	*1,392*	*0.15*	*0.9*
Medium-human development countries						
Togo	54	34	46	1,326	0.18	3.4
Congo	51	14	90	2,404	0.92	0.1
Bangladesh	97	48	147	25,446	0.14	−1.3
Sudan	75	62	246	2,634	0.05	1.4
Lesotho	78	49	54			0.0
Bhutan	62	70	41	385		0.0
Lao People's Dem. Rep.	37	30	47	407	0.06	0.4
Comoros	96	98	51	81	0.08	4.0
Swaziland			40	385	0.09	−1.2
Papua New Guinea	42	82	31	2,426	0.18	0.4
Myanmar	72	64	89	9,200		1.4
Cambodia	30	17	69	674	0.04	0.6
Ghana	73	72	33	5,577	0.14	1.7

Exhibit X.1. (Continued)

Country Name (listed from lowest to highest HDI)	Percentage of the Population with Access to		Emissions & Pollution			
	An Improved Water Source[a] 2000	Improved Sanitation Facilities[b] 2000	Fine Suspended Particulates[c] 1999	Total Industrial Carbon Dioxide Emissions[d] 1999	Carbon Dioxide Emissions Per Unit of PPP$ GDP[d] 1999	Annual Deforestation[e] (Annual Percent Change) 1990–2000
Vanuatu	88	100	28	81	0.13	–0.1
India	84	28	89	1,076,989	0.42	–0.1
Morocco	80	68	29	35,838	0.38	0.0
Botswana	95	66		3,877	0.35	0.9
Namibia	77	41	53	128	0.01	0.9
Solomon Islands	71	34	31	165	0.16	0.2
Sao Tome and Principe			52	88		0.0
Nicaragua	77	85	42	3,756		3.0
Egypt	97	98	152	123,587	0.61	–3.4
Guatemala	92	81	59	9,673	0.21	1.7
Gabon	86	53	21	3,554	0.52	0.0
Mongolia	60	30	71	7,548	1.93	0.5
Equatorial Guinea	44	53		649		0.6
Honduras	88	75	49	5,027	0.30	1.0
Bolivia	83	70	106	11,241	0.62	0.3
Tajikistan	60	90	64	5,100	0.85	–0.5
Indonesia	78	55	102	235,625	0.42	1.2
South Africa	86	87	24	334,582	0.76	0.1
Syrian Arab Republic	80	90	102	53,359	1.06	0.0
Viet Nam	77	47	75	46,569	0.33	–0.5
Moldova, Rep. of	92	99	35	6,496	0.76	–0.2
Algeria	89	92	76	90,812	0.52	–1.3
Iran, Islamic Rep. of	92	83	71	301,434	0.91	0.0
El Salvador	77	82	43	5,771	0.19	4.6
China	75	38	87	2,825,025	0.67	–0.9
Cape Verde	74	71		139	0.06	–9.3
Kyrgyzstan	77	100	41	4,716	0.39	–2.6
Uzbekistan	85	89	83	116,607	2.16	–0.2
Armenia			85	3,078	0.36	–1.3
Sri Lanka	77	94	94	8,647	0.15	1.6
Ecuador	85	86	28	23,266	0.62	1.2
Turkey	82	90	54	198,494	0.54	–0.2
Albania	97	91	32	1,513	0.15	0.8
Dominican Republic	86	67	39	23,274	0.45	0.0
Grenada	95	97	25	213	0.33	0.0
Guyana	94	87	34	1,685	0.49	0.3
Tunisia	80	84	47	17,481	0.32	–0.2
Jordan	96	99	77	14,572	0.83	0.0
Azerbaijan	78	81	99	33,628	1.80	–1.3
Georgia	79	100	98	5,375	0.46	0.0
Turkmenistan			68	32,415	2.07	0.0
Maldives	100	56	49	465		0.0
Philippines	86	83	49	73,214	0.27	1.4
Paraguay	78	94	97	4,529	0.17	0.5
Lebanon	100	99	45	16,913	0.97	0.3
Peru	80	71	62	30,393	0.27	0.4
Fiji	47	43	34	725	0.18	0.2
Saint Vincent and the Grenadines	93	96	33	161	0.28	1.5
Oman	39	92	105	19,888	0.73	0.0
Jamaica	92	99	54	10,215	1.15	1.5

Exhibit X.1. (Continued)

Country Name (listed from lowest to highest HDI)	Percentage of the Population with Access to		Emissions & Pollution			
	An Improved Water Source[a] 2000	Improved Sanitation Facilities[b] 2000	Fine Suspended Particulates[c] 1999	Total Industrial Carbon Dioxide Emissions[d] 1999	Carbon Dioxide Emissions Per Unit of PPP$ GDP[d] 1999	Annual Deforestation[e] (Annual Percent Change) 1990–2000
Suriname	82	93	51	2,151		0.0
Kazakhstan	91	99	27	112,837	1.54	−2.2
Ukraine	98	99	35	374,307	2.09	−0.3
Thailand	84	96	76	199,659	0.56	0.7
Saudi Arabia	95	100	106	235,408	0.93	0.0
Romania	58	53	23	81,205	0.69	−0.2
Saint Lucia	98	89		322	0.40	4.3
Samoa (Western)	99	99		139	0.16	2.1
Venezuela	83	68	16	125,825	0.99	0.4
Dominica	97	83	28	81	0.21	0.8
Belize	92	50	23	619	0.55	2.3
Bosnia and Herzegovina				4,822	0.24	
Brazil	87	76	33	300,657	0.26	0.4
Colombia	91	86	25	63,640	0.23	0.4
Russian Federation	99		26	1,437,340	1.62	0.0
Mauritius	100	99		2,470	0.24	0.6
Libyan Arab Jamahiriya	72	97		42,770		−1.4
Macedonia, TFYR			33	11,377	0.95	0.0
Panama	90	92	53	8,251	0.52	1.6
Malaysia			24	123,653	0.69	1.2
Bulgaria	100	100	75	42,088	0.88	−0.6
Antigua and Barbuda	91	95	16	348	0.53	0.0
Median	*84*	*83*	*49*	*7,900*	*0.42*	*0.1*
High-human development countries						
Mexico	88	74	53	378,495	0.50	1.1
Trinidad and Tobago	90	99	24	25,087	2.45	0.8
Belarus	100		15	57,631	0.87	−3.2
Cuba	91	98	25	25,377		−1.3
Saint Kitts and Nevis	98	96	23	103	0.22	0.0
Latvia			22	6,588	0.43	−0.4
Bahamas	97	100	43	1,795	0.39	0.0
United Arab Emirates			78	87,976		−2.8
Croatia			37	20,790	0.59	−0.1
Kuwait			134	47,969	1.37	−5.2
Lithuania	67		29	13,242	0.51	−0.2
Qatar			67	51,699		
Chile	93	96	65	62,515	0.50	0.1
Costa Rica	95	93	38	6,119	0.16	0.8
Estonia			20	16,155	1.41	−0.6
Uruguay	98	94	173	6,548	0.23	−5.0
Slovakia	100	100	22	38,622	0.66	−0.3
Hungary	99	99	25	56,880	0.51	−0.4
Bahrain			70	19,012	2.00	
Seychelles				216		0.0
Poland			44	314,390	0.94	−0.1
Argentina			71	137,799	0.32	0.8
Malta	100	100		3,422	0.73	
Czech Republic			27	108,854	0.81	0.0
Brunei Darussalam			38	4,668		0.2
Korea, Rep. of	92	63	43	393,510	0.64	0.1

Exhibit X.1. (Continued)

Country Name (listed from lowest to highest HDI)	Percentage of the Population with Access to		Emissions & Pollution			
	An Improved Water Source[a] 2000	Improved Sanitation Facilities[b] 2000	Fine Suspended Particulates[c] 1999	Total Industrial Carbon Dioxide Emissions[d] 1999	Carbon Dioxide Emissions Per Unit of PPP$ GDP[d] 1999	Annual Deforestation[e] (Annual Percent Change) 1990–2000
Slovenia	100		36	14,425	0.48	–0.2
Singapore	100	100	41	54,260	0.66	0.0
Barbados	100	100	41	2,034	0.55	0.0
Hong Kong, China (SAR)			38	41,191	0.28	
Cyprus	100	100	55	6,020	0.43	0.0
Greece			47	85,946	0.53	–0.9
Portugal			34	60,002	0.37	–1.7
Israel			52	61,127	0.52	–4.9
Italy			33	422,719	0.32	–0.3
New Zealand			17	30,774	0.45	–0.5
Spain			40	273,668	0.37	–0.6
Germany			22	792,204	0.41	0.0
France			17	359,688	0.28	–0.4
Austria	100	100	33	61,365	0.30	–0.2
Luxembourg			18	8,024	0.41	
Finland	100	100	21	58,375	0.51	0.0
United Kingdom	100	100	19	539,337	0.41	–0.8
Ireland			23	40,414	0.41	–3.0
Denmark	100		23	49,658	0.35	–0.2
Switzerland	100	100	26	40,579	0.21	–0.4
Japan			33	1,155,164	0.38	0.0
Canada	100	100	22	438,628	0.57	0.0
United States	100	100	25	5,495,436	0.62	–0.2
Belgium			28	104,439	0.43	
Netherlands	100	100	37	134,641	0.34	–0.3
Australia	100	100	19	344,445	0.77	0.0
Sweden	100	100	15	46,580	0.24	0.0
Iceland			21	2,066	0.28	–2.2
Norway	100		21	38,710	0.31	–0.4
Median	*100*	*100*	*33*	*49,658*	*0.44*	*–0.2*

United Nations Human Development Index countries are included in the Exhibit only if they have data available.

[a]An improved source includes a household connection, public stand-pipe, borehole, protected well or spring, or rainwater collection. Reasonable access is defined as the availability of at least 20 liters per person per day from a source within one kilometer from the domicile.

[b]Improved sanitation facilities range from simple but protected pit latrines to flush toilets with a sewerage connection.

[c]Particulate matter less than 20 microns in diameter capable of penetrating the respiratory tract and causing damage. It is measured in micrograms per cubic meter and expressed as the population weighted average of all cities in the country with a population greater than 100,000.

[d]Carbon dioxide emissions are those stemming from the burning of fossil fuels and the manufacture of cement.

[e]Negative numbers indicate an increase in forest area.

Source: World Bank, World Development Indicators, 2003; The Little Green Book, 2003.

Selection X.1. Development and the Environment*

Recent years have witnessed rising concern about whether environmental constraints will limit development and whether development will cause serious environmental damage—in turn impairing the quality of life of this and future generations. This concern is overdue. A number of environmental problems are already very serious and require urgent attention. Humanity's stake in environmental protection is enormous, and environmental values have been neglected too often in the past.

This Report explores the two-way relationship between development and the environment. It describes how environmental problems can and do undermine the goals of development. There are two ways in which this can happen. First, environmental quality—water that is safe and plentiful and air that is healthy—is itself part of the improvement in welfare that development attempts to bring. If the benefits from rising incomes are offset by the costs imposed on health and the quality of life by pollution, this cannot be called development. Second, environmental damage can undermine future productivity. Soils that, are degraded, aquifers that are depleted, and ecosystems that are destroyed in the name of raising incomes today can jeopardize the prospects for earning income tomorrow.

The Report also explores the impact—for good and bad—of economic growth on the environment. It identifies the conditions under which policies for efficient income growth can complement those for environmental protection and identifies tradeoffs. Its message is positive. There are strong "win-win" opportunities that remain unexploited. The most important of these relates to poverty reduction: not only is attacking poverty a moral imperative, but it is also essential for environmental stewardship. Moreover, policies that are justified on economic grounds alone can deliver substantial environmental benefits. Eliminating subsidies for the use of fossil fuels and water, giving poor farmers property rights on the land they farm, making heavily polluting state-owned companies more competitive, and eliminating rules that reward with property rights those who clear forests are examples of policies that improve both economic efficiency and the environment. Similarly, investing in better sanita-

tion and water and in improved research and extension services can both improve the environment *and* raise incomes.

But these policies are not enough to ensure environmental quality; strong public institutions and policies for environmental protection are also essential. The world has learned over the past two decades to rely more on markets and less on governments to promote development. But environmental protection is one area in which government must maintain a central role. Private markets provide little or no incentive for curbing pollution. Whether it be air pollution in urban centers, the dumping of unsanitary wastes in public waters, or the overuse of land whose ownership is unclear, there is a compelling case for public action. Here there may be tradeoffs between income growth and environmental protection, requiring a careful assessment of the benefits and costs of alternative policies as they affect both today's population and future generations. The evidence indicates that the gains from protecting the environment are often high and that the costs in forgone income are modest if appropriate policies are adopted. Experience suggests that policies are most effective when they aim at underlying causes rather than symptoms, concentrate on addressing those problems for which the benefits of reform are greatest, use incentives rather than regulations where possible, and recognize administrative constraints.

Strong environmental policies complement and reinforce development. It is often the poorest who suffer most from the consequences of pollution and environmental degradation. Unlike the rich, the poor cannot afford to protect themselves from contaminated water; in cities they are more likely to spend much of their time on the streets, breathing polluted air; in rural areas they are more likely to cook on open fires of wood or dung, inhaling dangerous fumes; their lands are most likely to suffer from soil erosion. The poor may also draw a large part of their livelihood from unmarketed environmental resources: common grazing lands, for example, or forests where food, fuel, and building materials have traditionally been gathered. The loss of such resources may particularly harm the poorest. Sound environmental policies are thus likely to be powerfully redistributive.

Making decisions about some environmental problems is complicated by uncertainties about physical and ecological processes, by the long-term

*From World Bank, "Overview: Development and the Environment," *World Development Report* 1992 (New York: Oxford University Press, 1992), pp. 1–15. Reprinted by permission.

nature of their effects, and by the possibility of thresholds beyond which unexpected or irreversible change may occur. New evidence that the impact of chlorofluorocarbons (CFCs) on stratospheric ozone depletion is greater than earlier thought is a timely reminder of how little we know. Such uncertainties call for much greater attention to research and to designing flexible precautionary policies.

Because this Report is about development and the environment, it focuses primarily on the welfare of developing countries. The most immediate environmental problems facing these countries—unsafe water, inadequate sanitation, soil depletion, indoor smoke from cooking fires and outdoor smoke from coal burning—are different from and more immediately life-threatening than those associated with the affluence of rich countries, such as carbon dioxide emissions, depletion of stratospheric ozone, photochemical smogs, acid rain, and hazardous wastes. Industrial countries need to solve their own problems, but they also have a crucial role to play in helping to improve the environments of developing countries.

- First, developing countries need to have access to less-polluting technologies and to learn from the successes and failures of industrial countries' environmental policies.
- Second, some of the benefits from environmental policies in developing countries—the protection of tropical forests and of biodiversity, for example—accrue to rich countries, which ought therefore to bear an equivalent part of the costs.
- Third, some of the potential problems facing developing countries—global warming and ozone depletion, in particular—stem from high consumption levels in rich countries; thus, the burden of finding and implementing solutions should be on the rich countries.
- Fourth, the strong and growing evidence of the links between poverty reduction and environmental goals makes a compelling case for greater support for programs to reduce poverty and population growth.
- Fifth, the capacity of developing countries to enjoy sustained income growth will depend on industrial countries' economic policies; improved access to trade and capital markets, policies to increase savings and lower world interest rates, and policies that promote robust, environmentally responsible growth in industrial countries, will all help. . . .

Table 1 outlines the potential consequences for health and productivity of different forms of environmental mismanagement. Since environmental problems vary across countries and with the stage of industrialization, each country needs to assess its own priorities carefully.

Clean Water and Sanitation

For the 1 billion people in developing countries who do not have access to clean water and the 1.7 billion who lack access to sanitation, these are the most important environmental problems of all. Their effects on health are shocking: they are major contributors to the 900 million cases of diarrheal diseases every year, which cause the deaths of more than 3 million children; 2 million of these deaths could be prevented if adequate sanitation and clean water were available. At any time 200 million are suffering from schistosomiasis or bilharzia and 900 million from hookworm. Cholera, typhoid, and paratyphoid also continue to wreak havoc with human welfare. Providing access to sanitation and clean water would not eradicate all these diseases, but it would be the single most effective means of alleviating human distress.

The economic costs of inadequate provision are also high. Many women in Africa spend more than two hours a day fetching water. In Jakarta an amount equivalent to 1 percent of the city's gross domestic product (GDP) is spent each year on boiling water, and in Bangkok, Mexico City, and Jakarta excessive pumping of groundwater has led to subsidence, structural damage, and flooding.

Clean Air

Emissions from industry and transport and from domestic energy consumption impose serious costs for health and productivity. Three specific problems stand out for their effect on human suffering.

Suspended Particulate Matter

In the second half of the 1980s about 1.3 billion people worldwide lived in urban areas that did not meet the standards for particulate matter (airborne dust and smoke) set by the World Health Organization (WHO). They thus faced the threat of serious respiratory disorders and cancers (see Figure 1). If emissions could be reduced so that the WHO standards were met everywhere, an estimated 300,000 to 700,000 lives could be saved each year, and many more people would be spared the suffering caused by chronic respiratory difficulties.

Table 1. Principal Health and Productivity Consequences of Environmental Mismanagement

Environmental problem	Effect on health	Effect on productivity
Water pollution and water scarcity	More than 2 million deaths and billions of illnesses a year attributable to pollution; poor household hygiene and added health risks caused by water scarcity	Declining fisheries; rural household time and municipal costs of providing safe water; aquifer depletion leading to irreversible compaction; constraint on economic activity because of water shortages
Air pollution	Many acute and chronic health impacts: excessive urban particulate matter levels are responsible for 300,000–700,000 premature deaths annually and for half of childhood chronic coughing; 400 million–700 million people, mainly women and children in poor rural areas, affected by smoky indoor air	Restrictions on vehicle and industrial activity during critical episodes; effect of acid rain on forests and water bodies
Solid and hazardous wastes	Diseases spread by rotting garbage and blocked drains. Risks from hazardous wastes typically local but often acute	Pollution of groundwater resources
Soil degradation	Reduced nutrition for poor farmers on depleted soils; greater susceptibility to drought	Field productivity losses in range of 0.5–1.5 percent of gross national product (GNP) common on tropical soils; offsite siltation of reservoirs, river-transport channels, and other hydrologic investments
Deforestation	Localized flooding, leading to death and disease	Loss of sustainable logging potential and of erosion prevention, watershed stability, and carbon sequestration provided by forests
Loss of biodiversity	Potential loss of new drugs	Reduction of ecosystem adaptability and loss of genetic resources
Atmospheric changes	Possible shifts in vector-borne diseases; risks from climatic natural disasters; diseases attributable to ozone depletion (perhaps 300,000 additional cases of skin cancer a year worldwide; 1.7 million cases of cataracts)	Sea-rise damage to coastal investments; regional changes in agricultural productivity; disruption of marine food chain

Lead

High levels of lead, primarily from vehicle emissions, have been identified as the greatest environmental danger in a number of large cities in the developing world. Estimates for Bangkok suggest that the average child has lost four or more IQ points by the age of seven because of elevated exposure to lead, with enduring implications for adult productivity. In adults the consequences include risks of higher blood pressure and higher risks of heart attacks, strokes, and death. In Mexico City lead exposure may contribute to as much as 20 percent of the incidence of hypertension.

Indoor Air Pollution

For hundreds of millions of the world's poorer citizens, smoke and fumes from indoor use of biomass fuel (such as wood, straw, and dung) pose much greater health risks than any outdoor pollution. Women and children suffer most from this form of pollution, and its effects on health are often equivalent to those of smoking several packs of cigarettes a day.

Other Forms of Pollution

An estimated 1 billion people live in cities that exceed WHO standards for sulfur dioxide. Nitrogen oxides and volatile organic compounds are a problem in a smaller but growing number of rapidly industrializing and heavily motorized cities.

Soil, Water, and Agricultural Productivity

The loss of productive potential in rural areas is a more widespread and important problem, although less dramatic, than that evoked by images of advancing deserts. Soil degradation, in particu-

Figure 1. Urban air pollution: Average concentrations of suspended particulate matter, by country income group

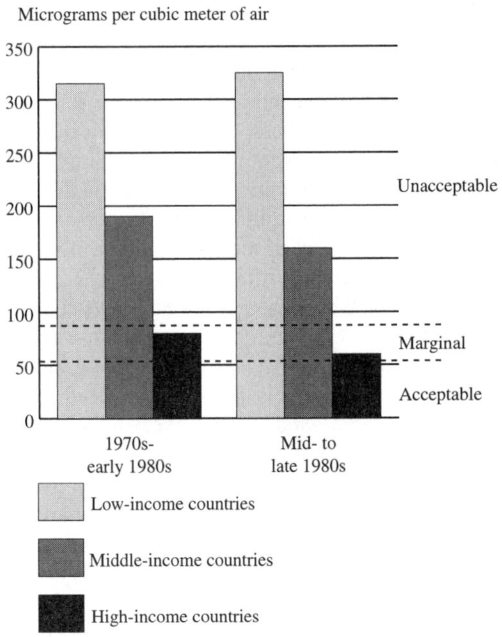

Micrograms per cubic meter of air

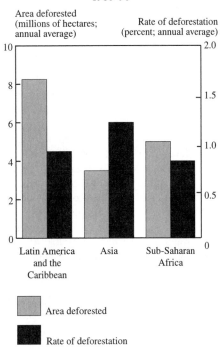

Unacceptable

Marginal

Acceptable

1970s–
early 1980s

Mid- to
late 1980s

Low-income countries

Middle-income countries

High-income countries

Note: Periods of time series differ by site. World Health Organization guidelines for air quality are used as the criteria for acceptability.
Source: World Development Report 1992.

lar, is the cause of stagnating or declining yields in parts of many countries, especially on fragile lands from which the poorest farmers attempt to wrest a living. Erosion is the most visible symptom of this degradation. Data on soil conditions are of low quality, but crude estimates suggest that in some countries the losses in productive potential attributable to soil depletion may amount to 0.5–1.5 percent of GDP annually. Erosion can also damage economic infrastructure, such as dams, downstream. Even when erosion is insignificant, soils may suffer from nutrient, physical, and biological depletion.

Waterlogging and salinization are serious problems in some irrigated areas and are often the result of policies and infrastructure that inadequately recognize the growing scarcity of water. The increasing conflicts over the use of water mean that in the future, additional growth in agricultural productivity will have to make do with more efficient irrigation and, in some regions, less water overall.

Agricultural intensification will continue as it becomes harder to expand the area of cultivation. High levels of inputs and changes in land use will cause problems for farm communities and other

parts of the economy. These problems, once confined mainly to the highly intensive agricultural systems of Europe and North America, are now increasing in such areas as the Punjab, Java, and parts of China.

Natural Habitats and Loss of Biodiversity

Forests (especially moist tropical forests), coastal and inland wetlands, coral reefs, and other ecosystems are being converted or degraded at rates that are high by historical standards. Tropical forests have declined by one-fifth in this century, and the rate has accelerated. As Figure 2 shows, in the 1980s tropical deforestation occurred at a rate of 0.9 percent a year, with Asia's rate slightly higher (1.2 percent) and Sub-Saharan Africa's lower (0.8 percent). The loss of forests has severe ecological and economic costs—lost watershed protection, local climate change, lost coastal protection and fishing grounds—and affects people's lives. African women have to walk farther for fuelwood, indigenous forest dwellers in the Amazon have succumbed to settlers' diseases, and 5,000 villagers in the Philippines were recently killed by flooding caused in part by the deforestation of hillsides.

Figure 2. Loss of tropical forests in developing regions, 1980–90

Area deforested
(millions of hectares;
annual average)

Rate of deforestation
(percent; annual average)

Latin America
and the
Caribbean

Asia

Sub-Saharan
Africa

Area deforested

Rate of deforestation

Source: FAO data.

Extinction of species is occurring at rates that are high by historical standards, and many more species are threatened because their habitats are being lost. Models that link species extinction to habitat loss suggest that rapid rises in the rate of extinction to levels approaching those of prehistoric mass extinctions may be difficult to avoid in the next century unless current rates of deforestation and other habitat loss are sharply reduced.

Greenhouse Warming

The buildup of carbon dioxide and other greenhouse gases will raise average temperatures on earth. The size of the effect remains unclear, but the best estimate of the International Panel on Climate Change (IPCC) is that average world temperatures may rise by 3° Celsius by the end of the next century under their "business as usual" scenario, with a range of uncertainty of from less than 2° Celsius to more than 5° Celsius. There is even more uncertainty about the consequences than about the extent of global warming. Although recent research has reduced fears that icecaps might melt or that the sea level might rise precipitously, there are still grounds for concern. Low-lying nations are at risk, and forests and ecosystems may not adapt easily to shifts in climatic zones. The consequences will depend both on whether policies are adopted to reduce emissions and on how effective economies are in adapting to rising temperatures. . . .

Economic Growth and the Environment

What pressures will economic growth place on the natural environment in the coming years? To assess this question, the Report explores a long-term projection of economic output. Under present productivity trends, and given projected population increases, developing country output would rise by 4–5 percent a year between 1990 and 2030 and by the end of the period would be about five times what it is today. Industrial country output would rise more slowly but would still triple over the period. World output by 2030 would be 3.5 times what it is today, or roughly $69 trillion (in 1990 prices).

If environmental pollution and degradation were to rise in step with such a rise in output, the result would be appalling environmental pollution and damage. Tens of millions more people would become sick or die each year from environmental causes. Water shortages would be intolerable, and tropical forests and other natural habitats would decline to a fraction of their current size. Fortu-

nately, such an outcome need not occur, nor will it if sound policies and strong institutional arrangements are put in place.

The earth's "sources" are limited, and so is the absorptive capacity of its "sinks." Whether these limitations will place bounds on the growth of human activity will depend on the scope for substitution, technical progress, and structural change. Forcing decisionmakers to respect the scarcity and limits of natural resources has a powerful effect on their actions. For example, whereas fears that the world would run out of metals and other minerals were fashionable even fifteen years ago, the potential supply of these resources is now outstripping demand. Prices of minerals have shown a fairly consistent downward trend over the past hundred years. They fell sharply in the 1980s, leading to gluts that threatened to impoverish countries dependent on commodity exports.

With some other natural resources, by contrast, demand often exceeds supply. This is true of the demand for water, not only in the arid areas of the Middle East but also in northern China, east Java, and parts of India. Aquifers are being depleted, sometimes irreversibly, and the extraction from rivers is often so great that their ecological functions are impaired and further expansion of irrigation is becoming severely limited.

The reason some resources—water, forests, and clean air—are under siege while others—metals, minerals, and energy—are not is that the scarcity of the latter is reflected in market prices and so the forces of substitution, technical progress, and structural change are strong. The first group is characterized by open access, meaning that there are no incentives to use them sparingly. Policies and institutions are therefore necessary to force decisionmakers—corporations, farmers, households, and governments—to take account of the social value of these resources in their actions. This is not easy. The evidence suggests, however, that when environmental policies are publicly supported and firmly enforced, the positive forces of substitution, technical progress, and structural change can be just as powerful as for marketed inputs such as metals and minerals. This explains why the environmental debate has rightly shifted away from concern about *physical limits* to growth toward concern about incentives for *human behavior* and policies that can overcome *market and policy failures.*

Figure 3 illustrates how rising economic activity can cause environmental problems but can also, with the right policies and institutions, help address them. Three patterns emerge:

Figure 3. Environmental indicators at different country income levels

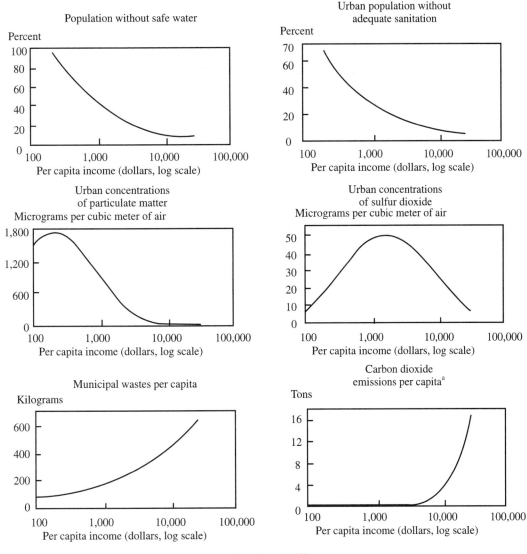

Note: Estimates are based on cross-country regression analysis of data from the 1980s.

a. Emissions are from fossil fuels.

Sources:World Development Report 1992, World Bank data.

- Some problems decline as income increases. This is because increasing income provides the resources for public services such as sanitation and rural electricity. When individuals no longer have to worry about day-to-day survival, they can devote resources to profitable investments in conservation. These positive synergies between economic growth and environmental quality must not be underestimated.

- Some problems initially worsen but then improve as incomes rise. Most forms of air and water pollution fit into this category, as do some types of deforestation and encroachment on natural habitats. There is nothing automatic about this improvement; it occurs only when countries deliberately introduce policies to ensure that additional resources are devoted to dealing with environmental problems.

- Some indicators of environmental stress worsen as incomes increase. Emissions of carbon and of nitrogen oxides and municipal wastes are current examples. In these cases abatement is relatively expensive and the costs associated with the emissions and wastes are not yet perceived as high—often because they are borne by someone else. The key is, once again, policy. In most countries individuals and firms have few incentives to cut back on wastes and emissions, and until such incentives are put into place—through regulation, charges, or other means—damage will continue to increase. The experience with the turnarounds achieved in other forms of pollution, however, shows what may be possible once a policy commitment is made.

Figure 3 does not imply an inevitable relationship between income levels and particular environmental problems; countries can choose policies that result in much better (or worse) environmental conditions than those in other countries at similar income levels. Nor does it imply a static picture; as a result of technological progress, some of these curves have shifted downward over recent decades, providing an opportunity for countries to develop in a less damaging manner than was possible earlier.

Policies for Development and the Environment

Two broad sets of policies are needed to attack the underlying causes of environmental damage. Both are necessary. Neither will be sufficient on its own.

- Policies that seek to harness the positive links between development and the environment by correcting or preventing policy failures, improving access to resources and technology, and promoting equitable income growth
- Policies targeted at specific environmental problems: regulations and incentives that are required to force the recognition of environmental values in decisionmaking.

Building on the Positive Links

Fortunately, many policies that are good for efficiency are also good for the environment. Policies that encourage efficiency lead to less waste, less consumption of raw materials, and more technological innovation. . . .

Removing Distortions. Some government policies are downright harmful to the environment. Notable here are distorted prices in general and subsidized input prices in particular. Subsidies for energy, for example, cost developing country governments more than $230 billion a year—more

than four times the total world volume of official development assistance. The former U.S.S.R. and Eastern Europe account for the bulk of this amount ($180 billion); estimates suggest that more than half of their air pollution is attributable to these distortions. The removal of all energy subsidies—including those on coal in industrial countries—would not only produce large gains in efficiency and in fiscal balances but would sharply reduce local pollution and cut worldwide carbon emissions from energy use by 10 percent. Other distortionary incentives have also had serious environmental consequences. Logging fees in a sample of five African countries ranged from 1 to 33 percent of the costs of replanting. Irrigation charges in most Asian countries covered less than 20 percent of the costs of supplying the water. And pesticide subsidies in a sample of seven countries in Latin America, Africa, and Asia ranged from 19 to 83 percent of costs.

Distorted incentives are often particularly evident in the behavior of state-owned enterprises. This is important because many sectors in which state enterprises are prominent—power generation, cement, steel, and mining—are heavy polluters; the "commanding heights" are also the "polluting heights." Thus, the environment can benefit if the managers of state enterprises are made more accountable and are exposed to the same competition as is the private sector.

Clarifying Property Rights. When people have open access to forests, pastureland, or fishing grounds, they tend to overuse them. Providing land titles to farmers in Thailand has helped to reduce damage to forests. The assignment of property titles to slum dwellers in Bandung, Indonesia, has tripled household investment in sanitation facilities. Providing security of tenure to hill farmers in Kenya has reduced soil erosion. Formalizing community rights to land in Burkina Faso is sharply improving land management. And allocating transferable rights to fishery resources has checked the tendency to overfish in New Zealand.

The most serious mistake that governments make in seeking to eliminate open access is to nationalize resources in the name of conservation. Nationalization has often reflected the failure of policymakers and aid agencies to distinguish between traditional common-property systems, which promote sound management of natural resources, and open-access systems that result in excessive exploitation. When land and water have been nationalized and traditional management arrangements abandoned, the environmental consequences have often been severe, as they were in the forests of Nepal.

Targeted Policies to Change Behavior

The policies described above are important, but they are not enough. Eliminating fuel subsidies will not be sufficient to end air pollution in Beijing or Mexico City. And it simply is not practical to find property-rights solutions for most of those environmental problems that adversely affect a large number of people "offsite"—air and water pollution, watershed destruction, loss of biodiversity, and the like. For these situations specific policies are required to induce or require resource users to take account of the spillover effects that their actions have on the rest of society.

Policies designed to change behavior are of two broad types: those based on incentives ("market-based" policies), which tax or charge polluters according to the amount of damage they do, and those based on quantitative restrictions ("command-and-control" policies), which provide no such flexibility.

Market-based instruments are best in principle and often in practice. They encourage those polluters with the lowest costs of control to take the most remedial action, and they thus impose less of a burden on the economy. A survey of six studies of air pollution control in the United States found that least-cost policies could reduce the costs of control by 45–95 percent in comparison with the actual policies implemented. Economic incentives have been used for years in indirect, or blunt, forms such as fuel and vehicle taxes (most OECD countries), congestion charges (Singapore), and surcharges on potentially damaging inputs such as pesticides and plastics (Denmark and Sweden). More specific charges, such as the newly introduced carbon taxes in some European countries, tradable permits for air pollution (in the United States), deposit-refund schemes for bottles and batteries (in several European countries), hazardous waste charges and performance bonds, which are under consideration in Bangkok, and surcharges on stumpage fees to pay for replanting, as in Indonesia, are growing in importance. Industrial countries have been slow to adopt market-based strategies, in part because environmentalists contended that degrading the environment was unacceptable at any price, but more importantly because corporations feared that they would have to adopt emissions standards *and also* pay charges on the remaining emissions. Most now agree that market-based instruments have been underutilized. They are particularly promising for developing countries, which cannot afford to incur the unnecessary extra costs of less-flexible instruments that have been borne by OECD countries.

Quantitative command-and-control instruments, such as specific regulations on what abatement technologies must be used in specific industries, have acquired a bad name in recent years for their high costs and for stifling innovation. But in some situations they may be the best instruments available. Where there are a few large polluters, as was the case in the industrial city of Cubatão in Brazil, direct regulation may be the quickest and most effective instrument. Management of land use in frontier areas is another example of situations that may require direct controls.

The appropriate choice among instruments will depend on circumstances. Conserving scarce administrative capacity is an important consideration. For many developing countries blunt instruments that avoid the need for detailed monitoring will be attractive. These may involve taxes or charges on polluting inputs rather than on the pollution itself. Also attractive will be policies that provide self-enforcing incentives, such as deposit-refund and performance-bond schemes.

Several lessons can be drawn from recent experience:

- *Standards should be realistic and enforceable.* Many developing countries have set unrealistically tight standards—often those of OECD countries—and have enforced them only selectively. This has wasted resources, facilitated corruption, and undermined the credibility of all environmental policies. Laws on the books and zoning charts on the walls of government offices are often a genuine indication of concern, but unless policies are implemented, they can give a false sense that serious problems are under control. Better to have fewer and more realistic standards that are truly implemented.
- *Controls must be consistent with the overall policy framework.* Many well-intentioned policies have been thwarted by other policies that pull in the opposite direction. Both China and Poland have had pollution taxes for years, but to no effect; state-owned enterprises were not interested in profitability. Land-use planning in Sub-Saharan Africa has usually failed in the face of policies that did not encourage intensification and off-farm employment. Brazil's concern about overfishing off the Bahia coast was undermined in the early 1980s by government subsidies for new nylon nets.
- *A combination of policies will often be required.*

Because environmental damage is frequently caused by different actors and for different reasons, a single policy change may not be enough. Reducing air pollution from vehicles in Mexico City, for example, will require mandated emissions and engine standards, fuel improvements, and gasoline taxes.

Reviewing Public Expenditures

Public expenditures can have a remarkable effect on the environment—for bad or for good. It is now clear that numerous public investments—often supported by development agencies, including the World Bank—have caused damage by failing to take environments considerations into account or to judge the magnitude of the impacts. Indonesia's transmigration program, Sri Lanka's Mahaweli scheme, and Brazil's Polonoreste projects are examples of large programs that caused unanticipated damage in earlier years. But equally important are design issues relating to individual project components—road alignments, the design of water systems, and the provision of access to forests and wetlands.

Beginning with analysis in the 1950s and 1960s of hydroelectric projects in the United States, considerable progress has been made in applying cost-benefit techniques to environmental concerns. Such analyses have tripled estimated returns for some forestry programs and halved returns on some hydroelectric and road projects, making the latter unattractive.

Most countries and aid agencies have recently introduced environmental assessment procedures. These are still early days for such arrangements; technical skills need to be developed, and lessons are being learned about the difficulties of incorporating assessment results, which are often nonquantitative, into decisionmaking. Making the process transparent has been found to be an important way of improving its quality and impact. Listening to local views has also proved essential; some lessons from the World Bank experience are that information must be shared with local people early in the life of the project and that comments from affected communities must be incorporated into project design.

Removing Impediments to Action

Even when straightforward ways of tackling environmental problems exist, governments have often found it difficult to translate them into effective policy. The reason for the gap between intentions and performance include political pressures, an absence of data and knowledge, weak institutions, and inadequate participation of local people in finding solutions.

Counteracting Political Pressures

Stopping environmental damage often involves taking rights away from people who may be politically powerful. Industrialists, farmers, loggers, and fishermen fiercely defend their rights to pollute or to exploit sources. Examples of the results include modification of proposed carbon taxes in Europe to assist energy-intensive industries, delay in the introduction of transferable fishing rights in Chile because of pressure from powerful fishing interests, and lack of progress almost everywhere in introducing irrigation charges. Those who are hurt when the environment is degraded, and who stand to gain most from sound policies, are often the poor and the weak. They may be less potent politically than the polluters whom governments must challenge.

A second reason for disappointing performance has to do with the inability of governments to regulate themselves. The problem arises partly because state bodies have conflicting social and economic objectives, which allow them to use resources less efficiently, and partly because of the inherent contradictions of being both gamekeeper and poacher. In the United States, for example, publicly owned municipal wastewater treatment plants are the most persistent violators of effluent discharge standards.

While private and public polluters may obstruct policy, other influences may persuade governments to set the wrong priorities. International pressures may favor issues of interest to donors rather than to developing countries. And there is always a tendency to focus on dramatic problems rather than chronic ones; few pressure groups, for example, lobby for improved sanitation or for reduced indoor air pollution. Moreover, governments may be pressed to address problems such as air pollution that affect everybody, including the rich, rather than problems such as fecal coliforms in rivers from which the rich can insulate themselves.

Improving Information

Ignorance is a serious impediment to finding solutions. Governments often make decisions in the absence of even rudimentary information. International initiatives are urgently needed to overcome a grave lack of knowledge in some areas, including soil depletion (especially in Africa), land productivity in and around tropical forests, and global atmospheric issues. Countries can reap large returns from investments in basic environmental data on exposure to emissions and unsanitary conditions, soil and water depletion, land capability, and loss of forests and natural habitat.

Understanding the causes and effects of environmental damage and the costs and benefits of action is the next stage. Following a careful analysis, authorities in Bangkok found that attacking lead and particulate emissions deserved the highest priority. The U.S. Environmental Protection Agency estimated that, as a measure for avoiding deaths, placing controls on unvented indoor heaters was 1,000 times more cost-effective than further tightening certain hazardous wastes standards. A study in southern Poland discovered that the benefits from reducing emissions of particulates would greatly exceed costs but that this would not be true of controls on sulfur dioxide.

Independent commissions have proved a useful way for governments to draw on technical expertise; a growing number of developing countries, including Hungary, Nigeria, and Thailand, are finding that ad hoc commissions can bring professional objectivity to highly charged issues. In Africa, national environmental action plans, which have already been completed for Lesotho, Madagascar, and Mauritius and are under preparation for seventeen other countries, are bringing technical experts and citizens' groups into the process of setting priorities and policies....

Involving Local People

Making choices between economic and social benefits and environmental costs often requires subjective judgments and detailed local knowledge. Neither governments nor aid agencies are equipped to make judgments about how local people value their environment. A participatory process is essential. Local participation also yields high economic and environmental returns in implementing programs of afforestation, soil management, park protection, water management, and sanitation, drainage, and flood control.

Development projects that have not built on the strengths of existing practices have often failed. Haiti's top-down reforestation program was unsuccessful until small farmers and community groups were allowed to choose what kinds of trees should be planted, and where. Then, instead of the target of 3 million trees on 6,000 family farms, 20 million trees were planted on 75,000 farms. A large irrigation project in Bali, Indonesia, that failed to recognize the advantages of traditional approaches to pest management had disastrous results. A follow-up project that built on indigenous strengths succeeded.

Involving people can be expensive and in some instances can paralyze decisionmaking, hold public investments hostage to unproductive NIMBY ("not-in-my-backyard") activism, and reinforce local power structures. Experience suggests that success is greatest when tasks are devolved selectively and on the basis of actual performance. Increasing responsibilities for local governments is an important part of this process. Public agencies need training in participatory approaches and a clear indication from senior management of the importance of participation.

Comment X.1. The "Environmental Kuznets Curve"

The middle row of Figure 3 of the preceding selection shows two types of air pollution that first increase and then decrease with per capita income. Because this is reminiscent of Kuznets's conjecture for income inequality (see section VIII.A in this book), this inverted-U relationship has become known as the "environmental Kuznets curve." (As the selection points out, the environmental Kuznets curve is not limited to air pollution, but at the same time there are some forms of environmental degradation to which it clearly does not apply.) The cause of the upswing of the inverted U is simply that greater output per head generates more emissions, all else equal. The cause of the downswing is more controversial. The conventional explanation is that richer consumers demand higher environmental quality, richer governments are better able to enforce regulations that yield the higher environmental quality their constituents demand, and more technologically advanced producers are better able to control their emissions. A more pessimistic explanation focuses on the composition of output. Richer countries produce more services relative to manufactures, and within manufacturing they tend to specialize in "cleaner" industries. Demand for the output of "dirty" industries is met by imports from poorer countries. If this latter explanation is correct, then at the global level economic growth of countries with per capita incomes above the "turning point" of the inverted U for a certain form of environmental degradation does not improve environmental quality but instead redistributes degradation to poorer countries. This point is made in more detail by Gilles Saint-Paul, "Discussion," in Ian Goldin and L. Alan Winters, eds., *The Economics of Sustainable Development* (1995).

Some evidence in favor of the conventional explanation of the downswing of the environmental Kuznets curve is contained in an article by Richard T. Carson, Yongil Jeon, and Donald R. McCubbin, "The Relationship Between Air Pollution Emissions and Income: U.S. Data," *Environment and Development Economics* (1997). They reason that since even the poorest U.S. state has a per capita income above most estimated "turning points" of the inverted U, per capita air pollutant emissions should decline monotonically with state per capita income. The data confirm their expectation. It is possible that this result obtains because dirty industries have moved from richer states to poorer states, or because richer states import the products of dirty industries from abroad to a greater extent. However, Carson et al. find that their result holds even when they include controls for industry mix in their cross-state regressions.

The paper by Carson, Jeon, and McCubbin appeared in an environmental Kuznets curve special issue of *Environment and Development Economics*. This special issue is an excellent source of additional information on the subject. We should also note that some scholars have challenged the evidence for the environmental Kuznets curve. For example, William T. Harbaugh, Arik Levinson, and David Molloy Wilson, "Reexamining the Empirical Evidence for an Environmental Kuznets Curve," *Review of Economics and Statistics* (August 2002), argue that new data cast doubt on the existence of environmental Kuznets curves for three types of air pollutants.

Selection X.2. North–South Trade and the Global Environment*

Why do developing countries tend to specialize in the production and the export of goods which deplete environmental resources such as rain forests (see Chichilnisky and Geoffrey Heal, 1991)? Do they have a comparative advantage in "dirty industries," and if so, does efficiency dictate that this advantage should be exploited? Is it possible to protect resources without interfering with free markets? Are trade policies based on traditional comparative advantages compatible with environmental preservation?

This paper proposes answers to these questions. It does so by studying patterns of North-South trade in a world economy where the North has better-defined property rights for environmental resources than the South.... It considers a trade model with two countries (North and South), two goods, and two factors.... The environment, which is one of the factors of production, is owned as unregulated common property in the South, and as private property in the North....

The paper considers a general completely symmetric case: a world economy consisting of two identical countries, both with the same inputs and outputs, and with the same endowments, technologies, and preferences. The two countries engage in free trade in unregulated and competitive markets. The countries differ only in the pattern of ownership of an environmental resource used as an input to production. I consider this case to demonstrate that lack of property rights alone can create trade, and that trade itself can exacerbate the common-property problem. No trade is necessary for efficiency when the two countries are identical, yet trade occurs when they have different property-rights regimes. In this context I establish two general propositions. First, the country with ill-defined property rights overuses the environment as an input to production, and these ill-defined property rights by themselves create a motive for trade between two otherwise identical countries. Second, for the country with poorly defined property rights, trade with a country with well-defined property rights increases the overuse of resources and makes the misallocation worse, transmitting it to the entire world economy. Trade equalizes the prices of traded goods and of factors worldwide, but this does not improve resource allocation. In the resulting world economy, resources are under-

priced; there is overproduction by one country and over-consumption by the other....

These results offer a new perspective on a current debate, initiated in 1992 by Lawrence Summers, a World Bank economist, about whether developing countries have a comparative advantage in "dirty industries" (see e.g., *The Economist,* 8 February 1992, Vol. 322, p. 66). If so, the argument goes, is it not efficient that they specialize in "dirty industries" and environmentally intensive production?

One response to this is that the apparent comparative advantages may not be actual comparative advantages, an issue which this paper addresses rigorously. They may derive neither from a relative abundance of resources nor from differences in productivity or preferences, not even from lower factor prices, but rather from historical and institutional factors: the lack of property rights for a common-property resource. In this context the South produces and exports environmentally intensive goods to a greater degree than is efficient, and at prices that are below social costs. This happens even if all factor prices are equal across the world, all markets are competitive, and the two regions have identical factor endowments, preferences and technologies. Under those conditions the trade patterns which emerge are inefficient for the world economy as a whole, and for the developing countries themselves. Developing countries are not made better off by specializing in "dirty industries," nor is the world better off if they do....

The problems described in this paper appear when societies that are still in transition between agricultural and industrialized economies trade with societies already industrialized. Many traditional societies had well developed systems for inducing cooperative outcomes in the use of shared resources. Laws to protect the citizens' property rights in running water were in operation in the United Kingdom in the Middle Ages. Japan had well developed systems for the management of traditional communal lands (*Iriaichi*). Other examples are the communal-field agriculture in the Andes and in medieval England, and the successful sea-tenure systems in Bahia, Brazil, before the arrival of outsiders (see Daniel Bromley, 1992). These traditional systems, however, appear to lapse in the period of transition between agricultural and industrial economies.

Today many environmental resources are unregulated common property in developing countries.

*From Graciela Chichilnisky, "North-South Trade and the Global Environment," *American Economic Review* 84 (September 1994): 851–853, 864. Reprinted by permission.

Examples are rain forests, which are used for timber or destroyed to give way to the production and export of cash crops such as coffee, sugar, and palm oil. Other examples include grazing land, fisheries, and aquifers, which by the nature of things must usually be shared property even when the land covering the aquifer is privately owned (see Partha Dasgupta, 1992). These are common-property resources whose ownership is shared with future generations. They are typically used as inputs to the production of goods that are traded internationally.

Recent studies show that 90 percent of all tropical deforestation is for the agricultural use of forests, particularly for the international market (C. S. Binley and Jeffrey R. Vincent, 1990; Torsten Amelung, 1991; Edward Barbier et al., 1991; W. F. Hyde and D. H. Newman, 1991). The Korup National Park between Cameroon and Nigeria, at 60 million years old, one of the oldest rain forests in the world and one of the richest in biodiversity, is exploited as an unregulated common-property resource for the production of palm oil, trapping, and other forest products sold in the international market (H. J. Ruitenbeck, 1990). So is the Amazon basin, which is cleared and used as a source of land for the production of cash crops, such as soy beans and coffee, for the international market.

In the now industrialized countries communal land was frequently observed prior to industrialization. Industrialization in England was preceded by the "enclosure" (privatization) of common lands (Cohen and Weitzman, 1975). Now, however, industrial countries have much better defined property rights for their resources than do developing countries. The United States has property-rights regimes for petroleum. These include laws to prevent the overexploitation of common-property resources such as the Conally "Hot Oil Act" of 1936 and "unitization" laws (Steven McDonald, 1971). Water, however, is still treated as common property in parts of Texas and California, leading to misallocation. Japan is well known for its protection of property rights in environmental resources, including even sunlight. Germany recently initiated a parallel system of national accounts which records the depreciation of environmental assets, effectively treating the accounting of national property on the same basis as that of private property. . . .

A main argument in favor of property-rights policies is that once these have been implemented, no market intervention is needed. Consider, for example, any policy which improves the property of Amazonian small farmers, such as rubber-tappers. This will change the supply function of Amazonian resources, reducing output at each price. In turn this will change the computation of comparative advantages and of gains from trade from agricultural exports based on deforestation of the Amazon. Production patterns shift, and export patterns will reflect more fully the social cost of deforesting the Amazon.

Examples of such property-rights approaches are provided by recent agreements involving debt-for-nature swaps (Ruitenbeck, 1990). Another example is provided by recent agreements between the United States pharmaceutical industry and Costa Rica. The spearhead of this project is a pair of ingenious efforts to exploit the forests to obtain medicinal products. A Costa Rican research institute (INBIO) is prospecting for promising plants, microorganisms, and insects to be screened for medical uses by Merck and Company, the world's largest drug company. Merck, in turn, is supporting the prospecting effort financially and will share any resulting profits with Costa Rica. Thus Costa Rica has acquired property rights over the "intellectual property" embodied in the genetic information within its forests. A similar initiative was taken by a small Californian company, Shaman Pharmaceuticals, which is tapping the expertise of traditional healers, "Shamans" or medicine people, in various parts of the tropics (see Chichilnisky, 1993). The company intends to promote the conservation of the forests by channeling some of its profits back to the localities whose medicine people provided the key plants. The theory behind both ventures is that everybody wins: the world gets new drugs, the pharmaceutical companies earn profits, and people in the localities are justly compensated for their "intellectual property" and their conservation and collection efforts.[1]

Similar examples hold for land resources. Recently the government of Ecuador allocated a piece of the Amazon the size of the state of Connecticut to its Indian population, a clear property-rights policy.[2] Under the conditions examined here, this policy should lead to a better use of the forest's re-

---

[1]Examples of successful medical discoveries from rain forests and other natural sources include widely used medicines such as aspirin, morphine, quinine, curare, the rosy periwinkle used to treat childhood leukemia and Hodgkin's disease, and (more recently) taxol.

[2]Indian groups will gain title to land in Pastaza Province, a traditional homelands area covering 4,305 square miles in eastern Ecuador. Ecuador's move is part of a wider trend in the Amazon basin. Achuar, Shiwiar, and Quiche Indians will soon administer an area where population density averages five people per square mile.

sources and to a more balanced pattern of trade between Ecuador and the United States.

References

Amelung, Torsten. "Tropical Deforestation as an International Economic Problem." Unpublished manuscript presented at the Egon-Sohmen Foundation Conference on Economic Evolution and Environmental Concerns, Linz, Austria, 30–31 August 1991.

Barbier, Edward B.; Burgess, J. C. and Markandya, Anil. "The Economics of Tropical Deforestation." *AMBIO,* April 1991, *20*(2), pp. 55–58.

Binkley, C. S. and Vincent, Jeffrey R. "Forest Based Industrialization: A Dynamic Perspective." World Bank (Washington, DC) Forest Policy Issues Paper, 1990.

Bromley, Daniel W., ed. *Making the commons work.* San Francisco: ICS Press, 1992.

Chichilnisky, Graciela. "Biodiversity and Property Rights in the Pharmaceutical Industry." Case study, Columbia University School of Business, 1993.

Chichilnisky, Graciela and Heal, Geoffrey M. *The evolving international economy.* Cambridge: Cambridge University Press, 1987.

Cohen, Jon S. and Weitzman, Martin L. "A Marxian Model of Enclosures." *Journal of Development Economics,* February 1975, *1*(4), pp. 287–336.

Dasgupta, Partha. *The control of resources.* Cambridge, MA: Harvard University Press, 1992.

Hyde, W. F. and Newman, D. H. "Forest Economics in Brief—With Summary Observations for Policy Analysis." Unpublished manuscript (draft report), Agricultural and Rural Development, World Bank, Washington, DC, 1991.

McDonald, Steven, L. *Petroleum conservation in the United States: An economic analysis.* Baltimore, MD: Johns Hopkins University Press, 1971.

Ruitenbeck, H. J. "The Rainforest Supply Price: A Step Towards Estimating a Cost Curve for Rainforest Conservation." Development Research Programme Working Paper No. 29, London School of Economics, 1990.

Comment X.2. *Empirical Studies of the Impact of International Trade on the Environment in Less Developed Countries*

Empirical studies of the impact of international trade on environmental quality in LDCs have mostly been inconclusive or suggested small effects. There appears to be a consensus that pollution-intensive industries expanded faster in lower-income countries during the 1970s and 1980s, but the contribution of international trade to this trend is not clear. Patrick Low and Alexander Yeats find that the share of the output of dirty industries in the exports of many LDCs increased between 1965 and 1988. On the other hand, Nancy Birdsall and David Wheeler find that within Latin America dirtier industries tend to be located in the economies that are less open to international trade. These studies are included in a book edited by Patrick Low, *International Trade and the Environment* (1992). Gunnar S. Eskeland and Ann Harrison, "Moving to Greener Pastures? Multinationals and the Pollution-Haven Hypothesis," *Journal of Development Economics* (February 2003), examine the pattern of foreign investment in Côte d'Ivoire, Mexico, Morocco, and Venezuela and find almost no evidence that foreign investment is concentrated in dirty industries. They also find no evidence that foreign investment in these countries is related to pollution abatement costs in more developed countries. Werner Antweiler, Brian R. Copeland, and M. Scott Taylor, "Is Free Trade Good For the Environment?," *American Economic Review* (September 2001), argue on theoretical grounds that we might not expect increased openness to trade to have a large effect on the pollution intensity of output in low-income countries. Even if dirty industries are attracted to LDCs by lax environmental regulation, this could be offset by a comparative advantage effect, whereby output becomes more concentrated in labor-intensive industries that tend to be cleaner than capital-intensive industries.

There is perhaps more evidence to support a connection between international trade and deforestation than there is for links between international trade and any other form of environmental degradation in less developed countries. A particularly ambitious attempt to establish such a link is Ramón López, "Environmental Externalities in Traditional Agriculture and the Impact of Trade Liberalization: The Case of Ghana," *Journal of Development Economics* 3 (June 1997). For villages in western Ghana during the period 1988–1989 López finds an overexploitation of biomass through a more than optimal level of land cultivated: fallow periods appear to be too short and the level of deforestation too high. A simulation of his model predicts that trade liberalization will exacerbate this problem, just as the selection by Chichilnisky would lead one to expect, but López has no direct estimate of the impact of trade liberalization on deforestation in Ghana.

Selection X.3. Deforestation and the Rule of Law in a Cross Section of Countries*

I. Introduction

The use of forests and other natural resources in developing countries has received growing attention from environmentalists, the media, and government decision makers. Concern for forests, particularly tropical forests, stems both from the recent recognition that they provide critical services to host nations and worldwide, and from reports that global forest cover is shrinking. Many observers have attributed this shrinkage to population growth, the process of economic development, and misguided government policies. Much of the economic literature on deforestation stresses different factors—the importance of property rights and the role of ownership security in promoting conservation of forests and other natural assets. This paper examines these hypotheses empirically by testing for relationships between deforestation and three possible causes: population pressure, growth in income, and insecure property rights as reflected in measurable legal and political attributes of countries. . . .

The causes of deforestation are not well understood. Popular discussions often mistake associated effects and proximate causes for underlying forces (Panayotou 1990). Deforestation in developing countries is sometimes attributed to slash and burn agriculture, logging, and demands for fuel wood, fodder, and forest products. Yet temperate forests in many developed countries also face growing demand for forest products, logging activity, and agricultural competition for land, but generally are not experiencing the rapid forest depletion and land degradation found in the developing world. . . .

Southgate, Sierra, and Brown (1991) have examined the effect of ownership security and found that security of tenure, as measured by the prevalence of adjudicated land claims, is negatively related to deforestation rates. In addition, there is ample case study evidence that enforcement of property rights is lacking in countries experiencing rapid deforestation. Leases to harvest from government forests in developing countries often are of very short duration so the harvester's self-interest does not provide sufficient incentive to conserve the economic value of the forest. Governments

could of course encourage conservation on forests they own by closely controlling the harvest and regeneration practices of concessionaires. However, the associated costs and benefits are such that they seldom choose to do so (Repetto et al. 1989, 23; Boado 1988, 176, 186–87). . . .

The present paper examines this property rights hypothesis indirectly, by testing for associations between deforestation and measures of political turmoil and repression. The potential role of these political factors in deforestation is summarized here and a more detailed discussion is presented in Section V. Conserving a forest to yield a stream of output in future years rather than consuming it immediately is an act of investment. Intuitively, investors will not forego current consumption for a future return without some assurance that the future benefit will be received by the party who makes the initial sacrifice. Such assurances normally result from legal contracts and the force of reputation. When legal and political institutions are volatile or predatory, the degree of assurance is lowered and the incentive to invest is diminished. The empirical analysis that follows tests for relationships between changes in forest cover and relevant political factors using data from a cross section of 120 countries.

As used here, deforestation is simply defined as a reduction in the land area covered by forests, using Food and Agriculture Organization (FAO) definitions of forested land (FAO 1988). . . .

II. Empirical Approach and Data Used

. . . The primary source of forest cover data is *An Interim Report on the State of Forest Resources in the Developing Countries* (FAO 1988). This source provides data on "total forest" cover for 129 countries in 1980 and 84 countries in 1985. Total forest includes land area covered by both closed and open forests.[1] A secondary source, FAO's *Production Yearbook,* reports "forest and woodland area," defined as land area under natural or planted stands of trees plus logged-over area that will be reforested in the near future. This source is available annually for most countries.

---

*From Robert T. Deacon, "Deforestation and the Rule of Law in a Cross-Section of Countries," *Land Economics* 70 (November 1994): 414–425, 427–429. Reprinted by permission.

[1]A closed forest includes broad-leaved, coniferous, and bamboo forests, with tree crown cover exceeding 20 percent of the land. An open forest consists of mixed forest/grasslands with at least 10 percent tree cover. See World Resources Institute (1992, 292) for further details on these definitions.

The *Interim Report* is considered the more reliable of the two and hence is used as the primary source of data on forest cover. The fact that this series is unavailable for many countries in 1985 is a drawback, however. In order to extend it, a statistical relationship between *total forest* and *forest and woodland area* was estimated using data on 84 countries for which both series are available. The estimated equation was then used to predict total forest cover in 1985 for the missing observations. The form of the equation used to predict total forest is motivated by postulating a general functional relationship between total forest, T, and forest and woodland area, w. This relationship, denoted $T(w)$, is then expressed as a second-order Taylor series expansion of T around 1980 values

$$T_1 = T_0 + T'(w_1 - w_0) + (T''/2)(w_1 - w_0)^2$$

where 0 and 1 represent values in 1980 and 1985. Ordinary least squares regression yielded the following estimates, with standard errors in parentheses,

$$T_1 = .9995T_0 + 1.2451(w_1 - w_0)$$
$$\quad (.0056) \quad\quad (.1510)$$

$$+ 10.2301(w_1 - w_0)^2$$
$$(1.9863)$$

$$R^2 = .998$$

$$N = 84$$

where T and w are measured as fractions of the land area of countries. The high R^2 is of course due to the close correlation between T_0 and T_1. As the other coefficient estimates clearly indicate, however, changes in total forest are strongly related to changes in forest and woodland area.

In addition, measures of population, national income, and country specific indicators of the rule of law—variables that indicate the degree of political stability and popular representation—are needed. Data on population were taken from Banks (1990) and data on income, actually gross domestic product, were taken from Summers and Heston (1991). Political/legal indicators were obtained from Banks (1990). Indicators of political and legal stability include frequencies of political assassinations, riots, major constitutional changes, guerrilla warfare, attempts at revolution, riots, and government regime changes. As explained later, measures of political representation were also examined, including type of government executive (military, elected, monarch), frequency of political purges, and existence of an elected legislature.

These variables are defined more precisely in Section IV.

Table 1 lists the 120 countries examined, 20 of which are defined as "high income" by the World Bank. It also partitions the overall sample into two deforestation groups, depending on whether countries lost more or less than 10 percent of their 1980 forest cover during 1980–85. This sample excludes countries with less than 500,000 population or having less than 1 percent of land area covered by forests in 1980. It may seem surprising to see Brazil, Indonesia, and the Philippines included among low deforestation countries, as they often appear prominently in discussions of worldwide forest conversion. While these three countries account for large absolute areas of forest loss per year, this is partly due to the fact that the total forest areas in these countries are large. Their percentage deforestation rates ranged from 0.5–0.9 percent per year during 1980–85. By comparison, average annual deforestation rates in Afghanistan, Cote d'Ivoire, and Haiti were 3.7–5.0 percent during the same time span.

In what follows, each of the three hypotheses of interest is examined in isolation, by testing for associations between deforestation rates and, alternatively, population growth, income growth, and political attributes. These simple tests are useful for determining the sensitivity of results to the choice of sample, the exact definition and lag structure of determining variables, and so forth. These results are then used to formulate a more general model that allows for the presence of all three influences at once.

III. Deforestation and Population Growth

Many cite population growth as the single most important cause of deforestation (Allen and Barnes 1985, 175; World Bank 1992, 26–29; World Rainforest Movement 1990, 78). Population growth often leads to migration to the forests by peasants seeking land to clear for subsistence farming. Population growth also increases fuel wood collection, which removes nutrients from the forest. If nutrient loss is sufficiently intense, the result is slowed regeneration and eventual degradation of forest cover.

Table 2 provides a simple test of this hypothesis, where the dependent variable is the proportionate rate of deforestation during 1980–85. Positive population growth is associated with deforestation but the effect is not immediate. Rather, the strongest association is with the rate of population increase five years earlier. In this simple model, a 1 percent

Table 1. Countries in Sample

High deforestation	Low deforestation		
Low and middle income countries			
Afghanistan	Albania	German D. R.	Papua New Guinea
Costa Rica	Angola	Ghana	Paraguay
Cote d'Ivoire	Argentina	Greece	Peru
Ecuador	Bangladesh	Guatemala	Philippines
El Salvador	Benin	Guinea	Poland
Gambia	Bhutan	Guyana	Portugal
Guinea-Bissau	Bolivia	Hungary	Romania
Haiti	Botswana	India	Rwanda
Honduras	Brazil	Indonesia	Senegal
Iraq	Bulgaria	Iran	Sierra Leone
Jamaica	Burkina Faso	Kenya	Somalia
Lebanon	Burundi	Korea, North	Sudan
Liberia	Cambodia	Korea, South	Swaziland
Malawi	Cameroon	Lao P. D. R.	Tanzania
Nepal	Cent. African Rep.	Madagascar	Togo
Nicaragua	Chad	Malaysia	Trinidad and Tobago
Niger	Chile	Mali	Tunisia
Nigeria	China	Mauritius	Turkey
South Africa	Colombia	Mexico	Uganda
Sri Lanka	Congo	Mongolia	Uruguay
Syria	Cuba	Morocco	Venezuela
Thailand	Czechoslovakia	Mozambique	Vietnam
	Dominican Rep.	Myanmar	Yugoslavia
	Ethiopia	Namibia	Zaire
	Fiji	Pakistan	Zambia
	Gabon	Panama	Zimbabwe
High income countries			
Israel	Australia	F. R. Germany	Spain
	Austria	Ireland	Sweden
	Canada	Italy	Switzerland
	Cyprus	Japan	United Kingdom
	Denmark	Netherlands	United States
	Finland	New Zealand	
	France	Norway	

Note: Excludes countries with fewer than 500,000 population. See text for definitions.

increase in population during 1975–80 is associated with a proportionate forest cover reduction of 0.24–0.28 percent during 1980–85.

The simple correlation between cross country population growth rates in 1975–80 and 1980–85 is fairly high, 0.86 in this sample. For this reason the model was reestimated with the 1980–85 population growth rate excluded. As the figures in the third and fourth columns indicate, this increases the significance of the lagged growth rate but has no appreciable effect on the coefficient estimates. The second and fourth columns of coefficients indicate that these results are largely unchanged when countries with relatively light forest cover

are dropped from the sample.[2] The general tenor of these results—that deforestation is associated with lagged population growth—does not change appreciably when countries are separated by income levels. Reestimating these models with high income countries excluded yielded coefficients that are slightly smaller in algebraic value than those in Table 2, but the change is not significant. Surprisingly, perhaps, the population growth coefficients are all larger in algebraic value when estimated for

[2]The countries excluded are Afghanistan, Burundi, Haiti, Iran, Iraq, Israel, Kenya, Lebanon, Niger, Pakistan, South Africa, Syria, Tunisia, and Uruguay.

Table 2. Deforestation and Population Growth (ordinary least squares estimates)

Countries in sample	All	Forest > 5%	All	Forest > 5%
Log change in population, 1980–85	−.0304 (−0.17)	.0009 (0.01)	—	—
Log change in population, 1975–80	.2593 (1.52)	.2815 (2.01)	.2357 (2.55)	.2814 (3.34)
Log change in population, 1970–75	.0575 (0.69)	−.0221 (−0.20)	.0544 (0.67)	−.0218 (−0.22)
Constant	.0274 (2.27)	.0188 (1.08)	.0270 (2.30)	.0188 (1.82)
R^2	.08	.14	.08	.14
N	112	98	112	98

Notes: t-statistics in parentheses. The dependent variable is the 1980–1985 change in the logarithm of land area classified as forest. The heading "Forest > 5%" indicates that forest cover in 1980 exceeds 5 percent of the country's land area.

Table 3. Deforestation and Income Growth (correlation coefficients)

	All countries	Forest > 5%	Low and middle income
Log change in per-capita GDP, 1980–85	−.1776	−.1061	−.1423
Log change in per-capita GDP, 1975–80	−.0642	−.0890	−.0110
Log change in total GDP, 1980–85	−.0917	−.0044	−.1066
Log change in total GDP, 1975–80	.0380	.0227	.0349
N	105	92	85

Notes: Low and middle income countries are identified in Table 1. See note to Table 1 for other definitions.

high income countries. That is, a given rate of population growth is associated with a higher deforestation rate if it occurs in a high income country than in a low income country. Again, the most significant association is with population growth lagged five years.

IV. Deforestation and Income Growth

Growth in measured national income is often identified as an important correlate, and sometimes as a cause, of deforestation. This is implicit in discussions that attribute deforestation to economic development strategies that promote conversion of forests to plantation agriculture and the production of cash crops for export (World Rainforest Movement 1990, 41, ff.). It also appears at the heart of proposals to revise national income to appropriately incorporate the consumption of natural assets. Those who advocate such revisions point out that an important share of measured GNP, particularly in developing countries, is actually consumption of natural capital such as forests (see Repetto et al. 1989, 4–9; Solorzano et al. 1991).

Table 3 presents evidence relevant to this hypothesis. These simple correlation coefficients indicate that, if anything, the association between deforestation and growth in measured income is negative—rapid deforestation accompanies slow, or negative, measured economic growth. Experimentation with different samples indicates that this lack of association is robust. Although not shown in the table, a negative relationship between income growth and deforestation exists for high income countries as well.

Of course this does not invalidate the proposition that some growth in measured income actually is consumption of forest capital. It may indicate, however, that any such relationship based on capital consumption is outweighed by the increase in demand for forest preservation that comes with increases in income. Alternatively, it may indicate the presence of a third factor that is positively related to both income growth and the maintenance of forest cover. A possible set of such factors is examined next.

V. Deforestation, Ownership Security, and the Nature of Political Systems

Forest cover is a form of capital that is productive in several land uses. Land continuously covered by forest can yield a sustained flow of minor forest products such as fruit, latex, rattan, oils, or grazing (Peters, Gentry, and Mendelsohn 1989). Alternatively, forested land can be harvested intermittently to obtain timber, in which case the standing biomass at any time is capital that enables future timber growth. If a forest is used for sustainable shifting cultivation, with relatively long fallow periods during which forest cover is allowed to increase, then the growing stock is a store of nutrients that can be harvested periodically. The latter two land uses are very similar. Both involve an investment period during which forest capital accumulates followed by harvest, either of timber or of nutrients for agriculture, and both allow the possibility for this cycle to be repeated indefinitely.

A Simple Model of Default Risk and Land Use

Poorly enforced ownership exposes standing forests and other kinds of capital to a form of confiscation or default risk and thereby discriminates against capital intensive land uses. Long fallow periods between harvests of nutrients are attractive only if the individual, family, or tribe has some assurance that a parcel of land and its forest cover will not be invaded by squatters, harvested by a timber company, or confiscated by a government official. The same point applies to land used to grow timber. Likewise, land that would be used to grow minor forest products if ownership were enforced might be deforested instead if ownership becomes insecure, in order to obtain timber or simply to make the land available for less capital intensive uses. In general, poorly defined ownership favors either the conversion of forested land to noncapital intensive permanent agriculture or its degeneration to wasteland. . . .

The Role of Political Factors in Ownership Security

Insecure property rights, either to assets or income streams, might arise from two sorts of political circumstances. First, government may lack the power, stability, and popular support to enforce laws of property. Absent reliable third party enforcement and predictable legal interpretations of property claims, the individual's incentive to invest is weak. While this argument seems straightforward when applied to privately held property, a similar argument can be made for assets nominally owned by government. When government lacks the ability to enforce controls on how government forests are used they tend to be treated as free ac-

cess resources. This is manifest in Latin America and elsewhere by the colonization of national parks and government forest reserves by squatters. Further, if the institutions of government are weak or short-lived, proposals for long-term investment in government-owned assets will lack credibility since the segments of society making the initial sacrifice will have no guarantee of receiving the ultimate reward. Measures of general lawlessness, guerrilla warfare, armed revolt, and rapid changes in laws or constitutions are used as empirical indicators of such instability.

Second, it is hypothesized that the average individual's ownership security tends to be weak in countries that are governed by the rule of individuals and dominant elites rather than the rule of law and anonymous institutions. In such circumstances, one's property claim may depend heavily on the favor of a specific individual or clique rather than the persistence of a set of political and legal institutions. If the clique is deposed, its allies may lose their property. For those who are not in favor with the ruling elite, property claims are even more problematic since those who control government may choose to enforce laws selectively and redistribute property toward themselves or their allies. Such redistribution need not be direct, it may take the form of opportunistic taxation or regulation. Accumulating capital in such circumstances may simply invite confiscation. Empirically assessing the degree to which a country is ruled by individuals as opposed to laws is approached by determining whether its governmental system exhibits attributes of popular representation, for example, whether its leaders are elected, whether a legislature exists, whether political opposition is tolerated, and so forth.

Empirical Results

This general set of hypotheses initially was tested in a very simple way. Data on the attributes of political and governmental systems were obtained in each country, and country averages were formed over 1980–85. These average political attributes were then compared for countries experiencing high versus low deforestation during 1980–85, using the sample of countries shown in Table 1. The ten variables selected to measure general lawlessness and governmental/legal instability are shown in Table 4. The mean number of political assassinations per million population is a measure of general lawlessness, and may also indicate government instability. Other variables are primarily indicators of instability in a given regime's grip on

Table 4. Deforestation and Measures of Lawlessness and Governmental/Legal Instability (mean political attributes by deforestation rate, 1980–1985)

	High deforestation countries, μ_H	Low deforestation countries, μ_L	t-statistic* $H_0: \mu_L < \mu_H$	$Pr > t$
Political assassinations**	.0822	.0264	0.94 (24)	.18
General strikes**	.0245	.0142	0.88 (34)	.19
Riots**	.0468	.0284	1.04 (28)	.15
Anti-gov't. demonstrations**	.0645	.0482	0.82 (49)	.21
Guerrilla warfare	.3333	.2051	1.31 (31)	.10
Revolutions	.3258	.1859	1.63 (29)	.06
Major government crises	.1439	.0684	1.08 (25)	.14
Coups d'état	.0303	.0384	0.39 (31)	.36
Major constitutional changes	.1136	.0705	1.41 (31)	.08
Government regime changes	.0727	.0436	1.08 (30)	.14
Number of countries	22	78	—	—

*t-statistic is for the one-tailed test $H_0: \mu_H \leq \mu_L$ versus $H_a: \mu_H > \mu_L$. Degrees of freedom are in parentheses.

**Per million population.

Notes: Excludes 20 countries classified as "high income" by the World Bank. A *high deforestation* country is one that lost at least 10 percent of the forest cover existing in 1980 during 1980–85. A *political assassination* is any politically motivated murder or attempted murder of a high government official or politician. A *general strike* is a strike of 1,000 or more workers aimed at national government policies or authority. A *riot* is any violent demonstration of more than 100 citizens involving the use of physical force. *Anti-government demonstrations* are peaceful gatherings of at least 100 people for the primary purpose of displaying opposition to government policies or authority. *Guerrilla warfare* is the presence of any armed activity, sabotage, or bombings carried on by independent bands of citizens or irregular forces and aimed at the overthrow of the present regime. A *revolution* is an attempted illegal or forced change in top government elite, or armed rebellion intended to gain independence from the central government. A *major government crisis* is a rapidly developing situation that threatens to bring the downfall of the present regime—excluding revolt aimed at such overthrow. A *coup d'etat* is a successful extra-constitutional or forced change in the top government elite and/or its effective control of the nation's power structure—including successful revolutions. *Major constitutional changes* reports the number of basic alterations in a state's constitutional structure, e.g., adoption of a new constitution that alters roles of different branches of government (minor constitutional amendments are excluded). A *government regime change* is any change in the type of regime, e.g., civilian, military, protectorate, in charge of government.

Source: A. S. Banks, *Cross-National Time-Series Data Archive,* SUNY Binghamton, 1990.

power or, as in the case of major constitutional changes, a measure of the frequency of changes in the basic legal structure regardless of regime.

All variables in Table 4 are defined in such a way that figures in the first column will exceed those in the second if the hypothesis is correct. This expectation is confirmed for nine of the ten measures. The differences are significant at 10 percent using a one-tailed test for frequencies of revolutions, guerrilla warfare, and major constitutional changes. Contrary to expectations, coups de'état are slightly more frequent in low deforestation countries, but the difference is small and insignificant. All high income countries were excluded in these comparisons. When high income countries are included the differences become much sharper: t-statistics rise for all comparisons except coups d'état, which falls to near zero, and six of the ten differences become significant at 10 percent.

The second set of tests concerns the effect of popular representation on deforestation. The variables used to measure representation in each country are defined in Table 5. The first three of these are self-explanatory. Regarding the fourth, the chief executive of government is a premier only if chosen by elected representatives. This indicates, jointly, that the selection process is democratic and that the legislative branch exercises substantial power, hence the degree of representation is high. Representation is thus weaker if the executive is not a premier. Frequent political purges indicate that opposition, and hence competition for political power, is not tolerated. Consequently, the first five measures are *larger* in less representative systems and are expected to be greater in high deforestation countries. The sixth, "Legislature is elected," is expected to be *smaller* in less representative governments, and hence smaller in high deforestation countries. Regarding the last measure, frequent changes in executive might plausibly indicate competition in the executive branch. If so, such changes should be more common in low deforestation countries. Alternatively, more frequent executive change might signal greater instability in government policy and hence greater deforestation. The comparison in Table 5 supports the former hypothesis, although the difference is not highly significant.

To summarize the results obtained, all seven comparisons are as expected. Only two of the dif-

Table 5. Deforestation and Indicators of Nonrepresentative Government (mean indicators by deforestation rate, 1980–1985)

	High deforestation countries, μ_H	Low deforestation countries, μ_L	t-statistic* H_0: $\mu_L < \mu_H$	$Pr > t$
Government executive is military	.2424	.0940	1.80 (27)	.04
Nonelected executive	.4394	.3184	1.11 (33)	.14
No legislature exists	.1742	.1410	0.49 (36)	.31
Executive is not a premier	.6136	.4124	1.79 (36)	.04
Political purges	.0909	.0620	0.74 (30)	.23
Legislature is elected*	.7879	.8419	0.72 (35)	.24
Changes in executive*	.1136	.1624	1.16 (50)	.13
Number of countries	22	78	—	—

*t-statistic is for the one-tailed test H_0: $\mu_H \leq \mu_L$ versus H_a: $\mu_H > \mu_L$, except in tests involving *Legislature is elected* and *Changes in executive* where the inequalities are reversed.

Notes: Excludes 20 countries classified as "high income" by the World Bank. A *high deforestation* country is one experiencing a loss of forest cover during 1980–85 exceeding 10 percent of the amount existing in 1980. *Government executive is military* indicates that the individual who exercises primary influence in shaping the country's major internal and external decisions is in the armed services. *Executive is not a premier* indicates that the executive is not drawn from the legislature of a parliamentary democracy. A *purge* is the systematic elimination by jailing or execution of political opposition within the ranks of the regime or the opposition. *Legislature is elected* indicates that a legislature exists and that legislators are chosen either by direct or indirect election. *Changes in executive* are the number of times in a year that control of the executive changes to a new individual independent of the predecessor. Other measures are self-explanatory.

Source: A. S. Banks, *Cross-National Time-Series Data Archive,* SUNY Binghamton, 1990.

ferences are significant at 10 percent, however, those for "military executive" and for "executive is not a premier." Again, the results become much sharper when high income countries are included. In this case four of the seven are significant at 10 percent.

The 17 political measures in Tables 4 and 5 clearly are not independent. To test their joint association with deforestation, a logit regression equation was estimated using the political measures as regressors and testing their joint ability to predict a categorical variable denoting high versus low deforestation countries. When all 17 measures are included and the sample includes all 120 countries, the chi square statistic indicates the regression is significant at a probability level of 0.02. All but four of the coefficients have signs that accord with the differences in means reported earlier, and none of the four with perverse signs approach significance. When high income countries are excluded, the probability of no relationship rises to 0.15. If variables with z statistics below 0.5 are excluded, however, the probability level falls to 0.02 and the number of perverse signs falls to one. Overall, then, the null hypothesis that these measures of political instability and nonrepresentation are not related to deforestation is rejected. . . .

VI. A Preliminary Synthesis

The preceding results are broadly consistent with the hypotheses that deforestation results both from population growth—and the increased competition for land and natural resources that accompany it—and from political environments that are not conducive to investment. . . . The political factors identified as correlates of deforestation were combined with population growth rates in a single regression equation for deforestation. In addition, . . . a variable was formed as the residual from a regression equation of the investment rate on political variables found important in explaining deforestation. This residual is intended to capture aspects of the investment climate not reflected in available political attributes.

Regression results are reported in Table 6. The sign patterns exhibited earlier are largely unchanged. The elasticity of deforestation with respect to lagged population change is reduced noticeably from the level shown in Table 2 (.23–.28), however, and its significance is reduced. As before, the association between deforestation and population growth is stronger in the full sample than in the sample that omits high income countries. Guerrilla warfare and revolutionary activity are correlated with one another, so including both in the same equation causes the coefficients of both to decline somewhat.[3] For each measure, the coefficients for 1980–85 and 1975–80 are of opposite sign and similar magnitude, which suggests that deforestation is responsive to changes in these variables. With other variables in the model the frequency of constitu-

[3]Simple correlation coefficients range from .47 to .72.

Table 6. Deforestation, Population Growth, and Political Attributes (OLS regression coefficients)

Sample	All countries		Low and middle income	
Population growth, 1975–80	.1744	.1860	.0704	.1247
	(1.84)	(2.21)	(0.60)	(1.27)
Guerrilla warfare, 1980–85	.0539	.0462	.0451	.0392
	(1.75)	(1.66)	(1.34)	(1.32)
Guerrilla warfare, 1975–79	−.0297	−.0156	−.0141	−.0024
	(1.00)	(0.63)	(0.43)	(0.08)
Revolutions, 1980–85	.0313	.0606	.0415	.0662
	(0.95)	(2.10)	(1.16)	(2.19)
Revolutions, 1975–79	−.0536	−.0597	−.0579	−.0636
	(−2.00)	(−2.38)	(1.92)	(2.34)
Constitutional changes, 1980–85	.0200	—	.0122	—
	(0.32)		(0.18)	
Constitutional changes, 1975–79	−.0339	—	−.0357	—
	(0.81)		(0.79)	
Military executive, 1980–85	.0220	—	.0192	—
	(0.66)		(0.55)	
Military executive, 1975–79	.0017	—	.0029	—
	(0.06)		(0.10)	
Executive is not a premier, 1980–85	.0177	.0168	.0227	.0207
	(1.25)	(1.29)	(1.42)	(1.43)
Investment residual	.0154	—	.0200	—
	(0.21)		(0.25)	
N	106	118	86	98
R^2	.21	.20	.19	.19

Note: Absolute values of t-statistics in parentheses.

tional changes and the presence of a military head of government becomes insignificant, though their signs are as expected. Again, the variable "executive is a premier" was included for 1980–85 only since its values in different time periods are highly correlated. The investment residual, included to capture unmeasured effects on investment incentives, is (perversely) positive but insignificant. It is unavailable for 12 countries so its inclusion alters the sample substantially. Figures in the second and fourth columns present estimates obtained by excluding political and other measures that lacked significance in the original regressions.

VII. Conclusions

The intent of this paper was to present descriptive statistical results and simple hypothesis tests on alternative causes of deforestation, particularly insecure ownership. Consistent associations were found between deforestation and political variables reflecting insecure ownership, and this is encouraging. The explanatory power of the model is fairly low, however, so firm conclusions would be premature. One likely reason for low explanatory power is the exclusion of relevant variables that presently are unavailable, hence an obvious task for continuing research is to obtain and examine additional data.

References

Allen, Julia C., and Douglas F. Barnes. 1985. "The Causes of Deforestation in Developing Countries." *Annals of the Association of American Geographers* 75 (2):163–84.

Banks, A. S. 1990. "Cross-National Time-Series Data Archive." Center for Social Analysis, State University of New York, Binghamton, September 1979 (updated to 1990).

Boado, Eufresina L. 1988. "Incentive Policies and Forest Use in the Philippines." In *Public Policies and the Misuse of Forest Resources,* ed. R. Repetto and M. Gillis. Cambridge: Cambridge University Press.

Food and Agriculture Organization (FAO). 1988. *An Interim Report on the State of the Forest Resources in the Developing Countries.* Rome: United Nations.

Panayotou, Theodore. 1990. "The Economics of Environmental Degradation: Problems, Causes, and Responses." Harvard Institute for International Development. Mimeo.

Panayotou, Theodore, and Somthawin Sungsuwan. 1989. "An Econometric Study of the Causes of Tropical Deforestation: The Case of Northeast Thailand." Discussion Paper No. 284, Harvard Institute for International Development.

Peters, Charles M., Alwyn J. Gentry, and Robert O. Mendelsohn. 1989. "Valuation of an Amazonian Rainforest." *Nature* 399 (June 29):655–56.

Repetto, Robert, William Magrath, Michael Wells, Christine Beer, and Fabrizio Rossini. 1989. *Wasting Assets: Natural Resources in the National Income Accounts.* Washington, DC: World Resources Institute.

Solorzano, Raul, Ronnie de Camino, Richard Woodward, Joseph Tosi, Vincente Watson, Alexis Vasquez, Carlos Villalobos, Jorge Jimenez, Robert Repetto, and Wilfredo Cruz. 1991. *Accounts Overdue: Natural Resource Depreciation in Costa Rica.* Washington, DC: World Resources Institute.

Southgate, Douglas, Rodrigo Sierra, and Lawrence Brown. 1991. "The Causes of Tropical Deforestation in Ecuador: A Statistical Analysis." *World Development* 19 (9):1145–51.

Summers, Robert, and Alan Heston. 1991. "The Penn World Table Mark V." *Quarterly Journal of Economics* 61 (May):225–39.

World Resources Institute. 1992. *World Resources, 1992–93.* New York: Oxford University Press.

World Bank. 1992. *World Development Report 1992: Development and the Environment.* Oxford: Oxford University Press.

World Rainforest Movement. 1990. *Rainforest Destruction: Causes, Effects, and False Solutions.* Penang, Malaysia: World Rainforest Movement.

Selection X.4. Determinants of Pollution Abatement in Developing Countries: Evidence from South and Southeast Asia*

1. Introduction

Developing countries, particularly those in Asia, are fast adopting industrial pollution control standards similar to those in developed countries. Some end-of-pipe water pollution control is already evident in many South and Southeast Asian economies. Formal regulation has been greatly hampered, however, by the absence of clear and legally binding regulations; limited institutional capacity; lack of appropriate equipment and trained personnel; and inadequate information on emissions. At present, the government-imposed "price of pollution" is nearly zero for many manufacturing facilities in these economies.

One would predict highly pollution-intensive production under such conditions. Our research, however, has uncovered strongly contradictory evidence. Despite weak or nonexistent formal regulation and enforcement, there are many clean plants in the developing countries of South and Southeast Asia. Of course, there are also many plants which are among the world's most serious polluters. What explains such extreme interplant variation? This paper reviews evidence drawn from three empirical studies which we conducted during 1992–94:

A case study of plants in two sectors in one country: fertilizer and pulping in Bangladesh;

A survey and econometric evaluation of abatement efforts by plants in one sector in four countries: 26 pulp and paper plants in Bangladesh, India, Indonesia and Thailand;

An econometric analysis of many plants across many sectors in one country: Indonesia.

We are particularly interested in policy-relevant variables which are not conventionally associated with environmental regulation. Formal regulation will undoubtedly remain weak for some time, but other determinants of plant-level abatement may provide useful tools for directly or indirectly inducing pollution control. Our analysis incorporates three sets of factors which are relevant for decisions affecting the pollution intensity of an industrial process: plant characteristics, economic considerations, and external pressure.

*From Hemamala Hettige, Mainul Huq, Sheoli Pargal, and David Wheeler, "Determinants of Pollution Abatement in Developing Countries: Evidence from South and Southeast Asia," *World Development* 24 (December 1996): 1891–1902. Reprinted by permission.

Relevant plant characteristics may include production scale, choice of technology, vintage, ownership, management quality, available human resources and technical expertise. Plants' responsiveness to pressure for abatement may also vary significantly with economic considerations: input prices, profitability, market characteristics, availability of information on abatement technology, and sources of financing. Finally, plants may adapt to external pressure from government regulators, buyers, investors, and neighboring communities which suffer damage from pollution. In our empirical studies, we have assessed the significance and relative importance of these factors in determining plants' environmental performance.

The rest of section 1 reviews the current extent of regulation in the study countries and presents some evidence on variations in plant-level abatement. Section 2 develops a conceptual framework for analyzing interplant variation. Our evidence to date is summarized in section 3, while section 4 discusses the implications.

(a) The Current State of Regulation

During the past two decades, many developing countries have instituted pollution-control systems which are similar, at least on paper, to those in developed countries. Quantity-based regulation has been nearly universal, with considerable cross-country variation in reliance on instruments such as effluent concentration standards, volume standards, and mandated installation of pollution control equipment. There has also been great variation in the strictness of monitoring and enforcement of regulations. Our study countries illustrate the existing range of regulatory experience in developing countries.

(i) Bangladesh. The environmental absorptive capacity of this densely populated, riverain country is very low; current environmental concerns focus on the impact of water pollution. Industrial facilities in pollution-intensive sectors such as food, wood pulping, chemicals, and fertilizer nearly always discharge their wastes into rivers which serve large downstream populations.

National regulation of industrial effluents has been weak, with severe shortages of supporting funds and trained personnel. Formal regulatory standards exist only for waste water. It therefore seems clear that formal monitoring and enforcement procedures have had little impact on plants' environmental performance in Bangladesh. In many cases, however, local communities have been able to identify and bring pressure to bear on plants whose discharges have caused fish kills, illness, and damage to irrigated paddy crops.

(ii) India. The formal regulatory structure in India presents a strong contrast to that of Bangladesh. National and state environmental management systems have been highly organized for over a decade. Air and water effluent concentration standards have been legislated for a large number of pollutants. The central government sets reference standards, but lacks legislative and enforcement authority over the individual states. Differences in local political, economic and environmental conditions have led to different degrees of enforcement of the reference standards. There is extensive emissions reporting by plants in some states, with a growing trend toward verification of reports by state-approved research laboratories and consulting firms. Formal sanctions such as fines and threatened shutdowns seem to have generated some abatement efforts at the plant level.

(iii) Indonesia. Indonesian waste-water regulation has only been in place since 1992, so implementation does not meet developed-country standards. Environmental management authority is decentralized, with different effective standards across provinces and uniform standards within provinces. The government's major water pollution control initiative to date is the PROKASIH (Clean Rivers) program. Although it is voluntary, it has produced a response which suggests that current and prospective environmental regulations are taken seriously by plant managers. Since 1990, PROKASIH has elicited substantial pollution reduction from plants in 11 provinces and 23 river basins. It has also apparently been taken by non-PROKASIH plants as a credible signal that the government is serious about combating industrial pollution.

(iv) Thailand. Thailand has had environmental guidelines and pollution standards for several industrial sectors since the early 1980s. The regulatory program has lacked credibility because industrial plants are simply asked to comply with standards without any serious pressure or legal enforcement.

Figure 1. Percentage of plants in the Pasig River Basin (Philippines) by BOD removal rates.

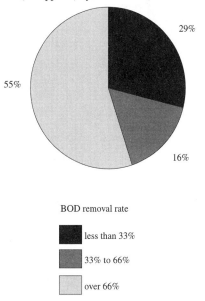

BOD removal rate

◼ less than 33%

◼ 33% to 66%

☐ over 66%

(b) Existing Variations in Abatement

Given the weakness of formal regulation in our sample countries, a conventional economic analysis would predict high emissions discharges in pollution-intensive sectors. If cost-minimizing polluters do not expect to pay for emissions, they should regard the environment as a free input and exploit it accordingly. Evidence gathered by World Bank field surveys and national regulators suggests, however, that such an analysis is far too simplistic.

Figure 1 shows the distribution of treatment rates of organic water pollution (BOD) by approximately 100 factories in the Pasig River Basin, Philippines.[1] These plants are all in the same region of the same developing country, operating under the supervision of the same national regulatory agency (DENR). Nevertheless, some are operating at or near high international standards while others are hardly cleaning their waste water at all.

[1]Biological Oxygen Demand (BOD) is one of the most commonly regulated water pollutants. Organic water pollutants are oxidized by naturally occurring microorganisms. These remove dissolved oxygen from the water and can seriously damage some fish species which have adapted to the previous dissolved oxygen level. Low levels of dissolved oxygen may also enable disease-causing pathogens to survive longer in water. The most common measure for BOD is the amount of oxygen used by microorganisms to oxidize the organic waste in a standard sample of pollutant during a five-day period.

Figure 2. BOD removal rates across a sample of Thai manufacturing plants.

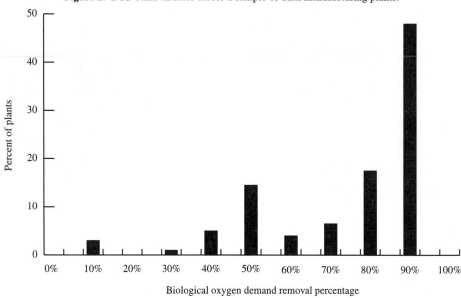

Biological oxygen demand removal percentage

Figure 3. BOD removal rates across a sample of the Philippines manufacturing plants.

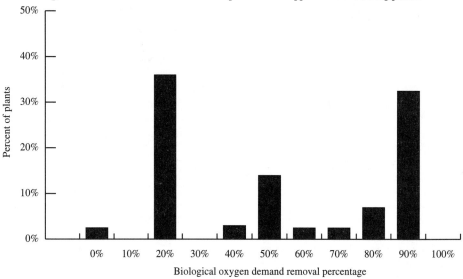

Biological oxygen demand removal percentage

Figures 2 and 3 compare samples of approximately 100 plants in the Metro Manila area (the Philippines) and the Bangkok region (Thailand: Suskawat and Ransig). The bar charts in the two figures depict the relative frequency of BOD removal rates in the two sets of plants, which were surveyed by the World Bank in the course of projects in these areas.

In the Philippines, DENR has overall regulatory authority. By contrast, Thailand's extremely "lais-sez-faire" approach to pollution control would seem to make it a likely candidate for "pollution haven" status. The average BOD reduction rate in Thailand is considerably higher than in the Philippines, however, and many Thai plants are running near OECD emissions standards. Approximately 50% of the plants are removing 90% of the BOD from the waste water stream, and 70–80% are removing over 70%. In the Philippines the distribution is less skewed, with about a third of the sample in each of the high, medium and low removal categories.

In Indonesia, the available plant-level data reveal the same pattern. Figures 4 and 5 show the distribution of effluent concentrations relative to US and Indonesian standards for large samples of Indonesian pulp and paper plants and textile mills.

While the US Environmental Protection Agency (EPA) is well staffed and has operated for over 20 years, the Indonesian national pollution control agency (BAPEDAL) is quite new, operates with a small staff and has little power to punish plants which are not in compliance with existing standards. Nevertheless, the actual distribution of In-

Figure 4. Distribution of BOD load intensity, Indonesian paper plants.

Figure 5. Distribution of BOD load intensity, Indonesian textile plants.

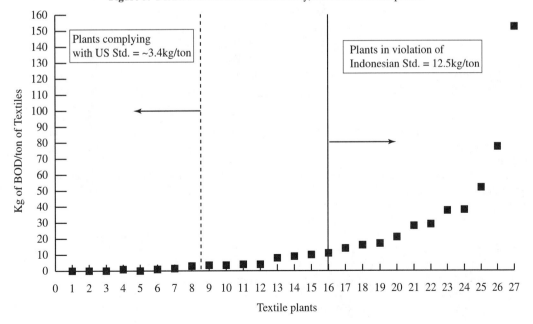

donesian plants is extremely broad, overlapping both US and Indonesian standards. Approximately two-thirds of the plants are in compliance with Indonesian standards, and one-third would be in compliance with US standards.

To summarize, the existing evidence does not conform to the predictions of conventional environmental economics. Pollution is undeniably an externality, and regulation in all our sample countries is quite weak by OECD standards. Cost-minimizing plants should all favor pollution-intensive production under these circumstances. Analysis of plant-level emissions reveals, however, a distribution of emissions reduction rates which overlaps typical OECD distributions. Average pollution reduction is clearly lower in the Asian developing economies, but more than a few plants are operating at or near world-class environmental performance standards.

2. The Economics of Industrial Pollution in Developing Countries: Some Hypotheses

The variation in pollution intensity of plants in developing countries, even in the absence of formal regulation, has led us to consider community pressure and environmental reputation as two potentially important factors influencing plants' environmental performance.

(a) Community Pressure

The recent literature includes many accounts of plants' response to community pressure in Asia. Cribb (1990) details several agreements reached by plants and communities in Indonesia. Khator (1991) uses several case studies to illustrate ways in which plants have responded to community pressure in India. In some instances, plants reduce their emissions by installing new treatment facilities. In other instances, they compensate the community indirectly by providing drinking water, blankets, or new facilities such as temples and community halls. Some plants, however, successfully refuse to address the pollution problem.

Khator notes that directly affected communities are usually the first to react to industrial pollution problems. Most activism begins with incidents such as fish kills, crop damage or the spread of disease, which can easily be associated with pollution from neighboring plants. Villagers' ability to organize and modify polluters' behavior is often limited, however, by a high illiteracy rate, lack of resources, or lack of influence over government officials. In addition, their capacity to pressure of-

fending plants is sometimes compromised by their dependence on those same plants for employment.

(b) Reputation

The ability and willingness of plants to respond to community pressure may also depend on reputation-related factors. Evidence from the United States suggests that large polluters have strong incentives to improve their environmental reputations through participation in voluntary cleanup programs. Arora and Cason (1995) find that large plants with high toxic releases have been more likely to participate in the US EPA's voluntary, highly publicized 33/50 program. Their results also suggest that the probability of joining such programs is enhanced by a plant's profitability and the competitiveness of the markets in which it operates. Arora and Cason argue that higher profits in imperfect capital markets enable some plants to finance voluntary cleanup, and that competitive markets prompt them to differentiate their products on environmental quality. Their results also suggest that such effects are more pronounced in consumer goods industries. . . .

3. Evidence from South and Southeast Asia

(a) A Case Study of Publicly Owned Plants in Bangladesh

This study by Huq and Wheeler (1993) draws on a 1992 survey of seven manufacturing plants in two sectors: fertilizer and wood pulp. The survey included four of the five urea fertilizer plants in Bangladesh, a superphosphate fertilizer plant and two large pulping facilities. All were public enterprises managed by the Bangladesh Chemical Industries Corporation (BCIC). They were of widely varying ages, and evenly distributed between urban and rural locations scattered throughout Bangladesh. The survey investigated process technologies, end-of-pipe treatment efforts, and the efficiency of general waste management. Results are summarized in Table 1, which categorizes plants by pollution intensity, abatement effort, relevant characteristics, location, and the nature of the surrounding community.

Weak vintage effects are suggested by Table 1, but the power of "clean technology bundling" is apparent: each of the four fertilizer plants was built with foreign aid, which was tied to technical assistance and equipment acquisition from the donor country. Each plant's environmental performance therefore reflects donor-country standards at the

Table 1. Plant and Community Characteristics Data from a Plant-Level Survey in Bangladesh

| Plant | Technology choice | | | Community | | | |
	Donor country	Year of installation (vintage)	Process pollution intensity	Cleanup effort	Local pressure	Identifiable	Job options
Urea Fertilizer Factory (UFF—Ghorasal, Narsingdi)	Japan	1968	Medium	High	High	Y	Medium
Polash Urea Fertilizer Factory (PUFF—Polash, Narsingdi)	China	1985	Medium	Medium	High	Y	Medium
Chittagong Urea Factory Ltd (CUF—Rangudia, Chittagong)	Japan	1989	Low	None	Zero	Y	High
Natural Gas Fertilizer Factory (NGFF—Fenchuganj, Sylhet)	Japan	1961	High	Medium	Low	Y	Low
Triple Superphosphate Complex (TSPC—North Patenga, Chittagong)	N.A.	1970	High	None	High	Y	High
Khulna Newsprint Mill (KNM—Khalishpur, Khulna)	Canada	1959	Medium	None	Zero	N	High
Sylhet Pulp and Paper Mill (SPPM—Chatak, Sylhet)	FRG	1975	High	High	Zero	Y	Low

Source: Huq and Wheeler (1993).

time of installation. The three Japanese plants constructed in 1961 (NGFF), 1968 (UFF) and 1989 (CUF) have been successively cleaner. The newest plant (CUF) has internalized environmental concerns to such an extent that there is little need for end-of-pipe (EOP) treatment. In contrast, the PUFF plant installed by China in 1985 has process technology and environmental performance similar to those of UFF, which was constructed by Japan in 1968.

In the absence of formal regulation, community pressure has apparently been quite effective in many instances. Negotiated settlements have included monetary compensation for damage to fisheries and paddy fields, and installation of EOP treatment equipment. Of the three plants which experienced pressure from adjacent communities, two undertook to clean up. The outlier in this context is TSPC, a highly polluting plant which has been identified as a major problem by the Bangladesh government. Its failure to respond to external pressure seems to reflect intractable management problems. Of the four plants where little local pressure was evident (CUF, NGFF, KNM, and SPPM),

only one (SPPM) undertook a substantial cleanup effort.

In all three instances where community pressure was evident (UFF, PUFF and TSPC), the plants were clearly identifiable polluters and other employment opportunities were plentiful. CUF was also clearly identifiable and operating in an area where employment opportunities were abundant. It did not face any local pressure, however, because it was already a very clean plant. The lack of community pressure on SPPM and NGFF, clearly identifiable as the only polluting facilities in a rural setting, may have been due to the scarcity of employment in their areas. In contrast, the location of the KNM plant among several other polluting facilities may have made it more difficult for the community to single out.

(b) A Crosscountry Survey of Paper and Pulp Plants

This section reviews the evidence from a survey of 26 pulp and paper plants in four countries (Bangladesh, India, Indonesia and Thailand) analyzed by Hartman, Huq and Wheeler (1995). The survey was sponsored by the World Bank and conducted by one of the authors (Huq) during a period of three months in 1992. The pulp and paper sector was chosen because it has both high pollution potential and alternative process technologies with highly varied pollution intensities. The sample was chosen to maximize variation in location- and ownership-related variables within the four countries. In Indonesia and Thailand the survey was conducted in Java and the Bangkok region, respectively; in India it spanned four states: Maharashtra, Kerala, Karnataka and West Bengal. The Bangladesh survey was a countrywide exercise.

The study focused on the degree to which plants had installed pollution-control technologies which were directly observable. This was the only feasible approach for a rapid survey, and it had the additional advantage of circumventing uncertainties about the quality of reported emissions data. As previously noted, emissions monitoring and reporting in the sample economies have been very weak in most cases. . . . Table 2 presents final regression results for the abatement effort equations, after nonsignificant variables have been dropped. Although degrees of freedom are modest, the results are quite strong.

(i) Formal and Informal Regulations. The results suggest that both formal and informal regulatory pressure have been significant determinants of abatement effort. As the formal regulation index increases, it is associated with a strong increase in the abatement effort index (ABI: scaled 0–36). Plants which experienced significant local pressure to abate score approximately 10 points higher on the ABI in Model I. Model II replaces the Pressure dummy with two hypothesized determinants of effective pressure: per capita income and the visibility of the plant (with relative invisibility proxied by location in a large city). Although the overall regression fit is not as good, it seems clear that these variables are robust instruments. Abatement effort rises strongly with national income per capita. In addition, plants operating "invisibly" in large urban/industrial clusters score nearly 12 points lower on the ABI.

(ii) Scale. Scale effects are tested with a quadratic specification in plant employment. The results suggest powerful scale economies for abatement, which apparently decline at the margin. They may also have significance for the analysis of community pressure. In local economies, large plants should be more visible and therefore more susceptible to pressure for cleanup. On the other hand, larger employers might expect more leniency from communities which value the jobs they provide. These results suggest that the combined effects of scale economies and visibility strongly outweigh any leniency effect.

(iii) Vintage, Process Technology. Age of plant has no measurable impact, probably because the survey's focus is on abatement at the end-of-pipe. Age of plant, however, may not be a good proxy

Table 2. Regression Results (dependent variable: Abatement Effort Index)

Variable	Model I (Adj. R^2 = 0.871)		Model II (Adj. R^2 = 0.752)	
	Coefficient estimate	t stat.	Coefficient estimate	t stat.
Intercept			−47.210	−2.69**
Community variables				
Degree of formal regulation	3.366	3.530**	2.991	1.926*
D [pressure]	9.676	2.341**		
Log [per capita income]			6.763	2.482**
D [big city location]			−11.946	−4.366**
Firm variables				
Employment	0.007	2.498**	0.004	1.956*
(Employment)^2	−1.04e^{-06}	−2.517**	−5.69e^{-07}	−1.834*
Competitive	3.487	1.723*	5.712	3.649**
D [state ownership]	−12.794	−2.798**		
D [clean technology]	−6.899	−1.912*		
No. of observations	22		20	

*Significant at 10% confidence level.

**Significant at 1% confidence level.

Source: Hartman, Huq and Wheeler (1995).

for equipment vintage in this survey, because many plants have replaced or improved their process technologies over time. The results do suggest that EOP abatement was not significantly more costly in older pulp and paper plants. As expected, they also show substantially less abatement effort—seven fewer ABI points—in plants whose cleaner process technologies already gave them a lower pollution intensity.

(iv) Competitiveness, Profitability. The results suggest an increase in the ABI of 4–5 points for each unit increase in management's assessment of plant competitiveness and profitability. This may reflect both greater availability of resources for financing cleanup and the superior implementation ability of well-managed plants.

(v) Ownership, Financing, Market Orientation. The results suggest that publicly owned facilities undertake far less abatement, even after controlling for vintage, efficiency and scale. Other things equal, SOE's score nearly 13 points lower on the ABI. Clearly, the bureaucratic shielding effect outweighed any soft budget constraint effect in the sample.

Multinational branch plants do not have higher ABI scores than their domestic private counterparts, ceteris paribus. In addition, the study finds no effect for export orientation or foreign financing of construction. These results certainly run counter to the conventional wisdom, but the latter seems to have been based on only a few anecdotes in any case.

(c) A Cross-sectoral Econometric Analysis of Indonesian Plants

This section draws on an econometric analysis by Pargal and Wheeler (1995) of organic water pollution (BOD) in Indonesian factories. The data are for 1989–90, when there was no effective national regulation of water pollution. This exercise therefore provided the opportunity to test a "pure" model of informal regulation, or community pressure, for a relatively large sample of manufacturing facilities located throughout the country.

As before, the analysis incorporated both economic factors and plant/firm-specific variables. It was possible to construct a relatively comprehensive data-base because the data collection system in Indonesia is one of the most efficient and comprehensive in the developing world. . . .

Regression results from the study of 243 Indonesian factories are presented in Table 3. The dependent variable is the log of annual BOD emissions. Since the log of output is incorporated on the right-hand side, the regressions can be interpreted as explaining variations in pollution intensity (or pollution per unit of output). The results are generally consistent with the findings of the four-country survey.

(i) Economic Variables. Although it is plausible to assume significant relations of complementarity or substitution for pollution with labor and energy, the results provide no supporting evidence. Complementarity with materials is consistent with the result for the Java dummy, which proxies higher transport costs for materials imported from the other Indonesian islands. This, however, is clearly a very crude index.

(ii) Plant/Firm Characteristics. These results are all consistent with the prior results, with the exception of plant vintage. They suggest higher pollution intensity for older plants, although the result does not have high significance. This may be because of the weak proxy used for plant vintage. As before, the results suggest very significant scale economies in abatement. Ceteris paribus, pollution intensity declines 0.35% for each 1% increase in output. Economic efficiency decreases pollution intensity; state ownership increases it; foreign ownership has no effect; and more visible plants are under significantly greater pressure to abate. The visibility effect is measured by two variables: the plant's share of total local manufacturing employment, and local degree of urbanization (measured by population density). Plants which are larger relative to the local economy pollute less, ceteris paribus; plants in more urbanized areas surrounded by other plants are able to pollute more. Because of the visibility effect it is harder to identify the plants which contribute to severe pollution exposure problems in cities.

(iii) Community Characteristics. As before, community per capita income has a very powerful effect on pollution intensity. Local education, although highly correlated with income, is still estimated to have an independent effect on pollution intensity. There is no independent estimate of community pressure in this case, but the mechanism is presumed to be the same as that discussed in the previous sections. . . .

4. Conclusions

(b) Policy Implications

The message of our results to date is an extremely hopeful one for sustainable development,

Table 3. Regression Results (dependent variable: Log BOD Load)

N = 243 Variable	Model [Adj R^2 = 0.3146]	
	Coefficient*†	t stat.
Intercept	31.580 (6.76)	4.67**
Economic variables		
Log [OUTPUT]	0.647 (0.19)	3.34**
Log [WAGE]	−0.740 (0.62)	−1.2
Log [FUEL PRICE]	−2.257 (2.42)	−0.93
D [JAVA]	−1.231 (0.55)	−2.23*
Plant/firm variables		
Log [VA/WORKER]	−0.325 (0.18)	−1.81*
LOG [AGE]	0.273 (0.17)	1.64
FOREIGN OWNERSHIP	−0.002 (0.01)	−0.27
STATE OWNERSHIP	0.017 (0.01)	2.64**
Community Variables		
Log [LOCAL EMPLOYMENT]	−0.352 (0.18)	−1.94*
Log [INCOME PER CAPITA]	−4.021 (0.91)	−4.41**
Log [% GT PRIMARY]	−1.072 (0.57)	−1.87*
Log [POP. DENSITY]	0.344 (0.17)	2.04*

*$H_0 \cdot b$ = 0 rejected with 90% confidence (two-tail).

**$H_0 \cdot b$ = 0 rejected with 99% confidence (two-tail).

†White heteroscedasticity-consistent standard errors in parentheses.

Source: Pargal and Wheeler (1995).

because several major policy trends appear favorable for environmental performance. The current wave of privatization implies declining significance for pollution-intensive public enterprises. Deregulation during the 1980s has presumably increased plant-level efficiency in the private sector, with significant reductions in pollution intensity. Rapidly spreading multinational facilities are relatively clean, and their performance is matched by otherwise comparable domestic plants. The equipment vintage effect may also have some importance. New facilities contribute a major share of output in rapidly industrializing economies, and our results provide some support for the proposition that many of these plants will be cleaner because they employ newer technology.

Our results on informal regulation also suggest that improvements in the quality of life will have an important impact. Post-primary education and per capita income are now advancing steadily in many Asian and Latin American countries, and this should lead to stronger local pressure on many polluting facilities.

The important role for informal regulation has several implications for environmental policy in developing countries. First, it is consistent with a model of local equilibrium pollution which reflects community differences, the market value of environmental reputation, and a number of insights from conventional environmental economics. Widespread informal regulation in a developing country represents a promising foundation for decentralized regulatory policy. Our results suggest that new formal regulatory systems may be able to build on local arrangements rather than replacing them at unnecessarily high cost.

Second, the economics of informal regulation have implications for formal regulation as well. Application of similar principles to national and state-level regulation would encourage the use of market-based instruments with regionally variable "pollution prices" associated with emissions charges or tradable emissions permits.

Third, and probably most important, our results suggest that community income and education are very important determinants of informal regulatory outcomes. Does this mean that "environmental injustice" is an important policy issue in developing countries? Income-based differences in pollution prices certainly reflect inequity in the distribution of income. As such, they may reflect a general problem of social justice. They do not necessarily imply additional "environmental injustice," however, because poor communities with limited resources may trade environmental quality against other social goods.

The effect of education on the price of pollution may, however, provide a stronger case. Poor communities with low levels of education and information may permit inappropriately high pollution, either because they are not aware of it, they cannot evaluate its consequences, or they are unable to organize to combat it. To compensate, formal regulation could be targeted particularly on the pollution control problems of poor communities. Alternatively, governments could try to raise environmental awareness while developing programs to empower poor communities.

References

Arora, Seema and Timothy Cason, "An experiment in voluntary environment regulation: Participation in EPA's 33/50 program," *Journal of Environmental Economics and Management,* Vol. 28 (1995), pp. 271–286.

Cribb, R., "Politics of pollution control in Indonesia," *Asian Survey,* Vol. 30 (December 1990), pp. 1123–1135.

Hartman, Raymond, Mainul Huq and David Wheeler, "Why paper mills clean up: Results from a four-country survey in Asia," Policy Research Department Working Paper (Washington, DC: The World Bank, 1995).

Huq, Mainul and David Wheeler, "Pollution reduction without formal regulation: Evidence from Bangladesh," Environment Department Working Paper, No. 1993–39 (Washington, DC: The World Bank, 1993).

Khator, Renu, *Environment, Development and Politics in India* (Lanham, MD: University Press of America, 1991).

Pargal, Sheoli and David Wheeler, "Informal regulation of industrial pollution in developing countries: Evidence from Indonesia," Policy Research Department Working Paper, No. 1416 (Washington, DC: The World Bank, 1995).

However defined, achieving sustainable development necessarily entails creating and maintaining wealth. Given the centrality of savings and investment in economic theory, it is surprising that the effects of depleting natural resources and degrading the environment have not, until recently, been considered in measurements of national savings. Augmented measures of savings and wealth in the national accounts are critical to conceptualizing and achieving sustainable development. . . .

Valuing depletion and degradation within a national accounting framework is an increasingly viable proposition, both as a result of the significant progress made in techniques of valuing environmental resources (for a recent example, see Freeman 1994) and as a result of the expanding foundation that theoretical developments are placing under the methods of "green" national accounting (Weitzman 1976, Hartwick 1990, Mäler 1991, and Hamilton 1994, 1996). The first cross-country application of these greener accounting methods to the measurement of net savings appears in Pearce and Atkinson (1993), who combine published estimates of depletion and degradation with standard national accounting data to calculate true savings for 20 countries. According to this measure many countries appear to be on unsustainable paths because their gross savings are less than the sum of conventional capital depreciation and natural resource depletion.

Enlarging the concept of net savings to include the depletion of natural resources is a reasonable way to extend traditional savings concepts. The depletion of a natural resource is, in effect, the liquidation of an asset and therefore should not appear as a positive contribution to net income or net savings. Although minor technical issues remain, the methods of valuing the discovery, depletion, and growth of commercial natural resources in the context of the System of National Accounts (SNA) are now well developed (Hamilton 1994 and Hill and Harrison 1994).

More problematic is the valuation of environmental degradation. While United Nations guidelines for environmental accounting favor valuation according to the cost of restoring the environment to its state at the beginning of the accounting period—the maintenance-cost method—theoretical

*From Kirk Hamilton and Michael Clemens, "Genuine Savings Rates in Developing Countries," *World Bank Economic Review* 13 (1999): 333–334, 338–348, 351–352. Reprinted by permission.

approaches suggest that the marginal social costs of pollution are a more correct basis for valuing emissions into the environment (United Nations 1993 and Hamilton 1996). . . .

Measuring Resource Depletion and Environmental Degradation

Building on the theory of green national accounting, this article provides a first set of calculations of genuine savings from a consistently derived and reasonably comprehensive time series data set on resource depletion and carbon dioxide emissions. Previous studies, such as Repetto and others (1989), Sadoff (1992), and Kellenberg (1995), deal with particular countries in depth. The calculations presented here necessarily trade off some amount of accuracy against wider coverage.

Data availability limits the adjustments to savings measures to the following: valuing resource rents for nonrenewable resources, valuing depletion of forests beyond replacement levels, and valuing the marginal social costs of carbon dioxide (CO_2) emissions.

The basic approach to calculating resource rents for nonrenewable resources is to subtract country- or region-specific average costs of extraction from the world price for the resource in question, all expressed in current U.S. dollars. Many world prices were derived from World Bank (1993): where multiple markets—for example, London and New York—are reported, a simple average of these market prices serves as the world price. So, for minerals the total resource rents are calculated as the world price minus mining costs minus milling and beneficiation costs minus smelting costs minus transport to port minus "normal" return to capital. Cost data are derived from U.S. Bureau of Mines (1987).

For crude oil, unit rents are calculated as the world price minus lifting costs. These lifting costs were estimated based on data from the Inter-American Development Bank (IDB 1981), International Energy Agency (IEA 1994b, 1995c, 1995d, 1996), Jenkins (1989), Sagers, Kryukov, and Shmat (1995), and Smith (1992).

Natural gas, although its international trade has soared in recent years, cannot yet be said to possess a single world price. A world price was estimated by averaging free-on-board prices from several points of export worldwide, after which the unit rents were calculated like those for oil. Production costs were taken from Adelman (1991), Cornot-Gandolphe (1994), IEA (1995d), Julius and Mashayekhi (1990), Khan (1986), Liefert (1988), Mashayekhi (1983), and Meyer (1994).

For hard coal a world price was calculated by combining data on steam and coking coals after adjusting for differences in heat content and quality. A world price for lignite was obtained by analyzing national-level differences in prices between hard coal and lignite in various countries and estimating a similar proportion of values to hold true with respect to the world price for hard coal. Unit rents for both hard coal and lignite were then calculated as for oil. Coal production costs were taken from Bhattacharya (1995), Doyle (1987), IEA (1994a, 1995b, 1995d, 1995e,), Tretyakova and Heinemeier (1986), and World Bank data.

For forest resources only rent on the portion of wood production that exceeds the country's mean annual increment in commercial wood mass was subtracted from savings. A price for the wood of each country was calculated based on the proportions of fuelwood, coniferous softwood, nonconiferous softwood, and tropical hardwood found in total annual production. Representative world prices were used for each type of wood, and a price for fuelwood was estimated using World Bank data. Unit rents were calculated by subtracting average unit harvest costs from the world price.

There are several further points to note about this methodology:

- From a theoretical viewpoint depletion estimates depend on scarcity rents, which should be measured as price minus *marginal* cost of extraction (including a normal return to capital). In practice, data on marginal production costs are almost never available, and practitioners (as evidenced by the green national accounting literature) fall back on using average extraction costs. This tends to overstate calculated resource rents and hence to understate genuine savings.
- Countries may or may not be selling their natural resources for internal consumption at world market prices, although they have good incentives to do so. Moreover, the use of uniform world prices tends to overstate rents for countries with lower-grade resources.
- Extraction costs are measured at a fixed point in time, which differs from country to country and resource to resource according to the availability of data. Extraction costs are held constant (in real terms) during 1970–94. World prices vary

over time, leading to corresponding variations in calculated rental rates.

- If the extraction cost data are region- rather than country-specific, the regional cost structure is applied to all of the producing countries in the region.
- Rents on minerals are generally viewed as accruing to the resource owner for the production of the crude form of the material in question, typically an ore. In practice, most mineral operations are vertically integrated to a considerable extent, and the only price and cost data are for refined forms of the materials. Measuring resource rents as described above for these vertically integrated mineral operations therefore implicitly ascribes to the resource rent any excess returns to capital for the milling and refining stages.

Table 1 presents the calculated average rental rates for several resources. The table also shows which cost components, subject to data availability, went into the calculation of rental rates. In most (but not all) cases an explicit rate of return on capital appears as a cost component. Missing cost components lead, of course, to overestimates of resource rents. In line with . . . green national accounting methods . . . , the country-specific unit resource rents in each year are multiplied by the quantities of resource extraction for each of the resources in Table 1 to arrive at the total value of resource depletion.

For tropical forest resources, valuing depletion is much more complicated. Where deforestation is occurring, the issue is essentially one of land use, with standing forests being one use among many for a particular land area. This suggests that the correct way to value deforestation is to measure the change in land value (which should represent the present value of the net returns under the chosen use for land); this is essentially the result in Hartwick (1992). . . .

Because data on the value of forested land before and after clearance are not widely available, deforestation is not treated explicitly, and forest depletion is simply valued as the stumpage value (price minus average logging cost) of the volume of commercial timber and fuelwood harvested in excess of natural growth in commercially valuable wood mass for that year. Harvest rates by country are as given in FAO (1994). The annual increment is estimated using World Bank data and Duvigneaud (1971), Lamprecht (1989), FAO/UNECE (1992), and Kanowski and others (1992). Stumpage rates come from World Bank data, Openshaw and Feinstein (1989), Kellenberg (1995), and oth-

Table 1. Rental Rates for Natural Resources
(share of world price)

Natural resource	Mean	Standard deviation	Cost components
Bauxite	0.61	0.13	Mining, milling
Copper	0.49	0.20	Mining, milling, smelting, 15 percent return on capital
Crude oil	0.65	0.26	Production costs
Forestry	0.45	0.13	Logging and transport
Gold	0.29	0.15	Mining, milling, transport, 15 percent return on capital
Hard coal	0.28	0.17	Mining and transport
Iron ore	0.58	0.24	Mining, beneficiation, transport
Lead	0.23	0.12	Mining, milling, smelting, transport, 15 percent return on capital
Lignite	0.38	0.17	Mining and transport
Natural gas	0.59	0.24	Production costs
Nickel	0.35	0.21	Mining, milling, smelting
Phosphate rock	0.26	0.14	Mining, milling, transport, 15 percent return on capital
Silver	0.31	0.22	Mining, milling, transport, 15 percent return on capital
Tin	0.35	0.16	Mining, milling, 15 percent return on capital
Zinc	0.21	0.13	Mining, milling, smelting, transport, 15 percent return on capital

Note: Values are for unweighted pooled data from 1985–94 (except silver and tin, 1975–94), excluding negative values.
Source: Authors' estimates.

ers; market prices are from FAO (1983, 1995), Openshaw and Feinstein (1989), van Buren (1990), Barnes (1992), and World Bank (1993).

The foregoing description of the valuation of forest depletion suggests that the calculations are quite rough. It should also be obvious that the values calculated pertain only to commercial exploitation, so that the values of biodiversity, carbon sequestration, and other uses are not captured.

Pollution damages can enter green national accounts in different ways. Although damage to produced assets (the damage to building materials caused by acid rain, for example) is in principle included in depreciation figures, in practice most statistical systems are not detailed enough to pick this up. The effects of pollution on output (damaged crops, lost production owing to morbidity) are usually not broken out explicitly, but because they are reflected implicitly in the standard national accounts, there is no need to adjust savings measures in this regard.[1] Traditionally, the key pollution adjustment is for welfare effects, valuing the willingness-to-pay to avoid excess mortality and the pain and suffering from pollution-linked morbidity. Because these marginal damage figures are locale-specific, no general treatment of pollution emissions is attempted in the following discussion.

[1]However, if the productive capacity of an asset, such as soil fertility, is damaged by pollution, then the loss in asset value should be deducted from savings.

The only social costs considered here, therefore, are for carbon dioxide. Data are readily available for this pollutant, and damages are global rather than strictly local. The basic emissions data employed are from the Carbon Dioxide Information and Analysis Center (CDIAC 1994), covering fossil fuel combustion and cement manufacture. The global marginal social cost of a metric ton of carbon emitted is assumed to be $20 in 1990, taken from Fankhauser (1994). Global damages are charged to emitting countries on the assumption that the property right to a clean environment lies with the pollutee—for example, we are assuming that the Comoros Islands have the right not be inundated as a result of CO_2 emissions elsewhere.

A key element missing in the calculations is any valuation of soil erosion, owing to the lack of comprehensive data sets on either physical erosion or its value. This is an important gap considering the significance of agriculture in most developing countries—erosion is considered to be a major problem in Sub-Saharan African countries in particular. A second missing element is fish stocks, where data problems, questions of ownership, and near-zero rental values resulting from overfishing all militate against including values of depletion.

Empirical Estimates of Genuine Savings

The traditional measure of a nation's rate of accumulation of wealth, as reported in the World

Figure 1. Genuine savings in Tunisia, 1970–94.

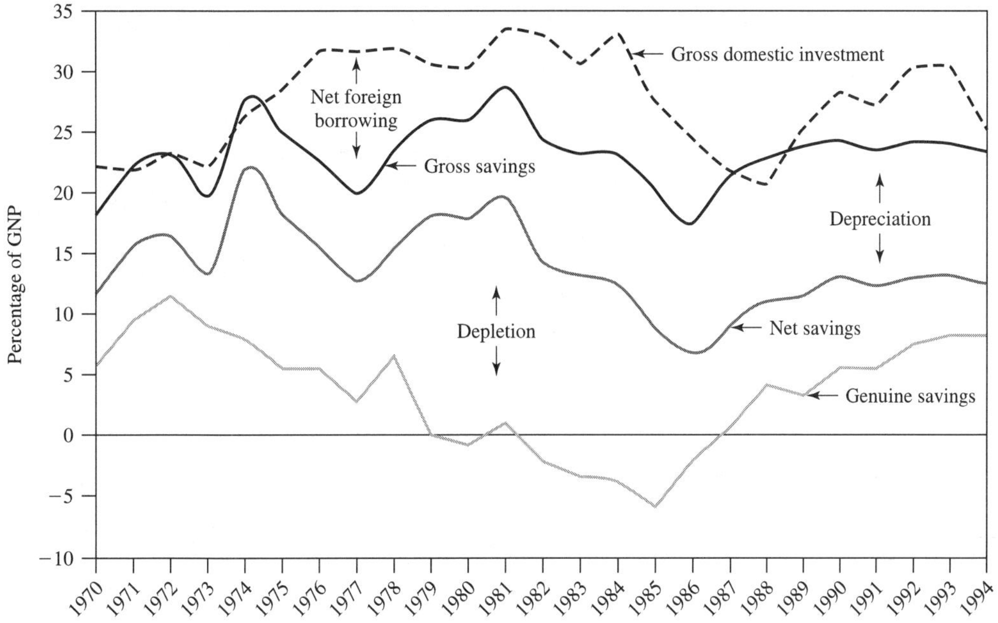

Source: Authors' estimates.

Bank's *World Development Indicators,* for instance, is *gross* savings (World Bank, various years). This is calculated as a residual: GNP minus public and private consumption. *Net* savings, gross savings less the value of depreciation of produced assets, is a first step toward a sustainability indicator. Measures of *genuine* savings address a much broader conception of sustainability than net savings by valuing changes in the natural resource base and environmental quality in addition to produced assets. Figure 1 presents the components of genuine savings as the share of GNP for Tunisia. Note that this calculation omits, for the moment, the effects of human capital investment.

The starting point in the calculation of genuine savings is just standard national accounting. The top curve in Figure 1 is gross domestic investment: total investment in structures, machinery and equipment, and inventory accumulation. Net foreign borrowing, including net official transfers, is then subtracted from this top curve to give gross savings: the difference between production and consumption over the year. Next, the depreciation of produced assets is deducted, yielding the curve for net savings. Finally, the bottom line is genuine savings, which is obtained by subtracting the value of resource depletion and pollution damages from net savings.

The basic national accounts data used to derive genuine savings rates are taken from the World Bank's *World Tables* (World Bank 1995). However, these data do not include the value of depreciation of produced assets. Unofficial estimates of depreciation, as calculated from perpetual inventory models, are taken from Nehru and Dhareshwar (1993). All of the data sets employed in this article—the *World Tables* data, the depreciation estimates, and the resource depletion and degradation calculations—have gaps in their coverage.[2]

The critical elements added by the green national accounting literature are recognition of natural resources as factors of production and of environmental amenities as sources of welfare. . . .

A calculation of genuine savings as a percentage of GNP reveals striking differences across the regions of the world. In many developing areas decisive moments in economic performance are reflected in large movements in the genuine savings rate, shown in Figures 2 and 3. These figures omit, for the time being, the effects of human capital investment.

The comparison of genuine savings rates reveals a disappointing trend for the countries of Sub-

---

[2]Resource extraction data in physical quantity are taken from the World Bank's Economic and Social Database.

Figure 2. Genuine savings as a percentage of GNP for selected regions, 1970–93.

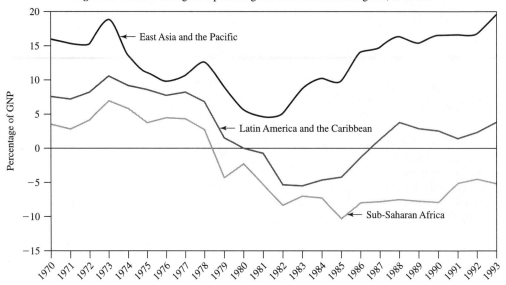

Source: Authors' estimates.

Figure 3. Genuine savings as a percentage of GNP for selected regions, 1970–93.

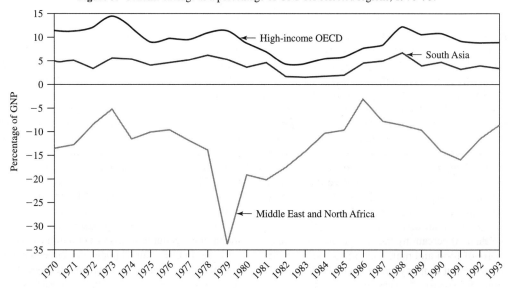

Source: Authors' estimates.

Saharan Africa (Figure 2). Here average genuine savings rates rarely exceeded 5 percent during the 1970s, followed by a sharp negative turn at the end of that decade from which they have never recovered. Despite a slight improvement in the early 1990s, regional genuine *dissaving* has recently been near 7 percent. Equally important, negative genuine savings rates have been accompanied by persistently low regional indicators of human welfare, including education, nutrition, and medical care (World Bank 1996b). The savings analysis highlights the fact that the situation *with regard to future well-being* is worse than might otherwise be thought: not only has Sub-Saharan Africa performed badly by conventional measures, it is clear that the wealth inherent in the resource stocks of these countries is being liquidated and dissipated.

The oil crisis also coincided with a period of decline in genuine savings throughout Latin America and the Caribbean, where figures had previously remained near 8 to 9 percent of GNP. In 1982, the year of Mexico's debt crisis, regional genuine savings rates dropped to negative 5 percent. As the region has emerged from the debt crisis, returned to democratic rule, and spurred the vigorous growth of the "jaguars," genuine savings rates have shown a consistently positive trend. They remain, however, well below 5 percent.

In stark contrast to the situation in Latin America and the Caribbean, the East Asia and the Pacific region has genuine savings rates sometimes topping 15 percent. However, the effects of important local pollutants, such as particulate matter in air, are not included in this calculation. Moreover, the 1997 financial crisis in this region shows that a robust savings effort is a necessary but not a sufficient condition for strong and smooth economic growth.

Consistently negative genuine savings in the Middle East and North Africa region stands out in figure 3. Regional total consumption as a share of GNP rose from around 50 percent in the 1970s to more than 70 percent by the end of the 1980s, and imports of food and manufactured goods flowed into the region as many current account surpluses of the 1970s turned into deficits in the 1980s (World Bank 1996a). However, the caveats about upward biases in the depletion estimates need to be considered when judging these figures: as the most resource-dependent economies, these countries exhibit the highest downward bias in estimated genuine savings rates.

South Asia exhibits moderately positive rates of genuine savings over the period. This is consistent with the moderate rates of economic growth that have characterized the countries in the region.

Finally, genuine savings rates in the high-income industrial countries (members of the Organisation for Economic Co-operation and Development—OECD), pushed upward by high investment, lack of dependence on natural resource depletion, and strong exports of high value-added goods and services, are near 10 percent for much of the period depicted. The recessions in 1982–83 and 1990 coincided with downward turns in genuine savings rates, but the volatility and high rates of genuine dissaving seen in other areas are consistently absent.

This picture of genuine savings rates is not complete, however. Just as standard measures of savings ignore asset consumption in natural resource capital such as forests, so can it be argued that they ignore investment in one of a nation's most valuable assets: its people.

Investing in Human Capital

The process of calculating genuine savings is, in essence, one of broadening the traditional definition of what constitutes an asset. Perhaps the most important of the additions to the asset base is the knowledge, experience, and skills embodied in a nation's populace, its human capital.

The world's nations augment the stock of human capital in large part through their educational systems, into which they collectively pour trillions of dollars each year. Standard national accounts label as an *investment* less than 10 percent of this amount, the portion that is spent on fixed capital, such as school buildings. Current (as opposed to capital) expenditures on education include teachers' salaries and the purchase of books, and are treated strictly as consumption. . . . This is clearly incorrect. If a country's human capital is to be regarded as a valuable asset, expenditures on its formation must be seen as an investment.

The effects of including human capital investment in the genuine savings calculation can be significant. In Chile, for example, current educational expenditures represented approximately 3.1 percent of GNP in the early 1990s (Figure 4). This level of investment helped to make genuine savings rates positive after the late 1980s. In 1993 and 1994 nearly one-half of the rents from natural resource depletion were, notionally at least, being reinvested in human capital.

Adjusting rates of genuine savings to embrace changes in human capital assets shifts regional genuine savings rates markedly upward (Table 2). In Sub-Saharan Africa accounting for education investment brings recent genuine savings rates close

Figure 4. Human capital and genuine savings in Chile, 1970–93.

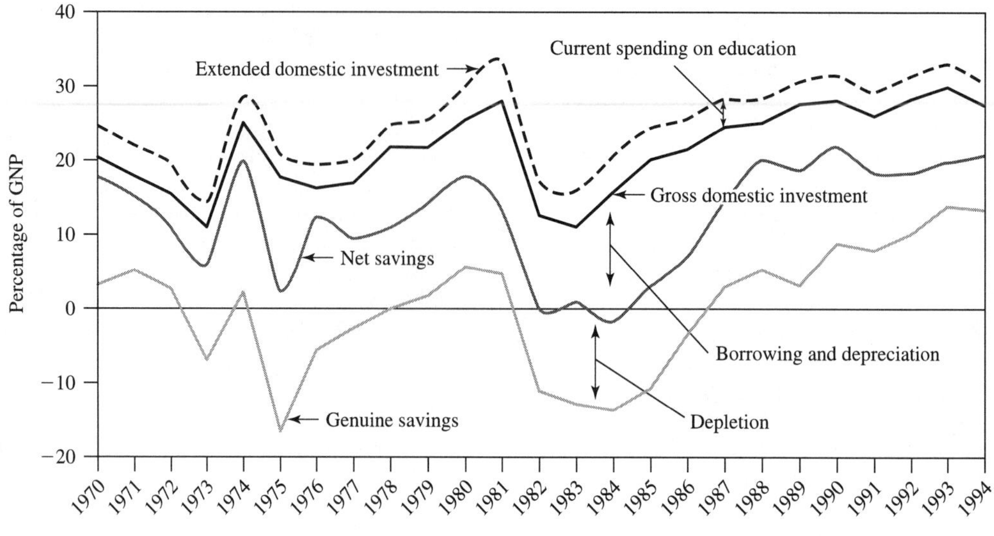

Source: Authors' estimates.

Table 2. Genuine Savings by Region and Income, 1970–93
(percentage of GNP)

Classification	Average		1990	1991	1992	1993
	1970–79	1980–89				
Region						
East Asia and the Pacific	15.1	12.6	18.6	18.7	18.7	21.3
High-income industrial countries	15.7	12.4	15.7	14.5	14.0	13.9
Latin America and the Caribbean	10.4	1.9	5.5	4.1	4.7	6.1
Middle East and North Africa	−8.9	−7.7	−8.8	−10.8	−6.6	−1.8
South Asia	7.2	6.5	7.6	6.3	7.1	6.4
Sub-Saharan Africa	7.3	−3.2	−3.8	−1.2	−0.6	−1.1
Income category						
Low	9.8	3.3	5.7	7.5	9.0	10.5
Middle	7.2	2.9	10.0	9.7	7.8	8.1
High	15.2	12.3	15.9	14.6	14.1	14.1

Note: Values include an adjustment for spending on education.

Source: Authors' estimates.

to zero. In the Middle East and North Africa genuine savings rates are consistently negative even after adjusting for education. Finally, high rates of education investment in high-income OECD countries and in East Asia and the Pacific sharpen the contrast between the genuine savings effort in these areas and across the rest of the globe. . . .

Conclusions

Savings rules have been criticized because they are concerned only with *weak* sustainability (see, for example, Martínez-Alier 1995).[3] One response to this criticism is to suggest that countries that fail the savings rule—exhibit persistently negative genuine savings—probably also fail to meet the criteria for *strong* sustainability, in the sense that critical natural assets are being depleted. It would be surprising if this were not the case. And as Pearce, Hamilton, and Atkinson (1996) argue, even if some amount of a critical resource must be preserved to meet the criteria of strong sustainability, savings rules are still required for the remaining resources if sustainability is to be achieved.

Thinking about sustainable development and its measurement leads naturally to a conception of the process of development as one of portfolio management. Prudent governments will not only consider natural resources as assets and pollution stocks as liabilities in the national balance sheet, they will also be concerned with the appropriate mix of produced assets and human capital.

Questions of the "appropriate mix" of assets are inherently questions about returns on the marginal investment. This marginal investment may be in better resource management, boosting the value of natural resources in the national balance sheet; it may be in pollution control, decreasing the size of the pollution liability to its efficient level; it may be in infrastructure, as has traditionally been the case; and it may be in primary education, as an essential building block in increasing human capital.

The policy implications of measuring genuine savings are quite direct: persistently negative rates of genuine savings must lead, eventually, to declining well-being. For policymakers, linking sustainable development to rates of genuine savings means that there are many possible interventions to increase sustainability, from the macroeconomic to the purely environmental.

---

[3]Pearce, Markandya, and Barbier (1989) define weak sustainability to mean that natural and produced assets are fully substitutable. Strong sustainability implies that at least some natural assets have no substitutes and so may need to be conserved if development is to be sustainable.

References

The word "processed" describes informally reproduced works that may not be commonly available through library systems.

Adelman, M. A. 1991. "U.S. Oil/Gas Production Cost: Recent Changes." *Energy Economics* 13(October):235–37.

Barnes, Douglas F. 1992. "Understanding Fuelwood Prices in Developing Nations." World Bank, Energy, Mining, and Telecommunications Department, Washington, D.C. Processed.

Bhattacharya, Subhes C. 1995. "Estimation of Subsidies on Coal in India." *Natural Resources Forum* 19(2):135–42.

CDIAC (Carbon Dioxide Information and Analysis Center). 1994. *Trends '93: A Compendium of Data on Global Change.* With accompanying magnetic media. Oak Ridge, Tenn.: Oak Ridge National Laboratory.

Cornot-Gandolphe, Sylvie. 1994. *Adequate and Secure Gas Supply for Europe: How to Meet the Growing Demand for Natural Gas?* Paris: International Energy Agency, International Center for Gas Technology Information.

Doyle, Guy. 1987. *China's Potential in International Coal Trade.* London: International Energy Agency Coal Research.

Duvigneaud, Paul, ed. 1971. *Productivity of Forest Ecosystems.* Paris: United Nations Educational, Scientific, and Cultural Organization.

Frankhauser, Samuel. 1994. "Evaluating the Social Costs of Greenhouse Gas Emissions." *The Energy Journal* 15(2):157–84.

FAO (Food and Agriculture Organization of the United Nations). 1983. *Forest Products Prices, 1963–1982.* Forestry Paper 46. Rome.

———. 1994. *Forest Products Yearbook 1993.* Rome.

———. 1995. *Forest Products Prices, 1973–1992.* Forestry Paper 125. Rome.

FAO/UNECE (Food and Agriculture Organization of the United Nations/United Nations Economic Commission for Europe). 1992. *The Forest Resources of the Temperate Zones.* Vol. 1: *General Forest Information.* New York: United Nations.

Freeman, A. M. 1994. *The Measurement of Environmental and Resource Values: Theory and Methods.* Washington, D.C.: Resources for the Future.

Hamilton, Kirk. 1994. "Green Adjustments to GDP." *Resources Policy* 20(3):155–68.

———. 1996. "Pollution and Pollution Abatement in the National Accounts." *Review of Income and Wealth* 42(1, March):13–33.

Hartwick, John M. 1990. "Natural Resources, National Accounting and Economic Depreciation." *Journal of Public Economics* 43(3):291–304.

———. 1992. "Deforestation and National Accounting." *Environmental and Resource Economics* 2(5):513–21.

Hill, Peter, and Anne Harrison. 1994. "Accounting for Subsoil Assets in the 1993 SNA." Paper presented to the London Group on National Accounts and the Environment, London, March 15–18. Processed.

IDB (Inter-American Development Bank). 1981. *Investment and Financing Requirements for Energy and Minerals in Latin America.* Washington, D.C.

IEA (International Energy Agency). 1994a. *Energy Policies of the Czech Republic.* Paris: Organisation for Economic Co-operation and Development.

———. 1994b. *Russian Energy Prices, Taxes, and Costs.* Paris: Organisation for Economic Co-operation and Development.

———. 1995a. *Coal Information 1994.* Paris: Organisation for Economic Co-operation and Development.

———. 1995b. *Energy Policies of Poland.* Paris: Organisation for Economic Co-operation and Development.

———. 1995c. *Energy Policies of the Russian Federation, 1995 Survey.* Paris: Organisation for Economic Co-operation and Development.

———. 1995d. *Middle East Oil and Gas.* Paris: Organisation for Economic Co-operation and Development.

———. 1995e. *Oil, Gas, and Coal: Supply Outlook.* Paris: Organisation for Economic Co-operation and Development.

———. 1996. *Energy Policies of Ukraine, 1996 Survey.* Paris: Organisation for Economic Co-operation and Development.

Jenkins, Gilbert. 1989. *Oil Economist's Handbook.* 2 vols., 5th ed. New York: Elsevier.

Julius, DeAnn, and Afsaneh Mashayekhi. 1990. *The Economics of Natural Gas: Pricing, Planning, and Policy.* London: Oxford University Press, Oxford Institute for Energy Studies.

Kanowski, P. J., and others. 1992. "Plantation Forestry." In Narendra P. Sharma, ed., *Managing the World's Forests: Looking for a Balance Between Conservation and Development.* Dubuque, Iowa: Kendall/Hunt Publishing Co.

Kellenberg, John. 1995. "Accounting for Natural Resources: Ecuador, 1971–1990." Ph.D. diss. Department of Geography and Environmental Engineering, Johns Hopkins University, Baltimore, Md.

Khan, Amar R. 1986. "The Prospects for Gas in Developing Countries." In Robert Mabro, ed., *Natural Gas: an International Perspective.* London: Oxford University Press, Oxford Institute of Energy Studies.

Lamprecht, Hans. 1989. *Silviculture in the Tropics.* Eschborn, Germany: Deutsche Gesellschaft für Technische Zusammenarbeit.

Liefert, William Mark. 1988. "The Full Cost of Soviet Oil and Natural Gas Production." *Comparative Economic Studies* 30(summer):1–20.

Mäler, K.-G. 1991. "National Accounts and Environmental Resources." *Environmental and Resource Economics* 1(1):1–15.

Martínez-Alier, Juan. 1995. "The Environment as a Luxury Good or 'Too Poor to be Green'?" *Ecological Economics* 13(1):1–10.

Mashayekhi, Afsaneh. 1983. "Marginal Cost of Natural Gas in Developing Countries: Concepts and Applications." World Bank, Energy Department, Washington, D.C. Processed.

Meyer, Sandra. 1994. *Natural Gas Statistics Sourcebook.* Tulsa, Oklahoma: Penn Well Publishing Co., Oil and Gas Journal Energy Database Publications.

Nehru, Vikram, and Ashok Dhareshwar. 1993. "A New Database on Physical Capital Stock: Sources, Methodology, and Results." *Revista de Analysis Económico* 8(1):37–59.

Openshaw, Keith, and Charles Feinstein. 1989. "Fuelwood Stumpage: Financing Renewable Energy for the World's Other Half." Policy Research Working Paper 270. World Bank, Policy Research Department, Washington, D.C. Processed.

Pearce, David W., and Giles Atkinson. 1993. "Capital Theory and the Measurement of Sustainable Development: An Indicator of Weak Sustainability." *Ecological Economics* 8(2):103–08.

Pearce, David W., Kirk Hamilton, and Giles Atkinson. 1996. "Measuring Sustainable Development: Progress on Indicators." *Environment and Development Economics* 1(1):85–101.

Pearce, David, Anil Markandya, and Edward Barbier. 1989. *Blueprint for a Green Economy.* London: Earthscan.

Repetto, Robert, William Magrath, Michael Wells, Christine Beer, and F. Rossini. 1989. *Wasting Assets: Natural Resources in the National Accounts.* Washington, D.C.: World Resources Institute.

Sadoff, C. W. 1992. *The Effects of Thailand's Logging Ban: Overview and Preliminary Results.* Bangkok: Thailand Development Research Institute.

Sagers, Matthew, Valeriy Kryukov, and Vladimir Shmat. 1995. "Resource Rent from the Oil and Gas Sector and the Russian Economy." *Post-Soviet Geography* 36(7):389–425.

Smith, Roger. 1992. "Income Growth, Government Spending, and Wasting Assets: Alberta's Oil and Gas." *Canadian Public Policy* 18(4):387–412.

Tretyakova, Albina, and Meredith Heinemeier. 1986. *Cost Estimates for the Soviet Coal Industry: 1970 to 1990.* Washington, D.C.: U.S. Department of Commerce, Bureau of the Census, Center for International Research.

United Nations. 1993. *Integrated Environmental and Economic Accounting.* Series F 61. New York.

U.S. Bureau of Mines. 1987. "An Appraisal of Minerals Availability for 34 Commodities." Bulletin 692. Department of the Interior, Washington, D.C. Processed.

van Buren, Ariane. 1990. *The Woodfuel Market in Nicaragua: The Economics, Sociology, and Management of a Natural Energy Resource.* Amsterdam: Centrum voor Studie en Documentatie van Latijns Amerika.

Weitzman, M. L. 1976. "On the Welfare Significance of National Product in a Dynamic Economy." *Quarterly Journal of Economics* 90(1):156–62.

World Bank. 1993. *Commodity Trade and Price Trends, 1989–91.* Baltimore, Md.: Johns Hopkins University Press.

———. 1995. *World Tables 1995.* Washington, D.C.

———. 1996a. International Economics Department data. Washington, D.C.

———. 1996b. *World Development Report 1996: From Plan to Market.* New York: Oxford University Press.

———. Various years. *World Development Indicators.* New York: Oxford University Press.

APPENDIX: HOW TO READ A REGRESSION TABLE

National accounts, social indicators, and other data have been accumulating for most less developed countries for more than 40 years. Writers on development frequently apply the technique of *multiple regression* to these data to estimate what they believe are underlying behavioral relationships among various economic, political, and social variables. They report their results in *regression tables.*

A number of selections in this book contain regression tables. Fortunately, lack of training in econometrics or statistics need not prevent the reader from understanding the important *economic* (as opposed to statistical) information contained in a regression table. The purpose of this Appendix is to show the untrained reader how to extract this information, using as an illustration a table adapted from the widely cited paper by Robert J. Barro, "Economic Growth in a Cross Section of Countries," *Quarterly Journal of Economics* 106 (May 1991): 407–43. The presentation applies to multiple regressions performed using a method called *ordinary least squares,* but the most important aspects of the discussion carry through even if other methods were used.

A regression table is read one column at a time. Each column reports an estimated relationship between the values of a *dependent variable,* y_i, and the values of a set of *explanatory variables,* $x_{1i}, x_{2i}, \ldots, x_{Ki}$, where i indexes *observations* and K is the number of explanatory variables. This estimated relationship takes the form

$$y_i = b_0 + b_1 x_{1i} + b_2 x_{2i} + \ldots + b_K x_{Ki} + e_i \tag{A1}$$

where the number b_0 is the *constant* or *intercept,* the numbers $b_1, b_2, \ldots, b_K$ are the *estimated coefficients,* and e_i is the *residual.* The quantity $b_0 + b_1 x_{1i} + b_2 x_{2i} + \ldots + b_K x_{Ki}$ is the *predicted value* of the dependent variable for observation i, so called because it gives the value of the dependent variable we would predict for observation i given knowledge of the values of the explanatory variables for observation i. It follows that the residual is simply the difference between the actual value of the dependent variable and its predicted value for each observation. By construction, the average or *mean* of the predicted values taken over all observations equals the mean of the actual values; equivalently, the mean of the residual is zero. As a consequence, if we know the estimated coefficients and the means of the dependent variable and the explanatory variables, we can compute the constant:

$$b_0 = \bar{y} - b_1 \bar{x}_1 - b_2 \bar{x}_2 - \ldots - b_K \bar{x}_K \tag{A2}$$

where the bar over a variable denotes its mean.

The estimated coefficients are the same for all observations because they are supposed to be estimates of underlying behavioral relationships between the dependent variable and the explanatory variables. The estimated coefficient b_1, for example, tells us that a one-unit increase in the value of the explanatory variable x_1 should cause the value of the dependent variable to increase by b_1 units, holding the values of all other explanatory variables constant. These estimated behavioral relationships are the most important economic information contained in a regression table.

With these preliminaries out of the way, we now turn to Table 1. In all regressions reported, an observation consists of the values of the dependent variable and the explanatory variables for one country for one time period. The number of observations used to estimate the coeffi-

Table 1. Regressions for per Capita Growth

	(1)	(2)	(3)	(4)
Dep. var.	GR6085	GR7085	GR6085	GR6085
No. obs.	98	98	98	98
Const.	0.0302	0.0287	0.0288	0.0345
	(0.0066)	(0.0080)	(0.0065)	(0.0067)
GDP60	−0.0075	−0.0089	−0.0073	−0.0068
	(0.0012)	(0.0016)	(0.0011)	(0.0009)
SEC60	0.0305	0.0331	0.0254	0.0133
	(0.0079)	(0.0137)	(0.0110)	(0.0070)
PRIM60	0.0250	0.0276	0.0324	0.0263
	(0.0056)	(0.0070)	(0.0077)	(0.0060)
SEC50	—	—	0.0183	—
			(0.0121)	
PRIM50	—	—	−0.0085	—
			(0.0064)	
g^c/y	−0.119	−0.142	−0.121	−0.094
	(0.028)	(0.034)	(0.027)	(0.026)
REV	−0.0195	−0.0236	−0.0189	−0.0167
	(0.0063)	(0.0071)	(0.0060)	(0.0062)
ASSASS	−0.0333	−0.0485	−0.0298	−0.0201
	(0.0155)	(0.0185)	(0.0130)	(0.0131)
PPI60DEV	−0.0143	−0.0171	−0.0141	−0.0140
	(0.0053)	(0.0078)	(0.0052)	(0.0046)
AFRICA	—	—	—	−0.0114
				(0.0039)
LAT.AMER.	—	—	—	−0.0129
				(0.0030)
R^2	0.56	0.49	0.56	0.62
$\hat{\sigma}$	0.0128	0.0168	0.0129	0.0119

Source: Barro (1991), pp. 410–413.

cients in each regression therefore equals the number of countries included in the analysis. (Barro included all countries for which data were available. They are listed in Appendix 3 of his paper.) In some regression tables in this book more than one time period per country is used in the estimation, so that the number of observations equals the number of countries multiplied by the number of time periods. In general, however, the units of analysis need not be countries. For example, in the regression tables included in Selection X.4 by Hettige et al., the units of analysis are manufacturing plants, and each observation consists of the values of the dependent and explanatory variables for one plant.

Let us focus on column (1). The dependent variable (dep. var.) is GR6085. (If the dependent variable were the same for all regressions it would be described completely in the title of the table rather than listed column by column.) We see from Table 2 that GR6085 is defined as the growth rate of real per capita GDP from 1960 to 1985. From Table 3 we see that the mean of GR6085 is 0.022: on average, per capita GDP grew by 2.2 percent per year from 1960 to 1985 in the sample of countries used in the estimation. Moving down column (1), we see that the number of observations (No. obs.) is 98: 98 countries are included in the sample. Next we see that the value of the constant (Const.) is 0.0302. Underneath this value is another number in parentheses. We will ignore all numbers in parentheses for now. After the constant begins the list of explanatory variables, all of which are defined in Table 2 and have sample means and standard deviations reported in Table 3. For example, GDP60 is defined as the 1960 value of real per capita GDP, and its mean is $1,920. The estimated coefficient for GDP60 is −0.0075. Moving down column (1), we can fill in all the explanatory vari-

Table 2. Definitions of Variables in Tables 1

GR6085 (GR7085): Growth rate of real per capita GDP
   from 1960 to 1985 (1970 to 1985).
GDP60 (GDP70, GDP85): 1960 (1970, 1985) value of
   real per capita GDP (1980 base year).
g^c/y: Average from 1970 to 1985 of the ratio of real
   government consumption (exclusive of defense and
   education) to real GDP.
SEC50 (SEC60): 1950 (1960) secondary-school
   enrollment rate.
PRIM50 (PRIM60): 1950 (1960) primary-school
   enrollment rate.
REV: Number of revolutions and coups per year
   (1960–1985 or subsample).
ASSASS: Number of assassinations per million
   population per year (1960–1985 or subsample).
PPI60DEV: Magnitude of the deviation of 1960 PPP
   value for the investment deflator (U.S. = 1.0) from
   the sample mean.
AFRICA: Dummy variable for sub-Saharan Africa.
LAT. AMER.: Dummy variable for Latin America.

Source: Barro (1991), p. 439.

ables and their estimated coefficients plus the dependent variable in equation (A1) above, obtaining

$$\text{GDP6085}_i = 0.0302 - 0.0075(\text{GDP60}_i) + 0.0305(\text{SEC60}_i) + 0.0250(\text{PRIM60}_i)$$

$$- 0.119(g^c/y)_i - 0.0195(\text{REV}_i) - 0.0333(\text{ASSASS}_i)$$

$$- 0.0143(\text{PPI60DEV}_i) + e_i \tag{A1'}$$

As an exercise, the reader may also want to use the means reported in Table 3 to verify that equation (A2) above holds given the numbers reported in column (1). Note that no coefficients are reported in column (1) for SEC50, PRIM50, AFRICA, and LAT. AMER. These explanatory variables were not included in the regression of column (1) but are included in subsequent regressions.

As we stated above, the coefficients in equation (A1') are supposed to be estimates of underlying behavioral relationships. Thus the coefficient on SEC60 indicates that an increase in a country's 1960 secondary-school enrollment rate of 10 percentage points (0.1) would raise its per capita GDP growth by roughly 0.3 percentage points ($0.0305 \times 0.10 = 0.00305$), all else equal. One common way to estimate the strength of a behavioral relationship is to ask how much effect an increase of one standard deviation in the explanatory variable has on the dependent variable. From Table 3 we see that the standard deviation of GDP60 is 1.81 ($1,810). Thus an increase of one standard deviation in GDP60 would reduce a country's per capita GDP growth by roughly 1.4 percentage points ($-0.0075 \times 1.81 = -0.0136$).

Continuing down column (1), we next see a value reported for R^2. R is the correlation coefficient between the actual and predicted values of the dependent variable. R^2 can be shown to equal the share of the variation of the dependent variable about its mean that is accounted for by the explanatory variables rather than by the residual. All else equal, the higher is R^2 the better. The number 0.56 in column (1) indicates that 56 percent of the variation in GR6085 can be "explained" by GDP60, SEC60, PRIM60, g^c/y, REV, ASSASS, and PPI60DEV.

$\hat{\sigma}$, sometimes labeled the standard error of estimate (s.e.e.), is the standard deviation of the actual value of the dependent variable from its predicted value, adjusted for the number of explanatory variables included in the regression. One can think of $\hat{\sigma}$ as the typical prediction er-

Table 3. Means and Standard Deviations of Variables

Variable	Mean	σ
GR6085	0.022	0.019
GR7085	0.016	0.023
GDP60 ($1,000)	1.92	1.81
g^c/y	0.107	0.053
SEC50[a]	0.10	0.14
SEC60	0.23	0.21
PRIM50[b]	0.65	0.39
PRIM60	0.78	0.31
REV	0.18	0.23
ASSASS	0.031	0.086
PPI60DEV	0.23	0.25
AFRICA (dummy)	0.276	0.449
LAT. AMER. (dummy)	0.235	0.426

[a]Sample of 95 countries.
[b]Sample of 97 countries.
Source: Barro (1991), p. 438.

ror. All else equal, the lower is $\hat{\sigma}$ the better. The number 0.0128 in column (1) indicates that the typical prediction error for GR6085 is roughly 1.3 percentage points, or slightly more than half its mean value.

In column (2) of Table 1 the dependent variable is changed from GR6085 to GR7085 but all the explanatory variables are kept the same. Comparing the estimated coefficients between columns (1) and (2), we can see that the relationships found for GR6085 are robust to a change in the time period over which growth is computed from 1960–1985 to 1970–1985. In column (3) the dependent variable is again GR6085, but two explanatory variables, SEC50 and PRIM50, have been added to the set used in column (1). We will discuss the regression results reported in column (3) later. In column (4) two *dummy variables,* AFRICA and LAT. AMER., have been added to the set of explanatory variables used in column (1). A dummy variable is a variable that takes the value 1 if a certain relationship is true (e.g., a country is located in Latin America) and 0 if that relationship is false. The estimated coefficients on dummy variables are especially easy to interpret: the numbers reported in column (4) indicate that, all else equal, a country's per capita GDP growth is 1.1 percentage points lower if it is located in sub-Saharan Africa and 1.3 percentage points lower if it is located in Latin America. Note that inclusion of these two dummy variables reduces the coefficients on most of the other explanatory variables (in absolute value) compared with column (1), indicating that some of their effects were actually attributable to special characteristics of Africa and Latin America.

We now turn to an explanation of the numbers in parentheses reported in each column underneath the constant and estimated coefficients. These are called the *standard errors* of the constant and estimated coefficients. We will denote by s_j the standard error of the estimated coefficient b_j. To understand the economic information conveyed by these standard errors we first need to introduce the idea that the regression (A1) can be thought of as an estimate of an unobserved "true" model (A3):

$$y_i = \beta_0 + \beta_1 x_{1i} + \beta_2 x_{2i} + \ldots + \beta_K x_{Ki} + \varepsilon_i \tag{A3}$$

where the numbers $\beta_0, \beta_1, \beta_2, \ldots, \beta_K$ are the *parameters* of the model (the "true" constant and "true" coefficients) and ε_i is the *error term* that accounts for random variation in the dependent variable that is not captured by the explanatory variables. We can then ask, what do the estimated constant and coefficients tell us about the values of the model parameters?

The answer is that, under certain assumptions, we can be roughly 95 percent confident that the true parameters are within 2 standard errors of their estimates. We can thus think of $2s_j$ as the "margin of error" for the estimate b_j. More precisely, we can state with a 95 percent degree of confidence that the value of β_j lies within $b_j - 1.96s_j$ and $b_j + 1.96s_j$:

$$b_j - 1.96s_j \le \beta_j \le b_j + 1.96s_j \tag{A4}$$

(A4) gives us the 95 percent *confidence interval* for the parameter β_j. The smaller is the standard error s_j, the narrower is the confidence interval, and the more information we can be said to have about the value of β_j. Ninety-five percent is the most common conventional level of confidence; the other conventional levels are 90 percent and 99 percent. To construct a 90 or 99 percent confidence interval we replace the number 1.96 in (A4) with 1.645 or 2.576, respectively. Note that greater confidence is associated with wider intervals, as we would expect.

For the interested reader we will indicate here how the confidence interval (A4) can be derived formally; other readers can skip this paragraph without loss of continuity. We begin by making the assumptions that ε_i is uncorrelated with the explanatory variables, is uncorrelated with itself across observations, and is *normally distributed* with mean zero and constant variance (i.e., the sampling distribution for ε_i follows the same bell-shaped curve centered around zero for all i). Under this assumption it can be shown that $(b_j - \beta_j)/s_j$, the ratio of the difference between an estimated coefficient and the corresponding parameter to the standard error of the coefficient, follows a t *distribution* with n-K-1 degrees of freedom, where n is the number of observations used in the regression. For most regressions reported in the selections in this book the number of observations relative to the number of explanatory variables is sufficiently large that the t distribution with infinite degrees of freedom (i.e., the normal distribution with mean 0 and variance 1) is an excellent approximation to the true t distribution. Ninety-five percent of the mass of this distribution falls within -1.96 and $+1.96$, so the probability that $(b_j - \beta_j)/s_j$ falls within -1.96 and $+1.96$ equals 0.95. Put differently, we can state with a 95 percent degree of confidence that

$$-1.96 \le \frac{(b_j - \beta_j)}{s_j} \le +1.96$$

Multiplying this inequality by s_j throughout, we get

$$-1.96s_j \le (b_j - \beta_j) \le +1.96s_j.$$

Subtracting b_j from all sides, multiplying throughout by -1, and switching the sides around yields (A4) above.

We now return to column (1) of Table 1 and reconsider our estimate of the effect of an increase in SEC60 of 10 percentage points on GR6085. Using (A4), we can find the 95 percent confidence interval for the "true" coefficient on SEC60:

$$0.0305 - 1.96(0.0079) \le \beta_{\text{SEC60}} \le 0.0305 + 1.96(0.0079),$$

$$\text{or} \quad 0.0150 \le \beta_{\text{SEC60}} \le 0.0460 \tag{A4'}$$

Using (A4') we can compute that the "true" model yields an effect of a 10-percentage point increase in SEC60 on GR6085 that lies within 0.15 and 0.46 percentage points. Our earlier estimate of 0.305 percentage points is, of course, the midpoint of this interval.

From (A4) we can see that, if b_j is positive, then if $b_j > 1.96s_j$ or $b_j/s_j > 1.96$ we can be (at least) 95 percent confident that β_j is positive. Similarly, if b_j is negative, then if $|b_j| > 1.96s_j$ or $|b_j|/s_j > 1.96$ we can be (at least) 95 percent confident that β_j is negative. Put differently, if the absolute value of the ratio b_j/s_j exceeds 1.96, we can be 95 percent confident that explanatory variable j has *some* impact on the dependent variable in the direction indicated by the estimated coefficient. If we cannot be at least 95 percent confident (or, sometimes, at least 90 percent confident), it is conventionally argued that explanatory variable j should not be considered to be part of the "true" model (A3). For this reason the ratio b_j/s_j, known as the *t statistic* for the coefficient b_j, is often reported in regression tables in parentheses underneath the coefficient instead of s_j. Note that if t statistics are reported instead of standard errors, the standard errors can be recovered by dividing the estimated coefficients by their t statistics. (It is customary to state that, if the absolute value of the t statistic for b_j exceeds 1.96, we can *reject the hypothesis that* $\beta_j = 0$. Equivalently, it is stated that b_j is *significantly different from zero at the 95 percent level*, or simply that b_j is *statistically significant*. We prefer not to develop the concept of hypothesis testing here.)

We now return for the final time to Table 1. We can easily compute that all estimated coefficients in columns (1) and (2) have t statistics larger than 1.96 in absolute value. This remains true in column (3) except for the coefficients on SEC50 and PRIM50, which have t statistics of 1.51 and 1.33 in absolute value, respectively. We can conclude that SEC50 and PRIM50 are superfluous explanatory variables, which is not surprising given the inclusion of SEC60 and PRIM60. In column (4) all estimated coefficients have t statistics that exceed 1.96 in absolute value except for the coefficients on SEC60 and ASSASS. The t statistic of 1.90 for the coefficient on SEC60 indicates that we can be 90 percent (but not 95 percent) confident that SEC60 has some positive impact on GR6085, while the t statistic of 1.53 (in absolute value) for the coefficient on ASSASS indicates that we cannot be even 90 percent confident that ASSASS has some negative impact on GR6085. We noted earlier that the addition of the dummy variables AFRICA and LAT. AMER. reduced the coefficients on most of the other explanatory variables (in absolute value). For SEC60 and ASSASS the changes were substantial enough so that by conventional standards inclusion of the former in the "true" model is now marginal and inclusion of the latter is no longer justified.

The reader who wishes to deepen his understanding of multiple regression can consult any econometrics text. Two popular texts are Damodar N. Gujarati, *Basic Econometrics,* 4th ed. (New York: McGraw-Hill, 2003) and Jeffrey M. Wooldridge, *Introductory Econometrics: A Modern Approach,* 2nd ed. (Cincinnati: South-Western, 2003).

INDEX OF SELECTION AUTHORS

INDEX

Acquired immune deficiency syndrome (AIDS), 185; Africa, 65; crisis, 14; development, 235; drugs, 218, 219

Adverse selection, 221–22, 310, 426

Afghanistan, 92, 95, 279, 280, 281, 604

Africa: agriculture and, 101, 104; divergence and, 128; economic development in, 498; economic growth in, 62–71, 88–89, 90–91, 93, 95, 96, 97; education in, 191, 192; environment and, 594, 596; foreign aid to, 315–16; income inequality, 473; industrialization and, 101, 103; microfinance, 320; population, 245; rural-urban migration in, 336, 337; typology of development in, 146–50; unemployment in, 368; urbanization, 336. *See also* East Africa; North Africa; South Africa; Sub-Saharan Africa; West Africa

Agency theory, 408

Agricultural household models, 383, 428–30

Agricultural productivity, 32; comparative advantage, economic growth and, 111–13; economic growth and, 103–5; factoral terms of trade and, 103–5; high-human development countries, 386–87; induced innovation, 397–98; inequality and, 461; in Lewis model of world economy, 108–10; low-human development countries, 384; medium-human development countries, 384–86; scale effects, 407; soil, water and, 590–91; strategies for increasing, 396

Agriculture, 3, 381–431; in Africa, 68; bimodal strategy, 382, 394–96; commercial, 405–6; crop yields and, 389; design of developmental strategies for, 394–99; development strategies and, 382; division of world into industry and, 101–3; economic growth and, 85, 86, 87–88, 398–99; elasticity of demand for goods,

111–12, 112, 114; income distribution and, 398–99, 400, 446; in Indonesia, 481–88; in Krueger's trade model, 151–54; land reform effects and, 407–14; marketing and, 405; in New World, 119; policies for, 400–402; postwar yields of, 95, 389; pricing policy for, 383, 401–2, 430–31; productivity of, 381–82, 384–87, 388–91; supply elasticity of production, 430–31; in Taiwan, 395; unimodal strategy, 382, 394–96. *See also* Rural sector; Rural-urban divide; Rural-urban migration

Aguas Argentinas, 350

Ahluwalia, Montek, 178

AIDS. *See* Acquired immune deficiency syndrome (AIDS)

Air quality, 589–90, 593

AK model, 154, 204, 297–99

Algeria, 91, 279, 280, 281

Amakudari, 546

Amazon Basin, 600

Argentina, 103, 121, 123, 231, 460; agriculture and, 112; capital flight from, 311; economic growth in, 90, 96, 98, 538; economic reforms in, 59; industrialization and, 102, 158; privatization in, 332; trade and, 170

Asia, 108; agriculture and, 101, 104; AIDS in, 231; economic growth in, 84, 88, 90, 97; education in, 259, 497; environment and, 594; industrialization and, 103; microfinance in, 320; population in, 248, 255; rural-urban migration in, 337; women in, 264, 265, 266, 276. *See also* East Asia; South Asia; Southeast Asia

Asian financial crisis, 41, 312

Assassinations, 523, 607

Australia, 92, 103, 105, 108, 109, 140, 159; income inequality in, 474; women in, 276

Automobile industry, 170, 565–66

Autonomy. *See* Embedded autonomy; State autonomy

Backwash, 102

Balanced growth, 73–74

Bangkok International Banking Facility, 313

Bangladesh, 140; economic growth in, 92; family planning programs in, 253; foreign direct investment and, 179; Grameen Bank of, 270, 320, 321–23, 324, 326, 328; infrastructure of, 497; microfinance in, 320–23, 324, 326; pollution abatement in, 612–13, 616–19; population in, 250, 251; technology transfer and, 172; women in, 267, 269, 270, 277, 278, 279, 280, 281, 282

Bangladesh Chemical Industries Corporation (BCIC), 616

Bangladesh Rural Advancement Committee (BRAC), 270–72, 324, 328

Bank Kredit Desa (Indonesia), 323

Banks: capital account liberalization and, 312; central, 567; China, 50

Barbados, 119, 355

Basic indicators, 21–26, 64

BEFIEX program, 564–65

Belgium, 111

Belize, 121

Big push, 73

Bimodal agricultural strategy, 382, 394–96

Biodiversity, 590

Birth rates, 86, 356. *See also* Fertility rates

Black markets, 162, 492, 523, 524, 525, 526, 528; recent trends, 37, 39

Bolivia, 59, 120, 306; business start-ups in, 511; education in, 194, 197; export subsidies and, 560, 567–69; microfinance in, 320, 321, 322, 324, 326

Botswana, 231, 237; ethnic diversity in, 528; political system of, 470

Brazil, 234; AIDS, 231; colonial, 118, 119, 123; deforestation in, 604; economic growth in, 87, 88, 90, 95, 96, 97, 98; economic reforms in, 59, 60; education in, 197, 202, 203, 204; environment and, 595, 596, 599; export subsidies and, 560, 564–66, 569; foreign aid to, 316; health in, 495; income inequality in, 473, 474;